# PRESIDENTIAL PROFILES
# THE JOHNSON YEARS

Chester Pach

An imprint of Infobase Publishing

**Presidential Profiles: The Johnson Years**

Facts On File, Inc.
An imprint of Infobase Publishing
132 West 31st Street
New York NY 10001

**Library of Congress Cataloging-in-Publication Data**

Pach, Chester J.
    The Johnson years / Chester Pach.
        p. cm.—(Presidential profiles)
    Includes bibliographical references and index.
    ISBN 0-8160-5388-X (acid-free paper)
    1. Politicians—United States—Biography. 2. United States—Politics and government—1961–1963. 3. United States—Politics and government—1963–1969. 4. United States—Politics and government—1969–1974. 5. Johnson, Lyndon B. (Lyndon Baines), 1908–1973—Friends and associates. 6. United States—History—1961–1969—Biography. 7. United States—History—1969—Biography. 8. United States—Biography. I. Title II. Presidential profiles (Facts On File, Inc.)
    E840.6.P43 2005
    973.923—dc22                                          2005043221

Text design by Mary Susan Ryan-Flynn
Cover design by Nora Wertz

Printed in the United States of America

VB Hermitage 10 9 8 7 6 5 4 3 2 1

This book is printed on acid-free paper.

# LIST OF CONTRIBUTORS

**Catherine A. Barnes**
Columbia University

**James L. Baughman**
Columbia University

**Miriam D. Bluestone**
Rutgers University

**Thomas J. Champion**
Rutgers University

**Joshua B. Freeman**
Rutgers University

**Steven L. Goulden**
University of Chicago

**Thomas L. Harrison**
Columbia University

**Joseph C. Holub**
University of California, Berkeley

**Frank H. Milburn**
Franconia College

**Thomas O'Brien**
New York University

**Donald K. Richards**
Rutgers University

**James L. Wunsch**
University of Chicago

# CONTENTS

# PREFACE

*The Johnson Years* is a revised volume in the Presidential Profiles reference series. It contains hundreds of biographies of individuals who made significant contributions to public policy and public life during the presidency of Lyndon B. Johnson. Many of the entries are for men and women who served in the Johnson administration. Quite a few others are for influential members of Congress, prominent state or local officials whose activities had national significance, and justices of the Supreme Court. A substantial number of biographies are of individuals who never held public office and who sometimes gained attention by challenging government actions. They include civil rights leaders, anti–Vietnam War activists, and social and cultural critics.

Each biography begins with the name of the individual, year of birth, and, if required, year of death, followed by the title of the most important office held, or the occupation or activity for which the subject was most noted during the Johnson years. The entry includes a detailed discussion of the individual's career, with emphasis on activities during the period from 1963 to 1969. Readers will also find important information about the subject's life and career before and after the Johnson years. Each entry calls attention to the individual's principal accomplishments or achievements as well as his or her influence on domestic or international affairs. The length of each profile is roughly equivalent to the importance of that individual during the Johnson years.

Many of these biographies are substantially revised versions of the entries that appeared in the original edition. Each has new information that carries the biography, as appropriate, up to the end of the individual's life, the end of his or her career, or the early 21st century. The release of many public documents and collections of personal papers during the past three decades and the publication of many excellent secondary works on various dimensions of the Johnson years have provided new information or new ideas and interpretations that have been incorporated into quite a few of the entries.

*The Johnson Years* also contains several valuable appendices. The chronology lists many significant developments in politics, civil rights, and the war in Vietnam, among other subjects. There is a roster of members of Congress who served while Lyndon Johnson was in the White House, as well as lists of officials in cabinet departments and major regulatory agencies, state governors, and justices of the Supreme Court. A selection of primary documents includes several of Johnson's major speeches and a transcript of one of his news conferences. Also included is an edited transcript of a telephone conversation that Johnson secretly recorded, one of hundreds of tapes that the Johnson Library in Austin, Texas, began releasing in the late 1990s. Also included in the primary documents are notes from a series of critical meetings between the president and his top national security advisers in July 1965 about expanding U.S. military involvement in the Vietnam War. The final appendix is a selected bibliography.

Although only one author's name appears on the title page, another historian made a substantial contribution to this book. Mitchell Lerner completed revision of most of the biographical entries in the first half of the alphabet before he turned over the project to me. As I completed my work, Owen Lancer, editor-in-chief of history and political science at Facts On File, was helpful, gracious, and patient. My wife, Mary Jane Kelley, and our children, Gregory and Lauren, endured my long hours of work and provided more help than they will ever know. I hope that *The Johnson Years* will be a valuable source of information to readers who are interested in a complex and controversial presidency and in a decade—the 1960s—that continues to fascinate.

—Chester Pach

# INTRODUCTION

A lthough the Johnson years ended in division and strife, they began in consensus. The stunned disbelief and shared grief following the assassination of President John F. Kennedy on November 22, 1963, dampened political conflict and created, if only briefly, a sense of national unity. Johnson worried about whether he would be equal to the challenges of the presidency at a time of national crisis, but he betrayed none of those private doubts when he spoke to a joint session of Congress after Kennedy's funeral. Instead, he expressed the sadness he shared with his fellow citizens and his determination to complete Kennedy's unfinished legislative agenda. "Let us continue," Johnson declared, as he urged passage of the civil rights bill and tax cut legislation as a memorial to Kennedy. Johnson also emphasized continuity by asking all of Kennedy's former advisers and cabinet officers to remain in their jobs. A substantial number did. Dean Rusk, Robert S. McNamara, and McGeorge Bundy became major figures in the formulation of the Johnson administration's national security policy while Richard Goodwin, R. Sargent Shriver, Nicholas Katzenbach, Orville Freeman, and Stewart Udall made important contributions to domestic policy.

Continuity in aims and advisers was not sufficient, however, to persuade some influential constituencies that Johnson would do what he professed. Liberals remembered Johnson's reputation as Senate Democratic leader in the 1950s, earned for the tactics he used in maneuvering legislation through Congress, and they worried that he would be more concerned about cutting deals than standing for principle. Northerners wondered whether Johnson's southern roots would mean that he would be all too willing to appease regional inter-

ests. African Americans feared that Johnson in the White House, as he had in the Senate, would provide only qualified support for civil rights.

Johnson acted quickly and forcefully to neutralize these suspicions. Only a day after Kennedy's assassination, Johnson met with Walter Heller, the chair of the Council of Economic Advisers, and asked him to tell his liberal friends not to believe the rumors that the new president was a conservative who was "likely to go back to the Eisenhower ways." Instead, Johnson declared, he was "a Roosevelt New Dealer" who found Kennedy "a little too conservative" for his taste. When Roy Wilkins, the head of the NAACP, came to the White House and asked the new president what accounted for his invigorated commitment to civil rights, Johnson replied that he now represented all the people, not just the voters of Texas.

Yet Johnson knew that his promises would mean little if he could not prove his effectiveness. He decided that he needed a quick victory in Congress, and he chose the income tax reduction bill, which Kennedy had proposed in January 1963. Kennedy maintained that a tax cut would stimulate the economy and produce substantial growth; Senate conservatives, however, balked at approving a measure that they thought would lead to higher budget deficits. Johnson drew on his exceptional skills at persuasion to assure legislators that he would do everything possible to reduce federal expenditures at the same time that he made the case that lower taxes would increase investment and produce more jobs. Johnson lobbied members of the Senate Finance Committee, which had been unwilling to clear the bill when Kennedy was in the White House. The committee soon voted its approval; the Congress concurred; and, on February 26, 1964, Johnson signed into law an $11.5 billion reduction in income taxes, the largest to that point in U.S.

history. At the signing ceremony, Johnson emphasized that Kennedy's inspiration had produced the tax cut. He knew full well that others would give him credit for the skillful leadership that had turned inspiration into legislation.

Johnson soon scored another major victory that had eluded Kennedy with the passage of the Civil Rights Act of 1964. The House gave its approval in early February by a large margin, but Johnson knew all along that the chief battle would be fought in the Senate. The president expected a filibuster, and a two-thirds vote was needed to terminate debate. Johnson adamantly opposed any significant modifications in the bill to secure Senate approval, lest he face charges that his southern background made him inclined to compromise or that he had to settle for less than Kennedy would have gotten. Johnson believed that the key to getting the required votes was the support of Senate Minority Leader Everett Dirksen (R-Ill.). Johnson courted Dirksen, making clear that he would allow the Republican leader to shape the legislation through a series of minor amendments provided that Dirksen, in turn, helped deliver the Republican votes needed to halt the debate. The filibuster lasted for 75 days, but the Senate voted cloture. The passage of the Civil Rights Act, which banned discrimination in public accommodations, was a masterly achievement, one that Johnson celebrated as an extension of basic American freedoms. Yet, privately the president feared that he would pay a fearful price in the form of a white backlash, which would eventually turn the South into a bastion of Republican strength.

Johnson achieved a third major triumph during his first months in office with the launching of the War on Poverty. The Kennedy administration had become interested in a new antipoverty effort, in part because of increasing public awareness of the persistence of widespread deprivation in the midst of general, national prosperity. In his influential book *The Other America* (1962), Michael Harrington drew wide attention to the issue, which he said was a national calamity that affected between 40 and 50 million people in innercity slums and rural backwaters, one that left them tormented, lonely, and hopeless. Civil rights leaders like Bayard Rustin, A. Philip Randolph, and Whitney Young emphasized that the average rate of unemployment for African Americans was much higher than that of whites and that many black workers with full-time jobs still did not earn enough to stay above the official poverty line.

Just before his death, Kennedy had said that he wanted to devise a program to deal with these problems. Johnson announced one that was far more ambitious than anything the Kennedy administration would have likely designed. He proclaimed in his first State of the Union address in January 1964, "This administration today, here and now, declares unconditional war on poverty in America." The president made clear that there would be many weapons in this war, including job training, education, and housing programs. Even before he had settled on any clear strategy, Johnson chose the program's director, informing a reluctant R. Sargent Shriver that he would head the War on Poverty only hours before the president announced the appointment. Johnson believed that the leadership of Shriver, who was the dead president's brother-in-law, would emphasize continuity between the Kennedy and Johnson administrations. At the same time, Shriver, who was director of the Peace Corps, had established a reputation with that popular program that would make him, in the president's words, "Mr. Poverty, at home and abroad." Once more Congress acted as Johnson proposed, creating the Office of Economic Opportunity in August 1964 and appropriating $1 billion for the first year of antipoverty efforts. Once more, Johnson asserted that he was advancing the national interest, since all Americans would benefit from an increase in self-sufficient and productive citizens, not dependent on government "doles."

The War on Poverty and the Civil Rights Act were parts of a breathtaking program of social reform that Johnson called the Great Society. In his commencement address at the University of Michigan on May 22, 1964, Johnson asserted that "the challenge of the next half century" was to use the abundance of American society "to enrich and elevate our national life." The Great Society, he explained, required an "end to poverty and racial injustice." But achieving those goals were only essential first tasks. "The Great Society is a place where every child can find knowledge to enrich his mind and to enlarge his talents. . . . It is a place . . . [to] renew contact with nature. . . . It is a place where men are more concerned with the quality of their goals than the quantity of their goods." Johnson's vision of a Great Society went far beyond the New Deal or Fair Deal or New Frontier by insisting that Americans could not only solve fundamental material problems but also raise the quality of life for all citizens. It assumed that the economy would continue to thrive and that a broad consensus of public opinion would believe that government's guiding hand would benefit all citizens. It would require an extraordinary national effort that would take decades to complete, but that would begin to produce significant improvements in the Johnson years. The president provided few specifics, but his agenda was clear. And the public reaction was widespread approbation. The Gallup poll showed that six months into his presidency, Johnson enjoyed the approval of 74 percent of Americans, only slightly below the 79 percent rating when the public rallied behind the new president after Kennedy's death.

Johnson saw the election of 1964 as an opportunity to secure the presidency in his own right, one that would free him from Kennedy's legacy. To do so, Johnson was determined to keep Robert F. Kennedy, the U.S. Attorney General, off the ticket as his running mate. During the spring of 1964, polls showed that Kennedy was far and away the first choice of Democrats for vice president. Kennedy and Johnson, however, had long had strained relations; the president worried that Kennedy, as vice president, would hardly be a subordinate figure in the new administration. Equally objectionable to Johnson was the likelihood that many observers would attribute his victory in November, if he won it, not to his accomplishments or to his appeal, but to the popularity of his running mate or, more generally, the Kennedys. Johnson maneuvered to diminish Kennedy's chances for the vice presidency without ever publicly ruling him out. Eventually, he announced that he would not select any member of his cabinet for the second spot on the ticket. Kennedy decided to run for the U.S. Senate from New York. Still fearful that Kennedy might somehow trigger a movement to draft him for the second spot, Johnson had the FBI track Kennedy's every move when the Democrats met at Atlantic City. Johnson revealed his choice of Senator Hubert H. Humphrey as his running mate only after the convention assembled. Widely popular, with a long record as a champion of liberal causes, Humphrey added strength to the ticket.

Johnson was also able to expand the consensus behind his leadership because of the unsettling candidacy of his Republican opponent, Senator Barry Goldwater of Arizona. During the early 1960s an ideological conservative movement in the Republican Party had gained notable strength in the South and West. Hostile to the moderate, eastern Republicans who had dominated the party since 1940, these conservatives opposed most social welfare measures at home and demanded uncompromising opposition to communism abroad. Extensive, early grassroots organizing allowed these conservatives to build their influence in local and state Republican organizations and prepare the way for Goldwater's successful campaign for the Republican nomination. Despite some difficulties in the early primaries, Goldwater prevailed over Henry Cabot Lodge of Massachusetts and New York governor Nelson Rockefeller by locking up more support among party regulars at a time when most convention delegates were not chosen in primaries.

Once his nomination was assured in early June after his victory in the crucial California primary, Goldwater did not moderate his conservative positions to try to broaden his support. He chose as his running mate an obscure member of Congress, William E. Miller (R-N.Y.), whose positions on most issues paralleled those of Goldwater. In his speech accepting his party's presidential nomination, Goldwater proclaimed, "Extremism in the defense of liberty is no vice." His words made even many Republicans cringe, as they seemed to confirm the persistent allegations that Goldwater had much in common with extreme right-wing groups like the John Birch Society. On the campaign trail, Goldwater continued to offer voters "a choice not an echo." He did not retreat from his criticism of such popular and well-established programs as Social Security and the Tennessee Valley Authority. He declared his opposition to racial discrimination, but he was one among very few Republican senators who voted against the Civil Rights Act of 1964, insisting that its enforcement would require an unconstitutional enlargement of federal power. Such unyielding fidelity to principle left the center of the electorate—including many independents and traditional Republicans—to Johnson. Prominent liberal and moderate Republicans—including Senator Jacob Javits (N.Y.), Governor George Romney (Mich.), and Rockefeller—refused to endorse the Arizona senator, while some top party leaders such as former president Dwight D. Eisenhower offered only lukewarm support.

Goldwater's bellicose rhetoric and loose talk about nuclear war also raised apprehensions that shifted votes to Johnson. Goldwater suggested that he was ready to wage hot war, not just cold war, to force the retreat of Communist power. He also seemed prepared to authorize nuclear strikes, not just conventional attacks. He once casually talked about lobbing an atomic bomb "into the men's room at the Kremlin," and he advocated giving U.S. commanders of North Atlantic Treaty Organization forces in Europe the power to decide whether to use tactical nuclear weapons in retaliation for an attack. He also called for increased U.S. military action, including the use of low-yield atomic weapons to defoliate jungles, to help win the war in Vietnam.

Johnson seized an opportunity to show that he would be firm but not irresponsible in meeting Communist challenges by authorizing retaliatory raids after North Vietnamese attacks on U.S. vessels in the Gulf of Tonkin in early August. For the first time, U.S. bombers openly hit North Vietnamese targets, and Johnson secured from Congress a resolution granting him broad authority to take whatever action was necessary to meet aggression and defend U.S. forces in Southeast Asia. Yet the Johnson administration suppressed information that revealed the second of the North Vietnamese attacks had never really occurred—that the initial reports of military action were equivocal or mistaken—so that the president would appear to have taken necessary, decisive, and proportionate action. If the point was not sufficiently clear, it was made even more bluntly when the Johnson campaign broadcast the infamous "Daisy commercial" on network television on Labor Day evening. The commercial began with a girl counting the petals that she plucked from a daisy, which suddenly became the countdown to a nuclear explosion. At the end, an announcer urged Americans to vote for President Johnson, as "the stakes are too high for you to stay home." Fears about Goldwater's finger on the nuclear button made many Americans think that Johnson was the only responsible choice for president.

Johnson won in a landslide. He captured 44 states and took 61 percent of the popular vote. His party also won a sweeping victory, gaining 37 seats in the House and two in the Senate. Democratic Party margins were overwhelming, with a 295-140 majority in the House and a 68-32 advantage in the Senate. The conservative coalition of southern Democrats and Republicans, which had often dominated recent congresses, could no longer command such influence. A revision of the House rules in early 1965 further reduced conservative clout. The

change gave Speaker John McCormack (D-Mass.) authority to bring to the floor legislation blocked by the Rules Committee, where conservatives had often prevailed. As a result of these changes, the conservative coalition was victorious on only 25 percent of all House roll-call votes in 1965, compared to 67 percent in 1963 and 74 percent in 1961. Johnson was able to secure from the 89th Congress a phenomenal 69 percent of his legislative proposals. The only ominous result of the 1964 election for Johnson and the Democrats was that Goldwater had carried five states in the Deep South, including four—Mississippi, Alabama, Georgia, and South Carolina—that had not voted Republican in a presidential election since Reconstruction.

Commanding majorities in both the House and Senate insured that Johnson would frequently get his way with Congress. But Johnson would never have succeeded so often or secured so much if he had not been a master of the legislative process. During his years in the Senate, Johnson had accumulated power that exceeded any previous majority leader. An important element of his success was what became known as the "Johnson Treatment," an array of techniques—including flattery, intimidation, manipulation, and overwhelming persistence—that he used to secure cooperation. As journalists Rowland Evans and Robert Novak explained in their book, *Lyndon B. Johnson: The Exercise of Power*, the Johnson Treatment

> could last ten minutes or four hours. . . . It ran the gamut of human emotions. Its velocity was breathtaking, and it was all in one direction. Interjections from the target were rare. Johnson anticipated them before they could be spoken. He moved in close, his face a scant millimeter from his target, his eyes widening and narrowing, his eyebrows rising and falling. From his pockets poured clippings, memos, statistics. Mimicry, humor, and the genius of analogy made the Treatment an almost hypnotic experience and rendered the target stunned and helpless.

As president, Johnson had even greater resources—more favors to provide, more threats to invoke—to make the Treatment effective. While he relied on congressional leaders and staff assistants to manage administration bills, he used his skills at persuasion to secure critical support, such as Dirksen's, or to help swing wavering or undecided legislators on close votes. In addition, Johnson kept close watch on most administration bills, frequently consulting with White House aides involved in liaison activities on Capitol Hill and giving them directions. Johnson, in short, committed a good deal of his energy, prestige, and expertise to insure that Congress acted more favorably and swiftly than it had since the New Deal.

Johnson's aim was nothing less than the greatest record of social reform in U.S. history. A rare confluence of circumstances, he believed, made it possible in the mid-1960s to move far beyond the achievements of the New Freedom of Woodrow Wilson or Roosevelt's New Deal. The economy was booming and there was broad confidence that prosperity and abundance had become constants of American life. There was also remarkable consensus behind Johnson's leadership, one of those unusual moments when a president had both the public and the congressional support to achieve ambitious social improvements. Johnson insisted in his State of the Union address in 1965 that a president "could not shape a new and personal vision of America," but only create one "from the scattered hopes of the American past." The Great Society, he declared, grew out of those earlier dreams and would benefit all Americans, providing rights and opportunities to those long denied them and a decent standard of living to those "still trapped in poverty and idleness and fear." Yet it would do far more as it enriched the lives of affluent Americans by rebuilding cities, protecting the environment, improving health care, and supporting the arts and humanities. As Johnson later told his biographer, Doris Kearns, "we have enough to do it all."

During 1965 Congress approved a torrent of legislation that defined the Great Society. Some of the most important programs were revisions of proposals that Kennedy or even Truman had previously sent to Congress. Medicare, for example, began as a Fair Deal proposal that Kennedy had later unsuccessfully tried to get through Congress. Johnson submitted a revised version of a plan to cover hospital costs for the elderly under Social Security and made it a top legislative priority. Congress actually gave the president more than he requested, adding provisions for paying physicians' fees and for providing medical care to the poor under Medicaid. Johnson also gained from Congress another program that eluded Kennedy, a major increase in federal subsidies for local school districts under the Elementary and Secondary Education Act. The Higher Education Act, which Congress approved

later that year, provided federal funds for library acquisitions and scholarship and loan programs. Johnson's commitment to these education measures was personal as well as political. He signed the first education bill in a one-room school in Johnson City, Texas, that he had attended as a child; he approved the Higher Education Act at his alma mater, Southwest Texas State College. In both ceremonies, Johnson asserted that education was the key to individual opportunity and that the new legislation would "swing open . . . the most important door that will ever open—the door to education." And there was much more new Great Society legislation in 1965, including an ambitious housing program, an expansion of national parks and wilderness areas, a liberalization of immigration law, and the creation of the National Endowments for the Humanities and for the Arts.

Another major part of the Great Society was the Voting Rights Act of 1965. In his State of the Union message in January 1965, Johnson had called for the elimination of "every remaining obstacle to the right and the opportunity to vote." Yet he hesitated to introduce new legislation that would have provided for federal intervention when localities barred minorities from the polls for fear of another prolonged civil rights battle in Congress—one he thought he might lose. Activists, however, forced his hand. Sheriff's deputies and Alabama state troopers beat back voting rights marchers who were leaving Selma for the state capital of Montgomery. Television networks interrupted their programming on the evening of March 7 to show the brutality that soon became known as "Bloody Sunday." Johnson used the opportunity to go before Congress and call for the enactment of legislation he had previously refrained from introducing. He invoked the words of the African-American spiritual as he explained that "really it is all of us, who must overcome the crippling legacy of bigotry and injustice. And we shall overcome." Johnson signed the Voting Rights Act into law in August, a measure that dramatically increased African-American political participation. In Mississippi, for example, black registration rose from less than 7 percent in 1965 to 59 percent in 1968.

For Johnson Congress could not act fast enough. At the beginning of 1965 the president predicted that his opportunity to create the Great Society would be brief. Each month he expected that his popular support would dwindle. Yet even

Johnson might have been surprised at how quickly the consensus that he had built in 1964 and 1965 collapsed during the last three years of his presidency. By 1966 the momentum in Congress behind the Great Society had slackened considerably. Even though the president usually got what he wanted on Capitol Hill, his proposals were generally not as bold or as sweeping as they had been in 1965. And discontent with his leadership increased. In mid-1966 the Gallup poll revealed for the first time that the president's approval rating had dipped below 50 percent. In the elections of 1966, the Republicans made sizable gains, increasing their representation by 47 seats in the House and four in the Senate.

Johnson's troubles occasionally arose from the ambition and innovation of some of his programs, such as the War on Poverty. The primary function of the Office of Economic Opportunity (OEO) was not to fight poverty with income supplements or federal employment. Instead it aimed at opening opportunities and providing skills that could help break the grip of poverty. The Job Corps, for example, furnished vocational training to young people who had left school, while the Work-Experience Program aided unemployed heads of household in finding jobs. Some programs, like Project Head Start, which prepared children from economically deprived families for school, became so successful that few, if any, political figures dared to criticize them. Yet the most innovative activity of the OEO—encouraging the participation of the poor themselves in local community action programs— was also the most controversial. The goal was to empower the poor—to give them some control over their efforts to escape poverty. These programs aroused strong opposition because they often bypassed local welfare agencies or challenged elected city officials. In 1965 the Conference of Mayors criticized community action; Chicago mayor Richard J. Daley, a critical political ally of the president, strongly opposed it. Two California mayors went even further. Sam Yorty of Los Angeles and John Shelley of San Francisco complained that the Community Action Programs were "fostering class struggle."

An even greater problem for Johnson was that Great Society programs raised expectations far beyond their ability to bring about social improvements. The number of people living in poverty declined substantially during the Johnson years,

falling from 19.5 percent of Americans in 1963 to 12.8 percent in 1968. Yet the poverty rate for African Americans, which stood at 34.7 percent in 1968, was far higher than that for whites, which was 10.0 percent. Despite a drop in the number of blacks who endured poverty, the conditions of life in predominantly African-American sections of many large cities hardly seemed changed. In 1966, when Martin Luther King, Jr., began a campaign for improved housing and economic opportunities for blacks in Chicago, he found that squalor and deprivation were commonplace and local authorities were uncooperative. Despite the achievements of the civil rights movement and the president's pledges to sweep away barriers to equal opportunity, strong and persistent racism meant that public services— schools, trash collection, police protection—were inferior or unreliable in Chicago's black neighborhoods. African Americans who tried to move to predominantly white neighborhoods found their ambitions frustrated by landlords, real estate agents, or financial institutions that simply would not rent, sell, or lend to blacks. When King led marches and rallies against segregated housing in Chicago during the summer of 1966, the demonstrators encountered hostile and violent white mobs. King compared the slums in Chicago and other cities to domestic colonies whose residents were "dominated politically, exploited economically, . . . [and] segregated and humiliated at every turn." The president's lofty rhetoric about waging war on poverty and ending discrimination oversimplified the enormous tasks of reconstructing American society in fundamental ways.

A combustible mixture of elevated expectations, frustrated aspirations, and smoldering resentment produced frightening explosions in many American cities. The first major riot occurred in August 1965 in the Watts section of Los Angeles, an overwhelmingly African-American neighborhood. The catalyst was a white police officer's arrest of a black man for a traffic offense. This apparently innocuous incident set off six days of violence that produced 34 deaths and $45 million in property damage. Scores of disturbances occurred in towns and cities across the country during the next two summers. The worst was in Detroit in July 1967, where 43 people died before federal troops could restore order. The president appointed a National Advisory Commission on Civil Disorders to explain the causes of the riots and propose solutions. The commission's report in March 1968 blamed the disturbances on "white racism," which produced "pervasive discrimination and segregation in employment, education and housing" and the growing concentration of African Americans in urban "ghettos, where segregation and poverty converge . . . to destroy opportunity and enforce failure." Despite the Johnson administration's array of social programs, the commission reached the alarming, basic conclusion that "our nation is moving toward two societies, one black, one white—separate and unequal."

Many civil rights leaders, such as King, Roy Wilkins of the NAACP, and Whitney Young, Jr., of the National Urban League, deplored the violence. Yet there were newly prominent African-American leaders who encouraged black resistance to white oppression and advocated self-defense against white violence. The black movement had begun to change at the time it had achieved its great victories with the passage of the Civil Rights Act of 1964 and the Voting Rights Act of 1965. For some members of the Student Nonviolent Coordinating Committee (SNCC), the main reason for a change in goals and tactics was the persistence and brutality of white resistance. In 1964 SNCC had sponsored Freedom Summer, a nonviolent, integrated effort to promote civil rights in Mississippi. Within days, local members of the Ku Klux Klan murdered three SNCC workers—James Chaney, Andrew Goodman, and Michael Schwerner—a frightening harbinger to a summer of bombings and beatings that the SNCC workers endured. The Mississippi Freedom Democratic Party (MFDP), an integrated alternative to the state's segregated regular party, could persuade the president and his advisers to offer it only two at-large seats at the Democratic national convention in Atlantic City in 1964, a compromise that the delegation angrily rejected. "I question America," proclaimed Fannie Lou Hamer, a disillusioned MFDP delegate. For some SNCC members the disillusionment led to rejection of the principle of nonviolence and the goal of integration. By 1967 SNCC had changed into an all-black organization with a new chair, Stokely Carmichael, who called for Black Power.

Black Power was an ambiguous, attractive, and alarming slogan. When Carmichael first popularized Black Power in the summer of 1966, he declared, "I'm not going to beg the white man for anything I deserve, I'm going to take it." Carmichael's assertiveness appealed to African Americans who were tired of waiting for rights, opportunities, or acceptance. He gained support from blacks who believed that they had to build independent power and who shunned cooperation with white leaders and institutions that they considered corrupt, oppressive, or irredeemably racist. Black Power also reflected the thinking of Malcolm X, the charismatic and controversial minister who had left the Nation of Islam shortly before his murder in February 1965. Malcolm X scoffed at civil rights, denounced integration as a manifestation of tokenism, and demanded that blacks take responsibility for their own communities and welfare. Black Power advocates also drew further inspiration from Malcolm X, as they made their slogan a call for black pride, awareness of black history and culture, and acceptance of black values and ideals.

Other groups committed to Black Power, such as the Black Panther Party, gave the slogan revolutionary overtones. Founded in Oakland in late 1966, the Black Panthers compared the condition of African Americans to colonial peoples and called for liberation through revolution, if necessary. Wearing black berets and leather jackets and openly carrying guns (which was legal at the time under California law), the Black Panthers patrolled Oakland streets to monitor police. Their defiant and confrontational actions gained national attention and helped them establish chapters in more than 30 cities by the end of the 1960s. The Black Panthers created a short-lived alliance with Carmichael and his successor as SNCC chair, H. Rap Brown. Brown had told a crowd in Cambridge, Maryland, in August 1967, "to burn this town down." The crowd did just that. Mainstream civil rights leaders denounced Black Power because of its violent or separatist connotations. Many fearful white citizens blamed Black Power supporters for riots in the streets. Whatever its exact meaning, Black Power represented a rejection of the liberal consensus.

Black Power contributed to a conservative backlash. The riots in Watts, Detroit, and other cities persuaded some Americans that law and order was disintegrating and that Black Power was both cause and symptom. Many whites—including some who had supported the efforts of the civil rights movement to end legal segregation—complained that African Americans were demanding too much, too quickly. Their reaction to the denunciations of white society and growing violence was in some sense like Johnson's when he learned about the outbreak of the Watts riot only five days after the signing of the Voting Rights

Act. "How could it be?" the president wondered. "Is the world topsy-turvy?"

Yet conservatives also blamed the Johnson administration for the social and racial turmoil. The unrest in inner cities helped to create the false impression that the War on Poverty was mainly a program to help African Americans, not a broad assault on deprivation in both rural and urban areas. Critics repeatedly alleged that Great Society programs benefited the few at the expense of the many, unlike earlier liberal programs, such as Social Security or unemployment insurance, that provided widespread benefits and were extremely popular. They also were quick to seize on the examples—and there were many of them—of the inadequacies, failures, or scandals in the War on Poverty and other social welfare programs. Public support for the Great Society plummeted during 1966. By the end of the year, according to the Gallup poll, Americans with an unfavorable view of Great Society programs outnumbered those with a positive opinion by 44 percent to 32 percent. The Johnson administration's first steps toward affirmative action in 1965 persuaded some whites that minority gains would come at their expense. Resentment also festered over the growth of the federal government—the transfer of power from Main Street to Pennsylvania Avenue—that gave federal officials or judges new authority to affect local schools, businesses, and social practices. Populist politicians began to exploit—and intensify—the resentment against "big government" that allegedly helped minorities while ignoring the interests of hard-working, law-abiding citizens. None was more successful than George C. Wallace, the governor of Alabama, who eventually proved that his populist polemics against demonstrators, militants, and liberal bureaucrats resonated with many working and middle-class voters outside the South.

The Supreme Court was another target of growing conservative criticism. Earl Warren's appointment as chief justice in 1953 marked the beginning of a period of exceptional judicial activism. The Court produced landmark rulings beginning in 1954 with the case of *Brown v. Board of Education* in which the justices unanimously declared that racial segregation in public schools was unconstitutional. During the early 1960s the Court banned mandatory prayer in public schools and required the reapportionment of congressional and state legislative districts according to the principle of "one person, one vote." In the area of the rights of

suspects in criminal investigations and trials, the Warren Court also broke new ground. A majority of the justices declared in the 1963 case of *Gideon v. Wainwright* that all criminal defendants had a constitutional right to an attorney. Three years later, the Court rendered one of its most important and familiar rulings in *Miranda v. Arizona*, which specified that police officers had to advise suspects they arrested in criminal cases of their right to remain silent and to have legal counsel. Warren maintained that the Court's actions reflected a view that government must be fair and follow procedures that insured the protection of the constitutional rights of all citizens. Yet many of these decisions aroused considerable controversy, including charges that the Court had gone too far in interfering with law enforcement efforts to bring criminals to justice. The most extreme opposition came from the John Birch Society, which organized a national campaign to impeach Earl Warren. While few Americans supported such a drastic step, many complained by the mid-1960s about activist judges who allegedly made rather than interpreted the law and whose power extended into local communities more directly and forcefully than ever before.

While domestic problems undermined the president's popularity, the Vietnam War was the biggest reason for the collapse of the broad support behind Johnson's leadership. Johnson turned what had been primarily an advisory mission since the creation of South Vietnam in 1954 into a major U.S. combat effort. He did so with an odd combination of reluctance and zeal. Johnson frequently expressed doubts about whether South Vietnam merited a major U.S. military commitment and whether one could succeed. Yet at the same time, he spurned diplomatic alternatives, dismissed and even ridiculed the counsel of advisers skeptical of U.S. bombing and the dispatch of troops, and tried to disguise his choices that deepened U.S. engagement in the hope of averting domestic dissent. The result was both disastrous and ironic: an onslaught of criticism of Johnson's leadership and of liberal politics more generally and the erosion of the Great Society—the programs Johnson prized more than any others—as Americans discovered to their bewilderment and distress that they could neither win the war in Vietnam nor the battle for social reform at home.

Johnson insisted that his policies in Southeast Asia continued and extended those of his predecessors —particularly Kennedy—and, to some extent, he was right. Truman had decided that Indochina was a "key area" whose loss to communism might bring the fall of other Southeast Asian dominoes. Eisenhower had committed U.S. prestige and power to the survival of South Vietnam and taken the lead in the creation of the Southeast Asia Treaty Organization (SEATO). Kennedy had dramatically enlarged U.S. aid to South Vietnam and increased the number of U.S. military advisers from 700 to 16,000. He had also shown no interest in negotiations as a solution to the expanding war in South Vietnam. It was easy for Johnson to believe that he had inherited a commitment to preserve the independence of South Vietnam. He did not have to think long or hard to reject the options of "pulling out" or pursuing negotiations for the neutralization of South Vietnam in favor of "putting in more U.S. forces" as "the only realistic alternative." Johnson augmented the U.S. military advisory force by more than 40 percent during the first year of his presidency. He also selected General William C. Westmoreland to direct the U.S. military effort and help reverse the gains that the National Liberation Front (NLF) was making in its guerrilla war against the South Vietnamese government. In early 1964 he also authorized intensified pressure against North Vietnam, including a program of covert operations, in retaliation for Hanoi's growing support of the NLF with troops and supplies. Johnson believed that all these actions, when compared to Truman's, Eisenhower's, and Kennedy's policies, amounted to "more of the same" and "doing the right thing."

Johnson also had his own distinctive reasons for taking strong action to defend South Vietnam. He tended to personalize political and international obligations, considering that they amounted to tests of his own resolve or effectiveness. Failing to meet the challenge of preserving South Vietnam, he thought, would carry severe political consequences. Johnson's greatest ambition as president was the establishment of the Great Society. Failure in Vietnam, however, could prevent him from securing his coveted reforms. Johnson remembered the vitriolic criticism that Truman had "lost China" following the victory of Mao Zedong's revolution in 1949. Charges of "losing Vietnam," he reasoned, would be fatal to his hopes for the Great Society. He used a crude, sexist analogy to explain the problem to his biographer, Doris Kearns. Johnson contrasted that "bitch of a war on the other side of the world" to "the woman I really loved—the Great Society." The two, however, were intimately connected. "If

I . . . let the Communists take over South Vietnam," he predicted, "then I would be seen as a coward and . . . would . . . find it impossible to accomplish anything for anybody anywhere." Yet if he made a major military effort in Southeast Asia that drained U.S. resources, he risked losing "everything at home." Striking the balance was critical.

Even as the Johnson administration increased U.S. aid and deepened U.S. involvement, the results were disappointing. McNamara returned from one of his frequent trips to Saigon in May 1964 and reported that the situation had worsened since his last visit. The NLF, he found, had increased the territory under its control and "held the initiative in military action." The South Vietnamese government was "fragmented" and beset with fundamental problems.

Johnson, too, was concerned about the prospects for success in South Vietnam, as we know from an important source of information that became available beginning in the late 1990s. The president recorded many of his telephone conversations, and the Johnson Library began to release those tapes three decades after the president left office. The tapes revealed facets of the president's personality and leadership, including his remarkable ability to secure consent, cooperation, or compliance, and his mastery of the intricacies of policies, that few Americans saw in his speeches and public appearances. The tapes also provide glimpses into the president's private assessments of issues and policies, and they show that he was deeply pessimistic about the war in Vietnam even as he deepened U.S. involvement. In a telephone conversation with McGeorge Bundy at the end of May 1964, the president declared. "I don't think it's worth fighting for, and I don't think we can get out. It's just the biggest damn mess I ever saw." Johnson insisted that SEATO obligated the United States to protect South Vietnam and so worried that withdrawal would undermine the nation's credibility by calling into question U.S. fidelity to treaties. In a conversation with Senator Richard Russell (D-Ga.) only a few minutes before his talk with McNamara, Johnson raised the specter of impeaching a president "that would run out." Yet sending in troops, he confided, "makes the chills run up my back." Russell offered no solution to the dilemma Johnson confronted and little solace. He warned the president that committing U.S. combat troops would be the start of "the most expensive venture this country ever went into."

During the campaign of 1964 Johnson was determined to prove that he could meet Communist challenges in Southeast Asia without bringing the United States any closer to war. He maintained that the retaliatory air raids that he ordered against North Vietnam in response to the Tonkin Gulf incidents were "limited and fitting. . . . We still seek no wider war." During the autumn of 1964 national security officials considered proposals for stronger U.S. military action, including sustained bombing of North Vietnam, but Johnson told voters that he did not want to get engulfed in an Asian war. He declared in a campaign speech at the University of Akron, "We are not about to send American boys 9 or 10,000 miles away from home to do what Asian boys ought to be doing for themselves."

Yet during the winter of 1964–65 Johnson made decisions that committed U.S. forces to war. Johnson's advisers provided frequent and alarming reports of continuing NLF military gains and chronic weaknesses in the Saigon government. The South Vietnamese were "not winning the war," Westmoreland bluntly asserted. "The conduct of the government," he added, was "characterized by inefficiency, corruption, disinterest, and lack of motivation." Westmoreland counseled caution about deepening U.S. commitments until the Saigon government had gained some stability. Yet by late 1964 many of Johnson's advisers insisted that the continuing weakness of the government made U.S. military action imperative. Although they did not expect the South Vietnamese government to "collapse immediately," they were keenly aware that it was "losing [the] game." A working group of the National Security Council proposed a graduated campaign of bombing North Vietnam, one that could signal U.S. determination to prevent a Communist victory. This "graduated squeeze" could be adjusted to intensify the pressure on Hanoi to reduce its support of the NLF guerrillas and negotiate an end to the war in the south.

Despite his continuing doubts about whether support of the Saigon government was worth sending "Johnson City boys out to die," the president approved his advisers' recommendations in early December. The first step involved bombing attacks against the supply routes in Laos that Hanoi used to send troops and military equipment to the NLF. A month later a second phase would begin, as U.S.

planes attacked targets in North Vietnam. Johnson hoped that the Saigon government would gain some stability by the beginning of this second stage. Yet even if the South Vietnamese were not able to do so, Johnson was prepared to authorize the bombing raids against North Vietnam, hoping that such escalation would provide greater incentive for the Saigon leadership to solve its political problems. Johnson insisted that his advisers take special care to preserve the secrecy of his December decisions. He joked that his policy for dealing with leaks would be "shoot at sunrise." In February 1965 the president ordered the beginning of the second phase of the escalation, justifying the commencement of bombing of North Vietnamese targets as retaliation for Communist attacks against a U.S. base at Pleiku. By early March, the bombing had become a sustained campaign, known as Rolling Thunder. On March 8 the first declared U.S. combat troops—two battalions of marines—came ashore to guard the U.S. air base at Danang.

Johnson made his decisions to commit U.S. forces to war even though there were was no strong or urgent political pressure to take action in South Vietnam. Some advisers, including Vice President Hubert H. Humphrey and Undersecretary of State George Ball, vigorously opposed escalation. So did Senate Majority Leader Mike Mansfield (D-Mont.), who had made several trips to South Vietnam and possessed considerable knowledge of Southeast Asian matters. Johnson listened to this skeptical counsel, sometimes with patience in the case of Ball, sometimes with irritation and even contempt, as in the case of Humphrey. Polls suggested that the American public was divided and uncertain about what to do in Southeast Asia, but most people did not consider Vietnam a major issue. Important allies counseled caution. French president Charles de Gaulle favored neutralization. The British and Canadian governments did not think that South Vietnam merited a major U.S. military commitment. Despite these international reservations, Johnson insisted that the failure to meet supposed obligations under SEATO would weaken U.S. credibility in the eyes of allies and adversaries. Despite his smashing victory in the November election, he feared a domestic backlash if South Vietnam collapsed without an intensified U.S. effort to prevent its defeat.

Johnson chose war in South Vietnam in part to preserve the political influence that would enable him to secure Great Society legislation from Congress. Yet he also recognized that frank and vigorous discussion about the war could jeopardize public support for domestic political reform. Johnson, for example, worried about "the psychological impact" of the deployment of marine combat troops. In a telephone conversation in early March 1965 the president asked McNamara whether the administration could announce the dispatch of "security battalions" instead of combat troops, but the secretary protested that there would be accusations of "falsifying the story." The president and his principal national security advisers, however, continued to insist in public statements that there had been no change in U.S. policy or objectives even though U.S. pilots and troops were fighting and dying in Southeast Asia.

The bombing of North Vietnam and the deployment of the marines quickly produced irresistible pressures for further escalation. At a news conference on July 28, 1965, the president announced that he had approved an immediate increase in U.S. troop strength to 125,000. "Additional forces will be needed later," he declared, "and they will be sent as requested." In discussing the growing war in Southeast Asia, Johnson emphasized that it was imperative "that our leaders speak with candor." In some ways, however, Johnson fell short of his own standard. Before his news conference, the president had approved an increase in U.S. forces in South Vietnam to 175,000 by the end of the year, but decided not to reveal that decision. Despite his reference to the need for additional deployments, he did not disclose that members of the Joint Chiefs of Staff had told him that success in Vietnam might require the commitment of hundreds of thousands of combat forces for several years. Johnson also announced his decisions in an afternoon press conference rather than a televised evening address in hopes of minimizing public discussion of the significance of his actions. This tendency to provide partial, misleading, or excessively optimistic information about administration policies had already produced charges of a credibility gap, a problem that intensified as more U.S. troops went to South Vietnam.

Westmoreland's desire to use heavy firepower and sophisticated military technology as keys to success on the battlefield led to a steady demand for more troops and equipment. By the end of 1966 385,000 U.S. forces were engaged in Southeast Asia. A year later troop strength stood at 486,000. U.S.

officials in Saigon and Washington emphasized progress, and many battles indeed produced success for American or South Vietnamese troops. Yet despite the steady increase in U.S. forces, the enemy held the initiative in the war. Nor had the bombing prevented an increase in the movement of enemy soldiers and supplies from North to South Vietnam. Occasional pauses in the air attacks did not produce negotiations that promised to halt the escalation or settle the conflict.

Maintaining public and congressional support for the war quickly became a major problem for the Johnson administration. In July 1965 only a handful of congressional critics spoke out against the growing commitment of U.S. forces. By early 1966 however, Senator J. William Fulbright (D-Ark.), the chair of the Foreign Relations Committee, openly questioned administration policies. In February Fulbright scheduled televised hearings that allowed several respected figures with long experience in national security affairs, such as Soviet expert George F. Kennan and retired general James J. Gavin, to criticize the administration's disproportionate investment in a distant nation with minor strategic significance or the effectiveness of Westmoreland's strategy of attrition. By early 1967 there were more skeptical voices on Capitol Hill, including senators Eugene McCarthy (D-Minn.), Frank Church (D-Idaho), George McGovern (D-S.Dak.), Robert F. Kennedy (D-N.Y.), and John Sherman Cooper (R-Ky.). Johnson also faced criticism from influential conservatives, such as Senator John Stennis (D-Miss.), who held hearings in an Armed Services subcommittee that he chaired that gave military leaders an opportunity to call for an even more powerful bombing campaign against North Vietnam. Polls showed that public support for administration policies steadily dwindled. By the middle of 1966 critics and supporters of Johnson's handling of the war had almost equal strength. By August 1967 those who disapproved of the president's policies in Vietnam outnumbered supporters by a margin of 54 to 32 percent. Like the critics on Capitol Hill, discontented citizens were divided between hawks and doves. While some people favored greater efforts to secure a negotiated settlement, others advocated increased military efforts to win the war. Johnson recognized the extent of his political difficulties when he told a group of educators in September 1967, "I am in deep trouble."

The growing controversy over the war and its mounting expense weakened support for the Great Society. In his State of the Union address in January 1966, the president proclaimed, "This nation is mighty enough, its society is healthy enough, its people are strong enough, to pursue our goals in the rest of the world while still building a Great Society here at home." Yet despite this prediction, appropriations for Great Society programs diminished as the cost of the war mounted. Johnson, at times, tried to manipulate budget figures to strengthen his case that Americans could afford "guns and butter." Yet he could not conceal the deepening budget deficits, aggravated, in part, by his own reluctance to seek to seek a tax increase to pay the costs of the war. The difficulties of financing antipoverty or education programs only increased liberal criticism of Johnson's war policies. Deploring the war expenses that were draining funds from "programs of social uplift," Martin Luther King, Jr., condemned the president's Vietnam policies in an influential speech in April 1967. King's criticism enraged the president, who insisted that the civil rights leader had no business discussing national security policy. But King only stated what the president knew all too well: that the escalating U.S. involvement in Vietnam, which the president had originally hoped would protect the Great Society, was instead harming it.

The president tried to diminish the mounting criticism by launching a major public relations campaign in the last half of 1967 to show that the United States was indeed making progress in Vietnam. Johnson insisted that "the administration's greatest weakness was its inability to get over the complete story about the war." He admonished his staff to "sell our product" and "get a better story to the American people." More than ever before, progress became the theme in news briefings in Saigon and Washington. The high point of the Progress Campaign occurred in November 1967, when Westmoreland gave a speech before the National Press Club in Washington in which he proclaimed that "we have reached the point when the end begins to come into view." If progress in the war continued at its current pace, Westmoreland said, U.S. troops could start coming home within the next two years. Such predictions helped Johnson reclaim some support in the polls, although more Americans continued to oppose rather than support administration policies in South Vietnam.

The Progress Campaign, though, did little, if anything, to diminish antiwar demonstrations. The antiwar movement was always diverse and frequently fragmented. Liberal organizations, such as the Committee for a Sane Nuclear Policy (SANE), organized rallies to press for a negotiated end to the war. Radical groups, such as the Students for Democratic Society, condemned what they said was an imperialistic or counterrevolutionary U.S. war and demanded the unilateral withdrawal of American troops. Although always a small minority, radical activists became more numerous and conspicuous following the escalation of the U.S. war effort as they organized campaigns to halt troop trains or encourage draft resistance. Much of this radical criticism called attention to the alleged larger failings of liberalism and maintained that the Vietnam War was a symptom of a political system that concentrated power in elite decision makers who put the interests of defense contractors or large corporate enterprises concerned with overseas markets ahead of the social needs of the American people. On October 21, 1967, 50,000 demonstrators, including many radical critics, conducted a March on the Pentagon to "confront the war makers." Johnson publicly defended the right to dissent, yet privately was certain that the protesters were encouraging the enemy to continue to resist in the expectation that public support for U.S. involvement in Vietnam would eventually collapse.

In early 1968 public support for Johnson's war policies did collapse during the Tet offensive, when the North Vietnamese and NLF launched their boldest attacks of the war. Enemy troops struck at 150 locations, including both large cities and isolated hamlets. Even the U.S. embassy in Saigon and the South Vietnamese presidential palace came under assault. In most cases, U.S. and South Vietnamese forces regained lost territory within hours or days and inflicted enormous casualties on enemy troops. In Hue and Khe Sanh, however, hard fighting lasted for weeks. The Tet offensive, which came while progress was still the main theme in the administration's public statements about the war, was a hard blow to Johnson's battered credibility. CBS news anchor Walter Cronkite spoke for many of his perplexed fellow citizens when he reacted to the news of the Tet offensive by asking, "What the hell is going on? I thought that we were winning this war." Polls showed a sharp decline in public approval for the president's handling of the Vietnam War. Critics outnumbered supporters by a margin of 63 to 28 percent.

The Tet offensive produced a major reconsideration of the Johnson administration's Vietnam policies. Even though he maintained that U.S. and South Vietnam forces had inflicted a stunning defeat on the enemy, Westmoreland asked for 206,000 additional troops to regain the initiative in the war. Westmoreland's request precipitated an intensive debate within the administration. Months earlier, McNamara had concluded that U.S. strategy was not working. The war, he believed, had reached a stalemate; further increases in bombing or combat troops would only raise the costs of war without breaking the deadlock, as the enemy could match any U.S. escalation. Johnson, however, rejected McNamara's counsel to stabilize the U.S. war effort in late 1967. Disenchanted and weary, McNamara left the administration at the end of February 1968 to direct the World Bank. The new secretary of defense, Clark Clifford, had previously supported Johnson's Vietnam policies. But in his first days in his new position, he reassessed his views, as he found that the Joint Chiefs of Staff could offer no assurances that even this proposed major increase in U.S. troop strength could assure a successful conclusion to the war. An international economic crisis that had weakened the dollar also made Clifford and other advisers worry that the cost of more troops would aggravate the financial problems that the war had helped cause. Other national security officials warned, too, that U.S. resources were spread too thin—that the huge commitment in Vietnam was creating vulnerabilities in other locations. The North Korean seizure of a reconnaissance ship, the USS *Pueblo*, just a week before the Tet offensive and the incarceration of its crew seemed to show that the United States had reached—or exceeded—the limits of its power.

Political considerations also affected administration strategic calculations. In late 1967 Senator Eugene McCarthy had announced his intention to run against Johnson as an antiwar candidate for the Democratic nomination for president. On March 13, McCarthy won 42 percent of the vote in the New Hampshire primary. Even though Johnson won the primary, McCarthy had exceeded expectations with his strong showing. Three days later a more formidable candidate, Senator Robert F. Kennedy, entered the race for the nomination. Johnson still believed that he could secure the nom-

ination, but he knew that he would face what might be a difficult and divisive contest. He could not command a consensus in his own party, much less in the country at large. As early as November 1967 Johnson had confided to Westmoreland that he was thinking of retiring at the end of his term. He worried about health problems, including how his family history suggested that he might not live another four years as president. The political strife over the administration's Vietnam policies surely moved Johnson closer to withdrawing from the race for the nomination. An additional impetus came from a group of senior advisers, commonly known as the "Wise Men," who met in late March to review the situation in Vietnam. While they had previously endorsed the president's policies, they now advised that "we can no longer do the job we set out to do in the time we have left and we must begin to take steps to disengage." This counsel was a bitter pill for the president to swallow. "Everybody is recommending surrender," he complained.

On the evening of March 31 Johnson finally reported the results of the administration's reassessment in a televised speech. Although he took no steps toward immediate disengagement, the president announced new restrictions on the bombing campaign in the hope that North Vietnam would reciprocate by agreeing to negotiations. And then the president added a conclusion that he had discussed with only a handful of advisers and friends. "With our hopes . . . for peace in the balance every day, I do not believe that I should devote an hour or a day of my time to any personal partisan causes," Johnson insisted. "Accordingly, I shall not seek, and I will not accept, the nomination of my party for another term as your president."

Johnson's announcement was one of a series of stunning and unsettling developments during the next several months. Soon after Johnson's withdrawal, Vice President Humphrey announced his candidacy for the Democratic presidential nomination. While McCarthy and Kennedy battled in the primaries, Humphrey concentrated on securing support in local and state party caucuses and conventions. Kennedy scored a critical victory in the California primary on June 4, but, minutes after speaking to jubilant supporters, an assassin mortally wounded him. Kennedy's murder was the second major assassination during the spring, occurring only two months after the death of Martin Luther King, Jr., in Memphis in early April. Those two murders—as well as the earlier killings of President Kennedy, civil rights leader Medgar Evers, and Malcolm X—led many people to wonder whether they lived in a "sick society" where violence and extremism rather than debate and elections settled political differences.

The Democratic National Convention in Chicago produced more violence and further anxieties. Antiwar activists had been preparing for months to protest the administration's Vietnam policies. Mayor Richard J. Daley and the Chicago police were determined to prevent any disruptions. Confrontations occurred each day in the city's parks and streets between protesters and police. The violence intensified the disputes inside the convention, as delegates heatedly debated the position they would take on the Vietnam War. Peace talks had begun soon after the president's March 31 speech, but they stalled over procedural issues and a North Vietnamese demand that the administration stop all bombing as a prerequisite to substantive talks. The McCarthy delegates, with some quiet encouragement from Humphrey forces, favored a complete bombing halt and intensified efforts to secure meaningful negotiations. But behind the scenes, Johnson used his influence to insure that the convention instead approved a plank that endorsed administration policies. Humphrey won the nomination as television networks showed scenes of the strife outside the convention. Most Americans blamed the antiwar activists for the trouble, even though an official investigation later concluded that a "police riot" had occurred, as law enforcement authorities exceeded their own guidelines about the use of force. Many Americans, too, thought the disorder both inside and outside the convention hall suggested that the Democrats were too disorganized and divided to govern.

The Republicans once again selected former vice president Richard Nixon as their candidate. Nixon called for "order in America," a message that won considerable support among those tired of demonstrations against the war and urban riots. He also said he would speak for "the great majority of Americans, the forgotten Americans, the non-shouters, the non-demonstrators . . . [who] work and save and pay their taxes." Capitalizing on the conservative discontent with Great Society programs that had shifted power from states and communities to the federal government, Nixon maintained that government social welfare policies had produced "an ugly harvest of frustrations, violence, and failure." He said that he favored new programs that gave everybody an "equal chance" without creating continuing dependency. Nixon also capitalized on the widespread disenchantment with the war and on Humphrey's association with Johnson's Vietnam policies, while suggesting, without specifics, that he would find a way to win the peace.

A third candidate, former Alabama governor George C. Wallace, also commanded substantial support. Early in the fall campaign, polls showed that Wallace might win 20 percent of the popular vote. His base remained in the South, and his strongest issue was dissatisfaction with an increasingly powerful federal government that promoted civil rights. Yet Wallace appealed to working and middle-class voters outside the South who thought that federal programs helped minorities at the expense of the majority. He made strident and sensational criticisms of faceless bureaucrats and "limousine liberals" who followed the ideas of "pointy-headed" intellectuals to engage in objectionable social engineering. Wallace said he spoke for the forgotten Americans, who were hard-working, law-abiding, and patriotic and who were tired of protests and riots.

The shadow of Vietnam hung over the campaign, especially as Nixon's early lead over Humphrey dwindled. In late September, Humphrey himself called for a complete bombing halt in hopes that it would get the peace talks moving. Johnson bridled over what he considered the vice president's disloyalty. But only a month later, he too was prepared to take the step that Humphrey had called "an acceptable risk for peace." On October 31 Johnson declared that he believed that the North Vietnamese were prepared to start productive talks and so he was halting the bombing. The president's dramatic announcement shifted many votes to Humphrey in the campaign's final days. But still the vice president fell short. Nixon, who remembered the pain of losing a close election in 1960, now felt the exhilaration of a narrow, but clear victory.

If Johnson had any hopes that his final weeks in office would produce a breakthrough at the peace table, those expectations vanished quickly. Negotiations in late 1968 indicated the depth of disagreement rather than the prospect of settlement. More than a half million U.S. troops remained in Southeast Asia. Casualties remained high; the talk about progress in the war a year earlier was a bitter memory.

Johnson left office remembered more for the war he said he despised than for the social programs that were so close to his heart. In March 1965, when he asked Congress to pass the Voting Rights bill, Johnson discussed what he hoped would be his legacy. "I do not want to be the president who built empires, or sought grandeur, or extended dominion," he declared. "I want to be the President who educated young children to the wonders of their world . . . who helped to feed the hungry . . . who helped the poor to find their own way and who protected the right of every citizen to vote in every election. I want to be the President who helped to end hatred among his fellow men and who promoted love among the people of all races and all regions and all parties. I want to be the President who helped to end war among the brothers of this earth." These lofty aspirations—as well as the failure to achieve them—were indeed what the Johnson years were all about.

# A

## Abel, I(orwith) W(ilbur)

**(1908–1987)** *president, United Steelworkers of America*

Born on August 11, 1908, in Magnolia, Ohio, Abel began work in the steel mills at age 17 and later helped start the first Steelworkers Organizing Committee (later renamed United Steelworkers of America) local at Canton Timkin Roller Bearing in 1936. The next year he was appointed a union staff representative and in 1942 was elected district director for the Canton, Ohio, area. When David J. McDonald succeeded Philip Murray as president of the United Steelworkers of America (USW) in 1952, Abel stepped into McDonald's old post as the union's secretary-treasurer. During the next 12 years Abel loyally served McDonald as USW second in command.

In the early 1960s Abel and other steelworkers grew increasingly critical of McDonald's leadership, which by late 1964 had failed to win an across-the-board wage increase in more than three years. USW district directors were also critical of McDonald's centralization of union power and his use of a small labor-management "Human Relations Committee" to secretly negotiate new contract settlements without the participation of the full USW executive board.

In December 1964 Abel announced his candidacy for the USW presidency. Running with district directors Walter J. Burke and Joseph Moloney (candidates for secretary-treasurer and vice president, respectively), Abel charged McDonald with "tuxedo trade unionism" because of his friendly relationships with some steel industry leaders. Abel promised "hard-nosed, arms-length bargaining" and a renewed rank-and-file role in union policy making. His insurgent campaign was supported by about half the USW district directors, including Joseph Germano, powerful head of the Chicago area's District 31, the largest in the union. Abel also won strong support from many black USW members and from another important but underrepresented "minority" in the union, the Canadian steelworkers. A hard fought two-month campaign culminated in unionwide balloting on February 9, 1965. In perhaps the most important ouster of an incumbent union president since the early postwar years, Abel defeated McDonald by some 8,000 votes out of 606,000 cast.

In the summer of 1965 Abel became embroiled in wage negotiations that involved the White House. The union had planned a strike for the end of August unless its wage demands were met. Since the 1959 steel strike was considered largely responsible for the 1960–61 Eisenhower recession, a nervous President Johnson interceded. Johnson, who held Abel in high regard, pressured both sides to compromise for the good of the country, and eventually obtained a settlement that gave the workers an increase of 40 cents an hour over three years without sparking a price hike. An enthusiastic Abel was effusive in his praise of Johnson's efforts, and wrote him saying, "We certainly think of you as our president."

During the first half of 1967 Abel helped negotiate the merger into the USW of the 40,000-member Mine, Mill and Smelter Workers Union, which had been expelled from the Congress of Industrial Organizations in 1949 on charges of Communist domination. With 80 percent of all nonferrous metal miners now in one union for the first time, the USW struck western copper mines July 15, 1967, in

**1**

what turned out to be a protracted nine-month conflict involving 37,000 union members, resolved only after federal intervention in the spring of 1968. The strike generated widespread support for the USW within the labor movement and helped Abel pass the union's first dues increase in 12 years at a special convention in March 1968.

During McDonald's presidency the USW had become somewhat aloof from other unions in the AFL-CIO. Abel sought to end this self-imposed isolation and move the union in a liberal direction, "into the mainstream of American labor." He spoke at the Americans for Democratic Action (ADA) convention in April 1965 and invited liberal union presidents A. PHILIP RANDOLPH and WALTER REUTHER to address the USW convention in September 1966. Abel also introduced a strong civil rights resolution at the convention and the next year served on the National Commission on Civil Disorders chaired by Illinois governor OTTO KERNER.

In the acrimonious dispute between Reuther and AFL-CIO president GEORGE MEANY over foreign policy issues, Abel sided with Meany. With Meany's approval President Johnson appointed Abel a member of the U.S. delegation to the United Nations in September 1967. Abel supported the president's conduct of the war in Vietnam and resigned from the ADA national board in February 1968 after that organization endorsed Senator EUGENE MCCARTHY (D-Minn.) for president. Four days after Johnson's decision not to run for reelection on March 31, Abel endorsed Vice President HUBERT HUMPHREY for the Democratic presidential nomination. In California Abel ordered local steelworker officials not to support Senator ROBERT F. KENNEDY (D-N.Y.) in the May primary. During the fall, sustained USW support for Humphrey helped the vice president carry Pennsylvania in the general election. Thereafter Abel remained an important labor advocate man in Democratic Party councils.

In 1968 and 1971 Abel signed collective bargaining agreements in basic steel without a strike. However, the settlements were preceded by massive company stockpiling and followed by widespread layoffs. To end this boom and bust cycle, Abel signed in March 1973 an Experimental Negotiating Agreement, which provided for binding arbitration of unresolved national contract issues, thus precluding industrywide strikes for the life of the four-year agreement. On January 10, 1977, Abel was rewarded for his lifetime of service with the Presidential Medal of Freedom, at the same ceremony where LADY BIRD JOHNSON received hers. He died in Malvern, Ohio, on August 10, 1987.

## Abernathy, Ralph D(avid)

(1926–1990) *secretary-treasurer, vice president, and president, Southern Christian Leadership Conference*

Abernathy, born on March 11, 1926, in Linden, Alabama, grew up in Marengo County, where his parents owned a 500-acre farm. He was ordained a Baptist minister in 1948, received a B.S. from Alabama State College in 1950 and an M.A. in sociology from Atlanta University in 1951. In that year Abernathy was named pastor of the First Baptist Church in Montgomery, Alabama, and he developed a close friendship with MARTIN LUTHER KING, JR., after King became pastor at the city's Dexter Avenue Baptist Church in 1954. The two ministers helped organize the historic Montgomery bus boycott. When King was chosen to lead the protest in December 1955, Abernathy emerged as his chief adviser and aide. In 1957 King was elected president and Abernathy secretary-treasurer of the Southern Christian Leadership Conference (SCLC), an organization they helped establish to further nonviolent direct action in the South. In 1961 Abernathy relocated to Atlanta, where he became vice president at large of the SCLC.

Beginning in March 1964 the SCLC supported a desegregation effort by the black community in St. Augustine, Florida. Abernathy was arrested on June 11 with King and 16 other protesters when the group demanded service at a segregated motel restaurant in the city. SCLC subsequently launched a campaign focused on Selma, Alabama, to secure voting rights for blacks. Abernathy joined many of the almost daily marches in Selma in January and February 1965 and was arrested with King on February 1, when they led a march to the county courthouse. He helped organize and was a participant in the famous march from Selma to Montgomery, which began on March 21, aided by President Johnson's decision to federalize the Alabama National Guard for their protection.

In June 1967 the Supreme Court upheld the contempt of court convictions of King, Abernathy, and six other ministers resulting from the 1963 Birmingham demonstrations. While serving their five-day prison terms beginning on October 30,

King discussed with Abernathy and other aides a plan to bring an interracial coalition of the poor to Washington to pressure the federal government into enacting far-reaching antipoverty legislation. Abernathy helped plan this Poor People's Campaign over the next few months. On April 4 King and Abernathy were in Memphis planning a march with other SCLC officials when King was murdered by a sniper while standing on the balcony of his motel room.

The day after King's assassination Abernathy was named his successor as president of the SCLC. He announced that the organization's first task would be to carry out the march King had planned in support of the virtually all-black Memphis sanitation workers union. A giant march occurred on April 8, and the strike was settled eight days later. That same month, the FBI opened an investigation into Abernathy's personal life that continued until 1974.

Promising that the SCLC would be "more militant than ever" while continuing to use nonviolent methods, Abernathy also went forward with the Poor People's Campaign planned by King. For three days beginning April 29, Abernathy led an interracial "delegation of 100" in conferences with congressional leaders and cabinet members in Washington to present the grievances and demands of the poor. The first group of nine caravans of poor people arrived in Washington on May 13 and began setting up an encampment called "Resurrection City" in Potomac Park near the Lincoln Memorial. Over the next month groups of poor persons attended sessions of

Ralph Abernathy (right) and Martin Luther King, Jr., at a press conference in Baltimore, 1965 *(Library of Congress, Prints and Photographs Division)*

Congress and committee hearings and demonstrated outside the headquarters of various government departments and agencies. President Johnson, however, refused to meet with Abernathy, even when aides suggested inviting him and CORETTA KING to the White House for breakfast, and ordered his aides to avoid promising generous federal aid, so as not to be seen as rewarding such disruptive protest.

The campaign showed signs of insufficient organization and disunity among staff leaders, and Resurrection City, which held 2,500 people at its peak, was plagued by inadequate facilities and some incidents of violence and crime. A Solidarity Day march on June 19 brought 50,000 supporters of the campaign to Washington. On June 23 the Interior Department refused to extend the permit for Resurrection City, and the next day the Washington police closed the encampment. Abernathy was arrested the same day while leading a demonstration on the Capitol grounds, and he remained in jail until July 13.

The Poor People's Campaign did secure an expanded food distribution program, changes in welfare eligibility requirements and new provisions for participation of the poor in local operations of several government agencies. But the campaign, as Abernathy admitted, had failed in its major goal of getting Congress "to move meaningfully against the problem of poverty" by adopting legislation for jobs, low income housing and a guaranteed annual income for the unemployed. Abernathy announced the end of the Washington phase of the campaign on July 16. In August he opened a new phase, leading demonstrations by poor people at the Republican National Convention in Miami Beach and the Democratic National Convention in Chicago.

Abernathy and the SCLC continued to emphasize the problems of poverty and unemployment over the next several years. He was also active in the antiwar movement, speaking at numerous peace rallies and marches. Abernathy resigned from the SCLC in 1977, returning to Atlanta as a Baptist minister. He died in Atlanta on April 17, 1990.

## Abrams, Creighton W(illiams)
(1914–1974) *commander, U.S. Military Assistance Command*

Abrams, who was born on September 15, 1914, in Springfield, Massachusetts, graduated from West Point in 1936. During World War II he distinguished himself as a tank commander, whom General

George Patton considered the best in the U.S. Third Army. He served in Korea in 1953 and 1954 and directed the federal troops that were put on alert in the South to prevent racial violence in the early 1960s.

President Johnson appointed Abrams deputy commander of the U.S. Military Assistance Command in South Vietnam in April 1967. One month later Abrams and presidential assistant ROBERT W. KOMER assumed responsibility for the South Vietnamese rural pacification program. By that time the program—originally designed to provide protection from Communist attack and give economic, social, and medical aid to the countryside—almost exclusively stressed local security. Under the plan large numbers of rural Vietnamese were moved to safe military areas. Critics estimated that the program resulted in the dislocation of over 2 million people.

In June 1968 Abrams succeeded WILLIAM WESTMORELAND as commander of the half-million American troops stationed in South Vietnam. Abrams's handling of the war was dictated in large measure by Johnson's March 1968 decision not to grant the military's request for substantial troop reinforcements and seek negotiations. Peace talks began in May 1968.

Abrams largely abandoned Westmoreland's use of large-scale "search-and-destroy" missions, and, instead, encouraged company-sized operations with 150 men or fewer. He also moved U.S. troops closer to cities and inhabited areas, protecting territory and people rather than sending them out into the countryside to find the enemy. At the same time, he emphasized the use of night patrols and B-52 attacks.

The president often consulted Abrams about the impact of peace negotiations on the military effort. In the fall of 1968 Abrams supported the Johnson decision to halt bombing North Vietnam as a prelude to substantive talks. During October he also negotiated the grants of weapons necessary to get the South Vietnamese to accept a halt and enter the peace talks.

During the Nixon administration Abrams oversaw the withdrawal of U.S. troops from Vietnam. He was named army chief of staff in June 1972. Abrams died in September 1974 of complications resulting from lung cancer surgery, the first army chief of staff to die in office. He was buried in Arlington National Cemetery with full military honors.

## Acheson, Dean G(ooderham)
**(1893–1971)** *foreign policy adviser*

Acheson, who was born on April 11, 1893, in Middletown, Connecticut, graduated from Harvard Law School in 1918. He served as private secretary to Supreme Court justice Louis Brandeis and then entered private law practice with the Washington firm of Covington and Burling. With the exception of a few months spent as undersecretary of the treasury in 1933, Acheson remained out of government until he was appointed assistant secretary of state in 1941. Four years later he became undersecretary of state. At this post Acheson helped plan the United Nations and formulate the Truman Doctrine for aid to Greece and Turkey and the Marshall Plan for the economic recovery of Europe.

Acheson left the State Department to return to his law practice in 1947 but became secretary of state in 1949. As secretary he implemented the containment policy toward the Soviet Union, which shaped the early American response to the cold war. Acheson returned to his law practice at the end of the Truman administration. Despite his advocacy of a strong cold war posture, he was attacked by conservative Republicans for "losing" China, pursuing a "no-win" policy in Korea, and "coddling" Communists in government.

Acheson served as a foreign policy adviser to President Kennedy during the 1961 Berlin and 1962 Cuban missile crises. In both these situations he took a hard-line stand that reflected his postwar philosophy. Acheson recommended the buildup of both nuclear and conventional forces in preparation for what he assumed would be a Soviet-American armed confrontation over Berlin and advocated bombing strikes against the Soviet missile installations discovered in Cuba.

In July 1965 Acheson and a small group of other foreign policy advisers known as the "Wise Men" counseled President Johnson that he needed to expand America's role in Vietnam in order to stave off Communist expansion, and that he needed to unite American public opinion behind him by offering detailed explanations about his policies. In March 1968, following the request of high military officials for over 200,000 additional ground troops for Vietnam, Johnson asked Acheson to assess the administration's war policy. Not trusting the briefings given by the Joint Chiefs of Staff, Acheson conducted his own investigation of the situation. Despite his earlier support of the war, Acheson con-

Dean Acheson (left) at a meeting of the president's consultants of foreign affairs, 1965 *(Photographed by Yoichi R. Okamoto; Lyndon Baines Johnson Library)*

cluded that he could no longer back the policy of seeking military victory. He believed that such a goal was impossible without the application of the nation's total resources and was not consistent with American interests. Acheson recommended that America get out of Vietnam as soon as possible because the public no longer supported the war. He reiterated his position at a meeting of the "Wise Men" on March 25 and 26.

Acheson died of a heart attack on October 12, 1971, in Sandy Spring, Maryland.

## Ackley, (Hugh) Gardner
### (1915–1998) *chair, President's Council of Economic Advisers; ambassador to Italy*

Gardner Ackley, who was born in Indianapolis, Indiana, on June 30, 1915, earned his Ph.D. in economics from the University of Michigan in 1940. A supporter of the New Deal, he worked for the Office of Price Administration during World War II and served for a

year with the Office of Strategic Services. After the war Ackley taught economics at the University of Michigan, becoming a full professor in 1952.

In July 1962 President Kennedy appointed Ackley to the President's Council of Economic Advisers (CEA). Like his colleague, CEA chair WALTER HELLER, Ackley was an enthusiastic proponent of the Keynesian "new economics," which held that the federal government could promote economic growth and maintain price stability through an activist fiscal policy. He played a key role in the formulation of the administration's wage-price guidelines, which were intended to keep wage increases below 3.2 percent a year and curb price increases as well. Ackley also supported the massive tax cut proposed by Kennedy and signed by President Johnson in February 1964. In November, upon the outgoing Heller's recommendation, Johnson named Ackley chair of the CEA.

Ackley's three-year tenure as chair coincided with a period of economic boom and large budget deficits incurred to finance the Vietnam War. He devoted most of his energy to fighting inflation, chiefly by exhorting business and labor to remain within the wage-price guideposts and by denouncing conspicuous violators of the standards.

The administration had mixed success in its anti-inflation campaign. When aluminum producers raised their price to 25 cents a pound in the fall of 1965, Ackley denounced the move as "inflationary." He argued that the latest rise brought the total price increase to 11 percent in 25 months, an unjustified rate since the industry's productivity was "substantially above the average for the economy." The administration's response went beyond exhortation when Ackley and Secretary of Defense ROBERT MCNAMARA announced on November 6 their intention to release 200,000 tons from the government's stockpile to force down the price of aluminum. On November 10 the producers rescinded their increase.

In January 1966 Bethlehem Steel also reduced a price increase of $5 a ton on structural steel products to $2.75 after Ackley and President Johnson attacked the original figure. In July the American Metal Corporation and the Molybdenum Corporation of America withdrew a 5 percent increase in the price of molybdenum in response to administration pressure. Ackley called the rollback "an act of industrial statesmanship." In December 1967 Ackley privately warned General Motors (GM) chair James Roche that the $61 increase in automobile prices planned by GM might provoke the administration into a public confrontation. "I believe I shook him up a little," Ackley wrote in a memo to Johnson. GM lowered the increase to $23.

Yet, as Ackley admitted in August 1966, the administration's wage-price program had suffered some "stunning defeats." In August 1966, August 1967, and December 1967, the major steel producers put into effect substantial price increases despite administration opposition. Ackley criticized the "inflationary" wage settlements that concluded the January 1966 strike of the Transport Workers Union in New York City and averted an American Airlines strike in October of the same year, but his admonitions proved futile in these instances.

Ackley contributed to the confusion surrounding the economic cost of the Vietnam War. In the fall of 1965 he projected the maximum possible increase in the cost of the conflict at $3 to $5 billion, while Senator JOHN STENNIS (D-Miss.) and Representative MENDEL RIVERS (D-S.C.), chairs of the Senate and House Armed Services Committees, were predicting $10 billion as a more likely figure. After consulting with Secretary of Defense McNamara, Ackley, in a speech before the American Statistical Association, dismissed the $10 billion estimate as unrealistic. In 1972, however, he said that the speech was "a major mistake."

Ackley played a vital role in persuading President Johnson to seek a tax increase in 1967 to curb inflation. As early as December 1965, Ackley had been quietly warning President Johnson that a tax increase would soon be necessary to restrain economic growth. Two years later, in testimony before the House Ways and Means Committee, Ackley said that the increase was necessary to stem a "hectic" expansion in the gross national product. Congress delayed passing the proposed 10 percent surtax until May 1968, however, when the administration agreed to compensating budget cuts.

In January 1968 Johnson appointed Ackley ambassador to Italy. (Ackley had spent a number of years in Italy studying the Italian economy.) Ackley remained at the post until August 1969, when he resigned and returned to the University of Michigan as a professor of economics. In 1982 he became president of the American Economic Association. He died on February 12, 1998, in Ann Arbor, Michigan.

## Agnew, Spiro T(heodore)

(1918–1996)  *governor, vice president of the United States*

Born on November 9, 1918, in Baltimore, Maryland, Agnew entered Johns Hopkins University to study chemistry. Because of a lack of money he transferred to Baltimore Law School, attending classes at night and working during the day. Following service in France and Germany during World War II, he returned to his law studies, earning his degree in 1947. Agnew began to practice law in suburban Maryland but was not successful and was forced to take jobs as an insurance claims adjuster and personnel manager for a supermarket chain.

Originally a Democrat, Agnew became active in Republican politics and local civic affairs on the advice of a law partner who assured him that his political prospects would be better in Maryland's small Republican Party than in the overcrowded Democratic field. In 1957 he was appointed to the Baltimore County Zoning Board of Appeals, but the Democratic majority on the board blocked his reappointment in 1960. Agnew, charging that the board members were trying to get rid of someone they could not control, used the incident to generate publicity and establish his reputation for integrity.

In 1962 Agnew was elected county executive of Baltimore County on a reform platform. During his tenure teachers' salaries increased, new schools were built, and the county's water supply and sewer systems improved. Although he had campaigned against racial bias in public places and sponsored a bill requiring equal accommodations in the county, Agnew changed his civil rights position while executive. Angered at their use of civil disobedience and demands for immediate change, he insisted that blacks work through government channels for gradual integration.

Agnew successfully ran for governor of Maryland in 1966. His victory was, in part, the product of dissension within the Democratic Party. Because of bitter infighting the two principal Democratic candidates split the liberal-moderate vote in the primary and the party's nomination went to George P. Mahoney, a wealthy contractor and segregationist. Against the ultraconservative Mahoney, Agnew attracted the support of blacks and liberals who viewed the Republican as the last line of defense against racism in the statehouse.

In addition, Agnew had secretly negotiated a deal with the chair of the liberal Montgomery County Democratic organization that resulted in the founding of a Democrats for Agnew Committee in the state's wealthiest county. Under the agreement Agnew allowed the Democrats to review all his position papers, promised not to campaign for local Republicans, assumed the financing of the organization, and promised local patronage appointments to supporting Democrats. Agnew carried the county, but the patronage agreement was not carried out because the Democrats found it politically compromising.

During his first year in office Agnew pushed several reform measures through the legislature: a budget making possible increased aid to antipoverty programs and local governments; an open housing law applicable to all but privately owned individual dwellings; repeal of the state law banning racial intermarriage; a graduated state sales tax; a liberalized abortion law, and the country's toughest state water pollution law.

By the spring of 1968, however, Agnew had reversed many of his liberal stands. He cut the state budget, particularly spending for health and welfare, and obtained new police powers, including the right to call out the militia in anticipation of an emergency. Agnew was increasingly angered by the tactics of the civil rights movement. Following 1967 riots in Baltimore he denounced militant blacks as "Hanoi-visiting, cater-wauling, riot-inciting, burn-America-down types." The next year he condemned the 1968 Poor People's March on Washington.

Agnew's shift to the right surprised many political observers. But others believed that Agnew had always been a conservative and had only looked liberal in contrast to Mahoney. Some attributed Agnew's shift to political pragmatism and a desire to take advantage of the conservative mood generated in part by the racial disturbances of 1967 and 1968. Still others attributed his swing to the right to his disillusionment with such Republican moderates as Michigan governor GEORGE ROMNEY and New York governor NELSON ROCKEFELLER.

An early backer of Rockefeller for the Republican presidential nomination in 1968, Agnew threw his support behind RICHARD M. NIXON when Rockefeller announced his withdrawal from the presidential race. Agnew placed Nixon's name in nomination at the Republican convention in August 1968, and the next day he became the party's vice presidential candidate despite being virtually unknown outside of Maryland. Nixon's choice of Agnew was generally attributed to his perception of the governor as a party "centrist." In Agnew's words, "I was the least offensive to all Republicans." In addition, Nixon hoped that Agnew's Greek background would appeal to many normally Democratic ethnic voters.

During the campaign Agnew became a blunt champion of "law and order." On a number of occasions his spontaneous remarks also made him the subject of ridicule. He lashed out against black militants and antiwar protesters, branded Democratic presidential candidate Senator HUBERT HUMPHREY (D-Minn.) "squishy soft on communism," called Polish-Americans "Polacks," and referred to a Japanese-American reporter as a "fat Jap." In the November balloting the Republican ticket received 43.4 percent of the popular vote; the Democratic ticket 42.7. The Nixon-Agnew team won 301 out of 538 electoral votes.

During his term in office Agnew became Nixon's "hard-line" spokesperson, attacking opponents of the

Vietnam War, reporters, and intellectuals. He also voiced the administration's belief that American values were threatened by the social turbulence and "permissiveness" of the period. Reelected with Nixon in 1972 Agnew resigned his office on October 10, 1973, following revelations that a Baltimore grand jury had uncovered massive evidence of personal corruption while he was governor and vice president. According to the report made public at his trial, Agnew, shortly after becoming governor in 1967, accepted payments from engineering firms in return for state contracts. The document also detailed an arrangement by which the presidents of two engineering firms made direct cash payments to Agnew while he was governor and vice president. According to the grand jury, these payments totaled about $100,000. Agnew pleaded nolo contendere to a lesser plea of income tax evasion at his October 10 trial. He was fined $10,000 and placed on three years unsupervised probation. He died on September 17, 1996, in Maryland.

## Aiken, George D(avid)
### (1892–1984) *member of the Senate*

George Aiken was born on August 30, 1892, in Dummerston, Vermont, and raised on a farm near Brattleboro, Vermont. After working in the nursery business, he was elected to the Vermont House of Representatives in 1930. He became speaker of the house in 1933 and two years later was elected lieutenant governor. Aiken was governor of Vermont from 1937 to 1941. He was elected to the U.S. Senate in 1940 and over the next 34 years had little difficulty winning reelection.

Aiken was generally associated with the moderate wing of the Republican Party, though his voting record was difficult to categorize. In the early 1960s he voted for the Kennedy administration's minimum wage and school aid bills. He opposed Medicare in 1962 but three years later voted for the Johnson administration's health care measure. In the mid-1960s Aiken's voting pattern remained unpredictable. The liberal Americans for Democratic Action gave him a 35 percent rating in 1965 and a 66 percent rating in 1966.

During the 1960s Aiken served on the Senate Foreign Relations and Joint Atomic Energy Committees. As the ranking Republican on the Senate Agriculture and Forestry Committee, his advocacy of the food stamp program was significant. This program, he argued, had greatly improved the health of many Americans who were "unable to get enough of the right kind of food to live decently." In 1964 Aiken helped win approval of an administration bill placing the food stamp program on a permanent footing. Long an advocate of federal aid to rural communities, Aiken sponsored legislation authorizing $55 million for the development of rural water-supply and waste-disposal systems in 1965. This measure was initially opposed by the Bureau of the Budget, but in August 1965 President Johnson endorsed the Aiken bill, which then passed both houses and became law.

In August 1964 Aiken, "with misgivings," voted for the Gulf of Tonkin Resolution giving the president broad authority to use military force in Southeast Asia. However, in April 1965 he denounced U.S. bombing of North Vietnam, arguing that it would stiffen rather than weaken the North's will to resist. In November of that year Aiken and four other senators conducted a "fact-finding" tour of South Vietnam and returned with a pessimistic appraisal of the situation. Aiken believed that the presence of U.S. troops in South Vietnam had prevented the North from overrunning the country, but he thought that in the long run the administration should seek a "political" rather than a military solution to the Vietnamese conflict. In a widely publicized speech delivered to the Senate on October 19, 1966, Aiken proposed that the U.S. declare that "we have 'won' [the war] in the sense that our Armed Forces are in control of the field and no potential enemy is in a position to establish its authority in South Vietnam." When an aide suggested to President Johnson that he follow Aiken's advice by declaring victory and withdrawing from Vietnam, the president was irate. A few years later, the aide reminded the president of the encounter, and asked why he had been so mad. LBJ responded, "I was afraid you and Aiken might be right."

Despite his opposition to an escalation of the war, Aiken continued to vote for bills to fund the military effort. To do otherwise, he believed, would be to disarm our troops in the field. He also suggested a change in strategy, urging the president gradually to redeploy U.S. forces along certain strategic enclaves, especially along the coast, where they could exist largely to prevent North Vietnamese offensives rather than work to redesign the southern society itself. He also called for the substitution of intensive reconnaissance to replace the massive bombing campaign. In May 1967 Aiken declared that the administration "cannot achieve an honorable peace in Vietnam" and called for the Republican Party to develop an alternative to President Johnson's policies. Little came of this appeal.

Despite his outspoken stand on Vietnam, Aiken remained an immensely popular figure in Vermont. In 1968 he won overwhelming victories in both the Republican and the Democratic primaries and was unchallenged in the general election.

Aiken urged the United States to begin pulling its troops out of Vietnam in May 1969; a year later he voted for the Cooper-Church Amendment barring the president from sending funds to maintain U.S. troops in Cambodia.

When Aiken retired from the Senate in 1974, he was 82 and the chamber's oldest member. He died in Vermont in 1984.

## Albert, Carl (Bert)
(1908–2000) *member of the House of Representatives*

Albert, who was born on May 10, 1908, in McAlester, Oklahoma, grew up in a poor family. He graduated Phi Beta Kappa from the University of Oklahoma in 1931 and received a Rhodes Scholarship to study at Oxford University, where he earned two law degrees. In 1941 Albert enlisted in the army, serving until 1946, when he was discharged at the rank of lieutenant colonel. In 1946, Albert won a seat in the U.S. House of Representatives from Oklahoma's impoverished Third Congressional District.

In Congress Albert consistently backed both social welfare measures and legislation favored by the oil industry, which was a major interest in his state. Albert uniformly supported the House Democratic leadership. From his earliest days as a representative, Albert later recalled, he carefully observed the operations of the House to familiarize himself with its procedures and with the voting patterns of its members.

Impressed by Albert's loyalty and diligence, Speaker Sam Rayburn (D-Tex.) and Majority Leader JOHN W. MCCORMACK (D-Mass.) tapped him to serve as majority whip in 1955. As whip his function was rounding up votes for positions favored by the House Democratic leadership. In January 1962, following the death of Rayburn, McCormack became speaker and Albert was chosen majority leader. His responsibilities in that post included devising Democratic floor strategy and speaking on behalf of administration programs.

As majority whip and later as majority leader, Albert shunned publicity and employed quiet, behind-the-scenes persuasion in his efforts to secure the passage of legislation. His critics believed that more forceful methods would produce greater results, but Albert felt that the representatives, and particularly the powerful committee chairs, could not be compelled to act as he wished and that the excessive use of pressure would create antagonism toward the Democratic leadership. Yet during the Johnson administration he sometimes used power rather than persuasion when important bills faced serious obstacles in the House. In 1964 President Johnson was pressing intensively for the passage of his antipoverty program but found resistance in the lower chamber. Albert spoke to the committee chairs who handled public works bills and suggested the possibility of blocking pending projects in the districts of those representatives opposed to the program. This step, observers believed, helped to secure the votes needed to pass the antipoverty bill in August 1964.

Albert was one of the leading legislative defenders of President Johnson's domestic programs. In October 1965 he praised the first session of the 89th Congress, which had adopted more administration bills than were usually passed in two sessions, as "the most significant in all our history." During March 1966, in reply to attacks on Great Society programs, Albert said that Republicans "have been blind for 35 years . . . blind in their opposition to progressive legislation; blind in their concern for human beings."

Believing that Congress should play a secondary role to the chief executive in the shaping of foreign policy, Albert was a strong supporter of administration foreign policy. Following the alleged attacks on American ships in the Gulf of Tonkin by North Vietnamese forces in August 1964, Albert was one of the first representatives whom President Johnson consulted. In January 1965 he opposed a House amendment to cut off aid to Egypt, asserting, "The issue here is whether a matter of major foreign policy should be determined by legislative action . . . without the advice, the information and the help of the president in his handling of this delicate international matter." He backed President Johnson's Vietnam policies, and many observers felt that Albert, as chair of the 1968 Democratic National

Convention in Chicago, ruled arbitrarily against the motions of delegates supporting the antiwar presidential candidacies of Senator EUGENE J. MCCARTHY (D-Minn.) and Senator GEORGE S. MCGOVERN (D-S.Dak.). And ironically it was Albert who read LBJ's message to the convention, declaring that he would not consider running for another term in office.

During the Nixon presidency Albert continued to back administration policies in Southeast Asia but opposed the Republican president's domestic programs. In the early 1970s he supported such congressional reforms as the recorded teller vote, the wider dispersion of House chairs, and disclosure of campaign contributions. In 1971 Albert succeeded McCormack as Speaker of the House. He subsequently came under attack from liberal Democrats for not articulating coherent policy alternatives to the programs of the Republican administration. Albert retired from Congress in 1977 and returned to Oklahoma. He died on February 4, 2000, in McAlester, Oklahoma.

## Alexander, Clifford L., Jr.
(1933– )  *chair, Equal Employment Opportunities Commission*

Clifford was born in New York City on September 21, 1933, and graduated from Harvard in 1955 and from Yale Law School in 1958. He served as assistant district attorney for New York County and then entered private law practice in New York City. Alexander worked in several antipoverty programs, including Haryou, Inc., [Harlem Youth Opportunities Unlimited] where he was executive and program director from 1962 to 1963. At the request of MCGEORGE BUNDY, Alexander joined the staff of the National Security Council in 1963. From 1964 to 1967 he successively held posts as deputy special assistant, associate special counsel, and deputy special counsel to the president, serving as an adviser to Johnson on various domestic problems, especially civil rights.

On June 27, 1967, Alexander became chair of the Equal Employment Opportunities Commission (EEOC), the agency established by the 1964 Civil Rights Act to help end job discrimination. With Senate confirmation of his appointment on August 2, Alexander became the first black to head the commission. Because the agency lacked the power to force industries to end discrimination and could use only conciliation to settle disputes, Alexander relied

on publicity and pressure to prompt businesses to hire minorities. In two October 1967 studies, for example, the commission reported the existence of widespread discrimination against African Americans in the drug industry and in white-collar jobs. During January 1968 Alexander held four days of hearings documenting discrimination in New York City's white-collar occupations, particularly in the financial and communications industries. At the conclusion of the investigation, he charged: "If future intentions were gauged by the past standard of performance, it would mean that Negroes and Puerto Ricans would probably be waiting until the year 2164 for a democracy to say what he or she shall have." Overall, Alexander led investigations in numerous industries, including movies, textiles, and utilities.

Alexander's efforts led to criticism from business and congressional leaders. In March 1969 Senator EVERETT M. DIRKSEN (R-Ill.) threatened to "get somebody fired" if the commission did not stop "punitive harassment" of business. On April 9 Alexander resigned as chair of the EEOC because of what he termed "a crippling lack of [Nixon] Administration support." However, he remained a member of the commission. Two weeks later Jerris Leonard, head of the Justice Department civil rights division, charged that the commission had been ineffective under Alexander, and without naming him directly, called for his resignation as a member of the agency. Alexander remained on the panel until August 8, when he resigned to become a partner in the Washington, D.C., law firm of Arnold & Porter. In September 1974 he made an unsuccessful attempt to win the Democratic mayoral nomination in Washington. In 1977 President Jimmy Carter appointed Alexander secretary of the army, a position he held until 1981, when he returned to private consulting.

## Ali, Muhammad
(1942– )  *professional boxer*

Muhammad Ali was born Cassius Marcellus Clay, Jr., on January 17, 1942, in Louisville, Kentucky. Encouraged at the age of 12 to take up boxing, Clay fought successfully for six years as an amateur. In 1960 he won an Olympic gold medal in the light heavyweight division and turned professional shortly thereafter. From the outset of his career Clay aroused and encouraged controversy by his bragging predictions of victory—often delivered in doggerel—and skillful bantering with sports writers.

The day after his stunning seventh round victory over heavyweight champion Sonny Liston in February 1964, Clay announced that he had become a Black Muslim and had dropped his "slave name" of Clay for the name Muhammad Ali. The next month the World Boxing Association (WBA) refused to recognize Ali as the heavyweight champion, ostensibly because of his zealous promotional efforts before the Liston fight. The WBA action, however, did not deter a Liston-Ali rematch in May 1965, which Ali won with a knockout in the first round.

During the next two years Ali defended his heavyweight crown eight times, scoring easy victories in each and building a reputation as one of the greatest heavyweight boxers in history. On April 28, 1967, in Houston, Texas, he refused induction into the army on the grounds that he was a full-time Black Muslim minister and, therefore, exempt from the draft. His feelings about the war in Vietnam were already widely known and quoted: "We [Muslims] don't go to wars unless they are declared by Allah himself. I don't have any personal quarrel with those Viet Congs." The same day that he refused induction, Ali was stripped of his world heavyweight title by both the WBA and the New York Boxing Commission, whose chair declared that Ali's "refusal to enter the service is regarded by the Commission to be detrimental to the best interests of boxing." His stand drew the animosity of many Americans; the governor of Maine said he should be "held in utter contempt by every patriotic American," and an American Legion post in Miami called him "an unpatriotic, loudmouthed, bombastic individual." After being denied conscientious objector status, Ali was convicted by a federal jury in Houston, Texas, on June 20, 1967 of violating the Selective Service laws after only 21 minutes of deliberation. He was given the maximum penalty of five years in jail and a $10,000 fine.

Following the verdict Ali's career went into a three-and-one-half-year hiatus pending legal appeals. During this period Ali's opposition to the draft and the Vietnam War provoked considerable animosity throughout the country. Conservative columnist WILLIAM F. BUCKLEY, JR., called for "someone to succeed in knocking sense into Clay's head before he's done damaging the sport." Many sports reporters also joined in condemning Ali's action.

As a result of increased public interest and intensive negotiations with officials, Ali returned to boxing in 1970. On October 26 he defeated Jerry Quarry in Atlanta in his first fight since 1967. Two months later Ali stopped Argentine heavyweight Oscar Bonavena, but in March 1971, in what was billed as the "Fight of the Century," he suffered his first ring defeat when he was outpointed by WBA heavyweight champion Joe Frazier in a fight that went 15 rounds in Madison Square Garden and earned $2.5 million for Ali.

On June 28, 1971, a unanimous U.S. Supreme Court voted to reverse Ali's draft conviction and prison sentence. The Court ruled that the Selective Service had refused to grant Ali conscientious objector status because of advice from the Justice Department that "was simply wrong as a matter of law."

Ali regained his world heavyweight boxing title on October 30, 1974, with an eighth-round knockout of George Foreman in Kinshasa, Zaire. After losing his title in 1978 to Leon Spinks, Ali became the only boxer to win the heavyweight title three times by reclaiming the belt from Spinks in a rematch six months later. Still, all the years of fighting had taken their toll, and in the early 1980s Ali was diagnosed with Pugilistic Parkinsonism, caused by repetitive trauma to his head.

## Alinsky, Saul D(avid)
### (1909–1972)  *social activist*

Born on January 30, 1909, in a Chicago slum tenement, Alinsky studied sociology at the University of Chicago, where he was awarded a graduate fellowship. After employment as a criminologist, Alinsky worked with John L. Lewis during the Congress of Industrial Organization's formative years. In 1938 he moved into "Back of the Yards," an Irish neighborhood behind the Chicago stockyards. There he formed the Back of the Yards Council and employed direct action tactics such as picketing and rent strikes to win concessions from meat packing companies, landlords and the local political machine. With the backing of philanthropist Marshall Field III, Alinsky founded the Industrial Areas Foundation in 1940. During the next two decades his foundation "contracted" to build community organizations in poor communities across the country. In the 1950s Alinsky received a contract from the bishop of Milan, later Pope Paul VI, to organize anticommunist labor unions in Italy.

Alinsky made his first attempt to organize the Chicago black inner city in 1960, out of which grew

The Woodlawn Organization (TWO) on Chicago's South Side. Organized in opposition to urban renewal plans, TWO developed into a multi-issue organization that Charles Silberman, author of *Crisis in Black and White*, described in 1964 as "the most significant social experiment going on among Negroes today."

More than any practical gain, however, Alinsky's activities served to connect people of all backgrounds to their larger society, and to empower them with the belief that democracy was indeed for all Americans. Sociologist Daniel Bell wrote of Alinsky that his work "attempts to give people a sense of participation and belonging [and] becomes important as a weapon against cynicism and despair."

Alinsky continued to make a name for himself in the civil rights arena. When, in the late 1950s, the Bay Area Presbyterian Churches organization invited him to come to Oakland to organize African Americans, the Oakland City Council passed a resolution banning him from the city, and another one approving the suggestion that he be sent a 50-foot rope with which to hang himself. Alinsky went anyway, to much success.

In 1965 the Rochester Council of Churches invited Alinsky to organize Rochester's black community. He created Freedom, Integration, God, Honor—Today (FIGHT), an organization that won some concessions from corporations in the hiring and training of blacks and formal recognition as the voice of Rochester's black poor. During FIGHT's struggle with Eastman Kodak over the corporation's job training program, Alinsky first sought to use stock proxies as a source of leverage against the company. In March 1967 FIGHT bought 10 shares of Kodak stock and sent out letters to 700 clergymen and civil rights organizations requesting that they persuade other shareholders to withhold their proxies at the April 25 stockholders meeting. Alinsky told Marion Sanders, who interviewed him for *Harper's Magazine*, that the proxies "turned out to be our major weapon in getting Kodak to deal with FIGHT."

Believing that social change would come from only a well-organized majority, Alinsky turned his attention to organizing the middle class, which he thought included almost 80 percent of America's population. In August 1968 he announced the establishment of the Mid-America Institute to train representatives of the middle class to organize in their own communities. The same year he launched an antipollution drive in Chicago. Alinsky outlined his strategy for middle-class organizing in *Rules for Radicals*, published in 1971. Until his death on June 12, 1972, Alinsky continued to train organizers at his institute.

## Allen, Ivan, Jr.
### (1911–2003) *mayor*

Allen was born in Atlanta on March 15, 1911, and graduated from the Georgia Institute of Technology in 1933. He then entered his father's successful office supply company in Atlanta. His aggressive entrepreneurial efforts enabled him to accumulate a large fortune. He played an active role in the affairs of the business community, culminating in his election to the presidency of the city's Chamber of Commerce in 1960.

Allen was also active politically. He served as executive secretary to Georgia governor Ellis Arnall immediately following World War II, and in 1954 he briefly entered the race for governor but withdrew when he failed to attract sufficient support. In a series of speeches associated with this abortive effort, Allen defended racial segregation as a fundamental part of the South's region way of life.

However, Allen's position on segregation changed during the next decade. He belonged to a dynamic, powerful, and politically active local business community that was more interested in promoting the economic growth of Atlanta than in defending traditional southern social mores. In 1961 Allen, as president of the Chamber of Commerce, was instrumental in behind the scenes negotiations between Atlanta business leaders and a student-led protest demanding integration, and he brokered an agreement that won the approval of both sides, although it took the direct intercession of MARTIN LUTHER KING, JR., to prevent a last-minute revolt by the protestors. He ran, with black support, in the 1961 Democratic mayoral primary against archsegregationist LESTER MADDOX and became Atlanta's mayor later that year.

Allen used his influence to integrate many of the city's public facilities, particularly after black and white college students staged antisegregation sit-ins in restaurants and hotels during the spring of 1963. In July of that year Allen, testifying before the Senate Commerce Committee, became the only major southern white politician to back the Kennedy administration's bill for the desegregation of public accommodations. The Atlanta mayor declared, "I am firmly convinced that the Supreme Court insists that the same fundamental rights must be held by every American citizen."

Allen was reelected in 1965 with 70 percent of the vote, but substantial tension between the city administration and the black community developed during his second term. The problems of the high rate of black unemployment and of segregated housing proved to be less tractable than those associated with the integration of public facilities. According to a National Opinion Research Center survey of 1966, only 3.8 percent of Atlanta's whites lived in integrated neighborhoods. An Equal Employment Opportunity Commission study the following year indicated the unemployment rate in the city's black neighborhoods was 15.5 percent in comparison to the overall city figure of 2.6 percent.

In Atlanta, as in northern cities, the persistence of these conditions, despite the gains of the civil rights movement, produced growing discontent. The shooting of blacks by Atlanta police officers sparked riots in 1966 and 1967. Allen gained national prominence in September 1966 by entering the violence-stricken areas and appealing to the rioters to disperse. Denouncing black opponents of nonviolence as vehemently as he had condemned segregationists in previous years, he charged that STOKELY CARMICHAEL and other leaders of the Student Nonviolent Coordinating Committee were responsible for inciting the disturbances and declared that "if Stokely Carmichael is looking for a battleground . . . he'll be met in whatever situation he creates."

But Allen had not abandoned his racial liberalism. He agreed with the conclusions of the 1968 report of President Johnson's National Advisory Commission on Civil Disorders, which cited poverty as the principal cause of urban riots. In March of that year he asserted, "We are responsible for the condition the Negro is in today." Allen supported the report's recommendation of massive federal programs to eliminate urban slums. A month later he reaffirmed his sympathy for the civil rights movement, stating that the assassination of Martin Luther King, Jr., "takes from Atlanta one of its greatest citizens."

In the summer of 1969 Allen supported President Nixon's proposals for sharing federal revenues with local governments, but the mayor said he did not think the amount of aid being offered was suffi-

cient to cope with urban problems. Earlier in the year Allen had announced that, for personal reasons, he would not seek reelection in 1969. He died in Atlanta, Georgia, on July 2, 2003.

## Allott, Gordon (Llewellyn)
### (1907–1989) *member of the Senate*

Born on January 2, 1907, in Pueblo, Colorado, Gordon Allott received his law degree from the University of Colorado in 1929 and five years later entered politics as chair of the Colorado State Young Republican League. During World War II Allott saw action with the U.S. Army Air Forces in the South Pacific. He won election as lieutenant governor of Colorado in 1950 and upset a popular Democrat for the U.S. Senate four years later. Allott voted against most of the Kennedy administration's domestic programs and led the Senate opposition to the president's wilderness preservation legislation. Allott's skill as a legislator was well known, and he was regarded by many of his colleagues as a master of the procedural process.

With the exception of civil rights legislation, Allott voted as a conservative Republican through the Johnson years. He supported cloture to end the southern Democrats' filibuster against the 1964 civil rights bill in June and spoke out in favor of the measure's controversial provision granting federal agencies the right to cut off funds to states or localities guilty of discriminatory practices. Allott remarked in June that the bill "represents nothing if we continue to use the taxes of this country for the benefit of one group." He supported the 1965 Voting Rights Act and the 1968 open housing law, although he voted for an amendment to the 1968 bill that would have limited its jurisdiction to apartments and condominiums.

Allott opposed much of the rest of the president's Great Society legislation. In January 1965 he condemned the aid to Appalachia bill, declaring that if it were enacted, "federal funds will gush forth without restraint of reason." He voted against Medicare in July 1965 and the effort to repeal Section 14(b) of the Taft-Hartley Act in October. He led an unsuccessful move to reduce appropriations for the administration's Model Cities program in September 1967, but he succeeded in cutting 4 percent from the Model Cities appropriation in July 1968. The Americans for Democratic Action (ADA) gave Allott a 42 percent rating on selected issues during the 1964 session dominated by the civil rights debate, but Allott's ADA rating fell to 15 percent or less in each of the next four years. The ADA's conservative counterpart, the Americans for Constitutional Action, gave Allott an 86 percent rating in 1968.

Allott supported appropriations for the U.S. war effort in Vietnam in 1965 and 1966. "Our aim must be directed more by our military leaders than civilians," Allott declared in opposition to "another Korean stalemate." In September 1967, however, Allott joined nine other senators in endorsing a proposal by Senate Majority Leader MIKE MANSFIELD (D-Mont.) that called for the United States to seek a negotiated settlement in Vietnam through the United Nations.

Allott worked against the appointment of Associate Justice ABE FORTAS as Chief Justice in 1968. In June he joined 18 other Republican senators in opposition to the Fortas nomination despite its endorsement by Senate Minority Leader EVERETT M. DIRKSEN (R-Ill.). Allott argued in September that the help Fortas gave the administration in drafting legislation to provide Secret Service protection for presidential candidates indicated his inability to separate his judicial responsibilities from the executive branch. Allott questioned the unusual decision of Chief Justice EARL WARREN to step down only upon the selection of a successor. Led by Senator ROBERT P. GRIFFIN (R-Mich.), the anti-Fortas forces succeeded in blocking the appointment. In December Warren agreed to retire after the inauguration of RICHARD M. NIXON.

Allott won the chair of the Senate Republican Conference (Policy) Committee in January 1969, becoming an official member of the party's Senate power structure. Despite appeals to his constituents based upon his seniority and prestige, Allott lost his campaign for reelection in 1972 to Floyd Haskell, a former Republican turned Democrat, who opposed the Vietnam War, by a mere 9,588 votes. He died in Englewood, Colorado, on January 17, 1989.

## Anderson, Clinton P(resba)
(1895–1975) *member of the Senate*

A native of South Dakota, Anderson, who was born on October 23, 1895, attended Dakota Wesleyan University and the University of Michigan. He was rejected for service in World War I because he was suffering from tuberculosis. At the age of 22 he set-

tled in New Mexico, where the climate helped him recuperate. Between 1918 and 1922 Anderson worked as a reporter for the *Albuquerque Journal* and helped uncover evidence relating to the Teapot Dome scandal. In 1922 he entered the insurance business and three years later became the owner of his own agency.

In 1933 the governor of New Mexico appointed Anderson to the post of state treasurer following the death of the incumbent. He later served as an administrator of New Deal relief and unemployment compensation programs in New Mexico, serving as head of the New Mexican Relief Administration during 1935, state representative of the Federal Emergency Relief Administration from 1935 to 1936, and chair and executive director of the Unemployment Compensation Commission of New Mexico from 1936 to 1938. Anderson won election to Congress in 1940 and served three terms. Early in 1945 he headed a congressional probe concerning food shortages; his report so impressed President Harry S. Truman that he appointed Anderson secretary of agriculture in the spring of 1945. Anderson held the post for three years. In this capacity, he worked closely with Truman and former president Herbert Hoover on the Famine Emergency Committee, which tried, with some success, to alleviate the international food shortage after World War II. He won election to the Senate in 1948 and served for the next 23 years.

During the 1960s Anderson's influence was based on his seniority, his important committee leadership, and his strong ties to both the Kennedy and Johnson administrations. Anderson was particularly close to President Johnson, with whom he established friendly relations when Johnson was serving in the Senate. Anderson was widely regarded as one of the more liberal members of a group of senators who wielded significant power. This liberal reputation was based on his support for the domestic legislation of the two Democratic administrations, his efforts to gain the passage of civil rights and social welfare bills by changing Rule 22 to allow the Senate to end filibusters with less than a two-thirds majority, and his sponsorship of Medicare legislation.

Between 1961 and 1964 Anderson, a ranking member of the Senate Finance Committee, and Representative Cecil R. King (D-Calif.) sponsored legislation to raise Social Security taxes to provide hospital care for the elderly. Their bill won the support of both the Kennedy and Johnson administrations but was defeated because of the stiff opposition of the American Medical Association and Representative WILBUR MILLS (D-Ark.), the conservative chair of the House Ways and Means Committee. Following the sweeping congressional victory of the Democrats in 1964, Representative Mills abandoned his opposition, and a version of the King-Anderson bill became law in the summer of 1965. In 1964 Johnson also appointed Anderson to direct a commission to oversee the reconstruction of Alaska after a devastating earthquake and tidal wave.

Anderson became chair of the Senate Aeronautical and Space Sciences Committee in January 1963 and held the post for nine years. He was an enthusiastic supporter of the space program and generously supported National Aeronautics and Space Administration (NASA) requests for increased funds. In 1967 Anderson chaired a Senate panel probing the causes of a January 27 launchpad fire that had killed three astronauts during a ground-flight simulation test, concluding that complacent management and "admitted overconfidence by NASA and North American [Corp.] based on past successes, proved fatal."

Anderson also maintained a long-standing interest in atomic energy. From 1959 to 1961 he chaired the Joint Congressional Committee on Atomic Energy and remained an influential member of that committee throughout the decade. He also championed the protection the nation's wilderness. His hard work paid off in 1963, when, after numerous defeats, Congress created the National Wildlife Preservation System.

Anderson supported the administration's Vietnam War policy, favored large-scale military appropriations, and opposed rigorous gun-control legislation. As a result of such stands, the Americans for Democratic Action, which had accorded Anderson an 80 percent rating in 1961, gave him only 21 percent in 1968.

In ill health, Anderson retired from the Senate in 1972. He died three years later at the age of 80.

## Anderson, Jack(son) Northman

(1922– )  *syndicated columnist*

Jack Anderson, who was born in Long Beach, California, on October 19, 1922, grew up in Salt Lake City, Utah, worked on the church-owned *Deseret News*, and briefly attended the University of Utah before serving as a civilian war correspondent during World War II. Drafted into the army in 1945, Anderson was discharged in 1947 and the same year obtained a job on the Washington staff of the widely syndicated muckraking columnist DREW PEARSON. Rarely credited for his contributions to the *Washington Merry-Go-Round* during the 1950s and early 1960s, Anderson was finally granted an equal byline with Pearson in 1965.

Inspired by his Mormon upbringing, Anderson began his journalistic career determined to ferret out corruption and further the cause of honest government. In doing so, he made powerful enemies; FBI director J. EDGAR HOOVER once commented that Anderson was "lower than the regurgitated filth of vultures." In June 1965 two employees of powerful Senator THOMAS DODD (D-Conn.) turned over to Anderson nearly 6,000 documents that indicated the senator had used his political influence to promote the private interests of Chicago public relations executive Julius Klein. The documents also revealed that Dodd had converted tax-free campaign contributions to his personal use. Anderson subsequently wrote 98 of over 100 columns concerning the Dodd affair that appeared under the Pearson-Anderson byline during the next few years. Dodd filed a 14-count, $5 million libel and conspiracy suit against Pearson and Anderson. The charges leveled against the Connecticut senator were so serious that on June 20, 1966, the Senate Select Committee on Standards and Conduct opened hearings on Dodd's misconduct. The committee's lengthy investigation resulted in Dodd's formal censure on June 23, 1967, by a vote of 92-5. In 1970 Dodd was unseated by Republican Senator Lowell Weicker.

Anderson also collaborated with Pearson on the best-selling 1968 book, *The Case against Congress*, an indictment of corruption in Washington that concentrated on abuses of power and privilege as well as the foibles of individual representatives. After Pearson's death in September 1969, Anderson took over the column, which by then was syndicated in 650 papers. The differences in journalistic approach between Pearson and Anderson were immediately evident. While Pearson had often reported mere personal gossip concerning public figures, Anderson sought to direct the column toward matters of greater substance. After Anderson took over *Washington Merry-Go-Round*, he instructed his assistants to keep their distance from politicians and avoid White House functions or social meetings with informants.

In 1972 Anderson was responsible for two journalistic "scoops," the publication of secret papers showing that President Nixon wanted the United States to "tilt" toward Pakistan in the India-Pakistan war over Bangladesh and a report by Anderson that the Justice Department had settled an antitrust suit in favor of International Telephone and Telegraph Corporation (ITT) at about the same time the corporation had pledged $400,000 to the forthcoming Republican National Convention in San Diego. That same year, he won the Pulitzer Prize for journalism. Subsequently, Anderson was active, through his columns, in probing the events surrounding the Watergate affair.

## Anderson, Robert B(ernard)

(1910–1989) *business leader, presidential adviser, secretary of the Treasury*

Anderson, who was born on June 4, 1910, in Burleson, Texas, grew up on a farm and taught high school after graduating from college in 1927. In 1932 he was elected to the Texas legislature on the same day he graduated from the University of Texas Law School. After serving as the state tax commissioner and chair of the Texas Unemployment Commission, Anderson became general attorney for the W. T. Waggoner estate, a huge conglomerate whose operations included livestock raising, oil refining, and the handling of stock and bond investments. He frequently appeared before Congress as a lobbyist for oil interests.

Anderson held several high positions in the Eisenhower administration: secretary of the navy from 1953 to 1954, deputy secretary of defense from 1954 to 1955, and secretary of the Treasury from 1957 to 1961. Eisenhower is alleged to have remarked, late in his second term, that he would have liked to see Anderson succeed him. During the Kennedy years he was a partner in the investment house of Loeb, Rhoades & Co., a director of several corporations and a member of a prestigious panel named by President Kennedy to study the U.S. foreign aid program.

Anderson was one of the first people President Johnson called in the aftermath of President Kennedy's assassination. Summoned immediately to Washington he spent four hours with Johnson on November 24, 1963, discussing economic policy. Anderson argued strongly that Johnson should pursue a conservative fiscal course by cutting the budget and abandoning the $11 billion tax cut pushed by Kennedy. Johnson chose to make spending cuts while maintaining the administration's commitment to the tax cut, which he signed in February 1964. He continued to rely on Anderson for advice. According to *Newsweek* magazine, "President Johnson frequently telephones Anderson in his handsome, 27th-floor offices at No. 1 Rockefeller Center or has him down to the White House for visits which rarely show up on the official callers list." In 1964 Anderson had enough influence with LBJ to persuade the president not to appoint Harvard professor Seymour Harris to the Federal Reserve Board, as John Kennedy had promised.

Anderson also often served Johnson as a diplomatic troubleshooter. In 1967 Johnson sent him to Egypt in a last-ditch effort to hold off war in the Middle East. The concessions Anderson was able to wrangle from President Gamal Nasser, however, were not enough to keep the peace. His most important assignment began with his appointment in April 1964 as special ambassador for the negotiations over the Panama Canal. After two-and-one-half years of negotiations, an agreement on the texts of new treaties governing the canal was reached in June 1967. Under the three proposed treaties the United States would surrender sovereignty over the Panama Canal Zone, and Panama's sovereignty over the zone would be "effectively" recognized. The existing canal would become the property of a U.S.-Panamanian authority. In 1970, however, a new Panamanian government rejected the three proposed treaties on the ground that the United States was granted a majority on the joint governing board. After his involvement with the canal question, Anderson devoted himself to his diverse business interests, including directorships in numerous corporations and the chairmanship of Robert B. Anderson & Co. Ltd.

In 1987 Anderson pled guilty to charges of avoiding taxes on more than $200,000 of income by operating an offshore bank. He was sentenced to one month in jail and five years probation. He died in New York in 1989.

## Arends, Leslie C(ornelius)

(1895–1985) *member of the House of Representatives*

Leslie Arends was born on September 27, 1895, in Melvin, Illinois, and attended Oberlin College.

After serving in World War I, he returned to Illinois as a farmer, and in 1935 became a member of the County Farm Bureau. He was elected to Congress that same year and served almost 40 years as the representative of a farming district south of Chicago. He became House Republican whip in 1943. His primary function as whip was to round up Republican votes on key bills for which a party position had been determined by the Republican Policy Committee.

During the Kennedy years Arends generally opposed the administration's domestic legislation. As the ranking Republican member of the House Armed Services Committee, he consistently voted for increased military appropriations, and generally sided with the Joints Chiefs of Staff in its disputes with Secretary of Defense ROBERT S. MCNAMARA.

Arends voted against the Johnson administration's Medicare, school aid, and poverty program bills. He supported the 1964 Civil Rights Act, however, and the administration's Vietnam War policy. In fact, after LBJ's decision in late 1965 to halt bombing in Vietnam, Arends encouraged him to restart it before the American military position suffered.

In January 1965 Representative GERALD R. FORD (R-Mich.) replaced Representative CHARLES HALLECK (R-Ind.) as House minority leader. Arends had supported Halleck, and Ford demanded that Arends be replaced as whip. House Republicans, however, voted 70 to 59 to retain him. Throughout his career, Arends maintained a reputation for being fair that carried over to both political parties. LBJ adviser LAWRENCE O'BRIEN praised Arends as one of a group of Republicans who rose above partisan politics; "They had their very strong views," O'Brien noted, "which didn't coincide with ours. But it was never personalized . . . and there was mutual respect and understanding."

Arends was a consistent supporter of President RICHARD M. NIXON. He opposed impeachment articles in the House Judiciary Committee until the president's guilt became clear. When Representative Ford became vice president in 1973, Arends made a nominal bid to become House minority leader. He was then nearly 80 years old, and Republicans chose JOHN S. RHODES (R-Ariz.) instead. Arends retired that year and was replaced by a Democrat. He died on July 17, 1985, in Naples, Florida.

—JLW

## Ashbrook, John M(ilan)

(1928–1982)  *member of the House of Representatives*

John M. Ashbrook was the son of a conservative, anti–New Deal Democratic representative from Ohio. Born on September 21, 1928, in Johnstown, Ohio, he received his A.B. from Harvard in 1952 and returned to Ohio. He graduated from Ohio State Law School and ran his family's central Ohio county weekly.

Unlike his father, Ashbrook became a Republican. In 1956 he defeated an incumbent Democrat for the Ohio House of Representatives and won reelection two years later. Ashbrook again defeated an incumbent Democrat, Representative Robert W. Levering, for the U.S. House in 1960. Reelected in 1962 Ashbrook became a member of the House Un-American Activities Committee (HUAC) the following January. Young and aggressive, he practiced the new, more strident anticommunist conservatism common in the southern and western wings of the Republican Party during the 1960s. Conservative journalist WILLIAM F. BUCKLEY, JR., a close associate, described Ashbrook as "by all odds the most exciting young man in the Republican Party" in the mid-1960s.

Ashbrook joined early in the effort to nominate conservative senator BARRY M. GOLDWATER (R-Ariz.) for president. In conjunction with political consultant F. CLIFTON WHITE and William Rusher, editor of Buckley's *National Review*, he formed the nucleus of what would be the Draft Goldwater for President Committee in September 1961. Ironically, Goldwater's subsequent nomination in July 1964 almost cost Ashbrook his House seat. In November he narrowly edged Levering, 51.5 percent to 48.5 percent, while Goldwater lost his district 57.5 percent to 42.5 percent. Ashbrook trailed the less conservative senatorial candidate, Robert A. Taft, Jr., by just under 13,000 votes.

Despite Goldwater's national debacle Ashbrook continued to support conservative causes. He served on the steering committee of the Committee of One Million against the Admission of Red China to the United Nations. Between 1966 and 1971 he chaired the American Conservative Union (ACU), a political education association established by conservatives following their January 1965 loss of the chair of the Republican National Committee.

In the House Ashbrook consistently opposed the Johnson administration's social welfare legislation. A member of the Education and Labor Committee, he boycotted a subcommittee's vote on the first elementary-secondary education bill in February 1965. He voted against operating funds for the War on Poverty in 1966 and 1967. In 1966 he defended the white minority government of Rhodesia. In 1968 the Americans for Constitutional Action gave Ashbrook a 100 percent rating on selected issues. Its liberal counterpart, Americans for Democratic Action, scored Ashbrook's voting record a "zero."

Ashbrook stood apart from the Ohio Republican organization. His independence almost cost him his seat in 1966 and denied him a role at the 1968 Republican National Convention. In December 1964 the Republican state legislature, unsympathetic to Ashbrook's interests, redrew his district and forced him into a 1966 reelection contest with another incumbent, Representative Robert Secrest (D-Ohio). Although the president and other high Democratic officials campaigned on Secrest's behalf, Ashbrook won 55 percent to 45 percent. Again, however, he ran behind the state Republican ticket, in this case by 13,000 votes. In Ohio's May 1968 presidential primary, Ashbrook opposed Republican governor JAMES A. RHODES, who wanted an uncommitted slate pledged to him. Ashbrook won in his own district. Like most other conservatives, he actively supported former vice president RICHARD M. NIXON for president. At the August National Convention Ashbrook unsuccessfully tried to persuade Rhodes into releasing the large Ohio delegation in Nixon's favor. "The boat's moving out," he pleaded, "and we're still on the shore." Rhodes, however, ignored Ashbrook's counsel and refused to climb onto the Nixon bandwagon.

Once president, Nixon quickly disillusioned Ashbrook. He castigated Nixon's welfare reform bill and new China policy, as well as the president's implementation of wage and price controls. Ashbrook ran against Nixon for the 1972 presidential nomination but failed to win over 10 percent of the vote in any primary or to capture a single delegate. Still, his challenge helped shape the coming conservative movement that would rally behind Ronald Reagan less than a decade later. Ashbrook died in Ohio on April 24, 1982, while campaigning for the Ohio Senate seat held by Democratic senator Howard Metzenbaum.

## Ashley, Thomas L(udlow)

(1923– ) *member of the House of Representatives*

Born on January 11, 1923, to an old, rich, and Republican Toledo family, Thomas L. Ashley earned his B.A. at Yale in 1948 and his LL.D. at Ohio State in 1951. Ashley worked briefly for Radio Free Europe, serving as assistant director of special projects. He resigned in 1954 and returned to Ohio to run for Congress. Running on the Democratic ticket, he won a narrow victory in a 1954 race for the U.S. House. Reelected without difficulty through the 1960s, he served on the Banking and Currency Committee and became a specialist in housing legislation. He secured federal funds for the rebuilding of downtown Toledo. In 1959 and 1961 Ashley was one of only two House members to vote against resolutions reiterating Congress's opposition to the admission of the People's Republic of China into the United Nations.

During the Johnson years Ashley voted for all major Great Society legislation and maintained a solid liberal record. In 1968, for example, the Americans for Democratic Action gave the Toledo Democrat a 100 percent rating on selected issues. But Ashley did not join those House liberals who frequently criticized Johnson's Vietnam policies.

As a member of the Banking and Currency panel, Ashley initiated legislation favorable to banking interests. In 1965 Congress sought to revise the vaguely phrased Bank Merger Act of 1960, which the Justice Department had interpreted as requiring bank regulatory agencies to obtain the attorney general's approval for bank mergers. The measure also sought to place mergers outside the authority of existing antitrust regulations. In a 1963 test case by the Justice Department, the Supreme Court had ruled that bank merger activity still fell under the guidelines set by the Sherman and Clayton Acts. In September 1965 Ashley proposed a House version of a bill authored by Senator A. WILLIS ROBERTSON (D-Va.) that effectively removed banks from the Sherman and Clayton laws. It compelled the Justice Department to follow what Ashley and others considered the more flexible anticoncentration guidelines established in the 1960 statute. The following month Ashley invoked a rarely used rule and called a special Banking and Currency Committee meeting in the absence and without the foreknowledge, of the chair, WRIGHT PATMAN (D-Tex.). As planned the Ashley bill—which Patman opposed—received committee approval. The full House delayed a vote until January 1966, and Patman persuaded Ashley to accept a mild rewording of his bill. The final measure, an amendment to the 1960 merger act, became law in February 1966 and closely resembled the original Ashley proposal.

Bank lobbyists considered the clarification of the 1960 merger statute to be a victory, a curb on Justice Department suits against ambitious bank mergers. The executive director of the Ohio Bankers Association endorsed Ashley for reelection and, in a letter to Ohio bankers, called the Toledo Democrat one of seven House members who has "shown an understanding of banking matters and a willingness to help develop sound laws on these subjects." Two Supreme Court decisions, however, later neutralized Ashley's labors. In separate 1967 and 1968 antimerger orders, the high court upheld the Justice Department's contention that the 1966 amendment, like its parent statute, had been too imprecisely worded to remove banks from previous antitrust legislation.

Ashley chaired the Banking and Currency Committee's International Trade Subcommittee and, with three other panel members, challenged a late 1966 Republican and southern Democratic attack upon the U.S. Export-Import Bank (Eximbank), which planned to participate in the financing of the Italian Fiat automobile company's proposed plant in the Soviet Union. Drawing upon CIA estimates of the facility's impact on the Soviet economy, a special four-member panel chaired by Ashley endorsed the loan in March 1967. Senate foes of Eximbank enacted a ban on support for the Fiat project, but in November the full House Banking and Currency Committee forced through a presidential waiver with the ban, thus effectively defeating the loan adversaries.

Ashley remained in the House during the Nixon years and helped draft the 1970 Omnibus Housing Act. His work was rewarded by the government's decision to build a new "model cities" town near Toledo. He was defeated in 1980 by Edward Weber, and he started a consulting firm in Washington D.C.

## Ashmore, Harry S(cott)

(1916–1998) *director, Center for the Study of Democratic Institutions*

The son of a Greenville merchant whose grandfathers served in the Confederate Army, Ashmore, who was born on July 28, 1916, began his career in journalism covering the local courthouse for the *Greenville Piedmont*. In the late 1930s he toured the poverty areas above the Mason-Dixon line to do a series on northern "tobacco roads." In 1941 Ashmore studied journalism at Harvard University as a Nieman fellow. Following wartime service he became associate editor of the *Charlotte* (N.C.) *News*, where he wrote editorials that advocated two-party southern politics, racial and religious tolerance, and the enfranchisement of African Americans. In 1948 Ashmore became executive editor of the *Arkansas Gazette* in Little Rock. In this position, he continued to play a leadership role in the fight for civil rights in the South. In fact, a compromise plan that he proposed in a December 1948 article became the basis for a civil rights program that Arkansas representative Brooks Hays proposed in 1949. Although the plan was defeated, largely by liberals who considered it too mild, it cemented Ashmore's reputation as one of the leading voices for racial equality in the South.

Under Ashmore's direction the *Gazette* supported the two successful gubernatorial campaigns of Orval E. Faubus in the 1950s. But in 1957 Governor Faubus ordered National Guards troops to Little Rock to prevent nine African Americans from integrating Central High School. The *Gazette* editorially denounced the governor and endorsed President Eisenhower's dispatch of federal troops to Little Rock to enforce implementation of the court order desegregating the school. "I'll give it to you in one sentence," Ashmore wrote. "The police have been routed, the mob is in the streets, and we're close to a reign of terror." Ashmore won national recognition for the support he gave to school integration in Little Rock, and the next year he won a Pulitzer Prize for the "forcefulness, dispassionate analysis and clarity" of his *Gazette* editorials.

In September 1959 Ashmore resigned as the *Gazette*'s executive editor to become a director of the newly founded Center for the Study of Democratic Institutions. The center, headed by educator Robert Hutchins, was supported by the Fund for the Republic, which in turn had been created by the Ford Foundation. The center assembled representatives of academia, government, the news media, business, and labor to examine "the major institutions of the 20th century in the light of their impact on the possibilities for the continued existence of democracy." At the center Ashmore concentrated his attention on race relations and the press, defending the growing militancy of the civil rights movement in the mid-1960s and arguing that the quality of the news media, especially television, would be enhanced if a national nongovernmental commission were established to annually review its quality and make recommendations for improvement.

Traveling on behalf of the center and with the authorization of the State Department, Ashmore visited North Vietnam in early January 1967. He was accompanied on the trip by *Miami News* editor William C. Baggs. Ashmore stayed in Hanoi for nine days and had a rare two-hour talk with President Ho Chi Minh. He reported on his return to the United States that damage inflicted by American bombing was "offset by the unifying influence" it had on the North Vietnamese people.

Upon his return from Hanoi, Ashmore reported to the State Department that Ho's conditions for the start of peace talks were the cessation of U.S. raids on North Vietnam and a halt to the buildup of American forces in South Vietnam. With Assistant Secretary of State WILLIAM P. BUNDY, Ashmore and Baggs drafted a note to Ho shortly after their return from Vietnam. According to Ashmore the letter modified previous U.S. conditions for "reciprocal restraint" on the part of Hanoi in exchange for a halt to the bombing of the North. The note also indicated that the United States would respect the Geneva Accords as the basis for the peace talks. The Ashmore-Baggs note was sent to Hanoi on February 5, 1967.

In September 1967 Ashmore published an article in *Center Magazine* charging that President Johnson had "effectively and brutally canceled" the Ashmore-Bundy peace initiative of January–February. According to Ashmore's article, "The Public Relations of Peace," Johnson had sent another note to Ho, dated February 2, but received by Hanoi on February 10, that nullified the effect of the Ashmore letter by insisting that any proposal for a de-escalation of the war go into effect at the end of the scheduled Tet truce on February 12.

In the ensuing controversy over the peace initiative, Bundy denied that Johnson's letter had contradicted the Ashmore note. Bundy said, "Mr. Ashmore yields to an understandable feeling that his own channel was the center of the stage. It was not; it was a very, very small part of the total picture." On September 18, 1967, Ashmore reiterated his view that the two letters were "inconsistent in tone and content. . . . The tone of ours is quite conciliatory. The tone of the president's is quite harsh." Senator J. WILLIAM FULBRIGHT (D-Ark.) noted the next day that the incident indicated that the United States could have entered into peace talks with

North Vietnam if it had been willing to consider "anything short of surrender" by Hanoi. The administration rejected the claim, and criticized Ashmore for meddling in government business. "These characters," State Department adviser GEORGE BALL later declared, "just wanted to get a Nobel Prize." Ashmore and Baggs collaborated on a 1968 book, *Mission to Hanoi*, which recounted their negotiations with Ho and the subsequent frustrations their peace efforts encountered in Washington. Although Ashmore continued to praise LBJ for his civil rights accomplishments, he blamed the president for losing sight of these aims in his quest for victory in Vietnam.

In 1974 a severe financial crisis compelled the center to eliminate its program of grants that enabled distinguished scholars to devote full-time to discussion and writing. In the midst of this crisis, Ashmore resigned. He went on to write or edit 14 books before his death on January 20, 1998.

## Aspinall, Wayne N(orviel)
### (1896–1983) *member of the House of Representatives*

Aspinall, the son of a fruit grower, was born on April 3, 1896, in Middleburg, Ohio, and raised in Palisade, Colorado. He studied at the University of Denver, where he received an LL.B. in 1925. After several years as a teacher and school administrator, Aspinall entered Colorado politics in 1930 and served in the state legislature until 1948, except for his years of service in World War II, which were spent with both the U.S. and British armies as a legal adviser. In that year he was elected to the House of Representatives from a large rural district in western Colorado. Assigned to the Public Lands Committee (later called the Interior and Insular Affairs Committee), Aspinall soon became an important figure in natural resources policy. He was a strong advocate of land reclamation projects and also favored a "multiple use" approach to resources development, combining recreation and commercial exploitation.

Aspinall became chair of the Interior and Insular Affairs Committee in 1959 and subsequently played a key role in all natural resources legislation. A strong opponent of what he called "conservation extremists," he helped delay and then weaken a wilderness preservation bill during the early 1960s. Observers also linked Aspinall to delays in the funding and construction of an irrigation project for

Navajo Indian lands in New Mexico. Environmentalists, commented the leader of the Sierra Club, had seen "dream after dream dashed on the stony continents of Wayne Aspinall."

The most important piece of natural resources legislation to gain Aspinall's attention during the mid-1960s was the Central Arizona Project (CAP), a $1.3 billion construction plan for facilities to divert Colorado River water to cities and farmlands in Arizona. Negotiations over CAP extended from 1963 to 1968, when Congress authorized the plan. Aspinall's main concern was to ensure that CAP would not deplete the supply of Colorado River water that the state of Colorado claimed. Therefore he worked for the addition of five irrigation projects to the CAP bill, all of which benefited his own Colorado district. Although three of the projects had previously received unfavorable reports from the Budget Bureau, the bill's sponsors accepted Aspinall's conditions in order to gain his support. The additional cost was $392 million.

Aspinall was less successful in other water-use conflicts of the mid-1960s. Vigorous opposition from Senator HENRY JACKSON (D-Wash.) quashed an Aspinall proposal to study the feasibility of augmenting the Colorado River flow by tapping the river basins of the Pacific Northwest. Aspinall also failed to put through legislation for the construction of two dams and a hydroelectric power station in the Grand Canyon section of the Colorado River. A massive lobbying campaign by the Sierra Club, a conservationist group, frustrated this plan in 1967.

Aspinall was a strong advocate of defense spending and the Vietnam War. These positions, as well as his stance on natural resources, helped him survive in conservative western Colorado. The Americans for Democratic Action gave Aspinall a "correct" rating of 57 percent for the mid-1960s. Redistricting in 1964 and 1966, however, increased the liberal and pro-conservation elements in his constituency. Aspinall was defeated in the 1972 Democratic primary by Alan Merson, a University of Denver law professor strongly supported by environmental and antiwar groups. He then returned to Palisade, Colorado, to practice law, where he remained until his death on October 9, 1983.

# B

## Baez, Joan
(1941–   ) *folksinger, pacifist*

Baez was born in Staten Island, New York, on January 9, 1941, and grew up in New York and California. In 1958 Baez began singing folksongs in the Boston area, then the center of a folk music revival. After successful appearances at the 1959 and 1960 Newport Folk Festivals, she signed a recording contract with Vanguard Records. Her first albums consisted mostly of traditional English and American

Political activist and folksinger Joan Baez, 1967 *(Library of Congress, Prints and Photographs Division)*

ballads and African-American spirituals, but she later began to perform contemporary songs and songs of her own composition as well. Baez rapidly became one of the country's most popular folksingers, helping to broaden the interest in folk music and serving in manner and dress as a model for many young women. She was one of the first American folksingers whose albums became best sellers; she was also one of the first popular performers to champion social activism in this period. "Action," she insisted, "was the antidote to despair."

Baez became increasingly involved in political activity throughout the 1960s. She was an active supporter of the civil rights movement and took part in a number of demonstrations, including the August 28, 1963, March on Washington, where she sang from the podium. Baez sang *We Shall Overcome* to a December 2, 1964, rally of several thousand Free Speech Movement supporters at the University of California, Berkeley, just before they occupied Sproul Hall, in a demonstration that first brought national attention to the growing student movement. She also sang at the first major national demonstration against the war in Vietnam, held in Washington, D.C., on April 17, 1965. In 1966 she walked arm in arm with Dr. MARTIN LUTHER KING, JR., during a march in Mississippi.

Baez was also a pacifist and in 1965 founded the Institute for the Study of Nonviolence in Palo Alto, California. She advocated the use of nonviolent tactics to oppose the war in Vietnam and was one of 350 people who announced in an April 14, 1966, advertisement in the *Washington Post* that they would protest the war by refusing to pay their federal income tax. Among the many antiwar activities Baez participated in were the "Stop-the-Draft-

Week" protests in Oakland, California, in October 1967. On October 16 Baez, her mother, and her sister, folksinger Mimi Farina, were among 125 picketers arrested at the Oakland Draft Induction Center. The arrested demonstrators received 10-day prison sentences. At the same center, Baez was again arrested on December 19 and received a 45-day sentence, which she began serving the next day. Baez was also a strong supporter of the United Farm Workers in their effort to unionize California agricultural workers. In 1968 Baez married David Harris, a leader of the Resistance, a draft resistance group. In 1969 she gave birth to their son, Gabriel; that same year, Harris began a three-year jail term for failing to report for induction into the army.

In 1967 and 1968 Baez made many speeches and television appearances urging resistance to the United States war effort in Vietnam, and she continued to be a vocal opponent of the war until its end. As one of a group of four Americans visiting North Vietnam in December 1972, she met with U.S. prisoners of war and was one of the few Americans other than the prisoners to be in Hanoi during the Christmas bombing raids. After the war she continued to use her music for political causes, singing at many benefits and protests, and, in 1979, she founded a human rights organization known as the Humanitas International Human Rights Committee.

## Bailey, John M(oran)
(1904–1975)  *chair, Connecticut Democratic State Committee; chair, Democratic National Committee*

Born on November 23, 1904, John M. Bailey grew up in Hartford, Connecticut, and received a B.S. degree from Catholic University in 1926. Politics became Bailey's life work in 1932, three years after he received his law degree from Harvard. In 1932 Bailey joined the Connecticut Democratic State Committee, and in 1946 he became its chair. Allying himself with former representative ABRAHAM A. RIBICOFF (D-Conn.). Bailey created a powerful Democratic organization, which by 1963 held both of the state's U.S. Senate seats and the governor's post. In national politics Bailey supported John F. Kennedy for the Democratic vice presidential nomination in 1956 and for the presidential nomination four years later. At the 1960 Democratic Convention, Kennedy managers charged Bailey with responsibility for rounding up delegate support in New England. He proved successful. Every delegate in the entire six-state region cast a vote for Kennedy, who won on the first ballot. As a reward for his labors, Kennedy named Bailey chair of the Democratic National Committee (DNC) in January 1961. More of a campaign strategist than an orator or ideologue, Bailey began detailed preparations for Kennedy's reelection in early November 1963.

After Kennedy's assassination Bailey continued as national committee chair, although President Johnson gave him only a minor part in the 1964 campaign. Bailey described his role at DNC as a "housekeeping job," overseeing the party's voter registration drive and aiding Democratic congressional candidates. Still, in this capacity he managed to increase the number of registered Democrats by approximately 2 million people. On September 11, 1964, Bailey signed, with his Republican counterpart Dean Burch, an agreement drafted by the Fair Campaign Practices Committee. The code called for both parties to concentrate on the "real issues" during the campaign, refrain from the defamation of opponents, and eschew appeals to racial or religious prejudice. Johnson won the election with 61 percent of the vote, while the Democrats increased their senatorial advantage by one and gained 37 seats in the House.

President Johnson displayed little interest in the functions of the DNC following the party's 1964 triumph and, in 1965, severely cut the committee's operations budget and eliminated its voter registration program. In the November 1966 elections the Democratic Party lost three Senate seats, 47 House districts and eight governorships to the Republicans. Despite the party's poor showing, Johnson ignored demands by some state Democratic officials to remove Bailey and instead reaffirmed his faith in the DNC chief in January 1967. The Democratic National Committee revived its registration program and sought to improve relations with state leaders. Still, Bailey had a hard time being taken seriously by many in the administration, who recognized that the president had little use for him since he had been an early Kennedy loyalist. By 1967 he had become, recalled one party leader, "just a figurehead."

In defense of the President, Bailey spoke out against critics of the Vietnam War. When Michigan governor and Republican presidential hopeful GEORGE W. ROMNEY complained in September 1967 of having been "brainwashed" during a Vietnam tour,

Bailey accused the governor of having "insulted the integrity" of General WILLIAM WESTMORELAND and Ambassador HENRY CABOT LODGE, both of whom had briefed Romney. Bailey charged Republicans the next month with playing "an opportunist game" on Vietnam. In January 1968 the party chair expressed his certainty that the president and vice president would win renomination.

When Johnson unexpectedly withdrew from the race on March 31, Bailey found himself without a candidate. He appeared representative of the "old politics" to the party's antiwar forces supporting the candidacies of Senator EUGENE J. MCCARTHY (D-Minn.) and Senator ROBERT F. KENNEDY (D-N.Y.). Bailey encouraged LBJ to reconsider his decision up until the 1968 Democratic National Convention, but to no avail. In his own state, where he had remained chair, Bailey confronted a well-organized McCarthy-for-President movement. As state chair he wanted an unpledged delegation to the national convention despite a 44 percent write-in vote for McCarthy in the primary. The McCarthy forces demanded 10 seats on the state's 44-member delegation, threatening to oppose Ribicoff for the Democratic senatorial nomination if Bailey denied them. On June 26, however, Joseph Duffey, chair of the state McCarthy committee, accepted Bailey's offer of nine delegates under orders from the candidate himself.

Bailey retired as national chair immediately after the August 1968 Democratic National Convention and returned to Connecticut as state leader. Duffey defeated Bailey's choice for the U.S. Senate in the August 1970 Democratic primary, but the Republicans defeated both Duffey and Representative Emilio Q. Daddario (D-Conn.), Bailey's candidate for governor, in the November general election. Bailey reasserted his influence four years later when he skillfully organized the landslide election of Ella Grasso as the first female governor of the state, which was ironic since a decade earlier he had been taken to task by Democratic leaders because of gender discrimination in the national Capital Democratic Club. Just six months after the election, John Bailey died in Hartford.

## Baker, Bobby (Robert Gene)
(1928–    ) *secretary to the Senate majority*
Bobby Baker, who was born on November 12, 1928, in Easley, South Carolina, came to Washington,

D.C. in 1943 at the age of 15 to be a Senate page, and by 1951 had become chief page for the Senate Democrats. Simultaneously he earned a college degree from George Washington University and then attended night law classes at American University. Senator Lyndon Johnson (D-Tex.) and Senator Robert Kerr (D-Okla.) became Baker's most powerful patrons. Appointed assistant secretary to the Democratic minority in 1953, Baker, dubbed "Lyndon Junior" by Senator ALAN BIBLE (D-Nev.), became secretary to the majority in 1955 when Johnson became Senate majority leader. In this role, he played a central role in helping advance legislation sought by Johnson, and appears to have played a particularly significant part in the passage of the 1957 Civil Rights Act.

With a sophisticated understanding of the traditions and procedures of the Senate and a shrewd knowledge of individual senators, Baker helped Johnson run the upper house. "Bobby Baker is my strong right arm," Johnson said in 1960. "He is the last person I see at night and the first person I see in the morning." It was Baker's task to round up senators to back measures favored by the leadership; the precision of his preliminary "head counts" was celebrated. Baker's ability to perform numerous favors for senators and others won him power and prestige on Capitol Hill, and his position as secretary-treasurer of the Senate Democratic Campaign Committee enhanced his influence. He also became a close friend to the Johnson family. Some Democrats outside the Senate establishment resented Baker's power; Senator JOSEPH CLARK (D-Pa.) identified him as "a protagonist of the conservative coalition." The new Senate majority leader, MIKE MANSFIELD (D-Mont.), kept Baker as majority secretary after 1961, but Baker worked more closely with his wealthy conservative sponsor, Kerr, than with his ostensible superior, Mansfield.

Baker also used his political connections to enrich himself: His net worth in 1963 was $1.7 million, although his annual salary was only $19,600. His financial machinations led to his political downfall in the fall of 1963, when a disgruntled business associate sued him, charging that Baker had "conspired maliciously" against his business. Amid accusations of "influence peddling" and rumors about his diverse sources of income, Baker was forced to resign as secretary to the majority in October.

Baker's wheeling and dealing began to unravel in late 1963, when the *Washington Post* reported that he was using his political connections to advance his business interests. During 1964 and 1965 the Senate Rules and Administration Committee carried out an intermittent investigation to uncover Baker's complex network of money-making ventures. His most lucrative investment was his interest in the Serv-U Corporation, a vending company dependent upon Baker's contacts for its business. Its chief customer was the aerospace industry, which relied heavily on federal contracts. Senator Kerr was chair of the Senate Aeronautical and Space Sciences Committee, and the head of the National Aeronautics and Space Administration (NASA), JAMES WEBB, was a former employee of Kerr's oil firm. Baker estimated his 28 percent interest in Serv-U to be worth $1 million.

In the case of the Mortgage Guarantee Insurance Corporation (MGIC), Baker's inside information and associations enabled him to earn handsome profits. Learning from his banking contacts that MGIC stock was about to soar in value, Baker bought $9,700 worth of stock from MGIC's president, Max Karl, in 1959. Subsequent stock splits and a favorable tax ruling from the Internal Revenue Service pushed the value of the shares to $145,000 by 1964. Karl admitted that there was "some question of the legality" of the sale of the stock before it was registered with the Securities and Exchange Commission, but he said that he had wanted "prominent stockholders" for MGIC and that Baker "knew a lot of people." Baker also made substantial sums by tipping off friends to MGIC and other opportunities in exchange for a share of the profits.

Baker traded on his official position and his access to political decision makers in a host of other ventures. Baker's political contacts figured prominently in the financing and patronage of the Carousel Motel in Maryland, of which he was a part owner. The motel became a center of Washington nightlife. Its grand opening party welcomed President Johnson and his wife, as well as busloads of Washington politicians. Rumors, however, of wild parties and illicit dealings cast a shadow over the hotel, and on the reputations of its owners. Baker joined Senator GEORGE SMATHERS (D-Fla.) in a Florida real estate project and invested in an Oklahoma bank recommended by Senator Kerr with funds borrowed from Kerr's own bank. He received fees for helping banks to gain charters, ocean freight forwarders to pass a licensing bill, and a Haitian slaughterhouse to obtain a license to export meat to the United States and Puerto Rico. He usually received compensation for his services in the form of legal fees paid to his Washington law firm, Tucker & Baker. Baker himself was never admitted to the District of Columbia bar.

The Rules Committee revelations made the Bobby Baker case an issue during the 1964 presidential campaign. A Baker associate, insurance agent Don Reynolds, testified that for the privilege of selling life insurance to Lyndon Johnson, he had been compelled by Johnson's aide, WALTER JENKINS, to buy advertising time on Johnson's Texas television station and give Johnson a hi-fi set. Throughout the scandal Johnson tried to dissociate himself from Baker, refusing to comment on the case except to call his former aide "no protégé of anyone." Republican presidential candidate Senator BARRY GOLDWATER (R-Ariz.) repeatedly claimed the scandal was symptomatic of the ethics of Johnson's Washington. Goldwater maintained that Bobby Baker was the issue that hurt Johnson "more than anything else." Still, LBJ managed to escape with relatively little damage.

Partisan politics also marked the Senate's Baker investigation. While the Rules Committee's Democratic majority endeavored to narrow the scope of the probe, the Republican minority sought to widen it. Committee Republicans accused the Democrats of conducting a "whitewash" and of sidestepping matters such as Baker's alleged use of "party girls" for political and business purposes. Several important revelations came not from the Rules Committee but from Senator JOHN WILLIAMS's (R-Del.) independent investigation. In May 1964 Williams proposed that the committee's inquiry be expanded to include senators as well as Senate employees and to probe improper campaign contributions. The Senate rejected the resolution, 42-33, after a bitter partisan debate.

The Rules Committee's report, issued in July 1964, found Baker "guilty of many gross improprieties." His business activities were "certainly in conflict with his official duties," the report said, but not in technical violation of conflict-of-interest statutes. The committee's three Republicans issued a dissenting report charging that "the full story has not been disclosed concerning Bobby Baker . . . because the majority prevented the investigation from proceeding." The report recommended amending Senate rules to require disclosure of financial interests by senators and Senate employees, but the full Senate turned aside the proposal. The Senate did approve, by a 61-19 vote, the creation of a six-member bipartisan committee to investigate future "allegations of improper conduct" by senators and Senate employees.

The Baker investigation did not end with the filing of the Rules Committee report in July 1964. In September Senator Williams charged that Baker and builder Matthew McCloskey had conspired to make an illegal $25,000 contribution to the 1960 Democratic campaign in order to secure for McCloskey's construction firm the contract to build the District of Columbia stadium. Williams's source was Don Reynolds, who claimed that the $25,000 was passed on through his insurance company as an overpayment by McCloskey on a performance bond for the stadium project.

The Rules Committee resumed hearings on the Baker matter after the November election. Baker appeared and, as he had done in February, refused to testify. McCloskey said that the $25,000 overpayment was an honest "goof." An FBI report challenged Reynolds's credibility. The committee—with the Republican minority objecting to the majority's "continuing effort to discredit witnesses"—found McCloskey had not been proven guilty of any wrongdoing but termed Baker's involvement "impropriety on his part as a public servant."

In January 1967 a U.S. District Court convicted Baker of income tax evasion, theft, and conspiracy to defraud the government. Baker was found guilty of, among other offenses, misappropriating $100,000 in campaign contributions he had solicited from savings and loan company executives anxious to defeat a tax proposal before the Senate Finance Committee. Baker started serving a one-to-three-year sentence in January 1971 and was paroled in June 1972.

—TO

## Baker, Howard (Henry), Jr.

(1925– ) *member of the Senate*

Born into a politically active family in Huntsville, Tennessee, on November 15, 1925, Baker was raised in the traditionally Republican eastern mountain enclave in Democratic-dominated Tennessee. Baker's father represented the state's second congressional district from 1951 until his death in 1964. The younger Baker received an LL.B. degree from the University of Tennessee in 1949 and became an affluent criminal and corporate lawyer.

Baker's father-in-law, Senate Minority Leader EVERETT M. DIRKSEN (R-Ill.), urged him to run for his father's congressional seat in 1964. Instead, Baker decided to seek the last two years of the term of Senator Estes Kefauver (D-Tenn.), who had died the previous year. He campaigned on a conservative platform, advocating a limited federal role in local education and in the enforcement of civil rights laws. However, Baker avoided identification with Republican presidential candidate Senator BARRY M. GOLDWATER (R-Ariz.). Baker lost the race to Democrat Ross Bass by 50,000 votes but received more votes than any other Republican in the history of Tennessee.

In 1966 Baker ran for a full Senate term against Governor FRANK CLEMENT. Baker adopted more moderate positions than he had in 1964 and sought to improve upon the 2 percent support among blacks that he had received in his first race. Receiving almost 20 percent of the black vote, Baker won the election by almost 100,000 votes and became the state's first popularly elected Republican senator.

During his first two years in the Senate, Baker compiled a fairly conservative record. According to *Congressional Quarterly*, he voted with the upper chamber's conservative coalition on 70 percent and 76 percent of key roll-call votes in 1967 and 1968. In 1967 he opposed a liberal effort to facilitate the invoking of cloture against filibusters. During the fall of the same year, Baker supported the conservative coalition in its effort to grant governors veto power over federal grants-in-aid to states and localities and worked hard in support of federal/state revenue sharing programs. He also helped arrange for Tennessee to become the home for the world's first nuclear breeder reactor plant. A consistent supporter of military expenditures, he backed the Sentinel antiballistic missile system in the fall of 1968.

However, on some major issues Baker deviated from a conservative voting pattern. In June 1967 he backed an amendment offered by Senator EDWARD M. KENNEDY (D-Mass.) to establish a maximum 10 percent population variation between the largest and smallest congressional districts beginning in 1968. The proposal was made during Senate debate over compliance with the Supreme Court's historic "one-person, one-vote" decision. Baker circulated among Republicans a statistical study indicating that equal-population districting would assist their party in the 1968 elections. He was also credited with helping to convince his father-in-law in 1968 to abandon his opposition to open housing proposals and support a compromise bill that exempted certain privately owned homes. He also had a fairly moderate record on environmental issues.

After Dirksen died in 1969 Baker sought to replace him as minority leader but lost by five votes in the Republican caucus to Senator HUGH SCOTT (R-Pa.). Scott defeated Baker again in 1971. In 1972 Baker won reelection with 62 percent of the vote. He would finally be elected minority leader in 1977, and then served as majority leader from 1981 to 1985. In 1973 he gained national attention as the ranking Republican on the Senate Select Committee on Presidential Campaign Activities, popularly known as the Watergate Committee. In that capacity, Baker, who had been a friend of President Nixon, slowly became convinced of his guilt. After leaving the Senate in 1985, he served as chief of staff to President Reagan from 1987 to 1988, and he was later appointed ambassador to Japan by President George W. Bush.

—MLL

## Baker, (John) Wilson

(1915–1975) *director of public safety, Selma, Alabama; sheriff, Dallas County, Alabama*

During the 1950s Baker, who was born on January 31, 1915, in Shallotte, North Carolina, served as a captain in the Selma, Alabama, police force, and, in 1963, he became its director, at a critical time in the civil rights struggle in the South. From January through March 1965 Rev. MARTIN LUTHER KING, JR.'s, Southern Christian Leadership Conference (SCLC) sponsored a series of demonstrations in Selma, culminating in a march from that city to Montgomery, to protest discrimination in the registration of voters and demand federal action to end it. Blacks constituted a majority of the population of Dallas County, of which Selma was the seat, but only 300 were registered to vote.

The white leadership of Selma, at that time, was divided. Many, including Baker and Mayor Joseph Smitherman, sought conciliation and peace. Although Baker asserted that he was a segregationist, he regarded himself as a professional police officer and attempted to negotiate with protest leaders and to use a minimum of force against illegal demonstrations. When, for example, a segregationist leader attacked Martin Luther King while he attempted to register at a Selma hotel in early 1965, Baker quickly interceded, and arrested the assailant

before King was seriously injured. The Rev. Hosea L. Williams, a SCLC leader, praised Baker for his restraining influence upon white "haters." As a result of his methods, Baker clashed with Dallas County sheriff JAMES G. CLARK, a militant segregationist who employed what the protesters and many other observers regarded as unnecessary and brutal violence to break up demonstrations.

In April 1965 Baker joined other city officials and local business leaders in sponsoring newspaper advertisements urging acceptance of the Civil Rights Act of 1964 and of equal voting rights for Negroes. Baker commented, "This is what we must do under the law, like it or not."

Baker challenged Clark in the May 1966 primary for the Democratic nomination for sheriff. Baker stressed his commitment to fair and efficient law enforcement, while the incumbent emphasized his belief that the civil rights movement was a Communist-inspired uprising. Thousands of blacks had been registered since the beginning of SCLC's activities in Dallas County, and civil rights leaders regarded the primary as an important test of their voting strength. Baker defeated Clark with the support of almost all of the new voters. Clark ran a write-in campaign in the general election and was again defeated by Baker. Assuming office in January 1967, the new sheriff announced that he would appoint a black deputy.

Baker was reelected sheriff twice and died on September 11, 1975, while still holding that post.

—MLL

## Baldwin, James A(rthur)

(1924–1987) *author*

Born on August 12, 1924, in New York City, the son of an indigent minister, Baldwin described his Harlem childhood as a "bleak fantasy." During his adolescence he tried preaching but gave up at age 17 and left home shortly thereafter relocating to Greenwich Village. Unable to sell his first two books, Baldwin at age 24 left for France, where in 1953 he finished *Go Tell It on the Mountain*, his highly praised novel of religious experience in Harlem. His most widely acclaimed work of the 1950s was *Notes of a Native Son*, a collection of personal essays that probed what one reviewer called "the peculiar dilemma of Northern Negro intellectuals who can claim neither Western nor African heritage as their own." During the early 1960s Baldwin was probably the most widely read and discussed black writer in America. In *The Crisis of the Negro Intellectual*, Harold Cruse characterized Baldwin as "the chief spokesman for the Negro among the intellectual class" during the early years of the decade. In May 1963 Baldwin arranged a meeting between President Kennedy and a dozen black leaders and artists.

In *The Fire Next Time*, two essays published in 1963, Baldwin argued that black people in America "are very well placed indeed to precipitate chaos and ring down the curtain on the American dream." He went on to predict that "if we do not dare everything, the fulfillment of that prophecy, recreated from the Bible in song by a slave, is upon us: 'God gave Noah the rainbow sign, no more water, the fire next time.' " Read in light of the 1965 Watts riot and later violence in inner cities across the nation, *The Fire Next Time* came to be regarded as a prophetic and insightful study of American race relations. In his history of the civil rights movement, Thomas Brooks wrote that no one else predicted the events "with such verve and before such a wide audience." It also earned him extensive scrutiny by the FBI, which resulted in a file of more than 1,700 pages.

Baldwin returned from Europe in March 1965 to participate in the march from Selma to Montgomery, Alabama, led by MARTIN LUTHER KING, JR. Although Baldwin lived abroad and devoted most of his energies to creative writing, he continued to take an active interest in the black movement in America. In February 1967 he resigned from the advisory board of *Liberator*, a black nationalist monthly he had been associated with since 1961, in protest against the magazine's publication of allegedly anti-Semitic articles. Baldwin also contributed the introductory essay to *If They Come in the Morning*, a collection of essays that assessed the significance of Angela Davis's trial, which was published in 1971. His writings also dealt increasingly with the topic of homosexuality. In fact, Baldwin's work as a whole focused more on conflict and the human condition than simply on the lives of African Americans. In 1983 he became a professor at the University of Massachusetts, and he died of cancer four years later in France.

—DKR

## Ball, George W(ildman)

(1909–1994) *undersecretary of state*

A specialist in European trade issues, Ball would prove to be one of the most influential foreign pol-

icy advisers of the decade. He was born on December 21, 1909, in Des Moines, Iowa. Following his graduation from Northwestern University Law School in 1933, he worked in several New Deal agencies before returning to Illinois to practice law. Ball reentered government service in 1942 in the Office of Lend-Lease Administration and in 1944 was appointed director of the U.S. Strategic Bombing Survey, a civilian group established to assess the effect of the air offensive against Germany. After the war Ball resumed private law practice and became a specialist on international trade. He was appointed undersecretary of state for economic affairs in January 1961; in November of that year he became undersecretary of state for economic affairs. In November he was promoted to undersecretary, which was the second-ranking position in the State Department.

During the Kennedy administration Ball was concerned primarily with the formulation of U.S. trade policy and with international problems in such areas as the Congo and Cuba, but he also became involved in the growing war in Vietnam. In 1961, when the administration was discussing policy options in Vietnam, Ball cautioned against the introduction of U.S. combat forces because he felt such a course would mire the United States in a war it could not win. He also believed that the United States was best served by devoting its resources to Europe, rather than Asia, and was highly critical of South Vietnamese leader Ngo Dinh Diem.

Ball's opposition to U.S. involvement in the war continued during the Johnson administration. Following the spring 1965 decision to increase troop commitments and launch regular bombing attacks upon North Vietnam, Ball wrote a memorandum titled "Cutting our Losses in South Vietnam," which argued for de-escalation and political compromise. Ball viewed South Vietnam as a "lost cause" because of the lack of popular support for the Saigon regime and the deep commitment of the Communists. He cautioned that continued troop increases would not assure victory.

Ball recommended that the administration hold forces at current levels while arranging a conference to negotiate a withdrawal. He recognized that America would lose face before its Asian allies, but he felt that the loss would be of short duration and that the United States would emerge as a "wiser and more mature nation." If this step were not taken, "humiliation would be more likely than the achievement of our objectives—even after we paid terrible costs."

In January 1966 Ball again wrote a memorandum to Johnson opposing the bombing of North Vietnam because that policy contained "a life and dynamism of its own" and could result in retaliation by Hanoi or involve the United States in a war with China. Drawing on his wartime experience he also argued that massive air strikes would strengthen, not weaken, North Vietnamese resolve.

Convinced that he could not change American policy, Ball left office in September 1966 to return to his law firm and to investment banking. He continued to advise President Johnson, however, particularly in the 1968 crisis with North Korea over their capture of the American spy ship USS *Pueblo*. He also served briefly as ambassador to the United Nations. In March 1968 Ball served as a member of the Senior Advisory Group on Vietnam. This gathering of what was commonly called the "Wise Men" had been called by President Johnson to advise him on the military's request for over 200,000 additional troops. In their high-level meetings Ball continued to press for de-escalation. A majority of Johnson's advisers, fearing the domestic social and political consequences of still another troop increase, now supported the point of view advanced for so long by Ball. On March 31 Johnson announced new restrictions on the bombing of North Vietnam in the hope of starting peace negotiations.

A quiet man who remained personally loyal to Johnson and Secretary of State DEAN RUSK, Ball's determined opposition to the war only became widely known after the publication of the *Pentagon Papers* in 1971. After leaving public service, Ball served as an investment banker until his death in 1994.

—EWS

## Barr, Joseph W(alker)

(1918–1996) *chair, Federal Deposit Insurance Corporation; undersecretary of the Treasury; secretary of the Treasury*

The son of an Indiana businessman, Joseph Barr, who was born on January 17, 1918, received his B.A. from De Pauw University and his M.A. degree in economics from Harvard University. During World War II he commanded a submarine chaser in the Mediterranean. He returned to Indiana after the war to help manage his family's businesses, which included grain elevators, farm equipment financing, real estate, and theater operations. Elected to the House of Representatives in 1958 as a Democrat from a traditionally Republican district, Barr served on the Banking and Currency Committee, where he concentrated on the balance of payments problem and helped write legislation creating the Inter-American Bank and the International Development Association. After being defeated for reelection in 1960, he was named an assistant to Undersecretary of the Treasury HENRY FOWLER.

In January 1964 President Johnson appointed Barr chair of the Federal Deposit Insurance Corporation (FDIC). The main tasks of the FDIC were to insure bank depositors against bank failures and to regulate those banks outside the purview of the Federal Reserve System and the Comptroller of the Currency, about one-seventh of all U.S. banks. Along with other banking regulatory officials, Barr came into conflict with controversial Comptroller James J. Saxon. Barr objected to Saxon's policy of liberally granting bank charters, and his office engaged in bitter disputes with Saxon's over various technical matters. In March 1965 Barr told Congress that 13 banks had failed since 1963, as compared with an average of only one or two a year over the previous 20 years. He dismissed fears of a rash of bank failures, however, stating that the assets of the failed banks amounted to only $113 million, a fraction of the $366 billion in total assets of all insured banks.

In April 1965 Barr became undersecretary of the Treasury at the request of Fowler, who had just become secretary of the Treasury. In addition to his administrative duties, Barr took chief responsibility for congressional relations, working to win approval for a broad range of administration proposals. He was a strong defender of the college-student loan program and a truth-in-lending proposal long held up by the Senate. The latter bill, requiring lenders to state clearly the interest and finance charges on consumer loans, was finally passed in July 1967.

Barr appeared before congressional committees on several occasions to promote the administration's campaign-finance reform plan, which involved federal subsidies for presidential and Senate campaigns and income tax credits for campaign contributions. The plan failed to pass during the Johnson administration. In March 1968 he called for approval of the administration's tax surcharge and implementation of budget cuts, both designed to curb inflation.

Following Fowler's retirement in December 1968, Barr served as secretary of the Treasury for the final month of the Johnson administration. In January 1969 he made headlines by criticizing wealthy Americans who were using tax loopholes to avoid paying taxes, singling out 155 individuals with incomes over $200,000 who had failed to pay any income taxes in 1966, 21 of whom had earned over $1,000,000. The firestorm of public protest encouraged Congress to pass a series of tax reforms in 1969, designed to ensure that the wealthiest Americans paid some taxes. After leaving the Treasury he became president of the American Security and Trust Company in Washington, D.C. He died of a heart attack on February 23, 1996.

—TO

## Bartlett, E(dward) L(ewis)

(1904–1968) *member of the Senate*

Although born in Washington, E. L. "Bob" Bartlett devoted much of his life to Alaska. He was born on April 20, 1904, in Seattle, Washington. He attended the University of Alaska; worked as a reporter at the *Fairbanks* (Alaska) *Daily News* from 1925 to 1933; and subsequently worked in the state as a gold miner, and as chair of the Unemployment Compensation Commission of Alaska, until the late 1930s. In 1939 President Franklin Roosevelt appointed him secretary of Alaska, and, from 1945 until 1959, he served as Alaska's nonvoting delegate to the U.S. Congress. There he lobbied effectively for Alaskan statehood, finally granted in 1959. That year he was elected to the Senate along with ERNEST GRUENING (D-Alaska). During the Kennedy years Bartlett compiled a liberal record and was one of a small bloc of liberals in the Senate to oppose creation of the privately owned Communications Satellite Corporation.

During the Johnson years Bartlett voted for school aid, civil rights, Medicare, and antipoverty legislation. His vote to end the filibuster on the 1964 Civil Rights Act was among the most critical in getting that landmark piece of legislation passed. Shipping and fishing were important Alaskan industries, and Bartlett, as a member, and, after 1967, as chair of the Merchant Marine and Fisheries Subcommittee of the Senate Commerce Committee, played an important role in shaping maritime legislation. In 1966 he won enactment of a bill providing federal aid for research and experimentation in the production of fish protein concentrate. He also won approval of a Coast Guard bill passed in June 1967, which appropriated $58 million more than the administration requested for the construction of five high-endurance Coast Guard cutters. The administration had asked for funds for only one such vessel.

As subcommittee chair, Bartlett clashed with the administration in shaping legislation to help the foundering U.S. merchant marine. In the fall of 1968 President Johnson pocket-vetoed a bill Bartlett sponsored creating an independent federal maritime administration within the executive branch. Earlier that year Transportation Secretary ALAN S. BOYD had proposed a scaling down of federal subsidies to the shipping and shipbuilding industries so that they would, in time, become competitive in world markets. Boyd admitted that this proposal violated previous agreements worked out with Bartlett, Commerce Committee chair WARREN MAGNUSON (D-Wash.), and other congressional leaders who favored substantial aid to American maritime industries. As a result of this conflict, no significant legislative program for the maritime industry passed during the Johnson administration.

Bartlett, who voted for the Tonkin Gulf Resolution of August 1964 soon earned a reputation as a critic of U.S. escalation in Vietnam. He was among 15 senators who sent a letter to President Johnson on January 27, 1966, calling for a continuation of the pause in the bombing of North Vietnam. In May 1968, however, Bartlett joined 16 Senate critics of the war who warned Hanoi that "they remained steadfastly opposed to any unilateral withdrawal of American troops from South Vietnam." He died in December 1968, while still in office, and was replaced by Ted Stevens. In 1971, Bartlett was honored by being the first politician to have a statue of his likeness built in the state Capitol Rotunda.

—JLW

## Battle, Lucius D(urham)

(1918–   ) *assistant secretary of state for educational and cultural affairs, ambassador to the United Arab Republic, assistant secretary of state for Near Eastern and South Asian affairs*

Lucius Battle was born on June 1, 1918, in Dawson, Georgia, and received his B.A. from the University of Florida in 1936. Following wartime naval service in the Pacific, he returned to Florida to earn a law degree in 1946. That year he also joined the State Department. From 1949 until 1953 Battle served as a special assistant to Secretary of State DEAN ACHESON. In 1956 he resigned from the foreign service to become vice president of Colonial Williamsburg. He rejoined the department in 1961 as special assistant to Secretary of State DEAN RUSK. In 1962 he became assistant secretary of state for educational and cultural affairs. By the time he was appointed ambassador to the United Arab Republic (UAR) in July 1964, he had acquired a reputation as a tough, effective administrator with little diplomatic experience.

Battle arrived at his post during a period of tension. In part, the friction resulted from America's Middle Eastern policy, and a refusal to grant Egypt long-term agricultural aid. Egypt's close contacts with the Soviet bloc strained relations still further. In addition, President Gamal Abdel Nasser had a personal dislike for President Johnson that hindered close communications between the two leaders.

Relations between the United States and the UAR became increasingly tense during November and December 1964, after mobs attacked the American embassy and Cairo shot down a U.S. oil company plane belonging to a close friend of Johnson. Misunderstandings caused the situation to deteriorate still further. Shortly after the plane crash Nasser received an incorrect report that Ambassador Battle had rejected an Egyptian request for more wheat. The account prompted Nasser to deliver a general attack on U.S. foreign policy on December 23. During his speech he personally insulted both Battle and Johnson. In reaction, the United States held up wheat shipments until June 1965. Battle eventually negotiated an agreement for the sale of $55 million worth of surplus U.S. agricultural products in January 1966.

Tensions between the two countries continued during 1965 and 1966 because of Washington's seemingly inconsistent policy toward Egypt. During these years Egypt attempted to improve relations and ensure future American aid by underplaying its role in Middle Eastern affairs and concentrating on national economic development. Although these actions had been recommended by the United States, neither Battle nor the State Department gave any indication of approval. Instead, the embassy continued to focus on Egypt's position in foreign affairs. The ambassador's attitude convinced Nasser to reassert Egypt's leadership in the Arab world, particularly in the struggle against Israel. Consequently, U.S.-UAR relations deteriorated further.

In January 1967 Battle was appointed assistant secretary of state for Near Eastern and South Asian affairs. He resigned the post in September 1968 to become vice president of the Communications Satellite Corporation. Battle became president of the Middle East Institute in 1973.

—EWS

## Bayh, Birch E(vans)
(1928–  ) member of the Senate

Bayh was born on January 22, 1928, in Terre Haute, Indiana, graduated from Purdue University's School of Agriculture, and then settled on a 340-acre farm outside Terre Haute in 1951. He won election as a Democrat to the largely Republican Indiana House of Representatives in 1954. Following the elections of 1958, a new Democratic majority in the state legislature chose the 30-year-old Bayh speaker of the House for the 1959–60 session. Simultaneously, Bayh studied law at the Indiana University School of Law, receiving his degree in 1960. In 1962 Bayh was elected to the Senate in a spectacular upset victory over the conservative Republican incumbent, Senator Homer E. Capehart.

As chair of the Judiciary Committee's obscure Subcommittee on Constitutional Amendments, Bayh became responsible for removing constitutional flaws in the procedure for presidential succession suddenly made apparent by the death of President Kennedy. In conjunction with Representative EMANUEL CELLER (D-N.Y.), chair of the House Judiciary Committee and with the support of President Johnson, Bayh introduced a constitutional amendment in January 1965 outlining the steps to be taken by the vice president, the cabinet, and Congress in case of presidential disability. The amendment also provided for the filling of a vice presidential vacancy by presidential appointment subject to congressional approval. The amendment passed both houses of Congress in the summer of 1965 and became the 25th Amendment after it was ratified by the 38th state legislature in February 1967.

Along with Senator SAM ERVIN (D-N.C.), Bayh led the fight against a constitutional amendment proposed by Senator EVERETT M. DIRKSEN (R-Ill.) that would have nullified the Supreme Court's decision barring prayer in public schools. In the Senate the proposed amendment fell short of the required two-thirds majority by nine votes in September

1966. As a substitute for the Dirksen amendment, Bayh offered a resolution stating it was "the sense of Congress" to encourage, but not require, "voluntary silent prayer and meditation" in public schools. The Senate rejected Bayh's proposal by a 52-33 vote.

Bayh supported the major civil rights and social welfare proposals of the Johnson administration. He also supported the president on Vietnam, although he did challenge specific elements of the conduct of the war that he found troubling, particularly the appointment of Rutherford Poats to the position of deputy administrator for the Agency for International Development. His overall voting record was that of a moderate liberal; *Congressional Quarterly* reported in 1964 that Bayh voted against measures favored by the conservative coalition of Republicans and southern Democrats 65 percent of the time. Reelected in 1968, Bayh was often in the forefront of constitutional and judicial action in Congress during the Nixon administration. He was instrumental in the passage of the 26th Amendment, which extended the franchise to 18 year olds; it also made him the first lawmaker since the beginning of the American republic to sponsor two constitutional amendments. He also led the Senate fight against confirming Clement Haynsworth and G. Harrold Carswell, Nixon's nominees to the Supreme Court in 1969 and 1970. Bayh was voted out of office in 1980, and he returned to the practice of law.

—TO

# Beirne, Joseph A(nthony)
(1911–1974) *president, Communications Workers of America*

Born on February 16, 1911, in Jersey City, New Jersey, Beirne began working for Western Electric in 1928 and became an important leader of its employees association during the 1930s. Initially resisting Congress of Industrial Organization (CIO) efforts to organize telephone workers, Beirne was elected president of the independent National Federation of Telephone Workers in 1943. He negotiated the first national contract with the American Telephone and Telegraph Company (AT&T) in 1946. Following the first nationwide strike the next year which saw over 300,000 workers walk off their jobs, he became president of the reorganized Communications Workers of America (CWA), which affiliated with the CIO in 1949. Beirne became a CIO vice president and, after the AFL-CIO merger in 1955,

a vice president of that organization. Throughout his years of leadership, Beirne stressed the importance of the union maintaining good ties with the community, and he became the first union leader to serve as chair of the United Way of America's governing board. He was also appointed by President Johnson to serve on the board of the Corporation for Public Broadcasting.

In 1957 Beirne helped expel the International Brotherhood of Teamsters from the labor federation, and during the early 1960s he thwarted Teamster efforts to raid the CWA. A strong Kennedy supporter, Beirne in 1960 proposed a broad AFL-CIO training program for Latin American unionists similar to one already operated by the CWA. President Kennedy backed the plan as a means of countering the influence of Cuban leader Fidel Castro in the region. The American Institute for Free Labor Development (AIFLD) was established in 1961 under government, AFL-CIO, and private corporate "sponsorship.

As president of the 440,000-member CWA, Beirne was a prominent figure in organized labor. Within his union, however, many considered him insufficiently aggressive toward AT&T. "A strike against the Bell System is like throwing pebbles at the Queen Mary," Beirne once remarked, noting that automation had reduced the system's vulnerability to work stoppages. In 1968 contract talks with AT&T, the CWA sought large wage increases well beyond the Johnson administration's anti-inflation guideposts. Beirne maintained that increased efficiency and automation would keep overall wage costs down. Reluctant to call a strike, Beirne finally did so because of strong rank-and-file pressure. On April 18 the CWA rejected the company's fourth and final offer and began the first nationwide telephone strike in 21 years. Although union members overwhelmingly supported the action, there was little disruption of phone service. Many female employees did not belong to the CWA, and supervisory personnel filled in for strikers. Direct dial communications were, for the most part, unaffected. Despite the phone company's success in maintaining services during the walkout, the Bell System agreed to a three-year 19 percent pay raise for CWA members on May 9, 1968.

An active Democrat, Beirne was one of several labor leaders who resigned in February 1968 from Americans for Democratic Action when the organization endorsed antiwar presidential aspirant Senator EUGENE MCCARTHY (D-Minn.). During the 1972 presidential campaign, however, Beirne defied AFL-CIO president George Meany's policy of neutrality to become secretary-treasurer of a national labor committee for Democratic candidate GEORGE MCGOVERN. He remained president of the CWA until his death on Labor Day in 1974. In 2001 Beirne was inducted into the U.S. Department of Labor Hall of Fame.

—MDB

## Bell, David E(lliott)

(1919–2000)  *administrator, Agency for International Development*

Born in Jamestown, North Dakota, on January 20, 1919, and raised in Palo Alto, California, Bell received an M.A. in economics from Harvard University. He joined the Bureau of the Budget briefly in 1942 and returned in 1945 following service in the U.S. Marine Corps. Between 1947 and 1953 Bell alternated between the Budget Bureau and the White House, specializing in drafting presidential budget messages and speeches on economic affairs. After helping with ADLAI STEVENSON's presidential campaign in 1952, Bell returned to Harvard and from 1954 to 1957, as a member of a Harvard-Ford Foundation team, assisted the government of Pakistan in formulating fiscal policies. He became a recognized authority on the economic problems of underdeveloped countries.

Bell was named Kennedy's director of the Bureau of the Budget soon after the 1960 election. He favored deficit spending when recession and high unemployment were the nation's major economic problems. While still working on Kennedy's controversial tax cut proposal in November 1962, Bell was appointed administrator of the Agency for International Development (AID). He assumed his new duties at the beginning of 1963.

Kennedy created AID in 1961 to coordinate and rationalize the allocation of money authorized for foreign aid. AID was intended to further a Kennedy foreign aid program that emphasized development rather than short-term assistance. As Bell stressed in 1965, "development assistance leads to permanent progress . . . and the earliest possible termination of economic assistance." AID was organized on a worldwide regional basis with missions attached to U.S. embassies. It paralleled the State Department in the economic field.

In early 1964 the Johnson administration inherited much of the congressional and public criticism of the Kennedy foreign aid program. Undersecretary of State GEORGE W. BALL, head of a panel studying the program, recommended that AID be abolished and its centralizing function be transferred to the State Department. Johnson decided to retain AID, but as an economy measure he instructed Bell to reduce by 1,200 the number of AID employees by the end of fiscal 1965.

Most of Johnson's reductions were made in economic assistance—funds for military projects were only slightly affected. The 1965 aid request of $3.38 billion was the smallest in the history of the program. In the years Bell served under Johnson, development assistance in loans and grants approached $1 billion in the annual foreign aid appropriation. The Alliance for Progress, a separate funding category, usually received about $500 million. Supporting assistance, which in 1960 amounted to approximately $1 billion, was cut to $369 million in fiscal 1966.

Bell concentrated development spending in those countries that showed the ability to benefit from development loans and a willingness to cooperate politically with the United States. Most of these nations—Brazil, Chile, Turkey, Nigeria, India, Pakistan—were large and politically sensitive. At the same time 14 nations no longer received supporting assistance grants because their economies were thought to be strong enough to dispense with such aid. Bell also encouraged participation from private sources and the governments of other developed countries. By emphasizing development Bell was also able to answer critics who charged that foreign aid contributed to the gold drain and the balance of payments problem. Speaking before the Senate Banking and Currency Subcommittee on International Finance in March 1965, Bell noted that "80 percent of the AID's expenditures last year represented not dollars going abroad, but steel, machinery, fertilizer and other goods and services purchased in the United States." Cutting AID appropriations "would primarily reduce U.S. exports, and would have only a very small effect on the balance of payments."

In January 1966 Johnson requested an additional $415 million for AID for the current fiscal year. Most of this money was part of a supplemental request for $13 billion to meet Vietnam costs. During the previous year AID had spent funds in

Vietnam that had been earmarked for other areas. Vietnam not only received more military aid—now computed as part of the Defense Department budget—than any other nation, but in fiscal 1967 it became the largest recipient of AID assistance. Much of the aid was in the form of short-term grants, which Bell had tried to eliminate from the foreign aid program. At the same time AID concentrated on development in Vietnam, attempting to build a modern economy in the midst of war. AID saw itself in a race with time, believing that the South Vietnamese would have the strength and will to defeat the Communists as soon as they possessed a functioning economy. More than in the past, therefore, AID assumed tasks of a military and political nature, and Bell frequently participated in Vietnam policy-making sessions. He decided to resign, however, in July 1966 to become the Ford Foundation vice president, in charge of its overseas programs. Bell was succeeded by AID deputy administrator William S. Gaud. Bell died of leukemia in September, 2000.

—JCH

## Bellmon, Henry

(1921–   ) *governor, member of the Senate*

Bellmon was born on September 3, 1921, near Tonkawa, Oklahoma, and became a farmer in the dry wheatfields of north central Oklahoma. Bellmon won a two-year term in Oklahoma's House of Representatives in 1946. In 1960 he became the state Republican Party's chair and in that post built a vigorous party organization. In 1962 Bellmon, a comparatively unknown political figure, launched a gubernatorial campaign in which he stoutly opposed an increase in the state sales tax. His Democratic opponent, W. P. Atkinson, was hampered by his advocacy of a one-cent sales tax increase and the disarray of his party following a bitterly divisive primary campaign. Bellmon campaigned as the common citizen's candidate, and his decisive victory margin of 76,000 votes made him the state's first Republican governor since Oklahoma's admission to the union in 1907.

Bellmon's victory on a "no new taxes" platform precipitated a major crisis in the state's public educational system. Oklahoma had had no general statewide tax increase since 1937, and its school system, struggling against rising postwar enrollments and increased operating costs, had by 1963 reached

"a critical plane" according to the National Education Association (NEA). Although Oklahoma ranked 37th in the nation in teacher's pay, Bellmon vetoed a proposed 1963 raise in salaries and campaigned vigorously against a sales tax increase scheduled to be put before the state's voters in April 1965.

In November 1964 Oklahoma teachers took a "professional holiday" to stress their dissatisfaction with state educational funding, and, in May 1965, after the defeat of the sales tax referendum, the NEA declared sanctions against the state for a school system that it termed "subminimal . . . in almost every area." Sanctions, in lieu of a strike, consisted of a warning to teachers in other states not to accept public-school jobs in Oklahoma and a "censure, through public notice, that Oklahoma, despite ample resources, maintains a subminimal pub-education program." Bellmon denounced sanctions as "disgusting, disgraceful and distasteful" and was chiefly concerned with the "black eye" that those sanctions gave to a state seeking to attract new industry and investment capital. In September 1965 the NEA lifted its sanctions, although it warned that it would continue to keep a watchful eye on the situation.

In December 1965 Bellmon announced "Operation Giant Stride," a plan to upgrade state social services, raise teachers' salaries by $800 over two years, raise the minimum wage for public employees, add to the highway program, and strengthen the state's public and mental health services. The plan, which Bellmon argued would not "strangle" Oklahoma's growth by raising taxes, died in a committee of the Democratic-controlled legislature.

Bellmon's fiscal conservatism and pro-industry attitude was reflected in his opposition to pollution-control expenditures in the mid-1960s. At a two-day national water conference in Washington, D.C., in December 1965, Bellmon expressed the view that the nation's waterways should be recognized in part to be repositories of waste, a policy that the Johnson administration had repudiated. "The objective of any pollution abatement program must be the attainment and preservation of usable water—not the elimination of waste discharges," Bellmon said. "Assimilation of waste is unavoidably one of the multipurpose uses that water must serve and this must be recognized by all."

Bellmon lost his bid for reelection to a second term in the Republican Party's 1966 gubernatorial primary. In August 1967 Bellmon was named chair of the Nixon for President Committee. In November 1968 he ran for the Senate and defeated three-term liberal incumbent senator A. S. MIKE MONRONEY (D-Okla.). In the Senate, Bellmon voted for school integration, civil rights, and the controversial Panama Canal Treaty.

A consistent supporter of Nixon administration programs, Bellmon was reelected to a second Senate term in 1974. Bellmon retired in 1980 and returned to Oklahoma. Six years later he was elected to a final term as governor.

—TJC

## Bennett, Wallace F(oster)

(1898–1993) *member of the Senate*

Born on November 13, 1898, in Salt Lake City, to parents who were Mormon pioneers, Wallace Bennett entered his family's plate and glass manufacturing business after graduating from the University of Utah. After serving as president of the National Association of Manufacturers (NAM) for 1949, Bennett was elected to the Senate as a Republican from Utah in 1950.

In the Senate Bennett espoused the same free enterprise views he had promoted for the NAM, opposing government restrictions on business and firmly defending "right-to-work" laws that allowed states to ban the union shop. He became an influential proponent of pro-business thinking on the Finance Committee and the Banking and Currency Committee, and Republican senators often looked to Bennett for conservative guidance on economic questions.

Bennett consistently opposed the social welfare programs of the Kennedy and Johnson administrations. He voted against Medicare, federal aid to education, the Model Cities program, and a minimum wage increase. In a minority report on a 1965 housing bill, Bennett denounced "new and enlarged urban programs, bulging with money, designed to step up the pace of creeping federalism." In July 1968 he argued that the answer to poverty lay in the involvement of business, rather than the federal government, in black inner cities.

Nevertheless, Bennett's overall voting record during the Johnson administration showed a gradual movement toward the Republican center. *Congressional Quarterly* reported that Bennett voted with the Senate's conservative coalition 92 percent of the time in 1961 and 94 percent in 1964 but on only 57 percent of key votes in 1966 and 67 percent in 1968. He supported the presidential candidacy of fellow-Mormon governor GEORGE ROMNEY of Michigan in 1964 and 1968, although it was more Romney's religious than his political affiliation that attracted him. Bennett voted for the Civil Rights Act of 1964, although he had opposed the cloture vote regarding this bill, the Voting Rights Act of 1965, and, the Civil Rights Act of 1968, but he favored an amendment to the latter exempting single-family homes from antidiscrimination coverage. He also was a strong supporter of U.S. involvement in the Vietnam War and high military spending.

Bennett was one of the few western senators to approve the administration-backed Coinage Act of 1965, which eliminated silver from nickels and dimes. In 1967 he finally relaxed his opposition to a truth-in-lending law to require merchants to furnish borrowers with full information about finance charges and interest rates. Maintaining that he had always favored full disclosure and opposed only the application of a single formula to many different types of credit, Bennett in July agreed to support a compromise version that exempted revolving charge accounts from the annual disclosure requirement. The compromise bill also exempted retail credit contracts when the finance charge was less than $10.

Bennett was one of five senators on the Finance Committee to vote against the administration's $11 billion tax cut in January 1964. Bennett preferred repeal of many excise taxes and a lowering of capital gains taxes. In 1965 he pushed through a depletion allowance of 10 to 22 percent for beryllium, rich deposits of which were located in Utah. Bennett backed the administration's tax increase when combined with spending cuts in 1968.

In October 1965 Bennett became vice chair of the Senate Select Committee on Standards and Conduct, the panel charged with investigating the ethics controversy revolving around Senator THOMAS DODD (D-Conn.). In April 1967 Bennett presented the committee's report recommending censure of Dodd for channeling campaign funds to his personal use. In February, however, Bennett had objected to Senator JOSEPH CLARK's (D-Pa.). "Bobby Baker amendment" to require senators to disclose all their assets and income. Bennett said that such a requirement came "perilously close to infringing upon the private affairs of a senator."

After defeating the Utah state coordinator for the John Birch Society in the Republican primary in

September 1968, Bennett won reelection over his Democratic opponent in November with 54 percent of the vote. During the Nixon years he acted as the administration's spokesperson on finance in the Senate. He retired from government service in 1974 and returned to Utah. He died in Salt Lake City on December 19, 1993.

—TO

## Berrigan, Daniel
### (1921– ) *antiwar activist*

One of six children, who was born on May 9, 1921, in Virginia, Minnesota, Daniel Berrigan moved with his family to Syracuse, New York, after his father was fired from his job on a railroad in Minnesota for his activity in the Socialist Party. At the age of 18 Berrigan applied for admission to the Society of Jesus. After his novitiate he studied philosophy and theology at Woodstock College in Maryland and Weston College in Massachusetts. He was ordained in 1952.

In 1953 and 1954 Berrigan served as an auxiliary military chaplain in Germany. After returning to the United States in 1954, he taught French and theology at the Jesuits' Brooklyn Preparatory School. Berrigan also led a chapter of the Young Christian Workers in work among Puerto Ricans living on Manhattan's Lower East Side. From 1957 to 1963 he was a professor of New Testament studies at Le Moyne College in Syracuse, where he attracted a dedicated group of young followers committed to pacifism and civil rights—one of whom was David Miller, later the first convicted draft-card burner.

Beginning in 1964 Berrigan fasted, picketed, sat-in, and spoke against the Vietnam War. In the summer of 1965 he helped form the interdenominational Clergy and Laymen Concerned about Vietnam. As a result of his antiwar activity, his superiors decided to send him to South America, apparently under pressure from the Archdiocese of New York, which was headed by the hawkish FRANCIS CARDINAL SPELLMAN. PRotests from liberal Catholics forced his recall after three months, and Berrigan resumed his organization of antiwar work.

On May 17, 1968, Daniel and eight other Catholics, including his brother, FATHER PHILIP BERRIGAN, walked into the draft board office in Catonsville, Maryland, and set fire to the draft records with homemade napalm. The Catonsville

Nine, as they came to be known, had selected the Catonsville draft board because it was housed in a Knights of Columbus hall and therefore symbolized, in their view, the collusion of the church and those directing the war. The Nine went to trial in October 1968 for conspiracy and destruction of government property. Daniel Berrigan and the others were found guilty, and he was sentenced to three years in prison. That same year, he was part of an American delegation to North Vietnam that orchestrated the release of three downed U.S. pilots. In April 1969, when he was to have begun serving his sentence, he went underground, later explaining that he had refused to accept the legal consequences of his lawbreaking because "there is no machinery of recourse with our law about this war." In August 1970 FBI agents apprehended him on an island off the Rhode Island coast, and he was sent to federal prison in Danbury, Connecticut, where he served 18 months. After his release, he continued to be active in protesting against the use of U.S. military force.

—TLH

## Bevel, James L(uther)
### (1936– ) *organizer and project coordinator for Southern Christian Leadership Conference*

James Bevel, born on October 19, 1936, in Itta Bena, Mississippi, became a Baptist minister in 1959 and shortly afterward joined the civil rights movement. While studying at the American Baptist Theological Seminary in Nashville, Bevel worked as an organizer for the Student Nonviolent Coordinating Committee (SNCC). In 1960 he helped organize a number of sit-ins, to protest segregated lunch counters in Nashville, and soon he became chair of the Nashville Student Movement. He would also prove to be a driving force in the continuation of the freedom rides in the South in 1961. In 1962 SNCC members joined with MARTIN LUTHER KING, JR.'s, Southern Christian Leadership Conference (SCLC),to protest the trial of freedom riders in Albany, Georgia. This was Bevel's first close contact with the SCLC; one year later, he joined King's organization as Alabama project coordinator.

Bevel was closely associated with King during the most important civil rights struggles of the mid-1960s. In April and May 1963 he helped organize the SCLC campaign to end segregation in Birmingham, Alabama. When Birmingham police jailed King and other leaders, Bevel played a leading role in organizing the famous "children's crusade," which helped capture nationwide sympathy. That same year, he took a leading role in organizing the March on Washington. Bevel also directed the statewide drive to register black voters in the spring and summer of 1965. Many of the marches that he led were broken up by police, and Bevel himself suffered cranial injuries at the hands of Selma police in March 1965. Bevel aided King at this time not only as an organizer but also as a contact with SNCC and other civil rights groups that increasingly objected to the nonviolent strategy of SCLC.

When King decided in 1966 to expand civil rights activity to northern cities, Bevel was to take charge of the SCLC Chicago program. His main task was to coordinate the activities of 100 neighborhood improvement and community action organizations in the city's large west side African-American neighborhood. Bevel soon came to believe that the neighborhood's condition resulted from "internal colonialism," which he defined as the efforts of business leaders and city officials to take money from blacks without reinvesting it in the black community. Attempting to reverse this pattern, he formed an association of welfare recipients in Chicago and directed a boycott of four local dairy companies that had refused to hire black workers. Bevel also helped organize several marches into all-white ethnic neighborhoods in May 1966, dramatizing black demands for an end to housing discrimination. The practical effects of the SCLC Chicago campaign were not great, but it did publicize the problems of black communities in the North.

In addition to his civil rights activities, Bevel became a strong opponent of the Vietnam War during the mid-1960s. As early as 1965 he urged the formation of an "international peace army" in which civil rights groups would share tactics and organizers with the antiwar movement. Bevel attacked U.S. involvement in Vietnam as a "war of oppression against a foreign colored people," paralleling the oppression of blacks in the United States. According to sources in SCLC, Bevel persuaded King in early 1967 to come out openly in support of the antiwar movement. This stand drew the criticism of several black leaders, including ROY WILKINS and WHITNEY YOUNG, who wanted to keep civil rights separate from issues of foreign policy. But Bevel continued working to bring the two together. In January 1967 he became head of the Spring Mobilization Committee to End the War in Vietnam, and he helped organize the large antiwar demonstrations of

Civil rights leader James Bevel in Selma, Alabama, 1965 *(Library of Congress, Prints and Photographs Division)*

April 15 in New York and San Francisco. In New York 125,000 participated, including King himself.

Bevel took a leave of absence from the SCLC in 1967 to devote himself to further antiwar activities. By the time of King's assassination in April 1968, however, Bevel had returned to the civil rights movement. He was present in Memphis when King died, and he led the march King had planned in support of the city's striking sanitation workers. One month later Bevel was a leader of the SCLC Poor People's Campaign in Washington, a series of demonstrations to demand greater government attention to poverty problems. He subsequently coordinated SCLC activities in Philadelphia and worked as an aide for RALPH ABERNATHY, King's successor as head of the SCLC. Bevel left SCLC in 1969, but he remained involved in various community movements.

—SLG

### Bible, Alan D.
(1909–1988) *member of the Senate*

Born on November 20, 1909, in Lovelock, Nevada, Bible served as attorney general of Nevada from 1942 to 1950. He was elected to the Senate in 1954 to fill the seat vacated by the death of Senator Patrick McCarran, a former law partner. Throughout the Eisenhower and Kennedy administrations he voted as a moderate Democrat and established himself as a very effective but "low-profile" senator. Bible's committee assignments attested to his broad range of influence: he sat on the Committees on Appropriations, Interior and Insular Affairs, Select Small Business, Special Committee on Aging and the Democratic Steering Committee and was chair of the District of Columbia Committee.

Bible had a mixed record of support for the Great Society measures of the Johnson era. He voted against imposing cloture during southern Democratic attempts to filibuster the Civil Rights Act of 1964 and the Voting Rights Act of 1965, but he favored those bills after cloture had been imposed. Bible's vote against cloture arose from his belief that the filibuster was the ultimate protection for small states against the large ones. He voted in favor of Medicare and the Economic Opportunity Act of 1964 but was one of only two western Democrats to vote against the creation of the Department of Housing and Urban Development in August 1965. Representing the "Silver State," Bible was one of nine senators to vote against the administration-backed Silver Coinage Act of 1965, which eliminated silver from all dimes and quarters. During the 89th Congress, according to *Congressional Quarterly*, Bible supported administration measures 65 percent of the time.

Bible took an active interest in policy on land management, parks, and recreation. He was appointed in September 1964 to the Public Land Law Review Commission to study public land laws and administrative policies. As chair of the District of Columbia Committee, Bible successfully managed a home rule bill through the Senate in July 1965, but the House passed an entirely different measure and the bill died in conference. Bible gave up his post as chair of the District Committee in 1968 and in 1969 was appointed chair of the Select Committee on Small Business. He resigned in 1974, and returned to the practice of law. He died in California on September 12, 1988.

—TO

## Biemiller, Andrew J(oseph)
(1906–1982) *director, Department of Legislation, AFL-CIO*

Born in Sandusky, Ohio, on July 23, 1906, Biemiller was a union organizer, Wisconsin state legislator, and a member of Congress before helping to pave the way for the merger of the American Federation of Labor with the Congress of Industrial Organizations in 1955. He subsequently became head of the AFL-CIO department of legislation and one of Washington's most influential lobbyists.

The AFL-CIO's basic political agenda was determined by its National Legislative Council under the leadership of Federation president GEORGE MEANY. Biemiller's department, staffed by five or six full-time lobbyists and several representatives of the major international unions, was charged with responsibility for carrying out the daily AFL-CIO lobbying effort on Capitol Hill. Biemiller's staff also maintained close relations with both the Kennedy and Johnson administrations. "We were in agreement with the White House on almost every piece of legislation," Biemiller later stated. "At least once a week I would compare notes with LARRY O'BRIEN, when he was in charge of congressional relations and then with [Harold] Barefoot Sanders who succeeded him. Occasionally, we would sit in on the White House legislative meetings and vote-counting operations."

During the Kennedy years Biemiller became a familiar figure on Capitol Hill, lobbying on behalf of the administration's worker training, education, and foreign aid bills. Biemiller's office also played an important role in winning enactment of the Johnson administration's civil rights, school aid, and antipoverty legislation. Biemiller and Nelson Cruikshank of the AFL-CIO department of social security successfully countered American Medical Association opposition to the Medicare bill that was enacted in the summer of 1965.

From time to time relations between the AFL-CIO and the Johnson White House were strained. Biemiller's office was critical of the administration for its failure to exert its full authority to win repeal of Section 14b of the Taft-Hartley Act, which permitted states to pass right-to-work laws banning the union shop. The AFL-CIO was also critical of the administration for its failure to maintain firm control over prices in exchange for labor's wage restraint in the mid-1960s and for the $6 billion in spending cuts that LBJ proposed in 1968 as part of a deal with conservatives to obtain a $10 billion tax surcharge as well. However, Biemiller and Meany steadfastly supported the Vietnam War policy.

Biemiller worked actively in Vice President HUBERT H. HUMPHREY's 1968 presidential campaign. During the Nixon years the AFL-CIO frequently found itself in an adversary position toward the administration. Biemiller played an important role in blocking the appointment of conservative southern judges Clement R. Haynsworth and G. Harrold Carswell to the U.S. Supreme Court. Biemiller died in Maryland on April 3, 1982.

—JLW

## Black, Eugene R(obert)

(1898–1992) *presidential adviser on Southeast Asian economic affairs*

Black, who was born on May 1, 1898, grew up in Atlanta. After graduating from the University of Georgia in 1918 and serving briefly in the navy during World War I, he began a successful career as an investment banker, first in Atlanta and later in New York. By 1933 he was vice president of the Chase National Bank of New York. Widely respected in the financial community for his judgment and international contacts, Black was appointed executive director of the World Bank by President Harry Truman in 1947. Three years later he became president of the internationally funded bank, which made loans to developing countries on a commercial basis. Black remained with the World Bank until 1963, administering it according to conservative, low-risk policies.

Black's contacts and experience made him an important link between the financial community in New York and the federal government in Washington. This was especially true during the 1960s. In 1963 Black served on a committee of business executives and public figures formed to study the U.S. foreign aid program; he endorsed the committee's report, which criticized the program and recommended cuts in foreign aid levels. In September 1964 President Lyndon Johnson appointed Black to a foreign policy advisory panel, and, in March 1965, Black joined a committee working on proposals for improvement of the foreign aid program.

Black moved from an advisory position to a more active foreign policy role in April 1965, when President Johnson put him in charge of the administration's economic program in Southeast Asia. Johnson, hoping to deflate criticism of increasing U.S. involvement in Vietnam, promised in an April 7 speech a massive American development and reconstruction effort in the area. He immediately chose Black as his agent to convince congressional skeptics that the program would be soundly managed. Black's main task was to arrange the creation of a multinational Asian Development Bank (ADB), which would provide investment funds and planning research staffs for Southeast Asian countries. Black enlisted the support of United Nations Secretary General U Thant, argued for the ADB before the House Banking and Currency Committee and represented the United States in negotiations over the bank's funding and charter. When the ADB was formally established in December 1965, Congress approved the requested $200 million appropriation with little resistance.

In addition to the ADB, Black helped organize other U.S. aid projects in Southeast Asia, including a Mekong River Redevelopment Commission. Such programs faded, however, as the U. S. military effort in Vietnam grew. By the late 1960s Black's direct involvement in foreign policy had declined, although he did represent the United States on an Asian trip in September 1968, specifically designed to encourage Cambodian prince Sihanouk to increase his support for American efforts in Vietnam. Earlier that year, Johnson had sent Black to the Middle East, where Egyptian president Gamal Abdel Nasser sent him home with subtle messages that he sought improved relations. In January 1969 President Johnson awarded him the Medal of Freedom, America's highest civilian honor.

Black did not break his ties with the business community because of his government activities during the 1960s. He remained associated with the Chase Manhattan Bank, which appointed him to its board of directors in 1963, and he also served on the boards of the New York Times Company, International Telephone and Telegraph, and several other large corporations. In 1969 he became president of the Overseas Development Council, a social and economic research organization funded by U.S. businesses and foundations. Black went into semi-retirement in 1970, resigning from most of his corporate positions. He died on February 20, 1992.

—SLG

## Black, Hugo L(afayette)

(1886–1971) *associate justice, U.S. Supreme Court*

Hugo Black, born on February 27, 1886, in Harlan, Alabama, graduated from the University of Alabama Law School in 1906 and then practiced law in Birmingham. Elected to the U.S. Senate in 1926 and again in 1932, he was an ardent supporter of the New Deal, and was nominated to the Supreme Court by President Franklin Roosevelt in August 1937. His appointment was greeted with concern from many, especially anti–New Deal Republicans, but also from progressive Democrats concerned by Black's membership in the Ku Klux Klan (a membership born of political necessity, which did not include Black's active participation in violence or intimidation). Justice Black took a broad view of government power in the economic sphere and voted to sustain New Deal regulatory legislation and to extend federal antitrust laws. He also, in perhaps his most infamous opinion, supported the military's right to evacuate Japanese-American citizens from the West Coast after the attack on Pearl Harbor in the 1944 *Korematsu vs. United States* decision. Four years later, he decided in favor of LYNDON JOHNSON in a contested primary for the Democratic Senate nomination from Texas.

His judicial reputation, however, was based primarily on his insistence that the Court should protect the individual liberties guaranteed by the Bill of Rights against government intrusion. Black argued that the Fourteenth Amendment made those guarantees fully applicable to the states as well as to the federal government, and he became the leading judicial advocate of the incorporation of the Bill of Rights into the Fourteenth Amendment. He also contended that the provisions of the Bill of Rights were absolutes that could not be infringed by government. Viewing the First Amendment as the core of individual liberty, Black insisted that it barred the government from placing "legal restrictions of any kind upon the subjects people could investigate, discuss and deny."

Justice Black initially set forth many of these views in dissent, but during the 1960s the ends he advocated were often adopted by the Court. Although a majority never subscribed to Black's position on "total incorporation" of the Bill of Rights, the Warren Court, on a case-by-case basis, gradually incorporated the major provisions of the Fourth, Fifth, Sixth, and Eighth Amendments into the Fourteenth. At the same time the Court liberalized its interpretation of the criminal rights guarantees in the Fifth and Sixth Amendments, thus adopting positions close to those advocated by Black.

The Court again adopted a point of view held earlier by Black when it asserted in March 1962 that federal courts could try state legislative apportion-

ment cases. In February 1964 Black wrote a majority opinion extending this ruling to congressional districting. The ruling held that such districts should be as equal in population as possible so that each person's vote in a congressional election would have equal worth.

Black's arguments for an absolutist approach to the First Amendment also helped move the Court to increasingly liberal positions on free speech, free press, and obscenity issues. During the 1950s Black had dissented in cases in which the majority upheld various subversive activities laws as necessary government regulations of speech and other liberties perhaps most notably in his lone dissent in the 1951 case *Dennis v. United States*, in which he supported the free speech rights of Communist Party leaders in the United States. By the mid-1960s the trend of Court decisions had changed. Black voted with the majority in June 1964 to nullify a federal law denying passports to members of the Communist Party. He also joined majorities that overturned a federal law making it a crime for a Communist Party member to serve as a labor union official in June 1965 and voided a set of New York State teacher-loyalty laws in January 1967.

Black believed that even libelous and obscene utterances were protected by the First Amendment. Consequently, he opposed all government censorship of allegedly obscene materials and urged the Court to protect even malicious criticism of public officials. The Warren Court never fully adopted these views, but it increasingly narrowed the definition of obscenity and raised the level of procedural safeguards in censorship systems throughout the 1960s. In a series of cases beginning in March 1964, the Court also expanded freedom of the press by ruling that a public official could not recover damages for a defamatory falsehood relating to his official conduct unless he could prove the statement was made with "actual malice."

In his last years on the Court, Black sometimes took positions that surprised many observers. He dissented in June 1965 when the majority voided a Connecticut anticontraceptive law as an invasion of the right to privacy. He said he could find no "right of privacy" in the Constitution. Black's literal approach also led him to take a narrow view of the Fourth Amendment's ban on unreasonable searches and seizures. Dissenting in a June 1967 case where the majority invalidated a conviction based on electronic eavesdropping, Black argued that the language of the

Fourth Amendment could not be extended to protect individuals from electronic bugging.

Black was a consistent supporter of the Warren Court's decisions against racial segregation and discrimination. In a sharply worded majority opinion in June 1964, Black held that the closing of public schools to avoid desegregation in Prince Edward County, Virginia, was unconstitutional. He voted to sustain the 1964 Civil Rights Act and joined the majority in June 1968 in upholding an 1866 federal law barring race discrimination in the sale and rental of housing and property.

Given this record Black startled legal commentators with several opinions in other civil rights cases of the mid-1960s. In March 1966 he dissented from a decision that voided a Virginia poll tax applicable to state elections on the ground that it was a violation of the Fourteenth Amendment's equal protection clause. Black accused the majority of writing its own notions of good government policy into the Constitution under the guise of equal protection. Although he had voted in 1961 and 1963 to void the convictions of nonviolent civil rights demonstrators, Black dissented in June 1964, when the Court overturned the trespass convictions of protesters who sat-in at a Baltimore restaurant. He dissented when the Court voided similar convictions growing out of nonviolent civil rights demonstrations in cases decided in December 1964, January 1965, and February 1966. Black finally spoke for a five-justice in November 1966 to sustain the trespass convictions of demonstrators who had gathered outside a Florida jail to protest the arrest of fellow demonstrators.

Black rejected the argument that these demonstrations were a form of free speech and assembly protected by the First Amendment. As he explained in one dissent, he believed that the First Amendment protected expression in any manner in which it could be "legitimately and validly communicated." But it did not give, people a "constitutional right to go where ever they want, whenever they please, without regard to the rights of private or public property or to state law." While some observers felt these votes signaled a shift toward conservatism on Black's part, others, including the justice himself, held that his opinions were consistent with earlier statements that government could regulate the place, though not the content, of speech.

In his remaining years on the Court, Black dissented in cases reversing the Warren Court's expansion of the rights of criminal suspects. After 34 years on the Supreme Court, Black resigned on September 17, 1971, because of poor health. He died a week later at the age of 85.

Virtually all legal scholars ranked Black as one of the greatest and most influential justices in the Court's history. Summarizing the views of many other analysts, John P. Frank said that "no other single individual has more sharply put his own personal imprint upon the law as declared by the Supreme Court from 1937 to the present day than Justice Black." Beginning in "lonely and persistent dissent," Professor Norman Dorsen noted, "Justice Black again and again marshalled arguments to convince the Court of his views on the First Amendment, reapportionment, due process and other issues. At the end, much of what he professed was accepted, and his profound contribution to constitutional law was assured."

—CAB

## Blake, Eugene Carson

(1906–1985)  *member of the clergy; secretary general, World Council of Churches*

Blake grew up in St. Louis, Missouri, where he was born on November 7, 1906. Educated at Princeton and Edinburgh University, Blake took over his first pastorate in 1932 in New York City. In 1951 he was elected to the first of a series of terms as the stated clerk of the General Assembly of the Presbyterian Church in the U.S.A., which became the United Presbyterian Church after a 1958 merger with another Presbyterian group. He served as a U.S. delegate to the World Council of Churches, and, between 1954 and 1957, he was the elected president of the National Council of Churches of Christ in the U.S.A., an organization of Protestant and Orthodox churches that took positions on social issues and furthered interdenominational cooperation.

Blake's official posts made him the most influential spokesperson of liberal American Protestantism. During the 1950s he publicly attacked McCarthyism for its infringement of human and civil rights and for an "anti-intellectualism . . . which tends to blur all distinctions except that of white and black." Speaking for the World and National Councils of Churches, he advocated a world peace program, specifically backing the United Nations, armaments regulation and reduction, and economic and technical assistance to the underdeveloped world. In the early 1960s Blake sought interdenominational cooperation in support of the civil rights struggle and initiated plans for the merger of some of the leading Protestant denominations.

Blake tended to stress the fundamental beliefs shared by all religions rather than their theological differences, partly because he believed that in the modern world all religion was threatened by atheistic communism and humanistic secularism. In addition, his social activism subordinated the particulars of theology to the Christian responsibility to work for the "transformation of society."

In the mid-1960s Blake continued to enlist widespread clerical support for the civil rights movement. In 1963 he spoke at the March on Washington, where he criticized many American Christians for "coming late" to their support for civil rights. He was named chair of the National Council of Churches' Emergency Commission on Religion and Race in 1964 and the following year served on a National Advisory Council for the administration's antipoverty program.

Exchanging the chief executive post in the Presbyterian Church for the secretary-generalship of the World Council of Churches in 1966, Blake represented a global constituency and could speak with greater authority on international issues, including the war in Vietnam. Having founded the National Emergency Committee of Clergy concerned about Vietnam in January 1966, he at first supported President Johnson's "policy of restraint," but by the end of the year, he admitted that there was some "suspicion" about the sincerity of U.S. peace initiatives. In April 1967 he asserted that U.S. activity in Vietnam constituted the "greatest danger to human survival with the . . . exception of [Communist China]." In addition, he contended that the war was "our excuse not . . . to win the war against poverty in our cities, not to establish racial justice in our nation."

Blake's dream for the unification of U.S. Protestant denominations seemed close to realization when, in May 1966, the Consultation on Church Union, which he had founded in 1962, issued a timetable leading to the merger of eight leading Protestant denominations before the end of the century.

Blake was replaced as secretary general of the World Council of Churches in 1972 by a black Methodist minister from Dominica, a choice that indicated the council's commitment to the underdeveloped countries. But many of Blake's efforts toward interdenominational unity went unfulfilled. Despite joint ventures with Rome in peace and relief work and Catholic attendance at World Council meetings, doctrinal differences prevented Roman Catholics from joining his organization. After stepping down as secretary general, Blake became active in Bread for the World, an organization that encouraged the U.S. government to help developing nations to increase their ability to grow their own food by following more stable economic principles. He continued his social activism until his death on July 31, 1985.

—JCH

## Blatnik, John A(nton)
(1911–1991) *member of the House of Representatives*

Born in Chisholm, Minnesota, on August 17, 1911, John Blatnik taught high school chemistry until 1939, when he became assistant county superintendent of schools. After service in World War II, he was elected to Congress from a northern Minnesota mining district in 1946. He gained a reputation during the 1950s as a strong supporter of clean water legislation and as a proponent of many large-scale public works projects, among them the St. Lawrence Seaway.

A liberal on social issues, he supported all civil rights legislation, including the Civil Rights Act of 1964 and the Voting Rights Act of 1965. Blatnik also backed Medicare, the Model Cities program, aid to mass transit, antipoverty programs, and comprehensive child-care facilities for the working poor. In 1968 the Americans for Democratic Action gave him a 75 percent rating and the Committee on Political Education, the political arm of the AFL-CIO, credited Blatnik with a 100 percent correct record on selected issues.

Although a prime force behind the development of federal water pollution control in the 1950s, Blatnik ceased to be a vigorous proponent of clean water legislation during the 1960s. Consequently, many of the pollution measures pushed through the Senate were dismembered by the pro-industry House Public Works Committee, where Blatnik had once skillfully supported reform. The reasons for this change were not clear, but critics suggested that it was the result of the federal Water Quality Control Administration's attempt to stop the Reserve Mining Company, the largest employer in Blatnik's district, from dumping industrial wastes into Lake Superior.

In late 1965, when a biologist at the National Water Quality Laboratory in Duluth reported that pollutants from the Reserve Mining Company were being spilled into Lake Superior, his superiors directed the scientist to stop research on the project. Although the reasons behind his order were never precisely determined, David Zwick, in his history of pollution legislation, *Water Wasteland*, implied that it was a result of fear that Blatnik, as chair of the powerful House Public Works Committee's Rivers and Harbors Subcommittee, would vote to cut off funds to the laboratory. According to Zwick, a man friendly to Blatnik and Reserve Mining was named assistant director of the Duluth laboratory in 1967. The issue of Reserve Mining's pollution continued into the 1970s. In March 1975, after a series of court fights, the U.S. Court of Appeals ordered Reserve Mining to plan to end water pollution "within a reasonable time." Blatnik retired from Congress in 1975 and was replaced by his longtime assistant James Oberstar. Blatnik worked as a consultant until his December 1991 death in Forest Heights, Maryland.

—EWS

## Bliss, Ray C(harles)
### (1907–1981) *chair, Ohio Republican State Central Committee; chair, Republican National Committee*

The son of German immigrants, Ray C. Bliss was born on December 16, 1907, in Akron, Ohio, and received his B.A. from the University of Akron in 1935. While establishing a lucrative insurance and real estate agency, Bliss filled various posts within the Akron Republican organization and in 1942 became chair of the Summit County Republican Central Committee.

In February 1949 state Republican leaders, disheartened by their party's poor showing in the 1948 election, elected Bliss chair of the State Central Committee. Bliss asked for and received a salary and staff commensurate with making his position a full-time job. Avoiding the spotlight, Bliss reorganized state and local party machinery. Except for two years—1958 and 1964—and the repeated election of one Democrat—Senator FRANK J. LAUSCHE (D-Ohio)—Bliss enjoyed striking success as party chair. Political observers credited Bliss with putting Ohio in the Republican column in the 1960 presidential

contest and with the Ohio GOP's impressive showing in 1962. National party leaders considered Bliss as chair of the Republican National Committee (RNC) in 1961 and 1964.

The Republican's disastrous showing in 1964 set the stage for Bliss's elevation to RNC chair in 1965. Bliss inaugurated a series of reforms designed to revitalize a party badly divided by internal factionalism. Under his direction the RNC sponsored workshops for state and local chair, and 20,000 party volunteers. He also convinced party leaders to begin soliciting small contributors through direct mail, and to establish a permanent national headquarters in Washington, D.C. Retired army general Lucius D. Clay became finance chair at Bliss's request, and the RNC raised $4 million in 1965 and a record $6 million in 1966. Author of a 1961 RNC study that urged a greater party effort in the larger metropolitan areas, Bliss encouraged liberal Republican candidacies in urban areas. In November 1965 Republicans won elections for mayor of New York and district attorney in Philadelphia.

More basic to the GOP's dilemma was an intense factionalism, which, if uncontrolled, threatened the party's very existence. In part because of his personality, Bliss quickly emerged as an excellent choice for RNC chair. A nervous man given to chain-smoking, Bliss disliked partisan speech-making and frequent press conferences. Instead, he fostered the creation of the Republican Coordinating Committee made up of an ideologically broad spectrum of former presidential candidates, governors, and representatives. Between 1965 and 1966, the Coordinating Committee issued 18 position papers couched in language bland enough to please Republicans of all persuasions. Anxious over the possibility of another heated campaign for the presidential nomination in 1968, Bliss maintained an early neutrality and forbade the RNC to pay for the airplane used by RICHARD M. NIXON in his extensive 1966 election tours.

The 1966 election signaled a Republican revival. The GOP gained three Senate seats, 47 House seats, and eight governorships. The party won control of 15 state legislatures—a gain of nine—a sign that the GOP's success had come "from the bottom up," as Bliss remarked. Paying far greater attention to the urban electorate, Republicans generally improved upon their 1964 tallies in Baltimore, Detroit, Boston, Chicago, and Los Angeles.

The August 1968 Republican National Convention marked the high point of Bliss's tenure as RNC chief. The convention proved an efficient operation, and, following Nixon's nomination, Bliss won reelection as chair. However, the Ohio politician played a minor role in Nixon's campaign and instead concentrated his efforts on state contests. Although the GOP failed to capture either house of Congress, the party won five more governorships.

Preferring a loyal spokesperson over a party technician, and mindful of Bliss's refusal to provide him with a plane in the 1966 campaign, President Nixon removed him as national chair in February 1969. Bliss declined Nixon's offer of a diplomatic post and retired to Akron to sell insurance while remaining a RNC member from Ohio. Bliss died in Ohio in August 1981.

—JLB

## Boggs, (Thomas) Hale

### (1914–1972) *member of the House of Representatives*

Born on February 15, 1914, in Long Beach, Mississippi, Boggs received his law degree from Tulane in 1937, and began his political career in 1939 as a member of the People's League, a business and professional organization funded to oppose corruption among Huey Long's political heirs. First elected to Congress in 1940 as a "reform" candidate, Boggs was defeated in 1942 but returned in 1946. He became one of Speaker Sam Rayburn's (D-Tex.) protégés and received a seat on the powerful House Ways and Means Committee in 1949. He became chair of the Ways and Means Subcommittee on Foreign Trade Policy in 1955 and the Joint Economic Committee's Foreign Economic Policy Subcommittee in 1957. Boggs strongly supported the Eisenhower and Kennedy administration's attempts to increase the chief executive's authority to lower tariffs. He called the Trade Expansion Act of 1962, which gave the president unprecedented tariff reduction authority, "one of the most significant events of the century." After the assassination of President Kennedy in 1963, Boggs was one of the first people that LBJ asked to serve on the Warren Commission, which investigated the shooting. "It was my total conviction," he later declared, "that we had found the truth—that Oswald had assassinated President Kennedy, that he had done so acting alone."

Boggs voted against the 1964 Civil Rights Act but received a standing ovation on the House floor on July 9, 1965, when he announced his support for the voting rights bill. Boggs again broke with most of his southern colleagues when he supported the 1968 Civil Rights Act, including its controversial open housing provision. As a result of his support for civil rights and antipoverty legislation. Boggs defeated his Republican opponent by only a small margin in November 1968. He also solidified his standing with President Johnson, with whom he had long had a good relationship.

As part of a congressional evaluation of America's long-range trade position, Boggs's Joint Economic Subcommittee on Foreign Economic Policy held hearings in July 1967 on the effects of the Kennedy Round of tariff negotiations. The subcommittee's report, which generally reflected Boggs's liberal trade stance, advocated new negotiating powers for the president, aid for industries injured by imports, an attack on tariff trade barriers, and trade preferences for less-developed countries.

The retirement of House Speaker JOHN MCCORMACK (D-Mass.) in 1970 and the subsequent elevation of House Majority Leader CARL ALBERT (D-Okla.) placed Boggs in line for the position of majority leader. Boggs was challenged by a group of reform-minded Democrats who supported Representative MORRIS UDALL (D-Ariz.). According to *The Almanac of American Politics*, Boggs used his position on the Ways and Means Committee to promise wavering representatives desirable committee posts. Boggs won an easy second ballot victory in January 1971, and the Ways and Means Committee rewarded many liberals with choice committee assignments. Boggs, who was generally considered the likely successor to Speaker of the House Carl Albert, disappeared on a campaign flight in Alaska on October 16, 1972. His seat would be taken by his wife, Lindy, who served another nine terms.

—DKR

## Bohlen, Charles E(ustis)

### (1904–1974) *ambassador to France, deputy undersecretary of state for political affairs*

Born on August 30, 1904, in Clayton, New York, Charles "Chip" Bohlen joined the foreign service in 1929, specializing in Soviet affairs. Bohlen was a staff member of the U.S. embassy in Moscow shortly after the establishment of U.S.-Soviet diplomatic relations in 1933. He served as Russian translator at the Teheran conference of 1943 and the Yalta and Potsdam conferences of 1945. In 1947 Bohlen wrote the original draft of the Marshall Plan speech, which was delivered by Secretary of State George C. Marshall in June. Despite objections from Senator Joseph McCarthy (R-Wisc.), who linked him with the "Truman-Acheson policies of appeasement," Bohlen was appointed ambassador to Moscow in 1953. In 1957 Secretary of State John Foster Dulles sent Bohlen to the Philippines amid rumors that the ambassador was being "exiled" because he disagreed with Dulles's Russian policies. In 1960 he became special assistant for Soviet affairs in the State Department.

During the Kennedy administration the new president asked Bohlen's advice on a wide range of foreign policy issues, including Laos, Cuba, and Berlin. However, Bohlen rarely participated in any one area of policy making for a long period of time. In August 1962 Kennedy appointed him ambassador to France. During the Johnson years Bohlen remained at his post in France. He tried to maintain good relations between the United States and France to set a time when French president Charles de Gaulle was critical of U.S. policies. Thus, when France announced its intention to pull out of the military structure of the North Atlantic Treaty Organization in 1966 and demanded the removal of American troops by April 1967, Bohlen advised Johnson to meet the conditions without delay, which the president did despite much opposition.

In 1966 Johnson asked Bohlen to return as ambassador to Moscow. Bohlen refused the appointment because, in his opinion, the tediousness of dealing with the Russians and the boredom Americans faced in that capital made a second term undesirable.

In December 1967 Bohlen was appointed deputy undersecretary of state for political affairs. In this post he was responsible for briefing other government departments on international developments and coordinating policy between these agencies. Never on close terms with Johnson, Bohlen opposed the continued bombing of North Vietnam on the grounds that it forced the Kremlin to increase its aid to North Vietnam and because the unpopular bombing policy alienated Western European public opinion.

During the Russian invasion of Czechoslovakia in August 1968, Johnson asked Bohlen's advice on possible American action. Bohlen counselled the president to adopt a low-key policy since any threat of active American intervention would lead to a confrontation with the USSR in which the president would be faced with the necessity either to back down or to escalate the crisis.

Bohlen retired from the State Department in January 1969. He died of cancer on January 1, 1974.
—EWS

## Bolling, Richard W(alker)
(1916–1991) *member of the House of Representatives*

Born in New York City, on May 17, 1916, Richard Bolling spent much of his boyhood in Huntsville, Alabama. After college and graduate work, he entered the army in 1941, and served until 1946, including a stint on the staff of General Douglas MacArthur in Japan. In 1947 he became the midwestern director for the Americans for Democratic Action. He ran for the House of Representatives in 1948 on a platform advocating repeal of the Taft-Hartley Act and was elected from Missouri's Fifth Congressional District over a Republican incumbent. Serving on the Joint Economic and the Rules Committees, Bolling, although a liberal with an urban constituency, became a protégé of Speaker Sam Rayburn (D-Tex.) during the later years of the Eisenhower administration. His early years in Congress marked him as having a strong liberal streak, as he supported increases in the minimum wage, expanding Social Security, and greater spending on public housing. Bolling was a leader of the successful effort in January 1961 to dilute the power of the conservative majority on the Rules Committee by expanding the body from 12 to 15 members.

A supporter of the antipoverty and civil rights legislation of the Johnson administration, Bolling played a key role in House passage of the Civil Rights Act of 1968. Title IV of this bill, as proposed by the administration, would have banned discrimination in the sale or rental of all housing; the vote on a compromise amendment introduced by CHARLES MATHIAS (R-Md.) to permit discrimination in the sale of individual homes (60 percent of the nation's housing) ended in a 179-179 tie. Bolling, temporarily presiding over the House, broke the tie and voted for the amendment on the grounds that only such a compromise version could pass.

Author of two critical studies of the House, *House Out of Order* (1964) and *Power in the House*

(1968), Bolling was the leading congressional advocate of internal House reform. Among his recommendations were full financial disclosure by members, limitations on conflicts of interest, and a weakening of the seniority system along with a strengthening of the role of the Speaker and the party caucus. Bolling backed the Johnson and Nixon administrations on the Vietnam War, sponsoring a successful motion to kill an amendment in August 1972 that mandated a halt to U.S. military activity by October 1. He retired in 1983 and remained in Washington, D.C., until his death in 1991.

—TO

## Bolton, Frances P(ayne) (Bingham)
(1885–1977)  *member of the House of Representatives*

A descendant of one of Cleveland's oldest and wealthiest families, Frances Bingham, who was born in Cleveland, Ohio, on March 29, 1885, married Chester C. Bolton, a steel executive, in 1907. She

Ohio representative Frances Payne Bolton  *(Library of Congress, Prints and Photographs Division)*

then devoted her time and a great deal of her money to a variety of progressive causes, including black self-help programs and the Tuskegee Institute. With a special interest in nursing, Bolton helped persuade the government to establish the Army School of Nursing during World War I. She participated in her husband's usually successful Republican campaigns for the House beginning in 1928.

Upon her husband's death Bolton succeeded to his suburban Cleveland seat in a special 1940 election and served consecutively for nearly 30 years. As a representative during World War II, she called for the desegregation, both by race and sex, of military nursing units. In 1949 she argued for the inclusion of women in the Selective Service System. Appointed to the House Foreign Affairs Committee, Bolton strongly advocated American entry into the United Nations and independence for colonial Africa. In 1953 she became the first woman appointed as a congressional delegate to the United Nations General Assembly. She also led efforts that resulted in the restructuring of committee procedure.

During the Johnson years Bolton was the ranking Republican member of the Foreign Affairs Committee. In her committee assignment she criticized America's foreign aid and Vietnam policies but consistently supported the administration on crucial votes. An energetic campaigner, Bolton won reelection in 1964 at age 79, running far ahead of the party's presidential ticket in her district. She handily won another term in 1966. In the drafting of civil rights legislation, she worked to include bans against sex discrimination.

Despite a longtime philanthropic connection with American blacks and a large African-American population in her district, her minority rights voting record during the 1960s was uneven. She voted for the 1964 Civil Rights Act and Voting Rights Act of 1965 but against the 1968 open housing law. In July 1968, however, she voted with a minority of House Republicans in favor of the Housing and Urban Development Act, which provided funding of housing units for the disadvantaged.

Blacks and blue-collar Democrats abandoned Bolton in 1968 and combined with opponents of the Vietnam War to deny her reelection. Representative CHARLES A. VANIK (D-Ohio), an antiwar liberal, ran against Bolton following a reapportionment of her Cleveland district by the Ohio legislature. With Bolton's age the silent issue of the campaign, Vanik defeated the veteran representative with 55 percent of the vote. She returned to Ohio, where she died on March 9, 1977.

—JLB

## Bond, (Horace) Julian

(1940–   ) *communications director, Student Nonviolent Coordinating Committee; Georgia House of Representatives member*

Bond, who was born on January 14, 1940, in Nashville, Tennessee, grew up on the campuses of Fort Valley State College in central Georgia and Lincoln University in Pennsylvania where his father, historian Horace Mann Bond, served as president. He enrolled in Atlanta's Morehouse College, an historically black institution, in 1957. When the sit-in movement began in February 1960, Bond cofounded the Committee on Appeal for Human Rights (CoAHR), which organized a series of student sit-ins in Atlanta. Bond was arrested in the first sit-in at the City Hall cafeteria in March, but he soon left sit-in campaigns to do communications and publicity work for CoAHR and to report for the *Atlanta Inquirer*, a newspaper Bond and other students founded in 1960. CoAHR coalesced with other student groups in April 1960 to form the Student Non-violent Coordinating Committee (SNCC), and, in the spring of 1961, Bond became communications director for SNCC. Working mainly at SNCC's Atlanta headquarters, Bond edited its newspaper, *The Student Voice*, prepared radio tapes and news releases for the press, and supervised publicity for SNCC voter registration and civil rights drives.

Early in 1965 Bond entered the Democratic primary for the Georgia House of Representatives in the 136th district, a new and predominantly black Atlanta district created as the result of a court-ordered reapportionment of the state legislature. Bond swept both the May primary and the general election in November. On January 6, 1966, four days before Bond was to be sworn in as a House member, SNCC issued a policy statement condemning the Vietnam War and expressing support for draft resistance. Bond endorsed the statement the same day. On the grounds that the statement was "un-American," the Georgia House voted 184-12 on January 10 not to seat him. Bond immediately filed suit in federal court to challenge his exclusion, but a three-judge court ruled 2-1 on January 31 that the House's action was constitutional. While this decision was on appeal to the Supreme Court, Bond

ran unopposed in a February 23 special election in his district but was again denied his seat by the House Rules Committee on May 23.

Bond ran a third time for the House seat in a September Democratic primary and this time won in a very close race. On September 8, just before the primary, he resigned from SNCC for "personal reasons." In later years Bond said economic necessity, the desire to start a new career, and SNCC's growing emphasis on the North rather than the South contributed to this decision. Bond won the November general election, and, on December 5, 1966, the Supreme Court ruled unanimously that the Georgia House had violated Bond's First Amendment right to free expression in expelling him for his antiwar statements. On January 9, 1967, Bond was finally sworn in as a member of the Georgia House of Representatives. During the year-long fight for his seat, Bond became a national political figure. He spoke at numerous antiwar rallies and in June 1966 was elected cochair of the National Conference for New Politics.

Bond was cochair of an insurgent delegation called the Georgia Loyal National Democrats at the Democratic National Convention in Chicago in August 1968. Before the Credentials Committee, Bond argued that Georgia's regular delegation, led by Governor LESTER MADDOX, should not be seated because blacks were excluded from any real participation in the regular Democratic Party in the state. A majority on the Credentials Committee recommended a compromise in which Georgia's votes would be split between the regular and insurgent groups. After a floor fight in which Bond's delegation came very close to unseating the regular delegation entirely, the convention accepted the compromise.

At the convention, Bond delivered one of two seconding speeches for the antiwar presidential candidate, Senator EUGENE MCCARTHY (D-Minn.), and, on August 29, Bond's own name was placed in nomination for the vice presidency making him the first African American to be nominated for the post by a major party. His nomination, Bond later explained, was "a diversionary effort" to extend the convention and give those who opposed the Vietnam War and the tactics used by Chicago police against antiwar demonstrators a chance to speak in protest. Bond received 48 1/2 votes for the nomination before withdrawing his name during the course of the balloting. Bond continued to serve in the

Georgia House of Representatives after 1968 and maintained an extensive speaking schedule as an advocate for a liberal political coalition of the black and white poor. He was elected to the Georgia Senate in 1974, and he remained until 1987. In 1998 he was elected chair of the NAACP.

—CAB

## Booth, Paul
(1943–   ) *national secretary, Students for a Democratic Society*

Booth, who was born in Washington, D.C., on June 7, 1943, was the son of a professional, politically involved couple. His father was chief of the Unemployment Security Bureau's Division of Program and Legislation and later a professor of social work at the University of Michigan. His mother was a psychiatric social worker in Washington, D.C., where Booth grew up. Both his parents were active in the Americans for Democratic Action. In 1962, while a first-year student at Swarthmore College, Booth was a delegate to the convention of the Students for a Democratic Society (SDS) in Port Huron, Michigan, and was elected vice president of the organization despite being, at age 19, one of the youngest delegates in attendance.

In the fall of 1964 Booth started the Peace Research and Education Project (PREP) in Ann Arbor, Michigan, an SDS-sponsored study of the problems involved in converting the economy from reliance on military spending. That summer, he helped organize a program in Boston designed to organize defense workers threatened by plant closings. With the escalation of the Vietnam War in 1965, however, the whole notion of "peace research" seemed pointless to Booth, and PREP was dropped. In the summer of that year, he moved to Oakland, California, where he worked as an organizer for an SDS Economic Research and Action Project (ERAP) in the inner-city area.

In the fall of 1965 SDS national leaders summoned Booth to Chicago to become national secretary and bring "order and politics" to the chaotic and directionless national office. During his one-year term SDS was the focus of national publicity. It had an unprecedented growth in membership and became large and influential.

In October 1965 the syndicated columnists Rowland Evans and Robert Novak accused SDS of drawing up a "master plan" to "sabotage the war

effort" by organizing systematic draft evasion. Senator JOHN STENNIS (D-Miss.) called on the government to "jerk this movement up by the roots and grind it to bits." The chorus of denunciation was joined by a number of other senators, and Attorney General NICHOLAS KATZENBACH threatened an official investigation. At this time SDS had no draft program beyond providing counseling for conscientious objectors, and Booth feared a "draft-dodging" image would hurt the organization. With SDS president CARL OGLESBY he flew to Washington, D.C., to hold a press conference at which he declared: "We are fully prepared to volunteer for service to our country and to democracy. We volunteer to go into Watts . . . to help the Peace Corps . . . to serve in hospitals and schools in the slums, in the Job Corps and VISTA . . . let us see what happens if service to democracy is made grounds for exemption to the military draft." The tone of the statement and the organization's slogan, "Build, Not Burn," disarmed many critics, but it provoked a strong reaction against Booth among many of the SDS rank and file who believed that the statement was excessively moderate and apologetic and did not attack the draft itself.

During Booth's term SDS formally severed its ties with its parent organization, the League for Industrial Democracy, and began to pursue an independent course. By April 1966 it claimed 5,000 members in 175 to 200 chapters. Most of these new recruits were young antiwar activists hostile to what they regarded as the "elitism" of the SDS "old guard." As a result, Booth found himself increasingly isolated by the end of his term. By that time he was involved independently with the National Conference for New Politics (NCNP), a coalition of antiwar and civil rights spokesmen organized to raise funds and manpower for the campaigns of Democratic insurgents in the primary elections of 1966. SDS did not endorse the NCNP, and at one point Booth was censured for giving the public impression that it did.

Booth subsequently took a job as an aide with the Packing House Workers Union in Chicago. In August 1968 he participated in the abortive efforts of the New Party to persuade Senator EUGENE MCCARTHY (D-Minn.) to run for president as an independent candidate in the fall elections. In 1969 he became president of Chicago's Citizen Action Program and he later became an organizer for the American Federation of State, County, and Municipal Employees.

—TLH

## Boutin, Bernard L(ouis)

(1923–    ) *deputy director, Office of Economic Opportunity; director, Small Business Administration*

Boutin, who was born on July 2, 1923, grew up in Belmont, New Hampshire. He graduated in 1945 from St. Michael's College in Vermont and returned to New Hampshire to work in his father's real estate and insurance business. In 1955 Boutin became active in New Hampshire politics as a Democrat; he served as mayor of Laconia, New Hampshire, until 1959, and as Democratic national committee member from New Hampshire until 1960. He was also coordinator of the 1960 Democratic presidential campaign in New Hampshire.

In 1961 President Kennedy appointed Boutin director of the General Services Administration, where he supervised the use and operation of government property. He served in this position until 1964. After a brief period as vice president of the National Association of Home Builders, Boutin returned to the federal government in 1965 as deputy director of the Office of Economic Opportunity (OEO). There he utilized his administrative experience to establish standards and distribute funds for a wide variety of community action programs sponsored by the OEO.

In May 1966 Boutin left the OEO to become director of the Small Business Administration (SBA). He took control of the SBA at a time when the agency had been without a director for one and a half years; some of its programs had been suspended, and speculation had grown that the SBA would be absorbed by the Department of Commerce. Boutin brought the agency back to life and restored its programs, including federally guaranteed loans to small businessmen. It was later revealed, however, that more than $1 million in SBA loans had been granted to a leasing company in New York connected to organized crime and that the loans had continued for a time even after the firm's background had become known. A memo, written for Boutin in January 1967, urged that the incident not be made public.

Boutin left the SBA in July 1967, returning to New Hampshire to serve as consultant to an electronics firm. In 1968 he managed President Johnson's write-in campaign in the New Hampshire Democratic primary; Johnson's relatively poor showing against antiwar candidate Senator EUGENE MCCARTHY (D-Minn.) destroyed Boutin's own hopes of running for governor in 1970. After serving briefly on the state board of education, Boutin was chosen in 1969 to be the first lay president of St. Michael's College, his alma mater.

—SLG

## Bowles, Chester

(1901–1986) *ambassador to India*

Chester Bowles was born on April 5, 1901, into a well-to-do Yankee family. During World War II he held a succession of administrative positions in Connecticut's rationing program before being appointed director of the federal Office of Price Administration in 1943. In 1948 Bowles was elected governor of Connecticut. When he lost his reelection bid in 1950, President Truman named him ambassador to India, where he served until 1953. From 1958 until 1960 Bowles was a member of the House of Representatives. In November 1959 he became the first nationally prominent liberal to endorse John F. Kennedy for president and served as the candidate's chief foreign policy adviser during the campaign.

Although mentioned as a possible candidate for secretary of state, Bowles was passed over because his liberal views angered many prominent politicians. Instead, he was named undersecretary of state in January 1961. While at the post he urged the president to reorient American policy to support the growing nationalist movements in the undeveloped nations. Bowles's views made enemies within the State Department and Congress while his frequent clashes with ROBERT F. KENNEDY lost him the support of the president. Particularly galling in the administration's eyes was the fact that Bowles had been an early critic of the Bay of Pigs invasion plan. In November 1961 he was ousted from his State Department position.

During the next year Bowles served as the president's special representative and adviser on Asian, African, and Latin American affairs but had little influence within the administration. Frustrated by his inability to reshape the foreign aid program or head off what he believed would be a major military involvement in Vietnam, he submitted his resignation in December 1962. Kennedy suggested that instead of leaving the administration, Bowles return to his former post as ambassador to India. Bowles accepted the offer with some reluctance, and was designated ambassador in April 1963.

When Bowles arrived in India, relations between the two countries were close because of India's general sympathy for the United States, America's continued economic aid, and its military assistance during the 1962 border war with China. However, despite Bowles's close personal friendship with Indian leaders, relations between the two nations declined during the remainder of the decade. The ambassador attributed this to President Johnson's inconsistent policies toward India, his use of aid as a weapon against nations opposing U.S. policy in Vietnam, and his failure to recognize the importance of India in Asia. All of this added up to the belief in India that the Johnson administration had decided to throw its support to their archrival, Pakistan.

During his tour one of Bowles's primary concerns was to increase long-term economic aid to India. In the spring of 1965 he submitted a detailed proposal for increased U.S. and World Bank assistance to enable India to achieve self-sustained growth within a decade. Although the administration received the initial report favorably, the plan was never put into effect. Instead, when full-scale war broke out between India and Pakistan in September 1965, the United States stopped all aid to both belligerents, thus alienating both of them.

When India's monsoons failed in 1965 and 1966, Bowles urged emergency aid to that country. Despite initial assurances from Johnson that wheat shipments would be forthcoming, the president granted the grain only grudgingly, releasing the shipments just days before the wheat was needed. Bowles attributed this conduct to Johnson's anger over the Indian government's opposition to the Vietnam War and the president's belief that the grain could be used to compel support for U.S. policy. Although there was some truth in this contention, LBJ also sought to break India of its dependency on American food aid and force it to modernize its economic and agricultural policies in such a way as to increase its self-sufficiency. Indians found U.S. policy confusing and irresponsible; one official termed it "something approaching sadism."

Bowles's second major concern while in India was the reorientation of America's Asian policy from a focus on Pakistan to one stressing the importance of India. During the postwar period the United States had funneled large amounts of economic and military aid to Pakistan in the belief that its strategic position near the Soviet and Chinese borders made its stability vital for the prevention of communist expansion in Asia. Bowles believed that this emphasis was inappropriate because that country did not share the U.S. democratic philosophy and because Pakistan had consistently used military aid not to protect itself from China but to attack India. Pointing out that India's large population and democratic tradition made it the keystone of a stable, democratic Asia, the ambassador recommended that the United States cut off large-scale military aid to Pakistan and begin supplying such assistance to India.

During his six-year tenure Bowles had little success in reorienting American policy. When war broke out between the two Asian countries in September 1965, Bowles again saw India attacked with U.S.-supplied weapons. The United States did cut off aid to Pakistan during the conflict but also stopped assistance to India. Despite Bowles's continued pleas, military aid resumed to Pakistan in 1967.

In January 1968 Johnson sent Bowles to Phnom Penh to discuss ways of curbing Communist use of Cambodian territory, which would eliminate the prospect of U.S. "hot pursuit" into Cambodia to attack Communist installations. On January 12 the United States and Cambodia agreed to strengthen the three-nation International Control Commission to police the Cambodian–South Vietnamese border. The United States also assured Cambodia that incursions were not American policy and promised to inform Phnom Penh of border violations rather than stage attacks. However, Bowles emphasized that the United States had the right of self-defense and would pursue Communist troops launching attacks from Cambodia if no other action were taken against them. Despite the January agreement the issue of "hot pursuit" was never resolved. The United States continued making secret raids into Cambodia and, in May 1970, staged a full-scale invasion of that country. Bowles remained a critic of the increasing American involvement in Asia, arguing that Asian nationalism made it unlikely that either the United States or the Soviet bloc would ever gain control of the region.

In April 1969 Bowles was replaced as ambassador to India. Two years later he published his memoirs describing his public life and outlining his ideas on foreign policy. He died in 1986.

—EWS

## Boyd, Alan S(tephenson)

(1922–   ) *member, Civil Aeronautics Board; chairman, Civil Aeronautics Board; undersecretary of commerce for transportation; secretary of transportation*

Boyd, who was born on July 20, 1922, in Jacksonville, Florida, served in the Army Troop Transport Command in World War II. He earned a law degree from the University of Virginia in 1948 and returned to his native state to practice law and to serve on state commissions dealing with transportation development and regulation. In May 1959 President DWIGHT D. EISENHOWER appointed Boyd to an unexpired term on the Civil Aeronautics Board (CAB). During the Kennedy administration, Boyd, a Democrat, chaired the board. As CAB head Boyd aided the commercial airline industry's recovery from a period of disappointing profits. Boyd sought to standardize airline industry fare reductions, and, during his term as chair, the CAB authorized subsidies to financially troubled lines for their less profitable runs between small cities. Boyd left the CAB to become undersecretary of commerce for transportation in June 1965.

Two positions taken by Boyd while at Commerce resulted in verbal confrontations with organized labor. Nine days after Boyd assumed his new post, Secretary of Commerce JOHN T. CONNOR selected him to chair a special interagency task force to study the nation's maritime industry. A preliminary report by the Boyd group, issued in September 1965, called for a reduction of the government's merchant fleet subsidy program and fewer legal restrictions on the industry's operation. The task force's tentative conclusions provoked strong denunciations by the industry's labor leadership, including JOSEPH CURRAN of the National Maritime Union. Speaking for the White House, Vice President HUBERT HUMPHREY disavowed the suggestions of the Boyd committee. Amid the threat of a nationwide rail strike in September 1965, Boyd angered the railway brotherhoods when he criticized "featherbedding" by railroad workers, calling for greater flexibility by rail union officials in the reassignment of workers removed from jobs due to modernization.

Boyd and other administration representatives began a campaign in January 1966 to establish a cabinet-level Department of Transportation (DOT). The Johnson administration sought to unify under one authority 35 government transportation agencies, ranging from the Coast Guard to the airline, rail, and federal highway commissions. The new department would also direct governmental policy on automotive safety, an issue of growing public concern after the recent publication of RALPH NADER's book, *Unsafe at Any Speed.* Boyd served on the five-member interagency committee that first recommended a Transportation Department to the president in September 1965, and Johnson endorsed the proposal in his 1966 State of the Union message. Although presidential counsel JOSEPH A. CALIFANO directed the congressional lobbying effort, Boyd was the most frequent witness before committees scrutinizing the administration's bill.

By the time Congress passed the DOT bill in October 1966, the new department's secretary possessed much less authority than the law's original authors had intended to grant him. AFL-CIO representatives successfully argued against transfer of the Maritime Administration to DOT, a union accomplishment some observers described as a major defeat for the administration. Despite the efforts of Boyd and Califano, regulatory agencies placed under the new department retained more autonomy than the White House had originally wished. Congress also curbed the secretary's control over transportation expenditures. The *Washington Post*'s Richard Harwood wrote that legislative leaders had so weakened the measure that the secretary of transportation had "authority to assign office space and little else."

Johnson named Boyd to serve as the nation's first secretary of transportation in November 1966, and the Senate confirmed his nomination two months later. Although 12th in cabinet seniority, Boyd led a department fourth in personnel and fifth in annual expenditures. Involved in a wide range of transportation issues, Boyd directed staff projects on airport modernization and air traffic control requirements. In June 1967 he defended appropriations for LADY BIRD JOHNSON's Highway Beautification Program before a Senate committee. As called for in the Highway Safety Act of 1966, Boyd issued state auto safety standards for driver education and alcoholism.

During its fight with Congress over the 1967 budget, the administration utilized Boyd's control over interstate highway funds to put muscle behind Johnson's tax surcharge. Boyd announced in February 1967 that $175 million of federal highway funds had been impounded by the president since November 1966 as an anti-inflation move. In October 1967 Boyd sent telegrams to all state governors warning that the budget issue between the administration and Congress "may have a profound effect on highway construction expenditures." The possibility existed, Boyd explained, that federal highway funds would have to be reduced from $4.4 billion to $2.2 billion in fiscal 1969.

DOT proved unable to revitalize passenger rail service. Congress declined to appropriate the full amount authorized in the High-Speed Ground Transportation Act of 1965, a measure designed to subsidize passenger railroad research and development costs. With the limited funds available in 1967, Boyd reported delays in the test runs of new models.

Boyd also devoted attention to the maritime industry and again antagonized ship industry labor officials. In May 1968 he proposed to restructure and reduce the government's subsidy programs as part of a comprehensive maritime proposal. As in 1965 the Maritime Committee of the AFL-CIO condemned Boyd's suggestion, with Curran calling it "inadequate, unimaginative and unsatisfactory." Again the administration dropped Boyd's plan and postponed further action to salvage the country's declining merchant fleet industry.

With President-elect Nixon's nomination of John A. Volpe as DOT secretary, Boyd returned to private life in January 1969 and became president of the Illinois Central Railroad. He subsequently served as the president of Amtrak and chair of Airbus Industries of North America.

—JLB

# Boyle, Tony (William) (Anthony)

(1904–1985)  *president, United Mine Workers*

Born on December 1, 1904, in Bald Butte, Montana, Boyle began working in the mines after he finished high school. He rose quickly through the United Mine Workers (UMW) ranks and in 1940 became president of the union's District 27, covering Montana and other western states. Boyle served as a regional director of the Congress of Industrial Organizations for two years and also represented the UMW on several government boards during World War II.

In 1948 Boyle moved to UMW headquarters in Washington, D.C., to become UMW president John L. Lewis's administrative assistant. Over the next decade Boyle won increasing power as the day-to-day administrator of the UMW. His power grew further when Lewis retired in 1960 and Thomas Kennedy became president. Boyle took over the presidential office upon Kennedy's death in January 1963.

Heir to a highly centralized union structure, Boyle faced both growing rank-and-file pressure for democratization of the UMW and charges of collusion with large coal operators. Postwar automation had been rapid, and the union's membership declined by more than 200,000 between 1950 and 1970. Although the UMW won substantial wage increases during the 1960s, unauthorized wildcat strikes increased dramatically, and Boyle was challenged for the presidency in 1964. Dissatisfaction with the central leadership's tight grip on union affairs stemmed from the UMW's failure to win improved mine safety standards or guarantees of stable employment.

In August 1967 the Supreme Court found the UMW guilty of violating the Sherman Antitrust Act because it had made large loans to the Western Kentucky Coal Company, enabling the company to monopolize Tennessee Valley Authority coal contracts. The collaboration issue mushroomed again when an explosion at a Consolidation Coal Company mine killed 78 miners in November 1968. Three weeks earlier the UMW and the company had been fined $7 million for conspiring with other large companies since 1950 to monopolize production. Following the accident Boyle praised Consolidation's safety record and stated, "As long as we mine coal, there is always this inherent danger." Boyle also said the UMW "will not abridge the rights of mine operators in running the mines. We follow the judgments of the coal operators, right or wrong."

Boyle's defense of the coal companies was unpopular among rank-and-file miners. Soon after the Consolidation explosion an organized militant challenge to Boyle's leadership emerged. In December 1968 West Virginia miners formed the Black Lung Association. Led by Arnold Miller, the group demanded state worker's compensation for miners suffering from pneumoconiosis, or black lung, a disease caused by the accumulation of coal dust particles. Joseph A. Yablonski, a member of the union's executive board and long a critic of Boyle's tight control of the union, announced his candidacy for

UMW president in May 1969. After a sometimes violent campaign Boyle won what Yablonski charged was a fraudulent election in early December 1969. On December 31, 1969, Yablonski and his wife and daughter were murdered in their Pennsylvania home. In 1972 the Department of Labor invalidated the 1969 election. In a subsequent election Boyle was defeated for UMW president by Arnold Miller, a Yablonski supporter. Boyle was convicted in 1973 for making illegal use of union funds. He subsequently tried to commit suicide with an overdose or drugs. Later that year he was convicted of conspiring to kill Yablonski and was sentenced to three life prison terms. He died of a heart attack on May 31, 1985.

—MDB

## Brademas, John
(1927–   ) *member of the House of Representatives*

During the Johnson years John Brademas earned a reputation as one of the leading advocates of federal aid to education. Born on March 2, 1927, in Mishawaka, Indiana, he graduated magna cum laude from Harvard University in 1949 and later earned a doctorate from Oxford University. He then taught political science at St. Mary's College in Notre Dame, Indiana. At the same time he gained practical political experience as an assistant in charge of research for ADLAI STEVENSON's 1956 presidential campaign.

First elected to Congress in 1958, Brademas represented the northern Indiana district that included the cities of Elkhart and South Bend. During the Kennedy and Johnson years, the Americans for Democratic Action rated Brandemas's "correct" voting record at 80 percent to 95 percent. Brademas sat on the House Labor and Education Committee, and, despite his relatively low seniority, became an influential spokesperson on educational affairs. His opinions on school legislation were particularly well regarded by the Democratic Study Group.

Brademas played an active role in winning approval of the 1965 Elementary and Secondary Education Act and two years later served as the successful floor manager of the bill amending the original legislation. In 1967 Brademas won approval of a bill authorizing federal assistance for international studies programs in American colleges and universities and for legislation extending the teacher corps

for three years. Brademas also won the praise of environmental groups for his support of legislation protecting estuaries and imposing water pollution controls.

Unlike a number of House liberals, Brademas was not an outspoken opponent of the Vietnam War during the 1960s. Beginning around 1970 he started voting for antiwar legislation while insisting that withdrawal of American troops from Vietnam be contingent on release of U.S. prisoners of war.

In 1971 Brademas sponsored comprehensive child-care legislation as part of a bill extending the Economic Opportunity Act. This major bill, passed by both houses, was vetoed by President Nixon. He remained in office until his defeat in 1980, and then became president at New York University.

—JLW

## Breathitt, Edward T(hompson) (Ned)
(1924–2003) *governor*

A lawyer from an old Kentucky family whose tradition of public service predated the Civil War, Breathitt, who was born on November 26, 1924, in Hopkinsville, Kentucky, served three terms in the state House of Representatives from 1952 to 1958. As state personnel commissioner from 1959 to 1960, he instituted a merit system for state civil service employees. He was appointed state public service commissioner in 1960 by Governor Bert T. Combs.

In 1963 he ran for the Democratic nomination for governor against A. D. "Happy" Chandler, a former Kentucky governor, U.S. senator, and commissioner of baseball, in what the *Washington Post* called "probably the bitterest campaign in Kentucky history." The foremost issues were a recently enacted 3 percent sales tax (which Chandler denounced and Breathitt supported) and Chandler's age, then 65. Breathitt defeated Chandler by a landslide in the Democratic primary. He faced a young, conservative lawyer, Louie B. Nunn, in the general election. During the campaign—the first in recent years in which the race issue had figured prominently in Kentucky politics—Breathitt was attacked for his supposed links to northern civil rights organizations and his presumed support of the Kennedy administration's policies on racial integration. With a record 870,000 votes cast on November 5, Breathitt narrowly defeated Nunn by 15,000 votes.

Shortly after taking office Breathitt confronted the problem of civil rights. Civil rights leaders argued that because of the closeness of the election Breathitt found it expedient to procrastinate on a state public accommodations bill outlawing segregation in public places. To bring pressure upon the governor and state legislature, 10,000 persons, led by MARTIN LUTHER KING, JR., marched on Frankfort in March 1964. A compromise resolution was passed on March 19 favoring voluntary integration of public facilities. Kentucky political observers doubted whether the governor could have secured passage of the original measure under any circumstances.

At the 1964 Democratic National Convention, Breathitt seconded the nomination of Lyndon B. Johnson. During the October 1964 Southern Governors Conference, he was among a minority of three who quashed GEORGE WALLACE's constitutional amendment to give the states and state courts sole jurisdiction over their public schools. Conference backing required unanimity.

In 1966 Breathitt proposed a state civil rights bill broader in scope than the 1964 federal Civil Rights Act. The employment section of the bill brought 90 percent of Kentucky labor under a provision that barred racial discrimination in employment. The federal law covered only 60 percent of the state labor force. The public accommodations section of the Kentucky measure applied to such businesses as bowling alleys and coin-operated laundries not covered under the federal measure. It was the first law of its kind south of the Ohio River. In signing the bill into law on January 27, 1966, Breathitt said it was "a moral commitment kept after a hundred years of hope deferred—a promissory note long overdue."

On January 27, 1966, the Kentucky legislature overwhelmingly adopted a tough new law designed to end strip mining abuses. Enactment of this sweeping measure, which coal operators said would put them out of business, was a major victory for Breathitt over the state's powerful coal industry. In 1967 Breathitt headed the President's Advisory Commission on Rural Poverty. The panel's report, released December 9, asserted that "rural poverty is so widespread, so acute, as to be a national disgrace, and its consequences have swept into our cities violently." Breathitt also championed various environmental causes during his years in office.

Constitutionally unable to seek reelection in 1966, Breathitt became vice president in charge of public affairs of the Southern Railway System. He died of a fibrillation of the heart on October 14, 2003.

—TJC

## Brennan, William J(oseph), Jr.
(1906–1997)  *associate justice, U.S. Supreme Court*

The son of Irish immigrants, Brennan was born on April 25, 1906, in Newark, New Jersey, and graduated from the Wharton School of Finance in 1928 and from Harvard Law School in 1931. He then joined a law firm in Newark, where he specialized in labor law. He was appointed to the state Superior Court in 1949, to the Appellate Division of the Superior Court in 1950, and to the state Supreme Court in 1952. President Eisenhower named Brennan to the U.S. Supreme Court in September 1956, and he began serving under a recess appointment that October. The Senate confirmed the appointment in March 1957.

In his early years on the bench, Brennan often played the role of a bridge-builder between the Court's liberal and conservative wings, writing narrowly based opinions to gather a majority. When a solid liberal majority developed in the early 1960s, Brennan became more activist and creative in his opinions and a leader in expanding individual rights and protecting them from government intrusion. Brennan believed in the idea of a living, evolving, Constitution, one that needed to constantly be interpreted to meet the changing needs of society. Brennan became known for his special dedication to First Amendment freedoms and to procedural fairness. In March 1962 he wrote the majority opinion in *Baker v. Carr,* holding that federal courts could decide cases involving legislative apportionment.

Brennan wrote some of his most important First Amendment opinions in the Johnson years. Speaking for a unanimous Court in March 1964, Brennan expanded the freedom of the press in *New York Times v. Sullivan,* holding that a public official could not recover damages for a defamatory falsehood relating to his official conduct without proving the statement was made with "actual malice." Later that year Brennan extended this ruling to cover cases of criminal as well as civil libel, and, in a February 1966 decision, he gave a broad definition to the term public official. In *Time Inc. v. Hill,* decided in January 1967, Brennan applied the same principle to invasion of privacy suits against the press by newsworthy persons. Brennan found in the 1965 case *Dombrowski v. Pfister* an exception to the general rule that federal courts will not intervene to enjoin threatened state court criminal proceedings. Federal courts could act, he held, when a defendant's First Amendment rights were endangered by the fact of state prosecutions.

Throughout the Warren Court years Brennan wrote the leading opinions in the difficult and divisive area of obscenity law. In the 1957 *Roth* decision Brennan held obscenity was not protected by the First Amendment and declared the test of obscenity was "whether, to the average person, applying contemporary community standards, the dominant theme of the material taken as a whole appeals to the prurient interest." The first major reexamination of the definition of obscenity came in June 1964 in *Jacobellis v. Ohio* with Brennan's opinion reaffirming the *Roth* test. He gave greater emphasis, however, to the notion that obscene material was utterly without redeeming social importance and said the community standards of the *Roth* test were national, not local, standards. In three March 1966 cases Brennan constructed a narrower test of obscenity and held that to be judged obscene a work had to meet each of three criteria: its dominant theme must appeal to the prurient interest, it must be patently offensive, and it must be utterly without redeeming social value.

Brennan's majority opinion in the 1966 case *Katzenbach v. Morgan* upheld a section of the 1965 Voting Rights Act designed to guarantee the right to vote to non-English-speaking Puerto Ricans. Brennan sustained the law holding that section five of the Fourteenth Amendment gave Congress independent authority to decide if certain conduct violated the amendment's equal protection clause. This new and broader interpretation of section five has been judged to hold the potential for a vast expansion of federal power.

Brennan also contributed to the Warren Court's criminal decisions. His majority opinion in a June 1964 case held the Fifth Amendment's privilege against self-incrimination applicable to the states. In a June 1966 decision Brennan rejected a claim that a blood test to determine if a defendant was driving while drunk, conducted over the defendant's protest, violated his Fourth and Fifth Amendment rights. Writing for an eight-man majority in May 1967, Brennan overruled a 1921 Court decision and extended the right of police to use evidence seized in lawful searches of suspects' homes.

Over the next several years Brennan wrote important opinions on the rights of welfare recipients, and he dissented from the Burger Court's decisions cutting back on the 1966 *Miranda* ruling. The

difficulties of formulating a clear and manageable definition of obscenity led Brennan to a sharp reversal of his position in 1973. Dissenting in two cases where the majority modified his *Roth* standards, Brennan wrote that except to protect juveniles and to prevent the obtrusive exposure to unconsenting adults, the First Amendment prohibited all attempts to suppress materials on the basis of their alleged obscenity. Legal scholar Laurence Tribe recalled, "If Chief Justice John Marshall was the chief architect of a powerful national government, then Justice William Brennan was the principal architect of the nation's system for protecting individual rights." He retired from the Court for health reasons in 1990, and he died on July 24, 1997.

—CAB

### Brewster, Daniel B(augh)
(1923– ) *member of the Senate*

Born on November 23, 1923, into a wealthy family in Baltimore County, Maryland, Brewster served four terms in the Maryland House of Delegates and two terms in the U.S. House of Representatives before being elected to the Senate in 1962. Supported by the Baltimore County Democratic organization, the most powerful faction in state politics outside the Baltimore city organization, Brewster won each of his campaigns effortlessly.

While in the House Brewster supported civil rights legislation, increases in minimum wage protection, and aid for housing and education. During the Kennedy years the Americans for Democratic Action gave him an average rating of 87 percent.

The senator continued to support many domestic social welfare proposals during the Johnson era, voting in favor of aid to education, mass transit, Model Cities and Appalachia, civil rights measures, and the antipoverty program. In 1966 Brewster drafted a bill to establish a bipartisan Commission on Political Activity of Government Personnel to review the Hatch Act of 1939. That act limited the participation of government workers in national and local politics. When Johnson signed the bill in the autumn of 1966, he appointed Brewster one of the commission members. The commission report, issued at the end of 1967, recommended an easing of restrictions on political activities of most federal employees but urged a strengthening of provisions intended to protect public workers from coercion by their superiors.

During the 1964 presidential campaign Brewster served as a stand-in candidate for Lyndon Johnson in the Maryland Democratic primary. Calling the primary a "ridiculous" exercise and an invitation to "irresponsible voting," Brewster ran a lackluster race against Alabama governor GEORGE WALLACE. Pitted against the flamboyant Wallace, Brewster received only 53 percent of the vote; Wallace polled a surprising 43 percent. Analyzing the reasons for Brewster's failure, the *New York Times* attributed the poor showing to a conservative backlash against the tactics used by civil rights demonstrators.

Following his unsuccessful bid for reelection in 1968, Brewster became the subject of several investigations involving charges of impropriety in the introduction of immigration bills. He was also charged with violating federal bribery laws while a senator. In September 1969 the Senate Select Committee on Standards and Conduct began a preliminary investigation into allegations that a number of senators, including Brewster, received gifts or campaign funds in return for sponsoring private immigration bills to help illegal Chinese immigrants escape deportation. Brewster denied the charges, and no action was taken on the matter.

Three months later, in December 1969, Brewster was indicted on 10 counts of having violated federal bribery laws by accepting payments "in return for being influenced" to vote against an increase in third-class bulk mail rates while he was a member of the Senate Post Office and Civil Service Committee. In 1972 Brewster was convicted on a lesser charge of accepting an unlawful gratuity—a charge that in effect he had taken money without corrupt intent. He was sentenced to two to six years in jail and fined $30,000 in 1973. A retrial was ordered on appeal, but, in 1975, he pleaded no contest to the charge and was fined $10,000. He returned to Glyndon, Maryland, after leaving the Senate.

—EWS

## Bridges, Harry (Alfred)

(1901–1990) *president, International Longshoremen's and Warehousemen's Union*

Bridges was born on July 28, 1901, in Melbourne, Australia. While working on a merchant ship, he entered the United States permanently when his vessel docked in San Francisco in 1920. He worked as a longshoreman and became involved in union activities. Bridges emerged in 1934 as the most important leader of the San Francisco longshoremen's work stoppage and the citywide general strike that immediately followed. As a consequence of his strike leadership, Bridges played a key role in the organization of Pacific Coast longshoremen and in 1937 was elected president of the CIO-affiliated International Longshoremen's and Warehousemen's Union (ILWU).

For more than a decade and a half after 1939, the Justice Department tried to deport Bridges on the grounds that he was or had been a Communist. In 1950 he was sentenced to five years in prison for allegedly lying under oath at his 1945 naturalization hearing that he had never been a member of the Communist Party. Three years later, the Supreme Court dismissed the indictment. He was reindicted on similar charges, but in 1955 a federal district judge ruled that the government had failed to prove its case, and the Justice Department decided to abandon its fight to deport him. In 1958 he was granted a U.S. passport.

In 1960 Bridges signed a five-and-one-half-year collective bargaining contract with the Pacific Maritime Association (PMA) that had a far-reaching impact on the nature of longshore work and the future of the ILWU. Known as the Mechanization and Modernization Agreement (M & M), the new contract traded longstanding ILWU work rules and production standards for a guaranteed 35-hour week and a $29 million pension fund. The new contract was widely hailed in business and academic circles as an important step toward an increase in labor productivity and job security.

During the mid-1960s the M& M Agreement created a number of problems for the ILWU and its leader. When the contract was signed in 1960, the PMA and the ILWU expected the 14,000-member Pacific Coast longshore workforce to shrink. Both the union and employers therefore agreed to the continuation of a category of semi-casual workers known as B-men, who did longshore work, usually the least desirable, but who were not beneficiaries of the new contract. In June 1963 most of these B-men were admitted to full standing in the union, but a predominantly black group of some 80 were expelled. The excluded longshoremen were dissidents and radicals, opponents of M & M. They sued both the ILWU and the PMA and enlisted the aid of a group of prominent writers, intellectuals, and civil rights leaders in their defense.

In August 1965 Bridges countersued some 15 B-men supporters, including writers Paul Jacobs, Harvey Swados, Herbert Gold, and Nat Hentoff. Bridges claimed that they had falsely accused him of being an autocratic labor leader practicing racial bias. Both suits proved inconclusive. However, the public dispute, along with the M&M agreement itself, damaged Bridges's reputation among many labor radicals of the 1960s.

The M & M Agreement was renewed for another five years in 1966. Because of the introduction of more efficient containerized cargo handling procedures, the ILWU became involved in a series of disputes with the Teamsters Union in the late 1960s. Both unions claimed jurisdiction over the loading of the truck-length containers, and a number of local jurisdictional strikes began in early 1969. These culminated in a half-year-long ILWU strike in 1971–72.

Although the ILWU took strong stands against the war in Vietnam and in favor of the farm workers' organizing drive, Bridges developed close ties to moderate and conservative Democratic Party figures in the mid-1960s. He backed the San Francisco mayoral candidacies of Jack Shelley in 1963 and Joseph Alioto in 1967. Most observers thought Alioto's appointment of Bridges to the powerful San Francisco Port Commission in 1970 marked "official" recognition of the union leader's place in the Bay Area establishment. Bridges retired in 1977. When he died in 1990, all the ports on the West Coast were briefly shut down, and ports in Hawaii and Alaska shut down for two hours simultaneous with his burial at sea.

—NNL

## Brooke, Edward W(illiam)
### (1919– ) *member of the Senate*

Brooke, whose father was a lawyer in the Veterans Administration, was born on October 26, 1919, and grew up in a prosperous black family in Washington, D.C. He received a bachelor of science degree from Howard University in 1941. After serving in the army during World War II, Brooke entered Boston University Law School, earning LL.B. and LL.M. degrees in 1948 and 1949. In 1950 Brooke ran for a seat from Roxbury in the Massachusetts legislature by entering both the Democratic and Republican primaries. He won the latter contest and thereafter remained a Republican. Brooke lost the

Massachusetts senator Edward W. Brooke, 1968 *(Library of Congress, Prints and Photographs Division)*

election and was defeated again in a 1952 bid for the state legislature.

For the next eight years Brooke practiced law. In 1960 he ran as the Republican candidate for Massachusetts secretary of state. He lost by about 12,000 votes, but his total vote of approximately 1.1 million impressed political observers in a state that was both strongly Democratic and 98 percent white.

In 1962 Brooke was elected state attorney general. He was reelected in 1964 with a plurality of almost 800,000 votes, one of the largest margins of victory of any Republican in the country that year. As attorney general Brooke gained prominence for his investigations of government corruption. A number of high-ranking politicians, including a former governor and two speakers of the house, were indicted. He also pressed for bills to reduce air pollution and protect borrowers against excessively high interest rates.

Brooke was identified with the liberal wing of the Republican Party. At its 1964 national convention in San Francisco, Brooke gave the seconding speech for WILLIAM SCRANTON. He declined to endorse conservative senator BARRY M. GOLDWATER (R-Ariz.), the convention's nominee.

Brooke declared his candidacy for the U.S. Senate in December 1965 immediately after incumbent Republican senator LEVERETT SALTONSTALL announced his plans to retire. In November 1966 he defeated former governor Endicott Peabody by more than 400,000 votes to become the first black since Reconstruction to win a Senate seat and the first African American in history to be elected to that body by popular vote.

Brooke supported civil rights legislation but did not attempt to play a leadership role in the area of civil rights despite the attempts of the Johnson administration to get him to play a larger role. During his senatorial campaign he denounced both STOKELY CARMICHAEL and LESTER MADDOX. Some liberals criticized him for being less outspoken than Peabody on behalf of antidiscrimination laws.

Before entering the Senate Brooke was mildly critical of the Johnson administration's Vietnam policies and favored a cessation of the bombing of North Vietnam. In January 1967 he visited Southeast Asia. While in Cambodia he vainly attempted to contact the North Vietnamese in an effort to ascertain the possibilities of a negotiated settlement to the war. Upon his return Brooke reversed his earlier view and stated, "It does not appear that suspension of the bombing in the North would, by itself, produce fruitful negotiations." Brooke's change of opinion was widely reported as a significant setback for antiwar forces in Congress.

One of Brooke's major interests was low- and middle-income housing. In August 1967 he said it might be necessary to establish a new low- and moderate-income housing division within the Department of Housing and Urban Development (HUD). Brooke complained that in the previous six years the Federal Housing Administration (FHA) had written insurance for only 40,000 low-income housing units, a figure he called "pitifully inadequate." Early in 1968 he introduced a bill to create the new division. The measure was not adopted, but a housing bill passed in 1968 required the FHA to expand its insurance program for low-income housing. He also played a role in developing the legislation that later became the 1970 Housing and Urban Development Act.

Like most Republican representatives Brooke favored the promotion of home ownership as a means of improving living standards and fostering individual responsibility. In November 1967 Brooke joined his Republican colleagues on the Banking and Currency Committee's Housing and Urban Affairs Subcommittee in praising a bill designed to aid low-income families in purchasing homes. They asserted that "the responsibility and self-sufficiency that is inherent in home ownership can be expected to make a marked contribution toward bettering a family's living standards and environment."

In July 1967 President Johnson appointed Brooke to the 11-member Special Advisory Commission on Civil Disorders, also known as the Kerner Commission. Its function was to investigate the causes of the urban riots that erupted during the summer of that year. The commission released its findings on February 29, 1968. It found no evidence of a conspiracy or of an organization behind the disturbances and blamed them on "white racism."

Brooke endorsed the Republican presidential candidacy of RICHARD M. NIXON in 1968 but subsequently disagreed with the new administration on a number of important issues. He opposed the president's nominations of Clement F. Haynsworth and G. Harrold Carswell for the Supreme Court in 1969 and 1970. During the early 1970s he consistently supported antiwar proposals, including the McGovern-Hatfield and Cooper-Church amendments. In 1972 he was reelected with 65 percent of the vote. After the *Boston Globe* raised some questions about his financial dealings, Brooke was defeated in his bid for a third term in 1978 by Democrat Paul Tsongas. Brooke remained in Virginia as a lawyer and chair of the National Low-Income Housing Coalition. Brooke received the Presidential Medal of Freedom in 2004.

—MLL

## Brower, David (Ross)

(1912–2000) *executive director, Sierra Club*

Brower who was born on July 1, 1912, in Berkeley, California, was first exposed to the wilderness on family camping trips to the Sierra Nevada Mountains. Intensely interested in nature, he discovered the butterfly *Anthocaris sara reakirtii broweri* at the age of 15. A member of the Sierra Club beginning in 1933, Brower became the San Francisco–based organization's executive director in 1952. "We do not inherit the earth from our fathers," he insisted, "We are borrowing it from our children."

After the death of its founder, John Muir, in 1914, the Sierra Club had been neither active nor effective in advancing the cause of conservation. Brower transformed the club into a successful political pressure group while furthering its traditional role as a proponent of wilderness values to the American public. The club's lavish photo books, produced under Brower's direction in the 1960s, brought an appreciation of the wilderness to large numbers of Americans and won sympathy for the organization's lobbying efforts on behalf of conservation legislation. During Brower's tenure the Sierra Club also became a national organization, increasing its membership from 7,000 to 70,000 and the annual budget from $75,000 to $3 million. It was easily the most powerful conservationist group in the country.

The Sierra Club's influence was at a peak during the late 1960s, aided by the Johnson administration's own commitment to highway beautification, recreation, and antipollution measures as integral elements in the Great Society program. In 1964 the club claimed some of the credit for the creation of the Land and Water Conservation Fund and the establishment of Canyonlands National Park, the first national park created since 1956. It also helped push through Congress the Wilderness Act of 1964, which established a National Wilderness Preservation System. The club's lobbying efforts culminated in 1968, when Congress established the North Cascades and Redwood National Parks. Congress also set up a wild-and-scenic rivers system and a national trails system. It was indicative of the club's influence in the 1960s that the Kennedy and Johnson administrations added 2.4 million acres to the National Park Service lands. Only 30,000 acres had been added in the 1950s. In addition, the club was responsible for blocking billions of dollars worth of construction projects that it considered a threat to the natural environment.

With Brower taking aggressive leadership the Sierra Club won its biggest victory in 1966 and 1967 by preventing the construction of two large hydroelectric dams on the stretch of the Colorado River that runs through the Grand Canyon. The victory was remarkable because the dams' proponents included the Interior Department's Bureau of Reclamation, the Colorado River Association, private power companies, and the entire congressional delegation of the seven states located in the Colorado Basin. Interior secretary STEWART UDALL first proposed the two dams in 1963 as part of an administration's Southwest Water Plan. The legislation

moved slowly in order to work out compromises among the various interests involved, including the seven states. Brower soon undertook a vast publicity and lobbying effort to stop the plan. In 1964 the Sierra Club published *Time and the River Flowing*, a photo book on the Grand Canyon, and it distributed copies of the $25 volume to every member of Congress. In the following year Brower testified for the first time in congressional hearings against the legislation. His remarks, reproduced as a pamphlet "Dams in the Grand Canyon—A Necessary Evil?" and a Sierra Club *Bulletin* editorial were widely distributed, sparking a massive letter-writing campaign.

In early 1966, when agreement on Colorado River legislation that would include the two dams seemed imminent, Brower stepped up the Sierra Club's campaign. On June 9, 1966, he attacked the dams in full-page ads in the *New York Times* and the *Washington Post*. The Internal Revenue Service (IRS) acted immediately to remove the club's tax-exempt status on the basis of its lobbying activity. The club charged that the IRS action was politically motivated and appealed the decision. Meanwhile, the ads generated what Senator THOMAS KUCHEL (R-Calif.) called "one of the largest letter-writing campaigns . . . in my tenure in the Senate."

The Brower strategy was successful. The administration withdrew its support of one of the dams in 1966 and of the second in 1967. The Colorado River bill was passed in 1968 but without authorization for the Grand Canyon dams. Representative MORRIS UDALL (D-Ariz.), a key supporter of the bill, said, in discussing the conservationists' campaign, that he could not think of "any group in this country that has had more power in the last eight years."

Despite the Sierra Club's victories Brower's campaigns were considered financially irresponsible by many in the club. In addition, his tendency to make decisions unilaterally brought criticism from the club's board of directors. Brower also wanted to expand the club's book series, although his colleagues pointed out that the club could not afford to increase production of books that had not been financially successful. Some critics described Brower as rigid and argued that he had unnecessarily alienated many potential allies in business and government. In 1969 the board of directors forced his resignation. Brower then founded the John Muir Institute for Environmental Studies and Friends of the Earth. The former was a research and educational organization, while the latter was devoted to lobbying on conservation issues and campaigning for political candidates. Brower headed both organizations. In 1982 he founded the Earth Island Institute, an organization that advances various causes related to peace, environmental protection, and social justice, and he was nominated for the Nobel Peace Prize three times. He died on November 5, 2000, in Berkeley, California.

—JCH

## Brown, Edmund G(erald), Sr.
(1905–1996) *governor*

"Pat" Brown was born in San Francisco, on April 24, 1905. He attended San Francisco public and parochial schools and took evening courses at the San Francisco Law School. Originally a Republican, he became a Democrat in 1939 and advanced his career in San Francisco through one of California's few solid party organizations. Brown was the city's district attorney in 1943 and was elected attorney general of California in 1950 and 1954. He was the only Democrat to hold statewide office in the early 1950s. In 1958 Brown broke the Republican stranglehold on the state by winning the governorship and carrying with him the first Democratic majorities in both houses of the legislature since 1889.

Brown's governorship coincided with a period of tremendous growth, during which California became the nation's most populous and wealthiest state. He claimed credit for passage of legislation that answered the needs of a greatly increased population. Brown's administration expanded the freeway system, the public schools, and jobless benefits and enacted consumer protection and fair employment practices legislation. Most important, it passed a $1.7 billion water plan, which provided water for populous but arid southern California, and a "master plan" offering some form of college education to all California high school graduates. He did so while at the same time eliminating a large debt that he had inherited from previous governors. Brown's record of "responsible liberalism" won him a dramatic reelection victory in 1962 over former vice president RICHARD NIXON, and, in 1964, Brown was chosen to put LYNDON JOHNSON's name into nomination at the Democratic National Convention. Nonetheless, in a state known for its fluid political loyalties, Brown could not always exercise control over his own party. The Kennedy administration looked to Democrat, Speaker of the California Assembly, JESSE UNRUH as its chief political liaison in the state, and Brown depended on an often uncooperative Unruh for the success of his legislative program. In addition, the governor often faced criticism from both the left and right of his party as well as from Republicans.

Brown's second term saw a drastic deterioration in both his popularity and in Democratic unity, as well as a marked decline in the success of his legislative program. The governor's feud with Unruh, the most powerful state legislator in the country, continued. The mid-1960s in California were characterized by a conservative political trend. Unruh early sensed this shift, but Brown remained publicly committed to liberal positions that undermined his popularity. He backed a 1963 fair housing law, and, when Californians voted to repeal the act by a 2-1 margin in 1964, Brown bluntly criticized the voters for their "bigotry." Brown's difficulties with conservatives increased in August 1965, when riots broke out in Watts, a predominantly African-American section of Los Angeles. Brown interrupted a vacation in Greece to return to Los Angeles. Following a restoration of order in Watts, he appointed an eight-member commission, headed by former Central Intelligence Agency director JOHN MCCONE, to investigate the causes of the riots and to recommend means to prevent their recurrence. Immediately, the Democratic mayor of Los Angeles, SAM YORTY, attacked one of the governor's appointments to the commission. Yorty and other conservatives blamed Brown's social welfare programs for raising poor people's expectations unrealistically, thereby making the riots possible.

By the election year of 1966, Californians, who were angered by the Watts riots, the student disturbances at the University of California's Berkeley campus, and a rising crime rate, apparently had concluded that Brown administration was responsible for the state's problems. The extent of Brown's difficulties were evident when he defeated Mayor Yorty in the June Democratic gubernatorial primary by only 375,000 votes out of more than 2.3 million cast. Meanwhile, his approval of President Johnson's Vietnam policy and his weak support of the National Farm Workers' organizing efforts in California hurt his credibility among liberals. His liberal standing was further damaged at the Democratic state convention in August when he unsuccessfully opposed adoption of a platform plank unreservedly supporting fair housing legislation.

Brown's Republican opponent in the general election was RONALD REAGAN. The governor's supporters were pleased with Reagan's primary victory over a moderate opponent, thinking that Brown could easily defeat an "ultraconservative" who lacked previous government experience. Yet anti-Brown feeling was so great that his chances of victory against any opponent were considered slim. Surrounded by angry liberals and radicals on his left and by a tough-talking Reagan on his right, the governor appeared indecisive. The Reagan campaign's portrayal of Brown as bumbling and weak was aided by the articulate speech and glamour of the Republican candidate. Reagan's attacks on professional politicians and the wastefulness of big government clearly appealed to the California electorate. Brown lost his reelection bid by almost a million votes out of approximately 5.4 million.

In March 1967 President Johnson appointed Brown head of a newly created National Commission on Reform of Criminal Laws. Brown remained a vociferous critic of his successor in the California governorship. He died in Beverly Hills, California, in February 1996.

—JCH

## Brown, Harold

(1927–  ) *director of defense research and engineering, Department of Defense; secretary of the air force*

Born on September 19, 1927, in New York City, Brown became a nuclear physicist interested in atomic weapons development. He was director of the University of California's Livermore Laboratory before joining the Defense Department as director of defense research and engineering in May 1961. He had also acted as a Pentagon scientific consultant and technical adviser to the Conferences for the Cessation of Nuclear Tests in 1958 and 1959.

As research director, Brown aided Secretary of Defense ROBERT S. MCNAMARA's attempts to find alternatives to the use of nuclear force. He developed the technical compromises necessary for military acceptance of the proposed multiservice bomber/fighter, the TFX. Brown, testifying before the House Appropriations Subcommittee in May 1963, advocated the use of chemical warfare as an

intermediate step between conventional and nuclear weapons. Several months later, in August 1963, he supported McNamara in asking Congress to ratify the nuclear test ban treaty.

Brown became secretary of the air force in September 1965. During his first two years in office, he acted as spokesperson for administration opposition to the expansion of bombing campaigns against North Vietnam. In a televised interview on May 22, 1966, and later in a speech on December 8, 1966, Brown conceded that bombing had reduced but not cut off infiltration from the north. However, he cautioned that Johnson did not want to widen raids to include Hanoi and Haiphong for fear of involving Communist China in a nuclear war.

Brown was one of Johnson's advisers who counseled de-escalation of the war following the military request for further massive troop buildups in February 1968. At the instruction of Secretary of Defense CLARK CLIFFORD, Brown and his staff, led by TOWNSEND HOOPES, developed three alternative strategies to the military proposal: (1) intensive bombing of the North, including attacks on Haiphong; (2) a concentrated effort against supply trails in the southern portions of North Vietnam; and (3) a campaign designed to substitute tactical airpower for a large portion of the search-and-destroy missions conducted by various ground troops in the South. Brown, believing that military victory was impossible at any price consistent with U.S. interests, supported the third position as the most likely to provide a strong negotiating posture. President Johnson, however, adopted the second proposal at the end of March.

In 1969 Brown resigned as secretary of the air force to become president of the California Institute of Technology. He served as secretary of defense under President Carter and, later, as chair of the Foreign Policy Institute of the Johns Hopkins University Paul H. Nitze School of Advanced International Studies.

—EWS

## Brown, H(ubert) Rap (Geroid)

(1943–  ) *chair, Student Nonviolent Coordinating Committee*

Brown, who was born on October 4, 1943, grew up in Baton Rouge and enrolled at Southern University in 1960. He spent the summers of 1962 and 1963 in Washington, D.C., where he joined demonstrations organized by the Nonviolent Action Group (NAG), an affiliate of the Student Nonviolent Coordinating Committee (SNCC). Brown quit school in 1964 and moved to Washington, where he became chair of NAG in the fall of 1964 and a neighborhood worker in a local antipoverty program during 1965. He began working as a SNCC organizer in Greene County, Alabama, in the fall of 1966 and was named SNCC's state project director in Alabama late that year. In May 1967 Brown was elected chair of SNCC, replacing STOKELY CARMICHAEL.

The militant Carmichael told reporters at the time of Brown's election that "people will be happy to have me back when they hear him." As SNCC chair Brown quickly captured media attention for his statements in support of Black Power, his condemnation of American society and government, and his advocacy of violence and revolution. He repeatedly accused white America of conspiring "to commit genocide against black people" and counseled blacks to "get yourself some guns." Brown called President Johnson a "wild, mad dog, an outlaw from Texas" who sent "honky, cracker federal troops into Negro communities to kill black people." He applauded inner city violence and called on blacks to celebrate August 11, the day the 1965 Watts riot had begun, as their "day of independence." He warned that the riots were only "dress rehearsals for revolution" and predicted that "the rebellions will continue and escalate." Violence "is necessary," Brown asserted. "It is as American as cherry pie."

Brown became controversial not only for his public statements but also for the role he allegedly played in instigating riots in 1967. Rioting erupted in Dayton, Ohio, in June and in East St. Louis, Illinois, in September shortly after speeches by Brown in each city. In a widely publicized incident Brown addressed a rally of blacks in Cambridge, Maryland, on June 24, reportedly telling his audience that they should get their guns and that they "should've burned . . . down long ago" a 50-year-old all-black elementary school in the city. Later that night a fire broke out in the school and quickly spread throughout the black business district, destroying nearly 20 buildings.

Brown was arrested in Washington on July 26 by federal officials and taken to Alexandria, Virginia, where he was rearrested by state authorities on a fugitive warrant, charged by Maryland with arson and inciting to riot. Released on bond on July 27,

Brown was again arrested in New York City on August 19 on a warrant issued by a federal court in New Orleans and charged with violating the Federal Firearms Act by carrying a gun across state lines while under indictment. He was also arrested in February 1968 for violating travel restrictions imposed on him by a federal judge while he was out on bond. Following the time of his July 1967 arrest, Brown spent various periods of time in jail while raising bail ranging from $10,000 to $100,000 on different charges.

Brown, who repeatedly insisted that the charges against him were trumped-up, was often singled out by proponents of a federal antiriot bill as one of their major targets. The 1968 Civil Rights Act included a section making it a crime to cross state lines with intent to incite a riot, and the controversial provision was popularly known as the "Rap Brown amendment." In May 1968 Brown was convicted of violating the federal firearms law and given the maximum sentence of five years and a $2,000 fine, but he was released on bond pending appeal.

From February to July 1968, while SNCC and the Black Panther Party were allied with each other, Brown served as the Black Panthers' minister of justice. That same year, he published his controversial autobiography and political manifesto, *Die, Nigger, Die*. He was replaced as SNCC chair in June 1968 but then reelected to the post in July 1969 at a meeting where SNCC also changed its name to the Student National Coordinating Committee. Brown's trial on the Maryland charges was scheduled for March 16, 1970, but was twice postponed when he failed to appear in court. Brown disappeared in March 1970, and in May he was placed on the FBI's 10-most-wanted list. He was not seen until October 1971, when he was shot and captured by police in New York City. The police charged that Brown had participated in the armed robbery of a Manhattan bar and was shot while trying to make a getaway. In March 1973 Brown was found guilty of armed robbery in New York and was sentenced to a term of five to 15 years. Maryland dropped its riot and arson charges against Brown in November when he pleaded guilty to a lesser charge of failing to appear for trial in 1970. After he was released in 1976, Brown, who had become a Muslim in prison and taken the name Jamil Abdullah Al-Amin, led the National Ummah, one of America's largest black Muslim groups. In 2000, after a shootout with

Atlanta policemen who had come to arrest him for theft, Brown was found guilty of murder and sentenced to life in prison.

—CAB

## Bruce, David K(irkpatrick) E(ste)
### (1898–1977) *ambassador to Great Britain*

Born on February 12, 1898, into a politically prominent Baltimore family, Bruce successfully employed his talents in law, politics, the diplomatic service, and business. Associated with the Bankers Trust Company and Harriman and Co., he was at one time the director of 25 corporations. After working in the Office of Strategic Services in the European theater during World War II, Bruce became one of the leading diplomats in Europe. He was the only U.S. diplomat to hold the three most important ambassadorships in Europe: he served as ambassador to France from 1949 to 1952, as ambassador to West Germany from 1957 to 1959, and as ambassador to Great Britain during the 1960s. He was greatly respected for his diplomatic skills; for a time in December 1960 Kennedy had considered him for secretary of state.

After Kennedy's assassination Bruce remained at his post at President Johnson's request. He not only represented Washington's views in London but spoke out on European affairs as well. A proponent of European integration, he attacked French president Charles de Gaulle in May 1966 as "ideologically reckless" for his repudiation of an integrated North Atlantic command structure and his demand for the withdrawal of American troops from France.

Bruce faced his most delicate task in communicating Washington's views to British prime minister Harold Wilson during Wilson's February 1967 talks with Soviet premier Alexei Kosygin in London. Wilson and Kosygin hoped to use their influence in Washington and Hanoi to extend the Tet cease-fire and to arrange negotiations aimed at ending the war in Vietnam. Acting on instructions from Washington, Bruce and U.S. envoy Chester Cooper indicated that the United States would stop the bombing of North Vietnam as a sign of good faith with the understanding that Hanoi would then give private assurances that infiltration of the South would cease. The United States in turn would stop augmenting its troop strength in Vietnam. Wilson and Kosygin were ready to act on this proposal, but presidential adviser WALT W. ROSTOW phoned

Bruce indicating that the United States had suddenly changed its position. The Johnson administration stated that would not stop the bombing until Hanoi promised to stop infiltration. The new White House policy effectively killed what was, at least to Harold Wilson, one of the most promising peace initiatives taken during the Johnson administration. In addition, Wilson was angry with Washington, because he, Bruce, and Kosygin had been put in an embarrassing position.

In July 1968 in London Bruce signed the nuclear nonproliferation treaty for the United States. He remained at his post until February 1969, having served the longest term of any U.S. ambassador to Great Britain. After his retirement Bruce agreed to consult with the State Department on a part-time basis. In 1970 he returned to full-time responsibilities as the U.S. representative at the Vietnam peace talks in Paris, and, in 1972, he went to Peking as liaison officer to the People's Republic of China. He died in Washington, D.C., on December 5, 1977.

—JCH

## Buckley, William F(rank), Jr.
### (1925–    ) *editor in chief,* National Review

Born on November 24, 1925, into a wealthy family in New York City, William F. Buckley, Jr., attended private schools in Great Britain and served in the navy during World War II. A year after his 1950 graduation from Yale, Buckley wrote *God and Man at Yale*, a best-selling condemnation of what he regarded as his alma mater's political and irreligious liberalism. In *McCarthy and His Enemies* (1954), he championed the anticommunist activities of Senator Joseph R. McCarthy (R-Wisc.).

By the mid-1960s Buckley had emerged as the intellectual leader of a new, postwar conservatism linking militant opposition to communism abroad with antagonism toward political liberalism at home. To provide a forum for conservative opinion, Buckley founded the biweekly *National Review* in 1955. Edited by Buckley and partially subsidized by his family, the *Review* became the conservative counterpart to the left-leaning *New Republic* and *Nation*. In the *Review*, a widely syndicated newspaper column begun in 1962, and in frequent debates and on lecture tours, Buckley argued against a host of programs and policies supported by liberals, including Social Security, U.S. membership in the United

Nations, and the federal judiciary's school desegregation orders. A vigorous critic of the Soviet Union, Buckley compared it to Nazi Germany and said he agreed with the proposition "Better the chance of being dead than the certainty of being Red."

Buckley supported conservative senator BARRY M. GOLDWATER (R-Ariz.) for president in 1964 but did not play a role in his campaign. In his columns Buckley strove to differentiate Goldwater's candidacy from the extreme, right-wing John Birch Society, which he deemed a threat to a genuine conservative political movement in America. At the same time, however, members of the Goldwater staff rejected Buckley's offer of assistance.

In 1965 Buckley championed conservative politics in the New York City mayoralty campaign. Running as the candidate of the Conservative Party, established with his assistance in 1962, Buckley hoped to frustrate the political ambitions of Representative JOHN V. LINDSAY (R-N.Y.), the Republican-Liberal Party mayoral candidate who had refused to endorse Goldwater in 1964. Declining to campaign in the traditional New York fashion—in the streets, eating blintzes and pizza—Buckley instead offered lengthy position papers and denunciations of Lindsay's grammar and the predominant social welfare philosophy of the nation's largest city. He criticized the city's budgetary policies and voting-bloc politics. Among other proposals Buckley offered tax relief for minority business enterprises, legalization of gambling, access to drugs by addicts with a doctor's prescription, compulsory work for able-bodied welfare recipients, and an elevated bicycle expressway along First Avenue. Although he failed to accomplish his principal objective, that of denying Lindsay's election, he succeeded in a secondary purpose of his campaign. With 13.4 percent of the vote, he exceeded Lindsay's tally on the Liberal Party line. He drew most of his support from Republican districts outside Manhattan.

Becoming something of a celebrity Buckley pursued his conservative campaign nationwide. Beginning in 1966 he hosted *Firing Line*, a syndicated television interview program in which he debated, with acumen and sarcasm, liberals and radicals. An early critic of both the civil rights and antiwar movements, Buckley attacked their militance and emphasis upon civil disobedience as subversive to an orderly and rational society. Still protesting his college's "liberal bias," Buckley ran for a seat on the board of the Yale Corporation in 1967. Former

deputy defense secretary CYRUS VANCE, a liberal Democrat, defeated him.

In 1968 Buckley supported former vice president RICHARD M. NIXON for president and managed his own brother's campaign for the U.S. Senate. Running on the Conservative Party line, James L. Buckley lost to Senator JACOB K. JAVITS (R-Lib.-N.Y.) in November, but an impressive display of voter support (16.7 percent) set the stage for James's successful senatorial campaign two years later. William F. Buckley held two largely honorific appointments in the Nixon administration. In 1972 he declared a "suspension of support" for Nixon because he differed with the president's policy of détente with the People's Republic of China and the Soviet Union and his planned budget deficit. He continued, however, to support Republican causes and candidates throughout the century, particularly RONALD REAGAN, through his magazine and also through his own prolific writing.

—JLB

## Bunche, Ralph J(ohnson)
**(1904–1971)** *UN undersecretary for special political affairs*

Born in Detroit, Michigan, on August 7, 1904, Ralph Bunche was orphaned at 13 and raised in Los Angeles by his maternal grandmother. He graduated Phi Beta Kappa from the University of California at Los Angeles and in 1934 received a Ph.D. in government and international relations from Harvard. During World War II Bunche entered the State Department, serving in the division of dependent area affairs, which dealt with colonial problems. In 1945, Bunche was one of the chief advisers to the U.S. delegation to the San Francisco Conference that drafted the charter of the United Nations, and, in 1947, he left the State Department to join the secretariat of the new world body.

In 1948 and 1949 Bunche helped mediate the Arab-Israeli war. For his efforts he was the first black man ever awarded the Nobel Peace Prize. Bunche served Secretary General Dag Hammarskjöld and his successor U Thant as a principal UN troubleshooter. In 1953 Hammarskjöld put Bunche in charge of establishing a UN agency to oversee the development and control of atomic energy. He supervised the UN's peacekeeping force at Suez in 1956 and in 1957 was promoted to UN undersecretary for special political affairs. In 1960 Bunche directed the UN's peacekeeping force in the Congo, returning in January 1963 to oversee the UN's capture of Elisabethville, Katanga, and the reunification of the Congo. In March 1964 he assumed control of the UN peacekeeping force on Cyprus.

Dr. Bunche often lent his international prestige to the U.S. civil rights movement. An early supporter of the Rev. MARTIN LUTHER KING, JR., Bunche, who first walked a picket line for the NAACP in 1937, spoke at the 1963 March on Washington and joined King on the Selma-Montgomery march in March 1965. However, Bunche opposed King's attempt to link the civil rights movement with those who opposed the growing war in Vietnam. In October 1965 Bunche suggested that King should "positively and publicly give up one role or the other, that of civil rights leader or that of international conciliator." Bunche's opposition to King's position received greater publicity when he announced at an April 10, 1967, news conference that "the two movements have little in common" and that he had convinced the NAACP board of directors to adopt language characterizing King's position as "a serious tactical mistake." King immediately denied advocating a merger of the movements and challenged the NAACP to assume a "forthright stand on the rightness or wrongness of the Vietnam War." On April 13 Bunche announced that King's statement "takes care of the issue to which my statement had been directed."

Declining health, "frustrations" with UN peacekeeping operations, and "the calamitous war in Vietnam" led Bunche to consider retirement in January 1967, but U Thant persuaded him to remain. Responding to the increasing number of plane hijackings throughout the world, Bunche met with the president of the International Airlines Pilots Association in February 1970 and discussed strategies to block attacks on civil aircraft. He also played a central role in negotiating a settlement to the dispute between Bahrain and Great Britain stemming for Bahrain's desire for independence. Bunche died on December 9, 1971, after several years of poor health.

—DKR

## Bundy, McGeorge
(1919–1996) *special assistant to the president for national security affairs*

McGeorge Bundy, a close adviser to both President Kennedy and President Johnson, was born in Boston on March 30, 1919, into a family that had included a Revolutionary War general, a prominent poet, and a president of Harvard. Bundy graduated first in his class at Yale in 1940 and the next year became a junior fellow at Harvard. In 1948 he went to work for the agency responsible for implementing the Marshall Plan but left government to join Thomas Dewey's presidential campaign. After Dewey's defeat Bundy became a political analyst for the prestigious Council on Foreign Relations.

In 1949 Bundy returned to Harvard to teach in the government department. At 34, he was appointed dean of the college of arts and sciences, the second-highest position at Harvard. Although a nominal Republican, he campaigned for John F. Kennedy in 1960. Following the election he was appointed the president's special assistant for national security affairs. During the Kennedy years Bundy was one of the president's closest advisers, counseling him on all important foreign policy decisions, including those on Berlin, Cuba, and Vietnam.

Unlike many of Kennedy's close associates, Bundy did not leave government following the assassination. Instead, asserting that he served the presidency, not the president, he remained at the White House as an adviser to Johnson, and quickly became one of LBJ's leading foreign policy advisers. Bundy considered himself a pragmatist and was, therefore, anxious to base American policy on reactions to specific situations rather than on what he believed were long-term commitments prompted by ideological abstractions. Consequently, much of his counsel was directed at advising the president of all possible policy options and in keeping choices open until a major decision was unavoidable.

Bundy frequently served as Johnson's personal representative on important fact-finding and troubleshooting missions. In May 1965 Johnson sent him to the Dominican Republic to find a solution to that nation's civil war. After the April landing of U.S. troops to prevent what the president thought would be a Communist takeover, Bundy helped initiate negotiations on the formation of a coalition government.

As the Johnson administration became increasingly absorbed by Vietnam, Bundy became an important force in policy formation. In early 1964 he was on the periphery of decision making, helping to direct the targeting of South Vietnamese torpedo-boat raids against the North. These missions, known as 34A operations, were theoretically independent efforts by the South Vietnamese, but they were in fact planned and initiated by the U.S. military command and high-level officials in Washington, and were at the heart of the controversial Gulf of Tonkin incident in August that proved critical in Johnson's escalation of the American military commitment to the war.

In late 1964 Bundy was an active supporter of the policy of military expansion of the war. Such proposals were generally kept quiet until after the presidential election, but behind the scenes Bundy was encouraging a greater role for American forces. "It seems to me at least possible," he wrote to LBJ in August, "that a couple of brigade-sized units put in to do specific jobs about six weeks from now might be good medicine everywhere."

By January 1965 Bundy had become convinced that the president would have to make a decision on further U.S. action within the near future. In his opinion both the military effort and the political situation in Saigon had deteriorated to such an extent that a major American commitment was necessary if South Vietnam were to remain a viable nation. The decision was, to Bundy, a litmus test of America's readiness to save the rest of Southeast Asia. He believed a formidable effort was important to maintain the world's trust in American willingness to prevent the spread of world communism.

Following a trip to Vietnam in early February, Bundy recommended that the Johnson administration implement the recommendation of a Working Group of the National Security Council that called for sustained bombing raids of North Vietnam. President Johnson concurred, and the bombing raids, called Operation Rolling Thunder, began in March. During the remainder of his stay at the White House, Bundy reviewed targets for the raids and became a leading spokesperson for the administration's policy in Vietnam.

After leaving the Johnson administration in early 1966, Bundy did not publicly criticize U.S. policy in Vietnam. But, in early 1967, he wrote a private letter to Johnson opposing further escalation of the war as counterproductive. During a symposium held at DePauw University in October 1968, Bundy, whose counsel had contributed to large-scale involvement in Vietnam, called for lowering the cost of the conflict and systematic reduction of the number of American troops there. That same year he was one of a group of foreign policy experts (dubbed the "Wise Men") brought to the White House for a few days of meetings to advise Johnson on the Vietnam War; to LBJ's dismay, the majority, Bundy included, suggested that it was time for the United States to begin to disengage.

Following his resignation from the White House staff, Bundy became president of the Ford Foundation. He pledged that the foundation's first priority would be to eliminate racial discrimination. During his tenure Ford authorized grants, totaling several million dollars, to train black leaders in the fields of education, social service, and politics. Among the most controversial of its grants was a large 1967 contribution to the Congress of Racial Equality. It was designed to increase black voter registration in Cleveland shortly before the election in which CARL STOKES was elected as the first black mayor of major city.

Bundy's other top priorities were the fiscal problems facing the nation's colleges and universities, which Bundy believed were caused, in part, by their conservative investment policies. To promote more aggressive investment of endowment portfolios, the foundation tied grants to the individual institution's income. The effort proved unsuccessful, especially after the stock market decline began in 1969.

Bundy remained at the foundation into the 1970s. During that period Ford made dramatic cuts in grants to meet a much lower level of investment income. He left Ford in 1979 and became a professor of history at New York University. Later, he served as chair of the Carnegie Corporation Committee on Reducing the Nuclear Danger, and a scholar-in-residence at Carnegie. He died on September 16, 1996.

—EWS

## Bundy, William P(utnam)

(1917–2000) *assistant secretary of defense for international security affairs, assistant secretary of state for Far Eastern affairs*

William Bundy, one of the prime architects of the Johnson administration's policy in Southeast Asia, was born on September 24, 1917, into a socially and politically prominent New England family. A brilliant student, he was educated at Groton and Yale, graduating from the latter in 1939. After serving in the army during the war, Bundy received his law degree from Harvard in 1947 and entered the prestigious Washington law firm of Covington and

Burling. Three years later he joined the Central Intelligence Agency, where he was put in charge of overall evaluation of international intelligence.

In 1960 Bundy became staff director of the President's Commission on National Goals, which had been founded to formulate broad, long-term objectives and programs. President John F. Kennedy appointed Bundy deputy assistant secretary of defense in charge of international security affairs in January 1961. At this post he was responsible for coordinating military aid programs throughout the world.

Although his role in Vietnam policy making was less well known than that of his brother McGeorge, William Bundy was an important figure in America's growing involvement in the war. In the fall of 1961 he was one of the officials who analyzed South Vietnam's request for a bilateral defense treaty and increased American military aid. Bundy recommended "an early, hard-hitting operation" to arrest Communist expansion. However, President Kennedy decided to send only more U.S. military advisers and equipment in November 1961.

He became assistant secretary of state for Far Eastern affairs in 1964, and he voiced some doubts about the growing American commitment to Vietnam. In one of his memos to the president he argued that the United States should, "Swing wildly . . . then bunt," meaning that the United States should launch a major bombing campaign against North Vietnam for a few days in order to generate pressure on them from internal and external sources, and then the United States could negotiate. The result, he acknowledged, would likely be a neutralist, coalition government in the South, leading to a Communist takeover. But the United States would "gain time to shore up the next line of defense in Thailand." The argument went nowhere, and, as it became clear that the administration was determined to continue its presence, Bundy continued to take an active role in shaping the details. As the political and military situation in Vietnam deteriorated in the fall of 1964, President Johnson ordered the National Security Council Working Group, led by Bundy and JOHN MCNAUGHTON, to review operations and make recommendations on the future course of the war. In its report, completed at the end of November, the group recommended aerial attacks on the North, their intensity to vary with the level of Communist infiltration and the pace of the war in the South. The panel based its recommendation on the belief that an American defeat in Vietnam would make the defense of the rest of Southeast Asia extremely difficult. Bundy did not support the domino theory, which held that if Vietnam fell the rest of Southeast Asia would shortly fall to communism. However, he calculated that a Communist takeover would be probable by the end of a decade.

The panel did not believe that the use of air power would settle the war but rather saw the bombing strikes as a means of upholding and improving South Vietnamese morale. In Bundy's estimation the prospect was "for a prolonged period without major strikes or escalation, but without any give by Hanoi." He rejected a negotiated settlement at this time because he believed it would neither lead to a stable peace nor help South Vietnamese morale.

Johnson adopted the committee's proposals in December 1964. These recommendations determined the course of the war until July 1965, when the administration committed extensive ground forces to the conflict. In the months that followed the decision to launch what was known as Operation Rolling Thunder in March 1965, Bundy was one of the officials responsible for choosing targets for the bombing campaign.

Despite his support of bombing Bundy was reluctant to back the large-scale introduction of American troops, fearing that the United States would have the same experience as the French in Indochina. However, once the decision was made he supported the position and eventually became a leading defender of the administration's policy.

During the years that followed the introduction of systematic bombing raids, Bundy helped formulate the conditions under which the United States would halt the attacks and begin peace negotiations. In May 1966 he submitted a memorandum to Secretary of State DEAN RUSK that served as a guideline for U.S. policy until 1969. In this paper, bombing was seen as a means of driving North Vietnam to the negotiating table. The United States would stop bombing only if North Vietnam agreed to limit infiltration and end Communist action in the South. A halt in return for an agreement to negotiate was considered unacceptable.

In the spring of 1967 Bundy opposed the continued escalation of the conflict, and particularly the proposed mining of Haiphong harbor, on the grounds that such action would not change Hanoi's position but would have an adverse effect on relations with U.S. allies. Further buildups, he believed, would also convince the South Vietnamese that the United States could win the war without their all-out support. Despite the lack of progress in the war, he argued against negotiations as useless and, instead, favored "sticking it out if necessary."

Bundy left the government in March 1969 to become a visiting professor at the Massachusetts Institute of Technology's Center for International Studies. In 1972 he became editor of *Foreign Affairs*. He retired in 1984 and died of heart disease in October 2000 in Princeton, New Jersey.

—EWS

## Bunker, Ellsworth
(1894–1984)  *ambassador to the Organization of American States, ambassador-at-large, ambassador to South Vietnam*

Born on May 11, 1894, in Yonkers, New York, Bunker joined his father's firm, the National Sugar Refining Company, following his graduation from Yale in 1916; he rose to become chair of the board in 1948. Three years later Bunker left private industry to become ambassador to Argentina. From 1952 to 1953 he served as ambassador to Italy and from 1956 to 1961 was ambassador to India. In 1962 and 1963 Bunker mediated disputes between the Dutch and Indonesians over West Irian and between the Saudi Arabians and Egyptians over Yemen.

Shortly after President Johnson appointed Bunker ambassador to the Organization of American States (OAS) in January 1964, the diplomat was assigned to help reestablish U.S.-Panamanian diplomatic relations, severed following an incident in which American troops fired on Panamanian rioters. By April Bunker had succeeded in reaching an agreement with Panama to resume diplomatic ties and discuss problems between the two countries.

In 1965 Bunker undertook a year-long mission in the Dominican Republic, then torn by a civil war. Fearing that the war would result in a takeover by Castro-allied leftists, President Johnson had ordered U.S. troops to that Caribbean country in April 1965. In May he sent a negotiating team headed by MCGEORGE BUNDY to try to persuade the factions to establish a coalition government, but the mission failed. Bunker arrived in Santo Domingo in June as a member of a three-man OAS peace mission. By winning the personal trust of leaders on both sides during the course of three

months of patient negotiation, Bunker was able to find a provisional president agreeable to all and to arrange terms for the surrender of rebel arms. Bunker also helped stabilize the provisional regime by convincing rightist plotters that Washington would not support a new coup. At the same time he demanded and received from the Johnson administration assurances that no matter what its reservations about the new government, it would not support a military takeover. For his conduct in this affair, Walter Lippmann called Bunker "America's most accomplished diplomat." That same year, Bunker briefly served as special envoy to Indonesia, working to stabilize U.S. relations with Jakarta. A series of difficult meetings with top Indonesian officials convinced him that relations were unlikely to improve in the immediate future, leading to an American decision to reduce its commitment to the South Asian nation.

Ambassador to South Vietnam Ellsworth Bunker *(Photographed by Yoichi R. Okamoto; Lyndon Baines Johnson Library)*

In April 1967 President Johnson named Bunker ambassador to South Vietnam, an appointment applauded by both "hawks" and "doves" in Congress and the press. Bunker's reputation as a disinterested mediator was severely damaged by his stay in Vietnam. While there he became, in the words of David Halberstam, "one of the three most resilient hawks in the Johnson administration." Bunker opposed bombing halts in the winter of 1967, which were designed to bring North Vietnam to the negotiating table, and he asserted that progress was being made in the conduct of the war even after the disastrous Tet offensive of January–February 1968. Bunker was a strong supporter of the regime of President Nguyen Van Thieu. Because of his prestige as a diplomat, this support carried great weight within the Johnson administration.

Bunker remained at his post during the early 1970s and employed his skills as a diplomat to coordinate U.S.–South Vietnamese bargaining strategy during the Paris peace talks. He was replaced by GRAHAM MARTIN in March 1973 and returned to Washington to assume the position of ambassador-at-large. After the Vietnam War ended, Bunker headed the U.S. team involved in the drawing up of the 1978 Panama treaty. He died in 1984.

—EWS

## Burdick, Quentin N(orthrup)
### (1908–1992) *member of the Senate*
The son of a pioneer family, Burdick, who was born on June 19, 1908, in Munich, North Dakota, graduated from the University of Minnesota Law School in 1932. While practicing in his father's law firm, he became active in the Nonpartisan League, which had been formed to aid small farmers. Burdick was elected to the U.S. House of Representatives in 1958 as the first Democratic representative in North Dakota's history. After the death of Senator William Langer (R-N.Dak.) in 1959, he won a special election to the Senate. According to *Congressional Quarterly*, Burdick supported Kennedy administration legislation on more than 65 percent of key roll-call votes and backed such administration measures as the Area Redevelopment Act and civil rights and public works bills.

During the Johnson administration Burdick supported administration legislation on over 60 percent of key roll-call votes. In the 1964 Senate election he defeated business executive Thomas S.

Kleppe with 58 percent of the vote, equaling President Johnson's total in the state. Burdick served on the Interior and Insular Affairs Committee and, in 1965, won the $300 million Garrison Dam and Diversion Project for his state. In 1967 he became chair of the Senate Environment and Public Works Committee. He also formed and co-chaired the Senate Rural Health Caucus, along with serving on the Special Committee on Aging and the Select Committee on Indian Affairs.

On January 27, 1966, Burdick was one of 15 senators who sent a letter to President Johnson calling for the continued suspension of air strikes against North Vietnam. He was also among a group of Senate critics of the war who issued a statement on May 17, 1967, warning Hanoi that dissent on the war was a minority view in the United States and that, while the group would still press for a negotiated peace, they steadfastly opposed any unilateral withdrawal of U.S. troops from South Vietnam.

Burdick remained in the Senate until his death, from heart failure, on September 8, 1992, in Fargo, North Dakota. His wife, Jocelyn, was chosen as his replacement.

—FHM

## Burns, John A(nthony)
### (1909–1975) *governor*
Burns, who was born on March 30, 1909, in Ft. Assinneboine, Montana, spent his youth in Hawaii and Kansas. He served as a captain on the Honolulu police force during World War II, working as the head of a counterespionage unit affiliated with the Federal Bureau of Investigation. Following the war he began to reorganize the territory's Democratic Party with the substantial support of the islands large Nisei population and the International Longshoremen's and Warehousemen's Union (ILWU), which fostered multiracial unionism and opposed Hawaii's oligarchic economic system. Burns won election as territorial delegate to the U.S. Congress on his third try in November 1956, and, once in Washington, he fought for Hawaii's application for statehood. He lost the July 1959 gubernatorial election to the incumbent territorial governor, Republican William F. Quinn, but, in a November 1962 rematch, Burns, recognized as the architect of Hawaiian statehood, easily defeated Quinn.

Hawaii experienced an economic boom during Burns's first term. A practitioner of "consensus" politics, Burns modeled himself after his close friend and congressional adviser, LYNDON B. JOHNSON, who sent Burns on diplomatic missions to Korea and Africa in the mid-1960s. He also served as the personal representative of President Kennedy to the South Pacific Commission Conference in 1962 as well as sitting on the National Governors' Conference Executive Committee from 1965 to 1966 and chairing the Western Governors' Conference from 1967 to 1968. Burns helped his protégés, many of them Japanese Americans, win elective office and contributed to reducing the state Republican Party to one of the weakest in the nation. Yet, despite Burns's close relations with business, labor, and Hawaii's ethnic minorities, opposition to increased taxes and government expenditures made his 1966 reelection victory difficult.

During his second term divisions arose within Democratic ranks. Critics charged that, while Burns encouraged the islands' economic expansion, he ignored pressures on the environment and gave greater attention to tourism than to the living needs of the people of Hawaii. Burns, whose optimistic vision of Hawaii included the eventual absorption of the Marianas, the Caroline and Marshall Islands, Guam, and American Samoa into the state, argued that there should be no limit on economic development, confident that the people of Hawaii could cope with the problems of prosperity.

Despite a serious primary challenge from his lieutenant governor, Thomas P. Gill, Burns was reelected again in 1970. However, after learning that he was suffering from cancer, he decided not to run in 1974. In the November election his chosen successor, Lieutenant Governor George Ariyoshi, was elected the nation's first nonwhite governor. Burns died on April 5, 1975.

—JCH

## Burton, Philip
(1926–1983) *member of the House of Representatives*

Burton, who was born on June 1, 1926, in Cincinnati, Ohio, moved with family to California in 1939. He served in World War II and in Korea, took a law degree in 1952 and soon became deeply involved in California's Democratic Party. Burton was elected to the California Assembly from a San Francisco district in 1956. In 1960 he was one of the few elected California officials to support student demonstrations against the House Un-American Activities Committee when it held hearings in northern California.

Burton was elected to the House of Representatives in 1964 from San Francisco's ethnically heterogeneous and liberal eastern district. His equally liberal brother John filled his vacated assembly seat, and together the Burton brothers won great influence among Bay Area liberals. In the late 1960s their faction in northern California's Democratic Party rivaled San Francisco mayor Joseph Alioto's for leadership in the party.

In the House Burton was among the earliest critics of American involvement in Vietnam, and he belonged to the handful of representatives who consistently dissented from Johnson administration policies there. In 1965 and 1966 he voted against Vietnam appropriation bills in the House and at the tumultuous 1968 Democratic National Convention Burton presented the minority platform position on Vietnam. Known as the McGovern-McCarthy-Kennedy plank, it called for an unconditional end to the bombing of North Vietnam.

Supported by Bay Area labor unions as well as peace groups, Burton was also an active backer of labor and welfare legislation. Assigned to the House Education and Labor Committee, Burton introduced an amendment in 1966 to that year's minimum-wage bill to extend minimum-wage and overtime protection to 700,000 federal employees. He was also a consistent advocate for welfare reform, black lung compensation for coal miners, and wildlife and parks conservation.

Burton often went further than fellow liberals on civil rights and civil liberties issues. In January 1966 he led 23 representatives who protested the Georgia state legislature's refusal to seat civil rights leader JULIAN BOND because of his antiwar views. Burton also favored the dissolution of the House Un-American Activities Committee. Unlike many congressional liberals he opposed the committee's investigation of the Ku Klux Klan. "No committee of Congress," Burton said in April 1965, "has the authority to determine whether or not any organization, including the Klan, will be proved to be un-American."

Burton, who continued to sponsor important labor and welfare legislation, was elected chair of the liberal Democratic Study Group in 1971 and was a leader in the movement for congressional reform. Known in the House for his effectiveness behind the scenes, he helped to abolish the House Un-American Activities Committee's successor, the House Internal Security Committee, by persuading all its Democratic members but the chair to resign. In 1974 he became chair of the powerful House Democratic Caucus. He died while still serving in Congress in San Francisco on April 10, 1983.

—MDB

## Byrd, Harry F(lood) (Sr.)

(1887–1966)  *member of the Senate*

Born in Martinsburg, West Virginia, on June 10, 1887, Byrd established himself as a successful apple grower in Virginia's Shenandoah Valley. He won a seat in the Virginia Senate and in 1925 was elected governor of the state. During his four-year term Byrd skillfully employed patronage to establish himself as the leader of a powerful Democratic political machine. For almost 40 years Byrd's rural-oriented organization based on county courthouses maintained nearly unquestioned control of Virginia's politics.

In 1933 Byrd was elected to the U.S. Senate, where he remained for over 30 years. Applying his principles at the national level, he opposed New Deal welfare spending programs and called for balanced budgets. By the late 1940s Byrd was a leader of the southern Democrat–Republican conservative coalition in Congress. His seniority enabled him to obtain the chair of the Senate Finance Committee in 1955. Other continually reelected candidates of his Virginia machine, such as Senator A. WILLIS ROBERTSON and Representative HOWARD W. SMITH, had also accumulated seniority, and with them Byrd was able to play an effective role in advancing his political agenda.

Beginning in 1952 Byrd tacitly endorsed Republican presidential candidates by declining to back the Democratic nominees, whom he regarded as dangerously liberal. Without his support, ADLAI STEVENSON lost the state in 1952 and 1956, and Senator John F. Kennedy (D-Mass.) likewise failed to carry Virginia in 1960. In Congress Byrd was a potent enemy of Kennedy's New Frontier measures. As chair of the Senate Finance Committee, he helped kill the administration's 1962 bill for expanding unemployment compensation benefits and played a major role in preventing the passage of

President Kennedy's Medicare bill during the same year. In 1963 Byrd held up in his committee a tax cut bill, designed to stimulate the economy.

President Johnson gave the Kennedy tax bill high priority in the early months of his administration. The deficits, which the measure would create, were anathema to Byrd. But by announcing, in his State of the Union message of January 8, 1964, that the budget for fiscal 1965 would be kept below $100 billion, Johnson convinced Byrd to let the Finance Committee vote on the tax cut bill, although the senator was still against it. On January 23 the committee voted, 12-5, with Byrd in opposition, to approve the measure. The Senate adopted it two weeks later. Johnson then submitted a budget with expenditures of $97.9 billion.

Byrd continued to be a staunch opponent of liberal presidential programs. In May 1964 he asserted that federal spending could be cut by $6.5 billion through the curtailing of such measures as the mass transit, air pollution, public works, aid-to-education, and housing programs. Byrd also opposed the civil rights bill of 1964 and the voting rights and Medicare bills of the following year.

However, Byrd proved a less effective opponent of welfare legislation during the Johnson administration than he had been in former years. Johnson was a skillful manager of Congress and his power increased as a result of the overwhelming Democratic victory in the 1964 elections. Therefore, the president succeeded in securing passage of a large majority of the Great Society programs he proposed in 1964 and 1965. During the latter year, for example, he pressured Byrd into granting prompt hearings for the Medicare bill, and the senator was thus unable to block the measure through stalling tactics, as he had done in the early 1960s.

As Byrd's power in Congress ebbed, his control over his state's politics also eroded. In the late 1950s a moderate group had coalesced within Byrd's machine in reaction to the senator's intransigent opposition to court-ordered school desegregation. That group grew in ensuing years as the moderate electorate in urban areas expanded and the size of the black vote increased. In 1964 the Virginia Democratic convention, in defiance of Byrd, endorsed President Johnson for reelection. Not only were the state's voters moving toward the political center, but many of Byrd's political lieutenants feared that continued failure to endorse Democratic national tickets would eventually reduce the party's strength in state and local elections.

Illness ended Byrd's career before he suffered any further setbacks. He resigned from the Senate because of poor health in November 1965 and died of a brain tumor on October 20, 1966.

—MLL

## Byrd, Harry F(lood), Jr.
(1914–   ) *member of the Senate*

Harry F. Byrd, Jr., was the son of U.S. senator Harry F. Byrd (D-Va.), whose organization dominated Virginia's politics from the late 1920s to the mid-1960s. The younger Byrd, who was born on December 20, 1914, in Winchester, Virginia, won election to the Virginia Senate in 1948 and served in that body until November 1965, when Governor Albertis S. Harrison appointed him to fill the U.S. Senate seat of his father, who had just retired because of illness. One year later he won election to his father's seat.

"Little Harry," as he was known in Virginia, proved as staunchly conservative as the senior Byrd. Throughout his political career he opposed civil rights measures and large government expenditures, especially for social welfare programs. As a state senator he favored reductions in taxes and unyielding resistance to school integration. In the U.S. Senate he strongly opposed President Johnson's Great Society programs. According to the *Congressional Quarterly*, Byrd voted against Johnson administration bills more often than any other Democratic senator in 1966, 1967, and 1968.

In October 1966 he offered an amendment to an antipoverty bill that would have banned aid to subversives and inciters of riots. Congress ultimately adopted a proviso that barred funds to anyone convicted of inciting riots. The following year he unsuccessfully proposed that the ceiling on the federal debt be lowered from $358 billion to $348 billion. In September 1968 he declared his opposition to President Johnson's nomination of Supreme Court associate justice ABE FORTAS to be chief justice, asserting that the Court had contributed to "the current permissiveness pervading the land."

Byrd ardently supported the U.S. war effort in Vietnam. In 1966 he offered an amendment to a foreign aid bill that denounced West Germany for indirectly aiding North Vietnam through economic assistance to the People's Republic of China. The Senate adopted the amendment, but it was dropped in a House-Senate conference. The following year he proposed an amendment to an Export-Import Bank bill to bar the bank from extending credits to any country trading with North Vietnam. The House revised the amendment so that it would apply only to Communist nations. During the same year the Senate adopted a Byrd resolution that advocated that the United Nations impose economic sanctions upon North Vietnam similar to those that the world body had applied to Rhodesia.

Primarily because of the growing number of moderate urban and black voters in the 1960s, the Byrd organization's control over Virginia politics declined. Furthermore, the younger Byrd did not exercise the strong leadership that had characterized the political work of his father, who died in October 1966. During the summer of 1966 the younger Byrd narrowly won the Democratic primary with 50.9 percent of the vote, while U.S. senator A. WILLIS ROBERTSON and U.S. representative HOWARD W. SMITH, both conservative stalwarts, lost. After a liberal won the 1969 Democratic gubernatorial primary, Byrd decided to abandon the party and run for reelection as an independent. Effectively exploiting opposition to school busing, he won election to a full term in 1970 with 54 percent of the vote, and was re-elected in 1976. He retired from the Senate in 1983.

—MLL

## Byrd, Robert C(arlyle)
(1917–   ) *member of the Senate*

Born on January 15, 1918, in North Willesboro, North Carolina, and orphaned at an early age, Robert C. Byrd grew up on a West Virginia dirt farm. He attended two state colleges and after eight years of night classes earned a law degree from American University in 1963, making him the first person to earn a law degree while serving in Congress. During World War II Byrd worked as a shipyard welder and briefly belonged to the Ku Klux Klan. In 1946 he won election to the West Virginia legislature and six years later became a member of the U.S. House of Representatives from Charleston. Twice reelected, Byrd defeated incumbent senator Chapman Rivercomb (R-W.Va.) in 1958 with 59.2 percent of the vote and quickly emerged as the most powerful Democrat in the state. Although he usually voted with the Senate Democratic leadership, in

1963 Byrd opposed the Kennedy administration's nuclear test ban treaty and civil rights bill.

Byrd joined the southern Democrats' filibuster against the 1964 civil rights bill and on June 9 gave the longest speech in opposition, lasting 14 hours and 13 minutes. Later, he would describe this stance as the worst mistake he had made in his career. He also opposed the 1965 Voting Rights Act. In September 1964 he joined a group of southern Democrats and Republicans who sought to overturn the Supreme Court's recent ruling requiring the reapportionment of state legislatures. Byrd endorsed Johnson in 1964 and won reelection in his own state with 67.7 percent of the vote.

Between 1961 and 1969 Byrd chaired the Appropriations Subcommittee on the District of Columbia. A self-proclaimed foe of welfare recipients "trying to get a free ride," Byrd frequently attacked the Aid-to-Dependent Children program and oversaw the creation of welfare inspectors for the district. However, he also approved appropriations for the hiring of additional teachers and social workers and construction of the city's first public pools in 30 years.

Although he did not oppose passage of the relatively mild Coal Mine Safety Act of 1966, Byrd declined, like most members of his state's congressional delegation, to take an active role in mine safety legislation. Coal mining was West Virginia's largest single employer. Indeed, the top leadership of the United Mine Workers in 1966 praised the coal operators' efforts to improve job safety. In his 1964 reelection campaign Byrd enjoyed overwhelming support from rank-and-file miners, although his finance chair was an executive vice president of the Consolidated Coal, the state's largest coal producer. Not until the Huntington, West Virginia, Mountaineer Mine No. 9 disaster of November 1968 did Congress consider major legislation to alleviate hazardous working conditions for miners.

According to *Congressional Quarterly*, Byrd voted with the administration on 57 percent of the tallies for which Johnson announced a position during the 1965 session of the 89th Congress. In February he supported the Appalachia Regional Development Act, an antipoverty aid measure that affected all of West Virginia. He voted for Medicare in July but against the Senate leadership's efforts to repeal Section 14(b), the open shop provision, of the Taft-Hartley Act.

During the 90th Congress Byrd voted with the majority of southern Democrats on 60 percent of the roll call votes. (In contrast he voted with the northern Democrats 31 percent of the time.) He opposed the consular treaty with the Soviet Union in March 1967 and voted against the confirmation of THURGOOD MARSHALL as an associate justice of the Supreme Court in August of the same year. However, he successfully sponsored an amendment in April 1967 that made persons eligible for reduced Social Security benefits at age 60.

Byrd denounced riots in northern cities and, in perhaps his most quoted statement of the Johnson years, declared in July 1967 that "brutal force" should be used to quell urban disturbances and that looters should be "shot on the spot." A Byrd amendment to the Crime Control bill in May 1968 denied federal employment for five years to anyone convicted of inciting a riot. After heavy rains in June 1968 turned "Resurrection City," the camp of thousands of poor brought to Washington to lobby for antipoverty legislation, into a quagmire, Byrd termed the temporary community a "festering sore which must be excised." He also generally supported the administration's foreign policy, including the war in Vietnam, although by the end of LBJ's term in office he was quietly expressing his concerns to the president that the United States had underestimated the strength of its foe.

In his first decade in the Senate Byrd established a reputation for tireless dedication to his Senate duties. He voted on 92 percent of all Senate roll calls during the 89th Congress and on 93 percent of the tallies during the 90th Congress. In January 1967 he defeated Senator JOSEPH CLARK (D-Pa.), a liberal, by a vote of 35 to 28 for the post of secretary of the Party Conference, the Democrats' third-ranking position in the Senate. Chosen again unanimously two years later, Byrd assumed many of the responsibilities assigned to the majority whip EDWARD M. KENNEDY (D-Mass.) and, in 1971, following his reelection in West Virginia, unseated Kennedy for the Senate Democrats' second-ranking leadership position. He became Senate Majority Leader in 1977 and remained at the top of the Democratic Party hierarchy until 1988. He has also held more leadership positions in the U.S. Senate than any other senator in history, and he has to date cast the most votes in the history of the Senate.

—JLB

## Byrnes, John W(illiam)

(1913–1985) *member of the House of Representatives*

Byrnes was born on June 12, 1913, in Green Bay, Wisconsin, and graduated from the University of Wisconsin Law School in 1938. He was appointed Wisconsin's special deputy commissioner for banking in that same year. Elected to the Wisconsin Senate in 1940, he was named majority floor leader in 1943. He won election to the House of Representatives as a Republican in 1944 and in 1947 gained a position on the Ways and Means Committee, where he built a reputation as a fiscal conservative. In 1959 Byrnes became chair of the House Republican Policy Committee after helping Representative CHARLES A. HALLECK (R-Ind.) depose Representative Joseph W. Martin (R-Mass.) as House Minority Leader.

During the Kennedy administration Byrnes was the leading House Republican spokesperson on economic policy and, according to the *New York Times*, "second only to Mr. Halleck as a power among House Republicans." Byrnes frequently led Republican efforts to reduce or eliminate Kennedy administration social welfare expenditures and was a vocal opponent of Kennedy's proposed $11 billion tax cut in 1963.

Byrnes remained in the vanguard of House Republican conservatism throughout the Johnson years. His voting record, as evaluated by the conservative Americans for Constitutional Action, ranged from 78 percent in favor of conservative positions in 1964 to 93 percent in 1967. He voted in favor of the Civil Rights Act of 1964 and the Voting Rights Act of 1965 but consistently opposed Great Society antipoverty programs.

Byrnes lost some influence when the Republican caucus that unseated Halleck as minority leader in January 1965 also adopted a rule barring a party leadership post to any ranking Republican on a legislative committee. Byrnes elected to drop his post as chair of the Republican Policy Committee and continue as senior Republican on the Ways and Means Committee.

In 1965 Byrnes spearheaded Republican opposition to the Johnson administration's proposed Medicare program. The Byrnes Plan, put forth as a substitute by the House Republican leadership, was similar to Medicare in certain respects but would have provided that health insurance for the aged be voluntary and be financed by individual contributions combined with subsidies from federal general revenues. The House rejected Byrnes's substitute, 236-191, in April and then passed the administration plan, 313-115. The final bill, however, incorporated an important element of the Byrnes Plan, whereby a person over 65 could purchase supplementary insurance covering doctors' bills as well as hospital costs. Byrnes then played a major role in the House-Senate conference committee that worked to resolve differences between the plans approved by both bodies. With his senior position on the Ways and Means Committee, Byrnes exerted greater influence on tax policy than any other House Republican. Although frequently opposed to tax measures proposed by the Johnson administration, the pragmatic Byrnes developed an effective working relationship with the committee's chair, Representative WILBUR D. MILLS (D-Ark.). Byrnes and Mills usually worked together to round up a consensus behind compromise measures.

Byrnes and the committee's Republicans often opposed various excise and luxury taxes favored by the administration. His most telling moment of resistance, however, came when President Johnson requested a 10 percent income tax surcharge in 1967. Byrnes joined Mills in holding up the tax increase for over a year until Johnson agreed to substantial budget cuts. Byrnes voted for the increase in June 1968 after it had been coupled with $6 billion in spending cuts.

Byrnes remained a key House Republican until his retirement in January 1973. He remained in Washington, D.C., practicing law until his death on January 12, 1985.

—TO

## Califano, Joseph (Anthony)

(1931–   ) *White House special assistant*

Born on May 15, 1931, in Brooklyn, New York, Califano graduated from Holy Cross in 1952 and took his law degree from Harvard Law School in 1955. That same year he joined the navy, where he served as a legal officer in the Defense Department. He went to work for the Defense Department in 1961. By 1965 he was special assistant to Secretary of Defense ROBERT S. MCNAMARA and had gained the attention of President Johnson and BILL MOYERS, who admired Califano's sharp analytical ability and his talent for devising clear proposals for solving governmental problems.

Califano was named a White House special assistant in July 1965. He quickly became one of LBJ's closest advisers and was given the authority to oversee the domestic legislative program. Califano, another aide recalled, "began to regularize the development of the legislative program in a way that it had not been before." He exerted particular influence in a few areas, especially issues involving urban life and the environment, but he played a behind-the-scenes role in almost every domestic initiative the administration produced.

On January 12, 1966, Johnson announced his intention to create a Department of Transportation. The president put Califano in charge of the legislation and told the cabinet the next day, "When Joe speaks, that's my voice you hear." The bill was an enormously complex piece of legislation involving some 30 autonomous and semi-autonomous agencies, including the Civil Aeronautics Board and the Interstate Commerce Commission. Its progress was slow because many members of Congress regarded many of the affected government activities, such as

highways, dams, and waterways, as valuable "pork-barrel" projects. After passage of the Department of Transportation bill in October 1966, Califano's power and prestige within the White House increased.

Unlike WALTER JENKINS or Moyers, Califano was never an "alter ego" to Johnson, nor did he attract significant public attention. Calling himself "the president's instrument," he was described by Secretary McNamara as "the man who, next to the president, has contributed more than any other individual in our country to the conception, formulation and implementation of the program for the Great Society."

After Moyers's departure from the administration on December 1966, Califano continued to expand the "task-force system" initiated by Moyers and RICHARD GOODWIN. He exercised White House control over the Department of Labor, various welfare programs within the Department of Health, Education and Welfare, the poverty program, the Agency for International Development program, and all aspects of foreign trade. Concerned with the legislative proposals of these agencies and with many of their day-to-day activities, Califano's role went well beyond guiding the administration's legislative program through Congress. In the Model Cities program, for example, Johnson told Califano he wanted a big, innovative housing program but that the response from housing officials had not been imaginative enough. Califano then helped to organize a task force to advocate the Model Cities plan, meanwhile overcoming resistance from housing officials who insisted the program was too large, and was too controversial to undertake in the first year of the new Department of

President Johnson and Joe Califano chart riot outbreaks in Washington, D.C., 1968 *(Photographed by Yoichi R. Okamoto; Lyndon Baines Johnson Library)*

Housing and Urban Development. A modified version of the Model Cities program, allocating $11 million for the project, was passed by Congress in 1966.

Throughout his White House career Califano concentrated on domestic affairs and made a conscious decision to avoid the issue of Vietnam. Although he had both the position and the expertise to become an authority on the war, Califano preferred to remain silent in order not to place himself in conflict with national security affairs adviser MCGEORGE BUNDY.

In 1969 Califano joined the law firm of Arnold and Porter in Washington. From 1970 through 1972 he served as general counsel to the Democratic National Committee. He served as secretary of health, education and welfare from 1977 until 1979, and, in 1992, he became president and chair of the National Center on Addiction and Substance Abuse at Columbia University.

—FHM

## Cannon, Howard W(alter)
### (1912–2002) *member of the Senate*

Cannon was born on January 26, 1912, in St. George, Utah, and earned a law degree from the University of Arizona in 1937. He served as an air force fighter pilot during World War II, receiving a number of decorations. Soon after the war he became a partner in a Las Vegas law firm. Cannon was the elected city attorney in Las Vegas from 1949 to 1957.

In 1958, following his victory in the Democratic senatorial primary, he opposed incumbent Republican George W. Malone. Malone's links were with mining interests of the northern and western areas of the state, interests that had long dominated Nevada's economy. Cannon's ties were to new, expanding, and politically more liberal industrial interests of the state's southern region. Aided by his war record, support from organized labor, and a national Democratic trend, Cannon attacked the conservatism of his opponent and defeated Malone with more than 56 percent of the vote. In the early 1960s Cannon established himself as a moderately liberal Democrat. According to *Congressional Quarterly*, he backed the Kennedy administration on 71 percent of the domestic roll call votes in the 87th Congress. Among other things, he supported trucking and airline deregulation and numerous water projects that promoted development in his home state.

After he won reelection in 1964 by a bare 48 votes, Cannon's support of the administration on domestic legislation dropped during the Johnson presidency, declining to 60 percent and 58 percent in the 89th and 90th Congresses. He did, however, vote for most of the administration's major civil rights bills and Great Society programs, including a crucial vote to break the southern-led filibuster of the 1964 Civil Rights Act. Cannon also defended President Johnson's Vietnam War policies. In the summer of 1967, when such prominent Senate Democrats as Senate Majority Leader MIKE MANSFIELD (D-Mont.) and Foreign Relations Committee chair J. WILLIAM FULBRIGHT (D-Ark.) condemned the bombing of North Vietnam near the Chinese border, Cannon asserted the military necessity of this strategy. His major legislative interests, stemming from his service in the air force, were aviation and the space program. He was, by preference, a member of both the Armed Services and the Aeronautics and Space Committees of the Senate. During the Johnson years he was also a general in the Air Force Reserve, a Senate adviser to the United Nations Committee on Peaceful Uses of Outer Space, and a member of the Board of Governors of the National Rocket Club.

Reelected in 1970, Cannon spoke out strongly for both the supersonic jet transport and the space shuttle program. He first received national attention during the fall of 1973 when, as chair of the Senate Rules and Administration Committee, he led that panel's consideration of President RICHARD M. NIXON's nomination of Representative GERALD R. FORD (R-Mich.) for vice president. The following fall, in the same capacity, he directed the investigation of President Ford's choice of NELSON ROCKEFELLER for the vice presidency. He lost a reelection bid in 1982 to Chic Hecht, a relative political unknown, and died in Las Vegas, Nevada, on March 5, 2002.

—MLL

## Carey, Hugh L(eo)
(1919–    ) *member of the House of Representatives*

Carey was born in Brooklyn, New York, on April 11, 1919. After winning a Bronze Star as an infantry officer during World War II, he entered St. John's Law School, receiving his degree in 1951. He then began work for his family's oil company, the Peerless Oil and Chemical Corporation. In 1960 Carey, a political unknown, ran for Congress in Brooklyn's 12th Congressional District, which had been gerrymandered in favor of the borough's only Republican representative. Attaching himself to the campaign of John F. Kennedy and endorsing aid to education and medical care for the aged, Carey defeated the incumbent Republican, Representative Francis E. Dorn, by a narrow margin. He won reelection in 1962 by only 383 votes, although subsequent victories came more easily.

Carey was a faithful supporter of the civil rights and social welfare programs of the Kennedy-Johnson administrations. Assigned to the Education and Labor Committee in 1962, he was a principal author and sponsor of the Elementary and Secondary Education Act of 1965, which authorized federal aid to education. Carey was a champion of aid to private as well as public schools; the 1965 law included some forms of assistance to parochial school students, but not to the schools themselves. Carey was also a strong advocate of the administration's antipoverty program and special aid for the handicapped.

Along with the other members of the Brooklyn congressional delegation, Carey labored to persuade the Johnson administration to sell the Brooklyn Navy Yard to New York City for development as an industrial park. The sale was finally consummated on January 24, 1969.

Carey ran for president of the New York City Council in the 1969 Democratic primary on a ticket headed by former mayor ROBERT F. WAGNER but lost in a very close race. He remained in Congress, moving to the Ways and Means Committee in 1970, until his election as governor of New York in 1974. He was reelected in 1978, and, in 1982, he resumed the practice of law in New York.

—TO

## Carlson, Frank
(1893–1987) *member of the Senate*

The son of Swedish immigrants, Frank Carlson was born in Concordia, Kansas, on January 23, 1893.

He grew a special hybrid "streamlined" wheat that he had developed on his north-central Kansas farm. He won the first of two terms in the Kansas House of Representatives in 1928. In 1934 he won election to the U.S. House. Reelected five times, Carlson supported the Roosevelt administration's farm-price support system but criticized most other aspects of the New Deal. He also supported the creation of a simplified federal tax code, various flood control measures, and greater support for agricultural interests. By the late 1940s he had clearly identified himself with the older Kansas Progressivism of William Allen White and Senator Arthur Capper. In 1946 Kansas voters elected Carlson governor; he won reelection two years later.

Carlson became a U.S. senator in 1950 and was returned to the upper house in 1956 and 1962. Identified at the time of his first Senate election with the party's liberal "Eastern Establishment" wing, Carlson was an early participant in the 1952 presidential nomination campaign of General DWIGHT D. EISENHOWER. Once president, Eisenhower received Carlson's loyal support. The Kansan served on the 1954 panel that urged the censure of controversial senator Joseph R. McCarthy (R-Wisc.) in 1954. During the Kennedy years Carlson opposed much of the New Frontier social welfare legislation but endorsed the president's foreign aid policy. In September 1963 he voted for the limited nuclear test ban treaty.

Carlson's record in the Johnson years was mixed. He opposed Medicare and favored reductions in annual War on Poverty appropriations, but he endorsed the president's "demonstration cities" program in August 1966. Under pressure from House Minority Leader EVERETT M. DIRKSEN (R-Ill.), Carlson twice voted to invoke cloture and cut off debate (an unusual step for a small-state senator) to aid enactment of the 1964 and 1968 civil rights bills.

A member of the Senate Foreign Relations Committee, Carlson was skeptical of Johnson's Vietnam policy. At the August 1964 hearings following the Gulf of Tonkin incident, he commented that the administration's growing participation in the Vietnam War "involves us in a situation from which it is most difficult to extricate ourselves." While Carlson voted for the Gulf of Tonkin Resolution and never joined the ranks of the Senate's Vietnam War critics, he occasionally called for peace negotiations. In a March 1968 debate following the

North Vietnamese Tet offensive, Carlson asked if the United States had not "reach[ed] a saturation point" at which "we have lost the support of the civilian population."

Carlson did not seek another term in 1968. He died in Concordia, Kansas, on May 30, 1987.

—JLB

## Carmichael, Stokely
(1941–1998)  *chair, Student Nonviolent Coordinating Committee; prime minister, Black Panther Party*

Carmichael, who was born on June 29, 1941, grew up in Trinidad and New York City and then enrolled at Howard University in Washington, D.C., in 1960, after rejecting scholarship offers from a number of other colleges. There he joined an affiliate of the Student Nonviolent Coordinating Committee (SNCC) known as the Nonviolent Action Group (NAG), which organized sit-ins and demonstrations to desegregate public facilities in the Washington area. Carmichael also participated in the 1961 Freedom Rides, and, following his graduation from Howard in 1964, he became a full-time worker for SNCC. During the 1964 Mississippi Freedom Summer, he served as project director in the state's Second Congressional District. Carmichael also became director in 1965 of a SNCC voter registration project in Lowndes County, Alabama, where he organized the Lowndes County Freedom Organization, an independent political party with a black panther as its emblem. His efforts in Alabama were somewhat successful, as Lowndes County saw the number of African-American registered voters grow from 70 to over 2,500. But there was another consequence, as the violence and brutality of southern racists radicalized Carmichael. His work in Alabama made him a symbol of the greater militance and emphasis on blackness that many SNCC members were advocating by 1965, and he was elected SNCC chair in May 1966, replacing John Lewis.

Little known outside of SNCC at the time of his election, Carmichael soon became a much-publicized and highly controversial figure. He first attracted nationwide attention on a June 1966 protest march in Mississippi. The march was begun by JAMES MEREDITH but continued by other civil rights leaders after Meredith was shot from ambush. When the march reached Greenwood, Mississippi,

Stokely Carmichael taking part in a demonstration outside the Capitol, 1967 *(Library of Congress, Prints and Photographs Division)*

Carmichael called for "Black Power." The phrase, voiced repeatedly on the rest of the march, quickly captured national attention and generated great debate over its meaning. A prominent advocate of Black Power, Carmichael gave his most complete statement of its meaning in *Black Power: The Politics of Liberation in America*, written with Charles V. Hamilton and published in November 1967. Black Power, the authors wrote, meant first that blacks would redefine themselves, developing a positive self-image based on a "recognition of the virtues in themselves as black people." Black Power also meant a rejection of the traditional civil rights goal of integration on the grounds that the goal was based on the erroneous notion that there was nothing of value in the black community and because it required acceptance of the white middle-class values and institutions that were actually the mainstays of racism. Within the framework of Black Power, blacks would "reject the racist institutions and values" of American society, "define their own goals," and establish independent organizations to serve as "power bases . . . from which black people can press to change local or nationwide patterns of oppression." This organized Black Power would result in control of community institutions by blacks where they were in the majority and "full participation" by African Americans in "the decision-making processes" affecting their lives. The slogan, and his interpretation of it, also symbolized growing tensions between Carmichael and Dr. MARTIN LUTHER KING, JR.

Aside from his advocacy of Black Power, Carmichael generated controversy for frequently denouncing the Democratic Party as the "most treacherous enemy the Negro people have," for opposing the Vietnam War, and for encouraging African Americans to resist the draft. Carmichael was also considered by some an instigator of inner-city riots. He was in Atlanta in September 1966, when riots broke out there and was arrested on charges of inciting to riot. He spoke at a symposium in Nashville in April 1967, and riots erupted less than an hour after he left the city. He was again in Atlanta during disorders in June 1967 and in Washington during April 1968 riots there. Whether Carmichael's presence encouraged the riots remained debatable, but Carmichael and his successor as SNCC chair, H. RAP BROWN, were the two figures most often cited as targets of antiriot bills by member of Congress who favored such legislation in the late 1960s.

Carmichael did not seek reelection as SNCC chair in May 1967, and, from July to December, he traveled extensively in Europe and Africa and made trips to North Vietnam and to Cuba. During his travels Carmichael adopted a revolutionary position that went beyond the program outlined in his book on Black Power. At a conference of the Organization of Latin American Solidarity held in August 1967 in Havana, for example, Carmichael said that American blacks were fighting to change the "imperialist, capitalist and racialist structure" of the United States "We have no other alternative," he proclaimed, "but to take up arms and struggle for our total liberation and total revolution in the United States." Carmichael also advocated guerrilla warfare and armed struggle at various times after his return to the United States, further inflaming the controversy that surrounded him.

In January 1968 Carmichael helped establish the Black United Front to organize Washington's blacks, and he began working as a community organizer in that city. When SNCC established an alliance in February 1968 with the Black Panther Party founded by HUEY P. NEWTON and BOBBY SEALE, Carmichael was named prime minister of the party. The alliance ended in July, but Carmichael stayed on as the Black Panther prime minister and was expelled from SNCC shortly afterward. He resigned from the Black Panther Party in July 1969, denouncing it for its "dogmatic" party line and its willingness to ally itself with white rad-

icals. Late in 1968 Carmichael left the United States and began living in self-imposed exile in Guinea. He continued to travel throughout the world, however, preaching black nationalism and African unity. In 1978 he changed his name to Kwame Turé, to honor two African leaders. He died in November 1998 in New York of prostate cancer.

—CAB

## Carpenter, Elizabeth S(utherland)
(1920–   ) *staff director and press secretary to Mrs. Lyndon B. Johnson*

Elizabeth Carpenter described herself as "a political animal by nature, a southerner by birth and a P. T. Barnum by instinct." The daughter of a building contractor, she was born Elizabeth Sutherland on September 1, 1920, in Salado, Texas. After her graduation from the University of Texas School of Journalism in 1942, she moved to Washington, D.C., where she became a close friend of Senator Lyndon B. Johnson and his wife LADY BIRD. In 1944 she married newspaper journalist Les Carpenter. Three years later she and her husband started the Carpenter News Bureau in Washington.

After Lyndon Johnson secured the Democratic vice presidential nomination in 1960, Elizabeth Carpenter served as an executive assistant to Johnson and as press aide to Lady Bird Johnson. According to historian ERIC GOLDMAN, she was "the most independent and outspoken member of the whole Johnson group" during his vice presidency.

Aboard Air Force One in the immediate aftermath of John Kennedy's assassination in Dallas on November 22, 1963, Carpenter wrote Johnson's first presidential message, which he delivered at Andrews Air Force Base in Washington the same day: "This is a sad time for all people. We have suffered a loss that cannot be weighed. I will do my best. That is all I can do. I ask for your help—and God's."

In December 1963 Carpenter was appointed Mrs. Johnson's press secretary. The first professional journalist ever to become press secretary to a first lady, she immediately took over all news functions concerning Mrs. Johnson from presidential press secretary PIERRE SALINGER. In 1964 she was instrumental in planning Mrs. Johnson's whistle-stop southern campaign tour three months after the signing of the Civil Rights Act in July. Between October 6 and October 9 the tour covered 1,682 miles, eight states, and 47 stops, and it garnered considerable publicity. In her book *Ruffles and Flourishes*, Carpenter later wrote: "Our star attraction [on the tour] was a southern-bred First Lady. We were supposed to blow kisses and spread love through eight states and make them . . . forget about Barry Goldwater."

Carpenter did an effective job, through frequent news briefing, or projecting Mrs. Johnson in the way she wished to appear—as a first lady with a specific set of interests, including beautification and conservation, that were ancillary but similar to those of the president's. She also impressed LBJ and his advisers, who valued her input on political matters.

Following the departure from the White House in 1969, Carpenter published *Ruffles and Flourishes*, a memoir of her years in the Johnson White House that was subtitled "the warm and tender story of a simple girl who found adventure in the White House."

—FHM

## Case, Clifford P(hilip)

(1904–1982) *member of the Senate*

Case was born on April 16, 1904, in Franklin Park, New Jersey, and grew up in Poughkeepsie, New York, where his father was pastor of a Dutch Reformed Church. He studied at Rutgers University and Columbia University Law School and joined a Wall Street law firm in 1928. A Republican, he entered New Jersey politics in 1937 and seven years later was elected Union County's U.S. representative. Case left the House in August 1953 to become president of the Fund for the Republic, but he resigned the following March to run for the U.S. Senate. Stressing his opposition to the investigative methods of Senator Joseph R. McCarthy (R-Wisc.) during the campaign, he narrowly defeated his Democratic opponent in the November 1954 election. In the Senate Case was one of the most progressive members of the chamber. His electoral candidacies frequently won the endorsement of the Americans for Democratic Action (ADA) and organized labor.

Case was a consistent critic of the growth of what he considered ultra conservative influence in the Republican Party in the early 1960s. In April 1963 he announced his support of New York governor NELSON ROCKEFELLER's presidential aspirations in the hope of preventing the nomination of Senator BARRY GOLDWATER (R-Ariz.) as the 1964 Republican candidate. At the Republican National Convention in July 1964, Case joined the forces behind Pennsylvania governor WILLIAM SCRANTON and fought to liberalize the party's platform. With the nomination of Goldwater and the adoption of a conservative platform, Case declared that he could not give his support to the national ticket.

While Republican liberals in other parts of the country often suffered political reprisals for their lack of loyalty to the party, Case's influence in New Jersey was not affected. His liberalism and pro-labor record were assets in the nation's most thoroughly urbanized state. The financial backing of some of the wealthiest members of the Eastern Republican Establishment helped make Case independent of New Jersey's weak Republican Party organization. After the failure of a conservative challenge to Case in the 1960 primary, his hold on the Senate seat was never again seriously contested.

The ADA gave Case a rating of 100 percent in both 1967 and 1968, and he scored nearly as high in other years. In 1965 and 1966 he was one of only three Republicans to oppose senator EVERETT DIRKSEN's (R-Ill.) efforts to overturn the Supreme Court's reapportionment ruling of "one man, one vote" through the adoption of a constitutional amendment.

Beginning in 1957 Case annually offered a bill to require members of every branch of government to publicly disclose their financial holdings and transactions and all their oral and written communications to regulatory agencies. The BOBBY BAKER scandal gave Case the opportunity to intensify his drive for higher standards of congressional ethics. In March 1964 he attacked the Senate Rules Committee for its "perpetuation of the double standard which Congress has long practiced, one standard for all others, another for its members." Case wanted the committee to question all senators on their business and financial dealings with Baker.

Long a proponent of a relaxation of cold war tensions, Case became deeply involved with foreign affairs when he joined the Senate Foreign Relations Committee in 1965. In September 1966 he was confirmed as a U.S. representative to the 21st session of the United Nations General Assembly. In June 1967 he visited South Vietnam. In his first two years on the Foreign Relations Committee, Case often voted in support of foreign military aid. By 1967, however, he had become highly critical of U.S. military intervention in Vietnam. In a Senate speech delivered during the fall of 1967, he emphasized President Johnson's lack of honesty in informing the Congress and the American people about the situation in Vietnam. Case was also disturbed that Johnson's Indochina policies affected the constitutional relationship between the legislative and executive branches.

Although Case supported RICHARD M. NIXON in the 1968 presidential campaign, he became a critic of Nixon's Vietnam policy and opposed the president's first two Supreme Court nominees. Case easily won reelection in 1972. He was defeated in his bid for reelection in 1978 and returned to his law practice while also teaching at Rutgers University. He died in New Jersey on March 5, 1982.

—JCH

## Cater, Douglass

(1923–1995) *White House special assistant*

Cater, who was born on August 24, 1923, in Montgomery, Alabama, served in the Office of Strategic Services during World War II. He graduated from Harvard in 1947, took his M.A. from that university the next year, and became Washington editor of the *Reporter* magazine in 1950. Cater met Senator LYNDON B. JOHNSON (D-Tex.) in 1952 and later wrote stories sympathetic to Johnson, describing the senator as a "politician's politician" and a "pragmatic centrist." At the beginning of the Kennedy administration, Secretary of State DEAN RUSK planned to make Cater assistant secretary of state for public affairs—the press relations post—but White House press secretary PIERRE SALINGER moved Roger W. Tubby into the job.

While national affairs editor of the *Reporter*, Cater wrote the 1964 book *Power in Washington*, which offered a closely reasoned and critical analysis of leadership problems within the Kennedy administration. Referring to Kennedy's inability to gain congressional passage of his legislative program, Cater characterized the administration as one of "courageous expectations and cautious operations."

On May 8, 1964, President Johnson named Cater a White House special assistant. At first his exact duties were not clearly defined; Johnson only advised him to "think ahead," and it was widely believed that Cater would become strictly a speechwriter and "idea" man. He began his White House career by ghostwriting Johnson's 1964 book *My Hope for America*.

During the 1964 presidential campaign Cater wrote speeches that focused on U.S. educational problems. As a result, Johnson began to think of Cater as his expert on education. Named chief White House liaison with the 1964 Task Force on Health and Education, Cater worked closely with Task Force chair JOHN GARDNER and U.S. commissioner of education FRANCIS KEPPEL to turn Task Force recommendations into the $1.3 billion 1965 education bill. Cater played a major role in shaping some 40 health and education bills that were passed by Congress in 1965 and 1966, including such measures as Medicare, elementary and secondary education, and the heart, cancer, and stroke bill. He also worked very closely on developing the Public Broadcasting System and various environmental and beautification reforms.

Cater sought ideas on health and education from both the government bureaucracy and the academic community. In addition he was the central point of access to the White House for the educational community. He was also a point of access to the president for congressional and executive officials in the educational policy process. Cater saw his role in government as that of increasing Johnson's interest in educational policy, "It is a nebulous role—not at all systematic. . . . I know the president's ideas and try to see to it that they are always considered. . . . I keep things moving."

In the winter of 1965–66 Cater was a major force in drafting the international educational and health bill, which President Johnson sent to Congress on February 2, 1966. Cater hoped the legislation would demonstrate Johnson's concern for worldwide health and education problems. As a collection of 40 measures designed to aid international health and education, the bill was to have cost $524 million in its first year but remained unfunded because of budget cuts due to the Vietnam War.

Described as "a unique combination of journalist, intellectual, academic, bureaucrat, political scientist and presidential confidant," Cater was one of the few specialists in an administration where aides and special assistants dealt with many governmental areas. On October 3, 1968, Cater resigned as White House special assistant to join Vice President HUBERT H. HUMPHREY's campaign staff. After the campaign, he turned to teaching, eventually becoming president of Washington College in Maryland. He died on September 15, 1995.

—FHM

## Celebrezze, Anthony J(oseph)
(1910–1998) *secretary of health, education, and welfare; judge, Court of Appeals*

Anthony J. Celebrezze was born in Italy on September 4, 1910, and grew up in the slums of Cleveland. He worked his way through Ohio Northern Law School laying track for the New York Central Railroad. After three years in the Ohio Senate, Celebrezze ran successfully for mayor of Cleveland in 1953. He proved highly popular with Cleveland voters, winning reelection five times by substantial majorities. As mayor he sponsored a $140 million urban renewal project and earned a reputation as an efficient city administrator. Kennedy appointed Celebrezze secretary of health, education and welfare (HEW) in July 1962. Celebrezze sought both to reorganize his massive department while lobbying for the administration's civil rights, aid-to-education, and Medicare bills.

Early in the Johnson presidency Celebrezze became involved in a dispute with other cabinet heads over the president's War on Poverty program. Celebrezze and Labor Secretary W. WILLARD WIRTZ objected to the creation of a separate anti-poverty agency headed by Peace Corps director R. SARGENT SHRIVER. In arguments before the president in March 1964, both secretaries insisted that their departments could and should absorb the functions of the Office of Economic Opportunity (OEO). But Johnson insisted on an independent agency for his poverty program. Celebrezze acquiesced in Johnson's decision and defended the OEO before congressional critics. To Republican House members critical of Shriver's elevation to "poverty czar," Celebrezze asserted in March 1964 that he found "no conflict whatsoever" between Shriver's agency and his own. "I have absolutely no fear," he added, that "the powers of any department are going to be usurped" by the OEO.

During Celebrezze's tenure as HEW secretary, Congress passed the most important body of social legislation since the New Deal. In June 1964

President Johnson receiving a hug from Anthony Celebrezze, 1965 *(Photographed by Yoichi R. Okamoto; Lyndon Baines Johnson Library)*

Congress finally approved the Kennedy-Johnson civil rights proposals that gave the HEW secretary broad powers to restrict funds from any federal program to states or institutions found violating desegregation guidelines. Congress also enacted the administration"s Medicare program in July 1965. Although Celebrezze testified for the measure, Assistant HEW secretary WILBUR J. COHEN wrote the final bill and conducted the administration's lobbying effort with House Ways and Means Committee chair WILBUR MILLS (D-Ark.).

The HEW chief proved more active in the administration's campaign for a comprehensive aid-to-education bill in the spring of 1965. Although Republican losses in the 1964 election had strengthened liberal ranks, the White House still needed to overcome traditional opposition to federal aid to private and parochial schools. In congressional hearings held in January 1965, Celebrezze gave a variety of arguments in defense of assistance to parochial education. To the most pronounced defenders of the separation of church and state, he pointed out that governments subsidized subways that people used to ride to church and funded libraries that private school children utilized to check out books for class.

Before the bill went to Congress, Celebrezze and other administration figures won the approval of most Catholic and public school representatives for the measure. Drafted by a presidential task force chaired by JOHN W. GARDNER, then president of the Carnegie Corporation, the bill provided sufficient aid to private institutions to prevent their leaders' outright opposition, while not granting a sum large enough to provoke protests from defending of public schools. The final bill, revised by Senator WAYNE MORSE (D-Ore.) and Cohen, overcame the greatest obstacles to passage by providing the most assistance to school systems in poverty-stricken areas. Congress approved the Elementary and Secondary Education Act in April 1965.

Johnson offered Celebrezze an appointment to the U.S. Sixth Circuit Court of Appeals in July 1965. Celebrezze, who had originally wanted a judgeship when Kennedy asked him to head HEW, immediately accepted the president's offer. Johnson named Gardner to succeed Celebrezze as head of HEW. He retired in 1980 and died on October 29, 1998.

—JLB

## Celler, Emanuel
(1888–1981) *member of the House of Representatives*

Celler, who was born in Brooklyn, New York, on May 6, 1888, graduated from Columbia College and Law School and then practiced law in New York from 1912 to 1922. In the latter year he won election to Congress from Brooklyn's 10th Congressional District, beginning a 50-year career in the House. A liberal Democrat, Celler consistently supported the domestic legislation of Democratic presidents from Roosevelt to Johnson. As chair of the House Judiciary Committee, Celler developed a special expertise in the fields of antitrust and civil rights. In 1949 he established a new judiciary subcommittee to focus on antitrust violations and monopolies. As the subcommittee's head Celler conducted widely publicized investigations during the 1950s into such areas as the steel industry, monopoly practices in baseball, and Justice Department consent decrees. He coauthored the Celler-Kefauver Anti-Merger Act of 1950 and was a main architect of both the 1957 and 1960 Civil Rights Acts. He was the subject of criticism and verbal abuse by Senator Joseph McCarthy (R-Wisc.) in the 1950s.

Celler's initiative in antitrust began to wane in the 1960s; from 1963 to 1970 his Antitrust Subcommittee averaged only five hearings or reports per Congress, compared with an average of 14 from 1955 to 1962. But Celler's role in civil rights expanded. He sponsored the Twenty-fourth Amendment, ratified in 1964, which abolished the poll tax in federal elections, and he was a principal author of the 1964 Civil Rights Act.

In 1964 Celler helped thwart efforts to adopt a constitutional amendment allowing prayer in public schools. An opponent of all such proposals, Celler held hearings on various prayer bills in the spring and brought in as witnesses constitutional lawyers who testified against the legislation.

Celler achieved a series of legislative victories in 1965. With Senator EDWARD KENNEDY (D-Mass.), he won passage of the Immigration and Naturalization Act, which ended the national origins quota system that dated to 1924. He helped secure approval for a law to prohibit gerrymandering of congressional districts, a measure he had favored for 15 years. He sponsored a constitutional amendment providing for the execution of the president's duties in the event of presidential disability and for

New York representative Emanuel Celler meeting with President Johnson, 1964 *(Photographed by Yoichi R. Okamoto; Lyndon Baines Johnson Library)*

filling a vice presidential vacancy. Adopted by Congress in July 1965, this act was ratified as the Twenty-fifth Amendment in 1967. Celler also managed the Voting Rights Act of 1965; after introducing the Johnson bill in March, he led the Judiciary Committee hearings on the proposal and secured House passage on August 3.

In 1967 Celler chaired the Special Committee on the Seating of ADAM CLAYTON POWELL, JR. When the House refused the committee recommendation that Powell be seated with censure, and voted instead to exclude him from the 90th Congress, Celler was one of the most vocal critics. That same year he introduced an administration-supported crime control bill that authorized federal funds to aid local law enforcement agencies. On the House floor the bill was amended to reduce federal control over the program. Celler unsuccessfully opposed the change, and he also failed to block House action on an antiriot bill

making it a crime to cross state lines with intent to incite a riot.

The Senate took no action on either bill in 1967, but, in May 1968, it adopted the Omnibus Crime Control Act. The measure included a federal grant program similar to that passed by the House, a provision authorizing court-supervised wiretapping and a relatively weak gun control section. Celler disliked the wiretap provision and wanted a stronger gun control measure, but the House passed the entire act on June 6. Celler labeled the law "a cruel hoax," destructive of constitutional liberties. On June 10 he introduced a much stronger administration bill for gun control that would ban mail-order sales of rifles and ammunition and require the licensing and registration of guns. His Judiciary Committee reported the bill favorably, but to secure passage of the mail-order ban, Celler was forced by House Rules Committee chair WILLIAM COLMER (D-Miss.) to drop the licensing and registration section. Congress passed the bill, without any registration requirement, in October 1968.

Celler also played a key role in the passage of the administration's Civil Rights Act of 1968, which barred racial discrimination in the sale and rental of approximately 80 percent of all housing and supplied protection for civil rights workers. After committee hearings Celler pushed the bill through the House in August 1967. Senate approval followed in March 1968, but the Senate tacked onto the act an antiriot provision of the sort Celler opposed. Celler nevertheless pressed for quick House action accepting the Senate version of the bill to insure that the open housing section, the core of the measure, would become law. The House finally adopted the Senate's bill on April 10, and it was signed into law the next day.

Celler's long legislative career was marred in its last years by charges of potential conflicts of interest, especially in the corporate and antitrust field, resulting from his long-standing connection with a New York City law firm. Celler was also scored for the way he ran the Judiciary Committee. A 1975 report by the RALPH NADER Congress Project, *The Judiciary Committees*, called Celler "a willful potentate" who "ran his committee as his personal fiefdom." Celler frequently bottled up controversial bills, such as abortion reform and proposals for amnesty for Vietnam War resisters, by refusing to refer them to a subcommittee or to hold hearings. He was also criticized for failing to seek larger appropriations and a larger staff to handle the committee's workload. In the 92nd Congress more than 5,000 bills and resolutions were referred to his Judiciary Committee to be handled by a 36-member staff, while the Senate Judiciary Committee, with far fewer bills to consider, had a staff of 204.

During the Nixon administration Celler fought an effort to impeach Supreme Court justice WILLIAM O. DOUGLAS and in June 1970 secured an extension of the 1965 Voting Rights Act. In his final years in the House, Celler led hearings on six major conglomerates and opposed both the Equal Rights Amendment and an amendment to prohibit busing for school desegregation. In June 1972 Celler was defeated in the Democratic primary in his district by Elizabeth Holtzman, a 31-year-old attorney, who charged that Celler had lost touch with his constituency. He returned to Brooklyn, where he continued to practice law. He died in Brooklyn on January 15, 1981.

—CAB

## Chafee, John H(ubbard)
### (1922–1999) *governor*

John H. Chafee was born in Providence, Rhode Island, on October 22, 1922. During World War II he left his studies at Yale for active duty with the marines in the South Pacific. Returning to Yale at the war's end, he earned a B.A. in 1947 and a law degree at Harvard in 1950. He reentered the marine corps to fight in the Korean conflict. Chafee won the first of three terms to the state General Assembly in 1956; he served as minority leader in the General Assembly from 1959 to 1962.

Rhode Islanders first elected Chafee governor in 1962. As a Yankee Republican in a state that was overwhelmingly Democratic and as an Episcopalian in a state with a high proportion of Roman Catholics (61 percent), Chafee entered the gubernatorial contest with obvious disadvantages. To overcome his narrow ethnic and political base, he ran a highly personalized campaign. One supporter claimed that Chafee shook hands with about one out of every eight Rhode Islanders, or about 130,000 people. He attacked incumbent Democratic governor John A. Notte, Jr., for advocating a personal income tax, and he promised to revive the stagnant state economy. In November Chafee defeated Notte by just under 400 votes out of about 325,000 cast. In his first term Chafee persuaded the Democratic legislature to approve his medical care for the elderly plan and to expand the state parks system. At his initiative the legislature raised the state sales tax by a half a percentage point. He also fought for antidiscrimination laws in housing and employment, and he developed the state park system.

In his second gubernatorial campaign Chafee ignored the Republican presidential nominee, Senator BARRY GOLDWATER (R-Ariz.), who ultimately polled only 19 percent of the vote in Rhode Island. Instead, his managers urged voters to "Vote Chafee First." As a result, Chafee captured 61 percent of the vote, while Johnson and Senator JOHN O. PASTORE (D-R.I.) demolished their opponents. Two years later Chafee won again, carrying every town and helping to elect a GOP lieutenant governor and attorney general for the first time since 1938.

Chafee participated in 1968 Republican presidential politics. An attractive vote-getter in a Democratic area, Chafee himself sought consideration for the Republican vice presidential nomination; but Rhode Island's small population and his identification with liberal Republicanism hurt his prospects.

Beginning in November 1966 he and other liberal and moderate Republican governors began working for the presidential nomination of Michigan governor GEORGE W. ROMNEY. When Romney withdrew from the race in February 1968, Chafee came out for New York governor NELSON ROCKEFELLER. At the Republican National Convention, the liberals saw the nomination go to former vice president RICHARD M. NIXON. Chafee was dissatisfied with Nixon's choice for vice president, Governor SPIRO AGNEW, and joined in a last-minute attempt to nominate Romney for the post. However, the effort failed.

In November 1968 Chafee lost his bid for reelection, in large measure because of his call for a state income tax. President Nixon appointed him secretary of the navy in 1969, where one of his first actions was the controversial decision to overturn a Navy Board of Inquiry, which had recommended the courts martial of some of the officers of the USS *Pueblo*. He held that office until 1972, when he lost a hard-fought senatorial campaign against incumbent senator CLAIBORNE PELL (D-R.I.). He was elected to the Senate in 1976 and served until his death of heart failure in 1999, in Bethesda, Maryland.

—JLB

## Chancellor, John W(illiam)

(1927–1996)  *director, Voice of America*

John Chancellor, who was born in Chicago on June 14, 1927, left high school in 1942 at the age of 15 and took a series of jobs in and around Chicago before entering the U.S. Army in 1945. After his discharge, Chancellor briefly attended the University of Illinois; in 1948 he joined the *Chicago Sun-Times*, where he rose from copy boy to feature writer. In 1950 he joined the staff of WNBQ, the National Broadcasting Company station in Chicago, as a broadcast reporter and covered the 1956 political conventions as a television reporter. He helped to earn his national reputation with his coverage of the 1957 conflict over the desegregation of Central High School, in Little Rock, Arkansas. He was also in Berlin in 1961, when the Berlin Wall was built, and he then returned to the city in 1989 to broadcast when it was torn down.

NBC News assigned Chancellor to its Vienna bureau in 1958 in the first of many overseas assignments that eventually took him to London, Rome, Paris, Brussels, and Moscow before he returned to the United States in July 1961 to become the host of NBC's popular *Today* program. He left, however, after 14 months, to return to covering politics. Chancellor covered the 1964 Republican National Convention in San Francisco as a floor correspondent and was arrested by police while broadcasting "live" during an altercation stemming from an attempt by Goldwater forces to restrict the movements of television correspondents.

On July 28, 1965, President Johnson appointed Chancellor to replace Henry Loomis as director of the Voice of America (VOA). As the radio news division of the United States Information Agency (USIA), the VOA broadcast in 38 languages and employed 2,500 people both in the United States and abroad. Chancellor took over VOA in September 1965 amid charges by veteran staff members that the organization's news credibility was being sacrificed to favor Johnson administration policy, especially in Vietnam. The first working journalist ever named to the post, Chancellor took pains to insure that the VOA accurately reported the news, including civil rights issues and the conflicts of opinion within the United States over Johnson's Vietnam policy. During his tenure Chancellor introduced a number of new programming techniques to give VOA broadcasts a crisper, less propagandistic style. "Nothing that we said at the USIA was ever untrue," he later explained, "but it was the arrangement of the truthful information that made the point."

Chancellor resigned his post as VOA director in May 1967 to return to active broadcasting. He covered the 1968 political conventions for NBC News. In August 1971 Chancellor was named anchor of the *NBC Nightly News*. He died on July 12, 1996.

—FHM

## Chavez, Cesar

(César Chávez)

(1927–1993)  *president, United Farm Workers Organizing Committee*

Born on March 31, 1927, in Yema, Arizona, Chavez left school in the seventh grade to become a full-time field worker in California. After taking part in several unsuccessful strikes of farm workers, he began to consider ways of organizing Mexican American in California. In 1952 he joined the new San José branch of the Community Service Organization

Cesar Chavez, founder of the National Farm Workers Association and president of the United Farm Workers Organizing Committee, 1966 *(Library of Congress, Prints and Photographs Division)*

(CSO), which fostered grassroots efforts to meet the problems of poor people. As a CSO worker, and later director, Chavez organized voter registration drives among Mexican Americans and set up services to provide information on such matters as immigration laws and welfare regulations. He left the CSO in 1962, when the organization turned down his proposal to create a union of farm workers.

With their meager savings, Chavez and his wife, Helen, immediately established the National Farm Workers Association (NFWA). There followed several years of painstaking organizational work in the fields and migrant worker camps of southern and central California. By 1965 the NFWA had a membership of 1,700 families, but Chavez still considered it too weak for a confrontation with employers. His hand was forced on September 8, 1965, when 800 Filipino grape pickers in Delano struck for higher wages. The striking

workers belonged to a separate organization, the Agricultural Workers Organizing Committee (AWOC), affiliated with the AFL-CIO. Chavez called a sympathy strike, which developed into an extended fight to win recognition from grape growers and other employers in California agriculture.

Under Chavez, the farm workers' strike had elements of both a labor struggle and a civil rights movement with strong religious overtones. To dramatize union demands for recognition, Chavez led 60 union members in a 300-mile march from Delano to Sacramento in 1966; the march ended with a demonstration of over 10,000 people in the state capital. Chavez himself fasted for 25 days in 1968, hoping to emphasize the nonviolent character of the movement. These and more traditional tactics—including picket lines and organizing work—increased the membership of the farm workers' union to 17,000 in the late 1960s. Chavez decided to affiliate with the AFL-CIO in July 1966, merging the NFWA with the AWOC to form the United Farm Workers Organizing Committee (UFWOC).

The drama of the strike and Chavez's personal magnetism brought together a broad coalition of national support, ranging from civil rights and church groups to traditional labor leaders. Senator ROBERT F. KENNEDY and WALTER REUTHER, leader of the United Auto Workers Union, appeared at farm workers' rallies; the UAW also contributed to the UFWOC strike fund. The farm workers' struggle soon became a defining issue in both California and national politics. Democratic governor EDMUND G. BROWN, SR.'s, sympathy for the growers cost him much liberal support in his state, while the farm workers' enthusiastic endorsement of Senator Kennedy helped increase his national standing. Chavez's actions also earned him the attention of the Federal Bureau of Investigation, which developed a 2,000-page file on his activities.

Gradually, publicity and labor unrest began to tell on the California growers. The first employers to acknowledge union demands were the growers of wine grapes, who marketed their own brands and were highly vulnerable to a boycott. Between April and September 1966 the major wine manufacturers of California signed contracts with the UFWOC recognizing the union as the sole bargaining agent of the grape pickers.

The growers of table grapes, who employed more workers and did not depend on brand names, continued to hold out against the union. Chavez responded by calling for a national boycott of table grapes, taking advantage of the fact that farm workers were not covered by the National Labor Relations Act. UFWOC organizers, led by union vice president Dolores Huerta, mobilized support in the North and East, where the boycott became an important liberal cause. After table grape sales had dropped by 20 percent, the major growers agreed in July 1970 to sign contracts with the UFWOC. Like the 1966 contracts, these provided for a minimum wage ($1.80 per hour), union hiring halls for grape pickers, and fringe benefits, including a health and social service fund.

A growing problem for Chavez was the relationship between the UFWOC and the Teamsters union, which also attempted to organize agricultural workers in California. An interunion agreement for the grape industry was reached in 1967, assigning field workers to the UFWOC and processing workers to the Teamsters. The conflict reappeared in 1970, however, when both unions turned their attention to the lettuce workers. A full-scale organizing war developed. According to most observers, the violence was generally directed by the Teamsters against the UFWOC. Employers generally favored the Teamsters, who did not insist on union hiring halls and accepted the importation of docile migrant labor from Mexico. The UFWOC suffered a serious setback in 1973, when the Teamsters began to take over expiring union contracts in the grape industry. Chavez imposed a boycott on lettuce and certain brands of wine, but this was less effective than the earlier grape boycott.

The position of the UFWOC improved again after August 1975 with passage of a California farm labor law. The law, sponsored by Governor Edmund G. Brown, Jr., and supported by Chavez, created a state board to which farm workers could petition for elections to determine which union would represent them. By the end of the years, most of the elections held under the law had been won by the UFWOC. This brought the transfer of a number of Teamsters contracts back to the UFWOC. The new law also left Chavez's most important weapon intact by permitting boycotts against growers who refused to negotiate with a union chosen by their workers. Chavez continued to lead protests into the 1980s, focusing on issues such as the use of toxic pesticides and various labor conditions. He died on April 23, 1993, in San Luis, Arizona.

—SLG

## Chomsky, Noam A(vram)
### (1928–   ) *linguist, social critic*

Chomsky, who was born on December 7, 1928, grew up in Philadelphia, the city of his birth. He was educated in linguistics at the University of Pennsylvania, receiving an M.A. in 1951 and a Ph.D. in 1955. A committed Zionist, Chomsky considered settling in Israel during the late 1940s; but his academic mentor, Professor Zellig Harris, persuaded him to continue his linguistic studies in the United States.

Chomsky became assistant professor of linguistics at the Massachusetts Institute of Technology (MIT) in 1955. His first book, *Syntactic Structures*, was published in 1957. A revision of his doctoral dissertation, Chomsky's book developed the concept of generative or transformational grammar. Language, according to Chomsky, is a basic human capacity; grammar, in his view, is the surface product of deeper, universal conceptual structures existing in the mind, which can use rules of logic and syntax to generate new thoughts and expressions. Chomsky's thesis challenged the dominant behaviorist school of linguistics, which viewed language entirely as a response to external stimuli. Arguing against this attitude Chomsky pointed out that children are able not only to repeat what they are taught but also to use words and grammatical rules in sentences they have never heard before.

As the founder of a major new school of linguistics, Chomsky gained wide attention in academic circles. He reached the rank of professor at MIT in 1961 and was named Ferrari P. Ward Professor of Foreign Literatures and Linguistics five years later. At this time he also carried his conflict with the behaviorists into broader areas of philosophy and psychology. In his book *Cartesian Linguistics*, published in 1966, Chomsky traced his view of humans' creative capacity back to the rationalist philosophers of the 17th century. He expanded on his faith in free individual development as an alternative to what he considered the behaviorist system of social control and manipulation.

Always a close observer of current events, Chomsky was drawn increasingly to political activism during the mid-1960s. He opposed the Vietnam War from its inception and soon broadened his criticism to include most aspects of U.S. foreign policy. In numerous articles in the *New York Review of Books* and other journals he attacked American foreign policy as the product of a bankrupt ruling class attempting to preserve itself by forcefully maintaining the economic and political status quo. His most influential essay, "The Responsibility of Intellectuals," appeared in 1966. Here Chomsky criticized such liberal intellectuals as WALT W. ROSTOW and ARTHUR SCHLESINGER, JR., for developing an elaborate justification of American foreign policy in the service of government and industry. Chomsky argued that the proper place for authentic intellectuals was outside the power structure and that their proper function was one of criticism and dissent. This essay and other political writings by Chomsky were collected in *American Power and the New Mandarins*, published in 1969.

Chomsky's strong opposition to the war in Vietnam and his support of the protest movement made him a major influence within the American New Left. He was a participant and frequent speaker at many demonstrations during the mid- and late 1960s, including the 1967 March on the Pentagon. He also served on the steering committee of Resistance, a national antiwar group. Chomsky praised the anarchist element in the youth rebellion of the 1960s but favored libertarian socialism as the best path to "a society in which freely constituted social bonds replace the fetters of autocratic institutions." In 1969 Chomsky was appointed to an MIT panel reviewing the university's support of two laboratories involved in defense-related research. The panel urged MIT to recommend a stronger civilian orientation for both laboratories.

Chomsky remained an important academic and protest figure during the 1970s, although his early defense of Pol Pot's regime in Cambodia alienated many supporters. He moved away from his originally strong support of Israel in the aftermath of the 1967 Middle East war, urging first a binational state in Palestine and later a separate state for Palestinian Arabs. He also has been a prolific critic of U.S. foreign policy, having written many books, including *The Political Economy of Human Rights* (1979), *Towards a New Cold War* (1982), *Free Trade and Democracy* (1993), and *Hegemony or Survival: America's Quest for Global Dominance* (2003).

—SLG

## Christian, George (Eastland)
(1927–2002)  *special assistant to the president, White House press secretary*
Christian was born on January 1, 1927, in Austin, Texas, and served with the marine corps during and after World War II. He graduated from the University of Texas in 1949 and the same year joined the Texas-based International News Service as a correspondent. In 1956 he became assistant to Price Daniel, then U.S. senator, later governor of Texas. Christian also served as an assistant to Daniel's gubernatorial successor, JOHN CONNALLY.

A longtime acquaintance of LYNDON JOHNSON, Christian joined the president's staff in May 1966 as an administrative assistant to White House press secretary BILL MOYERS and succeeded Moyers in January 1967.

Described by Stewart Alsop in his 1968 book *The Center* as a "self-effacing fellow, who follows orders—which may be the only kind of press secretary who can survive with Lyndon Johnson," Christian exerted little influence over policy decisions during the Johnson administration. By 1967 many reporters had begun to question Johnson's handling of Vietnam. When Moyers received a favorable press after leaving the White House because of his well-known "private" opposition to the war within the administration, Johnson himself praised Christian to reporters, insisting that press relations had in fact improved since Moyers's departure. However, relations between the White House and the media remained cool.

Christian and Johnson maintained good relations throughout their years in the White House. The press secretary was a regular figure at meetings of the National Security Council, and a presence in many key meetings about Vietnam, although he was there as an observer more than as a policy maker. Christian also urged Johnson not to run for reelection in 1968, warning him that it would divide the nation.

Christian left the White House after the inauguration of RICHARD M. NIXON and founded the public relations concern of Christian, Miller and Honts, Inc. He died in Austin, Texas, in November 2002.

—FHM

## Church, Frank (Forrester)
(1924–1984)  *member of the Senate*
Born on July 25, 1924, in Boise, Idaho, Frank Church, a 1950 graduate of the Stanford University Law School, practiced law in Boise until elected to the Senate in 1956, at the age of 32. During the Kennedy years, Church compiled a liberal record, voting for the administration's civil rights, school

aid, minimum wage, and Medicare bills. The Americans for Democratic Action gave Church uniformly high ratings during this period.

Church was a member of the Senate Foreign Relations and Interior and Insular Affairs Committees; he also served on the special Senate Committee on Aging. He had a special interest in conservation issues, and, in 1962, Church served as floor manager for a bill designed to protect several million acres of wilderness from commercial and highway development. A similar measure became law in 1964. In 1967 Church introduced legislation, passed a year later, that established a National Wild and Scenic Rivers System to protect eight designated rivers from pollution and commercial exploitation. Although conservationists generally praised his work in the Senate, they pointed out that over the years Church had vacillated on the question of whether the Snake River–Hells Canyon area in Idaho should be developed for hydroelectric power—a measure that conservationists had vigorously opposed.

During the Johnson years, Church supported major social welfare legislation. Unlike most liberals, however, he voted against gun control legislation in 1968.

As a member of the Senate Foreign Relations Committee, Church generally advocated reduced foreign aid expenditures. He called for a phasing out of aid to prosperous Western European nations and Japan. He also urged an end to military assistance to nations such as India, Pakistan, Greece, and Turkey that seemed likely to engage in future hostilities. He did, however, support Johnson's intervention in the Dominican Republic in 1965.

Church was critical of U.S. military involvement in South Vietnam and in 1963 opposed aiding the regime of Ngo Dinh Diem. In June 1965 he called for direct negotiations with the National Liberation Front, free elections in South Vietnam, and a scaling down of the U.S. war effort. Nevertheless, during 1965 and 1966 he voted for the supplemental arms appropriations bills necessary for sustaining the war effort. In May 1967 Church drafted a letter signed by 16 antiwar senators warning the North Vietnamese that "our objective is the settlement of the war at the conference table, not the repudiation of American commitments already made to South Vietnam or the unilateral withdrawal of American forces from that embattled country." In 1969 Church coauthored a bill to prohibit the use of U.S. ground combat troops in Laos and Thailand.

Conservatives in Idaho were bitterly opposed to Church's antiwar stand and his liberal voting record. In 1967 they began a movement to have him recalled, but Church gained a good deal of popular sympathy as a result of this challenge, and he swept to an overwhelming victory in the 1968 elections.

In 1970 Church and Senator JOHN SHERMAN COOPER (R-Ky.) sponsored an amendment passed by the Senate, but rejected by the House, to prohibit the president from sending U.S. combat troops into Cambodia without consent of Congress. He also served, in the 1970s, as chair of the Select Committee to Study Governmental Operations with Respect to Intelligence Activities, better known as the "Church Committee," which found serious problems with the power and conduct of the American intelligence community. He was defeated for reelection in 1980, and he resumed the practice of law in Maryland. He died on April 7, 1984, in Bethesda, Maryland.

—JLW

## Clark, Jim (James) (Gardner)
(1921–    )  *sheriff, Dallas County, Alabama*

Clark, who was born in 1921 in Elba, Alabama, was political protégé of Alabama governor Jim Folsom. He was the state's assistant revenue commissioner in Folsom's administration, and became sheriff of Dallas County in 1955. Clark gained national prominence during the first three months of 1965, when Rev. MARTIN LUTHER KING's Southern Christian Leadership Conference (SCLC) sponsored a series of demonstrations in Selma, Alabama. These actions culminated in a march from Selma to Montgomery to protest racial discrimination in the registration of voters and to demand federal action to end this practice. Blacks constituted a majority of the population of Dallas County, of which Selma was the seat, but only 300 were registered to vote.

WILSON BAKER, Selma's director of public safety, followed a conciliatory policy toward the demonstrators. Clark, a militant segregationist who denounced civil rights leaders as "the lowest form of humanity," dealt with the protestors in a harsher fashion. At one protest, for example, Clark violently arrested Amelia Boynton, a well-respected African American in the local community. Pictures of the arrest ran in the *New York Times* and the *Washington Post*, causing such a public outcry that one SCLS leader thanked Clark for "publicity services rendered." Responding to charges of Clark's brutality by protest leaders, a federal district judge on January 23 enjoined the sheriff from employing intimidation and harassment. On February 10 Clark and his posse led black children and teenagers, who had been peacefully demonstrating at the Selma courthouse, on a forced march into the Dallas County countryside. They used clubs and electric cattle prods against the demonstrators. That night King said, "Selma will never get right . . . until we get rid of Jim Clark." Later in the year Clark was fined $1,500 for violating the January injunction. On March 7 state troopers and Clark's forces lined up near the Edmund Pettis bridge and used teargas, nightsticks, and whips to block an attempted march from Selma to Montgomery. These incidents produced a national outcry that spurred Congress's passage of the Voting Rights Act of 1965.

Baker challenged Clark in the May 1966 primary for the Democratic nomination for sheriff. Baker stressed his commitment to fair and efficient law enforcement while the incumbent emphasized his belief that the civil rights movement was a Communist-inspired uprising. Thousands of blacks had been registered since the beginning of SCLC's activities in Dallas County, and civil rights leaders regarded the primary as an important test of the strength of the new voters. Baker, who received almost all of the black votes, defeated Clark. Clark ran a write-in campaign in the general election but again lost to Baker.

After his defeat Clark served as a speaker for the John Birch Society and other right-wing organizations.

—MLL

## Clark, Joseph S(ill), Jr.

### (1901–1990) *member of the Senate*

Clark was born on October 21, 1901, into a well-to-do Philadelphia family. He attended Harvard and the University of Pennsylvania Law School. Rejecting his family's Republicanism, Clark became a New Deal Democrat and served as deputy attorney general of Pennsylvania in 1934 and 1935. Following military service in World War II he became a leader of the Americans for Democratic Action (ADA) and entered Philadelphia politics as a reform Democrat. He broke the power of the Republican organization in the city by winning elections for city controller in 1949 and mayor in 1951. Clark's progressive

record won him a second term in 1955, but he left office the following year to wage a successful campaign for the U.S. Senate.

Clark was a Senate maverick. He demanded open conduct of Senate business and was a severe critic of the methods of Senate Majority Leader LYNDON B. JOHNSON. His independence reduced his influence, but Clark served as one of the most persistent congressional advocates for the ideas of the ADA and the Democratic Party's liberal wing. Not surprisingly, he often earned 100 percent ADA ratings for his congressional voting record. Clark introduced civil rights and antipoverty legislation, laying special emphasis on the needs of the cities. He was best known for his largely unsuccessful efforts to reform the Senate, recommending changes in the seniority and committee systems, abolition of the filibuster, and measures to increase Senate efficiency.

As an enemy of the Senate "Establishment," Clark consistently supported Senator CLIFFORD CASE's (R-N.J.) efforts to set standards of congressional ethics. Although Clark joined other Democratic members of the Rules and Administration Committee in refusing to widen the 1964–65 investigation into BOBBY BAKER's financial and political manipulations, he took advantage of the impetus provided by the case to support ethics legislation. In July 1964 he and Case unsuccessfully introduced a measure that would have required senators to disclose assets of $5,000 or more, provide data on their income and outside business associations, and list gifts worth more than $100. The Senate finally passed a code of conduct in 1968, but the measure was not as strong as Clark wanted.

Clark persisted in his efforts to increase congressional efficiency. He met with some success in March 1965 when Congress agreed to create a 12-member bipartisan committee to study the organization and operation of Congress in order to eliminate time-consuming minor functions. However, his proposal to include "rules, parliamentary procedure, practices and/or precedents" as part of the new committee's focus was defeated. In 1966 Clark cosponsored a resolution to increase House terms to four years and another to reduce Senate terms from six to four years, but both measures were unsuccessful.

A member of the Senate Labor and Public Welfare Committee, Clark often sponsored administration civil rights and antipoverty legislation. He believed, however, that administration funding requests for the War on Poverty were inadequate, charging in December 1966 that the president and Congress "starved" the program to fund the Vietnam War. In August 1966 he made a symbolic effort to postpone action on defense appropriations until consideration was given to the "demonstration cities" program. The Senate defeated his proposal by an 84-5 margin.

Clark became a member of the Senate Foreign Relations Committee in 1965. His views on foreign policy often conflicted with those of the administration. Clark was in favor of establishing friendlier relations with the People's Republic of China. In November 1965 and again in May 1966 he and Senator ROBERT F. KENNEDY (D-N.Y.) urged the Johnson administration to invite China to participate in the Geneva disarmament talks. He was a major critic of the administration's Vietnam policies. As early as April 1965 Clark claimed that his mail indicated overwhelming disapproval of the president's air attacks on North Vietnam. In March 1967 he attempted to add an amendment to a Vietnam War funds authorization that would have prevented use of the funds "to carry out military operations in or over North Vietnam or to increase the number of United States military personnel in South Vietnam above 500,000." Senator MIKE MANSFIELD (D-Mont.), the majority leader, was able to replace Clark's proposal with a less restrictive one. Believing that North Vietnam was exploiting congressional criticism of administration war policy or propaganda purposes, Clark and other antiwar senators warned Hanoi in May 1967 that they did not favor unilateral withdrawal of U.S. troops from Vietnam.

In April 1968 Clark was renominated by a narrow margin in the Democratic primary. His poor showing indicated that his stature, never very high among Pennsylvania Democrats and labor leaders, had deteriorated because of his sharp disagreements with the administration. An appealing young moderate, Representative Richard Schweiker (R-Pa.), defeated Clark in November, although the Democratic presidential candidate, Vice President HUBERT HUMPHREY, won Pennsylvania with 48 percent of the vote.

Between 1969 and 1971 Clark was president of the World Federalists, U.S.A. After 1969 he served as chair of the Coalition on National Priorities and Military Policy. He remained active in Democratic

Party politics, until his death on January 12, 1990, in Philadelphia.

## Clark, Kenneth B(ancroft)
### (1914–2005)  *educator, psychologist*

Clark was born on July 24, 1914, in the Panama Canal Zone, where his father was a passenger agent for the United Fruit Company. When he was five years old, his parents separated and his mother took him and his sister to live in Harlem. He attended New York City public schools, received a B.A. from Howard University in 1935, and earned a doctorate in experimental psychology from Columbia in 1940, the first African American to do so. From 1939 to 1941 he worked under Gunnar Myrdal on the Swedish sociologist's famous study of the Negro in America. Clark became an instructor in psychology

Educator and psychologist Kenneth B. Clark *(Library of Congress, Prints and Photographs Division)*

at City College in 1942 and 18 years later was granted tenure, making him the first black to receive a permanent teaching appointment in the city university system. In February 1966 he became the first black member of the New York State Board of Regents, and in 1969 he was elected the first African-American president of the American Psychological Association.

Clark specialized in childhood personality disorders and was particularly interested in those related to racial discrimination and the problems of inner city life. He published a report in 1950 suggesting that racial discrimination adversely affected the emotional development of white as well as black children as demonstrated especially by his famous doll test, in which African-American children as young as three years old, given dolls with black skin and dolls with white skin, described the white dolls with more positive characteristics. This report was cited by the U.S. Supreme Court in its 1954 decision ordering school desegregation. Following that decision Clark pointed out that, although New York City had not deliberately created a segregated school system, such a system had in fact emerged as a result of the city's segregated housing patterns. Throughout the 1950s Clark worked with a variety of groups, which urged the city's Board of Education to begin to integrate its schools, but the board was reluctant to act.

Unlike many civil rights leaders in the early 1960s, Clark opposed forced long-distance busing to achieve integration. Middle-class parents, he said, would not permit their children to attend schools in overwhelmingly black areas. According to Clark, poor blacks therefore should not wait passively for the arrival of integration. They would not receive help from the New York City Board of Education, an overgrown bureaucracy incapable of effecting real change in the quality of education. If blacks and Puerto Ricans wanted better schools, he said, they would have to assume for themselves the responsibility of school management.

Clark also urged blacks to develop a broad range of community service organizations to help compensate for feelings of powerlessness in the inner city. In June 1962 he helped organize Harlem Youth Activities Unlimited (HARYOU), a group that sponsored retraining and work programs for unemployed youths, dropouts, and delinquents. This group became a prototype for antipoverty organizations funded by the Johnson administration under legisla-

tion passed in 1964 and 1965. Many inner city residents picketed the Board of Education in support of the Clark plan. To qualify for increased federal funding, HARYOU in June 1964 merged with Associated Community Teams (ACT), another Harlem antipoverty group associated with Representative ADAM CLAYTON POWELL, JR. (D-N.Y.). When former Powell aide Livingston Wingate was elected director of HARYOU-ACT, Clark resigned from the board, charging that Wingate intended to use the agency to advance Powell's political influence. To Clark's regret, HARYOU-ACT, plagued by internal dissension and fiscal mismanagement, failed to become a force in Harlem life.

As an eloquent spokesperson for school decentralization, Clark was invited by a community parent group in October 1966 to draw up plans for the management of experimental Intermediate School 201 and three nearby primary schools in Harlem. He proposed that these schools be run by a group of parents and university educators rather than the city's Central Board of Education. The plan won the enthusiastic endorsement of Mayor JOHN LINDSAY, State Commissioner of Education James E. Allen, and most civil rights groups. It was denounced by ALBERT SHANKER, head of the United Federation of Teachers (UFT), who charged that establishment of autonomous neighborhood school boards would lead to the abrogation of teachers' rights and protection against punitive transfers. The Clark plan was rejected by the Board of Education on the grounds that it could not delegate authority to any outside agency. A HARYOU report released in February 1964 documented the "massive deterioration" of Harlem schools and pointed out that student performance in inner cities actually decreased with length of schooling. Late in 1966, however, the Ford Foundation proposed that teachers be given representation on neighborhood boards. The proposal won the tentative approval of the UFT and became the basis for the establishment of local boards in Harlem, the Lower East Side, and the Ocean Hill–Brownsville section in Brooklyn.

In April 1968 the Ocean Hill–Brownsville board announced the dismissal of 13 teachers, five assistant principals, and one principal from district schools. Three hundred teachers in the district walked off their jobs in protest, and in the fall the UFT called a series of citywide strikes that lasted nearly two and a half months. Clark was sympathetic to the Ocean Hill–Brownsville board and attempted to bring about a settlement through the offices of Commissioner Allen. As the strike wore on, however, Allen was forced to suspend the board and replace it with a special three-person state supervisory committee.

By the early 1970s Clark had become thoroughly disillusioned with the decentralization experiments in Brooklyn, Harlem, and the Lower East Side. Local boards, torn by internal dissension and excessively concerned with politics, had failed, he said, to improve the quality of education in the inner city. He continued, however, to consult with various private and public organizations on racial policies. He retired from City University in 1975 and died on May 1, 2005.

—JLW

## Clark, (William) Ramsey

(1927–  ) *assistant attorney general, deputy attorney general, acting attorney general, U.S. Attorney General*

Son of former U.S. Attorney General and Supreme Court justice TOM C. CLARK, Ramsey Clark who was born on December 18, 1927, in Dallas, Texas, received a B.A. from the University of Texas in 1949 and an M.A. in history as well as a law degree from the University of Chicago in 1950. He then practiced law in Dallas until he was named U.S. assistant attorney general in charge of the Lands Division in February 1961. In that post Clark cut in half a backlog of 32,000 pending cases and at the same time introduced economy measures that reduced the division's staff and budget needs. He also headed federal civilian forces at the University of Mississippi following court-ordered integration there in the fall of 1962 and traveled to several southern cities in 1963 to oversee school desegregation.

On February 13, 1965, Clark was appointed deputy attorney general, the second-highest position in the Justice Department. He helped draft the 1965 Voting Rights Act and was the coordinator of federal forces sent to Alabama in March 1965 to protect the civil rights march from Selma to Montgomery led by MARTIN LUTHER KING, JR. Following riots in the Watts section of Los Angeles in August 1965, Clark headed a presidential task force charged with developing programs to help rehabilitate the area and the means to eliminate the cause of the rioting.

Tall, gangling, and soft-spoken, Ramsey Clark became acting attorney general on October 3, 1966, with the departure of NICHOLAS KATZENBACH. He was named U.S. Attorney General on February 28, 1967, and, with his father administering the oath of office, was sworn in on March 10. Justice Clark shortly thereafter retired from the Supreme Court to avoid any appearance of conflict of interest.

As U.S. Attorney General, Clark helped draft the administration's civil rights proposals and secure passage of the 1968 Civil Rights Act. He stepped up enforcement of fair employment and school desegregation laws and in April 1968 filed the first desegregation suit brought by the Justice Department against a northern school district. He also fought against the federal death penalty, oversaw the opening of the first federal halfway house, and established first federal narcotics addict treatment unit.

When Martin Luther King was assassinated in Memphis, Tennessee, on April 4, 1968, Clark immediately went to the scene and then carefully followed the investigation of King's murder. In the spring and summer of 1968 Clark resisted pressured to try to prevent a planned Poor People's Campaign in Washington, and, instead, he and other Justice Department officials negotiated with Rev. RALPH ABERNATHY and other campaign leaders to arrange for the arrival and encampment of the protesters.

To combat organized crime Clark initiated special "strike forces:" teams of attorneys and investigators from key federal agencies who cooperated closely with local law enforcement agencies to investigate, indict, and prosecute organized crime figures in a single locale. Clark also centralized the federal antinarcotics program in 1968 by merging several existing government operations into a new Bureau of Narcotics and Dangerous Drugs. He repeatedly called for improving local police forces by means of more education and training and higher salaries for police officers. He oversaw the administration of a program of federal grants established in June 1968 to upgrade local police, courts, and jails. Clark also supported greater emphasis on rehabilitation in the federal prison system, opposed the death penalty, and spoke in favor of controversial Supreme Court decisions expanding the rights of criminal suspects. He was a strong proponent of gun-control legislation and worked for passage of stricter federal laws in the summer of 1968 following the assassinations of King and ROBERT F. KENNEDY.

Clark generally opposed the use of wiretaps and electronic surveillance on the grounds that they were an invasion of privacy, probably unconstitutional, and largely unnecessary and ineffective in fighting crime. When instances of electronic eavesdropping by the FBI were revealed in 1967, Clark instituted a review of all government cases where illegal eavesdropping might have tainted the evidence and then notified the appropriate court when such a case was discovered. In June he issued controversial guidelines sharply restricting the use of wiretaps and secret listening devices by federal agencies. J. EDGAR HOOVER reportedly considered Clark a "jellyfish" and the worst U.S. Attorney General he had served under as head of the FBI. He refused to permit bureau agents to participate in the new strike forces set up by Clark.

In testimony before a 1975 Senate Select Committee on Intelligence Activities, Clark stated that he "had authorized electronic surveillance on a good many embassies in the national security field." He denied knowledge of the FBI's COINTELPRO campaign to disrupt left- and right-wing political organizations. He did admit, however, that he had known that the bureau had undertaken some disruptive activities that went beyond the investigation or prevention of crime.

Late in 1967, following a wave of riots in the nation's cities, Clark established an Interdivisional Information Unit within the Department of Justice. The purpose of this group was to pool information from various sources on the activities of black militants who were thought to be inciting riots. Clark spoke out against Mayor RICHARD J. DALEY's April 1968 order to the Chicago police to "shoot to kill" arsonists and shoot to maim or cripple looters in future riots. Clark thought such a policy would aggravate the riot control problem; he advocated instead overwhelming police presence coupled with restraint and the minimal use of gunfire. Clark also opposed an antiriot bill passed as a rider to the 1968 Civil Rights Act.

Along with Selective Service administrator LEWIS B. HERSHEY, Clark issued a statement in December 1967 outlining the administration's policy on antidraft protests. While lawful protest activities would not subject registrants to any special administrative action by the Selective Service, the statement said that any violations of the draft law itself could result in early induction of registrants or legal action against the protesters. These guidelines met much criticism, as did Clark's authorization of the prosecution of Dr. BENJAMIN SPOCK and four

others who were indicted in January 1968 for conspiracy to counsel, aid, and abet young men to evade the draft. Clark later said that while he had "doubts about the Spock case," especially in its use of conspiracy charges, he felt his duty as U.S. Attorney General was to prosecute Spock and other Selective Service cases when the evidence showed a violation of the law.

Prior to the August 1968 Democratic National Convention in Chicago, Clark unsuccessfully tried to convince Mayor Daley to meet with leaders of the groups planning demonstrations during the convention and to allow the protesters some peaceful means of expressing their dissent. He also unsuccessfully opposed Daley's request that federal troops be stationed near the city on stand-by duty. Following clashes between police and protesters at the convention, Clark rejected all demands that he prosecute the demonstration leaders under the 1968 antiriot law. Instead he instructed the U.S. attorney in Chicago to begin a federal grand jury investigation of police actions during the convention and possible police violations of the protesters' civil rights.

Clark's liberalism became a center of controversy during the 1968 presidential campaign when Republican candidate RICHARD M. NIXON emphasized that he would begin to restore order and respect for law in this country" by appointing "a new Attorney General." After leaving office in January 1969, Clark joined a New York City law firm and soon became an outspoken opponent of the Vietnam War. He defended the Rev. Philip F. Berrigan and five others indicted in January 1971 on charges of conspiring to kidnap Secretary of State HENRY KISSINGER and to blow up the heating systems of federal buildings in Washington. In 1975 Clark also defended several inmates facing criminal charges stemming from the Attica prison uprising of September 1971. Clark made a highly controversial trip to Hanoi in the summer of 1972 on behalf of the International Commission of Inquiry to investigate charges of American bombing of non-military targets in North Vietnam. Running an unorthodox campaign in which he refused all contributions over $100, Clark won the New York Democratic primary for the U.S. Senate nomination in September 1974 but lost the November election. He later became the founder and chair of the International Action Center, a large antiwar organization, and continued his legal work on behalf of many high-profile and controversial clients.

—CAB

## Clark, Tom C(ampbell)

(1899–1977) *associate justice, U.S. Supreme Court*

Clark, who was born on September 23, 1899, in Dallas, Texas, received his B.A. and his law degree from the University of Texas. He spent several years in private practice and then served as civil district attorney in Dallas County, Texas, from 1927 to 1932. Known as a protégé of Senator Tom Connally (D-Tex.) and Representative Sam Rayburn (D-Tex.), Clark joined the Justice Department in 1937. Over the next six years he helped coordinate the wartime relocation of Japanese Americans and handled cases on war claims, antitrust, and war frauds. Named an assistant attorney general in 1943, Clark cooperated closely with a Senate committee headed by HARRY S. TRUMAN (D-Mo.) investigating the wartime mobilization effort. He supported Truman's nomination as the Democratic vice presidential candidate in 1944. Appointed U.S. Attorney General by Truman in May 1945, Clark became one of the President's closest advisers on domestic issues. He instituted 160 antitrust cases, gave Justice Department support to the expansion of civil rights in Supreme Court cases, and played a major role in the development of Truman's domestic anticommunist program. Truman nominated Clark as a Supreme Court justice in 1949. Although the appointment aroused controversy, it was confirmed by the Senate.

At the outset Clark did not show much independence on the Court. He usually took a conservative position, voting to uphold government regulatory authority and to sustain loyalty-security programs against constitutional challenges. In the 1950s, however, Clark displayed increasing independence and innovation in his decisions. Although he remained a conservative in the loyalty-security field throughout the Warren Court years, Clark supported Court rulings against segregation and was regarded as a "swing" vote between the Court's liberal and conservative blocs on other issues. While he often voted against expansion of defendants' rights, for example, Clark wrote the majority opinion in *Mapp v. Ohio* (1961), one of the Court's most significant criminal justice decisions, which ruled that evidence obtained by illegal searches were inadmissible in court. With his strong background in antitrust, Clark became the Court's expert in this area. He also established himself as a friend to the civil rights movement. In 1950, he supported the majority decision in *Sweatt v. Painter*, which ordered the desegregation of the University of Texas law school, and three years later he wrote the majority opinion in *Terry v. Adams*, which eliminated the all-white primary in Texas. In 1954 he joined the unanimous decision in *Brown v. Board of Education*.

Clark continued to support the government's position in loyalty-security matters during the Johnson years, but by then he was usually in the minority. In 1964 Clark dissented in a series of cases in which the Court invalidated state loyalty laws in New York and Washington and a federal law canceling the citizenship of naturalized Americans who returned to their native country for a period of three years or more. Clark objected when the Court in 1964 nullified a provision in the 1950 Internal Security Act denying passports to members of the Communist Party. He also dissented in 1965, when the Court voided a clause in the Landrum-Griffin Act barring Communist Party members from serving as labor union officials.

Loyalty-security had become a less contentious issue by the mid-1960s, however, and much more controversy was aroused by Court rulings in areas such as reapportionment and criminal rights. Although Clark had concurred in the Court's 1962 decision in *Baker v. Carr*, ruling that federal courts could rule on legislative apportionment, he rejected the "one-person, one-vote" standard established by the majority in two 1964 cases. Clark argued that while the Constitution required "rational" apportionment, it did not mandate exact "one person, one vote" districting.

In criminal justice cases Clark often dissented from the majority's expansion of defendants' rights. He was in the minority, for example, when the Court held in 1964 that the Fifth Amendment's privilege against self-incrimination applied in state as well as federal court proceedings. Clark also dissented in the landmark case of *Miranda v. Arizona*" (1966), in which a five-justice majority defined the constitutional limitations on the power of police to question criminal suspects and set out specific rules for police interrogations. Clark did not always place society's claims above those of a defendant, however. He wrote the opinion of the Court in a 1967 case that held that the use of electronic devices to record conversations was a search within the meaning of the Fourth Amendment. Clark was also sensitive to the possibility of publicity infringing on a defendant's right to a fair trial. He wrote the majority opinion in a 1965 decision overturning the state conviction of Texas financier Billie Sol Estes on swindling charges. Estes's trial had been televised, and Clark ruled that the televising of criminal trials could have a prejudicial effect on the judge, jurors, and witnesses. Similarly, Clark was the author of a 1966 decision reversing a defendant's murder conviction because of the "massive pretrial publicity" and the "carnival atmosphere," that had reigned during the trial. Clark also joined the majority in a 1967 decision extending to children in juvenile court proceedings the procedural guarantees, such as right to counsel, afforded adults by the Constitution.

In two 1964 cases Clark delivered the opinion for a unanimous Court upholding the public accommodations section of the 1964 Civil Rights Act. He also voted in 1966 to reinstate the federal conspiracy charges against 14 defendants alleged to have murdered three civil rights workers in Mississippi in 1964 after District Court judge W. HAROLD COX had dismissed the charges. In his opinion in that case, Clark urged Congress to adopt broader laws against racial violence. In 1967 he voted to invalidate antimiscegenation statutes.

Although Clark usually approved the Court's efforts to expand civil rights, he did not always condone the activities of civil rights demonstrators. In a five-to-four decision in 1964, Clark wrote the majority opinion holding that the public accommodations section of the 1964 Civil Rights Act barred state prosecution of demonstrators who had previously tried by peaceful means to desegregate the business places covered by the new law. However, this proved to be an exceptional decision for Clark. In 1966 he voted against reversing the breach-of-the-peace convictions of five blacks who had tried to integrate a public library in Louisiana. He voted to sustain the trespass convictions of demonstrators who had protested outside a county jail in Florida against the arrest of other civil rights demonstrators. Clark was also part of a five-member majority that in 1967 upheld the contempt-of-court convictions of MARTIN LUTHER KING, JR., and seven other black leaders who had led protest marches during the 1963 Birmingham demonstrations in defiance of a temporary restraining order.

In February 1967 President Johnson appointed Clark's son RAMSEY CLARK U.S. Attorney General. Justice Clark announced that he would retire from the Court at the end of that term to avoid any appearance of conflict of interest. After he retired in

June 1967, legal scholars, assessing Clark's 18 years on the bench, generally portrayed him as a highly productive member of the Court who had written some of its most important opinions. The major criticism leveled against Clark was that he had unduly emphasized the needs of government and society over the rights of defendants and of the individual, particularly in the loyalty-security field.

Clark remained active in the law following his retirement from the Supreme Court. He sat as a judge on the lower federal courts, served as head of an advisory committee of the National Commission on Reform of Federal Criminal Laws, and, from 1968 to 1970, was the director of the Federal Judicial Center, a research and training agency of the federal judiciary. Clark also headed an American Bar Association Committee that recommended in 1970 reform of disciplinary procedures for lawyers involved in misconduct. He died on June 13, 1977, in New York, New York.

—CAB

## Cleaver, L(eroy) Eldridge
(1935–1998) *leader, Black Panther Party*

Cleaver was born in a small town near Little Rock, Arkansas, on August 31, 1935. He grew up in Phoenix, Arizona, and in the Watts section of Los Angeles, where his parents separated. Cleaver spent much of the early 1950s in state reformatories and prisons for marijuana-related crimes. In 1957 he began a two- to 14-year prison term for assault with intent to murder. The next year Cleaver joined the Black Muslims and became a leader among Muslim prisoners campaigning for religious freedom. When Muslim founder ELIJAH MUHAMMAD and the charismatic minister MALCOLM X split in March 1964, Cleaver sided with Malcolm and renounced Muhammad's racial demonology. Expressing his ideological debt to Malcolm X, Cleaver later wrote: "I have, so to speak, washed my hands in the blood of the martyr, Malcolm X, whose retreat from the precipice of madness created new room for others to turn around in, and I am now caught up in that tiny space, attempting a maneuver of my own."

In mid-1965 Cleaver wrote to Beverly Axelrod, a prominent San Francisco attorney specializing in civil liberties cases, to request that she plead his case for parole. Axelrod took his case and also showed Cleaver's manuscripts to the editor of *Ramparts* magazine, which began publishing autobiographical essays and critical pieces by Cleaver on racial issues and revolutionary violence in June 1966. In February 1968 these articles were published in a book entitled *Soul On Ice*, which won immediate critical acclaim. The book became an immediate best-seller and established Cleaver as a leading literary advocate for black militancy in the late 1960s.

Supported by prominent literary figures such as NORMAN MAILER and with the promise of a job at *Ramparts*, Cleaver was paroled in December 1966. In February 1967 he first met HUEY P. NEWTON and BOBBY SEALE, the cofounders of the Black Panther Party. A short time later Cleaver joined the party as its minister of information.

On April 6, 1968, a 90-minute gun battle took place between the Panthers and the Oakland police, in which Panther treasurer Bobby Hutton was killed and four others, including Cleaver, were wounded. Cleaver's parole was immediately rescinded, and he remained in jail until June 12, when Superior Court judge Raymond J. Sherwin ordered him freed on $50,000 bail. The state successfully appealed Judge Sherwin's decision to the District Court of Appeals, which ruled that Sherwin had acted beyond his authority in ordering Cleaver's release. Cleaver exhausted his last legal remedy November 26 when U.S. Supreme Court justice THURGOOD MARSHALL denied his request for a stay to prohibit state officials from taking him into custody.

Throughout this appeal process Cleaver maintained his militant posture. The radical Peace and Freedom Party chose Cleaver as its presidential candidate in August 1968, and Cleaver campaigned on a program calling for an alliance of black and white radicals. In the fall he became embroiled in a dispute with California governor RONALD REAGAN and the State Board of Regents over a series of lectures he was slated to deliver at the University of California, Berkeley. Governor Reagan denounced Cleaver September 17 as an advocate of "racism and violence" and sought to prevent him from lecturing at Berkeley. Three days later the Regents voted to limit Cleaver to one guest lecture and censured the faculty Board of Educational Development for having "abused a trust" in approving Cleaver's lecture series. Over 2,000 students met September 24 and demanded that the Regents rescind their restrictions on Cleaver's appearances. On October 3 the faculty voted to repudiate the Regent's action, and four days later Berkeley chancellor Roger W. Heyns announced that a lecture hall would be made available to Cleaver but that no course credit would be given to those attending the series. After Cleaver's first lecture, Governor Reagan submitted a resolution to the Regents barring university facilities for "a program of instruction . . . in which Mr. Cleaver appears more than once as a lecturer." Although Reagan's resolution was rejected by the Regents on October 18, student demonstrations and sit-ins in support of course-credit status for Cleaver's lecture series took place October 23 and 24 and resulted in about 200 arrests.

Having exhausted all legal appeals, Cleaver fled the country on November 28, 1968. He lived in Cuba until July 1969 and then moved to Algiers, where he founded the first international section of the Black Panther Party in September 1970. Cleaver was expelled from the party in February 1971, after he attacked the national leadership's lack of militance.

By the mid-1970s Cleaver had moderated his political views considerably. He returned to the United States in November 1975 and voluntarily surrendered to federal authorities. After a long legal battle, the prosecution dropped the attempted murder charges, and he was placed on probation for assault. He later renounced many of his former positions, embraced religion and cold war anticommunism, and ran unsuccessfully for a Republican Senate seat in California. He died in Los Angeles in April 1998.

—DKR

## Clement, Frank G(oad)
### (1920–1969) *governor*

Clement, who was born on June 2, 1920, in Dickson, Tennessee, received a law degree from Vanderbilt University in 1942. Four years later he was appointed general counsel of Tennessee's Railroad and Public Utilities Commission, where he earned a reputation as the "people's champion" in rate case fights. The recognition he received in that post helped him to win a two-year term as governor in 1952. He was reelected in 1955 by an overwhelming margin, this time to a four-year term that reflected a change in the state constitution in 1953. Clement employed a Bible-quoting, evangelical campaign style that was popular in rural Tennessee. He once declared, "If you can't mix your politics and your religion, then something is wrong with your politics."

Although his electioneering style was old-fashioned, Clement was, in the 1950s, relatively liberal in the context of Tennessee's traditionally conservative politics. He successfully pressed the legislature to pass greatly increased appropriations for education and mental health and opposed the intrusion of private enterprise into the operations of the Tennessee Valley Authority. A racial moderate, he neither endorsed nor criticized the Supreme Court's 1954 school desegregation decision, and, in 1956, he sent the National Guard to Clinton to protect African-American children from white opponents of integration. Clement was expected to have a bright political future, and he received some consideration for the Democratic vice presidential slot in 1956. But his keynote address at his party's presidential nominating convention of that year was derided by some as excessively folksy and sentimental, and Clement was never again seriously considered for national leadership.

After a compulsory retirement from the Tennessee governorship, Clement was reelected in 1962 despite his opponents' efforts to attack him for personal and business associations with Billie Sol Estes, a Texas financier then under indictment for conspiracy and fraud. But the expansion of Tennessee's black electorate and the increasing strength of the state's Republican Party in the 1960s accounted, in large measure, for the thwarting of his two bids to enter the U.S. Senate. In 1964, seeking to complete the unexpired term of the late senator Estes Kefauver, he challenged Representative Ross Bass (D-Tenn.) in the Democratic primary. Although a racial moderate by the standards of the previous decade, during the campaign Clement criticized Bass for voting in favor of the Johnson administration's 1964 public accommodations bill. As a result, Bass won black precincts in such cities as Nashville and Memphis by ratios of 12 to 1. In addition, Clement's popularity among many voters had declined because of his support for a 3 percent sales tax on TVA electricity. Bass defeated Clement by almost 100,000 votes out of about 800,000 cast.

After this defeat Clement wooed black voters by appointing African Americans to important posts and sending out recruiting agents to locate qualified blacks for state jobs. He also enhanced his reputation with liberal voters by urging the legislature to abolish capital punishment and by pardoning all five men on death row in 1965 after the lower house had failed by one vote to repeal the death penalty.

In 1966 Clement won a rematch with Bass for the Democratic senatorial nomination. In the general election he faced Republican HOWARD W. BAKER, JR., whom Bass had defeated two years earlier. For almost a century after the Civil War, the strength of Tennessee's Republican Party had been concentrated almost exclusively in the antisecessionist, eastern third of the state. But since DWIGHT D. EISENHOWER's landslide presidential victory in 1952, the party had been gradually expanding its following in other areas of the state. Baker, a moderate, extended these gains. He competed with Clement for black voters, almost all of whom had been driven to the Democrats by the 1964 Goldwater campaign. Furthermore, Clement's revivalist campaign oratory was losing its appeal as the state became increasingly urbanized. He received only 40 percent of the ballots, while Baker polled 56 percent of the vote to become the first popularly elected Republican senator from Tennessee. Clement left office in January 1967. On November 4, 1969, at the age of 49, he was killed in a traffic accident in Nashville.

—MLL

## Clifford, Clark (McAdams)
### (1906–1998) *secretary of defense*

Clifford was born in Fort Scott, Kansas on December 25, 1906, and grew up in St. Louis, where he attended local schools. He won a law degree from Washington University in 1928, entered a prominent St. Louis law firm, and soon established himself as one of the city's leading attorneys. In June 1946 he was appointed special counsel to President HARRY S. TRUMAN.

As a close adviser to Truman, Clifford drew up the foreign policy memorandum that influenced the administration's increasingly tough policy toward the Soviet Union. He also helped draft the 1947 National Security Act and position papers for the Truman Doctrine to aid Greece and Turkey. In the domestic political arena Clifford plotted the strategy that aided Truman's election in 1948, convincing the president to appeal to the electorate as a New Deal liberal and urging the president to recognize the independence of Israel. In 1950 Clifford resigned his position as special counsel to the president to become a senior partner in a Washington, D.C., law firm. Clifford became a millionaire, advising major American corporations on their tax and legal problems.

When John F. Kennedy won the Democratic presidential nomination, Clifford, a supporter of

Senator STUART SYMINGTON (D-Mo.), joined the Kennedy staff as an adviser. In May 1961 Kennedy named Clifford to the Foreign Intelligence Advisory Board to oversee the activities of the agencies that had mishandled the Bay of Pigs invasion. He became chair of the panel in April 1963. He also played a critical role in brokering a compromise between JFK and leaders of the steel industry, when they threatened a price increase that the president opposed.

In November 1963 President Johnson called upon Clifford, an old and respected friend, to help organize and recruit a new White House staff. Clifford might well have attained a high-ranking position in the administration—he was offered the attorney generalship in 1967—but he preferred to maintain his prosperous legal practice. Nevertheless, Clifford soon became a member of President Johnson's inner circle of trusted advisers. In 1964 he helped the president deal with two embarrassing scandals, the first resulting from the business activities of former Senate majority secretary BOBBY BAKER and the second from the arrest on morals charges of White House aide WALTER JENKINS.

In the fall of 1965 Clifford visited Southeast Asia as chair of the Foreign Intelligence Advisory Board. During the trip, he later recalled, "the optimism of our military and Vietnamese officials on the conduct of the war . . . confirmed my belief in the correctness of our policy." Clifford opposed the 37-day halt in the bombing of North Vietnam beginning at Christmas 1965 because he felt that it "could be construed by Hanoi as a sign of weakness on our part." As an adviser to President Johnson at the 1966 Manila Conference, he remained convinced that the United States was winning the war and that its Vietnam policy was sound.

Clifford began to develop doubts about the war, however, in the summer of 1967, when he and General MAXWELL TAYLOR toured Southeast Asia at the request of the president. The purpose of this trip was to determine why America's Asian allies, New Zealand, Australia, and the Philippines, had sent only token detachments to assist U.S. troops in Vietnam. Clifford discovered that these nations were less troubled by Communist aggression in Vietnam than the United States was, despite the fact that they were seemingly more vulnerable. "I returned home," wrote Clifford, "puzzled, troubled, concerned. Was it possible that our assessment of the danger to the stability of Southeast Asia and the

Clark Clifford, 1963 *(Photographed by Yoichi R. Okamoto; Lyndon Baines Johnson Library)*

Western Pacific was exaggerated? Was it possible that those nations which were neighbors of Vietnam had a clearer perception of the tides of world events in 1967 than we?"

Clifford's doubts were not widely publicized, and when he was named secretary of defense in January 1968, it was generally believed, even by the president, that Clifford would advocate an even more aggressive U.S. military posture in Vietnam than his predecessor, ROBERT S. MCNAMARA.

Clifford was confirmed by the Senate January 30, 1968, and sworn in March 1. He assumed office during a critical moment in the war. On January 31, 1968, Communist guerrillas and their North Vietnamese allies launched the Tet offensive, a massive attack on South Vietnam's cities and military installations. Before being driven back, the Communists had overrun the ancient city of Hue, the cultural capital of South Vietnam, and had even penetrated the American embassy at Saigon. Some military experts thought the Tet offensive was the last desperate effort of a beaten enemy; to many others, however, Tet suggested that the United States and their South Vietnamese allies had made little progress in limiting the ability of the Communists to wage war.

On February 28, 1968, two days before Clifford assumed office, he was named chair of the President's

Ad Hoc Task Force on Vietnam. The ostensible purpose of the group was to determine how best to raise the over 200,000 additional troops for Vietnam that had been requested by the Joint Chiefs of Staff and General WILLIAM C. WESTMORELAND. In fact, at Clifford's request, the task force debated the need for these troops and the nature of the entire U.S. role in Vietnam. Among other members of the task force, General EARLE WHEELER, chair of the Joint Chiefs of Staff; WALT ROSTOW, special president assistant; and General Maxwell Taylor favored the troop request. Deputy Undersecretary of Defense PAUL NITZE, Undersecretary of State NICHOLAS KATZENBACH, and PAUL WARNKE of the Defense Department stood opposed. Clifford remained neutral, attempting to use the debate to develop his own position. "After days of analysis," he later wrote, "I could not find out when the war was going to end; I could not find out whether the new requests for men and equipment were going to be enough, or whether it would take more and, if more, when and how much; I could not find out how soon the South Vietnamese forces would be ready to take over. All I had was the statement, given with too little self-assurance to be comforting, that if we persisted for an indeterminate length of time, the enemy would not choose to go on."

The task force eventually recommended immediate deployment of 23,000 additional troops in Vietnam, approval of reserve call-ups, larger draft calls, and lengthened tours of duty to provide additional forces. In transmitting these recommendations to the president, Clifford made known his serious reservations about the entire U.S. Vietnam policy.

On March 28 Clifford met with Secretary of State DEAN RUSK, Walt Rostow, Assistant Secretary of State WILLIAM BUNDY, and HARRY MCPHERSON, a White House speech writer, to discuss a draft of a scheduled presidential address on Vietnam. McPherson presented a speech that called for a modest 15,000-man troop increase and made a pro-forma appeal to the North Vietnamese to negotiate. The draft made no mention of a bombing halt, which the North Vietnamese had declared a prerequisite for peace talks. Clifford proposed that an alternative draft be presented to the president that would include the suggestion that the United States stop all bombing north of the 20th parallel, with a promise of total cessation of the bombing if Hanoi refrained from attacking the South Vietnamese

cities. McPherson thought Clifford "brilliant" in convincing Rusk and Rostow to reverse their long-standing positions on the war.

President Johnson delivered a revised version of the draft when he spoke over nationwide television on March 31, 1968. His address included the stunning announcement that he would not seek another term as president. However, the speech did not end debate on Vietnam within the administration. Clifford aligned himself with W. AVERELL HARRIMAN and CYRUS T. VANCE, U.S. representatives to the Paris peace talks, who urged the president to order a total bombing halt to speed the negotiations with North Vietnam. Rusk, General Westmoreland, and General Taylor argued that the bombing remained a military necessity. In October President Johnson accepted the Clifford position and ordered a complete end to the bombing of the North. "I believe," Clifford later wrote, "the contribution I made to reversing our policy in that wretched conflict in Vietnam is very likely the most gratifying experience I have had."

Clifford left office in January 1969 and returned to his legal practice. In 1982 he became chair of First American Bankshares, which was secretly owned by the foreign Bank of Credit and Commerce International (BCCI). In 1992 he was indicted on charges stemming from BCCI's conduct and secret ownership of First American, but the charges were dismissed for health reasons. He died in 1998 in Bethesda, Maryland.

—JLW

## Coffin, William Sloane, Jr.
(1924–    ) *chaplain, Yale University*

Coffin was born in New York City on June 1, 1924. His father was vice president of the family furniture business, W. & J. Sloane, Inc., and his uncle, the Rev. Henry Sloane Coffin, was president of the Union Theological Seminary and a fellow of the Yale Corporation. After attending Phillips Exeter Academy Coffin entered Yale, but his studies were interrupted by four years of service as an officer in the army. He returned to Yale in 1947 and later spent a year at the Union Theological Seminary. There Coffin became a follower of the theologian Reinhold Neibuhr, whose doctrine of "Christian realism" justified and encouraged political activism. From 1950 to 1953 he worked overseas for the Central Intelligence Agency, specializing in Russian affairs. After completing theological studies at Yale, Coffin was ordained a Presbyterian minister in 1956. He served as chaplain at Phillips Andover Academy and Williams College before being appointed Yale University chaplain in 1958.

Coffin took part in a May 1961 Freedom Ride to Montgomery, Alabama, where he was arrested for breaching the peace in an effort to desegregate a bus terminal lunch counter. Two years later he was arrested in an effort to end segregation at a Baltimore amusement park, and, in 1964, he was again arrested in St. Augustine, Florida, during a similar demonstration. In addition to his civil rights activities, Coffin served as a training adviser to the Peace Corps during the early 1960s.

Beginning in 1965 Coffin was strongly critical of American conduct in Vietnam. He argued that "the war is being waged with unbelievable cruelty and in a fashion so out of character with American instincts of decency that it is seriously undermining them. The strains of war have cut the funds that might otherwise be applied to antipoverty efforts at home and abroad—which is the intelligent way to fight Communism." After first restricting his protests to letters and petitions, Coffin became acting executive secretary of the National Emergency Committee of Clergy concerned about Vietnam in January 1966.

By the fall of 1967 Coffin was counseling active resistance to the war and was one of the original signers of the September 1967 statement, "A Call to Resist Illegitimate Authority," which supported draft resistance and the refusal of troops to obey orders to participate in the war. On October 16 Coffin was the main speaker at ceremonies at the Arlington Street Church in Boston, sponsored by New England Resistance, during which draft-eligible men burned or handed in draft cards. Four days later Coffin was part of a delegation that turned over these and other draft cards to Justice Department officials in Washington. On the steps of the Justice Department he stated: "In our view it is not wild-eyed idealism but clear-eyed revulsion which brings us here," and concluded, "we hereby publicly counsel . . . refusal to serve in the armed services as long as the war in Vietnam continues."

For these and other acts Coffin, BENJAMIN SPOCK, Marcus Raskin, codirector of the Institute of Policy Studies, writer Mitchell Goodman, and Harvard graduate student Michael Ferber were indicted on January 5, 1968, for conspiring to "counsel, aid

and abet" young men to "refuse and evade service in the armed services." After a widely publicized trial all but Raskin were convicted on one conspiracy count, and, on July 11, 1968, they were sentenced to fines and two-year prison terms. The convictions were overturned a year later, when the First U.S. District Court of Appeals ruled that the trial judge, Francis J. W. Ford, had made prejudicial errors in his charge to the jury. Coffin and Goodman were ordered retried, while charges against Spock and Ferber were dismissed. On April 22, 1970, the charges against the two remaining defendants were dismissed at the request of the Justice Department. Coffin announced his resignation as Yale University chaplain in February 1975, effective the next year. In the 1980s, he served as pastor of the prestigious Riverside Church in New York. He later became the president of SANE-Freeze, one of the nation's largest peace organizations, and continued to write and lecture on topics such as race, peace, and the role of church in society.

—JBF

## Cohen, Wilbur J(oseph)

(1913–1987) *assistant secretary, undersecretary, and secretary, Department of Health, Education and Welfare*

Wilbur Cohen was born on June 10, 1913, in Milwaukee, Wisconsin. After graduating from the University of Wisconsin in 1934, Cohen went to Washington as an assistant to his former economics professor, Edwin Witte, the executive director of President Franklin D. Roosevelt's cabinet committee on economic security. Cohen helped draft the 1935 Social Security Act and served for many years thereafter as technical adviser to the Social Security Board. Cohen was considered by many as the nation's leading authority on Social Security: "A Social Security expert," remarked one senator, "is a man with Wilbur Cohen's telephone number." Cohen was professor of public welfare at the University of Michigan from 1956 to 1961. In January 1961 President Kennedy named Cohen assistant secretary in the Department of Health, Education and Welfare (HEW) and charged him with responsibility for winning congressional approval of HEW legislation.

Cohen formulated and guided through Congress more legislation than any other department official in the 1960s. He was active in facilitating passage of some 65 bills relating to education, child welfare, social security, consumer protection, civil rights, mental health, and water resources planning. During the Kennedy years, however, he failed to win enactment of two of the measures most prized by the president: the Medicare bill linking medical care for the aged to the Social Security system and the administration's education bill authorizing federal aid to elementary and secondary schools.

The passage of both bills became feasible following the November 1964 elections, in which the Democrats increased their majorities in the House and Senate. Cohen played a key role in the passage of the Medicare bill, mobilizing the strength of organized labor to counteract the opposition of the American Medical Association. He also served as liaison between the White House and Representative WILBUR D. MILLS (D-Ark.), who as chair of the House Ways and Means Committee formulated the bill, which became law in the spring of 1965.

Cohen and Commissioner of Education FRANCIS KEPPEL and White House aide DOUGLASS CATER played a significant part in working out the compromise between public, private, and parochial school groups that expedited passage in the fall of 1965 of the Elementary and Secondary Education Act. Under the compromise, the National Education Association, representing a million public school teachers, agreed to permit some form of public assistance to sectarian schools, while the National Catholic Welfare Conference settled for substantial but less than equal participation of parochial schools in the various aid programs.

Cohen was promoted to HEW undersecretary in April 1965 and three years later succeeded JOHN GARDNER as head of the department. He continued to fight for causes related to societal health and welfare, including consumer protection, Native American health programs, substance abuse programs, and Public Health Service grants. With the approval of President Johnson, Cohen issued a sweeping order reorganizing the public health divisions of his agency in March 1968. Along with Gardner, Cohen had come to believe that the commissioned officer corps of the Public Health Service (PHS) could not be expected to adopt innovations necessary for effective administration of federally financed health programs. Under Cohen's order a new assistant HEW secretary for health and scientific affairs assumed authority over many of the functions of the PHS. Cohen also brought the National Institutes of Health, the National Institute of Mental Health, and the National Library of Medicine under control of a new agency called the Health Services and Mental Health Administration.

Cohen left Washington in January 1969 to become dean of the University of Michigan School of Education. In 1980 he left Michigan and became a professor at the LBJ School of Public Affairs at the University of Texas. He died in South Korea on May 17, 1987, while attending a conference on aging.

—JLW

## Colby, William E(gan)
(1920–1996) *official, Central Intelligence Agency*
The son of a career army officer, Colby, who was born on January 4, 1920, in St. Paul, Minnesota, was raised in a series of military posts in the United States and China. Following his graduation from Princeton in 1940, he enrolled in Columbia Law School but left a year later to enter the army. During the war Colby became a member of the Office of Strategic Services and served on missions in France and Norway. In 1947 he received his law degree from Columbia. Colby practiced law in New York for two years before joining the staff of the National Labor Relations Board.

When the Korean conflict broke out in 1950, Colby joined the Central Intelligence Agency (CIA). Under cover of diplomatic title he served the agency as an embassy attaché in Stockholm from 1951 to 1953 and as first secretary and special assistant to the ambassador to Italy from 1953 to 1958. In this later assignment Colby worked with Italian political parties to block the expansion of the Italian communist movement.

Colby was named first secretary of the American embassy in South Vietnam in 1959. As CIA station chief in Saigon, he helped develop the strategic hamlet program and directed the organization of Montagnard tribesmen to aid U.S. special forces.

In 1962 Colby was appointed head of the Far East division of the clandestine services, where he presided over the CIA's expanding programs throughout Southeast Asia. Using a private army of more than 30,000 tribal warriors, the agency launched a secret war against the Communists in Laos. It also organized commando-type raids into China and North Korea and conducted bombing operations with its own airline, Air America. Because the effort was not costly and American casualties were low, the operation was not widely known until the end of the decade.

As the United States became increasingly involved in South Vietnam, CIA activities in that area grew. In 1964 Colby oversaw the establishment of the Vietnam Counter Terror program. The operation, carried on solely by U.S.-organized CIA teams, used intimidation, kidnapping, and assassination against the Communist leadership. In 1967 the CIA began still another program, called Operation Phoenix, to coordinate American and Vietnamese attacks on the Communist infrastructure at the village level. Under the program 20,587 suspected Communists were killed in its first two and a half years.

Colby was sent to Saigon in April 1968 to assist ROBERT KOMER, director of Civil Operations and Rural Development Support (CORDS). This program was designed to "win the hearts and minds of the people" through the development of health and social services and the introduction of various economic programs to raise living standards. However, it was eventually coupled with Operation Phoenix and was generally accounted a failure. Colby became director of CORDS in November 1968 when Komer was made ambassador to Turkey.

In June 1971 Colby resigned his post and returned to Washington because of the serious illness of a daughter. He became director-controller of the CIA in January 1972 and was promoted to deputy director for operations in March 1973. At that post he was responsible for organizing the agency's covert actions and secret political operations. In August 1973 the Senate approved his nomination as director of Central Intelligence. A series of major congressional investigations of the agency began late the next year. Colby cooperated with these investigations, which revealed a number of controversial activities, including domestic spying and assassination attempts on foreign leaders. In November 1975 President Ford announced that Colby would be replaced by George Bush. Colby returned to the practice of law, and he became a leading spokesperson for the nuclear freeze movement. He died on April 27, 1996.

—EWS

## Coleman, James S(amuel)
(1926–1995) *sociologist*
A chemical engineer for the Eastman Kodak Company, Coleman who was born in Bedford, Indiana,

on May 12, 1926, began studying sociology as a pastime. He entered Columbia University in 1953 and two years later won a doctorate in his new field. He joined the faculty of Johns Hopkins in 1959.

A provision of the 1964 Civil Rights Act mandated that the U.S. commissioner of education undertake a study of the educational opportunities for minority-group school children. In the fall of 1965 Coleman began such a study and in July 1966 *Equality of Educational Opportunity*, the so-called Coleman Report, appeared. It is often considered the most important education study of the 20th century. The report, based on a study of 4,000 schools, and using data from over 600,000 students and teachers across the country indicated that de facto segregation was widespread throughout the United States. It also concluded that the quality of education for blacks was inferior to that provided to whites. Few blacks, relative to their numbers, attended college; twice as many blacks as whites dropped out of school; and with each succeeding grade, blacks fell further behind their white counterparts in reading ability.

The report indicated that black schools were overcrowded and run-down compared to white schools. However, Coleman attributed the backwardness of black children less to these factors than to the social and educational deficiencies of their environment and their teachers. Coleman and his staff concluded that academic performance was more closely related to the social composition of their schools and the student's comfort level within them, as well as to the student's family background, than to the specific operation of the school itself. Coleman proposed that the social handicaps afflicting black children might be compensated for if they were sent to middle-class white schools. White pupils, he argued, would suffer no appreciable educational loss from association with inner-city children.

His report was bitterly attacked by black leaders, who were coming to believe that efforts to upgrade the quality of inner-city schools should take precedence over attempts to integrate them. The national director of CORE, FLOYD MCKISSICK, condemned the report, saying it suggested, "Mix Negroes with Negroes and you get stupidity." A number of Coleman's fellow sociologists suggested that the report had been hastily compiled and was filled with statistical errors. Nevertheless, others supported it and a 1969 report by the New York State Department of Education tended to uphold Coleman's findings.

Coleman helped draft President RICHARD M. NIXON's 1970 message announcing a planned $1.5 billion appropriation to aid school desegregation in the North and the South. In the mid-1970s Coleman expressed pessimism about the progress of school integration. Court-ordered busing to achieve integration, he argued, had accelerated the migration of whites to the suburbs. He thought the prospect of improved educational opportunities for black children was declining. Coleman remained on the faculty of Johns Hopkins until 1973, when he returned to Chicago to continue his research. In 1981 he released his final report, *Public and Private Schools*, which argued that private schools were providing a better education than their public counterparts, even after family and social background issues were addressed. In 1991 he was elected president of the American Sociological Association. Coleman died in Chicago in March 1995.

—JLW

## Collins, John F(rederick)
### (1919–1995) *mayor*

Born on July 20, 1919, in the Roxbury section of Boston, John F. Collins received his law degree from Suffolk University in 1941. After duty in the Counter Intelligence Corps during World War II, he practiced law and served as a Democrat in the state House of Representatives. Ten days before a November 1955 contest for the Boston City Council, Collins contracted bulbar poliomyelitis. Despite the illness he won election to the council; the disease, however, confined him to a wheelchair for the next 15 years of an active political career. In November 1959 Collins ran as an independent and upset John Powers, a heavily favored organization Democrat, in the Boston mayoralty race.

Collins worked with considerable success to improve the city's financial condition. He cut the city budget and civil service lists and reorganized executive departments. Between 1960 and 1963 his administration reduced property taxes four times. The mayor won reelection easily in November 1963.

As a master builder Collins left a visible mark on his city. The mayor devised the "Prudential Law," passed by the legislature in January 1962 and subsequently copied by many other urban localities. It granted tax relief to the area's larger corporations for the construction of immense, multipurpose headquarters in areas facing economic stagnation

or decline. Collins reorganized the Boston Development Authority, which rebuilt vast sections of the city. One successful venture created a "walkway to the sea," consisting of architecturally distinct government structures and completely renovated buildings extending from Scollay Square to the waterfront. Other projects rebuilt the South Station and Copley Square areas. In August 1967 the city presented plans for a privately financed, $325 million capital improvement of the Back Bay section. In December the John Hancock Life Insurance Co. declared that it would construct a 60-story office tower as the project's central facility.

Despite a reputation for integrity, Collins became involved in an antipoverty project scandal in 1965. For two days in November the Labor Department froze funds for the Neighborhood Youth Corps because of charges that a Collins aide interfered for political reasons in the distribution of Youth Corps monies. A Labor Department investigation, however, failed to prove that Collins had in any way directly participated in the affair.

Collins faced major racial disturbances in Boston during the summer of 1967. Rioting began in Roxbury, a predominantly African-American section of the city, on June 2 after about 30 black mothers staged a sit-in to protest their treatment by a neighborhood city welfare office. Following their eviction by police, a major riot began. Mobs looted 25 stores and set two multiple-alarm fires. The police arrested almost 100, and 60 to 70 injuries were reported. On June 3 Collins termed the riot the "worst manifestation of disrespect for the rights of others this city has ever seen." Black leaders, however, blamed the police for inciting the lawlessness. The riots continued until June 6. The next day Collins told reporters that he would not seek a third term.

Although a Democrat, Collins chaired the Massachusetts Committee for the Reelection of President Nixon in 1972. The former mayor argued that the Bay State should support Nixon, the candidate overwhelmingly favored to win in November, if only for the sake of the state's future relations with Washington. In the general election Massachusetts was the only state carried by Senator GEORGE MCGOVERN (D-S.Dak.). Collins later taught urban affairs at the Massachusetts Institute of Technology, and he remained active in local political issues. He died on November 23, 1995.

—JLB

## Collins, (Thomas) Leroy

(1909–1991) *president, National Association of Broadcasters; Community Relations Service director, Commerce Department; undersecretary of commerce*

Born on March 10, 1909, in Tallahassee, Florida, Leroy Collins served in the Florida legislature for 16 years before becoming governor in 1954. Reelected to a four-year term in 1956, Collins opposed the Supreme Court's desegregation rulings but urged moderation to southern governors anxious to violate the Court's orders. Hailed by many commentators as "the voice of the New South," Collins chaired the 1960 Democratic National Convention. Between 1961 and 1964 he served as president of the National Association of Broadcasters and occasionally criticized the quality of television programs and advertisements.

Upon signing the 1964 Civil Rights Act, President Johnson appointed Collins director of the Community Relations Service (CRS), established by the new rights statute primarily to coordinate and expedite the enforcement of the law's public accommodations section through negotiation with local leaders. (As governor in 1957, Collins had called upon the federal government to create such an agency.) Collins's most notable role as CRS director came in March 1965 as the president's personal representative during the Selma, Alabama, voting rights demonstrations organized by MARTIN LUTHER KING, JR. On March 7 Alabama state troopers and sheriff's deputies physically beat back 500 civil rights activists setting out from Selma for Montgomery, the state capital, to protest the denial of voting rights to blacks. Collins arrived two days later and persuaded King not to risk another bloody confrontation by renewing the march as planned on March 10. He asked the rights leader to wait until a restraining order against the police had been obtained from Federal Circuit Court judge Frank M. Johnson. On March 10 King halted the march just short of the police line outside Selma, although some marchers criticized his acquiescence to Collins's plea. Following the expected favorable ruling from Judge Johnson, the march began again on March 21 and ended in triumph five days later. In Washington on March 25 Collins asked for a "respite" from future civil rights demonstrations in Alabama but added that the ultimate solution was "to correct the basic causes of the demonstrations" through legislation.

Collins left CRS in July 1965 to become undersecretary of commerce. Journeying to Los Angeles in August following the Watts riot, he arranged for the rehabilitation of the stricken areas through the release of $1.77 million of federal antipoverty funds, which had been held up because of a dispute between Mayor SAM YORTY and the local Office of Economic Opportunity. As the president's emissary, Collins participated in the August 1965 steel industry labor contract negotiations, although he did not play a role in the final settlement. He left the Commerce Department on October 1, 1966, to resume his law practice in Tampa, Florida.

In 1968 Collins campaigned unsuccessfully for the Senate seat vacated by Senator GEORGE SMATHERS (D-Fla.) losing in the general election to Republican Edward J. Gurney. Collins retired from politics to practice law in Tallahassee. He died on March 12, 1991.

—JLB

## Colmer, William M(eyers)

(1890–1980) *member of the House of Representatives*

Born in Moss Point, Mississippi, on February 11, 1890, Colmer taught public school until passing the bar in 1917. After interrupting his legal career to serve in World War I, he returned to the law and was elected district attorney of the second district of Mississippi in 1928. In 1932 he was elected to Congress, where he would remain for the next 40 years. Although Colmer supported the New Deal programs of the 1930s, he subsequently became an opponent of social welfare measures, and throughout his career he was a bitter foe of bills directed against racial discrimination. In 1948 he supported the segregationist Dixiecrat ticket in the South, which was headed by Strom Thurmond. In 1960 Colmer refused to support the presidential candidacy of John F. Kennedy because of the civil rights plank in the Democratic Party's national platform. For the rest of his career, Colmer fought against virtually any federal action that threatened to affect race relations in the South.

According to *Congressional Quarterly*, Colmer supported the southern Democrat–Republican conservative coalition on key votes between 64 percent and 92 percent of the time in the years from 1964 through 1968. Like many conservatives, he backed the administration's Vietnam policies. Favoring the prosecution of those who urged youths to evade the draft, he asserted during the spring of 1967 that "sedition, sabotage, and—yes—treason . . . are going on in the country today."

At the beginning of the Johnson administration Colmer was the second-ranking member of the powerful House Rules Committee, through which most bills had to pass on the way from their committee of original jurisdiction to the House floor. In 1966 the committee's chair, Representative HOWARD W. SMITH (D-Va.), lost his reelection bid, and Colmer became the panel's head in January 1967.

When Colmer assumed the committee chair, the House repealed the 21-day reporting rule, adopted two years earlier, which had facilitated the efforts of liberals to circumvent the traditionally conservative committee. Despite the repeal Colmer had less success in blocking liberal legislation than his predecessor. In the 90th Congress the liberals had a nine to six majority on the committee, and Colmer did not possess Smith's formidable parliamentary skills. In addition, before taking his new post Colmer had agreed to hold hearings on fixed days for the purpose of expediting the movement of legislation, a procedure that Smith never followed. Still, he could make things difficult for the administration, especially as it tried to push Great Society legislation; Colmer recalled one of Johnson's chief legislative aides, "voted against just about everything." As a consequence, LBJ and his staff made sure to always keep a very close eye on Colmer and the committee.

On occasion Colmer was able to employ his position as chair to influence the flow and content of legislation. In the spring of 1968, for example, the House Judiciary Committee reported out a gun control bill. He delayed the measure for three weeks until Representative EMMANUEL CELLER (D-N.Y.), chair of the Judiciary Committee, agreed to oppose any attempts to add registration and licensing amendments on the House floor.

In 1972 Colmer announced his retirement from political life. He returned to Mississippi, where he died on September 9, 1980.

—MLL

## Connally, John B(owden), Jr.
(1917–1993) *governor*

Connally was born on February 27, 1917, in Floresville, Texas, and grew up in a poor family near San Antonio. He attended the University of Texas

and was admitted to the Texas bar in 1938. That year he became an aide to Democratic Texas representative LYNDON B. JOHNSON. After serving in the navy during World War II, he managed Johnson's bitterly fought and narrowly successful campaign for the U.S. Senate in 1948.

In 1951 Connally moved to Fort Worth to become an attorney for Sid Richardson, who had made a fortune in the oil industry in the 1930s and in the manufacture of petrochemicals, electronic equipment, and defense-related hardware after World War II. In the process of managing Richardson's empire, Connally accumulated a wide range of Texas business connections and a network of corporate directorships in Richardson-owned firms.

Meanwhile, Connally remained closely linked to the ascending political career of Senator Johnson, who, in the 1950s, became one of the most powerful figures on Capitol Hill. In 1956 he played a key role in helping Johnson capture control of the dominant conservative wing of the Texas Democratic Party from Governor Allan Shivers. Four years later Connally directed Johnson's bid for the Democratic presidential nomination. When Johnson was elected vice president in 1960, Connally was named secretary of the navy by President Kennedy.

Connally served as navy secretary until December 1961, when he resigned to enter the Democratic gubernatorial primary in Texas. He faced bitter opposition from insurgent Democratic liberals, led by Senator RALPH YARBOROUGH, who reviled him as a pillar of the Texas business establishment. Heavily financed by many of the state's business interests and aided by his association with the Kennedy administration, Connally edged his liberal Democratic opponent in a primary runoff election in the spring of 1962 and went on to defeat his Republican rival the following November. He was in the presidential limousine in Dallas on November 22, 1963, when President Kennedy was assassinated. The governor suffered a serious chest wound but soon recovered.

During his three two-year terms as governor, Connally successfully promoted increased expenditures for education and for the mentally ill and retarded. In most other areas, however, his positions offended the intellectuals, labor unions, blacks, and Mexican Americans who formed the major elements of the state's liberal coalition. Connally favored voluntary desegregation but opposed the Kennedy-Johnson public accommodations bill as destructive of "one of our most cherished freedoms—the right to own and manage private property." He was an ardent supporter of President Johnson's Vietnam policies and denounced antiwar demonstrators as "bearded and unwashed prophets of doubt and despair."

Connally administered Great Society programs in Texas without enthusiasm, and he was the first governor to veto a War on Poverty project. He also actively defended the state's right-to-work law, which was vehemently opposed by the Texas AFL-CIO. The governor did not challenge the state's regressive system of taxation, and during his tenure in office the sales tax doubled without corresponding increases in taxes directed at the wealthy. The governor's conservatism, as well as his control over the state party, led to occasional tensions between Connally and Lyndon Johnson, although the two men maintained a working relationship throughout LBJ's years in the White House.

The most dramatic display of Connally's conservatism occurred in 1966, when a group of striking Mexican-American farm workers marched 400 miles from the Rio Grande Valley to Austin to ask the governor to support a minimum farm wage law. Connally drove about 30 miles out of the capital to meet them and explain his opposition to the measure. He then drove away and was not present when the marchers reached Austin. Senator Yarborough, on the other hand, symbolically walked with the marchers for several hundred yards. Texas political observers felt that the governor's handling of the matter had given an impression of personal arrogance and represented a serious political blunder.

Despite the opposition that he aroused, Connally's political position in Texas was strong throughout his governorship and particularly after the assassination of President Kennedy. The injury which he suffered in the presidential limousine generated a great deal of sympathy, but the most important consequence of the assassination for Connally was the accession of Lyndon B. Johnson to the presidency. Connally's association with the new president enhanced the governor's prestige. Furthermore, Johnson wanted left-of-center support and a united Texas Democratic Party in the 1964 national election. Therefore, he attempted to alter his role in Texas politics from conservative factional leader to party conciliator. Johnson was able to bring about a truce early in 1964 by deterring the conservatives from challenging Senator Yarborough's reelection bid. In return the liberals did not give full-scale sup-

port to Connally's primary opponent. Two years later Connally won reelection with little difficulty, capturing 72 percent of the popular vote. In 1968 the truce broke down because Johnson, by then a lame-duck president, had lost much of his influence, but Connally had already announced the previous fall that he would not seek reelection for a fourth term.

In the 1968 presidential election, Connally led the fight for the administration's Vietnam War plank in the party platform. He gave HUBERT HUMPHREY only lukewarm support in the election campaign. He was angered at the Democratic candidate for permitting the convention to drop the unit rule for delegate voting (traditionally a source of power for the Texas conservative establishment) and for refusing to even consider him as a vice presidential running mate.

In 1969 Connally returned to private practice with a leading Texas law firm. Two years later he entered the Nixon administration as secretary of the Treasury. In that post he played a major role in implementing President Nixon's wage and price control program. He resigned his cabinet post in May 1972.

Two months later, immediately after the Democratic National Convention had chosen Senator GEORGE MCGOVERN (D-S.Dak.) as the party's national standard bearer, Connally denounced the nominee's economic and military policies and endorsed President Nixon's reelection bid. He switched his allegiance to the Republican Party in May 1973. Later in the month Connally became a special adviser to the president but resigned after only two months. In July 1974 the Watergate grand jury indicted Connally for bribery and perjury in connection with an increase in federal milk price supports during his tenure as Treasury secretary. He was acquitted in April 1975. In 1980 he ran a brief campaign for the Republican nomination for president, but was unsuccessful. He returned to his career in law and real estate development, which included a bankruptcy declaration in the early 1980s that stemmed largely from the collapse of the oil market. Connally died in Houston on June 15, 1993.

—MLL

## Connor, John T(homas)
### (1914–2000) *secretary of commerce*

Connor was born on November 3, 1914, in Syracuse, New York, and graduated from Harvard Law

School. He joined the New York law firm of Cravath, de Gersdorff, Swaine & Wood in 1939. He went to Washington in 1942 to serve as general counsel for the Office of Scientific Research and Development, where he set up a program for the development and production of penicillin that involved a large number of government, university, and commercial laboratories. As special assistant to Secretary of the Navy James V. Forrestal from 1945 to 1947, Connor dismantled the military penicillin program to integrate it into the private economy.

Connor joined one of the largest drug manufacturers, Merck & Company, in 1947 as general attorney and became its president in 1955. He ably defended the firm before Senator Estes Kefauver's (D-Tenn.) investigation of the drug industry at the end of the 1950s. During his 10 years as president Connor expanded Merck's investments in foreign plants by 450 percent.

A founder and co-chair of the National Independent Committee for Johnson-Humphrey in 1964, Connor was appointed secretary of commerce by President Johnson in January 1965. His principal activities as commerce secretary lay less in the shaping of administration policy than in the selling of Johnson's programs to the business community.

Connor's chief preoccupation was the balance of payments deficit, which had averaged $3 billion annually from 1958 through 1964. A 15 percent tax on American investments abroad was seriously discussed within the administration as a possible antidote. Connor argued against this measure, and his success in substituting a program of voluntary business cooperation in reversing the dollar outflow, was the major achievement in his two-year tenure in office.

The voluntary approach involved Connor's asking the top management of each of the 500 largest U.S. corporations doing business abroad to improve its balance of payments position by 15 percent to 20 percent in 1965. He suggested several means: a company could increase its exports, raise capital from foreign sources, repatriate funds held abroad, or postpone planned investments overseas. Connor won a significant degree of business cooperation with the program, but its effect on the balance of payments was below expectations. The deficit for 1965 was $1.3 billion, down from $2.8 billion in 1965, but in 1966 the program reduced the deficit by only $900 million (compared to the anticipated $3.4 billion reduction).

On the whole Connor's voice carried less weight in economic policy councils than that of Secretary of the Treasury HENRY FOWLER or the chair of the Council of Economic Advisers, GARDNER ACKLEY.

During the aluminum price rise dispute between the industry and the federal government in the fall of 1965, Connor argued within the administration that the increase was not unjustified. He opposed the administration's decision to make a public confrontation and to use the sale of the government's aluminum stockpiles as an economic weapon. Connor was also unenthusiastic about the administration's 3.2 percent guidelines for wages and prices. And he was LBJ's only cabinet adviser to urge a tax increase in early 1966 to head off inflation. He played an important role, however, in the settlements of the East Coast dock strike in February 1965 and the General Electric employees' strike in October 1966.

Connor resigned as commerce secretary in January 1967 to become president of the Allied Chemical Corporation. He remained with the firm until his 1979 retirement. He died of cancer on October 6, 2000, in Massachusetts.

—TO

## Conte, Silvio O(cttavio)

(1921–1991) *member of the House of Representatives*

Born on November 9, 1921, in Pittsfield, Massachusetts, Silvio O. Conte graduated from Pittsfield Vocational High School in 1940 and briefly worked as a machinist for General Electric. A U.S. Navy seabee during World War II, Conte earned a law degree from Boston College in 1949. The following year he won election to the Massachusetts Senate and served there for eight years.

In 1958 Conte ran for the U.S. House in Massachusetts's First District against James MacGregor Burns, a Williams College political science professor, biographer, and close political associate of Senator John F. Kennedy. Despite a strong statewide Democratic tide, the bitterly fought struggle ended with Conte the victor with 55 percent of the vote. He easily won reelection in 1960 and 1962. The Democrats did not oppose his candidacy in 1964, 1966, or 1968.

Conte retained his office in a Democratic region largely because of his independent-minded, liberal Republicanism. He refused to endorse his party's conservative 1964 presidential nominee, Senator BARRY M. GOLDWATER (R-Ariz.), who netted only 25.9 percent of the vote cast for president in the first district. With other members of the liberal House GOP "Wednesday Club," Conte planned the removal of Representative CHARLES A. HALLECK (R-Ind.) and his replacement by Representative GERALD FORD (R-Mich.) as minority leader following the Goldwater defeat.

In his House votes Conte steered an especially nonpartisan course. During the 89th Congress, Conte supported the Johnson administration on 67 percent of all the votes for which the president had announced a position. In 1966 only one other GOP representative—Representative OGDEN R. REID (R-N.Y.)—supported Johnson more frequently. During the 90th Congress Conte voted with the Republican leadership 44 percent of the time, compared to a *Congressional Quarterly* average of 70 percent for all House Republicans.

Conte proved especially sympathetic to the Johnson administration's foreign aid programs. During Johnson's presidency he served on the House Appropriations Committee's Foreign Operations Subcommittee, the panel responsible for foreign aid authorizations. Although GOP members grew increasingly hostile to administration foreign assistance requests, Conte consistently defended the need for overseas aid. In December 1963 he attempted to restore $20 million cut by the subcommittee from the administration's request but lost in two separate votes. Later in the month only two Republican House members—Conte and Representative JOHN V. LINDSAY (R-N.Y.)—supported the president's request for a federal guarantee for the financing of trade with Communist nations. The measure passed, 189-158.

In late 1967 Conte broke with Johnson over U.S. military assistance to undeveloped nations. In November the House agreed to a Conte-sponsored ban on the use of military aid monies for "sophisticated" offensive weapons systems to all foreign assistance countries except seven bordering the Soviet Union and China. Conte feared the possibility of a Latin American or South Asian nuclear arms race. Johnson unsuccessfully tried to block the amendment.

Conte continued to be reelected by Massachusetts voters. He also consistently fought against attempts to restrict congressional powers, especially regarding the budget, opposing such measures as the 1985 Gramm-Rudman-Hollings Act and the Budget Reconciliation Act of 1974, along with proposals like a line-item veto for the president. Conte died on February 8, 1991.

—JLB

## Conyers, John, Jr.
(1929– ) *member of the House of Representatives*

Born on May 16, 1929, in Detroit, Michigan, Conyers served as an army officer during the Korean War and earned a law degree in 1958. He worked as Representative John Dingell's (D-Mich.) legislative assistant until October 1961, when he was appointed a referee for the Michigan Workmen's Compensation Department. During the early 1960s Conyers was also general counsel for the Trade Union Leadership Council (TULC), an influential organization of black unionists who pressed civil rights and minority representation demands within the UAW and other Detroit-area unions. After the Michigan legislature created a new, predominantly black congressional district in Detroit, Conyers declared his candidacy in January 1964. He was backed by a militant section of the TULC but opposed by most UAW officials, the Detroit Democratic Party organization, and the formal leadership of the TULC. After mobilizing a force of 2,000 volunteers Conyers defeated his black opponent by a narrow margin in the June 1964 primary. Easily elected in November, Conyers was one of six black members of Congress seated in January 1965 and was the first black representative appointed to the House Judiciary Committee.

Conyers helped sponsor the 1965 Voting Rights Act and later demanded its vigorous enforcement. In June 1966 he organized a group of eight northern representatives who traveled to Mississippi to observe the June 7 primary election there. At a press conference held the next day, Conyers stated that in his opinion the Voting Rights Act was being "minimally enforced" and that it would take 15 to 25 years "to have full voting at the present rate." He demanded that more federal registrars be sent to the South. During the summer of 1967 Conyers returned to Mississippi to encourage voting in four counties where black candidates were running for office. He was also one of the founders of the Congressional Black Caucus in 1969.

An honorary co-chair of the American Civil Liberties Union's national advisory board, Conyers strongly opposed legislation he regarded as anticivil libertarian. He denounced the District of Columbia Crime bill as "monstrous" in October 1966 and declared it "appropriate only in a most totalitarian society." Conyers said provisions in the bill making it easier for the police to detain suspects "returns us to a system of indiscriminatory [*sic.*] investigative arrests." He predicted that the section of the bill requiring mandatory minimum sentences would cause sympathetic juries to acquit guilty persons. Despite the objections of Conyers and other liberal Democrats, both the House and Senate passed the bill in October 1966. President Johnson pocket-vetoed the bill in November 1966.

An early opponent of the Vietnam War, Conyers was one of 16 Democratic members of Congress who signed a March 16, 1965, letter to President Johnson opposing the use of biological and chemical weapons in the Southeast Asian war. On May 5, 1965, he was one of seven representatives who voted against a supplemental Vietnam appropriation, and he continued to oppose funding of the conflict during the remaining years of American involvement in the war.

In January 1967 Conyers became the only black member of a special House committee appointed to investigate charges of misconduct brought against Representative ADAM CLAYTON POWELL, JR. (D-N.Y.). While he claimed that race had been part of the reason for Powell's investigation, he also insisted that it had not played a role on the committee itself. In January 1969, after Powell had been reelected by his Harlem constituency, Conyers helped formulate a compromise resolution that refrained from censuring Powell but fined him $25,000 for misuse of funds and stripped him of his seniority in the House.

Most of the unprecedented urban violence that Detroit experienced in July 1967 took place in Conyers's district. On July 24, one day after the rioting began, Conyers mounted a parked car and urged the crowd to return to their homes. He was hooted down, and two days later his district offices were sacked. On July 30 Conyers joined other black political leaders to demand an investigation of charges of police brutality during the riot.

During the 1968 presidential campaign Conyers chaired the National Committee of Inquiry, a group of nearly 1,000 prominent black leaders formed to make recommendations to black voters. On October 13 the group met and failed to endorse HUBERT HUMPHREY's presidential candidacy. At a news conference the next day, Conyers said the group would support Humphrey only if he took an unequivocal stand against the Vietnam War and made convincing pledges to help solve the problems of black people. Conyers continued to support the civil rights and antiwar movements during the Nixon years and afterward. He also played a key role in the successful fights against the confirmation of Clement Haynsworth and G. Harrold Carswell as Supreme Court justices in 1969 and 1970. He has also championed various hate crime and voter registration measures, consistently supported health care reforms designed to create universal health care, and wrote the Martin Luther King Holiday Act of 1983.

—DKR

## Cooley, Harold D(unbar)

(1897–1974)  *member of the House of Representatives*

Cooley was born on July 26, 1897, in Wilson, North Carolina. A graduate of the University of North Carolina and Yale Law School, he practiced law until a special 1934 election sent him to Congress. He became chair of the House Agriculture Committee in 1949 and became the chief congressional spokesperson for the Democratic Party's high price support policy. Cooley was the most loyal supporter of President Johnson in the North Carolina House delegation, and, as chair of the House Agriculture Committee, he introduced the administration's major farm bills. Cooley helped secure passage of a permanent food-stamp program in 1964 and successfully opposed conservative efforts to require states to pay half the costs. He managed the 1965 omnibus farm bill, one of the administration's biggest legislative victories, and wrote the provisions for a new cotton program included in the farm bill. The cotton provisions included direct income-support payments to farmers and an acreage diversion program to reduce production. Cooley also favored the administration's food distribution programs abroad. He helped push the administration's 1966 Food-for-Peace legislation through the House.

In the area of sugar legislation, however, Cooley did not side with the administration, since he had long been closely associated with Atlantic and

Gulf Coast cane sugar refiners and the Latin American exporting countries. In 1965 proponents of western beet sugar interests, who wanted to increase their production quotas, charged that foreign lobbyists exerted undue influence over Cooley, an accusation that he strenuously denied. Despite his difficulties with domestic producers, he arranged a compromise between them and the refiners in the Sugar Act of 1965. The measure increased the domestic quota immediately but granted the first 700,000 tons of the growth of the market above 9.7 million tons a year to foreign imports exclusively. In addition, Cooley successfully persuaded the administration to drop its plans to impose a special import fee on sugar.

Early in 1966 the North Carolina legislature reapportioned the state's congressional districts, and, in the November elections, Cooley was upset by a youthful Republican challenger, James C. Gardner, who had stressed Cooley's advanced age during the campaign. Cooley subsequently retired to his tobacco farm. He died in Wilson, North Carolina, on January 15, 1974.

—JCH

## Cooper, John S(herman)
### (1901–1991) *member of the Senate*

Cooper, who was born in Somerset, Kentucky, on August 23, 1901, began his political career in Kentucky's state legislature after earning a B.A. from Yale and a law degree from Harvard. In 1930 he became a judge at the county level. For several years in the 1940s and 1950s, he served on the circuit court, gaining a reputation as the "Poor Man's Judge." During this period he also served as a UN delegate, as ambassador to India and Nepal, and, most important as U.S. senator. Cooper won special elections to fill Senate vacancies in 1946, 1952, and 1956 although he lost two regular Senate elections held during that period. During these years, he was one of the strongest congressional critics of the tactics of his fellow Republican, Joseph McCarthy (R-Wisc.). Elected to his first full term in 1960, Cooper's. liberal voting record led President Kennedy to call him "an outstanding Republican."

Cooper considered himself a champion of small business and agriculture. During Senate hearings on a coal mine safety bill backed by the United Mine Workers, he testified on behalf of the operators of small mines. His amendment in March 1966 to render safety laws inapplicable if found "not to contribute to the safety of small mines" was defeated. He objected to legislation in April 1965 authorizing the Federal Trade Commission to regulate cigarette advertising as an unjustified expansion of the agency's power. He was successful in attaining greater state and local control over the Volunteers in Service to America (VISTA).

Cooper was one of three Republicans on the Senate Rules and Administration Committee who investigated presidential aide BOBBY BAKER in 1964. Cooper called the investigation "a whitewash" and opposed the committee's decision to block further hearings. His proposal for the establishment of a Senate Select Committee on Standards and Conduct passed in July 1964, and he was named to the committee in July 1965. He also served on the Warren Commission that investigated the assassination of President John F. Kennedy.

Cooper was a leading Republican critic of U.S. involvement in Vietnam. President Johnson sent him, along with AVERELL HARRIMAN and Secretary of State DEAN RUSK, to the Philippines to meet with President Ferdinand Marcos in the administration's widely publicized "peace drive" of January 1966. Later that month Cooper criticized the renewed bombing of North Vietnam. In August 1967 he supported Senator MIKE MANSFIELD's (D-Mont.) proposal to bring the matter before the UN and in a Senate speech called for the United States to make the first move toward negotiations by unconditionally ending the bombing of North Vietnam. He joined Senator ERNEST GRUENING (D-Ala.) and Senator WAYNE MORSE (D-Ore.), two of the Senate's leading doves, in protesting a capitol safety bill that prohibited orderly demonstrations on the Capitol grounds. During the February 1968 hearings on the Gulf of Tonkin Resolution, Cooper stated he did not believe that the incident had been provoked by the United States but that the nature and scope of the attack had not been sufficient to justify the adoption of the original resolution in 1964.

In 1970 Cooper and Senator FRANK CHURCH (D-Idaho) sponsored an amendment prohibiting the use of U.S. troops in Cambodia. Cooper, at age 71, retired from the Senate in 1972. After leaving the Senate, he served as U.S. ambassador to the German Democratic Republic. John Cooper died in Washington, D.C., on February 21, 1991.

—MDB

## Cox, Archibald
### (1912–2004) *U.S. Solicitor General*

Born on May 17, 1912, in Plainfield, New Jersey, and a graduate of Harvard College in 1934 and of Harvard Law School in 1937, Cox spent several years in private practice in Boston. He then held several government posts during World War II, including that of an attorney in the Solicitor General's office from 1941 to 1943 and associate solicitor in the Department of Labor from 1943 to 1945. In the latter year Cox began teaching at Harvard Law School, becoming a professor in 1946. His writings on labor law over the next 15 years established him as an expert in the field. Cox chaired two wage stabilization commissions during the Korean War, arbitrated both New England and national labor disputes during the 1950s, and served as a consultant to Senator John F. Kennedy on labor legislation. He headed a research and speech-writing team for Kennedy during the 1960 presidential campaign and was named U.S. Solicitor General by Kennedy in December 1960.

As U.S. Solicitor General, the third-ranking post in the Justice Department, Cox was responsible for all U.S. government litigation in the Supreme Court and decided which cases the government should appeal. Brilliant and self-confident, Cox was known as a tireless worker and an efficient administrator. In both briefs and oral arguments before the Supreme Court, Cox was thorough, precise, and effective.

Cox had intervened in the case of *Baker v. Carr* in 1961, and, in March 1962, the Supreme Court ruled, as he had urged, that federal courts could try legislative apportionment cases. The U.S. government again appeared as a friend of the Court in suits challenging the legislative districting in six states in November and December 1963. Cox argued that in all six cases the current apportionment should be found unconstitutional. The Court agreed with him in its June 1964 ruling and went on to mandate a "one-person, one-vote" standard for apportionment. In August 1964 Senator EVERETT M. DIRKSEN (R-Ill.) introduced a bill to stay federal court action in state legislative apportionment cases for periods of up to four years. Cox joined in the negotiations to work out a compromise measure to replace the Dirksen proposal. Although an alternative bill was developed, it was filibustered in the Senate in August and September 1964.

In October 1964 Cox argued in the Supreme Court in support of the constitutionality of the public accommodations section of the 1964 Civil Rights Act. The Court unanimously upheld the law in December 1964. He also took the lead role in *Buckley vs. Valeo*, which helped reform the nation's campaign finance system. Cox resigned as solicitor general in July 1965 after arguing 67 cases in the Supreme Court, more than any other living person. He went back to teaching at Harvard Law School but returned to the Supreme Court to argue several cases as a private attorney. In January 1966 he joined Attorney General NICHOLAS KATZENBACH in urging the Court to sustain the 1965 Voting Rights Act.

In May 1968 Cox was appointed head of a five-member commission to investigate the causes of disturbances at Columbia University that spring. The commission held 21 days of hearings. Its October 1968 report strongly criticized the university administration for conveying an "attitude of authoritarianism" in its dealings with students. The Cox Commission also scored the New York City police for using excessive force against students in the April demonstrations and condemned the disruptive tactics used by the students as a threat to a free university.

In later years Cox represented welfare clients in several significant Supreme Court cases involving the rights of welfare recipients. He was named special prosecutor for the Watergate case by Attorney General Elliott L. Richardson, one of his former law students, in May 1973. When Cox subpoenaed the secretly recorded audiotapes made by President Nixon, the president refused, and ordered Richardson to fire him. The attorney general resigned rather than carry out the order, as did his assistant, Attorney General William Ruckelshaus. The order was then carried out by the U.S. Solicitor General, Robert Bork. This event, which became known as the "Saturday Night Massacre," helped turn public opinion against the president. Cox returned to teaching law at Boston University and Harvard, and he remained a leading voice in calling for campaign finance reform and government ethics laws. Cox died in Brooksville, Maine, on May 29, 2004.

—CAB

## Cox, W(illiam) Harold
### (1901–1988) *U.S. district judge, Southern District of Mississippi*

Cox was born on June 23, 1901, in Indianda, Mississippi, and graduated from the University of Mississippi. He practiced law in Jackson, Mississippi, from 1924 to 1961 and was active in local Democratic politics. At the urging of Senator JAMES EASTLAND (D-Miss.), who was an old and close friend of Cox's, President Kennedy appointed Cox to a district court judgeship in Mississippi in 1961. Cox quickly emerged as a strongly segregationist jurist whose rulings obstructed the activities of the Justice Department and civil rights workers in the South.

Cox did order the integration of a Jackson restaurant chain in January 1966, and in a suit for damages against the Ku Klux Klan brought by relatives of an African American who was murdered in 1966, the judge condemned the murder and directed a verdict for the plaintiffs. These were exceptions, however, to Cox's usual pattern of rulings in civil rights cases. On March 6, 1964, he voted to uphold the constitutionality of Mississippi's voting laws in a Justice Department suit challenging the statutes as discriminatory. The *New York Times* reported on March 9, 1964, that Cox referred to blacks trying to register to vote in Canton, Mississippi, as "a bunch of niggers" and said they were "acting like a bunch of chimpanzees." The remarks prompted an unsuccessful attempt by NAACP official AARON HENRY and other Mississippi civil rights leaders to have Cox disqualified from handling any more civil rights cases. It also sparked a failed impeachment drive, led by New York senator Jacob Javits.

During a suit involving voter discrimination in Clarke County, Mississippi, Cox wanted perjury charges pressed against two black witnesses he felt were lying. After a probe by the Federal Bureau of Investigation, the Justice Department advised Cox that there was no basis for prosecution. When Cox insisted on the prosecution, Attorney General NICHOLAS KATZENBACH ordered the U.S. attorney in Mississippi not to sign indictments against the two blacks. Cox responded in October 1964 by holding the local U.S. attorney in contempt of court and threatening Katzenbach with the same. In January 1965 the Fifth Circuit Court overturned Cox's action. The judge dismissed a Justice Department suit to integrate a Gulf Coast beach in March 1966, asserting that the beach was privately owned, and, in December, he voted to hold federal school desegregation guidelines unconstitutional.

Cox's most famous case grew out of the murder of Andrew Goodman, Michael Schwerner, and James Chaney, three civil rights workers who were reported missing on June 21, 1964. After a massive federal investigation their bodies were uncovered six weeks later in an earthen dam near Philadelphia, Mississippi. In January 1965 a federal grand jury in Jackson indicted 18 people, including the county deputy sheriff, for the murders on charges of violating federal civil rights laws. A month later Cox dismissed most counts of the indictment, causing an outcry among civil rights activists. The U.S. Supreme Court unanimously reversed Cox's decision and reinstated the charges in March 1966. The charges were again dropped for technical reasons at the Justice Department's request, but a new indictment against 19 men was handed down in February 1967. In October an all-white jury convicted seven of the defendants. Cox sentenced them to prison terms ranging from three to 10 years, but he also made all the sentences "indeterminate," thus qualifying all seven for immediate consideration for parole. Cox died while still in office on February 25, 1988.

—CAB

## Cramer, William C(ato)

(1922–2003) *member of the House of Representatives*

Born on August 4, 1922, in Denver, Colorado, William Cato Cramer moved at age three to St. Petersburg, Florida, with his family. After serving in the navy during World War II, Cramer graduated from the University of North Carolina Phi Beta Kappa in 1946. He earned his law degree in two years at Harvard. Returning to St. Petersburg Cramer successfully led the revitalization of the long-dormant Pinellas County Republican Party. In 1950 he won election to the state House of Representatives and served as minority leader. Four years later the 32-year-old Cramer became the first Republican representative elected from Florida since 1875. He easily won reelection through the 1960s. His early success and statewide partisan labors made him, journalist Neal Peirce observed, "virtually the founding father of the present-day Republican Party in Florida."

In the House Cramer almost always voted with conservatives. He opposed the 1964 Civil Rights Act and annual appropriations for the administration's antipoverty program. Cramer also voted against such Great Society measures as highway beautification, food stamps, mass transit, and model cities. The Americans for Democratic Action gave him zero ratings for the 1965, 1966, and 1968 sessions. In an unusual move, however, Cramer supported the 1965 Voting Rights Act that prohibited voting practices that discriminated against minorities. Only one other southern Republican shared Cramer's position.

Cramer played an important role in framing the final draft of the 1968 Civil Rights Act on open housing. During the first debates on the bill in August 1966 and amidst the third consecutive summer of racial rioting in the cities, he offered an amendment making it a crime to travel in interstate commerce with the intention to incite a riot or commit an act of violence. The Cramer amendment passed by an overwhelming 389-25 margin. When the Senate failed to take action on the parent open housing measure, he presented his original amendment as a separate bill in early 1967. Cramer and his cosponsors pressured Judiciary Committee chair EMMANUEL CELLER (D-N.Y.), who originally opposed the proposal, into holding hearings on the measure. The Celler panel reported favorably on the bill, which the House passed in July 1967 by a 347-70 vote. Defending his legislation, Cramer declared in July that it was "aimed at those professional agitators," traveling from city to city, who "inflame the people . . . to violence and then leave the jurisdiction before the riot begins." Again the Senate failed to act, but the final open housing law, passed in April 1968, included Cramer's provision. Cramer, who had never planned to vote for an open housing bill, supported the measure because of his own part in its preparation. Also in 1968, Cramer successfully sponsored an amendment that expanded the Federal Aid Highway Act.

Until 1970 Cramer all but dominated the Florida GOP. Beginning in 1964 he represented the state on the Republican National Committee, and its chair, RAY C. BLISS, appointed Cramer to the GOP's policy-making National Coordinating Committee. The 1966 election of a Republican governor, CLAUDE R. KIRK, JR., however, opened a contest for control of the state party. In 1970 Kirk, himself a candidate for reelection, worked against Cramer's primary campaign for the senatorial nomination. Cramer won, but both he and Kirk were defeated in the November general election. Cramer returned to Florida, but he continued to play a part in Republican politics on both a state and national level. He

died in St. Petersburg, Florida, on October 18, 2003.

—JLB

## Cronkite, Walter L(eland)
(1916–  )  *CBS News correspondent*

Cronkite, who was born on November 4, 1916, in St. Joseph, Missouri, attended the University of Texas at Austin for two years while simultaneously working as the state capital reporter for the Scripps-Howard Bureau in 1935 and 1936. During World War II Cronkite had a distinguished career as a correspondent for United Press International. He joined the Columbia Broadcasting System in July 1950 as a member of the network's Washington staff and soon became one of its most important correspondents, acting as anchor for the 1952 and 1956 political conventions. Cronkite also served as moderator for such popular CBS programs of the 1950s as *You Are There* and the *Morning Show*. He became the anchor of the *CBS Evening News* in April 1962. In September 1963, the broadcast expanded from 15 to 30 minutes.

During the mid-1960s Cronkite's ratings dropped as a result of the popularity of NBC's Huntley-Brinkley news program, and he was removed from his customary position as anchor for the 1964 political conventions. His eclipse was temporary, however.

The Vietnam War was one of the most important stories that Cronkite covered during the 1960s. By the middle of the 1960s a majority of Americans said that television was their principal source of news. Cronkite won considerable praise for his balanced reporting, although, privately, like many Americans, he supported the Johnson administration's policies when the first declared U.S. combat troops went to South Vietnam in 1965. Cronkite's views about the war gradually shifted, especially after the enemy's Tet offensive, which began on January 30, 1968. Cronkite visited Vietnam and witnessed some of the heavy fighting. On February 27, in a special, prime-time report, Cronkite declared that the war was a stalemate and that the United States would most likely have to accept a negotiated settlement. Johnson despaired, "If I've lost Cronkite, I've lost the country."

During the August 1968 Democratic National Convention held in Chicago, Cronkite angrily described on the air police attacks on demonstrators

Walter Cronkite seated at his desk for *The Morning Show,* 1954 *(Library of Congress, Prints and Photographs Division)*

and journalists. Subsequently, he conducted an interview with Chicago mayor RICHARD DALEY in which Daley stated that the riots were led by "hard-core" radicals.

Renowned for a relaxed manner and a lucid style that was especially evident during "live" events, Cronkite's evening news program was broadcast by over 200 affiliated stations and led the competition with an estimated audience of 26 million by 1973. For years he was known as "the most trusted man in America." He retired from CBS in 1981, but remained active in the television field on many levels.

—FHM

## Curran, Joseph E(dwin)

(1906–1981) *president, National Maritime Union*

Born in New York City on March 1, 1906, Curran went to sea at the age of 16. In 1935 he led a strike aboard the S.S. *California.* The ship's crew was eventually fired, but an East Coast maritime's strike in their support, although unsuccessful, led to the formation of the National Maritime Union (NMU). Curran was elected the first NMU president in 1937, a post he held for the next 36 years. Virtually all of the other top union posts were held by Communist Party members who had been leaders in organizing the union. Curran worked closely with them until 1946, when he began a successful purge of Communist influence from the union. In that year he allied himself with a group of NMU officials who recently had been expelled from the Commu-

nist Party in a successful effort to defeat Maritime Union officials still close to the party and amended the union constitution to specifically prohibit the membership of any Communists. Later purges led by Curran eliminated other opposition leaders, including his earlier allies.

In October 1960 Secretary of Labor James P. Mitchell, acting under provisions of the 1959 Landrum-Griffin Act, brought suit to have Curran's 1960 reelection invalidated because of election irregularities. The following year Mitchell's successor, ARTHUR J. GOLDBERG, dropped the suit in return for a stipulation in which Curran admitted some charges and agreed that future elections would be held in accordance with the law.

The deterioration of the U.S. passenger and merchant fleets was one of Curran's main concerns during the Johnson administration. Curran supported government regulations that required the preferential use of U.S. ships as one way of preventing the further decline of U.S. shipping. In February 1964 he supported a boycott by the International Longshoremen's Association (ILA) of U.S. wheat being shipped to the Soviet Union. The boycott was called after the federal government waived a requirement that 50 percent of the wheat be shipped in U.S. vessels. The ILA, the NMU, and the Seafarers' International Union (SIU) jointly demanded that the grain firms be forced to abide by the original 50 percent requirement and that guarantees be given that none of the wheat would be transshipped to Cuba. The boycott ended after nine days, when President Johnson agreed that in the future 50 percent of the grain shipped to the USSR would be carried in U.S. ships, although contracts already signed would not be changed.

In July 1964 President Johnson appointed Curran to a new, predominantly non-government Maritime Advisory Committee, headed by Secretary of Commerce JOHN T. CONNOR. A subcommittee of this group, headed by labor arbitrator Theodore W. Kheel, recommended in June 1965 that the then current system of operating subsidies for U.S. merchant and passenger ships be continued and extended. On October 4 another group, the all-government Interagency Maritime Task Force, established June 10 and headed by Undersecretary of Commerce ALAN S. BOYD, recommended the elimination of subsidies for passenger vessels, a gradual phasing out of cargo preference laws, and an "application of maximum automation [to U.S.

ships] at as fast a rate as technology will permit."
The Task Force report was immediately and unanimously rejected by the Maritime Advisory Committee, and Curran called for the resignation of Maritime Committee administrator Nicholas Johnson, who backed the Task Force program. Shortly thereafter, Vice President HUBERT H. HUMPHREY declared that the Task Force report was not official administration policy. Although on November 30 the Advisory Committee accepted with few changes its subcommittee report, President Johnson did not propose any new maritime policy that year, as he had originally intended to do.

Three years later, however, the administration did offer a new program, presented to a congressional subcommittee in May 1968 by Boyd, who was then serving as the first secretary of transportation. The new plan included an end to passenger ship subsidies, reform of the merchant fleet operating subsidy program to limit it to legitimate national defense needs, and the transfer of the Maritime Administration to the Department of Transportation. Curran, who headed the AFL-CIO Maritime Committee as well as the NMU, condemned Boyd's proposal. Following widespread criticism of the administration proposal, Congress took no action on it.

In February 1966 Curran, SIU president Paul Hall and ILA president THOMAS W. GLEASON announced that their unions would boycott foreign ships that traded with North Vietnam. In August of that year Curran backed WALTER P. REUTHER in opposing an AFL-CIO Executive Committee resolution commending the American Institute for Free Labor Development (AIFLD), an AFL-CIO sponsored group that worked with Latin American trade unions. Reuther's brother Victor had earlier charged that the AIFLD had close ties to the Central Intelligence Agency. The AFL-CIO Executive Committee passed the resolution by a vote of 23-2.

In June 1966 Curran was reelected to his 13th term as NMU president, running unopposed on the ballot. A strong anti-Curran ticket led by James Morrissey contested other union offices, and Morrissey himself won one-third of the vote for secretary-treasurer. The opposition group charged that there had been election irregularities and illegal restrictions on candidates. In September Morrissey was badly beaten outside of the NMU headquarters. Secretary of Labor W. WILLARD WIRTZ brought suit in December, asking for a new election under changed rules that allowed members other than

those who had served at least one full term as a salaried union official to run for national office. On April 18, 1968, federal judge CONSTANCE BAKER MOTLEY ruled that the election procedures had violated the Landrum-Griffin Act and ordered a new election, to be supervised by the secretary of labor. In this election Curran, running against three opponents, was reelected by a 17,395 to 4,891 vote, and his full slate of supporters was victorious.

Curran retired as NMU president in March 1973. He died on August 14, 1981.

—JBF

## Curtis, Carl T(homas)
(1905–2000) *member of the Senate*

Curtis was born near Minden, Nebraska, on March 15, 1905, and practiced law in Minden beginning in 1930. He was elected to the U.S. Senate from Nebraska in 1954 after having served in the lower house of Congress since 1939. Representing a largely rural and consistently conservative state, Curtis was one of the Senate's most frequent opponents of social welfare programs during the 1950s and early 1960s.

Curtis opposed almost all of the Johnson administration's Great Society programs, and according to *Congressional Quarterly*, he never voted against the southern Democrat–Republican conservative coalition on more than 3 percent of the key roll-call votes during any year of President Johnson's tenure. He did, however, support the cloture vote in favor of the 1964 Civil Rights Act.

While opposing domestic spending measures, Curtis did not criticize large military expenditures. In 1964 he dissented from the majority of his colleagues on the Government Operations Committee's Permanent Investigations Subcommittee, who contended that the government had been paying Western Electric excessive profits for work on missile contracts farmed out to subcontractors. Three years later, during a debate on raising the national debt ceiling, Curtis asserted that domestic civilian spending, not the military budget, was responsible for increases in the debt.

Curtis supported the administration's Southeast Asia policies and voted in favor of supplementary funds for conducting the Vietnam War. In 1968 he successfully proposed an amendment to a National Aeronautics and Space Administration (NASA) funding bill that barred NASA, with certain exceptions, from using research and development monies at colleges where antiwar demonstrators had blocked U.S. Armed Forces recruiters from campus.

Curtis was a consistent supporter of the Nixon administration. Even after the president, in August 1974, revealed his participation in the Watergate coverup, Curtis refused to call for his removal. In 1975 he became chair of the Senate Republican Conference. He retired in 1979 and returned to Lincoln, Nebraska, to practice law. He died on January 24, 2000.

—MLL

## Curtis, Thomas B(radford)
### (1911–1993) *member of the House of Representatives*

Thomas Curtis was born on May 14, 1911, in St. Louis and grew up in Webster Groves, a nearly suburb. After graduating from Dartmouth College and Washington University Law School, he joined his father's law firm in 1935. He made a number of unsuccessful bids for public office before his election to Congress in 1950 as a Republican from Missouri's Twelfth District, which encompassed most of suburban St. Louis County. Joining the House Ways and Means Committee in 1953, Curtis gradually established himself as a leading Republican congressional spokesperson on economic policy. During the Kennedy administration, Curtis's resolute fiscal conservatism led him frequently to oppose welfare, defense, and revenue measures that he believed contributed to unbalanced budgets.

As a member of the Joint Economic Committee and as second-ranking Republican on the Ways and Means Committee, Curtis was often at odds with the Johnson administration on economic issues. He was a vigorous opponent of the Kennedy-Johnson Medicare program, which financed medical care for the aged through the Social Security system. In January 1965 Curtis sponsored the American Medical Association's (AMA) alternative "eldercare" plan. The AMA plan would have made the program voluntary for those over 65; it would have been financed by individual contributions and matching state and federal grants and administered by the states. The Ways and Means Committee rejected the AMA-Curtis proposal in favor of the Kennedy-Johnson version.

Curtis often carried his opposition to federal spending beyond that of many conservatives, who usually backed compromise appropriations bills and considered military spending an imperative. In March 1964 he voted against salary increases for federal employees and in June opposed raises for federal judges and members of Congress. He also voted against the appropriations for foreign aid and the Departments of Labor and Health, Education and Welfare. In July 1966 Curtis was one of only two members of Congress to oppose a $17 billion authorization for military procurement and research.

Refusing to support higher taxes in lieu of spending cuts, Curtis was against many of President Johnson's revenue-raising requests. He opposed the "interest equalization tax," a levy on foreign securities intended to cut the balance of payments deficit by making it more expensive for foreigners to borrow in the United States. Curtis said in July 1967 that the tax "merely serves to becloud the real problem—excessive government spending abroad."

Curtis was an opponent of Johnson's 10 percent tax surcharge in 1967 and 1968. In October 1967 he voted with the majority of the Ways and Means Committee in refusing to enact the surcharge until the administration made significant spending cuts. In June 1968, after budgetary reductions had been made to satisfy the committee's majority, including the ranking Republican, Representative JOHN BYRNES (R-Wisc.), Curtis still opposed the tax increase on the ground that the cuts had not been specified.

Curtis was a moderate supporter of the Johnson administration's civil rights program. He voted in favor of the Civil Rights Act of 1964 and the Voting Rights Act of 1965 but opposed open housing legislation in 1968. He played a major role in the 1965 revolt of younger House Republicans against the leadership of Representative CHARLES HALLECK (R-Ind.). Curtis and the other "Young Turks" voted to replace Halleck as minority leader with Representative GERALD FORD (R-Mich.). Curtis also introduced the amendment in March 1967 to expel Representative ADAM CLAYTON POWELL, JR. (D-N.Y.) from the House. The measure passed, 307-116.

Curtis retired from the House to run for the Senate in 1968, but he was defeated by Missouri attorney general Thomas Eagleton. In 1972 he became chair of the Corporation for Public Broadcasting and served as chair of the Federal Election Commission in 1975–76. He died in Michigan on January 10, 1993.

—TO

## Cushing, Richard J(ames)
(1895–1970) *Roman Catholic archbishop of Boston*

Cushing, was born on August 24, 1895, and grew up in Boston. After studying at Boston College and St. Joseph's Seminary in Brighton, Massachusetts, he was ordained a priest in 1921. The following year Cushing was assigned to the Boston office of the Society for the Propagation of the Faith, a fundraising agency for Catholic missions throughout the world. He soon distinguished himself as a resourceful organizer, drawing in unprecedented contributions. In 1929 Cushing became director of the society; 10 years later he was elevated to auxiliary bishop, assisting Boston archbishop William Cardinal O'Connell. When O'Connell died in 1944 Cushing was chosen to succeed him as head of the Boston archdiocese, the third-largest in the United States. Pope John XXIII made Cushing a cardinal in 1958. In the tradition of "brick and mortar" prelates, Cushing directed a $250 million construction program that substantially increased the number of Catholic schools, hospitals, and churches in the Boston area. He was important as a supporter of the liberal currents of Catholic thought aimed at "renewal" of the church during the 1960s. He sought frequently to foster interfaith contacts and won a rare ovation at the Second Vatican Council in 1962 for his strong defense of religious freedom. Cushing also supported modernization of the Mass in 1964 and urged a greater role for the laity in church affairs. As the controversy over birth control developed during the mid-1960s, he encouraged discussion and the presentation of pro-contraceptive views, but he refrained from taking an open stand against the Vatican position.

Cushing gained political recognition during the early 1960s as a confidant and strong supporter of President John F. Kennedy. A longstanding friend of the Kennedy family, he helped raise funds for Kennedy's presidential campaign, spoke at the inauguration in 1961, and officiated at the president's funeral in 1963. Cushing's association with the Kennedy family continued through the mid-1960s; he officiated at the funeral of Senator ROBERT F. KENNEDY (D-N.Y.) in 1968 and braved the displeasure of the Vatican as well as of many Catholic laypersons by defending the marriage of JACQUELINE KENNEDY to the divorced Aristotle Onassis.

In political and social matters, as in secular affairs in general, Cushing frequently took controversial positions. A strong anticommunist, he endorsed the John Birch Society in 1960 but later withdrew his support when he learned that the society was critical of Presidents Kennedy and Franklin D. Roosevelt. Cushing was a strong advocate of civil rights and urged Bostonians to accept school integration in 1963 and 1964. However, he opposed a black school boycott in 1964, and some observers criticized him for not doing enough to change the attitudes of white Catholics in ethnic areas. After supporting the Vietnam War during the mid-1960s, Cushing urged an end to American involvement in 1968.

Cushing's retirement in September 1970 marked the end of a 122-year period during which Irish Catholics had dominated the church organization in Boston. His replacement as archbishop was the Spanish-speaking Humberto Medeiros, chosen because of the growing number of Latin American immigrants in Boston's Catholic community. On November 2, 1970, shortly after his retirement, Cushing died of cancer.

—SLG

## Daley, Richard J(oseph)

(1902–1976) *mayor*

Richard Daley, who was born on May 15, 1902, began his political career as a precinct captain in Bridgeport, an Irish working-class neighborhood on Chicago's South Side. He rose steadily in the Cook County Democratic organization. After holding state and city offices, he became chair of the county Democratic Central Committee in 1953 and mayor of Chicago in 1955. As party chief and mayor, Daley filled the thousands of patronage jobs at his disposal with loyal Democrats. With solid ties to both business and labor and considerable influence over the large black vote, Daley built a political organization that made him the nation's most powerful mayor. His contribution to John F. Kennedy's 1960 electoral victory in Illinois first established him as a formidable political force. His reputation grew in 1964, when President Johnson carried Illinois by 800,000 votes. His influence with the federal leadership also meant an expansion of federal funds for Chicago under his tenure. The city underwent a massive building program, an expansion of public services, increases public transit and public housing, and urban renewal programs.

Chicago's housing patterns were among the most segregated in the North when MARTIN LUTHER KING, JR.'s, Southern Christian Leadership Conference announced in January 1966 a campaign to make Chicago an "open city." On July 13 Daley and King met to discuss the newly formed Chicago Freedom Movement's demand for city action to end racial discrimination in housing. Two days later rioting broke out on the West Side, and the National Guard was called in to restore order. Daley charged on July 15 that some of Dr. King's staff members "came in here and have been talking for the past year of violence."

After a meeting later the same day with civil rights leaders, Daley and King jointly announced a "peace plan" that featured sprinklers on fire hydrants and portable swimming pools for the West Side. In August King led a series of open-housing marches into white ethnic neighborhoods in suburban Cicero and on Chicago's Southwest Side. Mayor Daley called a "summit conference" of the city's business, religious, political, and civil rights leaders on August 26 to come up with a plan to end housing and job discrimination in Chicago. The conference reached an agreement on September 3, but the settlement lacked effective enforcement provisions. Three months later, when the immediate crisis had passed and Dr. King had left Chicago, Alderman Thomas Keane, who led the Daley majority in the City Council, announced, "There is no summit agreement."

After the assassination of Dr. King in Memphis on April 4, 1968, rioting occurred for three days on Chicago's West Side. Daley announced at an April 15 news conference that in the future Chicago police were "to shoot to kill" arsonists and "shoot to maim or cripple" looters. The statement aroused a storm of controversy. At a news conference the next day, New York mayor JOHN V. LINDSAY stated, "We are not going to shoot children in New York City." The FBI "cautioned against over-responding to disturbances," and on April 17 Attorney General RAMSEY CLARK characterized Daley's instructions as "a very dangerous escalation of the problems we are so intent on solving." Daley revised his order on April 17.

Daley again stood at the center of national attention during the 1968 Democratic National

Convention, held in Chicago from August 26 to 29. Daley cooperated with state and federal agencies in the establishment of a 25,000-member security force. He also ordered construction of a barbwire and chainlink fence around the International Amphitheatre, the site of the convention. Some delegates resented having to produce identification at a series of checkpoints inside the International Amphitheatre, and during the convention at least two delegates were removed from the floor for refusing to produce credentials.

Clashes between Chicago police and antiwar demonstrators began the night before the convention officially opened, when 500 city police officers cleared 1,000 demonstrators from Lincoln Park. In his welcoming address the next evening, Mayor Daley promised that "as long as I am mayor of this city, there's going to be law and order in Chicago." Although Daley urged that Senator EDWARD KENNEDY (D-Mass.) declare his candidacy, the mayor's intransigent opposition to the youthful supporters of Senator EUGENE MCCARTHY (D-Minn.) made him a symbol of the "old politics."

On August 28 the most violent confrontation of the convention took place outside the convention hall. Inside the hall, Senator ABRAHAM RIBICOFF (D-Conn.) gained the floor to nominate Senator GEORGE MCGOVERN (D-S.Dak.) and denounce the "Gestapo tactics in the streets of Chicago." Ribicoff was jeered by the Daley-dominated Illinois delegation. In the *New York Times* James Reston wrote that "by the end of the night, Daley had become a symbol in the Convention of the opposition within the party to the turbulent conditions of American life."

In the immediate aftermath of the convention the established Democratic leadership with whom Daley was identified did little to gain the allegiance of the supporters of Senator McCarthy or the late Senator ROBERT KENNEDY (D-N.Y.). At an August 29 news conference Daley described the demonstrators as "terrorists" who had come to "assault, harass and taunt the police into reacting before the television cameras." Vice President Humphrey declared on August 31 that it was time to "quit pretending that Mayor Daley did anything that was wrong." Senator McCarthy refused to endorse Humphrey after the convention and on October 8 demanded reform of the party to prevent "another Chicago" as a condition of his endorsement. On election day Daley failed to deliver the Illinois electoral vote to Humphrey, but his organization nev-

ertheless survived the controversy. Daley was reelected mayor in 1971 with over 70 percent of the vote. He was reelected in 1975, although growing public criticism and a series of court rulings had begun to erode his power. He died in office in 1976.

—DKR

## Dawson, William L(evi)

(1886–1970) *member of the House of Representatives*

Dawson, who was born in Albany, Georgia, on April 26, 1886, became an attorney and Republican alderman from Chicago's South Side during the 1930s. He followed the path taken by many of his black constituents and switched parties in 1939. He was first elected to Congress in 1942 as a Democrat. Dawson was then the only black representative; in 1949 he became the first black to head a regular standing committee of Congress.

Dawson offered his constituents low-paying patronage jobs and help with their housing, welfare, and legal problems. Voters responded with overwhelming support for Dawson and his designated candidates. He used his influence to secure the 1955 Democratic mayoral nomination for RICHARD J. DALEY.

As head of the Committee on Government Operations, Dawson was responsible for investigating Billie Sol Estes, the Texas promoter who in 1962 was convicted of fraud in connection with Department of Agriculture grain storage and cotton allotment programs. Estes's name had been prominently linked with Vice President LYNDON B. JOHNSON. On October 12, 1964, Dawson issued a committee report that stated, "There is no evidence that the then Vice President participated in any way in the relationships between Billie Sol Estes and the federal government or its agencies other than routinely referring to the Department of Agriculture correspondence including complaints in which Estes was involved." Observers noted that the report was issued while Congress was not in session and only a few weeks before the presidential election. Dawson sponsored no major legislation during Johnson's years as president but generally supported administration policies.

During his first years in Congress Dawson had fought for a permanent committee to enforce the Fair Employment Practices Act, and he also worked to outlaw the poll tax and segregation in the armed forces. During the 1950s, however, he became increasingly withdrawn from civil rights activity. In February 1964 Dawson, along with Mayor Daley and the local chapter of the NAACP (a branch allegedly dominated by Dawson workers), denounced the successful boycott that had been organized by the Congress of Racial Equality and the Student Nonviolent Coordinating Committee to protest de facto segregation in Chicago's schools. In 1966 Dawson lent no support when Rev. MARTIN LUTHER KING, JR., and the Southern Christian Leadership Conference organized marches in white neighborhoods to protest Chicago's segregated housing pattern.

Angered by Dawson's apparent indifference to the civil rights movement, young blacks challenged him during each Democratic primary in the mid-1960s. Dawson decided not to seek reelection in 1970 and died in Chicago in November of that year at the age of 84

—JLW

## Dellinger, David

(1915–2004) *pacifist; editor,* Liberation

In the antiwar movement of the l960s, David Dellinger, who was born on August 22, 1915, in Wakefield, Massachusetts, represented an older generation of radical pacifists—those who had been involved in labor and community organizing in the

1930s, who had been conscientious objectors during World War II, and who had organized acts of civil disobedience and moral witness on behalf of peace and civil rights throughout the 1940s and l950s.

Dellinger graduated from Yale in 1936 and enrolled in Union Theological Seminary in 1939. In 1940, along with seven fellow students who had been living in voluntary poverty in Harlem and Newark, he refused to register for the draft. Although registration would have exempted him from any further military obligation under the automatic exemption granted members of the clergy, Dellinger felt the need for a dramatic act. He was sent to federal prison in Danbury, Connecticut, for a year. In 1943 he was again arrested for Selective Service violations and sentenced to two years in the penitentiary at Lewisburg, Pennsylvania.

After the war Dellinger organized a cooperative community, and, in 1948, he joined with A. J. MUSTE, DWIGHT MACDONALD, and BAYARD RUSTIN in organizing the Peacemakers, a group that called for resistance to peacetime conscription by means of civil disobedience and tax refusal. In 1956 Dellinger, Muste, and Rustin founded *Liberation* magazine, which became a forum for the rising agitation against nuclear arms and racial discrimination.

During the early stages of the Vietnam conflict, Dellinger favored an immediate withdrawal rather than negotiations. He also opposed the moratorium on militant action called by peace and civil

Portrait of the Chicago Seven, from left to right: Lee Weiner, John Froines, Abbie Hoffman, Rennie Davis, Jerry Rubin, Tom Hayden, and David Dellinger, 1969 *(Photographed by Richard Avedon; Library of Congress, Prints and Photographs Division)*

rights leaders in 1964 to ensure a Democratic victory in the presidential election. When President Johnson ordered the bombing of North Vietnam, Dellinger helped organize a coalition of peace groups, calling itself the Assembly of Unrepresented People, that sponsored a series of acts of civil disobedience in Washington in August 1965. Despite opposition to the demonstration from the NAACP and the Urban League, and lukewarm support from Students for a Democratic Society, 356 people forced the police to arrest them on the Capitol mall. Coinciding with the Vietnam Day Committee's attempt to block troop trains in the San Francisco Bay area, the arrests marked the first large-scale application of civil disobedience tactics to the antiwar movement.

In November 1966 Dellinger served as co-chair of the Spring Mobilization to End the War in Vietnam. The "Mobe" chose April 15, 1967 for demonstrations in New York and San Francisco. Over the next five months it organized churches, women's groups, universities, political clubs, and peace groups in an attempt to show that active opposition to the war was not limited to a handful of radicals but included vast numbers of Americans. The marches in April were the largest demonstrations against government policy in American history up to that time. It also served to convince LBJ and others within his administration that the antiwar movement, and Dellinger in particular, was directly tied to Hanoi.

Dellinger was involved in the demonstrations in Chicago during the Democratic National Convention in August 1968. The violence of these events formed the basis for a five-month court trial in 1969, at which Dellinger and seven others were charged by the federal government with conspiracy to riot. Dellinger was sentenced to five years in prison, although the decision was overturned on appeal. Dellinger remained active promoting pacifist causes throughout the next decades. He died on May 25, 2004.

—TLH

## DeLoach, Deke (Cartha) (Dekle)

(1920–   ) *assistant to the director, FBI*

DeLoach was born on July 20, 1920, and raised in Claxton, Georgia, a small town west of Savannah. After graduating from Stetson University in 1942 he joined the FBI and worked as an agent in Norfolk, Toledo, and Akron, where he carried out investiga-

tions of Communist Party members. Disliking the work he joined the navy in 1944. After the war DeLoach returned to the bureau and was assigned to the home office in Washington, D.C. There he carried out routine security checks of potential employees on atomic energy projects. He subsequently coordinated FBI activities with the work of the Central Intelligence Agency and the Office of Naval Intelligence.

During the early 1950s DeLoach made a favorable impression on J. EDGAR HOOVER, and as a result he made rapid progress within the bureau. In 1959 he was named assistant director for the crime records division, a post that, despite its title, entailed responsibility for managing the bureau's public and congressional relations. DeLoach was skilled at political in-fighting, had an ingratiating personality, and proved adept at muting congressional criticism of the bureau and its director. He also had access to FBI files containing a vast amount of personal information on individual members of Congress. To advance the bureau's reputation DeLoach often supplied news stories and information to friendly columnists and reporters.

In December 1965 DeLoach was promoted to the post of assistant to the director and assumed responsibility for all the bureau's investigative activities. In the meantime he had developed a close relationship with President Johnson. Indeed, on a variety of matters Johnson preferred to communicate with DeLoach than Hoover, which strained DeLoach's relations with the director. DeLoach was the only member of the bureau to have a direct line to the White House in his home.

DeLoach undertook a number of special assignments for the president. In the summer of 1964 he headed a special FBI squad that ostensibly had been organized to aid the Secret Service in protecting the president at the Democratic National Convention in Atlantic City, New Jersey. However, according to a 1976 report by the Senate Select Committee on Intelligence Activities, the FBI agents, using electronic surveillance, "bugged" the hotel room of Rev. MARTIN LUTHER KING, JR., and gathered a substantial amount of purely political information having little to do with security matters. This data was turned over to the president's aide, WALTER JENKINS.

DeLoach subsequently supervised an investigation of Jenkins who, in the fall of 1964, had been involved in a homosexual incident in the basement of a Washington YMCA. Johnson ordered the investigation in the belief that Jenkins had been the victim of a Republican plot. The FBI could find no such evidence, and Jenkins was forced to resign. It also convinced Johnson to request DeLoach perform more detailed investigations into the backgrounds of some of his advisers.

By 1966 President Johnson was becoming increasingly sensitive to criticism of his Vietnam War policy. In March of that year he ordered DeLoach to undertake an investigation of representatives whose criticism of the Vietnam policy, Johnson thought, had been motivated by contacts with foreign agents. In late October 1968 Johnson ordered DeLoach to begin investigating the relationship of Anna Chenault, a Chinese-born Republican socialite, and the Republican vice presidential nominee, SPIRO AGNEW. The president believed that Agnew, working through Chenault, had informed the South Vietnamese government that a Republican administration would be more receptive to its interests. He also believed that the Republicans had encouraged the South Vietnamese to sabotage the Paris peace talks.

Shortly after President Nixon assumed office, DeLoach's private line to the White House was removed. He nonetheless maintained relatively cordial relations with the new administration. Attorney General John Mitchell preferred to deal with DeLoach rather than Hoover on a variety of Justice Department matters.

DeLoach had hoped to succeed Hoover as FBI director. However, when it became apparent that the director was unwilling to retire, DeLoach accepted a lucrative offer to become an executive with Pepsico, Inc. He left the bureau in June 1970.

—JLW

## DePugh, (William) Robert B(olivar)

(1923–   ) *national coordinator, the Minutemen*
DePugh, who was born on April 15, 1923, in Independence, Missouri, headed Biolab Corporation, a producer of veterinary medicines. At the beginning of the 1960s, he organized the Minutemen, whose purpose was to train Americans to fight a guerrilla war in the event of a communist takeover by either invasion or internal subversion, both of which he regarded as imminent possibilities.

The Minutemen's existence first came to the attention of the general public in October 1961,

when an associate of DePugh's was arrested in Shiloh, Illinois, for illegal weapons possession. A *New York Times* survey one month later concluded that the organization was a very loose federation of small units with a total membership of only several hundred.

The Minutemen came to light again during the presidential campaign of 1964. The group backed the candidacy of Senator BARRY M. GOLDWATER (R-Ariz.) because, according to DePugh, President Lyndon B. Johnson was an "opportunist who would sell the United States out to the Communists or anyone else who would pay his price." After Goldwater's defeat DePugh asserted that communism could no longer be stopped by political means and that only the Minutemen's secret "underground army" could save liberty. In July 1966 he organized the Patriotic Party, but he conceived of it as "the political arm of a complete patriotic resistance movement."

During the next two years persons identifying themselves as Minutemen were arrested in New York, Connecticut, and other places on charges of conspiring and threatening to commit acts of violence against liberal and radical organizations and individuals. According to J. Harry Jones, Jr., author of *The Minutemen*, the organization's membership during this period was probably about a thousand. An informant in 1968 told the government that 19 Minutemen strike teams existed across the United States assigned to assassinate several prominent persons, particularly Dr. MARTIN LUTHER KING, JR., and to incite race riots in order to facilitate their takeover of the government.

DePugh's role in local Minutemen activities was difficult to ascertain because of the organization's decentralized structure and DePugh's contradictory statements, but he encouraged a climate of violence. For example, each issue of *On Target*, the Minutemen's newsletter, which he edited, announced under its masthead, "We guarantee that all law suits filed against this newsletter will be settled out of court."

In November 1966 DePugh was convicted for violations of the federal firearms act and the following February pleaded nolo contendere to another charge of violating that law. While appealing his first conviction DePugh was indicted in February 1968 for conspiring to rob banks in Seattle. Shortly before this indictment was returned, he went into hiding.

DePugh was captured by the FBI in New Mexico in July 1969 and was jailed several days later. In

February 1973 he was paroled after having served three-and-a-half years of an 11-year jail term. The Minutemen organization had virtually dissolved during his period of incarceration largely because its new leaders became convinced that Communists in the Justice Department had singled them out for persecution. DePugh did not attempt to revive the group after his release from jail. Instead, he became involved with other, smaller-scale extreme right-wing political activities.

—MLL

## Diggs, Charles C(ole), Jr.
(1922–1998) *member of the House of Representatives*

Charles C. Diggs, Jr., the first black representative from Michigan, was born on December 2, 1922, in Detroit. His father was a wealthy Detroit undertaker who also served for many years in the Michigan state Senate. Diggs attended the University of Michigan and Fiske University before entering the U.S. Army Air Forces in World War II. After the war he enrolled in the Wayne University Mortuary School from which he received a mortuary license in 1946. Diggs then entered the family business. He also worked as a disk jockey and news commentator on the family's weekly radio show broadcast. During the 1940s the elder Diggs was sentenced to a year in prison for accepting graft; this did little to hurt his popularity with his constituents, who returned him to the state senate; that body, however, refused to seat him. His son, seeking to vindicate the family name, ran for his father's seat in 1950 and won an overwhelming victory. Four years later he was elected to Congress.

Diggs represented a poor, predominantly black district in downtown Detroit. In the 1960s this area, cut up by superhighways and urban renewal projects, lost 19 percent of its population. The 1967 riots also contributed to the population decline, hastening the exodus of middle-class blacks from the district. Diggs's success in winning reelection depended less on his voting record (which reflected a high rate of absenteeism) than on the services he offered his constituents. His office expedited the delivery of Social Security checks, streamlined the processing of small business administration loans, and performed numerous minor legal services for voters. Diggs customarily spent half his time in Detroit and was a familiar figure at black social functions and funerals.

As a member of the House District of Columbia Committee, Diggs consistently advocated home rule for Washington. His view was opposed to that of Representative JOHN C. MCMILLAN (D-S.C.), the domineering committee chair. The two men rarely spoke, and Diggs had almost no influence over legislation. In 1972 Diggs became committee chair, and a home rule bill was subsequently reported out and became law.

Diggs was not conspicuous in the civil rights movement although he did attract notice when he attended the murder trial of Emmett Till, a young African American beaten to death by white racists in Mississippi in 1955. Nevertheless, as a senior member of Congress from a major industrial state, his presence commanded the respect of black leaders. In July 1967 Diggs, Representative ADAM CLAYTON POWELL, JR. (D-N.Y.), and FLOYD MCKISSICK, national director of the Congress of Racial Equality, were named honorary co-chairs of the National Conference on Black Power. The meeting, held in Newark, New Jersey, in the aftermath of that city's riots, brought together representatives from 197 black organizations who issued a plea for greater black independence in economic, social, and political affairs.

As a member of the House Foreign Affairs Committee, Diggs became an outspoken opponent of U.S. involvement in Vietnam. In April 1965 he denounced American use of gas warfare in Vietnam and in January 1966 was one of seven House Democrats who sponsored a conference on Vietnam. The meeting ended in a call for the continuation of the pause in U.S. bombing of North Vietnam and a plea for negotiations between the South Vietnamese government and the National Liberation Front.

During the Nixon years Diggs, the senior African-American member of Congress, was elected chair of the congressional Black Caucus, a group that sought to develop a cohesive legislative policy for the advancement of black Americans. He resigned in 1980 after being convicted of taking kickbacks, and he operated a funeral home in Maryland. He died in Washington, D.C., on August 24, 1998.

—JLW

## Dillon, C(larence) Douglas
(1909–2003) *secretary of the Treasury*

C. Douglas Dillon was the son of a Wall Street banker who made a fortune building Dillon, Read & Company into one of the country's largest investment firms. Born in Switzerland, on August 22, 1909, Dillon attended Groton and Harvard. After serving an apprenticeship with some smaller investment houses, he joined Dillon, Read as a vice president in 1938. He followed the company's president, James Forrestal, into the Navy Department in 1940 and saw action in the Pacific toward the end of the war.

As chair of the board of Dillon, Read after the war, Dillon supervised the firm's far-flung domestic and foreign holdings and doubled its investment portfolio in six years. He was an active Republican, working with John Foster Dulles in the 1948 presidential campaign of Governor Thomas E. Dewey and initiating a "draft Eisenhower" movement in New Jersey in 1951. In 1953 Eisenhower appointed Dillon ambassador to France. He remained there until 1957, when he was recalled to Washington to serve as deputy undersecretary of state for economic affairs. In 1959 he was promoted to undersecretary of state. In the State Department, he cofounded the Inter-American Development Bank. Dillon contributed heavily to the Republican presidential candidate, Vice President RICHARD M. NIXON, in 1960.

President Kennedy's selection of Dillon as secretary of the Treasury was a surprise to many and an indication of Kennedy' strong desire to have an advocate of "sound-money" in the nation's top economic post. Dillon remained the most influential member of Kennedy's economic policy-making team throughout the administration. His success in persuading the president to give priority status to the balance of payments deficit was crucial in shaping Kennedy's moderate fiscal course, which ruled out more activist solutions to the economy's problems. As Treasury secretary, Dillon devoted himself to alleviating the intractable payments deficit, to devising and promoting the Kennedy tax program, and to spearheading the Treasury's opposition to proposals for international monetary reform and lower interest rates emanating from the Council of Economic Advisers.

After two years of opposition Dillon became persuaded in late 1962 of the need for a massive tax cut to stimulate the economy. The House passed an $11 billion tax reduction bill in September 1963, but the Senate had not acted on the measure by the time of Kennedy's assassination in November. Dillon was instrumental in convincing President Johnson to push the tax cut in the Senate and to accompany it with spending reductions in order to forestall inflation and conciliate Senate conservatives. The Senate passed the tax bill in February 1964.

In March 1964 Dillon testified against a plan of Representative WRIGHT PATMAN (D-Tex.), chair of the House Banking and Currency Committee, to reform the Federal Reserve System. He particularly opposed a provision placing the secretary of the Treasury at the head of a new Federal Reserve Board. "Experience over many years and in many countries," Dillon said, "has taught us the wisdom of shielding those who make decisions on monetary policy from day-to-day pressures." He also spoke against a proposal permiting interest to be paid on checking accounts.

Because of his social background Dillon never achieved the rapport with President Johnson that he had with President Kennedy. In comparing the work of Dillon and his successor HENRY FOWLER on the tax cut in 1963 and 1964, Johnson remarked, "He [Fowler] was there night after night, while Doug Dillon was going to tea parties or putting on his white tie and tails."

Dillon resigned in March 1965 to return to private finance. He became president of the U.S. & Foreign Securities Corporation in February 1967. Dillon was a member of the Senior Advisory Group on Vietnam, commonly known as the "Wise Men," who advised Johnson in March 1968 to begin to disengage U.S. forces from the Vietnam War. In the same month, as head of the Advisory Committee to the U.S. Treasury on International Monetary Affairs, he urged a tax increase, warning that failure to do so would "endanger worldwide confidence in the dollar" and "risk a serious upheaval in the international monetary system." Arguing against federal spending cuts as a substitute for a tax increase, he declared, "There is no feasible substitute for tax action to curtail the inflationary excesses in domestic demand that are now spilling over into imports." He also served as chair of the U.S. and Foreign Securities Corporation from 1967 to 1984, director of the Council on Foreign Relations from 1965 to 1978, and vice chair of the council from 1977 to 1978. He died on January 10, 2003.

—TO

## Dirksen, Everett McKinley
(1896–1969) *member of the Senate*

Born in Pekin, Illinois, on January 4, 1896, Dirksen attended the University of Minnesota. Following service in the army artillery during World War I, Dirksen returned to his hometown of Pekin, to practice

Senator Everett Dirksen in a meeting with President Johnson *(Lyndon Baines Johnson Library)*

law. He won the first of his eight terms to the House of Representatives as a Republican in 1932, and, in 1950, he moved up to the Senate by defeating Senate Majority Leader Scott Lucas (D-Ill.). In the Senate Dirksen identified himself with the GOP's conservative Old Guard. He defended Senator Joseph R. McCarthy (R-Wisc.) and the charges the Wisconsin Senator made concerning the presence of Communists in the federal government. After McCarthy's decline in popularity, Dirksen moved toward the more moderate Republicanism of President DWIGHT D. EISENHOWER and won the president's endorsement in his successful campaign for reelection in 1956.

Sponsored by the party's conservative leadership, Dirksen became Senate minority whip in January 1957 and two years later won the GOP Senate leadership post. An artful persuader, he established an unusual degree of unity among his Republican colleagues. Dirksen willingly gave up his own prestigious committee assignments to younger members.

In the early 1960s President Kennedy needed Senate Republican support in order to overcome the opposition to his legislative program among conservative southern Democrats. Although the minority leader endorsed little of the president's New Frontier legislation, he demonstrated a consistent loyalty to the administration on major foreign policy questions. Dirksen provided the necessary Republican votes for the ratification of the limited nuclear test ban treaty in September 1963.

Dirksen's influence over Senate Republicans proved crucial to the enactment of the 1964 Civil Rights Act. Throughout 1963 Dirksen had opposed President Kennedy's request for a federal guarantee to blacks of the right to use public accommodations. However, congressional liberals, spurred on by the increasingly active civil rights movements in 1963 and 1964, insisted upon a strong public accommodations section in the legislation. The House passed a version of the administration's bill in February 1964 that not only included the accommodations provision but also contained a strict "fair employment" section as well. Dirksen disapproved of both parts of the House measure.

Senate supporters of the bill needed Dirksen to persuade Republican members to end the southern Democrats' filibuster against the bill by invoking cloture and forcing a vote. In early May 1964 Dirksen agreed to negotiate with Senate majority whip HUBERT H. HUMPHREY (D-Minn.) and Attorney General ROBERT F. KENNEDY on the accommodations and fair-employment sections. The three legislators labored over the bill, and their revised version of the measure allowed the federal government to intervene only where a "pattern" of discrimination existed; otherwise, antidiscrimination suits would be left to individuals. Local agencies, where in operation, would be given time to work out the problems.

Arguing for an "idea whose time has come," Dirksen helped persuade 27 GOP senators, including many traditional opponents of cloture, to vote to cut off debate on June 10, 1964. Nine days later the Senate passed the compromise bill by a vote of 73 to 27, with only six Republicans in opposition. Dirksen received nationwide praise for his role in the enactment of the civil rights law. Senate Majority Leader MIKE MANSFIELD (D-Mont.) declared on June 19 that passage of the measure represented Dirksen's "finest hour."

The Republican leader's triumph, however, lacked the endorsement of Senator BARRY M. GOLD-WATER (R-Ariz.), the front-runner for the 1964 Republican presidential nomination. Dirksen had pleaded with Goldwater, a personal friend, to support the civil rights bill. After Goldwater failed to do so, he condemned the Arizona Republican's opposition to the measure in a Senate speech June 19. Goldwater's stand outraged Republican leaders with a strong commitment to civil rights and in part inspired Pennsylvania governor WILLIAM W. SCRANTON's last-ditch fight against Goldwater for the nomination.

Dirksen dismissed Scranton's personal plea for support on June 22 and resolved, with other midwestern GOP leaders, that no one could stop Goldwater. Dirksen's decision, in agreement with the majority of the Illinois delegation to the Republican National Convention, seriously weakened any lingering effort by party moderates to halt the Goldwater bandwagon. Dirksen agreed to nominate his colleague before the convention on July 15, and the Illinois delegation cast 56 of its 58 votes for Goldwater.

In the 1965 legislative session President Johnson skillfully took advantage of his large congres-

sional majorities to enact a wide range of Great Society legislation, most of which Dirksen unsuccessfully fought with great rhetorical vigor. Senate liberals still sought his assistance, and he worked for the passage of the administration's 1965 Voting Rights Act. Dirksen engineered one of the president's few legislative defeats in the 1965 session by leading a filibuster in October against the repeal of Section 14(b), the open shop provision, of the Taft-Hartley Labor Relations Law. Johnson frequently consulted with Dirksen, however, continuing a friendly relationship that dated back to their days as rival Senate leaders. The Americans for Democratic Action accused the administration in November 1965 of being "soft" on Dirksen, whom it claimed exercised "exorbitant influence" for a leader of only 32 senators.

Dirksen suffered two important legislative defeats in the mid-1960s. In September 1966 a Dirksen amendment to overrule the Supreme Court's recent decision against prayer in the public schools failed in the Senate for want of a two-thirds majority. Senate liberals also frustrated Dirksen's efforts in 1964, 1965, and 1966 to reverse the Court's decisions requiring state legislative apportionment on a basis of population only. After repeated defeats in Congress Dirksen and Senator ROMAN HRUSKA (R-Neb.) encouraged the formation of a "Committee for Government of the People." The committee urged state legislatures to petition Congress to call a constitutional convention to nullify the Court's reapportionment ruling. By the spring of 1967, 32 state legislatures had drawn up petitions, but the antireapportionment group failed to win the approval of three-fourths of the state assemblies—the number required to force Congress to act.

Dirksen projected a colorful if conservative image for the Republican congressional leadership. He gained national news coverage for the GOP by holding weekly press conferences with House Minority Leader GERALD R. FORD (R-Mich.). Capitalizing on his well-known grandiloquence, the Senate Minority Leader became the first senator to make a commercial record album in December 1966. A collection of patriotic readings, *The Gallant Men*, proved popular with both radio disc jockeys and the general public and won the senator a Grammy Award from the record industry in February 1968.

Dirksen steadfastly defended Johnson's foreign policy. He denied charges by Republican vice presidential candidate WILLIAM E. MILLER in September

1964 that the United States had agreed not to invade Cuba following the 1962 missile crisis. When, in August 1964, President Johnson asked for congressional sanction for military action against the North Vietnamese following the Gulf of Tonkin incident, Dirksen unsuccessfully sought to waive all committee testimony and to move instead to an immediate vote in favor of the White House resolution. Dirksen also gave an unqualified endorsement to the administration's military intervention in the Dominican Republic in April 1965.

Dirksen vehemently fought efforts by Ford and other Republican leaders to charge the administration with having mismanaged the war. When Ford criticized Johnson's trip to the Manila Conference in the fall of 1966 as "a political gimmick," Dirksen angrily decried the House leader's comments. "You don't denounce the commander in chief before the whole, wide world," he remarked in October. Indeed, by late 1966 Johnson received greater support on Vietnam from Dirksen than from Senate Majority Leader Mansfield.

Following the 1966 elections Dirksen found his control over his ranks increasingly tenuous. Younger and more liberal colleagues, many of whom wanted to make the war an issue in the 1968 election, joined the Republican Senate ranks. Although no one directly challenged Dirksen for his leadership post, Senator THRUSTON B. MORTON (R-Ky.) formed an unofficial coalition of moderate, antiwar Republicans who stood opposed to Dirksen's wholehearted endorsement of Johnson's foreign policy. Although Dirksen obtained sufficient votes to pass a compromise open housing bill in 1968, his prestige suffered when he supported Johnson's nomination of ABE FORTAS as chief justice in June 1968. Freshman senator ROBERT P. GRIFFIN (R-Mich.) led an intra-party revolt which forced the minority leader to withdraw his endorsement in late September, effectively destroying Fortas's chances of confirmation.

Dirksen chaired the Party Platform Committee at the Republican National Convention in August 1968. Accepting the Illinois designation as favorite son candidate for the presidential nomination, Dirksen deliberately forestalled the candidacy of Senator CHARLES H. PERCY (R-Ill.), who had expected to receive the delegation's endorsement. Dirksen withdrew his name on the eve of the convention and voted for the winning candidate, former vice president RICHARD M. NIXON.

Dirksen encountered greater difficulty than expected in his 1968 reelection, winning only 53 percent of the vote against an unknown and underfinanced opponent. He was unanimously reelected minority leader in January 1969, but Dirksen played a declining role in the party's national leadership over the last months of his life. He died on September 7, 1969, in Washington, D.C.

—JLB

## Dixon, Paul Rand(all)
### (1913–1996)  *chair, Federal Trade Commission*

Born on September 29, 1913, in Nashville, Tennessee, Paul Rand Dixon attended Vanderbilt University and received his law degree from the University of Florida in 1938. He immediately joined the staff of the Federal Trade Commission (FTC) as a trial attorney. Except for wartime naval service Dixon remained with the commission until 1957, when he was named chief counsel and staff director of Senator Estes Kefauver's (D-Tenn.) Antitrust and Antimonopoly Subcomittee. Under Kefauver and Dixon the subcommittee carried out a series of highly publicized investigations of big business abuses, most notably price-fixing by drug companies and identical bidding by manufacturers of heavy electrical equipment. The Justice Department followed up the latter study, obtaining convictions against 45 of the colluding executives, seven of whom received jail terms in the most spectacular business scandal of the decade. Sponsored by Kefauver, Dixon was appointed chair of the FTC by President Kennedy in 1961.

During the Kennedy years Dixon took the FTC beyond the defense of small business and into the area of consumer protection, especially in his attack on misleading advertising. In line with LYNDON JOHNSON's suggestion soon after he became president that regulatory agencies concentrate on "helping, not harassing" business, Dixon began to temper his approach. In a speech to the Advertising Federation of America in February 1965, he blamed false advertising on a "few bad apples" within the industry. He conceded that the FTC "has, on occasion, been overly meticulous, that it has fought wars where wars could have been better settled by persuasion." He announced that the FTC was no longer "trying to accumulate scalps" and was returning to what Woodrow Wilson intended it to be, "a clearinghouse for the facts by which both the public mind and the managers of great business undertakings shall be guided." In August 1966 Dixon vehemently opposed the creation of a cabinet-level department of consumer affairs. To improve consumer protection he recommended increasing the FTC budget.

Following the surgeon general's 1964 report linking cigarette smoking to cancer and other diseases, Dixon fought for restrictions on cigarette advertising and health warnings on cigarette packages. In July 1965 Congress passed the Federal Cigarette Labeling and Advertising Act, which superseded the FTC's more stringent regulations. The law required all cigarette packages to contain the warning: "Caution: Cigarette Smoking May be Hazardous to Your Health." In June 1967 the FTC submitted a report to Congress urging tighter restriction of cigarette advertising.

Congress in October 1966 passed a "truth-in-packaging" bill, which Dixon had favored since 1961. The law required manufacturers to provide consumers with specific information about a package's contents in order to guard against deceptive packaging and labeling practices. It directed the FTC and the secretary of health, education and welfare to issue regulations for that purpose.

Dixon maintained that corporate concentration was the greatest threat to free enterprise in the United States. "I'd be scared to death if we had only 20 large companies in the country," he told *Forbes* in July 1966. "We have 200 now, and our job is to see that they don't eat each other up." Nevertheless, the FTC under Dixon gradually devoted a decreasing portion of its budget to antimerger activity. In 1959 the commission spent approximately $1 million, or 16.9 percent of its budget, in this area; in 1968 it spent $1.35 million, or 8.8 percent. Its Bureau of Textiles and Furs, by comparison, received 9.3 percent of the budget in 1959 and 10.5 percent in 1968. The period 1960–69 saw the greatest corporate merger wave to date in American history. In 1960–66 there were 1,664 mergers annually; by 1967–69 an average of over 3,600 mergers took place each year, 80 percent of which involved conglomerates. During Dixon's chairmanship, from 1961 through 1969, the FTC issued 56 complaints against mergers.

In January 1969 a team of law students, organized by consumer advocate RALPH NADER, published a 185-page study of the FTC. Harshly critical of the commission and Dixon, it charged that "alco-

holism, spectacular lassitude and office absenteeism [and] incompetence by the most modest standards" were "rampant" at high levels of the FTC staff. The team accused the commission of inadequate protection of the consumer, "collusion with business interests," secrecy, and partisan politics in the hiring of staff.

The study criticized a decline in FTC enforcement activity and the increasing emphasis by the FTC on "voluntary" compliance on the part of industry. It maintained that the commission's powerful enforcement tools, such as its right to seek preliminary injunctions and criminal penalties, were "under-used and ill-applied." The investigators, whose forays into the commission's headquarters during the summer of 1968 had earned them the nickname of "Nader's Raiders," blamed most of the FTC's shortcomings on Dixon and called for his resignation.

Dixon issued an eight-page rebuttal, which characterized the study as "a hysterical, anti-business diatribe and a scurrilous, untruthful attack on the career personnel of the Commission." In May 1969, at President Nixon's request, an American Bar Association (ABA) panel undertook a study of the FTC. The 16-member panel, headed by Philadelphia lawyer Miles Kirkpatrick, issued a report in September whose conclusions largely paralleled those of the Nader team. The panel said its study had shown that although the FTC had been armed with a rising budget and increased staff, "both the volume and force of FTC law enforcement have declined during this decade."

President Nixon replaced Dixon as FTC chair with Caspar Weinberger, who took office in January 1970. Dixon continued to serve as an FTC commissioner throughout the Nixon administration.

—TO

## Doar, John M(ichael)

(1921–   ) *assistant attorney general in charge of Civil Rights Division*

Doar was born on December 3, 1921, in Minneapolis, Minnesota. After graduating from Princeton and receiving his law degree from the University of California, Berkeley, Doar practiced in New Richmond, Wisconsin, from 1950 to 1960. A Republican, Doar entered the Justice Department in the spring of 1960 and remained there for seven years. As first assistant in the Civil Rights Division from 1960 to 1964, Doar traveled extensively in the South to oversee Justice Department civil rights litigation, conduct investigations, and help resolve such crises as the integration of the University of Mississippi in September 1962 and of the University of Alabama in September 1963.

In December 1964 Doar became head of the Civil Rights Division following BURKE MARSHALL's resignation. In that position he supervised all Justice Department cases dealing with civil rights and continued to spend much of his time in the South, often turning up during critical situations.

In March 1965, when MARTIN LUTHER KING, JR., led a march from Selma to Montgomery, Alabama, to protest the denial of voting rights to blacks, Doar was present throughout the march to help coordinate the federal government's activities and to see that court orders barring state authorities from interfering with the march were followed. Doar went to Bogalusa, Louisiana, in July 1965 after several months of civil rights demonstrations there had flared into racial violence. As President Johnson's personal representative Doar met with rights leaders and with local and state officials, and he initiated a legal suit against the Ku Klux Klan to prevent it from harassing civil rights workers. Doar was also in Canton, Mississippi, on June 23, 1966, when the local police ordered some 250 people who were part of a protest march going to Jackson, Mississippi, to move away from their campsite. When the marchers refused to leave, the police fired tear gas at them, and Doar made a futile effort to restrain the police as they moved in with clubs to clear the area.

Doar personally led the Justice Department's prosecution in two major cases against defendants charged with the murder of civil rights workers in the South. On March 25, 1965, at the end of the Selma march, Viola Liuzzo, a civil rights worker from Detroit, was shot 20 miles outside of Selma. In his first criminal case in the Justice Department, Doar prosecuted the three Klan members believed responsible for her murder under an 1870 federal law making it a crime to conspire to violate an individual's civil rights. In December 1965 an all-white jury in the federal district court in Montgomery, Alabama, found the three men guilty of violating the law, and each received the maximum 10-year sentence. It was the first conviction in Alabama for the death of a civil rights worker. Doar also headed the prosecution of 18 defendants charged with

conspiracy in the June 1964 killing of three civil rights workers near Philadelphia, Mississippi. Once again Doar, who had been the first federal official notified of their disappearance, won his case. On October 20, 1967, another all-white federal jury in Meridian, Mississippi, convicted seven of the defendants.

Doar resigned from the Justice Department in December 1967 to become executive director of the Development and Service Corporation, a private company formed to redevelop New York's Bedford-Stuyvesant ghetto. He also served as president of the New York City Board of Education in 1968 and 1969, emerging as an advocate of decentralized control of schools. In December 1973 Doar was appointed majority counsel to the House Judiciary Committee for its inquiry into the impeachment of President Richard Nixon. After Nixon's 1974 resignation, he returned to private practice in Washington, D.C.

—CAB

## Dodd, Thomas J(oseph)
### (1907–1971)  *member of the Senate*

Born in Norwich, Connecticut, on May 15, 1907, Thomas Dodd graduated from Providence College in 1930 and Yale Law School three years later. He worked for two years as an FBI agent and then served in the Justice Department as a special assistant to the U.S. Attorney General. After World War II he was named executive trial counsel at the Nuremberg war crimes tribunal.

Dodd twice unsuccessfully sought the Connecticut gubernatorial nomination in the late 1940s. Elected as a Democrat to the U.S. House of Representatives in 1952, he lost a U.S. Senate election to incumbent senator Prescott Bush (R-Conn.) in 1956. He won a Senate seat in 1958, running on a strong anticommunist platform. Named to the Judiciary and Foreign Relations Committees, Dodd supported Kennedy administration legislation on over 60 percent of all major issues. He maintained a militant stand against communism throughout his public career.

Reelected to the Senate in 1964, Dodd continued to serve on the Foreign Relations and Judiciary Committees. In March 1964 he called for efforts to turn the Vietnam War against North Vietnam and deplored "the querulous, faint-hearted chorus of those who always ask the price of victory." The next year he charged that the antiwar movement was run by Communists.

In domestic politics Dodd was a liberal, supporting the Johnson administration's Medicare and civil rights bills. It was his reputation as a liberal, combined with President Johnson's desire to keep Senator HUBERT HUMPHREY (D-Minn.) guessing, that led to press speculation that Dodd would be LBJ's running mate in the presidential election 1964. In 1965 his Juvenile Delinquency Subcommittee conducted hearings on stricter gun control legislation, and Dodd introduced a bill to restrict importation of military surplus weapons. In May 1968 the Senate rejected a Dodd amendment to the Omnibus Crime Control and Safe Streets Act that would have barred mail-order sales of rifles and shotguns while permitting any state legislature to exempt its state from the prohibition.

On June 20, 1966, the Senate Select Committee on Standards and Conduct, chaired by Senator JOHN STENNIS (D-Miss.), opened hearings, at Dodd's request, on charges of official misconduct against the senator. In their newspaper columns DREW PEARSON and JACK ANDERSON had alleged that Dodd had accepted favors from business executives, double-billed the Senate for official and private travel, converted over $100,000 in tax-free campaign contributions to his personal use, and used his influence to promote the private interests of Chicago public relations executive Julius Klein. Earlier, Dodd had filed a 14-count, $5 million libel and conspiracy suit against both Anderson and Pearson.

The Stennis committee hearings carried over into 1967 and focused on Dodd's misuse of campaign funds. In March Dodd defended his financial dealings, calling himself a victim of "trial by press" and one of the poorest members of Congress. However, on April 27 the committee unanimously recommended that the Senate censure Dodd for conduct that "is contrary to accepted morals, derogates from the public trust expected of a senator and tends to bring the Senate into dishonor and disrepute."

On June 23, 1967, the full Senate formally censured Dodd by a vote of 92-5. The censure was only the seventh in the Senate's history. Dodd retained seniority and his position as chair of the Juvenile Delinquency Subcommittee and vice chair of the Internal Security Subcommittee.

Campaigning as an independent for reelection in 1970, Dodd was unseated by moderate Republi-

can senator Lowell Weicker (R-Conn.). Dodd died in May 1971 in Old Lyme, Connecticut.

—FHM

## Dominick, Peter H(oyt)
### (1915–1981) *member of the Senate*

Peter Dominick was born on July 7, 1915, in Stamford, Connecticut. His father, Gayer, was a partner in the family brokerage firm of Dominick and Dominick, Inc. After receiving undergraduate and law degrees from Yale, Dominick was admitted to the New York bar in 1940. He served as a pilot in the U.S. Army Air Forces during World War II and then moved to Denver, where he practiced law and became active in Republican politics. After an initial defeat in 1954, Dominick was elected two years later to the Colorado House of Representatives and reelected in 1958. In 1960 Dominick defeated incumbent Democratic Representative Byron L. Johnson to win a U.S. congressional seat and was elected to the Senate two years later, defeating another incumbent, Democrat John A. Carroll. During the Kennedy administration Dominick generally took conservative stands in Congress, opposing the expansion of domestic federal programs but strongly supporting the military.

Although he supported both the Civil Rights Act of 1964 and the Voting Rights Act of 1965, on most issues before Congress, Dominick continued to take a strongly conservative position. He voted against the 1964 proposal for medical care for the elderly and tried to amend the 1965 antipoverty appropriations bill to give governors a veto over proposed community action programs, which Dominick called "the focus of infection" in antipoverty activities. His amendment was defeated by a narrow margin, and Dominick voted against the final bill, which passed the Senate, 46-22. That year Dominick was also one of only 12 senators to oppose a bill providing aid to depressed areas.

In 1966 he opposed the Model Cities program and in 1967 and 1968 he unsuccessfully introduced an amendment to transfer the preschool child development Head Start program from the Office of Economic Opportunity to the Department of Health, Education and Welfare. According to *Congressional Quarterly*, Dominick supported the conservative coalition on 79 percent of the votes on which it formed in the 88th Congress, 81 percent of such votes in the 89th Congress, and 70 percent of such votes in the 90th Congress.

Dominick was a member of the steering committee of the anticommunist Committee of One Million, which strongly opposed admitting the People's Republic of China to the UN. An officer in the Air Force Reserve, Dominick supported the U.S. bombing of North Vietnam and in 1967 argued that the mining of Haiphong harbor should be considered. In 1968 he successfully introduced an amendment to the Senate version of the administration tax surcharge bill to prevent countries over 90 days in arrears on debts to the United States from redeeming dollars for gold. (Dollars presented would be credited to their debt.)

A strong supporter of pro-business legislation, Dominick received a 100 percent rating on selected votes from the National Associated Businessmen, Inc., in 1968. In 1964 he had opposed a reduction in the oil depletion allowance and was the only Senate opponent of the extension of the Renegotiation Act, which permitted the government to regain "excessive profits" made by private defense and space contractors. Dominick also successfully opposed AFL-CIO efforts in 1965 to repeal Section 14 (b) of the Taft-Hartley Act, which in effect would have outlawed state right-to-work laws. He also voted against the 1966 increase in corporate income taxes and the increase in telephone and automobile consumer taxes.

Dominick was reelected to the Senate in 1968, defeating former Colorado governor Stephen L. R. McNichols with 58.3 percent of the vote. In 1972 he served as chair of the Republican Senatorial Campaign Committee. He was defeated for reelection in 1974 by Gary W. Hart, a Democrat who had managed Senator GEORGE MCGOVERN's (D-S.Dak.) 1972 presidential campaign. After his defeat he served as ambassador to Switzerland and then returned to Colorado. He died on March 18, 1981, in Hobe Sound, Florida.

—JBF

## Douglas, Paul H(oward)

(1892–1976) *member of the Senate; chair, Joint Economic Committee*

Douglas was born on March 26, 1892, in Salem, Massachusetts, and raised in rural Maine. He worked his way through Bowdoin College. After earning a Ph.D. in economics from Columbia University in 1921, Douglas became a leading figure in the University of Chicago's department of eco-

nomics. As a labor economist he published several influential books, of which the most important were *Real Wages in the United States (1890–1926)* and *The Theory of Wages.* During the depression Douglas served on state and federal advisory panels and helped draft the legislation that became the Social Security Act. During this period Douglas gained a national reputation as a New Deal liberal. After a short tenure in the Chicago City Council, Douglas enlisted in the U.S. Marine Corps at the age of 48 and saw action in the Pacific.

With strong backing from both Illinois liberals and Chicago's Democratic machine, Douglas won election to the Senate in 1948. During the 1950s Douglas worked closely with the Americans for Democratic Action (ADA), the NAACP, and organized labor in generally unsuccessful attempts to advance civil rights legislation, close tax loopholes, increase Social Security and minimum wage coverage, and modify Senate Rule XXII to end southern filibusters by imposition of cloture. In the early 1960s Douglas stood slightly to the left of President John F. Kennedy. He helped the administration pass a $389 million area redevelopment bill early in 1961 but voted against Kennedy's 1962 tax revision package because he considered the 7 percent investment tax credit a new and unnecessary concession to big business.

Although Douglas criticized the 1964 Kennedy-Johnson tax bill for what he considered its failure to contain major progressive reforms in the tax code, he voted for the measure in February 1964 after successfully organizing Senate opposition to a House provision that would have lowered the effective capital gains tax by $200 million a year.

Douglas was a leading opponent of Senator EVERETT M. DIRKSEN's (R-Ill.) attempt to delay implementation of recent Supreme Court rulings requiring both houses of a state legislature to be apportioned on the basis of population alone. In August 1964 Dirksen and Senate Majority Leader MIKE MANSFIELD (D-Mont.) jointly sponsored a proposal that would have delayed enforcement of the Court's rulings until January 1, 1966, thus giving reapportionment opponents time to organize in support of a constitutional amendment negating the recent judicial orders. Beginning on August 13, Douglas and five other liberal senators began a "mild" filibuster to stop passage of the Dirksen-Mansfield measure. (A mild filibuster allowed other Senate business to continue uninterrupted.) After a

Dirksen-sponsored cloture motion failed on September 10, the Senate ended the impasse when Mansfield offered a nonbinding "sense of the Congress" amendment September 24 urging district courts to give state legislatures six months to comply with the Supreme Court's reapportionment decision. The Mansfield amendment passed the same day by a vote of 44-38.

The next year Dirksen again tried to delay court-ordered reapportionment, this time by working for passage of a constitutional amendment allowing one house of any state legislature to be apportioned on a basis other than population. Douglas again rallied liberal and urban senators and defeated Dirksen's measure on August 4, 1965. With only 59 votes Dirksen's constitutional amendment fell seven short of the required two-thirds.

Another important legislative victory for Douglas was the establishment after a long fight of the Indiana Dunes National Lakeshore. Since the late 1950s Douglas had worked for the preservation of Lake Michigan's Indiana sand dunes, which were frequently visited by Chicago-area residents. He met stiff opposition from Bethlehem and National Steel, which planned to establish new mills there, and from some Indiana public officials who favored a new lake port and more industrial development. Chief among his opponents were Senator Homer Capehart (R-Ind.) and Representative CHARLES HALLECK (R-Ind.). Faced with a difficult reelection campaign in 1966, Douglas asked House and Senate Democratic leaders to expedite passage of the bill. A compromise measure, which rearranged somewhat the size and shape of the proposed park, passed the House October 14. The Senate followed suit October 18, and President Johnson signed the law November 5, 1966.

Douglas strongly supported civil rights, consumer protection, and Great Society legislation during the mid-1960s. In fact, Douglas had been unhappy when LYNDON JOHNSON became president, convinced that LBJ would oppose all civil rights reforms. His ADA rating averaged 98 percent in 1964, 1965, and 1966. Douglas also backed President Johnson's war policies in Vietnam. (In 1954 he had advocated the use of American air power to aid the French garrison beseiged at Dien Bien Phu.) He voted in favor of the Tonkin Gulf Resolution in August 1964 and in each succeeding year voted for the administration's full appropriations request.

Forty-seven-year-old Republican business executive CHARLES H. PERCY defeated Douglas for reelection in 1966 after a hard-fought campaign in which the incumbent's support of open-housing legislation emerged as the principal issue. Douglas lost votes in Cook County's ethnic suburbs after MARTIN LUTHER KING, JR., led a series of demonstration marches in favor of open housing during the summer of 1966. At the same time Douglas lost votes among affluent liberals for his continued defense of the war. Percy's candidacy was indirectly aided in September by the unsolved murder of his daughter in the family's Kenilworth, Illinois, home. Douglas immediately called a two-week halt to his campaign. Most observers thought the tragedy produced a sympathy vote for Percy.

Immediately after his election defeat, Douglas was appointed chair of the National Commission on Urban Problems by President Johnson. The commission report, finished in December 1968, sharply criticized the administration and the Department of Housing and Urban Development for their failure to provide promised low-cost housing. Johnson disagreed with the findings of the panel and refused to officially accept the report.

With former president DWIGHT D. EISENHOWER and General Omar Bradley, Douglas also served as the organizing chair of a Committee for Peace and Freedom in Vietnam. The committee was formed in 1967 to back Johnson's Vietnam policy, but, after the release of the *Pentagon Papers* in 1971, Douglas reassessed his defense of the war and came to the conclusion that his vote in favor of the Tonkin Gulf Resolution in 1964 had been based on "deception" by Johnson administration officials. From 1966 to 1969 Douglas served as a professor at the New School for Social Research. He remained in Washington, D.C., until his death there on September 24, 1976.

—NNL

## Douglas, William O(rville)
### (1898–1980) *associate justice, U.S. Supreme Court*

Born on October 16, 1898, into an impoverished family in Maine, Minnesota, and raised in Yakima, Washington, Douglas worked his way through Columbia Law School, graduating in 1925. He became a leading expert on corporate and financial law while a professor, first at Columbia and then at Yale Law School from 1927 to 1936. He was named a member of the Securities and Exchange Commission in 1936 and its chair the next year. Appointed to the Supreme Court in March 1939, Douglas used his expertise to write some of the Court's important opinions in cases on corporate reorganization, antitrust, and patent law.

These contributions, however, were eventually overshadowed by Douglas's strong defense of individual rights and his support for a broad reading and strict enforcement of the guarantees in the Bill of Rights. He was especially solicitous of First Amendment rights, eventually taking an absolutist approach toward freedom of speech, of the press, and of religion. He repeatedly dissented from cases where the majority allowed what he considered infringements of these rights. Although the Court never adopted Douglas's view of the First Amendment, many of the positions he espoused in dissent in areas such as criminal rights, reapportionment, and citizenship became established doctrines of the Supreme Court.

With Justice HUGO BLACK, Douglas insisted that the First Amendment prohibited all government regulation of allegedly obscene materials, and the two justices reaffirmed this view in obscenity decisions in June 1964 and March 1966. Douglas also joined in concurring opinions in two 1964 cases that urged the Court to hold that there was an absolute right to criticize—even maliciously—the conduct of public officials. In May 1964 Douglas wrote the Court's five-member majority opinion overturning a federal law canceling the citizenship of naturalized Americans who returned to their native land for a three-year period. Dissenting in a 1958 decision, Douglas had expressed the view that Congress could not take away American citizenship; in a May 1967 decision the Court adopted his position that citizenship could be relinquished only voluntarily.

Douglas's majority opinion in a January 1966 ruling barred the city of Macon, Georgia, from withdrawing as trustee of a local park as a device to permit the park to exclude blacks. From 1961 on Douglas concurred in decisions overturning the state convictions of civil rights demonstrators. When the Court changed course in November 1966 and upheld the trespass convictions of demonstrators who had gathered in protest outside a Florida jail, Douglas wrote the dissenting opinion and asserted that a jail could be a proper place for protest.

In favor of a broad interpretation of the Bill of Rights, Douglas joined in Warren Court decisions expanding the rights of criminal defendants. He wrote the majority opinion in an April 1965 case holding it a violation of the Fifth Amendment's privilege against self-incrimination for a state judge or district attorney to comment during a trial on a defendant's refusal to take the stand. Douglas again wrote for the Court in January 1967, when it ruled that self-incriminating statements made by public employees who had been threatened with dismissal if they invoked their Fifth Amendment rights were inadmissible at trial. Generally supporting tight restrictions on police searches, Douglas was the sole dissenter from a June 1968 decision upholding the right of police to stop and frisk persons for weapons when the action seemed necessary for the safety of the police officer and others present.

In a famed and controversial opinion for the Court in the June 1965 case of *Griswold v. Connecticut*, Douglas overturned an anticontraceptive law because it invaded a right to marital privacy, which he said was guaranteed by the Constitution. In an expansive reading of the Bill of Rights, Douglas found this right to privacy in the "penumbras, formed by emanations" from the specific guarantees of the First, Third, Fourth, Fifth, and Ninth Amendments. Douglas was also a foremost exponent of using the guarantee of equal protection to guard the rights of the poor and other disadvantaged groups as well as racial minorities. His majority opinion in a March 1966 case invalidated a poll tax for state elections on the ground that it was a denial of equal protection to make affluence a qualification for voting. In May 1968 Douglas also overturned a Louisiana law that denied illegitimate children certain rights given to legitimate offspring, insisting upon equal treatment of the two groups.

From 1967 on Douglas repeatedly dissented when the Court refused to hear cases challenging the constitutionality of the Vietnam War. He adhered to his absolutist views of free speech and religion, voted to sustain the rights of debtors, welfare recipients, and illegitimate children, and objected to Court rulings in the 1970s that narrowed the rights of criminal defendants. A controversial justice, Douglas was applauded by liberals and radicals for his willingness to hear antiwar cases, his concern for the environment, and his protection of individual rights and freedoms. Conservatives often criticized his public and private behavior, however. When he was married for a fourth time in 1966 to a 23-year-old woman, there was an attempt to impeach him for having an allegedly bad moral character. In 1970, in the wake of the Senate's rejection of two Nixon nominees for the Supreme Court, Representative GERALD R. FORD (R-Mich.) led an impeachment effort against Douglas on grounds of alleged improprieties in his professional conduct and writings. A House Judiciary subcommittee cleared Douglas of all charges in December 1970. He had avoided a similar fate two decades earlier, when his stay of execution in the case of Julius and Ethel Rosenberg aroused strong criticism.

Douglas often disagreed with other justices who said the Court's workload was too heavy. As a conservationist and naturalist, he spent much of his free time hiking, mountain climbing, and traveling. A frequent public speaker and a prolific author, Douglas wrote numerous articles and essays on the environment, on his many travels, and on international affairs. He retired from the Court in November 1975 after a stroke he had suffered at the beginning of the year left him unable to participate fully in the Court's work. He was replaced by John Paul Stevens. At the time of his retirement, Douglas's 36 years on the Court made him its longest-serving member ever.

Although criticized by some for being too doctrinaire and result-oriented, Douglas has been ranked highly by most legal analysts. Called "a bridge from an old liberalism to a new" by legal scholar John P. Frank, Douglas won special recognition for his zealous protection of the rights of the individual against the power of government. He died in January 1980 and was buried in Arlington National Cemetery (a controversial event, after biographers claimed that he had invented a military record in order to do so). Still, his influence on the courts, and on American life in general, was irrefutable.

—CAB

## Dylan, Bob

### (1941–  ) *musician*

Dylan was born Robert Allan Zimmerman on May 24, 1941. He grew up in a middle-class family in Hibbing, Minnesota, a declining mining center. In high school he led a rock-and-roll band, and during a short stay at the University of Minnesota he began publicly performing folk music. In the winter of 1960–61 Dylan came to New York City, partially to fulfill his desire to meet the then seriously ill folksinger Woody Guthrie. In New York Dylan joined a growing circle of folk musicians performing in small Greenwich Village clubs. He first received wide attention in September 1961 when *New York Times* music critic Robert Shelton favorably reviewed one of his appearances.

By the time Dylan's first record album appeared in March 1962, he had begun to write songs at a rapid rate. Over the next 15 years he produced hundreds of songs. Many of his early songs dealt with social themes. Some, like "A Hard Rain's A-Gonna Fall," described a fundamental corruption Dylan saw pervading U.S. society. Others chronicled specific cases of injustice, particularly violence and discrimination against blacks, or commented on the arms race, fallout shelters, or the blacklist.

In the civil rights and peace movements, and in the cultural awakening of the early 1960s, Dylan found hope that a new spirit was beginning to emerge. When the singing group Peter, Paul, and Mary recorded Dylan's song "Blowin' in the Wind," it became a best-selling record, introducing Dylan's writing to millions of listeners and turning the song itself into something of an anthem for supporters of the civil rights movement. Dylan himself performed at several civil rights rallies, including the August 28, 1963, March on Washington, where he sang a song about the murder of Medgar Evers.

From the start of his career Dylan was a controversial figure. Many early press accounts of him were hostile, and, in June 1963, he walked out of a scheduled appearance on the *Ed Sullivan Show* when CBS refused to allow him to sing a song parodying the John Birch Society.

Recording and performing frequently, Dylan had become a major influence on millions of young Americans by 1964, especially after the release of his popular album *The Times They Are A-Changin.* For his largely white, middle-class audience, Dylan articulated a growing if inchoate dissatisfaction with the existing society, chronicling the plight and struggles of the poor, the abused, and the victims of discrimination. His songs often had a lyricism and grace that transcended the norm of much popular music. By writing about such a wide range of subjects, Dylan helped expand the range and depth of popular music in general.

By late 1964 Dylan was turning away from explicitly political themes and, as a result, was strongly criticized by many political activists. At the Newport Folk Festival the following summer, Dylan began performing with an electrified backup band. The reaction from both audiences and critics was sharply divided, with many vehemently denouncing this departure from a supposedly "pure" folk tradition. But Dylan's popularity continued to grow.

While Dylan's writing was less explicitly political, his vision of America was if anything more scathing than ever. In *Highway 61 Revisited*, an album released in 1965, Dylan portrayed a country in which everything, including war and death, had been reduced to a commodity to be packaged and sold, while bewildered liberals responded by giving "checks to tax-deductible charity organizations." The hit single, "Like a Rolling Stone," cemented his status as one of the leading voices of his generation.

Following several hit records and successful tours of America, Europe, and Australia, Dylan was seriously injured in a motorcycle accident in upstate New York in August 1966. After a period of seclusion Dylan began releasing records again in late 1967, but he did not resume regular public performances until 1974. By the middle of the decade he had again achieved considerable popular success, which he maintained throughout a long career. He won a Grammy Award in 1975 for best artist, following the release of the popular album *Blood on the Tracks*. Overall, he would record 43 albums, with more than 57 million copies sold, on his way to becoming one of America's most influential musicians. Dylan, wrote *Rolling Stone* magazine, "not only revolutionized popular music by incorporating poetry into his compositions, he also helped create a more inclusive and progressive social consciousness in American culture."

—JBF

# E

## Eastland, James O(liver)

(1904–1986) *member of the Senate*

Born on November 28, 1904, and raised in Mississippi, Eastland was admitted to the state bar in 1927 and served in the state House of Representatives from 1928 to 1932. He spent the next nine years practicing law and running his family's 5,400-acre cotton plantation in Sunflower County, Mississippi. Eastland was appointed U.S. senator from Mississippi for 90 days in 1941 to fill a vacancy and then won election to the Senate in his own right in 1942. Eastland was reelected continuously after that, and developed a reputation as a protector of agricultural, especially cotton, interests and as an opponent of labor, social welfare, and civil rights legislation. With the support of LYNDON JOHNSON the Mississippi senator became chair of the Judiciary Committee in 1956 and used that post to forestall passage of several civil rights bills in the late 1950s. In 1954 Eastland declared: "Segregation is desired and supported by the vast majority of the members of both of the races in the South." Eastland opposed the Kennedy administration's farm bill in 1962 and its minimum wage, school aid, Medicare, and civil rights proposals. He did support a compromise administration-backed drug safety bill in 1962.

Eastland opposed virtually all of President Johnson's antipoverty programs, school aid bills, aid to urban mass transit, Medicare, and a housing and urban development bill. Although he voted against the 1965 Appalachian Regional Development Act, Eastland supported an extension of the measure in 1967, when 18 counties in northeastern Mississippi were included in the measure. Eastland also supported the 1966 Auto Safety Act and one aid-to-higher-education bill in 1968. As chair of the Senate Immigration and Nationality Subcommittee and a longtime foe of immigration law reform, however, he voted against a 1965 act ending the national origins quota system, both in committee and on the Senate floor.

As chair of the Judiciary Committee, which had jurisdiction over civil rights legislation, Eastland had the power to bottle up civil rights bills. As of 1964 the Judiciary Committee, while he was chair, had never voluntarily reported out a civil rights bill, and, in 1966, Eastland claimed to have defeated 127 such bills during his Senate years. To keep Eastland from blocking the Johnson administration's civil rights measures, the Democratic leadership won Senate approval of a motion to place the 1964 Civil Rights Act directly on the Senate calendar, bypassing the Judiciary Committee altogether. The 1965 Voting Rights Act and later civil rights bills were referred to the Judiciary Committee but with orders from the Senate to report the measures back by set deadlines. Eastland objected to both maneuvers and claimed that the time-limit provisions amounted to "legislative lynching."

Eastland also opposed the appointment of THURGOOD MARSHALL to the Supreme Court and of CONSTANCE BAKER MOTLEY to a district court judgeship. He was a strong critic of Black Power advocates and supported federal antiriot legislation. When the Judiciary Committee, meeting a Senate deadline, reported out a bill to protect civil rights workers from injury and intimidation in November 1967, Eastland denounced the move, claiming that the bill would give "added protection to roving fomenters of violence, such as STOKELY CARMICHAEL and H. RAP BROWN." He voted to add an antiriot provision to the 1968 Civil Rights Act.

Eastland was floor manager for the cotton title of an administration-backed farm bill in 1964. The cotton section provided for subsidies to domestic textile mills to decrease the price they paid for domestic cotton. This bill, which he successfully steered through the Senate, was designed to make domestic cotton competitive in price, thus aiding both the textile industry and cotton farmers. Eastland's own cotton plantation became a source of increasing controversy in the Johnson years. Civil rights activists criticized the fact that Eastland received over $100,000 per year in cotton price supports and diversion cash payments from the government. In July 1965 a representative of the Mississippi Freedom Labor Union denounced the working conditions of black sharecroppers on Eastland's plantation in testimony before a House Education and Labor Subcommittee. In July 1967 a team of six physicians who had investigated malnutrition in Mississippi reported to a Senate Labor and Public Welfare Subcommittee that conditions in the delta region, where Eastland's plantation was located, approached starvation. Eastland and his colleague Senator JOHN C. STENNIS (D-Miss.) immediately denied that there was mass malnutrition in the Mississippi delta.

An outspoken anticommunist, Eastland supported Johnson's policy in Vietnam, and, as chair of the Senate Internal Security Subcommittee, he repeatedly searched for evidence of domestic communism. He suggested that the June 21 disappearances of three civil rights workers, later found murdered near Philadelphia, Mississippi, might be a communist-inspired "hoax." During Judiciary Committee hearings on the 1965 Voting Rights Act, Eastland claimed that the Mississippi Freedom Democratic Party was communist-influenced. In the committee's 1967 hearings on antiriot bills, he contended that "all these riots follow the same pattern. They follow the tactics used by the Communist party all over the world." Eastland criticized the Supreme Court's rulings on internal security laws and in 1968 sponsored a wide-ranging internal security bill designed to circumvent many of the Court's decisions. The bill, which was not acted on by Congress that year, included provisions to extend the life of the Subversive Activities Control Board (SACB) and authorize the SACB to hold hearings to determine if organizations were communist-action groups. It also barred members of such groups from union membership and employment in defense facilities or public schools receiving federal funds and eliminated federal court jurisdiction over the actions of congressional committees.

Eastland repeatedly denounced the Court's decisions on civil rights, criminal law, and reapportionment. In 1964 he supported efforts to delay the implementation of the Court's "one-person, one-vote" ruling. A strong law-and-order advocate, Eastland complained that the Court's criminal decisions "bound and gagged the dedicated lawman in a web of tangled and twisted legalities so that he is better armed with a law book than a night-stick." He voted for the 1968 Omnibus Crime Control and Safe Streets Act and against a 1968 law banning mail-order and out-of-state sales of rifles, shotguns, and ammunition. In an effort to change the Supreme Court's line of decisions, Eastland opposed the appointment of Associate Justice ABE FORTAS as chief justice in 1968.

Eastland, who was elected to his fifth Senate term in a landslide victory in 1966, held a reputation for fairness in his role as Judiciary Committee chair. He decentralized the committee, which had amassed the largest budget and staff of any congressional committee by 1971, leaving subcommittee chairs with a great deal of autonomy. With the notable exception of civil rights measures, Eastland assigned bills to subcommittees on the basis of subject matter and precedent, generally did not try to hold bills in full committee, and rarely delayed legislation approved by a subcommittee even when he opposed it.

During the Nixon years Eastland supported all of Nixon's Supreme Court appointments, including the nominations of Clement F. Haynsworth and G. Harrold Carswell. He voted against the Equal Rights Amendment, home rule for the District of Columbia, and fought busing for school desegregation. He remained a strong supporter of the war in Southeast Asia, voting against the Cooper-Church amendment to limit American military involvement in Cambodia in June 1970. He retired in 1978 and returned to Mississippi. He died in Doddsville, Mississippi, on February 19, 1986.

—CAB

## Eckstein, Otto
(1927–1984) *member, Council of Economic Advisers*
Otto Eckstein was born on August 1, 1927, and emigrated with his family from Germany in 1939. He

completed his elementary and secondary education in New York City, entering the army after graduation in 1946. Eckstein received his B.A. from Princeton in 1951 and his Ph.D. in economics from Harvard in 1955, when he joined the Harvard faculty. His first two books concerned the government's role in water resource development. A skilled economic forecaster, Eckstein served as a consultant to the Rand Corporation from 1957 to 1964 and was technical director of the Joint Economic Committee of Congress in 1959. During the Kennedy administration he served as a consultant to the Treasury Department and the Council of Economic Advisers (CEA). President Johnson appointed him to the CEA in September 1964.

Like the other CEA members during the Kennedy and Johnson administrations, Eckstein was an exponent of Keynesian economics, which held that the federal government could effectively combat inflation or recession with an alert fiscal policy. Eckstein had criticized the conservative economic policies of the Eisenhower administration and admonished Kennedy not to let the balance of payments problem weaken a vigorous antirecession program. During the Johnson administration inflation, not recession, was the primary danger. In 1967 Eckstein called for a temporary tax increase to curb inflation fueled by spending on the Vietnam War and Great Society programs. He argued that relying solely on monetary policy to control inflation was crippling the housing and construction industry because of high interest rates. In 1964 he pushed LBJ to oppose a rate increase by aluminum firms, a fight that the president won easily. The following year he opposed an increase in the minimum wage, arguing that it would stifle economic growth, especially in the South.

Eckstein left the CEA in February 1966 and returned to Harvard. He remained a prominent liberal economist throughout the decade. In the fall of 1968 he headed a special study group on inflation for Democratic presidential candidate HUBERT HUMPHREY, which acknowledged that the administration's wage-price "guideposts" policy had failed and suggested a conference with labor and management to come up with "a set of principles of responsible wage and price behavior." He later cofounded Data Resources, Inc., an economic forecasting company. He died of cancer in 1984.

—TO

## Edwards, William Donlon (Don)
(1915–   ) *member of the House of Representatives*

Edwards, who was born on January 6, 1915, in San José, California, attended Stanford University Law School from 1936 to 1938 but never received a degree, although he passed the bar exam in 1940. From 1940 to 1941 he served as an FBI agent. After World War II he founded the Valley Title Company and became a millionaire. In 1962 Edwards won a seat in the U.S. House of Representatives from the overwhelmingly Democratic Ninth Congressional District of California, which included San José.

Edwards compiled one of the most liberal records in Congress during the middle and late 1960s. In 1965 and 1966 he was chosen national chair of Americans for Democratic Action. He was a consistent supporter of President Lyndon B. Johnson's Great Society programs and civil rights measures, while opposing the administration's escalation of American military involvement in Southeast Asia. In May 1965 Edwards joined six other representatives in voting against a supplementary defense authorization bill for the Vietnam war. Two years later he was one of three members of the lower house who opposed a defense procurement and research authorization bill that provided funds for the war.

In 1965, 1967, and 1968 Edwards unsuccessfully introduced motions against the appropriation of funds for the House Un-American Activities Committee (HUAC). During floor debate in February 1965 he asserted that the panel's existence was unconstitutional because of "its practice of investigating with no legislative purpose but exclusively for the purpose of exposure, and . . . its practice of holding legislative trials in violation of Section 9, Title I of the Constitution proscribing bills of attainder."

In 1971 Edwards became chair of the Judiciary Committee's Subcommittee No. Four—also known as the Civil Rights Oversight Committee. In that post he successfully pressed for House passage of a constitutional amendment guaranteeing equal rights to women. In July 1974 he voted in favor of all of the five articles of impeachment against President RICHARD M. NIXON considered by the Judiciary Committee. He retired from Congress in 1995 and returned to California.

—MLL

## Eisenhower, Dwight D(avid)
### (1890–1969) *president of the United States*

The third of seven sons, born on October 14, 1890, in Denison, Texas, to a farming family, Dwight D. Eisenhower grew up in Abilene, Kansas. There he was nicknamed "Ike" and worked at a variety of jobs in order to support his brothers' college education. In 1915 Eisenhower graduated from West Point. He served as a tank instructor during World War I and remained in the army after the armistice. During the 1930s he worked under U.S. Army chief of staff Douglas A. MacArthur, following him to the Philippines, where his superior went to reorganize the islands' defenses.

On the eve of America's entry into World War II, Eisenhower returned from the Philippines and quickly received a series of promotions that led to his command of Allied forces in the European theater. He oversaw the Allied invasions of North Africa in 1942, Sicily and Italy in 1943, and Normandy in 1944.

Eisenhower resigned as army chief of staff in February 1948 to become president of Columbia University. In 1951 he assumed command of the forces newly organized under the North Atlantic Treaty Organization (NATO). One year later Eisenhower won the Republican presidential nomination as the candidate of the GOP's "Eastern" or "internationalist" wing in a contest against conservative senator Robert A. Taft (R-Ohio). The most popular war leader since Ulysses S. Grant, with a pleasing public personality and an easy grin, Eisen-

hower handily defeated his Democratic opponent, ADLAI E. STEVENSON, in 1952 and again in 1956.

In foreign affairs Eisenhower ended one war and prevented outright American participation in others. In July 1953 he secured an armistice in the Korean War. A year later he rejected counsel favoring the deployment of U.S. air power on the side of the French in Indochina. To prevent further communist territorial advances, his secretary of state, John Foster Dulles, negotiated regional mutual security agreements modeled after the North Atlantic Treaty Organization (NATO) in Asia and in the Middle East.

After the 1954 Geneva Conference held to resolve the Indochina conflict, Eisenhower supported the South Vietnamese regime of Ngo Dinh Diem. He acquiesced in its decision not to permit free elections for the reunification of Vietnam, a violation of the Geneva Accords, because of fear that the Communists would win. Instead, the United States supplied the Diem regime with military assistance, which it hoped would assure political stability. Eisenhower also ordered small contingents of U.S. military advisers to assist in the training of the South Vietnamese army.

Although a career army officer Eisenhower sought to reduce defense expenditures. His "new look" military budgets reduced defense appropriations at the expense of conventional "limited" army and navy systems. In his January 1961 Farewell Address, Eisenhower warned of the dangers to a democratic society from a "military-industrial complex" consisting of "an immense military establishment and a large arms industry." During the Kennedy presidency he called for cuts in the defense budget and reduced troop commitments to NATO.

In the political arena Eisenhower's own high standing did not rejuvenate the Republican Party. Younger and independent voters who faithfully voted for the general would not extend their support to his adopted party. During his presidency the percentage of registered Republicans declined. The GOP lost control of Congress in 1954 and through the end of his presidency never regained its majority. He did, however, maintain a good working relationship with many Democrats, including Senate Majority Leader LYNDON JOHNSON, especially on matters related to foreign policy.

To the end of his life, Eisenhower remained the most popular leader in the Republican Party. In the months preceding the 1964 Republican National

General Eisenhower meeting with President Johnson aboard Jetstar, 1965 *(Photographed by Yoichi R. Okamoto; Lyndon Baines Johnson Library)*

Convention, reporters and presidential aspirants repeatedly sought his views on the GOP presidential nomination. The former president followed a confusing and somewhat contradictory course in the final stages of the contest for the 1964 Republican presidential nomination. Following the June 2 California primary, the nomination of conservative senator BARRY M. GOLDWATER (R-Ariz.) appeared inevitable unless a broad coalition of moderate and liberal Republicans united behind a single candidate openly backed by Eisenhower. The general urged Pennsylvania governor WILLIAM W. SCRANTON to challenge Goldwater. Believing that the former president would endorse him, Scranton prepared his declaration of candidacy for the June 7 edition of the nationally televised *Face the Nation* program.

At the last moment, however, Eisenhower's first Treasury secretary, George Humphrey, persuaded his old chief not to act on Scranton's behalf. Humphrey argued that Goldwater, whom he supported, would likely gain the nomination regardless of Scranton's candidacy and that Eisenhower would risk his own prestige in a hopeless cause. The general called Scranton and withdrew his offer. As a consequence the Pennsylvania governor delayed his announcement and gave a confusing performance on *Face the Nation*. Four days later, after Goldwater voted against cloture in the Senate debate over the civil rights bill, Scranton decided to run with or without the former president's help. Goldwater, however, won the nomination easily.

Eisenhower endorsed the Vietnam policies of President Lyndon B. Johnson. In private discussions with the president, he counseled strong military action to achieve victory in Vietnam. He also resented the rising and spirited protests against American involvement in Vietnam. In March 1966 Eisenhower suggested imprisonment for draft-card burners "at least for the war's duration." In October 1967 he joined former president HARRY S. TRUMAN and other political and academic leaders in the formation of the Citizen's Committee for Peace and Freedom in Vietnam, organized as a counterpart to the numerous antiwar committees established in the preceding months. In December Eisenhower reiterated his belief in the "domino theory" that he himself had first propounded. Withdrawal from South Vietnam, he warned, meant that "it will only be a question of time before every country up to the borders of India falls under the Communist heel."

As a retired general of the army, Eisenhower frequently answered questions about strategy in Vietnam. In September 1966 he called for "as much force as we need to win." Tactical nuclear weapons, he later confided to former presidential adviser Arthur Larson, should be employed if the Communist Chinese army entered the war in Southeast Asia.

Ironically, opponents of American involvement in Vietnam seized upon Eisenhower's own words to buttress their arguments. Some presented his concept of a "military-industrial" complex as a cause for the tragic Asian conflict. The North Vietnamese also repeated Eisenhower's frank admissions of their popularity compared to the Diem regime during the 1950s.

Ike's popular standing remained high during the 1960s, and the reputation of his presidency actually rose among intellectuals. During the decade he ranked second only to the incumbent president among the Gallup poll survey lists of the "most admired living Americans." In January 1968 Eisenhower actually outpolled Johnson. Previously attacked by many scholars, his presidency earned praise from historians who were disenchanted with the "imperial presidency" and its interventionist foreign policy and more appreciative of the smiling general's unifying leadership style.

In July 1968 Eisenhower endorsed RICHARD M. NIXON, his running mate in 1952 and 1956, for the 1968 Republican presidential nomination. He denied earlier speculation that he "never really liked or supported or really believed in Nixon." Three weeks later, on the eve of the national convention, Eisenhower suffered a severe heart attack from which he never recovered. He died less than three weeks after his former vice president finally assumed the presidency.

—JLB

## Eisenhower, Milton S(tover)
**(1899–1985)** *president, Johns Hopkins University; chair, President's Commission on the Causes and Prevention of Violence*

Milton Eisenhower, a younger brother of DWIGHT D. EISENHOWER, was born on September 15, 1899, in Abilene, Kansas, graduated from Kansas State University in 1924, and immediately entered government service. Between 1926 and 1941 he held important posts in the Department of Agriculture.

Eisenhower worked for the War Relocation Authority and the Office of War Information until 1943, when he was named president of Kansas State College of Agriculture and Applied Science. He became president of Pennsylvania State University in 1950 and of the Johns Hopkins University in 1956. Meanwhile, he continued to offer his services to the government. In 1945 he helped reorganize the Department of Agriculture, and, from 1946 to 1948, he was chair of the U.S. National Commission for the United Nations Economic and Social Council.

Milton was his brother's admired and trusted adviser during the 1950s. He worked on Dwight's presidential campaigns, served as a member of the President's Committee on Government Organization, and was credited with initiating changes in Latin American policy that later developed into the Alliance for Progress. In Kennedy's first year in office, Eisenhower served on the Tractors for Freedom Committee, which unsuccessfully tried to trade agricultural tractors to Cuban leader Fidel Castro in exchange for the release of prisoners captured in the Bay of Pigs invasion.

Eisenhower was a key member of the Republican Party's liberal "brain trust." Beginning in September 1963 he headed the Critical Issues Council of the Republican Citizens Committee. He worked with 24 Republican intellectuals and experts who produced analyses and proposed alternative national policies to those advocated by the Kennedy and Johnson administrations. Eisenhower was responsible for a study on Panama that recommended construction of a new canal by conventional methods (i.e., without the use of nuclear devices), a toll increase for the existing canal, and larger payments to the Panamanian government. Republican moderates hoped that the council's recommendations would be included in the party's 1964 platform, but the work was attacked by party conservatives, and Senator BARRY GOLDWATER (R-Ariz.) tried to disband the council. Goldwater eventually met with Eisenhower in June 1964 and said that he agreed with the findings of all the studies except those on civil rights. Eisenhower nominated moderate Pennsylvania governor WILLIAM SCRANTON at the Republican National Convention. The delegates chose Goldwater and ignored the Critical Issues studies in drafting the party's platform.

President Johnson often sought Eisenhower's advice, particularly on Latin American questions. From 1965 to 1970 Eisenhower worked on the President's Commission for an Atlantic-Pacific Interoceanic Canal Study. An early proponent of educational television, he accepted appointment to the board of directors of the Corporation for Public Broadcasting in March 1968. Eisenhower resigned this post in June when the president asked him to head the Commission on the Causes and Prevention of Violence.

President Johnson formed the Commission on Violence immediately after the assassination of Senator ROBERT F. KENNEDY (D-N.Y.) and a few months after the shooting of MARTIN LUTHER KING, JR. The panel spent $1.6 million and employed as many as 100 staff members to produce a comprehensive study of violence. The 13-member commission held public hearings and created task forces to study seven major areas: individual acts of violence, group violence, assassinations and political violence, the effects of violence in the mass media, firearms, the criminal justice system, and the history of violence. Scholars were recruited to conduct research studies on specific issues and subjects related to the seven major areas, which the committee promised not to edit. Released as "Reports to the Commission" and not as "Reports by the Commission," these included the controversial Walker report, which charged the Chicago police with responsibility for much of the violence at the Democratic National Convention in August 1968.

The statement on campus unrest, issued in June 1969, was the first to carry the commission's policy seal. Eight more followed throughout the year, and the final report was presented on December 12, 1969. In their papers the panel members asserted that the United States was the most "criminogenic" of politically stable Western nations, its law enforcement and criminal justice systems ineffective, and its efforts to eliminate the social causes of crime inadequate. The commission concluded that the crime rate accelerated in the 1960s in part because of the rising expectations engendered by government social welfare programs and the mass media. Only the establishment of a police state could eliminate crime, said Eisenhower, but a national commitment of at least $20 billion annually might reverse the upward trend in the crime rate. The committee specifically recommended gun-control legislation, better police training, and efforts to provide full employment, reduce narcotics addiction, improve housing and schools, and restructure the urban tax base. Eisenhower's only notable disagreement with other members of the commission was his dissent from the seven-to-six majority statement of December 8, 1969, that condemned all massive civil disobedience, including nonviolent action.

Eisenhower was unhappy that President RICHARD M. NIXON failed to act on the commission's recommendations, but he wrote that the panel's work educated the public and may have influenced the next generation of legislators. President emeritus of the Johns Hopkins University since 1967, Eisenhower temporarily took over active leadership of the school in 1971 and 1972. The next year he was named chair of the President's Commission on International Radio Broadcasting. He died on May 3, 1985.

—JCH

## Ellender, Allen J(oseph)
### (1890–1972) *member of the Senate*

Ellender was born in Montegut, Louisiana, on September 24, 1890. After a career as a farmer-lawyer and city and district attorney, Ellender was elected to the Louisiana House of Representatives where he served for 12 years, the last four as speaker. Though he entered the legislature as an opponent of Huey Long, they formed an alliance in 1929, when Ellender joined Long's defense in his impeachment trial. After Senator Long's assassination in 1935 the Long organization slated Ellender for the Senate vacancy. In office Ellender was appointed to the Agriculture Committee and coauthored the Agricultural Adjustment Act of 1937. In January 1951 Ellender became chair of the Agriculture and Forestry Committee and in 1955 used his position as chair to secure new sugar import quotas more favorable to Louisiana's sugar industry. He supported the Kennedy administration's 1961 feed grain bill, which removed price support protection from farmers who declined to participate in the government's acreage retirement program.

Ellender was a leader of the southern opposition to the Civil Rights Act of 1964. He supervised one of the three Senate filibuster teams and warned

in his final speech on the civil rights bill that "its passage will bring on more strife than one can contemplate." However, once the bill became law Ellender broadcast a statewide appeal for "calm and reason" in Louisiana and called for resistance only "within the framework of the orderly processes established by law." In 1965 Ellender continued to oppose civil rights legislation and replaced Senator RICHARD RUSSELL (D-Ga.) as the leader of the southern resistance to the 1965 Voting Rights Act. When some southern senators, including his colleague Senator RUSSELL LONG (D-La.), showed signs of wavering, Ellender vowed to speak against the bill "as long as God gives me breath."

Ellender clashed with the Johnson administration in 1964 over the administration's new cotton commodity program. In opposition to an administration bill that created a new cotton price and acreage system and subsidized domestic textile mills, Ellender introduced a measure, written by the American Farm Bureau Federation, to reduce the price support from 32.47 cents to 30 cents a pound and to eliminate the cotton mill subsidy. The administration regarded this bill as excessively hard on many of the small cotton farmers of heavily Democratic portions of the Southeast. Ellender opposed the administration's cotton provisions in committee but supported the bill on the Senate floor, where he managed to cut the program's duration from four to two years. Ellender also clashed with the administration that same year over the increasing American involvement in Vietnam. "We should never have gone in there," he told the Foreign Relations Committee in March. "We should get out."

Ellender was floor manager for the administration's food stamp measures of 1964 and 1967. When the program came up for renewal in March 1967, the administration asked for at least a three-year extension, but the House would agree to appropriate money for only one year. The bill was tied up in a House-Senate conference for three months until Ellender persuaded House conferees to compromise on a two-year extension in September. Ellender resigned as chair of the Agriculture Committee in January 1971 to become chair of the Appropriations Committee. At his death on July 27, 1972, Ellender was also president pro tempore of the Senate and third in the line of presidential succession.

—DKR

## Epstein, Jason

(1930–  ) *founder,* The New York Review of Books

Born on August 25, 1928, in Cambridge, Massachusetts, Jason Epstein graduated from Columbia University in 1949. In 1951 Epstein took a job as an editor of Doubleday & Co., where he began Anchor Books, the first important line of quality paperbacks. In 1958 he left Doubleday to become a senior editor and vice president of Random House.

With a reputation as a powerful and enterprising editor committed to serious literature, Epstein built an extensive network of friends and contacts among writers and literary critics. In the early 1960s he discussed with some of these intellectuals the possibility of starting a newsprint paper for book reviews on the model of the *Times Literary Supplement* of London. A prolonged newspaper strike in New York in early 1963, which shut down the *New York Times Book Review,* freed a great deal of advertising money, readers, and reviewers to help Epstein realize his project. With the aid of Robert B. Silvers, a former editor of *Harper's* and the *Paris Review,* the poet Robert Lowell and Lowell's wife, Elizabeth Hardwick, *The New York Review of Books* began publication in February 1963. Silvers and Barbara Epstein (Jason Epstein's wife) were named as the editors; Hardwick was designated as an advising editor and Epstein and Lowell as members of the journal's board.

*Review* contributors soon included some of the most eminent members of the American literary world: F. W. Dupee, NATHAN GLAZER, PAUL GOODMAN, IRVING HOWE, Alfred Kazin, DWIGHT MACDONALD, NORMAN MAILER, and SUSAN SONTAG. Beginning regular biweekly publication shortly after its debut, the review characteristically ran long interpretative literary and political essays rather than straightforward book reviews. The Vietnam issue arose in its pages for the first time in 1964 with an article by I. F. STONE. This was followed in late 1965 by articles and reviews on Vietnam from HANS MORGENTHAU, Joseph Kraft, Bernard Fall, and Jean Lacouture—all expressing opposition to the U.S. escalation of the war.

During the late 1960s *The New York Review* became the country's most influential publication of America's liberal-radical intellectual community. From 1965 until the end of the decade it devoted more space to American involvement in Southeast Asia than to any other topic, and it featured such systematic critiques of American foreign policy as NOAM CHOMSKY's influential antiwar article, "The Responsibility of Intellectuals." In April 1966 Epstein himself contributed "The CIA and the Intellectuals," an exposé of liberal anticommunism in the 1950s and early 1960s. It followed *Ramparts* magazine's revelation that the CIA had been involved in funding the National Student Association.

The New York City teachers' strike in the fall of 1968 split the New York intellectual community, with *Commentary* and *Dissent* on the side of the teachers' union and *The Review* on the side of black proponents of community control of the schools. In a series of articles on the strike, Epstein responded to the charge made by the union and its supporters that anti-Semitism was behind much of the black community's hostility to the union. "Undoubtedly," he wrote, "there have been expressions of anti-Semitism on the part of the various black demagogues, and as the largely Jewish UFT [United Federation of Teachers] insists on pitting its strength against the black community, there will be more. Yet it seems to have become the policy of the union, whenever such slanders have been committed by blacks, to amplify them in a way that suggests that the Nuremberg rallies are about to be resumed in the Abyssinian Baptist Church."

In the fall and winter of 1969 and 1970 Epstein covered the trial of the "Chicago Eight," then under federal prosecution for their roles in the 1968 protests at the Democratic National Convention. His articles on the tumultuous courtroom events were printed in *The New York Review* and later published in rewritten form in *The Great Conspiracy Trial* (1970).

Epstein continually denied having great editorial influence over *The Review,* insisting that it was the unique product of its writers and editors. But in his history of the journal, *Intellectual Skywriting,* Philip Noble suggested that Epstein was in fact a predominant influence behind *The New York Review.* Epstein remained active in intellectual publishing over subsequent decades. In 1982 he started *The Library of America,* which released elegant versions of classic American works, and four years later created *The Reader's Catalog,* which sold high-quality literature directly to readers. In 1988 he became the first recipient of the National

Book Award for Distinguished Service to American Letters.

—TLH

## Ervin, Sam(uel) J(ames), Jr.
### (1896–1985) *member of the Senate*

A graduate of the University of North Carolina and of Harvard Law School, Ervin, who was born on September 27, 1896, practiced law in his hometown of Morganton, North Carolina, and served three terms in the North Carolina Assembly between 1923 and 1933. He was a judge on the Burke County Criminal Court from 1935 to 1937, on the North Carolina Superior Court from 1937 to 1943 and on the state Supreme Court from 1948 to 1954. He was appointed to the U.S. Senate in June 1954 and easily won election to three full terms. With legal and constitutional issues as his main interest, Ervin established a reputation as the Senate's expert on the Constitution and built a conservative record on most domestic and foreign policy issues.

A member of the Senate Judiciary Committee, Ervin was a leader in the fight against civil rights legislation during the 1960s. In hearings on civil rights proposals, Ervin frequently engaged administration witnesses in lengthy debates on the constitutionality and fairness of the bills. On the Senate floor he repeatedly offered major amendments to delete or seriously weaken various titles of civil rights acts. Ervin always contended that while he opposed racial discrimination, the federal laws designed to end it were unconstitutional invasions of states rights and individual personal and property rights.

As a result of his strict interpretation of the Constitution, Ervin built a liberal record on civil liberties issues. As head of the Judiciary Committee's Constitutional Rights subcommittee after 1961, Ervin conducted hearings on the rights of mental patients, military personnel, Indians, and federal employees. He successfully sponsored the 1964 District of Columbia Mental Health Act, which included a patient's bill of rights; the 1964 Criminal Justice Act, providing free legal counsel to indigent defendants in federal courts; and the 1966 Bail Reform Act, making it possible for federal criminal defendants who could not afford bail to be released pending trial. He also introduced the Military Justice Act of 1968, which reformed much of the court-martial system. In March 1968 he persuaded the Senate to agree unanimously to his amendment adding an "Indian Bill of Rights" to the 1968 Civil Rights Act.

An advocate of strict separation of church and state, Ervin spoke out against a constitutional amendment to allow prayer in public schools in September 1966. His speech contributed to the defeat of this proposal in the Senate. He regularly introduced bills to authorize taxpayer suits challenging federal aid to religiously affiliated schools and hospitals. The Senate passed such a bill in 1966 and again in 1967, but the House failed to act. Ervin also sponsored legislation to protect the right to privacy of federal employees. Again his proposal was adopted by the Senate in 1967 but died in the House.

However, Ervin opposed many of the Warren Court's rulings expanding the rights of criminal suspects, and he backed a section of the 1968 Omnibus Crime Control and Safe Streets Act designed to override several of those decisions. He also fought the appointment of THURGOOD MARSHALL to the Supreme Court in 1967 and the nomination of ABE FORTAS as chief justice in 1968 on the ground that both were judicial activists likely to support Court trends he opposed.

A supporter of the war in Vietnam and a conservative on military and defense issues, Ervin also opposed much social welfare legislation. Although he voted for the 1964 Economic Opportunity Act and aid to elementary and secondary schools in 1965, he opposed programs such as Medicare, Model Cities, aid to mass transit, child-care, and Project Headstart. He supported environmental legislation but voted against gun control, financial disclosure for members of Congress and labor legislation such as the 1966 Mine Safety Act. He also played a leading role in the Senate investigation of labor racketeering.

In later years Ervin led the fight against the Equal Rights Amendment and against Nixon administration anticrime proposals authorizing preventive detention and "no-knock" policy entry. He conducted hearings on army surveillance of civilians and on invasions of privacy caused by the use of computers and data banks. With a folksy, Bible-quoting, story-telling style, Ervin won national prominence in 1973 when he headed a seven-member Senate committee set up to investigate the Watergate scandal.

He retired from the Senate in January 1975. He returned to North Carolina to practice law and died in Winston-Salem on April 23, 1985.

—CAB

## Evans, Daniel J(ackson)

(1925– )    *governor*

Born in Seattle, Washington, on October 16, 1925, Evans received his B.S. and M.S. degrees at the University of Washington and then worked as a civil engineer in Seattle. In 1956 he was elected to the state House of Representatives, where he served twice as the Republican minority leader. In 1964 he vacated his safe seat to wage an uphill campaign for governor. In the September primary of that year, Evans, a moderate Republican, defeated a conservative pro-Goldwater candidate, Richard Christensen, by 100,000 votes. Though not previously well known, Evans countered the Democratic landslide of 1964 to defeat two-term incumbent Albert Rossellini in the general election. His campaign, run independently of the Goldwater presidential bid, proposed a "Blueprint for Progress," a 35-point program promising increased spending for education and welfare, coupled with inducements for industrial expansion, the reform of archaic administrative structures, and the abolition of the lucrative fee-appraiser system, one of the governor's choicest patronage plums.

Governor Evans's initial problem was to establish legislative reapportionment to accord with the 1964 "one person, one vote" Supreme Court ruling. Evans induced the recalcitrant Democratic-controlled Washington state legislature to enact an acceptable reapportionment plan in 1965. He also secured the total or partial passage of 24 of his 35 blueprint proposals after his first year.

After the Republican Party's devastating defeat of 1964, Evans argued that reviving the party could be best accomplished by gaining control of state houses and exercising strong leadership at that level. With Evans serving as the party's chief tactician in the 1966 elections, the GOP gained control of 25 governorships, a net gain of eight over the previous year.

Evans had become an advocate of the "new federalism" by 1967. In that year he called for state government to "reassume its rightful responsibilities" in coping with local problems and to end its reliance on centrally administered federal solutions.

He stressed that the states rather than the federal government could best devise solutions to economic and social problems. His 1968 keynote address at the Republican National Convention prompted a *Time* cover story praising the "creative federalism" outlined in his speech.

Evans's first term as Washington governor saw the enactment of air and water-pollution controls, the preservation of recreation areas, the initiation of a $242 million school-building construction program, and the increase of state grants to localities to restore strength to the lower levels of government. Evans won reelection in 1968 by defeating Washington state attorney general, John J. O'Connell, with 54 percent of the vote. During this term a special legislative session in 1970 focused on the environment, producing a set of bills designed to foster cleaner air and water, restore landscape destroyed by strip mining, protect endangered lands, and create the nation's first department of ecology. He was reelected to his third term in 1972. In 1983 Evans was appointed to the U.S. Senate after the death of then-senator HENRY JACKSON, and remained in that office until 1989.

—TJC

## Evers, (James) Charles

(1922– )    *field secretary, Mississippi NAACP*

Evers was born on September 11, 1922, and grew up in Decatur, Mississippi. He received a B.A. from Alcorn A & M College in 1950. He moved to Philadelphia, Mississippi, the next year and established several successful businesses, including a funeral parlor, hotel, cafe, and taxi service, all of which catered to the local black community. Evers also worked closely with his brother Medgar, who became state field secretary for the NAACP in 1954. As a result of his civil rights work, white segregationists put such severe economic pressures on Charles Evers that he was forced to leave Mississippi in 1956, and moved to Chicago.

Medgar Evers was assassinated by a sniper outside his home in Jackson, Mississippi, on June 12, 1963. Charles returned to the state immediately and asked the NAACP to let him succeed his brother as the organization's Mississippi field secretary. Assuming the job on June 16, Evers worked in campaigns to desegregate public accommodations and register black voters, concentrating on McComb, during 1964. He was arrested in Jackson in June 1965 for

Mrs. Medgar Evers and Mr. Charles Evers, wife and brother of slain activist Medgar Evers, and Mrs. Ruby Hurley (left) address a meeting for the NAACP, 1963 *(Library of Congress, Prints and Photographs Division)*

leading demonstrations to protest a special state legislative session called to rewrite Mississippi's voting and registration laws.

Following passage of the federal Voting Rights Act in August 1965, Evers moved his office to Fayette in Jefferson County, one of several predominantly black counties in southwest Mississippi. From the fall of 1965 through early 1967 he organized highly effective boycotts by the black communities in Natchez, Fayette, Port Gibson, and other towns in the area. In each place black demands included the integration of schools, hospitals, and public accommodations, increased employment of blacks by city agencies and private businesses, the use of courtesy titles for blacks by city employees, and black representation on juries and school boards. A boycott of white merchants, mass marches, and picketing continued in each town until black demands were met. At the same time Evers and NAACP state president AARON HENRY organized local NAACP chapters and took advantage of the federal voting rights law to increase dramatically voter registration

among blacks. Between 1963 and 1971 the number of blacks registered in Mississippi rose from 28,000 to over 250,000. Evers also became close with Lyndon Johnson during this period. He would later call LBJ "one of the greatest presidents this country has ever had.

When JAMES MEREDITH was shot on June 6, 1966, while on a protest march from Memphis, Tennessee, to Jackson, Mississippi, Evers joined national civil rights leaders in continuing the march. However, Evers repudiated a strongly worded march manifesto issued June 8, declaring it "too critical of President Johnson." He also complained that the highly publicized march could "turn into another Selma, where everyone goes home with the cameramen and leaves us holding the bag." After other march leaders announced that they would encourage black voter registration while en route to Jackson, Evers supported the march's objectives and labeled the protest a "good thing." Evers led demonstrations in Natchez in February and March 1967 to protest the murder of a local

NAACP official. He also led marches in Jackson in June after police shot and killed a black delivery man during disturbances at Jackson State College.

Evers ran for Congress in a 1968 special election to fill the seat vacated by JOHN BELL WILLIAMS after he became Mississippi governor in January. Running against six white opponents, Evers won a plurality in the February 27 election but lost the runoff on March 12 by over 40,000 votes. He supported Senator ROBERT F. KENNEDY (D-N.Y.) in his bid for the Democratic presidential nomination in 1968, serving as state cochair for the Kennedy campaign in Mississippi. Evers campaigned for Kennedy in California and was with the senator when he was assassinated on June 5.

The regular Mississippi Democratic Party selected Evers in July 1968 as one of four blacks in its 68-member delegation to the August Democratic National Convention (DNC). Evers rejected the offer as "tokenism," helped organize a biracial challenge delegation, the Loyal Democrats of Mississippi, and testified before the DNC Credentials Committee. On August 20 the committee voted overwhelmingly to unseat the regular state delegation and give all of Mississippi's convention seats to the challengers. Following the convention Evers

was chosen the Democratic national committee member from Mississippi.

Evers remained a shrewd entrepreneur as well as a tireless activist and organizer in Mississippi. He repeatedly argued that economic independence, with increased black employment and black-owned businesses, was a crucial underpinning for black political advancement in the South. In 1966 Evers opened the Medgar Evers Shopping Center in Fayette, and, in 1970, he added a motel with a restaurant and lounge to the complex.

Evers ran for mayor of Fayette in 1969, organizing a strong drive to get out the black vote. He won the May 13 Democratic primary, was unopposed in the June election, and resigned his post as NAACP state field secretary before he was sworn in as mayor on July 7. The first black mayor of a biracial community in Mississippi since Reconstruction, Evers successfully lobbied with the federal government, foundations, and businesses to secure grants and new industry for Fayette. In April 1971 he was nominated to run for governor by the Loyal Democrats, but he was defeated in the November election. He remained Fayette mayor until 1981 and then served again from 1985 to 1989.

—CAB

## Farmer, James L(eonard)

(1920–1999) *national director, Congress of Racial Equality*

Farmer, who was born on January 12, 1920, in Marshall, Texas, received a bachelor of divinity degree from Howard University in 1941 but refused ordination as a Methodist minister because the church was then segregated in the South. Instead he became involved in civil rights. He was race relations secretary for the Fellowship of Reconciliation and program director for the NAACP. Farmer was a founder of the Congress of Racial Equality (CORE), created in the early 1940s as an interracial organization to fight racial discrimination by means of nonviolent direct action techniques. He became national director of CORE in February 1961 and in May launched the Freedom Rides, a protest that helped desegregate interstate transportation facilities and that won for both CORE and Farmer a major place in the civil rights movement. During 1963 Farmer led antisegregation demonstrations in several North Carolina cities and in Plaquemines, Louisiana, where state troopers hunted for him door to door, interrogating people with electric cattle prods, until Farmer escaped in the back of a hearse driven by a local funeral director. He also served as cochair of the 1963 March on Washington.

Farmer refused to endorse a July 1964 statement, issued by the leaders of several other civil rights organizations, that called for a "moratorium" on mass demonstrations during the 1964 presidential campaign. Farmer asserted that "people must be allowed to protest" and said CORE would engage in "all the necessary nonviolent action" to support the challenge of the Mississippi Freedom Democratic Party (MFDP) against the seating of the regular Mississippi delegation at the Democratic National Convention in August 1964. CORE workers led a round-the-clock vigil outside the convention hall in Atlantic City while the MFDP's challenge was being considered.

In January 1965 the all-black Voters League in Bogalusa, Louisiana, invited CORE to aid in a campaign for desegregation and increased black employment in the town. Farmer joined the highly publicized protests in April, leading mass marches to the city hall on April 9 and 20. Vice President HUBERT H. HUMPHREY reportedly intervened in late April and convinced Farmer and CORE to accept a mediation effort and halt their demonstrations. During the Bogalusa demonstrations Farmer defended CORE's controversial association with the Deacons for Defense, a black self-defense group that often supplied protection against intimidation and assaults to civil rights workers in Louisiana. After reaffirming CORE's own commitment to nonviolence, Farmer stated that CORE had "no right to tell Negroes in Bogalusa or anywhere else that they do not have the right to defend their homes. It is a constitutional right."

At its July 1965 annual convention CORE delegates adopted a resolution calling for the withdrawal of U.S. troops from Vietnam. Although a pacifist and opponent of the Vietnam War, Farmer objected to the resolution on the grounds that the peace and civil rights movements should remain separate. He organized a successful effort to retract the resolution before the convention's end. The same convention endorsed a continuation of the civil rights drive in Bogalusa, and the campaign there was resumed on July 7. Farmer returned to the city and led 600 people in a silent march on July 11. The demonstrations continued into early August, eventually bringing Louisiana governor JOHN J. MCKEITHEN and JOHN DOAR, head of the Justice Department's Civil Rights Division, to Bogalusa to try to resolve the crisis. The Bogalusa campaign finally ended with desegregation of local restaurants and theaters, the employment of two black police officers, and a beginning of school desegregation under court order.

CORE announced in December 1965 that Farmer would resign as national director on March 1, 1966. Farmer explained that he was planning to establish and head a private agency, the National Center for Community Action Education, which would oversee a nationwide program to improve literacy and job skills among unemployed minorities. Farmer had submitted a proposal for this project to the Office of Economic Opportunity (OEO) in August 1965, and he later said he had received "assurances" from OEO before he left CORE that OEO would fund the center. By July 1966 OEO had not approved a grant for the project, and Farmer announced he was abandoning his plan for lack of funding. In July 1966 Farmer was named a consultant to New Jersey's antipoverty program, and in September he joined the faculty of Lincoln University as a professor of social welfare.

Farmer was a member of the Black Independents and Democrats for Rockefeller, organized in July 1968 to support New York governor NELSON ROCKEFELLER for the presidency. In the same year, Farmer ran for Congress with Republican and Liberal Party endorsements in Brooklyn's 12th Congressional District but lost in the November election to Democrat Shirley Chisholm. During the 1968 presidential campaign Farmer had opposed RICHARD NIXON, calling his civil rights record "apathetic at best and negative at worst." Despite that criticism, Farmer was appointed an assistant secretary of health, education and welfare in February 1969. He served in that post until December 1970. In 1975 Farmer broke with CORE over what he regarded as CORE's excessively pro-leftist positions. He died on July 9, 1999, in Fredericksburg, Virginia.

—CAB

## Fauntroy, Walter E(dward)

(1933–    ) *vice chairman, District of Columbia City Council*

Fauntroy was born on February 6, 1933, and attended Washington public schools. He graduated from the Yale Divinity School in 1958. The following year he became pastor of Washington's New Bethel Baptist Church. In 1960 Fauntroy was made the Washington bureau director of the Southern Christian Leadership Conference (SCLC), and in that post he became a close friend of MARTIN LUTHER KING, JR. Fauntroy was a coordinator of the March on Washington in 1963 and the demonstrations in Selma, Alabama, for voting rights in 1965. In 1966 he also founded and served as the president of the Model Inner City Community Organization, a group committed to inner-city neighborhood development. In 1966 Fauntroy also acted as the vice chair of President Johnson's Conference on Civil Rights, titled "To Fulfill These Rights." On September 6, 1967, the 34-year-old Baptist minister was appointed vice chair of the Washington city council by President Johnson.

While serving on the council, Fauntroy remained active in the civil rights movement. He joined with STOKELY CARMICHAEL in January 1968 in an attempt to create a "Black United Front" of moderate and radical leaders to formulate a unified black political program. The next month Fauntroy refused to bow to the demands of Representative William J. Scherle (R-Iowa) that he resign his council seat or cease his support of the Poor People's March planned by the SCLC for later in the spring of 1968. In the aftermath of Martin Luther King's assassination that year, Fauntroy urged Carmichael to disavow his call for insurrection. He appealed to blacks to refrain from rioting and later toured part of Washington with Senator ROBERT F. KENNEDY (D-N.Y.). In February 1969 President Nixon accepted Fauntroy's resignation from the District city council.

Fauntroy served as national coordinator of the ongoing Poor People's campaign in 1969. In March 1971 he was elected as the District of Columbia's first nonvoting congressional delegate. A leading advocate of Washington home rule and the election of the city's mayor. He served 10 terms in this position, and was one of the founders of the Black Congressional Caucus in 1969. In 1977 he founded the National Black Leadership Roundtable, to bring together leaders of African-American organizations across society, and, six years later, he helped organized the 20th anniversary March on Washington.

—TJC

Rev. Walter Fauntroy (second from right) and others protesting the arrest of Dr. Martin Luther King, Jr., in Albany, Georgia, 1962  *(Library of Congress, Prints and Photographs Division)*

## Findley, Paul
(1921–  ) *member of the House of Representatives*

Born in Jacksonville, Illinois, on June 23, 1921, Paul Findley, publisher of *The Pike Press*, a small county weekly, represented a prosperous farming district in west central Illinois. After entering Congress as a Republican he consistently called for balanced budgets and opposed Kennedy administration domestic programs.

During the Johnson years Findley voted against the antipoverty, Medicare, and federal aid to education bills as well as most legislation favored by organized labor. As a member of the House Agriculture Committee, he denounced government price supports, acreage allotments, and market quotas. He also opposed granting Communist-bloc nations credits to purchase American grain. He expressed no objections, however, to transactions with those nations involving immediate payment.

For a conservative midwestern Republican, Findley's opinions in foreign affairs were unorthodox. A passionate defender of NATO, Findley argued that world peace and order depended on a strong union between European democracies and the United States. He advocated giving America's NATO allies a larger decision-making role, particularly with regard to the use of nuclear weapons.

In the spring of 1967 Findley proposed that the United States threaten North Vietnam with nuclear attack to force it to the negotiating table. However, by the fall he began questioning the legality of

American involvement in Vietnam and helped draft a petition calling for a congressional reexamination of the Gulf of Tonkin Resolution. Findley thought American involvement in Vietnam a "fundamental mistake" but nonetheless voted for war appropriations and opposed efforts to set a rigid timetable for withdrawal of American troops from the conflict. He would later be one of the architects of the War Powers Resolution of 1973, which attempted to restrain the power of the executive branch to conduct military operations.

Throughout the 1960s the liberal Americans for Democratic Action (ADA) rated Findley among the most conservative members of congress. During the Nixon years, however, the ADA reported that Findley was beginning to vote more frequently with congressional moderates. He was defeated in 1982, and he was then appointed to the Board for International Food and Agricultural Development. He also served as chair for the Council for the National Interest, and a leading critic of American policy in the Middle East, especially its close relationship with Israel.

—JLW

# Fisher, Adrian S(anford)

**(1914–1983)** *deputy director, Arms Control and Disarmament Agency*

Born on January 21, 1914, in Memphis, Tennessee, a Princeton and Harvard Law School graduate, Fisher served as law clerk to Supreme Court justice Louis Brandeis in 1938 and Justice Felix Frankfurter in 1939. After wartime service in the U.S. Army Air Forces he became assistant executive officer to the assistant secretary of war and served as technical adviser to the American judges at the Nuremberg trials. After the trials Fisher joined the Washington law firm of Covington and Burling and later became vice president and counsel of the Washington Post Company.

President Kennedy appointed Fisher deputy director of the newly formed Arms Control and Disarmament Agency in October 1961. Within the agency he directed the gathering of basic data necessary for the presentation of a partial nuclear test ban proposal offered in Geneva in August 1962. During the July 1963 Moscow negotiations that led to the signing of a partial test ban treaty in August of that year, Fisher acted as adviser to Kennedy's personal representative, W. AVERELL HARRIMAN. Later that

summer he helped guide the administration's battle for ratification, which was completed in September.

Fisher continued at his post throughout the Johnson administration. During this period he alternated with WILLIAM FOSTER as delegate to the 17 Nation Disarmament Conference, which was attempting to formulate agreements on a comprehensive test ban, a freeze on weapons development, a nonproliferation accord, and the destruction of existing weapons. Fisher offered major statements on three of these issues. On March 17, 1964, he outlined the reasons for the U.S. rejection of the Soviet plan, known as the "Gromyko Umbrella," for the scrapping of all but a limited number of strategic missiles in the first stage of complete disarmament. He warned it would produce radical shifts in the current East-West military balance, did not provide for verification to assure that additional missiles were not retained by a party of the treaty, and was linked to a demand for the dismantling of all foreign bases, including those Western bases that had become an integral part of the East-West military balance.

Two days later Fisher submitted the U.S. proposal for a "Bomber Bonfire." Under the plan the United States was prepared to destroy 480 operational B-47 jet bombers if the USSR would destroy an equal number of TU-16 "Badger" bombers. The Soviet Union rejected it as an attempt to pass off the retirement of obsolete aircraft as disarmament.

Fisher presented President Johnson's proposal for a freeze on nuclear missiles and bomber forces in April 1964. Under this plan the freeze was to be applied to all long-range, ground-launched, surface-to-surface missiles, all sea-launched missiles, many large strategic bombers, and long-range, air-to-surface missiles. Verification was to be assured by a variety of measures including permanent international inspection of all strategic airfields, missile launching sites, and research and production centers. Worn or damaged missiles were to be replaced on an inspected one-for-one basis, but no improvement of missiles was to be permitted. The Soviet Union rejected the plan on the grounds that it would not "get rid of one missile or bomber" and would require inspection measures that would open the USSR's strategic forces to Western military espionage.

In August 1965 the United States, in conjunction with several other Western delegations, tabled a nonproliferation treaty designed to prevent the spread of nuclear weapons to nonnuclear states. This proposal faced serious opposition from both the Soviet Union and the major U.S. allies. The

Russians objected to the provisions of the early drafts that would have permitted the United States to give nuclear weapons to its North Atlantic Treaty Organization (NATO) allies under the proposed Multilateral Nuclear Force. On the other hand, America's allies, particularly Germany, insisted that the present defense system with it assurance of American nuclear protection, be maintained. In addition, the members of the European Atomic Energy Community (Euratom) objected to the treaty provision for inspection of nuclear facilities by the International Atomic Energy Agency (IAEA), believing that inspection by an agency that contained Communist bloc personnel would be tantamount to legalized espionage. Many nonnuclear nations also opposed the treaty for fear that they would be unprotected in a nuclear age.

Over a three-year period Fisher and Foster worked out drafts acceptable to all parties. Fisher, in particular, developed those provisions necessary to obtain Euratom approval. On January 18, 1968, Fisher was able to announce an agreement on a treaty. As a result of his negotiations with Euratom, a provision was made allowing each non-nuclear power to negotiate an agreement with the IAEA either individually or together with other nations on the terms of inspection. Under the treaty the NATO alliance was protected by the article reaffirming the right to individual and collective self-defense. This statement was vague enough to satisfy NATO demands and yet fulfill Soviet requirements that nuclear weapons not be given to U.S. allies, particularly West Germany. In addition, the document gave nonnuclear states assurance of protection from nuclear attack by stipulating that the nuclear powers in the UN Security Council would "have to act immediately in accordance with their obligations under the United Nations charter" if such an attack occurred.

In January 1969 Fisher left government service to return to private law practice and to accept the position of dean and professor of international law and international trade at Georgetown University Law Center. Fisher died in 1983.

—EWS

## Fitzsimmons, Frank E(dward)
(1905–1981) *president, International Brotherhood of Teamsters*

Born on April 7, 1906, in Jeannette, Pennsylvania, Fitzsimmons left school at 17 to help support his family. He worked for over 10 years as a truck driver in Detroit, where he joined International Brotherhood of Teamsters (IBT) Local 299, headed by the young JIMMY HOFFA. Fitzsimmons's organizing abilities impressed Hoffa, and he became business manager of the local in 1937. Three years later he was elected vice president of Local 299 and in 1943 became secretary-treasurer of the IBT Michigan Conference. In 1961, after Hoffa had become president of the IBT, Fitzsimmons was made an international vice president and joined the union's executive council.

Fitzsimmons built his career in the IBT as a loyal assistant to Hoffa. He supported the aggressive Teamster leader in his struggle to assert his personal authority over the union's powerful regional directors. After Hoffa was convicted of jury-tampering and misuse of union pension funds, he named Fitzsimmons his successor. In 1966 a national Teamsters convention elected Fitzsimmons general vice president of the IBT, a post newly created to fill any vacancy in the presidency. Such a vacancy occurred in March 1967, when Hoffa lost his last appeal and went to prison. Fitzsimmons immediately took over his functions as head of the two-million-member union, the largest in the United States.

The change in command came at an awkward time for the Teamsters. Union leaders were in the midst of renegotiating the national trucking industry contract, and talks with employers were thrown into confusion by Hoffa's departure. Less than a month after taking control, Fitzsimmons had to face a national lockout by trucking employers. He proved to be a skillful negotiator, however, and achieved a settlement in April 1967 that many union officials considered better than anything Hoffa could have gained. Trucking employers agreed to a wage increase of 5 percent (later raised to 6 percent) for each of the next three years.

With the contract crisis resolved Fitzsimmons turned to internal union affairs. His quiet, unassuming style contrasted so strongly with Hoffa's flamboyance that some observers doubted the new leader's ability to withstand the pressures of union politics. Fitzsimmons did survive, but only by introducing important policy changes in the IBT. At a meeting of union officials in May 1967 he promised to abandon the tight centralization enforced by Hoffa, returning power over local affairs to the regional union heads and area joint councils. From then on such matters as strike authorization and complaints against trucking firms or union officials were decided "through channels," that is in area offices rather than at the national union headquarters. Much of the dissatisfaction that had troubled the IBT under Hoffa subsided as a result.

One continuing problem of the union under Fitzsimmons was the reportedly close connections between organized crime and high IBT officials. Such contacts had grown during the presidency of Hoffa and his predecessor, Dave Beck. During Fitzsimmons's tenure, according to Justice Department officials, they gravitated to the regional level of the union. Fitzsimmons denounced such reports as "slanderous," but they persisted during the late 1960s, especially charges that Fitzsimmons had given organized crime leaders virtual control over union pension funds.

Desiring to counteract the bad publicity focused on the IBT, Fitzsimmons formed the Alliance for Labor Action (ALA) with the United Auto Workers in 1968. The ALA was presented as a "massive program in social and community action," including efforts to organize minority workers. But the new organization damaged relations between Fitzsimmons and the AFL-CIO, which viewed the ALA as an attempt to raid the membership of other unions. Eventually Fitzsimmons won the recognition that he sought by establishing close ties with the Nixon administration. He endorsed the wage-price freeze of August 1971 and remained on the president's wage board even after other labor leaders had quit. In 1972 he supported Nixon for reelection.

Fitzsimmons was elected president of the IBT in his own right in July 1971; at the end of the year, Nixon released Hoffa from serving the rest of his sentence on the condition that he refrain from union activity until 1980. Hoffa soon began a campaign to regain the IBT presidency, but he disappeared mysteriously in July 1975. No evidence was found to connect Fitzsimmons with Hoffa's disappearance, and he was easily reelected in 1976. He died of lung cancer on May 6, 1981, and was replaced by Roy Williams.

—SLG

## Flowers, Richmond
(1918–   ) *attorney general, Alabama*

Flowers, who was born on November 11, 1918, in Dothan, Alabama, practiced law until his election to the Alabama Senate in 1955. In 1962 Flowers was elected Alabama's attorney general on a segregationist platform. GEORGE WALLACE was chosen Alabama governor the same year. Flowers and Wallace soon broke ranks over integration of the Alabama schools. Flowers opposed Wallace's "segregation forever" slogan and the governor's promise to defy a court order mandating the integration of the University of Alabama. He warned that such defiance would provoke violence. Alabama's "soul," he said in his own inaugural speech, "will soon be laid before the world. God grant that we may not be ashamed of it."

Attorney General Flowers pursued a civil rights course that made him, as Andrew Kopkind wrote in the *New Republic*, "an agent of the changes Wallace dreaded." He intervened directly in the deeply controversial 1965 trial of Thomas L. Coleman for the slaying of white civil rights worker Jonathan Daniels. Daniels, a New Hampshire seminarian, was shot upon his release from a Fort Deposit jail after an arrest during civil rights picketing. Flowers, who relieved the county prosecutor, was initially "shocked and amazed" that Coleman's grand jury indictment was for manslaughter and not first-degree murder. When the all white jury acquitted Coleman, Flowers declared, "now those who feel they have a license to kill . . . have been issued that license. It is our duty to do what is necessary to retrieve it."

In October 1965 another all-white jury found Ku Klux Klan member Collie LeRoy Wilkins not guilty of the March 25, 1965, slaying of Mrs. Viola Liuzzo, another northern white civil rights worker who was murdered following the Selma-to-Montgomery march. Flowers again relieved the county prosecutor. When this jury voted for acquittal, he termed the verdict "a complete breakdown of justice and law and order." The killers were later tried and convicted in federal court for violating Liuzzo's civil rights. *Life* magazine lauded Flowers for "laying his political career on the line in the pursuit of due process."

During Flowers's four years as Alabama's attorney general, he achieved national fame as a racial moderate and enemy of Governor George Wallace. He began a gubernatorial campaign in the fall of 1965 (against Mrs. Lurleen Wallace, running as her husband's surrogate in a state that barred consecutive reelection) but was given little chance for success. He placed his electoral hopes in the hands of the state's newly enfranchised African Americans. To win their 200,000 votes, Flowers canvassed urban slums and rural shantytowns. Appealing to the small middle-class black community and the militant poor, he promised significant African-American appointments to state jobs, housing aid, and the removal of the Confederate flag from atop the capitol. He emphasized the need for industrial development and improved educational opportunities. Flowers freely admitted that his campaign was designed to attract black support, "Sure I solicit the Negro vote. I'm promising equal opportunity, equal education and good jobs for every citizen in this state." Flowers's candidacy marked the first time in modern Alabama history that a major candidate was not a segregationist. His campaign, though it softened the rhetoric of Alabama's racial debate, was unsuccessful. Flowers polled only 18 percent of the vote, while Mrs. Wallace's 52 percent majority forestalled a runoff.

On August 2, 1968, a federal grand jury in Birmingham indicted Flowers on charges of extortion conspiracy. He was convicted in 1969 and sentenced to eight years. After his appeals failed, he began serving his sentence in 1972, but he was paroled in the fall of 1974. He later received a presidential pardon.

—TJC

## Fong, Hiram L(eong)

(1906–2004) *member of the Senate*

Born on October 15, 1906, in Honolulu, Hawaii, Fong worked his way through the University of Hawaii and Harvard Law School to become a successful lawyer and millionaire business executive. Fong won election to the Hawaiian territorial legislature in 1938 as a Republican and served as speaker of that body between 1948 and 1954. In the same period he secured a working relationship with the powerful International Longshoremen's and Warehousemen's Union (ILWU).

A Republican, Fong was elected to the U.S. Senate in Hawaii's first general election as a state in July 1959. He later won designation as the state's senior senator and the longer term of office. In the Senate he tended to take more liberal stands on domestic issues than on foreign policy and was leading sponsor of civil rights legislation. Despite the disastrous performance of Senator BARRY GOLDWATER (R-Ariz.) as the Republican presidential can-

didate in the November elections, Fong won reelection to the Senate by a comfortable margin.

Fong was accorded modest ratings of from 30 percent to 40 percent on his voting record by both the liberal Americans for Democratic Action and the conservative Americans for Constitutional Action. In August 1964 he sponsored gun control legislation, and throughout the Johnson administration he fought for stringent regulations. A member of the Senate Special Committee on Aging, he was one of only a few Republicans to support Johnson's 1965 proposal to set up an Administration on Aging as part of the Department of Health, Education and Welfare. In 1965 he also worked to win passage for new immigration legislation, which eliminated many of the old restrictions against Asians, and successfully sponsored an amendment to the voting rights bill, which provided for poll watchers in voting districts where provisions of the bill had become effective.

In September 1968 Fong joined two other Republicans and four southern Democrats on the Senate Judiciary Committee in voting against Johnson's nomination of Supreme Court justice ABE FORTAS to be chief justice. The Fortas nomination was finally defeated by a Senate filibuster in October.

Fong endorsed the candidacy of RICHARD M. NIXON at the 1968 Republican National Convention. Consistently voting for large defense appropriations, Fong's unstinting support of Nixon's Vietnam policy hurt his popularity in Hawaii and weakened his relationship with the ILWU. Nonetheless, the ILWU and his personal organization—the Republican Party in Hawaii had become almost totally ineffective—carried him to a narrow reelection victory in 1970. He retired from Congress in 1977, and returned to Hawaii to direct numerous business interests. Fong died of kidney failure in Kahaluu, Hawaii, on August 18, 2004.

—JCH

## Ford, Gerald R(udolph)

(1913–   ) *member of the House of Representatives*

Gerald R. Ford, who was born on July 14, 1913, in Omaha, Nebraska, grew up in Grand Rapids, Michigan. He earned his B.A. at the University of Michigan, where he played center on the varsity football team. Declining offers from professional teams, he went to Yale Law School, graduating in

1941, and served in the navy during World War II. In 1948 Ford upset an incumbent representative in the GOP House primary and easily won election 12 times each time with over 60 percent of the vote. In January 1959 he supported Representative CHARLES A. HALLECK (R-Ind.) in his campaign for the House minority leadership, but four years later he defeated Halleck's candidate to chair the House Republican Conference Committee. He frequently supported the Kennedy administration's foreign and defense policies but remained opposed to most New Frontier domestic legislation.

On November 29, 1963, President Johnson appointed Ford to the seven-member commission headed by Chief Justice Earl Warren to investigate the assassination of John F. Kennedy. After the panel's report became public in September 1964, Ford defended its conclusions and in 1965 coauthored *Portrait of the Assassin*, which supported the Warren Commission's contention that Lee Harvey Oswald acted alone in the president's murder.

The Republicans' disastrous showing in the 1964 elections convinced many House members that their leadership needed a new image. They convinced Ford to oppose Halleck, although both the Indiana Republican and he shared similar voting records. The conservative Americans for Constitutional Action gave Halleck an 86 percent rating and marked Ford 83 percent right on the same issues. But younger House Republicans considered Halleck inattentive to their views, and liberal members strongly condemned his unofficial coalition with southern Democrats. Ford promised his colleagues a more open and positive leadership that would make every member "a sixty-minute player." By a vote of 73 to 67, Ford unseated Halleck on January 4, 1965. However, the party caucus then defeated Ford's candidate for minority whip, PETER H. B. FRELINGHUYSEN (R-N.J.), and elected Leslie Arends.

Ford worked to end the House Republicans' silent partnership with southern Democratic committee chairs, which prevented important legislation from reaching the House floor. Instead, the new minority leader wanted Johnson's Great Society proposals brought out of committee in order to permit House Republicans a chance to vote for or against the legislation. He urged his colleagues to offer positive alternatives to White House legislation. "If the Southern Democrats vote with us, fine," he wrote in January 1965, "but they will be voting for a Republican position." And despite his

legislative position, he maintained good working relations with most Democrats, including the members of the Johnson administration, on domestic issues.

The new strategy failed during the 89th Congress because the massive Democratic majority enabled the president's party either to defeat, or, when necessary, to incorporate Republican amendments into Great Society legislation and then assume full credit for each bill's enactment. During the Ways and Means hearings on the Medicare bill, Committee Chair WILBUR MILLS (D-Ark.) agreed to amendments covering the cost of doctors' services and drugs in the measure proposed by the committee's ranking Republican, Representative JOHN W. BYRNES (R-Wisc.). Reported out of committee with the Byrnes provisions, a narrow 70-68 majority of GOP House members voted for Medicare in July 1965. Ford alone of Michigan's nine-member Republican congressional delegation voted against the law.

The Republican gain of 47 House seats in November 1966 gave Ford an opportunity to demonstrate his leadership. Through hard work and an honest, easygoing personal style, he could usually bridge the geographic and ideological differences among House Republicans. He endorsed the policy recommendation of Representative CHARLES E. GOODELL (R-N.Y.) and Representative ALBERT H. QUIE (R-Minn.) to replace programmed federal assistance to localities with a "block grant" appropriation to the states. After a vigorous lobbying campaign, the administration defeated the Republican effort to include the block grant system in the May 1967 education aid bill. However, the House agreed, for the first time, to implement the block grant method in the Crime Control and Safe Streets Act in August 1967. In May 1967 Ford again expressed the need for ending the conservative coalition, "to drive Southern Democrats into the arms of the administration—where they belong." But during the 90th Congress the coalition enjoyed a vigorous revival. According to *Congressional Quarterly*, the coalition won only 25 percent of the votes on selected issues in 1965 and 32 percent in 1966; yet, in 1967, its margin of victory rose to 67 percent.

During the debate on the war in Vietnam Ford established a reputation for partisanship that strained relationships both with the White House and Senate Minority Leader EVERETT M. DIRKSEN (R-Ill.). On July 29, 1965, the minority leader revealed to reporters that at a White House briefing Senate Majority Leader MIKE MANSFIELD (D-Mont.) had expressed strong reservations over the president's plan to escalate the war in Vietnam. Three days later Johnson angrily assailed Ford as a man "who broke my confidence." When in April 1966 Ford accused the administration of "shocking mismanagement" of the war, Dirksen, who strongly endorsed Johnson on Vietnam, also publicly rebuked the House leader. Ford then agreed to inform Dirksen in advance of any future criticisms he made of the war and deferred to the Illinois senator for the presentation of the foreign affairs segment of their joint Republican "State of the Union" address in January 1967.

However Dirksen rarely reviewed Ford's prepared texts, and the House leader continued to assail Johnson's war policies as secretive and excessively cautious. A frequent advocate of intensive bombing, Ford asked in an August 1967 House speech, "Why are we pulling our best punches in Vietnam?" He said that he could find "no justification for sending one more American" soldier to Vietnam until the president established a sea quarantine against North Vietnamese ports and ordered air strikes against "all known oil storage targets and military and industrial bases in North Vietnam."

Ford proved equally militant when northern cities became the scene of violent race riots. Following racial disturbances in Los Angeles, Chicago, and Springfield, Massachusetts, he called for an investigation of subversive influences within the civil rights movement. In his January 1967 GOP "State of the Union" message, Ford asked that persons crossing state lines with the intent to riot be liable to federal prosecution.

In the spring of 1968 Ford confronted the first challenge of his leadership when a group of liberal Republicans led by Goodell and Quie defied Ford's opposition to the open housing bill, which had just passed the Senate with Dirksen's assistance. Goodell and Quie persuaded 77 Republican members to announce support for the measure, compelling Ford to endorse the bill just before the final vote.

Ford opposed Johnson's request in January 1967 for an income tax surcharge and instead advocated reductions in nonmilitary programs. He warned that Johnson's tax increase "could be a depressant which could trigger a very serious economic recession." In June 1968, however, Ford agreed to the administration's compromise tax package when Johnson agreed to reduce federal expenditures by $6 billion for fiscal 1969 and impose a 10 percent surcharge.

Ford served as permanent chair at the August 1968 Republican National Convention. As in 1960 and 1964, he received brief consideration as the party's vice presidential candidate. Hoping for a Republican majority that would make him Speaker of the House, Ford campaigned hard for the GOP in 1966 and 1968. He remained the minority leader during the Nixon administration until December 1973, when he succeeded SPIRO T. AGNEW as vice president. Upon the resignation of President Richard M. Nixon in August 1974, Ford became the 38th president of the United States. After losing a close bid for reelection to Georgia governor Jimmy Carter in 1976, Ford moved to California, but he continued to stay active in the political arena through writings, lectures, and other public appearances.

—JLB

## Ford, Henry, II
(1917–1987) *chair and chief executive officer, Ford Motor Company*

Born in Detroit, Michigan, on September 4, 1917, Henry Ford II was the grandson of the legendary industrialist Henry Ford and the son of Ford Motor Company president Edsel Ford. The young Ford attended Yale University and served in the navy during World War II. He was released from service in August 1943 and began an apprenticeship in top management under the tutelage of his 80-year-old grandfather, who had resumed control of the company following the death of Edsel Ford that May. He became president of Ford in 1945 at the age of 28. Unlike his grandfather, who was an autocratic manager and a bitter foe of unionism, the younger Ford developed a more flexible policy toward the demands of the United Automobile Workers (UAW). As company president, one of his first decisions was to fire the head of the Ford Service Department, who his grandfather had hired to stop the growth of unions at Ford. In the immediate postwar era he began a sweeping reform of the administrative structure of the company, hiring a specially recruited "Whiz Kid" management team, which included future defense secretary ROBERT S. MCNAMARA, to modernize the firm's inefficient managerial system and production techniques. To a large extent Ford adopted the more decentralized structure of its giant rival, General Motors.

*Fortune* magazine reported in 1964 that on the basis of total sales Ford was the fourth-largest corporation in the nation, ranking second in the auto industry behind General Motors. Ford had its best year in 1965 and its second best in 1968, when its earnings reached $626 million. Profits were much lower in 1967 because of a UAW strike in September and October. Henry Ford II, who denounced the work stoppage as "totally unjustified" and a "bludgeon against the public interest," agreed to a wage settlement providing an estimated 91-cent-an-hour increase in wages and fringe benefits over the next three years. This package substantially exceeded the Johnson administration's then current 3.2 percent wage guidelines. The settlement also included, for the first time, a guaranteed-annual-income plan under which a worker with seven years service would be entitled to 52 weeks income at 95 percent of take-home pay in the event of a layoff. Although the union's membership ratified the new contract on October 25, local plant disputes, centering on unresolved shopfloor grievances and the pace of work, continued in 33 of 101 Ford bargaining units. Full production was not resumed until November 10.

Along with the rest of the auto industry, Ford vigorously opposed the enactment of auto safety standards in 1966 and 1967. He labeled the safety campaign, sparked by consumer advocate RALPH NADER, "a harassment to the automobile industry." In December Ford criticized many federal motor vehicle safety regulations as "unreasonable, arbitrary and technically unfeasible" and said that enforcement could shut down some Ford plants. Between September 1966 and September 1967, Ford had to recall 531,000 cars because of safety defects. In response to critics who blamed the profusion of automobiles for environmental pollution and the declining quality of city life, Ford said in July 1966: "As far as urban transportation is concerned, what people want is clear. They have voted overwhelmingly in favor of the automobile. . . . The city's problems cannot be solved by encouraging transit at the expense of the automobile."

A lifelong Republican, Ford joined 25 other business leaders in September 1964 to form a National Independent Committee for Johnson and Humphrey. In January 1966 he urged U.S. industry to invest in combating poverty and aiding education as a form of "good business." "The poor simply are not very good customers for our products," he pointed out. During the Johnson administration he often led business efforts in support of Great Society programs. His support (along with 21 other executives) for the Model Cities program in October 1966 was said by *Congressional Quarterly* to have been a "key factor" in the acceptance of the measure by Congress. During 1967 and 1968 Ford headed a group of 500 business executives whose lobbying proved crucial to the passage of Johnson's 10 percent tax surcharge in June 1968.

Ford headed a National Alliance of Businessmen (NAB) effort in January 1968 to promote the federal government's Job Opportunities in the Business Sector (JOBS) program. The purpose of JOBS was to expand opportunities for the chronically unemployed by giving subsidies to businesses hiring such workers. He died from Legionnaire's disease on September 29, 1987.

—TO

## Forman, James
### (1928–2005) *executive secretary, Student Nonviolent Coordinating Committee*

Born on October 4, 1928, in Chicago, and a 1957 graduate of Roosevelt University, Forman became executive secretary of the Student Nonviolent Coordinating Committee (SNCC) in October 1961. Described by one observer of the civil rights movement as "personable, canny" and "erudite," Forman established an administrative structure for SNCC and participated in its demonstrations against segregation in Albany, Georgia, in December 1961 and in Danville, Virginia, in June 1963. He also helped organize voter registration drives in Greenwood, Mississippi, and Selma, Alabama, in 1963.

Forman participated in January 1964 demonstrations to desegregate public accommodations in Atlanta, Georgia. He and SNCC chair JOHN LEWIS led a January 18 protest outside a segregated restaurant in which 78 were arrested. Forman himself was arrested in demonstrations at another segregated restaurant on January 27. During the next few months he helped plan the 1964 Mississippi Freedom Summer, a project to increase black voter registration and to establish freedom schools and community centers for blacks in that state. He helped train the student volunteers for the project and directed SNCC's national office which was moved from Atlanta to Greenwood, Mississippi, for the summer. Forman accompanied the delegates of the Mississippi Freedom Democratic Party (MFDP) to the Democratic National Convention in Atlantic City in August 1964, where they challenged the seating of Mississippi's regular Democrats. When the party leadership offered the MFDP a compromise in which it would receive two "at-large" seats in the convention, Forman urged the delegates to reject the proposal, which they did. Forman and SNCC also supported the MFDP's unsuccessful 1965 challenge to the seating of Mississippi's five representatives in Congress. These experiences helped convince Forman that the movement could not rely on white liberals within the government.

SNCC and the Southern Christian Leadership Conference cooperated in an intensive voter registration drive in Selma, Alabama, beginning in January 1965. During the campaign MARTIN LUTHER KING, JR., suggested a march from Selma to Montgomery to protest the denial of voting rights to Alabama blacks. Forman opposed the idea because he felt that mass marches "create the impression" that the people were forcing change while in fact they achieved almost nothing. The march began March 7 but was quickly routed when state troopers attacked the demonstrators at the Edmund Pettus Bridge in Selma. Forman, unwilling to let such violence successfully end the protest, joined a second attempt to begin the march, which was also turned back at the bridge on March 9. The next day Forman joined in a demonstration in Montgomery, organized by students from Tuskegee Institute to protest the police attacks in Selma, in which the protesters marched to the state capitol and staged a sit-in on its steps until 2 a.m. Forman led another march on the capitol on the 16th, but the 600 marchers were attacked en route by state and county police wielding ropes, nightsticks, and electric cattle prods. Forman, King, and John Lewis led a March 17 demonstration of 1,600 people. When they reached the courthouse, several of the rights leaders conferred with the local sheriff and JOHN DOAR of the Justice Department, reportedly reaching an agreement that harassment of orderly demonstrations would be ended so long as rights leaders obtained parade permits for all future marches in Montgomery. Forman and local students continued demonstrations in the city until March 21, when the final march from Selma began. For-

man, whose commitment to nonviolence had been tactical rather than philosophical at the time he joined SNCC, later wrote that the Montgomery protests, especially the March 16 demonstration and the police attack, "snapped" his "ability to continue engaging in nonviolent direct action."

Forman was voted out as executive secretary of SNCC at a staff meeting in Kingston Springs, Tennessee, in May 1966. According to his account in *The Making of Black Revolutionaries*, he had wanted to leave the post since the fall of 1964 to give himself more time for reading, analysis and writing, and to rebuild his health. (Forman had nearly died of a bleeding ulcer in January 1963 and had recurrent health problems after that.) At the same meeting SNCC adopted a resolution introduced by Forman to stop using integrated field teams, and elected STOKELY CARMICHAEL chair over John Lewis. Forman supported Carmichael's election on the grounds that his greater militance and his emphasis on blackness represented the direction in which SNCC should move. He also supported the Black Power concept expounded by Carmichael after his election.

Forman remained active in SNCC as administrator of its national office during the leadership transition and as its director of international affairs after the spring of 1967. He attended the National Conference for a New Politics held in Chicago over Labor Day weekend in 1967. There he supported the organization of a black caucus at the Conference and the caucus's demands for 50 percent of the delegate votes and for endorsement of a statement condemning Israel as an aggressive, imperialist power. Addressing the conference on September 3, Forman argued for separate political action by blacks, asserting that blacks "have the responsibility to wage our own war of liberation as we see fit" and the "right to define the manner in which we will fight our aggressors." Forman was named minister of foreign affairs of the Black Panther Party in February 1968, when the party and SNCC formed an alliance. The alliance fell apart in July 1968, and Forman resigned his party post because of policy differences with the Panthers on questions of security, structure, and organizational discipline.

In April 1969 Forman presented a "Black Manifesto" at a Detroit conference on black economic development called by the Inter-religious Foundation for Community Organization. The Manifesto called for the establishment of a permanent

National Black Economic Development Conference (NBEDC). It demanded that white churches give $500 million to the NBEDC as reparations for their past wrongs to blacks, with the money to be used for educational, cultural, and industrial programs in the black community. NBEDC was set up as a permanent organization, and, throughout the summer, Forman presented the demand for reparations at the headquarters or conventions of various religious denominations. NBEDC named Forman the director of its programs of community organization in 1970. He later served as president of the Unemployment and Poverty Action Council. In the 1980s he turned back to education, earning a master's degree from Cornell University and a Ph.D. from the Union Institute, in African and African-American history. He died of cancer on January 10, 2005.

—CAB

## Fortas, Abe
(1910–1982) *associate justice, U.S. Supreme Court*

Born on June 19, 1910, in Memphis, Tennessee, Fortas worked his way through Southwestern College in Memphis, receiving his B.A. in 1930. Three years later he graduated from Yale Law School, where he had been editor in chief of the *Yale Law Journal.* He then taught at the school from 1933 to 1937. During those four years he also worked part-time for the Agricultural Adjustment Administration and the Securities and Exchange Commission (SEC). From 1937 to 1946 Fortas successively held posts in the SEC, the Public Works Administration, and the Department of Interior, serving as under-secretary of the interior from 1942 to 1946.

With several other New Dealers he then formed Arnold, Fortas & Porter, which soon became one of Washington's most prestigious and prosperous law firms. With a predominantly corporate practice, Fortas was known for his effectiveness in corporate counseling, antitrust litigation, and practice before administrative agencies. He and his firm also developed a reputation for handling, often without charge, some important civil liberties and individual rights cases. In 1954, serving as court-appointed counsel, he won a landmark ruling from the District of Columbia Court of Appeals that broadened the criminal insanity rule. Again as court-appointed counsel, Fortas represented Clarence Earl Gideon before the Supreme Court in 1963 and got a unanimous Court to overturn a 1942 decision to rule that the states must supply counsel to an indigent defendant accused of a serious crime.

Fortas successfully represented LYNDON JOHNSON in legal proceedings following his controversial victory in the 1948 Texas Democratic primary. The incident launched a long, close friendship between the two men, and Fortas became Johnson's confidant and one of his most trusted advisers. Johnson's first phone call following John Kennedy's assassination was to Abe Fortas. Fortas helped organize the Warren Commission, which investigated Kennedy's assassination, and advised Johnson on appointments, speeches, legislation, and foreign policy. He also participated in strategy conferences during the 1964 presidential campaign. When WALTER JENKINS, a top White House aide, was arrested on a morals charge in the fall of 1964, Fortas attempted to keep the story out of the news media and then advised Johnson on how to handle the situation. During the 1965 Dominican crisis, Fortas, who had close relations with a good friend of Dominican president Juan Bosch, acted as a back-channel emissary for LBJ and conducted a number of quiet meetings with Bosch to try to resolve the crisis.

In 1964 Fortas refused an offer to be named U.S. Attorney General, preferring to keep his role as Johnson's unofficial adviser. In July 1965, when ARTHUR GOLDBERG resigned from the Supreme Court to become ambassador to the UN, Fortas also turned down a nomination to a Court seat. On July 28, however, when Johnson told Fortas he was going to announce his appointment as associate justice that day, Fortas acquiesced. Fortas's nomination was well received, and the Senate confirmed his appointment on August 11.

On the bench Fortas was usually in accord with the liberal, activist justices of the Warren Court. He was part of the five-member majority in the June 1966 *Miranda* decision, which placed limits on police interrogation of criminal suspects. Writing for the Court in the May 1967 case of *In re Gault,* Fortas extended to children in juvenile court proceedings many of the constitutional protections required in adult trials. He also joined the majority in two June 1968 decisions. One upheld the right of police to stop and frisk persons for weapons under certain circumstances. The other barred the exclusion of individuals from murder trial juries because of their objections to capital punishment.

Fortas voted repeatedly to sustain civil rights claims. He supported, for example, a March 1966 decision holding unconstitutional a Virginia poll tax for state elections and a June 1968 ruling that an 1866 federal law prohibited racial discrimination in the sale and rental of housing and other property. Fortas's majority opinion in a March 1966 case upheld the federal prosecution, under an 1870 civil rights law, of 17 persons accused of involvement in the murder of three civil rights workers in Mississippi in June 1964. In February 1966 his opinion for the Court overturned the breach-of-the-peace convictions of five blacks who had tried to integrate a public library in Louisiana. Fortas dissented in November 1966 and June 1967 cases in which the majority voted to sustain convictions of civil rights demonstrators.

Fortas's opinion for a unanimous Court in June 1966 reversed the contempt-of-Congress conviction of a former labor union officer who had refused to answer questions before a House Un-American Activities subcommittee. In two 1967 cases Fortas voted to invalidate a Maryland loyalty oath law for public employees and a set of New York State teacher loyalty laws as violations of the First Amendment. He dissented, however, in January 1967, when the Court extended to invasion of privacy suits the rule that erroneous statements had to be made deliberately or recklessly before the press could be held liable. Fortas also voted in favor of a March 1966 ruling that "titillating" advertising could be used to convict a publisher of obscenity, although the materials sold might not in themselves be obscene.

On June 13, 1968, Chief Justice EARL WARREN sent the president a letter of resignation. Announcing Warren's retirement on June 26, Johnson nominated Fortas as chief justice and Homer Thornberry, a judge on the U.S. Court of Appeals for the Fifth Circuit and a longtime Johnson associate, for Fortas's seat. Eighteen Republican senators, led by ROBERT P. GRIFFIN (R-Mich.), declared shortly afterward that they would try to block confirmation of the appointments. Aside from the alleged impropriety of Fortas's advisory relationship with Johnson, opponents of the nominations objected to having a "lame-duck" president choose the new chief justice and charged Johnson with cronyism in making his selections. In mid-July Fortas made an unprecedented appearance at the Senate Judiciary Committee hearings on his nomination. Unfriendly questioning by several senators, including STROM THURMOND (R-S.C.), made it apparent that hostility to liberal Warren Court decisions and Fortas's own position on several controversial issues contributed to the opposition to his confirmation.

In September it was disclosed that Fortas had received $15,000 for teaching a nine-week course in the summer of 1968 at American University Law School. The money had been raised by one of Fortas's former law partners from five prominent business executives, one of whom had a son involved a federal criminal case. The Senate Judiciary Committee reported out Fortas's nomination on September 17, by an 11-6 vote, but a coalition of Republicans and conservative Democrats launched a filibuster against the appointment when it came up for Senate consideration late that month. A vote for cloture failed on October 1, and the next day Johnson withdrew Fortas's nomination at the justice's request.

Justice Abe Fortas joking with President Johnson, 1965 *(Photographed by Yoichi R. Okamoto; Lyndon Baines Johnson Library)*

Chief Justice Warren then agreed to stay on until the new president named his successor.

During the next Court term Fortas wrote several significant opinions expanding First Amendment and criminal rights. On May 4, 1969, *Life* magazine reported that in 1966 Fortas had accepted—and then several months later returned—a $20,000 fee from the family foundation of Louis E. Wolfson, a wealthy industrialist who had since been imprisoned for selling unregistered stocks. The article touched off heavy criticism and talk of impeachment proceedings against Fortas. On May 15 Fortas announced his resignation from the Court, making him the first justice ever to resign under the pressure of public criticism. At the same time he made public a long letter to Chief Justice Warren setting forth the details of his involvement with Wolfson and insisting that he was innocent of any wrongdoing. Fortas eventually returned to the private practice of law at Fortas & Kovan in Washington, D.C., and died on April 5, 1982.

—CAB

## Foster, William C(hapman)
(1897–1984) *director, Arms Control and Disarmament Agency*

William C. Foster was born on April 27, 1897, in Westfield, New Jersey. Prior to his appointment as director of the U.S. Arms Control and Disarmament Agency in September 1961, Foster had a varied career in government, serving as undersecretary of commerce, administrator of the Economic Cooperation Administration, and deputy secretary of defense during the Truman administration. He left government for private industry after DWIGHT D. EISENHOWER's 1953 election, and, from 1953 to 1961, he served as an executive for a number of large chemical corporations. In 1958 Foster headed the U.S. delegation to the abortive disarmament conference with the Soviet Union.

As head of the U.S. Arms Control and Disarmament Agency, Foster was responsible for running an autonomous department formed to coordinate and develop disarmament and nuclear testing policy. During the Kennedy administration he advised the president on a wide range of disarmament policy decisions. He helped draw up major arms control statements, including the proposal for "General and Complete Disarmament in a Peaceful World," delivered at the UN in September 1961, and the

partial test ban treaty tabled at Geneva in August 1962. Acting with a number of high-level government officials, Foster coordinated the administration's fight for ratification of the partial nuclear test ban treaty in September 1963.

In conjunction with his deputy ADRIAN FISHER, Foster negotiated the 1968 nonproliferation treaty, designed to prevent the spread of atomic weapons to nonnuclear powers. This proposal, first tabled at the 18 Nation Disarmament Conference in August 1965, faced serious opposition from both the Soviet Union and U.S. allies. The Russians objected to the provision that would have permitted the United States to give nuclear weapons to NATO under the proposed Multilateral Nuclear Force (MLF). On the other hand, members of the European Atomic Energy Community (Euratom) objected to inspection of nuclear facilities by the International Atomic Energy Agency, believing that inspection by an agency that contained Communist-bloc personnel would be tantamount to legalized espionage.

Although major Soviet objections were satisfied when the Johnson administration abandoned the MLF proposal in December 1966, Foster spent the next year negotiating the final terms of the treaty. Because of illness, Foster was not present at the climax of the negotiations. Early on the morning of January 18, 1968, the United States and the Soviet Union finally announced in Geneva that they had reached an agreement on a nonproliferation treaty.

Foster left government service in January 1969 and became president of Porter International Company in 1970. He died on October 14, 1984.

—EWS

## Fowler, Henry H(amill)
(1908–2000) *secretary of the Treasury*

Fowler was born on September 5, 1908, in Roanoke, Virginia. Following his graduation from Yale Law School in 1934, Henry Fowler became a counsel to the Tennessee Valley Authority, the first of many government positions he held under Democratic administrations. He served on several federal agencies and wartime boards until 1946, when he entered private law practice in Washington, D.C. He rejoined the government during the Korean War, becoming director of the Office of Defense Mobilization. During the Eisenhower administration, Fowler resumed his prosperous law practice and also served on the Democratic Advisory Council, an arm of the Democratic National Committee designed to outline party positions on national issues.

During the Kennedy years Fowler served as undersecretary of the Treasury. He devoted much of his attention to winning passage of the administration's tax program, the centerpiece of which was the $11.5 billion tax cut in 1963 and 1964. Fowler left the Treasury to return to his law practice in March 1964.

One year later, while he was representing the Automotive Manufacturers Association in the industry's campaign to repeal the auto excise tax, Fowler, became secretary of the Treasury. Johnson's first choice for the position, utility executive Donald C. Cook, had turned down the job. Fowler's nomination went through the Senate "without a ripple," *Business Week* wrote, noting his "complete acceptance by the most powerful men in Congress and his solid reputation with the nation's top-most business executive and bankers."

Fowler was not as strong or independent a Treasury secretary as his predecessor, C. DOUGLAS DILLON, had been during the Kennedy administration. He was completely loyal to President Johnson and faithfully represented the administration through the twists and turns of Johnson economic policy.

Assuming office during a period of general economic prosperity, Fowler had to face the problems of inflation and the balance of payments deficit, both of which were exacerbated by massive spending on the war in Vietnam. His immediate predecessors on the Kennedy-Johnson economic policy-making team had administered the popular Keynesian policies of tax incentives and tax cuts to spur economic growth. Fowler had to apply the bitter side of the Keynesian prescription: tax increases to slow down the economy and curb inflation.

Reluctantly, Fowler argued before Congress in October 1966 for the suspension of the 7 percent investment tax credit, which had been passed in 1962 to stimulate business investment in plant and equipment. "This is not offered as a revenue measure, or a tax increase measure or a tax reform measure," he said. "Its purpose is clearly and simply to suspend a stimulant to forces that are proving inflationary in the current economic situation." Congress suspended the credit in October and also temporarily ended certain methods of accelerated depreciation of

Secretary of the Treasury Henry Fowler in the Cabinet Room of the White House, 1967 *(Photographed by Yoichi R. Okamoto; Lyndon Baines Johnson Library)*

commercial buildings. Only six months later, however, Fowler sought restoration of the credit because of the administration's alarm over the abrupt slowing down of business investment.

In August 1967 Fowler began a 10-month battle to win passage of the administration's anti-inflationary 10 percent tax surcharge. Declaring that costs for the Vietnam War were running in excess of $22 billion a year, Fowler strongly appealed to the House Ways and Means Committee for taxing authority "to finance a war . . . with no clear prospect of an early ending." Besides the threat of inflation, Fowler said, the surcharge was needed "to avoid the risk of excessively high interest rates and limited credit in particular sectors, such as housing." He also pleaded that Congress "join with the President in making every possible expenditure reduction—civilian and military—short of jeopardizing the nation's security and well-being."

The administration's request, however, was held up in the committee, which voted in October 1967 to set the bill aside until the administration came up with a specific plan to cut spending. Fowler made another strong plea for the surcharge before the committee in November, in the wake of the devaluation of the British pound. He stressed that the soundness of the dollar depended on Congress's prompt action to reduce the deficit and control inflation. But the Committee's powerful chair, Representative WILBUR

MILLS (D-Ark.), found the administration's new proposal to cut the budget by only $4 billion unacceptable, and the impasse over the tax increase continued.

Fowler continued his fight for the tax surcharge in the first half of 1968, testifying before the House and the Senate repeatedly and mobilizing prominent business leaders behind the measure. Passed by the House in February and the Senate in April, the tax increase, combined with $6 billion in spending cuts, won final approval from the House-Senate conference in June. The "hero" of the lobbying effort, according to *Congressional Quarterly*, was Fowler, "who literally pursued bankers and businessmen around the world to seek out their support for the measure."

Fowler's other major concern as Treasury secretary was the balance of payments deficit. The deficit, aggravated by the expense of the Vietnam War, continued unabated throughout the Johnson years. Fowler was the leading proponent within the administration of the "go-slow" approach to the problem, while commerce secretary JOHN T. CONNOR advocated a more far-reaching plan. Johnson adopted Fowler's advice; for the most part the administration's balance of payments program was limited to the interest equalization tax on foreign securities and exhortations to corporations to place voluntary restraints on their overseas investments. In 1968, after the devaluation of the pound exacerbated the dollar crisis, Fowler presented a more stringent program to Congress on behalf of the administration. A proposal to tax U.S. citizens traveling in foreign countries proved highly unpopular, however, and Congress did not act on the plan.

Fowler resigned as Treasury secretary in December 1968 and joined the investment banking firm of Goldman, Sachs & Co. He died of pneumonia on January 3, 2000.

—TO

## Freeman, Orville L(othrop)
### (1918–2003) *secretary of agriculture*

Freeman, who was born in Minneapolis, Minnesota, on March 9, 1918, graduated from the University of Minnesota in 1940 and joined the marine corps. After his discharge he returned to Minnesota to earn a law degree. During the late 1940s he collaborated with HUBERT H. HUMPHREY, then mayor of Minneapolis, to make the Democratic–Farmer-Labor

Party (DFL) Minnesota's dominant political force. Freeman was elected governor on the liberal DFL ticket for three two-year terms beginning in 1954.

Initially a backer of Hubert Humphrey's 1960 presidential candidacy, Freeman turned to Senator John F. Kennedy following Humphrey's withdrawal and offered him crucial support at the Democratic National Convention. Briefly considered by Kennedy for the vice presidency, Freeman accepted an appointment as secretary of agriculture after he lost a bid for a fourth gubernatorial term in November, largely because of his decision to call out National Guard troops to prevent the outbreak of violence during a heated strike at a meat-packing plant. In his capacity as agriculture secretary, Freeman had an unusual amount of authority since President Kennedy had little interest in farm issues.

Agriculture was an extremely sensitive post because of the inability of previous administrations to solve the "farm problem": chronic overproduction, an average income for farmers lower than the national average, and an unceasing migration of rural population to the cities. In its efforts to increase farm income through price supports and storage of surpluses, the Agriculture Department had the second-highest budget of any federal department and thus became the target of sharp congressional criticism. Freeman sought to solve the dilemma by a reimposition of traditional Democratic agricultural policy on a more rigorous and comprehensive scale. Higher price supports, he argued, would temporarily raise farm income, while stringent acreage and production limitations would reduce surpluses and ultimately ensure higher prices for farm products. Freeman's policies aimed at maintaining the small farm family, historically a source of Democratic strength, or at least developing alternate nonfarm job opportunities in rural areas.

Freeman was partially successful during the Kennedy years. Farm income rose while acreage limitations and food relief programs abroad reduced surpluses. However, the secretary was unable to win full authority to impose marketing controls, and the opening of the Soviet market to U.S. wheat in late 1963 only partly offset Freeman's inability to expand the West European market for American farm products. In addition, the number of farms and the proportion of farmers in the total population continued to decline. Few were pleased with the progress of the farm program. Urban Democrats resented its expense and charged that it mainly enriched wealthy farmers. Republicans, the advocates of free enterprise, favored the gradual elimination of controls. In addition, southern Democrats, who were avid proponents of price supports, hesitated to add to the power of the secretary and the federal government.

In the area of price supports, controls, and surpluses, Freeman continued the Kennedy policy during the Johnson years although the new president took a much greater interest in farming issues, and doubted the secretary's abilities as a politician, hence lessening Freeman's authority. The most important piece of legislation and a major victory for Freeman was the Food and Agriculture Act of 1965. This omnibus farm bill established price support and production control programs for the major crops (cotton, wheat, and feed grains) for a four-year period. Under the law farmers would retire a portion of their land devoted to high surplus crops and put it into soil-conserving uses. Most significant, price-support levels were reduced in order to keep prices competitive on the international market, while the government offered direct cash payments in order to offset any large loss of income to small farmers. In addition, the secretary now had the authority to take administrative action to increase production. Still, the bill moved through a recalcitrant Congress more because of the efforts of President Johnson than because of Freeman.

Another result of the effort to reduce farm surpluses had been the expansion of food distribution programs abroad, but by 1966 production controls had succeeded to a great degree in limiting surpluses. With the growing awareness of world food shortages and famine conditions in India, the administration no longer viewed the Food for Peace program as a vehicle for the disposal of surpluses; under 1966 legislation it did become a form of foreign aid with more precise requirements and objectives. Recipient nations were now generally expected to pay for their food purchases in dollars instead of in local currencies. In addition, their willingness and ability to carry out "self-help" programs to meet food requirements determined the amount of goods they would receive. In 1966 Freeman announced acreage allotment increases for a number of crops to meet commitments abroad, including a 30 percent increase for wheat.

Because of the passage of the omnibus farm bill and Johnson's considerable skill in handling Congress, Freeman was able to expand the scope of

department activities. One of the most ambitious new programs was the effort to combat hunger in the cities and impoverished rural areas as part of President Johnson's War on Poverty. Despite the budgetary pressures caused by the Vietnam War, food programs were among the fastest growing outlays in the entire U.S. budget during the Johnson administration, rising from about $836.7 million in fiscal 1965 to a fiscal 1970 projection of $1.5 billion at the end of 1968. The authorizations managed to get through the agriculture committees, dominated by southern Democrats, because northern liberals, as the price for their backing of the generous price-support programs, demanded the inclusion of food programs as part of legislative farm packages.

The food stamp program, which was introduced in 1961 on an experimental basis, became permanent in 1964 and subsequently expanded to reach larger numbers of Americans. Under the plan people whose incomes met the department's eligibility requirements bought stamps for less than they were worth and then redeemed them for food at full value in participating grocery stores. In many parts of the country food stamps replaced direct distribution programs, which made available only a limited number of surplus commodities free to the poor. Still, direct distribution of surpluses to institutions expanded as did school lunch and milk programs. Freeman also championed the school breakfast program for poor elementary school children.

As agriculture's sphere of activity increased, criticism from both sides of the political spectrum intensified. Freeman, long the object of conservative attacks, now faced pressure from liberal groups. In 1965 the U.S. Civil Rights Commission cited department officials for discrimination against black southern farmers. This led Freeman to appoint three African Americans to the committees that administered federal farm programs in their respective states. Freeman's role in opening what he called "the second front of this war," the task of feeding South Vietnam and increasing its agricultural production, earned him the enmity of antiwar activists. The dramatic rise in domestic food prices in 1966, caused in part by the Vietnam War, forced him to defend farmers against consumer complaints. Freeman put most of the blame for increased costs on middlemen and exonerated the farmers, who, in fact, had gained little during the inflation.

The food stamp program also came under attack. In October 1967 there were reports that thousands of southern blacks, once surplus commodity recipients, faced starvation because they were too poor to purchase food stamps. The National Advisory Commission on Rural Poverty report, issued in December 1967, underscored the relationship between rural poverty and urban discontent and charged that the department and other government agencies had done too little to aid the rural poor. It recommended that the government revise the food stamp program, improve the quality and availability of services up to the level found in the cities, and provide jobs and a guaranteed income. In April 1968 the Citizen's Board of Inquiry into Hunger and Malnutrition in the United States, which had been organized on the recommendation of United Auto Workers president WALTER P. REUTHER, scored the food stamp program as a "nightmare for the hungry." Stating that the department was interested chiefly in making crop producers richer and had "little interest in feeding people," the board recommended that food programs be transferred either to the Office of Economic Opportunity or to the Health, Education and Welfare Department.

Freeman agreed that not enough had yet been done to eliminate hunger and put the blame for the problem on members of Congress, local officials, and the department bureaucracy, which was slow to change its old habits and sense of priorities. In testimony before the House Agriculture Committee on June 12, 1968, Freeman admitted that he had underestimated the severity and extent of hunger in the United States. By December 1968 he was able to announce a liberalization of the food stamp program.

Although Freeman's tenure as secretary of agriculture witnessed a dramatic reduction in farm surpluses and a rise in prices, his farm policy failed to reverse the historic decline of the American farm family. The number of farms decreased from 3.9 million in 1960 to 3.1 million in 1967, and farmers as a percentage of the total population declined from 8.7 percent to 5.4 percent. In the process farming continued to evolve into agribusiness. The small farmers the administration had pledged to protect lost much of their political strength.

Freeman stepped down in January 1969 with the inauguration of a Republican administration. In 1970 he became president of the Business International Corporation. In 1985 he returned to Washington to practice law, but he eventually returned to Minnesota as Visiting Scholar at the Hubert Humphrey Institute of Public Affairs at the University of Minnesota. He died in Minneapolis on February 20, 2003.

## Frelinghuysen, Peter H. B.
### (1916–   ) *member of the House of Representatives*

Frelinghuysen was born on January 17, 1916, in New York City into a prominent family that produced three U.S. senators and a secretary of state, Frelinghuysen graduated from Princeton University and Yale Law School. In 1952 he won election to Congress from New Jersey's most Republican district, a wealthy suburb of New York City. A moderate Republican, Frelinghuysen supported civil rights legislation and a large international role for the United States. He was a member of the House Foreign Affairs Committee and the Education and Labor Committee, becoming the ranking Republican on the latter in 1963. He was especially active in attempting to modify Kennedy's proposed federal aid to education program.

In 1964 Frelinghuysen persistently attacked President Johnson's proposals for an antipoverty program, arguing that the creation of an Office of Economic Opportunity (OEO) would concentrate excessive and unnecessary authority on the federal level. He drew up an alternative Republican antipoverty bill that delegated greater authority and economic responsibility to the states, gave greater emphasis to education and training, and eliminated the OEO and a federal Job Corps. After the passage of the administration bill, Frelinghuysen, as head of the Republican Task Force on Economic Opportunity in 1965, charged that the War on Poverty was an "administrative shambles" and held hearings in hopes of getting a "full-scale budgetary analysis."

In 1965 Frelinghuysen left the Education and Labor Committee for seats on the Republican Committee on Committees and the Republican Policy Committee. However, he failed to win separate contests for minority whip and chair of the House Republican Conference despite the support of recently elected minority leader Representative GERALD FORD (R-Mich.) and the demands of eastern liberals and moderates for representation in the House leadership.

By 1967 Frelinghuysen sat only on the House Foreign Affairs Committee. He made numerous trips abroad and emerged as a major House Republican spokesperson on foreign policy. An internationalist, he supported President Johnson on approximately 80 percent of roll-call votes concerned with foreign policy. At the August 1968 Republican National Convention, Senator EVERETT DIRKSEN (R-Ill.), the Senate minority leader, asked Frelinghuysen to draft a compromise Vietnam plan for the senator to offer to the convention. Presidential candidate RICHARD NIXON and New York governor NELSON ROCKEFELLER found an early plank too critical of President Johnson for not leaving key Vietnam decisions to the military but were satisfied with Frelinghuysen's draft, which stressed Vietnamization of the military effort and defense of the South Vietnamese population rather than territorial gains. The Frelinghuysen draft was adopted as part of the Republican national platform.

Because of his unswerving support of Nixon's Vietnam policy, Frelinghuysen's popularity in his affluent home district began to erode in the early 1970s, and he decided not to seek reelection in 1974. He returned to Morristown, New Jersey, to his law practice.

—JCH

## Friedan, Betty
(1921– ) *president, National Organization for Women*

Born on February 4, 1921, in Peoria, Illinois, and a graduate of Smith College, Friedan gained national attention in 1963 with the publication of *The Feminine Mystique.* An immediate best seller, her book argued that in the years after World War II a "mystique" promoted by advertisers, educators, women's magazines, and psychologists had convinced American women that fulfillment for them lay only in a life of domesticity. Living solely as wives and mothers, however, women abandoned any efforts at self-realization or personal achievement and submerged their own identities in that of their husbands and children. The result was not happiness but what Friedan called "the problem that has no name"—a sense of emptiness and malaise and a lack of personal identity. Controversial and influential, Friedan's study was both a portent of and a contributor to the women's liberation movement.

Friedan lectured extensively on the position of women over the next several years, and in October

1966 she founded the National Organization for Women (NOW) to press for "true equality" for women. As NOW's first president, Friedan helped build an organization that emphasized education, legislation, and court action to win equal rights for women. During 1967 and 1968 NOW members picketed the *New York Times,* charging that its use of "Male" and "Female" headings in classified advertisements discriminated against women. NOW also brought a suit against the Equal Employment Opportunities Commission (EEOC) for permitting such column headings and pressured the EEOC to step up its enforcement of Title VII of the 1964 Civil Rights Act, which prohibited sex discrimination in employment. Under Friedan's direction, NOW lobbied for the repeal of antiabortion laws in New York State and for passage of the Equal Rights Amendment in Washington. NOW also instituted court cases in various states to challenge state protective labor laws applicable only to women.

Friedan stepped down as NOW's president in 1970 but remained a prominent advocate of women's rights. She issued a call for a "Women's

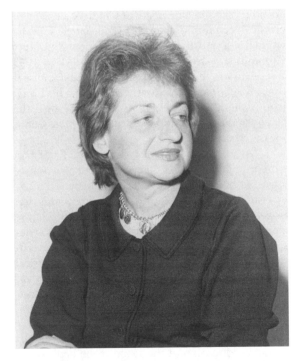

Betty Friedan, founder of the National Organization for Women *(Library of Congress, Prints and Photographs Division)*

Strike for Equality" to be held on August 26, 1970, the 50th anniversary of the Nineteenth Amendment. The result was the first nationwide protest for women's rights since the suffrage movement. In July 1971 Friedan helped organize the National Women's Political Caucus to work for equal representation of women with men at all levels of the political system. In 1973 she became director of the First Women's Bank and Trust Company. She was also a leader in the effort to obtain an amendment to the U.S. Constitution guaranteeing equality for women. She has remained an active figure for women's rights.

—CAB

## Friedman, Milton
(1912–    ) *economist*

Economist Milton Friedman was the foremost academic apostle of free market economics and iconoclastic critic of the Keynesian theories prevailing among government economists in the 1960s. Born in Brooklyn, New York, on July 31, 1912, Friedman grew up in Rahway, New Jersey, and graduated from Rutgers University in 1932. He did graduate work in economics at the University of Chicago, a citadel of classical economic theory. In the late 1930s he worked as a statistician with the National Resources Committee, a federal agency. From 1941 to 1943 Friedman was the principal tax research economist at the Treasury Department. After obtaining his Ph.D. from Columbia University in 1946, he joined the faculty at the University of Chicago, where he taught for the next three decades.

Within the academic community Friedman won prominence with his persistent and provocative advocacy of the quantity theory of money, or "monetarism" as it became known. According to this theory, the dominant factor in the economy is the amount of money in circulation, not, as the Keynesians held, the fiscal policy of the federal government. Friedman marshaled considerable empirical support for this theory in *The Monetary History of the United States* (1963), in which he correlated contractions in the money supply with the occurrence of economic recessions and depressions.

At the center of Friedman's history was a radical reinterpretation of the cause of the depression: he blamed the economic collapse not on the instability of the private market but on the monetary authorities, who allowed the money supply to shrink

when it should have been expanded. His chief policy prescription was to strip the Federal Reserve of its discretionary control over the money supply and mandate that the supply be increased at the steady rate of 4 percent every year.

Friedman coupled his promotion of monetary, rather than fiscal, manipulation with a vigorous attack on virtually all government interference with the private market. He favored the elimination of most federal regulatory agencies, arguing that the best guarantee of prosperity and consumer welfare was the unfettered price system. He believed that Social Security should be abolished and called for the abandonment of minimum-wage legislation on the ground that such a wage floor increased unemployment. In place of antipoverty programs and other welfare state efforts, Friedman favored a "negative income tax," which would provide direct cash payments to people whose income fell below a certain level. He defended the negative income tax as a cheaper and more direct approach to the problem of poverty than government social programs.

During the 1964 presidential campaign Friedman served as chief economic adviser to the Republican presidential candidate, Senator BARRY M. GOLDWATER (R-Ariz.). In an October interview Friedman declared that the senator and he agreed on the need to reduce federal spending on nonmilitary programs, to lessen government regulation of business activity, and to reduce taxes by 5 percent in each of the next five years. They advocated the tax cuts in order to restrict government activity and free the private sector, not as a contra-cyclical economic device, which had been the rationale behind the Kennedy-Johnson $11.5 billion tax cut enacted in February 1964. Goldwater did not endorse all of Friedman's proposals, particularly the economist's call for a free-floating exchange rate for the dollar and the elimination of all barriers to free trade.

For most of his career Friedman operated as a conservative gadfly outside the centers of economic policy making. By the mid-1960s, however, he began to reach a wider audience with the publication of his theory of political economy in *Capitalism and Freedom* in 1962 and of his monetary history the next year and then with the commencement of a triweekly *Newsweek* column beginning in 1966. The coming to power of a Republican administration in 1969 paralleled a growing national respect for Friedman's views. The next several years saw the implementation, or attempted implementation, of several of his favorite proposals, including the all-volunteer army, the publication by the Federal Reserve of regular reports on the growth of the money supply, and the Nixon administration's Family Assistance Plan, an unsuccessful attempt to enact the negative income tax. In 1976 he received the Nobel Memorial Prize for economic science, and he became a senior research fellow at the Hoover Institution in California the following year. He later joined President Ronald Reagan's Economic Policy Advisory Board.

—TO

## Fulbright, J(ames) William
(1905–1995) *member of the Senate*

J. William Fulbright was born on April 9, 1905, and raised in Fayetteville, Arkansas, where his family was economically and socially prominent. He graduated from the University of Arkansas in 1925 and studied at Oxford under a Rhodes scholarship until 1928, when he returned to the United States to take a law degree at George Washington University. After serving with the Justice Department and teaching law at George Washington, Fulbright joined the law faculty of the University of Arkansas in 1936. From 1939 to 1941 he served as president of that university.

In 1942 Fulbright was elected to the House of Representatives, and two years later he went to the Senate, where he remained for three decades. During 1946 he sponsored a law that set up the international educational exchange program bearing his name. In 1954 Fulbright defended the program against Senator Joseph McCarthy's (R-Wisc.) charges of communist infiltration and cosponsored the censure resolution against the Republican senator. It was McCarthy who first used the nickname "Half-bright," although Fulbright refused to respond to such personal smears. Through the influence of his friend LYNDON JOHNSON, Fulbright became chair of the Senate Foreign Relations Committee in 1959.

During the early 1960s Fulbright used his position to advocate a reappraisal of the basic tenets upon which Soviet-American diplomacy had been conducted. He asked the United States to abandon its ideological struggle with the Soviet Union and conduct diplomacy in terms of traditional great power rivalry. Pointing out that a militant cold war philosophy endangered America's domestic inter-

ests, Fulbright urged America to divert its energy from diplomatic confrontation to solving social problems at home. His own domestic record included a history of opposing civil rights for African Americans, including voting against the 1964 Civil Rights Act and 1965 Voting Rights Act, and signing the "Southern Manifesto," which defended segregation.

Fulbright was an enthusiastic supporter of Lyndon Johnson after Kennedy's assassination and during the first months of 1964 backed his foreign policy, including his actions in Vietnam. While calling for a reassessment of Vietnam policy, Fulbright asserted that given the unstable political and military situation the United States had no choice but to support the South Vietnamese government and its army "by the most effective means available." The senator ruled out a negotiated settlement as impractical because South Vietnam's military setbacks had left it in a weak bargaining position.

At the request of President Johnson, Fulbright introduced the Tonkin Gulf Resolution in the Senate on August 6, 1964. The resolution, prompted by a series of reported North Vietnamese attacks on American warships patrolling the Gulf of Tonkin, gave the president almost blanket authority to conduct the war as he wished. In debates on the proposal, Fulbright defended the measure against critics, such as Senator GAYLORD NELSON (D-Wisc.) and Senator WAYNE MORSE (D-Ore.), who feared that it would lead to a large-scale military involvement without congressional control. He refused to accept a Nelson amendment that stated, "Except when provoked to a greater response, we should continue to attempt to avoid a direct military involvement in the Southeast Asian conflict." However, Fulbright assured the Senate that the amendment was an accurate reflection of Johnson's policy. The upper house passed the resolution with only two dissenting votes on August 7.

In later years Fulbright termed his support of the Tonkin Gulf Resolution the most humiliating experience of his public career. The senator attributed his unquestioning support of the president's request to his belief that his old friend would not deceive him and to his desire to see Johnson elected president in 1964. Believing that the election of conservative senator BARRY GOLDWATER (R-Ariz.) would lead to a dangerous escalation of the cold war, Fulbright later said he had not wished to jeopardize Johnson's victory by engaging in a divisive policy debate.

During February 1968 Fulbright held closed hearings to determine if the United States had provoked the Tonkin Gulf incident, if North Vietnam had actually attacked U.S. ships, and if the administration had misled Congress into passing the Tonkin Gulf Resolution. The probe uncovered evidence suggesting that the second of two alleged attacks may not have taken place, and questioned the administration's claim that the ships had not been involved in any operations against North Vietnam. Appearing on national television, Fulbright charged that the resolution was introduced under "a completely false idea of what had happened" and that his own support was "based upon information which was not true." Although he denounced the resolution, Fulbright did not attempt to have it repealed at that time because he believed that some senators who opposed the war would feel compelled to support the president on this issue. The resolution was eventually repealed in 1970.

After Johnson had ordered systematic bombing of North Vietnam in the spring of 1965, Fulbright publicly voiced his doubts about U.S. policy in Vietnam. In a speech in March and a memorandum sent to the president in April, he questioned the administration's belief that a defeat in Vietnam would lead to Communist Chinese expansion throughout Southeast Asia. Fulbright suggested that the conflict in Vietnam was a nationalistic movement rather than the result of Chinese aggression.

Fulbright's first major dissent from administration foreign policy occurred in a debate over U.S. intervention in the Dominican Republic, where a civil war had broken out between leftists and a rightist military junta. Alleging the danger of a Communist takeover, the president had sent American troops to the island in April 1965. Johnson said that the move was necessary to protect American property and lives and to prevent another Cuba in the Caribbean. Fulbright warned that the indiscriminate use of force in civil wars and against national movements might actually push developing nations toward communism. Fulbright's criticism resulted in an open break between the president and the senator.

Fulbright's criticisms of the administration's Vietnam policy grew increasingly blunt during the Foreign Relations Committee hearings in February 1966. He used the televised probe to suggest alternatives to Johnson's policies and to make the public aware of the larger issues involved in the Vietnam dispute. During the opening days of the hearings, the nation heard testimony from such respected military and diplomatic figures as James Gavin and GEORGE KENNAN. These experts on national security questioned the strategic need for U.S. involvement in Southeast Asia and cautioned that continued escalation could involve the United States in a war with the People's Republic of China. Throughout the investigation Fulbright tried to introduce larger issues into the discussion, asking witnesses about the propriety of drawing a peaceful people into a struggle about which they cared little and the ethics of a technologically advanced great power systematically destroying a developing nation. The debate was inconclusive, but it served the educational function Fulbright had intended.

In a series of lectures given at Johns Hopkins University in April 1966, Fulbright delivered his most critical examination of American foreign policy. The senator stated that America was in danger of succumbing to the "arrogance of power which has afflicted, weakened and in some cases destroyed, great nations in the past." He denounced the administration's rhetoric, which portrayed the war in terms of a moral crusade, and questioned whether the continued American presence in Vietnam was not a result of prideful reluctance to accept a solution short of victory. He warned that the war was destroying plans for social reform, endangering relations with old allies, and having a corrosive effect on the American spirit. The lectures were published in 1967 as *The Arrogance of Power*, which became a best seller.

In his book Fulbright outlined the steps he would take to achieve peace. He suggested that the United States cease bombing North Vietnam and reduce military activity in the South to facilitate truce negotiations. The belligerents could then draw up plans for self-determination in South Vietnam and for an eventual referendum on the reunification of the North and South. If the proposed conferences failed to produce agreements, the senator believed that the United States should consolidate its military forces in defensible areas in South Vietnam and maintain them there indefinitely.

By the end of the decade Fulbright had emerged as the preeminent symbol of congressional discontent with the war. Furthermore, he believed that the Senate had abrogated its responsibility for foreign affairs and had left policy making in the hands of presidents who increasingly abused their power. Fulbright, therefore, led the fight in Congress to restrict presidential action in foreign affairs and attempted to make the Foreign Relations Committee a watchdog and counterbalance to the powerful executive. However, he was unable to prevent the continued expansion of the war in the late 1960s and early 1970s. In 1974, after five full terms in the Senate, Fulbright lost the Arkansas Democratic primary. Political observers attributed his defeat by Arkansas governor Dale Bumpers to the senator's preoccupation with foreign affairs at the expense of his constituents' domestic interests. He remained in Washington after his defeat until his death on February 9, 1995.

—EWS

# Galbraith, John Kenneth

(1908–    ) *economist*

Galbraith, who was born on October 15, 1908, in Iona Station, Canada, grew up in rural Ontario. He studied agricultural economics at the Ontario Agricultural College, the University of Toronto, and the University of California, Berkeley, where he earned his Ph.D. in 1934. After several years teaching economics at Harvard and Princeton, Galbraith entered government service in 1940 and soon rose to be deputy administrator of the Office of Price Administration (OPA). His vigorous enforcement of comprehensive price controls brought growing criticism from business and congressional leaders, finally prompting Galbraith's resignation in 1943. He continued to serve in other government agencies through 1948. Galbraith also worked at this time as a contributing editor to *Fortune* magazine.

In 1949 Galbraith returned to Harvard as professor of economics. He established a reputation as an iconoclastic critic of accepted economic theories during the 1950s with two important and widely read books—*American Capitalism: The Concept of Countervailing Power* (1952) and *The Affluent Society* (1958). Both works attacked the traditional view of the economy as a free market. Galbraith claimed that the system actually depended on a balance of powerful interests: large corporations, labor unions, and government agencies. The role of the small consumer, in Galbraith's view, had been eliminated by the development of sophisticated advertising techniques to manipulate consumer desires. In *American Capitalism* Galbraith was optimistic about the ability of the U.S. economy to sustain a stable growth rate. *The Affluent Society*, however, concentrated on the system's shortcomings: the growth of

private consumption at the expense of public services, the persistence of poverty amid affluence, and the danger of inflation resulting form the ceaseless stimulation of consumer buying.

In addition to its critique of the free market, Galbraith's analysis differed from the work of more traditional economists in its emphasis on the importance of political decisions in shaping the economic system. "Galbraith knows power and is drawn to it," commented one political scientist. This attitude appeared not only in Galbraith's writings but also in his lifelong involvement in liberal politics. In 1952 and 1956 he served on the campaign staff of Democratic presidential candidate ADLAI STEVENSON. During the late 1950s Galbraith shifted his support to Senator John F. Kennedy (D-Mass.) and became an important member of the intellectual circle that later helped make policy in the Kennedy White House. After serving briefly as an economic and foreign policy adviser to the administration, Galbraith was appointed ambassador to India in March 1961. Among his most important tasks there was supervision of U.S. aid to India during the Chinese-Indian border conflict of 1962. Galbraith also visited South Vietnam in late 1961 at President Kennedy's request and sent back a report critical of the ruling Diem regime. A diary that Galbraith kept during his two years of diplomatic service was published in 1969 as *Ambassador's Journal*.

In mid-1963 Galbraith left government service to resume his faculty position at Harvard. He devoted the next four years largely to completing his third major economic work, *The New Industrial State*. Published in 1967, Galbraith's new book sought to explain the workings of the industrial system that produced the aberrations discussed in *The*

*Affluent Society*. Of all forms of capitalist enterprise, Galbraith claimed, only the large corporation can satisfy the massive financial and organizational demands of modern technology. The survival of such corporate giants, he pointed out, depends on careful planning at every step—the purchase of materials, production, and sales. Galbraith argued that effective control of corporate planning lay in the hands of managers and skilled technicians, a group he called the technostructure. In the highly complex and integrated organizations of modern business, according to Galbraith, neither formal owners nor outside forces such as government or stockholders can exercise real power.

The model of balanced economic forces that Galbraith had proposed in *American Capitalism* thus gave way in *The New Industrial State* to a view of separate forces operating with the same purpose—the development of technology and expansion of production in directions determined by corporate planners. The flaw of this system, Galbraith argued, was its inability to meet social needs that failed to coincide with the requirements of corporate growth; among these he included a clean environment, satisfactory cultural opportunities, and public services. In the absence of adequate checks on corporate power within government or labor, Galbraith turned to a third group: the "educational and scientific estate" of university teachers and students. These intellectuals, he urged in *The New Industrial State*, could re-emphasize the aspects of life submerged in the corporate drive for production. Galbraith maintained that society could no longer ignore intellectual pressures, pointing out that corporations rely on universities for the educated managers of the technostructure. Eventually, he speculated, the government might be persuaded to regulate corporate power by nationalizing some of the largest corporations and introducing a system of wage and price controls. Like Galbraith's earlier books, *The New Industrial State* gained wide public attention; by the end of 1967 it had become a national best seller. He returned to many of these themes in his 1973 work, *Economics and the Public Purpose*.

Though he never reentered government service after the Kennedy administration, Galbraith remained active in politics during the mid and late 1960s, especially as a critic of the Vietnam War. Testifying before the Senate Foreign Relations Committee in 1966, he rejected the view that "Vietnam is a testing place of American democracy . . . or that it is strategically or otherwise important to U.S. interests." In April 1967 Galbraith was elected president of Americans for Democratic Action. At that time he called for a bombing halt of North Vietnam and intensified efforts at negotiations, charging that the administration was seeking a "military solution" to the conflict. During the 1968 presidential primaries Galbraith supported antiwar senator EUGENE MCCARTHY (D-Minn.), for whom he gave a seconding speech at the Democratic National Convention. He also spoke out frequently on financial issues at this time, urging reform of the tax structure and a "national system of income guarantees and supplements" for poverty groups.

Galbraith remained an influential writer and liberal spokesperson during the early 1970s. Testifying before the congressional Joint Economic Committee in 1972, he argued against proposals for a ceiling on taxes and federal project spending. He attributed the nation's economic difficulties to the Nixon administration's "game plan," which in his view called for "a serious recession, or a serious inflation, or a moderate amount of both" to maintain stability. Galbraith also became a strong advocate of women's rights, pushing through a feminist statement at the 1971 convention of the American Economic Association. Galbraith retired from his Harvard faculty position in 1975. He continued his writing and speaking about political and economic issues, and served as president of the combined American Academy and Institute of Arts and Letters from 1984 to 1987.

—SLG

## Gardner, John W(illiam)

(1912–2002) *secretary of health, education and welfare*

Born on October 8, 1912, in Los Angeles, California, John W. Gardner, a psychologist with a doctorate from the University of California, taught at Connecticut College for Women and at Mt. Holyoke College. Following service in World War II with the Office of Strategic Services, Gardner joined the Carnegie Corporation, one of the nation's leading foundations. In 1955 he became the corporation's president. Gardner was particularly concerned with the problem of maintaining standards of excellence during an era of mass education; many of the programs that he encouraged were directed toward that end.

During 1964 Gardner served as chair of a presidential task force studying the problems of federal aid to primary and secondary schools. The group suggested that "an agonizing tug-of-war over the church-state issue" might be avoided if federal funds to schools were disbursed on the basis of a selective formula related to the economic condition of each area. This became the basis of the 1965 Elementary and Secondary Education Act. In late July of 1965 President Johnson named Gardner, a Republican, to succeed ANTHONY J. CELEBREZZE as secretary of the department of health, education and welfare (HEW).

Shortly after he assumed office Gardner faced charges from members of Congress, the NAACP Legal Defense Fund, and other civil rights groups that HEW lagged in its efforts to integrate schools and hospitals. The Southern Regional Council pointed out that only 5.2 percent of African-American students in 11 southern states were attending integrated schools in 1965. In February 1966 the Civil Rights Commission criticized HEW for lax enforcement of Title VI of the 1964 Civil Rights Act, which barred racial discrimination in any federally assisted program or activity.

Gardner issued a new set of guidelines for all federally assisted schools and hospitals in March 1966. The guidelines stipulated percentage rates of desegregation expected in the South for the 1966–67 school year and mandated the closing of small, inadequate schools that African Americans and other minorities attended. They also called for an end to discrimination in the hiring of teachers and to segregation in hospital facilities. The guidelines did not apply to de facto segregation in cities outside the South.

Southern representatives objected vehemently to the guidelines, charging that they established a quota system in violation of the Civil Rights Act of 1964. In an effort to placate this criticism, Gardner wrote to southern governors, members of Congress, and school officials in April to assure them that HEW was not attempting to impose a specific degree of "racial balance" or to require "instantaneous desegregation." But during the remainder of the year, HEW began to cut off funds for institutions not meeting the department's stipulations, and by early 1967, 34 school districts and 54 hospitals, mostly in the Deep South, had lost federal funds.

In January 1967 Gardner announced the imminent termination of federal aid to Alabama because its governor, GEORGE C. WALLACE, had refused to permit integration of the state's welfare and mental health programs in accordance with Title VI. A year later the U.S. Supreme Court upheld Gardner's cutoff of funds. In May 1967 Gardner announced that the power to force compliance with Title VI was being transferred from HEW subdivision administrators, including U.S. commissioner of education HAROLD HOWE, to a new Office of Civil Rights.

As head of HEW Gardner drew up plans early in 1966 for the reorganization of the public health divisions of his agency. Gardner believed that the U.S. Public Health Service could not effectively manage federally financed health programs. He proposed that a new assistant HEW secretary for health and scientific affairs assume that responsibility along with coordination of the activities of the National Institute of Health, the National Institute of Mental Health, and the National Library of Medicine. This program was implemented by Gardner's successor, WILBUR J. COHEN.

After conferring with President Johnson in December 1966, Gardner announced that he was planning a major organizational reform of HEW. The eight major department bureaus and agencies, he stated, would be organized into three subcabinet departments: the health, the education, and the individual and family services departments.

Testifying before a Senate subcommittee in August 1966, Gardner responded to complaints that the administration was not spending enough money on the cities by warning of an American habit "of spending a lot of money to still our anxieties." He said that a "master plan" for urban areas was more important than the expenditure of large sums of money. The administration's Demonstration Cities program, he said, provided the beginnings of such a plan.

On January 3, 1967, Gardner offered new federal standards to reduce the quantity of car-exhaust pollutants. The plan proposed a requirement that 77 percent of hydrocarbon and 68 percent of carbon monoxide emissions be eliminated in 1970 automobiles. In justifying the measure Gardner estimated that "one billion gallons of gasoline annually pollute the atmosphere" as a result of motor vehicle use. The following July he backed a Federal Trade Commission recommendation for stronger health warnings on cigarette packs. Gardner stressed that such a step was particularly necessary to prevent young people from smoking.

As HEW secretary, Gardner controlled federal grants to institutions of higher education. He encountered criticism from educators for opposing general institutional grants and, instead, favoring categorical aid for the initiation of innovative projects. In October 1967 one educational lobbyist commented, "the trouble with this thinking is that in many instances the federal government is the only possible source of funds. If programs aren't sustained by it they will die."

In January 1968 Gardner resigned unexpectedly amid reports that he had clashed with President Johnson over U.S. involvement in Vietnam. Gardner denied these rumors, but they persisted. During 1968 he became chair of the National Urban Coalition, a privately supported antipoverty organization. In July, shortly after assuming that post, he spoke before the National Governors Conference and asserted that greatly increased federal spending would be required to solve the problems of the cities. In August 1970 Gardner announced the formation of Common Cause, which he described as a nonpartisan citizens' lobby. The new group, which Gardner headed, was designed to seek social and political reforms and to counter partisan and corporate influence in government. He continued to push for political reforms, especially campaign finance legislation and disclosure laws, and he became a professor of public service at Stanford University in 1989. He retired in 1996. He died of cancer in Palo Alto, California, in 2002.

—JLW

## Garrison, Jim

(1921–1992) *district attorney, Orleans Parish, Louisiana*

Garrison, who was born on November 20, 1921, in Dennison, Iowa, earned a law degree from Tulane University in 1949. That year he was admitted to the Louisiana bar and began his practice in New Orleans. He served as assistant district attorney for New Orleans from 1954 to 1958. In 1962, shortly after he became district attorney for Orleans Parish, he undertook an investigation of vice and crime in New Orleans's French Quarter. Late in the year the New Orleans Criminal District Court denied Garrison's request for additional funds for his investigation. Garrison alleged that "racketeering influence" had affected the court's decision. In February 1963 Garrison was convicted of defaming the judges and

sentenced to four months in prison and fined $1,000. Late in the year, however, the U.S. Supreme Court overturned the conviction.

In October 1966 Garrison began an investigation of the John F. Kennedy assassination. In February 1967 he announced that Kennedy had been murdered by a group of New Orleans conspirators. Four days later David William Ferrie, a former airline pilot and prime Garrison suspect, was found dead in his New Orleans apartment. New Orleans coroner Dr. Nicholas Chetta stated that Ferrie had died of a ruptured blood vessel in the brain, a finding confirmed by an autopsy. Garrison questioned the results of the autopsy and suggested that Ferrie had committed suicide. "Evidence developed by our office," said Garrison, "had long since confirmed that he was involved in events culminating in the assassination of President Kennedy. Apparently we waited too long."

Garrison announced on February 24 that his staff had "solved" the assassination but that he would need months or even years to "work on details of evidence" and to make arrests. Yet only days later Garrison ordered Clay L. Shaw, retired director of the New Orleans International Trade Mart, arrested for "participation in a conspiracy to murder John F. Kennedy." Garrison charged that during 1963 Shaw, alias "Clay Bertrand," Lee Harvey Oswald, and Ferrie had planned the assassination. Shaw denied that he knew Oswald or Ferrie and through legal appeals sought to prevent Garrison from bringing him to trial. While the Shaw case was making its way to the U.S. Supreme Court, Garrison attempted to develop an elaborate account of the assassination. He proposed that Oswald had been a CIA operative and implied that he had been framed by the agency. He suggested that a number of Cuban exiles working for the CIA and "having a venomous reaction from the 1961 Bay of Pigs episode" had actually murdered the president.

Garrison's allegations received extensive coverage as well as strong criticism in the news media. In June 1967 the National Broadcasting Company, in a special television broadcast, charged that Garrison was intimidating potential witnesses and had offered them bribes to secure cooperative testimony. The *New York Times* reported that two Louisiana convicts had asserted that Garrison's office had offered them their freedom if they would cooperate with the investigation.

In December 1968 the U.S. Supreme Court refused to bar Garrison from prosecuting Shaw.

The trial began Jan. 21, 1969. A key prosecution witness, Perry Russo, testified that in September 1963 he had heard Ferrie, Oswald, and Shaw discuss the assassination. Under cross-examination Russo confessed that he had previously been hypnotized to help strengthen his recollection of Oswald and Shaw. The jury acquitted Shaw after 50 minutes of deliberation on March 1, 1969. The *New York Times* called it one of the most disgraceful chapters in the history of American jurisprudence. Garrison vowed that he had "just begun to fight" and had Shaw arrested on March 3 for perjury, charging that he had lied under oath in denying having known Oswald and Ferrie. Shaw in turn sued Garrison for $5 million in damages stemming from his prosecution.

Although Garrison endured strong public criticism, he won reelection to another term as district attorney in November 1969. In May 1970 a federal judge ordered Garrison to cease his prosecution of Shaw. The U.S. Supreme Court upheld this order in 1972. Shaw's suit against Garrison was delayed for several years and remained unsettled when Shaw died in 1974.

During the early 1970s Garrison had to contend with his own legal problems. In December 1971 a federal grand jury indicted him on charges that he had taken bribes to protect New Orleans gambling and pinball machine interests. He was acquitted in September 1973. He also won acquittal in March 1974 on charges of federal income tax evasion. He attributed his prosecution in these matters to a government conspiracy to prevent him from pursuing his investigation of the Kennedy assassination.

In December 1973 Garrison was narrowly defeated for a fourth term as district attorney in the Democratic primary in New Orleans. He then returned to private legal practice. In 1978 he was elected to the Louisiana Fourth Circuit Court of Appeals. He published his recollections of the investigation in a 1988 book, *On the Trail of the Assassins*, which served partially as the basis for the controversial 1991 film, *JFK*, which Oliver Stone directed. Garrison had a cameo role in the movie. Despite the attention the book and the film garnered, his claims have been widely repudiated, and his own reputation suffered. He died of cancer on October 21, 1992.

—JLW

## Geneen, Harold S(ydney)
(1910–1997) *chief executive officer, International Telephone and Telegraph Corporation*

Born on June 11, 1910, in Bournemouth, England, Geneen spent much of his youth in a Connecticut boarding school, leaving at age 16 to become a page on the New York Stock Exchange. After acquiring a degree in accounting from New York University in 1934, he worked for an accounting firm for eight years. From 1942 to 1946 he was chief accountant for the American Can Company, from 1946 to 1950 comptroller of the Bell and Howell Company, and from 1950 to 1956 vice president and comptroller of the Jones and Laughlin Steel Corporation.

Geneen won his reputation as a master manager by his performance as executive vice president of Raytheon Manufacturing, which he joined in 1956. Dividing the large electronics concern into 12 semiautonomous units, Geneen applied a system of strict financial control and constant monitoring of each division by top management. Raytheon's earnings quadrupled in three years.

Upon assuming the presidency of International Telephone and Telegraph (ITT) in 1959, Geneen reorganized the communications carrier to conform to his "I want no surprises" dictum. With his aptitude for figures and sharp business acumen, he stood at the center of a system of long-range planning and relentless monitoring of business operations, which became his managerial trademark. Having transformed the management by 1963, Geneen embarked on an aggressive program of mergers and acquisitions that radically altered the nature of ITT itself.

Fearful of nationalization and growing competition overseas, Geneen worked with the investment bankers Lazard, Freres to expand and diversify his company's U.S. holdings. The purchase in 1965 of the Avis car rental firm for $52 million was ITT's first big acquisition. Other major purchases were the housing developer Levitt and Sons in 1966 for $92 million, Pennsylvania Glass and Sand in 1968 for $112 million, Rayonier in 1968 for $293 million, and Continental Baking in 1968 for $279 million. The acquired companies, along with a wide variety of smaller units absorbed by ITT, had in common only high earnings and high growth potential. Such acquisitions boosted ITT's stock value and made it still easier for ITT to expand, since it almost always paid the stockholders of the acquired companies in ITT stock. By 1974 ITT comprised several hundred companies with annual revenues totaling $8.5 billion.

Geneen encountered his greatest setback when he attempted to acquire the American Broadcasting Company (ABC). ABC's stockholders approved ITT's $400 million offer in April 1966, and the Federal Communications Commission (FCC), after extended hearings, approved the combination one year later by a four-to-three vote of the commissioners. The Department of Justice, however, refused to permit the giant merger. Challenging the FCC's judgment in the federal courts, the department opposed the merger, charging that ITT's international interests might prejudice ABC's news operations, while ABC as a whole could not retain its autonomy in the face of "pervasive, centralized control" by ITT. The department found Geneen's contention that ABC needed a capital infusion from ITT dubious. On January 1, 1968, Geneen canceled the planned merger.

During the Nixon administration Geneen's attempt to take over the Hartford Fire Insurance Company produced another antitrust suit by the Justice Department. The revelation of ITT's tactics in opposing the suit, particularly the publication by columnist JACK ANDERSON of a memo written by an ITT lobbyist connecting the settlement of the suit with an ITT promise to contribute $400,000 toward the 1972 Republican National Convention, resulted in a scandal of major proportions for the Nixon administration. The corporation was also embarrassed when a congressional committee disclosed that ITT had offered funds to the Central Intelligence Agency to sabotage the election campaign of Chilean president Salvador Allende.

Geneen stepped down as CEO of IT&T in 1977, although he remained chair of the board of directors until 1979, and he remained on the board until 1983. He continued to be active in the business world, however, until his death in Manhattan in 1997.

—TO

## Genovese, Eugene (Dominick)

(1930–    ) *historian*

Born on May 19, 1930, and raised in Brooklyn, New York, Genovese received a B.A. from Brooklyn College, and M.A. and Ph.D. degrees in history from Columbia University. From 1958 to 1963 he taught at Brooklyn Polytechnical Institute and in 1963 became an associate professor of history at Rutgers University in New Brunswick, New Jersey. At Rutgers he was faculty adviser to the campus chapter of Students for a Democratic Society.

At a Rutgers University antiwar "teach-in" on April 23, 1965, Genovese declared, "Those of you who know me know that I am a Marxist and a socialist. Therefore, unlike most of my distinguished colleagues here this morning, I do not fear or regret the impending Viet Cong victory in Vietnam. I welcome it." Genovese's declaration became the major campaign issue of the 1965 New Jersey gubernatorial election. Republican candidate Wayne Dumont demanded that Rutgers, New Jersey's state university, fire Genovese. His opponent, Democratic governor RICHARD J. HUGHES, differed with Genovese's views, but defended his right to free speech. Hughes declared that he was "determined to preserve academic freedom in the broadest sense." Both the University Board of Examiners and a state assembly committee found that Genovese had violated no state or university regulations, and the Examiners report, released August 6, found no ground for dismissal.

The Genovese case won national publicity in the fall of 1965. In October Senator ROBERT F. KENNEDY (D-N.Y.), campaigning for Hughes, said that pressure to oust Genovese "would sound the death knell of higher education in the state." That same month former vice president RICHARD M. NIXON, on a campaign swing for Dumont, attacked Kennedy and supported the call for Genovese's ouster. In a letter to the *New York Times* Nixon said, "Any individual employed by the state should not be allowed to use his position for the purpose of giving aid and comfort to the enemies of the state." (In the November 2 election Hughes was reelected by 350,000 votes, a record plurality for a New Jersey gubernatorial race.) After the November election former senator BARRY M. GOLDWATER (R-Ariz.) said that Genovese's remarks "come closer to treason than academic freedom."

Genovese published his first book, *The Political Economy of Slavery*, in 1965. He argued that slavery in the antebellum South had created a "premodern" society ruled by a small planter class increasingly at economic, ideological, and moral odds with northern bourgeoise society. By stressing that slavery was more than "simply a system of economic compulsion," but rather the basis of a paternalist system of social, economic, and psychological relations between whites and blacks, Genovese stood counterposed to most liberal historians of the 1960s who were primarily interested in describing the exploitation and resistance of blacks under slave conditions. He further developed these themes in his later book, *Roll, Jordan, Roll,* a best seller that was widely regarded as one of the definitive books about American slavery.

Genovese argued that the task of all historians, including those who identified themselves as socialists, was objectively and accurately to explain the past. During the late 1960s he was especially critical of other radical historians whom he thought moralistic and willing to sacrifice historical perspective for relevance. Although Genovese remained a critic of the Vietnam War, he was highly critical of the New Left for what he considered its "fantasies of revolutionary apocalypse" and its undiscriminating attacks on the universities and professional societies.

After leaving Rutgers in 1967 Genovese taught at Sir George Williams University and the University of Rochester. He continued to publish new works on slavery, establishing himself as one of the leading historians of the South and one of the most widely known and respected Marxist historians in the United States.

He also served as president of the Organization of American Historians and founder and president of The Historical Society.

—JBF

## Gilligan, John J(oyce)

(1921–  ) *member of the House of Representatives*

Born on March 22, 1921, in Cincinnati, Ohio, John J. Gilligan earned a B.A. from Notre Dame University in 1943 and won a Silver Star at Okinawa during World War II. After receiving a master's degree in literature from the University of Cincinnati in 1947, Gilligan taught English at Xavier University and sold insurance. In 1953 he won election on an independent reform ticket to the Cincinnati City Council and six years later won the first of three terms to the council as its sole Democrat.

Two years after losing the Democratic nomination for an at-large seat in the U.S. Congress in May 1962, Gilligan unseated the incumbent in the first district, Representative Carl W. Rich (R-Ohio). As past president of the Cincinnati Catholic Interracial Council, Gilligan organized a large volunteer force of civil rights and labor movement activists

for his campaign. LYNDON JOHNSON handily won in Cincinnati, helping to carry in Gilligan, who won with 51 percent of the vote. Only twice before in the 20th century had the overwhelmingly Republican First Congressional District elected a Democrat to Congress.

During the 89th Congress Gilligan consistently supported the Johnson administration. According to *Congressional Quarterly,* he opposed the president on only 5 percent of the votes for which the White House announced a position. Gilligan voted for the Vietnam War supplemental appropriation in March 1966 but joined 77 other House Democrats in an open statement urging the president to limit military operations and to negotiate a settlement. As a member of the House Interstate and Foreign Commerce Committee during the nationwide airline strike, Gilligan voted against a bill that would have forced the airline machinists back to work in August 1966. In October he helped to weaken the "truth-in-packaging" law, which standardized manufacturers' packaging and quality standards. Reportedly in deference to Procter and Gamble, a large employer in his district, Gilligan won the inclusion of an amendment that modified governmental regulations proposed by Senate sponsor PHILIP A. HART (D-Mich.).

As the 1966 elections drew near, Gilligan faced two major obstacles to his reelection. First, the Republican legislature had reapportioned his district in December 1964 to increase its Republican makeup. Second, former representative Robert Taft, Jr., scion of the district's most famous family, opposed him for reelection. Gilligan skillfully publicized the benefits to his district from the administration's new legislation. He also called attention to a $750 million defense contract for a local plant and federal grants for area housing and cultural programs. But in the election, which the *Washington Post* described as "an all-out, no-holds-barred battle between two able, articulate exponents of 1966 conservatism and liberalism," Taft rode a strong Republican trend in Ohio to win with 53 percent of the vote. Gilligan ran well, however, capturing 18 percent more of the district's vote than the Democratic candidate for governor.

In late 1967 the leaders of the Ohio Democratic Party and the state AFL-CIO persuaded Gilligan to challenge incumbent senator FRANK J. LAUSCHE (D-Ohio) in the primary. In eight general election campaigns since 1944, Lausche had only lost once, but his consistent conservatism had thoroughly antagonized the state's labor leadership. The Ohio AFL-CIO's Committee on Political Education (COPE) provided Gilligan with the money and manpower needed to overcome Lausche's traditional popularity. Both the state party committee and COPE gave Gilligan unprecedented preprimary endorsements. Gilligan easily defeated his older opponent by a margin of 10 percent of the vote.

Gilligan organized an attempt at the August 1968 Democratic National Convention to include a platform plank that advocated peace in Vietnam based on an unconditional cessation of U.S. bombing of the North. Under pressure from the White House, however, convention delegates rejected the proposed.

Gilligan's prominent role in the peace-plank debate led Ohio COPE, which strongly supported the administration's conduct of the war, to delay its general election endorsement and withhold financial support for his Senate campaign until late September. Antiwar senator EUGENE J. MCCARTHY (D-Minn.) made a rare appearance on Gilligan's behalf in October. Ohio's attorney general, William B. Saxbe, the Republican nominee, waged a folksy, mildly "law and order" campaign and received the full support of the state's efficient Republican organization. Gilligan lost by 100,000 votes.

Gilligan briefly retired from politics to return to his Cincinnati insurance agency. In 1970 he won election to the governorship, only to lose it four years later to former governor JAMES A. RHODES (R-Ohio). He subsequently worked for the Agency for International Development, before becoming director of the Institute for Public Policy at the University of Notre Dame. In 1992 he returned to Cincinnati, where he taught at the University of Cincinnati Law School.

—JLB

## Gilpatric, Roswell L(eavitt)
(1906–1986) *deputy secretary of defense*

Born in New York City on November 4, 1906, Gilpatric graduated from Yale Law School in 1931 and then joined the New York law firm Cravath, de Gresdorff, Swaine & Moore (later Cravath, Swaine & Moore). Gilpatric was appointed assistant secretary of the air force in May 1951 and, in October, was promoted to undersecretary. In 1953 he resigned and returned to his law firm.

Gilpatric served on two task forces on national defense established by John F. Kennedy after his presidential nomination, and, following Kennedy's election, he was appointed deputy secretary of defense. Gilpatric headed a task force appointed by Kennedy in April 1961 that issued a series of recommendations for a moderate increase in American involvement in Vietnam. He was also a member of ExComm, Kennedy's chief advisory body during the 1962 Cuban missile crisis.

Gilpatric had originally planned to serve in his post at the Defense Department for only two years, but his involvement in the TFX controversy delayed his resignation. Testimony before the Senate Permanent Investigations Subcommittee showed that Gilpatric's former law firm had done extensive legal work for General Dynamics Corporation, winner of the TFX fighter/bomber contract, both before and after Gilpatric left the firm to join the Department of Defense. Some subcommittee members charged that the firm's connections with General Dynamics made improper Gilpatric's involvement in the TFX decision. However, on November 20, 1963, the subcommittee gave Gilpatric an informal 5-4 "vote of confidence," and a Justice Department investigation likewise cleared him of charges of conflict of interest.

President Johnson announced Gilpatric's resignation on January 9, 1964. Gilpatric rejoined Cravath, Swaine & Moore as a senior partner and was elected to the board of directors of several major corporations and cultural institutions. On September 9, 1964, Johnson appointed Gilpatric one of 16 members of a nonpartisan advisory panel on national security.

Two months later Johnson appointed Gilpatric the chair of a panel to study ways of halting the spread of nuclear weapons. The Gilpatric panel report was secret, but according to a July 1, 1965, article in the *New York Times*, the report recommended that the United States give up the proposed multilateral nuclear force if necessary to achieve an accord to halt the spread of nuclear weapons. According to the *Times*, the recommendations and the secrecy surrounding them created considerable controversy within the administration. The State Department was reported to have been critical of the report, while the Department of Defense and the Atomic Energy Commission approved it.

In November 1965 a White House citizens committee headed by Gilpatric and Massachusetts

Institute of Technology dean Jerome Wiesner urged a three-year moratorium by the United States and the Soviet Union on the production and deployment of antimissile missile systems to avoid a new arms race. The report was submitted to the White House Conference on International Cooperation.

After leaving the government Gilpatric wrote a number of articles on disarmament, foreign policy, and military affairs. He was one of LBJ's "Wise Men," a distinguished group of foreign policy experts who advised the president on foreign policy, especially regarding Vietnam. In subsequent years he was an active opponent of the development of an antiballistic missile system. He remained active behind the scenes in American foreign policy until his death in 1986.

—JBF

## Ginsberg, Allen
(1926–1997) *poet*

Born in Newark, New Jersey, on June 3, 1926, Ginsberg grew up in difficult circumstances. His mother, Naomi Ginsberg, an emigré from Russia and a Communist in her youth, died in 1956 after many years of paranoia and long confinement in a mental hospital. Her son's painful memory of her deterioration was reflected in the poem "Kaddish for Naomi Ginsberg" (1961). Ginsberg entered Columbia University in 1943 on a scholarship and graduated in 1948. While at Columbia he was part of a circle that included writers Jack Kerouac and William S. Burroughs. In 1953 Ginsberg moved to San Francisco, where he worked for a short time as a market research consultant before quitting to devote himself to his poetry. Ginsberg became a leading figure in the literary movement known as the San Francisco Renaissance. His 1956 poem "Howl" was one of the Beat Generation's major documents. It also earned Ginsburg a trial for obscenity violations. That same year, the publication of his book, *Howl and Other Poems,* helped make him a national figure among an emerging artistic movement.

In 1960 Ginsberg began experimenting with drugs under the guidance of TIMOTHY LEARY. Three years later he returned from a visit to India chanting a Hare Krishna mantra and preaching the superiority of yoga and meditation over drugs, but he continued to regard psychedelics as useful aids to personal awareness and illumination. In June 1966

Beat poet Allen Ginsberg leading a demonstration in Greenwich Village, New York City, 1965 *(Library of Congress, Prints and Photographs Division)*

he testified in support of the liberalization of the laws against non-addictive psychedelics before a Senate subcommittee on narcotics. Ginsberg informed the senators that LSD had enabled him to stop hating LYNDON JOHNSON as a criminal and to pray for the president instead.

As a correspondent for the *Evergreen Review,* Ginsberg visited Cuba in 1965. He was quickly deported by Fidel Castro's regime, however, after he publicly condemned the government's persecution of homosexuals. On a tour of Eastern Europe in 1965 Ginsberg was expelled by the Czechoslovak government because, according to Ginsberg, it was embarrassed by the enthusiasm with which young people in Prague received a "bearded American fairy dope poet."

Back in the United States Ginsberg saw his role as one of bridging the gap between political radicals and hippies. In the fall of 1965 he proposed "flower power" to antiwar demonstrators in California as a means of neutralizing harassment from the police and the Hell's Angels motorcycle gang. He was also an organizer of the first Human Be-In, in Golden Gate Park in San Francisco in January 1967. Later in the same year he was arrested, with Dr. BENJAMIN SPOCK and others, in New York City for blocking the steps of a draft board office. During the 1968 Democratic National Convention in Chicago, he was teargassed while chanting a mantra at the Lincoln Park Yippie Festival of Life. He continued writing into the next decade, and won the 1974 National Book Award for his *The Fall of America.* His criticism of numerous U.S. government actions also earned him a large FBI file. Never moving from the Lower East Side of New York, he remained an active presence in the arts world until his death from liver cancer on October 5, 1997.

—TLH

## Ginzburg, Ralph
(1929–  ) *publisher*
Born on October 28, 1929, and raised in Brooklyn, New York, Ralph Ginzburg graduated from the City College of New York in 1949 and held a variety of newspaper and magazine jobs before he began publication in 1962 of *Eros*, a quarterly "joyfully [devoted to] the subjects of love and sex." An energetic promoter, Ginzburg sent out brochures seeking subscriptions to the magazine on a mass basis. They claimed that recent Supreme Court rulings had liberalized the law on obscenity and that *Eros* "takes full advantage of this new freedom of expression. It is *the* magazine of sexual candor." The Post Office received some 35,000 complaints about the advertisement, reportedly the largest number in its history.

An expensive and handsome hardcover magazine, *Eros* went through four editions in 1962 before Ginzburg was indicted for violating the federal obscenity statute that prohibited sending obscene literature through the mails. The indictment focused on the fourth issue of *Eros*, which included a photo-essay depicting a nude interracial couple, and two other Ginzburg publications, an issue of *Liaison: The Biweekly Newsletter of Love* and *The Housewife's Handbook of Selective Promiscuity*, a purported journal of one woman's sexual history. Ginzburg, a self-styled crusader for human liberation, went to trial before a judge in a federal district court in Philadelphia in June 1963. He contended that the publications were not obscene under the

standards established by the Supreme Court. Many commentators later evaluated the works as tame compared to publications that became generally available in the early 1970s. The judge, however, found Ginzburg guilty and sentenced him to a five-year prison term and a $42,000 fine.

A U.S. Appeals Court upheld his conviction in November 1964, and Ginzburg, with support from the American Civil Liberties Union, appealed to the Supreme Court. On March 21, 1966, in a controversial five-to-four decision, the Supreme Court also affirmed Ginzburg's conviction. Justice William Brennan's majority opinion held that "pandering" in the sale of materials and the use of "titillating" advertising that emphasized the works' sexually provocative aspects could be used to convict a publisher of obscenity even if the works themselves might not be legally obscene. Specifically, the Court noted that Ginzburg sought to have his publications mailed with postmarks from towns with names that carried some sexual innuendo, such as Intercourse, Pennsylvania, and Middlesex, New Jersey. They also noted that his advertising emphasized sexual imagery and promised a refund if the book was confiscated by the Post Office for its sexual nature. The decision was widely considered a reversal of a Court trend liberalizing the definition of obscenity. Many editors and legal experts questioned the validity of determining obscenity on the basis of the promotional techniques used rather than on the merits of the work itself.

While this case was on appeal, Ginzburg became embroiled in another controversy. He had begun publishing *Fact* magazine early in 1964, and in the September-October issue for that year, Ginzburg published a lead article on the mental competency of Republican presidential candidate BARRY GOLDWATER (R-Ariz.). Ginzburg had sent a questionnaire to every psychiatrist in the country. The majority of the approximately 20 percent who responded, he reported, considered Goldwater psychologically unfit for the presidency. Many psychiatrists denounced as unprofessional those colleagues who participated in this long-distance diagnosis. In September 1965 Goldwater filed a $2 million libel suit against Ginzburg and *Fact*, charging deliberate character assassination. Following a May 1968 trial in New York City, the jury found for Goldwater and awarded him $75,000 in punitive damages.

After the March 1966 Supreme Court ruling on his obscenity conviction, Ginzburg sought to have his prison sentence vacated or suspended, but he only succeeded in getting it reduced from five to three years. He spent eight months in a federal prison in 1972 before being paroled. After *Fact* magazine folded in 1968, Ginzburg published the periodicals *Avant Garde*, beginning in 1969, and *Moneysworth*, beginning in 1971.

—CAB

## Glazer, Nathan
(1923–   ) *sociologist*

Born in New York City on February 25, 1923, Glazer graduated from the City College of New York in 1944 and did advanced work in anthropology and linguistics at the University of Pennsylvania. After World War II he began a long association with *Commentary* magazine, serving as an assistant editor for a short time. In 1962 Glazer received his Ph.D. in sociology from Columbia University.

In 1948 Glazer collaborated with David Riesman and Reuel Denney on a research project in mass communications that resulted in a widely read book on social adjustment, *The Lonely Crowd: A Study of the Changing American Character* (1950). Between 1955 and 1960 Glazer was, successively, a lecturer at the University of Chicago, a staff member of the Fund for the Republic's "Communism in American Life" project for which he wrote *The Social Basis of American Communism* (1961), and a visiting professor at the University of California, Berkeley, and at Bennington and Smith Colleges. In 1963 Glazer coauthored with DANIEL PATRICK MOYNIHAN *Beyond the Melting Pot: The Negroes, Puerto Ricans, Jews, Italians and Irish of New York City*, a highly influential study of the persistence of racial and ethnic identity in modern America.

As a student at City College, Glazer had been a socialist, and, until the end of the 1950s, he was associated with the moderate left. Over the next few years, however, Glazer moved politically to the center. He related the evolution of his thought to two experiences of the 1960s. The first was the year he spent in Washington in 1962 and 1963 as an urban sociologist with the Housing and Home Finance Agency, where he helped initiate some of the domestic projects that became the nucleus for the federal government's antipoverty program. There, Glazer later explained, he developed a respect for bureaucracy and its ability to reconcile many complex social and economic interests. The second

experience was his participation in some of the events surrounding the student revolt at the Berkeley campus of the University of California, where he was a faculty member from 1963 to 1969. During the Free Speech Movement (FSM) in the fall of 1964, Glazer attempted to play a mediating role between the student rebels and the university administration in the initial stages of the confrontation. He advised the students that University president CLARK KERR could not afford to compromise with them over their principal demand for the unconditional right of political advocacy on campus.

At the Berkeley Academic Senate's decisive December 8, 1964, meeting, Glazer was a leader of the minority faculty group opposed to FSM. He seconded an amendment permitting student "speech or advocacy provided it is directed to no immediate act of force or violence . . .," which Glazer later defined as including such acts of civil disobedience as those carried out by the campus civil rights movement. His motion was defeated by a large majority, and the Berkeley faculty passed in its place a pro-FSM motion barring any university restriction on "the content of speech or advocacy." In the next several months Glazer and fellow Berkeley faculty members Lewis Feuer, Seymour Martin Lipset, and Paul Seabury published a series of articles in *Commentary*, the *Reporter*, and the *New Leader* attacking the FSM as an attempt to destroy what they viewed as a university's legitimate democratic authority.

Throughout the 1960s Glazer intensified his criticism of student radicalism in numerous speeches and articles, most of which were republished in his book *Remembering the Answers* (1970). In his view campus unrest posed a threat to the very existence of the university by attempting to transform it into a vehicle for direct political ends. To the charge that the university was already deeply involved in such political activity as war-related research, Glazer replied that these were marginal functions that could be reformed away; student radicals, he said, really wanted to destroy the university as a center for unbiased and unconstrained research and teaching.

Apart from his concern for the survival of the university, Glazer admitted that he found it progressively harder in the late 1960s to support attacks on existing institutions. Increasingly pessimistic about the possibility of social reform and deliberate government planning, Glazer broadened his criticism of the ideological left to include more pragmatic liberals and many of the liberal programs he had once favored. In the pages of *Commentary* and *The Public Interest*, he wrote disapprovingly of demands for equality in economic power and social status, and he speculated that the breakdown of traditional modes of behavior and social control threatened liberal democracy in the West. In 1969 Glazer became professor of education and social structure at Harvard University. He remained at Harvard for an extensive teaching and writing career.

—TLH

## Gleason, Thomas W(illiam)

(1900–1992) *president, International Longshoremen's Association*

Born in New York City on November, 1900, Gleason began working on the New York docks in 1915 and four years later joined the International Longshoremen's Association (ILA). In 1953 he was appointed to the specially created post of union general organizer by newly elected ILA president William V. Bradley. Gleason was elected president of the ILA's Atlantic Coast Division and executive vice president of the union in 1961. After serving as chief negotiator during a 1962–63 longshoremen's strike, Gleason challenged Bradley for the ILA presidency. On the eve of the July 1963 election, Bradley withdrew from the race to take a salaried position as president emeritus, and Gleason became the new head of the ILA.

In the fall of 1963 Gleason agreed to cooperate with a Kennedy administration proposal to sell wheat to the Soviet Union after the government agreed that 50 percent of the grain would be transported in U.S. vessels, unless such ships were unavailable. On February 12, 1964, the Maritime Administration issued a waiver to the Continental Grain Corporation permitting it to ship 62 percent of a million-ton Soviet wheat purchase in foreign ships on the grounds that several U.S. ships offered for Continental's use were actually "unavailable" because they were either too large for Soviet ports or otherwise unsuitable.

Gleason and Seafarers' International Union (SIU) president Paul Hall reacted to the waiver by denouncing the entire policy of grain sales to the USSR. They said that they had agreed to cooperate with the sales only because the 50 percent provision would provide work for U.S. sailors and longshoremen. On February 17 Gleason ordered ILA mem-

bers to refuse to load any Soviet-bound wheat, and both the SIU and the National Maritime Union (NMU) announced their support for the action. Following conversations between President Johnson and AFL-CIO president GEORGE MEANY and negotiations between union leaders, including Gleason, and Secretary of Labor W. WILLARD WIRTZ, a new agreement was reached, and the boycott ended February 25. Under the new agreement, all future wheat sales to the Soviet Union would be subject to a mandatory 50 percent U.S. shipping requirement, but existing contracts would be permitted to stand. A union demand that the 50 percent requirement be extended to other types of U.S. trade with Communist countries was to be considered in future government union discussions.

The settlement ending the 1962–63 Atlantic and Gulf Coast longshoremen's strike postponed the resolution of the shippers' demand for a reduction in the size of work gangs by referring it to the government for study. In July 1964 the Labor Department issued a report supporting the shippers' desire for the elimination of unnecessary hiring while also upholding the ILA's insistence on increased job security. Although there was no nationwide bargaining, the New York contracts generally helped set the pattern for other ports. The ILA and the New York Shipping Association, however, were unable to agree on a new contract, and, on October 1, Gleason's union struck Gulf and Atlantic ports. President Johnson immediately invoked the Taft-Hartley Act, and, following the issuance of a court order, the strikers returned to work.

On December 16 the ILA and the New York shippers agreed on a new four-year contract. It included a phased reduction in work gang size, an annual guaranteed minimum wage for full-time longshoremen, an increase in the size of the dues checkoff, increases in wages and benefits, and an agreement to seek the elimination of registration of longshoremen by the New York Waterfront Commission. Although Gleason called the agreement "the best contract we ever had," there was considerable rank-and-file opposition to it, particularly to the provision reducing the size of work gangs. As soon as the contract terms were announced, sporadic wildcats began. On January 8 New York longshoremen voted to reject the contract, and, three days later, 50,000 longshoremen in Gulf and Atlantic ports walked off their jobs.

After an intense campaign by Gleason and other ILA officials, the New York longshoremen reversed their stand and, on January 21, approved the pact by a wide margin. However, union and management in many other ports failed to reach agreements, and the strike continued under the ILA policy that if one port were closed, all ports would be closed.

In an effort to end the costly strike, President Johnson named an informal committee of Wirtz, Secretary of Commerce JOHN T. CONNOR, and Senator WAYNE MORSE (D-Ore.) to make proposals for a settlement. The union rejected the committee recommendations but agreed on February 12 to resume work in ports that had already agreed to new contracts. By February 17 the strike was restricted to several southern ports. All longshoremen were back to work by mid-March. When the new contract provisions reducing gang size actually took effect on April 1, 1966, longshoremen in New York again walked off their jobs in a series of wildcat strikes, which were ended only after court restraining orders were issued.

Gleason was a strong supporter of U.S. military activity in Vietnam. Starting in the fall of 1965, he helped the U.S. government eliminate cargo-handling problems in the ports of Saigon and Cam Ranh Bay. In February 1966 Gleason, Hall, and NMU president JOSEPH E. CURRAN proposed a boycott of ships from countries trading with North Vietnam. In 1969 he was elected vice president of the executive council of the American Federation of Labor and Congress of Industrial Organizations. He later served on President Reagan's Maritime Advisory Committee. During the Nixon administration Gleason became publicly identified with the pro-war "hard-hat" faction of organized labor. In 1983 he was named chair of the AFL-CIO's International Affairs Committee. He died on December 24, 1992.

—JBF

## Glenn, John H(erschel)

(1921–    ) astronaut

John Glenn was born in Cambridge, Ohio, on July 18, 1921. He became a naval pilot in the marine corps in 1943 and saw action in the Pacific, where he won several medals. He remained on active duty during the Korean War and later became a naval test pilot. In 1957 he set a speed record in the first nonstop, transcontinental supersonic flight.

In April 1959 Glenn and six others were selected from 110 military test pilots to become the first American astronauts. On February 20, 1962, Glenn became the first Project Mercury astronaut to orbit the earth, circling the globe three times in just under five hours. Glenn's flight allayed fears that America lagged hopelessly behind the Soviets in the space race and made him a national hero. Several days after his flight Glenn addressed a joint session of Congress in support of the space program's long-range goals, saying that "exploration and the pursuit of knowledge have always paid dividends in the long run." A New York Times writer called Glenn "the Administration's star witness on Capitol Hill."

During the last half of the 1960s Glenn became a close friend of the Kennedy family. "The fact is," White House aide Larry O'Brien recalled, "that the Kennedys generally and the president specifically became very much enamored with John. He was very much a hero to them." Encouraged by Attorney General ROBERT F. KENNEDY and national Democratic strategists, Glenn resigned from the space program on January 16, 1964, and the following day announced that he would seek the Democratic nomination for a U.S. Senate from Ohio. Glenn won his first political test in Columbus on January 20 when the Ohio Democratic convention adjourned without endorsing incumbent senator STEPHEN M. YOUNG (D-Ohio) who had asked for the convention's bucking and had delivered the keynote address. Glenn appeared the likely victor against the aged Young, but, on March 30, he announced his withdrawal from the race because of a severe head injury suffered in a bathroom fall, which affected his sense of balance. In explaining his decision the former astronaut said that he did not want to run just as a well-known name. He retired from the marines in 1965, as a colonel, and focused on politics.

In June 1968 Glenn became chair of the newly formed Emergency Committee for Gun Control, a coalition of groups formed to build public pressure for tough firearms control. Two days later he testified before the Senate Judiciary Committee's Juvenile Delinquency Subcommittee in favor of President Johnson's registration and licensing proposals.

Glenn ran unsuccessfully for the Senate in 1970. He won his third attempt and took his seat in January 1975. Glenn delivered the keynote address at the 1976 Democratic National Convention. Prior to the convention he was a candidate for the vice presidential nomination, but former Georgia governor Jimmy Carter chose Senator Walter Mondale (D-Minn.) as his running mate. He vacated his seat in 1998 and returned to Ohio. Later that year, as part of Shuttle Mission STS-95, the Shuttle Discovery, Glenn and six other astronauts spent nine days orbiting the Earth, making him the oldest person to travel in space.

—MDB

## Goddard, James L(ee)
(1923–   ) *commissioner, U.S. Food and Drug Administration*

Born on August 24, 1923, James L. Goddard grew up in the small industrial cities of Alliance and Warren, Ohio. He attended three colleges before earning his M.D. degree from George Washington University in 1949. Soon after his internship Goddard gave up a smalltown practice in western Ohio for public health administration. He received an M.S. in public health from Harvard in 1955. Through the 1950s Goddard worked for federal, state, and county health agencies in Colorado, New York, North Carolina, and Washington. In leadership positions he established a reputation for being an assertive, skilled, and imaginative administrator. He became the first civil air surgeon of the Federal Aviation Agency in 1959 and assistant U.S. surgeon general and head of the U.S. Public Health Service's Communicable Disease Center at Atlanta in 1962, becoming the youngest person to hold the position at that time.

In January 1966 Secretary of Health, Education and Welfare JOHN GARDNER made Goddard commissioner of the Food and Drug Administration (FDA). First organized in 1907, the FDA watched over the product safety of food and drug manufacture and distribution. The increase in the quantity of pharmaceutical products and the 1962 Kefauver-Harris Act regulating the drug industry greatly added to the FDA's tasks. By 1965 the agency faced widespread public criticism; private companies as well as consumer groups criticized agency delays in testing new drugs. Indeed, shortly after assuming office Goddard himself termed the FDA "lax, if not grossly negligent" in certain cases.

Like several prominent regulatory agency heads during Johnson's presidency. Goddard spent his first months in office castigating industries falling within his province. At an April 1966 gathering of the Pharmaceutical Manufacturers Association (PMA), he expressed dismay at the drug companies' "clear attempts to slip something by us." Goddard declared that the drug industry was more concerned with profits than product safety, and suffered from a "disease" beyond the cure of drugs, that of irresponsibility. Also in April, he warned the American Association of Advertising Agents against making "false claims." In May Goddard criticized the "general carelessness about the basic principles of sanitation," which, he said, the FDA had found in many food processing plants.

Under Goddard the FDA moved quickly in response to selected problems. Drug recalls grew by almost 75 percent in his first year alone. In April 1966 the FDA began a systematic inquiry into the possibility of harmful pesticide residue levels in foods. Goddard alleviated the backlog of agency testing by commissioning the National Academy of Science and the National Research Council to review some 4,000 drugs marketed between 1938 and 1962. These and other steps raised the once low morale of the FDA staff.

In August 1966 Goddard lifted a FDA stipulation requiring that producers of oral contraceptives recommend a two-year limit to users. Goddard found "no adequate scientific data at this time" indicating that "the Pill" was "unsafe for human use." A special FDA investigating panel, however, called for more research into the subject.

Goddard held office at a time of widespread drug use, especially on college campuses. Concern mounted when the news media reported tales of the bizarre effects of the hallucinogenic LSD. In an April 1966 letter to 2,000 university administrators. Goddard said LSD has "profound effects on the mental process" and is "dangerous in exceedingly small amounts." He told college officials to be wary of the appearance of these and other drugs on campus.

In an October 1966 address at the University of Minnesota, Goddard advocated the removal of penalties for the possession of marijuana. He told two congressional committees, that he did not "condone the use of marijuana" but reasserted his opposition to criminal action against marijuana smokers—as opposed to dealers.

In February 1968 Goddard testified on behalf of an administration bill that made possession of certain illegally obtained drugs, including LSD, a federal offense. He endorsed the measure reluctantly, declaring that "it would be unwise" to risk branding "a number of young people just entering adulthood as criminals" because they possessed "a small amount of drugs for personal use." But the president and federal law enforcement agencies, Goddard stated, wanted federal criminalization, and "their judgment on the need for this provision is one which I respect."

Goddard quit the FDA July 1, 1968. FDA Bureau of Medicine chief Herbert L. Ley, Jr., a Goddard appointee, succeeded him. Goddard went to Atlanta and worked for ETP Tech., Inc., a private medical and industrial systems analysis company. He left ETP in 1970 to advise the Ford Foundation on population problems. In 1972 he became board chair of the Ormont Drug and Chemical Company of Englewood, New Jersey. The following year he founded Omega Associates, a consulting firm, in Atlanta.

—JLB

## Godwin, Mills E(dwin), Jr.
### (1914–1999) *governor*

Born on November 19, 1914, in Chuckatuck, Virginia, Godwin served in the Virginia House of Delegates from 1947 to 1952 and then in the state senate from 1953 to 1961. As a member of the legislature, he was a stalwart supporter of the conservative Democratic machine of U.S. senator HARRY F. BYRD. The organization had dominated the state's one-party politics since the late 1920s, implementing policies of "pay-as-you-go" financing, frugal public spending, and racial separation. When the machine unsuccessfully promoted massive resistance to school integration in the late 1950s, Godwin defended those positions in the state senate.

In 1961 Godwin received the machine's endorsement for the lieutenant governorship in the Democratic primary and attacked his more moderate opponent for being soft on integration and for joining with the labor union movement in opposing the state's right-to-work law. Godwin won by an unusually small margin for a machine-backed candidate. The result reflected the post–World War II expansion of the state's more moderate urban population. Hoping to become the state's chief executive, Godwin moved toward the political center while serving as lieutenant governor, particularly after the state Democratic convention weakened Byrd's grip on the party in 1964 by endorsing President LYNDON JOHNSON for reelection against the senator's wishes.

When Godwin campaigned for governor in 1965, he abandoned his defense of segregation, asserting that the issue had long since been settled and advocated substantial expansion of public services. Capturing the support of liberals and of much of the weakened Byrd machine, he easily won the primary. Godwin then defeated Linwood Holton, the Republican candidate, with 47.9 percent of the vote to his opponent's 37.7 percent.

During his tenure as governor Godwin broke with some of Byrd's longstanding policies. In 1966 he successfully pressed the state legislature to pass Virginia's first sales tax—a step that Byrd had always opposed—as a device for financing new state programs. With the aid of revenue received from that levy, Virginia moved from last among the states in school expenditures per pupil in 1961 to a figure close to the national average a decade later. Godwin introduced a system of community colleges that increased college enrollment in the state from 64,000 in the mid-1960s to 150,000 in 1973. He also sponsored a state mental health program. He jettisoned Byrd's sacrosanct "pay-as-you-go" financing by proposing an $81 million bond issue, which the voters approved in 1968. During the same year Godwin appointed a blue-ribbon commission to revise the state constitution.

Godwin was constitutionally barred from seeking reelection in 1969. In that year Republican Linwood Holton, Jr., was elected to succeed Godwin. Switching to the Republicans, Godwin successfully ran for governor on its state ticket in 1973, making him the first governor in the United States to serve as both a Democrat and a Republican. During his second term, he oversaw the revision of the state constitution, reinstated the death penalty, and reorganized the penal system. He died in Richmond on January 30, 1999.

—MLL

## Goldberg, Arthur J(oseph)
### (1908–1990) *associate justice, U.S. Supreme Court; ambassador to the United Nations*

Goldberg was born on August 8, 1908, into a large family on Chicago's West Side. After working his way through college and law school. Goldberg practiced labor law and then served with the Office of Strategic Services during World War II. In 1948 he became general counsel for the United Steelworkers of America (USW) and in 1955 played a major role in merging the Congress of Industrial Organizations and the American Federation of Labor. Goldberg was the principal author of the AFL-CIO ethical practices code and helped guide the USW negotiations during the 116-day steel strike in 1959 and 1960.

As Kennedy's choice for secretary of labor, Goldberg gave the office new influence by forcefully asserting the "public interest" in labor-management disputes and on occasion intervening directly to recommend strike settlements. Goldberg encouraged USW president David J. McDonald to accept a modest steel contract in early 1962 and helped President Kennedy apply public pressure on the steel corporations when they unexpectedly raised prices in April. As secretary of labor he directed most of the administration's legislative attention to ameliorating the recession and lowering the level of unemployment. During 1961 and 1962 he suc-

cessfully fought for the Area Redevelopment Act to aid "depressed areas," an increase in minimum wage and social security benefits, an extension of state unemployment benefits and the passage of the $435 million Manpower Development and Training Act.

Kennedy appointed Goldberg to the Supreme Court in August 1962. Although he remained on the bench for only 34 months, his opinions, according to legal scholar Henry J. Abraham, "left an imprint far out of proportion to the brief period he served." In an October 1963 opinion, Goldberg first raised the issue of the unconstitutionality of the death penalty on the basis of the cruel and unusual punishment and due process of law clauses. In March 1964 he voted with the Court's six to three majority in ruling that congressional districts must be composed of approximately equal populations. He voted with a majority holding state loyalty oaths invalid in June and in a separate case spoke for the Court in a decision ruling that denial of passports to members of the Communist Party was "unconstitutional on its

Justice Arthur Goldberg meeting with President Johnson aboard Air Force One, 1965 *(Photographed by Yoichi R. Okamoto; Lyndon Baines Johnson Library)*

face." In the same month Goldberg wrote the Court's landmark five-to-four decision in *Escobedo v. Illinois*, holding that confessions cannot be used in court if police question a suspect without allowing consultation with a lawyer or without warning the suspect that any answers may be used against him or her.

With Justice HUGO BLACK, Goldberg dissented from an October 1964 Supreme Court decision rejecting Senator BARRY M. GOLDWATER's (R-Ariz.) demand for equal free time on radio and TV to reply to an earlier televised speech by President Johnson on the international situation. In May 1965 Goldberg joined Black and Douglas in a dissent holding unconstitutional the government's curb on travel to Cuba. The next month he joined a majority of the Court in striking down Connecticut's 1879 law forbidding the use of birth control devices.

After ADLAI STEVENSON's death in July 1965, President Johnson sought to fill the United Nations ambassadorship he had held with another prominent figure. Upon JOHN KENNETH GALBRAITH's recommendation Johnson asked Goldberg to step down from the Supreme Court and fill the vacant UN post. Although Goldberg had already turned him down once, when LBJ broached the possibility of appointing him attorney general, Johnson told Goldberg he would have a direct hand in shaping American foreign policy and ending the Vietnam War. Goldberg accepted Johnson's offer and resigned from the Court July 28. "I thought I could persuade Johnson that we were fighting the wrong war in the wrong place," he recalled of his decision. "I would have loved to have stayed on the Court, but my sense of priorities was [that] this war would be disastrous."

On issues other than Vietnam Goldberg was able to play a significant role in developing and implementing American foreign policy at the United Nations. As part of an attempt to upgrade the world body into a forum for "negotiations" rather than "debate," Goldberg announced on August 16, 1965, that the United States would drop its demand that General Assembly voting rights be denied to the Soviet Union, France, and other states who had not paid their financial assessments for upkeep of the world organization. When the India-Pakistan war broke out in the late summer of 1965, Goldberg worked privately to secure a unanimous Security Council agreement on a cease-fire resolution demanding that both belligerents pull back to their original prewar frontiers. And in 1968 he

played a significant role in getting the Nuclear Nonproliferation Treaty approved by the United Nations.

Goldberg demonstrated a degree of independence from the State Department during the October 1966 General Assembly debate over the status of Southwest Africa. He introduced a resolution, prepared by the U.S. delegation at the UN, declaring that South Africa "forfeits all rights to continue to administer the territory." Goldberg's proposal, which was linked to formation of a new UN commission for Southwest Africa, was widely hailed by many of the new African and Asian states. However, the resolution put greater pressure on the South African regime than the U.S. State Department itself might have wished.

In the aftermath of the June 1967 Arab-Israeli war, Goldberg sought to avoid a UN condemnation of Israel apart from a general solution to the Middle East conflict. In July Goldberg helped defeat a Soviet-sponsored Security Council resolution condemning Israeli aggression. But during the fall he worked closely with Soviet UN ambassador Anatoly Dobrynin on behalf of a British resolution that asserted Israel's right to exist, while at the same time calling for its withdrawal from land occupied during the Six-Day War. The resolution, which served as the basic UN position on the Middle East conflict for the next six years, was adopted November 22, 1967.

The Vietnam War dominated Goldberg's UN tenure, and much of his work at the world body was directed toward finding a formula that might start negotiations between the United States and North Vietnam. Goldberg was unsuccessful in this task. The progressive escalation of the air war was Johnson's chief strategy for resolving the conflict. In turn, the bombing of the North proved the main stumbling block to the start of negotiations, and Goldberg, who was not privy to the highest levels of administration decision making, often found himself out of step with or unaware of American military and political policy in Southeast Asia.

Goldberg began his term at the UN by announcing that the United States would "collaborate unconditionally" with the Security Council in the search for an "acceptable formula" to restore peace in Vietnam. Hanoi rejected Goldberg's request for UN intercession on August 2, 1965, and reiterated its own conditions for an end to the conflict: an immediate halt of U.S. air attacks on the

North and withdrawal of all U.S. troops from the South. (Later North Vietnam modified its second condition to one merely calling for an end to the U.S. troop buildup). During the fall of 1965 Goldberg was involved in at least two other attempts to establish contact with the North Vietnamese, first through Communist UN delegations, and then in December through two Italian university professors who had recently returned from Hanoi. Both "peace feelers" collapsed.

Later in December 1965 Goldberg was part of a widely publicized Johnson administration "peace offensive." The United States declared a halt to the bombing of North Vietnam on December 24, and several high-ranking American officials, including Undersecretary of State AVERELL HARRIMAN, Vice President HUBERT HUMPHREY, and Goldberg met with foreign heads of state in an effort to open negotiations with Hanoi. Goldberg conferred with Pope Paul VI in Rome on December 29, with Italian premier Aldo Moro on December 30, and with French president Charles de Gaulle on December 31. These diplomatic moves proved fruitless, in part because of the Johnson administration's continuing commitment to the escalation of the air war.

In the fall of 1966 Goldberg made another effort, again only partially backed by the administration, to start negotiations through the United Nations. For the previous several months UN Secretary General U Thant had proposed that peace talks might begin on the basis of three points: (1) cessation of U.S. bombing of North Vietnam (2) de-escalation of the ground war in South Vietnam, and (3) inclusion of the National Liberation Front (NLF) in peace talks. On September 22 Goldberg delivered a major speech at the UN responding to the U Thant proposals. He declared that the United States was prepared to halt the bombing and begin de-escalation of all military activity in Vietnam "the moment we are assured, privately or otherwise," that the U.S. moves would be matched by a reduction of North Vietnam's war effort. Goldberg also declared that inclusion of the NLF in any subsequent peace talks would not prove an "insurmountable problem."

Although the Goldberg speech was couched in terms somewhat more conciliatory than previous U.S. proposals, President Johnson declined to characterize the presentation as either new or important. North Vietnamese premier Pham Van Dong rejected the Goldberg proposal on September 25 and empha-

sized that a prerequisite to any negotiations was a "definite and unconditional" end to the bombing of the North. On December 19 Goldberg called on U Thant to "take whatever steps you consider necessary to bring about negotiations leading to a cease-fire." But this appeal, which the *Pentagon Papers* described as "window dressing" to make up for the administration's decision not to declare a lengthy Christmas cease-fire, was rejected by U Thant December 30 when he declared that an unconditional cessation of the bombing was the "first and essential" part of any step toward negotiations.

Although Goldberg was excluded from White House decision making on Vietnam, he played a notable role in the March 1968 reassessment of American policy that reversed the escalation of the war and opened the way to negotiations with the North Vietnamese and the NLF. On March 15 Goldberg sent Johnson an eight-page memorandum arguing for a complete bombing halt in order to get talks started. Goldberg asserted that the efficacy of an unconditional pause "can best be determined by what actually happens during the talks rather than by any advance verbal commitments of the kind we have been seeking." Goldberg's proposal, along with a similar suggestion from ambassador to India CHESTER BOWLES, became an important basis for discussion by the Senior Advisory Group on Vietnam, commonly known as the "Wise Men," which undertook a reevaluation of U.S. policy during the latter part of March. Goldberg participated in many of these discussions, at one point seriously deflating the military assertion that the recent NLF–North Vietnamese Tet offensive had been an enemy defeat. Along with former secretary of state DEAN ACHESON, former presidential special assistant MCGEORGE BUNDY, and General MATTHEW RIDGWAY, Goldberg was among those who successfully argued for a bombing halt and de-escalation of the war at the decisive meetings on March 25 and 26.

Goldberg submitted his resignation as ambassador on April 25, 1968. Johnson accepted his departure in a letter that failed to praise the former Supreme Court justice for his UN service. Goldberg joined the New York law firm of Paul Weiss, Rifkind, Wharton and Garrison. Former undersecretary of state GEORGE BALL succeeded Goldberg as chief U.S. representative at the UN.

Goldberg became active in domestic politics after his resignation. In October 1968 he assumed command of HUBERT HUMPHREY's presidential campaign in New York State. He joined other attorneys in appealing the conspiracy conviction of BENJAMIN SPOCK, WILLIAM SLOAN COFFIN, JR., and three other antiwar activists in January 1969. He spoke at the October 15 Moratorium Day protests against the war and, in December 1969, he joined with ROY WILKINS and 25 other prominent citizens in a "searching inquiry" into recent clashes between the police and members of the Black Panther Party. In 1970 Goldberg challenged NELSON ROCKEFELLER for the New York governorship but failed to unseat the three-term incumbent. He served as president of the American Jewish Committee in 1968 and chair of the Center for Law and Social Policy from 1968 to 1978. He remained active in political causes, especially those related to human rights, until his death from a heart attack in 1990.

—NNL

## Goldman, Eric F(rederick)

(1915–1989) *White House special consultant*

Goldman, who was born on June 17, 1915, in Washington, D.C., received his doctorate in history from Johns Hopkins in 1938, served a brief stint as a writer for *Time* and then joined the Princeton faculty in 1943. He gained prominence in 1952 with the publication of *Rendezvous with Destiny*, a book that traced two distinct and often contradictory traditions within the liberal reform movement in the United States—one concerned with protecting the individual from big government and big business, the other with using centralized power to aid human welfare.

Acting on the suggestion of one of Goldman's former students, then serving as a White House aide, President Johnson invited Goldman to the White House for a discussion in December 1963. Shortly afterward Goldman became a White House special consultant with the job of maintaining liaison between the White House and specialists and intellectuals outside the administration. Goldman ensured that opinions from a wide range of experts received a hearing at the White House. He scoffed at the suggestion made by some members of the news media that his appointment was as the token intellectual in the Johnson White House. Goldman described the president as a "restless, adventurous kind of man [who] assumes that talent, energy and brains can solve problems."

To dispel the lingering idea that Johnson was anti-intellectual, Goldman, in February 1965, conceived the idea of a White House Festival of the Arts, which was to be, in his words, "an outgoing, warm, colorful White House salute" to U.S. artists, writers, and social critics. The festival was also intended to show off the newly formed National Council on the Arts. The festival was scheduled at an unfortunate time—shortly after Johnson ordered the continuous bombing of North Vietnam and two months after U.S. military intervention in the Dominican Republic. These policies were extremely unpopular with many intellectuals. Johnson approved formal plans for the festival, to be held on June 14, 1965. The first hint that the gala would cause a furor came with publication of poet ROBERT LOWELL's open letter to the president declining the invitation because of Johnson's recent foreign policy actions. Lowell's gesture infuriated Johnson but won the support of many intellectuals and touched off a debate among the participating artists over whether they should attend the White House Festival. Goldman later wrote that in many instances "the LBJ [foreign] policy was not really being considered on its merits; it was being attacked in considerable measure out of snobbery, social and intellectual."

The White House Festival on the Arts convened on June 14 in an atmosphere of considerable tension. At one point *Newsweek* book critic Saul Maloff encountered novelist Saul Bellow and asked, "How can you stand up there and read from your book after what that man has done in Vietnam?" DWIGHT MACDONALD circulated a petition supporting Lowell's refusal to attend the festival. President Johnson appeared at the festival only briefly; his remarks were offhand and brusque.

After the White House Festival Goldman lost favor at the White House. Johnson had been offended, and his attitude hardened toward intellectuals who opposed his war policies. He also made some enemies at the White House, who resented what they saw as an attitude of superiority; Bess Abell, LADY BIRD JOHNSON's social secretary, recalled that Goldman "was always a problem, he was a prima donna." Goldman submitted his resignation on August 23, 1966, but it was not made public because Johnson, fearing that Goldman would write a book about the administration, wanted to underplay the historian's departure. On September 7, 1966, Goldman's resignation was finally announced to the press. His role within the administration was denigrated by White House press secretary BILL MOYERS, who said that "Goldman has spent most of his time working with Mrs. Johnson and Mrs. [Liz] Carpenter in the East Wing."

In 1969 Goldman published *The Tragedy of Lyndon Johnson*, as critical assessment of Johnson's character. He described the president as a man who "entered the White House unhailed, and functioned in it unloved. Only once did warmth and a degree of affection go out to him—when he told the country he was leaving the Presidency." In explaining the causes of this reaction, Goldman cited Johnson's lack of "likability," his limited preparation for the office of the presidency and his imperious, volatile personality. The book also suggested that LBJ was largely uninterested in foreign affairs, and that he was, in fact, leery of engaging with the outside world. He finally summed up Johnson as "the wrong man from the wrong place at the wrong time under the wrong circumstances."

Goldman returned to his teaching duties at Princeton in 1966. He remained at Princeton until he retired in 1985. He died on February 19, 1989, in Princeton, New Jersey.

—FHM

## Goldwater, Barry M(orris)
### (1909–1998) *member of the Senate*

Born on January 1, 1909, in Phoenix, Arizona, Goldwater was educated at Staunton Military Academy in Virginia and then spent a year at the University of Arizona. In 1929 he joined the family department store, Goldwater's, Inc., in Phoenix, becoming president in 1937. He served in the U.S. Army Air Forces during World War II and shortly thereafter won election to the Phoenix City Council. In 1952 he narrowly captured the Senate seat occupied by Majority Leader Ernest W. McFarland (D-Ariz.) and easily defeated him again six years later. During his second Senate term Goldwater

Senator Barry Goldwater meeting with President Johnson, 1964 *(Photographed by Yoichi R. Okamoto; Lyndon Baines Johnson Library)*

became the most prominent spokesperson for the new, more militantly anticommunist conservatism espoused by southern and western Republicans. In June 1960 he led the conservative attack upon the compromise platform agreement reached by Vice President RICHARD M. NIXON and Governor NELSON A. ROCKEFELLER (R-N.Y.), leader of the party's liberal eastern wing. And in 1961 he told a press conference that "sometimes I think this country would be better off if we could just saw off the Eastern Seaboard and let it float out to sea."

By the fall of 1963 Goldwater appeared to be the leading contender for the Republican Party's 1964 presidential nomination. A quietly efficient Draft Goldwater Committee, chaired by F. CLIFTON WHITE, had convinced many party strategists that the senator, opposed to the activist civil rights stance of the Kennedy administration, would sweep the South for the GOP. Many Goldwater enthusiasts also firmly believed that the potential but untapped conservative vote would turn out in large numbers if only the Republicans would avoid nominating a "me-too" contender who supported programs established earlier by Democratic presidential administrations.

Kennedy's assassination and the elevation of LYNDON B. JOHNSON to the presidency hurt Goldwater's presidential prospects. His support among Republican voters in public opinion surveys fell sharply, and Johnson's probable nomination dampened enthusiasm for a Goldwater-led "southern strategy." However, the strength of the Goldwater movement within the Republican Party effectively quashed any doubts he had about running. In January 1964 Goldwater officially announced his candidacy. Opposing what he regarded as the liberal tendencies of most Democratic and Republican leaders, Goldwater insisted that he offered "a choice, not an echo."

After deciding to run Goldwater restructured his campaign hierarchy. He relied primarily with Arizona friends—Denison Kitchel, Richard Kleindienst, and Dean Burch while relegating White to a subordinate position. Although Goldwater's managers had known the candidate for years and enjoyed his confidence, none had experience in national politics.

The first and most publicized primary, New Hampshire's, demonstrated the senator's vulnerability as a presidential aspirant. At first open and candid with journalists accompanying him, Gold-

water allowed them to quote him as giving preference to a voluntary Social Security program, a statement Rockefeller quickly attacked as destructive of the retirement system. Members of the Rockefeller staff unearthed a number of controversial Goldwater statements, including one that advocated giving control over the decision to use nuclear weapons to the NATO commander. Goldwater's inability to clarify his positions placed him on the defensive, but Rockefeller failed to benefit from the senator's difficulties. New Hampshire voters surprised everyone in March by writing in the name of ambassador to South Vietnam HENRY CABOT LODGE. The absent Lodge won first place with 35.5 percent of the total vote; Goldwater, with 23 percent, and then Rockefeller, with 20.6 percent, trailed far behind.

The consequences of his poor showing in New Hampshire appeared disastrous to Goldwater's chances for the nomination. Goldwater rebounded with consecutive primary victories in Illinois, Texas, Indiana, and Nebraska, but only against scant opposition. He withdrew from active campaigning in the May 15 Oregon contest to concentrate on the June 2 California primary. In Oregon Rockefeller upset the favored Lodge and thus ended any likelihood of the ambassador's nomination. The New York governor began his California drive two weeks before the vote with a clear lead in the polls. After a well-managed effort, however, Goldwater narrowly defeated Rockefeller and captured all 86 of California's convention delegates. Goldwater rapidly emerged as the clear front-runner for the nomination.

More than the California victory had made Goldwater the favorite. Through the spring of 1964, in a phenomenon largely ignored by their detractors, Goldwater supporters had attended unpublicized Republican precinct and district meetings to choose delegates to the national convention. This effort was not matched by the more passive Lodge and Rockefeller backers. F. Clifton White privately estimated that the California delegation, combined with those nonprimary seats already won, gave Goldwater about 555 first ballot votes, just 100 short of the number needed for the nomination. The spirited "grassroots" movement on Goldwater's behalf surprised many observers.

Goldwater's stand on civil rights added to divisions already apparent within the GOP. The senator opposed the 1964 Civil Rights bill on constitutional grounds and said that the measure's public accommodations and fair employment provisions would require a federal police force "of mammoth proportions" to enforce. Only six of his party colleagues joined Goldwater in opposition, while most GOP senators followed the lead of Senate Minority Leader EVERETT M. DIRKSEN (R-Ill.) in voting for the measure. Although Goldwater denied the charge, many construed his vote on the bill as a bid for southern support in the election.

Goldwater's civil rights vote had little effect on his nomination prospects. Four days before the convention opened, Governor JAMES A. RHODES (R-Ohio) released his 58-member delegation from its favorite-son status. Convention floor fights over delegate credentials and party platform planks soon demonstrated Goldwater's overwhelming strength. With 883 votes to 214 for Pennsylvania governor WILLIAM W. SCRANTON, Goldwater won the nomination on the first ballot on July 15.

Goldwater failed to heal the deep wounds created by the bitter preconvention contest. The intensity of the moderate-liberal attacks destroyed any consideration by Goldwater of immediate reconciliation. His managers had refused to compromise on platform amendments offered by the Scranton forces and by Governor GEORGE W. ROMNEY of Michigan. After the balloting Goldwater chose Dean Burch, an unknown, 36-year-old aide, to chair the Republican National Committee. He declined to consult with any party leaders, including Eisenhower and Nixon, over the vice presidential nomination, and chose the relatively obscure Republican National Committee chair, Representative WILLIAM E. MILLER (R-N.Y.) Goldwater's acceptance speech on July 16 gave revealing proof of his bitter mood. "Those who do not care for our cause," he declared, "we do not expect to enter our ranks in any case." In a direct challenge to party foes who had criticized his support from right-wing groups, he asserted that "extremism in the defense of liberty is no vice . . . moderation in the pursuit of justice is no virtue." Most of the convention cheered, but several leading members of eastern state delegations walked out in protest.

In August the senator attempted to reunite the party and win support for his campaign, but a leadership conference in Hershey, Pennsylvania, ended in failure. Governor Romney and Senator Kenneth B. Keating (R-N.Y.) refused to endorse his candidacy and ran their own reelection efforts apart from the presidential race. Rockefeller made only one appearance on the senator's behalf, although Eisen-hower, Nixon, and Scranton campaigned for the national ticket.

Because Goldwater's candidacy had become equated with dangerous, right-wing extremism, the fall campaign did not prove to be a liberal-conservative dialogue, as the candidate himself had anticipated. Johnson's campaign advertisements pictured Goldwater as the enemy of Social Security, world peace, and the northeastern section of the United States. By the contest's end Johnson portrayed himself as the true conservative. "I want to be conservative," he declared in Kansas, "without being a reactionary."

Goldwater sought unsuccessfully to generate support for his conservative proposals. Early in September he called for a 5 percent tax cut each year for the next five years. He favored the abolition of the draft though the creation of an all-volunteer army. Repeatedly he warned voters that "a government that is big enough to give everything that you need and want is also big enough to take it all away." In a series of tactless speeches he condemned the War on Poverty program while speaking in poor areas of West Virginia, attacked Medicare while addressing elderly voters in Florida, and reiterated in Tennessee a proposal (first made in August 1963) that the Tennessee Valley Authority should be sold to a private company. On the eve of the election most Republican candidates, regardless of their preconvention position, divorced their campaigns from the Goldwater-Miller effort.

Goldwater lost decisively to Johnson on November 3. The Republican nominee won 38.4 percent of the vote and carried only five Deep South states and Arizona. The GOP lost two Senate and 47 House seats. In the 1965 session massive Democratic majorities in Congress passed a series of administration social welfare proposals that Goldwater had strongly opposed.

Analyses of the 1964 election indicated that Goldwater won the votes of GOP loyalists who almost automatically voted Republican but that he failed to build significantly upon this hard core of support. A number of his statements, particularly his criticisms of Social Security and his comments indicating a casual attitude toward the use of nuclear weapons, caused a large number of moderate voters to identify him with extremist groups such as the John Birch Society. As a result he lost independent and marginal Republican backing. Only in the South, among those whites who opposed President

Johnson's civil rights legislation and the increasing power of the federal government over other issues that had traditionally been state and local concerns, did Goldwater win new support for the GOP. Goldwater's success in the South was a harbinger of a major shift in the South from traditional Democratic allegiance to Republican predominance.

Having relinquished his Senate seat for the presidential race, Goldwater all but surrendered his party leadership position in the election's immediate aftermath. He agreed to the removal of Burch as chair of the Republican National Committee in January 1965. Occasionally speaking out on foreign and domestic issues, Goldwater called for an expanded U.S. military role in Southeast Asia and condemned the administration's Great Society programs. In October 1967 he backed Nixon for the 1968 Republican presidential nomination, declining to support the more conservative governor RONALD REAGAN (R-Calif.).

In November 1968, he won election to the U.S. Senate. Becoming a less controversial but more respected figure within the GOP hierarchy, he urged Nixon to resign from office at the height of the Watergate crisis and later attacked Reagan's insurgent candidacy for the 1976 Republican presidential nomination. He was also a steady critic of America's policy in Vietnam, which he saw as not taking dramatic enough military steps to achieve victory.

Despite his repudiation by the voters in 1964, however, Goldwater is usually given credit for helping to pave the way for the new conservative movement, in particular the ascent of President Ronald Reagan in 1980. Ironically, he refused to join the Republicans of the New Right during the 1980s when they began to press for legislation that would limit the authority of the federal courts to curb organized prayer in public schools or to order busing for school integration, largely because he saw it as unconstitutional for the federal government to give orders to the court system. He later supported abortion rights and the inclusion of homosexuals in the military, both of which he believed were areas of personal morality that were not within the purview the federal government. He did not seek reelection to the Senate in 1986 and returned to Arizona. He died on May 29, 1998, in Paradise Valley, Arizona.

—JLB

## Goodell, Charles E(llsworth)
### (1926–1987) *member of the House of Representatives*

Born on March 16, 1920, in Jamestown, New York, Goodell received a law degree from Yale University in 1951 and took a master's degree in government there in 1952. After serving as a congressional liaison with the Justice Department in 1954 and 1955, he returned to Jamestown to practice law. Goodell won a special election for a congressional vacancy in 1959, and, during his first two terms, he established a moderate-to-conservative record. A backer of Representative GERALD R. FORD, (R-Mich.), Goodell was a leader in the January 1963 Republican rebellion that replaced Party Conference chair Charles B. Hoeven (R-Iowa) with Ford.

A second insurgency resulted in Goodell's elevation to the upper ranks of the House Republican policy makers. In January 1965 Goodell and several other younger House members managed the election of Gerald Ford over incumbent minority leader CHARLES A. HALLECK (R-Ind.) Ford planned to open up the leadership's decision-making process and to reward Goodell in particular by designating him chair of the GOP Policy Committee. The full GOP caucus, however, selected the more conservative representative JOHN J. RHODES (R-Ariz.) instead. Undaunted, Ford created a Planning and Research Committee in February and appointed Goodell its chair. He came to rely heavily upon its work. In August the Goodell committee released a "white paper" on President Johnson's Vietnam policy. Although it supported American participation, the report recommended that the United States end the war "more speedily and at a smaller cost while safeguarding the independence and freedom of South Vietnam." Beginning in 1966 Goodell and Representative ALBERT H. QUIE (R-Minn.) proposed a GOP Opportunity Crusade as an alternative to the administration's War on Poverty programs. It called for the states and private industry to assume a greater share of the antipoverty effort.

In his House votes Goodell compiled a record as a moderate Republican. Like most of his GOP House colleagues, he supported the 1964 and 1965 civil rights acts. He endorsed the Appalachian Regional Development Act once he won the inclusion of a small part of New York State in the program. However, he voted against the Economic Opportunity Act of 1964, which included many of the administration's antipoverty proposals. He also opposed the administration's 1965 Elementary and Secondary School Act. But he voted for Medicare in July 1965. During the spring of 1968 Goddell and Quie maneuvered Ford into coming out for the civil rights measure, which he had planned to work against.

Goodell supported the moderate wing of the Republican Party. He backed Pennsylvania governor WILLIAM SCRANTON's abortive campaign for president in 1964 and in 1968 supported the presidential candidacy of New York governor NELSON A. ROCKEFELLER. Later Goodell took part in the effort to draft New York mayor JOHN V. LINDSAY for vice president. Goodell campaigned for both Senator BARRY GOLDWATER (R-Ariz.) and RICHARD NIXON in their respective presidential campaigns.

In September 1968 Rockefeller named Goodell to fill the unexpired term of Senator ROBERT F. KENNEDY (D-N.Y.), who had been assassinated in June. Although New York State Democrats strenuously objected to the appointment of a Republican to fill a seat to which a Democrat had been previously elected, Goodell soon moved to the left to accommodate what he considered a far more liberal constituency. He became closely identified with opposition to the war in Vietnam and was an opponent of Nixon's domestic programs.

In the 1970 U.S. Senate election in New York, the Nixon White House repudiated Goodell in favor of his Conservative Party opponent, James L. Buckley. Goodell won only 24 percent of the vote in the subsequent three-way election in which Buckley triumphed. He returned to the practice of law in Washington, D.C., until his death there on January 21, 1987.

—MDB

## Goodman, Paul

(1911–1972) *social critic*

Goodman was born on September 9, 1911, and grew up in the New York City slums. He attended the City College of New York, where he was first attracted to the anarchist principles of Peter Kropotkin. He then studied at the University of Chicago, eventually receiving his Ph.D. in English there in 1955. During the 1940s and 1950s Goodman's wide-ranging intellect produced poetry, short stories, novels, and essays on sociology, linguistics, and city planning. His ideas

drew little attention until 1960, when he published *Growing up Absurd: Problems of Youth in the Organized System*, a sweeping indictment of modern American society that attributed the growing alienation of many young people to the bureaucratic dehumanization of the system itself.

*Growing Up Absurd* won a large audience among college students and intellectuals, and Goodman's many essays and books in the mid-1960s were an important influence on the growing student radicalism of the period. Goodman's ideas on restructuring education had special impact. In *The Community of Scholars* (1962) and in *Compulsory Mis-Education* (1964), Goodman argued that students were the "major exploited class" in the society. He suggested a wide range of experiments in educational reform, including the radical decentralization of the school system and integration of the work experience with academic life through widespread use of apprenticeship programs. Goodman's proposal for the creation of voluntary "mini-schools" in inner-city areas attracted substantial support in the mid-1960s. The Ford Foundation sponsored several such schools in 1967 and 1968.

Goodman was a vocal critic of the Vietnam War and actively supported draft resistance and civil disobedience. He was an editor of *Liberation*, a radical pacifist magazine, and a frequent contributor to the *New York Review of Books*. By the late 1960s, however, Goodman had grown increasingly critical of the New Left. Believing that it had failed to produce a creative leadership and a coherent body of thought, he doubted that the movement could significantly change American society. Goodman's disenchantment was reflected in his *New Reformation: Notes of a Neolithic Conservative* (1970). While still sympathizing with young people who were outraged by such "gut" issues as Vietnam, he was nevertheless distressed by their lack of interest in "fundamental" questions and by their anti-intellectualism and authoritarian tendencies. In the last years of his life, Goodman was also alarmed that many of his ideas had been misinterpreted. The proliferation of rural communes in the late 1960s owed much to Goodman's communitarian ideas, but he asserted that his anarchist principles were not intended to promote "dropping out," which he believed could never lead to basic social or political change.

Goodman died of a heart attack in 1972.

—JCH

## Goodwin, Richard N(aradhof)

(1931–  ) *presidential special assistant*

Born in Boston on December 7, 1931, Goodwin graduated first in his class from both Tufts University and Harvard Law School. After clerking for Supreme Court justice Felix Frankfurter and working for the House Interstate and Foreign Commerce Subcommittee on Legislative Oversight, he joined Senator John F. Kennedy's (D-Mass.) speechwriting staff in 1959.

Political writer Richard Rovere said that Goodwin could "write about anything . . . because . . . he knew about everything, or knew something about everything." During Kennedy's presidential campaign Goodwin set out to learn about Latin America. He later helped design the Alliance for Progress and, during Kennedy's first year in office, was one of the leading White House advisers on Latin American policy. After his appointment as deputy assistant secretary of state for inter-American affairs in November 1961, however, his influence declined. His ambitious manner and unwillingness to observe bureaucratic etiquette irritated State Department professionals. He was later named head of the small International Peace Corps secretariat. At the time of President Kennedy's assassination, he was scheduled to become a special presidential adviser on the arts.

Through BILL MOYERS, a key Johnson aide, Goodwin was one of the first members of the Kennedy staff to establish good relations with LYNDON JOHNSON. Johnson called Goodwin "one of the smartest men I've ever met" and reportedly said, "He's wonderful, that boy. He can cry a little. He cries with me whenever I need to cry over something." By March 1964 Goodwin had become one of the president's major speechwriters. At the same time he made important contributions to the administration's domestic program. He coined the term "Great Society," which so appealed to the president that it became the slogan for the administration, the Johnson equivalent of the New Deal and the New Frontier.

Goodwin recommended the establishment of a number of task forces to formulate programs for the Great Society. By June 1964, 14 task forces, each composed of about 12 to 15 intellectuals and experts, began to meet regularly. They helped formulate much of the administration's ambitious legislative program dealing with civil rights, poverty, and conservation in the mid-1960s.

Despite his access to Johnson, Goodwin had strained relations with some White House colleagues. Johnson aide JACK VALENTI said that Goodwin "had a larger dose of the ego disease than anyone I know," and historian ERIC GOLDMAN cited Goodwin's "chameleonlike air, the feeling that he was a good bit of an adventurer."

In December 1964 Goodwin gained the formal title of special assistant, with responsibility for urban affairs and the environment, but speechwriting continued to be his chief contribution to the administration. His best remembered speech was Johnson's celebrated address of March 15, 1965, which climaxed an explosive week of civil rights activity that focused on the voting rights drive in Selma, Alabama. In the speech Johnson adopted as his own the slogan of the civil rights movement, "We Shall Overcome." The president put the federal government on the side of civil rights activists in the southern states and called for immediate legislation that would eliminate all "illegal barriers" to the right of African Americans to vote.

Goodwin subsequently helped publicize Great Society programs, but when Johnson turned increasingly to Vietnam and ignored domestic issues, Goodwin felt less committed to the administration. Despite the president's protestations, Goodwin left the White House in September 1965 to accept a fellowship at the Center for Advanced Studies at Wesleyan University. The last speech he wrote for Johnson was the 1966 State of the Union message.

In April 1966 Goodwin wrote an article for the *New Yorker* attacking administration Vietnam policy as a series of blunders. A few months later the article was expanded into a book and published as *Triumph or Tragedy: Reflections on Vietnam*. Aside from a brief period in the winter of 1966, when he worked as JACQUELINE KENNEDY's attorney in her efforts to block the publication of William Manchester's *Death of a President*, Goodwin devoted his time to criticizing the administration and planning a strategy to defeat Johnson in 1968. Convinced that Johnson could be beaten, he consistently urged his friend, Senator ROBERT F. KENNEDY (D-N.Y.), to challenge the president in a primary election. Because Kennedy hesitated to enter the race, Goodwin, then a visiting professor of public affairs at the Massachusetts Institute of Technology, joined the antiwar campaign of Senator EUGENE MCCARTHY

(D-Minn.) in February 1968. When Kennedy announced his candidacy a month later, Goodwin, out of personal loyalty and a belief that only Kennedy could win, switched camps. After Kennedy's assassination in June Goodwin returned to McCarthy, even though he was aware that the senator could not win the Democratic nomination.

After the 1968 election Goodwin worked as a journalist and author. In 1988 he published *Remembering America: A Voice From the Sixties* in which he alleged that clinical paranoia may have accounted for President Johnson's obsession with the Vietnam War and intense resentments of antiwar critics.

—JCH

## Gordon, Lincoln
(1913–1996) *ambassador to Brazil, assistant secretary of state for inter-American affairs*

Born in New York City on September 10, 1913, Lincoln Gordon earned a Ph.D. from Oxford University in 1936 and taught in the government department at Harvard University before World War II. Gordon temporarily left his Harvard teaching post to serve as a government economist during the war. After the war he helped develop the Marshall Plan and consulted with the State Department while resuming teaching and research. In 1950 he decided to devote all of his time to public affairs. Gordon worked with the North Atlantic Treaty Organization under both the Truman and Eisenhower administrations. Between 1952 and 1955 he handled economic matters in the London embassy.

When John F. Kennedy became president Gordon, a liberal Democrat, became more prominent in policy-making circles. Partly because of some research experience in Brazil, Gordon joined a Latin American task force organized by Kennedy only a few weeks after the November 1960 election. Chaired by Adolf A. Berle, Jr., the task force recommended a Latin American policy that found its expression in the Alliance for Progress. To a considerable degree, Kennedy's subsequent Latin American policy reflected Gordon's views more than Berle's. While both wanted to counter the appeal of communism with open U.S. support of democracy and social change, Berle proposed giving assistance to political parties ideologically compatible with the United States, even if these parties were not in power. In contrast to Berle's argument

for democratic "subversion," Gordon thought it simpler and more effective to pressure existing governments to democratize their countries through the promise of economic aid. Gordon remained influential in planning foreign economic policy and worked on the economic features of the Alliance for Progress. In August 1961 Gordon was appointed ambassador to Brazil.

Gordon's first three years in Brazil were tumultuous. President João Goulart's administration faced a slowdown in the economic growth rate coupled with accelerating inflation. In the meantime the right wing in the Brazilian Congress and the military plotted against him while leftists pressured him to lead a Brazilian revolution. Relying on his influence in the labor unions, Goulart decided to side with the left in a power struggle with the right. On March 13, 1964, Goulart announced before a Rio crowd of 125,000 the nationalization of private oil companies and the expropriation of "underutilized" estates and promised to revise the constitution, grant suffrage to illiterates, and impose rent controls.

Gordon felt that a Communist takeover was imminent. U.S. economic aid was cut off. North American business leaders in Brazil and agents of the Central Intelligence Agency (CIA) helped organize and finance anti-Goulart civic demonstrations. Gordon assured Brazilian military conspirators that the United States was ready to support a new government. Recognizing the overwhelming military odds arrayed against him, Goulart left Rio de Janeiro on April 1. Both President Johnson and Secretary of State DEAN RUSK sent congratulatory telegrams to the new military government. The secretary described the coup as a "move to ensure the continuity of constitutional government." Some observers took the administration's obvious satisfaction with the coup as representative of a new Latin American policy fashioned by Johnson's assistant secretary of state for inter-American affairs, THOMAS C. MANN. The Johnson-Mann policy encouraged stable government and deemphasized issues of democracy and civil liberties.

Gordon soon became discouraged with the new Brazilian regime. The "institutional act," which allowed the chiefs of the armed forces to arrest whomever they pleased, and reports of torture were at odds with Gordon's concern for constitutional processes, which initially had led him to oppose Goulart. The U.S. embassy's political counselor persuaded Gordon not to resign, arguing that Gordon could use U.S. influence to support the moderate wing of the Brazilian military and return the country to constitutional government. Gordon accepted the argument and soon developed what North American scholar Roger W. Fontaine called an "intimate, unprofessional relationship" with Brazilian president Humberto Castelo Branco. Eschewing the nationalism prevalent within the Brazilian right, the Castelo Branco government enthusiastically supported U.S. foreign policy. Brazil broke diplomatic relations with Cuba, sent troops into the Dominican Republic in 1965, and promised to participate in the Vietnam War if the conflict widened.

Gordon soon became a defender of the Castelo Branco government. In 1964 and again in 1966 he was able to secure for Brazil $150 million loans through the Agency for International Development (AID). At the end of 1964 the United States and Brazil announced a $1 billion economic aid program. The largest U.S. foreign aid recipient in the hemisphere, Brazil rewarded Gordon's faith by cutting inflation and achieving high annual growth rates. Gordon's emphasis on monetary stabilization, however, ignored the drop in real wages in Brazil to 1962 levels by 1966, the reversal of the land reform process, and the curtailment of development projects in the poor regions of Brazil. Furthermore, Castelo Branco failed to heed Gordon's advice that he build a popular political base. Continued political repression belied Gordon's belief that Castelo Branco would eventually restore civil liberties.

In January 1966 Gordon replaced Jack Vaughn as assistant secretary of state for inter-American affairs and United States coordinator for the Alliance for Progress. Because of his experience in Brazil, Gordon evolved a new conception of the possible role of the military: a military that not only opposed communism but fostered economic development through the medium of a dedicated apolitical technocracy. Technical economic concerns and a self-proclaimed pragmatism characterized the Johnson-Gordon Latin American policy. With the exception of Brazil and a few other nations, however, Gordon was dissatisfied with the economic performance of the Latin American countries. Although he tried to maintain Alliance for Progress funds, criticism of its poor record shifted money out of Latin America into Asia and Africa.

Gordon resigned in January 1967 to become president of the Johns Hopkins University. In 1971 he resumed an academic life of teaching and research. He died on February 26, 1996.

—JCH

## Gore, Albert A(rnold)
### (1907–1998) *member of the Senate*

A country school teacher who was born on December 26, 1907, in Granville, Tennessee, Gore studied law at the Nashville YMCA's night law school. He won election to Congress as a New Deal supporter from Secretary of State Cordell Hull's old district in 1938. A liberal, Gore backed his populist oratory with diligent study of economic issues. After his election to the Senate in 1952, Gore matched the outspoken liberalism of his fellow Tennessean, Senator Estes Kefauver (D-Tenn.). Gore and Kefauver were two of the three senators from the states of the Old Confederacy who, in 1956, refused to sign the Southern Manifesto protesting the Supreme Court's decision banning school segregation. He did not mind challenging LYNDON JOHNSON; in fact, in 1961 Gore led the successful fight against the newly elected vice president's request to preside over future caucuses.

Along with Senator PAUL DOUGLAS (D-Ill.), Gore was the most determined crusader for tax reform in the Senate. In the Finance Committee and on the Senate floor, they waged a long series of usually unsuccessful battles to close tax loopholes that benefited corporations and wealthy individuals.

Gore was the foremost liberal opponent of President Kennedy's $11 billion tax cut, which passed the House in September 1963. He argued in a letter to the president that tax reform should take priority over tax reduction and that such a massive tax cut would fuel a conservative movement to curb spending on social programs. Gore also criticized the economic thinking behind the tax cut, which reduced rates for corporations and the rich as well as average earners, as representative of the "trickle-down" theory of former president Herbert Hoover.

Gore continued to oppose the bill even after President Johnson made Senate passage of the tax cut the leading item on his legislative agenda in early 1964. He was the only liberal on the Finance Committee to vote against the tax bill. In a 23-page minority report Gore denounced the bill as one of the "most ill-considered bills ever to come before Congress for serious consideration." He said that it would create more inequity, had "no resemblance to true tax reform" and was the "embodiment of fiscal folly" because it would increase debt and cut revenues in prosperous times. Defeated in most of their attempts to add reform amendments to the bill, Gore and Douglas did succeed in deleting a House-passed provision lowering the capital gains tax. In February the Senate also adopted a Gore amendment increasing taxes on foreign earnings of Americans living abroad. The tax-cut bill, providing for a $11.5 billion annual tax cut, passed the Senate on February 7 and was signed into law on February 26.

Gore and Douglas consistently lost in their attempts to reduce or eliminate the 27 1/2 percent oil depletion allowance, a primary target of tax reformers. "The oil and gas lobby," Gore said in April 1965, "is the most diabolical influence at work in the nation's capital. It has for years succeeded in blocking the assignment of public-spirited members to the tax-writing committees of the House and Senate, and also intervened in the election of leaders and assistant leaders of both Houses."

Characterizing the tax system as "a morass of favoritism," Gore tried to eliminate tax preferences enjoyed by philanthropic foundations and by corporation executives profiting from stock options. He also fought the 7 percent investment tax credit, passed in August 1962 in hopes of spurring businesses to modernize plants and equipment and create jobs. To Gore it was another expensive loophole. His March 1966 proposal to suspend the investment tax credit for two years in lieu of excise tax increases was turned down in the Senate by a 75-to-10 vote. In April 1968 Gore voted in favor of President Johnson's 10 percent income tax surcharge.

Gore's overall voting record, although hardly the most liberal in the Senate, was nevertheless unusually liberal for a southern senator. (The Americans for Democratic Action gave him an average score of 58 for the Johnson years.) Moreover, his ideological zeal and his debating fervor made him conspicuous in the Senate's liberal camp. In September 1964 Gore introduced the first Medicare bill to pass either House. He backed the bulk of Johnson's Great Society social welfare programs, voted against the school prayer amendment in September 1966, and favored the gun control laws enacted in September 1968.

Gore had a mixed record on civil rights measures. Although generally a supporter of legislation to end racial discrimination, he voted against the Civil Rights Act of 1964 because of its provision for withdrawal of federal funds from programs administered in a discriminatory fashion. He called the provision a "sledgehammer" that would punish the innocent in an attempt to pressure recalcitrant state or local officials. Reelected in 1964 Gore voted in favor of the Voting Rights Act of 1965 and the open housing Civil Rights Act of 1968, although he voted for an amendment to weaken open housing coverage in the sale of certain single-family homes.

A champion of liberal monetary policies, Gore frequently attacked "Johnson high-interest rates." He unsuccessfully appealed to the president not to reappoint WILLIAM MCCHESNEY MARTIN chair of the Federal Reserve Board in 1965. Gore also argued against the appointment of HENRY FOWLER as secretary of the Treasury.

A member of the Foreign Relations Committee, Gore was an early and consistent critic of the Vietnam War. Claiming that U.S. involvement damaged relations with the Soviet Union, he proposed a cease-fire in May 1965. In October 1967 Gore called for the United States to "honorably extricate" itself from "the morass in Vietnam" by accepting the neutralization of Southeast Asia. He subsequently joined Senator J. WILLIAM FULBRIGHT (D-Ark.) in claiming that the administration had falsely presented the Tonkin Gulf incident of 1964 as an act of North Vietnamese aggression in order to gain congressional approval for war measures.

The results of the 1968 presidential election, in which Democrat HUBERT HUMPHREY won only 28 percent of Tennessee's votes, foreshadowed the difficulty Gore's outspoken liberalism caused him in his 1970 reelection fight. Gore maintained his progressive stance in the first two years of the Nixon administration, attacking the appointment of David Kennedy as secretary of the Treasury and voting against Nixon's nomination of southerners Clement Haynsworth and G. Harrold Carswell to the Supreme Court. One of the chief targets of the Nixon administration in the congressional elections of 1970, Gore lost to representative William E. Brock in a bitter ideological contest.

In September 1972 Gore became chair of the Island Creek Coal Company, the nation's third-largest coal producer. He died on December 5, 1998, in Carthage, Tennessee.

—TO

## Graham, Katherine

(1917–2001) *president, Washington Post Company*

Katherine Meyer, the daughter of banker and *Washington Post* publisher Eugene Meyer, was born in New York City on June 16, 1917, and grew up in Washington, D.C. She attended the University of Chicago and began her journalism career in 1938 as a reporter for the *San Francisco News*. In 1940 she married Philip Graham, a young lawyer who took control of the *Washington Post* in 1948, after her father's retirement. Graham became head of the Washington Post Company when her husband committed suicide in 1963. By this time the company's holdings also included two television stations, one radio station, and the weekly magazine *Newsweek*.

Under Graham the Washington Post Company expanded by acquiring an additional radio station, a new television station, and part ownership of the *International Herald-Tribune*. Graham became best known not as an empire-builder but rather as a skilled manager who could attract and keep talent in her various enterprises. One of her most important decisions was to appoint Benjamin Bradlee managing editor of the *Post* in 1965, replacing Alfred Friendly. Bradlee himself was a practiced talent scout and brought many new faces onto the newspaper's editorial staff, which doubled in size between 1963 and 1970. Largely because of these policies, the *Post* became Washington's leading daily and an influential outlet for opinion, rivaling the *New York Times* for influence on the East Coast. Daily circulation topped 500,000 in 1970, giving the *Post* a larger share of the Washington-area readership than the *Times* enjoyed in New York.

Graham's rule in dealing with her employees was to give them a free hand in determining editorial policy and news coverage and to support them against outside attack. Despite her friendship with high officials of the Johnson administration, she made no objection to *Newsweek*'s critical coverage of the Vietnam War during the mid- and late 1960s. When Vice President SPIRO AGNEW criticized the Washington Post Company in 1969 for "monopolizing" public information outlets, Graham pointed out that each of the company's enterprises functioned "autonomously."

The *Washington Post* supported Lyndon Johnson and HUBERT HUMPHREY in the presidential elections of 1964 and 1968. During the early 1970s the *Post* became involved in unprecedented controversies, beginning with its publication of the *Penatagon Papers* in 1971. Graham supported this action and also seconded Bradlee in backing *Post* reporters Robert Woodward and Carl Bernstein during their investigative reporting about the Watergate scandal. For its role in reporting Watergate, the paper won a Pulitzer Prize in 1974. Graham retired as publisher in 1979 and turned the company over to her son, Donald Graham. In 1998 her memoirs, *Personal History*, won a Pulitzer Prize. She died in Boise, Idaho, on July 17, 2001.

—SLG

## Green, Edith S(tarrett)

(1910–1987) *member of the House of Representatives*

Born on January 17, 1910, in Trent, South Dakota, Green moved with her family to Oregon in 1916. A teacher and radio commentator before her election to Congress in 1954, Green represented most of Portland and some of its suburbs. She served on the House Education and Labor Committee and chaired its Subcommittee on Special Education. Green was a consistent supporter of Kennedy administration programs and sponsored major college aid bills in the early 1960s.

While continuing to play an important role in education legislation, Green increasingly favored greater state and local control over federal education funds. With support from southern Democrats she sponsored a successful amendment to a March 1967 education bill to allow states to distribute appropriations for supplemental education centers. While defending the extension of the Teacher Corps in June 1967, she led an effort to shift control of the corps from the federal government to local school systems.

Green also sponsored a local control provision in a bill that restructured the Community Action Program (CAP), which was part of the Johnson administration's War on Poverty. Called the "bosses and boll weevil" amendment because it appealed to rural southern and big city Democrats, the new law required that the CAP boards be composed of one-third public officials, one-third poverty-area representatives, and one-third business, labor, and civic organization representatives. The measure helped prevent southern Democrats from supporting Republican proposals to transfer Office of Economic Opportunity funds to other agencies.

In 1964 she refused to endorse an amendment to the Civil Rights Act that added protection of women to the already listed categories of race, color, religion, or national origins, largely because she suspected that it was designed to kill the bill. That it passed anyway, however, could not have been much of a disappointment to Green, who had been an author of the Equal Pay Act and had sat on the President's Commission on the Status of Women.

On several occasions Green voiced her opposition to the Johnson administration's Vietnam policies. In May 1965 she was one of seven representatives who voted against a $700 million military appropriation for the war. She also caused the administration problems in the passage of the Elementary and Secondary Education Act because her firm belief in the need to maintain a separation of church and state led her to oppose providing any aid to religious schools. Johnson aide LAWRENCE O'BRIEN recalled, that Green, "had firm views as to the role of government in education. This is something that you had to accept and understand. She wasn't amenable to maneuvering. What might happen sometimes where a person may not feel that deeply or be that involved, you'd say, 'Come on. You can go along with us.' You couldn't have that kind of discussion with Edith." In the end only skillful political maneuvering by administration officials enabled them to maintain her support.

Green, who grew increasingly conservative in the late 1960s and early 1970s, continued to concentrate her energies on education matters until her retirement from Congress in 1974. She returned to Oregon as a professor of government at Warner Pacific College and remained in Portland until her death on April 21, 1987.

—MDB

## Greenberg, Jack
(1924–  ) *director-counsel, NAACP Legal Defense and Educational Fund*

Greenberg was born on December 22, 1924, in New York City and graduated from Columbia College and Law School. He joined the Legal Defense and Educational Fund of the NAACP in 1949. Greenberg argued one of the five cases involved in the Supreme Court's 1954 decision *Brown v. Board of Education*, which held racial segregation in public schools unconstitutional. He served as chief assistant to the fund's director-counsel THURGOOD MARSHALL during the 1950 and was selected the new director when Marshall resigned in October 1961. Under Greenberg's direction the fund successfully defended thousands of civil rights demonstrators and won court orders to desegregate several major southern universities in the early 1960s.

In December 1964, with some 3,000 sit-in prosecutions still pending in the South, Greenberg won a ruling from the Supreme Court that the 1964 Civil Rights Act barred state prosecution of peaceful sit-in demonstrators. The Legal Defense Fund also brought the first court suit under the public accommodations section of the 1964 act and secured a federal court order requiring LESTER MADDOX to serve black customers in his Atlanta restaurant. Over the next several years Greenberg and the fund initiated numerous legal actions to ensure full implementation of the 1964 law, especially its equal employment opportunity provisions. The NAACP Legal Defense Fund also made a major effort to ensure the implementation of the Voting Rights Act, of 1965.

A leading exponent of the strategy of using litigation to achieve social change, Greenberg launched new fund campaigns in 1965 for the expansion of prisoners' rights and for the abolition of capital punishment. As part of its prison reform effort, the fund brought suits challenging disciplinary procedures, inadequate medical care, and censorship of mail in prisons. Along with the American Civil Liberties Union, the fund appealed a series of criminal convictions where defendants had received the death penalty, arguing that the death penalty was both cruel and unusual punishment in violation of the Eighth Amendment as well as racially discriminatory. By 1968 the campaign had achieved what Greenberg called a temporary "de facto abolition" of capital punishment. In that year there were no executions. The fund's effort ultimately led to a 1972 Supreme Court decision, *Furman v. Georgia*, in which the death penalty was held unconstitutional when the sentencing authority was free to decide between death and some lesser penalty. (In 1976 the Supreme Court affirmed that the death penalty per se was not unconstitutional.) Greenberg also founded the National Office for the Rights of the Indigent (NORI) in 1967 to protect the rights of the poor in court. With Greenberg as its director and with a million dollar grant from the Ford Foundation, NORI, like the Legal Defense Fund, sought cases likely to set legal precedents affecting large numbers of the poor.

Throughout the 1960s Greenberg oversaw several Supreme Court cases that successfully challenged various devices used to delay school desegregation. He repeatedly pressured the Department of Health, Education and Welfare to take stronger action to speed public school desegregation and to cut off federal aid to state welfare programs administered in a racially discriminatory manner.

In 1969 Greenberg argued the case of *Alexander v. Holmes* in which the Supreme Court ordered an end to segregated school systems "at once." During the Nixon years Greenberg publicly criticized the administration for maintaining policies that he alleged encouraged delay in school desegregation. Overall, Greenberg argued 40 civil rights cases before the Supreme Court. He later became a professor, and then a dean, of Columbia Law School.

—CAB

## Gregory, Dick

(1932–  ) *comedian, social activist*

Born on October 12, 1932, Gregory grew up in poverty in St. Louis. He ran track for his St. Louis high school and attended Southern Illinois University on an athletic scholarship. After serving in the army and drifting through several jobs, Gregory began his career as a comedian in 1958 at a black nightclub in Chicago. He remained largely unknown outside of black audiences until 1961, when he appeared at the Chicago Playboy Club as a replacement for a white comedian. He was so successful in his limited number of appearances that the Playboy Club offered him a contract extension from several weeks to three years. By 1962 he had become a national figure, with television appearances, comedy albums, and a large network of supporters from blacks and whites alike. In his comedy routines, he provided ironic commentary on many social issues.

Gregory became involved in civil rights in November 1962, when he spoke at a voter registration rally in Jackson, Mississippi. He became friendly with Medgar Evers, leader of the Mississippi NAACP, and subsequently toured the South, speaking at civil rights rallies and demonstrations. When local governments in Mississippi stopped distributing federal food surpluses to poor blacks in areas where the Student Nonviolent Coordinating Committee had taken an active role in voter registration campaigns, Gregory chartered a plane to bring in several tons of food. Gregory dropped out of the nightclub circuit entirely in 1966 to devote himself to college appearances aimed at encouraging student activism. During the late 1960s he became increasingly involved in opposition to the Vietnam War. Other issues, such as environmental protection and the rights of American Indians, also drew his attention.

Always an individualist, Gregory did not identify himself with any single civil rights or peace organization. However, his celebrity status enabled him to act alone for the causes he espoused. In November 1967 he began a series of fasts, lasting from 40 to 80 days, to dramatize his stand on the war and other issues. He also led antiwar demonstrations in Chicago during the 1968 Democratic National Convention and was jailed for crossing police lines—his 20th arrest since 1962. In 1967 Gregory ran a write-in campaign against RICHARD DALEY in the Chicago mayoral election, gaining 22,000 votes. A second write-in campaign during the Democratic presidential primaries of 1968 brought him 150,000 votes. In 1969 Gregory attended the World Assembly of Peace in East Berlin, protesting "racism as the prime cause of war."

Gregory's independent crusading drew mixed reactions from other black leaders. JAMES FARMER, former head of the Congress of Racial Equality, praised Gregory for stimulating the political interest of many blacks. But WHITNEY YOUNG of the National Urban League claimed that Gregory could do more good in the entertainment industry, opening new opportunities for black performers and writers. "There are many activists, but only one Dick Gregory," Young pointed out.

Gregory, in fact, reduced his political activism after 1969, partly for financial reasons. He resumed his nightclub performances in 1970 but left show business again in August 1973. This transition reflected a change in Gregory's life style; he moved with his family from Chicago to a farm outside Boston and devoted himself to pursuing a "natural" life, including a vegetarian diet, breathing exercises, and running.

Gregory published a number of books at various stages of his career, including *From the Back of the Bus* (1964), *Write Me In* (1968), and *Dick Gregory's Political Primer* (1972). In 1996 he returned to comedy, in a critically acclaimed show, *Dick Gregory Live*.

—SLG

## Griffin, Robert P.

(1923–   ) *member of the House of Representatives, member of the Senate*

Robert Griffin, who was born in Detroit on November 6, 1923, graduated from the Central Michigan College of Education in 1947. He earned a law degree from the University of Michigan and then cofounded a law firm in Traverse City, situated in the less-populated, northwestern tier of the state's lower peninsula. Defeating a conservative incumbent in the 1956 Republican primary for the House of Representatives, Griffin won in November and had no difficulty securing reelection through 1964. A specialist in labor law, he served on the Education and Labor Committee. Griffin gained a recognition unusual for a second-term representative when he cosponsored the Landrum-Griffin labor reform law in 1959.

In January 1963 Griffin and several other younger GOP colleagues plotted the first of two successful challenges to the party hierarchy. With Representative GERALD R. FORD (R-Mich.) as their candidate, the younger Republicans ousted Party Conference chair Charles Hoeven (R-Iowa), who had the support of House Minority Leader CHARLES A. HALLECK (R-Ind.). Two years later the Griffin faction elected Ford over Halleck to the top GOP House post.

Griffin's House voting record resembled that of most of his fellow Republicans. In the 1965 session, according to *Congressional Quarterly*, Griffin opposed key White House–endorsed legislation on 49 percent of all roll-call votes, a tally that closely matched that of most other GOP representatives. Yet unlike Ford and the majority of his party, Griffin voted for Medicare in April 1965 after endorsing the unsuccessful Republican substitute.

In May 1966 Governor GEORGE W. ROMNEY appointed Griffin to the seat left vacant by the death of Senator PAT V. MCNAMARA (D-Mich.). Griffin, faced the popular and outgoing former governor G. Mennen Williams in the fall elections. Strongly supported by Romney, Griffin defeated Williams by just under 300,000 votes.

As in his early House career, Senator Griffin soon violated the tradition that new members of a legislative body should defer to their party leadership. When President Johnson proposed to elevate Associate Justice ABE FORTAS to chief justice in June 1968, Griffin organized conservative opposition to the nomination in defiance of Minority Leader EVERETT M. DIRKSEN (R-Ill.), who supported Fortas.

Griffin himself attacked the nomination on three counts. First, the senator claimed in July that Johnson engaged in "cronyism" by choosing Fortas, an old political friend and White House counselor. Second, Griffin argued that the president, as a "lame duck," had improperly negotiated with Chief Justice EARL WARREN in an unprecedented and "obvious[ly] political maneuv[er]" to *create* a vacancy." (Warren had stated that he would not retire from the Court until the Senate confirmed his successor.) Dirksen angrily denied Griffin's first two objections as "frivolous, diaphanous gossamer." In September Griffin revealed that Fortas had received $15,000 for teaching a nine-week course at American University Law School in the preceding summer. His fee, Griffin added, had been paid by five "former business associates or clients" of Fortas and his old law firm; Griffin charged that this payment represented a conflict of interest.

By September Fortas's promotion appeared doomed. The Judiciary Committee recommended his nomination, 11-6, but Griffin, who was not a committee member, then organized a filibuster against it. In early October the Democratic leadership sought to end the debate through a cloture vote; with a 45-43 vote it failed to obtain the required two-thirds margin. By then Dirksen had surrendered to Griffin and voted against cloture. Fortas thereupon withdrew his name. For the first time since 1930, the Senate had failed to confirm a presidential Supreme Court nomination. President RICHARD M. NIXON nominated Warren Burger as Warren's successor in May 1969.

Eleven months after his victory in the Fortas nomination dispute, Griffin became Senate minority whip, the second-youngest in congressional history. Despite his position he occasionally opposed the Nixon administration on major votes. His reassertion of the Senate's right to reject a Supreme Court nominee added to the Senate Democrats' determination not to approve two of Nixon's high court appointments. Griffin himself voted against the confirmation of Clement F. Haynsworth, Jr., in October 1969. Winning reelection in 1972 he remained minority whip and improved his relations with the executive branch upon Gerald Ford's succession to the presidency. He was defeated in 1978 and returned to Michigan to the practice of law. He become an associate justice of the State Supreme Court 1986, and retired eight years later.

—JLB

## Griffiths, Martha W(right)

(1912–2003)   *member of the House of Representatives*

Born on January 29, 1912, in Pierce City, Missouri, Martha Wright graduated from the University of Missouri in 1934, married Hicks G. Griffiths, and secured her law degree from the University of Michigan in 1940. Griffiths served as a purchasing agent for the U.S. Army during World War II. After the war she and her husband started a private law practice in Michigan with G. Mennen Williams. In 1948 Williams became governor, and Griffiths won election to the state legislature. Griffiths held the office until 1952, when she made an unsuccessful bid for a congressional seat. Two years later she was elected to Congress from Detroit's mostly middle-class 17th Congressional District. Somewhat conservative by Michigan Democratic standards and lacking the close United Auto Worker ties of other Detroit Democrats, Griffiths became quite popular

Representative Martha Wright Griffiths in front of the Capitol, 1970  *(Library of Congress, Prints and Photographs Division)*

in the previously Republican district and won reelection by large majorities.

Throughout her congressional career Griffiths worked for laws to prohibit sex discrimination. She fought successfully for the inclusion of an antisex discrimination provision in the Civil Rights Act of 1964. The original administration bill included a section outlawing racial discrimination in employment. Hoping to ensure the section's defeat, southern Democrats introduced an amendment to forbid job discrimination on the basis of sex as well. Griffiths and other women in the House saw the conservative ploy as an opportunity to offer legal recourse to women denied employment because of their sex. Without the amendment, Griffiths said, "white women will be last at the hiring gate." When the Johnson administration, in its unsuccessful 1966 civil rights bill, proposed making racial discrimination in jury selection unlawful, Griffiths added an amendment to forbid any distinction on the basis of sex. The bill won approval in the House but died in the Senate because of its controversial open housing provisions. She also made headlines that year when she wrote an airline executive who had fired a flight attendant after she got engaged. "Just exactly what are you running," she wrote, "an airline or a whorehouse?"

Griffiths was a founding member of the National Organization for Women in 1966 and helped publicize data on women's employment and earnings. Dissatisfied with the Equal Employment Opportunity Commission's enforcement of sex discrimination laws, she asked President Johnson to replace its members in 1967.

Somewhat idiosyncratic in her voting, Griffiths was not among the administration's most ardent supporters. She was, however, a leading advocate of its unsuccessful 1967 rat control bill. "If you're going to spend $75 billion to try to kill off a few Viet Cong," she told Congress, "I'd spend $40 million to kill the most devastating enemy that man has ever had." She cast the House's only dissenting vote on a 1966 administration narcotics bill. She called it a "bribe" for addicts since it allowed them to voluntarily commit themselves to medical institutions for long-term treatment in lieu of serving a prison term. She was the first woman on the House Ways and Means Committee, and usually supported WILBUR MILLS (D-Ark.) the committee chair. However, in 1965, when the Johnson administration proposed to reduce the 10 percent automobile excise tax in stages to 5 percent in 1967, Griffiths called for elimination of the levy altogether. Mills argued that it provided necessary revenues, but he offered a compromise, later enacted, under which the tax was reduced gradually and allowed to expire in 1969.

Although she voted for the administration's requests for Vietnam War appropriations, Griffiths grew critical of the war toward the end of the Johnson years. Asked in a 1968 interview what she would do in Johnson's place, Griffiths replied, "I'd call Ho Chi Minh and tell him I was bringing the boys home." She voted for the 1970 Cooper-Church amendment prohibiting the use of U.S. troops in Cambodia.

Griffiths was a leading proponent of the Equal Rights Amendment, and its approval by Congress in 1972 was, according to Representative GERALD FORD (R-Mich.), "a monument to Martha." She retired from office in 1974, but continued working for the ERA in state referenda. She returned to Michigan, where she served as lieutenant governor from 1982 to 1991. She died in Amarda, Michigan, on April 22, 2003.

—MDB

## Griswold, Erwin N(athaniel)
(1904–1994) *member, U.S. Civil Rights Commission; U.S. Solicitor General*
Born on July 14, 1904, in East Cleveland, Ohio, Griswold graduated from Oberlin College in 1925. He received a bachelor of laws degree from Harvard Law School in 1928 and a doctor of laws degree the next year. From 1929 to 1934 he worked as an attorney in the solicitor general's office. Griswold taught at Harvard Law School beginning in 1934 and established a reputation as an expert in federal taxation and conflict of interest laws. As dean of the law school from 1946 to 1967. Griswold raised the quality of the student body, revamped the curriculum, and improved the fund-raising activities and physical plant of the school.

In April 1961 President Kennedy appointed Griswold, a registered Republican, to the U.S. Civil Rights Commission. An investigative body established in 1957, the commission made numerous recommendations in the early 1960s for stronger federal legislation in such areas as voting rights, school desegregation, the protection of civil rights workers, and employment and housing discrimination. Many of the commission's proposals became

part of the 1964 Civil Rights Act and the 1965 Voting Rights Act. Following passage of these statutes the commission also monitored their enforcement, and its reports frequently recommended greater federal action to ensure fill implementation of the laws.

Griswold resigned his posts on the commission and as dean of Harvard Law School when President Johnson appointed him solicitor general on September 30, 1967. Known for his rather taciturn and gruff manner, Griswold was in charge of all U.S. government litigation in the Supreme Court as solicitor general. In briefs and oral argument before the Court in March and May 1968, Griswold urged the justices to reject a claim that the government must turn over transcripts of any illegal eavesdropping to a defendant and his or her attorney. He told the Court that if such a claim were upheld, the government might have to drop some prosecutions against alleged spies for fear that its counterespionage methods would be disclosed to foreign governments. The Supreme Court by a five-to-three vote rejected Griswold's arguments in a March 1969 decision.

In September 1968 Griswold also filed a brief in a case involving a divinity student who had turned in his draft card in protest against the Vietnam War and had then lost his deferment in accordance with an October 1967 order from the Selective Service director to local draft boards. In an unusual move Griswold presented both the Selective Service System's view that the order was legal and the Justice Department's position that the directive might violate both the draft law and the Constitution by using the draft to punish antiwar dissenters. The Supreme Court's December 1968 ruling called the local draft board's action "basically lawless" and upheld the right of an individual to challenge in court the loss of a statutory draft exemption.

Griswold remained as solicitor general during the Nixon administration, and he argued several important Supreme Court cases involving school desegregation, court-ordered busing, and the constitutionality of antiabortion laws. Griswold also argued on behalf of the government that the *Pentagon Papers*, a detailed report chronicling U.S. involvement in the Vietnam War, should not be allowed to be published by newspapers for reasons of national security. Eighteen years later, he wrote a story for the *Washington Post* in which he admitted that he had been wrong. He resigned as solicitor general on June 26, 1973, to join a Washington law firm. He died on November 19, 1994.

—CAB

## Gronouski, John A(ustin)
### (1919–1996) *U.S. Postmaster General, U.S. ambassador to Poland*

Gronouski was born on October 26, 1919, in a small Wisconsin hamlet and raised in Oshkosh. He earned a Ph.D. in economics from the University of Wisconsin in 1955 and two years later joined the faculty of Wayne State University. In 1960 the governor of Wisconsin named Gronouski state commissioner of taxation.

President John F. Kennedy named Gronouski to succeed J. Edward Day as postmaster general in August 1963. He was the first cabinet member in history to hold a Ph.D. and the first of Polish extraction. Gronouski partially reduced a massive Post Office deficit by cutting back on overtime, closing the philatelic agency, and ordering large-volume mailers to presort their mail according to ZIP code numbers. However, he accomplished little in speeding the delivery of mail.

Gronouski faced a Senate Judiciary subcommittee inquiry into questionable Post Office practices and abuses in February 1965. Under a Post Office mail surveillance program, certain letters were delivered only after Post Office officials had noted all information on the envelope. Henry B. Montague, chief postal inspector, testified that the mail of about 1,000 companies and individuals was currently under surveillance—a procedure Gronouski defended as useful in solving crimes. Subcommittee chair EDWARD V. LONG (D-Mo.) charged the Post Office was denying citizens their right to privacy and won a pledge from Gronouski to "tighten and centralize" the mail surveillance program.

Senator Long also charged that the Post Office was turning over to the Internal Revenue Service the mail of delinquent taxpayers, but Gronouski testified that he had discontinued the practice. The Senate subcommittee did not discover that the Central Intelligence Agency (CIA), rather than the Post Office, continued not only to intercept but also to open first-class mail sent from the Soviet Union to American citizens. According to the report of the *Presidential Commission on CIA Activities within the United States* (1975), CIA officials in April 1965 considered briefing Gronouski but decided against it,

fearing that Gronouski's pledge to Senator Long would put him into conflict with their agency.

In the summer of 1965 President Johnson ordered the Post Office and other federal agencies to hire youths as summer replacements for regular workers on vacation. Administration critics charged the Post Office with hiring youths recommended by members of Congress and paying them salaries above the $1.25 an hour set by the president.

Despite the controversies swirling about the Post Office, President Johnson appreciated Gronouski's skill as a political campaigner, particularly in Polish-American neighborhoods. "I never heard any adverse comment regarding him in the White House," recalled Johnson aide LAWRENCE O'BRIEN. Late in the summer of 1965, Johnson named Gronouski ambassador to Poland. Over the next two and a one-half years, Gronouski, in his ambassadorial capacity, held a number of discussions in Warsaw with the ambassador from the People's Republic of China. (The United States and China did not have formal diplomatic ties, and the Warsaw talks, dating from 1958, constituted the only regular diplomatic contact between the two countries.) The discussions concerned Vietnam, disarmament, and a possible Chinese-American cultural and scientific exchange program.

In May 1968 Gronouski resigned his diplomatic post to campaign for HUBERT HUMPHREY. In September 1969 he became dean of the Lyndon B. Johnson School of Public Affairs at the University of Texas. He remained at the LBJ School until his retirement in 1989, when he returned to Wisconsin. He died there in 1996.

—JLW

## Groppi, James
### (1930–1985) *adviser, Youth Council of the Milwaukee NAACP*

Born on November 16, 1930, Groppi grew up on Milwaukee's South Side . He attended Milwaukee's St. Francis Seminary, where he was ordained as a priest in 1959. Groppi became interested in civil rights at this time owing in part to the discrimination against blacks that he witnessed in the seminary. After serving as an assistant pastor in an Italian section of Milwaukee, he was transferred to the predominantly black St. Boniface parish in 1963. He also became adviser to the youth council of the local NAACP.

Groppi's first active involvement in civil rights came in 1963, when he joined the March on Washington. The following year, he participated in several voter registration marches in Mississippi and worked with the Council of Federated Organizations on various civil rights–related activities. In 1965 he supported a school boycott by Milwaukee blacks protesting segregation in the city's educational system, and became the adviser to the Milwaukee chapter of the National Association for the Advancement of Colored People. On this occasion he came into conflict with his church superiors in Milwaukee, who opposed clerical participation in the boycott. Groppi was arrested several times in Milwaukee during the mid-1960s for leading or participating in civil rights demonstrations.

In 1967 Groppi and the youth council of the Milwaukee NAACP began to push vigorously for a local open-housing law. When rioting erupted in the city's predominantly black section during late July and early August, Groppi blamed the outbreak on the city government's continued refusal to act against discrimination in housing and education. On August 28 Groppi and the NAACP Youth Council began a series of open-housing demonstrations in Milwaukee. Lasting into late November, the protests attracted national attention as the most extensive campaign in the United States against housing bias. Most of the marches that Groppi led passed through the city's South Side, provoking violent while counterdemonstrations. After one clash on September 11, Milwaukee mayor Henry Maier claimed that "the city verged on civil war." The largest of the marches involved 2,300 people, including civil rights workers and clergy from seven midwestern states.

On September 13 Milwaukee archbishop William Cousins abandoned his earlier neutrality to support Groppi's demand for a municipal open-housing law. Other religious groups, including the American Lutheran Church, also gave their support. As a result of the open-housing campaign, the Milwaukee City Council passed a measure on December 13 outlawing discrimination in certain types of housing. This ordinance was the basis for a strict open housing code.

Groppi left the Milwaukee NAACP youth council in November 1968, in order to concentrate on "militant social action involvement" within the St. Boniface parish. He remained active, however, in the city's civil rights movement. In September 1969 he led a group of students and welfare recipients which occupied the Wisconsin State Assembly chamber to protest reductions in state welfare payments. This action alienated Groppi from many of his liberal supporters, who objected to the "disruptive" tactics of the demonstrators.

Groppi was transferred from the St. Boniface parish in June 1970 to the racially mixed Milwaukee parish of St. Michael. In 1972 he entered the Antioch Law School in Washington, D.C., driving a taxi part-time to support himself. Groppi was excommunicated and banned from performing priestly functions when he married in May 1976. In 1979 he returned to driving a bus for the Milwaukee County Transit System in the summer of 1979. He died in 1985.

—SLG

## Gross, H(arold) R(oyce)
(1899–1987)  *member of the House of Representatives*

Born on June 30, 1899, in Arispe, Iowa, H. R. Gross served overseas in the U.S. Army in World War I. After working on various newspapers from 1921 to 1935, he became a radio news commentator. Elected to Congress as a Republican in 1948 from Iowa's agricultural third district, Gross distinguished himself as an isolationist, a backer of high farm subsidies, and a conservative critic of what he considered government extravagance. He waged his campaign for government frugality through Republican and Democratic administrations alike and often denounced Congress for excessive staff and committees, unnecessary travel at taxpayers' expense, and too frequent recesses. His votes against the Eisenhower and Nixon administrations were so frequent that Minority Leader GERALD FORD (R-Mich.) remarked, "There are three parties in the House: Democrats, Republicans, and H. R. Gross."

Gross was a vigorous opponent of the liberal domestic and international programs of the Kennedy and Johnson administrations. *Congressional Quarterly* reported that Gross voted against measures favored by the Johnson administration more than any other representative in 1965, 1967, and 1968. He was the only Iowan to vote against Medicare in April 1965 even though Iowa was the state with the second-largest percentage of citizens over 65. An opponent of foreign aid since he voted against extending the Marshall Plan in April 1949,

Gross labeled the Peace Corps "a haven for draft dodgers" in 1961 and called the Arms Control and Disarmament Agency "a wanton waste of the taxpayers' money" in April 1965. He opposed a $200 million U.S. subscription to the Asian Development Bank in February 1966.

Gross was best known for his maverick forays against what he considered prodigal spending in government. Only 10 days after the assassination of President Kennedy, Gross protested spending money to provide Secret Service protection for the president's widow and children, and complained that the U.S. taxpayer should not have to pay for the eternal flame at JFK's grave in Arlington National Cemetery. In July 1964 Gross successfully proposed an amendment to the Land and Water Conservation Act to prohibit issuance of free passes to members of Congress or government officials for admission to areas covered in the bill. He voted against every congressional pay raise, and, in March 1964, he managed to defeat a proposed pay increase for federal employees by demanding a roll-call vote on the measure. Congress rejected an amendment that Gross proposed in June 1965 to delete a $35,000 appropriation for elevator operators in the House's Rayburn Building, whose elevators were automatic. He was one of only two members to vote against a military pay increase in October 1967. Gross continued to act as a budgetary watchdog through the Nixon administration. He once criticized Secretary of the Interior Walter J. Hickel because the secretary installed $56.25-a-yard carpeting in his office. Gross was not a candidate for reelection in 1974. He remained in Virginia until his death on September 22, 1987.

—TO

## Gruening, Ernest H(enry)
### (1887–1974) *member of the Senate*

Born in New York City on February 6, 1887, Gruening graduated from Harvard Medical School in 1912 but chose to become a journalist. He edited several liberal publications in the 1920s and 1930s and wrote a widely read account of the Mexican Revolution. Gruening opposed U.S. military intervention in Latin America and was an early advocate of racial equality and birth control. In 1924 he headed public relations for Senator Robert LaFollette's Progressive Party presidential campaign.

Franklin D. Roosevelt appointed Gruening director of territories and island possessions in 1934.

As governor of Alaska between 1939 and 1952, he pressed for construction of the Alcan Highway, antidiscrimination legislation aimed at protecting Alaska's Indians, a tax system designed to weaken the influence of absentee interests, and for Alaskan statehood. Elected Alaska's first senator in 1959, Gruening supported most Kennedy administration programs.

Gruening, who had long worked for more federal aid to Alaska, was angered that victims of the March 1964 Alaskan earthquake were required to pay higher interest on federal loans than were foreign aid recipients. Through his efforts federal expenditures following the earthquake were increased and the Housing and Finance Administration was authorized to purchase Alaskan bonds. He also claimed that Alaska suffered from inadequate transportation facilities because of its exclusion from federal highway programs while a territory. As a result of his efforts, appropriations were made in May 1966 for maintenance as well as construction of Alaskan highways.

Gruening had been a strong proponent of family planning since the 1920s, when he had worked with birth control advocate Margaret Sanger. He introduced a bill in April 1965 to create Offices for Population Problems in the Departments of State and of Health, Education and Welfare. As chair of the Government Operations Subcommittee on Foreign Aid Expenditures, Gruening held hearings on birth control services currently provided by federal and private agencies to determine whether the proposed offices would duplicate existing services. The hearings gained wide publicity for birth control ideas and had the effect of increasing the efforts of existing agencies. Later Gruening became convinced that his bill was obsolete, and he did not report it for Senate action. Instead, he released a study in January 1966 criticizing the government for lagging behind private agencies in providing family planning services.

Gruening was one of the earliest congressional critics of U.S. involvement in Vietnam, voicing opposition to the Johnson administration's policies in a March 1964 Senate speech entitled "The United States Should Get Out of Vietnam." In August 1964 he and Senator WAYNE MORSE (D-Ore.) cast the only votes against the Tonkin Gulf Resolution, which allowed the president to take "all necessary measures to repel further attacks. . . and to prevent further aggression." Gruening later denounced the resolution as a "blank check to the President." He and Morse consistently voted against the administration's requests for military appropriations for Southeast Asia, often forming the only opposition to such expenditures.

Gruening stated repeatedly that Southeast Asia was not essential to American security and held that the United States was acting in violation of the 1954 Geneva Accord and the UN Charter. Calling for negotiations with Hanoi, he and Morse assailed the bombing of North Vietnam in February 1965. In January 1966 he was among 16 senators who sent a letter to Johnson asking for an end to the air attacks. On March 1, 1966, Gruening was the only senator to support Morse's proposal to repeal the Tonkin Gulf Resolution. At the same time the Senate rejected, by a vote of 75 to 2, his amendment to prohibit sending draftees to Southeast Asia unless they volunteered for service there.

Gruening became one of the few senators to associate himself with the early antiwar movement. In April 1965 he addressed the first large demonstration in Washington against the war, which was sponsored by a coalition of groups including Students for a Democratic Society. He later protested a Capitol safety bill in September 1967, which did not include permission for orderly demonstrations on the Capitol grounds.

During the 1960s Gruening advocated strict congressional review of American foreign aid expenditures. He opposed most foreign military assistance, especially in Latin America, where he thought it was used for purposes at variance with those of the Alliance for Progress. Gruening's efforts to tighten congressional supervision of foreign aid proved generally unsuccessful, but, in the mid-1960s, he won modification of administration foreign aid bills on occasion. Gruening thought Communist influence pervasive in Indonesia, and his September 1965 amendment to cut off all aid to that country, unless deemed "essential" by the president, won Senate approval. He successfully introduced a measure in July 1966 that required the United States to use its voting power to prevent loans by the World Bank and its affiliates to countries already suspended from U.S. aid because of expropriation of American property. Gruening's August 1967 amendment to bar aid to any country breaking diplomatic ties to the United States also won Senate approval. (The proposal was directed against the Arab states, which had broken relations

with the United States following the Arab-Israeli war in June 1967.)

Gruening, 81, lost the 1968 Democratic senatorial primary to 38-year-old Mike Gravel, a real estate broker who emphasized state rather than national issues. Gravel's victory was in large measure attributed to the widespread showing of a sophisticated documentary film advancing the young challenger's candidacy. In the November general election Gruening's name was not on the ballot, but he nevertheless received a statewide write-in vote of 15 percent. Gruening continued to actively oppose the Vietnam War and in 1972 campaigned for Senator GEORGE MCGOVERN (D-S.Dak.) for president. Gruening died in Washington, D.C., on June 26, 1974.

—MDB

## Guy, William L(ewis)
(1919–  ) *governor*

Born in Devils Lake, North Dakota, on September 30, 1919, Guy worked as a farmer and taught agricultural economics at North Dakota State University. He entered politics as a Democrat and became assistant majority floor leader in the North Dakota House of Representatives from 1958 to 1960. In 1960 Guy became the first Democrat in 16 years to be elected governor. Guy was reelected to his second two-year term in 1962 and reelected in 1964 to his first four-year term. In 1962 he was chosen as the first chair of the Midwest Governors' Conference. Four years later he was elected chair of the National Governors' Conference.

When Guy took office in 1961, North Dakota faced a declining population primarily because of its almost total dependence on agriculture. In an effort to diversify and industrialize, Guy sought to reduce the state's high electric power rates by building three cooperative power plants on the Missouri River. Despite this effort the amount of new industry in the state did not significantly increase. Guy faced the problems of limited gubernatorial powers and a consistently Republican-dominated legislature. Nevertheless, he raised the state's biennial budget from $75 million to $283 million during his tenure, modernized the state government, reformed the tax system, established area mental-health clinics, expanded nursing-home facilities, consolidated school districts, and reduced the state's penitentiary population by almost 50 percent through revised probation and parole techniques. Guy said that "the most significant development" of his governorship was the start of a comprehensive resource plan for the Red River and its tributaries.

In May 1966 Guy was the first governor in the nation to veto Office of Economic Opportunity (OEO) programs in his state. He defended his action saying that "during this wartime inflationary period we should not permit indiscriminate expenditures of OEO funds for programs of questionable value." In September 1967 Guy was among a group of 20 "distinguished Americans" who observed South Vietnam's election, which, Guy said, was "as moving and profound an example of the desire for self-determination as can be found anywhere." As chair of the 1967 National Governors Conference, Guy expressed hope that the conference would pass a Vietnam resolution "in favor of the commander in chief." He became a member of the 1968 Humphrey-for-President Committee and won reelection to his second four-year term in November 1968.

In 1973 Guy retired to become an insurance company executive. He was narrowly defeated by five-term incumbent senator MILTON YOUNG in a 1974 Senate bid in a controversial election that saw him defeated by 186 votes after a recount.

—TJC

# H

## Habib, Philip Charles

(1920–1992) *counselor for political affairs, U.S. embassy, Saigon; deputy assistant secretary of state for Far Eastern affairs*

Habib's background was very different from that of most foreign service officers of his generation. Born in Brooklyn, New York, on February 25, 1920, Habib worked as a shipping clerk in Flatbush before attending the University of Idaho. After receiving his doctorate in economics from the University of California in 1952, he joined the diplomatic corps and became deeply involved in Asian affairs, serving in South Korea before being assigned to South Vietnam as counselor for political affairs in May 1965. He was named deputy assistant secretary of state in July 1967 for East Asian and Pacific affairs.

In March 1968 Habib participated in the policy discussions to advise the president on the military's request for over 200,000 additional ground troops following the communist Tet offensive in South Vietnam. At these meetings Habib recommended that the increase be denied because it would continue South Vietnamese reliance on U.S. power and delay the development of needed South Vietnamese military independence.

At the end of the month, when the president called together his Senior Advisory Group of Vietnam, commonly known as the "Wise Men," to study the request, Habib was one of three government officials to deliver a briefing. In what the *Pentagon Papers* described as "an unusually frank" report, Habib, who had accompanied General EARLE WHEELER on the mission to Saigon that had resulted in the troop request, told the group that the South Vietnamese government was generally weaker than had been realized as a result of the Tet offensive. He

also outlined the problems that resulted from corruption and the increase in refugees. As a result of these briefings and the fear of the domestic consequences of further troop increases, the group advised President Johnson to begin disengagement from the war.

In May 1968 Habib accompanied the U.S. delegation to the Paris peace talks as adviser on Vietnamese affairs. As the highest-ranking career diplomat in the delegation, Habib was an important link between the Johnson administration's delegation, led by W. AVERELL HARRIMAN and the Nixon administration's group, later headed by HENRY CABOT LODGE. In November 1969 Habib became head of the U.S. delegation at Paris. He was appointed ambassador to South Korea in September 1970. He remained in Korea until his retirement in 1974. In 1981 President Reagan appointed him special envoy to the Middle East, where he helped to arrange a cease-fire in Lebanon, and later helped persuade Ferdinand Marcos to relinquish power in the Philippines. He died in France on May 25, 1992.

—EWS

## Hall, Gus

(1910–2000) *general secretary, Communist Party U.S.A.*

Hall was born Arvo Gustav Halberg on October 8, 1910, in Iron, Minnesota, a small town in the Mesabi Range. His father was a Finnish immigrant and charter member of the American Communist Party, which Hall joined at 17. He was a leader of the Little Steel strike in Warren, Ohio, and after serving in the navy during World War II he became a member of the party's National Executive Board.

Hall briefly served as Communist Party national secretary after Eugene Dennis was jailed in 1950, but was himself imprisoned from October 1951 to March 1957 under the Smith Act for conspiring to teach and advocate the violent overthrow of the government.

In 1959 Hall was elected general secretary of the Communist Party and took over the leadership of an organization shattered by government repression, factionalism, and disillusionment. In June 1961 the Communist Party again came under legal attack when the Supreme Court ruled that under the 1950 Internal Security Act (McCarran Act) the Communist Party had to file registration documents, including a complete list of its members. Simultaneously, the Court ruled that being an active member of the party could be a crime under the Smith Act. Hall immediately announced that the party would not register with the government, and in March 1962 Hall and party national secretary Benjamin J. Davis were indicted for failing to register the party.

A Supreme Court ruling that invalidated parts of the McCarran Act led the Justice Department in May 1966 to request the dismissal of the charges against Hall. Hall called the court's decision "a blow against the longest political-legal vendetta in our history" and said that with the decision "it will be possible to be more openly active in all fields."

In the early 1960s the Communist Party had been cautious and defensive, but during the years after 1963 it became increasingly active politically. In June 1964 a Berkeley, California, youth group dominated by Communist Party members, the W.E.B. DuBois Club, expanded into a national organization. Although not openly endorsing President Johnson in 1964, Hall tacitly did so by calling on Communists to "join with all democratic forces to defeat the ultra-right Goldwater coalition."

In February 1966 Hall announced the publication of a new Communist Party draft program that said peaceful coexistence between communist and capitalist countries was possible. He called for the eventual formation of a new electoral party that would include all "the forces arrayed against monopoly." The new party would work for socialism through the ballot and constitutional amendment, but until such a party could be formed, the Communist Party would continue to seek change through the two-party system. The party generally supported liberal Democrats in the 1960s, especially

in those areas of its greatest strength: New York, Illinois, and California.

Hall was reelected general secretary in June 1966 at the first Communist Party convention in over six years. No longer under government orders that had long restricted his travels, he visited Europe and the Soviet Union in 1966 and attended the November 1967 Moscow celebration of the 50th anniversary of the Bolshevik Revolution.

Although rarely sponsoring rallies or demonstrations in its own name, the Communist Party was active in the civil rights and antiwar movements and advocated a third-party ticket for 1968. Members of the party participated in the August 1968 National Conference for New Politics, but the conference failed to endorse any national slate. The August 1968 Soviet invasion of Czechoslovakia sharply divided Communist Party members in the United States. New York State chair Gilbert Green and the majority of the West Coast party opposed the invasion. Hall supported it, arguing that force was necessary to avert a "counter-revolutionary takeover." His position was eventually accepted by the party, although several prominent members resigned in the aftermath of the dispute. Hall was unanimously reelected general secretary in May 1969 and in 1972 was the Communist Party presidential candidate. He continued to take an active role as party leader, author, and occasional presidential candidate, collecting almost 37,000 votes in 1984. He also received subsidies from Moscow to help with party activities, including a $2 million contribution in 1987. He died in Manhattan on October 13, 2000.

—JBF

## Halleck, Charles A(braham)
(1900–1986) *member of the House of Representatives*

Born on August 22, 1900, in Demotte, Indiana, Charles A. Halleck earned B.A. and LL.B. degrees from Indiana University. Following admission to the state bar in 1924, he entered Republican politics. Halleck won a special election to fill a House vacancy in 1935 and served successively until his retirement in 1969. He loyally campaigned for his fellow Republican members, rose steadily on House seniority lists, and became House Majority Leader following the election of Joseph W. Martin, Jr. (R-Mass.) as Speaker in January 1947. In January 1959 Halleck unseated Martin as House GOP leader.

Halleck's triumph marked the end of a cooperative relationship in the House between the Republican leadership and Speaker Sam Rayburn (D-Tex.). To gain his victory Halleck promised to oppose House Democrats in a partisan manner, an easy task for the Indiana Republican who frequently characterized himself as a "gut fighter." During the early 1960s he led the powerful Republican–southern Democratic conservative coalition, which defeated much of the Kennedy administration's legislative program.

As a precondition for the support of many younger Republican House members against Martin, Halleck had promised to rejuvenate the House Republican Conference (Policy) Committee and give it a new and enlarged role. Some Republicans, however, continued to express dissatisfaction with the policy-making procedure, and, in January 1963, Representative GERALD R. FORD, JR. (R-Mich.) challenged Halleck's choice for chair of the Conference Committee. Ford recruited enough support from younger members, both liberal and conservative, to win the position by eight votes.

Halleck abandoned his resolute partisanship to support the Johnson civil rights bill in 1964. While Representative WILLIAM MCCULLOCH (R-Ohio), ranking Republican member on the Judiciary Committee, helped draft the House version, Halleck persuaded a sufficient number of his conservative GOP colleagues to join with northern Democrats to overcome the opposition of House southerners to the bill. In February 1964 the House overwhelmingly passed the administration's bill, 290 to 130, with 78 percent of the Republican members voting for the measure.

The House version included federal employment and public accommodations guarantees which Senate Minority Leader EVERETT M. DIRKSEN (R-Ill.) opposed. Only after three months of negotiation with the bill's proponents did the Senate Republican leader agree to support the House bill. Though Dirksen received nationwide praise for his role in the enactment of the measure, Halleck's acceptance of the accommodations and employment provisions had forced the senator's hand. White House strategist LAWRENCE F. O'BRIEN later called Halleck "the unsung hero" in the passage in the 1964 Civil Rights Act. Despite this and a few other examples of close cooperation with the White House, Halleck and President Johnson had a fairly distant working relationship, and LBJ at times

seemed to take a particular interest in defeating him when it was known they were at odds on a bill; "Don't you ever let Halleck beat me up there," LBJ told one representative in the spring of 1964.

Like Dirksen, Halleck endorsed the presidential candidacy of Senator BARRY M. GOLDWATER (R-Ariz.). The Indiana Republican seconded Goldwater's nomination at the July 1964 Republican National Convention and defended the senator in the general election campaign. Johnson defeated Goldwater in November with 61 percent of the vote, and the GOP lost 37 seats in the House.

Halleck proved a belated casualty of the Goldwater debacle. In December 1964 Ford announced that he would challenge Halleck for the House GOP leadership. Both representatives held conservative voting records. The conservative Americans for Constitutional Action gave Halleck an 86 percent rating and Ford 83 percent on selected issues. Yet, Halleck appeared less responsive to younger and more liberal members, many of whom opposed the party's covert alliance with southern Democrats. He was also hurt by the fact that he had been a leading voice in Republican opposition to Medicare, which many felt had hurt the party with the American voters. In a secret ballot, Ford defeated Halleck by a vote of 73 to 67. "I've been through adversity before," Halleck complained after the tally, "but I've never had to run in a beauty contest." Halleck fell into relative obscurity after January 1965 and rarely participated in House debates. He retired in 1968. He returned to Indiana, where he died on March 3, 1986.

—JLB

## Hamer, Fannie Lou
(1917–1977) *vice chair, Mississippi Freedom Democratic Party*

The daughter of sharecroppers, Hamer who was born on October 19, 1917, grew up in rural Sunflower County, Mississippi. Her first contact with the civil rights movement came in 1962, when she led a group of 26 blacks attempting to register to vote in Ruleville, the county seat. Not only was the attempt unsuccessful, but Hamer was jailed and beaten, and her family was evicted from the farmland where they had worked for 18 years. After this experience Hamer joined the Student Nonviolent Coordinating Committee (SNCC) and worked to register black voters in Mississippi. In 1964 she helped organize Mississippi Freedom Summer, a massive voter registration drive sponsored by SNCC and other national civil rights organizations. At this time she was among the founders of the Mississippi Freedom Democratic Party (MFDP), formed to give newly registered black voters an alternative to the state's white-run regular Democratic Party.

Hamer gained national attention at the 1964 Democratic National Convention, where the MFDP attempted to unseat the regular Mississippi delegation. In hearings before the convention's credentials committee, MFDP representatives claimed that the state Democratic organization did not support President Johnson and did not represent black voters. Hamer electrified the convention when she told how police had repeatedly beaten her in jail after her first attempt at voter registration. Despite widespread sympathy for the MFDP, the credentials committee voted to recognize the regular Democratic delegation. At Hamer's urging the MFDP rejected a compromise offer to seat two MFDP representatives as "special delegates." If the MFDP wasn't seated in its entirety, she told a television audience, "I question America."

The 1964 convention was an important event in the growing disillusionment of many civil rights activists with their white liberal allies. When SNCC leader STOKELY CARMICHAEL called for "Black Power" in 1966, Hamer supported him and spoke at several rallies that promoted black separatist principles. Nevertheless, she worked in Mississippi to broaden the base of the MFDP through cooperation with integrationist and white liberal groups, including the NAACP and the state AFL-CIO. In 1968 the MFDP joined with these groups to form a faction called the Loyal Democrats, which again challenged the regular Mississippi Democrats for recognition at the party's national convention—this time successfully. Appearing before the 1968 Democratic National Convention as a delegate, Hamer received a standing ovation.

Hamer continued to serve the MFDP as vice chair after 1968, working for the registration of black voters and the election of black office seekers. Largely as a result of these efforts, nearly 60 percent of all black Mississippians were registered to vote in 1973. By this time Mississippi had more black elected officials (145) than any other southern state. She also remained active with the National Council of Negro Women and other southern civil rights groups and helped to organize the National Women's Political Caucus in the 1970s. She died on March 14, 1977 in Ruleville, Mississippi.

—SLG

## Harlan, John Marshall
### (1899–1971) *associate justice, U.S. Supreme Court*

Born in Chicago on May 29, 1899, Harlan graduated from Princeton University, studied at Oxford as a Rhodes scholar, and received a degree from New York Law School in 1924. He joined a prestigious Wall Street law firm in 1923, becoming a partner in 1931. His practice dealt primarily with corporate and antitrust cases. Harlan also served as an assistant U.S. attorney in the Southern District of New York and as special prosecutor in a New York State investigation of municipal graft in the 1920s. During World War II, he served with the bomber command of the U.S. Army Air Forces, rising by the end of the war to the post of division head in the U.S. Group Control Council for Germany From 1951 to 1953 Harlan was chief counsel for the New York Crime Commission. He resigned from his law firm when President Eisenhower named him a judge on the U.S. Second Circuit Court of Appeals in January 1954.

Grandson and namesake of Supreme Court justice John Harlan, Harlan was himself appointed to the high court in November 1954, and his nomination was confirmed in March 1955. On the bench Harlan developed a close personal and intellectual relationship with Justice Felix Frankfurter, and, following Frankfurter's retirement in August 1962, he became the leading spokesperson on the Court for a philosophy of judicial restraint. Harlan's views were frequently at odds with those of the Warren Court's liberal, activist majority, and he dissented from many of its rulings on criminal rights, reapportionment, and the powers of state and congressional investigating committees.

Harlan had a deep respect for precedent and rarely voted to overturn past Court decisions. He was also strongly committed to the principles of federalism embodied in the Constitution. Insisting that the Supreme Court should play only a limited role in the governmental system, he favored giving broad recognition to the powers of the federal executive and legislature and of state and local governments. Harlan argued that state criminal proceedings, for example, only had to meet a test of "fundamental fairness" under the Constitution, and he therefore dissented in June 1964, when the majority held the Fifth Amendment's privilege against self-incrimination applicable to the states. Harlan also objected to the June 1966 *Miranda* decision, in which the Court set out rules governing police interrogation of arrested suspects. His dissenting opinion argued that the majority was departing from settled constitutional doctrine and creating unnecessary difficulties for law enforcement agencies. Harlan concurred, however, when the Court in May 1967 extended certain constitutional safeguards such as the right to counsel to juvenile court proceedings. He also joined in a December 1967 ruling requiring police to obtain a judicial warrant before using electronic eavesdropping devices.

Harlan frequently voted to sustain federal laws against claims that they violated individual rights. He dissented, for example, in June 1964, when the Court invalidated a federal law denying passports to members of the Communist Party. Although he ordinarily supported congressional power to act against domestic Communists, Harlan did join in a November 1965 decision that held it a violation of the Fifth Amendment to require Communist Party members to register with the government under the 1950 Subversive Activities Control Act.

Harlan was equally wary of invalidating state legislation on constitutional grounds. He entered a sharp dissent to a March 1966 Court decision that held a Virginia poll tax for state elections unconstitutional. He also disagreed with the majority when, in May 1968, it overturned state laws mandating different treatment for legitimate and illegitimate children. In June 1965, however, Harlan concurred when the Court overturned a Connecticut law prohibiting the use of contraceptives by married couples.

In dealing with obscenity legislation Harlan used a stricter standard when judging the constitutionality of federal rather than state laws. Since the states, he argued, had primary responsibility for protecting public morals and welfare, they should be given more leeway than the federal government in regulating expression that was allegedly obscene. As a result Harlan voted repeatedly to sustain convictions under state obscenity statutes but often favored reversal in federal obscenity cases, such as the March 1966 *Ginzburg* decision.

Although Harlan opposed most of the major trends on the Warren Court, he united with his more liberal colleagues in major decisions outlawing racial segregation. He also voted to sustain the public accommodations section of the 1964 Civil Rights Act in December 1964 and major portions of the 1965 Voting Rights Act in March 1966. Harlan had voted to reverse the state convictions of civil rights demonstrators in several cases in the early 1960s, but by 1964 he had changed course and joined in opinions by Justice HUGO BLACK arguing to uphold such convictions. He also dissented in May 1967, when the Court voided a California constitutional amendment that had nullified earlier legislation prohibiting racial discrimination in housing.

Harlan opposed extending the Supreme Court's jurisdiction into new areas and argued that state or federal legislatures, not the courts, were the proper forums for dealing with many political and social issues. He had dissented in March 1962, when the Court overturned a 1946 precedent and held that federal courts could try cases on legislative apportionment. Harlan also objected to February and June 1964 decisions in which the majority set forth a "one-person, one-vote" standard for congressional and state legislative apportionment. In his dissenting opinion in the latter case, *Reynolds v. Sims,* Harlan summarized his objections to much of the Warren Court's activism. He labeled "mistaken" the view "that every major social ill in this country can find its cure in some constitutional 'principle,' and that this court should 'take the lead' in promoting reform when other branches of government fail to act." The Court, he added, as a judicial body, should not "be thought of as a general haven for reform movements."

In his final years on the Court, Harlan dissented when the majority overturned state residency requirements for welfare but joined in another decision holding that welfare recipients had a right to a formal hearing with constitutional safeguards before their benefits could be terminated. His opinion for the Court in a June 1971 case held that the First Amendment protected an individual who wore a jacket inscribed with a vulgarity condemning the draft. Later the same month, however, he dissented in the *Pentagon Papers* case when the Court upheld the right of newspapers to public materials from a classified government study on the origins of the Vietnam War. Harlan resigned from the Court on September 23, 1971, because of ill health. He was replaced by William Rehnquist. Harlan died in Washington on December 29, 1971.

Although Harlan took positions that could be classified as "liberal" in certain cases, his judicial philosophy led him to dissent from many of the liberal rulings of the Warren Court. Yet, even legal scholars who disagreed with Harlan's views had great respect for a jurist who, as Professor Alan Dershowitz said, "always brought sagacity and honesty to the deliberations of the Court." Nearly blind during his last seven years on the bench, Harlan continued to work unstintingly and to act as the "conservative conscience" on a liberal, activist Court. Many observers commented on Harlan's devotion to the Court and to the Constitution, and virtually all praised the consistently high quality of his opinions. Lucid, thoroughly reasoned, and learned, those opinions won Harlan a reputation as "the leading scholar" on the Warren Court and its best legal craftsman.

—CAB

## Harriman, W(illiam) Averell
(1891–1986) *undersecretary of state for political affairs, ambassador at large, chief U.S. representative to the Paris peace talks*

W. Averell Harriman, President Johnson's representative to the Vietnam peace talks, was heir to the Union Pacific Railroad fortune amassed by his father. Born in New York City on November 15, 1891, he graduated from Yale University in 1913 and then joined his father's business. By 1932 he had become chair of the board of the Union Pacific. During his first years in business he also embarked on a number of financial ventures, including ownership of a shipyard and establishment of an investment bank. Turning to international finance in the early 1920s, Harriman was among the first Americans to seek business concessions from the Soviet government.

Harriman entered Democratic Party politics and held a series of business advisory posts during the New Deal. In 1941 Franklin D. Roosevelt sent him to London as the president's special representative to the British government. In 1943 he went to Moscow. After service as ambassador to the Soviet Union, Harriman became secretary of commerce in 1946. From 1949 to 1950 he helped administer the Marshall Plan. Harriman was elected governor of New York in 1954 but lost his bid for a second term to NELSON ROCKEFELLER in 1958. His attempts to win national office also failed when he

ran unsuccessfully for the Democratic presidential nomination in 1952 and 1956.

During the Kennedy administration Harriman served in various State Department positions as the president's chief diplomatic negotiator. In 1962 he helped formulate the Laos Accords guaranteeing the neutrality of that Southeast Asian country. One year later he went to Moscow to negotiate the partial nuclear test ban treaty.

In 1965 President LYNDON JOHNSON appointed Harriman ambassador at large with the principal duty of handling Southeast Asian affairs. During 1965 and 1966 Harriman traveled around the world seeking support for U.S. Vietnam policy while sounding out the possibilities of a negotiated settlement of the war. When Johnson's announcement of a partial bombing halt of North Vietnam in March 1968 led to the opening of preliminary peace talks two months later, Harriman went to Paris as chief U.S. negotiator.

During the opening months of the conference, talks revolved around two main issues: Hanoi's insistence on a total American bombing halt as a precondition for serious discussions and Saigon's refusal to enter negotiations in which the National Liberation Front (NLF) participated. Johnson refused to halt bombing completely without assurances that North Vietnam would respect the demilitarized zone, cease shelling major South Vietnamese population centers, and promise a withdrawal of its troops from South Vietnam. Hanoi rejected these demands and continued to insist on a total U.S. bombing halt. However, major attacks did diminish in June and July. Harriman then recommended that the lull be regarded as a signal that North Vietnam had accepted the U.S. preconditions. Despite the ambassador's recommendation, Johnson still declined to stop all bombing. After four months without progress, in September the president finally gave his approval of a halt upon the "unilateral understanding" that if America stopped bombing, North Vietnam would respect the demilitarized zone. In November the United States ended the bombing of North Vietnam. Johnson announced that in exchange for a bombing halt, Hanoi had agreed to the participation of the South Vietnamese government at the Paris talks, while the United States had approved a role for the NLF.

The negotiations in Paris during the last weeks of the Johnson administration bogged down in procedural difficulties. In January 1969 HENRY CABOT LODGE succeeded Harriman as chief U.S. negotiator.

W. Averell Harriman (left) and Dean Acheson of the "Wise Men" at a meeting in the Cabinet Room, 1967 *(Photographed by Yoichi R. Okamoto; Lyndon Baines Johnson Library)*

During the Nixon administration Harriman continued to press for a complete U.S. withdrawal from Vietnam on a fixed schedule and in 1970 scored the Cambodian invasion as an unwarranted expansion of the war. In 1971 he urged Congress to use its power of the purse to end the conflict. In 1978 he became the senior member of the U.S. delegation to the UN General Assembly's Special Session on Disarmament. He also continued to serve as an unofficial U.S. representative to the Soviet Union. He died in New York on July 26, 1986.

—EWS

## Harrington, (Edward) Michael
### (1928–1989)  *chair, Socialist Party*

Michael Harrington was born on February 24, 1928, in St. Louis and educated by Jesuits at St. Louis University High School and at Holy Cross College. In 1951 he moved to New York, where he began drifting toward socialism. After spending a year working with the Catholic Worker movement, Harrington joined the Young People's Socialist League and eventually became a leader of the Socialist Party. In the early 1960s he became convinced that the anticommunist, socialist movement of which he was part could be most effective by working within the Democratic Party in an effort to "realign" it in a more progressive direction.

Harrington was active in civil liberties, civil rights, and peace groups throughout the 1950s and early 1960s. His 1962 book, *The Other America: Poverty in the United States*, was important in directing public attention toward the large number of people living in chronic poverty within the "affluent society." These people, Harrington claimed, especially the elderly and the rural poor of Appalachia, had become invisible to the larger society. The poor, as he described them, were not just a segment of Americans without money, but actually constituted "a separate culture, another nation with its own way of life." President Kennedy read Harrington's book in the fall of 1963, shortly before he ordered the

Council of Economic Advisers (CEA) to begin planning an antipoverty program.

On President Johnson's first full day in office, CEA chair WALTER HELLER advised Johnson that four days earlier Kennedy had approved the planning of a major antipoverty program. The new president gave the project his highest priority, and, on January 8, 1964, in his first State of the Union address, Johnson declared an "unconditional war on poverty in America."

Later that month poverty program planners asked Harrington to Washington. With Paul Jacobs, a former union organizer and West Coast radical, and Peace Corps official FRANK MANKIEWICZ, Harrington began two weeks of meetings with high government officials to prepare proposals for the new program. In their final memo Mankiewicz, Jacobs, and Harrington argued that the elimination of poverty would require major changes in the allocation of government resources and certain basic structural changes in society. Newly appointed poverty program head SARGENT SHRIVER incorporated part of the memo in his report to Johnson, who at the time responded favorably.

As U.S. involvement in Vietnam escalated, Harrington became involved in the growing antiwar movement. In October 1965 he spoke in a national, telephone-linked network of college teach-ins, calling for a more open policy toward the People's Republic of China and a negotiated settlement of the war in Vietnam. Harrington, however, had little sympathy for the Vietnamese Communists, from whom he felt the antiwar movement should publicly dissociate itself, and he opposed a unilateral U.S. withdrawal. As a member of the ad hoc committee arranging the November 27, 1965, antiwar march in Washington, Harrington convinced Dr. BENJAMIN M. SPOCK, spokesperson for the Committee for a Sane Nuclear Policy, to direct the demand for a negotiated settlement to Hanoi as well as Saigon and Washington.

His opposition to U.S. policy in Vietnam led Harrington to support Senator EUGENE MCCARTHY's (D-Minn.) 1968 presidential primary campaign. However, when Senator ROBERT KENNEDY (D-N.Y.) announced his candidacy on March 16, 1968, Harrington switched his support to Kennedy, who he thought could attract broader support around a more far-reaching program. At Kennedy's request Harrington briefly campaigned during the May 1968 California primary fight. Following Kennedy's

assassination Harrington supported the Democratic candidate, Vice President HUBERT HUMPHREY.

Harrington served on the National Executive Committee of the Socialist Party throughout the Johnson administration and wrote two books, *The Accidental Century* in 1965 and *Towards a Democratic Left* in 1968 during this period. In 1968 he became chair of the Socialist Party. Harrington was an outspoken critic of repression in the Soviet Union, and, in January 1966, he joined an international protest against the arrest and conviction of dissident Soviet writers Andrei D. Sinyavsky and Yuli M. Daniel.

During the New York City teachers' strikes of May and September-November 1968, Harrington supported the United Federation of Teachers (UFT) fight against the community school board in the predominantly black Ocean Hill–Brownsville section of Brooklyn. Harrington argued that the city's school decentralization experiment was fundamentally an attempt by the Ford Foundation, the Urban Coalition, and the New York City Board of Education to manipulate growing Black Power sentiment to preserve the status quo. According to Harrington, the final result would be "black control of black misery and white control of the nation's wealth." In 1973 he formed the Democratic Socialist Organizing Committee in the hopes of uniting the left wing of the Democratic Party, the progressive elements of the Socialist Party, the labor unions, and disillusioned former radicals. He also continued to write until his death from cancer in 1989.

—JBF

## Harris, Fred R(oy)
(1930–   ) *member of the Senate*

Harris was born on November 13, 1930, in Walters, Oklahoma, and spent his youth on a farm in the southwestern part of the state. After completing college and law school at the University of Oklahoma, he entered the state senate in 1956 as its youngest member. Within three years he became chair of its Democratic caucus. In the state legislature he helped to create the Oklahoma Human Rights Commission to prohibit discrimination in state employment.

Harris entered the primaries for the Democratic gubernatorial nomination in 1962 but finished a poor fifth. However, in a special election in 1964 to fill the remaining years of the term of the late Democratic senator Robert Kerr, Harris defeated Senator J. Howard Edmondson (who as governor had appointed himself to fill the vacant seat) in the Democratic primary. In November he edged out the Republican candidate, popular football coach Bud Wilkinson, by 20,000 votes. Harris's upset victory was attributed to the 1964 Johnson landslide, endorsement by the powerful Kerr family, and strong support from Oklahoma's Indian voters. (Harris's wife, LaDonna, was of Irish and Comanche descent). In the campaign Harris endorsed Johnson's Great Society programs and characterized his own political views as "good Oklahoma common sense."

Harris compiled a more liberal voting record than his powerful predecessor. He favored most of the Great Society programs, including antipoverty bills, rent subsidies, Model Cities, and aid to education but voted against Medicare. He also supported Senator EVERETT DIRKSEN's (R-Ill.) unsuccessful attempt to circumvent the Supreme Court's "one person, one vote" ruling by a constitutional amendment. Harris supported the body of civil rights legislation enacted during the Johnson years. He also established himself as a strong advocate of Indian rights.

Harris did not oppose the Vietnam War during Johnson's tenure. However, in 1967 he criticized the Central Intelligence Agency (CIA) for its infiltration of university activities abroad and urged the president to forbid the agency from using any university project as a cover for CIA activities.

In 1968 Johnson appointed Harris to serve on the President's Advisory Commission on Civil Disorders. After the Commission issued its report in March 1968 citing lack of jobs as a major cause of disorders, Harris supported a bill to appropriate $10 billion over four years to provide for 2.4 million jobs. On April 11, 1968, Harris became co-chair with Senator WALTER MONDALE (D-Minn.) of the United Democrats for Humphrey.

In the years following 1964 Harris moved steadily toward a more pronounced liberalism, a trend that continued during the Nixon administration. His rating by the American for Democratic Action rose from 59 percent in 1968 to 83 percent in 1969 to 100 percent in 1970. However, his Oklahoma constituency was becoming increasingly Republican and conservative, and Harris did not run for reelection in 1972. Instead he waged an unsuccessful campaign for the Democratic presidential nomination on a platform espousing a "new populism" to curb the power of the major corporations and equalize individual wealth and income. He moved to Corrales, New Mexico, and became a professor of political science at the University of New Mexico in 1976.

—TO

## Harris, Oren

(1903–1997) *member of the House of Representatives*

Harris, who was born on December 20, 1903, in Belten, Arkansas, graduated from Cumberland University Law School in Tennessee in 1930. He was elected district prosecuting attorney of Arkansas's 13th judicial district in 1936. Four years later he was elected to the U.S. House of Representatives after defeating the incumbent in the Democratic primary. As a member of the House Interstate and Foreign Commerce Committee, to which he was appointed in 1943, Harris sponsored a bill in 1949 exempting independent natural gas producers from the rate and service regulations of the Federal Power Commission (FPC). A similar measure passed Congress but was vetoed by President Harry S. Truman.

In 1956 Harris became chair of the Commerce Committee. Five years later he once again introduced a bill to relax FPC controls on natural gas producers, but it died in the House. During the same year he successfully opposed a Kennedy administration bill that he believed would increase the president's control over the Federal Communications Commission. In 1959 he also chaired hearings into allegations of bribery in the music industry, an outgrowth of the House investigation of corrupt broadcast practices that began with scandals involving rigged quiz shows.

The Commerce Committee had jurisdiction over legislation pertaining to federal regulatory commissions. Harris often opposed what he claimed were excessive grants of power to those agencies, and he was widely regarded as friendly to the private interests regulated by the commissions. In 1964 the Commerce Committee, under Harris's guidance, weakened a bill introduced the previous year to expand the Securities and Exchange Commission's (SEC) policing power over securities trading. The Senate had passed the bill in July 1963. But as reported out by Harris's committee in May 1964, the measure was modified to exempt insurance companies, which had lobbied strongly against the bill, from SEC jurisdiction. The final bill, which President LYNDON B. JOHNSON signed in August 1964, incorporated the Commerce Committee's amendment.

In February 1964 the committee began consideration of a bill, supported by Harris, to eliminate the Interstate Commerce Commission's powers over the rate-setting activities of railroads and water carriers for agricultural and fishery products. The measure aroused strong opposition from various interests, particularly the water carriers. They contended the railroads would cut their rates below cost on routes where rail and water transportation were in competition and make up for the resulting losses by raising rates in areas where water transport was not available as an alternative to railroads. As a result of this opposition, the bill that Harris supported did not pass.

During the first two months of 1965, Harris's committee held hearings on the illegal distribution of barbiturates and amphetamines. The panel reported out a bill to strengthen federal control over pharmaceutical companies for the purpose of curb-ing the diversion of those drugs from legal channels. While business leaders generally opposed increased government supervision over their operations, the drug industry almost unanimously supported this measure. He also sponsored a number of bills to help improve medical care, including a law that created regional medical programs to coordinate efforts to combat strokes, heart disease, and cancer.

In July 1965 President Johnson nominated Harris to be a federal district judge in Arkansas, and the Senate confirmed the nomination in August. Harris resigned from the House to assume the judgeship in February 1966. He died in Arkansas on February 5, 1997.

—MLL

## Harris, Patricia R(oberts)
### (1924–1985)  *U.S. ambassador to Luxembourg*

The first black woman to be appointed a U.S. ambassador, Harris, who was born on May 31, 1924, in Mattcon, Illinois, attended Howard University, where she graduated summa cum laude in 1945. An

Ambassador Patricia Roberts Harris making an appearance on *Meet the Press,* 1971  *(Library of Congress, Prints and Photographs Division)*

early civil rights activist, she participated as a student in the campus chapter of the NAACP and joined sit-ins at segregated restaurants in the Washington, D.C., area. After graduation Harris held a number of jobs, including assistant director of the American Council on Human Rights, before attending George Washington University Law School. Following her graduation she worked as an attorney for the Justice Department and taught law at Howard University.

In July 1963 President John F. Kennedy appointed Harris to the unpaid position of co-chair of the National Women's Committee for Civil Rights, where she worked to create support among women's groups for civil rights legislation. She also served at that time on the District of Columbia advisory committee to the United States Commission on Civil Rights.

LYNDON JOHNSON named Harris to the Commission on the Status of Puerto Rico in March 1964. One year later, in May 1965, she became U.S. ambassador to Luxembourg. Harris served at the post until August 1967, when she resumed her teaching career. In 1966 and 1967 she also served as alternate representative to the United Nations.

Following the assassination of Senator ROBERT KENNEDY (D-N.Y.) in June 1968, President Johnson appointed Harris a member of a commission to probe the causes of violence in the United States. When the commission report, issued in December 1969, condemned massive civil disobedience, including nonviolent action, and stated that even nonviolent civil disobedience could lead to "nationwide disobedience of many laws and thus anarchy," Harris issued a dissenting opinion. She maintained that civil disobedience, when there was a willing acceptance of the penalty, "can represent the highest loyalty and respect for a democratic society. Such respect and self-sacrifice may well prevent, rather than cause violence."

In February 1969, while Harris was serving as dean of Howard Law School, law students occupied the school as a protest against grading policies and lack of student participation in implementing academic decisions. In reaction, Harris obtained a court injunction against the students. At the end of February she resigned, charging that the university had placed her in an untenable position by negotiating with the students without her knowledge.

A lifelong Democrat, Harris had seconded the presidential nomination of Lyndon Johnson at the 1964 Democratic National Convention and campaigned for his election. With the backing of party regulars and labor, she was elected chair of the credentials committee for the 1972 Democratic National Convention over the objection of reform elements. In 1977 she became the first African-American woman to serve in a presidential cabinet, when President Carter appointed her secretary of the U.S. Department of Housing and Urban Development. Two years later she became secretary of the Department of Health, Education and Welfare. She ran unsuccessfully for mayor of Washington, D.C., in 1982. She died in Washington, D.C., on March 23, 1985.

—EWS

## Hart, Philip A(loysius)
### (1912–1976) *member of the Senate*

Born on December 10, 1912, in Bryn Mawr, Pennsylvania, Philip Hart attended Georgetown University. After receiving his law degree from the University of Michigan in 1937, he began private practice in Detroit. Seriously wounded during World War II during the invasion of Normandy, Hart returned to law practice after the war and entered government in 1949 as Michigan's corporation and securities commissioner. In 1953 he became legal adviser to Governor G. Mennen Williams, a former law school classmate, and was elected lieutenant governor in 1954 and 1956. With strong labor support Hart ran successfully for the Senate in 1958. In that and subsequent campaigns Hart was also aided by the inherited wealth of his wife, the former Jane Briggs, daughter of Walter Briggs, auto-parts millionaire and owner of the Detroit Tigers baseball team.

A member of both the Judiciary Committee and Commerce Committee, Hart compiled one of the most liberal records in the Senate. The conservative Americans for Constitutional Action, for example, gave Hart and six other senators "zero" ratings for their voting records in 1966. He was a consistent supporter of the Great Society social programs of the Johnson administration. Not a flamboyant advocate, Hart became known as a quietly effective legislative technician with a special interest in civil rights, consumer protection, and antitrust matters. For these efforts, as well as his commitment to principles and honesty in government, he earned the nickname the "Conscience of the Senate." A strong defender of the Civil Rights Act of 1964, Hart served as floor manager of the Voting Rights Act of 1965.

In the wake of the 1967 urban riots, Hart criticized congressional attempts to enact "antiriot" legislation. A provision of the Civil Rights Act of 1968 making it a crime for individuals to use interstate facilities for the purpose of inciting a riot passed the Senate, 82-13, in March 1968 with Hart in the minority. Hart was the floor manager for the civil rights provisions of the same omnibus bill, which provided federal protection for persons trying to exercise their civil rights and prohibited discrimination in the sale or rental of about 80 percent of the nation's housing.

Hart's most notable victory in the field of consumer protection was the passage of "truth-in-packaging" legislation by Congress in October 1966. During the Kennedy years he had held extended hearings before the Judiciary Committee's Subcommittee on Antitrust and Monopoly, which investigated misleading packaging and labeling practices such as short-weighting and unsatisfactory contents designation. The purpose of the 1966 law, enacted after repeated rebuffs, was to aid consumers in making price and value comparisons of some 8,000 products sold in supermarkets and drug stores.

Hart became chair of the antitrust subcommittee following the death of Senator Estes Kefauver (D-Tenn.) in August 1963. The flamboyant Kefauver had conducted headline-making investigations into industrial concentration and big business abuses like price-fixing and bid-rigging. Under the more reserved, judicious Hart, the subcommittee's activities attracted less attention. Hart held frequent hearings, but the volumes of testimony produced little immediate action. Where Kefauver's investigations sometimes resembled exposés and resulted in indictments, Hart's were general studies of a more academic character.

Hart was hampered by the fact that a majority of his subcommittee did not share his enthusiasm for antitrust action. After Kefauver's highly publicized hearings on drug prices in June 1961, Senator JAMES EASTLAND (D-Miss.), chair of the Judiciary Committee, had assigned conservatives to fill vacancies on the antitrust subcommittee. The subcommittee's practice of voting to issue subpoenas to secure information from businesses, an important investigatory tool under Kefauver, fell into disuse under Hart. Although he was disturbed by the great

conglomerate merger wave of the 1960s, Hart could not get a committee majority to favor strengthened antitrust laws. Instead he often used hearings and prolonged study as a device to stall attempts to provide antitrust exemptions for certain industries.

During the 1960s Hart moved slowly away from an identification with an anticommunist foreign policy. As late as May 1964 he had encouraged Cuban exiles in their efforts to overthrow the Castro regime, but, three years later, in August 1967, he was one of only six senators to vote in favor of a $3.5 billion cut in the defense budget. Beginning in December 1968 Hart led the battle against the Sentinel ABM (antiballistic missile) program.

Although Hart was not an early opponent of the Vietnam War, his wife, Jane, became active in the antiwar movement and was among those arrested for holding a religious service at the Pentagon in November 1969. Hart emerged as a member of the Senate's antiwar bloc during the Nixon administration. He died in office on December 26, 1976, in Washington, D.C. In 1978 the third of the Senate office buildings was dedicated and named after him.

—TO

## Hartke, R(upert) Vance
### (1919–2003) *member of the Senate*

Vance Hartke was born on May 31, 1919, in Stendal, Indiana, and raised in a small mining town in southwestern Indiana. After receiving his law degree from Indiana University, he practiced law in Evansville. Hartke was active in local Democratic Party politics and in 1955 was elected mayor of the city. Four years later he was elected the first Democratic senator from Indiana in 20 years. Hartke was a strong supporter of Kennedy administration domestic legislation. He served on the powerful Senate Commerce and Finance Committees but, because of his low seniority, did not play an influential role in their operations.

Hartke won reelection in 1964 with 55 percent of the vote. He supported Johnson administration civil rights, education, Medicare, and antipoverty bills. By 1965, however, Hartke began to have doubts about the administration's Vietnam War policy. In January of 1966 he drafted a letter sent by 15 other senators urging President Johnson not to resume the bombing of North Vietnam. The next month Hartke delivered his first major speech opposing escalation of the conflict. LBJ responded by dismissing him as a, "two-bit mayor from a two-bit town." Nevertheless, in March he voted for a $13 billion arms appropriations bill that included funding for the war. In 1967 he wrote *The American Crisis in Vietnam* but withheld publication for a year, fearing that it would hurt Democratic prospects in Indiana during a presidential election year.

During his 1964 campaign Hartke received large cash contributions from a Chicago-based mail order firm. A year later he requested and won appointment to the Senate Post Office Committee, where he worked to forestall planned postal increases for third-class mail. Hartke's opponents charged that he was guilty of conflict of interest. This, coupled with his outspoken opposition to American involvement in Vietnam led many observers to consider his reelection in 1970 problematical. Hartke managed to defeat his opponent, but the election was so close that Hartke's claim to his seat was not finally settled until the U.S. Supreme Court ordered a ballot recount 18 months after the election. He was defeated in his quest for reelection in 1976, and settled in Falls Church, Virginia, to practice law. In 1996 he lobbied for a riverboat casino project on behalf of a client and ran afoul of local electoral laws. He was convicted of two offenses and put on probation. He died on July 27, 2003.

—JLW

## Hatfield, Mark O(dum)

(1922–   ) *governor, member of the Senate*
Hatfield, who was born on July 12, 1922, in Dallas, Oregon, graduated from Williamette University and taught political science there from 1949 to 1956. During the same period he also proved remarkably adept as a practical politician, winning election to the Oregon House of Representatives in 1950 and the Oregon Senate in 1954. He became secretary of state in 1957 and two years later became governor, the youngest in Oregon's history.

Oregon was a state with a strong progressive tradition, and Hatfield was able to maintain his popularity while supporting the civil rights movement, backing legislation for the construction of community colleges, and advocating public rather than private hydroelectric power development in the Columbia River basin. He opposed state right-to-work laws and blocked a proposed effort by the legislature to impose a state sales tax.

In 1960 Hatfield nominated Vice President RICHARD M. NIXON for president at the Republican National Convention; four years later Hatfield was the convention's keynote speaker. Early in 1964 Hatfield supported New York Governor NELSON ROCKEFELLER for president, but he campaigned for Senator BARRY GOLDWATER (R-Ariz.) after the Arizona senator won the Republican nomination that year.

During the early 1960s Hatfield emerged as a promising future candidate for the Republican presidential or vice presidential nomination. In 1964, however, he began to attack U.S. involvement in the Vietnam War, and, as a result, his standing within the Republican Party declined sharply. In April 1966 Hatfield was the only one of 50 governors meeting at the Governors Conference in Los Angeles to vote against a resolution of support for American policy in Vietnam. When he ran for the Senate in 1966, Hatfield only narrowly defeated Representative Robert Duncan (D-Ore.), a supporter of the war.

During the Johnson years, Hatfield, lacking seniority, had little influence in the Senate. He generally voted with moderate Republicans in matters of domestic policy. The Americans for Democratic Action gave him a 54 percent rating in 1967 and 71 percent in 1968.

In April 1967 Hatfield and Representative Donald Rumsfeld (R-Ill.) called for an end to the draft and its replacement by an all-volunteer army. Hatfield argued that the draft was inherently unjust and that a volunteer army would be a superior fighting force. The Hatfield-Rumsfeld bill failed, but it marked the beginning of an effort that culminated in the abolition of the draft in 1973.

In 1968 Hatfield supported Nixon for president, but, after the election, he attacked the administration for its Vietnam War policy. In 1970 Hatfield and Senator GEORGE S. MCGOVERN (D-S.Dak.) cosponsored a widely publicized but unsuccessful amendment setting April 30, 1971, as a cutoff date for appropriations for American combat troops in Vietnam. He was also a supporter of arms control and disarmament reforms, culminating in 1992 with the passage of legislation he authored calling for an end to U.S. nuclear testing. He was not a candidate for reelection in 1996, and returned to teaching history and political science at Portland State University in Oregon.

—JLW

## Hawkins, Augustus (Freeman)

(1907–   ) *member of the House of Representatives*

Hawkins, who was born on August 31, 1907, in Shreveport, Louisiana, moved to California with his family in 1918. After a successful career in real estate and pharmacy, he was elected to the Assembly in 1934, and served in that body for 28 years, narrowly failing to win election as its speaker in 1959. In 1962 Hawkins won a seat in the U.S. House of Representatives, making him the first African-American representative in Congress from a western state.

A black representative from the predominantly black areas of south central Los Angeles, Hawkins was a New Deal Democrat who was particularly concerned with the problem of poverty in his district. On the House floor and in the Education and Labor Committee, he consistently backed President Johnson's Great Society programs and civil rights measures. After the 1965 riots in the Watts area, which was part of his district, large amounts of federal money went to aid his constituents, and his influence in Congress increased proportionately. In 1965 he opposed an effort to narrow the scope of the administration's open housing bill, and, the following year, he criticized an attempt to restrict community participation in antipoverty programs. A consistent liberal, Hawkins received a "correct" rating of 94 for his House voting during the 1960s from the Americans for Democratic Action.

Hawkins's views on foreign policy matters were shaped largely by his estimate of their effect upon his district. During the latter years of the Johnson administration, he became a critic of the Vietnam War on the ground that it drained funds from domestic social welfare programs. In 1966 Hawkins voted for supplementary funds for the war, but he was among 72 representatives who signed a statement urging efforts toward a peaceful settlement.

In 1969 Hawkins and 12 other black representatives organized a black caucus in the lower chamber; he was chosen vice chair of the group. Five years later Hawkins was the House sponsor of the Humphrey-Hawkins bill, which proposed to guarantee federally funded jobs to all unemployed persons. He also succeeded in obtaining an honorable discharge, retroactively, for the 167 black members of the army's 25th Infantry Regiment who were dishonorably discharged after being falsely accused of public disturbance in Brownsville, Texas, in 1906.

He was not a candidate for reelection in 1990 and retired to Los Angeles.

—MLL

## Hayden, Carl T(rumbull)

(1877–1972) *member of the Senate*

Carl Hayden was born in Tempe, Arizona, on October 2, 1877, 35 years before Arizona achieved statehood and served in Congress longer than any other member in U.S. history. After graduating from Stanford University in 1900, Hayden served as a council member and county sheriff. He was elected to the U.S. House of Representatives in 1912 and then to the Senate in 1926 with a brief period of interruption while he served as a major during World War I. During his first 21 years in office Hayden did not make a single speech on the Senate floor, yet he became known as a dogged champion of legislation to improve roads and irrigation in Arizona.

Hayden supported Kennedy administration legislation on nearly 70 percent of all major issues, according to *Congressional Quarterly*. Because he chaired the Appropriations Committee, Hayden was one of the most powerful senators. During the period between President Kennedy's assassination in November 1963 and Lyndon Johnson's inauguration in January 1965, Hayden was president pro tempore of the Senate and third in line for presidential succession after House Speaker JOHN MCCORMACK (D-Mass.).

Hayden supported President Johnson on Medicare and Social Security issues. He also supported the creation of the national park system, the protection of national forests, educational and health programs for native Americans, and American cold war resistance to the Soviet Union. He also supported LBJ's civil rights program, although he did so only after Johnson agreed to his demand to support a central Arizona water project. Throughout the 1960s he was a leader in the fight to gain passage of legislation to provide southwestern states with water for land reclamation and irrigation. During this period he faced strong opposition from Senator THOMAS H. KUCHEL (R-Calif.) and other influential California legislators who believed such legislation would reduce the supply of water their state received from the Colorado River.

In 1967 the Senate passed the Central Arizona Project (CAP), but the House took no action on the measure. The next year Congress passed the $1.3 billion Colorado River Project, which included the Arizona project and other land reclamation legislation. The $892 million authorized for the Arizona project allocated water from the Colorado River to the arid but populous region around Phoenix and Tucson via a 400-mile series of dams and aqueducts. In addition to the water-diversion system, the bill also provided for a joint public-private thermal power plant.

*Congressional Quarterly* described the Colorado River Project as "the largest reclamation program ever authorized in a single piece of legislation." It was subjected to some of the most intense lobbying in Senate history. At the bill's signing on September 30, 1968, President Johnson took note of the architect of the legislation and declared a "Carl Hayden day."

Hayden declined to seek reelection in 1968. He returned to Arizona, where he died in January 1972 at the age of 94.

—FHM

## Hayden, Thomas (Emmett)

(1939– )   *radical, antiwar leader*

Hayden was born on December 11, 1939, in Royal Oak, Michigan. After attending parochial schools he went to the University of Michigan in 1957 on a tennis scholarship. Majoring in English, he became editor of the student paper, *The Michigan Daily*. He was largely apolitical, however, until 1960, when he was inspired by John F. Kennedy's presidential campaign. In May 1960 Hayden attended a civil rights conference sponsored by the recently revitalized Students for a Democratic Society (SDS), and that fall he helped organize VOICE, a University of Michigan student group affiliated with SDS that soon became its largest chapter.

After graduating from Michigan Hayden was hired in the fall of 1961 as one of two paid SDS field secretaries. Working out of Altanta, he wrote articles and a pamphlet, "Revolution in Mississippi," about the southern civil rights movement. Hayden himself was beaten in McComb, Mississippi, in October 1961, and that December he was arrested with 10 others in a Student Nonviolent Coordinating Committee (SNCC) effort to desegregate Albany, Georgia, transit facilities.

Hayden wrote the initial drafts of the manifesto produced by the June 1962 SDS convention at Port Huron, Michigan. The Port Huron Statement became the most widely known formulation of New Left ideology. "We, are people of this generation, bred in at least modest comfort, housed now in universities, looking uncomfortably to the world we inherit," the Port Huron Statement declared. At the same convention Hayden was elected to a one-year term as SDS president.

Hayden helped plan and carry out an SDS experiment in community organizing, the Economic Research and Action Project (ERAP), which began in September 1963 supported by a $5,000 donation from the United Auto Workers. The following summer Hayden himself joined an ERAP group in Newark, New Jersey. Attempting to apply SNCC tactics in the North, Hayden and other SDS members spent two years in a predominantly black Newark neighborhood trying to develop local organizations and community campaigns on a broad range of issues. The Newark project, the most successful and longest lasting ERAP effort, ended following the July 1967 Newark riots.

In December 1965 Hayden joined Professor STAUGHTON LYND and U.S. Communist Party theoretician Herbert Aptheker on a 10-day trip to North Vietnam. During a 90-minute interview, the North Vietnamese premier, Pham Van Dong, told the Americans that in spite of President Johnson's December 20 statement that the administration would knock on all doors in the quest for peace, the United States had made no direct contact with North Vietnam. Hayden was one of 41 Americans who attended a September 1967 conference with high-level representatives of the National Liberation Front of South Vietnam (NLF) in Bratislava, Czechoslovakia. At the conference the possibility of the release of American prisoners held by the NLF was discussed. After another trip to Hanoi the next month, Hayden returned to Indochina, and, in ceremonies in Phnom Penh, Cambodia, three American POWs were turned over to Hayden by a NLF representative on November 11 as an indication of sympathy with the American antiwar movement and with American blacks. (Two of the three prisoners were black.)

In January 1968 Hayden attended an International Cultural Congress in Havana. In April of that year, when students at Columbia University occupied campus buildings, Hayden came to the campus to lend his support and became a leader of students in one of the five occupied buildings, Mathematics Hall.

Hayden, along with other antiwar leaders, had come to believe that it was necessary to move from protests to active resistance, and, in June 1968, wrote, "What is certain is that we are moving towards power—power to stop the machine if it cannot be made to serve humane ends."

Hayden and Rennie Davis, another SDS leader, helped organize the August 1968 antiwar demonstrations at the Chicago Democratic National Convention as project directors for the National Mobilization Committee to End the War in Vietnam. Police attempts to disperse the demonstrators received worldwide publicity. According to Mobilization Committee chairman DAVID DELLINGER, the use of force by police and Hayden's belief that some form of violent resistance would be necessary combined to make Hayden "ambivalent" about the agreement among demonstration organizers that the protesters should remain nonviolent even if attacked. On August 29 Hayden told a Grant Park rally, "It may be that the era of organized, peaceful and orderly demonstrations is coming to an end and that other methods will be needed."

In March 1969 Hayden, Davis, Dellinger, and five others were indicted for conspiracy to incite a riot and crossing state lines to incite a riot in connection with the Chicago events. Their widely publicized trial ended with Hayden and four others convicted on one count, and the seven defendants and their two lawyers receiving prison terms for contempt of court. (The case of the eighth defendant, Black Panther leader BOBBY SEALE, had been severed from the trial earlier.) Both the convictions and the contempt sentences were eventually reversed. Hayden continued to be an important radical leader throughout the early 1970s and organized and led the Indochina Peace Campaign. He was elected to the California Assembly in 1982 and the state senate in 1992. He retired in 1999.

—JBF

## Hays, Wayne L(evere)

(1911–1989) *member of the House of Representatives*

Hays, who was born in Bannock, Ohio, on May 13, 1911, grew up in rural southeastern Ohio. After graduating from Ohio State University in 1933, he taught high school history and public speaking for several years in Flushing, Ohio. In 1939 he was elected mayor of Flushing and served three terms.

He also served one term (1941–42) in the Ohio Senate. In 1948, after two years as a county commissioner, Hays won election to the House of Representatives from Ohio's 18th Congressional District, a semi-rural area in the southeastern part of the state dominated by dairy farming, coal mining, and steel production.

Known in Congress for his abrasive personality and frequent verbal attacks on his colleagues, Hays first gained attention during the early 1950s for defending tax-exempt foundations against charges that they had communist connections. He remained a strong opponent of the House Un-American Activities Committee, which investigated allegedly subversive groups, through the mid-1960s. Hay also became active in fostering international contacts through his membership on the House Foreign Affairs Committee. He viewed the Fullbright-Hays Act of 1961, which expanded the international educational exchange program, as his most notable legislative achievement. As chair of the Foreign Affairs Subcommittee on State Department Organization and Foreign Operations, Hays made yearly trips to Europe during the 1960s to attend the parliamentarians' conference of the North Atlantic Treaty Organization. He was also a strong anticommunist and vehement critic of peace advocates during the Vietnam War.

Hays sponsored relatively little substantive legislation during his long congressional career, although he did play fairly significant roles in obtaining the passage of the 1961 foreign aid bill and cast a key vote on the 1964 farm bill, in order to gain concessions from the Johnson administration on other legislation. He concentrated instead on accumulating institutional power through his seniority and committee positions. Especially important in this respect was his membership on the House Administration Committee, which determined the budgets of all other House committees (except Appropriations) and oversaw the travel and office expenses of all representatives. During the mid-1960s Hays rose from third in seniority to senior Democrat on the committee. He was also chair of the Administration Subcommittee on Contracts, which played an important part in the 1966 investigation of spending irregularities on the staff of Representative ADAM CLAYTON POWELL, JR. (D-N.Y.). A report issued by Hays's subcommittee in January 1967 concluded that Powell had improperly placed his wife on the congressional payroll and that

Powell's staff members had charged personal travel expenses to the House Labor and Education Committee, of which Powell was chairman. The report was subsequently used by other representatives in an effort to strip Powell as chair of his committee and ultimately to unseat him.

Following the Powell investigation the Administration Committee received an increased budget and was assigned primary responsibility for investigating ethics violations in the House. Hays's subcommittee was enlarged and renamed the Subcommittee on Contracts and Ethics. Hays thus played a major role in both setting congressional budgets and determining whether they were misused.

During the late 1960s Hays began to use his growing power against other House committees and individual representatives whose actions he disliked. Opponents of the Vietnam War were likely to face funding cuts and increased scrutiny of their spending; in 1969 Hays halved the budget of a House Government Operations subcommittee that had compiled a report critical of the Johnson administration's land-reform policy in Vietnam. Hays's power—and his unpopularity in Congress—increased when he became chair of the Administration Committee in 1971. He gained a reputation as a "bully" who openly threatened representatives and congressional staff members. One representative referred to him as, "the meanest man in Congress." His aggressive behavior made him feared in the House, but it also frustrated his efforts to rise further; shortly after taking control of the Administration Committee, he lost a bid to become House majority leader.

One political observer noted in 1972 that "nothing short of a major scandal would depose Hays." Such a scandal occurred in 1976, when Elizabeth Ray, a member of Hays's staff, charged that Hays had kept her on the congressional payroll solely for her sexual services. In investigation revealed that Hays had hired Ray as a secretary, with a $14,000 annual salary, even though as she admitted, "I can't type, I can't file, I can't even answer the phone." Faced with charges similar to those he had investigated against others, Hays relinquished his committee positions at the urging of the House Democratic leadership. In September 1976 he resigned from Congress. He returned to Ohio, where he became a member of the Ohio House of Representatives until 1980. He died in Wheeling, West Virginia, on February 10, 1989.

—SLG

## Hearnes, Warren E(astman)
(1923–   ) *governor*

A native of southwestern Missouri who was born on July 27, 1923, and a graduate of the United States Military Academy, Hearnes served in the Missouri House of Representatives from 1951 to 1961. He was that body's majority floor leader from 1957 to 1961. In 1960 he was elected Missouri's secretary of state, and, in 1964, Hearnes upset the state's old-line Democratic Party hierarchy by defeating its candidate in the gubernatorial primary. Hearnes won the general election by 303,000 votes.

As a result of his defeat of the party's establishment, Hearnes entered office with considerable power. Between 1965 and 1968 he submitted 80 bills to the legislature. Only one, a measure designed to permit private school students to attend certain public school classes, failed to pass. Hearnes was able to increase expenditures by more than any other governor in Missouri's history, but spending remained below that of other states of roughly the same size.

His major achievement was to increase aid to local schools, which rose 161 percent during his eight-year tenure as governor. He also instituted a network of regional clinics for the mentally retarded and increased Missouri's spending for prisons and for mental and public health facilities. Hearnes established a toll-road authority to provide a source of revenue for the construction of new highways and launched an unprecedented building program that exceeded $150 million. He authorized state welfare aid to families with unemployed fathers living at home and secured public accommodations legislation. Hearnes also created a Department of Community Affairs, an Air Conservation Commission, and a state-financed council on the arts during his governorship. This expansion of state services was achieved without a state tax increase, although much of it would not have been possible without the increased levies obtained by his predecessor.

Hearnes was one of the first prominent Democrats to raise public doubts about President LYNDON B. JOHNSON's domestic programs. His relationship with the president quickly collapsed, and throughout his term he and Johnson fought about the appropriate role of the federal government in implementing reforms in the states. In July 1968 he responded to the assertion of JOHN GARDNER, chair of the Urban Coalition, that "a great deal more" federal spending would be needed to cure the problems of the cities. Hearnes argued that "we have jobs in my state, but you have people who won't go five miles to work, and they are the ones who are hollering loudest for welfare." In 1968 Hearnes became the first Missouri governor elected for a second term, winning the election with over 60 percent of the popular vote. Still, his fights with LBJ and his own political enemies took a toll, and he was less successful in passing legislation. After leaving office, he was defeated in a bid for the Senate, and he then served as the executive director for Southeast Missouri Legal Services. He retired in 1997.

—TJC

## Hébert, F(elix) Edward
### (1901–1979) *member of the House of Representatives*

Hébert was born in New Orleans on October 12, 1901, and was a newspaper journalist from 1918 to 1940. He helped expose corruption in the administration of Louisiana governor Richard W. Leche in 1939. Capitalizing on his reputation as a Democrat Hébert successfully ran for Congress from New Orleans's Congressional First district in 1940. In subsequent elections he faced little if any opposition. A member of the southern Democratic bloc, Hébert opposed liberal domestic programs and supported the 1948 presidential campaign of Senator STROM THURMOND (D-S.C.), who ran on the States' Rights Democratic ticket. As chair of the House Armed Services Special Investigations Subcommittee, Hébert led an investigation of Defense Department procurement procedures in 1951, and, in 1959, he probed defense industry use of retired officers as lobbyists and salespeople. Hébert, a strong supporter of the military, opposed the Kennedy administration's attempt to impose stronger civilian control over the Pentagon. He clashed with the administration over its 1962 effort to reorganize and reduce the National Guard and U.S. Army Reserve. In 1963 he supported the development of the RS-70 bomber, which the Department of Defense opposed.

In January 1964 testimony before the House Armed Services Committee, Secretary of Defense ROBERT S. MCNAMARA reasserted the administration policy stressing missile systems over piloted aircraft. In the 1965 defense procurement budget he requested only $5 million for the study of a new bomber to "follow on" the retirement of the exist-

ing fleet. However, Air Force chief of staff general CURTIS E. LEMAY publicly supported the "follow on" bomber, as did presidential candidate senator BARRY M. GOLDWATER (R-Ariz.), who made it a campaign issue. During the House debate in February 1964, Hébert praised LeMay and attacked McNamara for ignoring the judgment of professional military officers, saying "the beardless striplings of the whiz kids are superseding the judgment of the people who have devoted and dedicated their lives to the country in uniform." In the final budget, passed March 9, 1964, $52 million was included for the bomber project.

In 1966 McNamara and Hébert again clashed over the need for a new bomber when Hébert's subcommittee issued a report critical of McNamara's decision to phase out the B-52 and not develop a new strategic bomber. The secretary of defense charged that the report, which included heavily censored testimony, was "shockingly distorted," and that it incorrectly implied that McNamara was acting against the judgment of the Joint Chiefs of Staff.

Hébert and McNamara also clashed over the reorganization of Army reserve forces. On December 12, 1964, McNamara announced a plan to merge the Army Reserve into the National Guard and, at the same time, reduce their combined strength from 700,000 to 550,000. Under the plan reserve officers would have applied for new commissions from the guard, and high federal officials, including members of Congress, would have been barred from participation in ready reserve units. (Seventy-nine representatives were active reservists.)

Reservists immediately protested the McNamara plan, and Hébert criticized the secretary of defense for not consulting with Congress or seeking new legislation before ordering the reorganization. He charged that McNamara had "defied" the law and shown "contemptuous disregard of Congress." On May 15, 1965, the two men held a joint press conference to announce an agreement under which McNamara would delay the reorganization to allow time for congressional review and "supporting legislation." After three days of hearings that August, Hébert's subcommittee postponed consideration of the matter until the next year, effectively blocking the merger until then.

In 1966 McNamara again sought approval of the merger plan, and again he was temporarily blocked by congressional opposition. That July Hébert introduced a far-reaching reserve reorganization bill that permanently prevented any merger. In spite of administration opposition the bill finally passed Congress and became law in November 1967.

A strong supporter of the war in Vietnam, Hébert was an early advocate of bombing North Vietnam. The draft lottery system, proposed by President Johnson in March 1967 to counter criticism that the draft was being used as punishment for antiwar protestors, met with Hébert's vigorous opposition. When, during May 1967 hearings on the proposed draft system, Assistant Attorney General Fred M. Vinson, Jr., stated that the First Amendment fully protected people speaking against the draft, Hébert responded that in such cases he would "forget the First Amendment."

Hébert was an opponent of the Civil Rights Act of 1964 and the Voting Rights Act of 1965 as well as the War on Poverty and Model Cities programs. During hearings in August 1968 on the behavior of federal troops during the 1967 Detroit riots, Hébert criticized Lieutenant General John L. Throckmorton, commander of the federal units, for ordering National Guard troops to keep their weapons unloaded and to fire only if ordered by an officer. The next year Hébert called the report of the President's Advisory Committee on Civil Disorders "propaganda ad nauseum."

Hébert continued to advocate large military spending during the Nixon administration and in 1971 became the chair of the full Armed Services Committee. He was not a candidate for reelection in 1976 and returned to New Orleans, where he died on December 29, 1979.

—JBF

## Heller, Walter W(olfgang)
(1915–1987) *chair, Council of Economic Advisers*

Born in Buffalo, New York, on August 27, 1915, Heller earned a Ph.D. in economics from the University of Wisconsin and served in the tax research division of the Treasury Department during World War II. He left the Treasury in 1946 to teach economics at the University of Minnesota but took a leave of absence in 1947 to become chief of finance of the United States military government in Germany. Heller also supplemented his campus teaching with service as a consultant to the Treasury Department and the Minnesota Department of Tax-

ation. From 1955 to 1960 he was an economic adviser to Minnesota governor ORVILLE FREEMAN.

Appointed chair of President Kennedy's Council of Economic Advisers (CEA), Heller an influential advocate of Keynesian economics, which held that the federal government must engage in active fiscal stimulation of the economy in order to achieve rapid growth and full employment. Arguing that the economy was being hampered by insufficient aggregate demand caused by the "fiscal drag" of heavy taxation, Heller persuaded President Kennedy to propose a major tax cut to promote economic expansion. Kennedy's tax reform package, totalling a net reduction of $11.2 billion, passed the House in September 1963 but had not reached the Senate floor by the time of Kennedy's death in November.

The chief obstacle to the tax cut when President Johnson took office was Senator HARRY FLOOD BYRD (D-Va.), chair of the Senate Finance Committee and one of the leading fiscal conservatives in the Senate. An opponent of unbalanced budgets, Byrd agreed to relax his opposition to the tax cut only after Johnson promised that he would keep the federal budget under $100 billion. As signed into law February 26, 1964, the Revenue Act of 1964, among other provisions, reduced personal income tax rates from the existing range of 20 percent–91 percent to 14 percent–70 percent and cut the corporate income tax from 52 percent to 48 percent.

Under Heller the CEA also developed the first voluntary wage-price guidelines system. Heller left the CEA in November 1964 to resume teaching economics at the University of Minnesota. He continued to speak out on economic matters, criticizing the aluminum price rise in November 1965 as "unjustified," "inflationary," and not warranted by the industry's productivity and profit performance. The price rise was subsequently rescinded under heavy administration pressure. In 1966 and 1967 Heller endorsed a tax increase accompanied by an easing of monetary restraints. He was also the major spokesperson for a plan by which the federal government would restore a portion of income tax revenues to the states, which, unlike most federal grants-in-aid, would have "no strings attached." Heller had proposed this plan, later called "revenue-sharing" or the "Heller Plan," in June 1960 and again in 1964. President Johnson was reportedly enthusiastic about the plan but dropped it from his legislative program when news of it leaked prematurely to the press. Heller continued his unofficial advocacy of the idea throughout the Johnson and Nixon years. In October 1972 President Nixon signed into law a revenue-sharing bill appropriating $30.2 billion to the states over a five-year period. He remained at the University of Minnesota until his death in June 1987.

—TO

## Helms, Richard M(cGarrah)

(1913–2002) *deputy director for plans, deputy director, and director, Central Intelligence Agency*
Richard Helms, director of the Central Intelligence Agency (CIA) during the late 1960s and early 1970s, born on March 30, 1913, in St. David's Pennsylvania. After receiving his secondary education in Europe, Helms entered Williams College, where he graduated in 1935. For the next seven years he worked as a correspondent for the United Press and as advertising director of the *Indianapolis Times*. Commissioned a lieutenant in the navy in 1942, Helms was transferred to the Office of Strategic Services one year later. After his discharge in 1946 he remained in intelligence work and in 1947 helped organize the CIA.

During the 1950s and 1960s Helms became one of the CIA's key staff officers, working on covert operations and recruiting and training top agents. Helms was involved in the agency's illegal domestic surveillance operations, including the project to photograph and open overseas mail arriving in New York, and he took part in planning schemes to assassinate such foreign leaders as Patrice Lumumba and Fidel Castro.

From April 1965 until June 1966 Helms served as deputy director of the CIA under Admiral WILLIAM RABORN. Because Raborn had little experience in intelligence operations or foreign affairs, he relied heavily on his subordinate. During Raborn's term in office relations with other departments deteriorated and morale within the CIA declined. Reacting to criticism of the agency, President Johnson appointed Helms director in June 1966. The president hoped that the appointment of an experienced CIA executive would improve morale and would result in needed organizational and management reforms.

While Helms was director of the CIA the agency was involved in numerous projects designed to ensure the establishment and preservation of friendly foreign governments. For example a con-

gressional investigation in 1975 and 1976 revealed that the CIA had become deeply involved in Chilean domestic politics despite Helms's sworn testimony otherwise. During that country's 1964 presidential race the CIA underwrote slightly more than half of the cost of the Christian Democratic Party campaign and mounted a massive anticommunist propaganda drive designed to forestall the election of the Marxist candidate, Salvador Allende. The intervention enabled the moderate Christian Democrat, Eduardo Frei, who was unaware of CIA's action, to win a clear majority in the election instead of the expected plurality. In the five years following that election, the CIA conducted a variety of covert activities designed to strengthen Chile's moderate parties. These actions included monetary support of political and intellectual groups, establishment of leftist splinter parties to draw support away from Allende, and continued propaganda and liaison activities with Chile's internal security and intelligence services to meet any threat posed by leftists. The total cost of CIA involvement in Chile during those years was $2 million. CIA activity in Chile culminated in 1970, when President Nixon instructed Helms to attempt to prevent Allende from taking power after winning the election that year. The agency, therefore, supported a group of military plotters planning a coup. The plot collapsed in the fall of 1970.

During Helms's tenure the CIA was also involved in numerous domestic activities that were illegal under the agency's charter, which forbade CIA operations in the United States except to protect intelligence sources. Acting at the request of President Johnson, the CIA and FBI coordinated activities in 1966 to determine whether there was any foreign influence in the social protest movements of the late 1960s. Under the program the CIA, at the request of the FBI, investigated Americans traveling abroad, expanded its mail-opening operations to include leading black activists and Vietnam War dissenters, and supplied the FBI with a steady stream of unsolicited information.

Under continued White House pressure the CIA also developed its own Operation Chaos to investigate possible foreign links with domestic dissidents. Acting on the premise that to investigate foreign infiltration the agency had to know if each person in an organization had any connection with foreigners, the CIA amassed files on 10,000 U.S. citizens and groups and indexed 300,000 names in agency computer records. CIA officials realized that these activities were in violation of the agency's charter, and, in a February 1969 letter to HENRY KISSINGER, Helms cautioned that Chaos reports were to be kept top secret.

The CIA established two additional projects to monitor dissident groups. In 1967 the agency, citing the need to obtain early warning of protest demonstrations that might threaten its facilities, set up Project Merrimack to infiltrate Washington-based peace and black activist groups. That year it also established Project Resistance to obtain background intelligence information on campus radical groups. In each case the CIA collected general information on radical leadership, funding, and policies, as well as data on prospective demonstrations.

Throughout the 1950s and 1960s the CIA was involved in covert funding of academic and philanthropic organizations. This action remained virtually unknown until 1967, when *Ramparts* magazine disclosed CIA funding of the National Student Association. In response to the storm of criticism that followed, President Johnson organized a committee composed of Helms, Undersecretary of State NICHOLAS KATZENBACH, and Secretary of Health, Education and Welfare JOHN GARDNER to review the relationship between the agency and U.S. educational and voluntary groups with overseas operations. The committee report, made public on February 23, 1967, was not critical of CIA action. However, the panel recommended that federal agencies stop covert financial assistance to U.S. educational or private voluntary organizations and suggested that CIA funding of U.S.-based groups end by December 31, 1967. Although Johnson adopted the recommendations as policy, they were not issued as executive orders or enacted into law and so had no firm legal status.

The 1975 Senate Select Committee on Intelligence Activities reported that these recommendations had a profound effect on the CIA's clandestine operations. The agency withdrew support from a large number of organizations, transferred some projects to other sources of funding, and financed continuing efforts by giving key projects large grants before the December 1967 deadline, thus ensuring their existence for a number of years. Although the agency instituted a series of reforms, the Senate Committee found that these were "aimed at preventing further public disclosure which could jeopardize sensitive CIA operations. They did not

represent significant rethinking of where boundaries ought to be drawn in a free society."

Although President Johnson had appointed Helms director in the hope that he could carry out needed reforms of the intelligence community, little progress was made in making the organizations more efficient or in preventing their continued expansion. Uninterested in management, Helms did not attempt to coordinate the activities of the intelligence agencies. In addition, the politically astute director realized that because he was not of cabinet rank, he lacked the power to make changes opposed by the State Department or the Pentagon.

In 1967 and 1968 Helms commissioned studies of the CIA and federal intelligence activities. They found that the various intelligence agencies were duplicating one another's efforts. Much of the information gathered was useless and merely served to obscure more important data, according to these reports. Helms, however, did not press for reform, fearing that to do so would risk Pentagon hostility and jeopardize funding for covert operations with which he was particularly concerned.

Shortly after the 1972 election Helms was replaced as CIA director, ostensibly because of his failure to institute the needed reforms. Helms had also not endeared himself to President Nixon by refusing to be intimidated into helping to cover up the Watergate break-in. Helms was appointed ambassador to Iran in January 1973. He remained in Iran until 1977 and then returned to the United States as a consultant. He died in Washington, D.C., on October 22, 2002.

—EWS

## Henry, Aaron E(dd)

(1922–1997) *president, Mississippi Conference of Branches of the NAACP; president, Council of Federated Organizations*

Henry was born in Coahoma County, Mississippi, on July 2, 1922, and grew up in Clarksdale, Mississippi. He opened a drugstore there after receiving a degree in pharmacy from Xavier University in 1950. Two years later he organized and became president of the Clarksdale branch of the NAACP. In 1960 he was named president of the state Conference of NAACP Branches and was arrested in 1961 for participating in the Freedom Rides, organized by the Congress of Racial Equality. It was the first of 38 arrests for Henry, all in the name of advancing the cause of civil rights. That same year he organized a boycott of stores in the Clarksdale, Mississippi, area that refused to hire black workers and discriminated against black customers. He and six others were arrested, although the charges were later dropped. Henry concentrated his efforts on securing voting rights for Mississippi blacks, especially after the Council of Federated Organizations (COFO) was established in the spring of 1962. A coalition of the NAACP and other civil rights groups in the state, COFO was set up to conduct a unified voter registration campaign in Mississippi. As COFO president, Henry helped organize voter registration projects, often in the face of repeated harassment and arrest. He ran for governor in the November 1963 "Freedom Ballot," a mock election sponsored by COFO to demonstrate the magnitude of black disfranchisement in Mississippi. Some 80,000 blacks voted in the election.

COFO organized the 1964 Mississippi Freedom Summer Project, an undertaking that brought over 1,000 volunteers into the state to set up community centers, teach in "Freedom Schools," and work on voter registration. The main vehicle for political work was the Mississippi Freedom Democratic Party (MFDP), founded at a statewide convention in April 1964 and intended as an alternative to the segregationist regular Democratic Party in the state. Henry was temporary chair of the new party at the convention and worked during the summer on the "freedom registration," which enrolled over 60,000 people as party members. In August Henry presided at a second MFDP state convention, which selected a 68-member delegation to send to the Democratic National Convention meeting later in the month. Henry was chair of the group that traveled to Atlantic City to challenge the seating of Mississippi's regular delegation.

The MFDP challenge posed an explosive dilemma to Democratic Party leaders. Through Vice President HUBERT HUMPHREY and former Pennsylvania governor David Lawrence, President Johnson proposed to split both Mississippi delegations and divide their votes equally. The MFDP rejected this proposal and in the next three days won support from many liberal Democrats. Henry, FANNIE LOU HAMER, and other MFDP delegates described Mississippi conditions to the Convention Credentials Committee. A proposal offered by Representative EDITH GREEN (D-Ore.) to effectively oust the Mississippi regulars and replace them with

the MFDP delegation was defeated when Johnson expressed his opposition.

Finally on August 25 Humphrey and United Auto Workers president WALTER REUTHER proposed another compromise offering to seat as regular delegates Henry and the Reverend Edwin King, a white minister active in the MFDP. The rest of the delegation was to be seated as "honored guests." King and Henry favored the proposal, and the Credentials Committee quickly adopted the Humphrey-Reuther plan, but the MFDP delegation as a whole voted against the compromise. Aided by sympathetic delegates from other states, MFDP members made their way into the convention seats reserved for the Mississippi regulars. In the end the fight over the MFDP at the convention left many civil rights activists embittered with both Democratic Party liberals and their own more moderate leaders like Henry.

In the fall of 1964 Henry was one of four candidates nominated by the MFDP to run for Congress. When the state election commission ruled that the candidates could not be included on the regular ballot, the MFDP organized an independent November election in which Henry received nearly 37,000 votes in his district. The MFDP then challenged the seating of Mississippi's five regular representatives in Congress in January 1965 and asked that its representatives be seated instead. The national NAACP favored a congressional investigation of Mississippi elections but did not endorse the MFDP's effort to seat its own members in Congress. Probably because of this, Henry was the only one of the MFDP candidates who did not join the congressional challenge. The challenge was eventually rejected by the House in September 1965, by a 228-143 vote.

In April 1965 the national office of the NAACP said it was officially withdrawing from COFO. Henry, who had been elected to the NAACP's national board of directors in January, joined in the announcement. Except for Henry's key role, the NAACP had not been heavily involved in COFO. The organization had been staffed primarily by members of the Student Nonviolent Coordinating Committee (SNCC), and the NAACP decided to end its affiliation in 1965, apparently because SNCC was becoming more radical and because policy-making differences appeared in COFO.

Henry remained active in voter registration work, however. Following passage of the federal

Voting Rights Act in August 1965, the NAACP, led by Henry and state field secretary CHARLES EVERS, took advantage of the law to step up registration efforts among Mississippi blacks. While Henry repeatedly called for more federal examiners and for a stronger federal effort in the state, the NAACP's registration drive helped increase the proportion of voting-age blacks registered to vote from 6.7 percent in 1964 to 32.9 percent in 1966. Henry and Evers continually expanded their program, and, in 1967, 12 blacks won election to state offices in Mississippi.

After the regular state Democratic Party chose only four African Americans to be part of its 68-member delegation to he 1968 Democratic National Convention, Henry again helped organize a challenge delegation, the Loyal Democrats of Mississippi. He was elected state chair of a biracial coalition, which included the NAACP, the MFDP, the state Teachers' Association, and the state AFL-CIO, among others. The Loyal Democrats delegation to the convention won the endorsement of all the major contenders for the Democratic presidential nomination. With Henry as its chair, the insurgent delegation presented its case to the Credentials Committee, which voted overwhelmingly to unseat the regular delegation and give all of Mississippi's convention seats to the challengers.

In February 1969 Henry became a member of a national party committee, headed by Senator GEORGE S. MCGOVERN (D-S.Dak.), charged with reviewing delegate selection procedures and other rules for the 1972 Democratic National Convention. He ran for a seat in the state legislature in 1971 but lost the election by about 400 votes. Henry became a member of the Democratic National Committee in 1972 and was state campaign manager for the party in that year's presidential election. He co-chaired the Mississippi delegation at the Democratic National Convention in 1976 and was elected to the Mississippi House of Representatives six year later. He retired in 1996 and died in Mississippi the next year.

—CAB

## Hershey, Lewis B(laine)

(1893–1977) *director, U.S. Selective Service system*

Lewis B. Hershey, a career army officer, served as director of the Selective Service under all presidents from Franklin Roosevelt to RICHARD NIXON. Born in Steuben County, Indiana, on September 12, 1893, Hershey served in Europe during World War I as a member of the National Guard and entered the regular army in 1920. He became secretary and executive officer of the Joint Army and Navy Selective Service Committee from 1936 to 1940. Following the enactment of draft legislation in 1940, President Franklin D. Roosevelt appointed him deputy director then, in 1941, director of the Selective Service System. In that later position, Hershey was responsible for planning the system under which millions of American men were inducted into the armed forces to fight in World War II, Korea, and Vietnam.

During the late 1960s Hershey was the target of intense criticism by members of the antiwar movement, who charged that he encouraged local draft boards to punish students protesting U.S. involvement in Vietnam by nullifying their deferments, thereby making them liable for immediate induction into the armed forces. In the fall of 1965, 10 University of Michigan students convicted of trespassing in an October 15 sit-in demonstration at the Ann Arbor draft board were declared delinquent by the board and reclassified 1-A. The decision was widely denounced. "The draft," said Representative EMANUEL CELLER (D-N.Y.), "was never intended to be used as a vehicle of castigation." Hershey stated that protesting U.S. policy in Vietnam was not in itself a cause for reclassification but that "deliberate illegal obstruction of the administration of the [draft] law by registrants cannot be tolerated." He made this policy explicit in an October 26, 1967, letter to local draft boards, urging that registrants violating draft laws be drafted as soon as possible. Before issuing the letter Hershey stated that he had consulted with the White House. On January 19, 1970, the U.S. Supreme Court, in a unanimous decision, ruled that the Selective Service lacked the authority to speed up the induction of men who violated draft regulations.

In several appearances before congressional committees, Hershey defended the system that he had helped plan. In June 1966 he came before the House Armed Services Committee to answer charges that the draft discriminated against those who could not be deferred because they were too poor to attend college. Hershey defended the deferment system, asserting that the United States "paced the world in technological advance" because thousands of men had been granted deferments to receive training as scientists and engineers. Hershey pointed out that 56 percent of those who entered college eventually entered military service, compared to only 46 percent of those who did not attend college. Hershey did, however, favor a change in the law, making it possible to draft men 26 to 34 to eliminate the temptation to stay in college to escape military duty.

Important changes were made in the way the Selective Service system operated in the late 1960s. Although Hershey had long opposed a draft lottery, because it would reduce the discretionary powers of local draft boards, he acquiesced in President Johnson's order to devise such a system in March 1967. Appearing before a congressional subcommittee that month, Hershey announced his opposition to the lottery, but stated, "When the quarterback calls the signals that is the way I play them."

In February 1968 Hershey announced another major change in the draft law. Speaking on behalf of the National Security Council, Hershey abolished all deferments for graduate students except for those in medicine and dentistry or for those who had completed two or more years of graduate study by June 1968.

Because of the growing unpopularity of the draft, Hershey became an inviting target for politicians running on an antiwar platform. Senator EUGENE MCCARTHY (D-Minn.), campaigning in the spring of 1968 for the Democratic presidential nomination, charged that Hershey, like FBI director J. EDGAR HOOVER, had grown so powerful that he was beyond the reach of public control. Vice President HUBERT HUMPHREY, the Democratic presidential nominee, in the fall also declared that he would replace Hershey as head of Selective Service. When Lyndon Johnson held his final news conference at the National Press Club, he jokingly told reporters that he had asked Hershey, "to get in touch immediately with each of you."

In February 1970 Hershey stepped down as director to become an adviser to President Richard M. Nixon on personnel mobilization. Secretary of Defense MELVIN R. LAIRD announced the end of the draft three years later. Hershey, 79, a four-star general and the oldest man on active duty, retired in March 1973. He died on May 20, 1977, in Angola, Indiana.

—JLW

## Hesburgh, Theodore M(artin)

(1917–   ) *president, University of Notre Dame; member, Civil Rights Commission*

Born in Syracuse, New York, on May 25, 1917, and ordained a Roman Catholic priest in 1943, Father Hesburgh taught theology at Notre Dame before becoming the school's president in 1952. He upgraded the academic reputation of Notre Dame, long famous for its football teams, and secularized its faculty and administration. Under his stewardship the campus more than tripled in size and doubled in enrollment. Active in national education circles, Hesburgh was appointed by President DWIGHT D. EISENHOWER to the newly formed United States Commission on Civil Rights (CRC) in November 1957.

In the early 1960s he was one of the most vocal members of the CRC in urging the adoption of comprehensive civil rights legislation. He also furthered the Catholic Church's ecumenical movement by working with representatives of other religious groups on an international as well as a national level.

During the Johnson administration Hesburgh served on a large number of boards and committees beside the CRC, including the National Science Board and the President's General Advisory Committee on Foreign Assistance. He was a trustee of the Rockefeller Foundation and the Carnegie Foundation for the Advancement of Teaching. He also served as permanent Vatican City representative to the International Atomic Energy Agency in Vienna from 1956 to 1970. However, Hesburgh remained best known for his work on the CRC.

While the early period of government-sponsored civil rights activity concentrated on discrimination against U.S. citizens, particularly blacks, Hesburgh brought the condition of Mexican migrant workers to national attention in December 1968. Serving as acting chair of the CRC, he issued a report asserting that Mexicans working in the lower Rio Grande valley of Texas received low wages and were forced to live under conditions of "near slavery" or "peonage." The report criticized the state police and officials of Starr County for assisting local employers in breaking migrant workers' efforts to organize. The employment of migrants also left a large number of local citizens unemployed.

Hesburgh took a "hard line" against the campus disorders of the late 1960s. At a conference on racism sponsored by the National Student Association at Notre Dame in December 1968, Hesburgh met with student leaders. The students, admitting that Hesburgh had accomplished much in fighting racism in the United States, charged that his approach was not sufficiently radical and that he had done little to deal with the problem at Notre Dame. Not only were there too few black students at the school, they claimed, but maintenance of the U.S. Army's Reserve Officer Training Corps (ROTC) on campus contributed indirectly to furthering a "racist" war in Vietnam. Hesburgh did not agree with the students' logic and insisted that ROTC would remain a part of the Notre Dame curriculum.

In February 1969 Hesburgh announced a "get-tough" policy for dealing with possible campus disorders at Notre Dame, which earned the praise of President RICHARD NIXON. Named chair of the CRC in March 1969, Hesburgh later came into conflict with the president over Nixon's policy of "benign neglect" in the civil rights field. Angered by Nixon's use of busing as a campaign issue, Hesburgh resigned his post in November 1972 following the president's reelection. In 1979 he was appointed ambassador to the 1979 UN Conference on Science and Technology for Development by President Carter, becoming the first priest to serve in an official diplomatic role for the United States. He resigned from Notre Dame in 1987, and, seven years later, he became the first priest to serve as an overseer at Harvard University, where he remained until his 1996 retirement.

—JCH

## Hickenlooper, Bourke B(lakemore)
(1896–1971) *member of the Senate*

Born in Blockton, Iowa, on July 21, 1896, and a former state legislator and Iowa governor, Hickenlooper served in the Senate from 1945 until his retirement in 1969. While in Congress Hickenlooper compiled what the *New York Times* described as a "moderately conservative" voting record. During the 1950s and 1960s the senator supported defense, business, and military assistance bills as well as most civil rights legislation. In the 1950s he was a defender of Senator Joseph McCarthy, although more because of the political advantage he gave to the Republicans than out of a genuine ideological affinity. Hickenlooper opposed many foreign aid bills and in 1962 successfully added a controversial

amendment to a foreign aid measure that prohibited aid to countries that did not reimburse Americans for property they had nationalized.

Reflecting the strongly held work ethic of many of his constituents, Hickenlooper voted against such domestic welfare measures as aid to education, Medicare, and the Johnson administration's antipoverty program. From 1966 to 1968 the liberal Americans for Democratic Action gave Hickenlooper a rating of zero percent. Hickenlooper was a supporter of the war in Vietnam, although a critic of the way President Johnson was conducting it. Hickenlooper charged the president with not doing enough to win a military victory. In 1964 he cosponsored the Gulf of Tonkin Resolution, although he claimed that the president needed no such endorsement from Congress to respond militarily, and, in 1968, he urged LBJ not to order a bombing pause.

Many conservatives strongly opposed the Soviet-American consular treaty of 1967 because they felt that the establishment of Soviet consulates would increase the possibilities of Soviet espionage and correspondingly complicate the job of the FBI in controlling such activities. Hickenlooper, the ranking minority member of the Senate Foreign Relations Committee, initially opposed the treaty but changed his position before the vote. As chair of the Republican Policy Committee, he worked to maintain Republican support for the Johnson administration's policy in Vietnam. He retired in 1969 and returned to Iowa. He died in Shelter Island, New York, on September 4, 1971.

—EWS

## Hill, Herbert
(1924–2004) *labor secretary, NAACP*

Born on January 24, 1924, in New York City, Hill left New York University in the 1940s to become a union organizer among steel workers. He began to work for the NAACP in 1948 and became the organization's labor secretary in 1951. He also served as a consultant to Representative ADAM CLAYTON POWELL, JR., (D-N.Y.) on the House Labor and Education Committee.

Beginning in the late 1950s Hill pressed both big business and big labor to give black workers greater access to the job market, especially through training programs leading to skilled work. He demanded that the Kennedy administration enforce fair hiring practices among defense contractors, and he pressured many of these companies into promising racial equality in employment. Hill also attacked a number of labor unions, including the International Ladies Garment Workers Union, for restricting minority membership in the higher-paying skilled locals.

As the job market continued to expand during the mid-1960s, Hill increased his efforts to gain what he viewed as a fair share of employment for minority workers. In 1964 and 1966 he led protest campaigns against promotion practices at General Motors and U.S. Steel. The entertainment industry also became a target of Hill's criticism, both for discriminating against black actors and technicians and for portraying blacks in terms of "outworn stereotypes." Hill's main conflict of this period, however,

was with the labor unions, particularly those in the highly skilled and high-paying construction industry.

Hill repeatedly attacked the building trades unions for restricting minority membership. With the expansion of housing construction in the 1960s, civil rights groups demanded the creation of training programs designed to qualify blacks for apprenticeships and, eventually, for full-fledged construction jobs. This clashed, however, with the desire of many union officials to limit entry into their trades, both to maintain wages and to minimize unemployment in the event of a slump. In response to this practice, civil rights leaders called for a reform of union hiring-hall practices and, failing this, public supervision of apprenticeship programs. Union leaders in turn viewed these demands as an assault on union

NAACP leaders holding a poster against racial bias in Mississippi; from left to right: Henry Moon, Roy Wilkins, Herbert Hill, and Thurgood Marshall, 1956 *(Library of Congress, Prints and Photographs Division)*

independence, reminiscent of earlier attempts at "union-busting."

Hill used several tactics in attempting to gain concessions from union leaders. In 1963 he led a nationwide campaign of sit-ins and demonstrations at publicly funded construction projects that did not meet NAACP standards of fair employment. This campaign, continuing into the late 1960s, was sometimes marked by violence. Hill also sued to block public funds from projects that refused to change their hiring practices, and he filed complaints with the Equal Employment Opportunity Commission against a number of unions for maintaining segregated locals.

All this effort, however, did not bring proportionate results. An NAACP suit to halt state- and city-supported construction in New York failed in 1963. The same year civil rights groups in Cleveland signed an agreement with the local plumbers' union, intended to increase black membership in apprentice programs, but Hill withdrew the NAACP and Urban League from the pact in 1966, claiming that the union continued to discriminate against blacks. A "biracial screening committee," set up encourage minority employment in the New York building trades, also collapsed after a short time. One consequence of Hill's agitation was an effort by national union leaders to increase minority membership by "voluntary" means, such as disseminating information on training programs. Both the AFL-CIO and the Alliance for Labor Action, comprising the Teamsters and United Auto Workers, endorsed this approach in the late 1960s. However, Hill dismissed such programs as ineffectual "tokenism" in the absence of "sanctions, time-tables and enforcement apparatus."

Hill's activity with the NAACP during the 1960s helped loosen the traditional alliance between civil rights groups and labor. "I have given up long ago trying to satisfy Herbie Hill," stated AFL-CIO president GEORGE MEANY at the height of the labor–civil rights conflict. In response to labor criticism, Hill wrote that "you must create a crisis to get something done." Most observers thought his efforts important in making the problem of job discrimination a major civil rights issue during the Johnson years. He also authored an *NAACP Labor Manual* that analyzed workplace discrimination and offered advice to African Americans about how to respond effectively, which became so popular among NAACP chapters that it ensured the perpetuation of his ideas long after he stepped down as secretary.

Hill also promoted the development of black literature in the United States. He edited and introduced two volumes of writings by black authors: *Soon, One Morning: New Writing by American Negroes* (1963), and *Anger and Beyond: The Negro Writer in the United States* (1966). Hill turned to teaching later in his career and became a professor at the University of Wisconsin. He died on August 15, 2004.

—SLG

## Hill, Lister
### (1894–1984) *member of the Senate*

Hill, who was born on December 29, 1894, came from a wealthy family that dominated the politics of Montgomery, Alabama, where his father was a prominent surgeon. In 1923, after serving as president of the Montgomery Board of Education, Hill won a special election to fill a vacant seat in the U.S. House of Representatives. In the House Hill supported New Deal programs, particularly the Tennessee Valley Authority, which played a crucial role in promoting the economic growth of northern Alabama. He ran for a vacant Senate seat in 1937 as an ally of President Roosevelt and with urban and labor support, he defeated his right-wing opponent, who reflected the views of the Ku Klux Klan.

After World War II Hill's primary legislative interests were in the areas of medicine and mental health. His major legislative accomplishment was the Hill-Burton Act of 1946, which provided federal grants for hospital construction and which Congress extended and expanded in subsequent decades. Hill became chair of the Senate Labor and Welfare Committee in 1955. In that post and as chair of the Appropriations Committee's subcommittee for health and welfare agencies, he was able to substantially increase federal health expenditures.

In 1956 he also signed the "Southern Manifesto," which pledged to utilize "all lawful means" to resist the school integration ordered by the Supreme Court in *Brown v. Board of Education, Topeka, Kansas.*

Hill narrowly averted an electoral defeat at the hands of a conservative Republican in 1962. From that year onward he adjusted his voting record to conform more closely to the views of his rural and more conservative constituents by opposing social welfare measures primarily directed at the problems of urban groups.

During the Johnson years Hill supported such rurally oriented programs as the Appalachia aid bill in 1965 and a 1966 bill to provide federal planning grants for the establishment of rural community development districts. But he voted against the housing and urban development bill of 1965, a rent supplement bill for low-income families in 1966, and the 1967 Demonstration Cities bill. In addition, Hill opposed repeal of the "right-to-work" clause of the Taft-Hartley Act in 1965 and a minimum wage bill in 1966.

Hill consistently opposed the Johnson administration's civil rights measures. In 1964 he led one of the three platoons established by southern Democratic senators to filibuster against the president's civil rights bill. Two years later he participated in Senate debate over school desegregation guidelines issued by the Department of Health, Education and Welfare under the 1964 Civil Rights Act, stating that the guidelines established racial quotas contrary to the provisions of that law. In 1967 Hill held up the Teacher Corps bill in his Labor and Welfare Committee until the Senate killed the president's open housing bill in September.

Hill continued to press for health legislation in the mid-1960s. In 1965 he offered an amendment to a supplemental appropriations bill to provide educational funds for the deaf. The following year Hill introduced an administration bill granting new authority to plan public health services on the state level, and he successfully offered an amendment to the measure specifying that state health services must be established and maintained for persons confined to mental institutions. In 1967, as chair of the Appropriations Committee's Health and Welfare Subcommittee, he proposed an appropriations bill amendment increasing Public Health Service funds for the treatment of chronic diseases. The Lister Hill Center at the National Institutes of Health, which he helped create, was named for him in 1968.

Over the years Hill was the leader of successful efforts to retain the essentially rural orientation of the Hill-Burton Act, which was designed primarily to fund the construction of hospitals in the countryside rather than the modernization of old, urban hospitals. A series of Hill-Burton amendments supported by Hill in 1964 provided greater assistance for city facilities but was criticized as insufficient by a number of health officials. In 1967 Hill agreed to meet many of the needs of urban hospitals, but no action was taken in 1967 or 1968 pending a report of the President's National Advisory Commission on Health Facilities.

In January 1968, at the age of 73, Hill announced that he would not run for reelection, and the following year he retired to Montgomery. He died of pneumonia in Montgomery on December 21, 1984.

—MLL

## Hoff, Philip H(enderson)
### (1924–   ) governor

Born on June 29, 1924, in Greenfield, Massachusetts, Hoff was a lawyer and former Democratic precinct worker who served in the Vermont House of Representatives from 1961 to 1962. He faced no primary opposition in his 1962 gubernatorial bid. His opponent in the general election, incumbent governor F. Ray Keyser, Jr., was hampered in his reelection attempt by his failure to reduce the income tax and increase state funding of local schools. Despite Vermont's reputation at the time as a national stronghold of conservative Republicanism, Hoff defeated Keyser by 1,348 votes, becoming the state's first Democratic governor in 109 years. He was reelected in 1964 and again in 1966.

During his tenure as governor Hoff promoted the growth of the state's economy by attracting new electronics industry, building highways, and expanding the winter ski-resort and summer-home businesses. Much of this expansion was attributable to Hoff's successful venture in importing two-million kilowatts of low-cost electrical power from Canada. Hoff termed this 1966 arrangement, in a state where power rates were the highest in the country, "New England's opportunity of the century." He also oversaw a dramatic expansion of the size and role of the state government; during his tenure the state budget grew by 116 percent and federal receipts rose by 191 percent. He also established the Vermont Commission on Women, to advance the rights of the women of the state.

In December 1966 President Johnson appointed Hoff to the Public Land Law Review Commission to study the nation's public land laws, practices, and problems. The commission's report, issued after five years of study, was termed by the New York Times "a predictable . . . tapestry of compromise." Shortly after the March 1968 Kerner

Commission report had predicted the increasing polarization of American society along racial lines, Hoff and New York City mayor JOHN V. LINDSAY developed a New York–Vermont summer project that brought black and white children from inner-city neighborhoods to Vermont homes for an experiment in interracial living.

In March 1968 Hoff became the first governor to give his unequivocal support to Senator ROBERT F. KENNEDY's (D-N.Y.) presidential bid. Two months after the assassination of Kennedy, Hoff transferred his support to Senator EUGENE MCCARTHY (D-Minn.) and helped draft the minority Vietnam peace plank at the 1968 Democratic National Convention. In September 1968 Hoff announced that he would not seek reelection. He won the Democratic nomination for the U.S. Senate in September 1970 but was defeated as Senator Winston L. Prouty (R-Vt.) captured his third term by winning 59 percent of the vote. He later served as chair of the state Democratic Party, and, in the 1980s, he won a seat in the state senate.

—TJC

## Hoffa, James R(iddle)

(1913–1975) *president, International Brotherhood of Teamsters, Chauffeurs, Warehousemen and Helpers of America*

Hoffa, who was born on February 14, 1913, in Brazil, Indiana, left school at 15 to help support his family. He soon became involved in union activity among freight handlers in Detroit; by 1931 he had gained control of Teamsters Local 299, the largest local in the union. During the 1940s Hoffa held a series of positions in the Michigan organization of the International Brotherhood of Teamsters (IBT) and managed the Central States Drivers Council, which organized long-haul truck drivers in the Midwest. In 1952 he became an international vice president of the IBT when his ally, Dave Beck, took control of the union. With a firm power base in the South and Midwest and growing influence in the East, Hoffa soon became the strongest of the union vice presidents. When indictment for tax fraud and embezzlement forced Beck's resignation in 1957, Hoffa succeeded him as president of the 1.5 million member IBT, the nation's largest union.

During the early and mid-1960s Hoffa worked to increase his authority over the traditionally autonomous regional Teamsters leaders. Local offi-

cials were encouraged to "call Jimmy" for strike authorization and financial support, bypassing the union's area joint councils and regional offices. IBT conventions in 1961 and 1966 approved changes in the union's constitution that increased Hoffa's power at the expense of local as well as area leaders. Such centralization enabled Hoffa, who had helped to introduce areawide trucking contracts in the 1940s, to press for the first national contract in the trucking industry. This agreement was signed in January 1964, bringing improved fringe benefits for Teamsters and a wage increase of about 8 percent over three years.

The IBT prospered under Hoffa, growing in size to more than 2 million members in the late 1960s. But his methods provoked internal opposition. Most of the union's vice presidents disliked Hoffa's unwillingness to delegate authority and his strict control over their own activity; several resigned in 1964. Automobile haulers in a number of eastern cities struck in June of that year against the national trucking contract, the provisions of which they disliked. Philadelphia Teamsters were especially rebellious. A truckers' strike began there against Hoffa's resistance in June 1965, and a Philadelphia local of the IBT sued to block payment of Hoffa's personal expenses from the union treasury. Reports of dissension within the union continued during the following years despite official denials.

More important to Hoffa at this time, however, were his legal difficulties. Because of reported connections between the IBT and organized crime, Justice Department officials had been watching him closely since the early 1950s. In 1961 the Senate Permanent Investigations Subcommittee accused Hoffa of misusing union funds and helping racketeers take control of a New York Teamsters local.

The following year government efforts to convict Hoffa on charges of taking "shakedown" payments from employers ended in a mistrial in Nashville, Tennessee; but in March 1964 he was found guilty of jury-tampering in the Nashville trial. Four months later another jury convicted him of fraud and misappropriation of union funds to finance a Florida land-development project. The two verdicts resulted in sentences totaling 13 years in prison. Hoffa spent much of his time in the mid-1960s fighting these convictions. The Supreme Court rejected his last appeal in December 1966, with Chief Justice EARL WARREN dissenting and condemning the government's use of an informant to gain the jury-tampering conviction.

Hoffa began serving his sentence in the Lewisburg Federal Penitentiary in March 1967, in the midst of negotiations for renewal of the national trucking contract. Control of the IBT passed to FRANK FITZSIMMONS, a loyal assistant of Hoffa who had been chosen general vice president in 1966. Hoffa did not immediately resign the union presidency, and there was speculation that he continued to control the IBT from prison. He made several unsuccessful attempts to gain release on parole. In June 1971 Hoffa finally resigned his several Teamsters offices, allowing Fitzsimmons to be elected president one month later. The following December he was pardoned and released from prison by President Nixon, with whom Fitzsimmons had established close ties. The terms of his release, however, prevented Hoffa from engaging in union activity until the end of his sentence in 1980.

In July 1975 Hoffa disappeared from a restaurant parking lot in Bloomfield Hills, Michigan, evidently a murder victim, at a time when he was planning to reenter Teamster politics. His body was never found, and, in 1983, he was declared legally dead.

—SLG

## Hoffer, Eric

### (1902–1983) *longshoreman, philosopher*

Longshoreman-philosopher Eric Hoffer was a popular thinker on current issues and a controversial celebrant of the American way of life. Born on July 25, 1902, in the Bronx, New York, Hoffer was blind from age seven to 15 after an accident. He became a voracious reader after regaining his sight but had had little formal education when he left New York for California in 1920. For the next two decades Hoffer worked as a migrant farm laborer and at times as a dishwasher, lumberjack, and gold prospector, reading extensively in his spare time. In 1943 he began steady work as a longshoreman on the San Francisco docks.

Hoffer won wide acclaim in 1951 with the publication of his first book, *The True Believer: Thoughts on the Nature of Mass Movements*. In this study of political fanaticism, Hoffer characterized the "true believer" as "a guilt-ridden hitchhiker who thumbs a ride on every cause from Christianity to Communism." In his description, fanaticism came from lack of self-confidence, which drove people to search for something to hold dear that was not a part of themselves. He continued to write in his spare time, publishing in 1955 *The Passionate State of Mind*, a collection of 300 epigrams, and in 1963 *The Ordeal of Change*, a series of essays whose central theme was that drastic social change was a profoundly disturbing experience and the dominant fact of modern life.

Hoffer's writings during the 1960s were collected in another slim volume, *The Temper of Our Time* (1967). In his familiar aphoristic style he voiced opinions on a range of subjects he had covered before: the role of the juvenile mentality in the making of history, idleness and creativity, and the relationship between intellectuals and the masses. Hoffer excoriated the "intellectual" for "loathing of the common man" and hostility toward America. "Rule by intellectuals," he wrote, "unavoidably approaches a colonial regime."

The most controversial essay was "The Negro Revolution," originally published in November 1964. Hoffer's sweeping denunciation of black activism earned him a storm of criticism from African Americans and liberals. "The Negro revolution is a fraud," he declared. "It has no faith in the character and potentialities of the Negro masses. . . . It wants cheap victories and the easy way." He added, "Individual achievement cannot cure the Negro's soul. . . . That which corrodes the soul of the Negro in his monstrous inner agreement with the prevailing prejudice against him." He criticized black nationalism and emphasized that "community building" was the only means by which African Americans could attain a desirable identity.

Hoffer developed a well-publicized relationship of mutual admiration with President Johnson. Hoffer vigorously supported the Vietnam War and frequently praised Johnson, whom he predicted would be "the foremost president of the 20th century." The president invited Hoffer to the White House for a half-hour talk in October 1967. In June 1968 Johnson appointed him to the National Commission on the Causes and Prevention of Violence, where his disagreements with other members attracted widespread attention. He challenged sympathetic accounts of black rage and frustration in inner cities and asserted that African Americans could do more to help themselves. Commission member Judge A. Leon Higginbotham attacked Hoffer's stand as being based on racism. In December 1969 Hoffer joined the commission's seven-to-six majority that condemned all massive civil disobedience, including nonviolent action.

In May 1968 Hoffer became a sponsor of the National Citizens for Humphrey Committee. He continued to write and speak out until his death on May 21, 1983. His ninth book, an autobiography, was published shortly after his death.

—TO

## Hoffman, Abbie
### (1936–1989) *antiestablishment leader*

Hoffman, who was born on November 30, 1936, in Worcester, Massachusetts, was expelled from high school at 17 for striking a teacher. Yet he managed to complete his secondary education and to attend Brandeis University, from which he graduated in 1959. He received an M.A. in psychology from the University of California, Berkeley, in 1960 and went to work as a psychologist at a Massachusetts state hospital. Hoffman was an early adherent of the New Left, working on H. Stuart Hughes's Massachusetts senatorial peace campaign in 1962 and later with the Student Nonviolent Coordinating Committee in Georgia. He also wrote frequently for the underground press, including the *East Village Other*, the *L.A. Free Press*, and *The Realist*.

By 1967 Hoffman had abandoned formal politics and had begun to present himself as an advocate for what he viewed as a growing counterculture of drugs, rock bands, and sexual freedom. He was particularly intrigued with the possibilities of guerrilla theater as a means of transforming this counterculture into a revolutionary movement. In 1967 he played a major role in orchestrating several protest performances of this genre, among them an invasion of the New York Stock Exchange, in which participants tossed money from the visitors' gallery to the brokers on the trading floor. In October 1967 Hoffman and JERRY RUBIN captured the attention of the media at the antiwar march in Washington, D.C., when they led a ceremony to "levitate" the Pentagon off its foundation. Late in 1967 Hoffman joined with Rubin, Ed Sanders of a rock group called the Fugs and Paul Krassner, editor of *The Realist*, to create the Yippies, or Youth International Party. In a book entitled *Revolution for the Hell of It* published in 1968, Hoffman defined the Yippies' concept of revolution as street theater, satire, confrontation, put-ons, stealing—anything that displayed irreverence for property and the Establishment. The Yippies' immediate goal was to communicate an alternative way of life to the young. "Long hair and freaky clothes are total information," he wrote. "It is not necessary to say that we are opposed to—. Everybody already knows. . . . We alienate people. We tear through the streets. Kids love it. They understand it on an internal level. We are living TV ads, movies, Yippie!"

During the summer of 1968 Hoffman and his fellow Yippies planned a massive "festival of life" in Chicago to coincide and contrast with what they interpreted as the "festival of death" at the Democratic National Convention. Their purpose, according to Hoffman, was to "make some statement, especially in revolutionary-action terms, about LBJ, the Democratic Party, electoral politics and the state of the nation." Largely in response, the FBI opened a security investigation of Hoffman, which would eventually run beyond 4,000 pages. They came to Chicago along with hundreds of other protestors from the National Mobilization Committee and Students for a Democratic Society. They applied for permission to use city parks for rallies and for overnight sleeping, but Chicago city officials denied them the right to remain in the parks after 11 p.m. On August 23 the Yippies opened their festival by setting up camp in Lincoln Park and nominating a pig for president in the Chicago civic center. Two days later the police drove them out of Lincoln Park after the 11 p.m. curfew, beating many in the process. The following evening, at about the same time the Democratic convention formally opened, an even larger confrontation took place with several injuries sustained by both demonstrators and police. The remaining days of the convention were full of similar disorder, much of it caught by television cameras or by news photographers.

In March 1969 Hoffman was one of eight persons indicted by a federal grand jury in Chicago in connection with the 1968 disorders. The "Chicago Eight," as they came to be known, were the first defendants tried under the antiriot provisions of the 1968 Civil Rights Act, which made it a federal crime to cross state lines to incite a riot. After a tumultuous trial five of the eight, including Hoffman, were convicted. In November 1972 the verdicts were overturned by an appeals court on the grounds that the judge in the case had been antagonistic and had committed legal errors.

In 1971 Hoffman wrote *Steal This Book*, a do-it-yourself manual of "rip-offs," including instructions on how to shoplift, cheat the telephone company, and make bombs. In 1973 he was arrested for allegedly selling three pounds of cocaine to three New York City police officers. He went underground to avoid imprisonment. He emerged in 1980, and, after a brief prison stint, he became politically active again, speaking frequently at college campuses and elsewhere. He committed suicide in Pennsylvania in April 1989.

—TLH

## Holifield, Chet (Chester) (Earl)
### (1903–1995) *member of the House of Representatives*

The son of a farmer, Holifield was born on December 3, 1903, in Mayfield, Kentucky, and grew up in Arkansas but ran away from home at 17 and settled near Los Angeles. He became interested in politics during the depression and by 1938 was district chair of the California Democratic Central Committee. Holifield won election to Congress in 1942 with nearly 60 percent of the vote.

During his long tenure in Congress, Holifield represented California's 19th Congressional District, a predominantly blue-collar area in Los Angeles County with a large Mexican-American community. He was one of the founders of the House's liberal Democratic Study Group and served as its chair in 1960. In 1946 President Truman appointed him to the Special Evaluation Committee on Atomic Bomb Tests at Bikini Atoll, sparking an interest that remained throughout his political life. Alternating as chair of the Joint Committee on Atomic Energy with Senator JOHN O. PASTORE (D-R.I.) in the 1960s, Holifield was a strong backer of the Kennedy administration's fallout shelter and public power proposals. He also served as a congressional adviser to numerous international conferences on the uses of atomic energy, nuclear weapons testing, and disarmament. He was an early critic of the internment of Japanese Americans during World War II and of the House Committee on Un-American Activities. He also played a role in establishing both the Department of Transportation and the Department of Housing and Urban Development.

Holified was a consistent supporter of the programs of President LYNDON B. JOHNSON. According to *Congressional Quarterly*, he never opposed administration positions on more than 5 percent of key House roll call votes during any year of the Johnson presidency.

However, after 1965 Holified came under increasing criticism from liberal House colleagues. One reason was his support of President Johnson's Southeast Asia policies. In 1966 he joined 77 other Democratic representatives in signing a statement that supported supplementary appropriations for the Vietnam War, and in succeeding years he continued to support strong military measures to resolve that conflict.

Furthermore, Holifield's role on the Joint Atomic Energy Committee often pitted him against certain liberal positions. He worked closely with military and quasi-military agencies and consistently supported Pentagon appropriations requests. In 1967 he opposed the efforts of civil rights groups to bar the construction of an Atomic Energy Commission facility in Weston, Illinois, on the ground that housing discrimination was practiced in the area.

In 1971 Holifield exchanged his Joint Committee position to chair the Government Operations Committee. In February 1974 he announced that he would not seek reelection. He engaged in clothing sales until his death from pneumonia in San Bernardino, California, on February 6, 1995.

—MLL

## Holland, Spessard L(indsey)
### (1892–1971) *member of the Senate*

Spessard L. Holland, who was born on July 10, 1892, in Bartow, Florida, practiced law and then served as judge and state legislator, before becoming governor of Florida from 1941 to 1945. He was appointed to the U.S. Senate to fill an unexpired term in 1946 and thereafter had little difficulty winning reelection. During the 1960s he served on the Senate Agriculture, Appropriations, and Aeronautical and Space Sciences Committees. Despite his seniority he never attained the chair of a major committee. Like many southern conservatives he generally opposed the Kennedy administration's social welfare policies. Similarly, during the Johnson years he voted against the antipoverty, Medicare, and school aid bills, while supporting the administration's Vietnam War policy. Holland, one of Johnson's legislative aides recalled, "was a nice, gentlemanly fellow who I don't recall supported us in any meaningful way."

Holland was a vigorous opponent of administration efforts to permit greater numbers of non–Western European immigrants into the country. "Why for the first time," he asked in 1965, "are the emerging nations of Africa to be placed on the same basis as our mother countries, Britain, Germany, the Scandinavian nations, France and other nations from which most Americans have come?" Despite these objections the administration won congressional approval in 1965 of a liberal revision of the immigration quota system.

As chair of the Senate Agriculture Credit and Rural Electrification Subcommittee, Holland successfully opposed administration efforts to reduce appropriations for the Soil Conservation Service, which was of particular benefit to southern farmers. Throughout the 1960s he also opposed efforts of Senate liberals and the administration to dismantle the "bracero" program, which permitted low-paid Mexican and Bahamian laborers into the United States to harvest citrus fruit and vegetables. This program benefited Florida, California, and Arizona farm employers.

Although Holland opposed most civil rights legislation, he differed from many of his southern colleagues on the question of the poll tax. As a state legislator Holland had helped abolish the Florida poll tax in 1937, and in every congressional session since 1949 he had introduced a bill proposing a constitutional amendment to outlaw the tax nationwide. Many southern states used the poll tax to prevent poor blacks from voting. Because of the powerful opposition of many southern senators, Holland's bill was not reported out of the Senate Judiciary Committee until 1962. That year it won the support of the Kennedy administration and passed both houses of Congress despite the opposition of both southern conservatives and certain civil rights groups. These organizations, which included the NAACP, argued that the Holland bill "would provide an immutable precedent for shunting all further civil rights legislation to the amendment procedure."

By February 1964 three-quarters of the states had ratified the measure, making it the 24th Amendment to the Constitution. The fear that Congress had committed itself to the cumbersome amendment process to rectify all abuses of civil and voting rights proved unfounded. Congress passed a Civil Rights Act in 1964 and, a year later, a Voting Rights Act. Holland voted against both measures.

He retired in 1970 to Bartow, Florida, where he died of a heart attack on November 6, 1971.

—JLW

## Hoopes, Townsend (Walter)
(1922–2004) *deputy assistant secretary of defense for international security affairs, undersecretary of the air force*

Hoopes was born on April 28, 1922, in Duluth, Minnesota, and graduated from Yale in 1944. He worked as a newspaper editorial writer before becoming assistant to the chair of the House Committee on Armed Services in 1947. Eighteen months later Hoopes was appointed assistant to the secretary of defense.

Although engaged in private business during the Eisenhower and Kennedy administrations, Hoopes was a frequent consultant to the White House and the State and Defense Departments. In 1957 he served as executive secretary of the Rockefeller brothers' panel that produced a report on defense policy and strategy. This study advocated the abandonment of nuclear "massive retaliation" as the nation's prime defense policy and recommended the development of "gradual deterrence and flexible military response."

In January 1965 President Johnson appointed Hoopes deputy assistant secretary of defense for international security affairs. While at this post he was primarily concerned with questions of military aid in the Near East and South Asia.

Although aware of the problems developing in Vietnam, Hoopes was not centrally concerned with them and, by his own admission, was "not at the center of policy, but on the near periphery." By the end of 1965 Hoopes had become skeptical of the administration's goal of a military victory through a limited war and particularly of the effectiveness of the policy of achieving this aim through the intensive bombing of North Vietnam. In December he wrote his superior, JOHN MCNAUGHTON, suggesting that the bombing had been "singularly inconclusive" and that any attempt to step up the operation would unify the Communist world and draw increasing criticism from U.S. allies. Instead of escalation, Hoopes suggested that the United States limit its military objectives to the holding and pacification of certain defined cities and ports that could be made secure with the current level of U.S. and South Vietnamese combat forces. McNaughton told Hoopes that he agreed with the general thrust of the message, but he remained confident that the United States would eventually achieve victory because of its military superiority.

One month later Hoopes sent a memorandum to Secretary of Defense ROBERT S. MCNAMARA repeating his argument for a bombing halt and pointing out that the military's major argument for bombing—that it prevented the death of countless American troops—was false. McNamara did not answer the memorandum.

Hoopes was far more successful in presenting his case to CLARK CLIFFORD, the incoming secretary of defense. In a personal letter to Clifford dated February 1968, Hoopes called military victory in Vietnam a "dangerous illusion" and suggested a bombing halt and reduction in ground troops as a prelude to a negotiated settlement. One month later Hoopes reiterated his position in a report he prepared for a task force Clifford had formed to brief him on Vietnam. These reports, along with others from such officials as PAUL NITZE and PAUL WARNKE helped convince Clifford that disengagement was necessary. Clifford, in turn, was one of the advisers who eventually persuaded Johnson to announce restrictions on the bombing of North Vietnam in March 1968.

Hoopes left government service in 1969. That year he wrote a book, *The Limits of Intervention*, that described his experiences during the Johnson administration and traced the steps that led to de-escalation. He later became executive director of the American Association of Publishers. He remained a prolific writer after his retirement and became a Senior Fellow at Washington College in 2003. He died on September 20, 2004, in Baja, California.

—EWS

## Hoover, J(ohn) Edgar

(1895–1972) *director, Federal Bureau of Investigation*

J. Edgar Hoover served as director of the FBI under every president from Coolidge to Nixon.

Hoover was born on January 1, 1895, and raised in Washington, D.C. After graduating at the head of his class at Central High School, he went to work for the Library of Congress. He also attended night law school at the George Washington University. After receiving his law degree in 1916, Hoover served as a clerk in the Justice Department. In 1919 he was named special assistant to U.S. Attorney General A. Mitchell Palmer, who was then engaged in rounding up hundreds of alleged Communists and revolutionaries for possible deporta-

tion under the provisions of the Sedition Act. As head of the newly created General Intelligence Division of the Justice Department's Bureau of Investigation, Hoover was successful in his efforts to deport two well-known anarchists, Emma Goldman and Alexander Berkman. His efforts paid dividends; American membership in the Communist Party, estimated to have been 80,000 before 1919, soon fell below 6,000.

In 1921 Hoover was appointed assistant director of the Bureau of Investigation (the name was changed to the Federal Bureau of Investigation in 1935), and, in 1924, he was named director. At the time he assumed the directorship, the bureau had been demoralized by revelations linking it to the scandals of the Harding administration. Hoover improved morale and recruited an honest and disciplined staff.

During the 1920s the bureau had rather limited investigatory powers, and its agents lacked authority to make arrests or carry arms. In May 1932 Congress passed legislation giving the bureau authority to investigate bank robberies, kidnapping, and extortion cases where use of the telephone was involved. Bureau agents were also empowered to carry guns and make arrests.

During the 1930s J. Edgar Hoover became a national hero as the press recorded the exploits of bureau agents—"G men"—who arrested "Baby Face" Nelson, John Dillinger, "Pretty Boy" Floyd, and other crime figures. Hoover also built the bureau into a major police resource and educational center. He established a national fingerprint file, an efficient crime laboratory, and a training school for local police officers. In 1939 President Roosevelt further increased FBI authority, giving the bureau the power to investigate espionage and sabotage. This authority was subsequently affirmed in directives issued by President Truman.

After World War II information gathered by FBI agents played an important part in the prosecution of Julius and Ethel Rosenberg and Alger Hiss. The bureau also became increasingly involved in the investigation of the American Communist Party. By the end of the 1950s investigation of Communist subversion was popularly viewed as one of the FBI's most important responsibilities.

By the early 1960s Hoover headed a 13,000-employee agency, which absorbed about 40 percent of the Justice Department's budget. Hoover maintained close relations with influential members of

Congress, including Speaker of the House JOHN MCCORMACK (D-Mass.) and Representative John J. Rooney (D-N.Y.), chair of the House Appropriations subcommittee that was responsible for approving Justice Department budgets.

Hoover was also long accustomed to dealing directly with the White House on major policy questions. However, in the Kennedy years he was obliged to communicate first with his nominal superior, Attorney General ROBERT F. KENNEDY, and the two often clashed. Hoover thought the U.S. Attorney General exaggerated the importance of organized crime, and the FBI director was also reluctant to comply with Kennedy's order that the bureau hire African-American agents. Despite these differences, Kennedy approved FBI requests to wiretap an Alabama Klan leader and black protest leaders MALCOLM X and MARTIN LUTHER KING, JR. After JFK's death, Hoover quickly ingratiated himself with the new president and once again opened direct channels of communication.

Following the assassination of President Kennedy the FBI conducted an extensive investigation and, in December 1963, issued a five-volume report that concluded that Lee Harvey Oswald, without accomplices, had murdered the president. In September 1964 the Warren Commission upheld this finding. The commission suggested, however, that the assassination might have been prevented had the bureau informed the Secret Service that the FBI file on Oswald indicated that he was a potential assassin. In 1975 a Senate inquiry into domestic intelligence activities disclosed that the FBI had received a letter from Oswald threatening to blow up the Dallas police station if its agents did not stop questioning his wife about Oswald's Cuban and Soviet contacts. The FBI had withheld his letter from the Warren Commission, and there was widespread speculation that Hoover had had the letter destroyed to protect the bureau's reputation.

Robert Kennedy resigned as U.S. Attorney General in September 1964 and was succeeded by NICHOLAS KATZENBACH. Hoover and Katzenbach clashed over a number of issues, particularly wiretapping. Kazenbach left the department the next year to be replaced by RAMSEY CLARK, whose relations with Hoover were also difficult. Clark organized "regional strike forces" to bring representatives from several federal law enforcement agencies together to fight organized crime in specific target cities. Hoover, mistrustful of other agencies, refused

FBI director J. Edgar Hoover *(Photographed by Yoichi R. Okamoto; Lyndon Baines Johnson Library)*

to permit his agents to participate because he did not wish them to be responsible to anyone outside the bureau. Clark, in turn, attempted to restrict the FBI's use of wiretapping, and between 1966 and 1968 the number of taps authorized by the attorney general declined from 107 to 43.

In July 1966 Hoover ordered an end to the bureau's secret mail-opening program and its practice of illegal break-ins, so-called "black-bag jobs." Since 1948 bureau agents, without warrants, had broken into homes and offices to photograph or seize documents necessary to aid ongoing investigations. Several attorneys general knew of FBI break-ins to plant secret listening devices, but Hoover apparently did not inform any other high-ranking government official. At the same time, however, the bureau continued to receive information from a Central Intelligence Agency (CIA) mail-opening program.

During the early 1960s the FBI came under attack for its failure to protect civil rights workers in the South. Rights leaders claimed that Hoover was a segregationist at heart who had little sympathy for their movement. In 1975 congressional testimony Katzenbach admitted that much of the voting rights work that should have been done by the FBI was performed instead by young civil rights lawyers. Hoover consistently maintained that the FBI was an investigative, not a peace-keeping organization, which therefore could not assist the civil rights workers. In June 1964, however, three civil rights workers were slain in Meridian, Mississippi. In response to the public outcry, and pressure from President Johnson, Hoover flew to Jackson, Mississippi, to open a new field office. Over 150 FBI agents began an investigation, and, through the aid of an informer, uncovered the bodies of the murder victims. The bureau agents eventually arrested a deputy sheriff and a Ku Klux Klan member who were charged with violating the civil liberties of the slain workers.

In September 1964 Hoover sent a memorandum to 17 FBI field offices directing them "to expose, disrupt and otherwise neutralize" the activities of "white-hate" organizations, including the Ku Klux Klan, the Alabama States Rights Party, the American Nazi Party, and several other groups. Efforts to "neutralize" these organizations were part of COINTELPRO, the program under which the FBI had earlier attempted to disrupt the activities of the American Communist Party and the Socialist Workers' Party. Both Katzenbach and Clark later denied knowing of COINTELPRO, which in the late 1960s was predominantly directed against civil rights, Black Power, and New Left organizations.

Hoover believed that the activities of a number of civil rights leaders should also be investigated; no one troubled him more than Martin Luther King, Jr., who was particularly critical of the bureau's failure to protect civil rights workers. Hoover also regarded King as a dangerous rabble-rouser and as an associate of Communists and subversives. Since the late 1950s the FBI had been investigating King and his Southern Christian Leadership Conference. In May 1962 the bureau placed King in section "A" of its reserve index; this meant that in a national emergency King was to be rounded up and detained. In October 1963, with the approval of Attorney General Kennedy, the FBI began tapping King's home telephone. The tap remained until April 1965, when Katzenbach ordered it removed. However, the bureau continued to plant "bugs" to monitor King's conversations.

In November 1964 Hoover called King "the most notorious liar in the country." Later that month, shortly before King was to receive the Nobel Peace Prize, the FBI sent the black leader a note suggesting that he commit suicide, and in an effort to break up King's marriage, the bureau sent

his wife tape-recorded evidence of her husband's alleged infidelity. Copies were also sent to the White House. Hoover also pressured Marquette University into canceling a plan to award an honorary degree to King in 1964. On December 1, 1964, King and Hoover met privately. Thereafter, King muted his criticism of the bureau, which nevertheless continued to leak information about his personal life to the press.

The FBI investigated other black leaders, including STOKELY CARMICHAEL, H. "RAP" BROWN, and the Reverend ELIJAH MUHAMMED. The bureau also attempted to disrupt the Student Nonviolent Coordinating Committee, the Congress of Racial Equality, and the Nation of Islam. In response to the 1967 wave of urban rioting the bureau initiated a campaign against those who had allegedly stirred up the trouble. Agents were directed to compile a "rabble-rouser" (later known as the "agitator") index. When the Black Panther Party came to prominence in 1968, Hoover called the group the "greatest threat to the internal security of the country." FBI offices were instructed to develop programs to cripple the group, and a particular effort was made to increase dissension between the Panthers and their rivals.

FBI efforts to disrupt New Left organizations began in May 1968. The FBI had no exact definition of the New Left, but an April 1968 memorandum suggested that it had "strong Marxist, existentialist, nihilist and anarchist" overtones. The bureau undertook to discredit New Left leaders by having them arrested on drug charges or by sending their parents or parents' employers anonymous letters about their activities. The bureau also engaged the Internal Revenue Service to audit the tax returns of some new leaders.

While president, Lyndon Johnson requested a number of favors of the bureau. In the summer of 1964 a team of agents went to the Democratic National Convention in Atlantic City, ostensibly to guard the president, but actually to gather intelligence on potential political opponents. In March 1966 the bureau, on orders from the president, investigated members of Congress whose criticisms of the administration's Vietnam policy Johnson thought had been motivated by contacts with foreign agents. Johnson also believed that Mrs. Claire Chennault, a Washington socialite, and Republican vice presidential nominee SPIRO AGNEW were attempting to sabotage the Paris Peace talks. Johnson ordered an FBI investigation of Agnew and Chennault, but then decided to keep the findings secret for political reasons.

In 1964 Johnson waived mandatory retirement for Hoover; President Nixon did likewise in 1971. "He had gotten beyond the norm," Johnson aide LAWRENCE O'BRIEN recalled. "It was really a dangerous situation in a lot of ways, because he was beyond authority even from the White House. He was in a position that was downright scary." During the Nixon administration officials argued that the FBI was not sufficiently aggressive in its campaign against antiwar organizations, and they consequently encouraged the CIA to infiltrate and disrupt these groups.

Hoover's reputation declined in the last years of his life following revelations of widespread illegal activities carried out by the bureau. He died on May 2, 1972.

—JLW

## Howe, Harold, II

### (1918–2002) *U.S. commissioner of education*

Harold Howe was born on August 17, 1918, and grew up in Hartford, Connecticut. He attended the Taft School and graduated from Yale in 1940. After naval service in World War II Howe received a master's degree from Columbia University in 1947. During the 1950s he served as principal of high schools in Massachusetts and Ohio. In 1960 Howe was appointed superintendent of the Scarsdale, New York, school system, where his innovative methods impressed Parent-Teachers Association member JOHN W. GARDNER, who was later appointed Lyndon Johnson's secretary of health, education and welfare (HEW). In 1964 Howe become director of the Learning Institute of North Carolina, a private organization that dealt with education problems, especially those related to poverty and segregation.

On the recommendations of both Gardner and outgoing Education commissioner FRANCIS KEPPEL, President Johnson appointed Howe commissioner of education in December 1965. Howe took office in January 1966 at a time when the power and prestige of the Office of Education (OE) had grown as a result of the passage of Johnson administration education bills.

During his tenure as commissioner, Howe's greatest efforts focused on segregation. At a March 7, 1966, news conference, he listed strict guidelines for southern school districts to follow in order to qualify for federal funds granted under the 1965 Elementary and Secondary School Act. His action was initiated to implement Title VI of he Civil Rights Act of 1964, which prohibited racial discrimination in any program or activity receiving federal assistance.

The March HEW guidelines required that between 15 percent and 20 percent of the African-American students in a school district attend desegregated schools; that school district officials mail "free choice" notices to all pupils, who could then decide which schools they wished to attend; and that a "significant start" be made in the integration of school faculties. Howe also indicated that the Office of Education planned greater emphasis on compliance reviews, field visits, and investigations. He set May 6 as the deadline for compliance.

In April Alabama governor GEORGE WALLACE declared that his state would not submit to the OE guidelines because they violated "the historic right of school boards to handle their own affairs and . . . the historic right of academic freedom." Howe reiterated that school districts failing to meet the May 6 desegregation deadline would be subject to "deferral of [federal] funds." On May 7, 1966, the OE announced that 255 southern school districts had failed to file pledges of compliance with the guidelines, but that 1,489 districts in 17 southern and border states had done so.

In a June speech at Columbia University, Howe expressed his displeasure with the slow pace of desegregation and accused U.S. educators of having a "blind faith in gradualism." He declared that schools remained almost as segregated as they had been in 1954, at the time of the Supreme Court's *Brown v. Board of Education* decision, which outlawed "separate but equal" public education. Howe called upon school administrators to consider redrawing school district boundaries and confederating with neighborhood districts "even though political boundaries may remain unchanged." He insisted that educators must be willing to sacrifice their jobs for desegregation.

Howe's strong support of desegregation angered many southern members of congress. At a September 1966 House Rules Committee hearing, Representative L. MENDEL RIVERS (D-S.C.) denounced him as an "idiot" and a man who "talks like a Communist." Others derisively called him the "Commissioner of Integration." There was also considerable friction within the administration over Howe's position. In April 1966 HEW secretary John Gardner attempted to soften opposition to the guidelines by assuring southern governors, representatives, and school officials that HEW was not ordering a specific degree of "racial balance" or requiring "instantaneous desegregation" of school faculties. At an October press conference President Johnson acknowledged that there had been "some harassment and some mistakes" in civil rights enforcement.

On October 19, 1966, Congress passed a bill amending the 1965 Elementary and Secondary Education Act. The law's civil rights provision restricted Howe's authority to defer funds to school districts not complying with Title VI of the 1964 Civil Rights Act. The OE was only permitted to hold funds to schools for up to 60 days pending a hearing and for another 30 days after the hearing. The expanded elementary education act mainly benefited schools in poorer states, providing them with an estimated $343 million for fiscal 1968.

In May 1967 Secretary Gardner announced that civil rights enforcement power within HEW would be transferred to the newly created Office for Civil Rights, headed by Gardner's special assistant, F. Peter Libassi. Gardner said that he had "complete confidence" in Howe and that "nothing in this change should be taken as a reflection on his standing within the Administration." However, many observers felt the move was an attempt to round up support of southern Democrats for the 1967 school assistance bill. The measure, authorizing $9.2 billion for fiscal 1969–70, was signed into law on January 2, 1968.

Shortly before his retirement as commissioner, Howe stated that progress in the integration of public schools had been "minimal." The United States, he said, still faced a racially divided school system with "some 85 percent of Negro youngsters in the South still [attending] almost fully segregated schools." In a January 9, 1968, interview with Norman C. Thomas, author of *Education in National Politics,* Howe described his role at the OE as "kind of a middle-level crossroads at the top of the bureaucracy." He acknowledged that during the 1960s "much policy development in education has moved from here [Office of Education] to the White House."

On January 12, 1968, Howe resigned to join the Ford Foundation as a director of education pro-

grams in India. In 1982 he became a senior lecturer at Harvard University, where he remained until his retirement in 1994. He died on November 29, 2002, in Hanover, New Hampshire.

—FHM

## Howe, Irving
### (1920–1993) *literary critic; editor,* Dissent

Irving Howe, the son of immigrant parents from Eastern Europe, was born on June 11, 1920, and raised in the slums of the East Bronx. He graduated from the City College of New York in 1940. During the 1940s and 1950s Howe emerged as a leading American literary and social critic. A prolific writer on a broad range of subjects, he was a frequent contributor to *Partisan Review* and other "little magazines." He wrote or coauthored 11 books over a 15-year period and edited 11 more. Among his works were *The U.A.W. and Walter Reuther* (1949), *William Faulkner: A Critical Study* (1952), *Politics and the Novel* (1957), and, with Lewis Coser, *The American Communist Party: A Critical History* (1957). At the same time Howe pursued an academic career as professor of English at Brandeis University from 1953 to 1961 and at Stanford University from 1961 to 1963. In 1963 he was appointed distinguished professor of English at Hunter College of the City University of New York.

As an adolescent during the depression, Howe had been a Trotskyite. In the 1940s he was a member of the Workers Party (later called the Independent Socialist League), a small socialist group that combined revolutionary opposition to both capitalism and communism under the difficult circumstances created by World War II and the East-West polarization of the postwar era. By the early 1950s, however, Howe no longer regarded this position as tenable, and he left the organization, arguing for critical support of the West in the cold war. In 1953 Howe and several other like-minded socialists founded *Dissent,* a journal "devoted to radical ideas and the values of socialism and democracy." During the 1950s *Dissent* defended the civil liberties of American Communists and criticized the celebration of American society by many formerly radical intellectuals.

In the 1960s Howe saw *Dissent* as the organ of an informal and loosely knit group of intellectual members of the "democratic left." It would be, he hoped, a bastion of defense for left-wing political views, while at the same time it would resist being subjugated by a Moscow-directed communism. As editor, Howe thought American social democrats could best influence national politics by working within the Democratic Party. During the early 1960s, when the civil rights movement was growing, Howe shared with many young radicals in the New Left the hope that the Democratic Party could be "realigned" on a more liberal basis through a "new politics" coalition of black, labor, liberal, and church groups.

Political differences between the democratic left and its youthful allies soon emerged over two issues. The first involved what attitude the civil rights movement should take toward the Democratic Party. Howe favored continued work with the party, and he opposed those in the Mississippi Freedom Democratic Party (MFDP) who rejected the compromise offered to them on their credentials challenge at the 1964 Democratic convention. (The compromise, sponsored by HUBERT HUMPHREY and WALTER REUTHER, would have seated two members of the MFDP but left the segregationist regular Mississippi Democrats in possession of their convention seats.) Howe criticized those in the Student Nonviolent Coordinating Committee and the Students for a Democratic Society who sought to organize a new political movement outside of and opposed to the Democratic Party. He described these radicals as "those who, in effect, want to 'go it alone' " with "a strategy of lonely assault, which must necessarily lead to shock tactics and desperation." He also aroused controversy with a 1963 essay in Dissent that criticized James Baldwin and Ralph Ellison for failing to embrace African-American militancy in their writings.

The gulf between Howe and the New Left widened further by the explosive Vietnam issue. Critical of Washington's conduct of the war in the mid-1960s, Howe favored a bombing halt and a negotiated peace but supported maintenance of a U.S. military presence in South Vietnam in order to prevent a massacre of anti–National Liberation Front elements. He thought much of the antiwar movement "apocalyptic," and he opposed its use of civil disobedience, violence, and resistance to the draft. In an important 1965 article in Dissent entitled "New Styles in Leftism," Howe described adherents of the New Left as "desperadoes" and "kamikaze radicals" who subordinated ideology to personal style, gave explicit or covert support to Communist regimes in developing nations, and rejected the "intellectual heritage of the West, the

tradition of liberalism at its most serious, the commitment to democracy as an indispensable part of civilized life." After the Democratic National Convention in August 1968, Howe supported the presidential candidacy of Hubert Humphrey.

With the decline of the New Left after 1970, Dissent turned its attention to the emergence of what Howe called a "new conservatism" among those academic intellectuals associated with Commentary and the Public Interest. With other Dissent authors, Howe defended economic liberalism and social egalitarianism and called for a heavier commitment of the nation's wealth to traditional welfare and education programs. Howe supported the presidential candidacy of GEORGE MCGOVERN (D-S.Dak.) in 1972 and was closely associated with the left-liberal Democratic Socialist Organizing Committee chaired by MICHAEL HARRINGTON in the mid-1970s. A prolific author, Howe published World of Our Fathers in 1976, a best-selling social history of the immigrant Jewish community in New York. He remained active in both political and literary circles, although his influence waned and he confessed to feeling out of place with the newer generation of literary critics. He died on May 5, 1993.

—TLH

## Hruska, Roman L(ee)
### (1904–1999) member of the Senate

Roman Hruska was born on August 16, 1904, in David City, Nebraska. A former county official and U.S. representative, Hruska resigned his House seat in 1954 to fill a Senate vacancy created by the death of Hugh Butler. A representative of perhaps the most Republican state in the nation, Hruska was an opponent of most foreign aid proposals and of many domestic social welfare measures such as Medicare, aid to education, and the Johnson administration's antipoverty program. He did, however, favor foreign military aid and supported efforts to continue the appropriation of funds for Radio Free Europe and Radio Liberty, stations that broadcast news to Communist-bloc countries. He also supported a number of civil rights measures, including the 1964 Civil Rights Act. In 1968 the conservative Americans for Constitutional Action gave him a 100 percent rating, while the Americans for Democratic Action gave him a 7 percent score.

Hruska was a constant supporter of business and defender of "free enterprise." As a member of the Judiciary Committee's Antitrust and Monopoly Subcommittee, he scored the 1961 subcommittee report that found price-fixing policies in the drug industry. In 1964 the senator objected to subcommittee hearings on the increased number of mergers in the United States. As a representative of an agricultural state whose economy, depended on cattle raising and feed grain production, Hruska consistently backed price supports and measures to limit imported meat.

Hruska was a strong opponent of gun-control legislation and in the late 1960s made several successful attempts to weaken antigun measures. "On gun control," one representative recalled, "he was almost so hostile that it was not possible to have any effective discussion on the issue." In conjunction with Senator JAMES EASTLAND (D-Miss.), he led a 1966 filibuster in the Judiciary Committee against Senator THOMAS DODD's (D-Conn.) strong gun-control bill. The proposal would have prohibited interstate mail-order sales of pistols and other concealable weapons to individuals and tightened restrictions on sales of shotguns and rifles. In order to get some legislation to the Senate floor, Dodd was forced to accept Hruska's bill, which restricted only the mail-order sale of pistols and revolvers. The bill was reported out of committee in 1970 but died before being considered by Congress.

In 1968 Hruska successfully fought to delete from the omnibus crime control and safe streets bill a provision prohibiting the mail-order sale of rifles and shotguns. As an alternative measure he unsuccessfully offered a proposal that would have permitted the sale of hand guns but required the purchaser to file an affidavit stating that he was eligible to own a gun. The affidavit would have been sent to the police along with a description of the weapon but not its serial number. Hruska's proposal, supported by the National Rifle Association, was rejected by the Senate. Congress passed the Omnibus Crime Control Act in June 1968. He later played a formative role in the 1972 Organized Crime Control Act, which included RICO, the federal antiracketeering legislation used against organized crime. He later chaired the Commission on the Revision of the Federal Appellate Court System.

Hruska was a supporter of the Johnson administration's Vietnam policy but opposed the use of U.S. combat troops in either Laos or Thailand. In 1970 he gained notoriety during the hearings on the nomination of Federal District judge G. Harrold Carswell to the Supreme Court when he remarked that mediocre people deserved representation on the high court. He retired in 1976 and returned to Omaha, Nebraska, where he died on April 25, 1999, due to complications from a broken hip.

—EWS

## Hughes, Harold E(verett)
### (1922–1996) *governor*

Born on February 10, 1922, near Idobrae, Iowa, and raised in rural poverty, Hughes had a troubled early life, which included a seven-year struggle with alcoholism following his service in World War II. On the brink of suicide in 1952, he instead turned to religion and Alcoholics Anonymous and pulled his life together. He became a trucking association executive in the mid-1950s and decided to run for a seat on the Iowa Commerce Commission in 1958 when that body failed to investigate his complaints about lax enforcement of the state's trucking laws. Hughes won the seat and remained a member of the commission until his election as governor in 1962. As a Democrat in a traditionally conservative Republican state, his victory was a product of the gradual transition of Iowa from a rural to a semi-urban state with urban problems.

As governor, Hughes instituted a number of important reforms: legalization of liquor by the glass, legislative reapportionment, government reorganization, tax reform for the elderly, utility regulation, penal reform, repeal of capital punishment, creation of a vocational-technical school system, and industrial safety legislation. He also led an intensive industrial promotion effort, which included "Sell Iowa" trips to major U.S. cities and countries abroad.

In 1967 Hughes was criticized for his insensitivity to black issues. During the riots in the black neighborhoods of Waterloo, the governor called in troops and walked the streets of the community in an attempt to quiet tensions. Shocked at the physical conditions and spiritual bitterness he found there, he admitted his previous lack of concern and began a program to alleviate these conditions. Hughes expanded the state Civil Rights Commission and supported a state open-housing law. In addition, he convinced Iowa's business and religious leaders to establish a civic task force and employment programs and to raise several hundred thousand dollars to implement them.

During the early years of U.S. involvement in the Vietnam War, Hughes was a backer of Johnson's policy and in 1965 organized a governors' tour to Vietnam to build support for the president. However, by 1966 he was beginning to have doubts about U.S. foreign policy. These misgivings prompted him to support Senator ROBERT F. KENNEDY (D-N.Y.) as a presidential candidate in 1968. When Kennedy was assassinated the governor backed antiwar candidate Senator EUGENE MCCARTHY (D-Minn.) and nominated him at the Democratic National Convention in Chicago. During the same period Hughes worked for reforms in the selection of convention delegates.

Because Hughes spent so much of his time campaigning for McCarthy, he did not devote close attention to his own campaign for the U.S. Senate and won by fewer than 7,000 votes. His narrow victory was attributed not only to his work for McCarthy but also to the accumulated antagonism caused by his raising taxes and increasing the state budget by 150 percent. In addition, Hughes insisted on running his campaign on two controversial issues—his opposition to the Vietnam War and civil rights.

In the Senate Hughes concerned himself primarily with Vietnam and the problem of alcohol and drug abuse. He often discussed his own difficulties with alcohol and privately attempted to aid representatives who had similar problems. In 1970 he successfully championed the Comprehensive Alcohol Abuse and Alcoholism Prevention, Treatment and Rehabilitation Act, which was better known as the "Hughes Act." This law established the National Institute on Alcohol Abuse and Alcoholism, offered incentives for hospitals to treat alcoholics, and made federal monies available to the states to establish and support community-based treatment programs. Hughes continued to work for party reform and in 1972 was mentioned as a dark-horse candidate for the Democratic presidential nomination. He retired from the Senate in 1975 to devote his time to religious work. He later founded a religious retreat in Maryland and continued to call for aid to those struggling with alcohol or drug dependencies. He died on October 23, 1996, in Glendale, Arizona.

—EWS

## Hughes, Howard R(obard)
(1905–1976) *industrialist, business leader*

Born on Christmas Eve 1905, to a wealthy Houston family, Howard Hughes, Jr., became a multimillionaire at the age of 18, when he inherited the estate of his father, who owned an oil-well drilling equipment business. With an estimated income of $2 million per year, Hughes turned to filmmaking in the 1920s and 1930s. In 1937 he purchased Trans World Airlines (TWA). A pilot himself, in 1935 he set a land-speed record of 352 miles per hour in his newly developed plane, the H-1. In 1952 Hughes assumed a reclusive, mysterious and rumor-filled existence, traveling frequently throughout the world.

During the 1960s Hughes was involved in antitrust lawsuits and countersuits concerning his absentee directorship of TWA. As a result of poor management and rigid contractual obligations, TWA was controlled during the early 1960s by several prominent financial lending institutions and an independently minded board of directors. Although Hughes still owned 78 percent of TWA stock, his position was weakened to the extent that in May 1966 he abruptly and without public explanation sold his shares for $546.5 million in what was then the second-largest stock transaction in U.S. history.

After the TWA sale Hughes began buying large amounts of land and property in Nevada. He purchased the Desert Inn complex in Las Vegas, part of which the used as a fortresslike headquarters for his business operations. He also acquired the Sands Hotel, the Frontier Hotel, Las Vegas television station KLAS-TV, Alamo Airways, and numerous properties in and around the city. In 1968 Hughes tried to buy another casino house, but when the Justice Department made preliminary investigations into possible antitrust violations, he withdrew his bid.

Rumors about Hughes circulated constantly to the effect that he was involved with organized crime or that he was dead and his name was being kept alive by the Hughes company. The Hughes empire in Nevada was run through an ex-FBI agent, Robert Maheu, who had never actually met Hughes. In 1973 Maheu linked Charles G. Rebozo, a close friend of President RICHARD NIXON's to a $100,000 political contribution that Hughes made in 1969 and 1970. Rebozo did not turn over the money to the Republican campaign committee but, according to Rebozo, kept it in a safe deposit box and later returned it to Hughes. A 1975 Senate committee implicated Maheu in an alleged 1961 CIA plot to assassinate Cuban leader Fidel Castro.

Hughes became involved in a bitter controversy in 1968, when the Atomic Energy Commission

(AEC) conducted a series of underground nuclear tests at its Nevada test site. Because of his extensive landholdings in the Southwest, Hughes appealed to the AEC on April 21 to postpone the tests, ostensibly so his own experts could conduct an "independent study" of the possible consequences. The AEC refused the request and subsequently denied a Hughes organization statement that a nuclear device detonated on January 19, 1968, had triggered an earthquake near Salt Lake City, 200 miles northeast of the test site.

In May 1968 *Fortune* magazine estimated Hughes's fortune at $1–1.5 billion, making him, with J. Paul Getty, one of the two wealthiest Americans. By 1970 his Nevada landholdings alone were worth $250 million.

In 1972 Hughes was the victim of a well-publicized hoax involving publication of a fake biography based on supposedly exclusive interviews with Hughes himself. His extensive political influence was highlighted during the 1973 Senate Watergate hearings when James McCord, convicted as a participant in the Watergate conspiracy, revealed a 1972 scheme to burglarize the offices of Las Vegas *Sun* owner Hank Greenspun to obtain damaging information about a unnamed presidential candidate. The plot involved the burglary team escape to Central America in a private plane owned by Hughes. Greenspun stated that the attempted burglary's real purpose was to obtain hundreds of memoranda pertaining to Hughes's antitrust problems with the Justice Department over his extensive landholdings in the Southwest. He later worked with the CIA in an attempt to recover a sunken Soviet submarine off the coast of Hawaii, by allowing his ship, *Glomar Explorer,* to try to raise it under the cover story that it was drilling for manganese nodules on the ocean floor. He died in an airplane on April 5, 1976, on his way to a Houston hospital.

—FHM

## Hughes, Richard J(oseph)

(1909–1992) *governor*

The son of a New Jersey Democratic politician, Hughes, who was born in Florence, New Jersey, on August 10, 1909, received his law degree in 1931 and began working for the Democratic Party in Mercer County. After losing a congressional election in 1938, Hughes was appointed assistant U.S. attorney for New Jersey in 1939. He was appointed to a county judgeship in 1948 and promoted to the appellate division of New Jersey's Superior Court in 1957. Financial and family responsibilities forced him to resign and resume his law practice the same year. In February 1961 a conference of state Democratic Party leaders chose Hughes as the party's gubernatorial candidate. A large urban turnout enabled him to upset former secretary of labor James P. Mitchell in the 1961 New Jersey gubernatorial race.

Hughes's 1965 reelection campaign received national attention when his GOP opponent, Wayne Dumont, demanded that Rutgers history professor EUGENE GENOVESE be fired for stating at an April 23 teach-in, "I do not fear or regret the impending Viet Cong victory in Vietnam, I welcome it." Investigations by the University Board of Examiners and a special state assembly committee revealed that Genovese had broken no state or university regulations. Hughes, although describing Genovese's view as "outrageous," declared that he was "determined to preserve academic freedom in the broadest sense." On election day Hughes defeated Dumont by an unprecedented 350,000-vote plurality; for the first time since 1911, the Democrats also gained control of the state senate.

One issue that occupied Hughes during both of his terms as governor was the state's apportionment system, which dated back to 1776. In November 1964 the New Jersey Supreme Court ordered reapportionment of the state legislature on a "one-person, one-vote" basis. After a prolonged conflict with the legislature over formulation of the reapportionment plan, Hughes accepted a proposal for the calling of a state constitutional convention in March 1965. The convention eventually agreed on a formula that enlarged both houses of the state legislature and redrew New Jersey's 15 congressional districts. The reapportionment measure was enacted by Hughes in June 1966. In the elections of November 1967, Democrats lost their recently won majorities in the enlarged New Jersey House of Representatives and Senate, severely restricting Hughes's freedom of action during the remainder of his second term.

Another problem that Hughes faced during the mid-1960s was reform of the state's tax structure. When Hughes first assumed office in 1962, New Jersey was the seventh wealthiest state but one of the last in per capita state revenue. In 1966 Hughes proposed a state income tax. Opposition from the powerful Essex County and Hudson County Democratic organizations left the governor one vote short of a legislative majority, and in April Hughes agreed with the state assembly to a substitute 3 percent sales tax.

Hughes took an active and controversial role in the racial violence that affected many New Jersey towns in July 1967. After Newark mayor Hugh Addonizio phoned Hughes on July 14 requesting state police and National Guard units, Hughes personally went into the city with the troops. Touring the affected areas he called the disturbances "criminal insurrection" and expressed shock at the "holiday atmosphere" among the rioters. President Johnson quickly made it clear that he was unwilling to provide federal aid, for fear of appearing to have given in to black rioters. On July 15 Hughes discussed the underlying problems of Newark's black community with a group of black leaders. He also met with a second group of community leaders, who presented evidence of brutality by National Guard troops and state police. Hughes and Addonizio were criticized for "inflammatory statements" that allegedly led to the formation of white vigilante groups. On July 16 Hughes contended that brutality charges were based on "hearsay" and "mostly second-hand information" but promised that "justice will be done" when the facts were made clear. Declaring on July 17 that "the restoration of order is accomplished," Hughes ordered the withdrawal of most of the guard.

Eight other New Jersey communities experienced racial violence during July 1967. The most serious incidents occurred in Plainfield, where a white police officer was shot with his own gun and beaten to death by about 30 people on July 16. The same day 46 semiautomatic rifles and ammunition were stolen from the Plainfield Machine Company. After Hughes proclaimed "a state of disaster and emergency," 300 heavily armed National Guard troops and state troopers conducted a house-to-house search for the weapons in selected black sections on July 19. Many blacks whose homes were searched complained of extensive property damage, and, on July 21, the state's American Civil Liberties Union director denounced the action. On July 25 Hughes appointed an eight-member, cabinet-level interdepartmental panel to develop programs to ease the state's urban problems. Hughes chaired a special panel of the 1967 President's Commission on Civil Disorders, which investigated the difficulties

suffered by residents and businessowners in riot-prone areas who sought to obtain property and liability insurance. On January 27, 1968, the group issued a report recommending that tax concessions be included in a program to ease the slum insurance crisis.

Hughes strongly supported the Johnson administration's foreign policy. At the 1966 National Governors Conference he amended the general resolution of support for the nation's global commitments to include a specific reference to Vietnam. In September 1967 Hughes observed the South Vietnamese elections and returned to announce that he had found no evidence of fraud or wrongdoing. That same year, in June, Hughes helped in the selection of Glassboro, New Jersey, as the location of the first meeting between President Johnson and Soviet premier Alexei Kosygin. He also encouraged LBJ to run for reelection in 1968, even after the president announced that he would not do so.

At the 1968 Democratic National Convention Hughes chaired the Credentials Committee, which was forced to resolve challenges to the seating of 15 delegations. Most of these were settled at committee meetings, but four, involving Texas, Georgia, Alabama, and North Carolina, went before the convention. The most dramatic controversy arose over the Georgia delegation, where the liberal slate led by JULIAN BOND challenged the seating of the regular delegation headed by Governor LESTER MADDOX. In an attempt to settle the dispute, Hughes suggested seating both delegations and splitting the state's vote.

Returning to New Jersey after the convention as a "lame duck" governor, Hughes supported former governor Robert Meyner's unsuccessful comeback attempt in 1969. He returned to private law practice in 1970. In November 1973 Hughes was named chief justice of the New Jersey Supreme Court. He remained on the court until his retirement in 1981. He died of heart failure in Boca Raton, Florida, on December 7, 1992.

—DKR

## Humphrey, Hubert H(oratio)
(1911–1978) *member of the Senate, vice president of the United States*
The son of a South Dakota druggist, Humphrey, who was born on May 27, 1911, in Wallace, South

Vice President Hubert Humphrey *(Photographed by Yoichi R. Okamoto; Lyndon Baines Johnson Library)*

Dakota, was profoundly influenced by his Democratic father's reverence for William Jennings Bryan and Woodrow Wilson. He was a star debater and class valedictorian in high school but had to leave the University of Minnesota early in the depression to help out in his father's drugstore. He became a registered pharmacist and managed the store, while his father participated actively in South Dakota politics. Humphrey returned to the University of Minnesota in 1937, earned in B.A. in 1939 and an M.A. in political science from Louisiana State University a year later. His master's thesis, entitled "The Political Philosophy of the New Deal," was a glowing tribute to Franklin D. Roosevelt's response to the depression.

Humphrey abandoned his teaching career to plunge into Minnesota politics. He played a key role in the 1944 merger of the Farmer-Labor and Democratic Parties and won election as mayor of Minneapolis the next year. As mayor he waged an antivice campaign, created the first municipal fair employment practices commission in the United States, expanded the city's housing program, and took an active part in settling strikes. Reelected in 1947, Humphrey helped organize the liberal, anticommunist Americans for Democratic Action (ADA) and fought a successful battle to purge the communist faction from the Democratic–Farmer-Labor Party. He gained national attention at the 1948 Democratic National Convention with a stirring oration in favor of a strong civil rights plank.

"Our demands for democratic practices in other lands will be no more effective than the guarantees of those practiced in our own country," he told the crowd "I do not believe that there can be any compromise on the guarantee of civil rights." In November 1948 Minnesota voters elected Humphrey to the Senate over the conservative Republican incumbent.

Humphrey quickly moved into the vanguard of the Senate's liberal minority, promoting a wide variety of social welfare, civil rights, tax reform, and pro-labor legislation. The first bill he introduced was a proposal to establish a medical care program for the aged, which was finally enacted in revised form as Medicare in 1965. The Senate's powerful conservatives, however, disapproved of Humphrey's aggressive debating style and effusive liberalism, and their hostility reduced his effectiveness.

Gradually he eased his way into the Senate "establishment," toning down his fervid ideological approach and working closely with the Democratic leader, Senator LYNDON JOHNSON, who used Humphrey as his liaison with liberals and intellectuals. Humphrey, moreover, was as anticommunist as many conservatives. He introduced the Communist Control Act of 1954, which outlawed the Communist Party. In foreign affairs he softened his anticommunism with Wilsonian idealism. He became a leading advocate of disarmament and the distribution of surplus food to needy nations. His natural enthusiasm and his commitment to the causes that he championed earned him the nickname, "The Happy Warrior."

Humphrey's first run for the presidency began in January 1959 and ended in May 1960 with his defeat in the West Virginia primary by Senator John F. Kennedy. Humphrey reached the peak of his legislative influence during the Kennedy administration. As assistant majority leader, or majority whip, he became the administration's most aggressive ally in the Senate, working tirelessly to win passage of Kennedy programs. In the process he helped to enact several measures, such as the Peace Corps and the nuclear test ban treaty, that he himself had long promoted.

In the aftermath of President Kennedy's assassination, Humphrey helped smooth the transition to the Johnson administration by advising the new president and serving again as his link to liberals and intellectuals, many of whom viewed Johnson with apprehension. In his last year as majority whip he labored energetically to pass the $11.5 billion tax cut in February 1964, an economic stimulus he had called for in 1962. Humphrey was the floor manager of the landmark Civil Rights Act of 1964, the fruition of his career-long advocacy of the cause of equal rights. He organized the pro–civil rights senators, maintained flagging morale throughout the frustrating struggle, persistently cultivated Senate Minority Leader EVERETT M. DIRKSEN (R-Ill.) and engineered the compromise with the Republican leader that finally broke the 75-day southern filibuster on June 10.

At the Democratic National Convention in August, Humphrey was at the center of another civil rights imbroglio: the battle between the all-white regular Mississippi delegation and the insurgent Mississippi Freedom Democratic Party (MFDP) over which group should represent the state's Democrats at the convention. Humphrey arranged a compromise that allowed the MFDP two votes as a special at-large delegation. Neither of the Mississippi parties accepted the plan, but it accomplished its primary purpose, which was to head off a mass southern walk-out or an embarrassing floor fight. Chosen by Johnson as his vice presidential running mate, the ticket won election in November in a Democratic landslide.

Humphrey's ascension to the vice presidency marked the end of an extraordinarily prolific 15 years in the Senate, during which he had introduced nearly 1,500 bills and resolutions. In his new post he spoke to a wider audience but with diminished authority, despite the numerous outlets President Johnson gave him for his kinetic energies. He become chair of the President's Council on Economic Opportunity, the Peace Corps Advisory Council, the National Aeronautics and Space Council, and the President's Council on Youth Fitness. In addition, Humphrey performed his constitutional duty to preside over the Senate and was Johnson's representative at a multitude of ceremonial functions.

Nevertheless, Humphrey's primary role was to sell administration policy to Congress and the public. Through his familiar ebullient lobbying and exhortation, he had a hand in the passage of much of the social legislation he had been identified with for years: Medicare, voting rights, aid to education, immigration reform, housing and rent supplements, and Model Cities. But his most controversial cause by far was public defense of Johnson's Vietnam policy.

At the beginning of his vice presidential tenure, he earned the president's displeasure by arguing within the National Security Council (NSC) against a hard-line policy in Vietnam. The issue before the NSC in February 1965 was what form of retaliation the United States should take for the Communist attack on the U.S. compound at Pleiku. In the heated discussions Humphrey was opposed to U.S. military escalation, arguing in particular against an air strike while Soviet premier Kosygin was in Hanoi and questioning the effectiveness of trying to bomb North Vietnam to the negotiating table.

A few days later Humphrey, in a private memorandum to Johnson, outlined his doubts about the administration's Vietnam policy. Maintaining that escalation and a military solution were the "Goldwater position" and that the public would not understand why grave risks were justified to support the "chronic instability in Saigon," he urged the president to "cut losses" and apply his famous political talents to attain a Vietnam settlement. Moreover, Humphrey said, escalation would jeopardize other policies to which the administration had committed itself: "United Nations, arms control and socially humane and constructive policies generally."

Angered by Humphrey's dissent at the NSC meeting and alarmed at the vice president's expression of his opposition on paper, Johnson excluded Humphrey from the foreign policy decision-making councils of his administration for a year. Humphrey returned to prominence in the foreign policy area in February 1966, when Johnson sent him on a 14-day journey to nine Asian nations, including South Vietnam. The trip was a vital turning point for Humphrey, marking the renewal of Johnson's confidence in him as foreign policy spokesperson and roving ambassador.

Beginning with his Asian trip Humphrey outdid other administration officials in his public enthusiasm for and optimism about the Vietnam War. Upon his return Humphrey said that "the tide of battle in Vietnam has turned in our favor." Humphrey also assailed critics of the war, a task he frequently assumed over the next three years. He denounced a proposal by Senator ROBERT F. KENNEDY (D-N.Y.) to include the National Liberation Front in a future coalition government, comparing the idea to "putting a fox in a chicken coop." The zest with which Humphrey now defended the war and attacked its critics did much to alienate many of his former allies among liberals and intellectuals.

The issue of the war haunted Humphrey during his 1968 presidential campaign as did the lack of support he received from the president for his campaign. The strong showing of the antiwar candidate, Senator EUGENE MCCARTHY (D-Minn.), in the New Hampshire primary revealed the extent of the divisions over Vietnam within the Democratic Party. President Johnson's withdrawal from the race later in the month left Humphrey as the candidate of the party's center, while the assassination of Senator Robert Kennedy in June left McCarthy with the allegiance of most of the party's antiwar wing by the time of the Chicago convention in August.

Backed by organized labor and party regulars, Humphrey won the nomination in August. But the circumstances of his selection made it a Pyrrhic victory. The convention was a tumultuous affair, punctuated by bitter floor fights over delegates' credentials and the content of the Vietnam plank in the platform. A majority voted to endorse Johnson's policies, but heavy-handed security by Chicago mayor RICHARD DALEY's personnel within the hall and clashes between police and young antiwar protestors outside intensified the emotional rifts within the party and associated the Democrats with violence and chaos in the eyes of the public. McCarthy's refusal to endorse Humphrey until the last week in the campaign symbolized the divided condition in which the party confronted the Republicans.

According to public opinion polls taken in September, Humphrey was far behind Republican candidate RICHARD NIXON and appeared headed for a crushing defeat. (A Gallup poll taken between September 20 and 22 indicated that 43 percent of the voters favored Nixon, 28 percent backed Humphrey,

and 21 percent chose Alabama governor GEORGE C. WALLACE.) Plagued by constant heckling, a disorganized campaign, and his identification with an unpopular war, Humphrey struggled along with little progress until he delivered a Salt Lake City speech on September 30, in which he pledged to stop the bombing of North Vietnam and institute a cease-fire if elected. This moderate departure from administration policy gave the campaign its first push forward. Humphrey took the offensive, campaigning indefatigably and attacking Nixon vigorously. Despite a massive voter registration drive on his behalf by organized labor, his effort fell short by an extremely narrow margin on election day. Nixon won with 43.4 percent of the popular vote compared to 42.7 percent for Humphrey and 13.5 percent for Wallace; Nixon had 301 electoral votes to Humphrey's 191 and Wallace's 46. Later evidence would reveal that the Nixon campaign had undermined LBJ's peace efforts in Vietnam out of fear that they would propel Humphrey to victory.

After teaching at the University of Minnesota and Macalester College, Humphrey returned to the Senate in 1971. He made his third unsuccessful run for the presidency in 1972, losing the nomination to Senator McGovern. Humphrey was reelected to the Senate in 1976, and briefly sought the Democratic nomination for the presidency. The post of deputy president pro tempore of the Senate was created for him and he held it from January 5, 1977, until his death from cancer in Waverly, Minnesota, on January 13, 1978.

—TO

## Innis, Roy Emile Alfredo

(1934– ) *national director, Congress of Racial Equality*

Innis, who was born on June 6, 1934, on the island of Saint Croix, spent his childhood in the Virgin Islands. He moved to New York as an adolescent and attended City College after serving in the army. In 1963, while working as a chemistry research assistant in a New York hospital, Innis joined the Harlem chapter of the Congress of Racial Equality (CORE), a civil rights organization. He soon became an important leader of Harlem CORE, rising in October 1965 to chapter chair. In July 1967 Innis was elected second vice chair of the national CORE organization. He became CORE's acting national director one year later, after the previous director, FLOYD MCKISSICK, resigned for health reasons. The national CORE convention in September 1968 confirmed Innis as head of the organization. In 1967 he also helped create the Harlem Commonwealth Council (HCC), an investment group designed to encourage African-American independence and stability in Harlem. He also served as the founder and coeditor of the *Manhattan Tribune* newspaper.

Innis's rise in CORE resulted from his position as a leading advocate of Black Power, which he embraced as a result of his impatience over the progress of civil rights during the early 1960s. Innis's conception of Black Power stressed preservation of a distinct black culture and greater reliance on black resources in the struggle for equality. In 1966 he and other Harlem CORE members concluded that the fight for integration of New York City schools was a failure and decided to press for community control over neighborhood schools. At this time Innis proposed an amendment to the New York

State constitution providing independent school boards for predominantly black areas. This was the first significant instance when integration was replaced by black separation as a civil rights goal. Innis had earlier formed a "black male caucus" as the chief policy-making body of the Harlem CORE, causing white members to leave the chapter. At the CORE national convention of 1966, he fought successfully for a resolution defining the organization's goal as "racial coexistence through Black Power."

By 1968 Innis, belonged to the organization's moderate wing. Radicals such as Brooklyn CORE chair Robert Carson viewed the destruction of American capitalism as a necessary part of black liberation and demanded that CORE reject funds from foundations and other "establishment" sources. Innis countered these arguments with proposals for a program of "black capitalism," translating his separatist philosophy into economic activity. Government and foundation money, he argued, should be used to finance black-controlled businesses in inner-city areas. In 1967 Innis succeeded in attracting federal funds to the Harlem Commonwealth Council, which encouraged the growth of small industries in Harlem and sought to employ jobless workers. CORE also urged Congress to pass a community self-determination act to attract private capital into inner-city neighborhoods through tax incentives and matching federal funds. In general, however, the level of outside help for black enterprise remained far below the expectations of CORE.

Innis's rise to the CORE leadership in 1968 was a victory not only for political moderates but also for those who wanted to give the 180,000-member organization a tighter, more centralized structure. The 1968 CORE convention, which confirmed

Innis as national director, also voted measures to give the organization's central office greater control over local chapters. A yearly assessment of $100 per chapter was levied for the central treasury. This gave Innis greater influence but also provoked the secession of many chapter heads and organizers who disagreed with his policies. The organization was further reduced in size by a new provision that barred whites from active membership.

Despite these organizational reforms, CORE lost influence within the civil rights movement during the late 1960s. Black Power, with its emphasis on self-help, focused attention on smaller groups— community organizations, black student groups, black caucuses in churches, and professional societies. CORE's local chapters, reduced to appendages of the central office, developed little significant activity of their own. Innis himself remained active in community affairs, especially in Harlem. He also became an international figure, as Innis led a delegation on a tour of African nations in 1971, and, two years later, he became the first American to attend the Organization of African Unity (OAU) in an official capacity. He won national attention in 1973 by debating physicist William Shockley on the allegation that blacks are genetically inferior to whites in intelligence. He continued to champion a diverse array of causes, including gun ownership, drug prevention, and immigrant rights, and gradually moved with CORE to embrace more conservative positions. He broke with the Democratic Party in 1998 and became a libertarian.

—SLG

## Inouye, Daniel K(en)

(1924–    ) *member of the House of Representatives, member of the Senate*

Inouye was born in Honolulu on September 7, 1924. Upon graduation from high school in 1942, he enlisted in the Japanese-American 442d Infantry Regiment, which became famous in World War II for its heroism and high casualty rate. Inouye, who lost his right arm in combat in Italy, rose to the rank of captain by the time of his discharge in 1947.

After studies at the University of Hawaii and George Washington University Law School, he practiced law in Honolulu. Between 1954 and 1958 he won elections to both the territorial House of Representatives and Senate. During this time he helped JOHN BURNS build the Democratic Party

into the territory's dominant political machine. When Hawaii became a state in 1959, Inouye stepped aside to allow one of Hawaii's "elder statesmen," Oren Long, to seek a U.S. Senate seat. Winning election to the U.S. House of Representatives instead, Inouye inherited the Senate post in 1962 when Long announced his retirement. As in most of his campaigns, the November 1962 contest against a Republican opponent resulted in a lopsided victory for Inouye.

Inouye's voting record received high marks from the Americans for Democratic Action. He solidly supported civil rights, poverty, and Medicare legislation, but he occasionally voted against bills that organized labor supported. This reflected his friendly relations with Hawaii's sugar and pineapple growers and his differences with the powerful International Longshoremen's and Warehousemen's Union (ILWU). Although the ILWU was one of the major components of Democratic power in Hawaii, Inouye, whose tremendous popularity made him less dependent than other Democrats on ILWU support for reelection, constantly tried to prevent the union from dominating the party. He also sought a relaxation and redefinition of antitrust laws, arguing that only monopolistic corporations could compete with other nations. He also maintained excellent relations with President Johnson, who had actively supported the Hawaii statehood bill as majority leader in the Senate. In 1968 Johnson urged presidential nominee HUBERT HUMPHREY to choose Inouye as his running mate. But Humphrey chose Senator EDMUND MUSKIE (D-Maine) instead.

A loyal Democrat concerned with maintaining party unity, Inouye generally supported President Johnson's Vietnam policies and delivered the keynote address at the 1968 Democratic National Convention. That November he won reelection to the Senate with 88 percent of the total vote. Under the Nixon administration, Inouye became more critical of the Vietnam War, and, in 1970, he voted for the Cooper-Church Amendment. He came to national prominence as a member of the Senate Watergate Committee in the summer of 1973. In 1975 he became the chair of the Select Committee on Intelligence, and, in the late 1980s, he served on the select committee that investigated alleged secret arms sales by the Reagan administration to the Nicaraguan contras.

—JCH

# Jackson, Henry M(artin)

(1912–1983) *member of the Senate*

Jackson, who was born in Everett, Washington, on May 31, 1912, was a University of Washington law school graduate. He became prosecuting attorney of Snohomish County, Washington, in 1938 and won election to the House of Representatives two years later, where he maintained one of the most liberal voting records in Congress. He won a seat in the U.S. Senate in 1952 by defeating the Republican incumbent Harry Cain. In the upper house Jackson continued to support liberal domestic legislation, but his major interest turned to military and foreign policy matters as well as to nuclear energy. He became best known for his vociferous insistence, as a member of the Armed Services Committee, upon the maintenance of American military superiority over the Soviet Union. Some political observers attributed Jackson's interest in military affairs and support of large defense expenditures to the presence of major defense industries in his state, especially the Boeing Corporation. By the late 1950s some detractors called him the "senator from Boeing."

Jackson expressed reservations about some of the Kennedy administration's efforts to control the arms race with the Soviet Union. In 1961 he opposed the bill creating the Arms Control and Disarmament Agency and two years later had doubts about the limited nuclear test ban treaty, although he ultimately backed it. Jackson criticized the Pentagon's November 1962 decision to award General Dynamics, rather than Boeing, the contract to build the swing-wing TFX fighter/bomber, and he initiated a 1963 Senate investigation of the matter.

Jackson succeeded Senator CLINTON P. ANDERSON (D-N.Mex.) as chair of the Interior and Insular Affairs Committee in 1963, and in that post he was able to increase his influence in the Senate. The panel had jurisdiction over bills pertaining to federal power projects, the use of public land, land reclamation, mining, and other matters closely related to economic growth. As chair of the committee, Jackson was able to promote the rapidly expanding economy of his home state. Furthermore, his position enabled him to start or stop major resource development projects in every other state, and he used this power to win support in the Senate for his positions on bills beyond the purview of the committee.

The Interior Committee was also responsible for introducing conservation bills, and Jackson won generally favorable comments from groups interested in promoting such measures. In 1964 he spearheaded congressional passage of the Wilderness Act, which limited entrepreneurial activity in wilderness areas. Three years later he began work on a bill to establish federal guidelines for protecting the quality of the environment, a measure that passed as the National Environmental Policy Act in 1969. He also sponsored the Alaska and Hawaii Statehood Acts.

Although Jackson criticized Johnson administration officials who predicted imminent victory in the Vietnam War, charging that they were creating false hopes that might ultimately cause disillusionment, he was one of the most enthusiastic supporters of the president's Southeast Asia policies. In 1965 he asserted that the war represented one episode in the long post–World War II struggle against world communism and that appeasement in Vietnam would lead to other setbacks for the West. Beginning in 1966 he stressed his belief that the

People's Republic of China was America's major enemy in Vietnam and that the war was part of China's effort to dominate all of Asia. Initially confident of America's ability to win a military victory in Southeast Asia, he subsequently placed much of the blame for Vietnam reverses upon the domestic peace movement.

By 1968 Jackson's position on the war had created a wide gulf between himself and many other liberals. Highly critical of the antiwar candidacies of Senator ROBERT F. KENNEDY (D-N.Y.) and Senator EUGENE J. MCCARTHY (D-Minn.), he supported Vice President HUBERT H. HUMPHREY's bid for the Democratic presidential nomination in 1968 and coordinated Humphrey's effort to win convention delegates in the state of Washington.

In December 1968 Jackson declined President-elect RICHARD M. NIXON's offer to appoint him secretary of defense. He backed the Nixon administration's Southeast Asia policies and voted for construction of the Safeguard Antiballistic Missile System in 1969 and the supersonic jet transport, a Boeing project, in 1970. He also identified himself with support of Israel and the rights of Soviet Jews, and an opponent of the president's policy of détente. He did support improved relations with China, and, between 1974 and his death in 1983, he made four official visits to China. In 1972 Jackson competed in the race for the Democratic presidential nomination but was eliminated after the first few primaries. He gave only nominal endorsement to the party's ultimate choice, Senator GEORGE S. MCGOVERN (D-S.Dak.), an opponent of the Vietnam War. Four years later Jackson again entered the contest for the Democratic presidential nomination but dropped out of the race. He remained in office until his death of a ruptured aorta in Everett, Washington, on September 1, 1983.

—MLL

## Jackson, Jesse L(ouis)

(1941–   ) *national director, Operation Breadbasket*

Jackson was born on October 8, 1941, in Greenville, South Carolina, and grew up in poverty. He attended a segregated high school in Greenville and graduated from the predominantly black Agricultural and Technical College of North Carolina at Greensboro in 1964. Jackson became active in civil rights as president of the college student body and led a campaign of sit-ins in Greensboro to desegregate public facilities in 1963. While participating in the Selma voter registration drive of 1965, he came into contact with the Southern Christian Leadership Conference (SCLC) and its leader, MARTIN LUTHER KING, JR. Jackson later described King as "my father figure, my brother figure and my teacher."

After the Selma campaign Jackson enrolled in the Chicago Theological Seminary, where he was ordained in 1968. While studying in Chicago he worked as an organizer for the SCLC, helping to increase cooperation among local civil rights and community groups and developed a reputation as an inspired figure that would remain with him throughout the rest of his long career with the movement. When King decided to open a civil rights drive in Chicago in early 1966, he chose Jackson to supervise the campaign's economic activities. These soon developed into Operation Breadbasket, an effort to improve the economic position of blacks through the coordinated use of black purchasing power. Working through a network of community and church groups, Jackson urged Chicago blacks to buy the products of black-owned companies and to boycott stores that refused to carry these products or practiced racial discrimination in hiring. Within five months nine Chicago companies had signed agreements promising to increase the number of black employees.

The early success of Operation Breadbasket encouraged King and Jackson to extend the program beyond Chicago. In late 1966 Jackson became the head of national Operation Breadbasket, which covered 16 cities. The program's greatest achievement came in 1968, when a 14-week black boycott of the A&P food chain forced the company to sign an agreement providing for increased hiring of blacks and the display of black-manufactured products in its stores. The pact also promised that A&P stores in black neighborhoods would use the services of black truckers, advertisers, and other small business owners.

In April 1968 Jackson was standing next to King in a Memphis motel when King was assassinated. Jackson continued to work for the SCLC after King's death. In May he went to Washington to help organize the Poor People's Campaign, a series of demonstrations and lobbying efforts aimed at increasing federal antipoverty funds. In 1969 Jackson organized a highly successful Black Expo in Chicago, which publicized achievements in business and culture. The interest generated encouraged him to make Black Expo an annual event. Conflicts eventually developed, however, between Jackson and RALPH ABERNATHY, King's successor as SCLC leader. Jackson wanted more authority in the SCLC than Abernathy was willing to give him; Abernathy, in turn, wanted control over Operation Breadbasket funds, which Jackson used in 1971 to finance the Black Expo. In December 1971 Jackson left the SCLC, followed by most of the organization's Chicago chapter.

Jackson immediately founded a new Chicago-based organization, Operation PUSH (People United to Save Humanity), to continue his work. The program's emphasis remained on black economic self-help. In addition to sponsoring the annual Black Expo, Operation PUSH negotiated "covenants" on the hiring of black workers with several large corporations. Although active in Chicago Democratic politics, Jackson urged a reorientation of the civil rights movement from political activism to community economic development, claiming that blacks needed greater financial resources to take advantage of the political rights won in the 1960s. He subsequently created PUSH-Excel, a branch of PUSH devoted to educational and voter registration issues. He ran for the Democratic Party's nomination for president in 1984, and, although unsuccessful, it led to the creation of his political organization, the Rainbow Coalition.

—SLG

## Javits, Jacob K(oppel)
(1904–1986) *member of the Senate*

Javits was born on May 18, 1904, and raised on New York's Lower East Side. He held part-time jobs while studying law at New York University. After his admission to the bar in 1927 he and his older brother established a law firm specializing in bankruptcy and corporate reorganization.

A supporter of Fiorello La Guardia, Javits joined the Republican Party during the 1930s. In 1946 he received the party's nomination in an Upper West Side congressional district. Javits ran on a liberal platform and was the first Republican to carry the district since 1920. In the House of Representatives Javits generally voted against the Republican majority on important bills.

Javits defeated Democrat FRANKLIN D. ROOSEVELT, JR., in a race for New York State attorney general in 1954. Two years later he won the Republican senatorial nomination and defeated New York City mayor ROBERT F. WAGNER, JR. by almost half a million votes. In the Senate Javits continued to compile a liberal voting record. He attempted to strengthen the Civil Rights Act of 1960, and, in 1961, he offered an amendment to expand the number of workers covered by minimum-wage legislation. The following year he cosponsored with Senator CLINTON P. ANDERSON (D-N.Mex.) an administration-backed Social Security Medicare bill. In 1962 he won his reelection bid by almost one million votes.

Javits, who accomplished the rare Republican feat of carrying New York City in the 1962 election, fared well in the city because of his liberal voting record and Jewish heritage. His party label also enabled him to carry easily the traditionally Republican upstate region. As a result, he was one of the most successful vote-getters in New York State's history. But in the Senate Javits's liberalism and combative style prevented him from becoming part of the upper chamber's Republican leadership. He tried to compensate for his lack of influence by serving on as many committees and subcommittees as possible and by expressing his views on a wide range of issues. Johnson aide LAWRENCE O'BRIEN later recalled, "Jack Javits was unique in the Senate. He was a nominal Republican with an R next to his name through his whole career in the Congress, but in reality he was a liberal. And that cost him in terms of influence in the Senate. He was not looked upon with favor by his Republican colleagues, and he was not considered really part of the Democratic liberal wing because he had the R next to his name."

According to *Congressional Quarterly*, Javits was among the two leading Republican opponents of the Senate's conservative coalition from 1964 through 1967. He consistently supported President LYNDON B. JOHNSON's civil rights measures and generally backed his Great Society programs. When the administration proposed a bill to create a domestic peace corps, which died in the House, Javits not only actively supported it but attached a rider to it outlawing public funds for any segregated facilities. He was also one of few senators who, in 1963, supported the March on Washington organized by civil rights leaders. He was sometimes more liberal than the administration itself. In April 1966 he introduced an amendment to the president's housing legislation that expanded the Demonstration Cities program to permit the participation of more than one neighborhood in eligible cities. The following July Javits opposed appropriations for work on a proton accelerator at Weston, Illinois, because of alleged housing discrimination in the area.

Despite his liberal beliefs, he criticized the Democratic left for what he regarded as its inclination to look to the federal government for the solutions to all social ills. The senator stated that he favored attacking national problems through a partnership of government and business. In April 1964 he criticized a majority report of the Labor and Public Welfare Committee's Employment and Manpower Subcommittee that advocated an increase of federal expenditures by at least $5 billion a year to increase demand in proportion to rising labor productivity. The following August Javits opposed a temporary, retroactive tax on the purchase by Americans of foreign securities, arguing that it would "erect an artificial wall to the free flow of private capital." Two years later he supported a bill providing for U.S. participation in the Asian Development Bank but said that he did not "believe that sufficient emphasis on the development of private enterprise is indicated . . . in the operation of the Bank."

In 1965 and 1966 Javits supported administration policy in Vietnam while stressing, as he stated in February 1966, that he favored "limited objectives and limited military force." Early in the following year Javits began to express strong reservations about the war, and, in October, he joined 22 other senators in supporting a resolution that urged an intensified effort to find a peaceful solution to the conflict.

Javits was a strong supporter of Israel. At the end of the June 1967 Mideast war he asserted that the United States "must not stand by as Israel is asked to pull back from positions gained through the expenditure of so much blood and heroism . . . until it is made certain that Israel's future security is guaranteed."

During the mid-1960s Javits was a close political ally of New York governor NELSON A. ROCKEFELLER. In 1964 Javits supported the governor's effort to win the Republican presidential nomination. Later he declined to endorse conservative senator BARRY M. GOLDWATER (R-Ariz.), the party's ultimate choice. Two years later Rockefeller proposed Javits as a vice presidential nominee to run with Michigan governor GEORGE ROMNEY in 1968. This suggestion gained some support within the party, but as Romney's hopes for the nomination faded so did the senator's chance to become the first Jew to run on a national ticket. In 1968 Javits endorsed another unsuccessful bid by Rockefeller to win the Republican presidential nomination. This time he supported the party's eventual nominee, RICHARD M. NIXON. During the same year Javits won reelection to the Senate in a three-way race with a plurality of over 1 million votes.

In 1970 Javits backed the Cooper-Church Amendment to bar funds for U.S. forces in Cambodia. During the same year he supported efforts to repeal the Gulf of Tonkin Resolution. He was also an early supporter of reining in the executive branch in its conduct of foreign policy, helping to push through the War Powers Act of 1973 over President Nixon's veto. Some opponents of the Indochina war, however, felt that the senator was not sufficiently outspoken in his criticism of the conflict. During the late 1960s and early 1970s Javits was also a leading advocate of consumer protection legislation. In 1970 he and Senator ABRAHAM RIBICOFF (D-Conn.) cosponsored a bill to establish an independent Consumer Protection Agency. He was also the principal author of the Pension Reform Act of 1974, which helped protect retirement pensions. In 1974 Javits was reelected with a margin of less than 400,000 votes. He was defeated for reelection in 1980 and returned to the practice of law. He served as an adjunct professor of public affairs at Columbia University. He died in West Palm Beach, Florida, on March 7, 1986.

—MLL

## Jenkins, Walter W(ilson)
(1918–1985) *White House special assistant*

Jenkins, who was born on March 23, 1918, in Jolly, Texas, attended the University of Texas at Austin and then joined Representative LYNDON B. JOHNSON's (D-Tex.) staff in 1939. During Johnson's Senate years, Jenkins served as his general office manager, personnel chief, private secretary, and administrative assistant.

After Johnson became president in 1963, Jenkins was named a White House special assistant. He occupied a unique position on the Johnson staff with a wide range of duties, including those of general manager, chief of payroll and personnel, congressional liaison, and adviser on domestic policy. Jenkins sat in on all cabinet meetings and was one of the few special assistants authorized to sign the president's name to letters. He did the screening for many high-level appointments, controlled access to LBJ, and served as the sounding board for many of the president's early decisions.

Once described as a "faceless anonymous servant," Jenkins first received national attention during the 1964 Senate Rules and Administration Committee investigations into the business affairs of former Senate majority secretary ROBERT "Bobby" G. BAKER. One of Baker's associates in a life insurance business. Don B. Reynolds of South Carolina, had twice sold $100,000 life insurance policies to Lyndon Johnson. In return for this favor, Jenkins allegedly requested that Reynolds purchase advertising time on the Johnson-owned television station, KTBC-TV. In a sworn affidavit Jenkins stated that he "had no knowledge of any arrangements by which Reynolds purchased advertising on the television station." Over strong Republican opposition, the Rules and Administration Committee voted to end the Baker probe on March 25, 1964, before Jenkins could be called to testify.

On October 7, 1964, Jenkins was arrested in a Washington, D.C., men's room on a charge of "indecent gestures." He had been arrested in a YMCA bathroom in what advisers told Johnson was "a compromising position" with another man. LBJ was stunned: "It shocks me as much as though my daughter committed treason," he told the deputy attorney general. He resigned his post as White House special assistant on October 14. News of the arrest was suppressed by major Washington newspapers at the request of CLARK CLIFFORD and ABE FORTAS, who appealed to the editors not to publish the story for "humanitarian" reasons. Only after Republican Party national chair Dean Burch had issued a statement that "the White House is desperately trying to suppress a major news story," did United Press International release the full details.

Coming just before a national election and on the heels of the Bobby Baker scandal, the news provoked considerable anxiety in the White House. Because Jenkins had access to the highest classified material in the White House, Johnson ordered a probe by the FBI. The bureau reported to the pres-

ident on October 22 that it could find no evidence that Jenkins had violated national security.

Emphasizing the issue of "government morality," the Republican national ticket sought to make the Jenkins incident a major campaign issue. Presidential candidate senator BARRY GOLDWATER (R-Ariz.) lamented Lyndon Johnson's "curious crew," and vice presidential candidate representative WILLIAM E. MILLER (R-N.Y.) stated that U.S. security had been violated by the presence of Jenkins in the White House.

After waiting a full week to comment on the Jenkins matter, President Johnson, on October 24, 1964, called the Jenkins incident "unfortunate" and "distressing." However, the full impact of the Jenkins resignation had already been muted somewhat by the fall from power of Soviet premier Nikita Khrushchev on October 14 and the detonation of Communist China's first nuclear device on October 16.

After his resignation Jenkins returned to Texas, where he took a job with the Johnson-owned radio and television stations. He died in 1985.

—FHM

## Johnson, Harold K(eith)
(1912–1983)  *chief of staff, U.S. Army*

Born in Bowesmont, North Dakota, in 1912, Johnson graduated from the United States Military Academy in 1933. He served with distinction in numerous capacities during World War II, including three years as a Japanese POW, and then graduated from the Command and General Staff School at Fort Leavenworth in 1947, remaining as a teacher until 1949. During the Korean War he served as the plans and operations officer of the I Corps, Far East Command. After graduating from the National War College in 1953, he directed the Joint War Plans Branch, Office of the Assistant Chief of Staff, until 1955. Five years later he was promoted to permanent brigadier general and was the commandant of the Command and General Staff College until 1963, when President Johnson selected him as army chief of staff.

In naming him as chief of staff, President Johnson bypassed 31 lieutenant generals and 12 four-star generals who outranked him in seniority of all members of the Joint Chiefs of Staff. Johnson was initially most unwilling to see the United States become deeply involved in Vietnam. In February 1965 Johnson told two *New York Times* reporters that he feared U.S. involvement in Vietnam would be worse than in Korea. The enemy, he stated, would begin using sanctuaries against which the United States would be unable and unwilling to employ its full power.

In February 1965 Communist guerrillas attacked the American bases at Pleiku and Qui Non. In retaliation the United States began bombing North Vietnam. One of the important questions the general had to consider was whether the United States should commit combat troops to the war. General WILLIAM C. WESTMORELAND, commander of the U.S. Military Assistance Command in Vietnam, had already urged that two battalions of combat-ready marines be sent to help defend the air base at Da Nang. This request was approved by the president while General Johnson was still in Saigon. Westmoreland, however, wanted more troops and the power to maneuver them anywhere in the South. On the other hand, U.S. ambassador MAXWELL D. TAYLOR feared that an initial commitment would only lead to further requests until the United States found itself deeply involved in a difficult Asian land war. If U.S. troops were sent, Taylor said, their role should be limited to the defense of strategic coastal bases, General Johnson, in his report of March 14, sided with Westmoreland in recommending that one division of combat troops be sent to South Vietnam's central highlands. He also suggested stepped-up bombing and removal of some of the restrictions on targets in the North, proposals that were approved by the White House. He was also critical of LBJ's policy of gradual escalation, which he believed did not do enough to mobilize the American people or the nation's war-making capacity. He also urged a greater effort to create and support a legitimate government in South Vietnam. Johnson also deeply disliked the president's lack of public candor in his public statements about U.S. policy in Vietnam. Johnson reacted with rage when he heard the president state in an afternoon news conference on July 28, 1965, that he had approved an increase in U.S. troop strength in Vietnam to 125,000 even though he had actually authorized a ceiling of 175,000. Johnson was so infuriated that he drove to the White House prepared to resign, only to change his mind at the last minute.

In July 1965 General Johnson brought together a group of talented young officers to work on a report entitled *Pacification and Long-Term Development of South Vietnam.* Completed in March 1966, the report recommended that the United States revive and modify its earlier effort to win the loyalty of the South Vietnamese peasants. It noted that there had been considerable conflict among the various U.S. agencies involved in earlier rural pacification efforts and recommended that the U.S. ambassador to South Vietnam become the sole manager of all nonmilitary U.S. activities in that country. According to the *Pentagon Papers,* many of the recommendations of this report were never implemented, but "the influence of the study was substantial" in reviving the rural pacification programs.

In August 1967 Johnson appeared before the Senate Preparedness Subcommittee to advocate heavier bombing of North Vietnam. He stated that he expected to see "very real evidence of economic and social progress" in South Vietnam and that with an addition of 45,000 more American troops and heavy bombing, the United States could have the war well in hand within 18 months and could begin bringing home its troops.

General Johnson retired in July 1968 to become a director of Genesco, Inc. He was succeeded as army chief of staff by General Westmoreland. He remained active writing and speaking until his death on September 24, 1983, in Washington, D.C.

—JLW

## Johnson, (Claudia Taylor) Lady Bird
(1912–   ) *first lady*

As a small child Claudia Alta Taylor was given the nickname Lady Bird when her nurse, Alice Tittle, described the two-year-old as being "as pretty as a lady bird." She was born on December 22, 1912, in an antebellum mansion on the Texas-Louisiana border, the daughter of a wealthy Texas merchant and landowner. Her mother died after a fall in September 1918. After taking a degree in journalism from the University of Texas in Austin, she married LYNDON JOHNSON in November 1934. Johnson was then executive secretary to a Texas member of congress. Johnson won a runoff election to Congress in 1937, and he and Lady Bird began a 30-year political career in Washington.

In her early years as a politician's wife, Lady Bird tried to avoid the limelight. Still, she was effective in a quiet way, especially after her husband left his seat in Congress to serve in World War II, leaving Lady Bird to manage his office in his absence. She also helped to stabilize their financial standing, by using money left to her by her mother to purchase a failing radio station in Austin in 1942. Relying on her hard work and business skill, as well as her husband's political connections, the station slowly grew until it became the basis for a diverse and highly profitable communications company.

As LBJ continued to progress up the political ladder, Lady Bird grew more and more involved with his operations. She actively campaigned for him in his successful quest for the Senate in 1948. When Lyndon had a heart attack in 1955, Lady Bird performed many of the tasks that the new majority leader was unable to do. In the 1960 election, Lady Bird traveled more than 35,000 miles in support of the Democratic ticket of her husband and John F. Kennedy. In 1963, when JFK was assassinated in Dallas, Lady Bird became the nation's first lady.

Lady Bird Johnson came to the White House in 1963 with a background as both a business and a political professional. During the administration she stressed her role as wife and mother, summing up her advisory duties with the phrase, "I infiltrate." But according to historian and former White House special assistant ERIC GOLDMAN, "a good many important figures, in and outside the White House, were advanced, eased out, or went up or down in influence depending on the impression they left on Lady Bird Johnson."

During the 1964 political campaign Mrs. Johnson undertook a widely publicized five-day, eight-state, 1,682-mile, whistle-stop campaign trip through the South in an effort to lure potential Goldwater votes for the president despite his signing of the Civil Rights Act the previous July. It was the first time that a first lady had ever campaigned on her own.

Lady Bird Johnson stealing a laugh with her husband *(Photographed by Yoichi R. Okamoto; Lyndon Baines Johnson Library)*

After the election Mrs. Johnson used the White House as a public forum for bringing environmental issues to national attention. In February 1965 she created the First Lady's Committee for a More Beautiful Capital, chaired by Secretary of the Interior STEWART UDALL. In October of the same year, at Mrs. Johnson's urging and under pressure from President Johnson, Congress passed the Highway Beautification Act, which the president declared "does not represent all we want, or all we need, or all the national interest requires. But it is a first step." The measure, which was widely known as "Lady Bird's Bill," authorized use of federal funds to help states control billboards and junkyards along noncommercial sections of interstate and primary highways. In addition, $80 million was appropriated over a two-year period to pay 75 percent of compensatory costs to billboard and junkyard owners. The Highway Beautification Act also gave $240 million in federal funds to the states over two years for landscaping and roadside development. She also served as the honorary chair of the National Head Start Program.

In the middle and late 1960s Mrs. Johnson ranked at or near the top of the Gallup poll's list of "most admired" women. She accompanied the president on many overseas trips and was considered a goodwill asset. However, during the late 1960s, when the Vietnam War provoked strong reactions throughout the nation, Mrs. Johnson was occasionally the target of antiwar protests and demonstrations. In a widely publicized incident at a January 1968 White House luncheon, singer Eartha Kitt accused the Johnson administration of

Lyndon Baines Johnson taking the oath of office aboard Air Force One hours after the death of President Kennedy as his widow, Jackie Kennedy, looks on, 1963  *(Photographed by Cecil Stoughton; Lyndon Baines Johnson Library)*

sending "the best of this country off to be shot and maimed." The next day Mrs. Johnson said she regretted that "only the shrill voice of anger and discord" had been heard at the luncheon. In March 1968 Mrs. Johnson was instrumental in helping the president make his decision not to seek reelection to the presidency.

Two years after leaving the White House, Mrs. Johnson published *A White House Diary*, an informal view of her years as first lady. In 1971 she was appointed to a six-tear term on the Board of Trustees for the University of Texas. Following Lyndon Johnson's death in 1973, she involved herself in the operations of the Johnson Library in Austin and the prosperous LBJ ranch in Johnson City, Texas. She also maintained her strong interest in the environment.

—FHM

## Johnson, Lyndon B(aines)
(1908–1973)  *president of the United States*

Lyndon Johnson, whose grandfather was a populist member of the Texas state legislature and whose father was a cattle speculator, was born on August 27, 1908, on a farm in the rugged hill country of south-central Texas, near Austin. He attended local public schools, graduated from Southwest Texas State Teachers College in 1930, and the next year became secretary to a Texas representative. While in Washington Johnson got advice to pursue a political career from Representative Sam Rayburn (D-Tex.), a close political confidant and later Speaker of the House of Representatives. In 1934 he married Claudia Alta Taylor, known as LADY BIRD, who was a steadying influence on the sometimes mercurial Johnson.

In 1935 President Franklin Roosevelt appointed Johnson as Texas state administrator of the National Youth Administration, a New Deal relief agency for young people. The job also provided Johnson with a wide political base for a successful congressional campaign in 1937. He ran on a strong New Deal platform rooted in a personal relationship with Roosevelt, who Johnson later declared "was like a Daddy to me." But after 1938 Johnson, like many other southern representatives, became more conservative. His political career was interrupted by service with the U.S. Navy in World War II. In 1948 he won a bitterly fought Democratic senatorial primary runoff election by 87 votes out of 1 million cast. The outcome, which was marred by charges of fraud and corruption, earned Johnson the nickname "Landslide Lyndon." He then easily defeated his Republican opponent in the general election.

Befriended by powerful Senator RICHARD RUSSELL (D-Ga.), a member of the Senate "establishment," Johnson rose quickly through the Senate hierarchy, winning the post of minority leader in 1953 and majority leader two years later. In 1955 he made a rapid recovery from a massive heart attack.

As majority leader, Johnson established a near-legendary reputation for his command of the legislative process and his assessment of the needs, ambitions, and weaknesses of individual senators. He was also well known for his willingness to work with moderate Republicans, including President Eisenhower, with whom he shared a close working relationship. As his own national ambitions increased, Johnson's political stance moved from conservative to moderate. He guided through Congress a number of programs that the Republican administration opposed and helped gain passage for the Civil Rights Acts of 1957 and 1960, despite considerable southern resistance. The civil rights bills, however, had been dramatically weakened in order to hold the coalition of moderates from both parties together. Johnson thus won a political victory by denying Republicans the ability to take credit for a civil rights bill, while at the same time not alienating the conservative southerners in his own party.

Johnson's 1960 presidential strategy was to remain aloof from the primaries in the hope that the announced candidates, Senator John F. Kennedy (D-Mass.) and Senator HUBERT H. HUMPHREY (D-Minn.), would either drop out of the race or become deadlocked before reaching the convention. However, Kennedy soon won a series of primary victories, and big-city political machines, labor unions, and black voters in the party moved solidly behind his candidacy. Johnson formally announced his own candidacy for the Democratic presidential nomination on July 5, but eight days later Kennedy won the nomination at the Los Angeles convention on the first ballot.

With the presidential nomination secured, Kennedy surprised his northern liberal and labor backers by selecting Johnson as his running mate in order to attract southern and western votes in the general election. Johnson's nomination was generally considered to be a critical factor in the Kennedy-Johnson victory over Vice President RICHARD M.

NIXON and HENRY CABOT LODGE in the November election.

As vice president, Johnson chaired the National Aeronautics and Space Council and the President's Committee on Equal Opportunity. He also served as chair of the Peace Corps Advisory Council. He also visited some 34 countries on trips many observers likened to Johnson's domestic campaign swings. Despite the publicity Johnson won on these trips, his 30 months as vice president were frustrating. He later told biographer Doris Kearns that the vice presidency "is filled with trips around the world, chauffeurs, men saluting, people clapping, chairmanships of councils, but in the end, it is nothing. I detested every minute of it."

In both 1962 and 1963 there were persistent rumors, denied by President Kennedy, that Johnson would be dropped from the 1964 Democratic ticket. This possibility seemed more real when ROBERT G. BAKER, secretary to the Senate majority and a Johnson protégé, was charged with having used his influential post to advance several business enterprises.

On November 21, 1963, President Kennedy flew to Texas with Johnson on a precampaign swing designed to reconcile rival factions of the Texas Democratic Party. The next day Kennedy was assassinated while riding in a Dallas motorcade. At 2:39 p.m. the same day, Lyndon Johnson was sworn in aboard Air Force One as the 36th president of the United States. In a brief address to the nation that evening at Andrews Air Force Base in Washington, Johnson said, "This is a sad time for all people. We have suffered a loss that cannot be weighed. . . . I will do my best, that is all I can do. I ask for your help and God's."

Recognizing that his most important contribution during the crisis of succession would be to exercise his authority prudently and confidently, Johnson initiated a series of conferences with congressional leaders, urged anguished Kennedy staffers to stay at their posts, and talked to several heads of state gathered for his predecessor's funeral. Acutely conscious that he was a Texan during a time of profound national anger after Dallas and that he was also the first southern president since Woodrow Wilson, Johnson immediately sought to allay northern fears about his presidency. On November 27 he addressed a packed and tense joint session of Congress and in a moving speech urged the earliest possible passage of Kennedy's civil rights bill as a memorial to the late president. "We have talked long enough in this country about equal rights," said Johnson. "It is time now to write . . . it in the books of law." Two days later Johnson appointed a prestigious bipartisan commission, chaired by Chief Justice EARL WARREN, to investigate the assassination of President Kennedy.

By the end of 1963 Johnson had decided on his legislative strategy for the next year: passage at all costs of the Kennedy civil rights bill and the late president's $11 billion tax cut to stimulate the economy. In addition, Johnson decided to add a third measure to his list of "must pass" legislation: an antipoverty measure that would be the first major legislation of his own administration. Although the new president inherited a Congress that had repeatedly frustrated Kennedy, Johnson proved adept at bending the legislature to his will. As majority leader in the 1950s and now as president, Johnson was a brilliant legislative tactician. His well-known ability to spur on his friends and persuade his enemies became known as the "Johnson treatment," a technique, according to the New York Times, that "consisted of a combination of cajolery, flattery, concession, arm-twisting and outright wooing, all applied by Mr. Johnson with an endless succession of phone calls."

Johnson first turned his attention to passage of the long-stalled, $11 billion tax cut. His principal opponent in the Congress was Senator HARRY BYRD (D-Va.), conservative chair of the Senate Finance Committee. After much discussion with Johnson, Byrd agreed that if the new budget stayed below $100 billion he would allow the Finance Committee to approve the bill. Johnson submitted a $97.9 billion budget in January 1964 and publicized his commitment to economy in government by personally turning out unneeded White House lights. The Finance Committee soon approved the tax cut, and the Senate passed it in February by a vote of 77 to 21. The same month Johnson informed Senate Democratic leaders MIKE MANSFIELD (D-Mont.) and Hubert Humphrey that he was willing to sacrifice all Senate legislation to break the prospective southern filibuster on the equal accommodations and equal employment civil rights bill. Meanwhile, civil rights groups, labor unions, liberal organizations, and church bodies lobbied furiously and effectively all through the spring of 1964. Johnson let Humphrey and Mansfield do much of the day-to-day work in getting the legislation passed, but he worked on a national level as well, working to convince the American public of the importance of this reform in order to put pressure on southern conservatives. A southern filibuster lasting 75 days was finally broken when Senate Minority Leader EVERETT M. DIRKSEN (R-Ill.) announced that he would vote for cloture. The Senate vote to end debate passed June 10, and Johnson signed the historic 1964 Civil Rights Act on July 2.

Johnson moved beyond Kennedy's legislative program with his "declaration of an unconditional War on Poverty" in his 1964 State of the Union address. He initially requested $1 billion to fund the new Office of Economic Opportunity (OEO) under the command of former Peace Corps director SARGENT SHRIVER. The OEO administered a wide range of services directed at making the poor employable. Many were highly controversial, especially the Community Action Program and Volunteers in Service to America, both of which soon developed politically activist orientations. Though the OEO never had a budget of more than $2 billion a year, it was the centerpiece of Johnson's Great Society domestic legislative program.

Although Johnson was widely praised for his legislative triumphs in 1964, he was fearful that the Kennedy wing of the Democratic Party had not fully accepted him as president. The mutual animosity between LBJ and ROBERT KENNEDY was well known, and some of JFK's advisers who had stayed on to serve Johnson were beginning to express their unhappiness with the new president. Trying to placate the liberal wing of the party, Johnson selected Minnesota senator Hubert Humphrey as his running mate in the presidential campaign in 1964. The selection of Humphrey, in turn, completed the process of reconciling liberals, especially those in the civil rights movement and in labor, to Johnson's leadership of the party.

Nominated by acclamation at the Democratic National Convention in August 1964, Johnson faced conservative senator BARRY GOLDWATER (R-Ariz.) in the November election. Attacking Goldwater as a political reactionary, Johnson campaigned as the candidate of a broad liberal consensus on domestic social issues. Meanwhile, Democratic Party political advertisements played skillfully upon the widely held view that Goldwater was a "trigger-happy" militarist. In contrast, Johnson campaigned as a peace candidate and rebuffed any suggestion that he was considering an escalation of the war in Vietnam. "We are not about to send American boys

President Johnson as he listens to a tape sent by Captain Charles Robb from Vietnam, 1968 *(Photographed by Jack Kightlinger; Lyndon Baines Johnson Library)*

nine or ten thousand miles away from home to do what Asian boys ought to be doing for themselves," he told voters. As the candidate of moderation, Johnson won the support of many independents and Republicans. Not even the October arrest of Johnson's closest aide, WALTER JENKINS, on a morals charge stemmed the impending Johnson landslide.

On election eve Johnson told a confidant, "It seems to me tonight . . . that I have spent my whole life getting ready for this moment." The next day he swamped Goldwater by 43 million to 27 million—the greatest vote, the greatest margin, and the greatest percentage (over 61 percent) in American history. Johnson captured 486 electoral votes to Goldwater's 44, all of which were from the Deep South and Arizona. Equally important was the enormous gain made by the Democrats in Congress. They captured two additional Senate seats and gained 37 in the House. This gave liberal and moderate Democrats majorities in both houses of Congress for the first time since the heyday of the New Deal.

These rare majorities enabled Johnson to pass a phenomenal 69 percent of his legislative program during the 89th Congress. Two Kennedy measures, Medicare and aid to elementary and secondary education, passed in the first half of 1965. The new Congress also liberalized the immigration law, increased antipoverty funds, and added substantially to the amount of land protected by the national parks and wilderness areas. It also began enactment of consumer protection and environmental pollution laws. These measures, as well as other domestic reforms, were part of what LBJ called the "Great Society," his ambitious program for improving the quality of American life and extending equal opportunity to succeed to all citizens.

Johnson's most dramatic moment as a legislative leader also came in 1965. After a series of tumultuous civil rights demonstrations in Selma, Alabama, the president appeared before a joint session of Congress to throw the weight of the government behind the demands of the demonstrators in Alabama for a new and stringent voting rights law. Taking as his own the refrain of the popular movement anthem, "We shall Overcome," Johnson asked for immediate passage of a federal Voting Rights Act that would end southern discrimination against black voters. Passage of the landmark bill five months later led to the enfranchisement of some 3.5 million new black voters within the decade, but it also marked the high point of collaboration between the federal government and the civil rights movement. In each summer beginning with 1965, racial rioting exploded in the cities of the North and West. Some in the movement demanded "Black Power," and a white backlash sentiment grew evident among many of the same lower-middle-class and working-class whites who had stood at the center of the Johnson consensus. After a 1966 open housing measure failed to pass, the president moved cautiously in the civil rights area, appointing a series of commissions to study the causes of rioting and violence but proposing little new legislation. It was not until April 1968, in the wake of the assassination of MARTIN LUTHER KING, JR., that Congress passed a strong open housing bill.

During the same years in which Johnson demonstrated his mastery of the domestic legislative process, he was becoming increasingly involved with foreign affairs. In January 1964 widespread rioting broke out in the Panama Canal Zone. The Panamanian government suspended diplomatic relations with the United States and demanded a revision of the 1903 Canal Zone treaty. Johnson walked a moderate line on the issue, resisting demands for military intervention but refusing to negotiate a new treaty under threat of violence in Panama. When order was finally restored, LBJ and Panamanian president Roberto Chiari agreed to talks about the status of the Panama Canal Zone, which culminated in the eventual American decision to turn control over to Panama a decade later. "Let's make a fair treaty with the Panamanians," the president told his chief negotiator, ROBERT ANDERSON. "Let's be very sure that it is fair to them and fair to us. And the second thing is, let's try to make a treaty that can be used as a model of how a big country like ours ought to enter into treaty relationships with smaller countries and countries less secure than ours."

In April 1965 Johnson faced another Latin American crisis when the Dominican Republic's ruling military junta was threatened by rebel forces. On April 27 the president announced that he had ordered the evacuation of U.S. citizens from Santo Domingo; the next day he revealed that 400 U.S. Marines had been dispatched to the city. As the number of troops there rose to 30,000, the president asserted that communist influence in the rebellion justified U.S. military intervention. Johnson came under vigorous criticism for his policy in the Dominican Republic, and Senator J. WILLIAM FULBRIGHT's (D-Ark.) Foreign Relations Committee conducted nine days of closed-door hearings on the crisis. Many liberals who supported the president's escalation of he war in Vietnam were nevertheless sharply critical of what they regarded reversion to "big-stick" diplomacy in Latin America.

Johnson's awkward handling of the Dominican crisis was soon overshadowed by the larger problem of Vietnam, but the Caribbean incident was significant because it furthered the belief, held especially among journalists and intellectuals, that the Johnson administration suffered from a "credibility gap." The president's problems arose in part from a penchant for secrecy and an overly sensitive mistrust of anyone who criticized his policies. "His almost desperate need for loyalty was the other half of the coin of [his] insecurity . . . ," wrote journalist David Halberstam. Johnson soon surrounded himself with loyalists from Texas like JACK VALENTI, Horace Busby, JOSEPH CALIFANO, and HARRY MCPHERSON. Among the most independent members of the Johnson staff was BILL MOYERS, but the youthful Texan left the administration in late 1966 in a dispute over the handling of Vietnam news.

In the first several months of his presidency, Johnson's chief concern in Vietnam was to continue the policy he had inherited from President Kennedy. He retained Kennedy's top foreign policy advisers—DEAN RUSK, ROBERT MCNAMARA, and MCGEORGE BUNDY—and relied heavily upon their advice in the conduct of the war. Johnson believed firmly in the "domino theory." Shortly after the assassination he told ambassador to South Vietnam Henry Cabot Lodge, "I am not going to lose Vietnam. I am not going to be the President who saw Southeast Asia go the way of China." Plans for an escalation of the war began in early 1964, when it became apparent to the White House that the South Vietnamese government could not hold its own against the National Liberation Front (NLF). In February 1964 the United States initiated a secret "Operation Plan 34A" by which it provided tactical support for South Vietnamese military action against the North. In April Johnson named General WILLIAM WESTMORELAND commander of the 20,000-man U.S. force in South Vietnam, and in June he appointed General MAXWELL TAYLOR as ambassador to South Vietnam to replace Lodge.

On August 4, 1964, two U.S. destroyers patrolling the Gulf of Tonkin off the coast of North Vietnam reported that they were under enemy attack. A few days earlier U.S. and North Vietnamese ships had fought a minor skirmish in the same area. Although Johnson soon received information suggesting that the reported attack might not have occurred or, if it had, had been grossly exaggerated, he withheld this information from the public and ordered retaliatory bombing of North Vietnamese coastal bases and oil depots. At Johnson's request Congress three days later passed the Tonkin Gulf Resolution, which gave the president broad authority to use military force throughout Southeast Asia "to prevent further aggression." The resolution passed both houses of Congress with only two dissenting votes. Subsequent evidence strongly suggested that no attack had taken place, and that problems with the ship's equipment, combined with poor weather conditions, led the American officers to erroneous conclusions.

Throughout the autumn of 1964 Johnson received reports that the NLF was tightening its hold on the South Vietnamese countryside. Taylor and Westmoreland urged the president to authorize systematic bombing of North Vietnam as a means of bolstering morale in the South and cutting infiltration from the North. Campaigning as a peace candidate in the fall, Johnson postponed action on their requests. Nevertheless, the actual decision to undertake the bombing of the North had been made as early as December 1964. "I suddenly realized that doing nothing was more dangerous than doing something," Johnson told Doris Kearns.

In February 1965 Communist guerrillas attacked the U.S. military compounds at Pleiku and at Qui Nhon. The attacks provided the pretext for Johnson to order retaliatory air raids on North Vietnamese military and industrial sites. By the end of the month, the bombing of the North had become continuous, though limited to targets outside the Hanoi area. Johnson also authorized the landing of two combat-ready marine battalions to defend the large airbase at Da Nang. On April 1 Johnson agreed to Westmoreland's request that he be authorized to use the troops for offensive actions anywhere in South Vietnam. By early June there were 50,000 American ground troops in Vietnam. Over the next two years Johnson agreed to almost all of Westmoreland's troop increase requests. By early 1968 there were over 500,000 American soldiers in Vietnam.

Backed by Bundy and McNamara, Johnson's escalation of the war took place in a gradual, step-by-step fashion. He chose this course for three reasons. First, Johnson and most of his civilian advisers feared that a major escalation would precipitate active Chinese intervention in the war. Second, they hoped that the relatively slow increase in the pressure on the North might force Hanoi to negotiate in order to prevent the terrible damage that large-scale bombing would inflict. Third, Johnson feared the domestic consequences of a rapid expansion of the war. In 1965 he worried that congressional conservatives would use the war as an excuse to reduce funding for Great Society programs. Later, after Johnson himself had begun to cut back on domestic social legislation, he feared that a dramatic escalation of the war would add to the growing list of liberal war critics.

During the years from 1965 to 1967 Johnson announced repeatedly that he favored negotiations with the North Vietnamese, and several bombing halts were called, ostensibly to facilitate the start of talks. Hanoi leaders did not respond to the president's numerous "peace feelers," in part because the Communists insisted upon an American commitment to an unconditional halt to the bombing of the North but also because they were convinced they were winning the war in the South. Meanwhile, the Joint Chiefs of Staff continually pressed Johnson for an expansion and intensification of the bombing, but Secretary of Defense McNamara grew increasingly skeptical over the diplomatic or military efficacy of continued air attacks. In a September 1967 speech delivered at San Antonio, Johnson promised to halt the air war indefinitely if North Vietnam agreed promptly to begin peace negotiations and not to "take advantage" of the bombing cessation to send men and material to the South. Since over 100,000 North Vietnamese troops had to be supplied in the South, Hanoi soon rejected the "San Antonio Formula."

As a result of the 1964 tax cut and the growing expenditures for the Vietnam War, the U.S. economy under Johnson enjoyed its longest period of sustained growth to that point in the postwar era. The gross national product increased by more than 7 percent per annum during the years 1964 to 1967. Meanwhile, both the inflation and unemployment rates remained at unusually low levels. At first Johnson tried to pay for the Vietnam War without cutting Great Society programs or increasing federal taxes, but by the end of 1965 he was forced to limit expansion of the antipoverty program because of the increasing cost of the war. As the price of the war escalated ($17 billion in 1967 alone), inflationary pressures increased throughout the economy. Johnson and his economic advisers tried to hold down wage and price increases by "jawboning" labor and management, but their appeals proved a failure by late 1966.

To stem the mounting inflation Johnson asked Congress for a 10 percent tax surcharge in August 1967. As Johnson had feared, congressional conservatives, led by Ways and Means chair WILBUR MILLS (D-Ark.), demanded substantial cuts in domestic social programs before they would support the tax surcharge. After several months of stalemate, Johnson reluctantly agreed to $6 billion in nondefense reductions. The surcharge finally went into effect at the end of 1968. Partially as a result of the delay, the federal budget deficit grew from $8.7 billion in 1967 to $25.2 billion the next year. This deficit added to inflationary pressures, and the Consumer Price Index, which had increased less than 3 percent per year until 1967, rose by 5 percent in 1968 and by even more in subsequent years. Most economists have concluded that Johnson's politically motivated underfinancing of the Vietnam War was a major contributing factor leading to the economic dislocations of the early 1970s.

As the Vietnam War dragged on and its domestic consequences began to make themselves felt, Johnson encountered ever growing antiwar sentiment. The students and intellectuals who protested the war as early as 1964 were joined by an increasingly large number of congressional liberals in 1966 and 1967. Even Vietnam War "hawks" grew dissatisfied with Johnson's conduct of the war because of the restraints he imposed upon the military. By 1967 the hostility of the protest movement had virtually barred Johnson from most public appearances except those held on military bases. He denounced his critics as "nervous nellies . . . blind to experience and deaf to hope," but Johnson was personally shaken when close associates like Moyers, McNamara, and Bundy shifted to a more "dovish" position. Meanwhile, the Republicans made large gains in the 1966 off-year elections. Johnson's personal approval ratio, as measured by the Gallup poll, dropped more than 30 points during the course of the war. By November 1967, 57 percent of the public disapproved of his handling of the conflict.

Johnson reached the decision to begin disengagement from the war only after the enemy's dramatic Tet offensive in early 1968 forced a reassessment of strategic thinking in the White House. Following the NLF's invasion of the South Vietnamese cities, General Westmoreland asked for over 200,000 more troops, but Johnson hesitated to fulfill this request. Instead, the president appointed his new secretary of defense, CLARK CLIFFORD, as head of a task force to study the proposal and examine its impact on the budget, public opinion and future prospects for negotiations. Clifford came to the conclusion that the war had to be wound down. By repeatedly reminding Johnson that the cost of victory had risen sharply and by rigorously challenging the optimistic reports from Saigon, Clifford helped check the momentum for increasing the war effort.

Johnson's simultaneously was receiving further evidence of public disenchantment with the war. In the New Hampshire primary Senator EUGENE MCCARTHY (D-Minn.), a vigorous critic of the war, ran a surprisingly strong race against the president in the March 12 balloting. Three days later Robert Kennedy announced he would enter the race for the Democratic Party's nomination on an antiwar platform.

Johnson relieved Westmoreland of his command on March 22. Shortly thereafter he convened at the White House an extraordinary informal advisory group, composed of such Establishment figures as DEAN ACHESON, GEORGE BALL, DOUGLAS DILLON, ARTHUR GOLDBERG, MATTHEW RIDGWAY, and Henry Cabot Lodge. After listening to detailed briefings, a solid majority of the group concluded on March 26 that Johnson had to begin to take steps to disengage from the war and open negotiations with the North Vietnamese.

Johnson went before a nationwide television audience on the night of March 31 to announce a partial halt to air and naval bombardment of North Vietnam. He called on North Vietnam "to respond positively and favorably to this new step toward peace." At the close of his speech Johnson stunned the nation by declaring, "I shall not seek and will not accept the nomination of my party for another term as your president." Three days later North Vietnam agreed to open negotiations in Paris, and the long-sought talks finally began in May.

Although Johnson had pledged to remain aloof from domestic politics in 1968, his influence on the campaign was considerable. He threw his still substantial influence behind the candidacy of Hubert Humphrey, thus helping the vice president to win the Democratic presidential nomination despite a series of primary victories by his two antiwar opponents. At the Democratic National Convention Johnson vetoed a compromise Vietnam plank, which favored an immediate halt in all bombing of North Vietnam. In the fall Johnson maintained a continued pressure on Humphrey to adhere to the administration's hard-line policy until late October, when Johnson himself announced a complete end to American bombing of North Vietnam. Many historians have speculated that if Johnson had softened his position on the war somewhat earlier, Humphrey might have won the presidential election in November.

After 37 years in Washington, Johnson retired to his Texas ranch following Richard Nixon's inauguration. In May 1971 he dedicated the $18.6 million Lyndon Baines Johnson Library complex on the Austin campus of the University of Texas. In November of that year his memoir, *The Vantage Point: Perspectives on the Presidency, 1963–1969*, was published to reviews that were generally critical of the book's blandness. During the next two years Johnson's health declined, and, on January 22, 1973, he died of a heart attack at his ranch.

Although most historians have applauded Lyndon Johnson's extraordinary skill in pushing through Congress the landmark civil rights and Great Society legislation of the mid-1960s, his reputation as president remained tarnished by the war in Vietnam. Eric Goldman saw Johnson as a "tragic figure" whose preoccupation with Vietnam destroyed the potential of his latter-day New Deal liberalism. ARTHUR SCHLESINGER, JR., offered a darker interpretation from the vantage point of the mid-1970s. He argued that Johnson's decision to escalate the Vietnam War without fully informing either Congress or the American people of his real intentions was a decisive step in the growth of an "imperial presidency" that Richard Nixon then sought to strengthen and institutionalize. His most recent biographer, Robert Dallek, portrayed Johnson as a "flawed giant," a leader whose desire to achieve sweeping domestic reforms collided with a determination to prevail in Vietnam that defied "good sense," a president who was "brilliant" and "highly effective," but also "deeply troubled."

—FHM, NNL

## Johnson, Paul B(urney), Jr.
### (1916–1985) *governor*

Johnson was born on January 23, 1916, in Hattiesburg, Mississippi. He practiced law in Jackson and Hattiesburg after receiving his law degree from the University of Mississippi in 1940. He served as an assistant U.S. attorney in Mississippi from 1948 to 1951 and won election as lieutenant governor in 1959 after being defeated in three previous attempts to win the governorship. In that post he joined Governor Ross Barnett in trying to block the court-ordered enrollment of JAMES MEREDITH at the University of Mississippi in September 1962. Johnson ran for governor in 1963 as an ardent segregationist, and, after defeating a more moderate candidate in the August Democratic primary runoff, he was easily elected in November.

After his strong campaign statements on segregation, Johnson startled many observers by delivering a far more temperate address at his January 1964 inauguration. Although he pledged to fight any authority he thought morally or constitutionally wrong, Johnson also promised that "hate, or prejudice, or ignorance will not lead Mississippi while I sit in the governor's chair." While Johnson continued to oppose integration throughout his term, his inaugural signaled a shift away from the tactic of defiance adopted by his predecessor. Concerned with improving the state's national image, Johnson repeatedly urged that efforts to oppose integration be limited to the courts, and he took a strong stand against public disorder and violence. He ended Barnett's policy of awarding state grants to the segregationist Citizens Councils. Johnson also allowed the State Sovereignty Commission, established in 1956 to fight for segregation, to fall into obscurity by never calling a meeting throughout his administration.

During Johnson's first year as governor a coalition of civil rights groups organized a Mississippi Freedom Summer Project to bring large numbers of civil rights workers into the state to conduct voter registration drives and establish freedom schools. Johnson condemned the project, at one point claiming that many project leaders had "Marxist backgrounds." However, when three rights workers disappeared near Philadelphia, Mississippi, on June 21, Johnson welcomed federal assistance in searching for them, promised full cooperation from the state, and urged area residents to aid in the search. He also ordered a state investigation of the series of bombings and shootings that plagued the McComb area that summer, and he played a major role in ending the violence there.

Johnson denounced the 1964 Civil Rights Act and opposed voluntary compliance with the public accommodations section of the law until it had been tested in court. He fought the Mississippi Freedom Democratic Party's (MFDP) challenge to the seating of the regular state delegation at the Democratic National Convention in August 1964. When the convention adopted a compromise by which the regular delegates would be seated if they took a loyalty oath and two MFDP representatives would be seated as at-large delegates, Johnson led the regular delegation in voting against the compromise and then in walking out. By October Johnson publicly supported Senator BARRY GOLDWATER (R-Ariz.) for the presidency, and Goldwater carried Mississippi in the November election with 87 percent of the vote.

In June 1964 Johnson called a special session of the state legislature to adopt a plan of tuition grants to private schools in an effort to circumvent court-ordered school desegregation. Johnson did not physically obstruct school desegregation, however, and he sent state police into Grenada in September 1966 to protect black youths who had been attacked by a mob when they entered the city's previously all-white public schools. Early in 1965 Johnson urged the state's white leaders to testify at U.S. Civil Rights Commission hearings on complaints of discrimination in Mississippi, and he made a surprise appearance himself when the commission opened hearings in February in Jackson.

Johnson opposed the 1965 Voting Rights Act. In June, while the bill was still pending in Congress, he called a special legislative session to rewrite the state's voting and registration laws. The MFDP led demonstrations against the special session in which over 800 protesters were arrested in Jackson that month. Most of the bills and amendments Johnson introduced were passed by the legislature and ratified by the state's voters in August. The legislation liberalized Mississippi's voting and registration laws. It was an attempt, as Johnson said, to put the state "in the most advantageous position possible" with respect to the federal voting rights law.

When MARTIN LUTHER KING, JR., and other civil rights leaders decided in June 1966 to continue a march from Memphis, Tennessee, to Jackson, Mississippi, begun by James Meredith, Johnson labelled the march "a very, very foolish thing," but promised police protection for the demonstrators. He reduced the number of highway patrol officers escorting the march on June 16, however, asserting that the state did not intend "to wet-nurse a bunch of showmen all over the country." Johnson increased the police escort again after the marchers were attacked by a mob in Philadelphia on June 21. He ordered the National Guard onto the campus of all-black Alcorn A&M College in April 1966, when demonstrations there led to some violence, and into Jackson State College in May 1967, when the school's black student body clashed with police.

Governor Johnson welcomed federal economic aid in Mississippi and generally approved grants from the federal Office of Economic Opportunity to community action programs throughout the state. In April 1966 a special presidential task force reported that Mississippi ranked second in per capita receipt of antipoverty funds. Despite such aid

Mississippi still had one of the lowest per capita income levels in the nation. A team of doctors who studied hunger and poverty in six Mississippi counties told a Senate Labor and Public Welfare subcommittee in June 1967 that nutritional and medical conditions in the state were "shocking" with many children facing starvation. Johnson then sent a team of prominent Mississippi doctors into the same areas and reported in August that, while there was malnutrition in some localities, the physicians had found no conditions approaching starvation. In fact, Johnson's years in office had seen some significant steps taken to improve the state's economy, including the creation of the Educational Research and Development Center and the development and improvement of the state's port facilities. Still, Mississippi lagged far behind most states in almost all economic measures.

Barred by the state constitution from seeking a second consecutive term as governor, Johnson ran for lieutenant governor in 1967. He placed third in a field of six candidates in the August 8 Democratic primary and was thus eliminated from the race. He returned to the practice of law, until his death of cardiac arrest on October 14, 1985, in Hattiesburg, Mississippi.

—CAB

## Johnson, U(ral) Alexis

(1908–1997) *deputy undersecretary of state for political affairs, deputy ambassador to South Vietnam, ambassador to Japan*

Born on October 17, 1908, in Falcen, Kansas, Johnson was a career diplomat with particular expertise in East Asian affairs. Joining the State Department in 1935, he served in Japan, Korea, China, and Manchuria before World War II. With the exception of a wartime assignment in Brazil and a tour of duty as ambassador to Czechoslovakia from 1953 to 1958, he continued to concentrate on East Asia throughout the postwar period. When President John F. Kennedy appointed him deputy undersecretary of state for political affairs an April 1961, Johnson became the highest-ranking career foreign service officer in the State Department. During the Kennedy and Johnson administrations. Vietnam was the central focus of Johnson's attention. He was an advocate of military intervention to prevent a communist takeover, urging this course as early as October 1961.

Johnson was appointed deputy ambassador to Vietnam in July 1964. While at that post he advocated immediate retaliation for Communist raids and continued increases in both bombing sorties and ground troop commitments. While in Saigon he was instrumental in getting the South Vietnamese government to accept these measures but he failed in his drive to strengthen local government and reform the Vietnamese army.

In January 1965 Johnson sketched a proposal for terminating the war while achieving military victory. Under this plan South Vietnam would agree to grant either amnesty and civil rights to insurgents or give safe passage to those wishing to go to the North. In addition the United States would offer a progressive reduction of military personnel, restoration of trade with North Vietnam, and participation of all parties in an American-sponsored development program for Southeast Asia. In return, the North would stop infiltration, cease support of National Liberation Front (NLF) insurgency, and agree to the neutrality of Laos. Negotiations were to be carried on between North and South Vietnam, but the NLF would not be recognized. This plan was never put into effect.

Johnson was one of the officials who advocated a bombing pause in December 1965 as a possible way of getting North Vietnam to negotiate. According to the *Pentagon Papers*, this pause was also meant as "a means of clearing the way for an increase in the tempo of the air war in the absence of a satisfactory response from Hanoi."

Johnson was active in areas beyond Vietnam, however. In early 1962 he played a significant role advising President Kennedy during the Cuban missile crisis. Earlier he had represented the United States in talks with China, held in Geneva.

Johnson succeeded EDWIN REISCHAUER as ambassador to Japan in July 1966. He left that post in January 1969 to become undersecretary of state for political affairs and in 1973 was appointed chief delegate to the Strategic Arms Limitation Talks (SALT). After leaving office he continued to speak and write about American policies toward Asia. In the 1980s he helped found the American Academy of Diplomacy, an association of former government officials who played prominent roles in American foreign policy. He died of pneumonia, in Raleigh, North Carolina, on March 24, 1997.

—EWS

## Jones E(verett) Leroi
(Imamu Amiri Baraka)
(1934–   ) *writer, black political activist*

Born on October 7, 1934, in Newark, New Jersey, Jones graduated two years ahead of his class at Newark's Barringer High School and received his B.A. from Howard University in 1953. After serving in the air force Jones settled in New York, where he did graduate work in comparative literature at Columbia and developed a reputation as an avant-garde writer. Jones's poetry, jazz criticism, and plays displayed an extraordinary sensitivity to black culture and to what he perceived as the debilitating effect of white society on black Americans. He published his first work, a collection of poetry, *Preface to a Twenty Volume Suicide Note*, in 1961. In *Dutchman*, winner of a 1964 Obie Award, Jones depicted a subway car confrontation between a sexually provocative white woman and a black intellectual whose middle-class appearance conceals an explosive hostility to white people.

In April 1965 Jones left his wife and their two children and moved to Harlem, where he founded the Black Arts Repertory Theatre, a multifaceted cultural center. A year later Jones moved the center to a dilapidated three-story building in Newark's Central Ward that he named Spirit House. In January 1968 he founded the Black Community Development and Defense Organization. *Ebony* characterized the group in 1969 as one "dedicated to the creation of a new value system for the Afro-American community" based on Afro-Islamic cultural principles. Members adopted the Kuwaida Muslim faith and Jones, whose early vocational aspiration had been the Christian ministry, became a Kuwaida religious leader and was addressed by members as Imamu Amiri Baraka, the name that he used publicly in the 1970s.

A 1960 trip to Cuba stimulated Jones's first political commitments. Upon returning he wrote of the contrast between the popular enthusiasm in Cuba and the "ugly void" of American life and described white Americans as an "old people" not needed by the "new people in Asia, Africa [and] South America." Jones exempted "the captive African," whom he described as "the only innocent in the bankruptcy of Western culture," from his indictment of American life.

In the Johnson era Jones became a symbol to many conservatives of the problems of Lyndon Johnson's Great Society reforms. LBJ's Office of Economic Opportunity offered financial support to many community programs, including one in Harlem that gave money to Jones's Black Arts theater. Jones used the money to produce plays such as *Jello*, in which a black valet employed by comedian Jack Benny turns against his employer and kills him, along with a number of other whites.

After his arrest on two counts of carrying concealed weapons during the July 1967 Newark riots, Jones's political influence in Newark increased. (P.E.N., the association of writers, and the United Black Artists came to Jones's aid when the sentencing judge stated that his disagreement with sentiments expressed in one of Jones's poems contributed to the length of Jones's prison sentence. The conviction was overturned in 1968.) While on bail he taught a course at San Francisco State College and met regularly with Ron Karenga, founder of the black politicocultural group US. Returning to Newark in January 1968, Jones helped create the Committee for a United Newark, a coalition of black and Puerto Rican community organizations that sought to secure political power for Newark's black and Puerto Rican population. In November 1969 the committee held a convention and nominated a slate of candidates for the June 1970 municipal elections.

During the campaign incumbent mayor Hugh Addonizio denounced Kenneth Gibson, the convention's mayoral candidate, as a "puppet" for black extremists, notably Jones, whose 1967 arrest made him a symbol of racial militancy. Gibson defeated Addonizio to become the first elected black mayor of a large East Coast city, and Jones was credited with a major role in the victory. Jones received national recognition at the 1972 National Black Political Convention, which he cochaired with Mayor Richard Hatcher of Gary, Indiana, and Representative CHARLES C. DIGGS, JR., (D-Mich.). In 1974 Jones rejected Black nationalism and announced his conversion to Third World Marxism. In 1975 he published a collection of poetry rooted in Marxist ideology, and continues to publish, as well as to teach at the university level.

—DKR

## Jordan B(enjamin) Everett
(1896–1974) *member of the Senate*

A wealthy North Carolina textile manufacturer and state Democratic Party fund-raiser, Jordan was born in Ranseur, North Carolina, on September 8, 1896. He chaired the Democratic state executive committee from 1949 to 1954. During that time he moved from the liberal faction of the party to its conservative wing. In April 1958 Governor Luther Hodges appointed him to fill a U.S. Senate vacancy, and, the following November, he was elected to complete the final two years of the term.

During the early 1960s Jordan compiled a conservative voting record, opposing most social welfare and civil rights measures. He became chair of the Senate Rules and Administration Committee in 1963. In the last days of the Kennedy administration, the panel began an investigation of the activities of ROBERT G. (Bobby) BAKER, secretary to the Senate majority, who had been accused in a civil suit of using his influence to obtain government contracts.

The Baker probe continued into 1964. The majority report, signed by Jordan, asserted that Baker had been guilty of "gross improprieties." But it dismissed allegations that had linked Baker's activities to prominent Democrats, including President LYNDON B. JOHNSON, who as majority leader had worked closely with Baker.

Don B. Reynolds, a former business associate of Baker, testified that Johnson had purchased life insurance policies from their firm in 1957 and 1961. He asserted that after both purchases Johnson aide WALTER W. JENKINS had suggested to him that the insurance company buy advertising on a Johnson family radio-television station and that Baker had urged him to buy a hi-fi set for Johnson. Jordan, who had been a strong Johnson-for-President supporter in 1960, questioned the veracity of Reynolds's testimony and, on January 31, 1964, stated, "There had been a lot of reckless talk about the President's part in all this."

Jordan generally voted against Johnson's domestic programs. According to *Congressional Quarterly*, he was the fourth- and tenth- most frequent Democratic senatorial opponent of administration-supported bills in 1966 and 1968, respectively.

In 1971 Jordan surprised many observers by announcing his opposition to the Vietnam War. The following year Representative Nick Galifianakis, who had a more liberal voting record than Jordan, defeated the incumbent in the Democratic senatorial primary. Jordan died on March 15, 1974, in Saxapahaw, North Carolina.

—MLL

## Kastenmeier, Robert W(illiam)

(1924–   ) *member of the House of Representatives*

Kastenmeier, whose father was a farmer and sometime court clerk, was born on January 24, 1924, in Beaver Dam, Wisconsin, and grew up near Madison in the district he would later represent in Congress. After serving in the Philippines during World War II, he studied law at the University of Wisconsin. Admitted to the bar in 1952, Kastenmeier became active in the state's revived Democratic Party and was narrowly elected to Congress in 1958. His majorities remained unimpressive until redistricting removed an affluent Republican suburb in 1963. Thereafter Kastenmeier, a strong liberal, was returned to office by comfortable margins, which grew as the Vietnam War escalated and Madison's university community became increasingly politicized.

Kastenmeier attempted to forge an alliance between liberal members of Congress and academics soon after his arrival in Washington. In 1960 he announced the formation of the "Liberal Project," a small group of representatives who joined with scholars from various fields to develop new liberal policies. *The Liberal Papers*, published by the project in 1962, urged a reappraisal of cold war foreign policy and recommended, among other things, admission of the People's Republic of China to the United Nations.

A consistent supporter of the Johnson administration's Great Society programs, Kastenmeier was a member of the Judiciary Committee and worked to strengthen the civil rights legislation passed in the mid-1960s. As chair of the Ad Hoc Advisory Committee on Voting and Civil Rights, he issued a report in January 1966 that called for more vigorous congressional action to implement the 1965 Voting Rights Act.

Kastenmeier was an early congressional opponent of the Vietnam War. Although he voted for war appropriations in 1965, in March of that year he and 15 other representatives wrote to President Johnson criticizing U.S. use of tear gas and defoliants in Vietnam. That summer Kastenmeier participated in an unsuccessful attempt to persuade the House Foreign Affairs Committee to hold public hearings on the war. Defeated in this effort, he then organized his own hearings on Vietnam in Madison. The meetings, at which more than 50 people spoke, resembled the campus Vietnam teach-ins of that April and May. The transcript of the hearings was published the following year as *Vietnam Hearings: Voices from the Grassroots.*

Kastenmeier joined 16 other representatives who sent Johnson a letter in December 1965 urging him not to bomb Hanoi and Haiphong. In January 1966 Kastenmeier and seven other House colleagues proposed contacts between South Vietnam and the National Liberation Front.

Maintaining a staunch liberalism in the early 1970s, Kastenmeier became a prominent advocate of prison reform legislation. During the 1974 House Judiciary Committee hearings on the impeachment of President Nixon he won national attention as a consistent proponent of Nixon's removal from office. He continued to advocate liberal causes and became an expert on copyright issues as well as the regulation of chemical and biological weapons until he was defeated for reelection in 1990 and returned to Wisconsin.

—MDB

## Katzenbach, Nicholas deB(elleville)

(1922–   )  *U.S. deputy attorney general, acting U.S. Attorney General, U.S. Attorney General, U.S. undersecretary of state*

Born in Philadelphia, Pennsylvania, on January 17, 1922, Katzenbach graduated from Princeton University in 1945. He received a degree from Yale Law School in 1947 and then was a Rhodes scholar at Oxford University for two years. He served two years working for the General Counsel's Office for the air force, and then, between 1952 and 1960, he taught at Yale and the University of Chicago Law School. Appointed assistant attorney general in charge of the Justice Department's Office of Legal Counsel in January 1961, Katzenbach was named deputy attorney general, the second-highest position in the Justice Department, in April 1962. He helped draft the Kennedy administration's foreign trade program and the Communications Satellite Act of 1962. In December 1962 he helped coordinate a government effort to assemble food and medical supplies needed to secure the release of prisoners captured during the April 1961 Bay of Pigs invasion of Cuba. Katzenbach was also concerned with civil rights questions, directing Justice Department operations on the scene during the crises over desegregation of the University of Mississippi in September 1962 and of the University of Alabama in June 1963. Katzenbach also acted as a major broker in the long negotiations with Congress over the 1964 Civil Rights Act.

Katzenbach worked closely with the Warren Commission in its investigation of President Kennedy's assassination, and, in September 1964, President Johnson named him to a four-member panel to advise him on execution of the commission's recommendation. When ROBERT KENNEDY resigned as U.S. Attorney General on September 3, 1964, Katzenbach, at Kennedy's urging, was named acting attorney general. President Johnson appointed him U.S. Attorney General on January 28, 1965.

Prior to the civil rights march from Selma to Montgomery, Alabama, which began on March 21, 1965, and was led by MARTIN LUTHER KING, JR., Katzenbach had the Justice Department seek a federal court order barring state officials from interfering with the demonstration. He kept in close touch with Justice Department aides in Alabama throughout the march. Working closely with congressional leaders of both parties, Katzenbach also drafted the Johnson administration's voting rights bill, introduced in Congress in March 1965, and then worked to secure its passage. It was Katzenbach who devised the controversial formula for measuring voter discrimination, which held that if a state used tests to establish voter eligibility and if fewer than 50 percent of all of its voting age citizens were registered to vote in 1964, it would be considered to be guilty of racial discrimination. Once the bill became law in August 1965, Katzenbach oversaw its enforcement and successfully defended its constitutionality in Supreme Court in January 1966. Both the U.S. Civil Rights Commission and rights leaders criticized Katzenbach's enforcement efforts, however, saying he should have sent more federal voting examiners into the South to increase black voter registration.

Katzenbach stepped up the Justice Department's efforts to achieve school desegregation for 1965–66. In December 1965 he issued guidelines for government agencies on cutting off funds, under provisions of the 1964 Civil Rights Act, to federally aided programs found to be practicing racial discrimination. Katzenbach played an important role in drafting the Johnson administration's 1966 civil rights bill, which included provisions prohibiting racial discrimination in housing and in the selection of juries and providing protection for civil rights workers. Although the bill passed the House, it died in the Senate in September 1966,

Undersecretary of State Nicholas Katzenbach in a meeting regarding Vietnam, 1968 *(Photographed by Yoichi R. Okamoto; Lyndon Baines Johnson Library)*

when its supporters were unable to end a filibuster against it.

Katzenbach helped write the administration's anticrime proposals of March 1965, and in the spring of that year he called for new legislation to aid in the fight against organized crime, supported curbs on interstate mail-order sales of firearms, and endorsed several proposals for federal prison reform. In July 1965 Katzenbach was named head of a presidential Commission on Law Enforcement and the Administration of Justice. The commission's February 1967 report recommended more than 200 measures to reduce the causes of crime and improve law enforcement at the local, state, and federal levels.

In the period when Katzenbach served as U.S. Attorney General, the FBI, a division of the Justice Department, engaged in a number of activities that clearly violated the law and others that were of questionable legality. These included the opening of first-class mail and the development of COINTELPRO, an effort to disrupt and discredit the Communist Party and Socialist Workers' Party and "white hate groups," particularly the Ku Klux Klan. In November 1975 testimony before a Senate Select Committee on Intelligence Activities, Katzenbach denied knowledge of the mail openings and COINTELPRO and held FBI director J. EDGAR HOOVER directly responsible. Katzenbach did admit that he had known of bureau efforts to disrupt the Klan in the South. He pointed out that Klan members were not "ordinary citizens seeking only to exercise their constitutional rights" but terrorists who threatened the lives of blacks and civil rights workers. He considered the FBI campaign against the Klan fully justified, even "magnificent."

Katzenbach also admitted that he had been aware that the FBI had wiretapped the home telephone of Martin Luther King. He ordered an end to the tap on April 1965, but the FBI tapped King's hotel bedrooms on three subsequent occasions without Katzenbach's approval. In 1966, after a bitter exchange between Katzenbach and Hoover on the question of wiretapping, Katzenbach concluded that "he could no longer effectively serve as Attorney General because of Mr. Hoover's obvious resentment of me."

Katzenbach was appointed undersecretary of state on September 21, 1966. He accompanied Secretary of Defense ROBERT S. MCNAMARA on fact-finding missions to South Vietnam in October 1966 and July 1967. Katzenbach headed several diplomatic missions abroad, including a 12-nation tour of Africa in May 1967, a January 1968 trip to Western Europe to explain the administration's new measures for improvement of the U.S. balance of payments position, and a July 1968 visit to India for a broad review of U.S.-Indian relations. He also toured Europe in October 1968 to demonstrate to Yugoslavia and other nations continuing American concern for European security following the August 1968 Soviet occupation of Czechoslovakia.

In February 1967, following disclosures that the CIA had secretly supplied funds for the overseas programs of the National Student Association and other private American organizations, President Johnson named Katzenbach to a three-member commission ordered to review these CIA activities. The commission, which was criticized by those who wanted full disclosure of covert CIA subsidies, reported that the agency had acted in accord with National Security Council policies established in the 1950s. On March 29 President Johnson followed the commission's recommendation that all covert government aid to private educational, philanthropic, and cultural organizations be barred.

Katzenbach was frustrated in his effort to introduce modern management techniques to the State Department, a reform which he believed would help restore the department's primacy among government agencies operating overseas. He did, however, work out personnel-sharing arrangements with various government agencies that were designed to broaden diplomats' experience with domestic problems and encourage a cross-fertilization of ideas between the Foreign Service and other government operations. Katzenbach resigned as undersecretary on November 8, 1968, following the presidential election, but he agreed to stay on in the State Department during the transfer of power to the Nixon administration. In his final year he was one of the chief advisers whom LBJ relied on in handling the crisis in North Korea, which seized the American spy ship USS *Pueblo* in January. In 1969 he joined the International Business Machines Corporation as vice president and general counsel. After many years of service with IBM, he joined the Board of Directors of WorldCom in 2002.

—CAB

## Kennan, George F(rost)
(1904–2005) *historian, diplomat*
Born on February 16, 1904, in Milwaukee, Wisconsin, Kennan graduated from Princeton University

in 1925 and joined the Foreign Service the following year. For the next two decades he served in nearly a dozen posts in Eastern and Central Europe, including two tours of duty in Moscow (1933–35; 1944–46) that secured his reputation as an expert on Soviet-American relations. In 1946, while in his second tour of duty in the American embassy in Moscow, Kennan received a telegram from Washington asking for an explanation of recent Soviet behavior. The result was the famous Long Telegram of February 1946, in which Kennan spelled out his views of the Soviet Union in 5,000 words and provided a basic framework for responding that would shape American foreign policy for the next half-century. Kennan saw the Soviets as driven not by ideology but by "the traditional and instinctive Russian sense of insecurity." Scared of contacts with the more advanced Western nations, Soviet leaders thus, in his view, justified their rule by exaggerating the U.S. threat, and hence depended on that threat for their survival. Soviet leaders, he concluded, "have learned to seek security only in patient but deadly struggle for total destruction of the rival power, never in compacts and compromises with it." He returned to these themes in a subsequent article "The Sources of Soviet Conduct," published in *Foreign Affairs* in 1947, in which he argued for a "long-term, patient but firm and vigilant containment of Russian expansive tendencies." These two pieces were formative in the creation of the doctrine of containment. As a result of his work in formulating the new policy, Kennan was named director of the State Department's policy planning staff in 1947. Kennan served briefly as ambassador to the Soviet Union in 1952 but was declared persona non grata by the Soviets because of his criticism of their treatment of Western diplomats. He formally retired from the Foreign Service in 1953 to take a post at the Institute for Advanced Study at Princeton, where he wrote several important works on Soviet-American relations.

In February 1961 President Kennedy named Kennan ambassador to Yugoslavia. Kennan, who had long advocated policies to weaken the internal unity of the Soviet bloc, sought to strengthen Yugoslavia's ties to the West. However, the American Congress, suspicious of economic cooperation with any Communist nation, undermined Kennan's efforts by restricting trade with Yugoslavia. He resigned his ambassadorship in May 1963 and later wrote that Congress was partly responsible for Soviet-Yugoslav reconciliation in the early 1960s.

Kennan resumed his academic career in July 1963 but returned to the public spotlight in the mid-1960s as an important critic of U.S. policy in Vietnam. In numerous articles and speeches and in testimony before several congressional committees, Kennan argued that Vietnam was not vital to American strategic or diplomatic interests. He warned that precipitous escalation of the war in Vietnam would destroy the possibility of a negotiated settlement and force a rapprochement between the Soviet and Chinese Communists. Although Kennan would later admit that his containment doctrine had been somewhat vague, he was now quick to criticize policy makers for applying it so broadly, rather than recognizing that he intended it to apply to a few critical regions and to rely on economic and political muscle as much as military.

Kennan's analysis received its widest hearing when Senator J. WILLIAM FULBRIGHT (D-Ark.) invited him to testify before a nationally televised session of the Senate Foreign Relations Committee in February 1966. Kennan charged that because of the administration's "preoccupation with Vietnam," Europe and the Soviet Union were not receiving proper diplomatic attention. Kennan argued that the United States had no binding commitment to South Vietnam and questioned whether American credibility or prestige would be seriously damaged by a withdrawal. Kennan counseled a minimal military effort to maintain a U.S. presence in Vietnam until a peaceful settlement could be reached. Always a European-oriented diplomat, Kennan "emphatically" denied the applicability of the "containment doctrine" to Southeast Asia while urging its retention in Europe. After the USSR invaded Czechoslovakia in August 1968, Kennan urged stationing 100,000 additional American troops in West Germany until the Soviets left Czechoslovakia.

Kennan was a strong proponent of a professional diplomatic corps that could generally function without concern for momentary domestic political pressures. He thought highly publicized summit conferences among heads of state generally unproductive and often disruptive of longstanding diplomatic relationships. In the late 1960s Kennan was also a severe critic of the student left, which he considered moralistic and anti-intellectual.

Kennan was inducted into the American Academy of Arts and Letters in 1964 and served as the academy's president from 1967 to 1971. He was also president of the National Institute of Arts and

Letters from 1964 to 1967. During the spring of 1967 Kennan assisted Svetlana Alliluyeva, daughter of the late Soviet dictator Joseph Stalin, when she was deciding to seek residence in the United States. Kennan read a manuscript copy of her autobiography and then met her in Switzerland after she had left the Soviet Union. Accompanying her to the United States, he urged Americans to accept Alliluyeva on her own terms, as a "courageous, sincere and talented" human being. He remained an active writer and speaker on matters related to foreign policy throughout the subsequent decades. He died on March 17, 2005.

—JCH

## Kennedy, Edward M(oore)

(1932–  ) *member of the Senate*

Edward Kennedy is the younger brother of President John F. Kennedy and Senator ROBERT F. KENNEDY (D-N.Y.). Born in Boston on February 22, 1932, he attended private schools in England and America before entering Harvard in 1951. In his first year he was suspended for cheating, but, after spending two years in the army, he returned to the university and graduated in 1956. He earned a law degree from the University of Virginia Law School three years later.

Kennedy had his first experience in practical politics when he served as manager of John Kennedy's 1958 senatorial reelection campaign. In 1960 he was put in charge of the Kennedy presidential campaign in the Rocky Mountain states.

Amid Republican and liberal accusations of "nepotism" and charges that the Kennedy family was attempting to start a political dynasty, Edward Kennedy announced his candidacy for the Senate in 1962. His opponent in the Democratic primary was Edward J. McCormack, Massachusetts attorney general and nephew of House Speaker JOHN MCCORMACK (D-Mass.). The voters' negative reaction to Edward McCormack's personal attacks on Kennedy's youth and inexperience contributed to an easy Kennedy victory in the Democratic primary. He went on to win the general election with 57 percent of the vote over the equally inexperienced George Cabot Lodge in a campaign that was billed as the "battle of the dynasties."

Unlike his older brother, who used the Senate as a stepping-stone to national office, Edward Kennedy was careful to fit smoothly into the Senate "Establishment" by courting such senior senators as JAMES O. EASTLAND (D-Miss.) and RICHARD B. RUSSELL (D-Ga.). Appointed to the Judiciary and the Labor and Public Welfare Committees, he supported President Kennedy on most major issues in 1963. He was presiding over the Senate on November 22 when word came that his brother had been assassinated in Dallas.

In 1965 Kennedy assumed his first important role as a senator, when he successfully managed passage of the Johnson administration's immigration bill, which abolished national origin quotas and allowed about 300,000 immigrants into the United States annually. In February he proposed authorization of a National Teachers Corps to provide financial incentives for instructors who volunteered to work in poverty areas. His idea was incorporated into a portion of the 1965 Higher Education Act. Unlike his older brother Robert, Edward Kennedy maintained generally good relations with President Johnson, who liked and respected him.

Edward Kennedy generally followed his brother Robert's cautious opposition to the Vietnam War. He recommended a complete overhaul of the Selective Service system at House Armed Services Committee hearings in 1966. He favored selection of men for the military by a national lottery, but his proposal was blocked by Senator Richard Russell and other conservatives until late 1969.

Kennedy's greatest impact was in his effort to focus national attention on the plight of Vietnamese refugees. As chair of the Senate Subcommittee on Refugees and Escapees, he became in his biographer Theo Lippman's phrase, "*the* American expert on the war's impact on the people of Vietnam." During the late 1960s he was a consistent critic of what he considered the administration's inhumane handling of the refugee problem. In August 1968 he condemned the war, called for a withdrawal of all U.S. and North Vietnamese troops from South Vietnam, and recommended increased political and economic aid to the South.

After Robert Kennedy's assassination during his 1968 presidential campaign, Edward Kennedy refused to run for the Democratic nomination or to accept a draft, despite pleas from his brother's liberal supporters and Chicago mayor RICHARD DALEY. Many saw him as a possible 1972 presidential contender until he was involved in a July 1969 automobile accident on Chappaquiddick Island, off Martha's

Vineyard, Massachusetts, in which a young woman drowned.

In 1969 Kennedy defeated Senator RUSSELL LONG (D-La.) for the post of majority whip, and the next year he was easily reelected to the Senate. Aided by a strong political organization in Massachusetts, a competent staff, and the lingering attractions of the Kennedy mystique, he emerged as one of the most powerful members of the Senate in the early 1970s. At the 1972 Democratic National Convention, Kennedy was the only Democrat to mention Lyndon Johnson in a speech, evidence of the decline of LBJ's reputation as much as the political security felt by Kennedy. Eight years later, he challenged incumbent president Jimmy Carter in the Democratic primaries, but went down to a surprisingly easy defeat. He remained in the Senate, where he became a champion of liberal causes, especially issues related to health care, minimum wage, and social welfare legislation.

—FHM

## Kennedy, Jacqueline (Lee Bouvier)

(1929–1994) *first lady*

Born on July 28, 1929, in Southhampton, New York, to wealth and social prominence, Jacqueline Bouvier briefly attended Vassar and the Sorbonne before graduating from George Washington University in Washington in 1951. First introduced to Senator John Kennedy (D-Mass.) in 1952, the couple was married on September 12, 1953, in one of the most publicized society weddings of that year.

During her husband's administration Mrs. Kennedy restored the White House as a period mansion of the 18th and 19th centuries. Her expertise in this area was highlighted on February 14, 1962, when she conducted an hour-long televised tour of the White House. Mrs. Kennedy was also instrumental in introducing various prominent writers, artists, and musicians to White House functions that had previously been restrictive and formal. She also set up a White House fine arts commission, hired a White House curator, and organized operas and concerts at the White House. "I think she cast a particular spell over the White House that has not been equaled," recalled one executive editor of the *Washington Post.* A trend-setter in fashion, Mrs. Kennedy proved to be a significant political and diplomatic asset to the president, especially during their trip to Paris in June 1961 and on a visit to

India she made alone in March 1962. So popular was the first lady in Europe that the president described himself, after they returned from France, as "the man who accompanied Jacqueline Kennedy to Paris—and I have enjoyed it."

Mrs. Kennedy accompanied the president to Texas in November 1963, and she was sitting beside him when he was shot to death in an open car on November 22. Later the same day she witnessed the swearing-in of President Johnson aboard Air Force One. Her dignified conduct and bearing during the aftermath of the assassination earned her worldwide respect and contributed to the power of the Kennedy mystique later in the decade. Throughout the 1960s Mrs. Kennedy remained among the country's most admired women and in 1965 and 1966 led the Gallup poll in that category. She also maintained a good relationship with the new president, Lyndon Johnson, who took great pains, for both personal and political reasons, to remain in contact with her.

Mrs. Kennedy's popularity remained undiminished until her October 1968 marriage to Greek shipping magnate Aristotle Onassis. Thereafter Mrs. Kennedy lived in France, Greece, and New York. After Onassis died in 1978, she returned to New York City as an editor for Doubleday. She died of cancer on May 19, 1994.

—FHM

## Kennedy, Robert F(rancis)

(1925–1968) *U.S. Attorney General, member of the Senate*

Robert Kennedy was the seventh of nine children, born on November 20, 1925, in a wealthy and politically ambitious Irish Catholic Massachusetts family. He graduated from Harvard in 1948 and the University of Virginia Law School three years later.

After managing his brother's successful Senate campaign in 1952, Bobby was appointed to the Senate Subcommittee on Investigations by Senator Joseph McCarthy (R-Wisc.). He resigned in 1953 after a series of disagreements with McCarthy and his staff, but he returned in 1954 after McCarthy's resignation. In 1955 he became chief counsel for the Democratic minority and wrote a report condemning McCarthy's investigation of alleged Communists in the army. In 1957 he was named chief counsel for Senator JOHN L. MCCLELLAN's (D-Ark.) Senate Rackets Committee, where he won national prominence for his investigations of Teamsters union leaders JAMES HOFFA and David Beck. He resigned in 1959 to manage his brother's presidential campaign.

Kennedy was chosen to be attorney general by the president-elect in December 1960. Although plagued through his tenure by criticism of his youth and inexperience, he attracted exceptionally competent lawyers to the Justice Department, launched a successful drive against organized crime, and became increasingly committed to the support of the civil rights of African Americans. Because he was the president's brother, he also assumed tasks well beyond his purview as U.S. Attorney General. During the 1962 Cuban missile crisis, for example, he helped secure a consensus on the decision to blockade Cuba and then negotiated with the Soviets on removal of the weapons.

Robert Kennedy was stunned by his brother's assassination in Dallas on November 22, 1963, and in the next few weeks delegated many of his respon-

sibilities at the Justice Department to subordinates. His last major action as U.S. Attorney General was to announce, in August 1964, the establishment of an Office of Criminal Justice to ensure that federal law enforcement was fair and objective, especially as it regarded the arrest system and the right of the poor to counsel.

Kennedy believed that he was a logical vice presidential candidate on a 1964 Johnson ticket. However, with Lyndon Johnson as president, a political rivalry that originated in the 1960 presidential campaign resurfaced. Johnson biographer Doris Kearns wrote: "There was between them a dislike so strong that it seemed almost as if each had been created for the purpose of exasperating the other." While Kennedy did have the support of many northern liberal political leaders, Johnson clearly did not regard him as necessary to ensure a November Democratic victory, particularly since Senator BARRY M. GOLDWATER (R-Ariz.), the likely Republican presidential nominee, appeared to be a

Former attorney general and New York senator Robert Kennedy meeting with President Johnson in the Oval Office, 1966 *(Photographed by Yoichi R. Okamoto; Lyndon Baines Johnson Library)*

weak challenger. In July Johnson circumvented a direct public confrontation with Kennedy, and a possible division of the Democratic Party, by announcing that he was eliminating all members of his cabinet from vice presidential consideration.

In August Kennedy announced that he would seek the U.S. Senate seat from New York held by Senator Kenneth B. Keating (R-N.Y.). In the initial stages of his campaign, Kennedy was widely criticized as a "carpetbagger" who merely sought the New York seat as a stepping-stone to the presidency. To dispel these doubts, and the reputation he had earned as a "ruthless" politician, Kennedy waged a vigorous statewide campaign that stressed his political liberalism and the importance of having a Democratic senator to influence a Democratic presidential administration. Aided by the Johnson landslide and by Keating's ineffectiveness as a campaigner, Kennedy won the November election by 719,000 votes. Still, the relationship between Kennedy and Johnson continued to decline; "he's mean, bitter, vicious," Kennedy told one reporter, "an animal in many ways."

In the Senate Kennedy was assigned to the Government Operations and Labor and Public Welfare Committees. Although he compiled a consistently liberal voting record, the day-to-day legislative process bored him. "They only take about one vote a week here," he once declared, "and they never can tell you in advance what it is going to be so you can schedule other things." As a senator, Kennedy used his great popularity to focus attention on the plight of the nation's minorities. Though an opponent of the idea of "Black Power" he strongly backed greater government antipoverty efforts and passage of new civil rights legislation. He further identified himself with black aspirations as a founder of the Bedford-Stuyvesant Restoration Corporation in Brooklyn's predominantly black neighborhood. In March 1966 he traveled to Delano, California, to publicly "break bread" with farm worker leader CESAR CHAVEZ, who was ending a 25-day fast dedicated to the reaffirmation of nonviolence in his movement.

In 1965 Kennedy said that he "basically" supported the Johnson administration's position on Vietnam. However, over the next three years he became increasingly critical of the administration policy. In February 1966 he recommended that the National Liberation Front (NLF) be "admitted to a share of power and responsibility in a future coali-

tion South Vietnamese government." In March of the next year he proposed suspending U.S. bombing of North Vietnam as part of a three-point plan to help end the war, but his proposals were immediately rejected by the administration. In November 1967 he made his strongest criticism of the war, asserting that the U.S. "moral position" in Vietnam had been undermined by the Johnson administration. "We're killing South Vietnamese," he said, "we're killing women, we're killing innocent people because we don't want to have the war fought on American soil."

By early 1967 many liberal Democrats hoped Robert Kennedy would oppose President Johnson in the next year's Democratic primaries. They sought Kennedy's candidacy as a means of de-escalating the war and of restoring and continuing in some measure the original administration of John F. Kennedy. Despite polls showing that Democrats favored him over Johnson, Kennedy repeatedly asserted that he would back the president for reelection in 1968. After Senator EUGENE J. MCCARTHY (D-Minn.) made a surprisingly strong showing in the March 12, 1968, New Hampshire primary, Kennedy announced that he was "reassessing" his position.

On March 16 Kennedy formally announced his candidacy for the Democratic presidential nomination, declaring, "At stake is not simply the leadership of our Party and even of our country. It is the right to the moral leadership of the planet." He also asserted that the New Hampshire results had removed the possibility of a "personal struggle" between himself and the president. Kennedy later called Johnson's March 31 decision not to seek reelection "truly magnanimous."

Kennedy was particularly anxious not to antagonize youthful voters or members of the antiwar movement, many of whom supported McCarthy. Throughout the campaign Kennedy was careful to maintain a surface cordiality, although Kennedy privately considered McCarthy vain and lazy. McCarthy openly regarded the New York senator as arrogant and opportunistic.

His broad national constituency of minorities, young professionals, and blue-collar workers reflected Kennedy's "extraordinary capacity to stress both the principle of equal access and the role of the law in gaining social cohesion," according to columnist Max Lerner. His candidacy, particularly among the disadvantaged, often assumed an evangelical fervor rare in American politics.

He easily won the Indiana primary on May 7 and the Nebraska primary, with 52 percent of the vote, one week later. However, the Oregon campaign turned bitter, with McCarthy asserting there would be "further involvements like Vietnam" if Kennedy were elected. Oregon had no large African-American or ethnic groupings and few blue-collar workers, and Kennedy's early role in the rackets hearings cost him the support of the state's powerful Teamsters union. McCarthy won the May 28 primary with 45 percent of the vote to 39 percent for Kennedy, who described his defeat as a "setback I could ill afford" and declared that he would "abide by the results" of the California primary. It was the first electoral defeat by any Kennedy in 29 contests.

Kennedy campaigned in California to the point of exhaustion, and he managed to put together a broad coalition of blacks, migrant laborers, and blue-collar workers. On June 4 Kennedy won the primary and its 172 delegates with 46 percent of the vote to McCarthy's 42 percent. Shortly after leaving the victory rally, he was shot and critically wounded by SIRHAN B. SIRHAN, an Arab alien. Kennedy died of his wounds on June 6, 1968. President Johnson declared a national day of mourning. The train bearing Kennedy's funeral procession from New York to Washington was reminiscent of those of Lincoln and Franklin Roosevelt, with thousands lining the railroad tracks to pay their respects as it passed.

—FHM

## Keppel, Francis
(1916–1990) *commissioner of education; assistant secretary of health, education and welfare*

Francis Keppel, son of a former dean of Columbia College, was born on April 16, 1916, in New York City. He attended Groton and graduated from Harvard in 1938. After studying sculpture in Rome for a short period following his graduation, he returned to Harvard University, where he served as dean of freshmen. Following the war he was assistant to the provost of the university. Keppel was named dean of the Harvard graduate school of education in 1948. Over the next 14 years he increased the size, endowment, and prestige of the school.

President John F. Kennedy chose Keppel to succeed Sterling M. McMurrin as commissioner of education in November 1962. Throughout 1963

Keppel worked on behalf of a number of Kennedy administration measures that passed shortly after the president's death. These included the Higher Education Facilities Act, the Library Services Act, the Vocational Education Act, and the Manpower Training and Development Act. Keppel also demonstrated a remarkable ability to mediate between the competing interests of the National Education Association (NEA), representing over a million elementary and secondary public school teachers, and the National Catholic Welfare Conference (NCWC) representing Catholic parochial schools.

Shortly after the 1964 presidential election, President Johnson suggested to Keppel that he undertake the delicate task of framing legislation, acceptable to both parochial and public schools groups, authorizing federal aid to elementary and secondary schools. Aided by WILBUR J. COHEN, assistant secretary of the Department of Health, Education and Welfare (HEW), and White House aides DOUGLASS CATER, JR. and LAWRENCE F. O'BRIEN, Keppel arranged a crucial compromise in which the NEA agreed to permit some form of public assistance to sectarian schools while the NCWC settled for substantial but less than equal participation of parochial schools in the various aid programs.

The administration bill stipulated that aid was to be distributed to local school districts on the basis of the number of children in each district who came from families with income under $2,000. It was left to state authorities to determine how much assistance should go to public, private, and parochial schools. The bill specifically authorized appropriations for private and parochial schools for library books and educational materials.

The Elementary and Secondary Education Act became law in April 1965. Keppel moved quickly to reorganize his office, recruiting a number of young and innovative staffers to deal with the heavy burden of administering the new law. As head of the Office of Education, Keppel was authorized under the 1964 Civil Rights Act to withhold federal aid to racially segregated school systems. He announced in April 1965 that the nation's 27,000 school districts would be required to desegregate by September 1967. He notified the Illinois Board of Education in October 1965 that federal funds totaling $34 million were being withheld from the Chicago public school system as a result of a complaint filed by a group representing 75 civil rights organizations.

Mayor RICHARD J. DALEY of Chicago, a power in Democratic Party politics, was incensed over the cutoff of funds and personally protested to President Johnson. The president sent Wilbur Cohen to Chicago to negotiate a compromise. The Chicago Board of Education agreed to establish a committee to review the drawing of school boundaries to alleviate segregation. The federal funds were then quickly released. This compromise was generally considered a defeat for Keppel. In September 1965 he was named assistant HEW secretary, ostensibly a promotion but really an effort by the Johnson administration to remove him from his politically sensitive post.

Keppel resigned from HEW in April 1966 to become chair and chief executive officer of the General Learning Corporation. He also served as vice chair of the New York City Board of Education and as a trustee of the Carnegie Corporation and the Russell Sage Foundation. In 1974 he became director of the Aspen Institute Program in Education for a Changing Society. He also chaired the National Task Force on Student Aid Problems, which became known as the Keppel Task Force, and, from 1978 to 1983, he served as commissioner of the National Commission on Libraries and Information Sciences. He died in New York in 1990.

—JLW

## Kerner, Otto
(1908–1976) *governor*

Kerner was born in Chicago on August 15, 1908. His father was a prominent Chicago judge who served on the U.S. Court of Appeals (7th Circuit). After receiving a law degree from Northwestern University in 1934, he practiced corporate law for many years in Chicago. In 1947 he was appointed U.S. district attorney for the northern district of Illinois. In 1954 Kerner won election as county judge for Cook County. In 1960, with the support of Chicago mayor RICHARD DALEY, he won the Democratic gubernatorial nomination and defeated incumbent William G. Stratton in the general election.

During his first term Kerner won legislative approval of a state fair employment practices act, a revision of consumer credit laws and the criminal code, the establishment of a state board of higher education, and a program of statewide mental health clinics. Under his leadership, in 1962 Illinois became the first state to ratify a constitutional amendment outlawing the poll tax as a condition for voting in federal elections. His legislative success was especially impressive considering that the state legislature was usually controlled by Republicans.

In 1964 Kerner won reelection, defeating his Republican challenger, CHARLES PERCY, by a substantial margin. During his second term Kerner had to deal with racial disturbances in Chicago and Cairo, Illinois. On August 14, 1965, he ordered 2,000 troops of the Illinois National Guard to stand by in Chicago armories to help, if necessary, in the suppression of rioting in the largely black Lawndale neighborhood of the city's West Side. City police managed to quell the riot without the use of the troops. In July 1966 Kerner, at the request of Mayor Daley, again dispatched soldiers to Chicago. This time 2,000 of them entered the riot area on the West Side to halt widespread looting and arson. On July 17 the governor toured the riot area; two days later the troops were withdrawn to the armories. Troops were not needed in Chicago during 1967, but, in July of that year, they were sent to suppress rioting in Cairo, a racially troubled town in southern Illinois.

In July 1967 President LYNDON B. JOHNSON named Kerner chair of a Special Advisory Commission on Civil Disorders to probe the causes of urban riots. New York mayor JOHN V. LINDSAY served as vice chair. In February 1968 the commission issued a report, popularly known as the Kerner report, that warned that "America is moving toward two societies, one black, one white—separate and unequal." The study attributed the rioting in black neighborhoods to poverty and despair resulting from racism. It called for sweeping reforms in federal and local law enforcement, welfare, employment, housing, and education and recommended massive federal appropriations to improve the quality of life in the ghettos. The report was hailed by many civil rights leaders, but President Johnson pointed out that it was unrealistic to expect multibillion dollar appropriations for black neighborhoods at a time when Congress was only reluctantly funding existing social welfare programs. He also resented that the report failed to discuss the achievements of the many programs that the administration had established to advance the cause of civil rights and to alleviate poverty. The Kerner report did not lead to the passage of major social legislation.

Governor Kerner was vacationing in Florida when rioting again broke out in Chicago's black neighborhoods following the April 4, 1968, assassination of the Reverend MARTIN LUTHER KING, JR. After consulting with Governor Kerner by telephone, Lieutenant Governor Samuel Shapiro ordered 6,000 National Guard troops into the city. On April 6 Johnson placed the National Guard troops under federal control while ordering 5,000 federal troops to assist them. By April 10 the riot had been quelled. The federal troops were withdrawn, and the National Guard was returned to state control.

In May 1968 Kerner resigned as governor to became a judge on the U.S. Court of Appeals (7th Circuit), the same post his father had held. In December 1971 Kerner was indicted on charges of bribery, fraud, conspiracy, and income tax evasion resulting from his purchase and sale of race track stock while governor of Illinois. During his trial a race track owner and a former Illinois state racing board chair testified that in 1962 Kerner and his revenue director, Theodore J. Isaacs, were given the opportunity to purchase race track stock at low prices. They made the purchase and then sold the securities for windfall profits. In exchange for the favor, Kerner intervened with the state racing board to ensure that the race track owner would be assigned prime dates on which to hold races. Kerner was convicted, and, in April 1973, he was sentenced to three years in prison and fined $50,000. He appealed his sentence on the ground that a federal judge could not be tried until first impeached. His appeal was dismissed by the U.S. Supreme Court, and, in July 1974, he began serving his sentence. In March 1975 the U.S. Parole Board granted Kerner release on medical grounds. After undergoing lung surgery for cancer, he died on May 9, 1976.

—JLW

## Kerr, Clark

(1911–2003)  *president, University of California*
Kerr, who was born on May 17, 1911, in Stony Creek, Pennsylvania, graduated from Swarthmore College in 1932 and then earned a Ph.D. in economics from the University of California, Berkeley. He taught at Stanford and the University of Washington in the early 1940s, acquiring a reputation as a leading private and federal mediator in labor-management disputes on the West Coast. In 1945 Kerr returned to the University of California to become the director of the Institute of Industrial Relations

at Berkeley. The author of a number of books on labor economics and industrial relations sociology, including *Unions, Management and the Public* (1948) and *Industrialism and Industrial Man* (1960), he argued that strikes and other forms of conflict would decline in a fully industrialized society.

In 1952 Kerr was appointed chancellor of the Berkeley campus, and, in 1958, he succeeded Robert Gordon Sproul as president of the seven-campus University of California. Kerr's tenure as president coincided with the rapid growth of California's higher education system, the nation's largest. He presided over a near doubling of the university's 50,000 student enrollment, the dramatic expansion of several campuses, and a growing consensus among scholars that the university's faculty and the quality of its research made it, perhaps, the most distinguished in the country. Kerr's growing reputation led, in 1964, to his selection by President Johnson to serve as part of a 14-member task force on educational reforms, a topic the administration considered important to their Great Society legislative package. The task force compiled a detailed report calling for a major overhaul of the educational system, including some specific reforms that the administration used as the basis for the Elementary and Secondary Education Act.

With the California higher educational system considered by many as a model for the nation in the early 1960s, Kerr achieved considerable influence as an educational theorist. His book *The Uses of the University* (1963) justified the role of the "multiversity"—a term coined by Kerr—in contemporary American society. Kerr argued that a great university of necessity catered to an elite but its existence was justified in a nation dedicated to egalitarianism by its role as a "prime instrument of national purpose," a "service station" for society. He pointed to the university's many "constituencies"—government, industry, faculty, students, and the general public—and described the university administrator's role as one of mediating among the demands of these groups.

Sproul, Kerr's predecessor, had maintained a virtual ban on student advocacy of political causes; even ADLAI STEVENSON was not allowed to speak on the Berkeley campus. Kerr, on the other hand, was regarded as a liberal when he assumed office, chiefly because of his role in fighting a special loyalty oath imposed on the faculty in 1949. As president, Kerr lifted a few of Sproul's restrictions, including a ban against communist speakers on campus—an action that earned him the Alexander Meiklejohn award for contributing to academic freedom from the American Association of University Professors.

Kerr's liberalization of university rules was put to the test by the growth in 1963 and 1964 of civil rights groups on the Berkeley campus who antagonized local citizens and businesses with aggressive campaigns against racial discrimination in hiring that often employed civil disobedience and resulted in arrests. These groups had become accustomed to using a "free speech" area, consisting of a section of sidewalk at the south entrance to the campus, as a place for recruiting and collecting funds. In September 1964 the campus administration asserted that the area was owned by the university and not by the city of Berkeley, as had long been assumed, and barred its use for the purpose of recruiting or fund raising for off-campus political actions. In the face of the ensuing student protest, Kerr defended the ban by contending that the mounting of political action directed at the surrounding community was incompatible with the university's educational purposes.

Student activists denounced the new ruling as a denial of their constitutional rights, and several campus groups joined together to form the Free Speech Movement (FSM) with the aim of opening up the entire campus to political advocacy. On September 29 students violated the ban by setting up literature tables without authorization. On October 1 campus police attempted to arrest a nonstudent who had also broken the ban by setting up a Congress of Racial Equality table in the Sproul Plaza area in front of the campus administration building. The police could not remove him from the plaza because of a massive 30-hour sit-in around the police car. The next day Kerr met with a delegation from the protesters, led by MARIO SAVIO. Informal agreements were reached that apparently resolved the students' most pressing grievances. When these understandings collapsed by late November, the FSM, charging bad faith, led a mass occupation of the administration building on December 2. Ignoring Kerr's advice to "let the students sit it out," Governor EDMUND G. BROWN ordered police to arrest them on December 3. The outraged response on campus was such that within a week Kerr and the administration were almost completely isolated. The Berkeley faculty voted overwhelmingly December 8 to grant the essence of the FSM's demands for free political activity on campus. The controversy lingered for several weeks with attempts by the regents to amend the settlement, but it was clear the students had won.

Continuing student activism at Berkeley made Kerr's role as a mediator between the university and state government impossible. In 1967 Kerr came into conflict with the newly elected governor, RONALD REAGAN, over the latter's proposals to cut the university's operating budget and to end free college education in California by imposing tuition fees. Kerr's resistance to these moves led the state Board of Regents to dismiss him as university president on January 20, an action that provoked widespread protest on campuses throughout the state. Afterward a spokesperson for the regents explained that Kerr's relations with the board had been "adversely affected" by his handling of the 1964 unrest at Berkeley and that they had "deteriorated further" since then.

No longer president, Kerr retained his teaching post in the university's School of Business Administration. He was also appointed to head a Carnegie Commission study on the future structure and financing of higher education. In 1968 the commission called for a federal civilian bill of educational rights that would guarantee a college education to any qualified student regardless of ability to pay. In subsequent years Kerr continued to press for equality of educational opportunity. During much of the Vietnam War era Kerr was a leading figure in the National Committee for a Political Settlement in Vietnam—Negotiations Now. He remained active in teaching, eventually settling in at the university's Institute of Industrial Relations and writing his memoirs about his controversial administrative period. Kerr died on December 1, 2003.

—TLH

## King, Coretta Scott

(1927–  ) *civil rights activist*

Coretta Scott was born on April 27, 1927, in Ferry County, Alabama. After graduating from a missionary high school in nearby Marion, she continued her education at Antioch College (where she and her older sister were the first full-time black students) and at the New England Conservatory of Music in Boston. In 1953 she gave up plans for a music career to marry MARTIN LUTHER KING, JR., a theology graduate student whom she had met in Boston. Both Mrs. King and her husband completed

Civil rights activist Coretta Scott King at a news conference in Newark, New Jersey, 1967  *(Library of Congress, Prints and Photographs Division)*

their studies in 1954 and returned to Alabama, where he took a position as minister in a black Montgomery church.

Mrs. King soon became deeply involved in her husband's civil rights activities, which began with the Montgomery bus boycott of 1955 and led to the creation of the Southern Christian Leadership Conference (SCLC) in 1957. She marched beside him in demonstrations, accompanied him on tours of Europe and Asia, and sang in numerous "freedom concerts" to raise money for the SCLC. At the same time she raised the couple's four children. Coretta King also made a place for herself in the peace

movement of the mid-1960s, serving on the Committee for a Sane Nuclear Policy and the National Mobilization to End the War in Vietnam. In 1962 she served as a delegate to the Geneva Disarmament Conference, representing the Women's Strike for Peace. In 1964 the Federal Bureau of Investigation, as part of its campaign of harassment against Martin Luther King, sent her a tape recording that purported to prove her husband's unfaithfulness. Mrs. King nevertheless remained with her husband and continued to support his work.

In April 1968 Mrs. King won national admiration for the dignity and fortitude with which she responded to her husband's assassination. Her conduct and her position as Martin Luther King's widow made her an important civil rights figure. On April 11 she took her husband's place in Memphis at the head of a massive, orderly demonstration in support of the city's striking sanitation workers. Her speech following the march stressed the theme: "We must carry on." In May and June 1968 Mrs. King participated in the Poor People's Campaign in Washington, organized by the SCLC to press for larger federal antipoverty expenditures. Speaking before the Lincoln Memorial, she urged American women "to unite and form a solid block . . . to fight the three great evils of racism, poverty and war." Shortly afterward she was named to the executive bodies of both the SCLC and the National Organization for Women.

In the late 1960s and early 1970s Mrs. King participated in numerous civil rights and peace rallies. In early 1969 she made a tour of Europe and India, during which she accepted the Nehru Award for International Understanding on behalf of her husband. Using money raised on the trip and other contributions, she established the Martin Luther King Memorial Center in Atlanta for the study of nonviolent social change. This soon became a source of dispute between Mrs. King and RALPH ABERNATHY, her husband's successor as head of the SCLC, who claimed that the funds absorbed by the center were sorely needed by the SCLC itself.

Mrs. King took little public interest in the 1969 trial of JAMES EARL RAY, her husband's accused assassin, but expressed her belief that the assassination resulted from a conspiracy extending beyond Ray. She still remained active in civil rights causes, but devoted much of her time and energy to the King Center, which would eventually house one of the largest collection of civil rights documents in the world. In 1974 she helped organize and chair the Full Employment Action Council, dedicated to both full and equal employment, and, in 1990, she was co-convener of the Soviet-American Women's Summit in Washington, D.C.

—SLG

## King, Martin Luther, Jr.
**(1929–1968)** *president, Southern Christian Leadership Conference*

King, who was born on January 15, 1929, grew up in Atlanta, Georgia, and was ordained in 1947 at the Ebenezer Baptist Church, which his grandfather had founded and where his father was then pastor. He received a B.A. from Morehouse College in 1948, a divinity degree from Crozer Theological Seminary in Chester, Pennsylvania, in 1951, and a Ph.D. in systematic theology from Boston University in 1955. King accepted his first pastorate in September 1954 at the Dexter Avenue Baptist Church in Montgomery, Alabama, one of the most prestigious black churches in the South. In December 1955 he was chosen to direct the black community's boycott of Montgomery's segregated buses. "The action had caught me unawares," he would later write. "It happened so quickly that I did not even have time to think it through. It is probable that if I had, I would have declined the nomination." As leader of the yearlong boycott, a protest which marked the beginning of an era of nonviolent direct action by southern blacks, King won national prominence. He helped establish the Southern Christian Leadership Conference (SCLC) early in 1957 to coordinate direct action protests in the South and was named its first president. King participated in the May 1957 Prayer Pilgrimage to Washington, which demanded desegregation and voting rights for blacks. In January 1960 he moved to Atlanta, site of the SCLC's headquarters, to become co-pastor at his father's church.

King encouraged the student sit-ins that began in the South in February 1960 and helped organize the Student Nonviolent Coordinating Committee (SNCC), which emerged from those demonstrations. He also supported the 1961 Freedom Rides, a protest aimed at desegregating transportation facilities, and was chosen head of a Freedom Rides Coordinating Committee organized in May. From mid-December 1961 through September 1962, King led an antisegregation campaign in Albany, Georgia. The Albany Movement was plagued by disunity among its local leaders and by insufficient planning and organization. Even though intensified demonstrations in the summer of 1962 attracted national attention, the campaign did not win substantial gains for the city's black population.

From the defeat in Albany, however, King and his aides learned valuable lessons, which they put to use in a desegregation drive in Birmingham, Alabama. Preceded by months of careful preparation, the Birmingham campaign began on April 3, 1963. King and the SCLC led a series of daily demonstrations and marches, which received nationwide publicity, especially when Birmingham's police began savage attacks on the demonstrators early in May. The campaign ended on May 10 after a desegregation agreement had been negotiated. The agreement brought only limited changes to the city, but the historic Birmingham demonstrations had a major national impact. They dramatized the problem of southern discrimination as never before, were crucial in forcing the Kennedy administration to call for strong civil rights legislation, and made King the key leader of the civil rights movement in the eyes of the general public. Following the Birmingham campaign King helped organize the August 28 March on Washington which brought together a quarter of a million people. The "I Have a Dream" speech he delivered there was one of the highlights of the day and became the best-known statement of King's vision of full equality for American blacks.

In all of these demonstrations King was guided by a philosophy of nonviolent resistance. He had first encountered the precepts of Gandhian civil disobedience while a student, and both the Montgomery boycott and a trip to India in February 1959 advanced King's understanding of and commitment to nonviolence. Throughout the 1960s King was the major proponent of nonviolent direct action within the civil rights movement. It allowed blacks, he said, to challenge segregation and discrimination but called on them to love and forgive their oppressors, to "struggle without hating." Nonviolence was a "creative force," for by remaining nonviolent in the face of white resistance and brutality, civil rights demonstrators transformed and redeemed their oppressors. To white opponents King declared, "We will match your capacity to inflict suffering with our capacity to endure suffering" and "in winning our freedom we will so appeal to your heart and conscience that we will win you in the process."

King joined in demonstrations against segregated public facilities in Atlanta in late 1963 and

President Johnson meeting with civil rights leaders in the Oval Office, from left to right: Martin Luther King, Jr., President Johnson, Whitney Young, and James Farmer, Jr., 1964 *(Photographed by Yoichi R. Okamoto; Lyndon Baines Johnson Library)*

early 1964 that were organized primarily by SNCC. Beginning in March 1964 King and the SCLC gave their support to a desegregation drive in St. Augustine, Florida. The almost daily demonstrations and marches were repeatedly attacked by crowds of whites. The campaign was intensified in May and June. When local police failed to provide protection for the demonstrators, King called for federal intervention but to no avail. By the end of June a stalemate had developed, and when Florida's governor appointed an emergency biracial committee to "restore communications" between the races, King agreed to a temporary truce. Following passage of the Civil Rights Act in July 1964, local black leaders secured federal court orders for desegregation of public facilities in St. Augustine, and a measure of desegregation was finally won in the city.

On July 18, when a riot erupted in Harlem, New York's mayor ROBERT WAGNER asked King to come to the city. King was criticized by Harlem leaders for conferring with Wagner and for touring the riot area without having contacted them first. His main recommendation—a civilian review board to investigate charges of police brutality—was rejected by the mayor. King abhorred the violence of the Harlem riot, but he said its sources lay in the economic and social deprivation blacks suffered in northern inner cities. He placed the blame for the rioting, as he would repeatedly in the future, on white society's failure to remedy inner city conditions.

Later that summer King toured Mississippi, encouraging blacks to enroll in the newly organized Mississippi Freedom Democratic Party (MFDP). He also supported an MFDP delegation when it challenged the seating of the regular Mississippi delegation at the August 1964 Democratic National Convention and testified before the credentials committee on the MFDP's behalf. When the convention refused full recognition of the group and voted for a compromise measure, however, King urged the MFDP delegates to accept it, but they overwhelmingly rejected the compromise. King also joined several other rights leaders in a July 1964 call for a moratorium on civil rights demonstrations until after the November elections, a call which SNCC and the Congress of Racial Equality (CORE) refused to endorse.

King went on a speaking tour of Europe in the fall of 1964. Shortly after his return in mid-October, it was announced that he had won the Nobel Peace Prize for 1964. While preparing for a trip to Oslo,

to accept the prize in December, King was attacked by FBI director J. EDGAR HOOVER as "the most notorious liar in the country" for allegedly having said that FBI agents would not act on civil rights complaints in the South because they were southerners. King replied in a telegram to Hoover that the FBI was not fully effective in the South but not because of the presence of southerners on its staff. He called Hoover's statement "inconceivable."

Later reports revealed that the FBI had been conducting an extensive program of surveillance and harassment of King that dated to the early 1960s. At the urging of J. Edgar Hoover, U.S. Attorney General ROBERT KENNEDY approved a wiretap on King's phone in 1963. Aside from numerous telephone taps and bugs in King's hotel rooms, the program of harassment included attempts to disrupt functions at which King was to appear. In late 1964 and early 1965 the agency anonymously sent King and his wife, CORETTA, two tape recordings that supposedly revealed instances of infidelity on his part and a letter implying that King should commit suicide. In testimony before the Senate committee, FBI officials acknowledged there had been no legal basis for these actions.

Awarded the Nobel Peace Prize on December 10, King returned to the United States ready to launch another major campaign, this time to pressure the federal government to act to secure voting rights for blacks. He chose to focus the campaign on Selma, Alabama, a Black Belt city where only 1 percent of the local black population was then registered to vote and where SNCC organizers had been at work during the previous two years. King announced a voter registration drive in Selma on January 2, 1965, and during the next two months he and other SCLC and SNCC leaders led almost daily marches to the county courthouse there. Thousands of demonstrators were arrested and many were assaulted by Sheriff JAMES CLARK and his volunteer posse. By the end of February a stalemate was developing, and King called for a mass march to Montgomery to present black grievances to Governor GEORGE C. WALLACE.

Wallace announced on March 6 that the demonstration would not be permitted. When some 500 people, led by SNCC's JOHN LEWIS and the SCLC's Hosea Williams, started the march the next day, they were met at the bridge leading out of Selma by Sheriff Clark, his posse, and state troopers. The demonstrators, given two minutes to disperse, were attacked with tear gas and by the posse on horseback using cattle prods and clubs. King, who was in Atlanta that day, vowed to return to Selma to lead a second march on March 9. The attack on the demonstrators received national publicity. While supporting marches occurred throughout the country, other civil rights leaders and scores of northern white clergy and sympathizers journeyed to Selma to join the next march.

A federal judge enjoined a march planned for March 9, and administration officials pressured King and his aides to abide by the injunction. When the 1,500 demonstrators crossed the bridge on the outskirts of Selma, they were met once again by state troopers who ordered them to disperse. After briefly kneeling in prayer King turned the marchers around and told them to go back to Selma. King denied charges that he had made a prior agreement with federal officials to halt the march at the bridge.

Whatever his reasons for turning back, King's decision marked a key turning point in his relations with black militants, especially the youths in SNCC. Well before Selma many members of SNCC had criticized King for being too cautious, too ready to compromise, and too closely allied to the federal government and the white establishment. By 1965 many SNCC workers were also questioning the efficacy of King's strategy of nonviolence. Before Selma King had served as a mediator between the militant and traditionalist wings of the black protest movement. After his new loss of credibility among the militants, it became far more difficult for King to play such a role.

On March 17 federal district judge Frank M. Johnson authorized the Selma march, and it began on March 21 under the protection of a federalized Alabama National Guard and army troops. Under the court order, only 300 people could march along the entire route, but 25,000 people came to Montgomery for the final leg of the march to the state capitol. Like Birmingham in 1963, the Selma demonstrations and march did not bring immediate improvement in the condition of local blacks. But Selma, and especially the March 7 assault on the demonstrators and the deaths of three civil rights workers during the campaign, aroused national protests that forced the federal government to act. On March 15 President Johnson addressed a joint session of Congress to decry the violence in Selma and announce that "We shall overcome." Johnson called for prompt passage of a voting rights bill to suspend the use of literacy tests and other devices that denied blacks the vote and to install federal registrars in the South and other areas where vote registration lagged. King was present on August 6 when Johnson signed the bill into law.

After Selma King began to speak out against American involvement in Vietnam, calling for a negotiated settlement from July 1965 on. By 1966 he was outspoken in his opposition to the war, and, in 1967, he openly identified himself with the antiwar movement. In addition to violating his precept of nonviolence, King argued that the war diverted money and attention from domestic programs to aid the black poor. He faced strong criticism from most other civil rights leaders for attempting to link the civil rights and antiwar movements. He also alienated President Johnson; at a White House conference on civil rights in June 1966, King was virtually ignored by administration officials and he found the federal government increasingly less receptive to appeals for aid or intervention in his campaigns.

Although King remained a resident of Atlanta, he also began giving greater attention to the problems of the black poor in northern inner cities. Early in 1964 he called for a federal "Bill of Rights for the Disadvantaged." The Watts riot of August 1965 reinforced King's conviction that massive federal aid to improve the economic and social conditions of blacks in the northern inner cities was needed. With an invitation from some local community groups, the SCLC began planning a drive in Chicago in the summer of 1965. On January 7, 1966, King announced the beginning of the Chicago Freedom Movement to end discrimination in housing, schools, and employment. King was in and out of Chicago over the next several months while his aides, led by the Reverend JAMES BEVEL, did the day-to-day organizing of the campaign. King announced on May 26 that a mass march on city hall would be held one month later, to be followed by "a long hot summer of peaceful nonviolence."

These plans were delayed when King learned on June 6 that JAMES MEREDITH, in the course of a protest march from Memphis, Tennessee, to Jackson, Mississippi, had been shot from ambush just over the Mississippi border. King rushed to Memphis and, on June 7, he, STOKELY CARMICHAEL, the newly elected chair of SNCC, and FLOYD MCKISSICK of CORE, announced they would continue the march. Despite an attack on the demonstrators by a white mob in Philadelphia, Mississippi, on June 21 and by police in Canton, Mississippi, two days later, the protesters reached Jackson and held a final rally at the state capitol on June 26.

The most notable feature of the Meredith march was the public divisions among civil rights leaders it revealed. A manifesto issued June 8 declared the march was "a massive public indictment and protest" against the failure of American society and government to fulfill blacks' rights. ROY WILKINS of the NAACP and WHITNEY YOUNG of the National Urban League refused to sign the manifesto, while King signed it with reluctance. During the march Carmichael called for "Black Power," a slogan that reflected the rising militance within SNCC. King deplored the slogan, which quickly captured national attention, arguing that it carried connotations of violence; he continued to speak out against Black Power after the march. He later softened his opposition somewhat, saying he supported the emphasis on black pride and the call for blacks to amass political and economic strength to achieve their legitimate goals. But King remained opposed to black separatism and encouragement of violence.

King returned to Chicago after the Meredith march. Following a rally attended by some 30,000 at Soldiers' Field on July 10, he led 5,000 marchers to city hall to present the movement's demands. King met with Chicago mayor RICHARD DALEY the next day. On July 12 a three-day riot broke out on Chicago's West Side. In late July King launched a series of marches into white ethnic neighborhoods in the city to protest housing discrimination. Continuing through most of August, the marches resulted in repeated assaults on the demonstrators by angry crowds of whites. The culmination came in late August, when negotiations between business leaders, civil rights officials, and government representatives led to a 10-point agreement, and the demonstrations were halted.

Although King hailed the agreement as a victory, most of SCLC's staff later admitted that the Chicago Movement did not really achieve its goals. King's biographer David Lewis labeled the agreement "little more than a good-will pledge from the city, business, and realtors" to act against housing discrimination. In the months after Chicago King publicly recognized that changes in black economic and social conditions would not come quickly. At the same time he became more of a political and economic radical. In the summer of 1967 King told

an interviewer he had abandoned his earlier ideas of step-by-step reform of American institutions. Now, he said, "I think you've got to have a reconstruction of the entire society, a revolution of values," which would involve the rebuilding of the cities, the nationalization of some industries, a review of American foreign investments, and the establishment of a guaranteed annual income. In his speeches and writings King continued to argue that nonviolent methods could bring real change, but he also displayed less optimism than in earlier years.

Following the Chicago campaign King's public stature began to decline. While traditional civil rights leaders condemned his antiwar statements and activities, the militants attacked King for his adherence to nonviolence and his refusal to endorse Black Power. He was also losing his base of support among northern whites. A growing number of white radicals, more sympathetic to black militants, considered King and his methods outdated. White liberals called for slowing down the pace of the civil rights movement. Others turned their attention to the Vietnam War, which for many remained part of the same struggle against an oppressive American government. Contributions to the SCLC declined. Even among King's supporters there was a growing conviction that his strategy could not be successfully applied to the problems of northern poverty and discrimination.

In June 1967 the Supreme Court upheld contempt of court convictions of King and seven other ministers resulting from the 1963 Birmingham demonstrations. While serving his five-day prison term beginning October 30, King discussed with his aides a plan to assemble an interracial coalition of the poor that would pressure the federal government into enacting new antipoverty legislation. He devoted the next several months to organizing the Poor People's Campaign, an effort designed to prove the continuing viability of nonviolence in addition to seeking a massive program of federal aid for the poor. The plans for the campaign, completed in February 1968, called for a mass march on Washington by poor whites, American Indians, and Mexican Americans as well as blacks. In Washington there would be daily nonviolent protests until Congress acted to guarantee jobs to all those able to work, a viable income for those unable to work, and an end to discrimination in housing and education. King's plans met strong opposition from government officials and hostility or indifference from other civil rights organizations.

In March 1968 King took time off from recruitment for the Poor People's March to aid a sanitation workers' strike in Memphis. He led a mass march in Memphis in support of the strikers on March 28. The demonstration ended in violence when some protesters broke away from the main crowd and began smashing windows and looting stores. Although the number involved in the violence was relatively small, King was troubled by the violence and angered when press reports focused on the incident, resulting in a storm of criticism from both blacks and whites. King was back in the city on April 3 to begin preparations for a second march. At about 6 p.m. the next evening, as he stood on the balcony outside his motel room in Memphis, King was shot by a sniper and died almost immediately. JAMES EARL RAY, arrested in London in June 1968 and extradited to the United States in July, was charged with King's assassination and pleaded guilty to the charge in March 1969. In later years Ray attempted to change his plea and secure a new trial. This plus the 1975 disclosures of FBI harassment of King led many of his former associates and others to call for a new investigation of King's assassination. In the end Ray's guilty plea was upheld eight times by various state and federal courts. A congressional committee concluded in 1978 that Ray was the killer but admitted that he may have had help before or after the assassination. However, the committee did not find grounds to suspect any government involvement. An independent Justice Department investigation in the 1990s came to the same conclusion.

King's unique position and leadership during much of his life were due in part, as David Lewis noted, to "forces external to himself." King lived in an era when the impulse toward social reform and black protest was rising and when many whites were willing to heed that protest. Still, King himself was a singular man, "a rare personality, endowed with an ample intelligence, great courage and convictions, and an arresting presence." Even as his influence declined in the last years of his life, King remained an unusual figure. He was seeking a solution to the problems of economic injustice for all the poor, not simply the black poor, at the time of his death. His opposition to the Vietnam War began well before the antiwar movement became respectable or popular and represented for King a broadening of his commitment to nonviolence from the national to the international level.

—CAB

## Kirk, Claude R(oy), Jr.
(1926–    ) *governor*

Claude R. Kirk was born on January 7, 1926, in San Bernadino, California, and grew up in Chicago and Montgomery, Alabama. During World War II Kirk served in the U.S. Marine Corps. After the war he received his B.S. degree from Duke and LL.B. from the University of Alabama. Starting with limited capital Kirk made his fortune between 1956 and 1962 by establishing a Jacksonville life insurance agency and shrewdly exercising stock options.

Kirk soon quit the insurance business for Republican politics. He had headed Florida's Democrats for Nixon in the 1960 presidential campaign and subsequently changed his registration to Republican. In 1964 Kirk campaigned as a conservative against Senator SPESSARD L. HOLLAND (D-Fla.) With only 36 percent of the vote, he ran far behind the Republican presidential and gubernatorial nominees in the state.

Two years later, however, Kirk became the first Republican governor of Florida since 1872. After a divisive primary the Democrats nominated the moderate-liberal mayor of Miami, Robert King High. Kirk branded High a captive of northern liberals and attacked proposed open housing legislation with the slogan "Your home is your castle—protect it." Defeating High 55 percent to 45 percent, Kirk ran well throughout the state; he fared poorly only in the predominantly black wards.

Kirk stirred controversy during his first days in office. He announced that a private detective firm paid through public voluntary donations would investigate organized crime and political corruption in the state. His move immediately set off a debate over the methods and scope of the agency's proposed work. Most Democratic officials and many law enforcement leaders condemned the hiring of the firm, with some referring to it as "the Governor's Gestapo." Although Kirk rejected these attacks, he reversed himself in May 1967. At his request the legislature agreed to the creation of a special state-financed and operated law enforcement bureau.

During the debate over the state anticrime force, Kirk scored an important political victory. In February a federal circuit court ordered a reapportionment of the Florida legislature and a special election in the redrawn districts. After a vigorous campaign Kirk and the state GOP scored impressive gains; they garnered 35 percent of the legislature's seats, thus making the best legislative showing of any Republican Party in the South.

The March elections reinforced Kirk's earlier desire to seek national office. Shortly after the balloting he hired public-relations consultant William Safire to boost his possible national candidacy. Aiming for a vice presidential nomination on a ticket that they then suspected would be headed by a liberal-moderate, Kirk and Safire decided to present an "ultra-conservative" image.

At the same time Kirk sought a national rather than sectional appeal. In April 1967 he criticized Governor Lurleen Wallace (D-Ala.) for suggesting that southern governors meet to formulate a strategy to combat federal court school desegregation orders. Kirk declared that his state "cannot join attempts to subvert or delay" the Supreme Court's edicts. He termed Wallace's proposal "divisive and unwise."

Having criticized Lurleen Wallace, the unpredictable Kirk personally greeted Black Power advocate H. RAP BROWN during another summer of racial turmoil. When Brown, who most whites associated with the spread of black rioting, came to Miami for an address in August, Kirk was on hand to meet him. "You're welcome here as long as you understand we don't want any talk about guns," Kirk declared. Brown declined Kirk's proffered hand. The governor's unusual performance gained him national attention.

Although he received still more publicity as the host governor of the August 1968 Republican National Convention in Miami, Kirk never came close to national office. His willingness to endorse Governor NELSON A. ROCKEFELLER for president and his feud with Florida GOP chair William Murfin denied him any control over the state's 34-member delegation. Ignoring Kirk, Murfin promised Florida's votes to RICHARD M. NIXON. Nixon, the convention's ultimate choice, never considered Kirk for vice president.

Racial violence in Miami marred the Republican gathering. Personal appeals by Kirk and civil rights leader RALPH ABERNATHY could not quell the disturbances. On the riot's second day Kirk offered local officials "whatever force is needed" and subsequently sent in units of the state highway patrol and 1,000 National Guardsmen.

In November 1968 Florida voters approved a new state constitution that endorsed Kirk. The governor had called the legislature back into session

three times in 1967 until it agreed to present the new constitution to the electorate. Replacing an 1885 charter, the new constitution provided limited home rule for cities and counties, consolidated state agencies, and required the legislature to meet annually.

The electorate grew disenchanted with Kirk after 1968, partly because of a scandal in the appropriation of state monies and a bitter 1970 GOP gubernatorial primary. He lost his reelection bid to Democrat Reuben Askew, a Pensacola lawyer. After losing his bid, he remained in Florida, campaigning unsuccessfully for senator, governor, and state education commissioner.

—JLB

## Kirwan, Michael J(oseph)
(1886–1970) *member of the House of Representatives*

Kirwan was born on December 2, 1886, in Wilkes-Barre, Pennsylvania, and served in the American Expeditionary Force during World War I. After a brief career in business he entered Youngstown, Ohio, Democratic politics as a city council member in 1932. Four years later he won the first of 16 terms in the House. With the unionization of the steel industry, the district's predominant Republicanism, which had dated back to the earliest years of the GOP, gave way to the New Deal's Democratic alliance with second-generation immigrants who worked in the area's iron and steel works. From the very start of his political career, Kirwan maintained strong ties with organized labor and consistently supported the national Democratic leadership. In 1947 he became chair of the House Democratic Congressional Campaign Committee, charged with the allocation of funds for congressional elections. He further enhanced his power by acquiring the number two position on the Appropriation Committee's Public Works Subcommittee during the Kennedy years.

Upon the death of Representative Clarence Cannon (D-Mo.) in May 1964, Kirwan succeeded to the Public Works Committee chair. A blunt, strong-willed figure, Kirwan tended to approve authorizations for the districts of fellow Democrats most faithful to the official party leadership. In his study of Congress Senator JOSEPH S. CLARK (D-Pa.) termed Kirwan "almost a czar" as committee chair. A *Cleveland Plain Dealer* reporter labeled the Youngstown representative the "Prince of Pork."

Kirwan had to defend his budgets against annual Republican attacks. He argued in July 1967 that Congress could not reduce funds for water resource development (reservoirs, canals, etc.)—a prime feature in the annual authorizations—without creating "critical water problems" for the future. At the same time, however, he successfully led the opposition to floor amendments to increase funds spent on water pollution control. Kirwan also lobbied for the creation of an aquarium in Washington, D.C. Finally, after exchanging nasty words with Senator WAYNE MORSE (D-Ore.) about the issue, Kirwan took to blocking Morse's projects as they came through the appropriations committee. Since the Johnson administration was working closely with Morse on education reforms, the president finally had to intervene and sign a bill allowing for funding of a Washington aquarium. A satisfied Kirwan relented, and the aquarium funding was subsequently removed.

Throughout his long House career Kirwan called for the construction of a canal to run 120 miles from Lake Erie to Ohio River, which would have run through his district. Nicknamed "Mike's Ditch," the proposed water route met with determined opposition. Pennsylvania officials and railroad lobbyists feared the loss of the Ohio-Pennsylvania interstate trade to the southern Mississippi Valley states. Both groups fought hard against the measure. Ohio's senior senator, FRANK J. LAUSCHE, also spoke against the waterway. Acknowledging the canal's popularity in the Youngstown, Painesville, and Ashtabula areas, Lausche otherwise found "no unity of opinion in Ohio about the desirability of the canal." But Kirwan persisted. Finally, out of respect to the veteran Ohio Democrat, the House agreed in a September 1966 voice vote to a $500,000 U.S. Army Corps of Engineers feasibility study. With Lausche in dissent, the Senate voted 61-4 in October to include the Corps of Engineers study in its public works appropriations. The canal scheme expired with Kirwan's death on July 27, 1970, in Bethesda, Maryland.

—JLB

## Kissinger, Henry A(lfred)
### (1923–   ) *State Department adviser*
Kissinger was born on May 23, 1923, into a middle-class Jewish family in Furth, Germany. Fleeing Nazi persecution, his family settled in New York City in 1938. He served in the army in World War II and was a district administrator with the military government of occupied Germany from 1945 to 1946. After obtaining his B.A. summa cum laude from Harvard in 1950, Kissinger continued graduate studies there while working as executive director of the Harvard International Seminar. He obtained his Ph.D. in 1954, writing his dissertation on European diplomacy during the era of the Congress of Vienna.

In 1954 Kissinger became study director of a Council on Foreign Relations project seeking to explore alternatives to the massive retaliation policy of the Eisenhower administration. The project report, published in 1957, accepted the view that the Soviet Union was an expansionist power seeking to undermine the stability of the West. However, it rejected Eisenhower's stress on all-out nuclear warfare to stem Soviet aggression and proposed instead a strategy based on the limited use of nuclear weapons at the onset of an international conflict. In Kissinger's view, "Limited nuclear war represents our most effective strategy against nuclear powers."

Kissinger's work at the Council on Foreign Relations brought him to the attention of NELSON A. ROCKEFELLER, who, in 1956, appointed him a director of a Rockefeller Brothers Fund special project formed to study the nation's major domestic and foreign problems. The project's final foreign affairs report, published as *The Necessity for Choice: Prospects of American Foreign Policy* (1961), warned against optimism over prospects for a Soviet American détente and stressed the need for a strategy centered on tactical nuclear weapons. It called for an expansion of a nationwide civil defense system and for a major increase in defense spending to meet the expected Soviet challenge.

Kissinger returned to Harvard as a lecturer in the government department in 1957 and eventually became a professor in 1962. From 1959 to 1969 he was director of Harvard's Defense Studies Program. Kissinger also served as a consultant to the Arms Control and Disarmament Agency from 1961 to 1967 and to the State Department from 1965 to 1969. Between 1961 and 1962 he was an adviser to the National Security Council but resigned because of his disapproval of Kennedy's Multilateral Nuclear Force (MLF) proposal.

Kissinger's writings during this period focused on America's relations with Europe. In *The Troubled Partnership: A Reappraisal of the Atlantic Alliance* (1965) and *American Foreign Policy: Three Essays* (1969), he denounced American policy as arrogant in its failure to consider European interests or consult Western allies. Kissinger stressed that the United States could not be the sole defender of the West.

In July 1965 ambassador to South Vietnam HENRY CABOT LODGE asked MCGEORGE BUNDY to appoint Kissinger as a State Department consultant to develop new ideas on the conduct of the war. Kissinger visited South Vietnam in October 1965 and, in the summer of 1966, published an article supporting U.S. policy in that country. He believed that a North Vietnamese victory would encourage further Communist expansion and demoralize Asia. He concluded that "a demonstration of American impotence in Asia cannot fail to lessen the credibility of American pledges in other fields."

In October 1966 Kissinger returned to South Vietnam to aid a program designed to instigate high-level defections from the North. Between June and October 1967 he served as a contact in "Pennsylvania," the code name for an indirect exchange of letters between Hanoi and Washington that was designed to exchange a U.S. bombing halt for Hanoi's agreement to promptly enter productive negotiations. The attempt failed but proved a prelude to other secret negotiations begun the following year.

While pursuing his academic and diplomatic activities, Kissinger also served as foreign policy adviser and speech writer to Nelson Rockefeller in his unsuccessful 1964 and 1968 bids for the Republican presidential nomination. In 1968 Kissinger helped draw up Rockefeller's Vietnam peace plan. The proposal, presented on July 13, envisioned a restoration of peace in four phases: (1) a troop pullback on both sides and the interposition between them of a neutral, international peace-keeping force; (2) the withdrawal of North Vietnamese and most allied troops from South Vietnam; (3) free elections under international supervision; and (4) direct negotiations between North and South Vietnam on reunification. The Rockefeller plan also proposed that the United States reduce search and destroy missions, cut back American personnel, and gradually turn the war over to the Vietnamese.

Kissinger became assistant to the president for national security affairs in 1969. Four years later he was appointed secretary of state. During the Nixon administration Kissinger played a vital role in shaping U.S. policy in Vietnam, opening up contacts with the People's Republic of China, establishing détente with the USSR, and initiating peace talks in the Middle East. His "shuttle diplomacy" helped broker disengagement agreements between Israel and Arab states in the aftermath of the 1973 war, winning him much praise. He also helped orchestrate the overthrow of the democratically elected government of Salvador Allende in Chile, famously explaining, "I don't see why we need to stand by and watch a country go communist due to the irresponsibility of its people. The issues are much too important for the Chilean voters to be left to decide for themselves." He further supported the secret bombings of Cambodia that wreaked havoc in the nation and helped destabilize the neutralist regime of Prince Norodom Sihanouk.

In 1973 he was joint winner of the Nobel Peace Prize for helping to negotiate an end to the Vietnam War. The other winner, Le Duc Tho of North Vietnam, refused the award since fighting still raged in his nation. After leaving office, Kissinger opened an international consulting firm and remained active in numerous foreign policy organizations and efforts.

—EWS

## Komer, Robert W(illiam)

(1922–2000) *presidential assistant for Vietnamese nonmilitary affairs, ambassador to Turkey*

Described as an ebullient, always optimistic man by journalist David Halberstam, Komer served as pacification program chief in Vietnam. Born on February 23, 1922, in Chicago, Illinois, Komer graduated from Harvard Business School in 1947 and then joined the Central Intelligence Agency. During the Kennedy administration he served as White House special assistant for nonaligned nations and often advised the president on disarmament policy.

As the United States became increasingly involved in the Vietnam War, Komer became one of the Johnson administration's chief advocates of the Vietnam pacification program. This effort, which President Johnson called "the other war" was an attempt to provide the Vietnamese rural population with local security and positive economic and social programs to win their active support. Dormant during the opening months of the Johnson administration, it gained new emphasis in February 1966. Komer was put in charge of coordinating the effort in Washington. He played a part in allocating Agency for International Development funds in

President Johnson meeting with his assistant for nonmilitary matters in Vietnam, Robert Komer, 1966 *(Photographed by Yoichi R. Okamoto; Lyndon Baines Johnson Library)*

sive, along with many other efforts. This new effort, known as Civil Operations and Revolutionary Development Support (CORDS), stressed security rather than positive social and economic proposals, which had been an important part of previous plans. Its goal became the relocation of all Vietnamese living in areas that could not be put or kept under military control. The result was the dislocation of large segments of the rural population: the program created hundreds of thousands of refugees. CORDS also orchestrated a program designed to coordinate intelligence resources and neutralize the Communist organization in the South by any means necessary, including kidnapping and murder. This effort, known as Operation Phoenix, accounted for the killing of almost 21,000 Vietnamese, according to CIA director William Colby. As a result, he came under criticism for planning political assassinations.

In October 1968 Komer became ambassador to Turkey. He resigned in April 1969 to become senior social science researcher for the Rand Corporation. He returned to government service in 1976, becoming undersecretary of defense under President Carter. He died in Arlington, Virginia, on April 9, 2002.

—EWS

Vietnam, expanding programs designed to train local political and military leaders for South Vietnamese hamlets, and attempting to define the goals of the pacification project. But, according to the *Pentagon Papers.* Komer's major contribution to the program was to raise the priority of pacification and other nonmilitary efforts within the administration.

Despite his continuing optimistic assessments of the pacification program, Komer soon criticized its organization and recommended that troops be committed to the effort. In May 1967 Johnson, angered at the program's failure to show visible results, ordered General WILLIAM WESTMORE-LAND to take it over. Komer, however, ran most of the day-to-day operations, including modernizing and reequipping South Vietnamese forces and repairing the damage caused by the 1968 Tet offen-

## Kuchel, Thomas H(enry)

(1910–1994) *member of the Senate*

Kuchel was born on August 15, 1910, into a family that had helped found the town of Anaheim, California, where he was born. He attended the University of Southern California Law School and in 1935 opened a law practice. In the following year Kuchel won his first electoral contest running for the California Assembly from Orange County. Following a number of terms in the state assembly and senate and wartime service in the navy, Kuchel was named state controller by Republican governor EARL WARREN in February 1946 and that November won election to a full term. After RICHARD NIXON was elected vice president in 1952, Warren appointed Kuchel to Nixon's U.S. Senate seat.

Beginning his Senate career as a conservative, Kuchel became known as a moderate and, by the early 1960s, was a target of attacks by right-wing California Republicans. His political moderation, however, was advantageous in a state where, despite a large Democratic majority among registered voters, ticket-splitting was common. Kuchel had substantial Democratic support in winning reelection in 1956 and 1962. By the early 1960s he held the highest elected office of any California Republican.

As the Senate Republican whip since 1959, Kuchel was responsible for getting out the Republican vote on issues on which the party position had been determined by the Republican Policy Committee. He also sat on the Senate Appropriations Committee and the Interior and Insular Affairs Committee. Although his voting record was a mixed one as evaluated by the Americans for Democratic Action (ADA), Kuchel clearly sided with the Republican liberal minority in the Senate on the most important domestic issues. In 1964, for example, he was the Republican floor manager for the civil rights bill and was one of only five Republicans to vote for Medicare. He also supported the Johnson administration's immigration reform bill in 1965. LBJ's chief legislative aide recalled Kuchel as "a unique Republican senator. With his voting record, his attitude toward our programs, Kuchel was, in his view, a friendly member of the Senate."

Just as in his home state, however, Senate conservatives criticized Kuchel more harshly than other liberals, partly because of his occasional expressions of contempt and irreverence for his colleagues. During Senator BARRY GOLDWATER's (R-Ariz.) 1964 presidential campaign, Kuchel openly mocked Goldwater's aspirations in front of other senators. According to journalist Neil McNeil, he coined his own version of the Arizonan's campaign slogan: "In your guts you know he's nuts." Kuchel's indiscretions, combined with his refusal to support Goldwater in the general election, led conservative Senator KARL MUNDT (R-S.Dak.) and Senator CARL CURTIS (R-Neb.) to attempt to replace him as minority whip in January 1965. However, the minority leader, Senator EVERETT M. DIRKSEN (R-Ill.), who had helped Kuchel win his post in 1959, quashed the maneuver. Dirksen personally liked Kuchel and believed it necessary to keep a liberal in a party leadership post.

In foreign affairs Kuchel favored international cooperation but urged a strong defense policy and energetic protection of U.S. interests. He firmly supported the U.S. role in the United Nations. He approved President Johnson's Vietnam policy, although he did not join with Republican conservatives in demanding an escalation of the conflict. Extremely critical of draft resisters, he characterized them in 1965 as "vile and venomous" and charged that their demonstrations would "sow the seeds of treason." Also in 1965 Kuchel proposed a successful amendment to the foreign aid bill that barred aid to any country that extended its jurisdiction for fishing purposes over any area of the seas beyond that recognized by the United States.

As the ranking Republican on both the Interior and Insular Affairs Committee and the Appropriations Committee's Public Works Subcommittee, Kuchel played a significant role in the passage of two important 1968 conservation measures, the Redwood National Park bill and the Colorado River basin bill. Kuchel consistently backed the Johnson administration's plan to save the world's oldest and tallest trees in northern California from the time the Redwood National Park bill was introduced in 1965. He helped work out a compromise satisfactory to lumber companies and California governor RONALD REAGAN, who originally opposed the park, by guaranteeing compensation to both the companies and the state of California for land appropriated for inclusion in the park. In addition, the park was enlarged and moved father south in response to pressure from conservationist groups. The Senate approved the compromise bill in 1967 and the House did likewise the following year. During debate on the Colorado River bill, Kuchel defended California's traditional claims to 4.4 million acre-feet per year of Colorado water. Although the final bill included the Central Arizona Project, a plan to divert the Colorado's waters to the arid urban centers of Arizona, California's claims were also guaranteed, even in the event of water shortages.

Since Kuchel's victory over a conservative challenger in the 1962 Republican primary, his position in the state party had deteriorated as conservatives gradually took over its organizational apparatus. Although many conservatives considered Kuchel a disloyal Republican for his relatively liberal views, his refusal to endorse fellow Republicans in general elections was more crucial to his decline. In 1962 he did not back Richard Nixon's gubernatorial candidacy. In 1964 Kuchel managed New York governor NELSON ROCKEFELLER's unsuccessful primary campaign, but he refused to campaign for either Goldwater or GEORGE MURPHY, who was running for the Senate from California. In the 1966 gubernatorial primary Kuchel backed George Christopher, the former mayor for San Francisco, and when Christopher lost to Ronald Reagan, Kuchel withheld his support from Reagan. Many California

Republicans planned to "punish" Kuchel when he sought reelection in 1968. However, political observers believed that Reagan and other party professionals only wanted to "scare" Kuchel, since his Senate seniority was valuable to California. Kuchel's primary opponent was the extreme conservative MAX RAFFERTY, the state's superintendent of public instruction. Assuming that he would win easily, Kuchel conducted a desultory campaign. He lost to Rafferty in June by 70,000 votes. In 1969 Kuchel returned to private legal practice with a Beverly Hills firm. He retired in 1981 and remained in Beverly Hills until his death on November 21, 1994.

—JCH

## Kunstler, William M(oses)

### (1919–1995) *civil rights attorney*

Born on June 7, 1919, in New York City, Kunstler attended Yale University and took a law degree at Columbia in 1948. During the 1950s Kunstler joined his brother in a successful legal practice. He gradually became involved in civil liberties cases toward the end of the decade. His most important case in this period was that of William Worthy, a black reporter for the Baltimore *Afro-American*, to whom the State Department had denied passport renewal following his visit to mainland China. Worthy later traveled to Cuba and was arrested for entering this United States without a passport when he returned. Kunstler represented him during his appeal and won. In the early 1960s Kunstler became deeply committed to the civil rights movement after he volunteered to defend freedom riders in Mississippi who had been arrested during their 1961 attempt to integrate interstate transportation facilities in the South.

In 1962 and 1963 Kunstler successfully appealed the conviction of the Reverend FRED L. SHUTTLESWORTH and other blacks who had challenged segregated seating on buses in Birmingham, Alabama. During the same years he tried unsuccessfully to win a court ruling favorable to Dewey Greene, an African-American student denied admission to the University of Mississippi. Later Kunstler served as special counsel for MARTIN LUTHER KING, JR., and the Southern Christian Leadership Conference. He was a member of the legal advisory staff of the Council of Federated Organizations, the coalition that directed the massive voter registration drive in Mississippi in the summer of 1964.

Kunstler also worked with the Mississippi Freedom Democratic Party and with the Student Nonviolent Coordinating Committee (SNCC).

In 1966 Kunstler defended SNCC chair STOKELY CARMICHAEL on charges arising out of the civil rights demonstrations in Selma, Alabama, the year before. During the same year Kunstler challenged the constitutionality of federal grand jury selection procedures in the Southern District of New York, arguing that the system of selection intentionally excluded members of minority groups. Kunstler was also part of the team hired by JACK RUBY, accused murderer of Lee Harvey Oswald, to participate in the trial to determine whether he was sane and therefore competent to hire and dismiss his own lawyers. Kunstler participated, without fee, in the October 1966 appeal that reversed Ruby's conviction in the Oswald murder. (Lawyers for Ruby successfully argued that undue publicity had biased the jury.) The next year Kunstler was Representative ADAM CLAYTON POWELL, JR.'s (D-N.Y.) chief defense lawyer in the representative's fight to prevent his expulsion from Congress, Kunstler argued that to remove Powell would unconstitutionally deprive his constituents of the representative of their choice. The Supreme Court eventually ruled that the House had violated the Constitution in excluding Powell from his seat. During the same year that he defended Powell, Kunstler also represented black leader H. RAP BROWN. Kunstler claimed that the $25,000 bail set in Brown's arraignment on federal charges of carrying a gun across state lines while under indictment was "excessive and outrageous." He also charged that the government's attempt to place Brown, then chair of SNCC, in solitary confinement was a "political maneuver." Kunstler's motion that the high bail violated Brown's constitutional rights was rejected by an appeals court. In May 1968 Brown was convicted of violating the Federal Firearms Act. Kunstler unsuccessfully urged suspension of Brown's five-year prison sentence and $2,000 fine because of the "horrendous gap between white and black people in this country."

By the end of the 1960s Kunstler had thoroughly committed himself to legal and political support of those in the civil rights and antiwar movements who sought radical change in American society. Kunstler thought the legal profession offered the possibility of a "dedicated life" in which the "worker-lawyer is the equivalent of the worker-priest." Kunstler received little money from his many clients in the late 1960s. Most of his income came from the Law Center for Constitutional Rights, which paid him about $100 a week plus expenses, and lecture fees that brought his annual income to approximately $20,000 a year.

Kunstler became the center of national attention in late 1969 and early 1970 when he served as counsel for the Chicago Seven, a group of antiwar activists accused of conspiracy to incite a riot during the 1968 Democratic National Convention. A Chicago jury later found none of the defendants guilty of conspiracy but five guilty of incitement to riot. Judge Julius J. Hoffman found all of the defendants, including Kun-

stler and his co-counsel, Leonard Weinglass, guilty of contempt of court. Kunstler was sentenced to over four years in prison for his courtroom behavior. The sentence was later suspended. In 1970 he also helped arrange a defense team for students and one faculty member charged with various riot crimes. The following year he represented Attica prisoners during and after an uprising at the upstate New York prison. His commitment to the defense of freedom of expression never wavered; he won cases defending the rights of American citizens to burn flags in 1989 and 1990 before the Supreme Court. He died of a heart attack on September 3, 1995.

—NNL

# L

## Laird, Melvin R(obert)

(1922–  )  *member of the House of Representatives*

Laird born in Omaha, Nebraska, on September 1, 1922, and grew up in Marshfield, Wisconsin, where his mother's family had extensive lumber interests. After graduation from Carleton College and wartime service in the navy, he won election to the Wisconsin Senate in 1946, filling the seat vacated by the death of his father. In 1952 Laird moved on to the House of Representatives, where he effectively represented the dairy and lumber interests which dominated his north central Wisconsin district. On national issues Laird presented himself as a "pragmatic conservative" with a strong interest in military affairs. His Book *A House Divided: America's Strategy Gap* (1962) advocated an augmented military establishment, reduced domestic spending, and closer coordination between U.S. foreign policy and military strategy. Laird was vice chair of the Platform Committee at the 1960 Republican National Convention and became committee chair at the 1964 convention. Although not a partisan of Senator BARRY GOLDWATER (R-Ariz.), he served as Goldwater's foreign policy adviser in the 1964 presidential campaign.

During the mid-1960s Laird, who was the second-ranking Republican on the Defense Subcommittee of the House Appropriations Committee, became one of the Republican Party's chief spokespersons on military affairs. Together with subcommittee member GERALD R. FORD (R-Mich.), he repeatedly criticized administration defense budgets, which he claimed covered the rising cost of the Vietnam War by cutting into strategic weapons development. Laird urged, instead, that Great Soci-

ety programs be reduced in scope. In 1967 he supported an administration proposal for a tax surcharge to finance increased military expenditures. He also opposed any negotiated settlement of the Vietnam conflict that would include Communists in the South Vietnamese government.

Laird's importance as a Republican spokesperson in military affairs helped him enter the party's congressional leadership during the mid-1960s. In 1967 he became chair of the House Republican Conference; he also served on the Republican Policy and Congressional Campaign Committees. Hoping to reinforce his argument for a cutback in federal domestic spending, Laird became an early advocate of revenue sharing. In 1967 he introduced a bill that sought to return 5 percent of federal income tax receipts to the states and provide federal tax credits for state and local taxes paid. The proposal failed, but Laird continued to push revenue sharing in subsequent years.

In 1968 Laird was a strong supporter of RICHARD M. NIXON's presidential candidacy. He served on the "key issues" committee of the Nixon campaign staff, and, in January 1969, he was named secretary of defense in the new administration making him the first member of Congress to hold that position. Laird remained at the head of the Defense Department for four years. During his tenure the military draft ended. It was Laird who, in 1969, was dispatched by President Nixon to Vietnam to order American military commanders to begin shifting the burden of the fighting from U.S. soldiers to South Vietnamese and to begin withdrawing U.S. troops from Southeast Asia. He would later oppose some of Nixon's strategies in Vietnam, including the invasion of Cambodia and the mining of Haiphong harbor. He continued his strong advocacy of strategic weapons programs, including the antiballistic missile system (ABM). He also moved away from the more centralized approach of his predecessors, giving the service secretaries and the Joint Chiefs of Staff more influence in the development of budgets and force levels as well as in tactics and strategy. Laird served as domestic adviser to President Nixon during the Watergate scandal. After leaving the White House staff in 1974, he became senior counselor for the Reader's Digest Corporation.

—SLG

### Lane, Mark
(1927–  ) *author, attorney*

Born in New York City on February 24, 1927, Lane graduated from Long Island University and Brooklyn Law School and then opened a law office in East Harlem in 1952. There he became known for his interest in civil liberties, opposition to the House Un-American Activities Committee, and concern for such community problems as narcotics addiction, slum housing, and police relations. Lane also participated in the civil rights movement, journeying south in June 1961 with Percy Sutton, president of the Manhattan branch of the NAACP, to assist the freedom riders.

As a founder of the East Harlem Democratic Club, Lane won a seat in 1960 in the New York State Assembly. In December 1961 he charged Speaker Joseph F. Carlino with conflict of interest in a $100-million fallout shelter program. The assembly (which voted against Lane 143 to 1) exonerated Carlino of wrongdoing. Lane decided not to seek reelection in 1962.

Lane attained national prominence in January 1964, when he volunteered to go before the Warren Commission, then investigating the assassination of President Kennedy, to defend the interests of Lee Harvey Oswald, Kennedy's alleged assassin. Oswald had himself been murdered by nightclub proprietor JACK RUBY before he could stand trial. Lane feared that the commission was disposed to pronounce Oswald guilty before hearing the defense. Oswald's mother accepted Lane's offer to defend her son's name, but the commission rejected Lane's request to appear on Oswald's behalf.

Lane then undertook his own investigation and appeared before the commission on March 4, 1964. He claimed that on November 14, 1963, eight days before the assassination, a meeting had taken place in Ruby's nightclub between Ruby, Bernard Weissman, the leader of a right-wing group hostile to Kennedy, and J. D. Tippit, the Dallas policeman allegedly slain by Oswald during his getaway. Lane implied that Oswald might have been framed, but he refused to disclose who had told him of the night club meeting nor was he able to prove that it had, in fact, taken place. In its final report the Warren Commission declared that Oswald, acting alone, had murdered the president.

Lane's rebuttal, *Rush to Judgment*, published in August 1966, became a best seller. A number of reviewers suggested that while Lane had failed to prove Oswald innocent, he had argued convincingly that the Warren Commission, through a preconceived determination to uphold a lone assassin theory, had overlooked or dismissed substantial evidence to the contrary.

Lane charged that the commission had failed to examine important witnesses in the matter of the alleged Ruby-Weissman-Tippit meeting. More important, he argued that ballistic evidence undermined the commission's claim that Oswald alone could have killed President Kennedy and wounded Texas governor JOHN B. CONNALLY riding in the same car. *Rush to Judgment*, along with a number of other books attacking the Warren Commission, raised doubts about the assassination that have persisted.

Lane became active in the antiwar movement in the late 1960s. His book *Conversations with Americans*, published in the fall of 1970, attempted to demonstrate in a series of interviews with veterans and deserters that U.S. troops in Vietnam had committed widespread atrocities. Lane, along with lawyer WILLIAM M. KUNSTLER, also served in the successful defense of Indian activists Dennis Banks and Russell Means during their trial and appeal stemming from the occupation of Wounded Knee, South Dakota, in 1973. He remained active as both a lawyer and an author over the next decades, writing a total of nine books and lecturing throughout the United States on political and legal subjects.

—JLW

### Lausche, Frank J(ohn)
(1895–1990) *member of the Senate*

The son of Slovenian immigrants, Frank J. Lausche was born in Cleveland, Ohio, on November 14,

1895. He worked as a street-lamp lighter, court interpreter, and semi-professional baseball player before receiving an LL.D. from a Cleveland law school in 1920. After nine years on the Cleveland municipal bench, Lausche won election as mayor on the Democratic ticket in 1941. Three years later he won the first of five campaigns for governor. Frugal with state funds and possessor of a cheery, nonpartisan campaign style, Lausche won support among the state's normally Republican majority. In the first of two successful campaigns for the U.S. Senate, Lausche unseated Senator George H. Bender (R-Ohio) in November 1956.

Lausche maintained his independence from the national Democratic leadership throughout the Johnson years. In July 1964 he helped engineer the administration's only defeat during the enactment of its War on Poverty program. Lausche amendments reduced rural poverty aid appropriations by 30 percent and deleted from the bill a section that would have created farm-development corporations to buy rural land at market value and then resell it in family size units. According to *Congressional Quarterly*, during the 89th Congress the conservative Ohio Democrat supported Johnson on only 46 percent of the roll call votes for which the White House announced a position. On votes indicating agreement with the Republican–southern Democratic conservative coalition in 1966, Lausche held by far the highest margin of support (87 percent) of any northern Democrat. Lausche voted for the 1964 and 1965 civil rights laws and for Medicare. However he opposed the formation of the Housing and Urban Development Department and endorsed the campaign of Senate Minority Leader EVERETT M. DIRKSEN (R-Ill.) to modify the Supreme Court's legislative reapportionment rulings. In August 1966 Lausche and Senator WILLIAM PROXMIRE (D-Wisc.) voted with Senate Republicans to reduce by one-third the White House's mass transit aid bill for fiscal years 1968 and 1969. By 1967 the Ohio Democrat's record of agreement on the positions endorsed by the Americans for Democratic Action fell to a career low of 8 percent.

As a member of the Senate Foreign Relations Committee, Lausche usually supported the foreign policies of the Johnson administration, although he voted against the administration's consular treaty with the Soviet Union in March 1967. Lausche castigated critics of America's intervention in Vietnam. In October 1965 he condemned the early antiwar

demonstrations as "substantially" the "product of Communist leadership" and decried the "countless youths" who unknowingly "are following the flags of Reds." Attacking Senator ROBERT F. KENNEDY (D-N.Y.) in April 1967, Lausche complained that "the President is being plagued and hit from every side" because he had been "following out his honest judgment." In March 1968 he criticized "these vitriolic condemnations of our country" arising from the war protests. In July he spoke out in favor of a House amendment to the fiscal 1969 Labor-Health, Education and Welfare appropriation that would have denied federal aid to any student convicted of using force to disrupt a university.

Lausche began to modify his stand on Vietnam in February 1968 following the enemy Tet offensive and the opening of the Foreign Relations Committee's hearings on the August 1964 Gulf of Tonkin incident. A secret committee report on Tonkin Gulf, Lausche admitted, "tends to prove" that Congress should not have condoned the president's aggressive response. During a March 1968 Senate debate on the war, Lausche proposed that the Senate repeal the Tonkin Gulf Resolution and called upon the military to adopt the defensive "enclave" strategy of Lieutenant General James M. Gavin.

Lausche, along with Senator STROM THURMOND (R-S.C.), led the effort to include an antiriot amendment to the 1968 civil rights bill. As proposed, the Lausche-Thurmond amendment made it a federal offense to travel by interstate commerce or to use interstate communications systems with the intent to participate in a riot. Their provision broadly defined both a riot and "intent"; the Senate modified and adopted their proposal by an 82-13 vote.

In one of the greatest upsets in Ohio politics, Lausche lost the May 1968 Democratic primary to former Representative JOHN J. GILLIGAN (D-Ohio). Inattentive to the state's organized labor leadership, Lausche infuriated the Ohio AFL-CIO in October 1965 by opposing the repeal of the "open shop" provision of the Taft-Hartley Act. In January 1968 Gilligan received the endorsements of the state AFL-CIO and the Democratic state committee. Well financed by the AFL-CIO, Gilligan waged an aggressive media campaign as "the Real Democrat," while Lausche appeared at numerous barber shops and business clubs, most of whose members were Republicans. With 55 percent of the vote, Gilligan decisively defeated Lausche, who retired from public life in January 1969. He died in Cleveland, Ohio, on April 21, 1990.

—JLB

## Leary, Timothy (Francis)
### (1920–1996) *psychologist, drug cult leader*

The son of an army officer, Leary was born on October 22, 1920, in Springfield, Massachusetts, and grew up in an atmosphere of devout Catholicism. After a year at Holy Cross College, a Jesuit school in Worcester, Massachusetts, and another year at the U.S. Military Academy at West Point, he began his studies in psychology at the University of Alabama. He received a B.A. from Alabama in 1942 and a Ph.D. in 1950 from the University of California, Berkeley. From 1950 to 1955 Leary taught psychology at Berkeley, and from 1955 to 1958 he was director of psychological research at the Kaiser Foundation Hospital in Oakland. While at Kaiser Leary developed a personality test that was widely used by private and governmental agencies, including the Central Intelligence Agency, and was later administered to Leary himself during one of his many incarcerations on drug charges.

In 1959 Leary became a lecturer at Harvard University. There he began to develop a perspective that viewed social interplay and personal behavior as stylized games. At the same time Leary and several other clinical psychologists at Harvard became interested in LSD as a consciousness-altering substance that produced hallucinatory effects which seemed to resemble schizophrenia. His firsthand experimentation began in Mexico in 1960, when a friend offered him a local hallucinogenic; "Five hours after eating the mushrooms it was all changed," he recalled. "The revelation had come. The veil had been pulled back." Leary began taking exploratory "trips" along with a colleague, Richard Alpert, a number of student volunteers, and occasional collaborators such as ALLEN GINSBERG, Richard Watts, Aldous Huxley, and Arthur Koestler. These experiments suggested the drug's usefulness in treating alcoholism and mental illness, but they also began to alter Leary's own perception of himself and of the world around him. He became an evangelist for LSD, claiming its users became aware of numerous levels of consciousness beyond what Leary called the everyday, ego, or game-level consciousness.

Leary's notoriety embarrassed the Harvard administration. In December 1962 a Harvard dean publicly accused him of conducting dangerous experiments with unprepared undergraduates. Leary, who denied the charge, was eventually fired from the university. After a brief attempt to continue his experiments in Mexico, he moved into a 60-room mansion on an estate in Millbrook, New York, which was owned by William Mellon Hitchcock, a millionaire sympathizer. There Leary set up the Castalia Foundation, a legal entity under which he carried on his work with psychedelic drugs. "All I'm about," he later said, "is empowering individuals to explore with your friends the great wonders and mysteries of life."

Leary soon lost interest in science and began to explore what he viewed as the redemptive potential of LSD. In 1965 he was formally converted to Hinduism during a trip to India. Upon his return in 1966 he founded the League for Spiritual Discovery, a quasi-religious cult that rejected the external physical world for an inner world of self-awareness. Also at this time Leary publicized his belief that psychedelic drugs and the lifestyle associated with them would produce a political and spiritual revolution in the United States by spreading spontaneously throughout the country. In 1967 he told an interviewer, "It will be an LSD country in 15 years. Our Supreme Court will be smoking marijuana. . . . There'll be less interest in warfare, in power politics." Casting his lot with the emerging hippie movement, Leary became an almost messianic figure for thousands of young people in search of spiritual experience. In January 1967 he spoke at the Human Be-in in San Francisco's Golden Gate Park. Dressed entirely in white and holding a daffodil, he told the audience of 20,000 to "turn onto the scene, tune into what's happening and drop out—of high school, college and grad school, junior executive, senior executive—and follow me, the hard way." This message was later shortened to the popular slogan: "Turn on, tune in, drop out."

In 1965 Leary and his 18-year-old daughter were arrested in Laredo, Texas, for possession of several pounds of marijuana. Tried on a charge of failure to pay tax on the drug, he was convicted and sentenced to 30 years in jail. He appealed the case, and, in 1969, the Supreme Court overturned the sentence on the grounds that the marijuana tax law required self-incrimination and was therefore unconstitutional. In 1970 Leary was again arrested on a marijuana charge, this time in California, and was convicted and sentenced to 10 years in jail.

Denied bail pending appeal, he entered the minimum security section of the California State Prison near San Luis Obispo. On the night of September 13, 1970, he escaped. The radical press reported that he had become a political revolutionary and that he had been aided in his escape by members of the Weathermen, an underground revolutionary group.

Shortly afterward Leary reappeared in Algiers, where he was granted political asylum by the Algerian government. He announced his intention to work with ELDRIDGE CLEAVER, the fugitive Black Panther leader. Soon under criticism by the Panthers for his continued use of LSD, Leary also antagonized the Muslim government of Algeria. He went to Switzerland in July 1971, where he was arrested and later released on $18,000 bail to await extradition hearings at the request of U.S. authorities. Leary then fled to Afghanistan, where local officials turned him over the U.S. narcotics agents. In April 1973 he was sentenced by a California court to from six months to five years for his 1970 escape. He was released in 1976, reportedly after providing the government with information against those who helped in his escape. In the 1980s he began to focus more energy on his writing, especially with regard to outer space, cyberculture, and death. He also went on a cross-country speaking tour with conservative figure G. Gordon Liddy. Leary died of cancer in May 1996; the next year, a portion of his essays were taken into space on a rocket.

—TLH

## LeMay, Curtis E(merson)
### (1906–1990) *air force chief of staff*

Curtis E. LeMay was born on November 19, 1906, in Columbus Ohio, and studied engineering at Ohio State University. He won a chance to study flying in the army, and rose through the ranks to become, at 37, a major general in the U.S. Army Air Corps. An innovator in the tactical use of massed bombers, LeMay played an important role in planning the B-29 raids that destroyed a large part of Tokyo in March 1945. Rejecting the traditional policy of daylight, precision bombing, LeMay loaded B-29 bombers with firebomb clusters and ordered the start of nighttime firebombing. By the end of the war, these tactics had destroyed 63 Japanese cities and killed half a million people. "All war is immoral," LeMay said of these new tactics, "and if

you let that bother you, you're not a good soldier." LeMay became the commander of the U.S. Air Force in Europe in 1947, directed the Berlin airlift for several months in 1948, and later that year became commanding general of the Strategic Air Command (SAC). During the 1950s the SAC bombers, bearing nuclear weapons, were the primary U.S. deterrent against Soviet attack.

By the time LeMay succeeded General Thomas D. White as air force chief of staff in 1961, he had become embroiled in a dispute with the Kennedy administration over the question of continued production of bombers. Although Secretary of Defense ROBERT S. MCNAMARA thought that in the missile age the bomber was becoming obsolete, LeMay argued that the United States needed a flexible attack system and that only bombers could "show the flag" by providing visible evidence of American striking power. LeMay had little difficulty winning congressional appropriations for research and development of the new RS-70 bomber, but McNamara diverted a substantial part of the funding to other purposes. He also did not endear himself to the Kennedys with his calls for a military strike to destroy the Soviet missiles in Cuba in 1962.

By 1964 LeMay admitted that Russian defense systems had rendered the RS-70 obsolete, but he insisted that the United States desperately needed a replacement for its aging fleet of B-52s. He also criticized the Defense Department for failure to keep pace with the Russians in the development of high-yield nuclear weapons. Testifying before the House Appropriations Defense Subcommittee in February 1964, he called for manufacture of a 100-megaton bomb.

Fearing that LeMay might become a serious political threat upon retirement, both Kennedy and Johnson extended his tour of duty. LeMay's attacks on administration policy won endorsements from conservatives like Senator BARRY GOLDWATER (R-Ariz.), who stated in 1964 that he "would rather put my faith in a man like General LeMay than a man like McNamara who puts his primary reliance on computers."

When he finally retired in 1965 to join the board of Network Electronics Corporation, LeMay began attacking the Johnson administration for its "no win" conduct of the Vietnam War. As a member of the Joint Chiefs of Staff, LeMay had long advocated massive air strikes against North Vietnam's ports, depots, and supply lines. "My solution to the problem," he wrote in 1965, "would be to tell them [the North Vietnamese] frankly, that they've got to draw in their horns and stop their aggression, or we're going to bomb them back into the Stone Age. And we would shove them back into the Stone Age with air power or naval power—not with ground forces." LeMay believed that bombing could effectively destroy the enemy's ability to make war and argued that the administration's restrictions on bomber runs were needlessly costing the lives of American military forces.

In October 1968 Alabama governor GEORGE C. WALLACE chose LeMay to be his vice presidential running mate on the American Independent Party ticket. During the campaign LeMay denounced President Johnson's decision to halt the bombing of North Vietnam and promised that if elected he would resume the air against the North. LeMay stated the United States could win the war in Vietnam without the use of nuclear weapons but that the United States should "use anything that we could dream up, including nuclear weapons if it was necessary." LeMay also declared that the nation had a "phobia" about the use of such force and that "the world won't come to an end if we use a nuclear weapon." These remarks, attacked by the major party candidates, placed Wallace on the defensive and harmed his candidacy.

To liberal and radical opponents of the war in Vietnam, LeMay typified the irresponsibility and amorality of the military mind—the "cave man in a jet bomber," I. F. STONE once called him. To his supporters, however, LeMay was a lone voice promising a victorious end to a long and humiliating conflict. He died on October 1, 1990, in Colorado Springs, Colorado.

—JLW

## Lemnitzer, Lyman L.
**(1899–1988)** *chair, Joint Chiefs of Staff; supreme allied commander, Europe*

After a distinguished career in a series of command positions in Europe and the Far East, General Lemnitzer, who was born on August 29, 1899, in Honesdale, Pennsylvania, was appointed army chief of staff in 1959 and chair of the Joint Chiefs of Staff in 1960. As chair Lemnitzer advised President Kennedy to proceed with the Bay of Pigs invasion in April 1961 and urged the commitment of American air and naval power to the operation. After the plan

failed he continued to push for action against Cuba, even advocating CIA-sponsored covert actions against the United States, designed to encourage public support for an invasion of Cuba. He also counseled the president on the necessity of a large-scale commitment of troops and weapons to win a war in Southeast Asia.

In January 1963 Lemnitzer replaced General Lauris Norstad as supreme commander of allied forces, Europe. During the 1964 Cyprus crisis, Lemnitzer served as President Johnson's personal envoy to Turkey, warning that country not to land troops on Cyprus. In August Lemnitzer, in his capacity as supreme allied commander, also successfully appealed to both Greece and Turkey to return troops intended for invasion forces to the North Atlantic Treaty Organization (NATO).

Like Lauris Norstad, Lemnitzer was a proponent of a Multilateral NATO Nuclear force (MLF) as well as an advocate of increasing conventional troops in the alliance. Following his predecessor's recommendation, Lemnitzer also championed the development of a multinational mobile unit designed to show a potential aggressor that the allies were capable of quick, united action.

Lemnitzer's plans were directly challenged by the French decision to withdraw from the military structure of NATO in 1966 to pursue an independent foreign policy and by threatened British and U.S. troop reductions made to ease those countries' foreign exchange problems. In 1967 Lemnitzer warned the allies of the implications of these moves. In the event of attack, the French withdrawal meant the earlier commitment of reserve forces and the possibility of earlier deployment of nuclear weapons. Lemnitzer scored the British and U.S. plans as adversely affecting the "credibility" of the deterrent force. Warning that the enemy's military capabilities were very substantial and its policy increasingly aggressive, he urged the continued buildup of forces in Europe. His pleas went unheeded until Russia's 1968 invasion of Czechoslovakia, after which allied commitments to NATO were substantially increased.

Lemnitzer retired from the army and from his position as commander of NATO in June 1969. In the 1970s he served on the Rockefeller Commission, which was charged with investigating allegations of CIA operations conducted within U.S. borders. He died on November 12, 1998.

—EWS

## Lewis, John R.

*(1940–   ) chair, Student Nonviolent Coordinating Committee*

Born on February 21, 1940, and raised in rural Alabama, Lewis became a Baptist minister at age 16. He was a seminary student in Nashville when the sit-in movement began in February 1960. Lewis joined the Nashville sit-ins that month, helped found the Student Nonviolent Coordinating Committee (SNCC) in April 1960, and participated in the Freedom Ride of May 1961. Elected chair of SNCC in June 1963, Lewis spoke at the March on Washington as the group's representative.

Lewis helped lead demonstrations in January 1964 to integrate public accommodations in Atlanta, Georgia. He led over 150 black high school students in a January 7 protest at the mayor's office and was arrested 11 days later in a demonstration outside a segregated restaurant. He was jailed again during antisegregation demonstrations in Nashville in April and May of 1964 and during a July 1964 march against voter discrimination in Selma, Alabama. Lewis also helped organize and raise funds for the Mississippi Freedom Summer of 1964, a project to encourage community organizing and voter registration among the states's black citizens. In July 1964 Lewis met with A. PHILIP RANDOLPH and the leaders of other rights organizations at a strategy conference in New York City. The meeting resulted in a call for a "moratorium" on mass civil rights demonstrations until after the 1964 presidential election. After consulting with other members of SNCC, Lewis refused to sign the call.

Following the election the Southern Christian Leadership Conference (SCLC), led by MARTIN LUTHER KING, JR., decided to make Selma, Alabama, its focal point for 1965. Beginning in January it cooperated with Lewis and SNCC, which had been active in Selma since early 1963, in an intensive voter registration drive. By March the two organizations had made little headway because of strong opposition from local whites, and King called for a march to Montgomery to protest the denial of voting rights to Alabama blacks. SNCC did not endorse the march because some members insisted that voter registration work in Selma should take precedence over mass demonstrations. Lewis supported the march, however, and, independent of SNCC, helped organize it. On March 7 Lewis and Hosea Williams of the SCLC led 500 marchers from the Brown Chapel in Selma to the Edmund Pettus Bridge leading out of town. There they met 200 state troopers and sheriff's deputies who ordered them to disperse. When the marchers failed to move, the troopers fired tear gas and attacked them with whips and nightsticks. Lewis suffered a concussion in the melee, yet he and Williams were able to lead many of the marchers back to Brown Chapel. Lewis then participated in marches in Harlem and in Montgomery to protest the violence in Selma and, on March 21, was a leader of the final march that did go from Selma to Montgomery.

During the summer of 1965 Lewis led other voting rights demonstrations in Mississippi and Georgia. He also helped plan the challenge brought by the Mississippi Freedom Democratic Party to the seating of the state's five representatives in Congress, a move that the House defeated on September 17. In January 1966 Lewis issued a SNCC policy statement that denounced the Vietnam War and supported those men unwilling to the drafted. He then helped found the Southern Coordinating Committee to End the War in Vietnam. Despite his opposition to Johnson's war policies, in February Lewis accepted an invitation to become a member of the President's Council for the White House Conference on Civil Rights scheduled for June.

Lewis was ousted as chair of SNCC in May 1966. During the previous year he had helped establish a SNCC policy that the organization and the civil rights movement should be led by blacks, but Lewis continued to support integration as the goal of the movement, with white participation in SNCC and nonviolence as the means of protest. By early 1966, however, many black members of SNCC were opposed to white involvement and were rejecting nonviolent tactics. Lewis faced criticism for these policy differences and also for having supported the Selma march and for being on the council for the White House Conference. At an all-night SNCC meeting near Nashville on May 14 and 15, Lewis lost the chair to the more militant STOKELY CARMICHAEL. At the same meeting, SNCC decided to stop using integrated field teams.

Lewis was named to a 10-member policy-making central committee in SNCC, and later that month he signed a statement in which SNCC withdrew from the White House Conference, charging that President Johnson was not serious about ensuring blacks' constitutional rights. On July 22 Lewis resigned from SNCC, by then identified with

Carmichael and "Black Power." Publicly, Lewis refused to take issue with SNCC, but privately he was distressed by the group's turn away from integration and nonviolence.

Lewis continued his civil rights work as a staff member of the Field Foundation in 1966 and 1967 and later as director of community organization projects for the Southern Regional Council (SRC). He worked in Senator ROBERT KENNEDY's (D-N.Y.) 1968 presidential campaign. In March 1970 he was named director of the SRC's Voter Education Project. In 1977 he was appointed by President Carter to serve as director of ACTION, the federal volunteer agency. He was elected to Congress from Georgia in 1986, where he still serves.

—CAB

## Lindsay, John V(liet)

(1921–2001) *member of the House of Representatives, mayor*

The son of an investment banker, Lindsay was born in New York City on November 24, 1921, and graduated from Yale in 1943. After serving in the U.S. Naval Reserve during World War II, he received his law degree from Yale in 1948. A leader of the New York Young Republican Club and an Eisenhower partisan, Lindsay worked as executive assistant to U.S. Attorney General Herbert Brownell from 1953 to 1956. He was first elected to Congress in 1958 as the representative from Manhattan's East Side "Silk Stocking" district. His strong support for civil rights and civil liberties legislation won him a reputation as one of the most liberal Republicans in Congress. In 1964 Lindsay was one of three Republican representatives who refused to support Senator BARRY M. GOLDWATER's (R-Ariz.) presidential campaign.

In New York City Lindsay's public image was untainted by ties to local political bosses and enhanced by his handsome appearance. Announcing his Republican candidacy for mayor in May 1965, he challenged the city's traditional liberal-labor Democratic Party alliance by pledging to professionalize and revitalize city government. Lindsay's chances of election advanced dramatically when he won the backing of New York's Liberal Party, which usually endorsed Democrats. He was aided further by the entry of WILLIAM F. BUCKLEY, JR., founder and editor of *National Review*, as a third candidate on the Conservative line.

Lindsay ran as a fusion candidate and attracted diverse support. While Democratic candidate Abraham Beame appealed to the longstanding Democratic Party loyalties of New York's white ethnic groups, a *New York Times* analysis later showed that both Lindsay and Buckley cut into that territory. Lindsay, however, found particularly strong support among blacks, Puerto Ricans, and reform Democrats, all of whom he courted strenuously. Backed politically and financially by Governor NELSON A. ROCKEFELLER, Lindsay spent a record $2.5 million in his campaign. Both the *New York Times* and the *New York Post* endorsed Lindsay, while the city's Central Labor Council backed Beame. Lindsay was the November 1965 election with a 45 percent plurality.

Even before he took office Lindsay faced the first crisis of his administration's stormy relationship with organized labor. The Transport Workers Union, whose contract was due to expire at midnight December 31, the hour Lindsay was scheduled to take office, demanded a 30 percent wage increase and a shortened work-week. Union president Michael J. Quill requested that Lindsay attend or send a representative to the December contract negotiations. Lindsay at first refused, saying that it was outgoing mayor ROBERT F. WAGNER's responsibility to settle the dispute. Furthermore, Lindsay was determined not to work through what he termed "the power brokers," such as New York Central Labor Council president Harry Van Arsdale. However, Wagner, Lindsay, and Quill later agreed to the appointment of a three-member mediation panel.

Lindsay's first counterproposal to the union's demands, made December 31, was flatly rejected by Quill, who thereupon called a subway and bus strike for the next morning. Lindsay pleaded with workers dependent on public transportation to remain at home unless their jobs were "absolutely critical," but auto traffic soon became chaotic, and New York experienced the "longest rush hour" in its history. The city's economy, particularly small business and the garment industry, was badly hurt by the walkout, and school operations were disrupted. The public backlash against the strikers helped doom efforts by the Johnson administration to repeal section 14(b) of the 1947 Taft-Hartley Act, which organized labor had been fighting against since its passage. Despite the support of the federal government, the reform movement ran into much opposition, and the New

York strikes only served to rally the antiunion supporters. The strike, Lindsay noted, was "the death warrant."

Considered by many observers the victim of his own idealism and inexperience, Lindsay settled the strike after 12 days when he agreed to a 15 percent pay increase for transit workers and conceded a $500 a year pension bonus. In reaching the settlement Lindsay did not consult his own Transit Authority, which had long opposed the special bonus. President Johnson criticized the agreement for violating anti-inflationary wage-price guidelines. When New York teetered on the edge of bankruptcy in 1975, many observers recalled the 1966 transit pact, and particularly its pension provisions, as a milestone on the city's slide toward fiscal insolvency.

With the strike behind him Lindsay began implementation of a program to reorganize city government. He recruited modern managers with national reputations, coordinated city functions by merging various agencies sharing similar operations into 10 "super-agencies," and tried to establish a "little city hall" in each of the five boroughs. His program encountered immediate resistance from council members and borough presidents, who sensed a threat to their power. His ambitious plans to rationalize and decentralize city government were only partially accomplished.

During Lindsay's first term in office the city budget grew from $3.8 to $6.1 billion. This 60 percent growth in expenditure was due primarily to a doubling of the welfare roles, a rapid increase in pension benefits, and a substantial rise in the number of city employees. These increased costs were met by the enactment in 1966 of a city income tax, a doubling of the subway fare, and an increase in state and federal assistance. Real estate tax revenues also rose substantially as a result of an apartment house and office building boom in Manhattan.

Lindsay worked to cultivate a warm relationship with New York's black and Puerto Rican communities. While racial violence erupted in other cities. Lindsay's personal appearance in Harlem's streets in August 1967 may have had a calming effect. Lindsay's conciliatory approach to racial disturbances was further highlighted in April 1968, when riots flared in Chicago and other cities after the assassination of MARTIN LUTHER KING, JR. After Chicago mayor RICHARD J. DALEY instructed police there to "shoot to kill" arsonists and to "shoot

to maim or cripple" looters, Lindsay pointedly told a news conference the next day, "We are not going to turn disorder into chaos through the unprincipled use of armed force. . . . We are not going to shoot children in New York City."

Though free from the serious racial violence that swept other large cities in the late 1960s, New York became increasingly polarized as minority group demands clashed with the interests of other groups. Identifying himself with social change and the needs of the black and Puerto Rican communities. Lindsay suffered from criticism that he was insensitive to organized labor and the white middle class. Despite his growing prominence as an advocate for massive federal aid to the cities, his local popularity among traditionally liberal groups declined. His effort to form a civilian review board to consider citizen complaints against the police department gained support from civil rights groups and liberals but bitter opposition from the Police Department and the Patrolmen's Benevolent Association. In a November 1966 referendum voters rejected the board by a two-to-one margin. Lindsay suffered another setback in February 1968, when his refusal to negotiate with the sanitation workers union led to a nine-day strike. The mayor called on Governor Rockefeller to use the National Guard to collect garbage, but instead Rockefeller appointed a mediation team that approved a wage increase that ended the strike on terms close to those proposed by the union.

Probably the most bitter controversy of Lindsay's first administration was the struggle over community control of city schools and the resulting teachers strikes of 1968. By 1966 nonwhite enrollment in the public schools had risen above the 50 percent level, while the city's teaching staff remained overwhelmingly white and heavily Jewish. Minority groups considered the schools unresponsive to their needs, but integration had proven an elusive goal in sprawling New York. Decentralization became an issue when Lindsay requested that the state legislature consider the city's five boroughs as separate districts in order to increase state aid. The legislature agreed, provided that Lindsay submitted a plan for decentralizing the system. While the highly centralized Board of Education was willing to implement administrative decentralization and establish local boards, parents and community activists in inner city areas sought much greater community control of these governing boards.

In July 1967 the Board of Education established three demonstration school districts whose boards gained some of the powers previously held by the central board. The United Federation of Teachers (UFT) agreed to such decentralization but opposed removing the power to hire and fire from the central Board of Education because of a fear that local school boards in nonwhite areas would undermine the job security and working conditions of the mostly white unionized teachers. In May 1968 the governing board of Brooklyn's Ocean Hill–Brownsville district ordered 13 tenured teachers transferred out of the district. Community boycotts and demonstrations protested the central board's ruling that the transfers were illegal, while UFT teachers in the district struck for the duration of the school year. The state legislature, pressured by community control advocates to adopt a citywide decentralization plan, passed a compromise after heavy UFT lobbying and voted to enlarge the Board of Education, enabling Lindsay to appoint pro-decentralization members.

The first of three fall UFT strikes began on the initial day of school when the Ocean Hill–Brownsville governing board refused to reinstate 10 of the 13 teachers dismissed in May. Lindsay sided with the governing board as the conflict divided increasingly on racial lines. Tension between non-whites and New York's traditionally liberal Jewish community flared as community control supporters accused the union of racism and the UFT denounced the governing board and its supporters as anti-Semitic. The final strike ended November 19, when the city agreed to reinstate the transferred teachers and turn the district over to a state trustee.

Lindsay supported Rockefeller for the Republican presidential nomination in 1968 and campaigned actively for him in the primaries. Some party liberals considered Lindsay a potential vice presidential candidate, but he refused to allow his name to be placed in nomination and made the seconding speech for SPIRO AGNEW at the Republican National Convention. He also became an outspoken critic of the war in Vietnam.

In 1969 Lindsay lost the Republican mayoral primary but won reelection as a Liberal in a four-way race. In 1971 he left the Republican Party and declared himself a Democrat, and, in 1972, he ran unsuccessfully in several presidential primaries. He left office in 1973. He then returned to his law practice, while also working as an author and a television commentator. He lost in his bid to win the Demo-cratic senatorial nomination in 1980. He died in South Carolina, on December 19, 2001.

—MDB

## Lodge, Henry Cabot, Jr.

(1902–1985) *ambassador to South Vietnam*

Henry Cabot Lodge, U.S. ambassador to South Vietnam during the Johnson presidency, was born on July 5, 1902, in Nahant, Massachusetts, into a distinguished family that included several cabinet members and powerful members of Congress. The young Lodge graduated from Harvard in 1924 and worked as a reporter and editorial writer for the *New York Herald Tribune* before entering the Massachusetts House of Representatives in 1933. He was elected to the U.S. Senate in 1936 and, with the exception of periods of army service in World War II, remained there for the next 15 years.

In 1951 Lodge helped persuade DWIGHT D. EISENHOWER to run for the Republican presidential nomination; he later managed the candidate's primary campaign. His work for Eisenhower forced him to ignore his own political career, and Lodge was defeated for reelection by Representative John F. Kennedy in 1952. During the remainder of the decade, the former senator served as ambassador to the United Nations. In 1960 he was the Republican Party's vice presidential candidate on a ticket headed by RICHARD M. NIXON. From August 1963 until June 1964 Lodge served as ambassador to South Vietnam.

While Lodge was in Vietnam, liberal Republicans opened a Lodge for President campaign designed to prevent conservative senator BARRY GOLDWATER (R-Ariz.) from capturing the 1964 Republican presidential nomination. Relying only on write-in votes, the Lodge forces won the March 1964 New Hampshire primary, and the ambassador temporarily emerged as the party's most popular candidate. His record, public exposure as UN ambassador, and personal appeal contributed to popular movements on his behalf in California, Colorado, and Oregon. However, Lodge refused to leave his post to campaign and disavowed the efforts on his behalf.

Lodge left his post as ambassador at the end of June 1964. By that time he had become alarmed at the possibility of a Goldwater nomination and so returned to campaign for Pennsylvania governor WILLIAM SCRANTON. His efforts failed as did his

Ambassador to South Vietnam Henry Cabot Lodge meeting with President Johnson in the White House, 1967  *(Photographed by Yoichi R. Okamoto; Lyndon Baines Johnson Library)*

eloquent plea for a Republican platform promising a "Marshall Plan" for U.S. cities. At the July Republican National Convention the party nominated Goldwater and adopted the Arizona senator's conservative platform.

At the request of President Johnson, Lodge toured North Atlantic Treaty Organization countries in August and September 1964 to acquaint their leaders with American policy in Vietnam. In February he became a presidential "consultant" on Vietnam and helped shape the decisions to launch an air war on North Vietnam and to make major ground troops commitments to the struggle. Lodge supported both of these measures on the grounds that the United States could not abandon a country it had promised to protect and that a defeat would encourage new communist aggression in Asia.

In July 1965 Johnson asked Lodge to serve a second tour in Vietnam. The ambassador, who had been a popular figure in that Southeast Asian country, replaced MAXWELL TAYLOR, whose relations

with the government and the opposition leaders had become increasingly strained. For LBJ, getting Lodge to join the team was a political coup, as it allowed him to associate his policies (and any potential fallout) with a prominent Republican. Even before assuming his post Lodge attempted to convince Washington to reemphasize the pacification program, which had been stressed in 1962 but had been subordinated to military considerations during the beginning of the Johnson administration. Lodge insisted that the military situation could be settled if the government secured the political support of the people. This, he believed, could be achieved only by a program designed first to provide protection and then to carry out economic and social reforms that would raise the living standards of the rural population of South Vietnam.

By late 1965 both Washington and Saigon had acceded to Lodge's request. The South Vietnamese government established the Revolutionary Development Cadres, financed by $400 million in Agency for International Development (AID) funds. Once the program had been established, the ambassador's involvement became inconsistent and irregular, particularly after February 1966 when Johnson put William Porter in complete charge of the effort. Lodge objected to a subordinate controlling the program and refused to support his recommendations or press for further administration backing. Despite the embassy's optimistic reports on the success of pacification, the program floundered. After Lodge left Vietnam the effort was restructured in hopes of improving its effectiveness, but rural pacification eventually proved a failure.

Because Lodge saw himself as a presidential adviser rather than as a manager of the American civil-military effort in Vietnam, he did not try to formulate an integrated program of U.S. involvement. He respected the American generals leading the war and so did not play an active role in making military decisions.

During the spring of 1966 Lodge became involved in efforts to end the conflict between the central government, led by Premier Nguyen Cao Ky, and the Buddhist-dominated Struggle Movement led by Tri Quang. Prompted by the regime's failure to set a definite date for elections and its dismissal of the leading Buddhist general, Nyugen Chanh Thi, the movement demanded the overthrow of Ky and the installation of a civilian government. By the end of March antigovernment Buddhists and sympathetic elements of the South Vietnamese army had gained control of Hue and Da Nang. Although Lodge supported Ky and termed the Buddhists' demands "a naked grab for power," he tried to prevent a head-on collision between the two groups. When conciliatory efforts failed, Lodge concurred in Ky's decision to use force. In early April the U.S. Military Assistance Command in Vietnam airlifted loyal South Vietnamese troops to Da Nang in an unsuccessful attempt to quell the disturbances.

To avoid heightening anti-American feelings, Lodge did not involve U.S. troops or equipment or use economic leverage in Ky's later attempts to end the protests. At the direction of the State Department, he maintained relations with both factions and urged moderation. When Ky again sent troops to the rebel cities against Lodge's advice, the United States gave no assistance and withdrew its military advisers from army units of both factions. The movement was put down by a combination of force

and negotiations in June 1966. Reacting to criticism that America should not be fighting for a country afflicted with petty political squabbles, Lodge defended American involvement, saying that the nation's strategic interest in the war lay "in avoiding World War III."

During the summer of 1966 the ambassador opened secret negotiations with Hanoi that were designed to explore the North's reaction to a possible bombing pause. In November Lodge relayed communications from Washington suggesting that the United States would halt bombing North Vietnam in return for a secret commitment from Hanoi "after some adequate period" to reduce its infiltration of South Vietnam. The proposed delay in the North's reaction was designed to give the impression that its withdrawal of troops was not related to the bombing pause. In December Lodge received word that Hanoi seemed ready to negotiate on American proposals. However, during the following days the United States resumed heavy bombing near population centers around Hanoi. Despite Lodge's attempts to halt the air strikes, they continued and the talks collapsed. Lodge resigned his post in April 1967.

In March 1968 Johnson asked Lodge to become a member of the Senior Advisory Group on Vietnam, convened to consider the military's request that over 200,000 additional troops be sent to Vietnam following the Tet offensive. During the group's meetings he was one of the members who was dissatisfied with current policy but who were still reluctant to vote for a dramatic change. The panel recommended rejection of the troop increase request and favored adoption of a policy of beginning to disengage from the war.

From April 1968 until January 1969 Lodge was ambassador to West Germany. He served as U.S. chief negotiator at the Paris peace talks between January 1969 and June 1970 and was then named presidential envoy to the Vatican. He remained in that position until he returned to Massachusetts in 1977. He died in Beverly, Massachusetts, on February 27, 1985.

—EWS

## Loeb, William
### (1905–1985) *publisher*

William Loeb, whose father had been private secretary to Theodore Roosevelt, was born on December 26, 1905, and grew up in fashionable Oyster Bay,

Long Island, New York. He attended the Hotchkiss School and graduated from Williams College in 1927, before enrolling for two years in Harvard Law School. He bought a share in New Hampshire's *Manchester Union Leader* in 1946 and gained full control of the newspaper two years later, using it as a forum for his conservative and often idiosyncratic views on U.S. politics. Ironically, considering the power he wielded in the state, Loeb never resided in New Hampshire, instead dividing his time between homes in Nevada and Massachusetts.

During the 1960 New Hampshire Democratic presidential primary, Loeb supported the candidacy of an obscure Chicago ballpoint pen manufacturer, Paul C. Fisher, over Senator John F. Kennedy (D-Mass.), whom he regarded as soft on communism. In the 1960 presidential campaign Loeb subjected Kennedy to repeated editorial attacks and after the inauguration in January 1961 called the new president "the No. 1 liar in the United States." Loeb was involved with antitrust litigation in the early 1960s that resulted in a fine of $3 million, which he borrowed in installments from the Teamsters union. Throughout the Kennedy years Loeb lent vigorous editorial support to Teamster president JAMES R. HOFFA in his running legal battle with Attorney General ROBERT F. KENNEDY.

In the 1964 New Hampshire Republican primary, Loeb supported conservative senator BARRY GOLDWATER (R-Ariz.). He reserved his strongest editorial invective for New York's governor NELSON A. ROCKEFELLER, whom he referred to as a "wife-swapper" and for Ambassador HENRY CABOT LODGE, JR., against whom Loeb held a longstanding personal grudge. Lodge, however, who was not even on the ballot, won the primary by 13,000 votes. That same year, he editorialized against the passage of the 1964 Civil Rights Act, calling it the forced association of a totalitarian state.

Loeb devoted much of the mid-1960s to restoring the popularity of the Republican Party in New Hampshire after the disastrous Goldwater defeat in 1964. In the 1966 Senate race Loeb induced an obscure candidate named Harrison R. Thyng, a retired brigadier general, to run on the Republican ticket against Senator THOMAS MCINTYRE (D-N.H.). According to biographer Kevin Cash, Thyng was portrayed by Loeb as a combination of "the Wright Brothers, Billy Mitchell, Eddie Rickenbacker, Alvin York and Rocky Marciano." McIntyre ignored Thyng during the campaign and ran exclusively against the editorial policies of William Loeb, winning the election by a comfortable 18,000-vote margin.

National interest concentrated on New Hampshire and William Loeb once again in the 1968 presidential primary. Loeb boosted RICHARD NIXON's candidacy on the Republican side, while referring to Senator EUGENE MCCARTHY (D-Minn.) as a "skunk's skunk." Loeb regarded the Minnesota senator as merely a stalking horse for Robert Kennedy's (D-N.Y.) presidential ambitions.

Loeb again had an impact on national politics in the 1972 primary and was instrumental in damaging Senator EDMUND MUSKIE's (D-Maine) candidacy when a highly personal *Union Leader* attack on Muskie's wife provoked a widely publicized emotional outburst from the senator. He reached the peak of his political power in 1972, when he helped Meldrim Thomson, an obscure Georgia native, capture the New Hampshire governorship, largely based on an antitax platform. He was also a fierce critic of the anti–Vietnam War movement, and, in 1971, refused to allow his paper to cover the Muhammad Ali–Joe Frazier fight because of his hostility toward Ali for refusing to serve in the army. Loeb withdrew support from President Nixon after Nixon's trip to the People's Republic of China and in the Republican primary supported Representative John Ashbrook (R-Ohio). Loeb released his most vehement attacks, however, against proposals for state income taxes. He was the state's most outspoken critic of any such tax legislation, criticizing it with such vigor that politicians regularly refused to even discuss it. He died of cancer in 1985, and his wife took over as publisher until 2000.

—FHM

## Long, Edward V(aughan)
### (1908–1972) *member of the Senate*

Born on July 18, 1908, in Whiteside, Missouri, Long was admitted to the Missouri bar in 1936. He was the city attorney in Bowling Green, Missouri, from 1941 to 1945, and was elected lieutenant governor in 1956. He was appointed to the Senate seat vacated by the death of Thomas C. Hennings (D-Mo.), and defeated his Republican opponent in a November 1961 special election.

Long was a moderate liberal who supported President Kennedy on over 60 percent of all administration-backed bills. Elected to a full term in 1962, he was particularly active in drug reform legislation and vigorously supported the 1962 Federal Food, Drug and Cosmetic Act, which required substantial evidence of a drug's effectiveness before allowing it on the market. However, Long generally disapproved of what he regarded as excessive federal intervention in private enterprise and acted to prevent two important Senate investigations into the drug industry during 1963.

Long, who had one of the highest absenteeism records in the Senate, generally supported major Johnson administration domestic and foreign policy legislation. Active in the fight for civil rights, he was a floor captain of the section of the 1964 civil rights bill reforming and extending the life of the Civil Rights Commission. In 1964 he sponsored two unsuccessful measures to authorize federal courts to hear suits brought by individuals against federal agencies and to make the surveillance of a citizen's mail by postal authorities a punishable act. Two years later Long sponsored the 1966 Freedom of Information Act.

In May 1967 *Life* magazine published charges that Long had used "his Senate subcommittee as an instrument for trying to keep [Teamsters president] JIMMY HOFFA out of prison." The article alleged that as chair of the Judiciary Committee's Administrative Practice and Procedure Subcommittee, which had been conducting an investigation of wiretapping and electronic eavesdropping by federal agencies, Long had tried to get Hoffa's conviction for jury-tampering and misuse of union pension funds reversed. The article further charged that Long had received $48,000 from Morris A. Shenker, Hoffa's chief counsel, and stated that Long had been influenced to take up the investigations of federal agencies by Teamsters union leaders. According to *Life*, the hearings had hurt the effectiveness of the Justice Department's drive against organized crime by discrediting governmental investigative agencies, particularly the Internal Revenue Service. It had been a major contention of Hoffa's attorneys that evidence against Hoffa had come from illegal federal wiretapping.

Long denied the charges on May 21, 1967. He admitted that he had accepted the funds but insisted that the payments—allegedly $2,000 a month for 1963 and 1964—were for nongovernmental cases referred to Shenker's firm. Long also declared that "big money interests in the East" were behind the charges. However, *Life* later contended that the actual figure paid to Long by Shenker was well over $100,000 and that Long had not practiced law during the entire time the payments were being made.

On October 25, 1967, the Senate Committee on Standards and Conduct cleared Long of charges stemming from the *Life* article. Committee Chair JOHN STENNIS (D-Miss.) stated that the committee had "found no facts" to show that payments for Shenker's legal services had any connection with Long's "activities as a member of the Senate." *Life* later called the committee's findings a "whitewash." The article's impact in Missouri was a major factor in Long's loss to Thomas Eagleton in the 1968 Democratic senatorial primary. After his defeat Long returned to private business. He died on his farm in Missouri on November 6, 1972.

—FHM

## Long, Russell B(illiu)
### (1918–2003) *member of the Senate*

As the eldest son of Huey Long, the Louisiana politician who dominated state politics in the 1920s and 1930s, Russell Long was marked for a political career. Born on November 3, 1918, in Shreveport, Louisiana, after law school and World War II naval service, he aided uncle Earl K. Long's successful gubernatorial campaign in 1947. The following year Russell Long was elected U.S. senator after a barnstorming effort reminiscent of his father's campaigns.

Long sought the membership in the Senate's "inner club" that his father had never secured. His entree was confirmed in January 1965, when Long was elected assistant Senate majority leader (majority whip). Most of his support came from southern Senators, but Long also won the votes of such liberals at CLINTON ANDERSON (D-N.Mex.) and PAUL DOUGLAS (D-Ill.). He was opposed by other Senate Democrats largely because of his opposition to civil rights, Medicare, the limited nuclear test ban treaty, and foreign aid legislation.

In 1965 Long reversed his position and voted for the Medicare bill. But before the bill reached the Senate floor, Long offered amendments to remove any time limit on a patient's hospital care and to provide for graduated Social Security payments on the basis of income. Long's amendments were introduced on the last day of the Finance Committee's hearings on the bill and approved by an 8-6 vote. Certain that their adoption by the Senate would kill

Medicare when it reached the House-Senate Conference, the American Medical Association supported Long's amendments. President Johnson learned of the amendments only after they had been accepted by the Finance Committee, but he successfully pressured the committee into reversing its vote. Ultimately Long worked for the bill's final passage.

Long vigorously supported the administration's policies in South Vietnam and the Dominican Republic. He defended the "domino theory," declaring in February 1965 that if the United States withdrew from South Vietnam "there will be no place to stop until we reach our own borders." Long supported the landing of U.S. troops in Santo Domingo, since "to stand aside" would be to "risk another Cuban-type Communist takeover." Despite his tough stance toward challenges in Latin America and Asia, Long supported the reduction of North Atlantic Treaty Organization forces in Europe.

Long's accession to the chair of the Finance Committee in January 1966 provided the Democratic leadership with the rationale for appointing four assistant whips. The appointments reflected the administration's disappointment with Long's performance as majority whip. Democratic senators were irritated at Long's unreliability and willingness to delay Senate business. In 1966 Long's Presidential Campaign Fund Act, permitting tax-payers to voluntarily allot $1 of their annual income tax payment to a campaign fund, was enacted as a rider to the Foreign Investors Tax Act. The next year Long and Senator ALBERT GORE (D-Tenn.) engaged in a protracted debate over the retention of the Campaign Fund Act. The debate delayed passage of the administration's bill to restore the 7 percent investment tax credit. His knowledge of, and involvement with, the federal tax codes were unequalled during his time; the *Wall Street Journal* would eventually refer to him as the fourth branch of government.

Louisiana senator Russell Long and President Johnson in deep conversation, 1964 *(Photographed by Yoichi R. Okamoto; Lyndon Baines Johnson Library)*

Senate Democratic irritation increased when, on May 18, 1967, Long announced that he would act as counsel for Senator THOMAS DODD (D-Conn.) in his defense against a Senate motion to censure. Long charged that "half the Senate" could not stand a similar investigation and requested a six-week delay in calling up the censure resolution so that he might prepare a "proper defense." The Senate leadership granted a three-week delay, making clear that the postponement was granted to accommodate Dodd rather than Long. Long defended Dodd in a rambling six-hour speech on June 16 and later offered an amendment to substitute for the censure an admonishment to Dodd to avoid any conduct "which might be construed" as derogatory to the ethics of a senator. The substitute was defeated and only four senators (Dodd included) joined Long in voting against the motion to censure. These incidents contributed to Long's loss of his majority whip post to Senator EDWARD M. KENNEDY (D-Mass.) in January 1969. In the 1970s he attracted some political criticism in his state for casting a vote in favor of the Panama Canal agreements under which the United States relinquished control of this waterway, and he was a constant advocate of employee stock option plans. In 1986 he was instrumental in the development of a dramatically simplified tax code. He was also a leading proponent of the earned income tax credit. He did not seek reelection in 1986 and returned to the practice of law. He died of a heart attack in Washington, D.C., on May 9, 2003.

—DKR

## Love, John A(rthur)

### (1916–2002) governor

John Arthur Love was born in Illinois in 1916, before his family moved to Colorado because of his father's tuberculosis. He earned a B.A. from the University of Denver, and then a law degree from the same school. During World War II Love twice won the Distinguished Flying Cross as a navy pilot. He then returned to Colorado in 1945.

He became a Colorado Springs attorney, who first entered public life in 1961, when he unsuccessfully sought a position as a county Republican chair. The following year he rose from almost total political obscurity to defeat David Hamil, a former speaker of the Colorado House of Repre-

sentatives and 1948 Republican nominee for governor, in a bitter gubernatorial primary. Although the incumbent, Democratic governor Steve McNichols, was favored to gain reelection in 1962, Love won in large measure because of the unpopularity of a regressive tax program passed under McNichols.

Love was a moderate Republican who reflected the political inclinations of the burgeoning Denver suburbs. Within 16 days of taking office in 1963, Love signed into law a personal income tax reduction of 15 percent. However, he so increased expenditures for education that in 1965 he was forced to ask the state legislature for a sales tax increase to balance the budget. He was a progressive on racial and social issues. In April 1966 Love signed an executive order declaring that the state would refuse to deal with any company that practiced racial discrimination. The most controversial action of his administration came a year later when he signed a bill giving Colorado what was then the most liberal abortion law in the country. He also signed into effect a law that downgraded the possession of small amounts of marijuana from a felony to a misdemeanor offense and enforced fairly strict air and water pollution standards.

Although the Colorado Republican Party was becoming increasingly conservative during the 1960s, Love sided with the moderate wing of the national Republican Party. He directed the short-lived presidential campaign of Pennsylvania governor WILLIAM SCRANTON in the Rocky Mountain states; although he supported Senator BARRY GOLDWATER (R-Ariz.) in the fall, he was among those liberal Republicans who insisted that the conservatives relinquish control of the party following the election. In 1968 Love again broke with Colorado conservatives when he supported the presidential candidacy of New York governor NELSON ROCKEFELLER.

Love was chair of the 1969 Governor's Conference and was reelected in 1970 to his third term as governor. In June 1973 he resigned the governorship to become President RICHARD M. NIXON's first federal energy administrator. He resigned six months later, complaining that he was frustrated by an inability to affect policy. He pursued numerous business interests as well as teaching at the University of Northern Colorado. He returned to Denver, where he died in January 2002.

—TJC

## Lowell, Robert (Traill Spence), Jr.
### (1917–1977) *poet, playwright*

A member of a famous New England patrician family, Robert Lowell was the great-grandnephew of James Russell Lowell. The poet Amy Lowell was a distant cousin. He was born in Boston on March 1, 1917, and began to write poetry in high school. His subsequent search for a poetic mentor took him from Harvard to Kenyon College, where he received a B.A. in 1940. At Kenyon and later at Louisiana State University Lowell studied under the southern poets John Crowe Ransom and Robert Penn Warren and converted to Roman Catholicism.

After U.S. entry into World War II, Lowell at first attempted to enlist (he was rejected as physically unfit because of his poor eyesight); but when drafted later he refused to serve because he opposed the Allied bombing of civilians that had occurred in the interim. As a result he served six months in prison. Not long after his release in 1944 his first volume of poetry, *Land of Unlikeness*, was published. In 1947 *Lord Weary's Castle* made Lowell one of the country's most highly honored poets, with a Pulitzer Prize, a Guggenheim fellowship, and an appointment as poetry adviser to the Library of Congress. He subsequently lectured in poetry and creative writing at the University of Iowa, Kenyon, and Boston University. His collections of poetry included *The Mills of the Kavanaughs* (1951), *Life Studies* (1959), and *For the Union Dead* (1965). In 1966 he published three one-act plays in free verse—"My Kinsman, Major Molineux," "Benito Cereno," and "Endicott and the Red Cross"—that were staged in 1964 and 1968. Over the years his writing evolved from a traditional, formalistic style to one that reflected greater variety and informality. Despite a series of mental breakdowns related to depression, he continued to produce quality works, and his influence on 20th-century poetry is beyond question.

In 1965 Lowell played an important role in opening the breach between the Johnson administration and a large part of the American artistic and intellectual community. When he was invited to attend a White House Festival of the Arts in May 1965, he refused in an open letter to the president, explaining that he could "only follow our present foreign policy with the greatest dismay and distrust." The letter was reported in the *New York Times* in a front-page story on June 3. At the same time Robert Silvers, the editor of the *New York Review of Books* (of which Lowell was a founder), sent a telegram signed by 20 distinguished writers and artists to the president supporting Lowell's actions. Other guests at the festival were thus placed in the position of having to join or repudiate Lowell. Many refused to attend as a result, and Johnson was furious. The festival's organizer, historian ERIC E. GOLDMAN, pronounced it an "unmitigated disaster" in the end.

In September 1967 Lowell was part of a group of 320 American professors, writers, ministers, and other professionals who signed a statement in support of draft resistance, which appeared in the *New Republic* and the *New York Review of Books*. The statement was entitled "A Call to Resist Illegitimate Authority." In October of that year Lowell was a leading participant in the March on the Pentagon to protest the war in Southeast Asia, and he figured prominently in NORMAN MAILER's subsequent account of the event, *The Armies of the Night* (1968).

Lowell was an enthusiastic supporter of Senator EUGENE MCCARTHY's (D-Minn.) campaign for the Democratic presidential nomination in 1968. He admitted that he admired McCarthy "first for his negative qualities: lack of excessive charisma, driving ambition, machinelike drive and the too great wish to be President." In 1971 Lowell moved to England, explaining his expatriation in a 1972 interview: "I'm not here in protest against conditions in America, though here there's more leisure, less intensity, fierceness. . . . After 10 years living on the front lines in New York, I'm rather glad to dull the glare." He died of a heart attack on September 12, 1977.

—TLH

## Lowenstein, Allard K(enneth)
### (1929–1980) *member of the House of Representatives*

Lowenstein, whose father was a prominent physician and restaurateur, was born on January 16, 1929, and grew up in New York. He studied at the University of North Carolina and Yale Law School, where he received an LL.B. in 1954. A committed liberal, Lowenstein quickly showed his talents as a political organizer. He served as president of the National Student Association during the early 1950s and directed student volunteers for Democratic presidential candidate ADLAI STEVENSON. He also worked as educational adviser to the American Association for the United Nations. In 1959 Lowenstein toured the UN trust territory of Southwest Africa;

his impassioned attack on South African rule in the area, *Brutal Mandate*, was published in 1962.

After directing the successful 1960 congressional campaign of reform candidate WILLIAM FITTS RYAN (D-N.Y.), Lowenstein taught political science at Stanford and North Carolina State University. He was also active in the civil rights movement, organizing student volunteers for voter registration work in Mississippi and advising the Southern Christian Leadership Conference on legal matters. In 1966 and 1967 Lowenstein served as a civilian observer of elections held in the Dominican Republic and South Vietnam.

A strong opponent of American policy in Vietnam, Lowenstein became convinced in early 1967 that the war could be ended only by denying President Johnson the Democratic Party's renomination. He became a pivotal figure at this time, linking Senator ROBERT KENNEDY (D-N.Y.) and other liberal Democratic leaders with the growing antiwar movement. Throughout the year Lowenstein worked to build "dump Johnson" sentiment in such liberal organizations as the Americans for Democratic Action and the California Democratic Council. He also helped organize the Conference of Concerned Democrats, which worked for the election of antiwar candidates. Beginning in the summer of 1967, Lowenstein searched for a well-known liberal whom antiwar Democrats could support against Johnson in the 1968 party primaries.

Lowenstein first approached Senator Robert Kennedy and Senator GEORGE MCGOVERN (D-S.Dak.), but both turned him down, believing that Johnson was unbeatable in the primaries. Later, Lowenstein unsuccessfully sought to interest such liberals as Representative DON EDWARDS (D-Calif.) and Senator FRANK CHURCH (D-Idaho). He finally turned to Senator EUGENE MCCARTHY (D-Minn.), a somewhat less prominent opponent of the war. McCarthy surprised Lowenstein and other antiwar Democrats in late October by agreeing to run.

Campaigning in hundreds of cities and campuses, throughout the country. Lowenstein and his followers threw their enthusiastic support behind McCarthy's candidacy. Student volunteers recruited and organized by Lowenstein played an important part in McCarthy's surprisingly strong showing in the March 1968 New Hampshire primary, which did much to persuade the president to withdraw from the race. In August 1968 Lowenstein helped form the Coalition for an Open Convention, a group that attempted unsuccessfully to block the nomination of Vice President HUBERT HUMPHREY and to insert a peace plank into the Democratic platform during the national convention. Though a leader of opposition delegates at the convention, Lowenstein later alienated many antiwar Democrats by supporting Humphrey in his campaign against Republican candidate RICHARD M. NIXON.

While organizing antiwar forces for the convention, Lowenstein himself ran as a peace candidate in a Long Island congressional district. After a vigorous campaign conducted largely by student volunteers, he defeated his conservative Republican opponent in November 1968 and entered the House of Representatives. As a first-term member of Congress Lowenstein compiled a consistently liberal voting record. With other junior legislators he attempted to reform the rigid House seniority system and to relax committee rules to allow for more rapid movement of legislation. Lowenstein also joined a bipartisan group of representatives including Paul McCloskey (R-Calif.), that coordinated strategy for measures to end the Vietnam War.

Lowenstein lost his bid for reelection in 1970, after the boundaries of his congressional district had been altered by the New York State legislature. He remained active in liberal politics, however, and in May 1971 was elected president of the Americans for Democratic Action. He also cooperated with Representative McCloskey and others in organizing a bipartisan voter registration drive aimed at newly enfranchised 18-to-21-year-olds, who were expected to increase the chances of peace candidates in coming elections. Viewed with hostility by the Nixon administration, Lowenstein was included on the White House "enemies list" compiled in 1971. After he was narrowly defeated in a New York Democratic primary race in June 1972, Lowenstein returned to teaching at the Yale School of Urban Studies; he moved to the University of Massachusetts in 1972 and New York's New School of Social Research in 1973. He was alternate U.S. representative for special political affairs in the United Nations with the rank of ambassador from 1977 to 1978 and was shot to death by Dennis Sweeney in New York, on March 14, 1980.

—SLG

## Luce, Henry R(obinson)

(1898–1967) *editor in chief,* Time *and Time Inc.; editorial chair,* Time Inc.

A Presbyterian missionary's son, Henry R. Luce was born on April 3, 1898, in Tengchow, China. He grew up in China and received a B.A. from Yale in 1920. Luce and Briton Hadden edited the *Yale Daily News* while in college and in 1923 founded *Time*, the weekly news magazine. Hadden died in 1929 but Luce and his publishing concern prospered with the notable additions of *Fortune* in 1930 and *Life* in 1936. In 1954 he started publishing *Sports Illustrated*, whose initial print order was a massive 550,000, which broke circulation records previously set by *Life*. By 1964 the circulation of all Time Inc. publications totaled about 13 million. Although Time had no editorial page, its influential news reportage clearly reflected the views of its editor in chief. "I am a Protestant, a Republican and a free-enterpriser," Luce once snapped at a critic, "which means I am biased in favor of God, Eisenhower and the stockholders of Time Inc.—and if anybody who objects doesn't know this by now, why the hell are they still spending 35 cents for the magazine?"

Luce retired as editor in chief in April 1964 but retained much of his authority over the magazine as editorial chair. As in previous presidential campaigns the Luce publications attempted to influence the outcome of the 1964 contest. Defense Secretary ROBERT S. MCNAMARA received highly favorable coverage in the hope that President Johnson would name him as his running mate. Early in the Republican race *Life* promoted dark-horse presidential contender Pennsylvania governor WILLIAM W. SCRANTON, whose brother-in-law served as president of Time Inc. When the Republicans nominated conservative senator BARRY M. GOLDWATER (R-Ariz.), Luce reluctantly abandoned his tradition of Republican campaign support. Although his wife, Clare Booth Luce, seconded Goldwater's nomination at the Republican National Convention in July and *Life* ran a two-part exposé of Johnson's personal finances in August, the magazine formally endorsed Johnson in September. Luce also personally praised much of the president's domestic social program. Still, his publications generally retained their positions as defenders of big business and free enterprise, and opponents of organized labor.

The Luce magazines encouraged American military intervention in South Vietnam. In an April 1964 speech Luce termed Vietnam "troublesome" but added that it represented an "entanglement in the cause of human freedom." The August 1964 Tonkin Gulf incident was covered as an unprovoked challenge to freedom of the seas in the Luce magazines, with their reports bolstered by confidential Defense Department information that seemed to justify the administration's military response. *Time* made Army general WILLIAM C. WESTMORELAND its "Man of the Year" in January 1966. Only after the Communists' February 1968 Tet offensive (one year after Luce's death) did Time-Life modify its support of the administration's Vietnam policy.

Luce was involved in more than just magazines, however. He oversaw the operations of numerous radio and television stations and published a series of popular books on science and history. When he retired, he had a net worth in excess of $40 million.

Luce retained a journalist's curiosity until his death. Despite his long association with the pro-Jiang Jieshi (Chiang Kai-shek) "China Lobby," Luce sought a visa to travel to the People's Republic of China in 1966. He died of a heart attack in Phoenix, Arizona, on February 28, 1967.

—JLB

## Lynd, Staughton (Craig)

(1929–    ) *historian, antiwar activist*

Lynd's parents were the sociologists Robert and Helen Lynd, who coauthored the classic *Middletown* and *Middletown in Transition*. Born in Philadelphia, Pennsylvania, on November 22, 1929, Lynd was a Quaker who lived for a time in the Macedonia Community in New York, which had been established by World War II conscientious objectors. He graduated from Harvard in 1951 and obtained a Ph.D. in history from Columbia in 1962. In 1966 he was appointed an assistant professor at Yale, where he became a noted historian of colonial America.

Throughout the 1960s Lynd was deeply involved in the civil rights and antiwar movements. He worked with the Students for a Democratic Society (SDS), was an editor of the radical historical journals *Liberation* and *Studies on the Left*, directed the Freedom Schools for the Mississippi Summer Project in 1964, and helped organize the nationwide teach-ins on the Vietnam War held in the spring of 1965.

Lynd was encouraged by the growing militancy and self-confidence of the antiwar movement, but he was an outspoken opponent of what he considered its reliance on the liberal wing of the American Establishment. Speaking at the Vietnam Day teach-in at Berkeley in May 1965, he attacked liberals, such as ARTHUR SCHLESINGER, JR., who were mildly critical of the conduct of the war, insisting that for the antiwar movement to ally itself with the liberals would amount to a "coalition with the Marines." In the June–July 1965 issue of *Liberation*, Lynd criticized BAYARD RUSTIN's proposal for a strategy of coalition within the Democratic Party. Recalling an SDS-sponsored antiwar march in Washington during April of that year, Lynd offered his own vision of nonviolent revolution: "It seemed that the great mass of people would simply flow on through and over the marble buildings, that our forward movement was irresistibly strong, that had some been shot or arrested nothing could have stopped that crowd from taking possession of its government. Perhaps next time we should keep going."

Late in 1965 Lynd accompanied antiwar activist TOM HAYDEN and Communist Party theoretician Herbert Aptheker on a highly publicized visit to North Vietnam. He returned in January 1966 to report on Hanoi's peace terms and on the effects of American bombing. Federal officials insisted that Lynd had broken the law by traveling in an area banned to U.S. citizens without government permission, and the State Department suspended his passport. Later, after a trip to London where he spoke at a rally in Trafalgar Square, Lynd's passport was canceled.

Lynd was an early proponent of the resistance strategy that began to emerge in the antiwar movement in 1966, which advocated the organization of large collective protests, rather than acts of individual defiance, in the hopes of inspiring a larger movement among draftees. In July 1966 a group of eight young men met with Lynd in New Haven and signed a statement pledging to "return our draft cards to our local boards with a notice of our refusal to cooperate until American invasions are ended." At the same time Lynd and SDS president CARL OGLESBY drafted a statement containing a broad list of acts of resistance that the signer was asked to encourage: sending medical aid to the National Liberation Front, obstructing troop movements, refusing induction, opposing orders to fight in Vietnam, and refusing to pay income taxes. Eventually Lynd

withdrew his statement in favor of a similar one drafted by Arthur Waskow and Marc Raskin of the Institute for Policy Studies in Washington. Entitled "A Call to Resist Illegitimate Authority," it was published in the *New York Review of Books* and the *New Republic* in September 1966. It received over 2,000 signatures by the end of the following year. Lynd was an enthusiastic supporter of the Resistance, an antidraft organization formed in the fall of 1967. With Michael Ferber, he later wrote *The Resistance* (1971), a history of the antidraft movement.

During this time Lynd was also an active scholar. His book *Class Conflict, Slavery and the United States Constitution* was published in 1967, and it was followed in 1968 by *Intellectual Origins of American Radicalism*. In May 1967 Lynd requested a leave of absence from Yale, with the understanding that he was leaving the Ivy League school to find a teaching post in the "inner city." He was attracted to Chicago and applied at the University of Illinois and Northern Illinois University but was rejected without explanation. In the fall of 1967 he was hired by Chicago State College. When the Illinois Board of Governors of State Colleges and Universities attempted to block the appointment, Lynd threatened a breach of contract suit and forced the board to back down. In March 1968 he helped form the New University Conference, an organization of university faculty and graduate students that set up radical caucuses in the academic disciplines.

In the 1970s Lynd devoted himself to the study of labor history and to community organizing in the Calumet area of south Chicago and northern Indiana. With his wife, Alice, he wrote *Rank and File: Personal Histories of Working-Class Organizers* (1973), and with Gar Alperovitz, *Strategy and Program: Two Essays toward a New American Socialism* (1973). In Chicago he became more and more involved in the struggles of organized labor, and in 1976 he graduated from the University of Chicago Law School, determined to become a labor lawyer. He ended up in Ohio, working in public legal services until his retirement in 1997.

—TLH

# M

## Macdonald, Dwight

### (1906–1982) *author and critic*

Macdonald was born on March 24, 1906, into a wealthy family in New York City. He graduated from Yale in 1928, worked as a staff writer for *Fortune* over the next seven years, and then became associate editor of *Partisan Review*, a journal that then combined radical politics with an avant-garde approach to the arts. In the late 1930s and 1940s Macdonald was successively a Trotskyist, anarchist, and pacifist. Always a prolific and witty essayist, he published his own "little magazine," *Politics*, from 1944 to 1949.

In the early 1950s Macdonald shifted his attention from politics to social-cultural reporting, chiefly in the pages of the *New Yorker*, for which he became a staff writer in 1951. Macdonald was a caustic critic of what he considered the suffocating spread of "mass culture" in American life. Many of his critical essays on culture and society were collected in *Against the American Grain*, published in 1962. The 1950s also saw the transformation of his political views, as his disenchantment with the Soviet Union sparked him to criticism, although he saved his most virulent barbs for his attack on mass culture.

Macdonald's long review-essay of MICHAEL HARRINGTON's *The Other American* in the *New Yorker* helped establish Harrington's exposé of poverty amid affluence as one of the most influential books of the decade.

Spurred by the growth of the civil rights and antiwar movements, Macdonald returned to political activism in the 1960s. He attended President Johnson's White House Festival of the Arts in June 1965 and circulated an antiwar petition among the guests there. Six months later Macdonald and other intellectuals protested the Soviet imprisonment of writers Andrei D. Sinyavsky and Yuli M. Daniel for their publication of allegedly anti-Soviet works abroad.

Macdonald defended the tactic of civil disobedience used by the antiwar and student movements. In October 1967 he participated in the March on the Pentagon, where he unsuccessfully courted arrest. Observing the scene at Columbia University the next spring, when a group of student radicals marched on Low Library, Macdonald likened the action to the start of the Russian Revolution. Applauding the sense of camaraderie evinced by the student takeover of university buildings, he concluded, "I've never been in or near a revolution. I guess I like them."

In the fall of 1968 Macdonald took part in a bitter exchange of letters with social critic Michael Harrington, whom he had once praised so highly, over the New York City teacher's strike. Writing in the *New York Review of Books*, he opposed the United Federation of Teachers (UFT) strike as one against community control and accused Harrington of misrepresenting the UFT's strike demands. Macdonald later called UFT president ALBERT SHANKER a "racist demagogue."

Describing himself as a "conservative anarchist" and described in turn by novelist Norman Mailer as "America's oldest living anti-Stalinist," Macdonald remained at the end of the 1960s one of the most prominent critics of contemporary society. He continued writing into the 1970s, although alcohol took its toll on him in the later years of his life. He died in 1982.

—FHM

## Maddox, Lester G(arfield)

(1915–2003) *governor*

After holding a variety of jobs, Maddox, who was born in Atlanta on September 30, 1915, opened a drive-in restaurant called the Pickrick in Atlanta, Georgia, in 1947. The restaurant, which refused service to blacks, expanded nine times over the next 15 years. As it prospered Maddox took an increasing interest in politics. He ran as a segregationist candidate for mayor of Atlanta in 1957 and 1961 and for lieutenant governor in 1962. Although he lost all three elections, his campaign for lieutenant governor made him well known throughout the state of Georgia.

Maddox received national attention in the summer of 1964, when he defied the provision in the newly adopted Civil Rights Act prohibiting racial segregation in public accommodations. When three black ministerial students tried to enter the Pickrick on July 3, they were chased away by Maddox, who brandished a gun, and by his white patrons, who carried ax handles. Similar incidents occurred when other blacks tried to enter Maddox's restaurant in July and August. The three ministerial students sued Maddox in federal court, and in what proved to be the first court test of the 1964 Civil Rights Act, a three-judge federal panel in Atlanta upheld the public accommodations law on July 22. The court ordered Maddox to desegregate his restaurant within 20 days. After this order was affirmed by Supreme Court justice HUGO BLACK on August 10, Maddox decided to close his restaurant rather than open it to blacks. Blaming President Johnson for his troubles and arguing that the civil rights law was an attack upon Americans' "right to the private enterprise system," Maddox picketed the White House and the Democratic National Convention in August. Early in 1965 he erected a monument in front of his former restaurant, opened a stand there which sold souvenir ax handles, which he occasionally autographed, and shifted from the restaurant to the furniture business.

Maddox announced his candidacy for the Democratic nomination for governor of Georgia in October 1965. He spent most of the next year conducting a vigorous grassroots campaign on a platform of support for segregation and opposition to alleged federal encroachment on state and individual rights. Maddox placed second in a field of five candidates in the September 14, 1966, Democratic primary. He then defeated former governor ELLIS G. ARNALL in the September 28 runoff even though Arnall, a racial moderate, had the support of most Georgia newspapers and the state's Democratic hierarchy. In the November election neither Maddox nor his Republican opponent, Representative HOWARD H. CALLAWAY (R-Ga.), received a majority of the popular vote. Georgia law required the state legislature to choose the governor in this situation. Even though Callaway had received about 3,000 more popular votes than Maddox, the legislature selected Maddox as governor by a vote of 182 to 66 on January 10, 1967.

Sworn in as governor the same day, Maddox delivered a moderate inaugural address. He promised not to close any schools to prevent desegregation and said no "extremist organization or group" would have "any voice or influence in any state program." He urged respect for federal authority, declared there was "no necessity" for any federal-state conflict, and said any disagreements should be solved "under the framework of the Constitution."

Considered a buffoon by many of his critics and a populist hero by his supporters, Maddox surprised most observers with his inaugural and with his actions during his first years in office. He quickly invited Alabama's former governor GEORGE C. WALLACE to address the state legislature, but he also met with President Johnson early in 1967, declaring afterward that he was "pleasantly surprised" to find Johnson "so knowledgeable." Maddox appointed blacks to local draft boards, to the Georgia Bureau of Investigation, and to various special commissions and interim legislative committees. He ordered an investigation of conditions in state prisons after four escaped black prisoners surrendered to him at the governor's mansion to tell him of penal conditions.

Maddox also accepted antipoverty funds from the federal government but denounced federal guidelines on school desegregation and praised a local school board when it again segregated black and white teachers despite the potential loss of federal funds. He criticized President Johnson's formation of a federal commission to investigate the cause of urban riots in 1967, saying government officials knew that the violence was "Communist inspired and directed." Maddox also challenged the need for greater federal spending to cure the country's urban problems and said the country should instead "start instilling" in the urban poor the spirit of initiative "that made this country great."

On August 17, 1968, Maddox announced his candidacy for the Democratic presidential nomination, declaring he represented the "conservative element of American society." He labeled the major aspirants for the nomination "socialists" and, in a nationally televised address, emphasized the need for a stronger American commitment to fight world communism and for greater law and order at home. His candidacy was generally considered inconsequential, however, and Maddox withdrew his name from consideration shortly before the balloting began at the August 1968 Democratic National Convention.

Meanwhile, in accordance with long practice in Georgia, Maddox and the state Democratic Party chairman personally selected the 107 members of Georgia's delegation to the national convention. They chose only six blacks and a few moderate or liberal whites. As a consequence, a coalition of blacks and white liberals organized a challenge delegation headed by state representative JULIAN BOND. The Convention Credentials Committee suggested two different compromises between the regular and the challenge delegations, but Maddox rejected both and then resigned as a delegate on the ground that he was then a candidate for the presidential nomination. On August 27 the convention accepted one compromise proposal under which both delegations would be seated and the Georgia vote split between them. Most of the regular delegation walked out after the compromise was voted, and Maddox left the convention shortly afterward, proclaiming that the party had been infiltrated by "socialists, beatniks, and misfits."

During the remainder of his term Maddox denounced federal school desegregation suits and met with several other southern governors to devise means to stop busing for school desegregation. He also urged a full American military victory in Vietnam and continued to warn against socialism and communism within the United States. While in Washington in February 1970 to testify at Senate hearings on a voting rights bill, Maddox created a furor by passing out his souvenir ax handles at the House restaurant. The state constitution barred Maddox from a second consecutive term as governor. After he lost a court suit to overturn this provision, Maddox ran for lieutenant governor in 1970. He defeated three opponents, including the incumbent, in the September Democratic primary and then won the November election.

As he completed his term as lieutenant governor under the administration of Governor Jimmy Carter, Maddox once again sought the top spot in Georgia state politics. He lost, though, in the election of 1974. He sought to become governor one more time in 1990, but finished last among five candidates in the Democratic primary. He never renounced his belief in racial segregation. He died on June 25, 2003, at the age of 87, after suffering many illnesses over several years.

—CAB

## Magnuson, Warren G(rant)
(1905–1981)  *member of the Senate*

Born in Moorhead, Minnesota, on April 12, 1905, and orphaned in infancy, Magnuson was raised by an immigrant Scandinavian family in Moorhead. At 19 he left home and settled in Seattle, where he received his law degree from the University of Washington in 1929. Elected to the state legislature in 1932, Magnuson sponsored the nation's first unemployment compensation law. He served as county prosecutor in Seattle from 1934 until his election to Congress in 1936.

In Congress Magnuson sought to generate public work projects to revive his state's economy. Water development programs soon became his dominant interest. He won election to the Senate in 1944 and continued to promote federally operated dams and power projects in the upper house. Strongly supported by organized labor, Magnuson fought against the more restrictive provisions of the Taft-Hartley Act in 1947 and introduced a bill in 1950 that restored the maritime union hiring hall. Because his state's economy relied heavily on federal defense contracts and resource development, Magnuson's seniority on key committees and ability to deliver federal programs made him an extremely valuable legislator. In 1955 he became chair of the powerful Senate Interstate and Foreign Commerce Committee (later renamed the Commerce Committee). He also served on the Appropriations Committee and the Aeronautics and Space Sciences Committee, In addition to liberal social legislation, Magnuson favored large defense expenditures. He and Senator HENRY JACKSON (D-Wash.) were sometimes called "the senators from Boeing."

During the early 1960s Magnuson continued to focus on legislation designed to boost Washington's economy, particularly its aerospace, shipbuilding, and extractive industries. However, his emphasis in committee began to shift to issues of broader national significance. In the Commerce Committee and later on the Senate floor, Magnuson figured prominently in the passage of the controversial public accommodations section of the Civil Rights Act of 1964.

The pace of Magnuson's activity continued to rise with the quickening legislative tempo of the mid-1960s. Magnuson was a longtime Senate ally and close friend of President Johnson, who was best man at his 1964 wedding. He introduced most of the Johnson administration's major consumer protection bills and guided them through the Commerce Committee and onto the Senate floor where, because of the Democratic majority and Magnuson's stature, they were usually assured of passage.

In January 1965 Magnuson introduced a bill requiring a health hazard warning and statement of tar and nicotine yields on all cigarette packs as of January 1966. His bill also prohibited the imposition of any other package warning requirements by government agencies and effectively banned warning requirements on advertisements. A stronger measure, sponsored by Senator MAURINE NEUBERGER (D-Ore.), which would have permitted the Federal Trade Commission to retain its authority to set labeling requirements and would have required uniform label and advertisement warnings, was defeated in committee despite support from Surgeon General LUTHER TERRY. The Magnuson bill, minus the provision for tar and nicotine yield, passed without difficulty and was signed in July. Many health and consumer organizations saw the act as a victory for the tobacco industry, which had launched a massive lobbying campaign against stiffer legislation.

Magnuson was more willing to use his influence to curb the manufacture of unsafe motor vehicles and tires. Mounting public pressure, aroused by the publication of RALPH NADER's *Unsafe at Any Speed* in 1965, propelled the Johnson administration and Congress into action on auto safety. Nader attacked the automobile industry for placing style and sales above safety and argued that the introduction of safety features could substantially reduce traffic casualties.

In March 1966 Magnuson introduced an administration bill authorizing the secretary of commerce to establish auto safety standards if, after two years, he concluded they were necessary. Responding to pressure from Nader and such senators as ROBERT KENNEDY (D-N.Y.) and ABRAHAM RIBICOFF (D-Conn.), Magnuson later agreed to make

the establishment of safety standards mandatory and to hasten the effective date for compliance. He also supported an amendment to include criminal rather than civil penalties for manufacturers found in violation of the law, but his was defeated 14–62. The House and Senate passed the bill without opposition. A tire safety bill, introduced by Magnuson in October 1965 and already approved by the Senate, was incorporated into the Auto Safety Act during the House-Senate Conference.

In accordance with the act a National Traffic Safety Agency (NTSA) was formed in November 1966. Its chair issued federal safety standards later that month, but car manufacturers, who had first favored a voluntary industry safety program and later supported discretionary federal standards, complained that they would be unable to meet the federal standards in the allotted time. In January 1967 the NTSA announced a revised set of standards, less stringent than those originally established. The new set shifted the compliance deadline from September 1967 to January 1968 and temporarily withdrew some of the original standards pending further study. To evaluate the NTSA's new standards, Magnuson held Commerce Committee hearings in March 1967 during which Nader accused NTSA of having a "protective attitude" toward the automotive industry. No further action was taken. Magnuson also criticized the president for requesting only $26 million of the more than $91 million authorized for the first year of safety programs.

In addition to the cigarette labeling and auto safety laws, Magnuson introduced numerous less significant consumer protection bills requested by the administration, most of which passed with little debate or opposition. These included the 1966 Child Protection Act authorizing labeling requirements on dangerous household items, the 1967 Flammable Fabrics Act Authorizing the establishment of flammability standards, and a 1967 law creating the National Commission on Product Safety. The commission's task was to review the adequacy of existing regulations and to identify hazardous products already on the market, although it was prohibited from listing them by brand name. Magnuson's 1966 "truth-in-packaging" bill also had the administration's backing and passed the Senate easily. However, it was diluted in the House, where manufacturers concentrated their lobbying efforts. Magnuson's original proposal, giving federal officials the authority to set standard weights and sizes for packages, was eliminated in favor of requirements for uniform labels indicating quantity. A radiation control bill and a gas pipeline safety bill, also introduced by Magnuson and passed in 1968, were similarly weakened by effective industry lobbying in the House.

Although heavily involved in consumer protection, Magnuson did not neglect his state's welfare. In 1966 he won a "sea-grant" college bill to aid oceanography research, and he was a major congressional advocate of increased federal aid to the merchant marine. He also worked to liberalize trade with the Soviet bloc. Hoping to increase U.S. trade with Asia, he called for recognition of the People's Republic of China. Of all federal programs affecting Washington's economic health, aerospace spending remained most crucial; consequently, Magnuson continued to champion the development of Boeing's supersonic transport jet. The effectiveness of Senators Magnuson and Jackson in promoting their state's interests was clearly demonstrated by Washington's share of public works funds, which in 1972 came to 15 percent of the national total.

Magnuson served as chair of the Democratic Senatorial Campaign Committee and was known in the Senate for his willingness to remain in the background so other Democrats more in need of publicity might benefit from the exposure. He appointed himself chair of the Commerce Committee's newly created Consumer Subcommittee in 1967, but after he won reelection in 1968 he stepped down in favor of Senator FRANK MOSS (D-Utah).

Magnuson supported Johnson's policies in Vietnam but opposed the war after RICHARD NIXON took office. In the early 1970s, he promoted a system of national health care. Despite his continued support for the supersonic transport, he championed environmental protection legislation. Magnuson was also a leading force in Congress behind the creation of Amtrak, the federal passenger rail system. He failed to win reelection to the Senate in 1980. He died on May 20, 1989.

—MDB

## Mahon, George H(erman)
(1900–1985) *member of the House of Representatives*

Born in Mahon, Louisiana, on September 22, 1900, George Mahon moved with his family from Louisiana to the high plains of west Texas in 1908.

After receiving his law degree from the University of Texas, Mahon entered politics and successively served as county attorney, district attorney, and Democratic representative from the rural 19th Congressional District. A supporter of Roosevelt and Truman administration foreign policy, defense, and agriculture programs, Mahon delivered few speeches during the course of his steady rise on House seniority lists. As chair of the Appropriations Committee's Department of Defense Subcommittee, Mahon urged greater military spending and opposed efforts by the Eisenhower administration to trim the defense budget. During the Kennedy years he endorsed increased defense expenditures sought by the White House.

With the death of Representative Clarence Cannon (D-Mo.) in May 1964, Mahon became chair of the full Appropriations Committee and thus became one of the most influential House leaders. As head of the committee that reviewed all budgetary requests made by the executive branch, he shared much of the authority Cannon had tended to monopolize.

Mahon proved a key congressional supporter of Johnson's Vietnam policy. Cooperating with the administration, he defeated efforts by congressional "hawks" in October 1965 to amend a defense appropriations bill with a clause denying U.S. aid to nations trading with North Vietnam. Six months later Mahon's committee approved the $13.1 billion supplementary budget request made by the Defense Department. "When we vote for this bill," Mahon proclaimed in March 1966, "I think we will show to the nation and to the entire world that the elected representatives of the people stand firmly together in resisting any program of appeasement."

Mahon failed to support many key measures in the president's domestic program. He opposed the 1964 Civil Rights Act, although he refused to join southern Democratic colleagues in advocating nonenforcement of the law's provisions. In the 1965 session he declined to support the Voting Rights Act, Medicare, and the aid-to-Appalachia program. However, in 1965 he voted with the White House in supporting repeal of the right-to-work provision of the Taft-Hartley Act and backed extending coverage of the minimum wage law to farm workers.

In the 90th Congress Mahon's disenchantment with Great Society programs grew more apparent. In January 1967 he appointed four conservative Democrats to the Appropriations Committee's

Labor, Health, Education and Welfare Subcommittee. Violence in northern cities provoked him to condemn calls by liberal Democrats for greater spending in inner cities. "A spending spree was not the answer to the riots." Mahon declared in July 1967, defending Congress's record in social legislation. Angered by the March 1968 report of the Kerner Commission, Mahon denounced its recommendations. Already engaged in the administration's fight for a surtax, Mahon rejected any increase in social spending. "If you can't pass a surtax of 10 percent," he asked, "how can you expect to cover the cost of massive new programs?"

In the area of defense spending, Mahon retained the leadership role that he had played during the Kennedy administration. He endorsed Secretary of Defense ROBERT S. MCNAMARA's proposal in 1967 for an antiballistic missile defense system (ABM) directed toward threats from Asia at an initial cost of $5 billion. To liberal critics of the system's expense, he replied that "those who speak of the ending of the conflict in Southeast Asia as the beginning of a time when we can have a mere skeletonized Defense Department are not thinking along realistic lines." The following month the House authorized the ABM expenditure.

During his years of service in the House, Mahon earned a reputation for personal integrity and hard work. As liberal senator WILLIAM PROXMIRE (D-Wisc.) noted in 1970, Mahon did not practice "pork barrel" politics for his west Texas constituency. Proxmire reported that Mahon's district was "not weighed down with Army bases or Air Force runways, although Texas has been the recipient of vast military and space contracts." Mahon did not seek reelection in 1978. He died on November 19, 1985.

—JLB

## Mailer, Norman

(1923–  ) *novelist, journalist*
Born in Long Branch, New Jersey, on January 31, 1923, Mailer grew up in Brooklyn, New York. He graduated from Harvard in 1943 with a degree in aeronautical engineering and served with the army in World War II. Out of his experiences in the infantry, Mailer wrote the 1948 best-selling novel *The Naked and the Dead.* In 1951 and 1955 Mailer published two novels, *Barbary Shore* and *The Deer Park.* The first concerned Mailer's disillusionment with commu-

nism, the second, the psychopathology of sexuality and power—two of Mailer's most important themes in later years.

In the early 1960s Mailer began a monthly column for *Esquire* magazine. His most significant article was called "Superman Comes to the Supermarket," a glamorization of John F. Kennedy as an existential hero. Many of Mailer's articles and columns on Kennedy were collected in his 1963 book *The Presidential Papers.*

Pressed for money, Mailer wrote a serialized novel in 1965 for *Esquire* called *An American Dream.* Utilizing the familiar Mailer themes of violence, sex, existential anguish, satanism, and magic, the novel was considered by many critics to be an imaginative vehicle for Mailer's own variant of Reichian psychology.

With the publication of his novel *Why Are We in Vietnam?* in 1967 and the Pulitzer Prize–winning *Armies of the Night* in 1968, Mailer returned to radical politics. Subtitled "History as Novel, the Novel as History," *Armies of the Night* was an exercise in subjective journalism that described the October 21, 1967, March on the Pentagon and Mailer's own participation in the antiwar demonstration. Combining a careful presentation of facts, first-person narration, and a spectacular mix of ideology and sensation, the work provided a biting but often moving description of the antiwar movement, its leaders, and the extraordinary tension that existed between the author's private ego and his public persona.

Mailer continued to mix journalism and personal narrative with another widely read 1968 book, *Miami and the Siege of Chicago.* This account of the two nominating conventions described Mailer's guarded respect for RICHARD NIXON and admiration for Senator EUGENE MCCARTHY (D-Minn.).

In the late 1960s and early 1970s Mailer also directed, edited, produced, and acted in three films—*Beyond the Law, Wild 90,* and *Maidstone.* "Existential" in the sense that they were unscripted and depended for their drama on the interplay among the actors, the films reinforced Mailer's self-generated image as "personage," an image nurtured by all his works since publication of *The Deer Park* in 1955.

In 1969 Mailer ran a seriocomic campaign for mayor of New York City. Columnist Jimmy Breslin ran on the same ticket for president of the city council. Advocating community control and statehood for the city, Mailer and Breslin won 5 percent of the vote in the Democratic primary held in June. In 1971 Mailer published *Of a Fire on the Moon*, a favorable account of the American space effort, and *Prisoner of Sex*, a searing attack on the women's liberation movement. He remained a prolific and important author through the end of the 20th century.

—FHM

## Malcolm X
### (1925–1965) *Black Muslims leader*

Malcolm X was born Malcolm Little in Omaha, Nebraska, on May 19, 1925. His father was a Baptist minister and organizer for Marcus Garvey's United Negro Improvement Association. After a move to Michigan and his father's death, Little migrated to Boston to live with a halfsister. He developed a reputation in the black ghettos of Boston and New York as a "hustler" and, in February 1946, received a prison sentence for burglary. In jail he discovered the teachings of Black Muslims leader ELIJAH MUHAMMAD. Released from prison in August 1952, he settled in Detroit, where he became assistant minister of Muslim Temple No. 1 with the name of Malcolm X. He was placed in charge of the Muslims's New York temple in 1954 and in 1963 became the Muslims's first "national minister."

A charismatic speaker and aggressive recruiter who employed his firsthand knowledge of the ghetto to build the Black Muslims organization, Malcolm emerged in the early 1960s as the Muslims's leading spokesman and heir apparent to Elijah Muhammad. He frequently described himself as "the angriest black man in America," and his call for self-defense appealed to many blacks impatient with the nonviolent integrationist strategy of the civil rights movement.

The first public indication of trouble between Elijah Muhammad and Malcolm X occurred in December 1963, when Muhammad silenced Malcolm for 90 days because Malcolm described President Kennedy's death as a case of "chickens coming home to roost." A rumor that Malcolm was suspended indefinitely from his leadership functions spread throughout the Muslims organization. On February 26, 1964, Malcolm telephoned Muhammad and asked for a clarification of his status.

Muhammad's reply did not satisfy Malcolm, and, on March 8, 1964, he announced that he was leaving the Nation of Islam to form an organization that would stress "black nationalism as a political

Black Muslims leader Malcolm X waits at a Martin Luther King, Jr., press conference, 1964 *(Library of Congress, Prints and Photographs Division)*

concept and form of social action against the oppressors." A month later he embarked on a five-week pilgrimage to Mecca and Africa, returning again to Africa later the same year. During his first trip abroad he wrote the well-publicized *Letter from Mecca* describing experiences with Caucasian Muslims that caused him to favorably reevaluate the role which white people in America might play in the struggle against racism. He also adopted the Arabic name El-Hajj Malik El-Shabazz.

According to Alex Haley, Malcolm's trips abroad "sorely tested the morale of even his key members" in his newly formed Organization of Afro-American Unity. Upon returning from his second trip abroad in September 1964, Malcolm sought to solve the financial problems of both his new organization and his family by accepting numerous speaking engagements. He also sought to establish a cooperative relationship with the civil rights movement. On February 3, 1965, he visited Selma, Alabama, during the voter registration drive there and, according to MARTIN LUTHER KING,

JR.'s, biographer, David Lewis, confided to CORETTA KING that he counted on his own militant reputation to "scare" white people to her husband's cause. In public he stopped labeling black integrationists "Uncle Toms."

The relationship between Malcolm X and the Black Muslims continued to deteriorate, and in early 1965 Malcolm reported several death threats. On February 14 Malcolm's home was firebombed. One week later, as he addressed a rally at the Audubon Ballroom in New York City, he was assassinated by men linked to the Black Muslims. The posthumous publication of his *Autobiography*, which detailed his rise from ghetto hustler to militant black spokesman, contributed to his reputation as a martyred symbol of African-American pride and militancy. So did Spike Lee's film *Malcolm X*, released in 1992.

—DKR

## Mankiewicz, Frank

(1924–   ) *Peace Corps director for Latin America*

The son of author and film writer Herman Mankiewicz, Frank was born on May 16, 1924, in New York City, and educated at the University of California at Los Angeles (UCLA), Columbia, and the University of California, Berkeley. He ran unsuccessfully for the California state legislature in 1950 on a Democratic ticket headed by Helen Gahagan Douglas. Mankiewicz remained involved in California politics through 1954, serving as chair of the state Democratic committee. In 1955 he received an LL.B. from UCLA and practiced law for the next six years in California. Mankiewicz joined the Peace Corps in 1962 as director of the organization's programs in Lima, Peru. In 1964 he became regional director of the Peace Corps for Latin America, returning to Washington to coordinate programs and supervise recruitment.

Mankiewicz first met Senator ROBERT KENNEDY (D-N.Y.) in 1965, when he was called upon to brief the senator for an upcoming Latin American trip. Six months later he left the Peace Corps to become Kennedy's press assistant. Mankiewicz's liberal political views sharpened during his service on the Kennedy staff. As the Vietnam War intensified in 1967, he joined other Kennedy aides and friends in urging the senator to challenge President LYNDON JOHNSON for the 1968 Democratic presidential nomination. When Kennedy entered the primary race in March 1968, Mankiewicz helped project the candidate's strong appeal to students and minority groups that contributed to Kennedy's impressive victory in the California primary of June 4. Like his fellow staff members, Mankiewicz was completely devoted to Kennedy and crushed by his assassination on the day of the California victory. It was Mankiewicz, as Kennedy's press secretary, who had to announce the senator's death in the early morning of June 6.

As the Kennedy staff disbanded, Mankiewicz sought another political channel for the support that the senator had accumulated. During the 1968 Democratic Convention he tried unsuccessfully to transfer Kennedy's delegates to Senator GEORGE MCGOVERN (D-S.Dak.), the presidential contender whom he viewed as closest to Kennedy on major issues. Mankiewicz also participated in pre-convention meetings between antiwar leaders and Democratic regulars who wished to negotiate a compromise Vietnam plank for the party's platform. These efforts to avoid a convention dispute over the war were frustrated by President Johnson's refusal to accept any platform statement that did not reaffirm administration policy on Vietnam.

Mankiewicz undertook a number of activities in the years that followed the 1968 campaign. Together with Tom Braden, he wrote a syndicated news column, which soon became known in Washington for its literary style and liberal outlook. Drawing on his earlier government experience, Mankiewicz accepted a $15,000 Ford Foundation grant in 1969 to study "the effects of Peace Corps community development projects in Latin America and the Caribbean." He also served on the board of directors of the Center for Community Change, a privately funded organization that aided self-help programs in low-income areas of the United States.

In 1971 Mankiewicz joined the McGovern staff and quickly gained a reputation as a shrewd campaigner who helped McGovern win his surprising primary victories. Mankiewicz's tactic was to saturate a small area with publicity and volunteers for a short time, then withdraw to analyze the experience and prepare for the next effort. This succeeded in the primaries but not in the national election. Insufficient funds and McGovern's "ultraliberal" image prevented Democratic campaigners from breaking through to the larger electorate, resulting in the overwhelming reelection of RICHARD NIXON.

Following the 1972 campaign Mankiewicz returned to journalism, this time as a television writer and producer. In 1973 he published a book on the Watergate affair, *Perfectly Clear: Nixon from Whittier to Watergate.* Five years later, he wrote, with Joel Swerdlow, *Remote Control: Television* and *The Manipulation of American Life.*

—SLG

## Mann, Thomas (Clifton)
*(1912–1999) assistant secretary of state for inter-American affairs, undersecretary of state for economic affairs*

Born on November 12, 1912, Mann grew up in the border town of Laredo, Texas, where he learned to speak fluent Spanish. Educated at Baylor University, he worked in the family law firm from 1934 to 1942. He then joined the State Department and gained expertise in Latin America and international economics. He became a Foreign Service officer in 1947. Except for one year in Greece, his career was concerned solely with Latin America. In 1957 he was named assistant secretary of state for economic affairs. Some of the changes that Mann and other officials in the Eisenhower administration helped to implement pointed the way toward Kennedy's Alliance for Progress. Mann served as ambassador to Mexico under Kennedy and with C. DOUGLAS DILLON revised U.S. economic policy toward Latin America. He encouraged the Latin Americans to control the production and, thus, the prices of their major exports. At the same time he realized that the United States had to exercise restraint in unloading its farm surpluses in Latin America, where they could drastically disturb the balance of internal markets.

When Johnson appointed Mann assistant secretary of state for inter-American affairs in December 1963, the president also gave him two other posts. He headed the Alliance for Progress and, as the President's special assistant, coordinated the Latin American policy of all departments. As Secretary of State DEAN RUSK said, Mann was "Mr. Latin America," with an extraordinary measure of authority in all aspects of hemisphere policy.

Mann's appointment was highly controversial. Many New Frontier liberals thought Mann far too accommodating to North American business and too preoccupied with the Communist threat in Latin America. Many recalled that in 1962 Mann (then ambassador to Mexico) had refused EDWARD M. KENNEDY's request to entertain Mexican Communists and leftists at the U.S. embassy. Senator HUBERT HUMPHREY (D-Minn.) advised against Mann's appointment. Others suggested that if Mann took charge of the Alliance for Progress Johnson's prestige would decline with both Latin Americans and Spanish-speaking voters at home. However, Mann's appointment was very popular with the North American business community. As Alphonse de Rosso of the Standard Oil Company of New Jersey later said, "Not until Tom Mann came back . . . did the business community feel that it was 'in' again with the United States government."

The new Latin American policy was soon known as the Mann doctrine. It consisted of four basic objectives: (1) to foster economic growth and to be neutral on internal social reform; (2) to protect U.S. private investments in the hemisphere; (3) to play down U.S. concern for the establishment of representative democratic institutions; and (4) to oppose communism. During Mann's tenure U.S. business investments in Latin America increased substantially, and the United States supported military governments more frequently and less critically than it had under the Kennedy administration.

Despite Mann's overall control of Latin American policy, President Johnson's domestic political concerns sometimes limited his authority. In January 1964 fighting broke out in Panama between Panamanian students and young North American residents of the Canal Zone over the flying of the Panamanian flag within the zone. When U.S. Canal Zone police killed some Panamanians during the riots, Panama broke off diplomatic relations, and Mann was dispatched as head of a peace mission to Panama. Although Mann suspected that Communists had exacerbated the conflict in the Canal Zone, he was not adverse to the Panamanian demand that the United States agree to "review" the 1903 treaty that established U.S. sovereignty in the zone. However, when the Organization of American States (OAS) worked out an agreement acceptable to Mann in March, Johnson publicly repudiated it. Johnson was conscious of the upcoming 1964 elections and did not wish to appear "weak" to Congress and the electorate. When the situation quieted in April, Johnson reestablished relations with Panama and in December agreed to renegotiate the canal treaty.

In February 1965 Mann became undersecretary of state for economic affairs but continued to advise Johnson on Latin American policy. When he urged the president to send marines into the Dominican Republic in April 1965, he was blamed for Johnson's failure to inform the OAS of the action. Along with MCGEORGE BUNDY and CYRUS VANCE, he left for Santo Domingo on May 15 to help set up a provisional government. Mann wanted to form a government acceptable to democratic groups within the Dominican Republic, but the mission ended in failure. ELLSWORTH BUNKER and the OAS successfully completed the task in September. Although he argued that the United States would have worked through the OAS "had no lives been in danger," Mann was heavily criticized in the press and left the government in April 1966. After spending some time as a visiting lecturer, he became president of the Automobile Manufacturers Association in 1967. He died on January 23, 1999.

—JCH

## Mansfield, Mike (Michael) (Joseph)
(1903–2001)  *member of the Senate*

After his mother died, Mansfield, who was born in New York City on March 16, 1903, was sent at the age of three to live with relatives in Montana. He served successively in the navy, army, and marines from 1918 to 1922, and for the next nine years worked as a miner and mining engineer in Montana. Mansfield received bachelor and master of arts degrees from Montana State University in 1933 and 1934. He remained there to teach Latin American and Far Eastern history.

Mansfield lost a Democratic congressional primary in 1940 but won a seat in the U.S. House of Representatives two years later. With his academic background in foreign affairs, the first-year representative was assigned to the Foreign Affairs Committee.

In 1952 Mansfield entered the Senate by defeating an incumbent Republican and was assigned a seat on the Senate Foreign Relations Committee the following year. In 1957 the Senate majority leader, LYNDON B. JOHNSON, selected Mansfield as his assistant, or whip. Johnson chose Mansfield because the latter was a political moderate who had good relations with powerful southerners who, at that time, dominated the Senate leadership. In January 1961 Johnson assumed the vice presidency, and the Senate Democratic Caucus chose Mansfield to succeed him. During the early 1960s observers credited Mansfield with helping to secure Senate passage of the controversial aid-to-education bill of 1961 and the mass transit and area redevelopment bills of 1963, all of which were blocked in the House.

The position of majority leader, although unrecognized by either the Constitution or in the Senate rules until after World War II, gave its occupant great potential power. By tradition the majority leader had nearly total control over the scheduling of bills and considerable influence over committee appointments and policy through the chairship of his party's steering and policy committees and of the full party conference. Johnson, a forceful and dominant leader, used all of the powers at his disposal to shape legislation and control the votes of his Democratic colleagues. He served as floor manager for almost every major bill and as the Democrats' chief strategist, parliamentarian, and whip when majority leader.

Mansfield had a different concept of the role of the majority leader. He had a mild-mannered and scholarly disposition, preferring to win votes by use of persuasion rather than cajolery or threats, which often were Johnson's most effective techniques. Indeed, he dismantled his predecessor's centralized system for exerting power over fellow Democrats. Instead Mansfield shared power. He left the arrangement of deals and the employment of pressure to his whips, first Senator HUBERT H. HUMPHREY (D-Minn.) and then Senator RUSSELL B. LONG (D-La.). He also generally avoided intricate parliamentary maneuvering and long sessions to enforce his will. Unlike Johnson, who led Senate Democrats with a Republican in the White House, Mansfield directed the Senate majority during the presidencies of fellow Democrats, Kennedy and Johnson, and so, at times, shared responsibility with the White House for steering legislation through Congress. Johnson especially used his Senate experience and network of congressional connections to guide administration bills through the upper chamber. Despite their long experience in working together on Capitol Hill, Mansfield said that his relationship with Johnson was never close because of their different personalities.

Mansfield established cooperative relationships across the aisle with Republicans. One instance in which he shrewdly secured Republican allies was during Senate consideration of the administration's civil rights bill in 1964. The majority leader left floor management of the bill to Humphrey. In his position above the battle, Mansfield forged an alliance with, the minority leader Senator EVERETT M. DIRKSEN (R-Ill.), whose support was essential for the bill's passage because of the opposition of southern Democrats. Mansfield endorsed Dirksen's amendments, most of which concerned minor or procedural issues. In return, Dirksen helped deliver enough Republican votes to produce a two-thirds majority that halted the southern filibuster and that guaranteed approval of the legislation that Johnson signed on July 2, 1964. At times, some liberal Democrats expressed discontent with what they saw as Mansfield's cautious leadership, but his cooperative relationship with Dirksen helped gain passage of the Voting Rights Act of 1965 and the Civil Rights Act of 1968.

Mansfield expressed consistent, but private opposition to Johnson's decisions to deepen U.S. military involvement in the Vietnam War. Beginning in late 1963, Mansfield regularly submitted memoranda to the president expressing his conviction that expanded military action could not secure the Saigon government and that the president should seek a negotiated solution, perhaps by reconvening of the Geneva Conference of 1954. Mansfield opposed the beginning of sustained U.S. bombing of North Vietnam and the commitment of U.S. ground troops in 1965. In a meeting between congressional leaders and the president in July 1965 just before Johnson announced a major increase in U.S. combat forces, Mansfield was the only legislator who voiced opposition to the president's policies. He insisted that U.S. interests did not justify a major military commitment to South Vietnam, that the American people would not support a prolonged war, and that the quest for military victory would only decimate the Vietnamese people.

Yet Mansfield did not express these criticisms publicly. He refused to join with Democratic colleagues, such a J. WILLIAM FULBRIGHT (D-Ark.), GEORGE MCGOVERN (D-S.Dak.), and FRANK CHURCH (D-Idaho), who broke with the president over the Vietnam War. Instead, Mansfield thought that his position as majority leader left him with less freedom to advocate policies at odds with the President's. He also hoped to maintain access to Johnson so that he would be able to continue to press for modifications in administration policies. Despite his impatience or even disdain, Johnson read Mansfield's memos and discussed the senator's proposed

alternatives of negotiation and disengagement, if only to refute or reject them. During a lengthy meeting on March 27, 1968, as Johnson considered a request from General WILLIAM C. WESTMORE-LAND for more than 200,000 additional U.S. troops in the aftermath of the Tet Offensive, Mansfield declared emphatically that there was strong opposition in the Senate to the dispatch of additional military forces to Southeast Asia and that he hoped that the president would find some way out of the current difficulties. His advice reinforced Johnson's decision to announce in a televised speech on March 31, 1968, a partial bombing halt of North Vietnam and a new initiative to secure negotiations.

After the election of Republican president RICHARD M. NIXON, Mansfield publicly dissented from administration policies. In 1972, he secured the approval of the Democratic Policy Committee for an amendment that would have required the withdrawal of U.S. military forces from Vietnam within six months. He also called on the Senate to play a more active role in the formulation of foreign policy. In early 1976, he announced that he would not seek reelection later that year. He served as U.S. ambassador to Japan from 1977 until the beginning of 1989. He died on October 5, 2001.

—MLL

## Marcuse, Herbert
### (1898–1979) *philosopher, social critic*

Marcuse was born in Berlin on July 19, 1898, into a prosperous family. After serving in the army during World War I, he earned a Ph.D. in literature from the University of Freiburg in 1922. When the Nazis came to power in 1933, Marcuse, who was Jewish, left Germany for Switzerland and taught in Geneva for a year. In 1934 he came to the United States and took a post as lecturer at Columbia University. There he was a colleague of the German neo-Marxist sociologists Max Horkheimer and Theodore W. Adorno at the Institute of Social Research, which they had moved from Frankfurt in 1933.

During World War II Marcuse served as a European intelligence analyst with the Office of Strategic Services (OSS). After the war, he worked for the State Department's Office of Intelligence Research and became chief of the Central European section. After establishing a reputation in this office as an expert on Soviet affairs, he lectured at the Russian Research Center at Harvard. From 1958 to

1965 Marcuse taught at Brandeis University, and then he joined the faculty at the University of California's San Diego campus.

Marcuse's first book in English was *Reason and Revolution* (1941), an interpretation of Hegel and Marx. Marcuse sought to refute the charge that Hegelian philosophy had helped pave the way for the rise of Nazism in Germany. He identified the fundamental antithesis in modern thought as one between Marx and Hegel, on the one hand, and the tradition of positivism on the other. In *Eros and Civilization* (1955) Marcuse attempted a synthesis of Marx and Freud. Assuming, from a Marxist standpoint, that under capitalism people were dominated and exploited not only by external oppressors but also by forms of consciousness that prevented them from liberating themselves, he turned to Freud for the social psychology he found lacking in Marxism. Marcuse argued that Freud had been correct only up to a point in his account of the history of civilization; while pre-modern history required social domination and instinctual repression in order to remove scarcity and lay the technological foundations for abundance, Marcuse insisted that advanced industrial societies now demanded more repression of sexual energies than was necessary. Human liberation required that sexuality be freed from what Marcuse called false renunciation and asceticism. In *Soviet Marxism* (1958) he applied much of this critique to the new system of authority created by Joseph Stalin and his heirs.

*One-Dimensional Man* (1964) was Marcuse's most influential work, and it contained his fullest critique of industrial society. In contrast to the utopianism considered possible in *Eros and Civilization*, it was permeated with a pessimistic fear that the "power of negative thinking," which Marcuse considered the sole source of creativity in social life, was threatened with oblivion. His thesis was that the technology of modern industrial societies had enabled them to eliminate conflict by assimilating the forces of dissent. Marcuse attributed this, in part, to affluence, which by satisfying human needs removed the reasons for protest and fostered identification with the established order. Ironically, in claiming that conflict had basically disappeared, Marcuse accepted the central argument of Daniel Bell and other theorists of pluralism and consensus. Like them he assumed that affluence and the institutions of the welfare state had domesticated the working classes and made the Marxist doctrine of class struggle inapplicable to industrialized societies.

Despite his rejection of classical Marxism, Marcuse thought that revolutionary protest was now in the hands of "the substratum of outcasts and outsiders, the exploited and persecuted of other races and other colors, the unemployed and unemployable."

*Eros and Civilization* and *One-Dimensional Man* were widely read by New Leftists in the 1960s. On a lecture tour of European countries in early 1968 Marcuse met with Rudi Dutschke, the leader of a student uprising at the University of Berlin. Later in the spring of that year Dutschke's name was prominently identified with the university rebellions in Paris, Rome, and New York. A rumor that Marcuse planned to bring Dutschke to San Diego as his graduate student brought a demand for his removal from a local newspaper. The university's faculty and administration came to Marcuse's defense, however, and he was retained.

The wave of international student protest in the late 1960s led Marcuse to revise his pessimistic perspective in *An Essay on Liberation* (1969). He now argued for the existence of revolutionary minorities capable of redeeming industrial civilization. These he identified as the student movement in the United States, the black population of the American inner cities, the Chinese cultural revolution, and the Castro regime in Cuba. In an earlier essay, "Repressive Tolerance" published in *A Critique of Pure Tolerance* (1967), Marcuse granted these revolutionary minorities the right to withdraw "toleration of speech and assembly from groups and movements which promote aggressive policies, armament, chauvinism, racial and religious discrimination or which oppose the extension of public services." Marcuse later said that he "would restrict expression only in the case of movements which are definitely aggressive and destructive." Despite his support for the student left, Marcuse insisted that he had "never advocated destroying the existing universities," which he said he regarded as in many cases "still enclaves of relatively critical thought and relatively free thought." Marcuse concentrated on questions of aesthetics in his later writings. He died in Starnberg, Germany, on July 29, 1979.

—TLH

## Marks, Leonard H(arold)
**(1916–   )** *director, U.S. Information Agency*
Born on March 5, 1916, in Pittsburgh, Leonard H. Marks, graduated from the University of Pittsburgh

Law School and taught law there for four years. In 1942, he became assistant general counsel of the Federal Communications Commission. He established a law partnership with Marcus Cohn in 1946. The two men specialized in communication law, and among the many radio and television stations they represented were those owned by LADY BIRD JOHNSON. In the fall of 1962 President Kennedy appointed Marks to a 13-member panel to establish and incorporate the Communications Satellite Corporation (COMSAT). He was elected to the board of directors of COMSAT in 1964.

Marks, an old friend of President Johnson's, served as the treasurer of the Johnson-for-President Committee in 1964. In July 1965 the president named him to succeed Carl T. Rowan as the director of the United States Information Agency (USIA). Rowan had resigned during a controversy over whether the agency's radio network, Voice of America, should present objective news reports and air the views of dissenters or serve as a propaganda vehicle and transmit only official viewpoints. At his confirmation hearing before the Senate Foreign Relations Committee, Marks avoided taking a position on this matter by asserting that the use of propaganda was not necessary for presenting the American way of life. Sworn in on August 31, 1965, he assumed control of a 12,000-person agency established in 1953 "to help achieve U.S. foreign policy objectives by influencing public attitudes in other nations."

One of Marks's major objectives was the expansion of USIA activities in Southeast Asia, where American military involvement was rapidly escalating. In September 1965 he asked a group of news executives, including CBS president Frank Stanton, to go to Saigon to study the USIA program in Vietnam. The following month he requested an additional $13 million for the agency's work in Indochina. More than half of the funds were to be used for building a powerful transmitter in Thailand, a project that Congress approved in 1967.

Meanwhile, the USIA's programs in Europe were being cut back, and the closing of the agency's London library in December 1965 aroused considerable opposition in America. In March 1966 the United States Advisory Commission on Information, established by law to counsel the USIA, issued a report criticizing the cutbacks. Marks promised that there would be no further library closings in Europe and pledged to try to bolster the USIA's efforts there.

Marks served as an adviser to the president and Defense Department on the Vietnam pacification programs in 1966. Following the South Vietnamese national elections in September 1967, Marks told the president in a private meeting that he favored U.S. withdrawal from Vietnam. He suggested that the elections, which observers certified as fair and free, could serve as justification that the United States had achieved its objectives and could limit its support for the Saigon government to military and economic aid. The president crossly dismissed the recommendation in what Marks described as his only dispute with Johnson during their long friendship.

In October 1968 Marks announced his resignation from the USIA to head a conference on the use of satellites for international communications. He later returned to his law practice in Washington.

—JLW

## Marshall, Burke

(1922–2003) *assistant attorney general in charge of the Civil Rights Division; chair, National Advisory Commission on Selective Service*

Born in Plainfield, New Jersey, on October 1, 1922, Marshall graduated from Yale University in 1943 and from Yale Law School in 1951. He became a member of the prestigious Washington, D.C., law firm of Covington and Burling in the 1950s, specializing in antitrust litigation. He was named assistant attorney general in charge of the Justice Department's Civil Rights Division in February 1961, and he played a key role in the development of the Kennedy administration's civil rights policies. Marshall also significantly increased the number of voting discrimination suits brought by the Justice Department. A quiet, cool, and skillful negotiator, he played a major part in the federal government's handling of racial crises such as the 1961 Freedom Rides and the spring 1963 Birmingham, Alabama, demonstrations. When the Justice Department met strong criticism for not doing more to protect civil rights workers in the South, Marshall answered the charges by insisting that the Constitution did not give the federal government the authority to act against all assaults on civil rights workers.

Marshall also helped draft the Kennedy civil rights bill submitted to Congress in June 1963 and negotiated with members of Congress on a compromise measure in October 1963. He worked for passage of the measure, which was signed into law on July 2, 1964, and then oversaw the Justice Department's efforts to ensure enforcement of the statute.

Marshall resigned his post on December 18, 1964, saying it "would not be wise" for the same person to have his job for more than one presidential term. He then spent several months aiding Vice President HUBERT H. HUMPHREY in his capacity as coordinator of the federal government's policies and programs in civil rights. Although he formally returned to private law practice in January 1965, Marshall joined top Justice Department officials in March of that year to oversee the federal government's activities during the protest march from Selma to Montgomery, Alabama, led by MARTIN LUTHER KING, JR. In February 1966 Marshall was appointed to a 28-member presidential council that prepared a special report and recommendations for the June 1966 White House Conference on Civil Rights.

President Johnson named Marshall chair of a National Advisory Commission on Selective Service in July 1966. Ordered to make a broad study of the draft, the commission issued a report on March 4, 1967, that found that the existing Selective Service system resulted in many inequities. The panel called for changes in the draft, including call-ups by an impartial and random process and the replacement of local draft boards with some 500 area centers, which would apply uniform classification standards. The report was one basis for Johnson's March 1967 proposals for reform of the Selective Service system.

In June 1965 Marshall joined the International Business Machines Corporation (IBM) as vice president and general counsel. He was named a senior vice president in 1969. In 1970, he joined the faculty of Yale Law School. He died in 2003.

—CAB

## Marshall, Thurgood

(1908–1993) *U.S. circuit judge, Second Circuit Court of Appeals; U.S. Solicitor General; associate justice, U.S. Supreme Court*

Born in Baltimore, Maryland, on July 2, 1908, Marshall graduated from Lincoln University and Howard University Law School before joining the NAACP as assistant special counsel in 1936. He was named special counsel in 1938 and, in 1940, became director-counsel of the newly created NAACP Legal Defense and Educational Fund. During his 23 years as head of the NAACP's legal program, Marshall directed the series of cases against segregated education that culminated in the 1954 Supreme Court decision *Brown v. Board of Education.* He also won court victories in suits challenging segregated housing, transportation, and recreational facilities and discrimination in voting and jury selection.

Marshall was named to the U.S. Second Circuit Court of Appeals by President Kennedy in September 1961, but because of opposition from southern Democratic senators, he was not confirmed until a year later. On the bench Marshall developed a reputation as a liberal jurist who curbed government authority when it infringed on individual liberties but gave the government broad powers in economic affairs.

President Johnson appointed Marshall U.S. Solicitor General in July 1965. The first African American to serve in that post, Marshall's chief areas of concern were civil rights and eavesdropping by government agencies. Marshall won Supreme Court approval for extension of the protection of the Voting Rights Act to Spanish-speaking citizens. He also persuaded the Court to confirm federal authority to indict defendants charged with the murders of civil rights workers Michael Schwerner, Andrew Goodman, and James Chaney and to overturn a California constitutional amendment prohibiting open housing legislation. Convinced that all electronic eavesdropping that involved an illegal trespass was unconstitutional, Marshall voluntarily informed the Supreme Court in two cases that the government had used electronic devices to collect information on suspects charged with violation of federal laws. He had no similar qualms about the use of government informers, however, and he successfully argued in the Supreme Court that the government's use of an informer did not invalidate the convictions of JAMES HOFFA and three other Teamster union officials for jury tampering. Marshall argued 19 cases for the government before the Supreme Court, winning all but five.

On June 13, 1967, President Johnson nominated Marshall as an associate justice of the U.S. Supreme Court to fill the vacancy created by the retirement of Justice TOM C. CLARK. Once again Marshall was the first African American appointed to this position. In announcing Marshall's nomination Johnson declared that this was "the right thing

Associate Justice Thurgood Marshall (on telephone) and President Johnson in the Oval Office, 1967 *(Photographed by Yoichi R. Okamoto; Lyndon Baines Johnson Library)*

to do, the right time to do it, the right man and the right place." The Senate confirmed the nomination on August 30 by a 69-11 vote, with all of the opposition coming from southern senators. Sworn in on October 2, Marshall joined the Court's liberal bloc. Legal scholars asserted that Marshall's best writing was in the area of his greatest expertise and concern: equal protection, due process and the First Amendment. As the majority of the Court became more conservative during the 1970s and 1980s, Marshall gained recognition for dissenting opinions that often reflected his long experience as an advocate of minorities and the poor.

Marshall was not actively engaged in the civil rights movement after 1961 because of the government positions he held, but his career exemplified that segment of the movement that relied primarily on the judicial process to win political and social advancement for blacks. In a May 1969 speech at Dillard University in New Orleans, Marshall criticized those blacks who advocated violence saying, "Anarchy is anarchy, and it makes no difference who

practices it, it is bad; it is punishable, and it should be punished." Younger black militants, in turn, criticized Marshall's and the NAACP's legal approach during the 1960s as ineffective "gradualism." However, Marshall remained a symbol of black achievement for his work in the NAACP and for the recognition he won in his various federal appointments. He retired from the Supreme Court in June 1991 and died on January 24, 1993.

—CAB

## Martin, Graham A(nderson)

(1912–1990) *ambassador to Thailand, special assistant to the secretary of state for refugee and migration affairs*

Martin, who was born on September 22, 1912, in Mars Hill, North Carolina, worked as a newspaper reporter and employee for several New Deal agencies before joining the foreign service in 1947. During the postwar period he served in various missions and was deputy U.S. coordinator for the Alliance for

Progress from 1962 to 1963. President Kennedy appointed him ambassador to Thailand in July 1963.

Martin became ambassador during the period when communist guerrilla attacks were increasing in Thailand and threatening to extend the Indochina war to that country. Convinced that the lack of adequate early American aid had led to a full-scale war in Vietnam, Martin was instrumental in securing and increasing U.S. military and civilian assistance to Thailand in 1964 and 1965. In January 1966, when armed insurgency increased, Martin convinced the Thai government to establish a counterinsurgency office and accept U.S. aid in setting up the program. Eager to start counteraction as quickly as possible, he initiated several pilot projects in separate areas in the hope that experimentation might uncover a successful method of defeating the guerrillas. People's Assistance teams, similar to those used in Vietnam, were started to improve villagers' welfare, demonstrate the government's interest, and provide security. Other efforts were made to increase protection and collect intelligence.

In January 1967 Martin admitted that the United States was building large air bases in Thailand to supply its troops in Vietnam, a fact that had been known to many observers for over a year. Martin was replaced as ambassador to Thailand by LEONARD UNGER in July 1967. He returned to Washington to become special assistant to the secretary of state for refugee and migration affairs. Martin served in that post until named ambassador to Italy in September 1969. In 1973 President Nixon appointed him ambassador to South Vietnam. He remained in Saigon until April 1975. His role in the U.S. evacuation at the end of the Vietnam War was highly controversial, as he favored delay in the removal of U.S. personnel and South Vietnamese who had worked for the U.S. government for fear of undermining support for the Saigon government. He served as a special assistant to Secretary of State HENRY A. KISSINGER before retiring in 1977.

—EWS

## Martin, William McChesney
(1906–1998) *chair, Board of Governors of the Federal Reserve*

Born in St. Louis on December 17, 1906, Martin was the son of a banker who had aided in the drafting of the Federal Reserve Act of 1913 and had become president of the Federal Reserve Bank of St. Louis. The product of a strict Presbyterian background, he graduated from Yale in 1928. Martin spent a year as a clerk at the St. Louis Federal Reserve Bank and then left to become head of the statistical department of a St. Louis brokerage firm. In 1931 he acquired a seat on the New York Stock Exchange to become his firm's Wall Street representative. Martin became president of the exchange in 1938 at the age of 31. While in the army during World War II, he served in an important administrative position with the Munitions Allocation Board and supervised much of the Russian lend-lease program.

President Truman made Martin a director of the Export-Import Bank in 1945 and appointed him assistant secretary of the Treasury in 1949. Two years later the president named him chair of the Board of Governors of the Federal Reserve. Independent of the national administration, Martin and the Federal Reserve pursued a conservative course designed to halt the threat of inflation by keeping interest rates high. Martin eased monetary policy somewhat during the Kennedy administration but still exerted a strong conservative pull on the course of economic policy. He generally supported Treasury secretary C. DOUGLAS DILLON in opposing the more liberal fiscal policies of WALTER HELLER, chair of the Council of Economic Advisers. In February 1963 President Kennedy appointed Martin to another four-year term as chair of the Federal Reserve Board.

As chief custodian of the nation's money supply, Martin was a figure of great controversy throughout the 1950s and 1960s. Conservatives praised him as a symbol of financial integrity, while liberals castigated him for his "tight money" policies. During the Johnson administration he let interest rates rise to the highest levels since the 1920s in an effort to curb the inflation fueled by a booming economy and Vietnam War spending.

In the first year of the Johnson administration, Martin reluctantly continued a relatively expansionary monetary policy in order to avoid undoing the stimulative effect of the $11.5 billion Kennedy-Johnson tax cut of 1964. Yet he was uncomfortable with the inflationary possibilities inherent in the economic boom of the mid-1960s. In June 1965 he gave a widely publicized speech in which he warned of "disquieting similarities between our present prosperity and the fabulous 20s." Martin drew a number of unsettling analogies between the contemporary boom and the prelude to the Great

Depression: large increases in private and international debt, the "uneasy" balance of payments situations in the United States and Great Britain and the instability of the dollar, which he equated with the British pound before its devaluation in 1931. The "stable dollar," Martin said, was "the keystone of international trade and finance" and of "economic growth and prosperity at home." Martin's speech was followed by a sharp drop in prices on the New York Stock Exchange.

In December 1965 Martin cast the deciding vote in the Federal Reserve Board's four-to-three decision to raise the discount rate from 4 percent to 4.5 percent. The rate increase was made just as the first inflationary pressures were being felt from the escalation of the Vietnam War, but while the Johnson administration was still forecasting only a limited rise in defense spending to pay for the conflict. Hence the change in monetary policy put Martin at the center of a major controversy. In raising its rate the Federal Reserve Board stated that the increase was made in order "to dampen mounting demands on banks for still further credit extensions that might add to inflationary pressures." Led by Martin, the Federal Reserve was strongly signaling the Johnson administration and the business community its belief that the economy needed to be slowed down. Its action marked the first time in five years that the Federal Reserve Board had openly dissented from Kennedy-Johnson economic policy.

The discount rate increase generated much protest from the White House and from the Congress. The president expressed "regret" at "any action that raises the cost of credit, particularly for homes, schools, hospitals, and factories." He "particularly" regretted that the board's action was not coordinated with administration policy and was taken before "the full facts" of the budget for fiscal year 1967 had been made available. Taking issue with Johnson, Chamber of Commerce president Robert Gerholz said that the business community should be grateful to Martin "for acting to check a dangerous inflationary condition."

AFL-CIO president GEORGE MEANY criticized the increase as "mistaken and costly" and suggested that presidential influence should be exerted to rescind it and that representation on the Federal Reserve Board should be broadened to include labor. Martin's most persistent adversary, Representative WRIGHT PATMAN (D-Tex.), denounced the move and called for Martin's resignation "to prevent the country from being thrown into economic chaos." Questioning Martin sharply at hearings before his Joint Economic Committee, Patman predicted that the rate rise would "destroy the savings and loan industry." During 1966 $2.4 billion was drained from savings and loan associations, which were forced to cut their mortgage lending by one-third. The result was a $6 billion decline in home building. Interest rates rose to the highest level since the 1920s.

Disturbed that monetary policy was being forced to battle inflation alone, Martin, in the spring of 1966, began urging a tax increase as the "logical way" to deal with inflation. He indicated that if a tax increase were not forthcoming, the Federal Reserve might have to take further action. Martin persisted in this exhortatory campaign for the next two years. When Johnson finally recommended a 10 percent tax surcharge in the summer of 1967, Martin advised the administration that a tax increase was no longer sufficient and should be combined with substantial budget cuts as well. He issued ominous public warnings of the dangers if an anti-inflationary fiscal course were not followed. "The nation is in the midst of the worst financial crisis since 1931," Martin declared in April 1968. "We are faced with an intolerable budget deficit and also an intolerable deficit in our international balance of payments. Both have to be corrected over the next few years or the United States is going to face either an uncontrollable recession or an uncontrollable inflation." In June 1968 Congress passed the 10 percent surtax along with a $6 billion spending reduction.

Despite their differences, Johnson appointed Martin to another four-year term as chair of the Federal Reserve Board in March 1967. At a time when the position of the dollar was deteriorating, the administration needed Martin, the symbol of the sound dollar, to reassure the financial community. In December 1968 President-elect RICHARD M. NIXON asked Martin to remain in his post until his term expired on January 31, 1970. He was a member of the board of many business and nonprofit organizations until his death in 1998.

—TO

## Mathias, Charles McC(urdy)
(1922–    ) *member of the House of Representatives*

Elected to Congress from a traditionally Democratic Maryland district that voted for conservative

Republicans on the national level, Mathias emerged as one of the Republican Party's more liberal spokespersons by the end of the decade. Prior to his election to the House in 1960, Mathias, who was born on July 24, 1922, in Frederick, Maryland, had been a practicing lawyer, city attorney, and member of the Maryland House of Delegates. During his early years in Congress, Mathias voted against many of President Kennedy's domestic proposals, including housing subsidies, area redevelopment, and aid to education. But in the mid-1960s he supported much of the Johnson administration's social welfare program including Medicare, aid for urban redevelopment, aid to education, and antipoverty programs.

While in the House Mathias was primarily concerned with District of Columbia affairs and civil rights legislation. As a member of the District of Columbia Committee, Mathias introduced legislation in 1963 to give the district a nonvoting delegate in the House as a step toward full voting representation. In 1965 he was one of four representatives to sponsor a proposal for a territorial form of government for the District with an elected assembly and a presidentially appointed governor. The bill was defeated, and a weaker measure providing for the election of a charter-drafting committee and the popular ratification of the charter was passed by the House.

As a member of the Judiciary Committee, Mathias helped shape the Civil Rights Act of 1964 and the Voting Rights Act of 1965. In 1966 he led the fight for a civil rights bill that included a ban on racial discrimination in the sale or rental of all housing. When intense opposition to the provision threatened to defeat the entire measure, Mathias sponsored a controversial compromise that exempted the sale of individual homes or small owner-occupied multiple dwellings from the law in an effort to save the entire proposal. The House passed the amended bill, but the Senate killed it by a filibuster in September.

In 1967 Mathias sponsored several major resolutions, including a proposal to create a select committee to watch over the standards and conduct of House members. He also called for disclosure and regulation of political spending. Concerned with protecting the privacy of citizens, Mathias opposed President Johnson's 1967 wiretap bill because of its lack of safeguards against abuses. That year he and seven other liberal Republican members of Congress proposed a five-stage plan to end the bombing of North Vietnam in return for de-escalation by Hanoi. By the end of the decade Mathias had accumulated a 78 "correct" rating from the liberal Americans for Democratic Action; the conservative Americans for Constitutional Action gave him a correct rating of only 15.

In 1968 Mathias challenged incumbent Daniel Brewster (D-Md.) for election to the U.S. Senate. Supported by many unions and even by several state Democratic leaders, Mathias defeated his opponent by 100,000 votes in November. In the Senate he supported many of President Nixon's domestic proposals but continued his opposition to delays in ending the Vietnam War and maintained his support for congressional reform. He retired from the Senate in January 1987.

—EWS

## McCarthy, Eugene J(oseph)
### (1916–   ) member of the Senate

Eugene McCarthy rose to unexpected prominence in the late 1960s as the foremost critic of President Johnson's Vietnam policy. The early successes of his unorthodox campaign for the presidency in 1968 helped drive Johnson from office and brought a corps of idealistic young volunteers from the antiwar movement into the Democratic Party, where they had a significant impact on American politics.

Born on March 29, 1916, in Watkins, Minnesota, McCarthy graduated from St. John's University in Minnesota in 1935. He taught economics and sociology at Catholic high schools and colleges for 13 years. He also spent nine months in a monastery as a Benedictine novice in 1942 and 1943. McCarthy was teaching sociology at St. Thomas College in St. Paul when he first entered politics as a supporter of HUBERT HUMPHREY's fight against the Communist-led wing of Minnesota's Democratic Farmer–Labor Party (DFL). After leading a successful drive to take control of the DFL in St. Paul and Ramsey County, McCarthy won election to the House of Representatives in 1948.

In the House McCarthy compiled a liberal, pro-labor voting record. He organized an informal caucus of liberal House Democrats—later institutionalized as the Democratic Study Group—that agitated for more ambitious legislative programs than those proposed by the Democratic leadership. He entered the Senate after defeating a Republican incumbent in 1958. With his scholarly demeanor and air of detachment, McCarthy stood apart from his colleagues in the Senate's liberal bloc. His voting record continued to favor positions endorsed by the Americans for Democratic Action, but he failed to exercise the leadership he had shown in the House, and he did not use his position on the powerful Finance Committee to advance the cause of tax reform as many liberals had hoped.

Early in the Johnson administration McCarthy emerged from the Senate shadows when administration figures began mentioning him as a serious vice presidential candidate. As a prospective running mate for Johnson, McCarthy's intelligence, grace, and attractiveness enhanced his complementary value as a northern liberal Catholic. Still, his candidacy was never taken seriously by LBJ, a fact that McCarthy recognized. He withdrew his name from the list of possible candidates shortly before the 1964 convention, leaving both men with feelings of resentment over the way the matter had been handled.

Aided by the publicity resulting from his vice presidential possibilities, McCarthy won reelection easily in 1964. His assignment to the seat on the Foreign Relations Committee Humphrey vacated gave him the long-desired opportunity to have a greater voice in the making of foreign policy. McCarthy stood out as a critic of U.S. policy in several important areas. Long an advocate of closer congressional oversight of U.S. intelligence agencies, he called for a "full and complete investigation" of the Central Intelligence Agency (CIA) in November 1965. "The role of the CIA in the Dominican Republic, Vietnam, Cuba and a number of other critical areas has raised serious questions about the relationship of the agency to the process of making and directing foreign policy," he said, adding that there was some evidence that the CIA had gone beyond its statutory purpose of collecting and evaluating intelligence.

McCarthy was also a veteran critic of the large volume of U.S. arms sales to undeveloped nations. He charged that such sales undermined other foreign policy goals, such as peace and disarmament, exacerbated world tensions, and led to the dangerous militarization of the developing World. Criticizing the Pentagon's effort to promote sales of U.S. weapons abroad, he warned in January 1967 that "we may be subsidizing weapons manufacturers to a dangerous and undesirable extent."

Through his opposition to the Vietnam War, McCarthy exerted a profound and dramatic impact on the course of American foreign policy. He was not an early dissenter, having voted for the Gulf of Tonkin Resolution in August 1964 and avoided any public criticism of Johnson's war policy until January 1966. At that time he joined 14 other senators in sending a letter to the president calling for continued suspension of air strikes against North Vietnam. The bombing, which had been halted during the holiday truce period, was resumed on January 31. McCarthy maintained that the bombing had not had a "beneficial political or diplomatic effect" in the past. He suggested that the war in Vietnam called for "a national debate . . . and a real searching of the mind and the soul of America."

Whatever his private doubts about U.S. policy, McCarthy remained mild and hesitant in his dissent throughout 1966. In March he said, "I think that the kind of escalation we now have, in which we're sending in more troops, is defensible on the part of the Administration," while "bombing civilian areas in North Vietnam" is a "change of substance" and "should be challenged." McCarthy indicated in May that the United States should stay in South Vietnam even if a newly elected government opposed the American presence.

In early 1967 McCarthy became more vocal in his opposition. "We should hesitate to waste our strength—economic, military, and moral—in so highly questionable a course," he said on February 25. Three days later he told a student audience that the war was "morally unjustifiable." In April he criticized President Johnson's use of General WILLIAM WESTMORELAND as a spokesperson for his Vietnam policy as a "dangerous practice" and an "escalation of language, method and emotions." He was particularly upset by Undersecretary of State NICHOLAS KATZENBACH's August 1967 defense of the Johnson administration's broad interpretation of the Gulf of Tonkin Resolution and Katzenbach's dismissal of the lack of a congressional declaration of war in Vietnam as a matter of "outmoded phraseology." An angry McCarthy was quoted by a *New York Times* reporter as saying. "This is the wildest testimony I have ever heard. There is no limit to what he says the President can do. There is only one thing to do—take it to the country." In October McCarthy published *The Limits of Power*, a strong critique of U.S. foreign policy.

After persistent urging by antiwar liberals, McCarthy announced on November 30 that he was running for the Democratic presidential nomination in order to further the campaign for a negotiated settlement of the war. "I am concerned," he declared, "that the Administration seems to have set no limit to the price which it's willing to pay for a military victory." He also voiced his hope that his campaign might alleviate "this sense of political helplessness and restore to many people a belief in the processes of American politics."

Dismissed by many as a futile and quixotic venture, McCarthy's New Hampshire primary campaign slowly gained momentum. The character and spirit of his race were decidedly unorthodox. Grassroots canvassing was carried out by legions of idealistic young volunteers instead of experienced party workers. The style of the candidate was equally novel. McCarthy wrote many of his own speeches, which were laced with wit and literary allusions. Yet he often frustrated his supporters and risked losing audiences with his flat, unemotional delivery. Besides the evil of the war, McCarthy stressed the grave danger of the growing power of the presidency, the erosion of the role of Congress in the making of foreign policy, and the alleged mendacity and arrogance of President Johnson.

McCarthy's unexpectedly strong showing in the March 12 New Hampshire primary won him recognition as a serious presidential contender. In light of the widespread assumption that the president would score an easy victory over his obscure opponent, McCarthy's winning 42 percent of the popular vote (Johnson received 49 percent) was not only a stunning moral victory for the antiwar candidate but also a revelation of Johnson's personal vulnerability: an NBC poll taken after the primary showed that more than half of the Democrats questioned had not known where McCarthy stood on the war.

The reverberations from McCarthy's New Hampshire upset quickly transformed the 1968 presidential campaign. Senator ROBERT F. KENNEDY (D-N.Y.) declared his own candidacy two days after the New Hampshire results were in, and, on March 31, President Johnson announced that he would not seek reelection. The president's withdrawal made McCarthy's victory over Johnson in the Wisconsin primary a few days later seem anticlimactic. On April 27 Vice President Humphrey formally entered the presidential race.

McCarthy and Kennedy were the major combatants in the remaining primaries. With their essential agreement on the key issues and their visceral dislike for each other, the focus of their contests became personal and bitter. McCarthy considered Kennedy opportunistic and ruthless, while Kennedy supporters charged that McCarthy had been a lazy senator and circulated controversial "fact sheets" accusing McCarthy of inconsistency in his voting record.

McCarthy could not match Kennedy's emotional appeal to minorities and blue-collar whites, and Kennedy won the majority of their primary contests. After Kennedy triumphs in Indiana and Nebraska, McCarthy revived his campaign with a victory in Oregon, but he lost the crucial California primary on June. The assassination of Kennedy on the night of the primary made McCarthy the leader of the Democratic Party left in opposition to Humphrey and the regular party organization.

As the convention approached, McCarthy attracted enthusiastic crowds everywhere, but he failed to seek or win the allegiance of many Kennedy delegates. The candidate himself showed a waning commitment to his cause and a fatalistic attitude about a Humphrey victory. At the Chicago convention in late August, Humphrey won the nomination with 1,760 delegate votes to McCarthy's 601 and Senator GEORGE MCGOVERN's (D-S.Dak.) 146. McCarthy was alienated by the circumstances of Humphrey's victory: the packing of the convention galleries with supporters of Chicago mayor RICHARD DALEY, the violence used by the Chicago police against young antiwar marchers, and the control of much of the delegate-selection process by the party machine. Unconvinced that Humphrey had changed his position on the war, McCarthy refused to endorse the nominee after the convention. He withheld his support until October 29, when he offered a lukewarm endorsement, stating that Humphrey showed "a better understanding of our domestic needs and a stronger will to act" than his Republican opponent, RICHARD M. NIXON.

McCarthy unexpectedly resigned from the Foreign Relations Committee in 1969 and retired from the Senate in 1971. He made lackluster runs for the presidency in 1972 and 1976, and for the Senate in 1982, but he never ignited the enthusiasm he had fired in 1968, partly because of his occasional indifference and enigmatic behavior. Even while he personally was attracting little support, however, national party politics revealed the far-reaching effects of the movement he had crystallized: the reform of Democratic Party procedures, the introduction of thousands of young people as a potent factor in electoral politics, and eventually the ending of the Vietnam War.

—TO

## McCarthy, Mary (Therese)
(1912–1989) *novelist, critic*

Mary McCarthy was born on June 21, 1912, in Seattle, Washington, and orphaned at the age of six when her parents died in the influenza pandemic of 1918. She and her three brothers were then placed in the care of their paternal grandparents, who arranged to have them looked after by a great uncle she later described as harsh and repressive. After five years McCarthy went to live with her maternal grandfather and grandmother in Seattle. Her grandfather, a prosperous lawyer, saw that she received a classical education at the exclusive Forest Ridge Convent in Seattle and the Annie Wright Seminary in Tacoma. McCarthy later described this upbringing in her vivid, autobiographical *Memoirs of a Catholic Girlhood* (1957).

McCarthy attended Vassar College, and after graduating in 1933 she took up residence in New York City, where she wrote book reviews for the *Nation* and the *New Republic*. In 1937 she joined the editorial staff of *Partisan Review*, for which she wrote theater criticism until 1948. During the 1940s and 1950s McCarthy contributed to a number of magazines. The more important of these writings, including essays on such wide-ranging topics as politics, travel, women, and literature, were collected in *On the Contrary: Articles of Belief: 1946–1961* (1961). In *Venice Observed* (1956) and *Stones of Florence* (1959) she combined commentary on contemporary life in these cities with history and art criticism. Her work also examined the role of intellectuals in addressing the problems of modern society.

McCarthy reached her largest audience through her fiction. In 1942 she wrote *The Company She Keeps*. This was followed by a short novel *The Oasis* (1949), a collection of short stories entitled *Cast a Cold Eye* (1950) and her full-length novels, *The Groves of Academe* (1952) and *A Charmed Life* (1955). *The Group* (1963), a fictional chronicle of eight Vassar girls from the class of 1993, became a best seller and a movie (1966).

In the late 1930s McCarthy had been associated with the group of leftist intellectuals around *Partisan Review*, who had broken away from the Communist Party orthodoxy and were briefly attracted to Trotskyism before moving toward some form of liberalism or democratic socialism in the 1940s. Summarizing this experience, McCarthy observed: "For my generation, Stalinism, which had to be opposed, produced the so-called non-Communist Left, not a movement, not even a sect, but a preference, a political taste, shared by an age group resembling a veterans' organization." Although she continued to describe her political taste as "libertarian socialist," she remained for the most part uninterested in political writing during the 1940s and 1950s.

With the escalation of the Vietnam War in 1965, McCarthy began to search for a way to contribute personally and dramatically to the antiwar effort. Early in 1966 Robert Silver, the editor of the *New York Review of Books*—which had given Jean Lacouture and Bernard Fall an early opportunity to present their views on the war to an important American audience—asked her to go to South Vietnam for the magazine. Despite her lack of experience as a reporter, McCarthy went to Saigon in 1967 and Hanoi in 1968. Her reports on these trips—published serially in the *New York Review of Books* and later in pamphlet form as *Vietnam* (1967) and *Hanoi* (1968)—were unique at the time. McCarthy was the first American novelist to go to Hanoi and only the second important literary figure to go to South Vietnam, having been preceded only by John Steinbeck, who supported the war. In her reports she renounced any claim of journalistic objectivity, declaring that she went "looking for material damaging to American interests." In particular, she deplored the Americanization of South Vietnam and the moral corruption that followed. Her impressions of North Vietnam, where she was a guest of the government, were generally sympathetic.

In 1973 McCarthy attacked David Halberstam for what she said was an inappropriate stress on the personal failures of high administration figures in explaining America's involvement in Vietnam. This article was republished, along with *Vietnam, Hanoi*, and a report on the trial of Captain Ernest Medina for his role in the My Lai massacre, in *The Seventeenth Degree* (1974). She died of cancer in New York on October 25, 1989.

—TLH

## McClellan, John L(ittle)

### (1896–1977) *member of the Senate*

McClellan, who was born in Sheridan, Arkansas, on February 25, 1896, entered private law practice at the age of 17. He served as city attorney of Malvern, Arkansas, from 1920 to 1926 and as prosecuting attorney of the state's seventh judicial district from 1927 to 1930. In 1934 McClellan was elected to the U.S. House of Representatives, where he supported most New Deal programs. He lost the Democratic senatorial primary four years later but won a Senate seat in 1942.

During the postwar years McClellan opposed civil rights legislation and compiled a generally conservative voting record. He first received national attention when, as the ranking minority member on the Government Operations Committee and its Permanent Investigations Subcommittee, he led Democratic protests against what he charged were committee chair Joseph McCarthy's (R-Wisc.) undemocratic methods. McClellan gained further attention as chair of the Select Committee on Improper Activities in the Labor and Management Fields, an ad hoc panel that investigated corruption in labor unions from 1957 to 1960. In 1959 he even proposed an amendment to a labor bill that gave union members the right to take union leaders to court for any of a number of reasons. LBJ and John Kennedy worked to defeat the bill, and, when it passed, Johnson got the bill rewritten by pointing out to southern Democrats that a section of it could be interpreted in such a way as to weaken the southern position on racial segregation.

By 1960 Senator McClellan had established a reputation as a stern, effective, and fair investigator, and for the next decade his senatorial career centered on his role as chair of the House Permanent Investigations Subcommittee. Despite his conservatism, he maintained a good personal relationship with the Kennedy family.

From February through November 1963 McClellan led the panel's investigation of reports of pressure and favoritism in the Defense Department's award of the multibillion dollar TFX (Tactical Fighter Experimental) swing-wing, fighter/bomber contract to General Dynamics. In September and October of the same year, Joseph Valachi, a convicted murderer and self-described former member of a crime syndicate, testified before the subcommittee on the structure and operations of organized crime in one of the panel's most publicized probes.

In September 1964 the subcommittee issued a report on its 1963 investigation of Texas business executive Billie Sol Estes. The probe had been launched to determine why Estes's illegally acquired cotton allotments had not been canceled by the Agriculture Department until after his arrest on other charges. McClellan issued a statement of individual views that reflected the position taken by the report of the panel's Democratic majority. He said that the department had demonstrated "timidity, vacillation and indecision" in the Estes affair but exonerated the Kennedy administration from major responsibility by commenting that "the prevailing system had been established and the procedures developed during previous administrations and over a long time." McClellan and his fellow Democrats also asserted that they had uncovered no evidence of favoritism within the Agriculture Department. The panel's Republican minority, on the other hand, charged that the department had given Estes special treatment.

In March 1964 the subcommittee issued a report, based on a 1962 investigation, that criticized the government's missile procurement policies. It asserted that excessive profits were being paid to companies for work that they farmed out to subcontractors and stated that money paid to other companies for subsystems "should not of itself generate profit." During the following year McClellan's panel and the House Banking and Currency Committee investigated an increase in federally insured bank failures and the "milking" of bank assets by criminal elements. As a result of these probes, legislation was introduced to tighten federal bank-regulatory procedures.

In February 1967 President Johnson proposed legislation to provide funds for the improvement of crime prevention and control methods at the state and local levels. The bill went to McClellan's Judiciary Committee's Subcommittee on Criminal Laws and Procedures. McClellan believed that a number of recent Supreme Court decisions had, through what he regarded as the unwarranted expansion of the rights of criminal defendants, seriously undermined the effectiveness of the criminal justice system. By the time the administration bill came to the Senate floor in May 1968, the subcommittee had added to it a number of provisions overturning some of those decisions.

One of the most important of the provisions declared that confessions were admissible if the trial judge ruled that they had been given voluntarily. This stipulation was a challenge to the Supreme Court's *Miranda v. Arizona* (1966) ruling, which barred interrogation of a suspect until informed of his or her rights. In floor debate McClellan argued that if the Supreme Court decisions were not reversed "the law-breaker will be further . . . reassured that he can continue a life of crime and depredations profitably with impunity." The subcommittee version of the crime bill also permitted wiretapping in many federal and state cases. The enactment of the Omnibus Crime Control and Safe Streets Act in June 1968 in essentially the form proposed by the subcommittee represented a major defeat for congressional liberals.

One of the factors contributing to congressional sentiment for stronger crime legislation was the rioting in black urban neighborhoods during the summer of 1967. In August 1967 the Permanent Investigations Subcommittee was selected by the Rules Committee to examine the causes of the disturbances. Some liberals opposed the choice on the ground that McClellan, because of his segregationist views and belief in vigorous law enforcement, would ignore what they felt were the underlying social causes of the riots. At the beginning of the panel's hearings the following November, McClellan added to their fears by stating that the subcommittee would examine the immediate causes of the riots. He also condemned "callous and deliberate disregard for law and order, spurred on by inflammatory speeches and proclamations of those who publicly advocate the use of violence." In 1968, as the hearings progressed, he denounced the Office of Economic Opportunity for granting funds to black street gangs.

In 1969 the subcommittee continued its probe of urban riots and also examined campus disturbances. In July McClellan introduced a bill to impose fines and jail sentences upon persons who disrupted federally assisted colleges. The following year the panel investigated terrorist bombings. In the same year McClellan proposed what became the Organized Crime Control Act of 1970, the most comprehensive law ever passed to fight organized crime.

In August 1972, after the death of Senator ALLEN J. ELLENDER (D-La.), chair of the Appropriations Committee, McClellan gave up his Government Operations chair to become head of the Appropriations panel. He died in Little Rock, Arkansas, on November 28, 1977.

—MLL

## McCloy, John J(ay)
### (1895–1989) *presidential adviser*

John J. McCloy, one of the architects of American foreign policy in the 1940s, was an adviser to Presidents Kennedy and Johnson during the 1960s. Born in Philadelphia, Pennsylvania, on March 31, 1895, McCloy graduated from Harvard Law School in 1921. He then worked in several New York law firms where he specialized in international corporate law. During World War II he served as a high-ranking member of the War Department and was one of a few advisers to President Truman, who encouraged him to seek political solutions before dropping the atomic bomb. McCloy resumed private law practice in 1946 but became head of the World Bank a year later. In 1949 he was appointed military governor and high commissioner for Germany. He left that country in 1952 and for the next nine years served as chair of the Chase Manhattan Bank. In 1962 he returned to private law practice, where he handled international legal problems for some of America's largest oil companies. From 1953 to 1965 he was also chair of the Ford Foundation.

During the opening months of the Kennedy administration, McCloy served as the president's principal disarmament adviser. Throughout the summer of 1961 he successfully negotiated terms for the resumption of East-West disarmament talks. McCloy also helped draft the legislation that led to the establishment of the U.S. Arms Control and Disarmament Agency in the fall of 1961. Following the October 1962 discovery of Russian offensive missiles in Cuba, McCloy took part in negotiations at the United Nations on the ground rules involving U.S. inspection of Soviet removal of weapons from the island.

In late 1963 LYNDON JOHNSON appointed McCloy to the Warren Commission, formed to probe the death of John F. Kennedy. The commission report, issued in September 1964, concluded that Lee Harvey Oswald had acted alone in assassinating President Kennedy. During the Johnson administration McCloy also served on government panels investigating ways of forestalling the spread of nuclear weapons and ensuring world peace. He did, however, turn down the president's request, in 1964, that he replace HENRY CABOT LODGE as ambassador in South Vietnam.

In April 1966 McCloy was appointed a special presidential consultant on the crisis precipitated by French president Charles de Gaulle's decision to withdraw his nation's troops from the North Atlantic Treaty Organization (NATO). It was an inspired choice. McCloy was held in high regard by most European leaders, while at the same time was known to be both a tough negotiator and a critic of General de Gaulle, thus assuaging those Americans who wanted to see LBJ adopt a tough line with the general. NATO unity was threatened again that summer when Germany announced its desire to renegotiate financial arrangements made to offset a U.S. balance of payments deficit brought about by the presence of American troops in Germany. Under existing agreements Bonn had purchased U.S. military goods to compensate for the drain. But West Germany, facing serious budget problems because of the rising cost of its welfare programs, suggested that its other pay-ments and services be considered as part of the com-pensation. The situation was inflamed still further by the British desire to withdraw some of its troops from Germany to stem its own currency drain and by a Senate resolution stating that the United States should take similar action.

To prevent a weakening of the alliance, Johnson proposed multilateral negotiations between Britain, West Germany, and the United States and asked McCloy to serve as American envoy to the October 1966 talks. Under the final plan announced in April 1967, the United States would redeploy its troops on a rotating basis with two of three brigades and four of nine fighter bomber squadrons returned to the United States, where they would maintain a high degree of readiness. To help offset the dollar deficit, Germany agreed to invest $500 million in medium-term U.S. government securities and promised to continue its policy of not converting dollars into gold.

In March 1968 Johnson asked McCloy to par-ticipate in the meetings of the Senior Advisory

Presidential adviser John McCloy at a meeting of the "Wise Men," 1965 *(Photographed by Yoichi R. Okamoto; Lyndon Baines Johnson Library)*

Group on Vietnam, commanded known as the "Wise Men" to consider the military's request that over 200,000 additional troops be sent to Vietnam. During the committee's meetings McCloy was among those advisers, along with Henry Cabot Lodge, Arthur Dean, and General Omar Bradley, who were dissatisfied with the existing policy but were reluctant to advocate a dramatic change. Nevertheless, the majority of the group recommended rejection of the troop buildup request and steps toward U.S. disengagement from the war.

In 1974 a Senate investigation of the petroleum industry revealed that since 1961 McCloy had been in the forefront of attempts to unite U.S. oil companies in their negotiations with the producing nations. He had also used his influence to obtain Justice Department approval for multicompany bargaining in 1971. McCloy's efforts proved fruitless because the shah of Iran insisted that the oil companies conclude separate price arrangements with the producing states. McCloy continued to serve as an informal adviser to the U.S. government officials until his death in Connecticut on March 11, 1989.

—EWS

## McCone, John A(lex)

### (1902–1991) *director of Central Intelligence*

John McCone was born into a prosperous San Francisco family on January 4, 1902. He graduated from the University of California in 1922 and over the next 25 years amassed a fortune in the steel and shipbuilding industries. During the Truman administration, McCone held several high posts in the Defense Department, where he helped in the creation of the Central Intelligence Agency (CIA). From 1958 to 1961 he served as chair of the Atomic Energy Commission.

Distressed over the agency's handling of the Bay of Pigs invasion, President Kennedy appointed McCone director of the CIA in September 1961. While at the agency, McCone focused his attention on improving the quality of intelligence work and developing new technological data collection systems. He also tried to coordinate the activities of the various intelligence services under the leadership of the director of central intelligence. However, his attempts were blocked by the Defense Department, which under ROBERT MCNAMARA had dominated the technological intelligence field.

He did, however, help restore the agencies morale and confidence after the humiliating events in Cuba.

He was also frustrated in a number of cases when the president ignored his advice; McCone pushed LBJ to make a more forceful response in Panama, when anti-American rioting broke out in the Panama Canal Zone in 1964, but Johnson turned to diplomacy instead. The president also ignored the director later that year when McCone cautioned him that the alleged attacks on American ships in the Gulf of Tonkin by North Vietnam were intended as defensive actions only.

Despite McCone's attempts to develop new intelligence-gathering techniques, the CIA's emphasis remained on covert activities. In 1962 the agency began a secret war in Laos and instituted counter-terrorist programs in Vietnam. It committed $3 million to the 1964 Chilean election to prevent Marxist Salvador Allende from winning the presidency. Throughout the decade, it also continued efforts to block the development of leftist governments in Italy and Greece. Until 1966 the CIA used private foundations to channel money to groups and projects the agency thought helpful to its mission. According to a 1976 congressional report, at least 14 percent of all grants over $10,000 given by 164 American foundations (excluding the Ford, Rockefeller, and Carnegie Foundations) were partially or completely funded by the CIA. Nearly one-half of those in the field of international activities involved agency funding.

Although McCone was director of the CIA, he may not have known about some of the agency's most controversial activities. These included the illegal opening of foreign mail sent to U.S. citizens and several unsuccessful attempts to assassinate such foreign leaders as Cuban premier Fidel Castro. In hearings before the Senate Select Committee on Intelligence in 1975, McCone testified that he had not authorized the efforts and had never even been informed of them. The committee reported that McCone probably had not known about the mail openings. However, because the system of executive command in the agency was purposely ambiguous (to permit "plausible denial"), McCone's role in the assassination plots remained undetermined by committee investigators.

As Johnson's chief intelligence officer, McCone became increasingly involved in Vietnam policy making. Although personally hawkish on the war,

McCone was fair in presenting the views of more dovish experts in the agency. McCone was reportedly one of the few high administration officials willing to give Johnson unbiased, often pessimistic reports on the progress of the war.

During the debate on the possible introduction of combat forces in Vietnam in the spring of 1965, McCone cautioned against the move unless it was accompanied by an expansion of bombing in the North. He believed that the war could not be won in the South. The United States could achieve victory only by inflicting such serious injury on North Vietnam that it would be forced to negotiate. Therefore, McCone said, the number of bombing raids would have to be vastly increased and targets expanded to include airfields, power stations, and military compounds. McCone's advice went unheeded. U.S. marines began offensive operations in April. Although raids were increased during May and June, they did not reach the high levels McCone advocated.

In April 1965 McCone resigned as director of the CIA because Johnson did not support his efforts to centralize intelligence operations. Four months later he headed an eight-member commission investigating the major riot in the Watts section of Los Angeles. The panel's report, submitted to California governor EDMUND G. BROWN in December 1965, found many causes for the disturbances: long-term frustrations, "the angry exhortation of civil rights leaders," and the publicity given federal antipoverty programs that did not fulfill the expectations they raised. To prevent future riots and improve living conditions among blacks and Mexican Americans, the committee recommended increasing educational and job-training programs and upgrading mass transit and health facilities in the slum area. It cautioned that only "a change in attitude" by both black and white communities would prevent racial violence in the future. The panel also discussed suitable tactics and strategies for dealing with racial disorders. Its report called for reliance on nonlethal deterrents and outlined rigorous procedures for riot training, which became a guide for police departments throughout the United States. McCone returned to private business after leaving the administration, eventually becoming a director of ITT. In 1983 he was a member of the Scowcroft Commission on U.S. strategic nuclear forces. He died on February 14, 1991.

—EWS

## McCormack, John W(illiam)
(1891–1980) *member of the House of Representatives*

McCormack, who was born on December 21, 1891, grew up in the poor, tight-knit Irish community of South Boston. He left school to go to work at age 13 after his father died. He passed his bar exams when he was 21. In 1917 McCormack was elected a delegate to the Massachusetts Constitutional Convention. Three years later he entered the state legislature and served there for six years. In 1926 McCormack ran unsuccessfully for the U.S. House of Representatives, but two years later he won a special election as a Democrat to fill a House vacancy.

In Congress McCormack was a strong supporter of New Deal programs and worked closely with the House Democratic leadership as a member of the important Ways and Means Committee. When House Majority Leader Sam Rayburn (D-Tex.) became Speaker of the House in 1940, McCormack moved into Rayburn's former post.

As majority leader, McCormack gained a reputation as an unswervingly loyal deputy of Rayburn. He made many political friendships in the House by helping obtain committee assignments for colleagues and influencing the scheduling of their bills. McCormack also became known for his sharply partisan debating style.

McCormack almost always backed the legislative positions of President John F. Kennedy. However, he was a devout Catholic with close ties to many of the church's high clerics, and, in 1961, he favored federal aid to parochial schools, a policy the president opposed. In January 1962, after the death of Rayburn, McCormack drew upon the political debts he had accumulated as majority leader to win election to the speakership. At age 70, he was the first Catholic and the second-oldest representative to be chosen for that post.

According to the *New York Times*, McCormack, despite the numerous ties he had established with his fellow representatives over many years, "never developed, either through disinclination or inability, the same sort of elaborate network of information and rewards that enabled Mr. Rayburn to keep the House a relatively tightly run political apparatus." Many of his associates, and particularly the younger liberals of the House, believed that he was not forceful enough to be an effective leader. Some thought McCormack too old to competently exercise the functions of his position. Nor did McCormack enjoy the trust of President Johnson, who liked him but had little respect for his political acumen.

McCormack's age, then 71, became the subject of considerable public discussion when the assassination of President Kennedy placed the Speaker first in line to succeed President LYNDON B. JOHNSON under the Presidential Succession Act of 1947. Some politicians and political observers felt that because of both age and ability McCormack was not competent to serve as the nation's chief executive, but the Speaker indignantly rejected suggestions that he resign his post. In 1964 the Senate proposed a constitutional amendment to provide for filling a vacancy in the office of vice president. The House did not act on the matter because, most observers believed, its members did not wish to offend McCormack. But the following year he indicated his support of the proposed 25th Amendment, and the House adopted it.

McCormack consistently backed President Johnson's domestic programs. As a militant anticommunist who believed the president should have a free hand in conducting foreign policy, he also supported the administration's military involvement in Vietnam. Early in 1966, during House debate over a supplemental defense authorization for the war, he stated that in supporting the authorization "I am also voting again for the [Tonkin Gulf] Resolution. . . . Thus, we will convey to the actual and potential enemy and also the rest of the world that America is united." As opposition to the war increased during the last years of the Johnson administration, liberal Democrats became increasingly critical of McCormack's unwavering support of the president's Indochina policies.

In a matter relating to the war, McCormack defended what he believed was the constitutionally prescribed independence of the legislature from the judiciary. During August 1966 federal district judge Howard F. Corcoran ordered the House Un-American Activities Committee (HUAC) to cease its investigation of persons aiding North Vietnam or the National Liberation Front. McCormack and other House leaders decided that HUAC's investigation should proceed. The Speaker commented, "The Constitution provides for three independent branches of government. If the judicial branch can enjoin the legislative branch, it could result in judicial control of the American government. . . ." The next day a three-judge federal court lifted Corcoran's order and a month later ruled that it lacked

jurisdiction to determine the constitutionality of the committee's hearings.

In the fall of 1969 Dr. Martin Sweig, a longtime aide of McCormack, and Nathan Voloshen, a friend of the Speaker's, were accused of employing their connection with McCormack to engage in influence-peddling. Sweig and Voloshen were indicted in January 1970. In May 1970, after U.S. attorneys cleared McCormack of any involvement in the matter, he announced that he would retire at the end of the year. He returned to Boston, where he remained until his death in 1980.

—MLL

## McCulloch, William M.
(1901–1980) *member of the House of Representatives*

Born on November 24, 1901, in Holmesville, Ohio, McCulloch earned a law degree from Ohio Northern University and practiced law in Piqua, Ohio. In 1932 he won the first of six terms in the Ohio House of Representatives. A Republican, McCulloch served as state house minority leader (1936–38) and speaker (1939–44). In a special election in 1947, he was elected to the U.S. House of Representatives. The ranking Republican on the Judiciary Committee by 1959, McCulloch worked closely with committee chair EMANUEL CELLER (D-N.Y.). After negotiations among the Ohio Republican, President Kennedy, and Justice Department officials, McCulloch gave crucial aid to the administration in drafting a comprehensive civil rights statute in the fall of 1963. The Judiciary Committee approved a bill coauthored by McCulloch in October 1963.

With the full support of President Johnson, McCulloch, House Minority Leader CHARLES A. HALLECK (R-Ind.), and liberal Republicans joined administration Democrats in winning full House approval for the committee's bill. Although he represented a rural, western Ohio district with a small (3 percent) black constituency, McCulloch championed the new civil rights legislation. "The belief in the inherent equality of man induces me to support this legislation," he declared in January 1964. Opponents of the measure failed to amend it, and, on February 10, it passed the House by a vote of 290 to 130. Of the GOP membership, over three-quarters supported the measure. The Senate modified certain provisions and passed the bill in June. The most far-reaching civil rights legislation since Reconstruction, it became law in July. "If any Republican deserves historically to be credited with a major input into civil rights," recalled LBJ adviser LAWRENCE O'BRIEN, "it's this fellow."

Except for civil rights, McCulloch was a traditionally conservative Republican. He wrote a mild civil rights plank for the 1964 Republican Platform Committee and supported the presidential candidacy of conservative senator BARRY M. GOLDWATER (R-Ariz.), who had voted against the 1964 civil rights bill. On positions preferred by the Americans for Democratic Action (ADA) during the Johnson years, McCulloch received generally low marks, ranging from 4 percent in 1964 to 13 percent in 1967. Local Democrats never mounted a serious challenge against McCulloch; in 1968, they declined even to field a candidate.

In July 1965 McCulloch offered a voting rights bill that, unlike the White House version, did not provide for federal voter registration machinery. Johnson's opposition to—and southern Democratic support for—the McCulloch substitute killed any chance of enactment. After a 215-166 defeat McCulloch endorsed the administration bill, and a majority of the GOP membership followed his example. McCulloch also accepted an "open housing" amendment to the 1966 civil rights bill offered by liberal representative CHARLES MATHIAS, JR. (R-Md.). As a result of the Mathias provision, Minority Leader GERALD R. FORD (R-Mich.) came out against the bill and assured its defeat. Despite Ford's opposition, McCulloch continued to seek a ban on discrimination in real estate transactions. In April 1968 a group of moderate Republicans led by representatives CHARLES E. GOODELL (R-N.Y.) and ALBERT H. QUIE (R-Minn.) rebelled against Ford's position and forced him to back a House bill, approved by McCulloch, that provided for an open-housing regulation. In recognition of McCulloch's civil rights record, Johnson appointed the Ohio Republican to two presidential commissions: one on civil disorders, chaired by Governor OTTO KERNER, and one on the causes and prevention of violence, chaired by MILTON S. EISENHOWER.

McCulloch kept a wary eye on the Nixon administration's enforcement of civil rights legislation and criticized the Republican president's proposed revision of the 1965 Voting Rights Act. He retired from the House in 1973. He returned to Ohio, where he resumed the practice of law. He died on February 22, 1980.

## McGee, Gale W(illiam)
### (1915–1992) *member of the Senate*

Gale W. McGee was born on March 17, 1915, and grew up in Nebraska. He graduated from Nebraska State Teachers College in 1936, earned an M.A. from the University of Colorado three years later, and took a Ph.D. from the University of Chicago in 1947, writing his dissertation in American diplomatic history. McGee accepted a professorship at the University of Wyoming in 1946, and he studied Soviet foreign policy for the Council on Foreign Relations in 1952 and 1953. Endorsed by Eleanor Roosevelt, McGee made his first campaign for public office in Wyoming's 1958 Senate race. He unseated a conservative Republican incumbent with 50.8 percent of the vote. During the Kennedy years McGee supported administration programs while taking few legislative initiatives on his own.

McGee won reelection in his normally Republican state in 1964 and proved equally loyal to the Johnson administration. He supported the 1964, 1965, and 1968 civil rights acts, Medicare, and the repeal of Section 14(b) of the Taft-Hartley Act. He also supported numerous environmental protection laws. A strong proponent of nonmilitary foreign assistance programs, McGee criticized congressional cutbacks in foreign aid in October 1968 as "a discouraging retreat from our responsibility" to aid nations "struggling to break free from the endless cycle of poverty and despair." That same year he published a book, *The Responsibilities of World Power*, that articulated his opposition to American isolationism and demanded that the United States accept its role as the leading actor on the world stage.

McGee gave consistent and vocal endorsement to American intervention in Vietnam. In a February 1966 debate over American participation in the war, McGee asked his colleagues to "look at the prize at stake" in Southeast Asia. "Three-hundred million people or more. Most of the rice in the world. Oil, tin bauxite and rubber. These would be sparkling diamonds in the resources of great powers."

In January 1968 McGee challenged a proposal by Senator ROBERT F. KENNEDY (D-N.Y.) that the U.S. halt the bombing of North Vietnam as an indication of American willingness to negotiate. Appearing on a television news program with Kennedy on January 21, McGee branded the New York senator's suggestion "totally irresponsible." The real issue in Vietnam, McGee declared two days later, was "stability in all Eastern Asia." As a

member of the platform committee at the Democratic National Convention in August, he defended
the majority plank on Vietnam, which endorsed the
president on the war. The party's antiwar faction,
McGee told the delegates, must "not hobble [the
next president] with restraints and particulars" that
would "complicate the task of negotiators."

As a partial consequence of his stand on the
war, McGee's Senate voting rating by the Americans
for Democratic Action fell from 90 percent in 1966
to 57 percent in 1968. Organized labor, however,
continued to give the Wyoming Democrat high
marks, with the AFL-CIO ranking him 90 percent
"correct" on its key votes in 1968. Early in January
1969, antiwar senator EUGENE J. MCCARTHY (D-
Minn.) stepped down from his place on the Senate
Foreign Relations Committee, and McGee, next in
seniority, assumed McCarthy's position. At the same
time, McGee became chair of the Senate Post
Office and Civil Service Committee. McGee
remained active after Johnson left office. He sponsored the Postal Reorganization Act in 1970, and,
two years later, he was part of a four-member American delegation to the United Nations. He was
defeated for reelection in 1976 by Republican Malcolm Wallop and became ambassador to the Organization of American States, and then an independent
consultant in Washington, D.C. He died in
Bethesda, Maryland, on April 9, 1992.

—JLB

## McGovern, George S(tanley)
(1922–  ) *member of the Senate*

The son of a Methodist minister, George McGovern was born on July 19, 1922, and grew up in
Mitchell, South Dakota. He excelled at debating in
high school and at Dakota Wesleyan University,
where he was twice elected class president. After
service as a bomber pilot during World War II,
McGovern trained for the ministry but abandoned
it to undertake graduate work in history at Northwestern University, where he began a sympathetic
study of the 1913–14 Colorado coal strike. Northwestern awarded him his Ph.D. in 1953.

From 1943 to 1953 McGovern taught history
and political science at Dakota Wesleyan, leaving to
become executive secretary of the state Democratic
Party. He was the only full-time organizer for the fee-
ble organization; South Dakota Democrats then held
only two out of 110 seats in the state legislature. Criss-

crossing the state alone in an automobile, McGovern
laboriously reconstructed the party apparatus. In the
1954 elections Democrats increased their representation in the legislature to 25 seats. Alongside the party
organization, McGovern built a personal following
as well. He ran for Congress in 1956 on a liberal platform, attacking the unpopular farm policies of Republican secretary of agriculture Ezra Taft Benson and
won an upset victory over the Republican incumbent.
Reelected in 1958 McGovern ran for the Senate in
1960 against the conservative senator KARL E.
MUNDT (R-S.Dak.) but lost to the incumbent in a
sharp ideological confrontation. Appointed by President Kennedy as director of the Food for Peace program, McGovern ran for the Senate again in 1962
and won by an extremely narrow margin.

McGovern was assigned to the Senate Agriculture and Forestry Committee and the Interior and
Insular Affairs Committee. Representing an agricultural state whose chief products were wheat and
beef cattle, McGovern fought for higher wheat
price supports and restrictions on imported beef.
He was the floor manager of the wheat title of the
1964 farm bill, which raised supports and made
acreage allotment voluntary instead of mandatory as
it had been in 1963. McGovern's espousal of higher
wheat prices frequently brought him into conflict
with Secretary of Agriculture ORVILLE FREEMAN,
an antagonist during his Food for Peace tenure.
McGovern also supported higher appropriations for
Food for Peace during the Johnson administration
and argued that its utility in disposing of agricultural
surpluses should not supersede its humanitarian
functions. He called for the removal of restrictions
on the program that prevented the United States
from selling or giving food to Communist nations.

Unlike fellow South Dakotan Karl Mundt,
McGovern was a strong supporter of the social welfare legislation of the Johnson administration. He
consistently voted for the civil rights enactments of
the period and said in June 1964: "What is usually
referred to as 'the race problem' is, in fact, . . . the
white problem . . . white racism." He displeased
organized labor, however, in October 1965 with his
vote to maintain the controversial "right to work"
section 14(b) of the Taft-Hartley Act. The strength
of the pro-business National Right to Work Committee in South Dakota influenced his stand. He
later admitted, "It was a straight political decision."
Although the balance of his voting record was pro-
labor, the AFL-CIO often cited this vote as an

explanation for their coolness toward McGovern's subsequent presidential candidacies.

McGovern's maiden Senate speech in March 1963 was a critique of U.S. Latin American policy, and he continued throughout the decade to denounce what he considered the militaristic bent of U.S. foreign policy and the burgeoning defense budget. He regularly voted to reduce defense appropriations and opposed much of the Pentagon's expensive new weaponry, including the air force's advanced manned bomber and the antiballistic missile system. He also sought to reduce military assistance to foreign countries.

McGovern was most conspicuous as an early, outspoken foe of the Vietnam War. He first criticized U.S. involvement in September 1963, although he did vote for the Gulf of Tonkin Resolution the following August. (The next day he inserted some second thoughts in the *Congressional Record:* "I do not want my vote for the resolution to be interpreted as an endorsement for our long-standing and apparently growing military involvement in Vietnam.") In January 1965 he called the war "a South Vietnamese problem . . . not basically a military problem but a political one." He proposed a negotiated solution, leading to gradual withdrawal of U.S. troops and the neutralization of Vietnam protected by a UN presence. He visited Vietnam in November 1965 and returned to call for a bombing halt and recognition of the National Liberation Front. In April 1967 he castigated U.S. policy makers for "distorting history to justify our intervention" and "backing a dictatorial group in Saigon against a competing group backed by a dictatorial group in the North." McGovern's attacks escalated during the Nixon administration, culminating in the unsuccessful McGovern-Hatfield amendments of 1970–71 designed to cut off all funding for the Vietnam War.

In the fall of 1967 the liberal antiwar activist ALLARD K. LOWENSTEIN tried to persuade McGovern to run in the presidential primaries against LYNDON JOHNSON. McGovern, who faced what he thought would be a difficult reelection contest in 1968, turned Lowenstein down, and suggested that he approach either LEE METCALF (D-Mont.) or EUGENE MCCARTHY (D-Minn.), two Senate "doves" who did not face election challenges the next year. To McGovern's surprise McCarthy accepted Lowenstein's offer to become the candidate of the "Dump Johnson Movement." Publicly, McGovern remained neutral during the early presidential primaries of 1968 but clearly favored Senator ROBERT F. KENNEDY (D-N.Y.) after the New York senator announced his candidacy in March.

Following Kennedy's assassination in June, a number of former Kennedy supporters and staff workers urged McGovern to run for the nomination. On August 10 he announced his candidacy, saying that he hoped to "serve as a rallying point for his [Kennedy's] supporters." In a 16-day campaign McGovern denounced the Vietnam War, advocated a "systematic reduction of our overgrown military-industrial complex," and the diversion of the resulting resources to the reconstruction of the cities and rural America. McGovern also criticized "empty-headed cries for law and order" for their "undertone of racism." In a climactic three-way televised appearance with McCarthy and Vice President HUBERT HUMPHREY before the 174-member California delegation on August 26, McGovern delivered a strong attack on U.S. policy in Vietnam, which many observers thought "won" the debate for his antiwar candidacy. Nevertheless, McGovern finished a distant third in the convention balloting with 146 votes, behind Humphrey with 1,761 and McCarthy with 601. McGovern then endorsed Humphrey and campaigned for him against RICHARD NIXON.

In the 1972 campaign McGovern made an early start and, by slowly winning support on a platform advocating immediate withdrawal from Vietnam and sweeping tax reform, won the nomination after an unexpectedly strong performance in the primaries. His support for a guaranteed annual income for American families alienated many middle-class voters, who saw him as too liberal for their tastes. He was defeated by a large margin in November. He was reelected in 1974, and, in 1976, President GERALD FORD appointed him a delegate to the United Nations General Assembly. Two years later, President Carter named him a United Nations delegate for the Special Session on Disarmament. He was defeated in his quest for reelection to the Senate in 1980, and then again in 1984 when he ran for the Democratic nomination for the presidency. He served as U.S. ambassador to the United Nations Food and Agricultural Agencies in Rome, Italy, from 1998 to 2001, and later as the United Nations Global Ambassador on World Hunger.

—TO

## McIntire, Carl

### (1906–2002) *anticommunist preacher*

The son of a Presbyterian minister, McIntire was born on May 17, 1906, in Ypsilanti, Michigan, and began his religious career by enrolling in the Princeton Theological Seminary. He departed, however, with scholar J. Gresham Machen, over what they saw as a "trend toward socialism and modernism." Machen and his followers then organized Westminster Seminary, which graduated McIntire in 1931 as an ordained minister. As pastor of the Presbyterian Church in Collingswood, New Jersey, McIntire took Machen's side when the denomination was split by modernist-fundamentalist quarrels in the 1930s. The Presbytery of New Jersey defrocked McIntire in 1935 for ecclesiastical disobedience and replaced him with a new pastor, but most of the congregation followed McIntire into his new Bible Presbyterian Church in 1936.

From this base McIntire waged a vociferous crusade in the ensuing decades against the leaders of the major Protestant denominations, whom he accused of having Communist tendencies. His chief organizational targets were the National Council of Churches and the World Council of Churches. Denouncing these bodies for their liberalism and their "apostasy," McIntire set up the American Council of Churches in 1941 and the International Council of Churches in 1948 to promote his brand of theological conservatism. He also established a college, seminary, and resort hotel in New Jersey to perpetuate his fundamentalist movement.

In the 1960s McIntire expressed his views through a weekly newspaper, *The Christian Beacon*, and *The 20th Century Reformation Hour*, a radio show broadcast daily over some 600 stations. His polemics by then encompassed a broad range of political and religious institutions. He criticized civil rights demonstrations, Social Security, fair-employment legislation, the United Nations, and the YMCA (for sponsoring teenage dances). He backed a constitutional amendment to permit prayer and Bible-reading in public schools and continued his defense of a literal interpretation of the Bible and his campaign against "modernism, liberalism and Roman Catholicism." He supported Israel in its 1967 war with the Arab states and was an enthusiastic advocate of escalation of the Vietnam War.

Beginning in 1964, 19 religious and civic groups petitioned the Federal Communications Commission (FCC) to deny license renewal for McIntire's radio station WXUR on the grounds that the station was a forum for anti-Catholic, anti-Semitic, and antiblack propaganda. The American Civil Liberties Union defended McIntire in the suit. In July 1970 the FCC voted 6-0 to revoke the license, saying that the station management had no regular procedure for reviewing its presentations on controversial issues. In 1973, the FCC ordered his stations taken off the air for his failure to provide a more balanced distribution of shows. He remained the pastor at the Bible Presbyterian Church for the next three decades until his death on March 19, 2002.

—TO

## McIntyre, Thomas J(ames)

### (1915–1992) *member of the Senate*

McIntyre, who was born on February 20, 1915, in Laconia, New Hampshire, became active in New Hampshire Democratic politics during the 1940s. He won a special November 1962 election held to fill the seat of the late senator STYLES BRIDGES (R-N.H.). He thereby became the first New Hampshire Democrat to be sent to the Senate since 1932. During his first year McIntyre generally supported the Kennedy administration's foreign and domestic policies.

McIntyre also supported key Johnson administration legislation, including the civil rights, antipoverty, Medicare, and school-aid bills. He also cast a critical vote in 1966 in favor of the administration's Model Cities program. He devoted substantial time to advancing New Hampshire interests in the Senate. As a member of the Armed Senate Services Committee, McIntyre opposed government efforts to close the naval base at Portsmouth. He also called for higher tariffs on textiles and shoes to protect New Hampshire industries that were hard-hit by foreign competition. At the same time he campaigned for liberalized oil import quotas to permit New Englanders to purchase fuel oil at lower prices.

As a member of the Senate Banking Committee, McIntyre sponsored the administration's truth-in-lending bill, which required banks to specify their interest rates on loans. Although most lending institutions opposed the bill, it passed both houses and became law in May 1968. McIntyre also worked to reduce fees charged by mutual funds and to allow commercial banks to sell mutual fund shares.

McIntyre stood for reelection in 1966 and faced a difficult test in predominantly Republican New

Hampshire. He was opposed by retired air force general Harrison Thyng, who had the support of WILLIAM LOEB, the arch-conservative publisher of the only major newspaper in the state. Tyng charged that the Johnson administration had failed to mount the aggressive military campaign he thought necessary to win the war in Vietnam. McIntyre defended the Johnson policy of gradual escalation and publicly challenged Thyng and Loeb to a debate. They declined, and his challenge, unusual for an incumbent, coupled with the fact that Republicans were badly divided, enabled McIntyre to win the election with 54 percent of the vote.

In February and March 1968 McIntyre was once again called upon the defend Johnson administration war policies, this time under attack from Senator EUGENE J. MCCARTHY (D-Minn.), the antiwar candidate who had entered the New Hampshire presidential primary. McIntyre and New Hampshire governor John King first ignored McCarthy's challenge to the president, but as McCarthy developed a powerful organization, they sharpened their criticism, charging that a vote for McCarthy was a vote for "weakness and indecision." On March 12, Johnson barely outpolled McCarthy, and the Minnesota senator was widely credited with a stunning upset. On March 31 Johnson announced that he would not seek reelection.

During the Nixon years McIntyre abandoned his support of the war and advocated legislation establishing a specific date for withdrawal of American troops from Vietnam. He also sponsored the bill in 1971 that created National Hunting and Fishing Day. He was defeated in his reelection bid in 1978 and retired to New Hampshire. He died in Palm Beach, Florida, on August 8, 1992.

—JLW

## McKeithen, John J(ulian)
### (1918–1999) *governor*

McKeithen was born on May 28, 1918, in Grayson, Louisiana. A lawyer, farmer, and protégé of the powerful Long political machine in Louisiana, McKeithen served in the Louisiana House of Representatives as Governor Earl Long's floor leader from 1948 to 1952. In 1954 McKeithen was named to the Louisiana Public Service Commission, where he remained until 1962. In January 1964 McKeithen defeated the former mayor of New Orleans and ambassador to the Organization of American States,

deLesseps S. Morrison, in a Democratic gubernatorial primary runoff. In that campaign McKeithen alleged that Morrison had made a deal with the NAACP for votes. This charge cost McKeithen the support of moderate and liberal Democrats, white and black, in the general election. Nor did he have the support of the Johnson administration, which resented his offer to endorse their presidential campaign in return for political favors. The Republicans nominated Charleton H. Lyons, a Shreveport oil executive and Goldwater supporter. McKeithen won the election, but his margin of victory was the smallest received by a Louisiana Democratic gubernatorial candidate in the 20th century.

McKeithen's first objective in office was to establish a good government image in order to enhance the state's attractiveness to industry. This effort was impeded by 1967 *Life* magazine allegations that the McKeithen administration had closed its eyes to widespread organized crime influence in Louisiana. As an inducement to industry, the state passed a series of "right-to-profit" laws, which extended tax credits to industrial users of natural gas and provided other business incentives. Partly owing to these measures, Louisiana's industrial growth more than doubled during McKeithen's tenure.

Although his campaign had been geared toward strongly pro-segregationist voters, McKeithen was a moderate on racial matters. He made the first significant appointment of blacks to government positions in the South, including the selection of two African Americans as judges. In April 1965 the Congress of Racial Equality (CORE) centered an intensive civil rights campaign on Bogalusa, Louisiana. In July McKeithen proposed a 30-day moratorium on demonstrations following months of severe racial tension and violence. His proposal, which earned him attention as a peacemaker, was rejected by black leaders. McKeithen termed that rejection a "tragic mistake." During the rest of his term the governor took no further significant actions on civil rights.

In 1966 McKeithen won adoption of a state constitutional amendment permitting a governor to succeed himself. He was reelected to his second term of office with 81 percent of the vote, the highest percentage in modern Louisiana history. During his second term McKeithen confronted the problem of busing to achieve racial balance. While specifically rejecting violence as a recourse to court directives, he wrote in August 1971 that he anticipated "using police power or whatever other power I have" to stop busing. He is also credited with the creation of a tough ethical code for public employees and with the reform of the prison system in Louisiana. In November 1972 State Senator J. Bennett Johnson, Jr., defeated McKeithen in his bid to fill the seat of the late U.S. senator ALLEN ELLENDER. After leaving office, he continued to practice law in Louisiana. He died on June 4, 1999.

—TJC

## McKissick, Floyd B(ixler)
(1922–1991) *national director, Congress of Racial Equality*

McKissick was born on March 9, 1922, in Asheville, North Carolina. After military service during World War II, he attended North Carolina College and was the first African American to study law at the University of North Carolina; in 1952 he became the first black in the school's history to receive an LL.B. McKissick opened a law practice in Durham, North Carolina, and soon became senior partner in the firm McKissick and Burt.

An ambitious lawyer, McKissick resented racial discrimination in the North Carolina bar and in local life. In one of his earliest fights he successfully represented his daughter in her attempt to enroll in an all-white school. During the 1950s he served as youth chair of the North Carolina NAACP, and, in 1960, he became legal counsel for the Congress of Racial Equality (CORE), a more militant civil rights organization. Much of McKissick's work during the early 1960s consisted of defending CORE demonstrators arrested while protesting segregation at public facilities in southern cities and working to integrate the local unions. McKissick also helped expand the network of CORE chapters in North Carolina. In 1962 he left the NAACP, which had fallen into a dispute with the North Carolina CORE over the planning and leadership of desegregation marches.

Beginning in 1963 McKissick's role in CORE was determined by the growing militance developing in the civil rights movement. Black activists were proud of their earlier struggles, but many were also impatient with the pace of civil rights progress and disappointed by the continued economic deprivation of American blacks. This unrest gave rise to a desire for greater black self-reliance and independence from white liberal supporters of civil rights. CORE responded to this sentiment by choosing McKissick, known as "a down-home black lawyer," to be national chair in June 1963; the unpaid position had earlier been held by whites.

McKissick himself was affected by the new currents in the civil rights movement and increasingly stressed the importance of black self-help and control over decision making in CORE. Speaking at the 1963 CORE convention, he claimed that civil rights litigation had gone as far as possible in the courts, leaving direct action as the only avenue of black advancement. In 1965 McKissick attempted to shift the organization's funding base from middle-class whites to blacks. He also invited the Black Muslims to speak for the first time at a CORE national convention in January 1966, dramatizing his commitment to separate black cultural development. The same convention elected McKissick CORE's national director after JAMES FARMER announced his departure from the organization. At this time CORE had a national membership of 180,000 in 200 local chapters.

Under McKissick's leadership CORE remained on the militant side of the civil rights spectrum. McKissick followed civil rights leader STOKELY CARMICHAEL in adopting the rhetoric of Black Power, calling blacks "a nation within a nation." The greatest support for black separatism came from CORE chapters in northern cities, and McKissick shifted the organization toward a stronger focus on urban poverty problems. He tried repeatedly to attract federal and foundation money for voter education, job training, and aid to black businesses in inner city areas. In a symbolic action McKissick moved CORE's national headquarters to Harlem in August 1966. He also became one of the strongest critics among black leaders of the Vietnam War, denouncing "black men going over . . . and dying for something they don't have a right for here."

Despite McKissick's policies, many CORE members were not satisfied with his leadership. Much of the tension within the organization resulted from its growing financial difficulties. The rise of Black Power sentiment had alienated many white financial supporters, and McKissick could not find adequate replacement funding in the black community. To avoid bankruptcy he was forced in January 1967 to curtail a number of CORE projects. This caused resentment in local chapters whose projects were affected and increased competition for remaining funds. Some militant CORE staffers also viewed McKissick as a follower rather than a leader of Black Power, and there were complaints that his southern background prevented him from relating to blacks in the northern inner cities. In September 1967 McKissick took a leave of absence from CORE. He resigned as national director in 1968 to be replaced by ROY INNIS, former head of CORE's Harlem chapter.

After leaving CORE McKissick established his own consulting firm, which dealt with poverty problems. He also planned and collected funds for a community in North Carolina called Soul City, intended to provide economic opportunities for rural blacks. Soul City never became what McKissick hoped, however, and, in 1980, the federal government assumed operational control of most of its holdings. He stayed on, however, as pastor at the local Baptist church until his death on April 28, 1991.

—SLG

## McMillan, John L(anneau)

(1898–1979) *member of the House of Representatives*

McMillan was born on April 12, 1898, and spent his childhood on a farm in South Carolina's tobacco region. He served in the navy during World War I and graduated from the University of North Carolina and then the University of South Carolina Law School in 1923.

Elected as a Democrat to Congress from South Carolina's Sixth Congressional District in 1938, McMillan assumed the chair of the House District of Columbia Committee in 1948. He also served as vice chair of the House Agriculture Committee, where he oversaw South Carolina's tobacco interests.

As chair of the District Committee, which was controlled by conservative southern Democrats, McMillan successfully blocked home-rule legislation through three presidential administrations. His opposition, which he said was based on constitutional principles, was often attributed by observers to a bias against black control of the city. (The District of Columbia ranked ninth in population among U.S. cities, with a 63 percent black majority.)

During the Kennedy administration McMillan voted with the conservative coalition on over 75 percent of all major issues; in 1963 he voted with the

conservatives on 100 percent of key issues. McMillan voted against Medicare, the 1964 Civil Rights Act, and the 1965 Voting Rights Act. He did, however, author a number of bills specifically designed to provide farmers with long-term loans of land and equipment from the government aid to farmers, including the 1971 Federal Land Bank and Intermediate Land Bank Act.

In 1965 President Johnson stated that "the restoration of home rule to the citizens of the District of Columbia must no longer be delayed." Over the next two years the House District Committee, in a series of highly intricate legislative maneuvers, managed repeatedly to block the administration's home-rule bill. Debate on the issue lasted until 1967, when the president, circumventing the committee, used the authority given him under a government reorganization act to change the city's form of government. Since 1874 Washington had been governed by Congress and a three-member board of commissioners selected by the president. Under the new plan the three commissioners were replaced by a single commissioner, a deputy commissioner, and a nine-member city council. The president appointed a black, WALTER E. WASHINGTON, to the newly created post of commissioner in September 1967.

In 1970 McMillan won a close primary reelection race. Two years later organized labor and black groups coalesced around a Democratic state legislator half McMillan's age, who defeated the 16-term representative. He returned to South Carolina after his defeat, where he remained until his death on September 3, 1979.

—FHM

## McNamara, Patrick V(incent)

(1894–1966) *member of the Senate*

McNamara was born on October 4, 1894, in North Weymouth, Massachusetts. A pipe fitter by trade, McNamara served as president of Detroit Pipe Fitters Local 636 of the American Federation of Labor for 20 years. As a member of the Detroit Board of Education, the relatively unknown McNamara defeated the incumbent Republican, Homer Ferguson (R-Mich.), in 1954 on a platform calling for repeal of the Taft-Hartley Act and federal aid to education. Named to the special Senate committee investigating labor (the Senate Rackets Committee) in 1957, McNamara quit in April 1958 and accused the committee of persecuting the labor movement. He criticized Senate Majority Leader LYNDON JOHNSON (D-Tex.) in January 1958 for holding too few Democratic caucuses, and in 1959 wrote an open letter to LBJ protesting the Senate's failure to push for unemployment reform.

McNamara became chair of the Senate Public Works Committee in 1963. He was also ranking Democrat on the Labor and Welfare Committee and the Special Senate Committee on Aging. During the Kennedy and Johnson years, he was a strong supporter of aid to education, wages-and-hours legislation, and medical aid for the aged. He proved an important figure in the passage of much of the early Great Society legislation. In January 1964 he sponsored an administration bill to extend minimum wage coverage and overtime provisions to 2.6 million additional workers. He was the floor manager in July for the administration's omnibus antipoverty program, the Economic Opportunity Act of 1964.

McNamara sponsored the Older Americans Act of 1965, which created an Administration on Aging in the Department of Health, Education and Welfare. This bill was strongly backed by the AFL-CIO, as was McNamara's unsuccessful attempt in September 1965 to repeal Section 14(b) of the Taft-Hartley Act. The controversial section of the law allowed states to outlaw the "closed shop." A cloture motion to end the filibuster against repeal was defeated, 45–47, on October 11. *Congressional Quarterly* reported that McNamara's voting record was among the four highest in support of President Johnson's proposals in 1964 and 1965. He died of a stroke on April 30, 1966.

—TO

## McNamara, Robert S(trange)

(1916–  ) *secretary of defense*

President Johnson considered Robert S. McNamara the most impressive member of his cabinet. McNamara, who served as secretary of defense from 1961 to 1968, was brilliant and controversial. He was a major architect of U.S. strategy in Vietnam, who eventually questioned the policies he had helped to create.

Born in San Francisco on June 9, 1916, McNamara graduated with honors from the University of California, Berkeley, in 1937 and the Harvard Business School in 1939. He worked briefly for a San Francisco accounting firm before returning to Har-

vard to accept a teaching post at the business school. In World War II he served with the Army Air Forces, where he helped develop the logistical system for mass bomber raids on Germany and Japan.

Following the war McNamara joined a group of talented young ex-army officers, later dubbed "the whiz kids," who worked for the financially troubled Ford Motor Company. As a Ford general manager and later as a vice president, McNamara helped revive the company with emphasis on strict cost-accounting methods. He supported the development of the Falcon, a compact economy automobile and the four door luxury version of the Thunderbird. Both were financial successes. In November 1960 McNamara was named the company president, the first man outside the Ford family to hold that position.

McNamara served in his new post only one month before President John F. Kennedy named him secretary of defense. During his first years in office he worked to modernize the armed forces and make the Pentagon more efficient by centralizing decision making in his own office. He also restructured Pentagon budgetary procedures to ensure that each service would coordinate budget requests to avoid costly duplication. McNamara refused to approve the development of costly weapons systems of unproven or dubious value. During 1961 and 1962 he would not spend funds appropriated by Congress for the development of the RS-70, an experimental air force bomber that he considered obsolete in the missile age. McNamara also resisted pressure from the navy to develop nuclear-powered surface ships, which he considered overpriced and of little strategic value.

When the air force and navy each requested permission to develop a new aircraft, McNamara instructed them to cooperate in the construction of an aircraft adaptable for both services. In November 1962 McNamara and his aides awarded the contract for the fighter/bomber, the TFX (tactical fighter experimental), to the General Dynamics Corporation. Because military officials found the Boeing Corporation's design preferable, McNamara and his aides were called before a Senate subcommittee to justify their selection. The TFX investigation, lasting nine months, embarrassed McNamara because it revealed long smoldering differences between civilians and the military in the Defense Department. McNamara's decision was upheld, but the TFX proved far more costly than Defense Department estimates and, because of various structural problems, did not perform up to expectations.

Although McNamara was a strong advocate of the 1963 nuclear test ban treaty and strategic arms limitation talks, his defense strategy called for improved U.S. nuclear capabilities. He favored an accelerated program to replace vulnerable liquid-fuel intercontinental ballistic missiles (ICBMs) with solid-fuel missiles, which could be widely dispersed and fired from submarines and underground silos. These new weapons would give the United States a "second-strike" capability, that is, the ability to absorb a nuclear attack while retaining the capacity to launch a devastating counterattack. McNamara welcomed the development of a Soviet second-strike capability, as he believed it would produce "a more stable 'balance of terror' " that would lessen the danger of nuclear war.

The secretary also advocated the development of a large, highly mobile strike force to permit the United States to deal with guerrilla or conventional wars without nuclear weapons. The Eisenhower administration's strategy of "massive retaliation," he argued, had limited U.S. ability to react in crisis situations while increasing the probability of nuclear confrontation. In developing a "flexible response" capability, McNamara won approval for a 300,000-man increase in U.S. fighting strength and authorization for a vast buildup in troop airlift capacity.

From his earliest days as vice president, LYN-DON B. JOHNSON thought McNamara the most talented member of the Kennedy cabinet. When he became president, Johnson was gratified that McNamara remained as defense secretary, particularly at a time when Vietnam was becoming a more troublesome problem. McNamara had first visited South Vietnam in 1962 and had declared upon his return that "every quantitative measurement we have shows that we're winning this war." At that time the United States had approximately 6,500 troops stationed in the area as advisers to the South Vietnamese armed forces. McNamara believed that the United States should commit itself to the defense of South Vietnam because a Communist victory there could lead to a Communist takeover of other Southeast Asian nations. He remained confident that the United States, with its enormous military power and its newly developed counterinsurgency techniques, could defeat the National Liberation Front (NLF) and its North Vietnamese allies.

Secretary of Defense Robert McNamara during a meeting in the Cabinet Room, 1968 *(Photographed by Yoichi R. Okamoto; Lyndon Baines Johnson Library)*

In March 1964 McNamara again visited South Vietnam. He made optimistic statements as he toured the country with the new premier, General Nguyen Khanh. Back in Washington, the secretary informed Johnson that "the situation has unquestionably been growing worse." In public McNamara promised Khanh "everything he needs," a pledge that suggested limits of neither time nor money. In a meeting with the National Security Council, McNamara indicated that increased aid could reverse the deterioration in the war within six months. By April 1964 McNamara was so closely identified with Vietnam policy that Senator WAYNE MORSE (D-Ore.) dubbed the conflict "McNamara's war." Despite his private reservations about the conflict, McNamara replied, "I am pleased to be identified with it and do whatever I can to win it."

By 1964 U.S. aircraft were aiding the South Vietnamese armed forces in carrying out covert raids on North Vietnam's coastal installations and attacks on infiltration routes in Laos and Cambodia. Despite these actions Communist forces threatened to overwhelm South Vietnam. Consequently, Pentagon strategists began drawing up plans for expanded U.S. intervention.

The president did approve new military action on August 4, 1964, when two U.S. destroyers were allegedly attacked by North Vietnamese gunboats in the Gulf of Tonkin. Admiral Ulysses S. Grant Sharp, commander in chief of U.S. Pacific forces, and members of the Joint Chiefs of Staff urged immediate retaliation against North Vietnam. President Johnson agreed. McNamara hurriedly sought verification of the attack before U.S. planes took action. Evidence of the night attack, based largely on radar and sonar readings, was equivocal. An attack two days earlier, whose certainty was never in doubt, made technicians inclined to interpret ambiguous electronic evidence as clear indication of North Vietnamese hostile action. McNamara telephoned Sharp in Honolulu and told him that he did not want to launch a retaliatory strike "until we are damn sure what happened." Sharp called back less than two hours later to say he was certain that the U.S. vessels had been attacked. Later investigations indicate, however, that the attack of August 4 never occurred. Nevertheless, President Johnson, with McNamara's support, ordered air strikes against North Vietnamese shipping and coastal installations. McNamara presented evidence of the attack to Congress, which on August 7 approved the Tonkin Gulf Resolution, giving the president broad power to "take all necessary measures to repel . . . further aggression" throughout Southeast Asia.

Throughout the fall of 1964 McNamara received reports of significant gains by Communist forces in South Vietnam. Some members of the Joint Chiefs favored a U.S. bombing campaign against North Vietnam as a way of destroying its will to support the war in the South. But General MAXWELL TAYLOR, the U.S. ambassador in Saigon, objected, arguing that the South Vietnamese government was too weak to risk a major escalation of the war. Taylor, however, insisted that additional military actions against North Vietnam would eventually be necessary. He agreed with General WILLIAM WESTMORELAND, the commander of U.S. forces in Vietnam, that the time was not yet right to expand the war.

After the 1964 presidential election many of Johnson's advisers, including McNamara, recommended a sustained bombing campaign against North Vietnam. In February 1965, the president used a Communist attack on a U.S. base at Pleiku as a pretext to justify retaliatory air strikes against the North. By the beginning of March, those retaliatory raids had become a systematic bombing campaign, known as Rolling Thunder. At the request of General Westmoreland, 3,500 Marines were also sent to help defend the airbase at Da Nang. Despite these moves, McNamara thought that the war would

come to an end through a negotiated settlement, but only after U.S. military action had proved that the NLF could not hope to win. After consulting with Westmoreland, McNamara endorsed the general's request that 175,000 troops be sent to Vietnam by the end of 1965. Johnson approved the recommendation but rejected, as politically unpalatable, McNamara's proposal for calling up the reserves. The president also deferred asking Congress for large appropriations sufficient to pay the costs of the war.

By November U.S. troops were engaged in major battles against North Vietnamese regulars in the Central Highlands. That month Westmoreland recommended that up to 400,000 troops be sent to Vietnam by the end of 1966. McNamara concurred but cautioned that "deployments of the kind I have recommended will not guarantee success. U.S. killed in action can be expected to reach 1,000 a month, and the odds are even that we will be faced in early 1967 with a 'no decision' at an even higher level." What McNamara had come to realize was that North Vietnam would counter a U.S. troop buildup by sending more of its own troops south.

At McNamara's urging, the United States initiated a halt in the bombing of North Vietnam in December 1965. The secretary argued that the bombing halt might induce North Vietnam to enter peace negotiations with the United States. If not, then more intensive bombing could be justified. General Westmoreland and the Joint Chiefs opposed the halt because they feared the North Vietnamese would take advantage of the lull to resupply their troops. The pause proved unproductive, and the bombing was renewed on January 31, 1966.

Bombing strategy was a continual source of conflict between McNamara and the military. The president, McNamara, Secretary of State DEAN RUSK, and MCGEORGE BUNDY retained the right to review all proposed bombing targets in North Vietnam. McNamara and his staff charged that the Joint Chiefs too often selected targets that were of dubious military significance. The Joint Chiefs, in turn, argued that McNamara placed unnecessary restrictions on U.S. air power.

In October 1966 McNamara visited South Vietnam for the eighth time. Publicly he was optimistic, stating that military progress "exceeded our expectations." Privately he had growing doubts. The air war had not forced North Vietnam into peace negotiations; U.S. troops had prevented a Communist victory but were now stalemated; casualties were high and prospects for a quick end to the war were nil. He was becoming increasingly sensitive to antiwar opinions, particularly those of Senator ROBERT F. KENNEDY (D-N.Y.). In a speech delivered in Montreal in the spring of 1966, McNamara seemed to question the wisdom of the U.S. military commitment. Referring to the government of South Vietnam, he stated, "We have no charter to rescue floundering regimes, who have brought violence on themselves by deliberately refusing to meet the legitimate expectations of their citizens."

Such statements were rare. For the most part McNamara continued to urge Americans to remain firm in their resolve to resist Communist aggression. He was, in turn, denounced by antiwar leaders, who considered his references to "body counts" and "search-and-destroy missions" ruthless and cold-blooded. McNamara, who had enjoyed his student days and brief career as a college teacher, was no longer welcome on many campuses. In a November 1966 visit to Harvard University, he was challenged to debate the war and was then hooted down. Yelling above the crowd, he recalled his student days, "I was a lot tougher and a lot more courteous than you. I was tougher than you and I am tougher today."

During 1967 McNamara became openly skeptical over the effectiveness of bombing the North to prevent resupply of Communist troops in the South. Hoping to find a more effective means of preventing infiltration by North Vietnamese regulars, McNamara announced that the United States would construct a barrier of barbed wire, mines, and electronic sensors south of the demilitarized zone. The barrier proved ineffective and was abandoned in 1969.

While concerned about the military conduct of the war, McNamara became increasingly interested in finding a way to end the conflict through a negotiated settlement. During the summer of 1967 McNamara, PAUL WARNKE, and PAUL NITZE drew up the "San Antonio Formula," a peace proposal offered privately to North Vietnam in August. The plan was a significant change in the U.S. terms for ending bombing and beginning negotiations. Prior to the communication the United States had offered to end the bombing if North Vietnam would stop its infiltration of the South. The San Antonio Formula modified this demand. It asked only for productive

discussions in exchange for an end to the bombing. The United States requested no specific guarantee from Hanoi that it would end its infiltration. The only condition made was that the United States reserved its right to act if it concluded that the North Vietnamese were taking advantage of the bombing lull. The proposal, made public in September, was rejected by North Vietnam in October. By the fall of 1967, McNamara had concluded that "we could not achieve our objective in Vietnam through any reasonable military means." His doubts about the bombing and his desire for a negotiated settlement led him in November to propose a policy of "stabilization," which included a freeze on U.S. troop levels, a transfer of greater responsibility to the South Vietnamese for ground combat, and a halt of the bombing of North Vietnam in order to secure negotiations for an end to the war. These recommendations raised the tension between the president and the secretary "to the breaking point."

In November McNamara announced that he would resign in February to become the president of the World Bank. In January 1968, a few weeks before McNamara left office, Communist forces launched a major offensive against Saigon, Hue, and many other South Vietnamese cities and hamlets. After intense fighting the Communists were driven out of the cities, but the Tet offensive seemed to confirm McNamara's pessimistic assessment of the war.

In response to the Communist offensive, the military requested more than 200,000 additional troops for the war. Johnson, concerned about the possible reaction to another increase, convened a senior advisory group on Vietnam to study the request. Although the panel favored approval of the troop request, McNamara's successor, CLARK CLIFFORD, recommended steps toward disengagement. Johnson accepted that recommendation and at the end of March announced restrictions on future bombing of the North and a renewed bid for negotiations.

McNamara remained at the World Bank through 1981, where he attempted to increase loans to developing nations and channel funds to programs directly related to the daily life of the poor rather than to large civil engineering projects, which had formerly been favored by the bank. During the 1980s, he advocated curbing the U.S.-Soviet nuclear arms race and criticized President Ronald Reagan's Strategic Defense Initiative (or "Star Wars"). In 1995 he published a memoir about his involvement with the Vietnam War, *In Retrospect*, and asserted that in making policy decisions about Vietnam, "we were wrong, terribly wrong." His memoir produced considerable public debate, including praise for candid evaluation of Vietnam decisions as well as criticism for belated acknowledgment of responsibility. He cooperated with filmmaker Errol Morris in a documentary, *Fog of War* (2003), about lessons drawn from his public career, including several derived from U.S. involvement in Vietnam.

—JLW

## McNaughton, John T(heodore)

(1921–1967)  *assistant secretary of defense for international security affairs*

Born in Bicknell, Indiana, on November 21, 1921, John T. McNaughton, a Rhodes scholar and Harvard University law professor joined the Defense Department in the summer of 1961 and dealt with arms control and disarmament issues. In July 1963 McNaughton served as a member of the diplomatic team that successfully negotiated a treaty with the Soviet Union barring above-ground testing of atomic weapons.

McNaughton was named assistant secretary of defense for international security affairs in June 1964. He maintained a close working and personal relationship with Secretary of Defense ROBERT S. MCNAMARA and soon became McNamara's chief assistant in developing strategy in Vietnam.

In September 1964, McNaughton completed at McNamara's request a "Plan for Action for South Vietnam," which aimed at reversing "the present downward trend" in the war. McNaughton maintained that the South Vietnamese government was not strong enough to carry out a successful pacification program. Accordingly, he proposed a significant expansion of U.S. military involvement in South Vietnamese rural pacification. In addition, his plan called for "a crescendo of . . . military actions," including naval pressures, mining of harbors, and air strikes against North Vietnam. Coming just a month after the alleged North Vietnamese attacks against U.S. vessels in the Gulf of Tonkin, the actions McNaughton outlined were designed to provoke a North Vietnamese military response. Such retaliation, McNaughton wrote, "would provide good grounds" for further U.S. military escalation.

The president and his national security advisers were not yet ready in September 1964 to approve U.S. bombing of North Vietnam or other actions aimed at eliciting a North Vietnamese military response. Concern about a South Vietnamese government "still struggling to its feet" caused them to defer provocative actions that carried excessive risk. Ironically, McNaughton may well have doubted the wisdom of his own recommendations. According to his deputy, DANIEL ELLSBERG, McNaughton privately expressed opposition to deeper U.S. military intervention in Vietnam and considered the sustained bombing of North Vietnam a dangerous course of action. Yet McNaughton never committed these thoughts to paper and continued to produce memoranda that proposed stronger U.S. military action.

In November 1964 McNaughton joined the National Security Council working group, headed by Assistant Secretary of State WILLIAM P. BUNDY, which was considering ways to deal with the deteriorating situation in South Vietnam. The panel recommended that the administration support "graduated military moves against infiltration targets first in Laos and then in North Vietnam," coupled with attempts to open negotiations with Hanoi and Peking. McNaughton preferred this option of the "slow squeeze" to the "fast and full squeeze" of heavy bombing because it would produce controlled escalation, allowing the president to adjust the level of bombing to military or political developments. Johnson accepted the committee's proposals in February 1965. These recommendations determined the course of the war until July of that year, when the administration committed extensive ground forces to the war.

Shortly after authorizing the sustained bombing of North Vietnam, President Johnson ordered U.S. combat troops to South Vietnam in March 1965. The mission of these forces, which at first was to guard U.S. bases, quickly became to search out and destroy the enemy. At this juncture McNaughton attempted to define U.S. goals in Southeast Asia: "70 percent—to avoid a humiliating U.S. defeat (to our reputation as a guarantor); 20 percent—to keep SVN [South Vietnam] (and then adjacent) territory from Chinese hands; 10 percent—to permit the people of SVN to enjoy a better, freer way of life; also— to emerge from crisis without unacceptable taint from methods used; not to 'help a friend' although it would be hard to stay in if asked out."

McNaughton doubted that the bombing of North Vietnam would force Hanoi to stop supporting the war in the South. He prepared a memorandum for McNamara that recommended a "massive increase" in U.S. ground forces, ranging from a minimum in South Vietnam to a maximum of 150,000 in both South Vietnam and Laos. Whatever the results of the war, McNaughton believed that it was "essential" that the United States "emerge as a 'good doctor.' We must have kept promises, been tough, taken risks, gotten bloodied, and hurt the enemy very badly." By the end of 1965, U.S. troop strength in South Vietnam had exceeded McNaughton's maximum level and stood at 184, 314.

In July 1965 McNaughton and McNamara, increasingly skeptical about the advantages of bombing the North, began planning, over the objections of the Joint Chiefs of Staff, for an extended bombing halt. A halt was initiated on December 24. McNaughton believed that the North would not yet consider negotiating but that the United States should at the very least "create a public impression of willingness 'to try everything' before further increases in military action." There was no satisfactory response from Hanoi, and the bombing was renewed on January 31, 1966.

McNaughton was one of a number of Defense Department officials who met with Secretary McNamara at weekly sessions to review a list of bombing sites in North Vietnam proposed by the Joint Chiefs of Staff. The military consistently argued that the civilian planners imposed illogical and arbitrary restrictions on the bombing. McNaughton countered that many of the requested military targets were of no strategic value and endangered the lives of civilians. He suggested that the bombing could be more effective if concentrated on infiltration routes south of Hanoi.

By May 1967 McNaughton became so alarmed by the growing public protest against the war that he wrote President Johnson to warn "of a feeling widely and strongly held that 'the Establishment' is out of its mind. The feeling is that we are trying to impose some U.S. image on distant people we cannot understand." He advised Johnson not to accede to a request from General WILLIAM WESTMORELAND for and additional 200,000 troops at a time when there were over 400,000 American soldiers already stationed in South Vietnam. At the same time McNaughton advised the president to press on with military, pacification, and political programs in the South and "drive hard to increase the productivity of Vietnamese military forces." The

United States had prevented a Communist victory in 1965, he said, but victory would ultimately depend on the South Vietnamese themselves.

In June 1967 McNaughton became secretary of the navy. On July 19, shortly before he assumed his new post, McNaughton, his wife, and younger son were killed in an airplane crash in North Carolina.

McNaughton received little attention in the press during his lifetime, but with the publication of the *Pentagon Papers* in 1971, he emerged as a controversial figure. To journalist Ralph Stavins, McNaughton was a man "torn between committing 'unbridled acts' of the most egregious sort and detaching the United States from an untenable situation. It would seem that his reason compelled him to urge a pullout but fear of being too weak to employ massive violence and his positive desire to wield power swayed him to betray his own reason." Robert McNamara, on the other hand, called him "a voice of reason" in the Pentagon, a restraining influence on the military whose persistent and informed opposition to the bombing in the North helped pave the way for its cessation in 1968.

—JLW

## McPherson, Harry C(ummings)
(1929–   ) *assistant secretary of defense for education and cultural affairs, special assistant to the president, special counsel to the president*

Harry McPherson was born on August 22, 1929, in the East Texas community of Tyler. After two years at Southern Methodist University, he transferred to the University of the South in Sewanee, Tennessee, graduating in 1949. McPherson dropped out of Columbia University—where he did graduate work in English literature—to join the air force in 1950. Following his discharge McPherson received a degree from the University of Texas Law School in 1956. The same year he took a job as assistant counsel to the Senate Democratic Policy Committee, chaired by Senator LYNDON JOHNSON. McPherson was named general counsel to the committee in 1961. In August 1963 he was appointed deputy undersecretary of the army for international affairs.

After Johnson became president, McPherson remained at his Pentagon post. In July 1964 he requested and was granted the post of assistant secretary for educational and cultural affairs, a job that appealed to his strong intellectual interests. In August

1965, McPherson was named special assistant to the president. In February of the next year he succeeded Lee C. White as special counsel.

McPherson provided the unswerving loyalty that the president demanded of his assistants, yet he was candid and forthright in his advice. He served as the president's personal lawyer, drafted many presidential executive orders, and worked with the Justice Department on legal matters concerning civil rights cases and presidential pardons. Along with special assistants DOUGLASS CATER and JOSEPH CALIFANO, McPherson acted as presidential liaison with several government agencies, coordinating education, antipoverty, and urban programs with the White House. Because of his intellectual credentials, he was often sent to college campuses to sound out the academic community's reaction to Great Society proposals. He eventually became the president's top speechwriter.

In his post as special counsel, McPherson saw most major bills that crossed the president's desk and commented on each of them. Of the 1968 Safe Streets Act, McPherson wrote the president: "I recognize that you must sign this bill. But it is the worst bill you will have signed since you took office. Title III, the wiretapping-eavesdropping provision, is extremely dangerous."

McPherson played an important role in the aftermath of the Tet offensive of 1968, as the president weighed a request from General WILLIAM C. WESTMORELAND for 206,000 additional troops. The president's advisers were divided, and McPherson agreed with Secretary of Defense CLARK CLIFFORD that there was insufficient public support for further escalation of the U.S. role in Vietnam and that the president should instead announce a new peace initiative. In a March 23, 1968, memorandum, McPherson recommended that the president, in his upcoming address on the Vietnam War, order the cessation of bombing north of the 20th parallel and announce that the U.S. would send representatives to Geneva and Rangoon to await a North Vietnamese response. McPherson believed that such an announcement would "show the American people that we are willing to do every reasonable thing to bring about talks." McPherson's proposals were incorporated into the March 31 speech. Johnson did announce new limitations of the bombing of North Vietnam and said that AVERELL HARRIMAN and LLEWELLYN THOMPSON would be available to go to Geneva "or any other suitable place" to begin peace talks.

At the end of the Johnson administration in 1969, McPherson entered private law practice in Washington.

—FHM

## Meany, George
### (1894–1980) *president, AFL-CIO*

Born on August 16, 1894, Meany, the son of an Irish-Catholic plumber, grew up in New York City. He entered his father's trade after high school and gained his first full-time union post at 28 as business agent of a plumbers' local in New York. Meany gradually rose within both the Plumbers Union and the American Federation of Labor (AFL), a national organization dominated by craft unions. In 1940 he was chosen secretary-treasurer of the AFL, and, 12 years later, he succeeded William Green as the organization's president. Meany's first major act as the head of the AFL was to negotiate a merger with the Congress of Industrial Organizations (CIO), a smaller grouping of unions organized chiefly on an industrywide basis. The merger took place in 1955, with Meany assuming the presidency of the united AFL-CIO; WALTER REUTHER, head of the United Auto Workers union (UAW) and former CIO president, took control of the new federation's Industrial Union Department.

With 12.4 million members in 130 affiliated unions, the AFL-CIO included more than 90 percent of the nation's trade unionists at the time of its creation. Meany himself, blunt-spoken and cigar-smoking, became the federation's chief policy maker on issues of both domestic and foreign politics. He was already known from his work in the AFL as a firm liberal and militant anticommunist. He endorsed the social welfare legislation of the Kennedy administration, but criticized President Kennedy—as he had President Eisenhower—for being "overly timid" in efforts to reduce unemployment. At the same time Meany gave unqualified support to anticommunist initiatives in U.S. foreign policy. In 1962 the AFL-CIO created the American Institute for Free Labor Development (AIFLD), which provided money and training to Latin American union leaders who agreed to oppose Communist politicians. Funded largely by U.S. government agencies, the AIFLD became an important instrument of U.S. policy in Latin America. During the mid-1960s it trained insurgent union leaders who helped overthrow anti-U.S. regimes in British Guiana and Brazil.

Meany's role within the AFL-CIO was limited by the organization's federal structure, which prevented him from influencing the bargaining strategies or strike decisions of member unions. His own concept of union integrity and independence made Meany a strong defender of union autonomy. Although he expelled the notoriously corrupt Teamsters union from the AFL-CIO in 1957, Meany generally referred complaints of union misdeeds to individual union leaders. Meany also resisted the demands of civil rights organizations that racial quotas be introduced in union apprenticeship programs to guarantee blacks a proportionate share of skilled jobs. The AFL-CIO leadership vigorously supported the Civil Rights Act of 1964, which banned discrimination in union locals and created a Fair Employment Practices Commission to investigate charges of bias. Yet Meany remained suspicious of activist civil rights groups and helped keep them at a distance from American labor. He repeatedly came into conflict with HERBERT HILL, labor secretary of the NAACP, who frequently charged AFL-CIO–affiliated union locals with excluding African Americans and other minority group workers from their membership.

The mid-1960s were years of unusually close cooperation between U.S. labor and government, embodied in the friendship between Meany and Johnson. Relations between the two were not cordial from the start, however. Meany had bitterly opposed the choice of Johnson as vice president in 1960; he viewed the Texan's congressional voting record on labor issues as "horrible." Only Johnson's determined advocacy of Great Society programs beginning in 1964 changed Meany's opinion. The Civil Rights Act, the $11.5 billion tax cut of 1963–64, and the Medicare plan of 1965 all had enthusiastic labor support. Meany also appreciated Johnson's willingness to approve an increase in the minimum wage in 1966, despite objections from the President's Council of Economic Advisers.

Another policy area where Johnson could count on Meany's complete approval was Vietnam. The growing conflict stimulated Meany's traditional anticommunism, and he went on record repeatedly in support of "all measures the Administration deems necessary . . . to secure a just and lasting peace." In addition to policy statements, the AFL-CIO provided equipment and training for South Vietnamese trade union leaders and also helped solve logistical problems at U.S. supply bases. Labor support on Vietnam became increasingly important for Johnson as opposition to the war grew in 1967 and 1968. Meany denounced war critics as "kooks" and "jitterbugs," accepting Johnson's assurances that the administration's war aims could be achieved without curtailment of Great Society programs. Opposition to the war among some union officials was easily put down at AFL-CIO conventions, which Meany controlled.

Labor's only legislative disappointment during the mid-1960s was its failure to gain repeal of Section 14(b) of the Taft-Hartley Act. This provision permitted states to pass "right-to-work" laws barring the union shop. Meany viewed elimination of 14(b) as "the number one legislative issue confronting the trade union movement," and Johnson promised to work for repeal in 1965. It soon became apparent, however, that the administration was not willing to fight hard enough to overcome conservative resistance in Congress. According to his biographer, Joseph C. Goulden, Meany rejected the alternative of making a deal with Senate conservatives, who offered to accept repeal in exchange for labor support of a bill aimed at blocking congressional reapportionment. Although Meany vowed "never to quit" in his opposition to Section 14(b), the measure remained in effect, forcing unions to fight open-shop legislation in a number of states.

Disappointment over 14(b) did not make Meany regret his support of Johnson in the 1964 presidential race or deny his support to Johnson in 1968. Meany endorsed the president for reelection as early as February 1967, praising Great Society legislation as "a record unsurpassed in any period of democratic government." When Johnson announced his unexpected decision not to seek reelection in March 1968, Meany immediately turned to Vice President HUBERT HUMPHREY, political heir to both the administration Great Society and the Vietnam War policies. The AFL-CIO vigorously supported Humphrey's candidacy in 1968 through computer-designed voter registration campaigns in 16 states and the massive distribution of literature. Noting Humphrey's rapid rise in popularity during the last part of the campaign, Meany later claimed that "if we had had another week we might have elected Hubert Humphrey."

Meany faced difficulties during the late 1960s not only in domestic politics but also on the policy-making Executive Council of the AFL-CIO. His main problem there was a growing conflict with Walter Reuther, head of the UAW and of the AFL-CIO Industrial Union Department. Reuther, more eloquent and outgoing than Meany, was his chief rival for leadership of the American union movement. As former leader of the CIO, he resented Meany's domination of the AFL-CIO's Executive Council. Reuther also clashed with Meany on a number of policy issues. Although opposed to the communist system, he disliked Meany's militant anticommunism, criticized U.S. policy in Vietnam, and favored relaxation of East-West tensions. Reuther protested in 1966, when Meany withdrew U.S. representatives from the International Labor Organization, a United Nations affiliate, after a Polish union leader had been elected president of the agency.

Another point of conflict between Reuther and Meany involved the growth of the union movement. Many observers noted during the 1960s that American labor was "resting on dead center." The membership of AFL-CIO–affiliated unions stagnated until 1964; it subsequently increased (from 12.7 million in 1964 to 15 million in 1968), but only at a rate equal to the expansion of the workforce. To stimulate union growth, Reuther repeatedly urged a large-scale organizing drive concentrating on farm laborers, white-collar employees, and workers in economically depressed areas. Meany, reflecting the traditions of craft unionism, showed less interest in organizing workers outside the "mainstream" of American labor; during the mid-1960s he suspended aid to the AFL-CIO–affiliated United Farm Workers Organizing Committee of CESAR CHAVEZ. Reuther objected to this fund cutoff and continued sending separate aid to Chavez through the UAW.

Relations between Meany and Reuther moved toward an open break in November 1966, when Reuther refused to attend a special Executive Council session to reaffirm the AFL-CIO stance in foreign affairs. Describing the federation as "the comfortable complacent custodian of the status quo," Reuther ordered UAW officials to resign their AFL-CIO positions in February 1967. In early 1968 the UAW began to withhold its dues from the AFL-CIO. Meany suspended the 1.6-million-member union from the federation on May 16, denouncing Reuther for failing to use the "democratic forums" the AFL-CIO provided for expression of dissent. Meany also criticized Reuther in September 1968 for joining Teamsters leader FRANK FITZSIMMONS

to form the Alliance for Labor Action (ALA). Meany viewed the new organization as an attempt to "raid" the membership of AFL-CIO unions, and he expelled the Chemical Workers Union from the federation when it joined the ALA in 1969.

With internal opposition largely eliminated from the AFL-CIO, Meany continued to control union policy during the early 1970s. The federation remained a strong supported of the Vietnam War under President RICHARD NIXON and withheld support from antiwar Senator GEORGE MCGOVERN (D-S.Dak.) in the 1972 presidential campaign. Meany initially cooperated in the Nixon administration's economic program but left the president's Pay Board in 1972, rejecting what he viewed as an overly restrictive wage policy. He eventually admitted that he had been wrong about the Vietnam War and complained that the federal government had misled the American people about U.S. policy in Southeast Asia. Meany remained president of the AFL-CIO until two months before his death on January 10, 1980.

—SLG

## Meredith, James H(oward)
(1933–  )  *civil rights activist*

Meredith, who was born on June 25, 1933, in Kosciusko, Mississippi, achieved fame in September 1962 as the first African American to enter the University of Mississippi at Oxford. His admission came after 15 months of litigation in federal courts, and it touched off a confrontation between the federal government and state officials who tried to prevent the court-ordered desegregation of "Ole Miss." Mississippi's governor Ross Barnett ended his resistance to Meredith's admission on September 30, 1962, but a riot erupted on the university campus that night and National Guard and army units had to be brought in to quell it. Meredith registered at the university on October 1, 1962, and had federal protection throughout his three terms there. He graduated with a B.A. in political science on August 18, 1963.

Meredith left Mississippi following his graduation but returned briefly in June 1966 for a march from Memphis, Tennessee, to Jackson, Mississippi. Then a second-year student at Columbia University Law School, Meredith said on May 31 that his march was intended to encourage voter registration among Mississippi's blacks and to "challenge the all-pervasive and overriding fear that dominates the day-to-day life of the Negro in the United States—especially in the South and particularly in Mississippi." He began his walk on June 5 accompanied by a few friends. The next day, about 10 miles over the Mississippi border, Meredith was shot from ambush along U.S. Highway 51. He suffered over 60 superficial wounds in the head, back and legs and was taken to a Memphis hospital for emergency surgery. On June 7 civil rights leaders MARTIN LUTHER KING, JR., FLOYD MCKISSICK, and STOKELY CARMICHAEL retraced Meredith's route. On their return to Memphis that evening, they vowed to carry on his march all the way to Jackson. The march was resumed on June 8. During its three-week course divisions among the leadership became increasingly apparent. While King continued to speak of interracial cooperation and nonviolence, Carmichael called for Black Power and urged self-defense rather than nonviolence when attacked.

Meredith himself returned to New York City on June 8 to recuperate. There he occasionally expressed some criticism of the way the march was run, but he rejoined the march on June 25 at Canton, Mississippi, and spoke at a final rally in Jackson on June 26. By the end of the march, however, Meredith's original protest had been overshadowed by indications of a schism among the major civil rights leaders.

Meredith, who was considered a loner and an individualist within the civil rights movement, expressed support for Carmichael and the Black Power concept in a television interview in August 1966. He asserted that America was "a military-minded nation" and that nonviolence was "incompatible with American ideas." In the same interview Meredith said he "fully" supported the war in Vietnam and considered it "one of the best things happening to the Negro."

After Harlem representative ADAM CLAYTON POWELL, JR. (D-N.Y.) was excluded from the House of Representatives on March 1, 1967, Meredith announced that he would run on the Republican ticket in a special election for Powell's seat scheduled for April. Meredith said he was acting in accordance with his "divine responsibility," but local black leaders almost unanimously opposed his candidacy. On March 13, after meeting with Floyd McKissick of the Congress of Racial Equality and Mississippi rights leader CHARLES EVERS, Meredith withdrew from the race. He went back to Mississippi on June 24, 1967, to complete the march

against fear he had initiated the year before. Meredith walked from the place where he had been shot to Canton, Mississippi, the town where he had rejoined the 1966 march.

Following his graduation from law school, Meredith entered business in New York City. In July 1969 he staged a walk from Chicago to New York to "promote Negro pride and positive goals in the black community." Meredith announced in June 1971 that he was moving back to Mississippi. He said that the racial atmosphere in the South had improved greatly and that on a "day-to-day basis," it was a "more liveable place for blacks." In February 1972 he entered the race for the Republican Senate nomination in Mississippi but lost in the July primary election. He was involved with several unsuccessful businesses, and his political views became conservative and, at times, extreme. Criticizing white liberals for most national problems, he worked on the staff of Senator Jesse Helms (R-N.C.) and supported David Duke, a former member of the Ku Klux Klan, for governor of Louisiana in the early 1990s.

—CAB

## Metcalf, Lee
(1911–1978) *member of the Senate*

Prior to his election to the Senate in 1960, Metcalf, who was born on January 28, 1911, in Stevensville, Montana, had served as a state legislator and associate justice of the Montana Supreme Court. From 1953 to 1961 he represented Montana in the House of Representatives, where he was a major supporter of conservation measures. In the lower house Metcalf was part of a group of liberals pushing for progressive social legislation and reform of congressional procedures. While in the Senate Metcalf supported most Kennedy and Johnson administration domestic programs.

During the 1960s the senator focused his attention on three major areas: education, the regulation of power companies, and conservation. In 1965 Metcalf steered the Elementary and Secondary Education Act, which gave aid to impoverished inner-city and rural schools, through the Senate. A year later he led efforts to extend G.I. Bill educational benefits to recent veterans and to improve vocational training programs.

Metcalf had long been an opponent of private utility companies because he believed they used excessive profits to subsidize conservative political activity and propaganda favorable to the industry. In 1967 he published *Overcharge*, a detailed examination of the industry. In his book the senator scored state regulation of the companies as a failure because the government did not have the resources to discipline the utilities. The following year Metcalf unsuccessfully introduced a bill to set up an office of consumers' counsel to represent the public before regulatory commissions.

In the field of conservation Metcalf unsuccessfully introduced the 1962 "save our streams" bill to protect recreational resources from destruction by federal highway development and sponsored the Senate version of the Wilderness Act, which led to the establishment of the National Wilderness Preservation System in 1964. One year later he worked for the passage of the Water Systems Act, which increased expenditures for watershed restoration.

During 1965 and 1966 Metcalf served on the Joint Committee on the Organization of Congress. The committee report, issued in July 1966, recommended a series of steps designed to reform and modernize the legislature. These included: curtailing the power of committee chairs; creating new committees to reflect growing public concerns; opening committee sessions to the public; and decreasing the workloads of individual senators. No action was taken on these measures in 1966.

During the late 1960s and early 1970s Metcalf continued to be a strong supporter of conservation and consumer legislation. In addition, he campaigned for reassertion of congressional authority over spending as a way of curbing excessive presidential power. Metcalf served in the Senate until his death on January 12, 1978.

—EWS

## Miller, George (Paul)

### (1891–1982) *member of the House of Representatives*

Miller, who was born on January 15, 1891, in San Francisco, represented California's Eighth Congressional District, which included southern Oakland, several of the city's suburbs, and part of rural Alameda County. Most of the district's voters belonged to white blue-collar families. In the 1940s, 1950s, and early 1960s, he compiled a moderately liberal voting record. Interested in scientific matters, Miller was chair of the House Merchant Marine and Fisheries Committee's Subcommittee on Oceanography in the late 1950s. In 1961 he became chair of the House Science and Astronautics Committee. In the latter post he enthusiastically supported the Kennedy administration's space program.

During the presidency of LYNDON B. JOHNSON, Miller generally backed administration policies. According to *Congressional Quarterly*, he never opposed the administration position on more than 5 percent of the key House roll call votes in any of the years of President Johnson's tenure. His support of the president's policies included approval of the conduct of the Vietnam War and of large military expenditures.

Miller continued to endorse large appropriations for the National Aeronautics and Space Administration during the Johnson administration. In 1967 the president awarded him the Goddard Prize for his contributions in the space field. Miller was also a staunch supporter of federal grants for scientific research. He was appointed to the House Select Committee on Government Research in September 1963. Early in the following year he stated that the panel's preliminary report of February 1964 did not give sufficient recognition to the important contributions of federally supported research programs in improving the quality of American life in the areas of transportation, medicine, energy production, and communications.

In the late 1960s and early 1970s Miller's views remained substantially unchanged, when many liberals were becoming increasingly disenchanted with the Vietnam War, large military budgets, unrestricted technological growth, and the space program. As a result Miller lost the 1972 Democratic primary in his district to a candidate who represented this trend.

—NLL

## Miller, Jack (Richard)

### (1916–1994) *member of the Senate*

Born in Chicago on June 6, 1916, Jack Miller and his family moved to Sioux City, Iowa, in 1932. He received his A.B. from Creighton University and his LL.B. from Columbia. Miller served as an instructor in the air force during World War II. Returning to Iowa, Miller practiced law in Sioux City and intermittently lectured on taxation law. Although largely unknown in the state despite six years in the Iowa legislature, Miller won the 1960 GOP senatorial nomination. With just under 52 percent of the vote, he narrowly upset Democratic governor Herschel Loveless, a victim of John Kennedy's poor showing in Iowa. Miller easily won reelection in 1966, carrying every county.

In the Senate Miller was a moderate conservative, voting with the majority of his Republican Senate colleagues on almost every issue. Like them he voted for the 1963 nuclear test ban treaty and the 1964 and 1965 civil rights acts. He opposed Medicare legislation in 1962, 1964, and 1965 and the 1968 Civil Rights Act. The conservative Americans for Constitutional Action gave Miller a "correct" rating of 78 for his Senate votes during the 1960s. Miller's predictability and unexciting personality led journalists David Broder and Stephen Hess to describe him as "a most anonymous Senator from Iowa."

Miller gained notoriety in the Senate for his submissions of last-minute amendments to bills without regard to the legislative strategy of the party hierarchy. This tactic annoyed Senate Minority Leader EVERETT M. DIRKSEN (R-Ill.), while Senator THRUSTON B. MORTON (R-Ky.) dubbed him "Jack-the-Amendment" Miller. Many Senate observers felt that Miller used amendments to make his position on many issues ambiguous, developing over the years "a voting record which can be used to prove almost anything." Miller himself viewed his position as "conservative in monetary and fiscal affairs" and "liberal in the areas of education and human rights." During the Senate voting on the committee investigation of former secretary to the senate majority BOBBY BAKER in April and September 1964, Miller offered amendments (later defeated) that explicitly called for an inquiry into President Johnson's alleged involvement.

In August 1964 and June 1965 Miller introduced provisions to the annual foreign aid bill that would have denied all U.S. assistance to United Nations–member states failing to pay their UN dues and assessments. About 96 percent of the nations receiving U.S. aid, Miller claimed in July 1966, would be affected by his legislation. That month the Senate finally agreed to a version of the Miller ban giving the president the right to waive the provision in the "national interest."

A September 1965 Miller proposal would have reversed the Democratic leadership's plan to weaken the stringent 1952 McCarran Immigration Restriction Act. By voice vote the Senate rejected Miller's

amendment to set a 290,000-person annual quota or entry limit. Miller eventually voted for the final, more liberal legislation, which eliminated most ethnic and racial quotas.

A member of the Armed Services Committee, Miller consistently backed an aggressive military policy in the Vietnam War. In September 1967 he told reporters that if an intensified bombing of North Vietnam "might shorten the war, even by one day, then we ought to take the risks." Later that month he and three other GOP Senate "hawks" criticized Senator JOHN SHERMAN COOPER (R-Ky.), the senior Republican on the Foreign Relations Committee, for favoring a halt to the bombing as a signal of America's willingness to negotiate. Similarly, near the end of the North Vietnamese Tet offensive in February 1968, when some party colleagues began to back away from their earlier support of the war, Miller recommended expanded bombing of the North.

At the August 1968 Republican National Convention, Miller strongly opposed the designation of Governor SPIRO T. AGNEW for vice president. Judging Agnew an obscure and weak addition to the national ticket, Miller and an unusual alliance of liberal and conservative party figures urged New York City mayor JOHN V. LINDSAY to run against the Maryland governor. Lindsay refused, and the anti-Agnew coalition nominated Michigan governor GEORGE W. ROMNEY, who lost by a wide margin.

Between 1969 and 1972 Miller steadfastly supported the incumbent Republican administration. Up for reelection in 1972, Miller underrated his opposition, congressional aide Dick Clark, and lost, with only 43 percent of the vote, in a stunning upset.

After leaving the Senate he was a judge of the U.S. Court of Customs and Patent Appeals from 1973 to 1982. He died on August 29, 1994.

—JLB

## Miller, William E(dward)
(1914–1983) *member of the House of Representatives; chair, Republican National Committee; Republican vice presidential candidate*

The son of a janitor, William E. Miller, who was born on March 22, 1914, in Lockport, New York, received a B.A. from Notre Dame in 1935 and a LL.B with honors from Union University Law

School in 1938. During World War II Miller served with U.S. Army Intelligence and in 1946 was an assistant prosecutor at the Nuremberg war crimes trials. In 1950 Miller won election to the first of seven consecutive terms in the House of Representatives as a Republican from a western New York district. As chair of the Republican Congressional Campaign Committee in 1960, Miller campaigned personally in 34 states. In November the GOP gained 22 seats. Miller received substantial credit for the party's success, and, in June 1961, he was elected chair of the Republican National Committee. In the next three years, Miller gave over 500 sharply partisan speeches in 49 states. Under his leadership the national committee eliminated a $750,000 debt and appropriated funds for "Operation Dixie," designed to make the Republicans more competitive in southern elections. In the 1962 elections, however, the GOP gained only two seats in the House and lost two in the Senate. Republicans replaced Democratic governors in Ohio, Pennsylvania, and Michigan, but losses in other states kept the number of GOP governors limited to 16.

Although the second-ranking Republican on the House Judiciary Committee, Miller played a limited role in Congress. Voting on only 33 percent of the roll call votes in 1964 and 41 percent in the 88th Congress, Miller held the lowest voting participation record of New York's 41-member delegation. A partisan representative, Miller supported the Kennedy and Johnson administrations on only 15 percent of the votes for which the White House announced a position in 1963–64. However, with the majority of his party colleagues in the House, Miller voted for the administration's civil rights bill in February 1964.

Miller remained neutral through the bitter struggle for the 1964 Republican presidential nomination. In January 1964 he announced that he would not seek reelection to Congress in November and would step down as party chair following the Republican National Convention in July. F. CLIFTON WHITE, a key lieutenant in the campaign of Senator BARRY M. GOLDWATER (R-Ariz.), claimed that Miller tended to favor the anti-Goldwater forces. Following Goldwater's victory in the June 2 California primary, however, Miller urged all party leaders to unite behind the Arizona senator and avoid a potentially divisive effort to deny him the nomination. Pennsylvania

governor WILLIAM W. SCRANTON, Goldwater's tentative choice for a running mate, declined to follow Miller's advice and waged a desperate month-long campaign for the nomination. Scranton's unsuccessful effort eliminated him from consideration by Goldwater for the vice presidential nomination.

Following his nomination on July 15, Goldwater chose Miller as his vice presidential candidate, and the Republican convention nominated the New Yorker the next day. In naming Miller, Goldwater hoped to aid his campaign in the South and among Catholic voters. Because of his advocacy of Operation Dixie while party chair, Miller enjoyed the support of southern delegates. Since Miller was a Roman Catholic, Goldwater believed that Johnson would feel compelled to choose Attorney General ROBERT F. KENNEDY, a Catholic, as his running mate to prevent defections by Catholic voters to the GOP. Because of the unpopularity of Kennedy's leadership of the Justice Department among many southerners, Goldwater thought that Kennedy's position on the ticket would increase his base of southern support. Johnson never wanted Kennedy as his running mate, and he gave only limited consideration to choosing EUGENE J. MCCARTHY, also a Catholic. When polls indicated that the president would overwhelmingly defeat the Goldwater ticket, he selected HUBERT H. HUMPHREY (D-Minn.), who had been his first choice all along.

Although well known among party professionals, Miller never overcame his lack of national recognition. His nomination represented another opportunity lost by Goldwater to placate bitter party liberals and moderates, for Miller held nearly as conservative a voting record as the Arizona senator. The presidential nominee justified his selection by saying that Miller's partisanship "drives Johnson nuts." Because of his running mate's qualities as a "gut fighter," Goldwater reportedly believed he himself could campaign on a more statesmanlike level.

Miller campaigned in 40 states and traveled over 40,000 miles for the national ticket. In August he attacked Johnson for his ownership of an Austin, Texas, radio-television station and alleged that the president had made more than $10 million as a result of favorable treatment by federal regulators when Johnson served in the Senate. The same month Miller criticized Johnson's brief military service during World War II. The Goldwater staff mildly rebuked him because of its fear that such attacks would provoke sympathy for the president. Undaunted, Miller turned his attention to Humphrey in September, describing his Senate record as "clearly one of the most radical in Congress." He denounced Humphrey's close ties with the liberal Americans for Democratic Action, which he declared "preaches a philosophy of foreign socialist totalitarianism." When Washington police in October arrested White House aide WALTER W. JENKINS on a morals charge, Miller derided the White House contention that "this type of man" did not "compromise national security."

Miller faced charges of conflict of interest in late September when columnist DREW PEARSON alleged that as a member of Congress in 1951 or 1952 Miller had offered then representative Frank Smith (D-Miss.) $350 to $500 a month as a public relations consultant for Lockport Felt Company if he voted for legislation favored by that upstate New York company. Miller owned a part of Lockport Felt and received an annual retainer of $7,500 from the company. He denied any wrongdoing and accused his Democratic detractors of "Gestapo tactics" and "sleazy, unsubstantiated smears." On October 1 Representative W. DON EDWARDS (D-Calif.) demanded a House investigation, but the Democratic leadership declined to pursue the charge. Edwards and others also criticized Miller for keeping one of his Buffalo, New York, law partners on his congressional payroll.

On November 3, 1964, Goldwater and Miller polled but 38.5 percent of the vote and carried only five southern states and Arizona. Two weeks after the election, Miller became a vice president of Lockport Felt. In 1968 he helped plan the campaign of Governor NELSON A. ROCKEFELLER (R-N.Y.) for the Republican presidential nomination, and he seconded Rockefeller's name at the August 1968 Republican National Convention. He opposed the nomination of Governor SPIRO T. AGNEW (R-Md.) for vice president. In 1975, Miller used his obscurity to become a celebrity when he appeared in a television commercial for the American Express credit card and asked, "Do you know me?" He was the first political figure to participate in a major national advertising campaign on television. He died of a stroke on June 24, 1983.

—JLB

## Mills, Wilbur D(aigh)
### (1909–1992) *member of the House of Representatives*

Mills, who was born on May 24, 1909, in Kensett, Arkansas, attended Arkansas public schools and Methodist-affiliated Hendrix College before entering Harvard Law School in 1930. He returned to Arkansas without receiving a degree in 1933, taking a job as a cashier in his father's bank. In 1934 he was elected county and probate judge for White County and remained in that post until his election to the House of Representatives in 1938. Mills was reelected in every subsequent election with little or no opposition.

Joining the tax-writing Ways and Means Committee in 1943, Mills industriously applied himself to his work, becoming by the 1950s the House's foremost tax expert. He compiled a moderate voting record and joined his southern colleagues in voting against all civil rights proposals. In late 1957 Mills became chair of the Ways and Means Committee; he was the youngest representative ever to hold that post.

The peculiar structure of the Ways and Means Committee and the committee's prestige and unique prerogatives within the House enabled Mills to exert extraordinary influence on the writing of tax laws. In addition to its economic responsibilities, the Ways and Means Committee also functioned as the Committee on Committees, doling out committee assignments to House members. Mills was at the center of this crucial process. The fact that Ways and Means, alone among House committees, had no subcommittees further centralized its legislative responsibilities in Mills's hands. Bills emerging from the committee, moreover, operated on the House floor under a "closed rule," meaning that no amendments were permitted; only total approval or absolute rejection was possible.

The result was almost always approval, in part because of Mills's impressive abilities. No member of Congress could match his vast knowledge of the tax laws. Most stood in awe of his mastery of the complex subject matter, and many owed their grasp of complicated bills to Mills's lucid explanations, which at times brought members of both parties to their feet in applause. Equally important to Mills's success on the floor of the House was his insistence on achieving a consensus in committee. He refused to report out controversial measures by narrow majorities, preferring to delay, remove, or water down controversial features until he had attained unanimity or a large majority. By compromising in the committee he managed to head off potential opposition in the House. Consistently smooth passage of measures introduced by Mills enhanced his aura of power. However, his fear that a defeat on the floor of the House would diminish that aura often led him to pursue a strategy of delay on important legislation until he felt assured of a safe majority.

Until 1965 Mills was the principal congressional obstacle to passage of the Kennedy-Johnson administration's Medicare program. Medicare, a plan to finance medical care for the aged through the Social Security system, had been bottled up in the Ways and Means Committee for almost a decade. Mills had basic doubts as to the fiscal prudence of the plan. He also worried that the measure could not pass the House. Even if he could have pushed the bill through the committee by a slim majority, he resisted doing so, fearing defeat on the floor of the House and the wrath of the medical establishment if he provided the decisive vote. The Senate finally approved Medicare in September 1964 as an amendment to a Social Security increase, but Mills engineered the amendment's defeat in the House-Senate conference the next month.

Mills ended his opposition to Medicare after the election of 1964 returned pro-Medicare majorities to the House and the Ways and Means Committee. Faced with its inevitable passage he shifted to support of the program and became its principal legislative architect.

The compromise legislation that Mills crafted in March 1965 was a response to a tactical shift on the part of House Republicans and the American Medical Association (AMA), the most vociferous and unrelenting foe of compulsory medical insurance for the aged. In addition to its traditional denunciation of Medicare as "socialized medicine," the AMA began to attack the program as inadequate because its proposed benefits covered hospital costs but not doctors' fees. Instead, the AMA proposed a plan that would provide subsidized, voluntary health insurance and pay hospital and physicians' costs and that would be available without charge to the poor. Representative JOHN BYRNES (R-Wisc.), ranking Republican on the Ways and Means Committee, offered yet another alternative, one financed through a combination of tax revenues and individual contributions, graduated according to income.

In a surprise move Mills combined elements of all competing plans into what he called a "three-layer cake." The first part of the plan paid for hospital and nursing home costs through increased Social Security taxes; the second part took care of doctors' fees through federal subsidies and monthly contributions by individuals; the third part—Medicaid—provided health care benefits to the medically indigent. "It took the most brilliant legislative move I'd seen in 30 years," said Assistant Secretary of Health, Education and Welfare WILBUR COHEN. "In effect, Mills had taken the AMA's ammunition, put it in the Republicans' gun, and blown both of them off the map."

On March 23 Mills's Medicare package passed the committee in a 17-8 straight party-line vote. He introduced the measure in the House on April 8. After defeating the Republicans' voluntary health plan by a 236-191 vote, the House passed the Mills proposal 313-115. Following Senate passage of a more extensive program in July, Mills eliminated most of the Senate additions in the House-Senate conference on the bill. Yet, in its final form Medicare was far more comprehensive than the limited versions he had opposed for years.

Mills again became the center of attention in 1967 and 1968 with his opposition to the administration's August 1967 request for a 10 percent tax surcharge to curb inflation. His demand that the tax increase be accompanied by $6 billion in budget cuts involved him in a 10-month confrontation with the Johnson administration. At the committee's hearings Mills questioned administration representatives as to why they had consistently underestimated expenses and overestimated revenues. In October the committee voted 20-5 to postpone action on the tax request until the administration had made sufficient budget cuts. Secretary of the Treasury HENRY FOWLER and Budget director CHARLES SCHULTZE returned to the committee in late November to pledge $4 billion in budget cuts, but Mills declared that the figure was not high enough and that his committee needed "more, particularly more specific, information" about administration spending plans before any increase would be enacted. The impasse continued through the first half of 1968. In June the administration finally agreed to the $6 billion reduction. The measure passed the Ways and Means Committee, and Mills steered it through the House by a 268-150 vote.

Mills's voting record was considerably more conservative in the second half of the 1960s than the earlier part of the decade. He voted for major measures favored by the liberal Americans for Democratic Action 69 percent of the time in 1964, 37 percent in 1965, 6 percent in 1966, 20 percent in 1967, and 8 percent in 1968. He backed the Vietnam War and consistently voted against civil rights bills. Although Mills favored a total overhaul of the tax code, he did manage to guide more limited tax reform legislation through Congress during the first year of RICHARD M. NIXON's presidency.

In late 1974 Mills resigned under pressure as chair of the Ways and Means Committee because of a scandal involving his relationship with an Argentine striptease dancer and his public confession of alcoholism and addiction to prescription drugs. He did not seek reelection to the House in November 1976. He died on May 2, 1992.

—TO

## Mink, Patsy T(akemoto)
### (1927–2002) *member of the House of Representatives*

Born in Hawaii of Japanese ancestry on December 6, 1927, Mink graduated from the University of Hawaii in 1948 and received a law degree from the University of Chicago in 1951. Mink found that no law firm would hire her, because of discrimination on account of race and sex, and so she began teaching business law at the University of Hawaii in the 1950s, while the state Democratic Party consolidated its near-dominance of the territory's politics. Mink was active in the Hawaii Young Democrats and became its president in 1956. She was elected to the territorial legislature in 1955 and entered the Democratic congressional primary in 1959. Unsuccessful in that attempt, Mink won election in 1964 as one of Hawaii's two representatives-at-large.

A consistent liberal, Mink was an enthusiastic supporter of President Johnson's Great Society legislation and won an Americans for Democratic Action rating of 100 percent in 1968. Mink usually voted in accordance with AFL-CIO preferences, which was not surprising since the International Longshoremen and Warehousemen's Union was a primary source of strength for Hawaii's Democrats. A member of the House Education and Labor Committee and the Interior and Insular Affairs Committee, Mink was particularly concerned with educational legislation. In 1965 she sponsored a successful bill for the construction of schools in the Pacific territories. Her proposal to use federal money to help maintain a 3 percent interest rate on private loans for college construction programs was incorporated into the 1967 Housing and Urban Development Act. Mink introduced a bill in May of 1967 to appropriate $300 million for public and private, nonprofit day-care centers. Her efforts on behalf of day-care programs continued beyond the bill's defeat and culminated in the Child Development Act of 1971, a measure that cleared Congress but was vetoed by President Nixon. She also sponsored legislation favorable to residents of U.S. possessions in the Pacific.

Mink supported early military appropriations for Vietnam. However, in March 1967, despite the dependence of Hawaii's economy on federal defense expenditures, she was one of 18 House members who supported a bill that would have prohibited the use of supplemental defense funds for Vietnam.

Mink won her bids for reelection easily and in 1970 ran unopposed in the newly organized second district. She became an increasingly vocal opponent of U.S. policies in Indochina and a congressional spokesperson for feminist issues. Mink entered the

Hawaii representative Patsy Mink, 1972 *(Library of Congress, Prints and Photographs Division)*

1972 presidential primaries but withdrew before the Democratic convention. After losing the Democratic nomination for the Senate in the party primary in 1976, Mink left the House when her term expired in 1977. She returned to the lower chamber in 1990 and held her seat until her death on September 28, 2002.

—MDB

## Mitchell, Clarence M.
(1911–1984) *director, Washington Bureau, NAACP*

Born on March 8, 1911, in Baltimore, Maryland, Mitchell, an African-American attorney, served as executive director of the National Urban League Office in St. Paul, Minnesota, from 1937 until 1941. During World War II, he worked for various federal agencies, including the Fair Employment Practices Committee, before joining the Washington bureau of the NAACP in 1946. In 1950 he became the bureau's director. His major function in that post was serving as the organization's lobbyist for civil rights measures in the legislative and executive branches of the federal government.

The NAACP and other civil rights groups criticized the administration of John F. Kennedy for its failure to introduce significant antidiscrimination bills in the early 1960s. Mitchell charged that the problem was not the absence of a strong constituency for such measures but the unwillingness of the president to press vigorously for civil rights laws. In 1962 and early 1963 he testified before congressional committees in favor of antibias riders to federal aid bills, but these provisos did not have administration support and were not passed by Congress. Kennedy introduced a civil rights bill in June 1963, but Mitchell denounced the administration's subsequent opposition to strengthening amendments added by a House Judiciary Committee subcommittee.

President LYNDON B. JOHNSON's strong efforts on behalf of civil rights legislation, however, were welcomed and supported by Mitchell and most other rights leaders. On Capitol Hill Mitchell lobbied intensively on behalf of the Civil Rights Act of 1964 and the Voting Rights Act of 1965. In March 1968 he worked closely with House Democratic leaders in an effort to overcome southern Democratic and Republican resistance to the administration's open housing bill, covering four-fifths of the nation's housing, which had already been passed by the Senate. Representative GERALD R. FORD (R-Mich.), the minority leader, wanted a House-Senate conference committee to modify the bill, which was stalled in the House Rules Committee. But Democratic managers of the bill, after meeting with Mitchell, decided to press for the administration version. The assassination of MARTIN LUTHER KING, JR., on April 4 helped generate the additional support needed to bring the bill out of the Rules Committee and pass it on the House floor.

Mitchell was a staunch defender of the administration's antipoverty program. Many Republicans charged that the urban riots of the summer of 1967 demonstrated the failure of the program and sought to reduce its budget. Mitchell denounced the attacks on the program as political opportunism and, contending that the riots stemmed from injustice, urged an increase in antipoverty funds.

Although some blacks regarded President Johnson's civil rights record as inadequate, Mitchell defended it in a speech to the NAACP Southeast Regional Conference in April 1968. He praised the president's contributions to the welfare of blacks, citing the civil rights acts of 1964, 1965, and 1968, the antipoverty program, and the appointment of two African Americans, ROBERT C. WEAVER and THURGOOD MARSHALL, as secretary of housing and urban development and Supreme Court justice, respectively. President Johnson, he asserted, "has given more successful leadership on civil rights than any other President of the United States."

Mitchell, supporting the Johnson administration and unsympathetic to the peace movement, backed Vice President HUBERT H. HUMPHREY's bid for the Democratic presidential nomination in 1968. In December 1968 he criticized President-elect RICHARD M. NIXON's plan to promote black-owned businesses. Some civil rights leaders, disagreed and supported the program. But Mitchell feared it represented "a desire on the part of some to shift away the government assistance to the private enterprise approach" under which the benefits would "trickle down" from wealthy entrepreneurs to the poor.

Mitchell regarded the Nixon administration's civil rights record as retrogressive. He opposed the president's 1969 effort to replace the Voting Rights Act of 1965 with a new bill, charging that the administration was seeking to stem the tide of civil rights progress in order to win southern segregationist support. Three years later he denounced the president's legislative proposals to limit busing as "the most blatant products of racism that I have seen in the federal government.

Mitchell retired from his position with the NAACP and returned to private law practice in 1978. He died of a heart attack on March 18, 1984.

—MLL

## Mondale, Walter F(rederick)

(1928– )   *member of the Senate*

Born on January 5, 1928, Walter Mondale grew up in the village of Ceylon, Minnesota, graduated from the University of Minnesota in 1951, and served in the army during the Korean War. He took his law degree from the University of Minnesota in 1956 and that same year began practice with the prestigious Minneapolis law firm of Larson, Loevinger, Lindquist, Freeman and Fraser. Mondale first entered politics in 1958 as campaign manager for Governor ORVILLE L. FREEMAN, who had been a partner in Larson, Loevinger. After serving for two years as a special assistant to the state's attorney general, Mondale was appointed by Freeman in May 1960 to fill out Miles W. Lord's unexpired term as attorney general. He was elected to a full term in November of that year and reelected two years later. In 1963 Mondale received national attention for filing an amicus curiae brief with the U.S. Supreme Court in defense of Clarence Early Gideon, a Florida convict who had petitioned the Court in order to establish the right of a defendant to free counsel. Mondale also played a leading role, as a member of the Credentials Committee at the 1964 Democratic National Convention, in devising a compromise in the dispute over the seating of the Mississippi Freedom Democratic Party, an integrated delegation that challenged the all-white regular Mississippi representatives.

In November 1964 Governor Karl F. Rolvaag appointed Mondale to the U.S. Senate seat vacated by Senator HUBERT H. HUMPHREY (D-Minn.) shortly after Humphrey's election as vice president. Mondale was assigned to the Senate Aeronautical and Space Sciences, Banking and Currency and Agriculture and Forestry Committees. Regarded as an activist liberal with a special interest in the disadvantaged, he supported Johnson administration policies on over 70 percent of all major issues.

In 1965 Mondale supported the Elementary and Secondary Education Act, the Voting Rights Act, and Medicare. The next year he introduced nearly 100 bills in the Senate, including an amendment to the administration's traffic and motor vehicle safety bill to require auto makers to shoulder more responsibility for safety defects in automobiles and to require public disclosure of such defects. In November 1966 Mondale defeated his Republican opponent, Robert A. Forsythe, by 100,000 votes and won a full term in the Senate.

Mondale remained one of the Senate's strongest advocates of automobile safety. In 1967 he expressed concern that car prices in 1968 would be substantially higher than those of 1967 and joined with consumer advocate RALPH NADER to protest the increases. Mondale declared, "One begins to wonder whether safety is being used as an excuse to raise prices or whether price increases are being used to promote opposition to future vehicle safety standards—or perhaps both."

Mondale led the fight for the open housing amendment in the 1968 civil rights bill, which in its modified form prohibited discrimination in the sale or rental of about 80 percent of the nation's housing. The open housing amendment was passed only after Senate Republican leader EVERETT M. DIRKSEN (R-Ill.) switched from opposition to support of the measure. After adoption of the amendment Mondale stated that it was "far stronger than we believed possible."

During the Nixon administration Mondale continued as one of the Senate's most prominent liberals. He won another Senate term in 1972. In 1977, he became vice president in the administration of President Jimmy Carter. When the Carter-Mondale ticket failed to win reelection, Mondale returned to private law practice but soon began seeking the Democratic nomination for president. As his party's presidential nominee, he lost in a landslide to Ronald Reagan in 1984. Mondale served as ambassador to Japan, from 1993 to 1996. He lost in a final run for the Senate in 2002, as a last-minute replacement for Minnesota's incumbent Democrat, Paul Wellstone, who had died in a plane crash just two weeks before the election.

—FHM

## Monroney, A(lmer) S(tillwell) Mike

(1902–1980)   *member of the Senate*

A 1924 graduate of the University of Oklahoma, Monroney, who was born on March 2, 1902, in Oklahoma City, was a political reporter for the *Oklahoma*

*News* from 1924 to 1928. He then ran the family furniture business in Oklahoma City. Elected to the House of Representatives in 1938, Monroney served six terms there before winning a Senate seat in 1950. In both chambers he supported most liberal domestic legislation and became known as an advocate of congressional reorganization and of aviation interests.

Chair of the Aviation Subcommittee of the Senate Commerce Committee, Monroney sponsored bills extending the federal aid-to-airports program, which passed Congress in 1964 and 1966. After an intensive two-year study, his subcommittee reported in January 1968 on current and anticipated problems in the national airport system and recommended new federal financing methods, including establishment of an airport trust fund. In June 1968 Monroney introduced the administration's airport development act, but Congress took no action that year on this or other proposals to relieve the problem of airport congestion. Monroney also supported development of the controversial supersonic transport (SST) and opposed efforts to decrease federal funding of the program.

In 1965 Monroney was a co-chair of the Joint Committee on the Organization of Congress, which conducted the first major review of congressional operations since 1946. The committee was barred from proposing changes in House or Senate rules, and its July 1966 report also avoided the controversial question of altering the seniority system. The report did, however, recommend many reforms in committee structure, procedures, and staffing, changes in Congress' work schedule, and other measures to streamline legislative operations, to evaluate and review the budget, and to regulate lobbyists. Monroney sponsored bills embodying most of the committee's recommendations in 1966 and again in 1967. Passed by the Senate, they were bottled up by the House Rules Committee through the end of the 90th Congress.

Monroney became chair of the Senate Post Office and Civil Service Committee in April 1965. He served as Senate floor manager between 1966 and 1968 for several bills raising postal rates and the salaries of federal employees and appropriating funds for the Post Office and Treasury Departments. In July 1965 he was named a member of the newly established Senate Ethics Committee and participated in its investigation of charges of misconduct by Senator THOMAS J. DODD (D-Conn.). Monroney supported the Sen-

ate's censure of Dodd for misuse of political funds in June 1967.

Monroney usually voted for the Johnson administration's domestic and foreign policy programs, supporting civil rights and Great Society measures and U.S. policy in Vietnam. Trying for a fourth Senate term in 1968, Monroney easily defeated four opponents in the August Democratic primary, but he lost the November election by some 33,000 votes to his Republican opponent. He worked as a consultant in the aviation industry before retiring in 1974. He died on February 13, 1980.

—CAB

## Montoya, Joseph
### (1915–1978)  *member of the Senate*

Montoya, the son of a county sheriff and politician, was born on September 24, 1915, in Penablanca, grew up in northern New Mexico. He studied at Regis College in Denver and Georgetown University, where he received an LL.B. in 1938. Montoya's political career began in 1936, when he won election to the New Mexico House of Representatives. He remained in the state legislature for 10 years and subsequently served four terms as lieutenant governor. Montoya was elected to the U.S. House of Representatives in 1957; he served in the House until 1964, when he defeated a conservative Republican to become the junior senator from New Mexico.

Montoya's main problem as both a representative and a senator was how to satisfy the diverse elements of his constituency, ranging from the liberal Spanish Americans and Indians of northern New Mexico to the conservative whites of Albuquerque and "little Texas" in southeastern New Mexico. He survived politically by establishing himself as a moderate and paying close attention to legislation that directly benefited his constituents. During the mid-1960s Montoya was a strong advocate of land reclamation projects, agricultural price supports, aid to small business, and vocational training programs for unemployed and migrant workers. On these and other issues he was an ally of Senator ROBERT BYRD (D-W.Va.), whose state resembled Montoya's in its chronic high unemployment and heavy dependency on federal aid. Montoya's Senate committee assignments—Agriculture and Forestry, Public Works, Small Business, and Government Operations—

enabled him to influence key aid legislation affecting New Mexico during the mid-1960s.

Montoya's political moderation made him a "swing" voter on many issues of national importance. The rating he received from the liberal Americans for Democratic Action ranged from 82 percent "correct" in 1965 to 36 percent "correct" in 1968. He was a member of the U.S. delegations to several inter-American conferences, and he supported the Alliance for Progress as a way to halt the spread of communism in Latin America. Yet he was an early critic of U.S. military involvement in Vietnam and consistently supported congressional attempts to limit the war. He also worked to limit military spending despite the heavy dependence of New Mexico industry on defense contracts and military installations. He also supported consumer protection; in 1969 he proposed creation of an independent agency for consumer affairs.

Montoya was reelected to the Senate in a hard-fought 1970 campaign with 52 percent of the vote. During the early 1970s he clashed repeatedly with the Nixon administration over agricultural policy. Montoya gained national prominence in 1973, when he was named to the Senate committee that investigated the Watergate affair. Beset by allegations of financial irregularities, he lost his bid for a third term in the Senate in 1976. He died on June 5, 1978.

—SLG

## Moore, Daniel K(illian)
### (1906–1986) *governor*

An attorney and jurist, Moore, who was born on April 2, 1906, in Asheville, North Carolina, was a judge on the North Carolina Superior Court from 1948 to 1958. After returning to private life as chief counsel for a paper company, Moore entered the June 1964 Democratic primary. Moore was pitted against Governor TERRY SANDFORD's handpicked successor, L. Richardson Preyer, and militant segregationist I. Beverly Lake. The primary provided a clear-cut battle between the state's liberals and conservatives. Preyer was the candidate of youthful progressives committed to policies in line with those of the national Democratic Party. Moore, with the backing of the state's oldline conservatives, defined his position as middle of the road in matters of racial and economic policy. Moore finished second, polling 34 percent of the vote. Preyer took 37 percent.

Because no candidate had won a majority, a runoff was held. Moore campaigned as a candidate of common sense surrounded by racial and economic extremists. He depicted Preyer as too radical for North Carolina and as compromised by his support from "tremendous financial interests" and "other special interests including the high leadership of the AFL-CIO and the NAACP." Moore promised to enforce any law passed by Congress but viewed the 1964 civil rights bill as a "mixed bag of legalistic nonsense." He pledged to bring a "calm, moderate approach" to the civil rights problem. In the runoff Lake endorsed Moore, who won by polling an overwhelming 62 percent of the vote. The *New York Times* viewed Moore's victory as having potentially national implications, "for it reflected a seething resentment against the racial policies set down by Washington." Moore easily won the general election in November.

In his January 1965 inaugural address Moore promised that, like former governor Sanford, he would continue to make education a top priority in his administration. He was soon involved in a major controversy over freedom of speech on state college campuses. In 1963 the North Carolina legislature had passed a law banning members of the Communist Party from speaking in state-supported educational facilities. In response the Southern Association of Colleges and Schools threatened North Carolina schools with loss of accreditation. In late 1965 Moore warned that "the public controversy arising from this law is damaging to the state." Although Moore had campaigned against repeal of the ban, he now proposed amending the law to give university officials "discretion in having speakers they deem proper." Backed by Moore the state General Assembly established a study commission on the issue. In a special legislative session held in November 1965, the assembly voted to substantially repeal the ban.

Moore also moved to curb the influence of the Ku Klux Klan in North Carolina. In August 1965 Klan members attacked civil rights workers in Plymouth, North Carolina. Moore immediately dispatched 100 highway patrol officers to the scene to prevent additional Klan members from moving into the area. He also met privately with Robert Jones, the "grand dragon" of the North Carolina Klan, to warn him that his followers should stay away from Plymouth. In early September Moore sent his administrative assistant and a civil rights aide to Plymouth, where they were instrumental in setting up a biracial committee. Demonstrations planned for early September were suspended after reports that progress was being made by the new panel. At Moore's request the state assembly passed legislation in 1967 making the burning of crosses without permission of the affected property owner a felony. The assembly also passed a law increasing the penalty for bombings directed against persons to 10 years minimum imprisonment.

Barred by the state constitution from seeking reelection, Moore was succeeded by Lieutenant Governor Robert Scott. A member of the North Carolina delegation to the 1968 Democratic National Convention, he was nominated for president as a favorite son candidate but withdrew his name on the first ballot. In 1969 Moore was named an associate justice of the North Carolina Supreme Court. He served until he reached the mandatory retirement age of 72 in 1978 and died on September 7, 1980.

—TJC

## Morgan, Thomas E(llsworth)
(1906–1995) *member of the House of Representatives*

A practicing physician, "Doc" Morgan was born on October 13, 1906, in Ellsworth, and grew up in the nearby depressed coal-mining districts of southwestern Pennsylvania, where his father was an organizer for the United Mine Workers. Following medical studies and an internship in Detroit, he became involved in Democratic politics in Fredericktown, Pennsylvania. By 1939 he had assumed leadership of the local organization. In 1944 Morgan was selected to run for Congress. Since his district was overwhelmingly Democratic, Morgan never faced serious opposition in subsequent general elections. Characterized as an "organization man" by the *New York Times*, he consistently voted with his party and was an especially vigorous advocate of measures favorable to organized labor. In 1958 Morgan became chair of the House Foreign Affairs Committee. Well liked by members of both parties, Morgan was a master of bipartisan politics, and he conceived of his role as that of the floor manager for Democratic foreign aid programs.

In early 1964 Morgan initiated a dispute with his Senate counterpart, J. WILLIAM FULBRIGHT (D-Ark.), over the form in which the administration should sub-

mit its annual foreign aid budget to their respective committees. Fulbright, preferring to use his Senate Foreign Relations Committee as a forum for the discussion of foreign policy, wanted to consider only economic assistance requests, leaving foreign military assistance to the Senate Armed Services Committee as part of the Defense Department budget. He also hoped to get four-year authorizations for development projects. Morgan, who represented a district with a high rate of unemployment, argued that military assistance helped make foreign aid packages more palatable to members of Congress and voters who resented spending U.S. dollars aboard. In addition, Morgan wanted two-year authorizations at the most, warning that longer authorization periods would deprive Congress of its control over foreign policy.

In 1966 President Johnson, bowing to Fulbright's pressure, asked Congress for permission to submit foreign military assistance as part of the defense budget, but the Congress decisively rejected the Fulbright proposal. In the same year Morgan managed the administration's aid budget more skillfully than Fulbright, whose relations with Johnson were already strained over the war in Vietnam. Morgan kept spending cuts to a minimum and won three-year authorizations for the development loan program and the Alliance for Progress. In 1967, however, Morgan could not prevent Congress, disenchanted with the conduct of the war in Vietnam and large budget deficits, from passing the lowest foreign aid authorization in history.

Morgan strongly supported President Johnson on most legislative issues and vigorously backed the Vietnam War. He followed a different course than Fulbright, whose committee undertook critical investigations of the war. Morgan's committee did not begin Vietnam hearings until 1971, and he did not announce his opposition to the war until 1972. Morgan did not seek reelection in 1976 and returned to his medical practice in Fredericktown. He died on July 31, 1995.

—JCH

## Morgenthau, Hans J(oachim)
(1904–1980) *political scientist*

Morgenthau was born on February 17, 1904, in Coburg, Germany, received a Juris Utriusque Doctor (doctorate of canon and civil law) from the University of Frankfurt in 1929, and two years later was appointed assistant to its faculty of law. In 1932 he went to Switzerland to teach German public law at the University of Geneva. He came to the United States in 1937 and taught law, history, and political science at Brooklyn College and the University of Kansas City before becoming a visiting professor of political science at the University of Chicago in 1943. He became a full professor at that university six years later. In 1950 Morgenthau was appointed director of the Center for the Study of American Foreign and Military Policy at the University of Chicago.

In the late 1940s and the 1950s Morgenthau, through the publication of *Politics Among Nations* (1948), *In Defense of the National Interest* (1951) and other books, became known as a proponent of the "realist" approach to foreign policy. Rejecting Wilsonianism, he argued that America should not seek to transform the world according to its own political ideals but should instead concern itself with the promotion of vital national interests. Believing that popular passions often interfered with patient pursuit of the fixed designs required in diplomacy, Morgenthau felt that democratic societies like the United States found it difficult to pursue a coherent, rational foreign policy founded upon a consistent sense of the national interest.

Writing in the November 1962 issue of *Commentary*, Morgenthau advocated the employment of any necessary means, including an invasion, to remove Soviet missiles from Cuba. He wrote that since the promulgation of the Monroe Doctrine, America had claimed Latin America as a sphere of influence and stated that "if the United States is unwilling—nobody doubts its ability—to protect one of its vital interests, regarded as such for a century and a half, is it likely to protect interests elsewhere . . . ? Mr. Khrushchev, in particular, cannot help but ask himself that question."

Morgenthau was an early critic of increasing U.S. support of South Vietnam. He believed that South Vietnam should have a low priority among U.S. global interests, and he questioned whether the administration of President DWIGHT D. EISENHOWER was backing the wrong side in a civil war after his visit to South Vietnam in 1955. A decade later, he asserted that escalating U.S. military intervention in Vietnam was contrary to the national interest. In an April 1965, *New York Times Magazine* article, he criticized the "crusading moralism" and the "falling dominoes" outlook that characterized Johnson administration policies in

Southeast Asia. Morgenthau concluded that a Communist South Vietnam would likely follow a Titoist course, maintaining considerable independence in foreign policy. "How adversely would a Titoist Ho Chi Minh governing all of Vietnam affect U.S. interests," Morgenthau asked. "Not at all," he declared.

Morgenthau was a prominent participant in a number of the early university teach-ins on the Vietnam War. On May 15, 1965, he criticized administration policy at a Washington, D.C., teach-in sponsored by the Inter-University Committee for a Public Hearing on Vietnam. His talk was transmitted via a special radio hookup to over 100 campuses. MCGEORGE BUNDY, special assistant to President Johnson on national security affairs, was scheduled to be the major defender of the administration, but he announced that he was unable to attend because of official business. Morgenthau told the teach-in audience that the government was creating a myth of North Vietnamese subversion of South Vietnam to justify American involvement in a civil war there. Two months later he finally faced Bundy on a special CBS television broadcast. Bundy contended that escalation or complete and immediate withdrawal were the only alternatives to the president's policy. Morgenthau declined to endorse withdrawal, asserting that the administration could find a face-saving way of extricating America from the conflict without overt surrender.

In November 1965 Morgenthau addressed a New York meeting of Clergy Concerned about Vietnam, and the following March he appeared before the Senate Foreign Relations Committee to urge abandonment of the policy of military containment of China. As the antiwar movement became increasingly powerful during the late 1960s, Morgenthau's prominence as an administration critic receded. In 1968 he served as a foreign policy adviser to antiwar presidential candidate senator EUGENE J. MCCARTHY (D-Minn.).

In 1968 Morgenthau joined the faculty of the City College of New York. Concerned with the problems of Soviet Jews, he attended the Brussels Congress on Soviet Jewry in February 1971. In August 1975, as chair of the Academic Committee on Soviet Jewry, he protested the suppression of nonpolitical Jewish publications in the USSR. He died on July 19, 1980.

—MLL

## Morse, Wayne (Lyman)

*(1900–1974) member of the Senate*

Morse was born on October 20, 1900, near Madison, Wisconsin, and majored in labor economics at the University of Wisconsin, graduating in 1923. In 1928 he received a law degree from the University of Minnesota. The following year Morse became an assistant professor of law at the University of Oregon, and, two years later, he was appointed dean of the University's law school.

During the 1930s Morse served as an arbitrator in West Coast labor disputes. In January 1942 he was selected as a public member of the National War Labor Board. Although generally sympathetic to the interests of labor, Morse resigned from the panel two years later in protest against what he regarded as excessive concessions to John L. Lewis's United Mine Workers.

Later that year Morse defeated the incumbent U.S. senator in Oregon's Republican primary and won the general election. On Capitol Hill Morse quickly established a reputation as an argumentative and individualistic liberal who frequently refused to modify strongly held views for the sake of legislative compromise. His opponents acknowledged his intelligence and legal expertise but criticized him as a rigid, humorless egotist who displayed a self-righteous and scornful attitude toward those who disagreed with him. His persistent tendency to antagonize his colleagues barred him from playing a major leadership role in the Senate, but his admirers regarded him as a fearless maverick who placed principle above expediency and who served as a watchdog against injustice.

Morse denounced the 1952 Republican national platform as "reactionary," and in October of that year he resigned from the party to become an independent. He persistently criticized the Eisenhower administration for showing excessive concern for the interests of big business and in April 1953 led a liberal filibuster against a bill giving the states title to offshore oil. Early in 1955 Morse joined the Democratic Party.

Morse was a strong advocate of the settlement of international disputes through multilateral cooperation and a system of world law. In 1946 he successfully pressed for American participation in the World Court. During the 1950s he criticized John Foster Dulles for bypassing the United Nations in his execution of American foreign policy.

In 1960 Morse made a brief, unsuccessful bid for the Democratic presidential nomination. Under

Oregon senator Wayne Morse meeting with President Johnson, 1967 *(Photographed by Yoichi R. Okamoto; Lyndon Baines Johnson Library)*

the Kennedy administration Morse for the first time belonged to the same party as the president. As chair of the Labor and Public Welfare Committee's Education Subcommittee, he promoted the Kennedy administration's education bills. But he did not give up his role as a gadfly, and during the summer of 1963 Morse led a liberal filibuster against an administration bill creating a privately owned communications satellite corporation.

During the middle and late 1960s Morse was best known for his opposition to President Johnson's escalation of American military involvement in Vietnam. In August 1964 he and Senator ERNEST GRUENING (D-Alaska) were the only members of Congress who voted against the Tonkin Gulf Resolution, which authorized the president to take all necessary steps to repel North Vietnamese aggression. He questioned the administration's account of alleged North Vietnamese attacks upon American naval vessels in the Tonkin Gulf. During Senate debate on the resolution, Morse suggested that the vessels may have been positioned to defend South Vietnamese ships that were shelling North Vietnamese islands.

In a Texas speech delivered in May 1965, Morse denounced both the United States air raids on North Vietnam, which had begun the previous February, and the subsequent dispatch of American combat troops to South Vietnam. He asserted that the conflict in the South was a civil war rather than an invasion by the North and that the United States was intervening on behalf of a despotic South Vietnamese regime with little popular support. On the Senate floor during the same month, Morse stated that "my government stands before the world drunk with military power" and that it was laying the foundation for "intense Asiatic hatred."

In February 1966 Morse condemned the administration for lawlessly pursuing hostilities without a congressional declaration of war and in violation of the charter of the Southeast Asia Treaty Organization, which he said provided for collective rather than unilateral action in Southeast Asia. He believed that either the United Nations or the SEATO nations should intervene to separate the Vietnamese combatants and reestablish peace.

On March 1, 1966, the Senate defeated a Morse amendment to repeal the Tonkin Gulf Resolution, which President Johnson had repeatedly cited as the legal authorization for his Vietnam policies. Critics of the senator contended that the amendment was an example of Morse's tendency to undercut his own cause by taking extreme positions regardless of political considerations. They noted that a number of senators who had reservations about the war but who did not want to totally repudiate the president had been forced to vote with the administration.

Another of Morse's major concerns was the defense of the civil liberties of the individual. In August 1965, as a member of the District of Columbia Committee, he opposed a D.C. crime bill that would have permitted three hours of interrogation of criminal suspects before arraignment. The bill sought to modify the Supreme Court's ruling in *Mallory v. U.S.* (1957), which barred "unnecessary delay" in the arraignment of criminal defendants. Morse stated that the measure abridged rights guaranteed by the Fourth, Fifth, Sixth, and Eighth Amendments. During the same month he sought to protect the rights of criminal defendants from the effects of prejudicial pretrial publicity without impinging upon freedom of the press by proposing restrictions on the comments of attorneys prior to trial. In May 1968 he opposed an omnibus crime bill that attempted to overturn several Supreme Court decisions broadly defining the rights of criminal defendants and that authorized wiretapping in a wide range of federal and state cases. Morse argued that the provisions overruling the Supreme Court

"could start us down the road toward a government by police state procedures" and that the wiretapping provisions could permit "total invasion of our homes through spying."

Despite his differences with Johnson over Vietnam, Morse worked closely with the administration in the field of labor legislation, on which he was considered an expert. In January 1966 Morse supported an unsuccessful effort to repeal Section 14(b)—the right-to-work clause—of the Taft-Hartley Act, which gave states the option of outlawing the union shop. But he did not believe that workers should have the right to strike if their action jeopardized the public interest. During July 1966, in the face of an airline strike, he proposed legislation to require airline workers to return to their jobs for 180 days and establish mediation procedures. The strike was settled before Congress acted. In May 1967 he introduced in the Senate an administration plan for ending a railroad strike that provided for compulsory arbitration. The plan was enacted in July, and President Johnson appointed Morse to head a panel assigned to settle the strike. The panel devised a settlement in September, and it took effect the following month after labor and management failed to reach a voluntary agreement.

In 1968 Morse was defeated in a reelection bid by Republican challenger Robert W. Packwood, who insisted that the senator's maverick tendencies had become so extreme that he had "forfeited any right" to remain in office. Four years later Morse won a Democratic senatorial primary but lost the election to incumbent Republican senator MARK O. HATFIELD. In 1974 Morse again won a senatorial primary. But on July 22, in the midst of his campaign, he died of kidney failure.

—MLL

## Morton, Thruston B(allard)
(1907–1982) *member of the Senate*

Morton was born in Louisville, Kentucky, on August 19, 1907, and he earned a B.A. from Yale University in 1929. He won election three times to the House as a Republican beginning in 1946 and voted with the GOP's liberal, internationalist wing. Morton supported General DWIGHT D. EISENHOWER for the 1952 Republican presidential nomination, and in January 1953, Eisenhower appointed him assistant secretary of state for congressional relations. Three years later Morton unseated Senator Earle C. Clements

(D-Ky.). In 1959 he won appointment as chair of the Republican National Committee, serving through the 1960 election. Morton opposed most of President Kennedy's domestic programs and in his 1962 senatorial campaign found himself a target of the national Democratic leadership. He won reelection with 52.8 percent of the vote.

Morton sought the middle ground during the Republican Party's divisive 1964 presidential campaign. Although respected by many party leaders, he declined to enter the presidential contest himself and in April withdrew his name as Kentucky's favorite son candidate. His move unintentionally aided Kentucky supporters of Senator BARRY M. GOLDWATER (R-Ariz.), who won 21 of the state delegation's 24 votes. Morton served as permanent chair of the July national convention, which nominated Goldwater. Following the Republican defeat in November, the Kentucky senator refused to join moderate and liberal party leaders demanding the ouster of National Committee Chair Dean Burch, a Goldwater appointee. "This is not the time for bloodletting," Morton remarked on the anti-Burch movement in December 1964. "Our Republican Party blood is too thin, and there is too little of it." However, in September 1965 Morton attacked the John Birch Society, which liberals had frequently associated with the Goldwater campaign, and accused the extreme right-wing group of "infiltrating" the GOP.

Morton voted against most of the Johnson Great Society programs. Although supporting the Appalachia Regional Development Act for his state, he opposed the Elementary and Secondary Education Act and efforts to repeal Section 14(b) of the Taft-Hartley Act. In both the Kennedy and Johnson administrations, Morton fought White House proposals for federal medical insurance for the elderly. He advocated a voluntary program financed through general federal revenues granted to the states, which would then share control of the program with private insurance companies. Morton, however, was the only Republican senator to support consistently the administration's campaign finance legislation in 1966 and 1967.

Morton voted for the 1964, 1965, and 1968 civil rights acts and insisted that the Republican Party actively seek the support of black voters. He told an Alabama party gathering in March 1966 that the GOP could not afford to place itself "on the right of the [southern] Democratic position on civil rights," explaining that "there just isn't much room on their right!" When in July 1966 a national Republican leadership group criticized Johnson for the "state of anarchy" in northern cities, Morton strongly condemned its action. Describing urban rioting as a "national tragedy" and the "worst domestic crisis since the Civil War," he denounced efforts to place violence in the cities "in the political arena." He proposed that an unrestricted $1 billion "anti-riot chest" be placed at the disposal of mayors for housing, welfare, education, and antipoverty programs. No other Republican leader joined Morton in his attack on the party leadership's report.

The 1966 elections added to the ranks of Senate Republican liberals and moderates, and Morton began the following year to challenge some of the positions taken by Senate Minority Leader EVERETT M. DIRKSEN (R-Ill.). Morton led the campaign for the ratification of the 1967 consular treaty with the Soviet Union, even though Dirksen had announced himself against the agreement as an unwarranted hazard to domestic security. Angry over the minority leader's stand, Morton overcame State Department reluctance to fight Dirksen and the powerful anticommunist "Liberty Lobby" in order to win Senate approval of the treaty in March by a 66-28 vote. Morton's success represented the first successful Republican challenge to Dirksen's Senate authority.

Following his activity on behalf of the consular treaty, Morton came out against the administration's Vietnam policies in 1967. Morton had never been one of the Senate's more militant or "hawkish" proponents of the Vietnam War, but he had supported Johnson in his escalation of American involvement in Southeast Asia. Conscious of a decline in the public's support for the war, Morton attempted to move the GOP away from any identification with Johnson's war policies. In August Morton called for a de-escalation of military operations, adding that "we're on a bad wicket and should try something else."

One month later Morton condemned America's war effort in stronger language. Responding to a comment by presidential candidate GEORGE W. ROMNEY that he had been "brainwashed" during a recent Vietnam tour, Morton declared on September 27 that the president himself had been "brainwashed" by the "military-industrial complex" into believing that a military victory could be achieved. Morton accused Johnson of having been "mistakenly committed to a military solution in Vietnam for the past five years, with only a brief pause" during the 1964 election "to brainwash the American people" with promises not to engage American troops. Morton asked for an indefinite halt to the bombing of North Vietnam and a curtailment of American military operations in South Vietnam. Dirksen, a loyal supporter of Johnson's Vietnam actions, sternly criticized Morton's address in an October speech.

Although Morton never challenged Dirksen for the Senate Republican leadership post, he appeared a likely opponent or successor following his success on the consular treaty and his break with the minority leader over Vietnam. Yet, Morton denied any interest in Dirksen's position, declaring it to be "a lousy job" and himself "too lazy to do the work." He pledged never to oppose Dirksen for the minority leadership. Weary of the Senate's pace and in poor health, Morton surprised the Washington community in February 1968 by announcing that he would not run for reelection in November. Instead, Morton urged New York governor NELSON A. ROCKE-FELLER to seek the 1968 Republican presidential nomination. Morton later served as an adviser in the unsuccessful Rockefeller campaign of that year. He retired to Kentucky in 1969, occasionally returning to Washington to lobby for banking and horse racing interests. He died on August 14, 1982.

—JLB

## Moses, Robert

(1888–1981) *chair, Triborough Bridge and Tunnel Authority; president, New York World's Fair Corporation*

Although his initial interest was in government reform and reorganization, it was as New York's "Master Builder" that Moses achieved fame. Born in New Haven, Connecticut, on December 18, 1888, he grew up in New York City in a wealthy family. After earning a B.A. from Yale University in 1909 and a Ph.D. in political science from Columbia University in 1914, he worked for the New York City Civil Service Commission. In 1924 he became head of the state park system, which he greatly extended with a series of magnificent new beaches, parks, and parkways. In 1934 Moses became New York City's first citywide commissioner of parks as well, and he continued to acquire new jobs until at one point he simultaneously held 12 different state and city posts.

A pioneer in the use of bond-issuing public authorities to finance and build public works, Moses achieved unprecedented power over public construction in New York City and much of the state and was virtually immune from criticism or control. However, in 1960, as a result of mounting opposition to his high-handed manner, he resigned his city posts to assume the presidency of the New York World's Fair, planned for 1964–65. Two years later, Governor NELSON A. ROCKEFELLER forced his resignation from his state posts as well, leaving him as head of only the World's Fair and New York's powerful Triborough Bridge and Tunnel Authority.

Even before the World's Fair opened, Moses had been involved in a controversy over charges of favoritism in the assignment of lucrative contracts and franchises. When the Bureau of International Exhibitions failed to sanction the fair, most European governments decided not to sponsor pavilions, leaving the fair with an unusually high proportion of corporate exhibitors.

When the fair was opened by President Johnson on April 22, 1964, the ceremonies were marked by the presence of civil rights demonstrators, protesting the plight of New York's black population. Almost 300 demonstrators, including JAMES FARMER and BAYARD RUSTIN, were arrested, but a threatened "stall-in" blocking approach roads failed to materialize. Leaders of the American Jewish Congress also appeared at the fair to picket an allegedly anti-Semitic mural displayed at the Jordanian pavilion.

Although attendance topped 27 million the first season, revenues were considerably below the projected figure and, combined with an extravagant operating budget, pushed the fair into a serious financial crisis. Moses initially tried to conceal the situation, claiming a surplus of $12 million at the end of the first year. But in January 1965 an audit revealed that the fair had a deficit of $17.5 million and would be unable to repay a $24 million loan from New York City. However, new bank loans were obtained, and the fair reopened April 21, 1965.

In spite of increased ticket prices and Moses's successful attempt to attract new exhibits, the fair closed on October 17, 1965, with a $10 million deficit. Bonds were repaid at one-third their face value, leaving $8.6 million for demolition and some park improvements—nowhere near enough money for the chain of parks Moses had initially envisioned as the fair's legacy.

In January 1966, shortly after his election as mayor of New York, JOHN V. LINDSAY proposed merging New York City's money losing Transit Authority, which ran subways and buses, with the Triborough Bridge and Tunnel Authority, which was accumulating large surpluses from automobile tolls. Moses opposed the plan and was able to muster enough support to easily defeat the proposal.

However, Governor Rockefeller, who had failed to support the Lindsay plan, the next year proposed a more extensive merger including the two agencies, the Long Island Railroad, the Penn Central commuter lines, and other transportation bodies to form a new Metropolitan Transportation Authority (MTA). Moses, promised a significant role in the new agency, agreed to support it. On March 1, 1968, the MTA was formed, headed by longtime Rockefeller aide William J. Ronan. Moses, however, was offered only a consulting job with no real power. After over four decades of public life, serving under six New York governors and five mayors, Robert Moses's career effectively ended. He died on July 29, 1981.

—JBF

## Moses, Robert P(arris)

(1935– )   *field secretary, Mississippi Student Nonviolent Coordinating Committee; director, Mississippi Council of Federated Organizations; director, Mississippi Freedom Summer Project*

Born on January 23, 1935 and raised in Harlem, New York, Moses received a B.A. from Hamilton College in 1956 and an M.A. in philosophy from Harvard University in 1957. He began teaching at Horace Mann, an elite private school in New York City, the next year. In the summer of 1960 Moses went to Atlanta as a volunteer for the newly organized Student Nonviolent Coordinating Committee (SNCC). He quit his teaching job in June 1961 to become a full-time SNCC worker, and, in July, he moved into Amite and Pike Counties in southwestern Mississippi to begin a voter registration drive.

The first member of SNCC to undertake a voter registration project, Moses quickly emerged as SNCC's most significant figure in Mississippi. He was named project director of the Council of Federated Organizations (COFO), a body set up by SNCC and other civil rights groups in Mississippi in the spring of 1962 to conduct a unified voter registration program in the state. Moses helped plan and oversee all registration work in Mississippi during

1962 and 1963 and joined directly in registration projects despite repeated arrests, jailings, and beatings. Moses also directed the November 1963 Freedom Ballot, a mock election sponsored by COFO open to all African Americans over 21. Intended to prove that Mississippi blacks did want the vote, the Freedom Ballot campaign brought some 80,000 blacks to its polling places.

Following the Freedom Ballott Moses urged COFO and SNCC to make a major voter registration effort in Mississippi during the summer of 1964. According to former SNCC executive secretary JAMES FORMAN, Moses argued that a concentrated civil rights drive, especially when aided by white student volunteers, would capture national attention and force the federal government to intervene in Mississippi to uphold blacks' civil and political rights. Moses also wanted to begin building viable community institutions among the state's blacks. His advocacy was in large part responsible for the organization of the 1964 Mississippi Freedom Summer Project. Moses served as director of the effort, which brought over 1,000 volunteers into the state to set up community centers, teach in "freedom schools," and work on voter registration.

Violence flared repeatedly throughout the summer. Three civil rights workers were murdered near Philadelphia, Mississippi, in June, and in October COFO reported that there had been at least 35 shootings, 80 beatings and assaults, over 1,000 arrests, and over 60 churches and homes burned or bombed. Very few blacks were actually registered to vote, and only half of the nearly 100 freedom schools and community centers established during the project continued after the summer. Although the immediate tangible results appeared limited, the project directed national attention to the brutality of the segregationist system in Mississippi and the violence used to maintain it.

The summer project was also the vehicle for organizing the Mississippi Freedom Democratic Party (MFDP). Founded in the spring of 1964, the MFDP was open to all citizens and was intended as an alternative to Mississippi's segregationist regular Democratic Party. Moses helped organize the party and the "Freedom Registration" drive, which enrolled over 60,000 people as MFDP members during the summer. In August the MFDP held county and district conventions and then a state convention in Jackson where delegates for the August Democratic National Convention were elected.

Moses accompanied the MFDP delegates to Atlantic City, where they challenged the seating of Mississippi's regular delegation at the convention. When the convention voted a compromise in which two MFDP members would be seated as at-large delegates and the regular Mississippi delegates would be seated if they took a party loyalty oath, Moses counseled the MFDP against acceptance. The delegates rejected the compromise by a vote of 60 to 4, and at Moses's suggestion, they staged a sit-in on the convention floor on the night of August 25.

By the end of the summer Moses had become uneasy about his role in the civil rights movement. As director of COFO and the 1964 Summer Project, Moses was often forced to make key decisions on policy and strategy. Always reluctant to exercise such leadership, he shared with many others in SNCC a strongly democratic, antileadership philosophy. SNCC, Moses once explained, was "in revolt not only against segregation but also against the type of leadership where you have had a select few to speak for the Negro people." He saw his goal as simply helping local people organize so they would be able "to speak for themselves." In addition, Moses's courage, ability, and hard work had made him an extremely respected figure among many SNCC members and Mississippi blacks by 1964. Quiet and reflective, Moses feared that a cult was growing around his name. To halt this development he left Mississippi and SNCC in 1965. He spent several years in Tanzania as a teacher, returning to the United States in 1976. In 1982 he received a grant under the MacArthur Foundation Fellows Program, which he used to establish the Algebra Project, a program for the teaching of college-preparatory mathematics in public schools. Moses maintained that the principles of family involvement and local participation that supported his civil rights work in Mississippi also sustained the educational reform of the Algebra Project.

—CAB

## Moss, Frank E(dward)

(1911–2003) *member of the Senate*

A devout Mormon, Moss was born in Holladay, Utah, on September 23, 1911. He received his law degree from George Washington University in 1937 and then worked for the Securities and Exchange Commission. In 1940 he won election as a Salt Lake City judge and served as a judge advocate in the U.S. Army Air Corps during World War II. He was Salt Lake County attorney until his election to the Senate as a Democrat in 1958.

A liberal with strong labor support, Moss won his Senate seat in 1958 with a plurality of 38 percent when a former Republican governor ran as an independent and split the state's traditionally conservative vote. An energetic representative of his state's natural resource interests, he served on the Interior and Insular Affairs Committee and was chair of its Subcommittee on Irrigation and Reclamation. In the early 1960s Moss advocated a cabinet-level department of natural resources. President Kennedy remarked at the time that Moss "has preached the doctrine of the wise use of water with, I think, more vigor than almost any other member of the U.S. Senate." Moss also cosponsored truth-in-lending legislation and favored controls on political campaign contributions. During his first term he began to work for the ban on television cigarette advertising. This brought him increased electoral support from those Utah Mormons for whom smoking is a sin.

Although Senator BARRY M. GOLDWATER (R-Ariz.) ran strongly in Utah in 1964, Moss had established his reputation as an able representative of his state's interests and was reelected with 57 percent of the vote. During his second term he continued to press for federal action on water use, an important issue for Utah. In 1967 he wrote *The Water Crisis*, in which he argued that the competition between federal and local authorities for jurisdiction exacerbated the water shortage crisis. Charging that "no one is in charge of the federal effort," Moss called again for a federal department of natural resources and for the establishment of "effective planning agencies for all water resource regions." He also worked with great success for the enlargement of Utah's parks.

Moss continued to urge government restrictions on cigarette advertising and was also active in other health-related issues. In June 1965 he cosponsored Senator ERNEST GRUENING's (D-Alaska) bill to establish offices of population problems in the Departments of State and of Health, Education and Welfare. He also called for the development of a national program of and standards for nursing homes and housing for the aged.

A liberal supporter of the Great Society's social programs, Moss was the chief Senate sponsor in 1965 of the Law Enforcement Assistance Act. In

1968 he proposed an amendment to the Safe Streets Act to grant federal aid for the improvement of local police departments. Although he voted for appropriations for the Vietnam War in 1966, Moss was one of 15 Democratic senators who sent a letter to Johnson in January of that year urging that he continue the suspension of air attacks on North Vietnam.

Moss's opposition to U.S. involvement in Vietnam grew in the early Nixon years. As a Democrat in a Republican state, he faced a difficult election in 1970, when the Nixon administration threw its weight behind his opponent, but he was able to win a third term with support from labor and antiwar groups. Moss remained active in the areas of resource development, consumer affairs, and health. He lost his reelection bid in 1976 and then returned to the practice of law. He died of pneumonia on January 29, 2003.

—MDB

## Moss, John E(merson)
### (1915–1997) *member of the House of Representatives*

Moss, who was born on April 13, 1915, in Hiawatha, Utah, ran a retail appliance business in Sacramento and was active in local Democratic politics before serving in the navy during World War II. After the war he joined his brother's real estate firm and won election to the California Assembly in 1948. Moss was first elected to Congress in 1952 from Sacramento County as a self-described "really liberal Democrat."

Moss was among the most consistent supporters of Johnson administration legislation, but his main interest was the reform of laws concerning public access to government information. In 1955 he became chair of the Government Operations Committee's newly created Foreign Operations and Government Information Subcommittee. One of the subcommittee's tasks was to conduct periodic investigations of government agency information procedures. Moss soon became convinced that the 1946 Administrative Procedure Act, which governed agency information disclosure, allowed federal agencies too much latitude in forming their own information policies and enabled them to withhold important information from the public.

In February 1965 Moss introduced a freedom of information bill to require federal agencies to open their files and records to the public. Specific exceptions to the bill included defense secrets, medical and personnel files, trade secrets, and similar documents. At the same time Moss's Government Information Subcommittee undertook a survey of the information policies of 105 federal agencies and discovered a wide variety of information procedures. The American Bar Association, members of the press, and civil liberties groups all supported the freedom of information bill, while most government agencies and many business groups opposed it. Moss, who described the bill as "moderate," acted as its floor manager in the House. Signed into law in 1966, the Freedom of Information Act was a landmark piece of legislation that has provided journalists, academics, public interest advocates, and citizens with a means to secure the release of government secrets.

Moss was also outspoken in 1965 congressional hearings on the use of lie detectors by the federal government in interrogation procedures. "People have been deceived by a myth that a metal box in the hands of an investigator can detect truth or falsehood," said Moss, who stated that he would "absolutely refuse to submit to a polygraph examination for any purpose." In 1966 he introduced a bill that would have prohibited the interstate shipment of eavesdropping and wiretapping devices, but no action was taken on the proposal.

As chair of the Commerce and Finance Subcommittee of the Interstate and Foreign Commerce Committee, Moss backed legislation of interest to labor and consumer groups. He protested that the health warnings required on cigarette packs by the Cigarette Labeling Act of 1965 were insufficient. In December 1967 he called for a federal investigation of the auto insurance industry by the Department of Transportation. He voted for repeal of the Taft-Hartley Act's "right-to-work" provisions, which allowed states to ban union shops, and opposed administration efforts to impose compulsory arbitration to force strikers in critical industries back to work.

Moss was an early supporter of the Vietnam War but later grew critical of its conduct. After an investigatory trip to Southeast Asia in 1966, Moss's Foreign Operations and Government Information Subcommittee reported that U.S. aid programs there were riddled with corruption. Moss came to oppose U.S. involvement in Indochina and voted for the 1970 Cooper-Church Amendment to limit the president's authority to continue the American military presence in Cambodia. He resigned as chair of the Government Operations Subcommittee when the 1970 Legislative Reorganization Act required him to relinquish one of his two subcommittee chairships. Nevertheless, he remained active in civil liberties legislation as well as in consumer affairs. He did not run for reelection in 1978. He returned to Sacramento to become chair of the board of a local bank. On December 5, 1997, he died from complications of asthma and pneumonia.

—MDB

## Motley, Constance Baker

(1921–2005) *associate counsel, NAACP Legal Defense and Educational Fund; state senator; president, Manhattan Borough; U.S. district judge, Southern District of N.Y.*

Born on September 14, 1921, in New Haven, Connecticut, Motley graduated from New York University and Columbia University Law School. She joined the staff of the Legal Defense and Educational Fund of the NAACP in 1945. She was a key attorney in numerous school desegregation cases handled by the fund, including *Brown v. Board of Education* in 1954 and the struggle to integrate the University of Georgia in 1961. Motley was also chief counsel for JAMES MEREDITH and won court orders for his admission to the University of Mississippi in September 1962. In September 1963 she directed the fund's legal efforts to prevent Governor GEORGE C. WALLACE from blocking school desegregation in four Alabama counties. Appointed associate counsel of the fund, its second-highest position, in October 1961, Motley also aided civil rights demonstrators in the South in the early 1960s. She successfully fought the May 1963 suspension of over 1,000 black public school students in Birmingham, Alabama, for participating in demonstrations there that spring. She also persuaded a federal court in November 1963 to declare unconstitutional an insurrection law carrying the death penalty under which four civil rights workers in Americus, Georgia, had been convicted.

Running as a Democrat early the next year, Motley won a special Manhattan district election to become the first black woman elected to the New York State Senate. In February 1965 she was chosen Manhattan borough president by the island's city council, and nine months later she won the general

borough election by a large margin. As borough president Motley repeatedly pressed for city and federal funds to rehabilitate housing and increase employment in Harlem. She also endorsed proposals to increase local community involvement in New York City planning boards and to improve educational facilities in the city. Motley represented the city on the march from Selma to Montgomery, Alabama, in March 1965.

President Johnson nominated Motley in January 1966 for a federal district court judgeship in the Southern District of New York. The Senate confirmed her nomination in August, and Motley became the first African-American woman appointed to the federal bench in American judicial history. In one of her first major decisions Motley issued a controversial April 1967 ruling that New York City public school students were entitled to be represented by an attorney at hearings on their possible suspension or expulsion. In April 1968 Motley invalidated the results of a 1966 election of officers in the National Maritime Union on the ground that eligibility rules for union candidates had been "unreasonably restrictive" and a violation of the Landrum Griffin Act. In 1982 she became the court's chief judge. Four years later, she became a senior judge. Motley died on September 28, 2005.

—CAB

## Moyers, Bill(y Don)

(1934–  ) *White House special assistant, White House press secretary*

Born in Tulsa, Oklahoma, on June 5, 1934, Moyers, the son of a laborer, grew up in Marshall, Texas. While a sophomore at North Texas State College he took a summer job in Senator LYNDON B. JOHNSON's Washington office and then, at Johnson's urging, transferred to the University of Texas at Austin, from which he graduated in 1956. After a year abroad at the University of Edinburgh, Moyers returned to take a divinity degree from the Southwestern Baptist Theological Seminary in 1959. The same year he rejoined Lyndon Johnson's staff and quickly advanced from personal assistant to executive assistant, helping to direct Johnson's vice presidential campaign and acting as liaison with the Kennedy political team. After the inauguration Moyers resigned from Johnson's staff to become publicity director of the Peace Corps. Moyers was successful in winning support for the Peace Corps from the Congress and the public. In January 1963 he was named deputy director.

In the aftermath of the Kennedy assassination Moyers left his Peace Corps post to again become one of Lyndon Johnson's most important advisers. In the early months of the Johnson administration, he acted as liaison with Kennedy administration holdovers, as well as chief interpreter of the unique Johnson "style."

During the first year of the new administration, Moyers and special assistant RICHARD GOODWIN organized and supervised 14 task forces established to focus on Great Society legislative proposals. In his memorandum to the president setting up guidelines for the task forces, Moyers made it a key provision that government officials be mixed with outside experts. His plan stood in marked contrast to the 1961 Kennedy task forces, which had consisted almost entirely of nongovernmental personnel and had created hostility within the federal bureaucracy.

Moyers's work on the domestic task forces was interrupted by the 1964 presidential campaign. According to Theodore White, Moyers was Johnson's "chief idea channel of the campaign." At the Democratic National Convention in Atlantic City, Moyers helped write the party platform, which included a strong civil rights plank. After the convention Moyers created what journalist Patrick

White House special assistant and press secretary Bill Moyers talking with President Johnson at the White House, 1965 *(Photographed by Yoichi R. Okamoto; Lyndon Baines Johnson Library)*

Anderson called "the most effective, most savage media campaign in political history." It was Moyers who approved the controversial one-minute "daisy" television advertisement that appeared only once on national television and showed, first, a girl plucking daisy petals and, next, a nuclear mushroom cloud. The ad was intended to leave the impression that Republican presidential candidate senator BARRY GOLDWATER (R-Ariz.) would be dangerously irresponsible as president. While neither Goldwater nor the Republican Party was mentioned in the commercial, the reaction in the Goldwater camp was one of outrage.

Following the election Moyers returned to his notably successful work on the task forces, which made their reports on November 15, 1964. Moyers's principal impact on the project was in creating the organizational framework within which the task forces could operate. He regarded the first six months of 1965, when bill after bill came from Congress for the president's signature, as the most rewarding period of his career in public service.

In July 1965, while still functioning as the president's special assistant, Moyers replaced GEORGE REEDY as White House press secretary. He took over the post after the legislative euphoria of 1964 and early 1965 had worn off and the president's relations with the press had begun to erode because of mounting criticism over U.S. involvement in the Vietnam War. One of Moyers's tasks was to divert media attention from the Johnson personality and to focus it on the administration's legislative successes. He was frequently given high marks by reporters for candor and for reducing the "credibility gap" between President Johnson and the press. However, Moyers also brought a high degree of political sophistication to his job as press secretary. In an interview in January 1966, Moyers declared that press conferences were held "to serve the convenience of the President, not the convenience of the press," and acknowledged that he had "planted" some questions at President Johnson's August 29, 1965, news conference "to make sure that the news [about steel negotiations] got out that day." As press secretary, Moyers said he preferred "informal conversations" between the president and reporters to "televised extravaganzas." Moyers also criticized the news media, declaring that President Johnson felt he was better served by radio and television than by newspapers. It was Moyer's belief that the press was often "poorly informed" and wrote "its opinion" rather than the facts.

During his nearly two years as press secretary, Moyers earned a reputation as one of the White House's most prominent "doves" on Vietnam. His doubts about the war were well publicized. Moyers's growing reputation as what Patrick Anderson called "the most powerful White House assistant of modern times" and his favorable press coverage led to inevitable friction with the president. (Significantly, in his 1971 memoir, *The Vantage Point*, Johnson accorded his former top aide only seven citations, two of which were footnotes.)

During 1966 Moyers was increasingly frustrated by the strains in his relationship with the president and by the enormous amount of detail work involved with the press secretary's job. He was also unable to obtain foreign affairs posts that he yearned for, such as undersecretary of state or executive secretary of the National Security Council.

Moyers resigned as press secretary in December 1966 to become publisher of the Long Island newspaper *Newsday*, the nation's largest suburban daily newspaper. He immediately hired such innovative editors and fresh writers as DANIEL P. MOYNIHAN and Pete Hamill in an effort to help the paper shed its conservative image.

After *Newsday* was sold to the Times-Mirror Co., Moyers wrote *Listening to America; a Traveler Rediscovers His Country*, a best-selling 1971 book based on his travels through the nation. Moyers later joined New York City's public television station, where he was host of the highly praised *Bill Moyers's Journal*. In May 1976 Moyers accepted a position with the Columbia Broadcasting System. He produced documentaries for both CBS and PBS and served as a commentator for NBC during the mid-1990s. Most recently, he was host of the weekly PBS program *Now*.

—FHM

## Moynihan, Daniel Patrick

(1927–2003) *assistant secretary of labor*

Born in Tulsa, Oklahoma, on March 16, 1927, Moynihan grew up in New York City. His father, a former newspaper journalist, deserted the family when Moynihan was 10. What had been a comfortable childhood abruptly became an uncertain life of poverty, forcing Moynihan to work to pay family expenses. Moynihan remained in school and graduated first in his class from Benjamin Franklin High in Manhattan in 1943. He worked briefly on the Hudson River docks, attended City College for a year, and then enlisted in the navy in 1944. After his discharge from the service, he won his bachelor's degree from Tufts University. He later took an M.A. from Tufts's Fletcher School of Law and Diplomacy and did graduate work as a Fulbright scholar at the London School of Economics. He eventually earned a Ph.D. in international relations from Syracuse University in 1961.

During the 1950s Moynihan served as assistant secretary and later acting secretary to New York governor W. AVERELL HARRIMAN. From 1958 to 1960 he was secretary of the public affairs committee of the New York State Democratic Party.

During the 1960 presidential campaign Moynihan wrote a number of position papers on urban affairs for John F. Kennedy. Shortly after he took office Kennedy appointed Moynihan special assistant to Secretary of Labor ARTHUR GOLDBERG. In March 1963 Moynihan was promoted to the post of assistant secretary of labor for policy planning and research. In this job he undertook an extensive study of employment problems throughout the country. During 1963 President Kennedy appointed Moynihan, SARGENT SHRIVER, James Sundquist and ADAM YARMOLINSKY to draft the legislation that became the 1964 Economic Opportunity Act.

In March 1965 Moynihan, Paul Barton, and Ellen Broderick released a Labor Department study called *The Negro Family: The Case for National Action*. Commonly known as the "Moynihan report," this study suggested that the high rates of juvenile delinquency and illiteracy among black children could be traced to the fact that in nearly 40 percent of black families the father was absent.

Moynihan and his coauthors suggested that African Americans stood little chance of improving their position in American society as long as their family structure was unstable. The report proposed that the federal government develop social welfare policies to make it possible for more black fathers to remain with their families. In June 1965 President Johnson, relying on Moynihan's report, delivered a speech at Howard University calling for a White House conference on problems in the black community. Many civil rights leaders, including FLOYD MCKISSICK and MARTIN LUTHER KING, JR., were critical of the report. They considered the report patronizing and condescending.

In June 1965 Moynihan resigned his Labor Department post to seek the Democratic nomination for president of the New York City Council. He was defeated and served for a time as an aide to New York City comptroller Abraham D. Beame in his unsuccessful mayoralty campaign against JOHN V. LINDSAY.

While active in politics Moynihan built a reputation in academic circles. In 1963 Moynihan and Nathan Glazer completed *Beyond The Melting Pot*, an important study that suggested that the various immigrant groups of New York City were not being assimilated but instead retained striking individual characteristics from one generation to the next. In October 1965 Moynihan won a fellowship to Wesleyan University, where he began work on an extensive study of the black family. In June 1966 he was named director of the Harvard–Massachusetts Institute of Technology Joint Center for Urban Studies.

In the spring of 1968 Moynihan served as an adviser to Senator ROBERT F. KENNEDY (D-N.Y.) in his quest for the Democratic presidential nomination; after Kennedy was assassinated Moynihan worked briefly on behalf of the candidacy of Senator EUGENE J. MCCARTHY (D-Minn.). He supported Vice President HUBERT HUMPHREY in the fall. Because Moynihan was generally associated with the liberal wing of the Democratic Party, his political and academic colleagues were surprised in December 1968, when he joined the Nixon administration as an assistant to the president for urban affairs. Moynihan won administration support for new legislation providing federal assistance to families with incomes below a fixed level. The assistance was intended to supplement or replace local welfare payments. But the proposed legislation met with considerable resistance from both liberals and conservatives and was defeated in 1970.

In a confidential memorandum to the president, Moynihan in February 1970 suggested that "the time may have come when the issue of race could benefit from a period of 'benign neglect.' " This statement was leaked to the press and created outrage among black leaders, who suggested that it reflected the administration's hostility to the pursuit of black social and political equality.

In 1970 Moynihan resigned from his post as a presidential assistant and returned to academic life as a sociology professor at Harvard University. In December 1972 he was named ambassador to India. In May 1975 he was appointed U.S. ambassador to the United Nations. A year later Moynihan resigned

and won the first of four terms as Senator from New York. He died on March 26, 2003.

—JLW

## Muhammad, Elijah
### (1897–1975) *leader of the Nation of Islam*

Muhammad was born Elijah Poole on October 7, 1897, in a tiny hamlet between Macon and Augusta, Georgia. His parents were ex-slaves turned sharecroppers, and his father also served as a Baptist preacher. Poole worked as a laborer from the age of nine and at 16 left home, eventually settling in Detroit, where he found work in the auto industry.

In 1931 Poole met W. D. Fard, a door-to-door seller of fabrics goods in Detroit's African-American ghetto. Fard founded the Temple of Islam, and by 1933 Poole was his most trusted lieutenant. After Fard mysteriously disappeared in June 1934, Poole, who took the surname Muhammad, claimed that he was Fard's designated successor. A leadership struggle ensued, and Muhammad moved to Chicago and established a new headquarters for what he now called the Nation of Islam. During World War II, Muhammad spent three years in jail after conviction for draft evasion. From prison he directed followers of the Nation of Islam, commonly called Black Muslims, and returned to Chicago in 1946 as their unchallenged leader. Stressing strict personal discipline, black pride, and racial separatism, the Muslims recruited actively in the nation's inner cities and prisons during the 1950s. Estimates of their membership varied from 50,000 to 100,000.

In the early 1960s the Muslims began to receive national attention when Muhammad allowed the charismatic MALCOLM X to establish himself as the organization's chief spokesperson and heir apparent. The two leading Muslims officially split on December 4, 1963, when Muhammad censured Malcolm for a statement made three days earlier describing President Kennedy's death as a case of "chickens coming home to roost." On March 8, 1964, Malcolm X, who reportedly was unhappy with Muhammad's condemnation of Caucasian Muslims and nonengagement policy in civil rights and political affairs, announced that he was leaving the Black Muslims to form an organization that would stress "black nationalism as a political concept and form of social action against the oppressors." Malcolm was shot to death on February 21, 1965, by assassins linked to the Black Muslims.

Although Muhammad strenuously denied responsibility for the assassination, law enforcement officials feared that Malcolm's supporters would attempt to retaliate. Five days after Malcolm's death the Black Muslims's national convention opened as scheduled in Chicago, and Muhammad received police protection comparable to that received by the president. At the convention Muhammad denounced Malcolm X as a "hypocrite" who "got just what he preached."

During the 1960s, the Muslims accumulated considerable wealth, including many businesses, a bank, and farmland, in their pursuit of a program of economic self-sufficiency. Muhammad faced persistent challenges from internal factions in the late 1960s and early 1970s, and frequent health problems limited his efforts to combat these dissidents. He died of congestive heart failure on February 25, 1975.

—DKR

## Mundt, Karl E(rnst)

(1900–1974) *member of the Senate*

Born in Humboldt, South Dakota, on June 3, 1900, Karl Mundt graduated in 1924 from Carleton College and then taught high school speech and social science in Bryant, South Dakota. After earning an M.A. in economics from Columbia University in 1927, he became chair of the speech department at Beadle State Teachers College in Madison, South Dakota, a position he held until 1936. He gained election to the House as a Republican in 1938. Appointed to the House Un-American Activities Committee (HUAC) in 1946, he became known as a staunch anticommunist. He gained national prominence as the acting chair of HUAC, which was then investigating the Alger Hiss case. That same year, Mundt, in cooperation with Representative RICHARD M. NIXON (R-Calif.) sponsored a bill requiring the registration of Communist-front organizations. It passed the House, although it never emerged from committee in the Senate. Some of its provisions, though, became part of the Internal Security Act of 1950.

In 1948 Mundt was elected to the Senate and continued his anticommunist efforts. In 1954 he served as the chair of the committee that conducted a probe into the allegations of Senator Joseph R. McCarthy (R-Wisc.) of communist influence in the U.S. Army. He voted against the Senate censure of

McCarthy three years later. During the Kennedy administration Mundt became a prominent critic of the Defense Department's conduct in awarding TFX fighter/bomber contracts and of the Agriculture Department's dealings with Billie Sol Estes.

Throughout the 1960s Mundt remained a powerful voice for the conservative views of his South Dakota constituents. He voted consistently with the conservative coalition of southern Democrats and Republicans, supporting that group over 80 percent of the time during the Johnson administration. Although conservative on most domestic issues, the senator backed civil rights measures, farm subsidy bills, and legislation for cooperation with allies.

In 1967 Mundt led Senate resistance to ratification of the U.S.-Soviet consular treaty, which detailed procedures for operating additional new consulates in the two countries. The agreement was opposed by a large number of conservatives because of its provision granting complete criminal immunity and extending diplomatic immunity to consular officials and employees. Mundt claimed that this would make the FBI's counterespionage job "more difficult" and questioned the propriety of the agreement in light of Soviet support of North Vietnam in the Indochina war.

Prior to the ratification vote the senator offered two amendments to the treaty. One would have authorized U.S. consular officials to distribute statements of U.S. policy to the Soviet press and would have provided for the number of U.S. journalists in the USSR to be equal to the number of Soviet reporters in the United States. The other sought to prevent the treaty from taking effect until U.S. combat forces were no longer needed in Vietnam or until the removal of U.S. troops from Vietnam was not being delayed by Soviet military aid to North Vietnam. The treaty was ratified without his amendments.

In January 1968 Mundt called for an investigation of the mission of the captured American spy ship *Pueblo*. In a closed session of the Foreign Relations Committee, held on January 28, he told Secretary of State DEAN RUSK that the administration had "bungled very badly" in permitting the *Pueblo* to operate near the North Korean coast and, if such close-in operations were necessary, in not providing protection for them.

In 1969 Mundt suffered a debilitating stroke that prevented him from appearing on the Senate floor or at committee meetings. However, the senator refused to resign. Two years later, in a precedent-setting decision, the Senate relieved him of his posts as ranking Republican on the Government Operations Committee and second-ranking minority member of the Foreign Relations and Appropriations Committees. Mundt died in the capital on August 16, 1974.

—EWS

## Murphy, George (Lloyd)
(1902–1992) *member of the Senate*

Although born in New Haven, Connecticut, on July 4, 1902, George Murphy grew up in Philadelphia, where his father coached track at the University of Pennsylvania. After briefly studying mining engineering at Yale, Murphy went into show business in New York as a dancer and Broadway performer. In the 1930s he starred in Hollywood musicals. Beginning in 1939, when he switched his party affiliation to the Republicans, politics and the entertainment industry became equally important and interconnected parts of his life. He was a founding member of the Screen Actors Guild and served two terms as its president. He battled alleged Communist subversion in Hollywood after World War II, was a delegate to the Republican National Conventions in 1948 and 1952, and directed entertainment for the Eisenhower inauguration festivities. He retired from films in 1952 to devote more time to work as a public relations executive for film companies and to assume a larger role in the California Republican organization, including a one-year term as state committee chair.

In December 1963 Murphy announced that he would seek the Republican nomination for the U.S. Senate. His candidacy was seen as an act of party loyalty since he would have to run against popular incumbent senator Clair Engle (D-Calif.), but Engle's death in July 1964 changed the odds in the November contest. Murphy's opponent was now President Kennedy's former press secretary, Senator PIERRE SALINGER (D-Calif.), who, after winning the Democratic primary, had been appointed by Governor EDMUND G. BROWN to complete Engle's term. Murphy brought legal suit in August seeking to invalidate the appointment on the ground that Salinger was not a qualified California voter. Although the suit failed, the "carpetbagger" issue served Murphy well. In addition, Salinger's vocal opposition to Proposition 14, an effort to repeal an unpopular state fair housing law, proved helpful to Murphy. Derided as a "song and dance man" by the Democrats, Murphy's show business personality appealed to Californians, and he slowly chipped away at his opponent's early lead in the public opinion polls. Some political analysts saw the professional Murphy campaign as one of the first to fully exploit the political potential of television. He defeated Salinger by 215,000 votes out of more than 7 million cast. Salinger allowed Murphy to replace him on December 31, 1964, so that he would have seniority over other newly elected senators.

Although Murphy described himself as a "dynamic conservative" in the Eisenhower tradition, his victory was interpreted as part of the right-wing revival in California politics, and he proved to be one of the most conservative members of the Senate. As of 1968, for example, the conservative Americans for Constitutional Action gave Murphy's cumulative voting record a score of 83. According to *Congressional Quarterly*, Murphy voted in disagreement with the Senate's conservative coalition on only 5 percent of key roll-call votes during 1965 and 1966. As a member of the Labor and Public Welfare Committee, Murphy often expressed conservative criticism of administration-sponsored antipoverty legislation, sharply attacking the "bureaucratic bungling" of the new programs. He vigorously sought to expand the role of the states in the management of federal programs and to give governors veto power over the allocation of federal funds in their respective states. In September 1965 Murphy broke his usual pattern by voting with the Labor and Public Welfare Committee majority to report a bill that would repeal state "right-to-work" laws, but in October he opposed a cloture vote to stop debate on the bill. As a member of the Labor and Public Welfare Committee's Migratory Labor Subcommittee, he sided with California's large farmers in 1966 in opposing the Labor Department's limitations on the importation of Mexican farm workers. In general, Murphy objected to the extension of national labor legislation to agriculture.

Murphy sometimes supported social welfare measures, as in April 1967, when he urged the president to take more vigorous action to combat hunger and, in May 1968, when he voted to expand the Department of Agriculture's food distribution program. In September 1968 he reversed his 1967 position on the Teacher Corps by voting for fund increases, stating that he was "now satisfied that the program is doing a good job."

In the late 1960s Murphy, an extreme hawk on the Vietnam War issue, criticized President Johnson for imposing too many restraints on the U.S. Army in the field. He later became a steadfast supporter of President Nixon's prosecution of the war. Despite growing disenchantment with the conflict among California voters, it was assumed that Murphy would be reelected easily. However revelations early in 1970 that he had been on the payroll of Technicolor, Inc., since he entered the Senate badly hurt his reputation. In the November election Representative John Tunney (D-Calif.), a moderate and an opponent of the war, defeated Murphy by nearly 600,000 votes. Murphy retired to Florida and died of leukemia on May 3, 1992.

—JCH

## Muskie, Edmund S(ixtus)
(1914–1996) *member of the Senate*

Muskie, the son of an immigrant Polish tailor, was born in Rumford, Maine, on March 28, 1914. He studied at Bates College in Lewiston, Maine, and at Cornell Law School, where he received an LL.B. in 1939. After naval service during World War II, he returned to Maine and won election to the Maine House of Representatives, serving two terms as a Democrat. In 1951 he left the legislature to become state director for the Office of Economic Stabilization.

Muskie first gained wide political attention three years later, when he won an upset victory in 1954 over the incumbent Republican governor. Although he won reelection in 1956 by a wide margin, Muskie's effectiveness as governor was limited by Republican domination of the state legislature. Rather than seek a third term in 1958, he decided to run for the U.S. Senate. Muskie defeated the Republican incumbent with 61 percent of the vote and became the state's first Democrat Senator since 1911.

Muskie began his Senate career inauspiciously, offending the powerful majority leader, LYNDON JOHNSON, by voting for an antifilibuster measure that Johnson opposed. As a result Muskie was denied the Foreign Relations Committee assignment he had requested and placed instead on the Banking and Currency, Public Works and Govern-

ment Operations Committees. Muskie sought to make the best of what he viewed as a bad situation by working conscientiously at his committee tasks. He soon became known in the Senate as an expert at formulating workable legislation and mobilizing support for it. Johnson himself, despite his initial hostility toward Muskie, later praised him as "one of the few liberals who's a match for the Southern legislative craftsmen."

As Muskie gained experience in the Senate, he discovered that his committee assignments were not as unfavorable as they had seemed at first. The Public Works Committee, in particular, involved him in environmental matters, which greatly concerned the voters in Maine's scenic and undeveloped areas. In 1962 he was named chair of the Public Works Subcommittee on Air and Water Pollution. By the time pollution became a major national issue during the mid-1960s, Muskie was the leading Senate authority in the field and the sponsor of several landmark environmental measures. These included the Water Quality Acts of 1963 and 1965, the Clean Air Act of 1963, and the Clean Rivers Restoration Act of 1966. All provided federal funds for pollution control programs and mandated the Interior Department and the Department of Health, Education and Welfare to set standards for pollutant emissions. Muskie was also instrumental in establishing new agencies to coordinate and encourage work on pollution control. These included the Federal Water Pollution Control Administration and the Environmental Quality Council, created in 1969 in the Office of the President.

In addition to his involvement in environmental issues, Muskie was a strong and steady supporter of President Johnson's Great Society programs. The liberal Americans for Democratic Action consistently gave him "correct" ratings of 85 percent to 90 percent. Muskie won the administration's gratitude in 1966 by successfully floor-managing the Model Cities Act, an urban development program that faced strong opposition from Senate conservatives and rural representatives. That year he was appointed assistant Democratic whip in the Senate, and in 1967 he became chair of the Democratic Senatorial Campaign Committee. On Vietnam policy Muskie generally followed the administration's lead during the mid-1960s, though leaning privately toward a more "dovish" position. In January 1968 he expressed reservations about the bombing of North Vietnam in a private letter to President Johnson. At the 1968 Democratic National Convention, however, he opposed the antiwar platform proposal, which demanded an unconditional bombing halt.

Despite his growing influence in the Senate and the development of national concern over environmental issues, Muskie remained little known outside Maine and Washington during the mid-1960s. Vice President HUBERT HUMPHREY thus gave Muskie national exposure for the first time by choosing him as his running mate in the 1968 presidential contest. Most political observers agreed that Muskie made a favorable impression during the campaign with his low-keyed approach and appeals for reasoned judgment on public issues. He was particularly effective in politely but firmly dealing with antiwar hecklers at his campaign appearances. Humphrey himself viewed Muskie as his "greatest asset" in the close race, and Democratic campaign manager LARRY O'BRIEN called him "a co-performer with Hubert." National polls indicated that Muskie was considerably more popular than Republican vice presidential candidate SPIRO T. AGNEW.

Muskie returned to his Senate duties after the narrow Democratic defeat in November 1968. He continued to concentrate on environmental issues and sponsored several pollution control bills during the early 1970s. His importance within the national Democratic Party was far greater than before, and he maintained a busy speaking schedule. During the 1970 congressional campaign Muskie gained wide approval with a nationally televised talk criticizing Republican claims that Democratic candidates were "soft on crime." He was an early contender for the Democratic presidential nomination in 1972 but lost to Senator GEORGE MCGOVERN (D-S.Dak.). He remained in the Senate until 1980, when he resigned to serve as secretary of state in the administration of President Jimmy Carter. He served on a panel chaired by former senator JOHN TOWER to investigate the Iran-contra scandal in 1987. He died in Washington, D.C., on March 26, 1996.

—SLG

## Muste, A(braham) J(ohannes)

(1885–1967) *minister, peace activist*

Born in Zierikzee, Netherlands, on January 8, 1885, Muste immigrated with his family to Grand Rapids, Michigan, at the age of six. After graduating from Hope College in 1905, he was ordained a Dutch Reformed minister in 1909. As his theological views

evolved, he became a pacifist who opposed U.S. entry into World War I. In 1918 he joined the Fellowship of Reconciliation, a nondenominational pacifist organization. He moved to Boston to work as a mediator in labor disputes, and he became a leader of the Lawrence, Massachusetts, textile workers strike in 1919. Two years later he became faculty chair of the Brookwood Labor College in Katonah, New York, and, in 1923, a vice president of the American Federation of Teachers, a union affiliated with the American Federation of Labor. During the Great Depression, he advocated revolutionary action by workers to achieve social justice. He was a committed socialist for the rest of his life, but by the end of the 1930s he had decided that any social revolution must be nonviolent.

"Nonviolence," Muste told a group on the eve of World War II, "is not apathy or cowardice or passivity." As executive secretary of the Fellowship of Reconciliation, he supported those who refused to cooperate with the Selective Service system during wartime and continued to oppose conscription after the end of World War II. He became highly influential in the postwar peace movement. He joined DAVID DELLINGER and BAYARD RUSTIN in founding *Liberation* magazine in 1956 and the following year became chair of the Committee for Nonviolent Action (CNVA). Muste's pacifism influenced MARTIN LUTHER KING, JR., who joined the Fellowship of Reconciliation in the early 1950s.

During the early 1960s, Muste opposed all nuclear tests and urged unilateral disarmament. He helped organize the 1961 San Francisco-to-Moscow Walk for Peace and was co-chair of the 1962 Hiroshima Day Committee and the United Easter Peace Demonstrations Committee in 1963.

Muste was an early and leading opponent of U.S. involvement in Vietnam and worked with various antiwar groups, including the War Resisters League and the National Mobilization Committee to End the War. In a June 1965 meeting, which he termed frustrating, Muste presented his views to Secretary of Defense ROBERT MCNAMARA while antiwar protesters distributed pamphlets in the Pentagon.

As chair of the Committee for a Fifth Avenue Peace Parade, Muste led several marches and demonstrations in New York in 1965 and 1966. At a draft-card burning rally in November 1965, he called for an expanded program of civil disobedience. He refused to pay his federal income tax in

1966 in order not to participate in the government's "serious crimes against humanity."

Muste and five other pacifists were expelled from South Vietnam in April 1966 for attempting to hold antiwar demonstrations there. Accompanied by two other members of the clergy, he traveled to Hanoi in January 1967. The three conferred with Ho Chi Minh, who, they said, had invited President Johnson to Hanoi for peace talks. Although the Defense Department maintained that only military targets had been scheduled for bombings, Muste later reported having seen residential sections of the North Vietnamese capital that had been bombed on December 13 and 14, 1966. The three urged an immediate, unconditional end to U.S. bombing of North Vietnam, warning that otherwise there could be no progress toward ending the war. Before his death on February 11, 1967, Muste described himself as "an unrepentant unilateralist, on political as well as moral grounds."

—MDB

# N

## Nader, Ralph

### (1934– ) *consumer activist*

The son of Lebanese immigrants, Nader was born on February 27, 1934, and grew up in a small Connecticut town where his father owned a restaurant. He attended Princeton University and Harvard Law School, where he edited the student newspaper, the *Record*. It was at Harvard that Nader became absorbed in the subject of auto safety, particularly the dangers of vehicle design. After receiving his law degree in 1958, he served a six-month stint in the army, traveled around the world as a freelance journalist, conducted a law practice in Hartford, Connecticut, and continued his campaign for stricter auto safety legislation in Massachusetts and Connecticut.

In 1964 Nader carried his campaign to Washington, D.C., as a consultant to Assistant Secretary of Labor DANIEL P. MOYNIHAN, who had been working on the issue of auto safety since the mid-1950s. Nader devoted a year to producing for Moynihan a 235-page report criticizing the government's role in highway safety. Moynihan used the report, which very few people read, to buttress his own efforts to win administration support for federal regulation of automobile manufacture. In May 1965 Nader left the Labor Department to write a book on the role of vehicle defects in automobile crashes. Simultaneously, he was associated, unofficially and without pay, with the Senate Government Operations Subcommittee on Executive Reorganization, which, under Chair ABRAHAM A. RIBICOFF (D-Conn.), was holding hearings on traffic safety. Nader supplied the subcommittee's staff director, Jerome Sonofsky, with ideas, technical information, and questions for witnesses.

Nader achieved some public recognition with the publication in November 1965 of *Unsafe at Any Speed: The Designed-in Dangers of the American Automobile*, a scathing indictment of the automobile industry for emphasizing style, speed, and comfort to the detriment of safety. By focusing on the dangerous features of automotive design, he intended to refute the prevailing belief that driver deficiencies were the main cause of automobile deaths and injuries. He detailed the various hazards of the "second collision" that occurred when a car's occupant was thrown against the interior of the vehicle after a crash and injured on protruding knobs, rigid steering wheels, and easily shattered windshields. Nader singled out for special attack the General Motors (GM) Corvair for having an unsafe rear suspension system and other dangerous defects. He castigated the Corvair design as "one of the greatest acts of industrial irresponsibility in the present century."

Nader won widespread public attention in March 1966, when he charged before Ribicoff's subcommittee that GM had initiated an investigation into his personal life in order "to obtain lurid details and grist for invidious use." More than 50 of his friends and relatives had been questioned by private investigators about his sex life and political beliefs. Nader also asserted that he had been followed, had received harassing telephone calls, and had had two suspicious encounters with young women who tried unsuccessfully to lure him to their apartments.

At first GM called Nader's charges "ridiculous," but a few days later the corporation acknowledged the investigation, labeling it "routine" and denying that it involved "harassment or intimidation." On March 22, in a nationally televised hearing, GM president James Roche appeared before the subcommittee and admitted that GM had initiated an investigation into Nader's private life and that there had been some harassment. He conceded that the probe was "most unworthy of American business" and publicly apologized to Nader. Roche denied that any girls had been employed as "sex lures," however. Ribicoff characterized the investigation as "an attempt to downgrade and smear a man," adding that the detectives had been unable to find "a damn thing wrong" with Nader.

In November 1966 Nader filed an invasion-of-privacy suit against GM for $26 million. He was awarded $425,000 in August 1970 in an out-of-court settlement. Nader said that he would use the money to monitor GM's activities in the safety, pollution, and consumer relations areas.

The revelation of GM's harassment of Nader aroused public indignation and gave an impetus to the campaign for federal regulation of automobile manufacture. Nader continued his persistent lobbying effort and participated in the drafting of the actual legislation. In the summer of 1966 the Traffic and Motor Vehicle Safety Act passed the Senate by vote of 76 to 0 and the House by 331 to 0. The new act was a strong law directing the secretary of commerce to prescribe detailed safety standards for all new cars, buses, trucks, and other motor vehicles. Nader applauded the bill's passage but voiced his disappointment that it did not contain criminal penalties for manufacturers who violated its provisions.

Nader's campaign for auto safety did not end with President Johnson's signing of the measure in September 1966. He became an active and critical watchdog of the National Highway Safety Agency, which was set up to promulgate safety regulations and ensure their enforcement. Before the first set of standards was issued on January 31, 1967, he charged that the agency showed "disturbing signs of being intimidated" by the auto industry. After they were issued he denounced the new regulations as being too lenient and "considerably weakened" to meet industry objections. Nader said the agency's leaders "did not compromise with the industry" but "surrendered to it." In March he criticized the auto manufacturers for "banding together" to claim that strict standards were impossible when in fact they were practicable and to exaggerate the costs of the safety improvements. The combination of harsh invective, a solid array of technical information, and an unwillingness to compromise became hallmarks of Nader campaigns.

The auto safety investigation was the first of many probes by Nader into areas where he believed citizens were being victimized. In mid-1967 he attacked the unwholesome conditions in intrastate meat-packing plants, which were not subject to federal inspection. Through publicity and congressional lobbying he contributed to the passage in December of the Wholesome Meat Act, which gave states two years to bring their inspection systems up to federal standards. Other Nader campaigns resulted in the passage of the Natural Gas Pipeline Safety Act of 1968 and the Coal Mine Health and Safety Act of 1969.

In the summer of 1968 a team of law students organized by Nader began an investigation of the Federal Trade Commission (FTC), the regulatory agency charged with the general responsibility of policing the market economy and protecting consumers. The investigators, whose invasion of the commission's headquarters in Washington earned them the nickname "Nader's Raiders," produced a 185-page report in January 1969 harshly critical of the FTC. They accused the commission of inadequate protection of the consumer, "collusion with business interests," secrecy, and lassitude. The group's effort led to the revitalization of the FTC under the Nixon administration.

The birth of Nader's Raiders, first institutionalized as the Center for Study of Responsive Law in 1969, signified the expansion of Nader's personal investigations into an organized network of well-educated young people working on behalf of the public interest. Inspired and guided by Nader, teams of his young followers labored to expose and correct corporate abuses and government failures in a host of new areas, including air and water pollution, antitrust enforcement, taxation, land policy in California, nursing homes, federal regulation agencies, and the U.S. Congress. They used Nader's techniques of investigation, exposure, lobbying, and litigation to galvanize movements for reform in these areas.

Nader himself occupied a position unique in American political life during the 1960s. His spartan lifestyle and his refusal to capitalize on his fame set him apart from other figures in public life and strengthened his image as a selfless champion of the public interest.

In 1996 Nader made the first of three consecutive runs as a third-party candidate for the presidency. In that first campaign and in his subsequent race in 2000, Nader was the nominee of the Green Party. His share of the vote in 1996 was less than 1 percent. Four years later, he garnered 2.7 percent and became the center of controversy over whether he lured sufficient votes away from the Democratic nominee, Vice President Albert Gore, Jr., to allow George W. Bush to win the decisive state of Florida in an extremely close election. In 2004 Nader, as an independent candidate, secured only 0.3 percent of the vote.

—TO

## Nelson, Gaylord A(nton)

(1916–2005) *member of the Senate*

Gaylord Nelson was born on June 4, 1916, in the small Wisconsin town of Clear Lake, where he grew up. His father was a country doctor and a devoted supporter of Senator Robert M. LaFollette's Progressive Party. After earning a law degree and serving in the Pacific during World War II, Nelson ran as a Republican in 1946 for a seat in the Wisconsin Assembly. He lost, along with many other followers of Senator Robert M. LaFollette, Jr., but was elected to the state senate as a Democrat in 1948. After 10 years service in the senate, Nelson was elected in 1958 as Wisconsin's first Democratic governor since 1932. As governor, Nelson attacked industrial polluters and launched an Outdoor Resources Acquisition Program, financed by a penny tax on cigarettes. The program committed the state to a $50 million land acquisition program to preserve wild and unspoiled areas against developers. He also carried out the first major reform of the state's tax system in 50 years, introducing a state sales tax. Nelson was elected to the U.S. Senate in 1962 over the incumbent Republican, Senator Alexander Wiley.

In the Senate Nelson supported the Great Society legislation of the Johnson administration, taking a special interest in the Teacher Corps, which he and Senator EDWARD M. KENNEDY (D-Mass.) cosponsored in 1965. Created as part of the Elementary and Secondary Education Act of 1965, the corps was designed to alleviate the shortage of teachers in poverty areas by training young volunteers and supporting them while they gained teaching experience in low-income districts. In September 1968 Nelson successfully introduced an amendment to raise the funding of the corps from $17 million to $31 million.

An early environmentalist, Nelson introduced the first legislation to ban DDT in 1965, but he was unable to find any cosponsors for the proposal. In the same year he introduced a bill to place a tax on strip mining to finance reclamation. As a member of the Senate Interior and Insular Affairs Committee, many of his efforts were directed against industrial pollution of the Great Lakes. He was particularly concerned about the activities of the Reserve Mining Company, which was dumping tons of waste from its taconite processing plant into Lake Superior. Since 1963 Nelson had fought to get a federal enforcement conference held on the matter. He finally succeeded in January 1969 when outgoing secretary of the interior STEWART UDALL signed the order for the Lake Superior conference. Nelson achieved recognition as the originator of Earth Day in April 1970. In October of that year the *New Republic* said of him, "Nelson . . . probably comes closest to being [the Senate's] resident national philosopher on ecology."

Influenced by consumer advocate RALPH NADER, Nelson became active in the campaign to legislate automobile and tire safety. He introduced a bill in February 1965 to authorize the secretary of commerce to prescribe safety standards for all automobiles sold in the United States. The standards were to be the same as those already required by the General Services Administration for the purchase of government vehicles. In April Nelson proposed a bill to mandate tire safety standards, claiming that "tire production was dominated by the automobile industry, which has a great incentive to reduce unit costs in every possible way." This "discourages the production of really high quality tires, which many motorists should be using." A revised version of Nelson's bill was introduced by Senator WARREN MAGNUSON (D-Wash.) and became the Tire Safety Act of 1966.

Nelson was one of the earliest Senate opponents of the Vietnam War. In the 1964 debate on the Gulf of Tonkin Resolution, Nelson proposed an amendment to clarify the intent of the resolution and prevent it from being used to justify later expansion of American involvement. He withdrew his amendment, however, after Senator J. WILLIAM FULBRIGHT (D-Ark.) assured him it was superfluous, and Nelson voted for the resolution. Unlike most antiwar senators, Nelson consistently voted against supplemental appropriations to pay for the war. From 1965 to 1968 only WAYNE MORSE (D-

Ore.) and ERNEST GRUENING (D-Alaska) joined Nelson in this form of opposition.

In November 1967 Nelson secured $20 million in tax relief for the American Motors Corporation (AMC). His amendment permitted AMC's losses to be carried back five years instead of three. Nelson said that the tax break was essential to enable the company, Wisconsin's largest employer, to continue to compete with the Big Three automakers and to give it "working capital at a most critical time in its recovery."

Nelson was reelected in 1968 with 62 percent of the vote, an impressive showing in a year when Wisconsin gave its electoral votes to RICHARD NIXON and also elected a Republican governor. He won another term in 1974, but lost his reelection bid in 1980. He later worked for the Wilderness Society. He died on July 3, 2005.

—TO

## Neuberger, Maurine (Brown)
### (1907–2000) *member of the Senate*

Born in Cloverdale, Oregon, on January 9, 1907, Maurine Neuberger graduated from the University of Oregon in 1929 and then worked as a physical education and English instructor in Oregon's public schools. She won election as a Democrat in 1950 to the state house of representatives. Her husband, Richard, had won a seat in the state senate two years earlier, and they became the first married couple to serve at the same time in the two houses of a state legislature. As a state representative, she sponsored bills on education and consumer protection. The Neubergers supported themselves as a journalistic team until Richard's election to the U.S. Senate in 1954. In Washington, she worked as his unpaid assistant, helping with research and public relations. When he died in March 1960, Maurine Neuberger was elected first to complete his unexpired term and then in November, to a six-year term of her own.

In the Senate she gained a reputation as an independent liberal and participated in a 1962 filibuster against the Kennedy administration's communications satellite bill because the new system was privately owned and operated. Neuberger sponsored a variety of reform measures, including an antibillboard bill and a tax amendment that allowed working women to deduct the cost of child care from their taxable income.

Neuberger wrote *Smoke Screen: Tobacco and the Public Health* in 1963. When the U.S. Surgeon General's report, linking smoking and lung cancer, was released in January 1964, she became a leading congressional advocate for legislation on smoking. Neuberger wrote the bill that required cigarette labels and ads to include the warning that "smoking may be hazardous to your health." She proposed that the Federal Trade Commission establish standards for the labeling and advertising of cigarettes and that the Department of Health, Education and Welfare research the effects of smoking, study methods of reducing its hazards, and conduct a national educational program on smoking. Her proposal in January 1965 that these regulations be made effective within a year was rejected unanimously by the Senate Commerce Committee in favor of a three-year grace period for cigarette companies. Neuberger was also a major supporter of an unsuccessful bill introduced in 1967 to require that warning labels for each brand of cigarettes include their tar and nicotine levels.

Along with "truth in packaging," Neuberger favored "truth in lending" and cosponsored a bill that would have required lenders to disclose the amount and rate of interest in advance. Although endorsed by President Johnson in January 1965, he did not press for the measure's passage and no action was completed on the bill.

Neuberger introduced a successful bill in 1966 to authorize the Housing and Urban Development Agency to study the scenic and economic effects of overhead powerlines. Her repeated attempts to add the Oregon Dunes National Seashore to the National Parks system were successfully opposed by Senator WAYNE MORSE (D-Ore.) and local developers despite support from the president.

In January 1966 Neuberger joined 15 other senators who sent a letter to Johnson calling for continued suspension of the air strikes against North Vietnam. Near the end of her term, the Subcommittee on the Health of the Elderly, which she chaired, held hearings on detection and prevention of chronic diseases and utilization of multiphasic health screening techniques.

She decided not to seek reelection to the Senate in 1966 because of the cost of financing her campaign. In February 1967, Johnson appointed her as the first woman to serve on the General Advisory Committee of the Arms Control and Disarmament Agency. Later that year, the president named her to the Consumer Advisory Council. She taught government at Boston University and Radcliffe College and then returned to Oregon, where she tutored elementary school children. She died on February 22, 2000.

## Newton, Huey P(ercy)
### (1942–1989) *leader, Black Panther Party*

Born in Monroe, Louisiana, on February 17, 1942, Newton was the son of a sharecropper and Baptist preacher who named him after Louisiana's flamboyant governor, Huey P. Long. Newton's family moved to California, and he grew up in Oakland. He graduated from Merritt College, a two-year institution, in 1965. He also took courses at the University of San Francisco Law School. Newton's education was interrupted in 1964 by a six-month prison term for assault with a deadly weapon. While attending Merritt, Newton met BOBBY SEALE, a fellow student who shared Newton's outrage over racial discrimination and police brutality. They borrowed the name of the black political party in Lowndes County, Alabama, that STOKELY CARMICHAEL had created and founded Black Panther Party for Self-Defense in October 1966, with Seale as chair and Newton as minister of defense.

Begun as a grassroots organization in Oakland, the Panthers sought to protect African Americans from police intimidation and violence and to improve conditions of life in the black community. They demanded improved housing, education, and employment opportunities. They also compared the condition of African Americans to colonial peoples and called for liberation through revolution, if necessary. Wearing black berets and leather jackets and openly carrying guns (which was legal at the time under California law), the Black Panthers patrolled Oakland streets to monitor police. The party was generally unknown outside the Bay Area until May 2, 1967, when 30 armed Panthers marched into the California State Assembly to protest a gun-control measure then under consideration. Such defiant and confrontational actions gained national attention and helped the Panthers establish chapters in more than 30 cities by the end of the 1960s.

The growth of heavily armed Panther groups also drew the attention of local police and the Federal Bureau of Investigation. According to the American Civil Liberties Union, police killed or wounded at least 24 Panthers in shootouts between 1967 and 1969. During this period, Newton called for revolutionary action and helped establish liaison with other radical groups, leading to the formation of the Peace and Freedom Party. Newton was the party's unsuccessful candidate in 1968 for a seat in the U.S. Congress.

One of the first casualties of police-Panther animosity was Newton himself; he was wounded in Oakland on October 28, 1967, in a shootout that left one police officer dead and another wounded. By the time that his trial for first-degree murder began in July 1968, Newton had become an international symbol of black oppression. Many supporters considered him a political prisoner, and demonstrators crying "Free Huey" repeatedly converged on the Oakland courthouse, where the trial was held. Newton, who claimed that he was unconscious as a result of a previous gunshot wound during the gun battle, was convicted of voluntary manslaughter. He spent two years in prison before his conviction was overturned by the California Court of Appeals, which found that the judge in the first trial had "omitted instructions" to the jury concerning Newton's claim of unconsciousness.

Released from prison in August 1970, Newton found the Panthers in disarray. Membership had dropped because of police harassment and factional quarrels, both within the Panthers and between them and other militant groups. It was later revealed that some of this strife resulted from letters forged by the FBI and accusations spread by infiltrators. Newton attempted to pull the party together by de-emphasizing violence and antipolice activity. He involved the Panthers in a number of community action programs, including free breakfasts for schoolchildren and health clinics for inner-city residents. The Panthers also supported the United Black Fund, a church organization that subsidized social services in poor neighborhoods.

Newton's turn to social action brought him into conflict with Panther education minister ELDRIDGE CLEAVER, who had fled to Algeria to escape imprisonment for a parole violation. Newton expelled Cleaver from the party in 1971. The FBI's Counterintelligence Program, which involved infiltration of the Black Panthers and efforts to sow dissension, was partly responsible for the fissure in the party.

Newton wrote *Revolutionary Suicide*, published in 1973. He also published a collection of interviews and speeches entitled *To Die for the People* (1972). Indicted for assault and murder, he fled to Cuba in

1974 to avoid trial. After returning to the United States three years later, two trials for murder ended in hung juries. In 1989 he was convicted of embezzlement of funds, which he used to support a drug addiction. On August 22, 1989, a drug dealer in Oakland shot and killed him.

—SLG

## Nitze, Paul H(enry)
(1907–2004) *secretary of the navy, deputy secretary of defense*

Born on January 16, 1907, in Amherst, Massachusetts, Paul Nitze worked as an investment banker in New York for Dillon, Read and Company. His career in government began in 1940, when he went to work for James V. Forrestal, his former colleague at Dillon, Read, who served first as assistant to President Franklin D. Roosevelt and then as undersecretary of the navy. After the end of World War II, Nitze helped prepare the legislation that established the Marshall Plan. In 1950, as the head of the State Department's Policy Planning Staff, he was the principal author of NSC-68, a comprehensive reassessment of U.S. national security policy. NSC-68 called for a major augmentation of U.S. military strength. When implemented after the outbreak of the Korean War, it led to a four-fold increase in defense spending.

As a member of the School for Advanced International Studies at Johns Hopkins University, Nitze was out of government service during the presidency of DWIGHT D. EISENHOWER. During the campaign of 1960 he was the head of John F. Kennedy's task force on national security problems. During the Kennedy administration Nitze served as assistant secretary of defense for international security affairs and, during the Berlin crisis of 1961, as head of a task force that planned strategy. As a member of the Executive Committee of the National Security Council, Nitze at first favored an air strike to remove Soviet missiles from Cuba but ultimately agreed that a blockade was the wisest course of action.

In October 1963 Kennedy appointed Nitze secretary of the navy. Believing that one of the keys to a successful defense policy was the effective management of the service's extensive technological capability, the secretary reorganized the Department of the Navy in 1966.

In an attempt to coordinate the technological capabilities of the air force and navy, Nitze was an early advocate of the multiservice TFX, the swing-wing fighter/bomber whose cost overruns and technological problems made it a controversial project during the 1960s and 1970s.

During April 1967 Nitze, worked closely with Secretary of Defense ROBERT MCNAMARA in the secretary's attempts to limit the bombing of North Vietnam. They proposed that the administration cease bombing above the 20th parallel, a plan rejected by President Johnson in the absence of what he considered enemy willingness to reciprocate.

In June 1967 President Johnson appointed Nitze deputy secretary of defense. Two months later Nitze joined Undersecretary of State NICHOLAS KATZENBACH, and Assistant Secretary of Defense PAUL WARNKE in writing a proposal modifying the administration's previous demand for North Vietnamese deescalation before peace negotiations could begin. The "San Antonio Formula," sent privately to Hanoi, stated, "The United States is willing immediately to stop all aerial and naval bombardment of North Vietnam when this will lead promptly to productive discussions." The North Vietnamese rejected the plan.

During the first days of March 1968, Nitze was a member of the Ad Hoc Task Force on Vietnam formed to study the military's request for over 200,000 additional ground troops following the Communist Tet offensive. Within this group Nitze was a strong opponent of further escalation. Arguing that the administration should view U.S. involvement in Vietnam in the wider context of U.S. interests elsewhere in the world, he cautioned that further troop increases could lead to direct military confrontation with China or jeopardize military commitments elsewhere.

Nitze hoped that the task force would conduct a complete reassessment of U.S. policy. But it failed to do so and, instead, endorsed a continuation of current policy and recommended the immediate dispatch of 22,000 troops to Southeast Asia, with the remainder of the military's requested increase held in reserve. When the president asked him to represent the Department of Defense at hearings about Vietnam before the Senate Foreign Relations Committee, Nitze prepared to resign, as he believed that he could not in good conscience defend current policy. CLARK CLIFFORD, who had recently taken over from McNamara as secretary of defense, refused to allow Nitze to resign. The depth of Nitze's objections to the administration's course in Vietnam had a profound effect on Clifford, who had previously been inclined to support the 200,000 troop increase. Clifford altered his position and helped forge a consensus among Johnson's national security advisers that led to the president's announcement in a televised speech of March 31 of a partial bombing halt and a new proposal to begin negotiations.

After leaving his position as deputy secretary of defense at the end of the Johnson administration, Nitze became a member in November 1969 of the U.S. delegation to the Strategic Arms Limitation Talks (SALT). He had reservations about the first SALT treaty, which was signed in 1972, and resigned from the Nixon administration in 1974 because of his objections to U.S. negotiating positions. In 1976 he helped establish the Committee on the Present Danger, which warned about Soviet advantages in the nuclear arms race. He served the Reagan administration as chief negotiator on intermediate-range nuclear forces (INF), but he was no longer involved in the negotiations at the time that RONALD REAGAN and Mikhail Gorbachev signed the INF treaty in 1987. Nitze's long government service ended in 1989, and he died on October 19, 2004.

—EWS

## Nixon, Richard M(ilhous)
### (1913–1994) *president-elect*

Nixon was born in Yorba Linda, California, on January 9, 1913, and grew up in Whittier, where he worked in the family grocery store and attended public schools and Whittier College. He graduated from Duke University Law School in 1937 and practiced law in Whittier until 1942, when he went to work for the Office of Price Administration in 1943 and then joined the U.S. Navy.

Soon after he left the service, Nixon won the Republican Party nomination for a seat in Congress from California's 12th district. He conducted an aggressive campaign in which he capitalized on anticommunist sentiment to defeat his liberal, incumbent opponent, Representative Jerry Voorhis. As a member of the House Un-American Activities Committee, Nixon gained national recognition in the sensational investigation of Alger Hiss, a former State Department official, which eventually led to Hiss's conviction on perjury charges. In 1950 he won a seat in the U.S. Senate by defeating Representative Helen Gahagan Douglas (D-Calif.) by a wide margin.

Nixon's rapid rise in national politics continued when he became the Republican vice presidential candidate in 1952. Nixon's youth, California roots, and appeal to party conservatives provided balance to a ticket headed by former general DWIGHT D. EISENHOWER, the choice of the Republican moderates and internationalists.

Elected in 1952 and reelected in 1956, Nixon gained more public exposure than most previous vice presidents. Partly because of Eisenhower's distaste for partisan politics, Nixon campaigned extensively for state and local candidates in election years. When Eisenhower suffered a major heart attack and a stroke, Nixon assumed many of the ceremonial duties of the presidency. He also acted as a liaison between the White House and Congress and traveled abroad as Eisenhower's representative. His "kitchen debate" in 1959 with Soviet premier Nikita Khrushchev contributed to his stature as an experienced cold war leader. By 1958, when he began to lay plans for a 1960 presidential race, polls showed that Nixon was already the choice of a majority of registered Republicans.

As the Republican nominee for president, Nixon tried to capitalize on his experience in governing in a close race with John F. Kennedy. Yet on many cold war issues, Nixon's position differed only slightly from Kennedy's. A decisive moment in the campaign occurred when Nixon met Kennedy in the first televised debate between the presidential nominees of the major parties. Although Nixon did well at presenting his positions on issues, he appeared tired and looked pallid—the result of a recent illness and poor makeup—compared to Kennedy, whose good looks and vigorous style appealed to viewers. Nixon believed that a mild recession, which reached a low point in October, also cost him precious votes. Nixon finished little more than 100,000 votes behind Kennedy, although he lost the electoral college by 303 to 219 votes.

Nixon ran a disastrous campaign for governor of California two years later. Rated an easy victor in the early polls, he lost to Governor EDMUND G. BROWN by 52 percent to 47 percent. The morning after the election Nixon offered a concession speech in which he attacked the news media for biased reporting. "You won't have Nixon to kick around anymore," he told the assembled reporters, "because, gentlemen, this is my last press conference." With his political career apparently over, Nixon left California in June 1963 for a lucrative law practice in New York City.

President Johnson meeting with Republican presidential nominee Richard Nixon, 1968  *(Photographed by Yoichi R. Okamoto; Lyndon Baines Johnson Library)*

Despite his two defeats Nixon still felt that he had a chance for the 1964 Republican presidential nomination. Immediately after Kennedy's assassination his support among Republican voters outranked all other potential candidates. Nixon decided not to actively seek the nomination; rather, he hoped for a convention deadlock between conservative senator BARRY GOLDWATER (R-Ariz.) and liberal New York governor NELSON A. ROCKEFELLER, both of whom campaigned in the primaries. At the National Governors Conference shortly after the June 2 California primary, Nixon asked both Michigan governor GEORGE W. ROMNEY and Pennsylvania governor WILLIAM SCRANTON to enter the race as last-minute "stop-Goldwater" candidates. Romney declined, but Scranton announced his entry into the race. Nixon welcomed Scranton's candidacy, which caused hard feelings in the Goldwater camp. Nixon quickly recognized that he had nothing to gain by maneuvering to block Goldwater's certain nomination.

Instead he devised a strategy that would lead to his own successful quest for the presidential nomi-

nation four years later. Although Nixon and his aides thought that Goldwater had no chance in the November election, they decided that Nixon should campaign vigorously for the national ticket after the Republican convention. Nixon would then be in a position to unify the party under his leadership.

Nixon carefully followed this strategy during the 1964 campaign. He appeared before the Republican National Convention and introduced Goldwater prior to the candidate's acceptance speech. Between September 30 and November 3 he conducted a 36-state, 150-stop speaking tour for the Republican candidate. Nixon, Goldwater recounted appreciatively in January 1965, "worked harder than any person for the [1964] ticket."

Nixon's law practice permitted him to make annual world tours that enhanced his image as a foreign policy specialist. *Reader's Digest*, published by political supporters of Nixon, reprinted his major foreign policy statements. During a visit to Saigon in 1964, Nixon charged that the Johnson administration was following a weak and inconsistent policy in South Vietnam and proclaimed that the U.S. goal must be military victory. The next year Nixon said the United States was "losing the war in Vietnam" and recommended an escalation of American air and naval activity in North Vietnam. In the 1966 off-year elections, Nixon campaigned hard for GOP congressional candidates. Of the 86 gubernatorial and congressional candidates whom he aided, almost 70 percent won.

In the race for the 1968 Republican presidential nomination, Nixon at first ran second in the polls to Governor Romney, who enjoyed the support of Rockefeller and other liberal GOP leaders. Through 1967, however, Romney's careless, impromptu remarks reduced his credibility as a national candidate. By the end of the year, media coverage of Romney's mistakes had cost the governor his lead over Nixon among Republicans and independents. In late February 1968, just two weeks prior to the first presidential primary in New Hampshire, Romney dropped out of the race. Three weeks later Rockefeller announced that he would not challenge Nixon.

Nixon's early 1968 campaign strategy called for a heavy emphasis upon foreign policy. Amid growing public concern over America's Vietnam policies, Nixon told a Hampton, New Hampshire, audience on March 5 that he would end the war, but he avoided details about how he would fulfill the promise. After President Johnson announced a halt in the bombing and the beginning of negotiations with the North Vietnamese, Nixon announced that he would temporarily refrain from discussing the war. He argued that to do so might jeopardize Vietnam peace talks scheduled to open in May.

During the spring Nixon took important steps toward the nomination. His "loser" image had been countered somewhat by overwhelming wins in the primaries against unofficial, makeshift campaigns for Rockefeller and California governor RONALD REAGAN, Nixon's two main competitors. In June Nixon secured the endorsement of senator STROM THURMOND (R-S.C.), which assured him substantial support from southern Republicans. Though ideologically closer to Reagan, Thurmond and Goldwater backed Nixon largely because polls clearly showed him to be the stronger candidate. In June Senator MARK O. HATFIELD (R-Ore.), the leading antiwar Republican and a liberal, endorsed Nixon. Hatfield's support gave credence to Nixon's presentation of himself as a party "centrist" standing

between the liberal Rockefeller and conservative Reagan.

With 692 delegate votes, 25 more than required, Nixon won the 1968 Republican presidential nomination on the first ballot. Nixon then surprised the convention by naming little-known Maryland governor SPIRO T. AGNEW as his vice presidential running mate. Nixon chose Agnew in part because he was acceptable to southerners and easterners. He also thought Agnew, who had denounced African-American leaders for allegedly contributing to a riot in Baltimore, would be useful in appealing to conservative voters, including those who might support a third-party candidate, Governor GEORGE C. WALLACE of Alabama.

Nixon entered the fall campaign with a strong lead in the polls. Division within the Democratic Party over Vietnam hampered its presidential nominee, Vice President HUBERT HUMPHREY, while Wallace campaigning as the candidate of the American Independent Party, threatened to take northern blue-collar votes from the Democrats. In mid-September Nixon led Humphrey and Wallace in the Gallup poll 43 percent-31 percent–19 percent, respectively.

In a year of widespread protest and violence, Nixon, like Wallace, searched for the votes of those Americans least identified with the tumult. In his acceptance speech Nixon spoke of "the forgotten Americans, the non-shouters, the non-demonstrators." Aiming his campaign at this group of voters, he made crime a major issue; he assailed the Johnson administration for allegedly favoring criminals and promised to fire U.S. Attorney General RAMSEY CLARK. Nixon and his trusted adviser John Mitchell shaped a $42 million campaign that they considered appropriate for a front-runner: meticulously planned, relatively unhurried, strongly based on television coverage and the avoidance of specific proposals on important issues.

Nixon's front-runner strategy was sharply challenged in early October, when Humphrey's campaign suddenly gained momentum. On September 30 Humphrey broke with administration policy on Vietnam and called for a halt to all American bombing missions over North Vietnam. A mild position compared to that of antiwar Democrats, it nevertheless became a rallying point for party "doves" opposed to Nixon.

Nixon's narrowing lead was further jeopardized on October 31, when President Johnson announced that the United States would halt the bombing of North Vietnam and broaden the Paris peace talks to include the National Liberation Front and the Saigon government. This "October Surprise," which the Nixon campaign had feared, whittled Nixon's lead over Humphrey, according to the Gallup poll, to just two percentage points on the eve of the election. In anticipation of a bombing halt, Nixon's adviser Mitchell had used Anna Chennault, a conservative Republican with ties to Asian leaders, to pass the word to the South Vietnamese government that it should not participate in any new peace talks and could anticipate better treatment under a Nixon administration. Johnson learned about Chennault's interference and questioned Nixon about it. But Nixon denied any involvement in Chennault's activities.

Nixon won the election, one of the closest in U.S. history, with 43.4 percent of the vote of Humphrey's 42.7 percent and Wallace's 13.5 percent. He narrowly captured New Jersey, Ohio, Illinois, and California, as well as most border, western and midwestern states to win 302 Electoral College votes. He also ran well in ethic working-class areas and in parts of the South.

Nixon devoted his first term as president to ending the U.S. war in Vietnam. He withdrew U.S. troops in increments while turning over combat responsibility to the South Vietnamese. At the same time that he implemented this strategy of Vietnamization, Nixon also occasionally and sharply escalated U.S. military action, including the dispatch of U.S. ground troops into Cambodia in April 1970 and the mining of North Vietnamese ports and intensified bombing in response to the enemy's Easter Offensive in 1972. Negotiations finally produced the Paris Peace Accords of January 1973, an agreement to withdraw U.S. combat troops and to return American prisoners of war. These accords, however, left fundamental questions about South Vietnam's future to further negotiations. Nixon called the Paris accords "peace with honor." Privately, however, administration officials expressed doubts about whether these agreements would really end the war.

Nixon won reelection in a landslide in 1972, but he was quickly embroiled in the Watergate scandal. When secret White House recordings revealed that Nixon had attempted to thwart the investigations into the scandal, he resigned the presidency on August 9, 1974. An unconditional pardon from his successor, President GERALD R. FORD, protected him from any criminal prosecution. Despite the ignominy of being the only president to resign, Nixon managed to refurbish his reputation by cultivating the image of a statesman with unique expertise in international affairs. He published several best-selling books and visited many countries. He suffered a stroke and died on April 22, 1994.

## O'Boyle, Patrick A(loysius)
(1896–1987) *Roman Catholic archbishop of Washington, D.C.; cardinal*

The son of Irish immigrant parents, O'Boyle was born on July 18, 1896, and grew up in Scranton, Pennsylvania. He was ordained in 1921 after graduating from St. Thomas College (later Scranton University) and St. Joseph's Seminary in New York. Assigned to work in several New York social service agencies, O'Boyle proved himself an able administrator; in 1947 New York archbishop FRANCIS CARDINAL SPELLMAN appointed him director of the city's Catholic charities. Later that year, O'Boyle was elevated to archbishop as leader of the new archdiocese of Washington, D.C. He became a cardinal in 1967.

O'Boyle was a strong advocate of civil rights. In 1951, before the Supreme Court decision barring segregation in public schools, he ordered the integration of Catholic schools and other institutions in his archdiocese. In 1963 O'Boyle organized the Interreligious Committee on Race Relations, which attempted to promote the economic advancement of Washington's inner-city blacks. He delivered an invocation at the 1963 March on Washington and pressed for a special declaration against discrimination at the Second Vatican Council in Rome. O'Boyle was also one of the few Catholic church leaders in the United States to create a special office in his archdiocese devoted to urban affairs. Some civil rights advocates criticized O'Boyle for not going far enough in opposing discrimination, especially in the social functions of Washington parishes. However, a 1965 *Washington Post* survey revealed great respect for the archbishop among African-American leaders.

Though O'Boyle was known as a "liberal" in secular affairs, he was a conservative on matters of religious ritual and doctrine. He opposed changes in the Mass, especially the substitution of English for Latin in 1964. During the late 1960s O'Boyle became involved in a heated controversy over birth control. A five-day student strike broke out in 1967 at Washington's Catholic University, a center of liberal Catholic thought in the United States, when O'Boyle ordered the dismissal of a theology professor for advocating the limited use of contraception. O'Boyle, who was chancellor of the university, relented after meeting with the board of trustees and allowed the professor's reinstatement.

When Pope Paul VI reaffirmed the church's traditional ban on birth control in 1968, O'Boyle strongly supported the Vatican position. This brought him into conflict with a number of priests in his archdiocese, who refused to counsel against birth control and signed a declaration recommending that Catholics use contraception "according to their consciences." O'Boyle eventually dismissed 40 dissenters from their priestly functions, an action that brought further protest and unrest in his archdiocese. In September 1968 several hundred worshippers walked out on a sermon he was delivering at Washington's St. Matthew's Cathedral. The dispute was settled only in 1971 by a Vatican decision affirming the correctness of O'Boyle's positions but allowing the priests to resume their functions without recanting their views.

O'Boyle spent his last years in office under a cloud of criticism and unpopularity. He offered his resignation in 1971 and retired as archbishop in March 1973. He died on August 10, 1987.

## O'Brien, Lawrence F(rancis)

(1917–1990) *special assistant to the president for congressional relations, U.S. Postmaster General*

O'Brien's father, a leader of the local Democratic organization, began training his 11-year-old son, born on July 7, 1917, in Springfield, Massachusetts, as a worker in Governor Alfred E. Smith's presidential campaign of 1928. The younger O'Brien continued his political involvement while taking night courses at Boston's Northeastern University. After graduating in 1942 and serving three years in the army, he reentered politics to manage the congressional campaign of his friend, Foster Furcolo. Defeated in 1946, Furcolo won two years later and invited O'Brien to accompany him to Washington as his administrative assistant. O'Brien remained with Furcolo until 1950, when he began working for Representative John F. Kennedy (D-Mass.)

As chief campaign organizer on the Kennedy staff, O'Brien managed Kennedy's successful senatorial drives of 1952 and 1958 as well as his 1960 presidential race. With great care and thoroughness O'Brien created a network composed largely of volunteers to handle everything from distribution of campaign literature to voter registration drives.

In January 1961 President Kennedy appointed O'Brien as his special assistant for congressional relations. This post was especially important for the new administration, which faced strong opposition to its legislative program from Republicans and southern Democrats on Capitol Hill. O'Brien brought central direction to the network of congressional liaison offices located in more than 40 federal departments and agencies, insisting that they work in concert for the president's legislative priorities. His efforts produced important successes for Kennedy's legislative program, including an increase in the minimum wage and an omnibus housing act.

President Johnson meeting with staff members Lawrence O'Brien (center) and Bill Moyers (right), 1965
*(Photographed by Yoichi R. Okamoto; Lyndon Baines Johnson Library)*

At President Johnson's urging O'Brien remained with the new administration as congressional liaison after the Kennedy assassination. As he recounted in his autobiography, *No Final Victories* (1974), O'Brien continued his lobbying efforts to carry through the remainder of Kennedy's legislative program and then to take advantage of the new opportunities for Johnson's Great Society legislation, which opened with the large Democratic congressional gains of 1964. Among the measures that he pushed strongly in 1965 were Medicare, aid to education, and the Voting Rights Act; at the end of the 1965 congressional session the administration could point to a record of 87 major bills proposed and 84 passed. O'Brien also served as Johnson's "eyes and ears" on important issues, traveling frequently around the country to gauge public opinion. He sent back early warnings of growing public concern over Vietnam, an issue that he considered partly responsible for Democratic losses in the 1966 congressional elections.

In November 1965, with a large part of the administration's legislative program either enacted or near passage, President Johnson appointed O'Brien U.S. Postmaster General. Although O'Brien continued to advise the president on legislative matters, he sought to be more than a "figurehead" in the Post Office Department and applied himself seriously to his new task. He soon became disturbed by what he viewed as antiquated postal facilities, inadequate promotion procedures, and high turnover among the large number of low-level minority group postal employees. In April 1967 he proposed a postal reform plan involving replacement of the existing Post Office Department with a nonprofit government corporation managed by a professional executive. Johnson did not publicly endorse O'Brien's proposal until his final days in office. Congress eventually gave its approval in 1970.

In early 1968 O'Brien joined the growing number of Democratic leaders who warned President Johnson that the administration's Vietnam policy could be a fatal political liability. During the New Hampshire primary campaign, he wrote several memos to the president urging a bombing pause and the phased reduction of American forces. After Johnson's withdrawal from the race in late March, O'Brien resigned as U.S. Postmaster General to direct the presidential campaign of Senator ROBERT F. KENNEDY (D-N.Y.). Using his tested campaign techniques, he organized the Kennedy primary drives in Indiana, Nebraska, Oregon, and California. All but the Oregon contest ended successfully for Kennedy, and O'Brien was optimistic about his candidate's chances for gaining the Democratic nomination when the campaign was cut short by Kennedy's assassination on June 5.

As the Kennedy staff disbanded, O'Brien shifted his support to Vice President HUBERT HUMPHREY, whose campaign he helped manage in the last weeks before the 1968 Democratic National Convention. During negotiations over the party platform, O'Brien attempted to preserve Democratic unity by working for a compromise Vietnam plank. This effort was frustrated, however, by Johnson's refusal to accept any statement that did not affirm administration policy. Although O'Brien had originally intended to leave the campaign after the Democratic convention, he changed his mind at Humphrey's request and accepted appointment as chair of the Democratic National Committee. Working to counter the Democratic disarray that followed the convention, O'Brien quickly created a campaign organization that dramatically narrowed the initial lead of Republican candidate RICHARD M. NIXON during the last weeks of the contest. Inadequate campaign funds continued to hamper the Democratic effort and played a major role, according to O'Brien, in Humphrey's narrow defeat.

In January 1969 O'Brien resigned from the Democratic National Committee to take a position with McDonnell and Co., a New York investment firm. He left seven months later and was again appointed chair of the Democratic National Committee in March 1970. O'Brien was an important Democratic spokesperson during the 1970 congressional elections, attacking Republican emphasis on the crime issue as "the politics of fear." He later helped implement reforms in the selection of delegates for the 1972 Democratic National Convention and presided over stormy debates at the convention itself. During the 1972 presidential primary campaign, O'Brien became the principal target of the Republican intelligence-gathering efforts that led to the Watergate scandal. In 1973 O'Brien again resigned as chair of the Democratic National Committee. In 1975 he became commissioner of the National Basketball Association, a position he held until 1984. He died on September 28, 1990.

—SLG

## O'Donnell, Kenneth P(atrick)

(1924–1977) *special assistant to the president*

The son of Irish-Catholic parents, O'Donnell was born on March 4, 1924, in Worcester, Massachusetts, and grew up in Boston. He served in the U.S. Army Air Forces during World War II and then graduated from Harvard University with a degree in politics and government. His relationship with John F. Kennedy dated from Kennedy's first race for Congress in 1946, when he served as a campaign aide.

O'Donnell served as one of Kennedy's chief political tacticians in the 1960 presidential campaigns. As appointments secretary during the Kennedy administration, O'Donnell's job gave him wide but often concealed powers. He controlled access to the president, allocated White House office space, served as liaison with the FBI and Secret Service, and helped dispense political patronage. He also handled the logistics of all presidential trips.

In November 1963 O'Donnell handled the political arrangements for President Kennedy's visit to Texas, which was designed to end the disruptive political feud between conservative and liberal factions of the Texas Democratic Party. In the aftermath of Kennedy's assassination, O'Donnell, despite interference from local officials, was instrumental in seeing that Kennedy's body was returned immediately to Washington aboard Air Force One.

O'Donnell, remained on the Johnson staff the longest of Kennedy's White House staff aides. While acknowledging that O'Donnell's first allegiance was to the political ambitions of ROBERT KENNEDY, Johnson needed O'Donnell as a link to the big-city Democratic leaders who were virtually unknown to the new president. Shortly before the 1964 Democratic National Convention, Johnson urged O'Donnell to act as liaison with Robert Kennedy and to request Kennedy's voluntary withdrawal from consideration for the vice presidential nomination on the Johnson ticket. O'Donnell refused to take any action because of his anomalous position as an assistant to Johnson and a supporter of Robert Kennedy. On July 30, 1964, Johnson announced a decision—clearly formulated with Kennedy in mind—to bar cabinet members from the vice presidential candidacy. During the 1964 campaign O'Donnell, who was still a White House aide, was named executive director of the Democratic National Committee and given the assignment of arranging Johnson's campaign schedule.

O'Donnell resigned from Johnson's staff on January 16, 1965. The next year he ran in the Democratic gubernatorial primary in Massachusetts, losing to Edward McCormack by nearly 100,000 votes. While Robert Kennedy supported O'Donnell, Senator EDWARD KENNEDY (D-Mass.), anxious not to alienate House Speaker JOHN MCCORMACK (D-Mass.), whose nephew he had defeated in the 1962 Senate race, remained neutral.

In 1968 O'Donnell actively supported Robert Kennedy's presidential candidacy. He collaborated with former White House special assistant David Powers on *Johnny, We Hardly Knew Ye*, a 1970 memoir that was particularly vivid in its description of the Irish-Catholic milieu from which the career of John Kennedy developed. O'Donnell died in 1977.

—FHM

## O'Dwyer, (Peter) Paul

(1907–1998) *member, New York City Council*

O'Dwyer came to the United States from Ireland in 1925, 18 years after his birth on June 19, 1907. After settling in New York City, he stopped using his first name. He met his brother, William, who had immigrated earlier, and followed his brother's example by studying law at night. He financed his studies by working on the Brooklyn docks. After graduating from St. John's University and passing the bar exam in 1931, he represented several labor unions. He actively supported the Zionist movement after World War II and was a strong advocate of civil rights for African Americans.

O'Dwyer ran for Congress from Manhattan's Upper West Side in 1948 with the backing of the Democratic and American Labor Parties, but he lost in a close race to incumbent representative JACOB K. JAVITS (R-N.Y.). In 1958 O'Dwyer, Eleanor Roosevelt, Herbert H. Lehman, and other liberal Democrats founded the Committee for Democratic Voters and launched the New York Democratic reform movement. O'Dwyer sought and failed to gain the New York Democratic senatorial nomination in 1962, but he won a seat on the New York City Council the following year.

O'Dwyer went South at the request of the Congress of Racial Equality in the summer of 1964. He defended civil rights demonstrators and worked with the Mississippi Freedom Democratic Party (MFDP). That August, as a New York delegate to the Democratic National Convention, O'Dwyer supported the MFDP's bid to be seated in place of the segregationist, regular Mississippi Democratic delegation (The Credentials Committee voted to seat the regular delegation and offered two at-large voting seats to Freedom Democratic Representative. The MFDP delegation voted to reject the compromise.)

O'Dwyer began a campaign for the Democratic nomination for mayor of New York in June 1965. In the September 14 primary he finished a distant fourth behind New York City controller Abraham D. Beame and two other candidates. (Beame lost the general election to the Republican-Liberal candidate, Representative JOHN V. LINDSAY.

In October 1966 O'Dwyer successfully defended Ernest Gallashaw, a 17-year-old black youth accused of fatally shooting an 11-year-old boy during racial violence that July in Brooklyn's East New York district. During the same year O'Dwyer also won a U.S. Supreme Court decision granting Puerto Rican citizens the right to take voting literacy tests in their native language.

A critic of U.S. policy in Vietnam, O'Dwyer was an early and important supporter of Senator EUGENE J. MCCARTHY's (D-Minn.) 1968 presidential campaign. O'Dwyer himself sought New York's senatorial nomination in a primary fight against Nassau County executive Eugene Nickerson, a supporter of Senator ROBERT F. KENNEDY (D-N.Y.), and Representative Joseph Y. Resnick (D-N.Y.), who supported Vice President HUBERT H. HUMPHREY. O'Dwyer was given little chance of victory. He continually attacked administration policy in Vietnam and pledged that even if McCarthy were defeated, "I would not support Humphrey. Period." O'Dwyer won a narrow victory in the June 18 primary.

O'Dwyer was a leader of the strong McCarthy group in the New York delegation to the Democratic National Convention in Chicago. During the August 28 platform debate, O'Dwyer spoke in favor of the minority plank on Vietnam, which called for an unconditional bombing halt, a negotiated U.S. withdrawal and urged the South Vietnamese government to negotiate a political reconciliation with the National Liberation Front. The administration's majority plank passed 1,537 to 1,041. That same night O'Dwyer was involved in a melee on the convention floor when New York delegate Alex Rosenberg refused to show security guards his credentials. O'Dwyer intervened when guards attempted to

expel Rosenberg. In the resulting commotion Chicago police came onto the convention floor, and both O'Dwyer and Rosenberg were briefly detained.

In New York O'Dwyer's senatorial campaign against Republican-Liberal incumbent Jacob K. Javits and Conservative Party candidate James L. Buckley focused on the Vietnam War. O'Dwyer called for a cease-fire and an end to the draft. He also called for community control of schools, free heroin distribution to registered addicts, and an end to "hypocritical talk" about law and order. O'Dwyer's refusal to endorse the national ticket continued until November 1 when, following President Johnson's announcement of a halt to the bombing of North Vietnam, he finally endorsed Humphrey. Four days later O'Dwyer lost by over a million votes to Javits, who continued his record as New York State's leading vote-getter. O'Dwyer remained active in public life and in 1973 was elected president of the New York City Council. In 1976 he ran unsuccessfully for the Democratic senatorial nomination. He died on June 23, 1998.

—JBF

## Oglesby, Carl
(1935– )  *president, Students for a Democratic Society*

Born in Akron, Ohio, on July 30, 1935, Oglesby attended Kent State University. He spent a year in New York's Greenwich Village and wrote three plays. In the early 1960s Oglesby—by then married and the father of three children—worked as a technical writer for the Bendix Systems Division in Ann Arbor, Michigan. In the fall of 1964 Oglesby wrote an article critical of U.S. policy in the Far East, prompting local members of Students for a Democratic Society (SDS) to contact him. Oglesby soon became active in SDS antiwar activity. At the SDS National Council meeting following the group's April 1965 antiwar rally in Washington, D.C., Oglesby proposed that SDS establish a research, information, and publication bureau. The proposal was accepted, and Oglesby was hired to staff the bureau.

Oglesby was elected SDS president at the organization's June 1965 convention. A member for less than a year, Oglesby was the first SDS president to come from outside the group that had revitalized the organization in the early 1960s. His election reflected the growing influx of midwestern and southwestern students attracted to SDS by its antiwar activities. Immediately after his election Oglesby traveled to South Vietnam and Japan to meet with antiwar groups.

During Oglesby's presidency SDS grew rapidly and established itself as the leading campus opponent of the escalating U.S. intervention in Vietnam. Although generally critical of national demonstrations, SDS endorsed the plans of the National Coordinating Committee to End the War for antiwar demonstrations on October 15–16, 1965. The demonstrators as well as criticism from several U.S. senators and Deputy Attorney General NICHOLAS B. KATZENBACH brought SDS far more publicity than it had ever previously received, and its chapter membership virtually doubled to an estimated 10,000 members. At a widely publicized press conference shortly after the demonstrations, Oglesby and SDS national secretary Paul Booth announced a proposal to exempt from military service men participating in alternative "service for democracy," but SDS itself later repudiated the plan, which had not been approved by its rank-and-file membership.

SDS participated in a major antiwar demonstration on November 27, 1965, in Washington. Oglesby delivered what was generally considered the day's most influential speech. He argued that the Vietnam War was a product of "American liberalism," which served as an ideological justification and defense of the "corporate state." The speech, which Oglesby later called "an attempt to describe imperialism without giving it that name," was reprinted and became one of the most popular pieces of SDS literature. In June 1966, in a change of position, Oglesby joined the new chair of the Student Nonviolent Coordinating Committee, STOKELY CARMICHAEL, in rejecting alternate service and calling for an end to the draft.

After leaving office in September 1966, Oglesby coauthored a critical study of U.S. foreign policy, *Containment and Change*, and in 1967 was one of three U.S. members of Stockholm-based International War Crimes Tribunal sponsored by Bertrand Russell. In June 1968 Oglesby again became active in SDS when he was elected to the eight-member National Interim Committee. Oglesby opposed both the Progressive Labor Party and those supporting the "Revolutionary Youth Movement" strategy, the two strongest factions in SDS. As a result he did not play a major role in SDS's split the next year. Since the 1970s Oglesby

has written articles and books about the American power structure, the role of the intelligence community in domestic politics, and the assassination of John F. Kennedy.

—JBF

## Okun, Arthur M(elvin)

(1928–1980)  *chair, Council of Economic Advisers*

Born in Jersey City, New Jersey, on November 28, 1928, Okun earned a B.A. from Columbia University in 1949 and a Ph.D. seven years later. He joined the economics department at Yale University in 1952 and quickly earned promotions, attaining the rank of full professor in 1963. He began working as a consultant for the Council of Economic Advisers (CEA) in 1961. He formulated "Okun's Law," which correlated each 1 percent decrease in the unemployment rate, when it was high, with a 3.2 percent increase in gross national product. Okun's estimate of a generally predictable relationship between employment and economic growth provided a statistical rationale for the CEA's advocacy in 1963–64 of a massive tax cuts to stimulate lagging demand.

Okun was made a member of the CEA in 1964 and appointed its chair in January 1968. An adherent of the Keynesian "new economics," Okun, like his predecessors WALTER HELLER and GARDNER ACKLEY, believed that the federal government could generate rapid growth and maintain price stability through an aggressive and alert fiscal policy. As early as January 1967 Okun had argued that the economy's main problem was not sluggishness but rising prices. His major efforts as CEA chair were directed against inflation, what had been exacerbated by the increase in the administration's spending on Great Society programs and on the Vietnam War while the president deferred seeking a tax increase and maintained that the economy could provide both "guns and butter." Okun thought the 10 percent tax surcharge, which Congress approved in May 1968, was essential, if belated.

Okun took a firm stand on the Johnson administration's second line of defense against inflation, the struggle to moderate industrial wage settlements and price rises. As part of the administration's reaction to Bethlehem Steel's announcement of a 5 percent across-the-board steel price rise in July 1968, followed by similar increases on the part of other major producers, Okun sent telegrams urging the steel companies to consult with the government prior to price decisions. When U.S. Steel, the largest producer, posted increases averaging 2 1/2 percent, Bethlehem and the other producers reduced their own increases to that level. Okun was a major figure in the administration's campaign of pressure and exhortation to curb auto prices following an announcement by Chrysler in September of an $89, or 2.9 percent, increase on its 1969 models. Chrysler lowered its increase to the government-recommended 2 percent level after Ford and General Motors held their 1969 increases to that amount. Okun left the CEA in January 1969 and became a senior fellow at the Brookings Institution. He died of a heart attack on March 23, 1980.

—TO

## Ottinger, Richard L(awrence)
(1929–    ) *member of the House of Representatives*

Ottinger's father founded U.S. Plywood Company and his uncle, Albert Ottinger, ran as a Republican against Franklin Roosevelt in the 1928 race for the New York governorship. Richard Ottinger, born in New York City on January 27, 1929, graduated from Cornell in 1950 and took a law degree from Harvard in 1953. Ottinger was a subregional director of the Peace Corps from 1961 until 1964, when he defeated the incumbent Republican representatives from New York's 25th district, spending over $200,000 of his family's money.

Representing the western half of Westchester County, Ottinger was an early congressional spokesperson for alleviating environmental problems. Ottinger's concern about pollution in the Hudson River led him to criticize the 1965 antiwater pollution bill as inadequate for the needs of New York State. The new appropriations authorized by the bill, he said, "will be little more than a sigh in a hurricane." When 1966 water pollution legislation required the development of interstate water basin plans, Ottinger, claiming that the other states involved would be only minimally affected, engineered a compromise that allowed New York and New Jersey the power to veto any plan for the Hudson. Ottinger testified in 1966 on the need for a federal study of the environmental effects of power lines and tried, unsuccessfully, to add 60,000 miles of gas-gathering lines to a 1967 gas pipeline safety bill. In 1968 he supported elimination of funds for the supersonic transport (SST) airliner.

Ottinger consistently supported the Johnson administration's foreign and domestic policies during his first two terms. He urged federal research on nonpunitive drug addict rehabilitation plans and in 1967 attempted, without success, to increase hospital construction funds. However, Ottinger was one of two representatives to vote against the 1967 military construction bill that appropriated funds for the Vietnam War. In June 1968 Ottinger offered an amendment to limit the president's power to increase the number of U.S. troops in South Vietnam, invade North Vietnam or other Southeast Asian countries, or use nuclear weapons there.

Ottinger also opposed Johnson's plan for compulsory arbitration of the 1967 railroad strike, which Congress approved. Ottinger denounced arbitration that denied the right to strike because, he said, it "takes away from the railroads involved in the dispute any incentive to bargain collectively."

Ottinger remained in Congress until 1970, when he ran for the Senate. He came in second in a three-way race against Republican CHARLES GOODELL and the victor, Conservative James Buckley. Ottinger returned to Congress in 1974, when he won election from Westchester's other congressional district, previously held by OGDEN REID. He retired from Congress in 1985 and became a professor at Pace University Law School later that year. He served as dean of the law school from 1994 until 1999.

—MDB

# P

## Passman, Otto E(rnest)

(1900–1988) *member of the House of Representatives*

Born in Washington Parish, Louisiana, on June 27, 1900, Passman, after establishing a successful restaurant supply business and serving in the U.S. Navy during World War II, was elected to Congress in 1946 from Louisiana. He consistently opposed civil rights measures and usually voted with the conservative coalition of southern Democrats and Republicans.

Passman became a member of the House Appropriations Committee in 1949. Six years later Committee chair representative Clarence Cannon (D-Mo.) appointed Passman to head the panel's Foreign Operations Subcommittee, which initiated congressional consideration of foreign aid appropriations bills. Dominating the subcommittee, Passman became the most powerful foe of foreign assistance programs on Capitol Hill. Passman once declared, "I don't smoke, and I don't drink. My only pleasure in life is kicking the shit out of the foreign aid program of the United States of America." With the support of Cannon he succeeded in sharply reducing Eisenhower and Kennedy administration annual foreign aid requests. In 1963 President Kennedy's assistance proposal was cut by 33.8 percent, the largest reduction since the beginning of the foreign aid program.

Cannon died in May 1964 and was replaced as Appropriations Committee chair by Representative GEORGE H. MAHON (D-Tex.). President LYNDON B. JOHNSON had been a colleague of Mahon in the Texas congressional delegation and the new chair, although not a friend of foreign aid, was amenable to administration influence. Furthermore, Mahon was determined to assert control of the committee and decided to begin by challenging Passman's previously unquestioned authority over foreign assistance bills. In addition, President Johnson used his extensive network of connections on Capitol Hill to undermine Passman's support on the foreign operations panel.

As a result, Passman's attempt to cut $515 million from the administration's $3.5 billion foreign aid request was rejected by the subcommittee in the spring of 1964 by a vote of seven to five. Ultimately, Congress voted to reduce the foreign aid program by only 7.6 percent.

The following year Mahon revamped the membership of the subcommittee to further reduce Passman's support on the panel. Again his efforts to substantially reduce foreign aid were rebuffed, and administration requests were cut by just 6.9 percent.

During the last three years of the Johnson administration, opposition to foreign aid increased as the cost of the Vietnam War placed pressure upon the remainder of the budget. In 1966 and 1967 Congress cut foreign aid requests by 13.3 percent and 28.8 percent, respectively. In 1968 the administration's proposed figure was slashed by 39.7 percent, which represented a record cut.

Passman, the floor manager of the 1968 aid bill, declared, "We believe this is a bill which should satisfy those of us who have been trying to bring the annual aid appropriations . . . down to a reasonable amount." He remained the most outspoken opponent of foreign aid in Congress and continued to have influence in that area. But Passman never regained the unchallenged power over assistance appropriations he had possessed.

Passman failed to gain renomination for a 16th term in Congress in 1976. He died of a heart attack on August 13, 1988.

—MLL

## Pastore, John O(rlando)

(1907–2000)  *member of the Senate*

Born on March 17, 1907, John Pastore grew up in Providence, Rhode Island. He graduated from Northeastern University Law School in 1931 and then launched a career in local politics. He was elected lieutenant governor of Rhode Island in 1944 and assumed the governorship one year latter, following the resignation of J. Howard McGrath. In 1950 Pastore became the first Italian American ever elected to the U.S. Senate.

A liberal Democrat, Pastore supported the Kennedy administration on most major issues. As chair of the Communications Subcommittee of the Senate Commerce Committee, he was active in the regulation of television and other broadcast media. In his post as vice chair of the Joint Congressional Atomic Energy Committee, Pastore was a vigorous supporter of the 1963 limited nuclear test ban treaty.

Pastore supported the Johnson administration on over 65 percent of all major issues. He led the Senate fight for Title VI of the 1964 Civil Rights Act, which prohibited racial discrimination in any program or activity receiving federal assistance. He voted for the 1965 Medicare bill, and he was a strong supporter of the President's Vietnam policies. In 1965 he lost a close fight for the post of majority whip to Senator RUSSELL LONG (D-La.).

Pastore delivered the keynote address at the 1964 Democratic National Convention in Atlantic City, New Jersey, and set the rhetorical tone for the presidential campaign to follow. Speaking of the "prosperity, preparedness and peace" of the Kennedy years and the previous "nine miracle months" of the Johnson administration, Pastore declared that Senator BARRY GOLDWATER (R-Ariz.) and the Republican Party had been "captured" by extremists. He urged the nation to keep a "safe" trigger-finger on the atomic bomb.

In 1966 Pastore introduced a resolution of support for the administration's efforts to achieve a nuclear nonproliferation treaty. He requested that

President Johnson meeting with Rhode Island senator John Pastore, 1967  *(Photographed by Yoichi R. Okamoto; Lyndon Baines Johnson Library)*

the treaty include a requirement for international inspection of nuclear facilities and recommended that the People's Republic of China (PRC) be included in disarmament talks. Later that year Pastore criticized the administration for rejecting "out of hand" a 1965 proposal by the PRC asking that both nations agree never to take the initiative in the use of nuclear weapons against each other.

Pastore was a consistent advocate of a strong national defense posture. He declared in 1967 that the United States "should move full-speed ahead on building an anti-ballistic missile system [ABM]" and said that if the country was able to spend $24 billion a year in Vietnam it could "certainly spend as much to insure the life and security of our American society." Later, Pastore supported the Nixon administration's ABM program.

In 1969 Pastore's Communications Subcommittee conducted widely publicized hearings on the effects of televised violence on children. He was reelected to the Senate in 1970 by a large margin. Pastore retired from the Senate at the end of his term in 1976. He died on July 15, 2000.

—FHM

## Patman, (John William) Wright
(1893–1976) *member of the House of Representatives*

Wright Patman adhered for a lifetime to the anti–Wall Street populism prevalent in the turn-of-the-century rural Texas of his youth. Born in Patman's Switch, Texas, on August 6, 1893, he worked as a tenant farmer while attending school. After earning a law degree from Cumberland University in Lebanon, Tennessee, he returned to Texas to practice law. He served in the U.S. Army during World War I and won election as a Democrat to the Texas state legislature, where he met Sam Ealy Johnson and his son Lyndon. After four years as district attorney in Texarkana, he won election in 1928 to the first of 24 consecutive terms in the U.S. House of Representatives.

In Congress Patman quickly emerged as the figure of controversy he was to remain for over four decades, becoming the most persistent legislative opponent of the concentration of economic power in the hands of major commercial banks and Federal Reserve officials. In the early 1930s, against the wishes of Presidents Hoover and Roosevelt, Patman pushed the bonus bill to provide

$2.2 billion to World War I veterans as an anti-depression measure. The bill finally became law in 1936 over Roosevelt's veto. Payment of the bonus did not alleviate the depression, and Patman blamed the Federal Reserve for nullifying its impact by doubling bank reserve requirements, thus cutting consumer purchasing power. Patman also championed small business owners in the depression, helping to establish the Small Business Administration and later insisting that they share in World War II defense contracts. He favored national economic planning and backed the Employment Act of 1946, a landmark measure that declared "maximum employment, production and purchasing power" permanent objectives of national policy. By the early 1960s Patman was conspicuous chiefly for his attacks on the power of giant commercial banks and the policies of the Federal Reserve Board. After becoming chair of the Banking and Currency Committee in 1963 he had a prominent forum in which to campaign for his unorthodox monetary views.

Patman repeatedly attacked the Federal Reserve for its policy of high interest rates. Charging that the resulting constriction of the money supply was the chief cause of high unemployment, he led forces calling for low interest rates to stimulate the economy. To check inflation he advised the Federal Reserve to raise bank reserve requirements rather than interest rates.

Although the Kennedy and Johnson administrations shared Patman's desire for lower interest rates to a degree, neither president endorsed his structural criticism of the Federal Reserve System nor his proposed solutions. The major shortcoming of the Federal Reserve, Patman argued, was its domination by powerful private banking interests. The two conspired to keep interest rates artificially high, he contended, swelling bank profits but injuring small business owners and farmers in need of cheap credit. Patman proposed a drastic restructuring of the Federal Reserve to end its "independence" from Congress and the White House and thus curb the influence of the financial community and enable the administration to coordinate fiscal and monetary policy. "I would have the monetary system in the charge of and directed by public servants, who owe no allegiance to any group," Patman said in November 1962. On the first day of every session Patman introduced his perennially unsuccessful Federal Reserve reform bill.

Patman's chief adversary was the chair of the Federal Reserve Board, WILLIAM MCCHESNEY MARTIN. When the Federal Reserve raised the discount rate from 4 percent to 4.5 percent in December 1965, Patman immediately denounced the move and initiated an investigation by the Joint Economic Committee, which he chaired in alternate years. Characterizing the Federal Reserve action as "arrogant" and a "complete betrayal of the will of the people," he subjected Martin to sharp questioning and called for Martin's resignation. Patman predicted that the rate increase would "destroy the savings and loan industry" and would "create poverty" and "harm education and hospitals." Martin defended the board's action as necessary to prevent inflation.

Another Patman foe was Comptroller of the Currency JAMES J. SAXON whose liberalization of banking regulation was welcomed by the large national banks. As the champion of the nation's small banks and savings and loan associations, Patman excoriated Saxon's initiatives and blocked his proposal to permit national banks to establish branches where states had prohibited branch banking. In March 1965 Patman introduced a bill that would have abolished the Office of the Comptroller of the Currency and consolidated all regulatory functions in the secretary of the Treasury.

Despite the highest interest rates in a generation during the Johnson administration, Patman refrained from any criticism of President Johnson himself. Patman had shared a desk with Johnson's father in the Texas state legislature and for the next 40 years took a paternal interest in the younger Johnson. He generally aided in the passage of programs favored by the president. For example, Patman pushed through the Banking and Currency Committee a Johnson-backed bill allowing the federal government to "pool" certain mortgages and other loan assets held by the government and sell the paper to banks. The government thus obtained cash to reduce the visible budget deficit. Patman hurried the measure through the committee after only a few hours of testimony.

Patman was also a strong supporter of Johnson's Vietnam policy and a backer of most Great Society social legislation, with the exception of civil rights bills. He voted against the Civil Rights Act of 1964 and the Voting Rights Act of 1965.

Patman's other major target was the tax-exempt foundation. Using his Small Business Committee

as a forum, in 1961 he began the most comprehensive investigation of foundations ever undertaken. In a series of reports issued over the decade, the committee detailed abuses and irregularities in the operations of the 534 foundations studied. In general, Patman found that many foundations were virtually unregulated and placed the pursuit of profits and tax avoidance above their philanthropic functions. In March 1968 Patman's sixth foundation report criticized the use of foundations by wealthy persons to avoid estate taxes. "As a result of the Treasury's inaction, ineptness and lethargy," he said, "the same old tax-dodging devices exist today that have been used for decades." Patman suggested that for the duration of the Vietnam War foundations contribute their gross receipts to the federal government "in support of our defense of democracy in Southeast Asia."

Patman's populist crusades made him a figure of great controversy and a maverick among committee chairs in Congress. On the Banking and Currency Committee, some members resented and even rebelled against his attacks on the financial establishment and his autocratic style as chair. A revolt occurred in 1965, when some committee members met without Patman's knowledge in a darkened committee room to approve a bill liberalizing bank mergers that Patman had been blocking. The incident infuriated Patman, who overturned the action on the ground that the dissidents had not followed committee rules. A compromise measure passed a few months later, with Speaker of the House JOHN MCCORMACK (D-Mass.) acting as a peacemaker, but bitter feelings remained on the committee.

Patman was unseated as chair by the House Democratic caucus in January 1975. In January 1976 Patman announced that he would not seek reelection. He died of pneumonia on March 7, 1976.

—TO

## Pearson, Drew (Andrew) (Russell)
(1896–1969) *syndicated columnist*

For more than three decades, Drew Pearson was a popular, sensational, and influential columnist who gained fame for exposing corruption in government. He was born on December 13, 1896, in Evanston, Illinois, where his father was a professor of English at Northwestern University. When his father accepted a faculty position at Swarthmore College, the family moved when Pearson was six years old. Pearson graduated from Swarthmore in 1919 and worked for several newspapers as a correspondent in Asia and Europe and as foreign editor of the *United States Daily* (the predecessor of *U.S. News and World Report*) before becoming a diplomatic correspondent for the *Baltimore Sun* in 1929. With journalist Robert Allen, he wrote a book, *Washington Merry-Go-Round* in 1931 and a sequel a year later that quickly led to a syndicated column by the same name. Pearson and Allen specialized in exposés of political figures and wrote in a muckraking style. By the time that Allen enlisted in the U.S. Army in 1942 and left Pearson to write by himself, the column has become a popular fixture in 350 U.S. newspapers.

Pearson ensured that his column remained popular by filling it with gossip on the private lives of public figures and acerbic criticism of his political targets. He never lost sight, however, of the issues behind Washington's personalities. During the 1950s Pearson was an important backer of many liberal causes, including the fight against Sen. Joseph McCarthy (R-Wisc.). In 1958 he was the first Washington journalist to expose the influence-peddling activities of presidential assistant Sherman Adams, and his column later investigated the close relationship between President Eisenhower and powerful business interests. After an exclusive interview with Soviet Premier Nikita Khrushchev in 1961, Pearson became an early advocate of East-West détente. He also criticized increasing U.S. aid to South Vietnam's Diem regime, which he blamed partly on the Catholicism of President John F. Kennedy.

Pearson's most important cause during the mid-1960s was his fight against Senator THOMAS DODD (D-Conn.). In more than 100 columns Pearson and his associate JACK ANDERSON accused Dodd of using his political influence to promote the private interests of Julius Klein, a Chicago public relations agent. The columnists also charged that Dodd had diverted tax-free campaign contributions to his personal use. In May 1966 Dodd filed a $5 million libel and conspiracy suit against Pearson, but it was subsequently dropped. On June 20 the Senate Select Committee on Standards and Conduct, chaired by Senator JOHN STENNIS (D-Miss.), opened hearings on Dodd's alleged misconduct. The committee's lengthy investigation resulted in Dodd's formal censure in June 1967 by a Senate

vote of 92 to 5. Dodd was unseated in 1970 by Republican challenger Lowell Weicker.

In 1968 Pearson collaborated with Jack Anderson on the best-selling book *The Case Against Congress,* an indictment of the corruption and abuse of power that he believed was common on Capitol Hill. By 1969 Pearson's newspaper column was syndicated by more than 650 papers, making it the most widely read in the United States. When Pearson died in September 1969, the column was taken over by Jack Anderson, who had been Pearson's associate since the late 1950s.

—FHM

## Pell, Claiborne (de Borda)
**(1918–  )** *member of the Senate*

Born in New York City on November 22, 1918, into a wealthy and prominent Newport family, Claiborne Pell attended the fashionable St. George's School, graduated from Princeton in 1940, and served in the U.S. Coast Guard during World War II. After being commissioned in the foreign service in 1946, Pell served in the U.S. embassy in Prague and the consulate in Genoa, Italy, as well as in the State Department during the next six years. He then became a limited partner with a prominent investment banking firm.

Pell first gained political recognition through his ability as a state Democratic fund-raiser and as a consultant to the Democratic National Committee from 1953 to 1960. After long-serving senator Theodore F. Green (D-R.I.) announced his retirement in 1960, Pell won the Democratic senatorial primary. A Protestant in a state that was 60 percent Catholic, Pell won the general election with a record 69 percent of the vote.

Named to the important Labor and Public Welfare Committee, Pell supported most Kennedy administration legislative programs, but his diplomatic background had given him a particular interest in foreign affairs. In February 1963 Pell was a member of a four-person Senate study group headed by Senator MIKE MANSFIELD (D-Mont.) that toured Southeast Asia and issued a report questioning the high level of U.S. military and economic aid to South Vietnam.

Regarded as a liberal, Pell supported Johnson programs on over 65 percent of all issues in the 88th, 89th, and 90th Congresses. He was named to the Senate Foreign Relations Committee in 1965.

Pell was instrumental in the passage of the 1964 National Arts and Cultural Development Act, which established a National Council on the Arts and provided for federal matching grants and non-professional groups to promote the arts. A member of the Rules and Administration Committee, which issued two 1965 reports on the investigation of the Senate Majority Leader former secretary ROBERT G. ("Bobby") BAKER, Pell proposed that all senators who were lawyers should list the clients of their firms with the U.S. Comptroller General.

Pell devoted much of his first term in the Senate to dealing with the decline of railway passenger service in the Northeast. He sponsored several Senate resolutions proposing an eight-state public authority to provide high-speed intercity rail service for the busy "Northeast corridor." Many conservative senators opposed Pell's plan because they believed it would involve excessive federal intrusion in the railroad industry. Pell was a strong supporter of the 1965 High-Speed Ground Transportation Research Act, which granted $90 million for research into advanced ground transportation systems.

Reelected to the Senate in 1966, Pell was a firm but not particularly vocal opponent of U.S. involvement in Vietnam. In May 1967 he warned that indefinite escalation of the war might lead to China's intervention and "the start of a domestic clamor to use nuclear weapons."

Pell won election to six Senate terms before retiring in 1997. He served as chair of the Senate Foreign Relations Committee from 1987 to 1995.

—FHM

## Percy, Charles H(arting)

(1919–   ) *member of the Senate*

Born in Pensacola, Florida, on September 27, 1919, Percy grew up in Chicago, after his family moved during his infancy. His father was a bank clerk who lost his job and declared bankruptcy during the depression. Percy worked to pay the costs of attending the University of Chicago. After graduating in 1941, he took a job with Bell and Howell, a manufacturer of cameras and photographic equipment. He returned to the company after two years in the U.S. Navy and rose quickly in executive positions. In 1949, at age 29, he became the youngest chief of a major U.S. business when he was appointed Bell and Howell's president. The company prospered until Percy's leadership, with sales increasing 12-fold by the time he left Bell and Howell in 1966.

Percy's involvement in politics began during the mid-1950s, when he worked as a fund raiser for the Republican Party in Illinois. In 1959 he chaired the party's Committee on Program and Progress, which formulated long-range policy proposals; with this experience he was chosen to head the Platform Committee at the 1960 Republican National Convention. A member of the party's moderate wing, Percy reluctantly supported the presidential candidacy of Senator BARRY GOLDWATER (R-Ariz.) in 1964. At the same time he gave up direction of Bell and Howell to run for governor of Illinois. He lost to incumbent OTTO KERNER by a narrow margin in the Democratic landslide of 1964.

Percy took the next opportunity to run for high office by challenging Senator PAUL DOUGLAS (D-Ill.) in 1966. The campaign developed into a closely watched contest. Percy criticized Douglas for his support of administration Vietnam policy and urged a negotiated peace settlement. Percy, like Douglas, called for a federal ban on racial discrimination in housing. He hoped his position, the reverse of his stand during the 1964 campaign, would help him make gains among African-American voters. Yet Douglas raised questions about the depth of Percy's commitment to civil rights and won large majorities in Chicago's predominantly black neighborhoods. The vigorous campaign was interrupted in September by the unexplained murder of Percy's daughter Valerie. Resumed after one month, the race ended in a victory for Percy, who gained 56 percent of the vote. Some observers claimed that the intensive publicity resulting from the murder and inquest helped Percy to win, although Douglas later admitted that Percy had already pulled ahead during the summer. Percy's strongest support came from suburban areas in northern Illinois.

In the Senate Percy soon became known as an aggressive newcomer who did not let his low seniority prevent him from gaining public attention. Frequently rumored as a potential presidential or vice presidential candidate, he fed speculation by making well-publicized statements on a wide variety of issues. Percy was especially critical of the administration's Vietnam policy. In early 1967 he urged "greater efforts" by the administration to achieve a negotiated settlement, claiming that previous U.S. peace offers were "simply too vague to be practical." He also introduced a "sense of the Senate" resolution demanding greater participation in the war by Asian allies of the United States. In late 1967 Percy made a trip to South Vietnam, gaining considerable publicity when he came under fire from the enemy in an abandoned village.

During his first term in the Senate, Percy maintained a moderate voting record and a reputation as a political independent. Percy's first important legislative effort was a 1967 proposal to provide federal aid for low-income homeowners through creation of a private, nonprofit mortgage loan corporation. Though over-ridden by Democrats on the Senate Banking and Currency Committee, the plan was later reformulated and incorporated into the Housing and Urban Development Act of 1968. In subsequent years Percy was one of the leaders in the unsuccessful fight for creation of a consumer protection agency. He also devoted considerable attention to the problems of elderly Americans as a member of the Senate Special Committee on Aging.

Percy won a second term in the Senate in 1972 with 62 percent of the vote. He considered seeking the Republican presidential nomination in 1976, but he decided not to declare his candidacy after GERALD FORD became president in 1976. Percy won a third term in 1978 and became chair of the Senate Foreign Relations Committee, when Republicans gained a majority in the Senate in 1981. He lost his seat, though, to Paul Simon in the election of 1984. After leaving the Senate, Percy headed a firm involved in trade and technology investment consulting.

—SLG

## Pike, James A(lbert)

*(1913–1969) Protestant Episcopal bishop of California*

Born in Oklahoma City, Oklahoma, on February 14, 1913, and raised in Los Angeles as a Roman Catholic, Pike studied for the priesthood but soon turned to a legal career. While serving in the U.S. Navy during World War II, he renewed his interest in religion and was ordained an Episcopalian priest in 1946. He served as dean of New York's Cathedral of St. John the Divine and as a professor of religion at Columbia University before becoming bishop of California in 1958.

Pike became well known for his iconoclastic views through numerous books and articles and his own television show. He advocated civil rights, supported the state of Israel and backed planned parenthood. He denounced book and film censorship and attacked the methods of the House Un-American Activities Committee. Pike also espoused extremely unorthodox theological ideas that prompted charges of heresy and, occasionally, communism from his conservative colleagues. Always independent and unpredictable, Bishop Pike sided with conservative Protestants in an attack on the Supreme Court's 1962 decision banning prayer in the public schools. In 1962 and 1963 Pike also worked with anti-Castro groups in the United States.

Pike was again embroiled in controversy when he headed the California Advisory Committee to the U.S. Civil Rights Commission (CRC). His committee issued a statement in January 1966 attacking the official government investigation of the 1965 Watts riot. Pike's group charged that the prestigious commission, headed by former CIA chief JOHN J. MCCONE, had "whitewashed" the role played by Los Angeles mayor SAM W. YORTY and police chief William H. Parker during the riot. Pike suggested that the CRC investigate "Negro complaints concerning police malpractices" and that the U.S. Housing and Urban Affairs Department "designate Los Angeles as an area for top priority attention" in its investigation of discrimination in housing. Mayor Yorty later accused Pike and his committee of turning its report into a political attack on the police.

As a result of Pike's skepticism about much Episcopal church doctrine—including the virgin birth, the Trinity, the incarnation, and the bodily resurrection of Jesus—charges of heresy were frequently raised against the bishop in the mid-1960s. Pike thought the church out of date theologically. In September 1966, for example, he announced plans to elevate a woman to ministerial status despite a resolution by the Episcopal House of Bishops banning women from serving communion. Partly because of the resulting furor, Pike decided to resign the bishopric of California to join the staff of the Center for the Study of Democratic Institutions as resident theologian.

At this time the House of Bishops refused demands for a heresy trial but issued a majority report chiding Pike for his "irresponsible" utterances and for his frequent "cheap vulgarization of great expressions of faith." Following the reprimand Pike moved further out of the mainstream of American Protestantism, meeting with mediums, for example, in efforts to contact his son, who had recently committed suicide. In September 1967 Pike published *If This Be Heresy* in defense of his beliefs.

In October 1967 Pike, as a member of the Clergy and Laymen Concerned about Vietnam, signed a statement promising "to aid and abet" American youths in resisting the military draft. He also remained active in the Southern Christian Leadership Conference and other civil rights groups.

While in Israel to gather information for a biblical study, Pike's car stalled in the desert. He died of exposure and his body was discovered on September 7, 1969.

—JCH

## Poage, W(illiam) R(obert) "Bob"
(1899–1987) *member of the House of Representatives*

Born in Waco, Texas, on December 28, 1899, Poage served in the U.S. Navy during World War I and then earned a B.A. from Baylor University in 1921 and a law degree in 1924. Poage practiced law and served for 12 years beginning in 1925 in the Texas state legislature. In 1936 he won election to the first of 21 consecutive terms in the U.S. Congress. As a member of the Agriculture Committee, he spoke for the interests of small farmers and criticized the policies of the Eisenhower administration, which he said forced farmers out of business.

While fighting to maintain high farm subsidies, Poage sought to hold down the cost of farm labor. In 1951 he helped establish the "bracero" program for the temporary migration of Mexican farm laborers into the United States. He called the program "the best kind of foreign aid" for Mexican families who might otherwise starve. Poage also opposed minimum wage standards for American farm workers and in 1959 declared a minimum wage "illegal, impractical, and immoral."

In the early 1960s Poage supported President Kennedy's efforts to require farmers to accept stiff controls over crop yields rather than acreage allotments before they could benefit from government price guarantees. Poage voted for both the original omnibus food and agriculture bill of 1962, which Congress rejected, and the compromise measure that became law on September 27, 1962.

After the electoral defeat of HAROLD D. COOLEY (D-N.C.) in November 1966, Poage became chair of the House Agriculture Committee. He used this position to oppose reforms in the food stamp program. During hearings in October 1967, Poage referred to food stamp recipients as "a bunch of

drones" and suggested that "maybe we have gotten too far away from the situation of primitive man" when the "drones" were killed. Poage's reluctance to enlarge the food stamp program led to clashes with citizens groups critical of the government's food assistance programs. After the Committee on School Lunch Participation and the Citizens Board of Inquiry into Hunger and Malnutrition in the United States issued widely circulated studies on hunger in America, Poage mailed letters to all the county health officers in the nation asking if they were aware of any cases of starvation or serious malnutrition in their districts. On June 16, 1968, the House Agriculture Committee issued its own "hunger study" based upon 181 replies to Poage's inquiry. According to the committee, the report "leads to the unmistakable conclusion that there is very little actual hunger in the United States but widespread malnutrition caused largely by ignorance as to what constitutes a balanced diet."

The committee's report ascribed the few instances of borderline starvation and hunger to parental neglect of infants, adding that most of these cases involved mentally retarded parents. When the report was issued Poage added, "There seems to be little or no evidence that substantial hunger in this country exists as the result of the refusal of assistance agencies, public and private, to give needed aid to those who are unable to work." Poage charged in July 1969 that a proposal to establish a free food stamp program would lead to "socialism."

Poage remained as chair of the Agriculture Committee until deposed in 1975 by younger Democrats who no longer believed that positions of authority should be allocated solely on the basis of seniority. He decided not to seek reelection in 1978. After leaving the House, Poage wrote books about Texas history. He died on January 3, 1987.

—DKR

## Pool, Joe (Richard)
(1911–1968) *member of the House of Representatives*

Born in Fort Worth, Texas, on February 18, 1911, Pool earned a law degree from Southern Methodist University in 1937 and served in the U.S. Army Air Force during World War II. After leaving the service, he practiced law and owned a mattress business. In 1952 he gained election to the first of three consecutive two-year terms in the Texas House of

Representatives. During his tenure in that body, he drafted a bill to outlaw sex and violence in comic books. In 1958 and 1960 he unsuccessfully sought election to the U.S. House of Representatives from Dallas. Two years later he won a seat in the House as an at-large Texas representative. Pool usually opposed Kennedy and Johnson administration domestic programs.

In January 1966 Pool, a supporter of intensified American military activity in Vietnam, introduced a bill imposing fines and prison terms upon persons convicted of giving material aid to a hostile foreign power or impeding the movement of armed forces personnel or materiel. The targets of the bill were antiwar activists who provided medical supplies and other aid to the National Liberation Front or North Vietnam or who blocked troop and military supply trains. Pool maintained such a law was necessary because existing statutes only covered such activities during declared wars.

Pool first gained national attention in August 1966, when he headed a House Un-American Activities Committee (HUAC) subcommittee investigating alleged Communist influence within the antiwar movement. On August 15, as the hearings were about to begin, a federal district court judge enjoined the panel from initiating its investigation on the ground that HUAC procedures violated the rights of witnesses. A constitutional confrontation between Congress and the judiciary was avoided when a three-judge appeals court dissolved the restraining order on the following day, minutes before Pool was prepared to begin hearings in defiance of the lower court.

The subcommittee went on to conduct a stormy four-day investigation. Antiwar activists subpoenaed as witnesses expressed contempt for the panel, while their sympathizers in the audience disrupted the proceedings. Arthur Kinoy, a lawyer for one of the witnesses, was dragged from the hearing room when he refused to sit down at Pool's behest. Administration witnesses opposed the bill as unnecessary and possibly unconstitutional.

On August 29 the full committee reported favorably on an amended version of Pool's bill, and the House passed the measure by a 275-64 vote on October 13. The Senate, however, did not act on the measure, HUAC reported out the bill again in May 1967, but the House did not take up the proposal.

Pool died of a heart attack on July 14, 1968.

—MLL

## Powell, Adam Clayton, Jr.

(1908–1972) *member of the House of Representatives*

Born in New Haven, Connecticut, on November 29, 1908, Powell earned a B.A. from Colgate University and an A.M. from Columbia University two years later. In 1937 he succeeded his father as pastor of Harlem's Abyssinian Baptist Church, the largest Protestant congregation in the country. During the 1930s and 1940s the younger Powell set up soup kitchens for the needy, organized a bus boycott that compelled the Transport Workers Union to accept black drivers, and used similar tactics to win concessions from the telephone company and Harlem merchants. In 1941 he became the first African American elected to the New York City Council and three years later won a seat in Congress as the representative from Central Harlem. The church, throughout Powell's long tenure in Congress, served as his political base.

As a representative in the 1950s, Powell was best known for his efforts to bar federal appropriations to state projects that practiced racial discrimination. The so-called Powell Amendment to a 1956 school construction bill seriously divided liberal Democrats because it forced them to choose between federal aid to education and de facto support of segregated school systems. ADLAI STEVENSON refused to support the amendment or to meet with Powell to discuss civil rights matters in general. As a result Powell broke party ranks in 1956 to support the reelection of DWIGHT D. EISENHOWER.

Powell's attendance record, among the worst in Congress, and his penchant for congressionally financed vacations abroad, were repeatedly condemned in the news media. Shortly before Powell became chair of the House Committee on Education and Labor in 1961, the *New York Times* wrote that his "miserable record as a legislator and his extreme absenteeism all tend to disqualify him as a reasonable and effective chairman." During his first years as chair, however, he headed a remarkably productive committee that reported out minimum wage, education, and antipoverty legislation generally favored by the Kennedy administration.

Powell's relations with President Johnson were at first cordial. Nevertheless, Powell's conduct as chair during 1965 and 1966 alienated liberal Democrats, organized labor, and the Johnson administration and contributed to his political demise. Powell's delay of the 1965 Elementary and

New York representative Adam Clayton Powell, Jr., talking with President Johnson, 1965
*(Photographed by Yoichi R. Okamoto; Lyndon Baines Johnson Library)*

Secondary Education Act threatened the passage of that legislation, angering President Johnson. In 1966 the poverty bill was delayed four months while Powell traveled and vacationed on the island of Bimini in the Bahamas. That same year Powell blocked legislation, strongly favored by organized labor, permitting "common site picketing." By September 1966 many members of Powell's committee were in open revolt not only over these matters but also over his alleged "capricious" dismissals of committee staff, his vetoes of legislation approved by subcommittee, and his misuse of congressional funds.

In September 1966 the Education and Labor Committee adopted 27 new rules making it difficult for Powell to delay legislation favored by the majority. Also in September, the usually inactive House Administration's Special Subcommittee on Contracts, under the chairship of Representative WAYNE HAYES (D-Ohio), began an investigation that culminated in a report demanding that Powell's wife, who lived in Puerto Rico, be removed from the congressional payroll.

Meanwhile, Powell was in contempt of court for his refusal to pay a $211,739 judgment (later reduced to $46,500) stemming from a defamation suit brought against him in 1960. Powell faced arrest if he returned to New York, but his influence remained strong in Harlem, and he was reelected in 1966.

Powell aroused additional controversy in the mid-1960s when he aligned himself with STOKELY CARMICHAEL and others in the Black Power move-

ment. As early as March 1963 Powell had demanded that blacks boycott all civil rights organizations (including the NAACP) "not totally controlled by us."

In January 1967, at the beginning of the 90th Congress, Powell was ousted from his committee chair and barred from taking his seat pending an investigation of his fitness to hold office. With the support of House Majority Leader CARL ALBERT (D-Okla.), Representative MORRIS UDALL (D-Ariz.) moved to seat Powell pending the outcome of the investigation. The motion was defeated by an overwhelming majority, with many northern liberals voting with Republicans and southern Democrats against the Harlem representative.

On February 23, 1967, a nine-member select House committee under Representative EMANUEL CELLER (D-N.Y.) reported that Powell had "wrongfully and willfully appropriated" public funds and had "improperly maintained his wife" on the congressional payroll. The committee recommended that Powell be censured for "gross misconduct," fined $40,000, and stripped of his seniority.

The House rejected the committee's recommendations on March 1, 1967, and—for only the third time in American history to that date and the first time in 46 years—voted 307 to 116 to exclude a duly elected representative. Representative Celler saw "an element of racism in the vote . . . accompanied by the hysteria that had resulted from the climate of opinion due to Mr. Powell's antics and peculiarities and swagger and defiance."

African-American leaders from around the country denounced the expulsion. FLOYD MCKISSICK, national director of the Congress of Racial Equality, called it "a slap in the face of every black in the country," while A. PHILIP RANDOLPH of the Brotherhood of Sleeping Car Porters said it was "a mockery of democracy without predecent." However, *Congressional Quarterly* reported that "the most notable aspect of the lobby action in the Powell affair was the lack of concerted effort in Powell's behalf by the organized civil rights lobby." ROY WILKINS, head of the NAACP, explained that "Powell never called on [the] civil rights movement . . . never invited [its] help."

In April 1967 a special election was held to fill Powell's seat; he was reelected by a margin of 7 to 1. The seat remained vacant for two years. In January 1969, after paying a $25,000 fine, Powell was permitted to return to the House, but he was stripped of all seniority. In June the Supreme Court ruled that Powell's expulsion had been unconstitutional. He was stricken with cancer that year, and before he could decide to retire from politics lost his seat to Charles B. Rangel, who narrowly defeated him in a June 1970 primary. Powell died two years later on April 4, 1972.

Powell was among the most controversial politicians of his time. To journalist Theodore White he was "the most egregious and frightening" exception to the general excellence of black elected officials. To Chuck Stone, Powell's chief congressional assistant, he was "a mercurial personality who wavered erratically between tub-thumping militancy and cowardly silence"—a man so driven by "hedonistic compulsions" that he undermined his role as a black leader. However, Julius Lester, a black author, remembered him as the man who once "gave blacks a national voice" when other were quietly submissive and deferential.

—JLW

## Price, Cecil R(ay)

(1938–2001)   *deputy sheriff, Neshoba County, Mississippi*

Price became chief deputy sheriff of Neshoba County, Mississippi, in January 1964. The following June three civil rights workers—Andrew Goodman and Michael H. Schwerner, whites from New York, and James E. Chaney, a black from Meridian, Mississippi—entered the county to investigate the recent burning of an African-American church, which was to have been used as a Freedom School in the Mississippi Summer Project. The three civil rights workers disappeared, and their bodies were discovered in August in a dam near Philadelphia, Mississippi, the county seat.

Although these events produced a national outcry, Mississippi authorities did not then bring any charges in connection with the case. In December 1964 FBI agents arrested Price, County Sheriff Lawrence A. Rainey, and 16 others. The Justice Department asserted that a plan to kill the three had been arranged by members of the Ku Klux Klan. Price was accused of detaining the victims in Philadelphia, recapturing them on a highway, and then turning them over to a lynch mob.

Price and the others were indicted under an 1870 statute for conspiring to injure citizens in the free exercise of federal rights. The indictment was struck down by Federal District judge W. HAROLD COX in February 1965, but his decision was overturned by a unanimous ruling of the U.S. Supreme Court in March 1966. New indictments were issued a year later, and, in October 1967, Price and six other defendants were found guilty in what was believed to be the first conviction in a civil rights slaying in Mississippi. Price received a prison term of six years.

The U.S. Supreme Court upheld the conviction in February 1970, and Price went to jail shortly thereafter. He served four and one-half years of his sentence before being released. After his release, he worked as a watchmaker, market manager, and truck driver. He died from a fractured skull suffered in an accidental fall on May 6, 2001.

—MLL

## Proxmire, (Edward) William

(1915–   )   *member of the Senate*

Born in Lake Forest, Illinois, on November 11, 1915, Proxmire earned a B.A. from Yale University and an M.B.A. from Harvard before doing intelligence work in the U.S. Army during World War II. He moved to Wisconsin in 1948 and won a seat in the state assembly two years later. In 1952 he made the first of three consecutive unsuccessful runs for governor. In a special election in 1957 to fill the U.S. Senate seat left vacant by the death of Joseph R. McCarthy (R-Wisc.), Proxmire won an upset victory. In the Senate he alienated Majority Leader LYNDON JOHNSON (D-Tex.) when, in February 1958, he criticized Johnson's "unwholesome and arbitrary power" and demanded more frequent party caucuses. During the Kennedy years Proxmire earned a reputation as a maverick liberal by combining an active opposition to the oil industry with fervid efforts to reduce government spending and balance the budget.

During the Johnson administration Proxmire was a member of the Senate Banking Committee, the Appropriations Committee, and the Joint Economic Committee. He was a leader in the 1964 battle waged by Senate liberals against Senator EVERETT M. DIRKSEN's (R-Ill.) proposed constitutional amendment to supersede the Supreme Court's "one-man, one-vote" decision. Proxmire orchestrated the liberal filibuster, which delayed Dirksen's bill and gave civil rights and labor groups time to build outside pressure against it. He continued a successful strategy of delay until the proposed amendment died with Dirksen in 1969. Proxmire was also the chief sponsor of a "truth in lending" law signed in May 1968, which required most lenders to disclose the actual amount of interest charged borrowers.

Proxmire supported the war in Vietnam in the mid-1960s and served as a member of the steering committee of the Committee of One Million against Admission of Communist China to the United Nations in 1965. On January 6, 1965, he stated that "it's a mistake to negotiate when losing." Yet, two years later, he criticized the Johnson administration for releasing public estimates of the cost of the war in Vietnam that were substantially less than actual expenditures. This error, he said, "destroyed all our economic policies." Proxmire opposed a tax increase to finance the war and urged instead that the budget be balanced by spending cuts, especially in the space and public works programs and by withdrawing four of the six U.S. divisions in Europe. He also asked Congress to restore the investment tax credit, which he had originally opposed in 1962.

Although he supported most Great Society programs, Proxmire was relentless in his efforts to reduce government expenditures, especially those he considered extravagant or wasteful. Although usually unsuccessful, he tried to trim funds for the Civil Aeronautics Board, the Federal Aviation Administration, and the National Aeronautics and Space Administration. He failed in 1967 to persuade the Senate to reduce the oil depletion allowance. That same year he urged abolition of the Subversive Activities Control Board, calling it a "ridiculous extravagance."

Proxmire's greatest success came in his eight-year struggle to kill the supersonic transport plane (SST). In November 1963 he was one of six senators to vote against the initial appropriation of $20 million for research and development. Proxmire was joined by 18 senators in his April 1967 attempt to delete funds for the SST from the Department of Transportation's budget. After the defeat of his amendment, Proxmire was the only senator to vote against the entire Transportation Department appropriation bill because it included the SST expenditure, which he called a "wasteful blunder." He played a major role in the Senate's eventual vote in 1970 to kill the project. He also persistently called attention to cost overruns in the C-5A cargo plane.

During the 1970s, Proxmire found new and, occasionally, sensational ways to publicize what he viewed as excessive government spending. He wrote two books on the subject, and, in 1975, he began giving out monthly "Golden Fleece" awards for what he considered notorious examples of government waste. After retiring from the Senate in 1989, he wrote a syndicated newspaper column and continued to pass out "Golden Fleece" awards. Because of the onset of Alzheimer's disease, he stopped writing the column in 1998.

—TO

## Quie, Albert H(arold)

(1923– ) *member of the House of Representatives*

Born in Dennison, Minnesota, on September 18, 1923, Albert H. Quie grew up on his family's dairy farm. A navy pilot during World War II, Quie received his B.A. from St. Olaf College in 1950. Four years later he won election to as a Republican the state senate and served there until a successful special U.S. House campaign in February 1958. Quie never encountered serious opposition in his reelection contests after 1958.

A party regular, Quie generally voted with the GOP leadership. In February 1964 he joined a majority of his GOP colleagues in support of the House version of the civil rights bill. In April Quie led the opposition to the bill permanently establishing the food stamp program, one of the president's 30 "priority" measures of the 1964 session. Yet, rather than reject the Democrats' idea altogether, Quie proposed that the states pay for 50 percent of the costs. The House rejected his amendment.

In 1965 Quie participated in the revolt against the leadership of Representative CHARLES HAL-LECK (R-Ind.) and ended in the selection of GER-ALD R. FORD (R-Mich.) as minority leader. Once elected Ford shared the leadership's policy functions. Beginning in 1966 Quie and CHARLES E. GOODELL (R-N.Y.) helped formulate and campaign for a comprehensive Republican alternative to the administration's War on Poverty programs. The two representatives accused the president of engaging the nation in an antipoverty war without a fully developed strategy. The Quie-Goodell proposal transferred many of the Office of Economic Opportunity's (OEO) programs to other, existing cabinet agencies. Another Quie measure required that at least one-third of OEO local community action board members be representative of, and chosen by, the poor, a provision aimed at limiting the OEO's patronage powers. Quie and Goodell also called for an increased state role in the programs and the "massive involvement of private enterprise." With the exception of the community board proposal, approved in September 1966, no action was taken on their ideas during the final years of the Johnson presidency.

Quie's own leadership role first became widely known in the debate over the 1967 federal aid-to-education bill. Through an amendment submitted in May, he sought to alter fundamentally the federal government's distribution of assistance funds. Quie's proposed measure provided for federal "block grants" to states rather than to affected localities; its proponents argued that bureaucratic "red tape" would be restricted by entrusting fund allocations to existing state authorities. Most Republicans and southern Democrats backed the Quie amendment. However, the administration strongly opposed the provision and rallied religious, civil rights, and educational organizations to its side. In late May the House forces defeated the proposal by a 168-197 vote. Although not original to Quie, the "revenue sharing" concept became a constant demand of the GOP House leadership during debates over the administration's Great Society legislation.

In the spring of 1968 Quie and Goodell pressured Ford into supporting an open housing bill. Their move represented the first—and one of the few—challenges to Ford's House leadership. Ford gave up his opposition to the bill just before the vote, after Quie and Goodell had announced endorsement of the bill by 77 GOP House members.

Quie left the House after he was elected governor of Minnesota in 1978. When his four-year term was over, he served on the President's Advisory Committee for Trade Negotiations and then as executive vice president of Prison Fellowship USA.

—JLB

# R

## Raborn, William F(rancis)

(1905–1990) *director, Central Intelligence Agency*

Born in Decatur, Texas, on June 8, 1905, Raborn graduated from the U.S. Naval Academy in 1928. In 1955 he became head of the Navy's Polaris submarine missile program and assumed responsibility for the construction of the first Polaris submarine base at Charleston, South Carolina. In January 1962 Raborn was named deputy chief of naval operations in charge of weapons development. He retired from the navy a year later to join the Aerojet General Corporation.

In April 1965 Raborn succeeded JOHN MCCONE as director of the Central Intelligence Agency (CIA). Shortly afterward, President Johnson asked Raborn for his opinion on U.S. strategy in the war in Vietnam. He favored increased bombing of North Vietnam but also suggested that the United States keep in mind the possibility of a bombing pause to bring the North Vietnamese to the negotiating table and "to exploit any differences on their side." The Johnson administration, did halt the bombing in May 1965 and for 37 days in December 1965 and January 1966, but these temporary pauses did not induce the North Vietnamese to negotiate.

Raborn served little more than a year as director of Central Intelligence, and he had difficulty establishing his authority in the eyes of intelligence professionals. CIA officers circulated stories about his ineptness or ignorance and considered him unsuited to his position. Raborn considered his greatest achievements were the reform of management procedures at the agency and the development of an efficient worldwide system of communications among CIA operatives. He resigned in June 1966

and returned to the Aerojet General Corporation. He died on March 3, 1990.

—JLW

## Rafferty, Max(well) (Lewis), Jr.

(1917–1982) *superintendent of public instruction, California*

Born on May 7, 1917, Max Rafferty grew up in New Orleans and Soux City, Iowa, and in 1931 moved to Los Angeles. An excellent student, Rafferty entered the University of California at Los Angeles (UCLA) two years later and became a member of the UCLA Americans, a right-wing campus group. He returned to UCLA after graduation to study at the School of Education, where he came to oppose the progressive education doctrines of John Dewey that were taught there. Beginning his teaching career in 1940, Rafferty rose through the ranks of the state education system, becoming superintendent of the Needles Unified School District in 1955 and earning an Ed.D. at the University of Southern California that same year. He turned Needles into one of the best school districts in the country, raising teachers' salaries to reduce turnover, initiating new programs for the gifted and for athletes, and making scholarships available to minority students. In 1961 Rafferty became superintendent of schools in La Canada, a suburb of Los Angeles.

Rafferty's political career began in the summer of 1961, when he delivered a speech called "The Passing of the Patriot" to a La Canada school board meeting. Rafferty blamed the education system for producing a generation of youth, the worst of whom were "leather-jacketed slobs" while the best were without "positive standards, with everything in doubt." He called for putting patriotism back into education in order to make "our young people informed and disciplined and alert—militant for freedom, clear-eyed to the filthy menace of Communist corruption . . . happy in their love of country." The speech elicited strong reactions, and reprints made Rafferty a celebrity among conservatives, some of whom urged him to run for the nonpartisan office of state superintendent of public instruction. Rafferty came in second in a field of nine in the 1962 primaries. With the backing of wealthy conservatives, he won the runoff election by 200,000 votes over a liberal opponent who had the solid support of the California educational establishment.

Despite his campaign oratory, Rafferty could do little to change the state's elementary and secondary education during his tenure. His power was limited by the liberal California Board of Education. Furthermore, as critics pointed out, Rafferty's programs did not differ greatly in substance from those of his "progressive" predecessors. His most significant changes were the adoption of grammar texts in the elementary schools and the introduction of compensatory education in fundamentals for potential dropouts. Liberals were pleased that Rafferty brought African Americans and Mexican Americans into his department. The best-publicized aspect of Rafferty's first years in office was his unsuccessful battle with the Board of Education to impose a "little censorship" over the books placed in California high school libraries.

As one of the most prominent figures in the California conservative revival, Rafferty became one of the best-known educators in the country. His reputation grew with a *Reader's Digest* reprint of the 1961 speech, a syndicated newspaper column begun in 1964, and the publication of his books, *Suffer, Little Children* (1962) and *What They Are Doing to Your Children* (1964). His arguments for greater discipline and patriotism in education won the approval of many Americans disturbed by the social changes of the 1960s. Many liberals agreed that the reintroduction of the phonics system and the substitution of classic literature for Dick and Jane stories might reverse the downward trend in elementary reading scores.

Despite the nonpartisan nature of his office, Rafferty endorsed the gubernatorial candidacy of conservative Republican RONALD REAGAN in 1966. Rafferty blamed Democratic governor EDMUND G.

BROWN and other liberals for the "weakness" that had made the University of California, Berkeley, "look more like a skid row than an institution of higher learning." Both Rafferty and Reagan successfully used Berkeley student unrest as a major campaign issue. Rafferty was reelected by a landslide of almost 3,000,000 votes. Following the election Rafferty, as an ex officio member of the University of California's Board of Regents, backed Reagan's attacks on student radicals and his removal of CLARK KERR as president of the university.

In February 1968 Rafferty took a long-predicted step by declaring his candidacy for the U.S. Senate. He hoped to unseat the only liberal California Republican still in high office, Senator Thomas Kuchel, who, in Rafferty's opinion, was not in the party's "mainstream." Governor Reagan decided not to choose sides in the primary contest, but Rafferty found many wealthy supporters to help him win a 70,000-vote victory. In the regular election against Democrat Alan Cranston, Rafferty campaigned as an enemy of the "four deadly sins" of violence, pornography, drugs, and lawlessness. But the defection of Kuchel followers to Cranston and revelations that Rafferty had avoided military service in World War II on a claim of physical disability ensured his defeat. Cranston won by over 350,000 votes.

Rafferty lost his 1970 reelection bid to Wilson Riles, a black he had appointed deputy superintendent of public instruction. In 1971 he became dean of the School of Education at Troy State University in Alabama. He died in an automobile accident on June 13, 1982.

—JCH

## Randolph, A(sa) Philip
### (1889–1979)  *president, Brotherhood of Sleeping Car Porters*

Randolph was born on April 15, 1889, in Crescent City, Florida, and became an excellent student who graduated from Cookman Institute in Jacksonville in 1907. After moving to New York City in 1911, he joined the Socialist Party and plunged into radical politics. With Chandler Owen, Randolph founded the *Messenger* magazine, which opposed World War I and later became a pillar of the Harlem Renaissance during the 1920s. A supporter of trade unionism, Randolph worked with a group of African-American Pullman porters to begin an epic 12-year struggle to organize the Brotherhood of Sleeping Car Porters. When the Pullman company signed a contract with the union in 1937, the cool and dignified Randolph became the most widely respected black leader of his time. In June 1941 Randolph's threat of a march on Washington by 100,000 blacks wrested from a reluctant Roosevelt administration an executive order banning racial discrimination in federal employment and in defense industries. Randolph's postwar protest campaign against segregation in the armed services helped pressure President Truman into issuing another executive order, in July 1948, ending segregation in the military.

In the late 1950s and early 1960s Randolph urged that the AFL-CIO make greater efforts to end discrimination within affiliated unions. He strongly supported the civil rights movement of that period and, with BAYARD RUSTIN, provided the initial impetus for a new March on Washington, which drew over 200,000 people to the capital in August 1963.

As the civil rights movement began to break into factions in the years after the march, Randolph aligned with those advocating legal tactics and integrationist goals. Reconciled by 1964 to what he considered a slow but steady AFL-CIO antidiscrimination effort, Randolph dropped his ties with the increasingly militant Negro American Labor Council (NALC) and gave his blessing to the formation of the A. Philip Randolph Institute. (The NALC soon withered away without Randolph.) Under Bayard Rustin's direction, the institute worked closely with the AFL-CIO to advance unionism among blacks and build a liberal-labor-black coalition within the Democratic Party, which Rustin and Randolph by then saw as the key to racial and economic progress. Fearful that the series of riots and demonstrations in the summer of 1964 would harm LYNDON JOHNSON's chances for election, Randolph joined with civil rights leaders ROY WILKINS, MARTIN LUTHER KING, JR., and WHITNEY YOUNG on July 29 to announce a "broad curtailment if not

A. Philip Randolph, president of the Brotherhood of Sleeping Car Porters, meeting with Lyndon Johnson, 1966 *(Library of Congress, Prints and Photographs Division)*

total moratorium" on mass demonstrations. Although not all in the movement accepted the moratorium, few protest demonstrations took place during the presidential campaign itself.

After the Student Nonviolent Coordinating Committee (SNCC) raised the "Black Power" slogan in June 1966, Randolph criticized the idea as a divisive and racist. He attacked SNCC for sponsoring a picket line at Luci Johnson's August 1966 wedding and in October 1966 joined with seven other moderate black leaders to "repudiate any strategies of violence, reprisal or vigilantism" and to "condemn both rioting and the demagoguery that feeds it." He again denounced riots in the summer of 1967 and in August joined with Bayard Rustin to reject SNCC's public defense of the Arabs in their June war with Israel. In the fall of 1968 Randolph supported the New York City United Federation of Teachers strike against the Ocean Hill–Brownsville Community School Board, although many in the black community supported the board as an experiment in greater local control of the schools.

Randolph was one of the strongest supporters of Representative ADAM CLAYTON POWELL, JR. (D-N.Y.) when the House sought to expel the Harlem representative in early 1967. Randolph valued Powell for the power he wielded as chair of the House Education and Labor Committee.

As part of his general social program, Randolph favored a larger federal role in economic affairs. In the fall of 1966 Randolph helped sponsor proposals for a $185 billion "Freedom Budget" designed to eliminate poverty in the United States in 10 years. The budget called for a guaranteed annual income, full employment, and greater federal funding of health, housing, welfare, and education programs. The budget was to be paid for by the "fiscal dividend" generated by a projected 5 percent annual rise in the gross national product. These budget proposals proved incompatible with the economic demands of the Vietnam War. In December 1966 Randolph attacked cutbacks in President Johnson's antipoverty program as a strategy designed to put the burden of the war on the white and black poor.

In September 1968 Randolph, aged 79 and ailing, resigned as president of the Brotherhood of Sleeping Car Porters, a union reduced by that year to a mere 2,000 members due to the postwar decline of the railroad passenger industry. He died on May 16, 1979.

—NNL

## Randolph, Jennings
### (1902–1998) *member of the Senate*

Born in Salem, West Virginia, on March 8, 1902, Randolph graduated from Salem College in 1924 and worked as a newspaper journalist before becoming a faculty member in the department of public speaking and journalism at Davis and Elkins College. Randolph was elected to the U.S. House of Representatives in 1932. In the House he was a strong supporter of New Deal domestic programs and a promoter of legislation for the development of civilian aviation. Randolph was defeated in the 1946 Republican electoral sweep. During the next decade he was an assistant to the president and director of public relations for Capitol Airlines. In 1958 Randolph was elected to fill a vacant Senate seat; two years later he won a full term.

During the early 1960s Randolph supported most Kennedy administration social welfare legislation. However, he devoted particular attention to measures that dealt with the economic problems of West Virginia. The state produced about 30 percent of the nation's coal, but mechanization of the mines after World War II created considerable unemployment. Randolph spoke in favor of area redevelopment bills in 1961 and 1963 and supported a worker retraining bill in 1961.

In 1964 and 1965 Randolph, as the second-ranking member of the Public Works Committee, was the Senate floor manager of the administration's Appalachian development bill for reviving the region's economy. In January 1965, responding to charges that the measure gave preferential treatment to one area of the country, he asserted that Appalachia had 8.5 percent of the nation's population but received less than 5 percent of public expenditures.

In April 1966 Randolph became chair of the Public Works Committee, a powerful post that gave him significant influence over the distribution of pork barrel legislation. He used his position to promote federal highway programs in West Virginia, a mountainous state with a poor road system. Randolph regarded a modern highway system as crucial to the state's economic growth.

The Public Works panel handled most air and water pollution legislation, and Randolph was accused by some observers of acting in collusion with coal operators and United Mine Workers officials in opposing strong antipollution laws. During testimony before the committee in 1967 on an air quality bill, Randolph challenged the Public Health Service's (PHS) recommendation that emissions of sulphur dioxide, a coal by-product, be strictly controlled. He contended that a PHS report on the effects of sulphur dioxide pollution was based on "vague" and "incomplete" evidence and successfully proposed an amendment that authorized the states, rather than the federal government, to establish emission standards for specific pollutants.

Randolph was also charged with backing a weak coal-mine health and safety bill in 1969. The operators' National Coal Association acknowledged that it had suggested many of the bill's provisions. Initially cool toward legislation for coal miners' "black lung" compensation introduced in 1970, Randolph subsequently took a more sympathetic position after miners staged wildcat strikes and demonstrations in support of such proposals. Randolph was also a leading advocate of the Twenty-sixth Amendment, which lowered the voting age to 18 after its ratification in 1971. Randolph retired from the Senate after the end of his term in 1985. He died on May 8, 1998.

—MLL

## Rankin, J(ames) Lee

(1907–1996) *general counsel, President's Commission to Investigate the Assassination of President Kennedy (Warren Commission)*
Born on July 8, 1907, in Hartington, Nebraska, Rankin received a law degree in 1930 from the University of Nebraska and then joined a law firm in Lincoln, Nebraska, becoming a partner in 1935. A Republican, he managed Thomas E. Dewey's presidential campaign in Nebraska in 1948 and headed a state committee for Eisenhower in 1952. From 1953 to 1956 Rankin served as assistant attorney general in charge of the Justice Department's Office of Legal Counsel. He was named U.S. Solicitor General in August 1956 and over the next few years argued important cases before the Supreme Court involving membership in the Communist Party and school desegregation in Little Rock, Arkansas. When a Democratic administration took over in January 1961, Rankin entered private practice in New York City.

In December 1963 Rankin was unanimously selected by members of the Warren Commission, investigating the assassination of John F. Kennedy, as its general counsel. Rankin supervised the investigation and the writing of the commission's final report. He assembled much of the panel's staff, examined and acted as the liaison between the commission and other government agencies, and between commission members and the staff. The Warren Commission's report, made public on September 27, 1964, concluded that Lee Harvey Oswald, acting alone, had killed President Kennedy. Although the report gained wide acceptance at the time of its release, it has since been the target of persistent and, at times, heated criticism. Until the mid-1970s, the government made no effort to reopen the investigation. Then, in the wake of disclosures that the Central Intelligence Agency (CIA) and the FBI had kept certain information from the commission, including the existence of CIA plots to assassinate Cuban premier Fidel Castro, the House of Representatives created a Select Committee on Assassinations to probe the murders of both Kennedy and MARTIN LUTHER KING, JR. In its final report issued in 1979, the committee concluded that the Warren Commission "failed to investigate adequately the possibility of a conspiracy to assassinate the President."

On December 2, 1965 Mayor-elect JOHN V. LINDSAY named Rankin New York City corporation counsel; he took office on January 1, 1966. With more than 300 attorneys working under him, Rankin was responsible for all litigation the city had to prosecute or defend, for giving legal opinions when necessary on the validity of actions taken by city departments, and for supervising legislation for submission to the city council and the state legislature. In December 1966 Lindsay also appointed Rankin head of a 17-member task force to draft a New York City program for the upcoming state constitutional convention. The task force's May 1967 report to the convention urged greatly expanded home rule powers for all cities and counties in the state. Rankin resigned as corporation counsel in June 1972 to enter private law practice with his son. He died on June 26, 1996.

—CAB

## Rauh, Joseph L(ouis)

(1911–1992) *lawyer; vice president, Americans for Democratic Action*
Born on January 3, 1911, Rauh, grew up in Cincinnati. After graduating in 1935 from the Harvard Law School, he served as law clerk to Supreme Court justices Benjamin N. Cardozo and Felix

Frankfurter. Rauh was an enforcement official for the Wage and Price Administration and worked on the staff of the army's Pacific Command during World War II. Returning to private law practice after the war, Rauh became an important defender of civil liberties and other liberal causes; among his clients were the United Auto Workers union, the Brotherhood of Sleeping Car Porters, and a number of Americans accused of Communist affiliations. In 1947 Rauh was one of the founders of the Americans for Democratic Action (ADA), a liberal anticommunist group. He was subsequently chief public spokesperson of the ADA and served the organization in several executive positions, including chair and national vice president. He also worked for the Democratic Party as a member—later chair—of the party's District of Columbia committee.

Rauh was a close friend and strong supporter of Senator HUBERT HUMPHREY (D-Minn.), whom the ADA favored for president in 1960. After the election of John F. Kennedy, Rauh and the ADA frequently criticized the new administration for failing to provide "dynamic, crusading leadership" in civil rights and other reform causes. Among the specific administration actions that Rauh attacked were proposals for the legalization of wiretapping in some cases and creation of a private corporation to operate the planned communications satellite system. Rauh also charged that federal funds continued to flow into racially segregated housing, despite administration promises to stop this practice.

As the pace of reform accelerated during the mid-1960s, Rauh became increasingly associated with the growing civil rights movement. In 1964 he began serving as general counsel of the Leadership Conference on Civil Rights, a coalition of national civil rights groups that lobbied in Washington for antidiscrimination measures. During the next several years Rauh played an important part in formulating and gaining passage of several landmark bills, including the Civil Rights Act of 1964, the Voting Rights Act of 1965, and the Fair Housing Act of 1968. In early 1964 Rauh became counsel for the Council of Federated Organizations (COFO), another civil rights coalition working to increase black voter registration in the South. He also served as adviser to the Mississippi Freedom Democratic Party (MFDP), a COFO offshoot that encouraged blacks to run for office in an attempt to break the power of the all-white regular Democratic organization in Mississippi.

In the summer of 1964 the MFDP chose an integrated group to challenge the seating of Mississippi's segregated regular delegation at the 1964 Democratic National Convention. Rauh accompanied the MFDP group to the convention and argued its case before the Credentials Committee. Emphasizing the refusal of the regular Mississippi Democrats to accept the political participation of blacks or to endorse President Johnson for reelection, he argued that the MFDP was an open party firmly committed to the president. A stream of witnesses called by Rauh, including civil rights worker FANNIE LOU HAMER, testified before the committee on police brutality and the victimization of blacks in Mississippi.

Rauh's presentation won widespread sympathy for the MFDP but failed to unseat the regular Mississippi delegation. Johnson, eager to avoid a split among southern Democrats, offered the MFDP two at-large convention seats plus assurances that the regular Mississippi delegates would be required to take a loyalty oath to the Democratic ticket and that future party conventions would prohibit discrimination in the selection of delegates. Rauh accepted the proposal, although he could not persuade most MFDP delegates to endorse what some of them called a "back-of-the-bus" arrangement.

In addition to his civil rights activities, Rauh was an energetic proponent of other liberal causes during the mid-1960s. In 1965 and 1966 he proposed and lobbied for legislation providing home rule for Washington, D.C., including an elected mayor and city council. Rauh was also one of the first liberal leaders to oppose the Vietnam War. In April 1965 he met with President Johnson and protested strongly against American bombing in Vietnam. Two years later he helped found Negotiations Now, a national antiwar group that circulated petitions calling for an immediate cease-fire and halt to U.S. bombing. Rauh's stand symbolized the division between liberals over the war issue. Humphrey, whom Rauh in 1965 had called "the finest man in American public life," gradually distanced himself from his former friend by his continued public support of U.S. Vietnam policy.

Rauh's political influence and his opposition to the war made him an important figure in the planning of antiwar strategy during the 1968 presidential campaign. Although initially doubtful that any peace candidate could defeat President Johnson, Rauh put himself firmly behind Senator EUGENE

MCCARTHY (D-Minn.) after he entered the race in November 1967. Besides gaining the ADA's endorsement of McCarthy, Rauh initiated negotiations between antiwar leaders and Democratic regulars over a compromise statement on Vietnam for the party's 1968 platform. After these efforts failed he directed McCarthy forces at the Democratic National Convention in challenging the seating of all-white (and pro–Vietnam War) delegations from several southern states. Among those successfully challenged were the Georgia and Mississippi groups, which had not reformed their selection procedures since 1964. Humphrey's nomination at the 1968 convention failed to bring Rauh back to his former loyalty; although the ADA favored Humphrey over Republican candidate RICHARD M. NIXON, Rauh took no notable part in the national campaign.

Rauh continued to work for liberal causes after the 1968 election, opposing the Nixon administration on many issues. In 1969 and 1970 he played an important part in arousing opposition to Nixon Supreme Court nominees Clement Haynsworth and G. Harrold Carswell. He also criticized the vice presidential appointment of Representative GERALD FORD (R-Mich.) in 1973, claiming that Ford had consistently worked against civil rights and social welfare legislation. In 1969 Rauh began serving as counsel for dissident members of the United Mine Workers union (UMW), who accused union leader TONY BOYLE of corruption and laxity in defending members' interests. Rauh's efforts helped reform candidate Arnold Miller win the UMW presidency in 1972 and spurred investigations that resulted in the conviction of Boyle and other UMW leaders for the 1969 murder of dissident leader Jock Yablonsky. Rauh died on September 3, 1992.

—SLG

## Ray, James Earl

(1928–1998) *convicted assassin of Martin Luther King, Jr.*

James Earl Ray, one of nine children, was born on March 10, 1928, in Alton, Illinois, and grew up in poverty. Ray left school in the eighth grade. After working at several jobs, he enlisted in the army in 1946. He served with the military police in Germany but was given a general discharge in December 1948 because of "ineptness and lack of adaptability to military service."

Over the next decade Ray drifted back and forth between Chicago and the West Coast. He was arrested several times and charged with vagrancy, burglary, and armed robbery. In 1955 he was found guilty of forging a Post Office money order and served three years in Leavenworth federal penitentiary. In October 1959 he was arrested for armed robbery in connection with a St. Louis supermarket holdup and was sentenced to 20 years at the Missouri State Penitentiary at Jefferson City. In April 1967 he concealed himself in a large breadbox being sent from the prison bakery and made a successful escape.

On April 4, 1968, Ray, registered at a rooming house across from the Lorraine Motel in Memphis, Tennessee, where MARTIN LUTHER KING, JR., was staying. Around 6:00 p.m. Ray shot the civil rights leader, as King was standing on the second floor balcony of his motel room. King was rushed to the hospital and pronounced dead. Ray fled the murder scene in a white Mustang. On April 20 Ray was placed on the FBIs 10 most wanted list.

On April 8 Ray had entered Canada, and on the 24th he obtained a Canadian passport. He flew from Toronto to London on May 6 and then, a day later, on to Lisbon. He returned to London on May 17. On June 8 Scotland Yard detectives seized Ray at Heathrow Airport in London. In July he was extradited and returned to Memphis, where he was charged with murder.

On March 10, 1969, Ray pleaded guilty to murdering King and was sentenced to serve 99 years in prison. Within days, however, Ray attempted to reverse his plea. Ray stated that he had sold the rights to his life story to journalist William Bradford Huie, to raise money for his legal defense. He charged that Huie and Percy Foreman, his attorney, had both pressured him to plead guilty. According to Ray, Huie had told him that a book about a man who did not kill King would not sell. Ray also stated that Foreman had promised that he would be pardoned after John Jay Hooker, Jr., son of a Foreman law associate, was elected governor of Tennessee. Ray later told one reporter that he had been "browbeaten, badgered and bribed into pleading guilty."

Foreman denied that Ray had been coerced into pleading guilty. He also suggested that Ray, a racial bigot, had slain Dr. King because "he wanted recognition and praise from his old inmates back at Jefferson City [site of the Missouri State Penitentiary]." Ray dismissed Foreman, but his new defense team was unable to win a new trial on appeal.

For the rest of his life, Ray maintained that he was part of a conspiracy to murder King. The key figure in the plot was someone named Raoul, and Ray wrote two books in which he insisted that others were involved. The House Select Committee on Assassinations concluded in 1979, however, that Ray was the lone shooter. The King family thought that Ray was part of a conspiracy and asked for further investigation into the murder. A report by the Justice Department concluded in 2000 "that the allegations relating to Raoul's participation in the assassination, which originated with James Earl Ray, have no merit."

Ray briefly escaped in 1977 from the Tennessee penitentiary where he was serving his sentence. In 1981 he survived a knife attack by several inmates. He died on April 23, 1998.

—JLW

## Reagan, Ronald (Wilson)
### (1911–2004) *governor*

Born into a poor family on February 6, 1911, in Tampico, Illinois, Reagan grew up in Dixon, and he later said that his childhood was "a Huck Finn idyll" in which he was never aware of deprivation. He worked as a lifeguard while in high school, and his earnings helped pay for his education at Eureka College, from which he graduated in 1932. Following graduation Reagan realized a childhood ambition by becoming a radio sportscaster in Iowa. He soon acquired a national reputation. In 1937, while covering the Chicago Cubs spring training on the West Coast, he received a film contract from Warner Brothers. Reagan subsequently appeared in over 50 movies, often playing the all-American "good guy" who fails to "get the girl."

After three years of service in a U.S. Army Air Forces film unit based in Hollywood during World War II, Reagan returned to his film career and played an active role in liberal Democratic politics. In 1947 he was elected president of the Screen Actors Guild, a position he held for five years. However, Reagan's political views gradually shifted to the right. He cooperated with motion picture industry efforts to purge actors alleged to have communist associations. In 1952 he married for the second time. His wife, actress Nancy Davis, encouraged his political activities. Reagan's film career began to decline by the mid-1950s. But from 1954 to 1962 he worked for the General Electric Company, hosting the company's weekly television series. He toured its plants and gave lectures to workers on the evils and big government and the advantages of the free-enterprise system. Though still a registered Democrat, Reagan campaigned for Republican presidential candidates in 1952, 1956, and 1960.

When Reagan became a Republican in 1962, he was already a popular figure among California's conservatives. He campaigned for John Birch Society member JOHN ROUSSELOT in the 1962 congressional elections. In 1964 he backed the senatorial candidacy of his Screen Actors Guild colleague GEORGE MURPHY, strongly supported an ultimately successful proposition to repeal a state open housing law, and served as co-chair of California Republicans for Goldwater. According to the *New York Times*, Reagan's television speech on behalf of Senator BARRY GOLDWATER (R-Ariz.), "drew more contributions than any other single speech in political history."

Reagan's Goldwater speech convinced many wealthy conservatives that he was a prime political prospect. Murphy's successful 1964 campaign showed that being an actor was not a political handicap and, in the age of television and image politics, might be an asset. In 1965 a group of California business leaders hired the public relations firm of Spencer-Roberts and Associates to help prepare a Reagan gubernatorial candidacy for 1966. Reagan toured the state, making a favorable impression on Republican voters, and, in January 1966, he announced his candidacy. He easily won the June primary against a former San Francisco mayor, George Christopher.

Public opinion polls showed Reagan far in front of the incumbent Democratic governor, EDMUND G. "PAT" BROWN, and the 1966 general election was bitter and sharply contested. The Democrats repeatedly emphasized Reagan's lack of experience in public office and his associations with "ultra-conservatives" and derided his show business background. The Reagan camp played down their candidate's relationship with the far right, and Reagan turned the other criticisms into advantages. He was far more self-assured and handsome on the television screen and in fielding questions before live audiences than was Brown, and he prided himself on being a "citizen politician." Throughout the campaign Reagan delivered essentially one basic speech—political writers called it "The Speech"—in which he blamed the professional politicians, specifically Brown, for the ills of modern society. His chief targets were high taxes and wasteful government, racial and student unrest, rising crime rates, and rampant immorality. Citing student unrest on the University of California's Berkeley campus and the Watts racial disturbances, Reagan charged that Brown was "soft" on militants and criminals. He attacked the waste in President Johnson's Great Society programs and offered, instead, a "creative society" in which an efficient and unobtrusive government would call upon individuals to contribute their special talents for the good of all. The professional Reagan campaign was a huge success; he defeated Brown by almost a million votes out of the approximately 5.4 million cast. As governor of the nation's largest state, Reagan immediately became a potential Republican presidential candidate.

Reagan and his staff were hampered in their first year in power by their lack of experience. Yet, Reagan was able to retain his political image as an economizer despite an inability to keep all his campaign pledges. Although he presented the legislature with a $5-billion budget—the largest in the state's history—and the biggest tax increases since 1959, he was able to blame the necessary taxes on the Brown administration, which had preferred not to impose them in the election year of 1966. Working in cooperation with Speaker of the Assembly JESSE UNRUH, a Democrat, Reagan made the increased taxes more palatable by shifting the burden from local property taxes to sales and income taxes and levies on banks and corporations. In addition, Reagan ordered freezes on hiring and the purchase of new state equipment and made well-publicized cuts in the state's mental hygiene and higher education programs. Among his conservative supporters only the most extreme turned against Reagan because of his new budget.

Liberals remained hostile to Reagan. Besides dissatisfaction with the budget cuts, they were angered by his plan to impose tuition at the University of California. They also opposed the Board of Regents' dismissal, at Reagan's urging, of university president CLARK KERR. The governor's proposals for escalating the Vietnam War and punishing war dissenters further alienated liberals. His remarks on the unimportance of redwood trees and the desirability of turning federally protected land over to individuals irritated conservationists. The governor also attacked welfare "cheats" and sided with California agribusiness growers in their opposition to farm workers' organizing activities.

Some of Reagan's measures, however, surprised many of his liberal critics. Though often charged with indifference to racial discrimination, he appointed a record number of minority citizens to top posts in his administration. In June 1967 the governor signed a liberalized abortion law and in August approved a gun-control bill that prohibited the carrying of loaded firearms in public. Despite his anti-conservationist views, Reagan was persuaded to agree to a federal plan to set up a Redwoods National Park in 1967. In addition, the governor strongly supported an automobile smog-control bill that made California's air pollution laws the strictest in the world.

In 1968 Reagan enthusiasts encouraged the governor to enter the race for the Republican presidential nomination, but he preferred to maintain noncandidacy status and planned to lead the California delegation to the national convention as a favorite-son candidate. Still, in the months before the August convention, Reagan issued position papers and toured the country as a party fund-raiser. He was particularly effective in the South. Despite his popularity among rank-and-file Republicans, his unwillingness to wage a campaign and RICHARD NIXON's string of unopposed primary victories reduced Reagan's chances of winning the nomination at the convention. He finally declared his candidacy on August 5 but could not get the support of prominent conservatives already pledged to Nixon. Following Nixon's nomination Reagan promised his complete support of the ticket and campaigned vigorously for his party's candidate. Political writer Lou Cannon noted that during the campaign Nixon borrowed heavily from those Reagan speeches that stressed the virtues of the American pioneer spirit and the need to reduce the role of government in the individual's daily life.

Reagan was easily reelected governor in 1970 and remained a highly popular figure in the Republican Party. In 1976 he challenged GERALD R. FORD for the party's presidential nomination and suffered a narrow defeat. Four years later, he won the nomination easily and defeated President Jimmy Carter in the November election.

Reagan's presidency was marked by sweeping, controversial, and unexpected changes. He aimed at restoring the effectiveness of U.S. international policies in the wake of the Iran hostage crisis and confidence in the U.S. economy, which was beset by high unemployment and inflation. The Reagan administration increased defense spending to record levels in peacetime, reduced spending on social programs, and cut taxes. After a severe recession that lasted until 1983, inflation declined dramatically and unemployment dropped as well, although budget deficits reached unprecedented levels. Reagan bluntly condemned the Soviet Union as an "evil empire," and Soviet leaders feared that the administration's military buildup might be the prelude to war. But the president moderated his policies toward the Soviets during 1984, and, in partnership with President Mikhail Gorbachev, who came to power in March 1985, made important strides toward ending the cold war. Despite a decline in his popularity during the Iran-contra scandal of 1986–87, Reagan left office with approval ratings in the polls of 60 percent. He considered his greatest accomplishment the restoration of national confidence, something he was able to do in part because of his abiding belief in American values and his ability to use televised speeches to inspire citizens.

In 1994 Reagan announced that he was suffering from Alzheimer's disease. He died in California on June 5, 2004.

—JCH

## Reedy, George E(dward)
### (1917–1999) *White House press secretary*

Born in East Chicago, Indiana, on August 5, 1917, Reedy worked as a congressional correspondent for United Press (UP) after his graduation from the University of Chicago in 1938. He served in the U.S. Army Air Forces during World War II before returning to the Washington bureau of what had become United Press International in 1946. In 1951 Reedy went to work on the staff of Senator LYNDON B. JOHNSON. The following year he became staff director of the Democratic Policy Committee, a position he held until 1960. When Johnson became vice president in 1961, Reedy was named his special assistant to coordinate speechwriting and press relations.

In March 1964 Reedy replaced Pierre Salinger as White House press secretary. Reedy had a close, but stormy relationship with Johnson. Johnson's relations with the news media deteriorated during Reedy's tenure, and the president often blamed his press secretary. Johnson on occasion berated Reedy in public, even complaining about Reedy's tousled hair and rumpled appearance. After Reedy told the

president about his reservations concerning deepening U.S. military involvement in Vietnam, Johnson decided to replace Reedy with BILL MOYERS in July 1965.

Reedy returned to the White House briefly as a special assistant in late 1965. He resigned in April 1966 to enter private business. In July 1966 President Johnson appointed him to the National Advisory Commission on Selective Service, a committee that recommended changes in the draft laws, including the establishment of a lottery system. Later Reedy wrote for various magazines and lectured on college campuses. In 1972 he was named Nieman Professor at Marquette University's College of Journalism.

In 1970 Reedy published *The Twilight of the Presidency*, a well-received book that lamented the increasing isolation of modern presidents. Describing the presidency as an "American Monarchy" and the White House as "a structure designed for one purpose and one purpose only—to serve the material needs and desires of a single man," Reedy likened life at the White House to that of a "barnyard," where below the president there was a distinct pecking order and a "mass of intrigue, posturing, cringing, strutting and pious 'commitment' to irrelevant windbaggery."

Reedy retired from teaching in 1990. He died on March 21, 1999.

—FHM

## Reid, Ogden R(ogers)
### (1925–　) *member of the House of Representatives*

An heir to the *New York Herald Tribune* fortune, Reid was born on June 24, 1925, in New York City and graduated from Yale in 1949. He worked on the *Tribune* until 1959, when President Eisenhower appointed him ambassador to Israel. Two years later New York governor NELSON A. ROCKEFELLER named Reid chair of the New York State Commission for Human Rights.

Reid first won election to Congress as a Republican in 1962 from a district encompassing the eastern two-thirds of Westchester County. Known for its wealthy suburbs, the area also included middle-class as well as impoverished sections. Since 1945 the district had experienced an industrial boom. Reid served on the Government Operations and Education and Labor Committees and soon established his political independence, voting against his party more often than not. Despite his liberal voting record, he backed Senator BARRY M. GOLDWATER's (R-Ariz.) presidential candidacy in 1964 but ran well ahead of Goldwater's tally in the traditionally Republican district.

A strong supporter of Johnson administration social legislation, Reid frequently sided with the Democrats on the Education and Labor Committee. He advocated large federal expenditures for education and was one of two Republicans on the committee in 1965 to favor repeal of Section 14(b) of the Taft-Hartley Act. Repeal would have made state "right-to-work" laws barring union shops illegal, but the attempt was defeated by a filibuster. Reid also proposed at this time to amend the 1964 civil rights bill to strengthen the powers of the Equal Employment Opportunity Commission in dealing with discrimination by labor unions. He also proposed to repeal the loyalty oath required for recipients of National Defense Education Act funds, but the effort died in committee.

Reid was a vigorous supporter of civil rights legislation and was one of a group of five Republicans to oppose the seating of the Mississippi congressional delegation in 1965. After Congress seated the delegation, the group issued a statement that the result "effectively condoned the disenfranchisement of more than 400,000 American citizens in Mississippi and missed an opportunity to rectify the wrong." Reid was among a group of northern representatives who observed the 1966 primary elections in Mississippi. They subsequently reported that the 1965 Voting Rights Act was being "minimally enforced."

Reid voted for the 1966 Vietnam War appropriations bill but questioned the Johnson administration's analysis of the situation there. In August 1967 he traveled to South Vietnam with a subcommittee of the Government Operations Committee. On its return the group warned that unless the government there made "substantive" economic reforms, "the advisability of continued U.S. involvement is questionable." A letter to Secretary of State DEAN RUSK signed by Reid and subcommittee chair JOHN E. MOSS (D-Calif.) urged a "firmer stand" on reform of the Vietnamese government and was very critical of the role of the Agency for International Development, whose officials, the letter said, "have too often attempted to avoid 'rocking the boat' rather than pressing for necessary reforms."

Reid's liberalism, though popular at general election time, created problems for him in his own party. He drew criticism from Republicans in 1968, when he accepted the designation of New York's Liberal Party in addition to the Republican nomination for reelection. In 1972 Reid followed the example of New York City mayor JOHN V. LINDSAY when he left the Republicans to join the Democratic Party. Reid backed GEORGE MCGOVERN for president in 1972 and was reelected as a Democrat despite the efforts of former ally NELSON ROCKEFELLER, who financed his opponent's campaign. Reid forfeited his congressional seat in 1974, when he declined to run, seeking instead the Democratic gubernatorial nomination. Democrats of longer standing within the party dominated the race, and Reid soon withdrew his candidacy. He was appointed as New York State's commissioner of environmental conservation in 1975 by Governor HUGH CAREY. He resigned that post in April 1976.

—MDB

## Reischauer, Edwin O(ldfather)
(1910–1990) *ambassador to Japan*

Born in Tokyo on October 15, 1910, of American missionary parents, Edwin Reischauer spent his formative years in Japan, coming to the United States to attend Oberlin College. In the United States Reischauer devoted himself to East Asian affairs, as a graduate student in Far Eastern languages at Harvard, as a Harvard instructor (1938–42), and then as a senior research analyst for the State and War departments (1941–42) and the army (1942–45). After the war he became the chair of the State Department's Japan-Korea secretariat and special assistant to the director of the Office of Far Eastern Affairs before resuming his Harvard career. Appointed associate professor of Far Eastern languages in 1946, he became professor of Japanese history in 1950 and director of the Harvard-Yenching Institute in 1956. While at Harvard he wrote several monographs on Asian history and collaborated with historian John K. Fairbank in producing a widely respected textbook, *East Asia: The Great Tradition* (1960). In his writings and public statements. Reischauer was critical of U.S. policy toward Japan, including the restrictions on Japanese trade and tacit approval of the Japanese government decision to push the unpopular Japanese-American Mutual Security Treaty of 1960 through the Diet.

Between April 1961 and July 1966 Reischauer served as U.S. ambassador to Japan. There his enormous personal popularity, based on his affinity for Japanese culture, served to strengthen ties between the two countries. In 1966 he resigned his post to return to Harvard.

During the Johnson era Reischauer became a leading academic critic of Asian policy. In January 1967 he appeared before the Senate Foreign Relations Committee to denounce the bombing of North Vietnam and call for a rethinking of the U.S. position in East Asia. Although Reischauer was a supporter of the administration's objectives in Vietnam, he called the bombing of the North a "psychological blunder" made in the mistaken belief that it would force Hanoi to negotiate. Reischauer advocated "prudent de-escalation of bombing" and suggested that it be replaced with a massive border blockade to prevent North Vietnamese expansion into the South. For a long-range Asian policy he proposed action guided by four goals: (1) minimizing military involvement; (2) avoiding formal alliances; (3) shunning sponsorship of political, social, or economic change because such sponsorship leads to "responsibility for the existence or nature of the regime;" and (4) not attempting to play the role of "the leader" in Asia. He also stressed the need for reconciliation between the People's Republic of China (PRC) and the United States.

In December 1967 Reischauer, along with 13 other scholars, issued a report that asserted a need to "deter, restrain and counter-balance" the PRC's power in Asia to prevent a major war. But along with "a firm and explicit set of deterrents to extremism," the scholars urged the establishment of "inducements to moderation." The report also recommended that limited experimental steps be taken to de-escalate the Vietnam War as an indication that "there is no inevitable progression upward." In January 1968 Reischauer signed a statement by Harvard's Ad Hoc Committee on Vietnam, which called on President Johnson to refrain from further escalation and to make "serious and sustained efforts, including de-escalation," to reach a negotiated settlement.

Throughout the 1960s and 1970s Reischauer continued to publish textbooks and foreign policy studies, including: *Beyond Vietnam: The United States in Asia* (1967); *Japan, the Story of a Nation* (1970); *East Asia: Tradition and Transformation* (1973); and *Toward the 21st Century: Education for a Changing*

*World* (1973). He retired from Harvard in 1981 and died on September 1, 1990.

—EWS

## Resor, Stanley R(ogers)
### (1917–   ) *secretary of the army*

Stanley R. Resor, born on December 5, 1917, into a wealthy New York family, attended Groton, Yale, and the Yale Law School. In 1955 he became a partner of the prominent New York law firm of Debevoise, Plimpton, Lyons and Gates. Resor left this firm in February 1965 to become undersecretary of the army. In June of that year, President Johnson named him to succeed Stephen Ailes as secretary of the army.

In his reorganization of the Pentagon, Secretary of Defense ROBERT S. MCNAMARA had stripped the secretaries of the army, navy, and air force of much of their planning and budgetary authority. Therefore, Resor was concerned more with administrative than with policy-making decisions.

On several occasions between 1965 and 1967 Resor testified before congressional committees on behalf of a plan proposed by McNamara to merge the Army National Guard with Army Reserve units. This plan, bitterly opposed by the Reserve Officers Association, met such extreme opposition on Capitol Hill that Congress passed a bill in 1967 formally prohibiting the Defense Department from implementing the merger.

Resor served as civilian head of the army during the critical period when the United States began committing large numbers of ground troops to the Vietnam War. Draft quotas were vastly increased to meet the demands of the war; the number of troops serving in the army rose from 961,000 in January 1966 to 1.5 million by June 1968. During this period several soldiers attempted to use court orders to enjoin Resor and McNamara from sending them to Vietnam to take part in what they argued was an illegal and immoral conflict. In November 1967 the U.S. Supreme Court in a six to two decision refused to intervene on behalf of these soldiers on the ground that it lacked jurisdiction in a case where the issues were primarily political and military.

On the evening of July 24, 1967, Resor, McNamara, General HAROLD K. JOHNSON and FBI director J. EDGAR HOOVER met with President Johnson and agreed that federal paratroops should be sent to Detroit because city police and National

Guard troops had been unable to halt rioting in the city's predominantly black areas. The paratroops succeeded in bring the situation under control, but the National Guard was widely criticized for its lack of discipline in dealing with the rioters. In response to this criticism, Resor testified before the Senate Armed Services Committee in February 1968 that the National Guard was being given special training and equipment to handle future civil disturbances.

Resor, a Republican and one of the few Johnson appointees retained by President RICHARD M. NIXON, continued as secretary of the army until the spring of 1971. During this period he faced congressional probes concerning the draft, atrocities in Vietnam, corruption in the management of officers' clubs, and charges that the army spied on American citizens.

—JLW

## Reuss, Henry S(choellkopf)
(1912–2002) *member of the House of Representatives*

The grandson of a Wisconsin bank president who had emigrated from Germany in 1848, Henry Reuss was born on February 12, 1912, in Milwaukee. He practiced law there after earning an LL.B. from Harvard in 1936. After wartime service with the Office of Price Administration and the army, Reuss resumed his law practice and served on the board of directors of several companies, including a Milwaukee bank. A Republican until 1950, Reuss switched to the Democratic Party in that year because he considered Senator Joseph McCarthy (R-Wisc.) "a disgrace to Wisconsin." He helped to organize an anti-McCarthy movement in the state and ran unsuccessfully for the offices of state attorney general in 1950 and U.S. senator in 1952. Reuss won election to the House of Representatives from Milwaukee's Fifth Congressional District in 1954 against a pro-McCarthy Republican incumbent, Representative Charles J. Kersten.

Reuss was a consistent congressional liberal and, in the Kennedy years, a reliable supporter of the president's legislative program. A member of the House Banking and Currency Committee and the Joint Economic Committee, Reuss became a House expert in the subjects of trade and finance and a sponsor of measures to protect the environment.

As chair of the International Finance Subcommittee of the Banking and Currency Committee,

Reuss became an active supporter of mechanisms to channel financial assistance to developing nations in the mid-1960s. In May 1964 Reuss was the floor manager for a bill to authorize a $312-million increase in the U.S. contribution to the International Development Association, which could provide credit on easier terms than its parent body, the World Bank. Reuss favored the multilateral approach to foreign aid partly because, he argued, it deflected bilateral diplomatic pressures away from the United States. He was also a consistent supporter of increasing U.S. contributions to the Inter-American Development Bank, which made "soft loans" to high priority development projects in Latin America.

Although a backer of Great Society social legislation, Reuss came to oppose the Johnson administration on the issues of the Vietnam War and the burgeoning defense budget. In January 1966 he suggested a continuation of the Christmas bombing pause and urged the president to recognize the National Liberation Front as the chief enemy belligerent and open negotiations with its representatives. Reuss was one of only seven members of Congress in October 1968 to vote against the entire defense budget, which contained an appropriation of $25.5 billion for the war in Vietnam.

Reuss was an early opponent of the supersonic transport plane (SST). In March 1964 he made an unsuccessful attempt to eliminate $24.7 million earmarked for research on the project. He continued to criticize the plane throughout the decade, arguing in July 1966 that "the convenience of a few VIPs in getting to their destinations a few minutes earlier is less a national priority" than the continuation of federal programs to aid the cities and combat water pollution. In August 1967 Reuss called upon the federal government to bring about a tenfold expansion of the nation's supply of low and moderate income housing.

Reuss responded to the breakdown in 1966 of the administration's 3.2 percent guideposts for annual wage increases by proposing that the Joint Economic Committee of Congress came up with its own guidelines after consulting with labor and management. He emerged during the Nixon years as one of the strongest advocates of wage-price controls. He retired from Congress at the end of his term in January 1983 and entered private law practice. He died on January 12, 2002.

—TO

## Reuther, Walter P(hilip)

(1907–1970) *president, United Automobile Workers*

Born in Wheeling, West Virginia, on September 1, 1907, Reuther was raised as a socialist in a family of German immigrants. After completing high school in Wheeling, Reuther moved to Detroit in 1927 and became a skilled tool and die worker at the Ford Motor Company. Reuther attended classes at Wayne University and campaigned actively for Norman Thomas's 1932 presidential candidacy. After being laid off at Ford, Reuther made an extended tour of Europe beginning in 1933, including an extended stay in the Soviet Union. After returning to Detroit in 1935, Reuther and his brothers Victor and Ray, plunged into organizational work for the fledgling United Auto Workers

United Automobile Workers (UAW) official Walter P. Reuther *(Library of Congress, Prints and Photographs Division)*

(UAW). Walter Reuther was first elected to the UAW executive board in 1936 but only achieved real power in the union after he helped organize 30,000 auto workers in Detroit after conducting a successful sit-down strike.

During the next decade, Reuther maneuvered to establish his leadership within the UAW. In a deeply divided union, Reuther severed his ties with socialists and communists and fought for control of the UAW. His adept handling of a 113-day strike against General Motors (GM) soon after the end of World War II insured him sufficient rank-and-file support to secure the UAW presidency in 1946.

During the next few years Reuther consolidated his control of the UAW, helped found the liberal Americans for Democratic Action and served as president of the Congress of Industrial Organizations from 1952 until its merger with the American Federation of Labor in 1955. Reuther also negotiated for the UAW a series of pacesetting collective bargaining agreements, which won for the union's membership substantially improved fringe benefits and higher real wages.

In September and October 1964 Reuther negotiated new collective bargaining agreements substantially exceeding the Johnson administration's 3.2 percent wage guideposts. Reuther first directed his union's pressure against Chrysler because he knew that the weakest of the big three auto makers, then enjoying its first significant profits in several years, would be reluctant to endure a strike. The Chrysler agreement, reached September 9, was later copied by Ford on September 18 and by GM on October 5. The new contracts increased retirement and insurance benefits, raised wages, and added 12 minutes a day relief-time and two more paid holidays. The final settlements totaled about 60 cents an hour and averaged 4.9 percent of the industry's labor costs. The White House, anxious for labor's support in an election year, called the contracts "reasonably close" to its wage guidelines.

Although Ford and GM had quickly agreed to the economic package Reuther negotiated at Chrysler, contract talks between the UAW and the two larger auto companies broke down over resolution of local plant disputes involving grievance procedures and working conditions. Ford and GM sought to absorb much of the new contract's increased labor costs through greater productivity, but local union negotiators resisted what they considered company "speed-ups." To head off a wildcat strike movement, Reuther authorized local strikes; he called GM working conditions below "the minimum standards of human decency." Ford was shut down for 20 days and GM for 31, but few important grievances were permanently resolved. Such disputes plagued the UAW's top leadership throughout the 1960s. In February 1967 a wildcat strike by a GM local in Mansfield, Ohio, stopped much of the corporation's production, idling 174,000 men in over 57 other plants. Reuther declared the strike illegal, called the local's leadership to Detroit, and ordered a return to work. When the strike continued in March, Reuther asked for a UAW executive board "seizure" of the local and ordered a resumption of work.

Another internal union problem faced by Reuther in the mid-1960s was the demand by skilled tool, die, and maintenance workers for wage parity with non-UAW craft unionists. At the auto union's May 1966 convention, leaders of the skilled trades were Reuther's most vocal opponents. To meet their criticism the UAW amended its constitution to give the skilled trades department, which contained less than 20 percent of the UAW's members, veto power over all national contracts. After a seven-week strike against Ford in September and October 1967 the union won a special 30-cents-an-hour wage increase for skilled workers. In return for this concession and other wage and benefit increases averaging 6 percent a year, the union agreed to a three-year ceiling of 18 cents an hour on automatic cost-of-living boosts. After Reuther made an unusual televised appeal, about 90 percent of the production workers and 70 percent of the skilled workers voted to approve the pact. Most of the contract provisions of the Ford settlement were later agreed to by Chrysler, GM, and American Motors.

As president of the politically active UAW Reuther served as a symbol of and spokesperson for the liberal wing of the Democratic Party during much of the 1960s. His union lobbied heavily for the Johnson administration's Great Society and civil rights legislation and contributed to Democratic electoral campaigns throughout the decade. At the 1964 Democratic National Convention Reuther played an important and controversial role as HUBERT HUMPHREY's agent in the fight over seating the Mississippi Freedom Democratic Party (MFDP). Reuther urged members of the MFDP to

accept a Humphrey-Johnson proposal that would seat the regular segregationist Mississippi delegation, give observer status to the MFDP, and seat two of its members as "delegates-at-large."

The MFDP rejected the proposal and JOSEPH RAUH, then acting as counsel for the Mississippi civil rights group, sought delay in the implementation of the plan so that he could take the issue to the convention floor. Reuther refused and virtually demanded that Rauh accept the Humphrey-Johnson plan regardless of MFDP opposition. The MFDP itself felt betrayed by Reuther and other liberals and later staged a sit-in on the convention floor. Rauh, who had long worked closely with the UAW, thought Reuther used too much "muscle" in the conflict, but Humphrey later praised the union leader as a "practical liberal" in the emotional dispute. In 1968 the UAW hierarchy solidly backed Humphrey for president, both before and after the Democratic convention in Chicago.

Reuther worked to advance liberal and labor causes in arenas outside of the Democratic Party as well. The UAW was primarily responsible for formation of a private Citizen's Crusade against Poverty in November 1965. Chaired by Reuther, the group directed over a million dollars in funds to a variety of civil rights and antipoverty organizations and to several urban organizing projects of the Students for a Democratic Society, (SDS). Reuther participated in the Selma to Montgomery voting rights march in early 1965 and in December flew to Delano, California, to pledge a UAW contribution of $5,000 a month to the National Farm Workers Association led by CESAR CHAVEZ. Reuther also contributed $50,000 in UAW funds to the Memphis, Tennessee, sanitation workers strike in April 1968 shortly after MARTIN LUTHER KING, JR.'s, assassination in that city. Following the July 1967 Detroit riots, Reuther joined HENRY FORD II and other prominent business and civic leaders in formation of a New Detroit Committee to help rebuild the city and improve minority employment and housing conditions.

During the mid-1960s Reuther clashed repeatedly with AFL-CIO president GEORGE MEANY over what Reuther considered the labor organization's "complacency" at home and rigid anticommunism abroad. Reuther supported President Johnson's conduct of the Vietnam War in its early phases but favored greater efforts toward negotiations and a bombing halt in 1966 and 1967. Relations between

Reuther and Meany deteriorated following a well-publicized attack by Victor Reuther on the AFL-CIO's American Institute for Free Labor Development. Using the UAW's May 1966 Long Beach convention for a platform, Reuther's brother charged that the institute's Latin American operations were largely funded by the CIA and supervised in a conspiratorial fashion by Meany's foreign affairs aide Jay Lovestone. (Later disclosures revealed that both Reuther brothers had accepted CIA funds in 1951 for distribution to West German trade unions.)

When in June 1966 Meany withdrew American representatives from the International Labor Organization (ILO) after a Polish Communist had been elected ILO president, Walter Reuther protested that the AFL-CIO president should have consulted his executive council before taking such unilateral action. Two months later Reuther characterized recent AFL-CIO statements on the Vietnam War and domestic dissent as "intemperate, hysterical and jingoistic." Reuther demanded a special meeting of the AFL-CIO Executive Council to review union foreign policy, but the UAW leader unexpectedly failed to attend the session when it convened in November 1966.

The UAW began to loosen its ties with the national AFL-CIO in December 1966 when Reuther announced that the auto union would "speak out on fundamental issues" if and when it found itself in disagreement with the parent labor organization. Reuther and other UAW officials resigned from their AFL-CIO posts in February 1967, and, in April, a UAW convention authorized the union executive board to formally withdraw from the AFL-CIO if it thought such action necessary. At the same time Reuther called on the national organization to launch an $87 million "national crusade" to organize white-collar employees and migratory and other poorly paid workers.

When the AFL-CIO took no action on Reuther's proposals in 1967, the UAW began to withhold its dues. The AFL-CIO formally suspended the 1.6-million member UAW in May 1968 and later issued a "white paper" denouncing Reuther for failing to use "democratic forums [within the AFL-CIO] to press his views." The UAW and the International Brotherhood of Teamsters subsequently formed an Alliance for Labor Action, which Reuther hoped would "revitalize" the labor movement. The alliance however disintegrated in the early 1970s.

Reuther, his wife, and four others were killed near Pellston, Michigan, on May 9, 1970, when their chartered jet crashed on landing.

—NNL

## Rhodes, James A(llen)
### (1909–2001) *governor*

Born on September 13, 1909, in Jackson, Ohio, James A. Rhodes quit Ohio State University after one semester to help support his family. Embarking upon a political career as a Republican, he served in several minor city positions in Columbus until 1943, when he won election as mayor. In 1952 Rhodes successfully ran for state auditor, serving in that position for a decade. Two years later, he failed to unseat then incumbent governor FRANK J. LAUSCHE in 1954.

Rhodes's impressive reelection campaign for auditor in 1960, in which he won by just under 700,000 votes, set the stage for a second gubernatorial campaign. In 1962 he defeated incumbent governor Michael V. DiSalle, a Democrat who had angered many voters by raising taxes in 1959. Republicans captured every other state office and retained control of both houses of the legislature.

Once elected, Rhodes proved faithful to the one pledge he had made to Ohio voters: not to raise taxes. To keep that promise and to eliminate a massive deficit inherited from DiSalle, he removed several thousand workers from the state payroll and reduced state expenses (exclusive of education) by 9.1 percent. The governor consistently presented a balanced budget to the legislature during his tenure in office. Newly elected conservative Republican governors RONALD REAGAN (Calif.) and CLAUDE R. KIRK, JR. (Fla.) sought out Rhodes's counsel when they prepared their first state budgets.

To fund extensive and popular highway and state university construction programs, Rhodes campaigned energetically, and usually with success, for state bond issues. Voters approved bond referendums in 1963 and 1965. In May 1967, however, the electorate rejected the governor's proposed Ohio Bond Commission, which would have transferred the right to issue state notes from the voters to a special state agency.

Rhodes devoted much energy to promoting tourism and bringing new industries to Ohio. As the state's sales agent, he traveled throughout the nation and most of the noncommunist world. In full-page ads in the *Wall Street Journal*, the Rhodes administration proclaimed, "Profit is *Not* a Dirty Word in Ohio." His efforts proved successful. In 1966 Ohio attracted an unprecedented $2.1 billion in new industry. Aided by the mid-1960s economic boom, the number of new companies relocating in Ohio increased five times between 1962 and 1966. "I don't say we invented industrial development," Rhodes remarked, "but we perfected it." To create a tourist industry for the state, Rhodes approved an impressive advertising campaign, which hailed "The Wonderful World of Ohio," and oversaw the rehabilitation of the state fair and parks system. The Ohio Development Department established a model for other state administrations to follow.

In the eyes of some observers, however, Rhodes's frugality starved state services. When measured against its capacity to pay in the late 1960s, Ohio ranked 48th among the states in educational support, 43rd in health care, and 38th in welfare expenditures. Running for reelection in 1966, Rhodes argued that his emphasis upon creating jobs had reduced the need for greater public welfare spending and had increased state revenues. His little-known Democratic opponent attacked the state's record in welfare programs but lost badly to the incumbent, who won 62.2 percent of the total vote. Rhodes refrained from a "no taxes" pledge during his 1966 campaign. As expected, he asked for, and received, a 1 percent increase in the state sales tax in 1967. The state remained, however, one of the largest in the nation without a personal income tax.

Republican Party leaders came to regard Rhodes as unpredictable, if not untrustworthy. At the June 1964 National Governors Conference in Cleveland, Rhodes approved a campaign to prevent the nomination of conservative senator BARRY GOLDWATER (R-Ariz.). However, the governor all but ended the presidential drive of Pennsylvania governor WILLIAM W. SCRANTON at the eve of the July convention by releasing the 58-member Ohio delegation to Goldwater. By then Rhodes recognized Goldwater's clear lead and determined not to weaken further the senator's fall campaign by aiding the desperate Scranton effort. His move came as a surprise to state party chair RAY BLISS and to Representative Robert Taft, Jr. (R-Ohio), who was running for the Senate. Rhodes publicly predicted that Goldwater's vote against the 1964 civil rights bill would win powerful voter "backlash" support and that the senator would carry Ohio. In fact, Goldwa-

ter lost the state by a million votes and Taft also went down to defeat.

Perhaps because of the 1964 debacle, Rhodes privately fought hard for the nomination of a liberal-moderate presidential candidate in 1968. He wanted New York governor NELSON A. ROCKEFELLER to win the nomination and urged Governor Reagan to enter the campaign in the hope that he would split the forces allied to former vice president RICHARD M. NIXON. At the August 1968 party gathering, he kept the Ohio delegation pledged to his "favorite son" candidacy on the first ballot. Despite his efforts, Nixon won the nomination on the first ballot.

Scandal, tragedy, and political defeat marred the last two years of Rhodes's second term. *Life* magazine published an April 1969 article connecting some of the governor's activities with Ohio mobsters. Professing his innocence, Rhodes ran against Representative Taft for the 1970 Republican senatorial nomination in the Ohio GOP's most bitter intraparty fight in a generation. Shortly before the primary, Rhodes ordered the Ohio National Guard onto the campus of Kent State University, scene of demonstrations protesting President Nixon's decision to order U.S. troops into Cambodia. Members of the guard shot into a crowd of protesters on May 4, killing four and wounding 11. The following day Taft narrowly defeated Rhodes for the nomination.

Barred from serving three consecutive terms as governor, Rhodes won another term in the state house in 1974 and then gained reelection in 1978. After a hiatus of four years, he sought the governorship once again but lost to Democratic incumbent Richard Celeste. Rhodes died on March 4, 2001.

—JLB

## Rhodes, John J(acob)

(1916–2003) *member of the House of Representatives*

John J. Rhodes was a native Kansan who rose to political prominence as an Arizonan. Born in Council Grove, Kansas, on September 18, 1916, he graduated from Kansas State University in 1938 and took a law degree from Harvard three years later. He served in the U.S. Army Air Forces during World War II and moved to Arizona after the war was over. In 1952 he won election to the U.S. House of Representatives as a Republican from Arizona's first district, which included Phoenix and the surrounding area. The population of Phoenix increased from just over 100,000 in 1950 to almost 600,000 in 1970, largely as a result of an influx of midwesterners and southerners with conservative political views. Rhodes's voting record in Congress paralleled the views of these constituents.

Rhodes favored a limited role for the federal government. He voted with the House's conservative coalition at least 80 percent of the time during the early 1960s. He generally opposed bills that the Kennedy administration supported during those years. He continued to vote with the conservative coalition during the Johnson presidency and opposed most of the administration's Great Society legislation. Although he voted against the Civil Rights Act of 1964, he supported the Voting Rights Act of 1965.

A staunch anticommunism guided his thinking on foreign policy issues. In 1964 he voted against allowing the sale of surplus farm goods to Communist countries. He supported each step of President Johnson's escalation of the Vietnam War and consistently backed large defense appropriations.

As ranking minority member of the Public Works Subcommittee of the House Appropriations Committee, Rhodes played a key role in Congress's passage in 1968 of a compromise bill establishing the Central Arizona Project to provide for the diversion of water from the Colorado River to arid areas around Phoenix and Tucson. The compromise included concessions that resolved many of the objections of California and the northwestern states, which had opposed the project for over two decades.

In 1965 Rhodes became a member of the House Republican leadership when he joined Representative GERALD R. FORD (R-Mich.) and other relatively young Republican representatives in a rebellion against Minority Leader CHARLES A. HALLECK (R-Ind.). The insurgents did not oppose the conservative views of Halleck but thought that he was not providing forceful leadership. The House Republican Conference chose Ford to replace Halleck in January 1965, and later in the month Rhodes was chosen to replace Representative JOHN W. BYRNES (R-Wisc.) as chair of the House Republican Policy Committee. The function of the committee was to recommend and enforce party positions on issues before the House.

Rhodes was a staunch supporter of the Nixon administration in the late 1960s and early 1970s.

When Representative Ford became vice president in 1973, Rhodes succeeded him as minority leader. During the Watergate scandal, Rhodes played an important role in persuading Nixon in August 1974 that the House would vote articles of impeachment. The next day Nixon announced his resignation. Rhodes retired from the House at the end of his term in January 1983 and then practiced law until 1997. He died on August 24, 2003.

MLL

## Ribicoff, Abraham A(lexander)
(1910–1998) *member of the Senate*

The son of poor Polish-Jewish immigrants, Ribicoff was born in New Britain, Connecticut, on April 9, 1910. He worked his way through New York University and the University of Chicago Law School as sales representative of a buckle and zipper factory. After receiving his LL.B. in 1933, he returned to Connecticut and opened a law practice. Ribicoff's political career began in 1938, when he won election to the Connecticut General Assembly. He served two terms in the state legislature and then became police court judge. Ribicoff ran successfully for the House of Representatives in 1948; he remained in Congress until 1952, when he lost a close race for the Senate. Two years later he was elected governor of Connecticut. Ribicoff won wide attention in the state house for his vigorous traffic safety program and his efforts to increase the efficiency of state government. He was reelected governor by a wide margin in 1958.

While serving in the House, Ribicoff had become close friends with Representative John F. Kennedy (D-Mass.). He was one of Kennedy's earliest supporters in national politics, working for both his vice presidential bid in 1956 and his presidential candidacy in 1960. Kennedy rewarded Ribicoff after the 1960 election by appointing him secretary of health, education and welfare (HEW), a position Ribicoff himself chose in preference to other, more prominent cabinet posts. Ribicoff remained in the cabinet for two years, spending much of his time in unsuccessful efforts to gain legislative approval for administration Medicare and aid-to-education proposals. His experience in HEW convinced him that the department's bureaucracy was too complex and unwieldy to handle the nation's social problems. Ribicoff resigned from the administration in 1962 and returned to Connecticut to run successfully for the Senate.

As a senator, Ribicoff remained interested in many of the problems that had confronted him as governor of Connecticut and secretary of HEW. He soon became known as a "cautious crusader," giving strong support to liberal causes but ready to compromise or defer action when necessary. In 1964 and 1965 he endorsed the Johnson administration's Medicare program, even though he objected to provisions that limited the length of coverage for specific medical problems. As chair of the Senate Government Operations Subcommittee on Executive Reorganization, Ribicoff held a series of hearings on traffic safety in 1965 and 1966. These hearings became a forum for the widely publicized conflict between U.S. auto company executives and consumer advocate RALPH NADER, who claimed that auto firms intentionally manufactured vehicles with important safety defects. Ribicoff generally supported Nader's position and used information collected in the hearings to push for a National Traffic and Motor Vehicle Safety Act. As passed in March 1966, the measure required the departments of Commerce and Transportation to establish federal safety regulations for all new domestic and imported cars.

Ribicoff again gained national attention in 1966, when the Subcommittee on Executive Reorganization conducted hearings on the problems of U.S. cities. Leaders of business, government, civil rights organizations, and labor unions appeared before the panel to discuss approaches to urban renewal. Ribicoff originally wanted to determine the impact of federal agencies and programs on inner-city areas; as the hearings progressed, however, he became increasingly interested in the possible role of private enterprise and community groups in reversing urban decay. After the conclusion of the subcommittee hearings, Ribicoff urged the upper chamber to initiate a major program of urban renewal. In January 1967 he introduced 13 bills in this area, including a $40 billion provision for inner-city housing renovation and a program of government loans and tax credits to attract industry into cities. The administration was reluctant to sponsor new domestic programs at this time, however, and Congress did not act on Ribicoff's proposals.

Ribicoff came out in mid-1968 in opposition to the Vietnam War, which he blamed for the administration's unwillingness to undertake new domestic spending. He supported the presidential candidacy of antiwar senator GEORGE MCGOVERN (D-S.Dak.) at the 1968 Democratic National Convention. Ribicoff further alienated Democratic Party leaders by denouncing, from the convention podium, the alleged "Gestapo tactics" of the Chicago police in handling demonstrators during the convention. Because the Connecticut Democratic Committee strongly supported the candidacy of HUBERT HUMPHREY, it gave Ribicoff relatively little support in his 1968 campaign for reelection to the Senate. He was nevertheless popular enough to win the election with 54 percent of the vote.

Ribicoff continued to champion liberal causes during the early 1970s. As a member of the powerful Senate Finance Committee, he fought unsuccessfully for welfare reform, including federalization of the welfare system and introduction of a guaranteed annual income. He also advocated several tax reform measures and urged creation of a Consumer Protection Agency; most of these proposals also failed to gain Senate approval or were frustrated by Nixon Administration inaction. He won a third and final Senate term in the election of 1974. After retiring from Congress, he practiced law in New York City. He died on February 22, 1998.

—SLG

## Ridgway, Mathew B(unker)
### (1895–1993) *retired army officer*

Ridgway was born into a military family, spent his professional life in the army, and became one of the most important U.S. military leaders of the 20th century. Born at Fort Monroe, Virginia, on March 3, 1895, Ridgway, like his father, became an army officer after graduating from West Point in 1917. He commanded the 82nd Airborne division in World War II and the 8th Army in the Korean War. In 1951 he succeeded General Douglas MacArthur as United Nations commander in Korea. Ridgway subsequently served as supreme commander of North Atlantic Treaty Organization forces in Europe and army chief of staff. In the latter position, he opposed the possibility of U.S. military intervention in Indochina in 1954.

During the Johnson years Ridgway was one of a number of military leaders, including General James M. Gavin and U.S. Marine Corps commandant David M. Shoup, who attempted to persuade the administration to limit U.S. involvement in Vietnam. In an article published in *Look* magazine in

April 1966, Ridgway proposed that the United States maintain a middle course between unilateral withdrawal from Vietnam and "all-out war." He believed that the United States should press for a negotiated settlement that would guarantee South Vietnamese security. Ridgway feared that increasing U.S. military involvement would lead to direct Chinese intervention. He opposed the suggestion of air force general CURTIS E. LEMAY that the United States bomb North Vietnam "back into the Stone Age." Ridgway wrote that "there must be some moral limit to the means we use to achieve victory." The use of nuclear weapons against North Vietnam, he said, would be "the ultimate in immorality." He thought that many advocates of expanded U.S. military intervention in Vietnam were misapplying the lessons of the Korean War.

In March 1968 President Johnson invited Ridgway and a number of prominent former government officials and military officers to the White House to advise him on Vietnam strategy. The panel, commonly known as the "Wise Men," reached the conclusion "that we can no longer do the job we set out to do in the time we have left and we must begin to take steps to disengage." Although Ridgway concurred in the conclusion of his colleagues, he thought that the Johnson administration should notify the Saigon government that it would have two years to create military forces capable of defending South Vietnamese independence and then the United States would begin to withdraw its troops. The advice of the Wise Men helped persuade the president to announce on March 31 new limits on the bombing of North Vietnam and a proposal to begin negotiations.

Ridgway died on July 26, 1993.

—JLW

## Rivers, L(ucius) Mendel

(1905–1970) *member of the House of Representatives*

Born in Gumville, South Carolina, on September 28, 1905, Rivers attended both the College of Charleston and the University of South Carolina School of Law without graduating from either. Nevertheless, he was admitted to the South Carolina bar in 1932. He won election to the House of Representatives in 1940 as a Democrat. He easily won 14 more consecutive terms, sometimes without opposition. He gained a seat on the Naval Affairs Committee, and, after the creation of the Department of Defense in 1947, the Armed Services Committee. Conservative on most issues, he often followed an independent course in national politics. He looked favorably on STROM THURMOND's (D-S.C.) Dixiecrat candidacy for the presidency in 1948; he supported DWIGHT D. EISENHOWER in the presidential campaigns of 1952 and 1956. A segregationist, he voted against civil rights legislation.

Rivers was an advocate of large military forces and a master of pork-barrel politics. He used his position on the Armed Services Committee to promote the construction of military facilities in his district. In the early 1950s Rivers succeeded in reopening two installations closed after World War II and during the next 13 years secured a marine corps air station, three air force installations, and a Polaris submarine base for his district. By the late 1960s military bases and defense-related industry accounted for 35 percent of the payroll in the Charleston area. Representative ROBERT SIKES (D-Fla.) once quipped that if Rivers put anything else in his district, "the whole place will sink completely from sight from the sheer weight of military installations."

Upon the retirement of Representative CARL VINSON (D-Ga.), Rivers became chair of the Armed Services committee in January 1965. Rivers viewed the committee as "the only official important voice the military has in the House of Representatives." Unlike his predecessor, Rivers met regularly with the committee's seven senior members, known on Capitol Hills as "the Junta."

As chair, Rivers first clashed with the Johnson administration over what he termed Secretary of Defense ROBERT MCNAMARA's "unilateral" decision to close unnecessary military bases. To counter McNamara's plan, Rivers added a provision to the 1965 Military Construction Authorization Act that subjected any base-closure plans to a veto by either chamber of Congress. President Johnson vetoed the measure, and Congress passed a new bill that included a provision giving the legislature 30 days to review base-closing plans submitted by the secretary. During the floor debate on this bill, Rivers stated that the executive branch was now convinced that Congress "must be a partner" in military affairs.

Rivers again differed with the administration in July 1965 by supporting the third major raise in military pay in three years, a 10 percent increase that doubled the Defense Department's request. During the House debate Rivers opposed an amendment submitted by Representative ROBERT KASTENMEIER (D-Wisc.) to alter the pay-increase scale in favor of junior officers and enlistees with two or three years of service. Rivers described the amendment as an abandonment of the "longevity principle" and dismissed as "fallacious" the argument that the pay increases in Kastenmeier's amendment might constitute a first step toward elimination of the draft. In 1967 Rivers supported another increase of 4.5 percent and successfully obtained a provision for automatic raises in military pay comparable to the upward adjustments in civilian federal employee's salaries.

Rivers vigorously defended the draft and the military's conduct of the war in Vietnam. In a Hartford, Connecticut, speech on August 11, 1965, Rivers called for turning "the conduct of the war over to those trained in war—the professional military men." He warned that unless the United States was willing to employ nuclear weapons against the People's Republic of China, an American victory in South Vietnam was "merely postponing the final victory of Red China." After North Korea seized the USS *Pueblo* in January 1968, Rivers asserted that the United States should do anything "including declaring war if necessary" to recover the ship. Rivers also advocated that strong measures be taken against opponents of the war and the draft. He described war protesters as "traitors" in May 1967 and maintained that antiwar protests "undoubtedly . . . mislead the enemy and prolong the war." Rivers continued as chair of the House Armed Services Committee until his death on December 28, 1970.

—DKR

## Robertson, A. Willis
### (1887–1971) *member of the Senate*

Robertson, born on May 27, 1887, in Martinsburg, West Virginia, served in the Virginia Senate from 1916 to 1922. For the next six years he was the commonwealth's attorney for Rockbridge County. In 1932 he won election to the U.S. House of Representatives, where he served until chosen to fill the unexpired U.S. Senate term of Carter Glass in 1946. Robertson was reelected for full terms in 1948, 1954, and 1960.

He was as conservative as his fellow-senator, HARRY F. BYRD, whose Democratic machine dominated Virginia's politics from the late 1920s to the

mid-1960s. Like Byrd, Robertson opposed extension of federal power, social welfare programs, and racial integration. But he was not on close terms with Byrd or the other organization leaders.

In 1959 Robertson became one of the leading spokesperson for Capitol Hill's southern Democrat–Republican coalition when he obtained the chair of the Senate Banking and Currency Committee. At the beginning of the Johnson administration he was also the sixth-ranking member of the Senate Appropriations Committee. Unlike Byrd, he gave nominal endorsement to Johnson's candidacy in 1964 as an act of party loyalty, but he persistently opposed administration programs in Congress. In 1964, 1965, and 1966 he was, according to *Congressional Quarterly*, among the seven Senate Democrats who most often voted against Johnson-supported bills.

Robertson was especially opposed to the administration's Great Society social welfare programs. In September 1964 he denounced the Appalachian development bill, asserting it would set a bad precedent because "every part of the country will want to have a piece of the pie." He argued that the best way to combat poverty was to reduce dependence on public welfare programs. During 1965 Johnson's public housing bill came before the Banking and Currency Committee, and, in June, Robertson attacked it as a measure that would "breed and foster reliance on the government and discourage private initiative." However, the committee reported the bill out favorably and it ultimately became law.

During the Johnson years Robertson was best known for the bank-related measures he was concerned with as chair of the Banking and Currency Committee. In 1964 the committee failed, as it had during the early 1960s, to report out a "truth-in-lending" bill, which would have required lenders to disclose in advance the actual amount of a borrower's commitment and the actual annual rate of interest Senator PAUL DOUGLAS (D-Ill.), a member of the Banking and Currency Committee and the sponsor of the bill, criticized Robertson for not permitting the committee to consider the measure.

The most controversial banking legislation handled by Robertson during President Johnson's tenure was a measure to revise the Bank Merger Act of 1960. In the spring of 1965 Robertson introduced a bill to prohibit the Justice Department from bringing antitrust action against banks involved in mergers approved by the appropriate federal regulatory agency. After objections were raised by small banks, the Banking and Currency Committee adopted an amendment offered by Senator WILLIAM PROXMIRE (D-Wisc.), which gave the Justice Department 30 days to challenge approved mergers. But the bill, which was eventually reported to the floor and which Robertson supported, exempted from antitrust action all of the six proposed mergers then being contested by the department. House Banking and Currency chair WRIGHT PATMAN (D-Tex.) regarded the bill as too favorable to large banks, and the measure did not become law until February 1966. The final version exempted only three of the proposed mergers from antitrust suits.

In 1966 William B. Spong, Jr., a moderate state senator, challenged Robertson in the Democratic primary. Spong charged that Robertson was a pawn of big banks and cited the incumbent's favorable attitude toward bank mergers. The accusation gained credence when the challenger was able to show that Virginia's banks were contributing heavily to Robertson's campaign. Robertson's prospects were also diminished by the growing number of urban and black voters, who were pushing the state's electorate toward the political center. Spong won the primary by 611 votes out of over 433,000 cast. After his loss Robertson resigned from the Senate and became a consultant to the International Bank for Reconstruction and Development. He died on November 1, 1971.

—MLL

## Roche, John P.

### (1923–1994) *White House special consultant*

Roche, who was born in New York City on May 7, 1923, graduated from Hofstra College in 1943 and served in the U.S. Army Air Forces during World War II. He received his doctorate from Cornell University in 1949 and the same year began teaching political science at Haverford College near Philadelphia. In 1956 Roche moved to Brandeis as professor of politics, later serving as the university's dean of the faculty of arts and sciences. While on the Brandeis faculty he wrote several political studies, including *Courts and Rights* (1961), *The Quest for the Dream: The Development of Civil Rights and Human Relations in Modern America* (1963), and *Shadow and Substance: Studies in the Theory and Structure of Politics* (1964).

In addition to his scholarly work, Roche served as chair of the Americans for Democratic Action (ADA) from 1962 to 1965. His period of leadership was one of growing dissatisfaction within the organization over U.S. involvement in Vietnam, culminating in an April 1966 ADA declaration deploring "the continuing intensification" of the war. Roche, a strong supporter of administration policy, opposed this trend. After a meeting of top ADA officials with President Lyndon Johnson in April 1965, Roche split openly with ADA vice chair JOSEPH RAUH, who opposed American bombing of North Vietnam. Roche resigned from the ADA in February 1968, when the organization endorsed Senator EUGENE MCCARTHY (D-Minn.) in his campaign for the Democratic Presidential nomination.

Roche's academic background and his strong support of administration policy in Vietnam made him an attractive candidate for a position as White House consultant. His appointment in September 1966 coincided with the abrupt resignation of historian ERIC GOLDMAN, who was popularly known as the White House "intellectual in residence." Yet Roche was not Goldman's replacement. White House aide BILL MOYERS had approached Roche weeks earlier about providing "another eye" on foreign affairs issues and "another hand" on domestic policy. Roche's appointment had yet to be announced when Goldman made critical comments about administration policy that appeared in newspapers. He quickly resigned, and newspaper reports described Roche as Goldman's successor, even though Moyers insisted that Roche's job was very different. Roche later declared that he "didn't think there was such a job as presidential ambassador to intellectuals." But if there was, he was the wrong person for the position because he "happened to have very little respect for most" intellectuals. Faced with vehement opposition to administration policy in the *New York Review of Books* and other influential periodicals, Roche attacked the "alienated intellectuals" of the "New York artsy-crafty set" as an isolated group of critics out of touch with American society. Many intellectuals, for their part, agreed with literary critic IRVING HOWE in viewing Roche's appointment as a sign of "official contempt" toward the academic community. Rather than trying to win support for administration policies from intellectuals, Roche spent most of his time in the White House as a speechwriter for the president. He also tried "to look around the corner," as the president once said, to provide a longer perspective on the effects of U.S. policies in Vietnam.

Roche left his White House position in September 1968, returning to his teaching duties at Brandeis. He also wrote a nationally syndicated news column. In 1973 he accepted an appointment as Henry R. Luce professor of civilization and foreign affairs at the Fletcher School of Law and Diplomacy. Roche's memoirs of his White House service, entitled *Sentenced to Life*, were published in 1974. He died on May 6, 1994.

—FHM

## Rockefeller, Nelson A(ldrich)
### (1908–1979) *governor*

Nelson Rockefeller was the grandson of John D. Rockefeller, the founder of the Standard Oil Company of New Jersey and one of the wealthiest men in the world. Born in Bar Harbor, Maine, on July 8, 1908, he was the third of six children of John D. Rockefeller, Jr., and Abby Greene Aldrich. While growing up, Nelson learned thrift, self-reliance, and a sense of social responsibility.

After graduating from Dartmouth College in 1930, Nelson worked in his family's Chase National Bank and leased space in the new Rockefeller Center in Manhattan. From 1935 to 1940 he was a director of the Creole Petroleum Corporation, a Standard Oil affiliate with large holdings in Venezuela. His experience in that post convinced him of the need for extensive economic assistance to Latin America to alleviate poverty and improve the political climate for investment by North American corporations.

Because of Rockefeller's interest in Latin America, President Franklin D. Roosevelt appointed him to head the Office of the Coordinator of Inter-American Affairs in 1940. Rockefeller held that post for four years and then became assistant secretary of state in charge of Latin American relations. After World War II Rockefeller established private organizations to promote Latin American economic development by providing technological aid and encouraging private investment.

From 1950 to 1951 he was an adviser to President HARRY S. TRUMAN on the implementation of the Point Four program. During the Eisenhower presidency Rockefeller served as undersecretary of health, education and welfare from 1953 to 1954 and as a special assistant to the president from 1954 to 1955.

In 1956 Rockefeller decided to seek the governorship of New York. For the next two years he cultivated Republican political contacts in his capacity as chair of New York's Committee on the Preparation of the State Constitutional Convention. Some Republicans believed that the Rockefeller name would prevent him from winning the election. The negative impact of Rockefeller's wealth upon his 1958 campaign, however, was reduced by the fact that the Democratic incumbent, Governor W. Averell Harriman was also a multimillionaire. Furthermore, Rockefeller's dynamic, self-confident, and quick-witted campaign style was a major asset against the uncharismatic Harriman. Outspending his rival by $1.8 million to $1.1 million and employing an exceptionally able staff, Rockefeller won the election by over a half-million votes.

Rockefeller introduced or expanded a broad array of civil rights, labor, and social welfare programs during the first five years of his governorship. He successfully pressed for civil rights legislation that barred discrimination in the areas of housing, lending, and public accommodations. Rockefeller established the state's first uniform minimum wage at $1.00 an hour in 1960 and increased it to $1.15 in 1962. State aid to education rose from $600 million to $1 billion. The state's middle-income housing program increased by more than tenfold. A vast program to enlarge the state university was begun. A school-to-employment program (STEP) to deter juvenile delinquency and a youth employment service (YES) were also created.

The high cost of many of these programs necessitated great increases in state expenditures. Since the state constitution mandated a balanced budget, Rockefeller asked for substantial tax hikes in 1959 and 1963. The 1963 request created considerable resentment among the voters because, during his reelection campaign of the previous year against Democrat Robert Morgenthau, the governor had pledged not to increase taxes.

From the time that he became governor, Rockefeller demonstrated that he was interested in seeking the presidency. As the governor of what was then the most populous state and a leader of the liberal, eastern wing of the Republican Party, he was a potentially powerful candidate. In 1959, however, Rockefeller determined that Vice President RICHARD M. NIXON had already positioned himself to secure the nomination. On December 26, 1959, Rockefeller issued a statement withdrawing his name from consideration for the party's presidential nomination in 1960. Yet Rockefeller intended to use his influence to shape the Republican platform. In July 1960, prior to the Republican convention, Nixon met with Rockefeller in New York City and offered the governor the vice presidential nomination. Rockefeller declined, but negotiated an agreement with Nixon in which they both announced their support for increased defense spending to meet Soviet challenges in the cold war and for accelerated efforts to raise standards of living and meet social needs, including the removal of "the remaining vestiges of segregation or discrimination in all areas of national life—voting and housing, schools and jobs." Outraged conservatives resented Rockefeller's efforts to use his influence to advance a liberal agenda.

After Nixon's defeat Rockefeller set his sights on the 1964 Republican presidential nomination. Polls showed that he was the front-running Republican candidate. But in May 1963, the recently divorced governor married Margaretta "Happy" Fitler Murphy, also recently divorced and almost 20 years his junior. His divorce and remarriage provoked an extremely unfavorable popular reaction that dogged Rockefeller for the remainder of the presidential race. Senator Barry M. Goldwater (R-Ariz.), the choice of Republican conservatives, made substantial gains against Rockefeller in the polls. In July 1963 Rockefeller attempted to halt his decline in popularity by issuing a stinging attack upon what he called the extreme right-wing elements in the party. He officially announced his candidacy in early November 1963.

Even after Kennedy's assassination, when Goldwater's southern-based strategy appeared threatened by the accession to the presidency of Texan LYNDON B. JOHNSON, Rockefeller's standing in the polls did not improve. He hoped to revive his prospects by a victory in the New Hampshire primary in March 1964 but finished third behind write-in candidate HENRY CABOT LODGE and Goldwater.

During the spring Rockefeller denounced Goldwater's opposition to civil rights and social welfare legislation as "the height of extremist folly" while concentrating his efforts on the May primary contest in Oregon. He won an upset victory in that state over Lodge, thereby destroying the latter's moderate candidacy. The one remaining primary was a winner-take-all contest in California. Even

with a victory there Rockefeller's nomination appeared unlikely, because Goldwater had done extremely well in nonprimary states. But the governor campaigned vigorously, charging that Goldwater's conservatism was outside of the party's "mainstream." On June 2 Goldwater defeated Rockefeller by 59,000 votes out of 1.1 million cast. Some observers attributed Rockefeller's narrow defeat to a revival of the remarriage issue that resulted when his wife gave birth to a son on the Sunday before the primary.

The governor withdrew from the contest on June 15 and threw his support to Pennsylvania governor WILLIAM SCRANTON, who had entered the race three days earlier as the last hope of Republican moderates and liberals. At the July Republican National Convention, Rockefeller endured booing from Goldwater supporters in the galleries as he spoke on behalf of the Scranton forces' platform proposals supporting civil rights legislation and criticizing extremist groups. Goldwater easily won the presidential nomination on the first ballot.

During the mid-1960s Rockefeller continued to press for liberal programs in New York State. In 1965 the State Commission on Human Rights was granted authority to bring complaints on its own initiative against any alleged discrimination in employment, education, housing, or public accommodations. The minimum wage increased to $1.60 in 1968. Rockefeller's vast network of social welfare programs was extended. In 1966 the state's Medicaid plan, the most ambitious of its kind in the nation, was launched. It provided free medical care for any family of four or more with an after-tax income of less than $6,000 a year. Almost a third of the state's 18 million residents were eligible for the program. In 1968 the maximum income for eligibility was reduced to $5,300. A Narcotics Addiction Control Commission was established in 1966 to provide treatment for addicts. It possessed authority to commit addicts for treatment regardless of their wishes. State aid for all levels of education amounted to $2.4 billion of the 1968–69 budget, a larger sum than the entire New York budget at the beginning of Rockefeller's governorship.

The Albany Mall project, a huge highway construction program and the creation of such planning agencies as the Metropolitan Transit Authority (established in 1968) entailed enormous expenditures, and the state budget increased from $1.7 billion in 1958–59 to $5.4 billion for 1968–69. At the beginning of his governorship, Rockefeller employed pay-as-you-go financing to meet the constitution's balanced-budget requirement. But tax revenues, even after they were enlarged by the creation of a state sales tax in 1965 and a hike in the state income tax in 1968, were insufficient to meet the cost of his programs. Therefore, the governor ultimately turned to bond issues for funds.

The constitution required voter approval for the sale of bonds backed by the credit of the state. In 1965 the electorate sanctioned a $1 billion bond issue to assist municipalities in eliminating water pollution, and two years later it endorsed a $2.5 billion transportation bond issue to build highways, airports, and mass transit facilities. The voters, however, did not always back bond proposals: in 1964 and 1965 public housing referenda were defeated at the polls.

To circumvent the risk of voter rejection of bond issues, Rockefeller's aides devised a plan to create quasi-independent agencies that would issue so-called moral obligation bonds. These institutions were responsible for redeeming the bonds, while the state assumed a moral, but not legally binding, commitment as their ultimate guarantor. The first such agency was the State University Construction Fund, established in 1962. A number of others were created in the mid-1960s, including the Urban Development Corporation, established in 1968 to promote the building of low-income housing. Some observers, including Democratic state comptroller Arthur Levitt, contended that this method of financing state projects was antidemocratic, of dubious constitutionality, and more expensive than voter-approved bonds.

The resentment created by the tax increases necessitated by Rockefeller's programs proved a significant problem in the governor's 1966 reelection bid. Polls taken early in the campaign showed him trailing Frank O'Connor, his Democratic opponent, by 26 points. The Rockefeller campaign organization reacted with a massive television advertising blitz. Between 3,000 and 4,000 television spots were shown on 27 commercial stations throughout the state. New York newspapers estimated that between $5 and $6 million were spent on the campaign, eight times the amount spent by the O'Connor forces and a new national record for any state election. Much of the money reportedly came from Rockefeller and his family. Rockefeller defeated O'Connor by approximately 400,000 votes in a four-candidate race.

In May 1966, as Rockefeller was launching his gubernatorial campaign, he stated that he was "completely and forever, without reservation" removing himself from contention for the 1968 Republican presidential nomination. He proposed a liberal slate consisting of Michigan governor GEORGE ROMNEY for president and Senator JACOB JAVITS (R-N.Y.) for vice president. But Romney's following dwindled after a series of campaign blunders in 1967, and he withdrew from the race in February 1968, two weeks before the first primary. Despite pressure to enter the campaign, Rockefeller reiterated his noncandidacy on March 21, 1968.

However, President Johnson's announcement at the end of the month that he would not seek reelection made a Republican victory in November seem more likely, and a number of party leaders began expressing a preference for Rockefeller as the most attractive candidate the Republicans could offer. On April 30 the governor reversed his position and offered himself as an alternative to Nixon, by that time the front-running candidate.

Rockefeller did not enter the Republican primaries. His strategy was to demonstrate through extensive personal and media campaigning that he was the most popular Republican among the general electorate. In May, June, and July he visited 45 states, addressing rallies and negotiating with uncommitted delegates and party leaders. Beginning in June he conducted an expensive television and newspaper campaign.

Against the advice of his campaign managers, who urged him to move toward the ideological center of the party, Rockefeller presented himself as a liberal Republican. He advocated a "universal compulsory national health insurance" plan, urged a vast program to "save and rebuild" the nation's cities, and eschewed use of the crime issue, asserting that "to keep law and order, there must be justice and opportunity." Unlike Nixon, Rockefeller presented in July the details of a Vietnam peace plan. It called for a gradual withdrawal of troops by both sides, free elections, and direct negotiations between North and South Vietnam that were to include the National Liberation Front "if it renounces force." Rockefeller's platform earned him considerable support from independent voters and liberals of both parties.

Goldwater's overwhelming defeat in 1964 worked against Rockefeller's candidacy four years later. Most Republicans thought that the strongest candidate would be someone, like Nixon, who was in the center of the party. They were unwilling to back the liberal Rockefeller, even though he fared better than Nixon in many presidential preference polls.

Rockefeller's negative image within the Republican Party was strengthened by his actions during a New York City sanitation workers strike early in 1968. He rejected a request of JOHN V. LINDSAY, mayor of the city and a fellow Republican, to send in the National Guard to collect garbage. Instead, the governor promoted a settlement of the dispute favorable to the union. Lindsay brought the matter to national attention and highlighted Rockefeller's close relationship with organized labor in New York State when he denounced the governor for "capitulation to extortionist demands . . . giving in to blackmail."

The final blow to Rockefeller's faint hopes for the nomination was a Gallup poll taken on the eve of the August Republican National Convention. The July 31 survey showed Nixon, for the first time, running better than Rockefeller against Vice President HUBERT HUMPHREY, the anticipated Democratic nominee. For Republicans who did not wish to endorse the governor in any case, the poll conveniently served to eliminate his only claim to the nomination. Nixon easily won a first ballot victory.

In 1970 Rockefeller won reelection to a fourth gubernatorial campaign by defeating former Supreme Court justice ARTHUR GOLDBERG with a 700,000 vote margin. The cost of the Rockefeller campaign was estimated at between $12 and $15 million, while the Goldberg forces reported spending $1.7 million.

During the early 1970s the governor shifted toward the right. In his January 1971 message to the legislature, he said that the state was approaching fiscal bankruptcy and could no longer either finance new programs or maintain old ones at former levels. The legislature immediately proceeded to cut Medicaid, welfare, and many other programs. During the next two years Rockefeller publicly "recanted" his views on government spending programs, denounced "welfare chiselers," and successfully advocated mandatory life sentences for certain categories of narcotics offenders. In 1971 he refused to negotiate personally with rebelling Attica state prison inmates and sent state troopers to quell the uprising.

Many observers regarded Rockefeller's change of views as representing a new presidential strategy aimed at winning conservative Republican support. When he resigned the governorship in 1973 to set up a study group called the Commission for Critical Choices, many believed that the new organization was intended to serve as a Rockefeller springboard to the presidency.

Yet Richard Nixon's resignation from the presidency dramatically altered national politics. After succeeding Nixon in August 1974, GERALD R. FORD nominated Rockefeller for the vice presidency, a position for which he won confirmation in December 1974. Ford sought the Republican presidential nomination in 1976, but faced a strong challenge from conservative RONALD REAGAN. As Ford tried to win support from the right wing of his party, Rockefeller became a political liability. In November 1975, Rockefeller announced that he did not wish to be considered for the vice presidency in 1976. After his term was over in January 1977, Rockefeller retired from politics. He died on January 26, 1979.

—MLL

## Rockefeller, Winthrop
### (1912–1973) *governor*

Winthrop Rockefeller, grandson of John D. Rockefeller, was born in New York City on May 12, 1912, into one of America's wealthiest families. He dropped out of Yale after three years, worked as a roustabout in the Texas oil fields, and, in January 1941, he joined the army as a private. After his discharge in 1946 as a lieutenant colonel, he worked for Socony-Vacuum. In 1953 he moved to Arkansas and bought a tract of land, which he later expanded into a 50,000-acre model cattle farm.

In addition to cattle raising, Rockefeller aided cultural, health, civic, and educational undertakings. In 1955 Governor Orval Faubus appointed him chair of the Arkansas Industrial Development Commission, where he helped bring much new industry to the state. During the 1957 Little Rock crisis Rockefeller publicly objected when Governor Faubus placed National Guard troops at Little Rock's Central High School to prevent nine black students from integrating classes.

Rockefeller unsuccessfully challenged Faubus for the governorship in 1964. Two years later he faced archsegregationist Jim Johnson in a second try for the state house. In a fiercely contested election Johnson's image as an intemperate segregationist drove thousands of independent and moderate Democrats and a majority of the black vote into Rockefeller's column. With 54 percent of the total vote, Rockefeller became the first Republican elected Arkansas governor since 1873.

As governor, Rockefeller's major objectives were to increase the state's financial commitment to education and to launch a major expansion of other social services. During his administration the state enacted its first general minimum wage statute and in 1969 substantially liberalized its abortion law. Rockefeller proposed to increase the state budget by 50 percent and place a heavier tax burden on the wealthy, but the Democratic-controlled legislature repeatedly rejected his tax-reform proposals by large margins.

Shortly after Rockefeller became governor, an investigation of the Arkansas prison system found "barbaric conditions" in existence at some state institutions. In February 1967 Rockefeller fired the superintendent and three wardens at the Tucker Prison Farm. In early 1968, after three human skeletons were found buried in crude wooden coffins at another prison farm, Rockefeller asked the state legislature to establish a Department of Corrections to carry out a thorough reform of the state prison system. A special session of the Arkansas legislature approved his proposals in February 1968.

Rockefeller won reelection to a second two-year term in 1968, but Dale Bumpers, a Democratic moderate, overwhelmingly defeated him when he ran again in 1970. Rockefeller died of cancer on February 22, 1973.

## Rockwell, George L(incoln)

(1918–1967) *commander, American Nazi Party*
The son of a vaudeville comedian, Rockwell was born in Bloomington, Illinois, on March 9, 1918. Rockwell spent much of his childhood on the road with his parents until their divorce in 1924. He entered Brown University in the late 1930s and did art work for the college's humor magazine.

Rockwell left Brown to join the navy in 1941. After the war he established a successful advertising agency. When the Korean War began he was recalled into the navy, eventually attaining the rank of commander. Until then Rockwell had been largely apolitical, but during the early 1950s he became interested in racist and anti-Semitic literature. After reading *Mein Kampf* he regarded himself

as a disciple of Adolf Hitler. In 1959 he organized a fascist group, which by 1960 called itself the American Nazi Party. He considered himself "the American Fuehrer."

Warning about an alleged Jewish-Communist conspiracy, Rockwell at different times advocated either the sterilization or extermination of American Jews. He also asserted the superiority of the "white race" and favored the deportation of blacks to Africa.

Rockwell frequently staged grotesque and provocative demonstrations. In one case he provided his supporters with gorilla suits and pro–civil rights placards. Often donning stormtrooper uniforms with swastika armbands, the Nazis received a hostile reception from even racist and extreme right-wing organizations. Throughout the period of Rockwell's leadership, the party's membership was tiny.

After New York City's parks commissioner had denied Rockwell a speaking permit on the grounds that the preaching of hatred might produce rioting, the U.S. Supreme Court upheld his right to speak in November 1961.

Whatever his constitutional rights, Rockwell often had difficulty in finding a forum for expressing his views. In October 1966 the Brown University student union withdrew an invitation to Rockwell after the university's president objected to the Nazi's appearance. In March 1967 the Idaho Board of Education vetoed an invitation from students at Idaho State University.

But Rockwell gained publicity by appearing at many major liberal and leftist political rallies, usually for the purpose of organizing counterprotests. His presence often produced violence and arrests. In January 1965 he was arrested for disturbing the peace outside a church in Selma, Alabama, where a civil rights meeting was being held. The following November he and other Nazis scuffled with persons carrying the National Liberation Front flag at an anti–Vietnam War demonstration in Washington.

In April 1965 Rockwell announced he would run for president. Later in the year he entered the Virginia gubernatorial contest, polling only a few votes.

Rockwell scored his greatest success in Chicago during open housing demonstrations led by Reverend MARTIN LUTHER KING, JR., in the summer of 1966. Many whites reacted violently to the demonstrations and some youths carried swastikas distributed by Rockwell and other Nazis. Apparently trying to follow up on his Chicago effort, he announced in December 1966 that his party would change its name to the National Socialist White People's Party and would replace its "sieg heil" slogan with "white power." But the Nazis made few converts in their attempt to identify themselves more closely with the "backlash" against the civil rights movement.

On August 25, 1967, Rockwell was shot and killed in Alexandria, Virginia, by a former Nazi who had been expelled from the party.

—MLL

## Romney, George W(ilcken)
### (1907–1995) *governor*

Born to an American Mormon family in Chihuahua, Mexico, on July 8, 1907, George W. Romney grew up in Texas and Idaho and attended the University of Utah and George Washington University. After working as a lobbyist for the aluminum and automobile industry, Romney joined Nash-Kelvinator in 1948. Six years later he became president of its successor firm, American Motors. His advocacy of the compact car over what he called "the dinosaur in your driveway" helped the company overcome severe financial problems.

Beginning in 1959 Romney became actively involved in statewide reform and Republican politics. He led the formation of "Citizens for Michigan," which successfully sponsored a new state constitution. He ended 14 years of Democratic rule in Michigan by winning election as governor in November 1962. Even before his election Romney had been considered a prospect for the 1964 Republican presidential nomination. Despite rank-and-file support within the GOP, Romney limited his political activities to Michigan. He maintained a strong civil rights record, but suffered a major political setback in November 1963, when the state legislature rejected his plan for a state income tax.

Following the California presidential primary on June 2, 1964, it appeared that the victorious conservative senator BARRY M. GOLDWATER (R-Ariz.) would capture the Republican presidential nomination. At the National Governors Conference in Cleveland the following weekend, former vice president RICHARD M. NIXON urged Romney to run against Goldwater. Governors NELSON A. ROCKEFELLER (R-N.Y.), WILLIAM W. SCRANTON (R-Pa.) and JAMES A. RHODES (R-Ohio) all promised to back the Michigan Republican's candidacy at the Republican National Convention in July. However Romney had pledged to run for reelection, and Detroit's two major newspapers strongly opposed a Romney presidential campaign. The governor decided not to oppose Goldwater, although he declared that the senator's nomination would "commence the suicidal destruction of the Republican Party." Romney refused to support Scranton's last-minute candidacy. He also refused to back Scranton-Rockefeller platform amendments on civil rights, nuclear arms policy, and right-wing extremism in the party. Instead, Romney presented his own amendments denouncing extremism without mentioning specific right-wing organizations supporting Goldwater and calling for the enforcement of the 1964 Civil Rights Act, which Goldwater had opposed. Although some Goldwater supporters privately urged endorsement of Romney's proposals as a friendly gesture to the party's liberal-moderate wing, the Arizona senator's high command refused to allow its delegates to vote for the Romney amendments. Michigan's delegation supported Romney as its favorite son, and the governor received 41 votes on the first ballot.

Following the convention Romney declined to endorse Goldwater and criticized the candidate's civil rights record and his campaign's alleged appeal to "white backlash" voters. In November Romney was the only Republican to win statewide election in Michigan, defeating his Democratic opponent by almost 400,000 votes, while Johnson carried the state by a million-vote margin. Soon after the election Romney renewed his criticism of the Goldwater campaign and in December demanded the resignation of Republican National Committee chair Dean Burch, a Goldwater appointee. Romney's victory enhanced his chances for the 1968 presidential nomination, but his unwillingness to endorse Goldwater and his failure to carry any other GOP candidates with him in 1964 damaged his standing among party conservatives and loyalists.

Between 1963 and 1966 Romney broke the decade-old stalemate between previous Democratic governors and their Republican legislators. Under his leadership Michigan acquired its first minimum-wage and construction-safety legislation, increased state aid to education, and avoided a fiscal crisis engendered by the need for comprehensive tax reform. The strength of Michigan's economy during Romney's tenure increased state revenues while reducing unemployment.

In his 1962 and 1964 campaigns Romney had appealed for votes in a nonpartisan manner similar to his efforts as leader of Citizens for Michigan. In 1966, however, Romney ran as a partisan Republican and overwhelmed his opponent with 60.5 percent of the vote. His landslide helped elect Senator ROBERT P. GRIFFIN (R-Mich.) and five new Republican representatives. In demonstrating his capacity for electing Republicans in a Democratic state, Romney emerged in November 1966 as the clear front-runner for the 1968 presidential nomination.

Romney's candidacy, however, suffered from political difficulties in Michigan. When rioting erupted in parts of Detroit's predominantly black areas on July 23, 1967, Romney maneuvered to shift responsibility to the White House. Romney hesitated at first to ask for federal troops to quell the riot. At the same time, some Republicans blamed the violence in Detroit, the latest in a string of racial disturbances, on the policies of the Johnson administration. The president worried that Republicans were trying to use the riots to score political points, and he insisted, when Romney did request federal intervention, that he specify that local and state forces were inadequate. Johnson dispatched army troops to Detroit, but declared in a televised statement that he regretted the action and took this step "only because of the clear, unmistakable, and undisputed evidence that Governor Romney of Michigan and the local officials in Detroit have been unable to bring the situation under control." Romney later claimed that "quibbling" over the phrasing of the request unnecessarily delayed the troops' arrival, and he asserted that Johnson had "played politics in a period of tragedy and riot." The Detroit riot was the worst of the 1960s, as it resulted in 43 deaths.

In the aftermath of the riot Romney decried the militancy of Black Power activists and declared that those who "preach revolution and preach the use of guns should be charged with treason." Yet in September he said that "the seeds of revolution have been sown in America more by our own failures and shortcomings than by any outside subversive ideology." Romney and state labor and automotive industry leaders unsuccessfully recommended to the state legislature a fair housing law and an emergency school aid appropriation for Detroit.

Difficulties of Romney's own making eventually derailed his bid for the presidency. The governor had been moving away from his earlier "hawkish" stand on Vietnam. In an August 31 Detroit interview, he defended his new position by asserting that during a 1965 Vietnam tour, "I just had the greatest brainwashing that anybody can get" from American officials on the scene. Supporters of the president's policies immediately attacked Romney's remark, while other governors on the 1965 trip with Romney refused to confirm his allegation of indoctrination by government officials. Although a few Republican leaders defended Romney, most found his remark indicative of an inability to deal with Vietnam or other foreign policy issues. On September 9 the *Detroit News* urged that Romney withdraw from the race and that Governor Rockefeller enter as his replacement. Richard Nixon, Romney's major opponent for the nomination, increased his standing among Republicans in the Gallup poll from 35 percent to 40 percent, while Romney's fell from 24 percent to 10 percent.

Romney fought hard to restore his lead and in November 1967 announced his formal candidacy. However, he never overcame the effects of his "brainwashing" statement. "Watching George Romney run for the presidency," Governor Rhodes remarked, "was like watching a duck try to make love to a football." Romney's campaign called for the restoration of old virtues and employed the slogan "George Romney Fights Moral Decay." He tried to capitalize on his controversial "brainwashing" remark by moving toward a distinctly antiwar position. On January 15, 1968, the governor proposed that the United States guarantee the neutralization of South Vietnam through a settlement between the Saigon government and the Communist insurgents. His antiwar strategy failed to generate support among Republican voters, and his own polls showed that, despite an active campaign, he would be overwhelming defeated by Nixon in New Hampshire's March primary. In February Rockefeller indicated for the first time, after reasserting his enthusiasm for Romney, that he would accept a "draft" for the nomination. Hurt by the growing sentiment for Rockefeller and his own poor showing in the polls, Romney withdrew his candidacy on February 28, 1968, less than two weeks before the first primary. At the Republican National Convention in August, Romney received Michigan's votes as its favorite son candidate on the first ballot.

Following Nixon's nomination at the convention, a group of party leaders opposed to Nixon's selection of Governor SPIRO T. AGNEW (R-Md.) for vice president persuaded Romney to allow them to nominate him as the anti-Agnew candidate. The abortive move against Agnew failed when most of the large state delegations supported Nixon's nominee. Romney received 178 votes to Agnew's 1,128. He served as secretary of housing and urban development in the first Nixon Administration. He died on July 26, 1995.

## Roosevelt, Franklin D(elano), Jr.
(1914–1988) *undersecretary of commerce; chair, Equal Employment Opportunity Commission*

The third son of Franklin Delano and Eleanor Roosevelt, Franklin D. Roosevelt, Jr., was born on August 17, 1914, on Campobello Island, Canada, and attended Harvard and the University of Virginia Law School. While in the navy during World War II, he earned a Silver Star. He won election to Congress from New York City in May 1949 as the candidate of the Liberal Party. After losing the Democratic gubernatorial nomination at the 1954 state convention to W. AVERELL HARRIMAN, Roosevelt agreed to run for state attorney general. He lost to Representative JACOB K. JAVITS (R-N.Y.). He resumed his New York law practice and alienated some supporters in 1956 by accepting a $150,000 legal retainer from Rafael Trujillo, the dictator of the Dominican Republic.

Early in 1960 Roosevelt campaigned for John F. Kennedy's presidential nomination. In the crucial West Virginia primary in May, he attacked Senator HUBERT H. HUMPHREY (D-Minn.) for not having served in the armed forces during World War II. In March 1963 he accepted appointment as undersecretary of commerce. In that position he helped negotiate the sale of $250 million worth of American wheat to the Soviet Union in the fall of 1963, Roosevelt also lobbied against efforts by Senate conservatives in late November 1963 that would have denied credit to Communist buyers. As chair of the federal-state Appalachian Regional Commission, he led in the planning of the area's economic revitalization; his group's work foreshadowed President Johnson's more ambitious War on Poverty in 1964 and 1965. He also contributed to the settlement of a long labor dispute involving the nuclear-powered ship *Savannah*. Yet to Roosevelt's dismay, Johnson passed over him in naming a successor to commerce secretary LUTHER D. HODGES in December 1964.

Instead, Johnson named Roosevelt the first chair of the Equal Employment Opportunity Commission (EEOC) in March 1965. Created by the 1964 Civil Rights Act and empowered to present "cease and desist" orders, enforceable in court, EEOC forbade employers and unions from discriminating against prospective employees or members on the basis of race, color, religion, national origin, or sex. Roosevelt approached his new task with enthusiasm. In August EEOC prohibited job listings in newspapers that required specific racial, religious, or ethnic backgrounds, although it put off a final determination on employment notices requesting a male or female only.

Roosevelt resigned from EEOC in May 1966 to run for the New York Democratic gubernatorial nomination. His hopes for the nomination depended upon a preconvention endorsement from Senator ROBERT F. KENNEDY (D-N.Y.), the state's most popular Democrat. Kennedy refused to support any candidate openly, however, and party leaders preferred New York City Council president Frank D. O'Connor, who had withdrawn from the 1965 mayoralty race in return for private pledges of assistance in the securing of the gubernatorial nomination. With no chance of defeating O'Connor at the upcoming state gathering, Roosevelt released in August a memorandum proving that a deal had been made between O'Connor and party leaders in 1965. Calling the convention a "boss-controlled masquerade," he withdrew from the race on August 25. O'Connor received the Democratic nomination two weeks later.

An angry Roosevelt agreed to run as the Liberal Party's candidate for governor in early September. The Liberal Party, the state's largest third party since World War II, had been Roosevelt's original base of support in his 1949 congressional race. But it had suffered recent setbacks in voter support. The state's new Conservative Party out-polled the Liberals in the 1964 senatorial and 1965 New York City mayoral elections. Denying the Democratic gubernatorial nominee its usual endorsement, Liberal Party leaders gambled that the once magical Roosevelt name would enable the party to recapture third place in the balloting.

Roosevelt himself hoped to poll between 1 million and 2 million votes and to reassert his name in state politics, laying claim to a more likely statewide victory on the Democratic line in 1968 or 1970. The Roosevelt campaign cost about $250,000, and the candidate appeared throughout the state. In November, however, Conservative nominee Pal Adams, an unknown Rochester college president whose committee spent about $40,000, narrowly out-polled Roosevelt, 510,023 to 507,234 votes. O'Connor had run a lackluster campaign, never escaping from Roosevelt's charge of "bossism," and lost to incumbent governor NELSON A. ROCKE-FELLER (R-N.Y.). Roosevelt's political career, once bright, then frustrated, had finally ended. He retired from active politics. He died on August 17, 1988.

—JLB

## Rose, Alex

(1898–1976) *president, United Hatters, Cap and Millinery Workers International Union; vice chair, Liberal Party*

Born in Warsaw, Poland, on October 15, 1898, Rose came to the United States in 1913 hoping to study medicine but became a millinery operator instead. He had been active in the Labor Zionist Organization and joined the "Jewish Legion" of the British army in 1918, serving in the Middle East for two years. Returning to the United States, he defeated a Communist-backed opponent and became the secretary-treasurer of his local in the Cloth Hat, Cap and Millinery Workers Union. By 1927 he had become a vice president, a position he retained when the union subsequently merged with the United Hatters of North America to form the United Hatters, Cap and Millinery Workers International Union in 1934.

In 1950 Rose was appointed president by the union's executive board and was subsequently elected to the post. "The class struggle is a thing of the past in my union and in many others," he said. During the 1950s the union loaned large sums to faltering hat manufacturers, purchased real estate in New York's millinery district and became the largest stockholder in the Merimac Hat Corporation, preventing its liquidation.

With International Ladies Garment Workers Union (ILGWU) president David Dubinsky and others, Rose assisted in forming the American Labor Party in 1936, offering New Yorkers the opportunity to support the New Deal without voting the Democratic, and therefore Tammany, line. When leftists won control of the party in 1944, Rose, who had served as state secretary until then, withdrew and helped form the Liberal Party. Dubinsky and Rose continued to support Democrats in most major elections. The Liberal Party ran candidates only in New York State.

In 1961 Rose and the Liberal Party helped incumbent mayor ROBERT WAGNER, who had repudiated his former Tammany supporters, win the backing of reform Democrats and thus gain reelection. The Liberals endorsed the Democratic slate in the 1962 state elections, in which NELSON A. ROCK-EFELLER won his second term as governor and Senator JACOB K. JAVITS (R-N.Y.) was reelected.

In the mid-1960s the party had a state enrollment of about 90,000, of which 50,000 were registered in New York City. In general elections the party often drew 400,000 votes on its ballot line. About one-third of its financing and most of its workers came from the ILGWU. Only a few districts maintained year-round clubs, however, and young activists found domination of the party by Rose and Dubinsky unattractive.

The party supported ROBERT F. KENNEDY's successful bid for the Senate in 1964 and also endorsed the national Democratic ticket. Following Wagner's announcement that he would not run for mayor in 1965, the Liberal Party turned to independent Republican representative JOHN V. LINDSAY. With Liberal backing Lindsay's fusion campaign attracted sufficient Democratic support to help him defeat Democratic controller Abraham Beame.

Charging "bossism" among Democrats, Rose refused to support the 1966 Democratic candidate for governor, Frank O'Connor. With some dissension the Liberals nominated their own choice, FRANK D. ROOSEVELT, JR., instead. Democrats contended that Rose's move was motivated by a desire to retain "Line C," the third line on the state ballot. But the Liberals were replaced as the state's third-largest party by the new Conservative Party, whose gubernatorial candidate outpolled Roosevelt.

In 1968 an ILGWU faction in the Liberal Party, charging that the organization was not democratically run, defied the party policy committee's endorsement of Javits for reelection and entered an opponent against the senator in the Liberal primary. Javits, however, easily won the contest. The Liberals also supported Senator HUBERT HUMPHREY's (D-Minn.) presidential candidacy in September.

Rose continued to dominate the party, which again played an independent role in 1969. Mayor Lindsay, who lost the Republican primary, nevertheless won reelection as a Liberal with 45 percent of the vote. Rose remained active in the party until his death on December 28, 1976.

—MDB

## Rostow, Eugene V(ictor)

**(1913–2002)** *undersecretary of state for political affairs*

Named for Eugene V. Debs, Rostow was born in New York on August 25, 1913. He earned an LL.B. from Yale University in 1937, worked briefly in private practice, and then joined the Yale Law School faculty in 1938. He served during World War II as a legal adviser in the State Department, where he worked for Assistant Secretary of State DEAN ACHESON. Returning to Yale after the war, Rostow soon gained a reputation as a prominent legal scholar. An article he wrote for the *Yale Law Journal* in 1945 helped persuade the federal government to restore the property and citizenship of Japanese Americans confined to detention camps during the war. Rostow's book *A National Policy for the Oil Industry*, published in 1948, aroused considerable controversy by calling for reorganization and increased government regulation of oil companies.

In 1955 Rostow became dean of the Yale Law School, a post he held for 10 years. During this time he supervised the development of an innovative curriculum. Rostow's goal was a "humane and broadly based" legal education relating law to history, economics, and other social sciences. Despite initial resistance from alumni, the new program was eventually considered a great success.

Rostow's academic career did not prevent him from maintaining the contacts he had developed in Washington during the war. Along with his brother Walt, he was an important link between the academic community and the federal government. In 1961 Rostow served on the Peace Corps Advisory Council and subsequently held a position as consultant to the State Department. He gave strong support to the foreign policy of the Johnson administration, defending American involvement in Vietnam and the 1965 invasion of the Dominican Republic.

Rostow began full-time government work in October 1966, when President Johnson appointed him undersecretary of state for political affairs. Rostow concerned himself largely with international financial matters. In January 1967 he visited India and other countries to confer on U.S. food assistance. He urged a "concentrated international effort in the war against hunger." In February 1968 he participated in a United Nations conference that recommended a system of preferential tariffs to encourage the growth of industry in developing countries. Rostow also represented the United

States in May 1968 in important negotiations over the financing of U.S. troops in West Germany; as a result of the talks the West German government agreed to reimburse the United States in 1969 for a large part of the cost of maintaining the troops. Rostow, meanwhile, continued to defend the Vietnam War, criticizing opponents of American involvement for stimulating a new isolationist spirit in the United States.

In January 1969 Rostow returned to Yale as Sterling Professor of Law and Public Affairs. During the Reagan administration, he served as director of the Arms Control and Disarmament Agency. He died on November 25, 2002.

—SLG

## Rostow, Walt W(hitman)

**(1916–2003)** *chair, State Department Policy Planning Council; special assistant to the president for national security affairs*

Rostow was one of three sons of a Russian-Jewish immigrant family. He was born in New York City on October 7, 1916, and named after the poet Walt Whitman. He attended Yale as an undergraduate and, following two years as a Rhodes Scholar at Oxford, received his Ph.D. from Yale in 1940. During World War II, he worked in the Office of Strategic Services, where he helped select bombing targets in Germany. He then worked briefly in the State Department and spent two years as the executive secretary of the Economic Commission for Europe. He returned to academic life in 1950, when he received a teaching appointment at the Massachusetts Institute of Technology (MIT). From 1951 to 1960 he was associated with MIT's Central Intelligence Agency (CIA)–backed Center for International Studies.

Rostow gained distinction for his work on economic development. His best-known book, *The Stages of Economic Growth: A Non-communist Manifesto* (1960), presented an economic interpretation of history that challenged Marxist theories of development. Rostow argued that economic growth was a multistaged process stimulated by a widespread desire for the improvement of life as well as the search for profit by the middle class. The past industrialization of Europe and the United States and the contemporary development of Asia, Africa, and Latin America followed similar patterns. After the creation of preconditions for growth in a formerly

President Johnson in conversation with his assistant for national security affairs, Walt Rostow, 1967
*(Photographed by Yoichi R. Okamoto; Lyndon Baines Johnson Library)*

traditional society, rapid growth in a few sectors such as railroads or textiles caused an economic "take-off" toward industrialization and modernization, while later maturation led to "the age of high mass consumption."

Rostow began advising Senator John F. Kennedy (D-Mass.) on foreign policy in 1958 and was active in Kennedy's 1960 presidential campaign. Kennedy appointed Rostow deputy special assistant to the president for foreign security affairs in the incoming administration. Rostow participated in the formulation of U.S. policy toward Laos and Vietnam, generally advocating a strong effort in fighting Communist insurgencies.

As part of a general November 1961 shuffle of foreign policy officials, Rostow transferred to the State Department as counselor and chair of the Policy Planning Council. In his new post he was in charge of long-range analysis and planning in a broad range of foreign policy areas, but was no longer centrally involved in the White House deci-

sion-making process. Kennedy had become concerned about Rostow's advice, as TOWNSEND HOOPES explained in his book, *The Limits of Intervention.* "Walt is a fountain of ideas; perhaps one in ten of them is absolutely brilliant," the president declared. "Unfortunately, six or seven are not merely unsound, but dangerously so."

In May 1964 President Johnson appointed Rostow to the additional post of U.S. representative to the Inter-American Committee on the Alliance for Progress (CIAP). Created in November 1963, CIAP was a special committee of the Organization of American States intended to provide Latin American countries with a greater say in the direction of the Alliance for Progress.

Although at this time Rostow did not directly participate in making high-level decisions on Southeast Asia, he exerted continued influence through State Department memoranda and—starting in June 1964—through direct access to the president. His most important contribution was what came to be known as the "Rostow thesis," which circulated widely among national security planners in the Johnson administration. Rostow restated his long-standing belief that externally supported insurgencies could be stopped only by military action against the source of external support. He considered North Vietnamese support for guerrilla action in the South critical, and he proposed a graduated bombing campaign against the North, designed to demonstrate that continued support of the National Liberation Front would result in heavy costs. Rostow believed that the North Vietnamese leadership ultimately would not risk destruction of their country's infrastructure—transportation systems, power facilities, and industries—in a U.S. bombing campaign that threatened to grow progressively larger.

In August 1964 the "Rostow thesis" circulated widely inside the administration. The Defense Department prepared a detailed critique. It concluded that serious difficulties were involved in attacks on North Vietnam and questioned whether domestic and international support could be rallied for such a program. Therefore, the report argued, acceptance or even public dissemination of the Rostow position was probably unwise. But, according to the authors of the *Pentagon Papers:* "These reservations notwithstanding, the outlook embodied in the 'Rostow thesis' came to dominate a good deal of Administration thinking on the question of pressures against the North in the months ahead."

As a National Security Council working group again reexamined the future direction of U.S. policy in Vietnam, Rostow contended in November 1964 that the United States had to convince the North Vietnamese of American determination to apply limited but sustained military pressure upon them until they ceased support of the National Liberation Front in South Vietnam. He urged the movement of a large retaliatory force to the Pacific area, the introduction of some U.S. ground troops in Laos and South Vietnam, and the initiation of a naval blockade and bombing against North Vietnam. These military measures, individually or in combination, would not work, Rostow asserted without the president's ability to send "a decisive signal" that the United States would not accept a South Vietnamese defeat and was prepared, over the long term, to apply pressure to end the guerrilla war. U.S. policy would not succeed without persuading the North Vietnamese "that we really mean it." Rostow's thinking helped shape recommendations, which the

president approved in February and March 1965, to begin a graduated campaign of sustained bombing against North Vietnam and to commit U.S. combat troops to the war in the South.

Rostow became increasingly and publicly identified with the administration's Vietnam policy in 1965. On arriving in Tokyo in April for a series of speaking engagements, he was met by 1,000 anti-American demonstrators. During this period of rising campus opposition to the war, Rostow defended the administration's position at a May 15–16 national teach-in on Vietnam, broadcast to over 100 colleges.

On March 31, 1966, President Johnson appointed Rostow special assistant to the president for national security affairs, succeeding MCGEORGE BUNDY, who had resigned to become president of the Ford Foundation. In this post Rostow worked closely with Johnson for the remainder of the administration on virtually all foreign policy issues. He selected the information to be presented to him, accompanied him on his foreign travels, and sat in on meetings with foreign leaders. Rostow genuinely admired the president, and, as criticism of U.S. policy in Vietnam grew, Rostow's continued optimism about the war and his willingness to defend it publicly led to an increasingly close relationship with President Johnson. (In September 1966 Johnson appointed Rostow's older brother, EUGENE V. ROSTOW, undersecretary of state for political affairs.)

Although CIA studies showed that the bombing had not reduced the rate of infiltration of troops and supplies from North Vietnam to the South, and the Hanoi government showed no serious interest in negotiations, Rostow remained optimistic about the war and the effectiveness of bombing. In May 1966 he advocated the expansion of the bombing to include destroying the petroleum facilities of North Vietnam. Rostow argued that a similar program—on which he had worked—had been effective against the Germans in World War II and would be equally effective against North Vietnam. Others, including the CIA, disagreed. After a period of hesitation in late May, Johnson approved the new air strikes, which included targets in the Hanoi-Haiphong area. In spite of initial reports of success, however, the program failed to limit the ability of the North Vietnamese to support the war in the South.

Throughout 1967 there was renewed conflict within the administration over the bombing campaign against North Vietnam. Most military leaders urged an extension of bombing and the elimination of existing restrictions. Many civilian officials, particularly Assistant Secretary of Defense for International Security Affairs JOHN T. MCNAUGHTON and Secretary of Defense ROBERT S. MCNAMARA, urged limiting the bombing to the southern panhandle of North Vietnam. In May Rostow, who attended the regular Tuesday meetings at which the president chose specific bombing targets, wrote an important memorandum indicating basic support for the McNamara-McNaughton position, although he argued that the option of future strikes in the Hanoi-Haiphong area had to be kept open. The president took a middle course and in July ordered a continuation of the "Rolling Thunder" bombing program along essentially existing lines, with only sporadic raids in the Hanoi-Haiphong area.

In June 1967 Rostow accompanied the president at the Glassboro, New Jersey, meeting with Soviet premier Aleksei N. Kosygin. That same month he worked closely with Johnson during the Arab-Israeli war. He also served on a special group headed by Bundy that Johnson established to work on both the immediate crisis and long-range solutions to the Middle East situation.

On November 1, 1967, an increasingly skeptical McNamara prepared a memo to the president in which he called for "stabilizing" the U.S. war effort in Vietnam, reexamining the ground fighting to try to reduce U.S. casualties, shifting a greater burden of fighting to the South Vietnamese army and instituting a bombing halt before the end of the year. Johnson gave the memo to Rostow and other senior advisers for comment. Rostow supported the first two proposals but opposed an unconditional bombing halt. Rostow insisted that halting the bombing would have the undesirable effect of moving administration policy off the "present middle position, . . . rationally using all power available" while avoiding provocative actions likely to lead to the intervention of the Soviet Union or the People's Republic of China. Recent diplomatic contacts had occurred with Hanoi representatives while U.S. planes struck targets in North Vietnam, he noted. Although those contacts had not led to the beginning of peace talks, Rostow remained hopeful. Rostow reminded the president that he had learned as an intelligence officer in World War II that it was often impossible to predict critical events. Until all possibility of peace talks vanished, the best course, he believed, was "holding steady to our present program." Johnson took a similar position.

Following the Tet offensive in late January and early February 1968, Johnson established a new group under incoming secretary of defense CLARK CLIFFORD to thoroughly reexamine Vietnam policy. Rostow drafted the directive to the group and participated in its deliberations. Rostow thought that the Tet offensive created an opportunity to shorten the war. He favored approval of General WILLIAM WESTMORELAND's request for an additional 206,000 troops, and he urged the president to consider mining North Vietnamese ports. He recommended a new peace initiative to accompany these military measures. Rostow's advice, however, was at odds with the counsel the president received both from his principal civilian advisers as well as the "Wise Men," senior military and political figures who had retired from their government positions. On March 31, the president announced new restrictions on the bombing of North Vietnam as well as a new initiative to begin peace negotiations.

In the final months of Johnson's term of office, overtures were made in Rostow's behalf to MIT and several other leading universities to secure for him a teaching position after his government service ended. These feelers were rebuffed, partially due to Rostow's role in the planning and conduct of the war in Vietnam. Rostow eventually accepted a position as professor of economics and history at the University of Texas at Austin, where a Lyndon B. Johnson School of Public Affairs was planned. In the final hours of his presidency, Johnson awarded Rostow and 19 others the Medal of Freedom, the country's highest civilian honor.

In Texas Rostow resumed teaching and writing and helped Johnson organize his foreign policy papers for inclusion in his presidential library. Rostow continued to defend U.S. military involvement in Vietnam. Rostow published *The Diffusion of Power, 1957–1972,* an account of the U.S. role in world affairs, which included some material on his own activities in the period covered. He died on February 13, 2003.

—JBF

## Rousselot, John H(arbin)

(1927–2003) *western district governor and national director of public relations, John Birch Society*

Born in Los Angeles on November 1, 1927, Rousselot operated a public relations consulting firm from 1954 to 1958. He served as director of public information for the Federal Housing Administration in Washington, D.C., from 1958 to 1960. In the latter year he was elected to Congress from a conservative suburban area of Los Angeles County. In April 1961 Rousselot acknowledged his membership in the ultraconservative John Birch Society. He went on to compile an ultraconservative voting record in the House during 1961 and 1962. His bid for reelection in 1962 was unsuccessful.

Early in 1963 Rousselot became the western district governor of the Birch Society. In the summer of 1964 he was appointed national public relations director of the organization. In his new position he used his congenial personality and public relations experience to attempt to modify the society's image as an irresponsible, extremist organization.

In the 1950s ROBERT H. W. WELCH, JR., the head of the society, had written that President Dwight D. Eisenhower was an agent of a world Communist conspiracy. Rousselot stressed that this assertion represented Welch's personal view and not the official position of the society. Rousselot also played down some of the membership's more bizarre views, such as their fear of a Communist plot to confine patriotic Americans to mental asylums. In addition, he created a professional and efficient public relations department, which placed Sunday supplements in major newspapers across the country and which sent society members and their sympathizers to speak before a wide range of civic groups.

The membership of the John Birch Society doubled from an estimated 40,000 in 1964 to 80,000 in 1966, partly because of Rousselot's efforts. But Rousselot did not succeed in altering the society's image, as most Americans considered it a radical organization of the extreme right. Rousselot's own statements reinforced that perception. In August 1964 he charged that 59 major leaders of the NAACP belonged to 450 "identifiable Communist fronts." Rousselot declared in July of the following year that the United Nations was created and controlled by Communists. He also believed that Chief Justice EARL WARREN should be impeached for his allegedly procommunist Supreme Court decisions.

In January 1967 Rousselot announced that he would soon resign his post to return to private business. In 1970 he again won a seat in the House of Representatives from Los Angeles County. Reelected five times, he lost his bid for another term in 1982. He worked briefly as a special assistant to

President RONALD REAGAN in 1983. He died on May 11, 2003.

—MLL

## Rubin, Jerry
### (1938–1994) *political activist*

Son of a bakery truck driver who became an official in his Teamsters union local, Jerry Rubin was born on July 14, 1938, and grew up in a middle-class neighborhood in Cincinnati. He attended Oberlin College briefly but quit school when he was offered a job as a sports reporter for the *Cincinnati Post*. He started taking courses at the University of Cincinnati and earned a B.A. in 1961. Rubin left Cincinnati shortly after finishing college and drifted for several years throughout Europe, India, and Israel. Early in 1964 he arrived in Berkeley and attended the University of California for six weeks before dropping out of school permanently.

In Berkeley Rubin quickly gravitated toward movements for political and social change. In the spring of 1964 he joined the local chapter of the Congress of Racial Equality and participated in a number of "shop-ins" at a Berkeley grocery store that refused to hire blacks. That summer he traveled with a group to Cuba in defiance of a State Department ban. During the fall he was active in the Free Speech Movement on the Berkeley campus.

In the spring of 1965 Rubin was a leading figure in the organization of a two-day teach-in held in late May. Over a continuous 36-hour period students and faculty heard a series of speakers, including NORMAN MAILER, Dr. BENJAMIN SPOCK, NORMAN THOMAS, and DICK GREGORY, denounce the Vietnam War. The teach-in established the Vietnam Day Committee (VDC), one of the largest and most active antiwar organizations in the country. As a leader of the VDC and its most prominent public spokesperson, Rubin acquired a reputation as a skilled organizer with a flair for winning the attention of the media. In August 1965 the VDC staged several unsuccessful, but well publicized, attempts to stop troop trains carrying Vietnam-bound soldiers as they passed through Berkeley. In October the VDC organized two large marches from Berkeley to the nearby Oakland Army Terminal. Both of the marches were halted and turned back by police at the Oakland city line. Rubin also served briefly during the fall of 1965 as *Ramparts* magazine editor ROBERT SCHEER's campaign manager in his unsuccessful attempt to gain the Democratic nomination for the House of Representatives from California's Seventh Congressional District.

After disputes with Scheer over campaign tactics, Rubin became increasingly concerned with developing and projecting a radical, self-expressive style of protest. In August 1966, when he was subpoenaed to appear before the House Un-American Activities Committee in Washington, he decided to use his appearance as an exercise in what he called "guerrilla theater." Rubin walked into the televised hearings wearing a Revolutionary War uniform. Despite his protests, the startled committee refused him permission to testify.

During the spring of 1967 Rubin entered the race for mayor of Berkeley and received 21 percent of the vote on a platform advocating legalization of marijuana and community control of the police. Following the election he moved to New York, where he became friends with a drug-oriented circle that included TIMOTHY LEARY, who pronounced him "Merry Jerry, the Lysergic Lenin, the grass Guevara, the mescaline Marx." Rubin also befriended ABBIE HOFFMAN. Together they were prominent organizers of the March on the Pentagon on October 21, 1967.

Rubin declared the march a victory. "We had symbolically destroyed the Pentagon . . . by throwing blood on it, pissing on it, dancing on it, painting 'Che lives' on it." Rubin was convinced that the antiwar movement was at root a generational conflict of youth in search of fun and excitement against their elders. On New Year's Eve 1967, Rubin, Hoffman, and Paul Krassner, editor of *The Realist*, devised the term Yippie, which they said applied to a member of the Youth International Party. There was no organization, however, to go with the name. Rubin and his collaborators used the Youth International Party as a term of convenience to represent what they said was a countercultural movement to escape what they called "white bread America." Rubin maintained that drugs, especially marijuana and LSD, were important means of purging minds of middle-class values and creating an alternative consciousness.

During that summer Rubin and his fellow Yippies planned a massive "festival of life" in Chicago to coincide and contrast with what they interpreted as a "festival of death" at the Democratic National Convention. The Yippies applied for permission to use city parks for rallies and for sleeping out overnight,

but Chicago city officials denied them the right to remain in the parks after 11 p.m. On August 23 the Yippies opened their festival by setting up camp in Lincoln Park and nominating a pig for president in the Chicago civic center. Two days later, after the 11 p.m. curfew, the police drove the Yippies out of Lincoln Park. The following evening, at about the same time the Democratic convention was formally opened, an even larger confrontation took place, and a number of injuries were sustained both by demonstrators and police. The remaining days of the convention were full of similar disorder, much of it caught by television camera. The Yippies were a small minority among the demonstrators in Chicago during the convention. But because of the media savvy and outrageousness of Rubin and other leaders, the Yippies got a disproportionate amount of news coverage.

Rubin and seven others were later indicted by a federal grand jury in Chicago in connection with the 1968 disorders. The "Chicago Eight," as they came to be known, were tried under the antiriot provisions of the 1968 Civil Rights Act, which made it a federal crime to cross state lines to incite a riot. Rubin said that he welcomed the indictment, calling it "the greatest honor of my life" and the "Academy Award of Protest." Following the tumultuous trial, five of the eight, including Rubin, were convicted. In November 1972 the verdicts were overturned by an appeals court on the grounds that the judge in the case had been antagonistic and had committed legal errors. In 1976 Rubin published *Growing Up (at 37)*; he asserted that both he and Hoffman had in fact gone to Chicago to disrupt the convention and the normal life of the city. The government's case in the Chicago Eight's trial, wrote Rubin, was "right in theory, wrong in specifics."

For a brief time in the early 1980s, Rubin got considerable publicity as he seemed to represent once more an important cultural transformation. He went to work on Wall Street as a stock broker, and the news media chronicled his transition from Yippie to Yuppie (young, urban professional.) Rubin died on November 28, 1994, after being hit by an automobile.

(TLH)

### Ruby, Jack
**(1911–1967)** *assassin of Lee Harvey Oswald*
Jack Ruby, born Jacob Rubenstein, was born, apparently, on March 25, 1911, in Chicago and grew up

in a troubled home. Ruby quit school at 16 and worked as a ticket scalper, a hawker of race-track tip sheets, and an organizer for the Scrap Iron and Junk Handlers Union. In the early 1940s he established the Spartan Novelty Company in Chicago. After service in the U.S. Army Air Forces, Ruby went to Dallas in 1947 to help his sister open a nightclub. He remained in Dallas, where he owned and managed various clubs for the next 16 years.

On the morning of November 24, 1963, Ruby made his way to the basement of the Dallas Police and Courts Building where Lee Harvey Oswald, the alleged assassin of President John F. Kennedy, was being held. At 11:20 Oswald, surrounded by police, reporters and camera operators, was being escorted to the car that was to take him to the county jail. Ruby approached, drew his pistol, and fired one shot into Oswald's abdomen. The shooting was witnessed by millions on live television. Oswald died within two hours.

Ruby said he had killed Oswald in a temporary fit of depression and rage over the death of the president. He denied that he had ever known Oswald or had been connected in any way with a plot to assassinate the president.

Ruby's defense team, headed by the flamboyant San Francisco attorney Melvin Belli, contended that the defendant could not get a fair trial in Dallas, but requests to move the proceedings were denied by Judge Joseph Brantley Brown.

In February 1964 after two weeks of difficult questioning in which the defense exhausted all its peremptory challenges, a jury was selected. All but two of the jurors had seen the shooting on television. During the trial, which began March 4, the defense pleaded that Ruby, suffering from psychomotor epilepsy, was not guilty by reason of insanity. Psychologists and neurologists for the prosecution contended the evidence, including electroencephalograms, introduced by the defense was insufficient to support the plea. On March 14 the jury found Ruby guilty and directed that he be sentenced to death. Belli called the proceedings a kangaroo court and charged that the Dallas "oligarchy wanted to send Ruby to the public abattoir . . . to cleanse this city of its shame."

In June 1966 a state court jury in Dallas ruled that Ruby was sane and competent to dismiss his lawyers. A new defense team, which included New York attorney WILIAM KUNTSLER took the case to the Texas Court of Appeals. In October 1966 that court's three judges—in separate opinions—agreed that Ruby's conviction should be reversed. The holding of Ruby's trial in Dallas had been in error, said the court, and it ordered that he be retried outside Dallas County.

Before he could be tried again, Ruby, who was suffering from cancer, died of a blood clot in the lungs on January 3, 1967.

Ruby consistently denied that he knew Oswald and that he was in any way connected to a plot to murder President Kennedy. Assassination theorists have nonetheless connected Ruby, despite the lack of evidence, to various conspiracies to kill Kennedy.

—JLW

## Rudd, Mark (William)
### (1947– ) *student leader*

Born on June 2, 1947, in Irvington, New Jersey, Rudd grew up in an upper-middle-class family. His father was in the real estate business and a lieutenant colonel in the U.S. Army Reserve. During his first year at Columbia, (1965–66) Rudd became active in a campus antiwar group, the Independent Committee on Vietnam. In the fall of 1966 he joined the newly formed Columbia chapter of Students for a Democratic Society (SDS). Rudd was among 46 people arrested at a large demonstration protesting Secretary of State DEAN RUSK's appearance at the New York Hilton Hotel in November 1967.

Throughout 1967 Columbia SDS was led by members of the so-called praxis axis, who stressed research, education, and propaganda, avoiding confrontations in hopes of building a broad base of student support. Rudd and others, labeled the "action faction," advocated more militant tactics. After returning from a three-week SDS trip to Cuba in February 1968, Rudd was elected chair of Columbia SDS. A week later, on March 20, members of the "action faction" threw a pie in the face of a Selective Service official speaking at Columbia, in spite of a previous SDS vote against any disruption. Rudd later said that this was the turning point in winning SDS over to more aggressive tactics.

SDS had long opposed Columbia's participation in the Institute for Defense Analysis (IDA), a 12-university consortium conducting weapons evaluation and research for the Department of Defense. The radical organization had more recently joined the opposition to Columbia's proposed new gym, to be built in city-owned Morningside Park. Plans for the gym included limited facilities for use by local residents. It rapidly became a symbol for many at Columbia and in the adjacent Harlem community of the university's alleged indifference to its poor, nonwhite neighbors.

On March 27 Rudd led a noisy demonstration inside Columbia's main administration building, Low Library, demanding severance of all university ties with IDA. The protest violated a recent university ban on indoor demonstrations, and, on April 22, Rudd and five others, the "IDA six," were placed on disciplinary probation after their request for an open hearing had been denied. That day, in an open letter to Columbia president Grayson Kirk, Rudd wrote: "We, the young people, whom you so rightly fear, say that the society is sick and you and your capitalism are the sickness. You call for order and respect for authority, we call for justice, freedom and socialism."

The next afternoon, following speeches by Student Afro-American Society (SAS) and SDS leaders, several hundred students marched to Low Library to demand an open hearing for the six students. Finding Low locked, part of the crowd went to the site of the gym. There, in a scuffle with police, one person was arrested. Returning to the campus, the students went to Hamilton Hall, where they vowed to stay and block the exit of a Columbia dean until the university cut all ties with IDA, canceled the gym project, and agreed to take no disciplinary action against the "IDA six."

Late that night, at the request of SAS leaders, the white students in Hamilton Hall left the building and occupied Low Library. Other students took over three more buildings during the next two days. Throughout the week-long occupation, Rudd was a key leader and chief spokesperson for the white protestors. (The black students in Hamilton acted independently.) The Columbia administration refused to agree to the demands, and faculty-initiated negotiations failed. At 2:30 a.m. on April 30, 1,000 New York City police, at Columbia's request, cleared the occupied buildings. 700 persons, 80 percent of them students, were arrested and 148 injured. Rudd himself avoided arrest.

Activists called a highly effective student strike and on May 1 formed an enlarged Strike Steering Committee, co-chaired by Rudd. Rudd and other SDS leaders wanted a continued focus on the original demands, but the faculty and the more moderate students among the 4,000 strikers were equally interested in restructuring the university. On May 17 Rudd was among 117 people arrested when community activists took over a Columbia-owned tenement from which tenants were being evicted.

At first, disciplinary proceedings for the April protests were begun only against Rudd and three others from the original "IDA six." On May 21 several hundred students marched to Hamilton Hall, where parents and lawyers of the four met with a college dean. When it was announced that the four were suspended for refusing to attend the meeting, the demonstrators decided to remain in Hamilton Hall until amnesty was granted to the participants in all of the recent protests. Police were again called, and at the building and in a later sweep of the campus, 68 persons were injured and 178, including Rudd, arrested. Rudd and 72 others were suspended from school, and Rudd's draft board was immediately notified that he was no longer eligible for a deferment. (He was later rejected by the army.)

Rudd ran for the SDS National Interim Committee in June but was elected only as an alternate. That fall, still suspended by Columbia, to which he never returned, Rudd went on several national speaking and fund-raising tours for SDS. At a December 1968 SDS conference Rudd supported a "Revolutionary Youth Movement" proposal that committed SDS to organizing working-class youth as well as students. Rudd was one of 11 coauthors of the "Weatherman" statement presented to the June 1969 SDS convention. When the organization split Rudd became a leader of the faction supporting and named for the statement. Rudd was a leader of the Weatherman "Days of Rage" demonstrations in Chicago in October 1969 and was later indicted for his role. Rudd vanished from public view until 1977. He turned himself in to both New York and Chicago authorities and was convicted of misdemeanor charges in both cities for his participation in the Columbia demonstrations and the Days of Rage, respectively. After working in construction in New Jersey, he taught mathematics at Albuquerque Technical Vocational Institute.

—JBF

## Rusk, Dean
(1909–1994) *secretary of state*

Rusk was born on February 9, 1909, in Cherokee County, Georgia. His father was a Presbyterian minister and his mother a schoolteacher. He graduated from Davidson College in 1931 and then studied at Oxford on a Rhodes scholarship. Returning to the United States in 1934, he joined the political science department at Mills College in California. Rusk became dean of the faculty in 1938.

While in the army during World War II Rusk became a protégé of General George Marshall. At Marshall's behest Rusk joined the State Department in 1946 as assistant chief of the division of international security affairs. In 1950 he was appointed assistant secretary of state for Far Eastern affairs, where he helped formulate policy on Korea and China.

Rusk left the State Department to become president of the Rockefeller Foundation in 1952. During his tenure he helped expand the foundation's projects in Asia, Africa and Latin America. President Kennedy selected him secretary of state in 1961. As secretary, Rusk advised the president on major crises in Berlin, Cuba, Laos, and the Congo. Rusk, however, had limited influence on the president's foreign policies. Partly that was because

Kennedy considered foreign affairs an area of personal responsibility. Kennedy also had only limited confidence in the State Department, where, he believed, bureaucratic rigidity and political orthodoxy often won out over creative thinking. Rusk's personality and his conception of his role as secretary of state also limited his influence. Rusk thought that he should serve as personal adviser to the president on foreign policy matters. For that reason, as well as his reserved personality, he sometimes did not offer detailed or vigorous explanations of his views in meetings of Kennedy's advisers. He served the president with energy and commitment, but Kennedy, at times, complained about his secretary of state's lack of assertiveness.

Rusk's influence increased once LYNDON JOHNSON became president. Johnson built his advisory system around Rusk, Secretary of Defense ROBERT MCNAMARA and presidential assistant for national security affairs MCGEORGE BUNDY (later WALT W. ROSTOW). He counseled the president on

Secretary of State Dean Rusk meeting with President Johnson concerning tension in the Middle East, 1967 (Photographed by Yoichi R. Okamoto; Lyndon Baines Johnson Library)

all important foreign policy matters. He was involved, for example in the decision to send U.S. marines to the Dominican Republic during a civil war to prevent a possible Communist seizure of power. He also tried to avert the outbreak of the Six-Day War in the Middle East in June 1967.

Rusk became one of the president's chief advisers on Vietnam. He helped Johnson make important decisions that deepened U.S. involvement in 1964–65. He saw the conflict in Southeast Asia as part of a global struggle to contain Communist influence, often comparing the situation in Vietnam to the war in Korea 15 years earlier. He also emphasized the importance of U.S. treaty commitments and the effect that a defeat in South Vietnam would have on U.S. credibility around the world. He insisted that U.S. success was imperative in South Vietnam in order to win the "psychological struggle for the conquest of minds and souls." The loss of Vietnam would mean "a drastic loss of confidence in the will and capacity of the free world to oppose aggression" and would bring the world considerably closer to a great power conflict, according to Rusk. Even though he was ambivalent about the commitment of U.S. ground troops to the war in early 1965, he was far more concerned about averting a defeat that he thought would have adverse, global implications for U.S. security.

Rusk insisted that the way to bring peace to Southeast Asia was simply for North Vietnam to cease what he considered its aggression against the South and withdraw its troops. He placed responsibility for the war—and its continuation—on the North Vietnamese and their unwillingness to negotiate. Although skeptical of bombing halts as a means to induce peace talks, he endorsed the extended pause in the air campaign that began just before Christmas in December 1965. Rusk hoped that Soviet pressure would encourage the North Vietnamese to make concessions. When they failed to do so, Rusk, who thought the administration "had gone the last mile," favored resumption of the bombing.

During the Johnson years Rusk emerged as a main public defender of the administration's Vietnam policies. In February 1966 he appeared at televised hearings of the Senate Foreign Relations Committee, chaired by Senator WILLIAM FULBRIGHT (D-Ark.), to explain administration policy. Rusk sought to refute Fulbright's charge that the conflict was a civil war in which the United States had no strategic interest by describing what he believed to be

a long-term pattern of Communist Chinese aggression. One year later, in an October 1967 press conference, he justified the U.S. presence as necessary to protect the region from the future threat of "a billion Chinese on the mainland, armed with nuclear weapons." Rusk often used the analogy of Munich to explain the American war effort in Vietnam. In a January 1967 letter to 100 student leaders, he maintained that the failure of the world community to stop aggression in Ethiopia, Manchuria, and Central Europe during the 1930s had resulted in World War II. "In short," he wrote, "we are involved in Vietnam because we knew from painful experience that the minimum condition for order on our planet is that aggression must not be permitted to succeed. For when it does succeed, the consequence is not peace, it is the further expansion of aggression. And those who have borne responsibility in our country since 1945 have not for one moment forgotten that a third world war would be a nuclear war."

In the aftermath of the enemy Tet offensive in January–February 1968, Rusk encouraged the president to make a new initiative to start productive negotiations. He had strong reservations about General WILLIAM WESTMORELAND's request for more than 200,000 additional troops. He worried that such a large increase would weaken U.S. forces committed to the North Atlantic Treaty Organization in Europe, weaken the U.S. economy, and discourage the South Vietnamese from making a stronger effort to maintain their own security. Although he remained persuaded that U.S. security required success in Southeast Asia, he also emphasized to the president the depth of the American public's discontent with the war. Johnson ultimately announced new limits on U.S. bombing of North Vietnam and a new proposal for peace talks in his televised address of March 31. Yet not until after the president completely halted the bombing of North Vietnam at the end of October 1968 did substantive negotiations begin.

After leaving office in January 1969, Rusk became a professor of international law at the University of Georgia. He died on December 20, 1994.

—EWS

## Russell, Richard B(revard)
### (1897–1971) *member of the Senate*
Richard B. Russell was born on November 2, 1897, in Winder, Georgia, and earned a law degree from

the University of Georgia in 1918. Three years later he was elected to the state assembly and became its speaker in 1927. In 1930 he won election as governor of Georgia, and, two years later, the voters chose him to fill a vacant U.S. Senate seat. He remained in the Senate until his death.

Russell supported many New Deal programs during his early years in Washington. He paid particular attention to the welfare of farmers, helping to pass legislation that created the Rural Electrification Administration and the Farmers Home Administration. He also played a major role in the creation of the first nationwide school lunch program. After World War II, however, he opposed most social welfare programs. He explained later, "I'm a reactionary when times are good. . . . In a depression, I'm a liberal."

Throughout his Senate career, Russell was an unrelenting foe of civil rights measures. By the late 1940s Russell was solidly established as the leader of the southern bloc in the Senate, and at the 1948 Democratic National Convention he had regional support for the party's presidential nomination. He refused, however, to join the Dixiecrat challenge to the national party after the nomination of President HARRY S. TRUMAN.

Russell was highly regarded by almost all senators. A member of a patrician family, he was known for his dignified bearing and courteous manner as well as for his formidable intelligence. Aided by this reputation and a single-minded dedication to his work, an intimate knowledge of parliamentary procedure, and his leadership of the powerful southern senatorial caucus, Russell became one of the most influential members of Congress in the 1940s and 1950s.

Russell reached the peak of his prestige in 1951, when he chaired an investigation of President Truman's removal of General Douglas MacArthur from his Korean command. The following year Russell made a serious bid for the Democratic presidential nomination but was hampered by his sectional identification and received only 294 out of 1,200 votes at the party's convention. Following the election, Russell decided not to seek the position of Senate minority leader. He did not want to abandon his opposition to civil rights, and he believed that his views would cost him support of some liberal and moderate Senate Democrats. Instead, he endorsed Senator LYNDON B. JOHNSON (D-Tex.), who became minority leader in 1953.

Russell became chair of the Senate Armed Services Committee in 1951 and in that position played a major role in national security affairs in the 1950s and early 1960s. Russell criticized the Eisenhower and Kennedy administrations for depending too heavily upon nuclear missiles. He succeeded in increasing appropriations for air force bombers during the Kennedy presidency. In that period he also led southern resistance to the Civil Rights Acts of 1957 and 1960 and directed a successful filibuster against a bill barring discriminatory use of literacy tests by voting registrars. In 1963 he declared his vehement opposition to the bill that President Kennedy proposed in June barring racial discrimination in public accommodations.

Russell remained an influential figure during Johnson's presidency. In addition to chairing the Armed Services Committee, he was then second-ranking Democrat on the Appropriations and Aeronautical and Space Sciences Committees. He also was a member of the Democratic Policy Committee and led the conservative majority on the Democratic Steering Committee, which distributed committee assignments. Early in 1965 liberal Democratic senators attempted to reform the Steering Committee, but Russell succeeded in preserving a slender conservative edge on the panel.

In 1964 Russell led the opposition during Senate consideration of the public accommodations bill that Kennedy had sent to Congress. Russell used his skills at parliamentary maneuver to delay the legislation and took part in a filibuster that lasted 75 days. On June 10, the Senate voted cloture, ending the longest filibuster in Senate history. Earlier in the year, Johnson had told Russell that he would not relent in his efforts to get the public accommodations bill through Congress. Russell had replied that the president might ultimately secure the legislation, but in doing so he would lose the South for the Democratic Party. Johnson nonetheless won a sweeping victory in the election of 1964. Yet he lost five southern states to Republican nominee BARRY GOLDWATER, clear indication that his vigorous support of civil rights was accelerating the erosion of what once had been the Democratic solid South.

Despite their disagreement on civil rights, Russell maintained a close relationship with Johnson, who frequently sought his counsel on many issues, including U.S. involvement in Vietnam. Even though he believed in the vigorous use of military power to protect national security, Russell was skeptical about the growing U.S. involvement in Vietnam. He anticipated that U.S. military intervention would lead to a costly war of indefinite duration that might escalate into a military confrontation with the People's Republic of China. As the military and political position of the Saigon government deteriorated, Russell told Johnson in a telephone conversation of May 27, 1964, that the situation in Vietnam was "the damn worst mess I ever saw." Yet as much as he wished to disengage, Russell could imagine no way to do so without incurring unacceptable political or strategic costs. On several occasions during 1964 and early 1965, Russell and Johnson shared their fears that Vietnam posed great risks while offering little prospect for the emergence of a stable, effective government that would facilitate U.S. withdrawal. After Johnson announced the dispatch of the first U.S. combat troops in early March 1965, Russell predicted in a telephone conversation with the president that the administration had started down a road with "no end." Yet despite his deep reservations, Russell supported the growing U.S. war effort, while calling for a powerful air campaign against North Vietnam that he hoped would be a key to victory.

After the National Liberation Front's Tet offensive early in 1968, Russell, believing that the time for a change in policy had come, declared that he would not support the sending of additional ground troops to Southeast Asia unless there was a drastic escalation of the air war. He said that the initial U.S. entry into the war was a mistake but that the United States could not abandon South Vietnam to the Communists.

Russell's personal influence in defense matters was largely responsible for the Senate's 1967 decision to drop administration-requested funds for a fleet of fast ships designed to give the United States a rapid transport capability in future wars. Fearing that such ships might encourage further entanglements like Vietnam, he commented, "If it is easy for us to go anywhere and do anything, we will always be going somewhere and doing something."

Although Russell wanted to avoid future American entry into similar wars and opposed the funding of military projects that would facilitate such involvement, he was a leading congressional advocate of defensive missile installations. In 1966 he played a key role in securing Senate approval of funds for production of the Nike-X, an extensive antiballistic missile system, which the Defense Department regarded as ineffective. The administration did not build the Nike-X system, but, in 1967, it supported a more modest Sentinel antiballistic missile (ABM) system for defense against a Chinese nuclear attack. Russell, still favoring the larger program, did not regard the threat of a Chinese attack as a serious possibility and ridiculed the proposal. But the following year, when the Sentinel ABM was presented as a defense against Soviet as well as Chinese missiles, Russell supported it as "the first step in a defense system against atomic attack from the Soviet Union," and the Senate appropriated construction funds.

In 1969 Russell stepped down as chair of the Armed Services Committee to head the Appropriations Committee. During the same year he became president pro tempore of the Senate. On January 21, 1971, while still a senator, he died of respiratory insufficiency after six weeks of hospitalization.

—MLL

## Rustin, Bayard
(1910–1987) *civil rights leader*

An illegitimate child, who was born in West Chester, Pennsylvania, on March 17, 1910, Rustin was raised by his grandparents. His grandmother belonged to the Society of Friends, and he was influenced by the Quakers' pacifist principles. Rustin later recalled that when traveling with his high school football team he was physically ejected from a restaurant because of his race and decided at that point never to accept segregation.

Rustin joined the Young Communist League (YCL) in 1936 because he believed that it was committed to peace and equal rights for blacks. He worked an organizer for the league and attended the City College of New York at night. Ruskin left the YCL in 1941 when, after the Nazi invasion of the Soviet Union, the Communists abandoned their opposition to World War II.

Upon leaving the YCL Rustin became a socialist and joined the Fellowship of Reconciliation (FOR), a pacifist nondenominational religious group opposed to the war and racial injustice. In 1941 he worked with A. PHILIP RANDOLPH, president of the Brotherhood of Sleeping Car Porters, in planning a march on Washington to demand fair employment practices in the nation's rapidly growing defense industries. In 1947 he helped organize and participated in the Congress of Racial Equality's first Freedom Ride into the South. At about the same time, he worked with Randolph's Committee to End Jim Crow in the Military, which helped secure President HARRY S. TRUMAN's executive order in 1948 prohibiting racial discrimination in the armed forces.

During World War II Rustin was a conscientious objector and served more than two years in jail. He became executive secretary of the War Resisters League in 1953 and in 1958 went to England to assist the Campaign for Nuclear Disarmament in organizing the first of its Aldermaston-to-London ban-the-bomb marches.

During the 1950s Rustin became one of the leading strategists of the civil rights movement. In 1955 he played a key role in organizing the Montgomery, Alabama, bus boycott led by MARTIN LUTHER KING, JR., and he subsequently drafted the plan for what became the Southern Christian Leadership Conference. In the late 1950s he served as an adviser to King.

Civil rights leader Bayard Rustin (left) with Cleveland Robinson before the March on Washington, 1963 *(Library of Congress, Prints and Photographs Division)*

In 1960 Rustin, acting on behalf of King and Randolph, organized civil rights demonstrations at the Democratic and Republican national conventions. When Representative ADAM CLAYTON POWELL, JR., (D-N.Y.) threatened to publicly denounce Rustin for his radical background and homosexuality, Rustin left the project and for the next two years was isolated from much of the civil rights movement.

During the winter of 1962–63, however, Randolph asked Rustin to draw up plans for a mass march on Washington. Rustin believed that blacks could overcome their second-class citizenship only if they went beyond demands for integration and stressed the need for fundamental economic and social reforms. The original plans for the march, which emphasized demands for federal action in the areas of jobs, housing, and education, reflected Rustin's views. But during the two months preceding the August 1963 demonstration, the march's leaders shifted their emphasis away from sweeping economic and social changes to attract a broad coalition in support of civil rights. The well-ordered, peaceful demonstration, of which Rustin was the chief organizer, drew 250,000 persons to Washington on August 25, 1963.

During the mid-1960s Rustin elaborated upon the strategy he had proposed during the early planning phase of the March on Washington. His program was presented most comprehensively in "From Protest to Politics: The Future of the Civil Rights Movement," an influential article that appeared in the February 1965 issue of *Commentary*. Rustin contended that the legal basis of American racism had been destroyed during the decade between the Supreme Court's school desegregation decision of 1954 and the Civil Rights Act of 1964 but that the desegregation of public accommodations was "relatively peripheral . . . to the fundamental conditions of life" of African Americans.

To effect basic change in the lives of blacks, Rustin continued, the civil rights movement had to extend its concern beyond race relations to fundamental economic problems. The private sector of the economy, he argued, could not fulfill the aspirations of blacks because it was not producing enough jobs. Furthermore, Rustin wrote, technology was eliminating unskilled jobs while creating positions that required professional training. The result, he said, was that the individual no longer could work his or her way up from the bottom of the economic ladder on personal initiative alone. He concluded that it was essential for blacks to promote federal programs for full employment, the abolition of slums, and the reconstruction of the educational system. To win such program, Rustin said, blacks should place less stress upon protest demonstrations and devote more attention to electoral politics.

Rustin argued that the great majority of blacks had much in common with white workers and that his proposals for federal action represented a program around which a majority coalition could be formed within the Democratic Party. The organized labor movement, Rustin asserted, was the major natural ally of the mass of poor blacks. He urged black organizations to work with the established AFL-CIO leadership to create such a coalition. Black separatism, he argued in a September 1966 *Commentary* article, was not a viable alternative because it would isolate blacks politically and foster antiblack sentiments.

In the mid-1960s Rustin, who had previously devoted most of his attention to behind-the-scenes organizing of civil rights protests, began to appear frequently before black, union, and liberal organizations to promote his political perspective. A tall, grey-haired figure with the appearance of both urbanity and athletic prowess, Rustin, who had cultivated a British accent in the radical days of his youth, was an imposing figure and a forceful speaker. Late in 1964 he became executive director of the newly created A. Philip Randolph Institute, an AFL-CIO–supported organization that attempted to place young blacks in union apprenticeship training programs and promote political proposals for the labor-liberal-black coalition, which Rustin thought LYNDON JOHNSON's landslide 1964 election victory had inaugurated.

Though Rustin generally supported the policies of President Johnson, he frequently criticized the administration's antipoverty program as inadequate. With other civil rights leaders and liberal economists, Rustin advocated a 10-year, $185 billion "freedom budget" by which the federal government could put all employable persons to work rebuilding inner cities, constructing hospitals and schools, and aiding other socially useful projects.

In 1968 Rustin strongly endorsed the presidential candidacy of Vice President HUBERT H. HUMPHREY. Noting the seating of JULIAN BOND and of the integrated Mississippi delegation at the Democratic National Convention, Rustin wrote in the September 21 New York *Amsterdam News* that

"the Negro-labor-liberal forces are clearly on top in the Democratic Party." He praised Humphrey as having an outstanding record in the area of civil rights and on matters pertaining to the welfare of workers. Rustin noted "the divisions among the progressive forces over Vietnam," but he attempted to minimize that issue, stating that the progressive coalition should not allow itself to become divided over the war because it "will end before long, but our problems at home will haunt us for generations if we do not act now."

Rustin's close relationship with the AFL-CIO, his support of coalition politics and his allegiance to integration set him apart from some black leaders in the late 1960s. In February 1964 he had organized a one-day New York City school boycott for integration led by Reverend Milton A. Galamison, a strike that was supported by most black leaders. But by 1968 many blacks had lost hope in the possibility of integration and were supporting the decentralization of the New York school system and black control of local school boards. During that year the United Federation of Teachers (UFT) went on strike when the black-controlled governing board of the Ocean Hill–Brownsville demonstration school district ordered 13 tenured teachers transferred out of the district. Rustin, who still staunchly supported integration and a black-trade union alliance, was one of the few prominent blacks who backed the UFT. A large number of blacks felt that the UFT and its president, ALBERT SHANKER, were hostile to their aspirations, and Rustin was widely denounced for his support of the union.

During the late 1960s and early 1970s, Rustin continued to oppose separatist tendencies. In 1969 he denounced college officials for capitulating to black student demands for black studies programs that he believed would not provide African Americans with economically usable skills. Philosophies of racial solidarity, Rustin argued in the January 1970 *Harper's Magazine*, had the unintended effect of strengthening the political position of segregationists and conservatives. In 1972 Rustin became a cochair of the Socialist Party–Democratic Socialist Federation (later known as Social Democrats, USA) a group dominated by trade union leaders and others who favored the type of black-labor union coalition that he advocated.

Rustin regarded President RICHARD M. NIXON as an opponent of blacks and workers. In 1970 he joined other blacks in denouncing a memo by

DANIEL P. MOYNIHAN, a domestic adviser to President Nixon, that urged "benign neglect" of racial issues. In a May 1971 article for *Harper's* he criticized the president's Philadelphia Plan, ostensibly designed to increase the number of construction industry jobs for blacks, as an antiunion device to increase the number of workers in the industry and place deflationary pressure on wages. He died on August 24, 1987.

—MLL

## Ryan, William Fitts

### (1922–1972) *member of the House of Representatives*

Born in Albion, New York, on June 28, 1922, Ryan earned a law degree from Columbia University in 1949 and worked as an assistant district attorney in Manhattan from 1950 to 1957. He helped found a reform movement in the late 1950s that challenged the Democratic Party leadership in Manhattan. He defeated the regular Democratic candidate in a primary fight in 1960 for the party's nomination for a congressional seat from the Upper West Side of Manhattan and then triumphed in the November election. After the 1960 census, the New York legislature approved a reapportionment plan that eliminated his district, a move that Ryan believed aimed at weakening the reform movement of which he was a part. Ryan sought election to the House in 1962 in an expanded, adjacent district. He defeated the regular Democratic candidate in the primary and then prevailed in the general election.

Ryan's outspoken liberalism reflected the political orientation of many of his constituents but often put him at odds with the vast majority of Congress. In March 1961, Ryan was one of only six House members who voted against appropriations for the House Un-American Activities Committee. Later that year, Ryan and a single House colleague spoke against a congressional resolution calling for the continued exclusion of the People's Republic of China from the United Nations. In 1962 he was one of only two House members who voted against postal restrictions on material that the U.S. Attorney General deemed communist propaganda.

A champion of civil rights, he challenged the seating of the Mississippi House delegation at the opening of the 89th Congress in January 1965. Acting on behalf of the Mississippi Freedom Democratic Party (MFDP), Ryan contended that the Mississippi House members had been illegally elected because African Americans in the state were systematically excluded from voting. The challenge was defeated in a key procedural vote, 276-149, and the Mississippi representatives were belatedly sworn in. Ryan called the large opposition vote an "historic achievement" and "a real warning to Mississippi for the future." The MFDP filed a new challenge on May 16, requesting that three of its members— elected in a MFDP-conducted "freedom vote"—be seated instead of the regular Mississippi delegation. The renewed challenge was bottled up by House clerk Ralph Roberts and then by the House Administration Committee until mid-September, when a group of 31 House members led by Ryan finally forced hearings on the issue. The Administration Committee recommended that the challenge be rejected, primarily on the ground that those initiating it had not been candidates in the contested election. The full House concurred on September 17 by a vote of 228-143.

When President Johnson requested the first supplementary appropriation specifically for funds to fight the Vietnam War on May 4, 1965, Congress approved in little more than two days. Ryan was one of only seven representatives to oppose the measure. Throughout the remainder of the Johnson administration, Ryan was among a small minority of representatives voting against all funds for the Vietnam War. "So long as the Congress continues to rubberstamp the war through the appropriations process," Ryan argued, "it is abdicating its responsibility for decision making and rational appraisal of executive policy . . . [and] the Administration will continue to rely on the possibility of military victory."

Ryan ran in a four-way Democratic primary for the 1965 New York City mayoral nomination, finishing third with about one-third of victor Abraham D. Beame's 327,934 votes. (Beame lost the general election to Republican-Liberal candidate representative JOHN V. LINDSAY. However, the next year Ryan was easily reelected to the House.

Ryan was a strong civil libertarian and continued to be a leader of the annual congressional fight to end appropriations for HUAC. Between 1961 and 1969 outright opposition to the committee grew to 123 votes. Ryan opposed a House measure, introduced after the April 1968 demonstrations at Columbia University, that denied federal aid to any student who willfully disobeyed a lawful college or university regulation. A modified Senate version of the measure was eventually adopted by the House.

Although best known for his opposition to American intervention in Vietnam, Ryan was also a consistent supporter of Israel. In 1965 he introduced an amendment that was incorporated into the Food-for-Peace appropriation that banned the sale of food to the United Arab Republic unless the president determined that it was in the national interest. During the June 1967 Middle East war, Ryan was critical of the United State's declaration of neutrality. The next year he opposed giving foreign aid to Jordan. Ryan served in the House until his death from cancer on September 17, 1972.

—JBF

## Salinger, Pierre E(mil George)

**(1925–2004)** *White House press secretary, member of the Senate*

Salinger, who was born on June 14, 1925, in San Francisco, served in the navy during World War II and graduated from the University of San Francisco in 1947. After jobs with the *San Francisco Chronicle* and *Collier's* magazine, he was hired by ROBERT F. KENNEDY as an investigator for the Senate Rackets Committee in 1957. He met Senator John F. Kennedy, who served on this committee, and became Kennedy's press secretary during the 1960 campaign. After the election, Kennedy chose Salinger as White House press secretary, making him, at age 35, the youngest person to date hold that job. Salinger, who had an easygoing manner and a good sense of humor, generally got along well with reporters. He encouraged Kennedy to approve an important change in news coverage by allowing live television and radio broadcasts of presidential press conferences.

After Kennedy's assassination President Johnson told Salinger, "I want you to stay with me as long as you can." Salinger stayed on until March 19, when he abruptly resigned as press secretary. He announced that he was running for the U.S. Senate in California the next day, which was the deadline for entering the race. Salinger sought the seat of Clair Engle (D-Calif.), who was ill with a brain tumor but still a declared candidate for reelection. Illness soon forced Engle to withdraw from the race, leaving Salinger and state controller Alan Cranston to contest the Democratic primary. Salinger won the primary election at the beginning of June by a substantial margin.

Following Engle's death, Governor EDMUND G. BROWN appointed Salinger to serve the remain-der of Engle's Senate term. Salinger took his seat in the upper chamber on August 5, 1964. In the November election, he lost to his Republican opponent, GEORGE MURPHY. He attributed his defeat to his opponent's shrewd use of the "carpetbagger" issue, since Salinger was a registered voter in Virginia at the time that he filed for the California race.

After leaving the Senate, Salinger turned to private business. He became vice president of National General Corporation in 1965 and served from 1965 to 1968 as vice president for international affairs at Continental Airlines.

During the presidential campaign of 1968, Salinger became a press aide to Senator Robert Kennedy (D-N.Y.). Following Kennedy's death in June 1968 he shifted his allegiance to Senator GEORGE MCGOVERN's (D-S.Dak.) unsuccessful bid for the Democratic presidential nomination at the Chicago convention. After McGovern's defeat Salinger once again returned to private business. He later moved to Paris, where he made frequent guest appearances on French television commenting on American developments. From 1979 until 1994, he was a correspondent for ABC News. He died on October 16, 2004.

—FHM

## Salisbury, Harrison E(vans)

**(1908–1993)** *assistant managing editor,* New York Times

Born in Minneapolis, Minnesota, on November 14, 1908, Salisbury began working for the United Press (UP) while attending the University of Minnesota. Following his graduation in 1930, he worked in UP bureaus in Chicago, Washington, and New York.

During World War II he reported from London and Moscow and then became the UP foreign news editor from 1944 until 1948. He joined the *New York Times* in 1949 and spent the next five years in Moscow as bureau chief, winning the 1955 Pulitzer Prize for international reporting for a series on the Soviet Union. In 1964 he became assistant managing editor of the *Times*. Salisbury wrote a number of books about the Soviet Union and international affairs during his years as a reporter.

In the mid-1960s Salisbury made repeated efforts to travel to North Vietnam, where few American reporters had visited since the escalation of U.S. military activity in Southeast Asia. During the summer of 1966 he traveled to several Asian nations in an unsuccessful effort to obtain a visa to enter North Vietnam.

Although the United States had been carrying out a sustained bombing campaign against North Vietnam since February 1965, attacks on the Hanoi area were at first relatively rare. On December 2, 1966, a new series of raids on Hanoi began, culminating in heavy bombing attacks on December 13 and 14. The North Vietnamese government charged that American planes had bombed nonmilitary targets and inflicted heavy civilian casualties. In mid-December, Hanoi issued a visa, and Salisbury became the first reporter for a major U.S. news organization to visit North Vietnam since the escalation of the war in 1965.

On December 25 the *New York Times* printed Salisbury's first dispatch. "Contrary to the impression given by United States communiques," Salisbury reported, "on-the-spot inspection indicates that American bombing has been inflicting considerable civilian casualties in Hanoi and its environs for some time past. . . ." The following day, in response to Salisbury's report, officials in Washington said that, although U.S. policy was to attack only military targets, American pilots had in fact accidentally struck civilian areas. On December 27 Salisbury reported that Nam Dinh, 50 miles southeast of Hanoi, had been repeatedly bombed since June 28, resulting in a large number of civilian casualties. "Whatever the explanation," he wrote, "one can see that United States planes are dropping an enormous weight of explosives on purely civilian targets." Salisbury's dispatches indicated that in spite of the intensive bombing, the North Vietnamese population seemed energetic and purposeful and the country's leadership appeared willing to fight a prolonged war if necessary.

Salisbury's reports began an intense debate over the bombing. President Johnson declared at a December 31 press conference that he regretted "every single casualty" in both North and South Vietnam and reasserted that the raids were aimed solely at military targets, with all efforts taken to avoid civilian casualties. Despite the president's assertion, much of the reaction to Salisbury's reporting focused on the credibility of the administration's explanations of its policies in Vietnam, an issue that plagued the president until he left the White House. Salisbury's dispatches were attacked by both government officials and other newspapers for failing to specify the sources of information on casualties and damage. *Newsweek* said of Salisbury's report of heavy civilian casualties in Hanoi, "To American eyes, it read like the line from Tass or Hsinsha." The *Washington Post* reported that the casualty figures Salisbury cited for Nam Dinh were similar to those appearing in a North Vietnamese pamphlet. Clifton Daniel, managing editor of the *Times*, responded that this was not surprising since "they both came from the same source—the North Vietnamese government."

Before leaving Hanoi Salisbury interviewed a leading official of the National Liberation Front of South Vietnam and North Vietnamese premier Pham Van Dong, who insisted that there could be no settlement unless "the United States put, unconditionally and for good, an end to the bombing and all hostile activity against the North."

For his reporting from North Vietnam, Salisbury received the George Polk Award for foreign reporting, a Sidney Hillman Award, and the Asia Magazine Award. The Pulitzer Prize journalism jury recommended that Salisbury be given the international reporting prize, but the advisory board voted 5-4 to reject the jury recommendation, a decision that was widely criticized.

In 1970 Salisbury became the editor of the *Times*'s new op-ed page. He left the newspaper when he reached the mandatory retirement age in 1973. He wrote many books, mainly on international topics, during the next 20 years. He died on July 5, 1993.

—JBF

## Saltonstall, Leverett
(1892–1979) *member of the Senate*

Leverett Saltonstall was a member of one of Massachusetts's oldest and most politically prominent families. Born on September 1, 1892, in Chestnut

Hill, Massachusetts, he graduated from Harvard in 1914 and Harvard Law School three years later. Saltonstall then served in the army during World War I. While practicing law in Boston after the war, Saltonstall entered state politics as a Republican and won election to the state legislature in 1922, eventually serving as speaker. He successfully ran for governor in 1938 and the U.S. Senate in 1944. In the 1950s Saltonstall was chair of the Armed Services Committee for two years and Republican whip from 1949 until 1957. Saltonstall was an internationalist in foreign affairs and a moderate on domestic issues. He had accumulated considerable seniority by the early 1960s, and he enjoyed considerable respect in the Senate. Yet Republicans eased him out of his position as party whip in 1957, and his influence on the GOP leadership in the Senate declined during the early 1960s.

Saltonstall voted for the Johnson administration's civil rights bill in 1964. In January 1965 he introduced an alternative to the administration's Social Security–financed Medicare bill. The Saltonstall measure called for a voluntary Medicare program for persons over 65 with incomes under $3,000 a year. Benefits were to vary according to the individual's choice of one of three plans. The program was to be administered by the states and financed by federal-state funds and graduated contributions by participants. Although his measure failed to pass, in July the Senate adopted a Saltonstall amendment to the Medicare bill making basic home-nursing benefits available to persons over 65 regardless of whether they had been hospitalized.

In February 1965 Saltonstall supported Senate Minority Leader EVERETT DIRKSEN's (R-Ill.) charge that senators advocating a negotiated settlement of the Vietnam War were "run[ning] up the white flag" of defeat. In June of the next year, Saltonstall asserted that, in widening the air war to include the bombing of Hanoi-Haiphong oil installations, President Johnson had acted "in the best interest of accomplishing our objective in Vietnam." He also declared that the air raids were worth the risk of Chinese intervention.

Pressure from the Massachusetts Republican Party, which supported the growing political aspirations of Massachusetts attorney general EDWARD BROOKE, led Saltonstall to announce his retirement from the Senate in December 1965. The next year Brooke won election to Saltonstall's old seat to become the first black to serve in the Senate since

Reconstruction. Saltonstall lived in retirement until his death on June 17, 1979.

—FHM

## Samuelson, Paul A(nthony)
(1915– ) *economist*

Paul Samuelson was the author of an immensely popular economics textbook and a prolific disseminator of Keynesian economic thought in both popular and professional journals. Although he did not take a position in the Johnson administration, he provided counsel on economic issues that helped shape the president's policies.

Born in Gary, Indiana, on May 15, 1915, Samuelson earned his Ph.D. in economics at Harvard University in 1941. He studied with Alvin Hansen, a prominent exponent of Keynesian theory. The British economist John Maynard Keynes had argued that the cycles of boom and depression characteristic of capitalism were not inevitable but could be moderated by government fiscal action. He urged deficit spending to combat economic slowdowns and heavy unemployment and a budget surplus when inflation was the primary threat. Adjusting interest rates was also a part of the Keynesian prescription for economic stability.

Samuelson promoted these modern concepts in his textbook, *Economics: An Introductory Analysis.* First published in 1948, it became the most widely read economics textbook in America, going through 18 editions during the next 56 years. Samuelson taught economics at the Massachusetts Institute of Technology, wrote often on current issues, and served as a frequent consultant to government agencies. Although he was reportedly the favorite economist of President John F. Kennedy, he declined an offer in late 1960 to chair the Council of Economic Advisers. Yet he often counseled Kennedy on economic issues, and the president frequently followed his advice.

Samuelson was not close to President Johnson, but he continued to be a leading shaper of public opinion on current economic issues through his column in *Newsweek.* He was an enthusiastic advocate of the massive tax cut proposed during the Kennedy administration and signed by President Johnson in February 1964. Samuelson praised the tax cut for its stimulative effect on the economy and foresaw a "long period of continuous growth, with rising living standards." He believed there would never be a recurrence of a great depression like that of the 1930s as long as there existed a government ready to intervene with the appropriate fiscal and monetary remedies.

In his column Samuelson offered the Johnson administration a steady stream of advice on how to meet the threat of inflation without bringing on a recession. Early in 1966 he urged a tax increase in order to forestall "demand-pull" inflation, that is, inflation caused by an excess of dollars in the hands of consumers. The administration did not raise taxes, however, and a year later, amid calls from a diverse array of economists for a tax increase, Samuelson changed his position and argued against raising taxes. In "An Open Letter to LBJ" in January 1967, Samuelson maintained that the time to raise taxes had passed and that to do so would bring "loss of momentum in this greatest of all peacetime economic expansions." "Too often in the past," he said, "governments have brought prosperity to end by a misguided concern for budget-balance ideology."

Late in 1967 Samuelson returned to advocacy of a tax increase. He argued that the threat of demand-pull inflation was paramount and could not be checked by the Federal Reserve's tight money policy alone. Nevertheless, Samuelson exhorted the government not to sacrifice its antipoverty and social welfare programs to fight inflation. "I favor a tax increase," he said in November 1967. "Let me make it clear that I do not favor it at any price. If its costs were a legislative deal to cripple important welfare programs, I would have to point out that a degree of open inflation is not the greatest evil." In June 1968 Congress passed a 10 percent tax surcharge accompanied by $6 billion in budget cuts.

Samuelson continued to promote his mainstream liberal economic thinking throughout the Nixon administration. In 1970 he was awarded the 1970 Nobel Prize for doing "more than any other contemporary economist to raise the level of scientific analysis in economic theory."

—TO

## Sanders, Carl E(dward)

(1925–   ) governor

Born on May 15, 1925, in Augusta, Georgia, Sanders began studying at the University of Georgia but enlisted in the U.S. Army Air Forces before he completed his degree. Following the end of World War II, he returned to the university and earned a B.A. and then a law degree. He practiced law in Augusta and began his political career in 1954, when he won election to the state House of Representatives. Two years later, he gained a seat in the state senate and became president pro tempore. Sanders became known as a racial moderate for the key role he played in the Senate's passage of "open school" bills, which barred the closing of the state's public schools as a device for avoiding integration.

In 1962 Sanders entered the Democratic gubernatorial primary against former governor Marvin Griffin, a white supremacist who vowed undying opposition to integration. Sanders's greatest strength was in the urban centers of the state, which were less inclined than the rural areas to resist federal pressure against segregation. Aided by a federal court decision in the spring of 1962 voiding the state's county unit voting system that had favored rural areas, Sanders defeated Griffin in the primary and subsequently ran unopposed in the general election.

As governor, Sanders did not support integration, and, in July 1963, he opposed the Kennedy administration's civil rights bill. Nevertheless, he emphasized his determination to keep the public schools open. When LYNDON JOHNSON assumed the presidency the following November and announced his intention to pursue Kennedy's programs, Sanders pledged his support in all areas but civil rights. At the Democratic National Convention of 1964, Sanders urged the Platform Committee to respect the local traditions of the South when considering racial matters.

Sanders's primary concern, however, was to promote the economic growth of Georgia. During his first year in office, he pursued this goal by successfully promoting bills to expand educational opportunities and to streamline the state's administrative apparatus. Believing that racial peace was essential to progress, he continued to oppose resistance to legally mandated integration and sought to compromise with civil rights groups. When civil rights demonstrations in Americus led to violence during the summer of 1965, Sanders urged the unyielding local administration to submit to mediation. In January 1966 the Georgia House of Representatives voted not to admit JULIAN BOND, a leader of the Student Nonviolent Coordinating Committee (SNCC), to his elected seat because he had opposed the Vietnam War and expressed support for draft resisters. Sanders, who was a supporter of administration war policy, opposed the exclusion of Bond, saying that it would make him a martyr and provoke SNCC demonstrations.

Barred by the state's constitution from running for reelection in 1966, Sanders considered challenging Senator RICHARD RUSSELL in the Democratic primary that year, but decided not to do so. In 1970 he entered the Democratic gubernatorial primary but lost to Jimmy Carter. He did not run again for public office and practiced law in Atlanta.

—MLL

## Sanford, (James) Terry
(1917–1998) *governor*

Sanford was born on August 20, 1917, in Laurinburg, North Carolina. He attended the University of North Carolina and, following wartime service in the army, returned there to earn a law degree in 1946. During the 1950s, he practiced law while becoming active in state politics as a Democrat. In 1960 Sanford won the governorship while calling for moderation on racial issues. As governor, his main achievements were in educational reform and expanded social services.

Constitutionally barred from seeking another term, Sanford returned to the practice of law in 1965. During the remainder of the decade, he continued his interest in education, which he considered a "vital tool" for economic development, the elimination of poverty and prejudice, and "the cultivation of all human capacities." At their July 1965 conference, U.S. governors adopted Sanford's "Compact on Education," which stressed the need for states to join the federal government in studying ways to improve education. That same month he was appointed to the National Advisory Commission on Education of Disadvantaged Children. He was also a member of the Carnegie Commission on Educational Television whose report, issued in January 1967, proposed the creation of a noncommercial educational television network funded by a federal tax on new televisions.

Sanford's other major concern during the decade was the strengthening of the states in the federal-state relationship. In November 1964 he urged a greater role for the states in supplying leadership and initiative to carry out federally sponsored programs. In April 1965 Sanford became director of a two-year study funded by the Ford Foundation and the Carnegie Corporation to determine ways of increasing the role of the states in educational reform.

In October 1967 Sanford completed the Ford Foundation study and outlined his program for the reform and revitalization of the states as a means of defending the nation's federal system against the "possible abuses of centralized power" and meeting "the challenge of the urban areas." He suggested a reform of state tax structures and recommended the use of state power as the only means of ordering urban growth and avoiding the "unordered piling up of problems upon problems."

In June 1968 Sanford was elected president of Urban America, Inc., a private, nonprofit city improvement group that rendered financial assistance and technical advice to sponsors of nonprofit housing developments. One month later he also became director of Esquire, Inc., a producer of educational films and books.

Sanford seconded the nomination of HUBERT H. HUMPHREY for president at the August 1968 Democratic National Convention and served as the national chair of the Citizens for Humphrey-Muskie committee. He became president of Duke University in December 1969. Sanford was the chair of the 1972 Democratic Charter Commission and was an unsuccessful Democratic presidential aspirant before supporting Senator GEORGE MCGOVERN's (D-S.Dak.) effort. He withdrew as a candidate for the 1976 Democratic presidential nomination in January 1976 to return to Duke University. He served in the U.S. Senate from 1986 to 1993. He died on April 18, 1998.

—TJC

## Saunders, Stuart T(homas)
(1909–1987) *chair and chief executive officer, Pennsylvania Railroad Company; chair and chief executive officer, Penn Central Transportation Company*

Born on July 16, 1909, in McDowall, West Virginia, Stuart Saunders attended Roanoke College in Virginia and Harvard Law School, from which he received his degree in 1934. After practicing law in Washington, D.C., for five years, he joined the legal department of the Norfolk & Western Railroad Company (N&W) in 1939. He moved up through the N & W's legal ranks and advanced to the company presidency in 1958. Under Saunders the N & W, a consistently profitable coal hauler, continued to perform well; in 1962 it realized a profit of over $65 million after taxes on a gross revenue of roughly $250 million. Saunders arranged the N & W's absorption of the Virginian Railway, the first railroad merger approved by the Interstate Commerce Commission in the 20th century. In October 1963 Saunders became chair of the board of the Pennsylvania Railroad Company, the nation's largest railroad.

Saunders worked to enlarge the Pennsylvania's income by expanding and diversifying its holdings. He supplemented the railroad's sizeable land holdings with extensive real estate investments in Florida, California, and the Southwest. Saunders concluded the Pennsylvania's purchase of the Buckeye Pipe Line Company, an 8,000-mile petroleum pipeline, and also bought a controlling interest in Executive Jet Aviation, a company providing charter service to business travellers.

The Pennsylvania gained the capital for these acquisitions partially through the sale of its own assets, such as its 98 percent interest in the Wabash Railroad and 25 percent in the N&W. In 1966 it sold the deficit-ridden Long Island Railroad to New York State for $65 million. Saunders built good stockholder relations with his policy of paying out high dividends; such payments increased in his first three years at the Pennsylvania from $6.8 million to $32 million.

Saunders's major task in the mid-1960s was the arrangement of the merger of the Pennsylvania with its largest rival, the New York Central. The proposed merger faced strong opposition from labor unions, the Department of Justice, small railroads, and Pennsylvania businessman Milton J. Shapp. On October 1, 1963, the day Saunders took over the Pennsylvania, Assistant U.S. Attorney General William Orrick declared that the government would oppose the merger because "the combination would eliminate a vast amount of beneficial rail competition" and endanger "the continued existence of several smaller railroads." The railway brotherhoods feared that workers would lose their jobs because of the merger. Shapp charged in May 1966 that the merger was "a legalized multibillion dollar swindle that would put the old robber barons to shame."

Saunders worked for four years to overcome the opposition to the merger. He argued that the merger was vital for the railroads' survival and would result in savings of $80 million due to greater efficiency. He won over the railway unions by promising to rehire all workers with five years seniority who had been furloughed between the spring of 1964 and the time of the merger. This

agreement cost $38 million in the two years after the merger. The Justice Department dropped its opposition in November 1967, after Saunders had promised that the merged railroads would also take over the bankrupt New Haven Railroad.

The government's shift was also the result of Saunders's assiduous cultivation of the Johnson administration. Saunders was an active supporter of administration policies within the business community. As co-chair with HENRY FORD II of the Business Committee for Tax Reduction he helped to rally support behind the Kennedy-Johnson $11.5 billion, tax-reduction bill in 1963–64. During the Johnson administration he served as chair of the National Alliance of Businessmen in the Philadelphia area, an administration inspired program to provide jobs for the unemployed. Saunders also served on the President's Advisory Committee on Labor Management Policy and was chair of the Department of Commerce Advisory Committee on Foreign Direct Investments. "I could not have gotten the merger through without help from members of the administration," Saunders said in January 1968 "They got the Justice Department to change its thinking."

The merger creating the Penn Central Transportation Company in February 1968 was the greatest combination in American history. The Penn Central had assets of $6.3 billion and annual revenues of almost $2 billion and was both the nation's biggest railroad and its largest landlord. *Saturday Review* named Saunders "Businessman of the Year" for 1968.

On June 8, 1970, the Penn Central's board of directors fired Saunders. Two weeks later the Penn Central filed for bankruptcy, at that time the largest corporate bankruptcy in American history. Among the reasons cited for its collapse were poor execution of the merger, bad management, expensive labor contracts, losses in the real estate market and jet subsidiaries, and the unprofitability of its commuter railroad divisions.

Under Saunders the Penn Central management had employed what *Fortune* magazine called "virtuoso bookkeeping" to conceal the company's losses from its shareholders, directors, and the financial community. By reporting sales of assets as normal income, counting uncollectable freight bills as earnings, listing operating expenditures as capital expenses, and by using other such devices, the Penn Central had inflated its profits by millions of dollars when it was actually losing money. Despite its cash shortage the company paid out $100 million in dividends in its first two years of operations.

In September 1975 Saunders and more than 50 other directors and officers of the bankrupt railroad agreed to pay $12.6 million to its shareholders, debenture holders, and trustees who had sued them for dereliction of duty in issuing false financial statements. Saunders later served as a consultant on transportation issues. He died on February 8, 1987.

—TO

## Savio, Mario
### (1942–1996) *leader, Berkeley Free Speech Movement*

Savio grew up in New York City, where he was born on December 8, 1942, to parents who had emigrated from Italy. After graduation from high school he entered Manhattan College, a school run by the Christian Brothers, but he found it "too parochial" and transferred to Queens College. At Queens he was president of the Fraternity of Christian Doctrine, and he spent the summer of 1963 in the Taxco area of Mexico, helping to build a laundry there to prevent cholera infection. In the fall of 1963 he transferred again, this time to the University of California, Berkeley, where he majored in philosophy.

At Berkeley Savio was dismayed by what he viewed as the depersonalized, regimented quality of the university's operations, and he was attracted to the flourishing student political activity around the campus. Briefly associated with the Young People's Socialist League, he read Marx and was particularly impressed with his concept of alienation as a human response to bureaucratic institutions. In the summer of 1964 Savio taught at one of the Mississippi Freedom Schools and worked as a voter registrar with the Student Nonviolent Coordinating Committee (SNCC). When Savio returned to Berkeley in the fall of 1964, he was elected chair of the University Friends of SNCC. Thus, it was as a leader of one of the several civil rights groups on campus that he took part in the free speech fight that fall.

The conflict arose initially over the university administration's revocation of students' rights to collect money or circulate petitions for political causes on a narrow strip of sidewalk at the south entrance to the campus. Savio and a number of others formed a committee to resist the ban. At first the coalition represented a wide spectrum of student

groups from socialists to Goldwater supporters. After conducting an unsuccessful legal protest, the United Front, as it was called, took direct action by setting up tables in violation of the ban. As a result, on October 1 Savio and seven other students were suspended from the university. That same afternoon Jack Weinberg, a nonstudent member of the campus chapter of the Congress of Racial Equality (CORE), was arrested for sitting at a table in front of the administration building. Students immediately sat down around the police car to prevent his removal. The sit-in attracted thousands, and Savio, speaking from the top of the police car, quickly emerged as the leader of the growing protest. While Weinberg sat in the police car surrounded by the crowd, Savio led a delegation to University president CLARK KERR, who agreed to negotiate the free speech issue, drop charges against Weinberg, and submit the case of the suspended students to a faculty committee, which would determine whether or not the suspensions should stand.

Preparing for a meeting of the university's Board of Regents that was to consider new political regulations and the case of the suspended students, the political groups broadened their base. The new organization called itself the Free Speech Movement (FSM), and Savio was a member to its steering committee. The Regents' meeting of November 20 disappointed student expectations, however, by stipulating that on-campus advocacy of "illegal" off-campus action—civil rights sit-ins—would make their advocates liable to university discipline. The FSM contended that this policy would subject students to double jeopardy, that is, to punishment by both the courts and the campus administration. The students were further aroused at the end of November when the administration, brought charges against Savio and three other FSM leaders for actions committed during the October 1–2 events. Interpreting this move as a hardening of the administration's position, the FSM called a mass rally on December 2. There Savio declared to a crowd of 6,000 that "there is a time when the operation of the machine becomes so odious, makes you so sick at heart, that you can't take part . . . you've got to put your bodies upon the gears and upon the wheels, upon the levers . . . and you've got to make it stop." With that, some 2,000 students occupied Sproul Hall, the administration building. Many, including Savio, elected to stay the night, and early in the morning police evicted and arrested 773 of them in what became the largest mass arrest in the history of California to that date.

On December 3 a campus strike began. It lasted five days and enlisted wide support. As a result, Kerr agreed to a liberalization of political regulations. On December 7 Kerr presented his proposals to 18,000 students and faculty at an outdoor amphitheater. He appeared to have gained some support for his cause of action. But when Savio approached the microphone to attempt to speak, he was grabbed by campus police and hustled off the stage. Although Savio was eventually allowed to speak, the incident angered the audience. At an FSM rally later that day, leading members of the faculty stood with Savio and other student leaders on the steps of Sproul Hall and told thousands of assembled students that "power is in your hands." The faculty, passed a resolution ending the administration's restrictions on political advocacy and demanding that disciplinary authority be taken away from the administration and given to the faculty. Their resolution endorsed most key points in the FSM platform.

The Regents of the University of California, meeting on December 18, refused to grant disciplinary authority to the faculty but acknowledged the primacy of the First and Fourteenth Amendments in future university regulations. They also appointed a new chancellor for the Berkeley campus, who eased a number of restrictions covering student political activity.

Despite the initial success of the FSM, the Berkeley campus administration regained the initiative in the spring of 1965 during the "filthy speech movement," when a group of students demanded the right to publicly display signs bearing vulgar language. By this time the FSM had become dormant, existing only as a committee of the 700 sit-in defendants whose cases were still before the courts. Moreover, there was little student interest in defending the "dirty word" group when its members were disciplined in April. Savio at first called for a protest, then unexpectedly announced that he was withdrawing from campus activity, saying that he did not wish to dominate the movement.

In June 1965 Savio was one of 155 students convicted on charges arising out of the December 2 sit-in. He received the most severe sentence of those convicted—120 days in jail. Forced to leave school for a time, Savio was denied readmission in November 1966 on the ground that he had violated rules prohibiting nonstudents from distributing leaflets on the campus. He participated nevertheless in a sit-in on November 30 protesting the administration's refusal to allow nonstudents to set up an antiwar table next to an authorized navy recruiting table in the student union. The police were called, and Savio and four other nonstudents were arrested. A large but unsuccessful student strike was launched on the following day. In January 1967 Savio was convicted with four others of creating a public nuisance and sentenced to 90 days in jail.

Savio remained for a while in the Berkeley area, but he withdrew from political activity. He taught at an alternative school in Los Angeles during the 1970s. He completed bachelor's and master's degrees at San Francisco State University in the mid-1980s and later taught mathematics and physics at Sonoma State University. He died of a heart attack on November 6, 1996.

—TLH

## Scheer, Robert

(1936–  )  *journalist, congressional candidate*
Scheer grew up in New York City, where he was born on April 14, 1936. He graduated from the City College of New York in 1958 and went to Syracuse University to study economics and public administration. In 1961 he moved to Berkeley, where he continued graduate studies without earning a degree.

During the early 1960s, Scheer became involved in radical politics. He visited Cuba and was impressed with the achievements of Fidel Castro's revolution. He published with coauthor Maurice Zeitlin *Cuba: Tragedy in Our Hemisphere*, which was critical of U.S. policy. He visited Southeast Asia in 1964 and the next year published *How the U.S. Got Involved in Vietnam*, a study that charged that U.S. officials failed to understand the grave problems of the Saigon government. In 1964 he became an editor of *Ramparts* magazine, where he helped expose the relationship between the Central Intelligence Agency and the Michigan State University's police training activities in South Vietnam.

Scheer became involved with the Vietnam Day Committee, centered at the University of California, Berkeley, and used that antiwar group as a base to challenge incumbent representative Jeffrey Cohelan (D-Calif.) in 1966 for the Democratic nomination in a congressional district that included Berkeley and surrounding areas. Although he sought the Democratic nomination in the primary, Scheer emphasized his radical politics. For a time, his campaign manager was the antiwar activist JERRY RUBIN. Scheer asserted that the Vietnam War was the outgrowth of American liberalism and that Cohelan, who had a strong liberal voting record and supported the Johnson administration's war policies, was blindly following the president. Scheer mobilized hundreds of enthusiastic precinct workers as he ran a grassroots campaign that appealed to campus and community activists and that built strength in the black community. Scheer maintained that his campaign was revitalizing democracy by restoring power to ordinary people.

The Scheer campaign attracted national attention and the concern of the Johnson administration. In April Postmaster General LAWRENCE O'BRIEN helped organize a testimonial dinner for Cohelan, at which he received the endorsement of Senator ROBERT F. KENNEDY (D-N.Y.) and Senator J. WILLIAM FULBRIGHT (D-Ark.). On the night of the primary, Johnson's press secretary, BILL MOYERS called election officials in the district several times to see how Cohelan was doing. Scheer lost the nomination, but he drew an impressive 45 percent of the vote. Cohelan admitted that he had won in spite of his position on the war rather than because of it.

An outgrowth of the Scheer campaign was the formation of the Community for New Politics (CNP) in Berkeley and the growth of a larger New Politics movement nationally. The Berkeley CNP was soon split over the issue of independent political action. A minority wanted the immediate creation of a third radical party, while Scheer and other CNP leaders favored continuation of work within the left wing of the Democratic Party. By January 1968, however, after the minority had succeeded in re-registering 100,000 California Democrats into a new Peace and Freedom Party, Scheer himself became an active participant in the new party. In 1970 he was the Peace and Freedom candidate for senator in California.

Scheer continued to be a prominent and prolific journalist. His books included *America After Nixon: The Age of the Multinationals* (1974) and *With Enough Shovels: Reagan, Bush, and Nuclear War* (1982). He conducted the infamous interview with Jimmy Carter published in *Playboy* magazine during the campaign of 1976 in which Carter revealed that he had frequently committed adultery in his heart. Scheer was a national correspondent for the *Los Angeles Times* from 1976 to 1993 and then a contributing editor.

—TLH

## Schlesinger, Arthur M(eier), Jr.
(1917–   ) *historian*

Schlesinger, whose father was a prominent historian, was born on October 15, 1917, in Columbus, Ohio, earned a B.A. from Harvard in 1938, and then joined his father in 1946 as a member of Harvard's history department. He won a Pulitzer Prize for the *Age of Jackson* (1945) and considerable acclaim for his multivolume biography (never completed) of Franklin D. Roosevelt. These works presented both Andrew Jackson and Roosevelt as pragmatic and successful proponents of progressive social change. Schlesinger combined his academic career with involvement in liberal politics. He was a founding member of the Americans for Democratic Action in 1947 and author two years later of *The Vital Center*, a call for a pragmatic, anticommunist, liberal politics that reflected the principles of that organization.

After backing ADLAI STEVENSON in 1952 and 1956, Schlesinger switched his support to John F. Kennedy in 1959 and helped recruit academic advisers for the new president's administration. Kennedy appointed Schlesinger a special assistant in January 1961 and assigned him, among other tasks to work on Latin America affairs. Schlesinger toured South America with Food for Peace director GEORGE MCGOVERN early in the year and argued for the Alliance for Progress as a means both to promote progressive democracy in the hemisphere and to counter the influence of Cuban-backed Communist movements. Although he opposed the Bay of Pigs invasion of Cuba as unwise, Schlesinger helped develop U.S. efforts to economically and politically isolate Fidel Castro's regime from other Western Hemisphere governments.

Two months after Kennedy's assassination Schlesinger resigned his post as a White House special assistant and began work on a history of the administration. His best-selling book, *A Thousand Days: John F. Kennedy in the White House*, was published in 1965 and won the Pulitzer Prize for biography the next year. The work celebrated the youth and vigor of the late president, his unsentimental liberalism, and the sophistication of administration policy makers. In 1966 Schlesinger became Albert Schweitzer Professor of Humanities at the City University of New York.

When the growing escalation of the war in Vietnam aroused debate in the American intellectual and academic community, Schlesinger first defended, albeit with qualifications, the Johnson administration's conduct of the war. At a May 15, 1965, Washington "teach-in" sponsored by opponents of the war, Schlesinger represented the administration in a debate with University of Chicago professor HANS J. MORGENTHAU. Schlesinger argued that the bombing of North Vietnam was counterproductive and advocated a negotiated settlement, but he nevertheless favored sending more troops to Southeast Asia.

Schlesinger's guarded defense of the war turned to a measured opposition by the middle of 1966. Late in the year he published *The Bitter Heritage: Vietnam and American Democracy*, which argued that the war must be stopped because of its "ugly side-effects" at home: "inflation, frustration, indignation, protest, panic, angry divisions within the national community, premonitions of McCarthyism." Schlesinger now favored a gradual de-escalation of the war, with an immediate halt to the bombing. In April 1967 he joined with liberals JOSEPH RAUH and JOHN KENNETH GALBRAITH to form Negotiations Now, a group seeking a million signatures on a stop-the-bombing petition.

Although aligning himself with the growing movement against the war, Schlesinger was careful not to lend his prestige to those in the New Left who attacked the entire thrust of U.S. postwar foreign policy. Schlesinger argued that American involvement in Vietnam resulted not from an inherently expansionary American foreign policy but out of a series of mistakes leading to a military-political quagmire. Writing in the journal *Foreign Affairs* in October 1967, Schlesinger attacked the revisionist historians and argued that because of the character of the Soviet state, the "most rational of American policies could hardly have averted the Cold War."

In 1967 Schlesinger first advised Senator ROBERT F. KENNEDY (D-N.Y.) to avoid a primary battle with President Johnson, instead urging that he throw his weight behind a peace plank at the Democratic National Convention. However, the historian-adviser reversed his position in November after Senator EUGENE MCCARTHY (D-Minn.) announced his candidacy for the Democratic presidential nomination. Schlesinger strongly supported Kennedy when he began his campaign in March. After Kennedy's assassination three months later,

Schlesinger was among those former Kennedy aides who threw their support to Senator George McGovern's (D-S.Dak.) short-lived bid for the Democratic nomination.

During the early 1970s Schlesinger was a leading academic critic of the Nixon administration. His influential 1973 work, *The Imperial Presidency*, attacked the growing centralization of power in the executive branch and cast into a somewhat darker light the increasing power exercised by such liberal presidents as Roosevelt, Kennedy, and Johnson.

—NNL

## Schultze, Charles L(ouis)
(1924– ) *director, Bureau of the Budget*

Charles Schultze was born on December 12, 1924, in Alexandria, Virginia, and earned his B.A. in 1948 from Georgetown University. Studying part-time over the next 12 years, Schultze earned his M.A. in economics from Georgetown in 1950 and his Ph.D. from the University of Maryland in 1960. Over the same period he alternated between college teaching and government service. From 1949 to 1951 he taught economics at the College of St. Thomas in Minnesota, returning to Washington for a year as an economist with the Office of Price Stabilization. For the next six years he was a staff economist on the Council of Economics Advisers. After teaching at Indiana University and the University of Maryland and writing two studies analyzing inflationary trends of the previous decade, Schultze joined the Bureau of the Budget as an assistant director in September 1962. He left in early 1964 but returned as head of the bureau in June 1965.

Schultze applied to the bureau the systems analysis procedures that Secretary of Defense ROBERT MCNAMARA had built into the operations of the Pentagon. Schultze employed the new management techniques to take the bureau beyond its traditional function of calculating government revenues and expenses and allocating resources among the various departments. He installed program evaluation experts in all government agencies to measure the performance as well as the cost of programs and suggest alternatives and improvements in the execution of particular jobs. The new method, known as the "planning-programming-budgeting system," was first used in the preparation of the fiscal 1968 budget. It gave the Budget Bureau a far more active role in the workings of the federal government. *Forbes* magazine praised the new budget as "the first attempt of the U.S. government to figure out in detail what it really is spending the tax dollar for."

As budget director, Schultze along with Secretary of the Treasury HENRY FOWLER and Council of Economic Advisers chairman GARDNER ACKLEY met regularly with President Johnson to shape economic policy. Like Ackley, Schultze was a proponent of the Keynesian "new economics," which held that an active fiscal policy on the part of the federal government was the key to economic growth and stability. During Schultze's tenure the main goal of Johnson's economic advisers was to curb the inflation growing out of spending on the Vietnam War and Great Society social programs.

In the second half of 1967, Schultze played a leading role in the administration's attempt to persuade Congress to pass an anti-inflationary 10 percent tax surcharge. In August 1967 he presented the administration's case for a tax increase before the House Ways and Means Committee. Schultze defended the surcharge as "temporary" and necessary to forestall a possible budget deficit of $25 to $35 billion. He said that "failure to act responsibly" would result in inflation, record-high interest rates, and a worsening of the country's balance of payments difficulties. Schultze also defended the administration's refusal to specify spending cuts until Congress had passed the tax increase.

The Ways and Means Committee rejected the tax rise without budget cuts by a 20-5 vote in October. In November Schultze returned to the committee with the administration's pledge to make $4 billion in budget cuts, but the committee's chair, Representative WILBUR MILLS (D-Ark.), rejected the new proposal as insufficient and not specific enough. The matter stood at an impasse when Schultze resigned from the Budget Bureau in January 1968. The 10 percent tax surcharge combined with $6 billion in spending cuts finally passed Congress in June 1968.

Schultze served as a member of Vice President HUBERT HUMPHREY's economic task force during the vice president's 1968 campaign for the presidency. After leaving the government Schultze became a senior fellow at the Brookings Institution and wrote lengthy analyses of the federal budget during the Nixon administration. He served as chair of the Council of Economic Advisers during the Carter administration.

—TO

## Scott, Hugh D(oggett)
### (1900–1994) *member of the Senate*

Scott, who was born in November 11, 1900, on a plantation in Fredricksburg, Virginia, once owned by George Washington, earned a law degree from the University of Virginia in 1922 and then worked as an attorney in Philadelphia. He entered politics as a Republican and served as Philadelphia's assistant district attorney from 1926 until 1941. He won the first of two consecutive terms in the House of Representatives in 1944. After serving for two years in the navy during World War II, he regained his congressional seat in the election of 1946 and held it for 12 years. In 1948 and 1949 Scott chaired the Republican National Committee, and in 1952 he joined DWIGHT EISENHOWER's personal staff, serving as a chair of the headquarters committee during the presidential campaign. General counsel to the National Committee from 1955 to 1960, Scott was first elected to the Senate in 1958.

Scott, who considered himself a moderate Republican, successfully challenged the conservative Old Guard leadership of the Republican Party in Pennsylvania. In 1962 he helped sponsor the young Representative WILLIAM SCRANTON (R-Pa.) as the Republican candidate for governor in a successful attempt to appeal to the state's electorate.

In 1964 Scott was disturbed by the success of conservative Senator BARRY GOLDWATER's (R-Ariz.) campaign for the Republican presidential nomination. Up for reelection, he feared that a Goldwater candidacy would lead to a big Democratic victory in November in which the Arizona senator would drag other Republicans down to defeat. Scott helped form a "stop-Goldwater" drive, and, in June 1964, after the collapse of New York governor NELSON A. ROCKEFELLER's campaign effort, he successfully urged Governor Scranton to oppose Goldwater for the nomination. In July Scott agreed to serve as Scranton's convention manager. As part of an attempt to weaken the Goldwater forces, Scott sought to add an amendment to the party platform repudiating "irresponsible" extremist groups, such as the John Birch Society, which was specifically named in the amendment. After a bitter convention floor fight, the measure was rejected. After Goldwater's nomination, Scott endorsed the entire Republican ticket, but kept his distance from the party's presidential nominee as he sought to retain his Senate seat. In Pennsylvania, where President LYNDON B. JOHNSON won a large majority, Scott narrowly defeated his liberal Democratic opponent, Genevieve Blatt. After the elections Scott urged replacement of the entire party leadership. For the next four years Scott worked to get the Republican National Committee to adopt moderate positions.

In the Senate Scott was careful to vote along the moderately liberal lines that he thought best reflected his constituency. Although Scott often voted with a small group of Senate Republican moderates, most of whom represented urban northeastern states, he also tried to keep close ties with the Republican majority. Therefore, he was able to play a more influential role in national Republican politics. He also maintained his influence in the Republican Party by occasionally taking up highly partisan issues. As a member of the Senate Judiciary Committee, Scott led Republican forces in 1964 in seeking to expand the investigation of former Johnson aide ROBERT "Bobby" BAKER.

Scott was especially conscious of his black constituency. In June 1964 he voted for cloture on discussion of Johnson's omnibus civil rights bill and supported the bill itself. In this case, unlike many times in the past, he was joined by a majority of Senate Republicans. In July 1965 Scott was one of only seven Republicans to vote for the administration's omnibus housing bill, which because it offered federal subsidies to low-income families, was condemned as "socialistic" by many Republicans. In 1968 he enthusiastically supported the open housing bill.

Scott generally supported the Johnson administration's Vietnam policies during 1965–67, although he, at times, warned against actions that might bring the People's Republic of China into the war. Still, Scott voted for the 1966 Vietnam War funds appropriations and never advocated unilateral U.S. withdrawal.

Although Scott originally backed Nelson Rockefeller for the 1968 Republican presidential nomination, he later worked hard for RICHARD NIXON. In September 1969 Scott was elected minority leader. In 1970 he was again narrowly reelected to the Senate. Charges that he had been receiving an annual fee from the Gulf Oil Corp., influenced his decision to seek another term in 1976. He practiced law in Washington, D.C., from 1977 until 1987. He died on July 21, 1994. (See *The Nixon Years* Volume)

—JCH

## Scranton, William W(arren)
(1917–   ) *governor*

Scranton was born into a wealthy Pennsylvania family on July 19, 1917, while his family was vacationing in Madison, Connecticut. He attended the Hotchkiss School and earned a B.A. from Yale in 1939. He began law school at Yale, but enlisted in the U. S. Army Air Forces in October 1941 before completing his studies. After World War II, he finished his law degree in 1946 and then joined a law firm in the city of Scranton. His work in Republican politics gained him an appointment in 1959 as special assistant to Secretary of State John Foster Dulles, a position that continued with Dulles's successor, Christian A. Herter. Scranton ran for Congress in 1960 and defeated his incumbent Democratic opponent. Two years later, he was a solid victor in the Pennsylvania gubernatorial election. His triumph soon led to speculation that he would seek the Republican presidential nomination.

During the spring of 1964 moderate Republicans turned to Scranton as a potential nominee as conservative senator BARRY GOLDWATER's (R-Ariz.) strength increased and other liberal or middle-of-the-road GOP candidates faltered. Scranton appeared the only candidate capable of rallying party moderates to halt the Goldwater nomination drive. Through the spring of 1964, however, Scranton had declared himself unavailable for the nomination. He had actively discouraged primary write-in efforts on his behalf and fared poorly in preference polls of Republican voters.

In the week following Goldwater's June 2 California primary victory, Scranton determined to seek the nomination, buoyed in part by what he thought was the endorsement of former president DWIGHT D. EISENHOWER offered in a June 6 meeting at the General's Gettysburg, Pennsylvania, farm. With national newspaper headlines announcing Eisenhower's support, the Pennsylvania governor prepared to make his candidacy official on the nationally televised *Face the Nation* program the next day. A few hours before the telecast, Eisenhower phoned Scranton and informed him that he could not be part of any "cabal" to stop Goldwater. In the ensuing confusion Scranton declined to announce his official candidacy. The telecast was, in the words of his own staff, "a complete and utter bomb." Four days later Scranton declared his candidacy, following Goldwater's vote against cloture in the Senate debate on the 1964 civil rights bill and a more encouraging telephone call from Eisenhower.

Despite his apparent irresolution Scranton's strength among Republican voters rose dramatically with his official entry in the campaign. His standing in Gallup polls of GOP members rose from, 5 percent in May to 15 percent in late June. Paired directly against Goldwater with no other candidates listed, Scranton led his rival 55 percent to 34 percent. The governor criticized Goldwater's "recklessness" and "philosophy of shoot-from-the-hip rather than think-from-from-the-head." Scranton strongly endorsed the 1964 Civil Rights Act, which Goldwater voted against. Although the Pennsylvania governor won endorsements from Rockefeller, Lodge, and much of the Republican "Eastern Establishment" and spent over $800,000 in a month-long search for convention support, he captured few of the more than 600 delegates already pledged to Goldwater. Scranton had hoped that key midwestern leaders would keep their delegations pledged to favorite-son candidates, but Ohio governor JAMES A. RHODES's release of his delegation to Goldwater on July 9 effectively ended the Pennsylvanian's dim prospects.

When the Republican convention met in San Francisco on July 13, Scranton's staff composed a highly controversial open letter to Goldwater demanding a public debate between the two candidates. The letter, which accused the Arizona senator's managers of regarding the delegates as "little more than a flock of chickens whose necks will be wrung at will," merely increased Goldwater's ranks. Goldwater won the nomination on the first ballot with 883 votes to Scranton's 214.

Although Scranton immediately endorsed and later campaigned for Goldwater, the bitterness of the pre-convention clash weakened the party's campaign effort. As late as June Goldwater had considered Scranton as his vice presidential running mate, but at the convention the Republican presidential candidate instead chose the little-known conservative representative WILLIAM E. MILLER (R-N.Y.).

After Goldwater's disastrous showing in November, Scranton called for the exclusion of right-wing and racial extremists from the GOP. In August 1965 Scranton warned that "there is a radical fringe which should never find a spiritual home in either of America's two great political parties, and the Republican Party ought to stop the hopeless task of trying to accommodate them." Barred by state law from a second gubernatorial term, Scranton told reporters in June 1966 that he would not

run "ever again for any public office under any circumstances." Scranton's unqualified renunciation removed him from speculation over the 1968 Republican ticket. Instead, in August 1967 he announced his support of George Romney for the presidential nomination.

Scranton visited the Middle East for President-elect RICHARD NIXON in December 1968. At the Jordan River he told reporters that the United States should follow a "more evenhanded" policy toward Israel and its Arab antagonists. His remark set off a protest by Israeli leaders, some of whom feared that the new administration would limit America's commitment to Israel. A Nixon aide denied that Scranton spoke for the incoming administration, yet the ex-governor refused to retract his comment and insisted that new administration correct "the impression in the Middle East" that the United States "is only interested in Israel." President GERALD FORD named Scranton ambassador to the United Nations in 1976, a position he held until January 1977.

—JLB

## Seaborg, Glenn T(heodore)
(1912–1999) *chemist; chair, U.S. Atomic Energy Commission*

Born on April 19, 1912, in Ishpeming, Michigan, to parents who were Swedish immigrants, Seaborg moved with his family to California when he was 10 and graduated from the University of California, Los Angeles, in 1934. He earned a Ph.D. in chemistry in 1937 from the University of California, Berkeley, and then joined the faculty there. He led a team of researchers that in 1941 discovered plutonium, the heaviest known element at the time, and which was a source of fissionable material for nuclear energy. He joined the Manhattan Project's work on the atomic bomb in 1941 and served on the Atomic Energy Commission's (AEC) general advisory board from 1946 to 1950. Returning to Berkeley after the war, his research uncovered several more transuranium elements. Seaborg won the 1951 Nobel Prize for chemistry and the AEC's 1959 Enrico Fermi Award.

President Kennedy appointed Seaborg to head the AEC in 1961, and he was soon involved in a controversy over the possible separation of the commission's operational and regulatory functions. Seaborg held that separation was possible within the agency at the management level, a position that the Joint Congressional Committee on Atomic Energy later approved. Following the resumption of nuclear tests by the Soviet Union in September 1961 he advocated resumption of U.S. atmospheric tests, but he testified in favor of the nuclear test ban treaty when Senate hearings were held in August 1963.

The responsibilities of the AEC, whose annual appropriations approached $2.5 billion, expanded greatly in the 1960s. In March 1965 Seaborg urged a subcommittee of the Joint Congressional Committee to approve a 15-year program for developing more powerful atom smashers at a proposed cost of $6 billion. The AEC announced its selection in December 1966 of Weston, Illinois, as the site for a 200 bev (billion electron volt) atom smasher to be built over the next eight years. He also told the committee in March 1965 that the AEC and the state of California had agreed to develop a prototype "seed-blanket" reactor, which might also include an experimental plant for desalination.

In January 1965 Seaborg told the Joint Congressional Committee that the United States should support Plowshare, an international program for developing peaceful uses of atomic energy. Warning of the dangers of nuclear proliferation in July 1965, Seaborg urged an agreement "to stop the spread of nuclear weapons to additional countries beyond the five that have them." The AEC withdrew authorization for private research into the gas-centrifuge method of obtaining enriched uranium in March 1967. This was viewed as part of the commission's effort to prevent nonnuclear nations from obtaining information on the techniques for producing fissionable atomic material. The United States would supply other nations' atomic fuel needs, Seaborg asserted. In June the AEC signed a contract to this effect with a private nuclear power plant in Sweden. The AEC agreed to process and supply enriched uranium for the plant, ant it was hoped that other nations might be dissuaded from building their own uranium plants.

In the late 1960s critics of the AEC raised questions about the health and safety of atomic workers and residents of areas near atomic plants. Hearings held by the Department of Labor indicated that uranium miners were suffering from a "cancer epidemic," and a near-disaster occurred in October 1966 at a Lagoona Beach, Michigan, plant. A nuclear reactor there overheated and began leaking radiation, leading some scientists to doubt the effec-

tiveness of existing safeguards. Another issue that aroused great public concern was the disposal of potentially dangerous radioactive waste. A 1966 national Academy of Sciences review condemned the AEC's disposal practices, but the AEC did not release this report to the public until 1970.

Seaborg remained chair of the AEC until 1971, when he returned to the University of California. He died on February 25, 1999.

—MDB

## Seale, Bobby (Robert George)
(1936–    ) *chair, Black Panther Party*

Bobby Seale was born into a poor family on October 22, 1936, in Dallas, Texas. The family moved several times before settling in Oakland, California. He dropped out of high school to enlist in the air force but was court-martialed and given a dishonorable discharge. After returning to Oakland, Seale finished high school and enrolled in Merritt College, a two-year institution. While attending Merritt, Newton met HUEY NEWTON, a fellow student

Bobby Seale (left) chair of the Black Panther Party and Huey Newton in a poster *(Library of Congress, Prints and Photographs Division)*

who shared Seale's outrage over racial discrimination and police brutality. They borrowed the name of the black political party in Lowndes County, Alabama, that STOKELY CARMICHAEL had created a few months earlier. In October 1966, they founded the Black Panther Party for Self-Defense, with Seale as chair and Newton as minister of defense.

Begun as a grassroots organization in Oakland, the Panthers sought to protect African Americans from police intimidation and violence and to improve conditions of life in the black community. They demanded improved housing, education, and employment opportunities. They also compared the condition of African Americans to colonial peoples and called for liberation through revolution, if necessary. Wearing black berets and leather jackets and openly carrying guns (which was legal at the time under California law), the Black Panthers patrolled Oakland streets to monitor police. The party was generally unknown outside the Bay Area until May 2, 1967, when 30 armed Panthers marched into the California Assembly to protest a gun-control measure then under consideration. Such defiant and confrontational actions gained national attention and helped the Panthers establish chapters in more than 30 cities by the end of the 1960s.

Though an all-black organization, the Panthers welcomed cooperation with white radicals. Seale sought to establish contacts with other radical movements. In 1968 the Panthers joined several white radical groups to form the Peace and Freedom Party.

Seale went to Chicago in August 1968 to participate in demonstrations at the Democratic National Convention; he later became one of the famous "Chicago Eight" who were indicted for violating the antiriot provision of the new Civil Rights Act. The trial, which began in 1969, became a radical cause célèbre. For his repeated outbursts against the judge, Seale was at one point ordered gagged and bound to his chair. On November 5 Seale was sentenced to four years in prison for contempt of court, and his case was severed from that of the others. The government later requested, however, that the charges against him be dropped.

With Newton in jail from 1968 to 1970 for the shooting of a police officer, Seale took a greater part in internal Panther affairs. In early 1969 he announced a drive to rid the Panthers of "provocateur agents, kooks and avaricious fools" seeking to use the organization for their own purposes. (It was

later revealed that the Federal Bureau of Investigation had, in fact, placed agents in the Panthers in an attempt to disrupt the organization.) In 1971 Seale went on trial in New Haven, Connecticut, on charges of ordering the 1969 execution of a Panther member suspected of being a government informer. The trial began in March and again aroused the anger of many radicals, who accused the government of trying to "get Bobby." When the jury failed to reach a verdict in May, the judge dismissed the charges against Seale, claiming that "massive publicity" made a new trial impossible.

Free from legal entanglements, Seale returned to Oakland and leadership of the Panthers. He cooperated with Newton in reorienting the party from "armed defense" to community action projects, such as health clinics for inner-city residents and a free breakfast program for school children. In 1973 Seale ran for mayor of Oakland as a Democrat, finishing second among nine candidates with 43,710 votes. Although the Black Panther Party ceased to exist by the early 1980s, Seale continued to be involved with various groups opposing political or social injustices.

## Shanker, Albert

(1928–1997)  *president, United Federation of Teachers; vice president, American Federation of Teachers*

Shanker was born on September 18, 1928, in New York City. He became politically active as a member of the Young People's Socialist League at the University of Illinois, where he earned a B.A. in 1949. While still a graduate student in philosophy and mathematics at Columbia University, Shanker began working in 1952 as a substitute teacher in the New York City school system. He soon abandoned his studies, took a permanent teaching position, and became active in the Teachers Guild, the New York affiliate of the American Federation of Teachers (AFT).

Shanker worked closely with AFT organizer David Selden to enlarge and strengthen the small union and was hired as a full-time AFT organizer in 1959. In March 1960 he helped merge a militant high school teachers group with the Guild to form the United Federation of Teachers (UFT). A one-day strike by 5,000 UFT members in November 1960 forced the New York City school board to hold a union recognition election the next year. The

UFT decisively won the election and, against the advice of Shanker and other leaders, successfully struck for higher wages in April 1962. These early strikes attracted 53,000 new members to the AFT, over half in New York City.

In May 1964 Shanker was elected UFT president. He negotiated in September of the next year a contract settlement that gave teachers an average annual increase of $800 in wages and benefits. Although wages were also involved in the negotiations for a new contract in 1967, it was primarily the inability to agree on noneconomic issues that led to a 14-day strike that September. The Board of Education sought to reduce teacher preparation time in elementary schools, change sick-leave provisions, and gain greater control over teacher assignments, while the UFT wanted an expansion of the More Effective Schools (MES) program for elementary school compensatory education, smaller teaching loads and classes, and authority for teachers to remove disruptive students from their classrooms.

The strike was settled on September 28, and the Board of Education agreed to set aside $10 million for the development of new programs for elementary schools but did not commit itself specifically to an extension of the MES program. On October 4 the UFT was fined $150,000 for violating New York State's recently passed Taylor Law prohibiting strikes by public employees. Shanker was convicted of contempt of court for violating an injunction barring the strike, and, on December 20, he began serving a 15-day sentence.

The 1967 strike, the first extended strike by New York's regular teachers, was followed within a year by a series of strikes over issues related to school decentralization. In July 1967 the Board of Education, under pressure from parents and community leaders in Harlem and elsewhere, had established three demonstration school districts in which local school boards were given some of the power previously exercised by the central board. The districts were all in predominantly poor, nonwhite neighborhoods, but they were widely viewed as a test for a possible future citywide school decentralization plan. One such plan was proposed in November 1967 by a panel headed by Ford Foundation president MCGEORGE BUNDY. The Bundy proposal would have given local school boards the power to hire new teachers and make future tenure decisions. Various government agencies and other private groups proposed other decentralization plans as well during

that winter and spring, encouraged by Mayor JOHN V. LINDSAY, who actively supported decentralization.

The UFT initially cooperated with decentralization planning, but it opposed any plan that eliminated central Board of Education control over the hiring and firing of teachers. The union feared that teachers' working conditions and job security would be threatened by powerful local school boards. In the existing experimental districts relations between the UFT and the local boards had seriously deteriorated during the 1967 strike.

In May 1968 the governing board of the largest of the three demonstration districts, Ocean Hill–Brownsville in Brooklyn, a predominantly African-American area, ordered 13 tenured teachers and six supervisors transferred out of the district. The district administrator, Rhody McCoy, charged that the 19 were trying to "sabotage" the decentralization experiment. The Board of Education said the transfers were illegal, but when it tried to overrule the local board, a series of community boycotts and demonstrations began. The UFT claimed that the transfers violated a contractual right to due process, and 350 teachers in the district struck for the last five weeks of the school year, demanding that the transfers be rescinded. In late May, in the middle of the Ocean Hill–Brownsville controversy, Shanker led a massive UFT lobbying effort in Albany that successfully defeated an attempt to pass a strong citywide decentralization bill, and a much weaker compromise measure was approved.

Beginning on September 9 the UFT called a series of three citywide strikes to protest the transfer of the Ocean Hill–Brownsville teachers and to seek changes in the Board of Education's interim decentralization plan. On the eve of the strikes Shanker said, "Decentralization is fine but not at the expense of the rights we have won and not with the smashing of the union." The final and longest of the strikes ended on November 19 with an agreement by the city to reinstate the transferred teachers and give authority over Ocean Hill–Brownsville to a state trustee.

Shanker was convicted of contempt of court in February 1969 for defying court orders during the 1968 strikes. He appealed his case to the Supreme Court on the ground that he had been denied a jury trial. The Court upheld the conviction, and Shanker began serving a 15-day sentence on May 15, 1970.

The 1968 strikes resulted in a dramatic increase in racial tension in the New York area. Shanker made a major issue out of alleged black anti-Semitism when he had the UFT reproduce and widely circulate anti-Semitic material originally distributed in the Ocean Hill–Brownsville area. His critics suggested the union's actions reflected white indifference or hostility to minorities, a charge that particularly rankled Shanker since he was a member of the Congress of Racial Equality and a participant in several civil rights demonstrations during the 1960s. Teacher-parent relations deteriorated when many parents, often with the help of nonstriking teachers, set up their own schools, sometimes crossing UFT picket lines or breaking into locked schools to do so. New York's liberal and intellectual communities were spilt over the strike.

Although Shanker emerged from the strike a controversial figure, the majority of the UFT membership strongly backed his leadership, and opposition groups within the union were isolated and ineffective. In addition to heading the UFT, Shanker was the most powerful figure in the UFT's parent union, the AFT, since he headed the largest local in the union. In 1974 Shanker was elected president of the union. He died of cancer on February 22, 1997.

## Sharp, Ulysses S. Grant, Jr.

(1906–2001) *commander of U.S. armed forces in the Pacific*

A distant relative of his namesake, Sharp was born in Chinook, Montana, on April 2, 1906. He graduated from Annapolis in 1927, commanded destroyers during World War II, and advanced through the ranks until in 1963 he became commander in chief of the U.S. Pacific Fleet. In July 1964 he was designated commander of all U.S. military operations in the Pacific.

On August 2, and again on August 4, 1964, U.S. ships in the Gulf of Tonkin reported attacks by North Vietnamese vessels. Evidence of the first attack was incontrovertible. But evidence of the second, based largely on radar and sonar readings, was equivocal. Secretary of Defense ROBERT S. MCNAMARA telephoned Sharp at his headquarters in Honolulu and told Sharp that he did not want to launch a retaliatory strike after the alleged second attack "until we are damn sure what happened." Sharp called back less than two hours later to say he was certain that the U.S. vessels had been attacked. Later investigations indicate, however, that the

August 4 attack never occurred. Nevertheless, President Johnson, with McNamara's support, ordered air strikes against North Vietnamese shipping and coastal installations.

In December 1964 the Joint Chiefs of Staff ordered Sharp to begin making plans for future air strikes against North Vietnam. National Liberation Front units attacked a U.S. military installation at Pleiku on February 7, 1965, and three days later shelled the American installation at Qui Nhon. American bombers once again attacked the North; Significantly, the raids were linked not to any particular incident but to "the larger pattern of aggression of North Vietnam." In a memorandum dated February 17, 1965, Admiral Sharp argued that the raids should be conceived of not as reprisals but as "pressure . . . to convince Hanoi and Peiking of the prohibitive cost of their program of subversion, insurgency, and aggression in Southeast Asia." In February air raids over the North were sporadic, but by mid-March they had become routine. Operation Rolling Thunder, the air war against North Vietnam, had begun.

On March 21 Sharp recommended that bombing be undertaken not simply to demoralize the North Vietnamese but to cut their strategic supply lines to the South. This proposal also won the approval of the Johnson administration.

During 1965 Sharp, along with General WILLIAM WESTMORELAND, commander of U.S. troops in Vietnam, urged a major expansion of the American involvement in the ground war. On February 24, 1965, Sharp urged the Joint Chiefs to immediately deploy two Marine battalions and one fighter squadron to South Vietnam to prevent the "tragedy" of a catastrophic Communist attack at Da Nang. This request was opposed by U.S. ambassador to South Vietnam MAXWELL D. TAYLOR, who argued that the deployment of combat troops would only lead to requests for more troops, and that two battalions would not significantly alter the military situation. Nevertheless, on March 8, 3,500 U.S. marines landed at Da Nang. In subsequent months Sharp supported requests by Westmoreland that troops be sent to various strategic bases along the Vietnamese coast and into the central highlands. Sharp requested another 75 battalions in December, and continued to call for additional troops in 1966 and 1967.

Throughout 1966 and 1967 Sharp recommended that the Johnson administration permit

American pilots to bomb a wider range of targets in North Vietnam–oil refineries, electric power stations, industrial plants, and the harbor at Haiphong. Gradually, the number of targets was increased. However, within the Defense Department, McNamara and other civilians doubted that bombing could effectively destroy the ability of the North to make war or send troops and material to the South. In the summer of 1966 McNamara proposed that a series of electric sensors and land mines be constructed near the Demilitarized Zone as a barrier to prevent infiltration of enemy troops from the North. Admiral Sharp denounced the idea as "impractical" and thought its implementation would be used to justify reduction or elimination of the air war.

Sharp consistently maintained that the North Vietnamese would negotiate only if they were incapable of waging war. Sharp opposed all the bombing halts called by the Johnson administration during the course of the war.

Sharp retired in the summer of 1968 to become a consultant to the president of Teledyne Ryan Aeronautics Company of San Diego, California. He criticized the Johnson administration and particularly Secretary McNamara for imposing restrictions on the use of force that, in his view, prevented a U.S. victory in Vietnam. The title of his 1978 book summarized his main argument: *Strategy for Defeat: Vietnam in Retrospect.* He died on December 12, 2001.

—JLW

## Shelton, Robert M(arvin), Jr.

(1929–2003) *imperial wizard, United Klans of America, Inc.; Knights of the Ku Klux Klan*

Born in Tuscaloosa, Alabama, on June 12, 1929, Shelton worked in a tire manufacturing plant and as a tire seller in the 1960s while serving as an Alabama officer of the Ku Klux Klan.

In the spring of 1960 he was ousted from his position and then formed a competing organization, known as the United Klans of America. Factional disputes led to defections to Shelton's new organization. Shelton also recruited new members angered by the growth of the civil rights movement in the early 1960s and the passage of the Civil Rights Act of 1964 and the Voting Rights Act of 1965. By the mid-1960s Shelton's United Klans was the largest and best organized of the Klan groups.

The B'nai Brith Anti-Defamation League estimated it had between 26,000 and 33,000 members.

Shelton stated that the fundamental purpose of the Klan was to preserve "white" civilization by resisting integration. He denied, however, that the Klan espoused violence, contending that the group pursued its goal by educating its members, supporting political candidates, and promoting white voter registration. Shelton tried to improve the image of the Klan by opening its meetings to outsiders and seeking middle-class recruits.

However, members of the various Klan groups were implicated in a number of acts of violence against civil rights workers in the mid-1960s. In March 1965 Mrs. Viola Liuzzo, a civil rights worker, was shot and killed in a car during the Selma to Montgomery march. Four members of the United Klans were arrested in connection with the murder.

President Johnson responded to the slaying and arrests by denouncing the Klan as a "hooded society of bigots," and the House Un-American Activities Committee (HUAC) began an investigation of the Klan in October 1965.

Shelton was the first witness called before the committee. He appeared but refused its request to produce Klan records. In January 1966 the committee cited him for contempt of Congress. The House supported the contempt citation the next month by a vote of 344 to 28, with most of the opposition coming from liberal representatives who had sought HUAC's abolition. In October 1966 Shelton was convicted in federal court and sentenced to one year in jail and a $10,000 fine. The following September, while Shelton was appealing the verdict, he was reelected imperial wizard at a national "Klanvocation" of the United Klans.

The U.S. Supreme Court upheld Shelton's conviction in January 1969, and he began serving his prison sentence the following month. By the time Shelton was released from jail in November 1970, the United Klans' membership had declined substantially from its peak. In 1987 a civil suit in Alabama against the United Klans arising from lynching of an African-American teenager resulted in a judgment of $7 million against the organization and the transfer of ownership of the United Klans's national headquarters to the mother of the victim. By the mid-1990s Shelton told a journalist that the Klan had forever vanished. Shelton died of a heart attack on March 17, 2003.

—MLL

## Shoup, David M(onroe)

(1904–1983) *commandant, U.S. Marine Corps*

Shoup, who was born on December 30, 1904, in Battle Ground, Indiana, attended DePauw University and enrolled in the Reserve Officer Training Corps mainly because it provided a stipend. Commissioned as a second lieutenant in the marines in 1926, he fought in the Pacific during World War II, earning the Medal of Honor for his heroic actions during the Battle of Tarawa in 1943. He became the marines' first fiscal director in 1953 and the corps's first inspector general of recruit training in 1956. In 1959 President DWIGHT D. EISENHOWER passed over nine generals with more seniority to nominate him as commandant of the marine corps.

In this position Shoup thought his main role was to insure that the marines were ready to undertake any mission that the president might ask them to perform. He did, however, offer advice on some policy matters. He thought the proposed invasion of Cuba, which President John F. Kennedy authorized in April 1961 at the Bay of Pigs operation, was militarily unfeasible because of the inadequacy of the troops. He also counseled against an invasion of Cuba during the missile crisis of October 1962, drawing on his experience at Tarawa to warn of unanticipated difficulties and high casualties. He also had reservations about the growing U.S. commitment to South Vietnam. In August 1963 he declared his support of the limited nuclear test ban treaty provided there was sophisticated equipment to monitor violations and resources available to resume atmospheric testing promptly, if necessary. Shoup retired from the marines in late 1963.

During the mid-1960s Shoup became a prominent critic of President Johnson's military policies in South Vietnam. Speaking in Los Angeles on May 14, 1966, he declared, "If we had and would keep our dirty, bloody, dollar-crooked fingers" out of the affairs of exploited nations like Vietnam, "they will arrive at a solution of their own," not one "crammed down their throats by Americans." In a radio interview with Representative WILLIAM F. RYAN (D-N.Y.) in December 1967, Shoup asserted that all of Southeast Asia was not worth "the life or limb of a single American." He described the war as a civil conflict between "those crooks in Saigon" and Vietnamese nationals striving for a better life. In December 1967 Shoup urged President Johnson to announce that American military operations would cease when peace talks started and to ask North Vietnamese president Ho Chi Minh to set the time and place for negotiations. He cautioned that the United States could achieve a military victory over North Vietnam but only by committing "genocide on that poor little country."

Increasingly, Shoup became critical of what he believed to be growing military interference in civilian policy-making decisions. In 1969 he warned that the military leadership of the United States was turning the country into a "militaristic and aggressive nation." He asserted that many of the policies of the Vietnam War were due to the military's desire for glory and that the lack of credibility in reporting the war could be traced to the "hocus pocus" of the armed forces. He died on January 13, 1983.

—EWS

## Shriver, R(obert) Sargent, Jr.

(1915– ) *director, Office of Economic Opportunity; ambassador to France*

Born on November 9, 1915, into a wealthy and socially prominent Maryland family, Shriver, grew up in Westminster Maryland, the place of his birth. He earned a B.A. from Yale in 1941 and a law degree three years later. After serving in the navy during World War II, he worked for Joseph P. Kennedy as assistant manager of the Chicago Merchandise Mart. Shriver married Kennedy's daughter Eunice in 1953 and served on the Chicago Board of Education from 1955 to 1960. During that period he became active in Democratic politics; when his brother-in-law, Senator John F. Kennedy, ran for president in 1960, Shriver served as a liaison between various offices of the campaign staff. He became the first director of the Peace Corps when it was established in 1961.

Shriver remained at the head of the Peace Corps until 1966. He assumed new responsibilities in 1964, however, in connection with President Johnson's War on Poverty. Eager to dramatize his commitment to improving the circumstances of the nation's poor, Johnson decided to create a new federal agency devoted entirely to poverty problems. Shriver, whose work with the Peace Corps had given him experience in setting up this type of innovative agency, was the president's choice to establish the new organization. On February 1, 1964, Johnson named Shriver director of the Office of Economic Opportunity (OEO).

Shriver not only had to launch the organization but also to define its role. Shriver, backed by

Johnson, argued that the antipoverty effort could not succeed simply by increasing the levels of federal assistance; new approaches were needed to mobilize public support and especially to stimulate the poor themselves. Shriver also recognized the necessity of pacifying the many members of Congress and state and local officials who feared that the OEO would develop into a huge, centrally directed "poverty bureaucracy."

These considerations were among those leading to the creation of OEO's Community Action Program (CAP), an effort to encourage participation by local leaders and poor people in the planning and execution of antipoverty projects. CAP supervisor Jack Conway, appointed Shriver's deputy in October 1964, channeled OEO funds into a number of community-based activities, ranging from job training and preschool education to health clinics and legal-aid services. Some of these projects were directed by local officials, others by community groups; most were experimental, and many failed

to achieve their objectives. Nevertheless, Shriver preferred community action to centrally administered forms of assistance, because the former involved a maximum number of politicians and civic leaders in the work of OEO.

At the height of antipoverty spending under the Johnson administration, community action projects absorbed over half of OEO's $2 billion budget. Other programs sponsored by OEO included the Job Corps, which provided work and training for unemployed teenagers, and VISTA (Volunteers in Service to America), which enlisted young people to work in projects helping Indians, migrant farm workers, the Appalachian poor, and other minority groups.

OEO began its work in 1964 amidst great official optimism. Problems soon arose, however, that opened the program to attack from both within and without. Increased military spending in Vietnam after 1965 meant that the amount of funds available to poverty projects remained static or

President Johnson and Sargent Shriver in a meeting, 1965 *(Photographed by Yoichi R. Okamoto; Lyndon Baines Johnson Library)*

declined. The OEO budget for 1967, originally set at $4 billion, was cut by Congress to $1.75 billion. Congress and critics lambasted the OEO's unorthodox programs and experimental efforts that sometimes did not produce results. Senator EVERETT DIRKSEN (R-Ill.), the Republican minority leader, denounced the antipoverty program as "the very acme of waste and extravagance and unorganization and disorganization."

In addition to such external criticism, OEO had to cope with internal bureaucratic conflicts that developed among agencies competing for the same antipoverty funds. The large number of politicians and community leaders whom Shriver had involved in the OEO became a liability when the time came to apportion the agency's limited budget. OEO itself, moreover, was constantly in conflict with the established federal and state bureaucracies that had administered assistance programs before the War on Poverty.

Among those most disillusioned with the War on Poverty were some of the poor themselves, especially those who had helped to organize community action projects. Encouraged by Johnson and Shriver to expect the rapid elimination of poverty problems, representatives of the poor were enraged to find these problems not only remaining but in some cases worsening. Many community workers blamed the shortcomings of the antipoverty program—including budget cuts and inadequate funding—on OEO and Shriver. Yet despite these criticisms and the difficulties OEO encountered, the poverty rate declined from 19 percent of the population in 1964 to 13 percent in 1968 partly because of the War on Poverty.

In February 1968 Shriver left the OEO to accept an appointment as ambassador to France. He served in that position until March 1970, when he took up private law practice in Washington and New York. In 1972 Shriver ran for vice president on the Democratic ticket with Senator GEORGE MCGOVERN (D-S.Dak.). He made an unsuccessful bid for the Democratic presidential nomination in 1976.

—SLG

## Shuman, Charles B(aker)

(1907–1999) *president, American Farm Bureau Federation*

Shuman was born in Sullivan, Illinois, on April 27, 1907, and grew up on the family farm. He earned a bachelor's degree in 1928 and a master's degree the

following year from the University of Illinois and began to participate in farm organization activities during the 1930s. He became the president of the American Farm Bureau Federation in 1954, a position he held for 16 years. An opponent of government controls on agriculture, he supported Secretary of Agriculture Ezra Taft Benson's policy of flexible price supports during the Eisenhower administration. He insisted, though, that the elimination of all price supports would be preferable and that farmers would flourish without government intervention.

The Farm Bureau, with a membership of 1.8 million farm families in 1968, was a far larger and more rapidly growing organization than its rivals, the National Farmers Union (NFU) and the National Grange. Although Shuman stated that the Farm Bureau's membership was representative of the American farming community, some observers noted that it included many whose wealth and large landholdings inclined them to oppose government controls. In contrast, members of the NFU and the Grange tended to own small and medium-size farms.

Shuman was a severe critic of President Johnson's secretary of agriculture, ORVILLE FREEMAN, who had also served under President Kennedy. Controls and price supports continued to constitute the central area of disagreement between Shuman and Freeman, who usually had the support of the NFU and the Grange. When Johnson and Freeman proposed in February 1968 to make price-support programs permanent in order to protect farmers with small holdings, Shuman charged that "the administration wants to continue to drive down farm prices and make farmers dependent on government subsidies for a large share of their net income."

Shuman also criticized the administration's program of providing technological farm aid to underdeveloped countries. In 1965 he said that a condition for such aid should be the willingness of recipient nations to "replace government management with a market price system." He added that "too often our foreign aid programs have been tied to social reform when the critical need was for economic reform."

In the heated political atmosphere of the 1960s, Shuman spoke out on issues not usually associated with traditional farm policy. At the Farm Bureau's national convention in December 1968, Shuman successfully urged the delegates to pass a resolution condemning the national boycott of California table grapes initiated by CESAR CHAVEZ's United Farm

Workers Organizing Committee. In addition, he suggested that Farm Bureau members not patronize stores agreeing to union boycott demands. The convention then voted to "strongly oppose extension of the National Labor Relations Act to agriculture." The convention also took a critical position on anti-war activists, advocating the expulsion from college of students who engaged "in lawlessness" and of faculty members who supported such activity and recommended reenactment of the loyalty oath requirement for recipients of federal scholarships.

As on previous occasions, charges that the Farm Bureau was a tool of big business surfaced in June and July 1967, when Representative Joseph Y. Resnick (D-N.Y.), chair of the House Agriculture Committee's Rural Development Subcommittee, sought to undertake an investigation of the organization. Resnick charged that the Farm Bureau, "the fifth largest lobby in Washington," had a substantial nonfarm membership and that is was "gigantic interlocking, nationwide combine of insurance companies with total assets of over $1 billion." Resnick pointed out that Shuman was also president of the American Agricultural Mutual Insurance Company and Farm Bureau Mutual Funds, Inc. In an official response the Farm Bureau's secretary-treasurer, Roger Fleming, argued that the insurance companies were developed to serve the needs of members. Fleming also stated that while Shuman actually headed six other organizations not cited by Resnick, he drew compensation only from his position with the Farm Bureau. Though unsupported by his subcommittee, Resnick conducted his own hearings in August in Chicago, Omaha, and Washington but with little result.

Shuman retired from the presidency of the American Farm Bureau Federation in 1970, but he remained active on the boards of a number of agencies and companies, including the Export-Import Bank, the Economic Development Administration, the Illinois Power Company, and the Chicago Mercantile Exchange. He died on October 24, 1999.

—JCH

## Shuttlesworth, Fred(die) L(ee)
(1922–   ) *secretary, Southern Christian Leadership Conference; president, Alabama Christian Movement for Human Rights*
Born on March 18, 1922, in Mt. Meigs, Alabama, Freddie Lee Robinson had his mother's surname

until she married William Nathan Shuttlesworth five years later. Ordained a Baptist minister in 1948, he was pastor to congregations in Selma, Alabama, and then in Birmingham. He helped organize the Alabama Christian Movement for Human Rights (ACMHR) in 1956 and, as its president, led efforts to integrate Birmingham's schools and buses. In September 1957, when he tried to enroll his daughters at an all-white Birmingham high school, a mob assaulted him with baseball bats and bicycle chains. Shuttlesworth also was a founder of the Southern Christian Leadership Conference (SCLC) in 1957 and became its secretary. Although he became pastor of a Baptist church in Cincinnati in 1961, Shuttlesworth remained president of the ACMHR, a leader of Birmingham's integration movement and an aide to SCLC president MARTIN LUTHER KING, JR. In May 1962 Shuttlesworth suggested that the SCLC join with ACMHR in an antisegregation campaign in Birmingham. His proposal led to the dramatic Birmingham demonstrations in the spring of 1963, in which Shuttlesworth played a key role.

Charging that Birmingham's white leaders had not lived up to the desegregation agreement reached in 1963, Shuttlesworth urged King to lead more demonstrations in the city during the spring of 1964. King declined to do so. Shuttlesworth joined in an SCLC integration campaign in St. Augustine, Florida that summer and was arrested in demonstrations at a segregated motel. He helped organize the march from Selma to Montgomery, Alabama, in March 1965 to protest voting discrimination in the state.

In August 1965 a dispute over Shuttlesworth's leadership developed within the congregation at his Cincinnati church. When Shuttlesworth's opponents accused him of being dictatorial and misusing church funds, he denied the charges and alleged that the opposition to him was part of an effort to discredit him within the civil rights movement. The controversy ended in January 1966 when several hundred of his supporters formed a new church in Cincinnati, and Shuttlesworth accepted their invitation to become its pastor. During riots in Cincinnati in June 1967, Shuttlesworth met with city officials in an effort to reach an agreement on black demands and prevent further violence.

Between 1958 and 1969 Shuttlesworth was a party in 10 Supreme Court cases involving civil rights. Altogether the Court overturned six of Shuttlesworth's convictions resulting from his role in the

1961 Freedom Rides and in various Birmingham demonstrations. In *New York Times v. Sullivan*, decided in March 1964, the Supreme Court also reversed a $500,000 libel judgment against Shuttlesworth, three other black ministers and the *New York Times*. The suit had resulted from a March 1960 advertisement in the *Times* that criticized Alabama officials and sought to raise funds for civil rights causes. However, in June 1967 the Court upheld contempt-of-court convictions stemming from the 1963 Birmingham demonstrations against Shuttlesworth and King. Shuttlesworth served a five-day sentence in Alabama in October 1967. Shuttlesworth remained active for many years in efforts to promote racial justice. In 2003–4, he served as interim president of the SCLC.

—CAB

## Simkin, William E(dward)

(1907–1992) *director, Federal Mediation and Conciliation Service*

Born in Merrifield, New York, on January 13, 1907, Simkin attended Earlham College and Columbia University. While teaching at the University of Pennsylvania's Wharton School of Business during the late 1930s he became an associate of Professor George W. Taylor, the well-known labor arbitrator. Simkin shortly thereafter began a lengthy career in the field of labor mediation, including service on the National War Labor Board and, later, an extensive private practice.

On February 2, 1961, President Kennedy appointed Simkin director of the Federal Mediation and Conciliation Service (FMCS). An independent agency within the executive branch, the FMCS was created by the Labor-Management Relations (Taft-Hartley) Act of 1947. The FMCS was notified of pending contract changes in collective bargaining agreements that affected interstate commerce. It was empowered to enter any case that developed negotiating problems, whether or not it was invited by the concerned parties. However, the FMCS did not have authority to enforce settlements—its only instruments were persuasion and the prestige of the federal government. Though primarily an administrator, Simkin personally intervened in a number of the more crucial labor negotiations that took place during the Kennedy administration and was usually successful in bringing both sides to agreement.

FMCS activity increased following President Johnson's settlement of the 1964 railroad strike. The service sought to keep settlements within the bounds of the administration's wage-price guidelines and, because of the Vietnam War, prevent strikes in industries essential to war production. In August 1966 Simkin estimated that his agency, with a staff of over 400 and a budget of $1 million, helped bring about 7,836 labor-management agreements in the fiscal year 1966.

Simkin believed that the mid-1960s marked a critical juncture in the history of labor arbitration. Contemporary labor disputes were, in his opinion, the most difficult since World War II. He felt that strikes were becoming obsolete—and even "useless" in some automated industries—making it imperative to develop new collective bargaining techniques. Simkin noted that, in order to avoid strikes and the pressure of "deadline bargaining," negotiators were finding it "wiser . . . to try out new bargaining procedures to maintain a continuing or longer-term dialogue." Concerned that his agency stay in the forefront of changes in collective bargaining techniques, Simkin developed a comprehensive training program for the FMCS staff. He also revived the practice, discontinued by the Eisenhower administration, of employing a panel composed of management and labor leaders to assist in the settlement of strikes.

Simkin participated in many important contract talks during the Johnson administration. The intervention of Simkin and Labor Secretary W. WILLARD WIRTZ in November 1965 sent striking McDonnell Aircraft workers at Cape Kennedy back to work in order to ensure that Gemini space shots planned for December would go off as scheduled. In April 1967 Simkin successfully mediated a nationwide dispute between the International Brotherhood of Teamsters and the trucking industry, and in July of the same year he helped end a three-month strike in the rubber industry. In April 1965 Simkin's intervention led to a temporary postponement of a strike deadline in the steel industry, but the White House was forced to intervene five months later when negotiations failed to produce a final settlement. The pact that was eventually agreed upon exceeded the administration's 3.2 percent wage-price guidelines. When 1966 negotiations in the electrical appliance industry, another important producer of war materiel, followed the same pattern, a large segment of the news media and many members of Congress demanded the enactment of legislation to ban strikes in industries vital to national security. Despite his own difficulties in these negotiations, however, Simkin repeatedly warned against compulsory arbitration and the forced settlement of strikes.

Simkin left the FMCS in 1969 to join the faculty of the Harvard School of Business Administration. Beginning in 1970 he was chair of the Federal Reserve System's labor relations panel, and, in the following year, he became chair of the State Department's Foreign Service Grievance Board. He died on March 4, 1992.

—JCH

## Sirhan, Sirhan B(ishara)

(1944– ) *convicted assassin of Robert F. Kennedy*

Sirhan Sirhan was born on March 19, 1944, in Jerusalem, then part of Palestine. He experienced the violence that occurred between Arabs and Jews in the struggle over the establishment of a Jewish state in Israel. Following the founding of Israel in May 1948 and the ensuing war between the new state and its Arab neighbors, Sirhan's family fled their home. In 1957 his family came to the United States.

Sirhan attended high school in Pasadena, California, and then entered Pasadena City College. He left the college in 1966. Sirhan hoped to become a jockey, and to gain experience he took a job as an exercise boy at the Hollywood Park Race Track. In September 1966 he was thrown from a horse and suffered head and back injuries. He was distressed over Israel's victory in the Six-Day War of June 1967. During the spring of 1968 Senator ROBERT F. KENNEDY (D-N.Y.), a supporter of Israel, became the focus of his rage.

In May 1968, as Kennedy campaigned in the California presidential primary, Sirhan considered assassinating him. On May 18 he wrote in his diary that "my determination to eliminate R. F. K. is becoming more of an unshakeable obsession . . . R. F. K. must die . . . Robert F. Kennedy must be assassinated before 5 June." (June 5 was the anniversary of the beginning of the Six-Day war.)

On June 4 Sirhan went to the Ambassador Hotel in Los Angeles, the Kennedy headquarters during the California campaign. Late in the evening, when it became clear that he had won the primary, Kennedy left his suite and made his way to the hotel ballroom to address his cheering campaign workers. After speaking briefly Kennedy headed for the press room, taking a shortcut through the hotel kitchen. Kennedy was shaking hands with the kitchen workers when Sirhan approached him. Shortly after midnight on June 5, Sirhan opened fire with a .22 caliber pistol. Kennedy, shot in the head and armpit, fell to the floor. Several others were also wounded, though none fatally. Roosevelt Grier, a former defensive tackle for the Los Angeles Rams and a Kennedy associate, wrested the gun from Sirhan and carried him from the room to protect him from the enraged spectators.

Early in the morning of June 6, 25 hours after the shooting, Kennedy died in Good Samaritan Hospital in Los Angeles. Sirhan was charged with first-degree murder. At his trial, which began January 7, 1969, defense attorneys argued that Sirhan had diminished mental capacity and therefore was not capable of the premeditation required to convict him of first degree murder. However, the admission into evidence of Sirhan's diaries with statements concerning the planned assassination damaged the defense case. On April 17 the jury found Sirhan guilty of murder. The judge sentenced him to death in the gas chamber.

Robert Kennedy's brother, Senator EDWARD KENNEDY (D-Mass.) requested that the death penalty be set aside, but Judge Herbert Walker, who had the power to reduce the sentence to life imprisonment, refused to do so. No date of execution was set for Sirhan pending the outcome of a Supreme Court decision concerning the constitutionality of capital punishment. In June 1972 the Supreme Court suspended all executions until state legislatures drastically revised their capital punishment statutes. This ruling led to the commutation of his sentence to life imprisonment.

—JLW

## Smathers, George A(rmistead)

(1913– ) *member of the Senate*

George Smathers, who became a close friend of President Kennedy and President Johnson, was born in Atlantic City, New Jersey, on November 14, 1913, and raised in Miami. Following his graduation from the University of Florida Law School in 1938, he entered private law practice and then became assistant U.S. district attorney for Dade County in 1940. After serving in the marines during World War II, he worked briefly as a special assistant to the attorney general of the United States. In 1946, he won the first of two consecutive terms to the House of Representatives.

In 1950 Smathers defeated the incumbent senator, Claude Pepper (D-Fla.), in the Florida Democratic primary. Smathers ran a sordid campaign in which he accused Pepper of being a Communist sympathizer. He referred to the senator as "Red" Pepper, who had a friendship with the Soviet leader, Joseph Stalin. Smathers also won the general election in November.

While in the upper house Smathers became one of a small group of senators who made committee assignments and could often decide the fate of legislation. The senator's power was based on his close friendship with Senate Majority Leader LYN-DON B. JOHNSON (D-Tex.), who appointed him head of the Senate Democratic Elections Committee in 1956. For the next two years Smathers used his position to distribute funds while building important political connections among powerful senators. During the early 1960s, Smathers voted against much of the Kennedy administration's domestic social legislation, despite his friendship with the president.

During the Johnson administration, Smathers advised the president on important legislative issues, such as the 1966 decision to suspend the 7 percent investment tax credit. He supported some important Great Society legislation, including Medicare and the Voting Rights Act of 1965.

During the Senate's 1964 investigation of BOBBY BAKER, Smathers was the only senator cited as having business connections with the former senate majority secretary, who was then under FBI investigation for fraud. Although Senate Rules Committee chair B. EVERETT JORDAN (D-N.C.) issued a statement exonerating Smathers of any impropriety in the matter, Smathers's handling of the incident caused many to question his business dealings. The senator announced that he had only a casual acquaintance with Baker, although both he and Baker had worked closely with Lyndon Johnson during the 1950s. He also issued conflicting statements on the profits he had made and confessed that he had lost his income tax returns for the year that could have provided him with the necessary information.

During the last part of the decade, the news media continued to question Smathers about his financial affairs. These investigations revealed banking and real estate transactions that, while not illegal, opened the senator to charges that he had used his influence to further his own business interests. In 1968 Smathers, coming under increased criticism for his business affairs, announced that for reasons of health he would not seek another Senate term. After leaving the Senate he practiced law in Washington, D.C.

—EWS

## Smith, Howard W(orth)
(1883–1976) *member of the House of Representatives*

Smith, who was born in Broad Run, Virginia, on February 2, 1883, first entered public life as the commonwealth's attorney for Alexandria, Virginia, in 1918. Four years later be became judge of the corporation court of that city and in 1928 was appointed judge of the state's 16th Circuit Court. Throughout the remainder of his career, he preferred to be known as Judge Smith, even though in 1930 he was elected to the first of 18 consecutive terms in the U.S. House of Representatives. In Congress, he sought to limit the federal government's powers in most domestic areas and preserve white supremacy.

Smith was one of the most powerful legislators on Capitol Hill once he became chair of the House Rules Committee in 1955. A conservative coalition of southern Democrats and Republicans had dominated the committee since the late 1930s. Most of the bills passing from their original committee to the House floor had to go through the Rules Committee, which determined the length and the terms of floor debate. As chair, Smith often used his power to prevent bills that he opposed from reaching the floor or, if released, to stipulate whether they could be amended.

During his first month in office President John F. Kennedy succeeded in winning House approval for the enlargement of the Rules Committee, with two of the three new seats going to moderate or liberal members. The expansion became permanent in January 1963. Yet the balance in the committee was nearly even, so Smith and his supporters were still in a position to halt or delay legislation that they opposed.

After LYNDON JOHNSON became president, Smith was less successful at obstructing administration measures. Relying upon a large network of friendships established during his years on Capitol Hill, Johnson was more effective than his predecessor in securing congressional support for his programs. During the first months of his presidency, he gained bipartisan backing for the civil rights bill which Kennedy had introduced. Smith denounced the bill as "unmatched in harshness and brutality . . . since the tragic days of Reconstruction." But because the measure was supported by the leadership of both parties, he felt compelled to allow the Rules Committee to clear the bill for floor consideration in January 1964. Smith, who continued to oppose the civil rights bill, proposed a successful amendment that barred discrimination on account of sex. He apparently hoped that this additional category of protection might lessen the chances of the bill's passage. Yet Smith had for years been a sponsor of an Equal Rights Amendment for women. Whatever his intention, once the Civil Rights Act of 1964 became law in July, Smith's action broadened the protections of legislation that he had tried to kill.

At the beginning of 1965 Smith's ability to block administration bills declined further. After the Democratic sweep in the November 1964 elections, the party's House caucus voted to back a 21-day rule. This proviso stipulated that if the Rules Committee did not send a bill to the floor within 21 days of its approval by the committee of original jurisdiction, the Speaker could permit the House to consider the measure. The House adopted the new rule in January 1965. President Johnson, who had strongly backed the measure, commented, "It could be better, but not this side of Heaven."

The 21-day rule was rarely invoked, but the mere threat of its employment proved effective in producing the release of a number of bills from the Rules Committee, and in 1965 Smith was not able to bury a single major administration proposal. The committee, for example, succeeded in delaying consideration of President Johnson's voting rights bill for five weeks. But when proceedings were initiated to apply the 21-day rule, the committee released the bill. The following year, when Smith was unyielding on a civil rights housing bill, the rule was employed to bring the measure to the floor.

While Smith was losing power in Congress, his political base in Virginia was also being undermined. A 1964 Supreme Court decision required the apportionment of legislative districts on the basis of population in order to give urban areas greater representation. In complying with this ruling, the Virginia General Assembly added a segment of the politically moderate Washington suburbs to Smith's district. In addition, the size of the black vote in Virginia increased because of the ratification by the states in 1964 of the constitutional amendment barring the poll tax and the passage of the Voting Rights Act of 1965. As a result, Smith was narrowly defeated in the 1966 Democratic primary by a liberal opponent. He resumed his practice on law after leaving Congress and died on October 3, 1976.

—MLL

## Smith, Margaret Chase
### (1897–1995) *member of the Senate*

After a varied career in business and local Republican politics, Smith, who was born on December 14, 1897, in Skowhegan, Maine, won election to the U.S. House of Representatives in 1940, filling a vacancy created by her husband's death. She served four full terms in the House. With her victory in the 1948 election, she became the first female Republican ever to serve in the Senate. Smith built a record as an independent on domestic issues. She made a powerful impression on June 1, 1950, in her first major Senate address, when she offered a "declaration of conscience" and denounced Senator Joseph R. McCarthy (R-Wisc.) for his tactics of "hate and character assassination." She took a special interest in military and defense matters and favored large and powerful armed forces. She won reelection in 1954 and 1960.

On January 27, 1964, Smith announced she would enter the race for the Republican presidential nomination to offer her party's voters a moderate candidate and to open the way for women in presidential politics. Insisting that her Senate duties remained her first responsibility, she spent little time campaigning and limited her spending to personal and travel expenses, which she paid herself. Smith ran a poor fifth in the first primary held in New Hampshire in March. She received nearly 26 percent of the vote in Illinois's April primary but again ran fifth in Oregon in May. She received 27 votes on the first ballot at the Republican National Convention in San Francisco.

In the Senate Smith retained her independent stance. In *Congressional Quarterly* surveys from 1964 to 1967, she was ranked as one of the top three

Republican supporters of the president's legislative program. Smith voted, for example, for civil rights, Medicare, aid to elementary and secondary schools, and several antipoverty programs. However, she opposed an urban mass transportation bill in 1964, voted to cut the appropriations for the War on Poverty in 1965, and opposed increased funding for other Great Society programs. She also voted against measures in 1967 and 1968 designed to increase financial disclosure by members of Congress. Although she later voted for the Equal Rights Amendment, Smith did not identify herself with the women's movement that gained strength in the late 1960s.

A member of the Appropriations Committee and the Aeronautical and Space Sciences Committee, Smith also headed the Senate Republican Conference from 1967 to 1972 and became the ranking Republican on the Armed Services Committee in 1967. She consistently supported spending for the Vietnam War. In March 1967, when a U.S.-USSR consular treaty was under consideration, Smith unsuccessfully proposed adding an "understanding" that it was the Senate's "hope" that no consulates would be opened until the war had ended. She explained that this was intended to be a Senate expression of disapproval of Soviet aid to North Vietnam. Smith usually supported Defense Department programs and appropriation requests, but she opposed the Safeguard antiballistic missile system in 1968 and 1969 on the grounds that it was ineffective, unnecessary, and a waste of resources.

Smith was unopposed for renomination to the Senate in the 1966 Republican primary in Maine, and she won the general election in November with 59 percent of the vote. Smith joined in Senate debate only infrequently and followed a policy of never announcing in advance how she planned to vote on an issue. Between June 1955 and July 1968 she set a Senate record for not missing any roll-call votes.

In a surprising upset, Smith was defeated in her bid for reelection to the Senate in November 1972. She died on May 29, 1995.

—CAB

## Sontag, Susan
### (1933–2004) *writer*

Sontag, who was born in New York City on January 28, 1933, attended high school in Los Angeles and entered the University of California, Berkeley, when

Writer and essayist Susan Sontag at a seminar, 1967 *(Library of Congress, Prints and Photographs Division)*

she was 15 years old. She transferred to the University of Chicago, receiving her B.A. in 1951.

She pursued graduate studies at Harvard and the University of Paris and, after a brief stint as an editor of *Commentary* magazine in 1959, taught philosophy at the City College of New York, Sarah Lawrence College, and Columbia University.

In 1962 Sontag began to publish criticism in literary journals and magazines, including *Partisan Review*, the *New York Review of Books*, *Evergreen Review*, and *Film Quarterly*, much of which was collected in *Against Interpretation* (1966). In this book's title essay she called for an end to the reductive analysis, or "interpretation," which she felt reduced the subject work of art to a mere example of the critic's preferred world view. "Interpretation," she insisted, "takes the sensory experience of the work of art for granted and proceeds from there. This cannot be taken for granted, now. . . . Ours is a culture based on excess, on overproduction; the result is a steady loss in sharpness in our sensory experience. . . . The function of criticism should be to show how [the work of art] is what it is, even that it is what it is, rather than to show what it means. In place of a hermeneutic we need an erotics of art."

This argument made Sontag a prominent champion of the "new sensibility" in the arts, and she became a celebrated critic during the 1960s. Through her erudite explanations of camp, underground films, pornography, and pop art, Sontag did much to transform accepted standards of aesthetic judgment and to justify the educated public's eagerness to respond to "style" and "experience" as aesthetic values in their own right. According to social historian William O'Neill, Sontag's abandonment of the old aesthetics helped legitimatize the breakdown in the distinction between high and low culture that was occurring in the 1960s. Although fiercely intellectual herself, Sontag's perspective welcomed the drive for sensual immediacy that characterized the counterculture and much of the New Left.

Sontag was a prominent opponent of the war in Vietnam. She signed the radical and widely circulated "Call to Resist Illegitimate Authority" in September 1967 and the next year publicly supported acts of draft resistance. During the same year she made a two-week visit to North Vietnam, later recorded in her essay "Trip to Hanoi." The account charted the changes in the consciousness of its highly cultured, ironic heroine, unwilling to think in terms of moral categories, yet learning finally to respond to what she viewed as the moral simplicity of the Vietnamese. Sontag was one of the few American leftist intellectuals visiting Hanoi to observe that North Vietnam was far from a model society, but on the whole she felt obliged to make allowances for the years of war and suffering endured by the Vietnamese people. Impressed by the nationalism of an embattled culture, she concluded her essay with a call on Americans to reinvent the radical patriotism of the Founding Fathers.

In the 1970s Sontag continued to produce many influential works, including an account of her own battle with cancer in *Illness as Metaphor* (1978). She died on December 28, 2004.

—TLH

## Sparkman, John J(ackson)
### (1899–1985) *member of the Senate*

Sparkman was born in Morgan County, Alabama, on December 20, 1899, to parents who worked as sharecroppers. He studied at the University of Alabama both before and after service in the army during World War I and earned a law degree in 1923, after which he worked as an attorney in Huntsville. He gained election to the U.S. House of Representatives in 1936 and supported many economic programs of the New Deal, especially the Tennessee Valley Authority, which played a major role in the development of northern Alabama.

In 1946, he won a special election to fill a vacant Senate seat. Although he opposed civil rights measures, he refrained from using demagogic rhetoric in his campaigns to exploit racial prejudice. While most of his southern colleagues on Capitol Hill after World War II opposed President Truman's Fair Deal programs, Sparkman supported many public works measures. As a member of the Joint Committee on Housing and the chair of the Banking and Currency Committee's Housing Subcommittee, he played an important role in the passage of almost all housing legislation during the late 1940s and 1950s. Sparkman was ADLAI E. STEVENSON's vice presidential running mate in 1952, and he campaigned vigorously in a losing effort.

Although he continued to oppose civil rights measures in the early 1960s, he backed most of the Kennedy administration's major proposed domestic measures.

In 1961 he was the Senate sponsor of the administrative omnibus housing bill. As chair of the Select Small Business Committee, Sparkman backed increased funding for the Small Business Administration in 1962 and 1963.

Partly because of the growing influence of Governor GEORGE C. WALLACE in Alabama politics during the middle and late 1960s, Sparkman voted against liberal domestic programs more frequently than in previous years. According to *Congressional Quarterly*, he never opposed the Senate's conservative coalition on more than 23 percent of key roll-call votes from 1964 through 1968. Yet he continued to endorse most administration housing bills. In 1964 he backed a bill to expand urban renewal and low-rent housing programs. The following year Sparkman introduced the most extensive housing and urban development bill since the Housing Act of 1949. The measure authorized the expenditure of over $7 billion and included a new and controversial rent supplement program to provide adequate living accommodations for the poor in private housing. Congress passed the bill in July.

In 1966 Sparkman, expecting stiff conservative opposition in both the Democratic primary and the general election, declined to sponsor the administration's hotly debated Demonstration Cities bill. He won both contests easily. In 1967 he succeeded former senator A. WILLIS ROBERTSON (D-Va.) as chair of the Banking and Currency Committee. In that position he opposed efforts to restrict the president's rent supplement program of 1967. The following year Sparkman backed President Johnson's bill for erecting and rehabilitating over 1.7 million housing units for low-income families. In May Sparkman asserted, during floor debate on the measure, that existing programs "have not reached down far enough to help those who need housing the most."

Sparkman's assumption of the chair of the Banking and Currency Committee influenced the fate of the administration's "truth-in-lending" measure, which Robertson had stalled in the committee for a number of years. Sparkman's support of the bill, which required lenders to provide full information about the cost of credit, facilitated its passage in 1967.

Sparkman endorsed administration foreign aid programs. He also backed the administration's Vietnam War policies. He defended Congress's 1964 passage of the Tonkin Gulf Resolution, which the president frequently cited as justification for American military involvement in Southeast Asia.

In 1972 Sparkman narrowly avoided a primary runoff against an opponent who accused him of being too close to big banking interests. Three years later he left his Banking and Currency post to succeed former senator J. WILLIAM FULBRIGHT (D-Ark.) as chair of the Foreign Relations Committee. He left the Senate at the end of his term in January 1979. He died on November 16, 1985.

—MLL

## Spellman, Francis J(oseph)
### (1889–1967) *Roman Catholic archbishop of New York*

Born in Whitman, Massachusetts, on May 4, 1889, trained in Rome, and ordained a Roman Catholic priest in 1916, Spellman became archbishop of New York in 1939. In 1946 he became a cardinal. His position in the Catholic hierarchy and his success at cultivating political connections, beginning with the administration of Franklin D. Roosevelt, made him a powerful and influential religious leader. A successful fund-raiser, he built churches and schools in New York and helped finance Catholic international missionary work. As military vicar for U.S. troops beginning in 1939, Spellman visited American forces around the world, thereby gaining him international and national prominence. His religious and political beliefs made him an ardent anticommunist, who advocated vigorous efforts to meet both international and domestic Communist challenges. He defended Senator Joseph R. McCarthy's efforts to find alleged subversives in government. He also

counseled the Eisenhower administration to support Ngo Dinh Diem, who emerged in 1954 as the leader of an anticommunist government in South Vietnam.

Spellman welcomed the election of John F. Kennedy, the first Roman Catholic to occupy the White House, but he disagreed with Kennedy on some important issues. He opposed the administration's proposed school aid program in 1961, since it would have made Catholic schools ineligible for federal assistance. He also objected to Kennedy's decision not to seek the establishment of full U.S. diplomatic relations with the Vatican.

Although a conservative on many theological issues, Spellman took positions that had the effect of advancing religious progressivism. In the late 1950s and early 1960s, Spellman, who had become the senior American cardinal, objected to the Vatican's efforts to intervene in the affairs of U.S. bishops. He defended some Catholic scholars who were the target of Vatican criticism. He used his influence in the Second Vatican Council to secure a declaration of religious liberty in 1965.

During the mid-1960s Spellman aroused controversy for his outspoken support of the war in Vietnam. Using language that was more extreme than any employed by the administration, he defended the conflict as "a war for civilization" and as "Christ's war against the Viet Cong and the people of North Vietnam." Early criticism of his position came from within the American Catholic community. In December 1965 Catholic college students picketed Spellman's New York office, demanding the end of "power politics in the church." The students protested Spellman's alleged suppression of three antiwar Jesuits, including Father DANIEL BERRIGAN, who had recently been transferred from New York to Cuernavaca, Mexico.

By 1966 Spellman's militant defense of the war had alienated him from large segments of the American religious community. His position was at odds with the peace initiatives of Pope Paul VI. In December the Vatican felt it necessary to state that the cardinal "did not speak for the pope or the church" on the war issue. Despite their disagreements, Pope Paul refused Spellman's October 1966 offer to resign as archbishop.

The intensity of Catholic antiwar demonstrations, often aimed at Spellman, increased in 1967. Cardinal Spellman died of a stroke in New York City on December 2, 1967.

—JCH

## Spock, Benjamin (McLaine)

(1903–1998) *co-chair, Committee for a Sane Nuclear Policy; co-chair, National Conference for New Politics*

Spock was born into a wealthy family in New Haven, Connecticut, on May 2, 1903. His father was a successful corporation lawyer, and his mother ran a home that Spock later characterized as "plain, repressed and strict." Spock studied medicine at Yale and Columbia and completed residencies in pediatrics and psychiatry. In 1933 he started a private practice that he continued until entering the navy during World War II

In 1946 he published *The Common Sense Book of Baby and Child Care*. An immediate success, it went through many editions and made him the best-known expert on child care during the last half of the 20th century. By the time of his death, "Dr. Spock," as his manual was commonly known, had sold 50 million copies, more than any other book except the Bible. He also reached a large audience with a regular column in *Ladies' Home Journal* and, later, *Redbook* magazine. During the 20 years beginning in 1947, he held positions, successively, with the Mayo Clinic, the University of Pittsburgh, and Case Western Reserve University.

Until 1960 Spock had taken public positions only on medical and public health issues, but that year he endorsed John F. Kennedy's presidential candidacy. After Kennedy's announcement in March 1962 that the United States was resuming nuclear testing, Spock accepted a previously rejected offer to become a national boardmember of the Committee for a Sane Nuclear Policy (SANE). The next year he was elected national co-chair of the organization.

Spock campaigned for President Johnson in 1964 and in January 1965 became a member of the National Advisory Council to the Office of Economic Opportunity. However, Spock became increasingly critical of the president after Johnson approved the beginning of sustained bombing of North Vietnam and the commitment of U.S. combat troops to South Vietnam shortly after his reelection. He first sent private letters to various administration leaders. Then on June 8, 1965, he spoke at a SANE-sponsored antiwar rally in New York's Madison Square Garden. Spock was a principal speaker at the November 27 march in Washington initiated by SANE, where he called on both the United States and North Vietnam to seek a negotiated settlement.

In 1966 SANE concentrated on generally unsuccessful campaigns to elect peace candidates, and Spock was a frequent campaigner. He was also one of the main speakers at a SANE demonstration held in Washington on May 15, 1966, in support of these candidates. Within SANE there was an often bitter debate over the extent to which the organization should cooperate with more radical elements in the antiwar movement. Spock favored a broadly inclusive and militant movement. Although SANE declined to work with the newly formed Spring Mobilization to End the War in Vietnam, Spock accepted the post of co-chair of the coalition's planned April 15, 1967 march. In a letter to A. J. MUSTE the wrote: "I now believe in leaning in the direction of recruiting more militant people into the peace movement rather than worrying over scaring off the timid ones. . . . I believe in solidarity." On April 15, Spock, the Reverend MARTIN LUTHER KING, JR., and Harry Belafonte led an estimated 300,000 marchers from New York's Central Park to the United Nations in the largest antiwar demonstration to date.

Spock was an early leader of the National Conference for New Politics (NCNP), founded in June 1966. At the August 1967 NCNP convention Spock was elected a co-chair of the group and shortly thereafter resigned his position with SANE. The NCNP convention was marked by numerous disagreements and voted not to run a national third-party slate in the 1968 elections. The NCNP itself dissolved within a year.

In the fall of 1967 Spock, recently retired from teaching, was increasingly active in opposition to the war. He was one of the original signers of "A Call to Resist Illegitimate Authority," published in September 1967, which supported draft resistance and the refusal of troops to obey "illegal and immoral orders." He was part of a group that visited the Justice Department on October 20 and handed over several hundred draft cards turned in by draft resisters. The next day he spoke at the antiwar rally that preceded a march on the Pentagon. On December 5 he was arrested with 263 others at the New York City Whitehall Induction Center in a civil disobedience action during "Stop the Draft Week."

Spock, Marcus Raskin, codirector of the Institute for Policy Studies, the Reverend WILLIAM SLOANE COFFIN, JR., Yale University chaplain, writer Mitchell Goodman, and Harvard graduate student Michael Ferber were indicted on January 5, 1968, for conspiring to "counsel, aid and abet" young men to "refuse and evade service in the armed services. . . ." In pretrial motions Spock's lawyer, Leonard Boudin, argued that the war in Vietnam was illegal. Therefore, under the precedents established at the post–World War II Nuremberg trials, Boudin contended, the defendants had committed no crime in advising potential draftees to refuse to participate in the war and in the war crimes committed as part of it. Judge Francis J. W. Ford ruled that the legality of the war or the draft was not relevant to the case. The trial, therefore, took place over the narrower legal issue of whether or not a conspiracy had existed. All of the defendants except Raskin were convicted on June 14, 1968, of one conspiracy count; they were sentenced the next month to fines and two-year prison sentences. However, on July 11, 1969, the First U.S. Court of Appeals set aside the verdicts, citing prejudicial error in Judge Ford's charge to the jury. Charges against Spock and Ferber were dismissed. Although Goodman and Coffin were ordered retried, charges against them were eventually dropped as well.

He continued his antiwar activities in the early 1970s, but became controversial in a new way, when Vice President SPIRO T. AGNEW asserted that Spock's counsel to parents had helped to create a climate of permissiveness that led to the counterculture and radical political protests. Spock rejected Agnew's charges. He remained engaged with social and public health issues as long as his health allowed. He died on March 15, 1998.

—JBF

## Staggers, Harley
### (1907–1991) *member of the House of Representatives*

Staggers was born in a log cabin on August 3, 1907, in Keyser, West Virginia, located in the rural, mountainous, coal-mining West Virginia district he later represented in Congress. He graduated from a small Methodist college in 1931 and held a variety of jobs, including county sheriff, before serving as a naval aviator during World War II. Staggers first won election to Congress in 1948 and was assigned to the Interstate and Foreign Commerce Committee in 1951. He compiled a liberal voting record and consistently supported the Democratic leadership.

Staggers, who once described himself as a "Johnson man," assumed the chair of the powerful Commerce Committee in 1966 and sponsored important administration legislation, most notably a series of health bills. Introduced by Staggers in March 1966, the Comprehensive Health Planning Act authorized coordination of public health services on a state and regional basis; it was signed in November, as were bills he introduced to appropriate funds for health training programs and hospital modernization. In March 1967 Staggers introduced the administration's major health legislation for that year, the "Partnership of Health" bill, which extended and expanded the Comprehensive Health Planning Act. It was signed in December.

Staggers also played a crucial role in the passage of the Johnson administration's 1966 Traffic Safety Act, which required the establishment of federal safety standards for vehicles that were intended for public highway use. Staggers, whose committee handled the bill, favored civil penalties for manufacturers who failed to notify owners and dealers of safety defects or who were found, during on-site inspections, to be in violation of portions of the act. However, Staggers considered criminal penalties unenforceable and opposed Representative THOMAS P. O'NEILL's (D-Mass.) amendment to add such penalties for violations by industry officials. Without criminal penalties, O'Neill said, the bill would repeat "the wishy-washy regulatory performance that has caused so much public disillusionment with the process of government." Staggers argued that "you cannot put a corporation in jail," and that viewpoint prevailed when O'Neill's proposal was defeated by voice vote in August. Enacted later in 1966, the Traffic Safety Act went beyond the administration's original plan and won praise from consumer advocate RALPH NADER, However, Nader also criticized the absence of criminal penalties.

Although Staggers opposed compulsory arbitration of labor disputes, he introduced the administration's bill to prevent a nationwide railroad strike in May 1967. The bill called for a 90-day strike delay during which a settlement would be sought—and if necessary imposed—by a mediation panel. Although the Senate approved the bill, Staggers joined a majority in the House in rejecting the imposition of a binding settlement. On June 15 the railroad unions agreed not to strike while a House-Senate Conference Committee headed by Staggers attempted to reconcile the conflicting versions of the bill. However, on July 13 the unions notified the committee that their no-strike pledge would be rescinded two days later. Members of the International Association of Machinists struck July 16. The next day the conferees agreed unanimously that they could not reach an agreement, and the Senate then reaffirmed its commitment to the original plan. By a vote of 244 to 148, the House overturned its earlier decision and gave its approval to the Senate version of the president's plan. Staggers maintained his opposition to the measure and said that "compulsory labor is foreign to America . . . it is a road America should never take." The strike ended on July 18 when Johnson appointed a five-person mediation board headed by Senator WAYNE MORSE (D-Ore.). Attempts to reach a voluntary settlement failed, and the board's recommendations went into effect into October.

In the early 1960s Staggers had begun to work on a bill to protect consumers from deceptive packaging in supermarket and drugstore products. His bill was enacted as the Truth-in-Packaging Act in November 1966. Staggers was also concerned with the Federal Communications Commission's "role as a guardian of the public interest" and during the 1968 presidential campaign held hearings on the application of the "fairness doctrine" to televised political debates. He supported a bill that would have suspended the "equal time" provision of the 1934 Communications Act for the 1968 presidential election, but the measure did not pass.

Staggers, who was a supporter of the Vietnam policies of the Johnson and Nixon administrations, remained in Congress into the 1970s. Near the end of his service in Congress, he was principal sponsor of the Staggers Rail Act of 1980, which led to partial deregulation of the nation's railways. He retired from the House in 1981 and died on August 20, 1991.

—MDB

## Stennis, John C(ornelius)

(1901–1995) *member of the Senate*

Born on August 3, 1901, in Kemper County, Mississippi, Stennis earned a B.S. from Mississippi State University in 1923 and an LL.B. from the University of Virginia in 1928. He served in the state legislature, as district attorney, and as a circuit judge. In 1947 he won a special election for a vacant U.S. Senate seat. He avoided inflammatory rhetoric about racial issues during the campaign. Throughout his Senate career, however, he voted against civil rights legislation. He also consistently favored a strong anticommunist foreign policy and opposed most social welfare legislation.

In the Senate Stennis, who was courtly and dignified, acquired a reputation for fairness and personal integrity that transcended his political outlook. He won public esteem in 1954, when he served on the committee inquiring into the conduct of Senator Joseph R. McCarthy (R-Wisc.) Believing that the maintenance of high standards of behavior in the Senate should supersede political partisanship, Stennis denounced what he considered McCarthy's vituperative and reckless allegations of Communist influence in American institutions. In November 1954 he became the first Democrat to call on the Senate floor for McCarthy's censure.

Eight years later, as chair of the Senate Armed Services Committee's Preparedness Investigating Subcommittee, he headed an investigation into what Major General Edwin A. Walker, a John Birch Society member, and Senator STROM THURMOND (D-S.C.) alleged was State Department and Pentagon "muzzling" of military officers. Many of Stennis's colleagues believed that his judicious handling of the probe prevented the matter from exploding into an emotional issue reminiscent of the McCarthy Era.

As a by-product of the Senate's investigation of the BOBBY BAKER scandal, in July 1964 the upper house established a Select Committee on Standards and Ethics to examine complaints of unethical conduct by senators and employees of the chamber. Because of his reputation for integrity, Stennis became the panel first chair in October 1965. During the next two years the committee investigated the case in Senator THOMAS DODD (D-Conn.), who was accused of improperly aiding a registered foreign agent, using campaign funds to pay personal bills, and billing trips both to the Senate and to private organizations. In April 1967 the committee, with Stennis's concurrence, recommended the censure of Dodd on the two latter charges. Two months later the Senate voted for censure on the campaign funds accusation while dropping the other charges.

Stennis at first had reservations about the deepening U.S. military involvement in the Vietnam War. Yet he consistently supported President LYNDON B. JOHNSON's request for troop increases and military appropriations. In a speech in early 1966,

Stennis expressed his political outlook when he stated, "Great Society programs with the billions they are gulping down should be relegated to the rear. . . . They should be secondary to the war." Favoring a prompt military victory, he asserted that North Vietnam and the National Liberation Front should be attacked "as often and whenever necessary" in order to avoid "a long, drawn-out and bloody war of possibly 10–15 years." In order to achieve victory in Vietnam, he was prepared to support the mobilization of military reserves and an increase in taxes. He also believed that the Johnson administration should ease restrictions on the bombing campaign against North Vietnam. In August and September 1967 he held hearings in his Preparedness Investigating Subcommittee in which military officers criticized the administration for failing to authorize raids against targets they deemed important.

Stennis also expressed concern about the possible consequences of the Vietnam War on the overall military strength of the United States. In August 1965, after the Preparedness Investigating Subcommittee had completed a one-year study of the combat readiness of the army, he contended that the war was rapidly draining the armed forces' stock of supplies. During subcommittee hearings in August 1966 he voiced the fear that the Vietnam War might establish a precedent for American entry into future conflicts without congressional approval and for the conduct of such conflicts with minimal legislative involvement.

Stennis often defended the Vietnam policies of the Nixon administration and protected Pentagon budgets from Senate colleagues who wished to cut proposed spending. In January 1973 two assailants shot and seriously wounded him. He recovered and served in the Senate until he retired at the end of his term in January 1989. He died on April 23, 1995.

—MLL

## Stevenson, Adlai E(wing), II

(1900–1965) *ambassador to the United Nations*

Stevenson was born in Los Angeles on February 5, 1900, and named after his grandfather, who had been vice president in the second administration of Grover Cleveland. He attended Princeton, Harvard, and Northwestern, earning a law degree from the last university in 1926. After several years of private law practice in a prominent Chicago firm, he became involved in government service at the beginning of the New Deal. He resumed his law practice in 1935, but became interested in foreign affairs and served as president of the Chicago Council on Foreign Relations. During World War II, he worked in the Foreign Economic Administration and then participated in the conference that organized the United Nations. He subsequently served on the staff of the U.S. delegation to the United Nations. In 1948, Stevenson ran for governor as a reform candidate, defeating his Republican opponent by a wide margin. He compiled an impressive record of progressive legislation and administrative reform during his four-year term as Illinois governor.

By the early 1950s Stevenson had become a prominent figure in the Democratic Party. In 1952 and 1956 he ran as the Democratic candidate for president, but lost to the overwhelmingly popular Republican candidate, DWIGHT D. EISENHOWER. After the failure of a draft-Stevenson movement at the 1960 Democratic National Convention, the former candidate played an important part in reconciling his party's liberal wing with the Democratic nominee, John F. Kennedy. Although he had hoped to be named secretary of state after Kennedy's election, Kennedy instead appointed Stevenson U.S. ambassador to the United Nations, a position that carried little policy-making responsibility. Lack of personal rapport between Stevenson and the new president, as well as the White House view that Stevenson lacked the toughness that Kennedy prized prevented him from gaining much influence. Stevenson was not consulted before the 1961 Bay of Pigs invasion. During the Cuban missile crisis, he played a dramatic role in a confrontation with the Soviet ambassador, who he trapped in a blatant lie once he displayed reconnaissance photographs of the Soviet missile bases. Yet he had no influence in shaping the administration's strategy during the crisis.

Shortly after Kennedy's assassination, Stevenson met at the White House with President Lyndon Johnson, who urgently requested the ambassador to remain at his post. Stevenson agreed and initially developed a good working relationship with the new president. Both men were approximately the same age and appreciated each other's political skills. Yet before long Stevenson realized he would have an even smaller role in shaping foreign policy under Johnson than he had under Kennedy. Stevenson again became little more than an administration spokesperson, reading speeches prepared by the

State Department and approved in advance by Johnson. He defended U.S. policy before the United Nations on such important occasions as the Panama Canal Zone riots of January 1964, the first U.S. bombing raids on North Vietnam in early 1965, and the U.S. troop landings in the Dominican Republic in May 1965.

As the Vietnam War escalated in 1965, Stevenson continued his public support of administration foreign policy. Friends and associates, however, reported that he had strong private doubts on U.S. actions in Southeast Asia. In September 1964 and January 1965 Stevenson cooperated with UN Secretary General U Thant in attempting to arrange exploratory talks with the North Vietnamese government in Burma; but this "peace feeler" was later rejected by the administration. Speaking before the American Newspaper Publishers Association in April 1965, Stevenson urged a "subtle shift" in U.S. diplomacy toward greater reliance on mediation through international organizations. In June 1965 writers PAUL GOODMAN, DWIGHT MACDONALD, and Harvey Swados visited Stevenson to urge him to repudiate American policy in Vietnam and join the growing antiwar movement. Stevenson refused, claiming that he was "on the [administration] team." Friends later reported, however, that Stevenson had tentatively made the decision to resign from his UN post.

In late June relations between Stevenson and the president deteriorated sharply when Johnson refused to read a speech prepared by Stevenson for celebrations marking the 20th anniversary of the signing of the UN Charter. The speech had been inadvertently leaked to the press, and Johnson ordered a new version prepared without consulting Stevenson. Friends indicated that Stevenson took the incident as a personal affront, confirming his decision to leave the UN. Before he could do so, however, Stevenson died of a heart attack during a London visit on July 14, 1965.

—FHM

## Stewart, Potter

(1915–1985) *associate justice, U.S. Supreme Court*

Born in Jackson, Michigan, on January 23, 1915, Stewart grew up in Cincinnati, Ohio. His father was a justice on the Ohio Supreme Court and his mother a prominent reformer. Stewart studied at Yale, earning a B.A. in 1937 and a law degree in 1941. He served in the navy during World War II and then practiced law with a prestigious firm in Cincinnati. He entered politics as a Republican; held several offices in Cincinnati; and, in 1954, became the country's youngest federal judge, when President DWIGHT D. EISENHOWER nominated him to the Sixth Circuit Court of Appeals. In October 1958, Eisenhower selected him for the U.S. Supreme Court, and the Senate confirmed the appointment in May 1959. Stewart did not side consistently with any faction on the Court. He sometimes said that he was not a liberal or a conservative, but a lawyer. He tended, on balance, to be a centrist who cast deciding votes in some important cases when the Court was closely divided, particularly during his first years as a justice.

When a solid liberal majority emerged on the Warren Court by the early 1960s, Stewart's position became less decisive, although he continued to follow a moderate and independent course. He voted to uphold individual rights that he found explicitly protected in the Bill of Rights. In what he sometimes said was his favorite case, *Rideau v. Louisiana* (1963), he wrote that a television broadcast of a suspect confessing to a murder charge amounted to "kangaroo court proceedings" that impaired the defendant's right to a fair trial. He dissented in other instances, as in *Griswold v. Connecticut* (1965), when the Court stuck down a state prohibition on the distribution of birth control information on the basis of a constitutional right to privacy. His opinions consistently upheld religious freedom. He dissented from the majority in 1961, which upheld the constitutionality of a Sunday closing law, declaring that it "compels an Orthodox Jew to choose between his religious faith and his economic survival. That is a cruel choice." The next year, he again dissented when the Court struck done school prayer laws.

During the mid-1960s, his opinions dealt with a variety of issues involving individual rights and criminal investigations. In a May 1964 ruling Stewart's majority opinion held that incriminating statements deliberately elicited by the police after indictment and in the absence of counsel were inadmissible in federal courts since the defendant's right to counsel had been violated. The next month, however, he dissented when the Court extended the right to counsel to a suspect under police investigation but not yet formally indicted or arraigned. He also objected to the Court's ruling that the First

Amendment's protection against self-incrimination applied to state cases. In a series of cases expanding criminal defendant rights over the next few years, Stewart repeatedly dissented, arguing that the rights of defendants should be balanced against the society's interests. He objected, for example, to the Court's June 1966 *Miranda* ruling, which placed limits on police interrogation of suspects. Stewart also dissented from a May 1967 ruling applying the procedural rights of the Fifth and Sixth Amendments to juvenile court proceedings. Writing the opinion of the court in a December 1967 case, however, Stewart overturned a 39-year-old precedent to hold that electronic surveillance was subject to the Fourth Amendment's guarantee against unreasonable searches and seizures and to require police to obtain judicial warrants before using electronic eavesdropping devices.

Stewart continued to support government security legislation, dissenting when the Court overturned a federal law prohibiting Communist Party members from serving as labor union officials in June 1965 and when it invalidated a set of New York State teacher loyalty laws in January 1967. In obscenity cases, however, Stewart took positions that expanded the scope of free speech. In his concurring opinion in a June 1964 case, for example, Stewart defined obscene material as "hard core pornography," a definition narrower in effect than the one supported by some of the Court's more liberal members. But Stewart aroused much hilarity and criticism by adding that while he could not define hardcore pornography, "I know it when I see it."

Stewart repeatedly dissented from Court rulings that legislative districts must be apportioned on an equal population basis. He objected in a February 1964 case to the application of this "one-man, one-vote" standard to congressional districting and argued that the Constitution had no provision determining the manner of apportionment of such districts. In a series of cases involving state legislative reapportionment beginning in June 1964, Stewart insisted that such state plans be rational and that they not frustrate the will of the majority of the electorate. But aside from this, Stewart thought districts could be drawn to reflect economic, geographic, and other interests in addition to population.

Justice Stewart also dissented in March 1966, when the majority voided a Virginia poll tax for state elections and in June 1966 when it upheld a provi-

sion in the 1965 Voting Rights Act designed to guarantee the right to vote to Spanish-speaking citizens. In December 1964 and February and November of 1966 he voted to uphold state court convictions of civil rights protesters. His majority opinion in a June 1967 case sustained the contempt-of-court convictions of MARTIN LUTHER KING, JR., and seven other black leaders resulting from the 1963 Birmingham demonstrations. However, Stewart also wrote the majority opinion in a June 1968 case that held that an 1866 federal law prohibited racial discrimination in the sale or rental of property and sustained the law's constitutionality under the Thirteenth Amendment.

When EARL WARREN retired from the Court in 1969, Stewart insisted that he should not be considered because he felt the new chief justice should be chosen from outside the Court. On the Burger Court Stewart was once again considered a "swing" justice between the new, more conservative members and the other liberal justices. Stewart's opinions, usually brief, lucid, and well reasoned, have earned considerable praise. He retired from the Court in 1981 and died on December 7, 1985.

—CAB

## Stokes, Carl B(urton)
### (1927–1996) *mayor*

Stokes, who was born on June 21, 1927, grew up in poverty in Cleveland, Ohio, the city of his birth. His father died when he was extremely young, and he and his brother, Louis, helped their mother support their family by delivering newspapers and clerking in neighborhood stores. Carl dropped out of high school at age 16 and served in the army during the Allied occupation of Germany. Later Stokes finished his secondary education and worked his way through four different colleges, earning a B.S. from the University of Minnesota in 1954. He received his LL.B. degree from Cleveland Marshall Law School in 1956. During the 1950s Stokes served as a liquor inspector and assistant city law director under Mayor ANTHONY J. CELEBREZZE. Active in Democratic politics and local civil rights organizations, Stokes served on the executive committees of the Cleveland NAACP and the county Democratic organization. In November 1962 he won election as the first African-American Democrat to the Ohio House of Representatives. He was reelected in 1964 and 1966.

In the mid-1960s Cleveland ranked 11th in size among American cities. As in other large northern cities, the minority population had grown dramatically. The black share of the city's population had risen from about 10 percent in 1940 to about 37 percent in 1965. The heavily polluted Cuyahoga River divided the city racially: blacks dominated the city's East Side neighborhoods while whites, including many second and third generation immigrants from eastern and southern Europe, lived in the western half.

Despite the increase in the city's black population, Cleveland's political officeholders remained overwhelmingly white. In 1963 civil rights groups began a protest over the de facto segregation of city schools. In April of the following year, 85 percent of the system's black school children boycotted classes. The success of the 1964 student boycott demonstrated the black community's capacity for effective action.

Stokes decided to run for mayor in 1965. He declined to oppose incumbent Democratic mayor Ralph S. Locher in the primary and instead ran in the general election as an independent. Two other candidates—both white—entered the 1965 race. Locher received the endorsement of the regular Democratic organization and both the city's major newspapers. Although Stokes won 97 percent of the black city vote, he narrowly lost the general election to Locher.

Little occurring after Locher's close 1965 victory suggested an easier campaign for him two years later. Rioting in the Hough section of Cleveland in July 1966 created serious doubts about the mayor's ability to deal with a turbulent racial crisis. The Locher administration's urban renewal program fell so far behind its original projections that the federal government reduced Cleveland's share of federal antipoverty funds. By early 1967 both of the city's dailies—the *Press* and the *Plain Dealer*—criticized the mayor and demanded new leadership.

In June 1967 Stokes announced that he would oppose Locher again. This time he entered the Democratic primary. A third candidate, former Lakewood mayor Frank P. Celeste, joined in the October primary. Locher easily won the endorsement of the city's Democratic machine. Celeste and Stokes joined in a series of debates throughout the city, thus assuring Stokes of needed exposure in white neighborhoods. In recognition of its candidate's telegenic appeal, the Stokes primary campaign spent an unusu-

ally large amount for television spots. The Cleveland chapter of the Congress of Racial Equality lent crucial assistance to the Stokes campaign by utilizing part of a $175,000 Ford Foundation grant to register blacks for the primary. The turnout in black neighborhoods averaged 15 percent higher on primary day than in white precincts. Stokes defeated Locher and Celeste with 52.7 percent of the total primary vote. He captured 96 percent of the black Democratic vote and between 12 percent and 15 percent of the party's white electorate.

In the month between the primary and general election, Stokes engaged in a bitter contest with Republican nominee Seth C. Taft, grandson of President William Howard Taft and cousin of Representative Robert Taft, Jr. (R-Ohio). An admirer of New York mayor JOHN V. LINDSAY, Taft sought to overcome his party's weak showing in previous mayoral elections and his family's political conservatism by emphasizing his own liberal Republicanism. Stokes, however, enjoyed the endorsement of both major dailies and greater financial support. In November he improved on his share of the white Democratic vote and defeated Taft by a thin margin. With the simultaneous election of Richard Hatcher as mayor of Gary, Indiana, liberal observers hailed the black politicians' triumph as the harbinger of a rising generation of high-level black officeholders.

Stokes enjoyed a series of personal triumphs as mayor in the spring of 1968. In the days following the assassination of Dr. MARTIN LUTHER KING, JR., he successfully staved off the racial troubles which plagued most other urban centers. On May 1 he announced an ambitious new plan for the reconstruction of Cleveland. With the full support of the city's business community Stokes's "Cleveland: NOW!" project aimed at a wide range of city problems over the next 10 years at an estimated cost of $1.25 billion. Less than a week later, Louis Stokes, the mayor's brother, won the Democratic nomination in the city's newly apportioned predominantly African-American congressional district.

Stokes's popularity proved short-lived, however. In July 1968 reports reached Cleveland police that a local book store operator, Fred (Ahmed) Evans, and his "Black Nationalists of New Libya" had gathered an arsenal of semiautomatic weapons with the intention of inciting the black community to riot. For reasons that remain unclear, shooting broke out on the night of July 23 between the Evans nationalists and police in the Glenville section.

Subsequent looting took place throughout much of the East Side. Within hours, nine people—including three police officers—lay dead.

Although Stokes had played the leading role in ending the Glenville riots, he faced a wave of criticism over the incident. The city council and local Fraternal Order of Police strongly condemned the mayor's exclusive use of black police officers in the resolution of the riot. The most devastating blow to the mayor's prestige, however, came with the revelation that Evans's New Nationalists had received $10,000 in "Cleveland: NOW!" funds. (Evans was found guilty of first-degree murder in May 1969.)

Stokes never again enjoyed the widespread popularity of April and May 1968. Several embarrassing appointments and adverse economic conditions beyond his control severely hampered Stokes's effectiveness. Stokes narrowly defeated a white Republican opponent in November 1969 but declined to seek a third term in 1971. In March 1972 Stokes announced that he had accepted a newscasting job with WNBC in New York City. He was a municipal judge in Cleveland from 1983 to 1994. He died on April 3, 1996.

—JLB

## Stone, I(sidor) F(einstein)

(1907–1989)   *editor,* I.F. Stone's Weekly

Born Isidor Feinstein, on December 24, 1907, in Philadelphia, Stone moved with his family to Haddonfield, New Jersey, as a teenager and began publishing his own newspaper, the *Progress.* He worked for a Camden newspaper while still in high school and entered the University of Pennsylvania in 1924, but dropped out in his junior year. He became an editorial writer for the *Philadelphia Record* and, then, in 1933, the *New York Post.* A socialist, he still wrote editorials praising the New Deal for the latter publication. During the 1930s, because of his concern about anti-Semitism, he changed his name to I. F. Stone. Between 1938 and 1952, he worked for the *Nation, PM,* and the *New York Daily Compass.* An opponent of the Truman administration's cold war policies, he supported Henry Wallace's 1948 Progressive Party candidacy. In 1952 he wrote *The Hidden History of the Korean War,* which challenged the prevailing view that North Korean aggression accounted for the outbreak of that conflict.

After *PM* folded in 1952, Stone was unable to find a job because of his controversial views. The following year he began publishing *I.F. Stone's Weekly,* an independent newsletter. Among the *Weekly's* first targets were Senator Joseph R. McCarthy (R-Wisc.), the House Un-American Activities Committee, and the practice of blacklisting alleged Communists and radicals.

Describing himself as a democratic socialist, Stone was an independent radical who avoided affiliation with organized political groups and spoke only for himself. In his role as a journalist he was also independent. His newsletter did not accept advertising, and Stone did all his own research, reportorial, and editorial work, while his wife handled the newsletter's business affairs. By 1963 his *Weekly* had a circulation of over 20,000.

Stone was best known for what his admirers believed was his iconoclastic skill in exposing the inconsistencies, mistakes, and hypocrisy of public officials and his ability to detect the early signals of changes in government policy. Although he was based in Washington, D.C., his information did not come from personal contacts with highly placed sources, of which he had few, or from official briefings, from which he was often excluded. Stone's journalistic method was the diligent sifting and comparison of government publications that were available to everyone but generally went unread.

During the early 1960s Stone criticized President John F. Kennedy's efforts to use military means to combat revolutionary regimes and movements. In April 1961 he warned that American support of the unsuccessful Bay of Pigs invasion and of the faltering effort of the Ngo Dinh Diem regime in South Vietnam to suppress the National Liberation Front (NLF) demonstrated the administration's failure to recognize that communism could be fought successfully only by responding to the aspirations of the people of the world's poor nations.

During the mid-1960s Stone's attention focused on the Vietnam War. Rejecting the U.S. contention that the NLF was an arm of North Vietnamese aggression, Stone wrote in February 1964, "The biggest obstacle to a settlement is the myth that the South Vietnamese war is an invasion, not a rebellion."

In August 1964 Stone questioned the administration's version of the events surrounding alleged North Vietnamese attacks on American military vessels in the Tonkin Gulf. He noted Senator WAYNE MORSE's (D-Ore.) contention that the vessels were on patrol near South Vietnamese ships that were shelling two North Vietnamese islands and were in a position to protect those ships. Stone also pointed out that during Senate debate on the Tonkin Gulf Resolution, which authorized the president to take all necessary steps to repel North Vietnamese aggression, neither Senator J. WILLIAM FULBRIGHT (D-Ark.) nor Senator RICHARD B. RUSSELL (D-Ga.), the chairs of the congressional committees that were briefed by the administration on the Tonkin incident, denied any of Morse's facts. He suggested that there was reason to doubt the administration's contention the U.S. vessels on routine patrol had been the targets of North Vietnamese aggression.

In March 1965 Stone used a close reading of a State Department White Paper to reveal what he said were contradictions in the argument for military intervention to support the South Vietnamese government. He compared the number of Communist-made weapons captured from South Vietnamese guerrillas listed in an appendix to the White Paper with what he learned from the Pentagon press office were the much larger quantities of American weapons seized by the rebels. Stone concluded that Communist nations supplied the insurgents with only a tiny fraction of their munitions. Stone also wrote that although the White Paper contended that about 75 percent of the NLF guerrillas who infiltrated South Vietnam from North Vietnam in the first eight months of 1964 were natives of the North, most of the guerrillas whose case histories were presented in the text and the appendices were from the South.

Next to Vietnam, the condition of American blacks was Stone's primary concern during the years of the Johnson presidency. In August 1966 he stated that the most urgent need of blacks was jobs and asserted that the growing nationalist sentiment among African Americans did not offer a realistic program to meet that need. But Stone still thought that the Black Power movement was an important source of self-respect and pride among African Americans and, ultimately, would help bring an improvement in race relations.

As opposition to the war in Vietnam mounted, Stone's *Weekly* became increasingly popular. But he incurred criticism when, after the Six-Day War of 1967, he urged Israel to take a more conciliatory position on the issue of resettlement of the Palestinian refugees. He argued that if Israel were not magnanimous in the wake of its overwhelming victory in that conflict, an Arab desire for revenge would spark future wars.

In December 1971 Stone announced that he would cease publication of his newsletter. At the same time he became a contributing editor to the *New York Review of Books*, for which he had been writing occasionally since 1964. He continued to write about political and social issues until his death on June 18, 1989.

—MLL

## Sullivan, Leonor Alice K(retzer)
(1902–1988) *member of the House of Representatives*

Born on August 21, 1902, Leonor Kretzer supervised the training of business machine operators in St. Louis, the city of her birth, before marrying Representative John B. Sullivan (D-Mo.) in 1941. She served as her husband's administrative assistant until his death in 1951. The St. Louis Democratic committee refused to slate her for her late husband's seat, and she sat out the special election. In the May 1952 primary election, however, she defeated seven Democratic rivals. In November she beat the Republican incumbent by a 2-to-1 margin. She was the first female member of Congress from Missouri.

In Congress Sullivan soon gained a reputation as a strong liberal on social issues, with a particular interest in consumer protection. In 1957 Sullivan played an important part in the passage at the Poultry Products Inspection Act. In 1959 she successfully included a food stamp plan in the administration's agriculture program, but Secretary of Agriculture Ezra Taft Benson withheld funds to implement it. Shortly after President Kennedy took office, Sullivan reminded him of his previous support for her food stamp plan and declared that Kennedy now was in a position "to prove that he meant it." Kennedy set up a pilot food-stamp program, and, in 1964, President Johnson signed the legislation that Sullivan had sponsored to establish a permanent program.

When the food-stamp program came up for renewal in 1967, opponents of the program supported a proposal to assess the states 20 percent of the program's cost. According to *Congressional Quarterly*, Sullivan believed this amendment was designed to scuttle the entire program, and she successfully opposed the measure on the House floor. When the bill reached the House-Senate conference, Agriculture Committee conservatives refused to compromise and kept the renewal measure in conference for more than two months. In retaliation, Sullivan led a coalition of northern Democrats who successfully defeated a peanut acreage bill favored by committee conservatives on August 21, 1967. A month later the conferees reported a compromise bill acceptable to Sullivan, and the peanut acreage bill was allowed to pass.

An early supporter of truth-in-lending legislation, Representative Sullivan introduced a House bill on July 20, 1967, which was stronger than either the administration's bill or the bill Senator WILLIAM PROXMIRE (D-Wisc.) had guided through the Senate earlier that month. Sullivan's bill, which went beyond simple disclosure of finance charges to include comprehensive credit protection for the consumer, became law in May 1968. Sullivan fought especially hard for the application of the rate disclosure principle to revolving charge accounts and opposed wage garnishment, which she termed "a successor to debtor's prison." When he signed the Consumer Credit Protection Act, President Johnson praised her fight "for a strong and effective bill when others would have settled for less." During the Nixon administration Representative Sullivan cosponsored a 1969 bill establishing a permanent office of consumer protection. She retired from Congress in 1977 and died on September 1, 1988.

—DKR

## Sullivan, William C(ornelius)

*(1912–1977) assistant director in charge of the Domestic Intelligence Division, FBI*

Born on May 25, 1912, on a farm near Bolton, Massachusetts, Sullivan earned a B.A. from American University, worked for the Internal Revenue Service, and joined the FBI in 1941. He worked in counterintelligence during World War II and steadily moved up the ranks of the bureau. During the 1950s he earned a reputation as a popular and entertaining speaker who lectured on the menace of communism in the United States. In 1961 he became assistant FBI director in charge of the Domestic Intelligence Division.

In the early 1960s Sullivan's division began investigating alleged Communist ties to MARTIN LUTHER KING, JR. J. EDGAR HOOVER, the director of the FBI, was an ardent opponent of civil rights who believed that King was a subversive who listened to Communist advisers. With the approach of the planned August 28, 1963, March on Washing-

ton, surveillance of King and others involved in the planning of that event intensified. On August 23 Sullivan reported that the Communist Party had not been able "to appreciably infiltrate, influence, or control" the civil rights movement. This conclusion outraged Hoover, who strongly believed otherwise, and Sullivan worried that his report had diminished his influence with the FBI director and might even cost him and others in his division their jobs. Sullivan hastily repudiated his earlier conclusion and wrote to Hoover that there was "an urgent need for imaginative and aggressive tactics to be utilized through our Counterintelligence Program . . . to neutralize or disrupt the Party's activities in the Negro field."

In October 1963 Attorney General ROBERT F. KENNEDY granted the FBI permission to wiretap King's home telephone. Sullivan then assumed control of a wide-ranging effort, utilizing wiretaps and "bugging," to gather information about King's private life. This information was subsequently leaked to select government officials including President Johnson. In an attempt to destroy King's marriage, the bureau sent his wife information concerning his extramarital affairs. In January 1964 Sullivan proposed that once King had been publicly disgraced, the bureau should promote its own black candidate to lead the civil rights movement. In November the bureau sent King a letter suggesting that he commit suicide.

Beginning in 1967 Sullivan's Domestic Intelligence Division also attempted to discredit ELIJAH MUHAMMED, H. RAP BROWN, and STOKELY CARMICHAEL and to disrupt the activities of the Southern Christian Leadership Conference, the Student Nonviolent Coordinating Committee, the Congress of Racial Equality, and other black groups it considered dangerous.

Sullivan was not exclusively concerned with subverting the civil rights movement or attempting to diminish the influence of what the bureau called inner-city "rabble rousers." By the fall of 1964 he had won permission from Hoover to neutralize the Ku Klux Klan and other "white hate" groups. It was also at Sullivan's urging that in May 1968 New Left organizations became targets of the bureau's COINTELPRO (or counterintelligence) campaign. Bureau agents faked documents to create dissension within various antiwar groups and sent intimidating letters to their leaders; the bureau also requested that the Internal Revenue Service audit the tax returns of key members of the antiwar movement.

Appearing before a Senate Select Committee in November 1975, Sullivan was asked whether members of the bureau ever questioned the fairness of COINTELPRO tactics. "We never gave any thought to this line of reasoning," he said "because we were just naturally pragmatic. As far as legality is concerned, morals or ethics [the problem] was never raised by myself or anybody else."

During the early Nixon years Sullivan maintained close relations with the administration. At the request of the president and National Security Advisor HENRY KISSINGER, Sullivan's office managed wiretaps placed on the phones of government officials and journalists to determine how secret information was being leaked to the press.

In June 1970 Hoover promoted Sullivan to the post of assistant director in charge of all investigative activities. By the fall of 1970, however, their relations had begun to deteriorate. At one point Sullivan suggested that the bureau was in decline because the director had surrounded himself with "cringing, frightened sycophants." Hoover then requested that Sullivan retire. Before doing so in October 1971, Sullivan turned over to the White House wiretap logs that Hoover could have used to blackmail the administration.

After leaving the bureau Sullivan worked for the Insurance Crime Prevention Institute and briefly for the Office of National Narcotics Intelligence. By the mid-1970s he had retired to his home in New Hampshire. He died in a hunting accident on November 9, 1977.

—JLW

## Sullivan, William H(ealy)

### (1922–   ) ambassador to Laos

A career foreign service officer, who was born on October 12, 1922, in Cranston, Rhode Island, William Sullivan specialized in East Asian affairs. Shortly after World War II he served in Bangkok, Calcutta, and Tokyo. In 1952 he was sent to Rome and in 1955 to The Hague before resuming his Far Eastern assignments as officer-in-charge of Burma affairs for the Department of State in 1958. In 1960 Sullivan became UN adviser for the Bureau of Far Eastern Affairs.

During the Kennedy administration Sullivan served as a member of the U.S. delegation to the 1961 Geneva conference on Laos. At the conference he was deputy to Ambassador W. AVERELL HARRI-

MAN, who led the delegation. In December Sullivan became acting head when Harriman left to assume the position of assistant secretary of state for Far Eastern affairs. During the spring of 1962 Sullivan worked with Harriman in a series of negotiations with Laotian leaders designed to gain acceptance of a neutralist coalition government in that country.

On February 24, 1964, President LYNDON B. JOHNSON appointed Sullivan chair of the Vietnam Working Group, a body formed to plan the possible escalation of the war and to coordinate policy decisions and statements between the Defense Department, the Central Intelligence Agency (CIA), and the U.S. Information Agency.

In June, Sullivan expressed deep concerns about the effectiveness of the South Vietnamese government. Sullivan explained that many Saigon leaders lacked confidence in U.S. intentions since they were keenly aware of congressional and media critics of greater commitment in Southeast Asia. Yet these South Vietnamese, according to Sullivan, also had "some fear of appearing to be American puppets" as the level of outside assistance increased. The result, he asserted, was the absence of "a single galvanized national purpose, expressed in the government leadership and energizing all parts of the country with a simple sense of confidence." Accompanying Sullivan's memorandum, which went to Secretary of State DEAN RUSK and Secretary of Defense ROBERT MCNAMARA, was a memorandum from Assistant Secretary of State WILLIAM BUNDY emphasizing the need to "lift morale in South Vietnam." Bundy suggested doing so by seeking approval of a congressional resolution, a draft of which he attached, giving the president broad authority to halt North Vietnamese aggression. The president chose not to submit this resolution in June. But two months later, after the incidents in the Gulf of Tonkin, the president secured congressional endorsement of a revised version of the resolution.

In December 1964 Sullivan became ambassador to Laos. There he controlled the secret U.S. war to assist anticommunist forces in Laos and to interfere with North Vietnamese efforts to utilize support routes in Laotian territory. Sullivan centralized the war effort under his command. As ambassador, Sullivan rather than the military, chose the bombing targets and the types of aircraft used. His control was so complete that Assistant Secretary of State William Bundy said, "There wasn't a bag of rice dropped in Laos that he didn't know about."

During his tenure Sullivan tried to impose two crucial conditions on American actions in Laos. He urged that the war be carried out in relative secrecy to avoid embarrassing either the neutralist leader Souvanna Phouma or the Soviets. He also insisted that no regular U.S. ground combat troops be allowed into Laos. Forces trained or directed by the CIA did play an important role in Laos.

Sullivan became deputy assistant secretary of state for East Asia in 1969. He served as U.S. ambassador to Iran from 1977 until 1979, leaving shortly after the revolution that overthrew Shah Mohammed Reza Pahlavi.

—EWS

## Sylvester, Arthur
(1901–1979) *assistant secretary of defense for public affairs*

Sylvester, who was born in Montclair, New Jersey, on October 21, 1901, graduated from Princeton University in 1923, and became, a year later, a reporter for the *Newark News*. He was the newspaper's Washington bureau chief when he accepted the position of assistant secretary of defense for public affairs in January 1961.

As the Defense Department's chief press officer, Sylvester earned credit for opening up the Pentagon to a wider flow of information and forcing officials who once would not be interviewed to answer questions. Yet Sylvester became a central figure in both the Kennedy and Johnson administrations not as an advocate of press freedom but as someone who continually clashed with journalists and who advanced the belief that the government had the right to withhold the news in certain critical situations. Following the Cuban missile crisis of 1962, Sylvester, in an informal interview, maintained that "the generation of news by the government" was "one weapon" to be used in a crisis situation. In a later statement he argued, "It's inherent in government's right . . . to lie to save itself when it's going up into nuclear war."

During the Johnson administration Sylvester continued to defend these ideas, exacerbating what critics called a "credibility gap" in reporting the Vietnam War. The worst incident in Sylvester's tempestuous relationship with journalists during the war came when he visited Saigon in July 1965. In a meeting with correspondents covering the war, Sylvester maintained that U.S. reporters should "get

on the team" and file stories that made U.S. policy look successful. His comments reflected his belief that the news media should serve as the "handmaiden" of government. If correspondents did not follow his advice, he threatened to apply pressure on their editors. Then he blurted out, "Look, if you think that any American official is going to tell you the truth, you're stupid." To emphasize the point, he put his thumbs in his ears, stuck out his tongue, and wiggled his fingers. His actions did much to confirm a widespread conviction among journalists that U.S. information officers in Vietnam could not be trusted to provide reliable information.

In January 1967 Sylvester resigned his position. He served as mayor of Cold Spring, New York, from 1977 until 1979. He died on December 28, 1979.

—EWS

## Symington, (William) Stuart
(1901–1988) *member of the Senate*

Symington was born on June 26, 1901, in Amherst, Massachusetts. He served in the army during World War I, and he attended Yale University, but left in 1923 without completing his degree requirements. He then began a successful business career that earned him the reputation of being a "doctor of ailing corporations" because of his ability to revive foundering enterprises and deal with labor problems.

During the Truman administration Symington held several important posts, including assistant secretary of war for air. In 1947, after the creation of the Department of Defense, he became the first secretary of the air force. Believing that the United States had to act from a position of military superiority to contain Soviet expansion, Symington became a leading proponent of increased defense spending. He particularly advocated the development of a large nuclear-equipped air force as the cornerstone of a modern defense system. In 1950, shortly before the Korean War, the secretary resigned to protest a series of economy-minded restructions on the size of the air force.

During the Korean War, he chaired the National Security Resources Board and the Reconstruction Finance Corporation. He resigned the latter position in 1952 to run for the Senate from Missouri. He unseated the Republican incumbent in a year when Republican candidates, including presidential candidate DWIGHT D. EISENHOWER, gained many notable victories. He won reelection to three more terms.

During the Kennedy years Symington continued to favor large military appropriations, especially for air power. He supported the development of the controversial TFX multi-service fighter/bomber in 1963.

Symington believed that it was important to contain communism in Southeast Asia, and he supported the dispatch of U.S. combat troops to Vietnam in 1965. Yet he also criticized the Johnson administration for imposing restraints on the air war by not allowing U.S. planes to bomb what military leaders considered important targets. He visited South Vietnam in September 1967 and found that U.S. pilots "quietly resented" what they considered restrictive rules of engagement that he believed "increased danger to their own lives" in an effort to limit North Vietnamese casualties. These restrictions on the use of air power helped persuade him that the war could not be won. In October he therefore urged a unilateral cease-fire aimed at initiating peace negotiations. During the next several months he also reappraised the effects of the war on U.S. security. He now reached the conclusion that the war was weakening the U.S. economy and endangering global commitments.

Throughout his career Symington had voted in favor of most foreign aid bills, but after 1967 he opposed those measures because of his belief that the United States was economically and militarily overcommitted throughout the world. He also voted against new weapons development projects because of the frequency with which they were changed or canceled.

During the Nixon administration Symington spoke out against extension of the war in Cambodia and Laos and demanded American troop withdrawals from Europe. Pointing out that many major military commitments of the 1960s and 1970s had been made through executive agreements without the knowledge or consent of Congress, Symington campaigned for the reassertion of congressional authority in foreign policy matters during the 1970s. He did not run for reelection in 1976. He died on December 14, 1988.

—EWS

# T

## Talmadge, Herman E(ugene)
### (1913–2002) *member of the Senate*

The son of Eugene Talmadge, the governor of Georgia during the 1930s and 1940s, Herman Talmadge was born on August 9, 1913, near McRae, Georgia. He earned a law degree from the University of Georgia in 1936, practiced law in Atlanta, and served in the navy during World War II. When his father died after being elected governor in 1946, but before being sworn in, he claimed to be the legitimate successor and held office briefly until the Georgia Supreme Court ruled his claim invalid. He won a special election, however, in 1948 to complete his father's term and then a full term of his own in 1950.

Although less flamboyant than his father, Talmadge still appealed to the racial fears of Georgia's white citizens. He insisted that the eradication of segregation would lead to the creation of a "mongrel race," a development that Communists allegedly desired. Barred by Georgia law from running for a second consecutive term as governor, he won a seat in the U.S. Senate in 1956. He consistently opposed civil rights legislation in the late 1950s and early 1960s and voted against most social welfare measures in the hope of limiting the power of the federal government to intervene in what he believed should be state or local concerns.

During the Johnson presidency he opposed many Great Society programs and voted against the Civil Rights Act of 1964.

In April 1965 Talmadge attacked the voting rights bill as "grossly unjust and vindictive in nature." In 1968 the administration offered an open housing bill, which included a provision protecting persons attempting to exercise their civil rights from injury, intimidation, or interference. Talmadge successfully offered an amendment to extend this protection to store owners or operators during civil disorders but voted against the final bill.

Talmadge gradually retracted from his defense of segregation and his appeals to racial fears as the number of black voters in his state increased. In 1966, speaking before a predominantly black Atlanta organization, he stated that there would be no more "race-baiting" campaigns in Georgia.

During the early years of the Johnson presidency Talmadge strongly supported the Vietnam War. In 1965 he denounced student opponents of the conflict as guilty of "treason and anarchy." The following year, speaking as a member of Congress's Joint Economic Committee, Talmadge urged restraint in domestic spending so that military needs in Indochina could be met. But in 1967 Talmadge stated that foreign aid and military spending were responsible for America's unfavorable balance of payments. The following year, citing graft and corruption in Vietnam, he expressed doubts about the worth of the administration's request for $480 million in aid to that country.

During the Nixon administration Talmadge criticized U.S. strategy for waging war in Southeast Asia. In 1969 he questioned the purpose of fighting a war that the government, in his view, was not attempting to win. Two years later he favored the withdrawal of American troops from Vietnam.

In the face of an enlarged black and urban electorate in Georgia, Talmadge became somewhat more disposed to support social welfare programs in the late 1960s and early 1970s. In 1971 he became chair of the Senate Agriculture and Forestry Committee and two years later was appointed to the Senate Select Committee to Investigate Presidential Campaign Activities, popularly known as the Watergate Committee.

Talmadge eventually faced ethical problems of his own arising from the misuse of campaign funds. After an investigation by the Ethics Committee, the Senate voted in 1979 to denounce him for financial misconduct. He lost his bid for a fifth term in the Senate in the election of 1980. He died on March 21, 2002.

—MLL

## Taylor, Maxwell D(avenport)
**(1901–1987)** *chair of the Joint Chiefs of Staff, ambassador to South Vietnam*

Born on August 26, 1901, in Keytesville, Missouri, Taylor attended West Point, graduating fourth in his class. During World War II he was artillery commander of the 82nd Airborne Division in the Sicilian and Italian campaigns and commander of the 101st Airborne in the Normandy invasion. From 1945 to 1949 he was superintendent of West Point.

During the next six years Taylor served in a number of command and staff positions before being named army chief of staff in 1955. In that post he criticized the Eisenhower administration's emphasis on massive nuclear retaliation and argued for strong ground forces capable of fighting conventional wars. Taylor presented his views to the public in *The Uncertain Trumpet*, published in 1959 after his retirement from the army.

After the Bay of Pigs failure, President Kennedy appointed Taylor to head an investigation of the Central Intelligence Agency's role in the unsuccessful Cuban invasion. In June 1961 he became a military representative of the president, and, in October of that year, he headed a mission to South Vietnam following a series of National Liberation Front (NLF) victories. To the surprise of many, he recommend the commitment of 8,000 American combat troops to the conflict although he suggested that their mission be disguised as flood relief. Taylor's troop recommendation was not carried out, but Kennedy did increase military aid and made contingency plans for the dispatch of combat troops.

In July 1962 Kennedy nominated Taylor for chair of the Joint Chiefs of Staff. A consistent supporter of administration policies, he provided crucial backing for the nuclear test ban treaty in congressional testimony during August 1963. In late

September, Kennedy sent Taylor and Secretary of Defense ROBERT S. MCNAMARA to South Vietnam to assess the military and political situation. They reported that the government of Ngo Dinh Diem was "becoming increasingly unpopular," but that "the military campaign has made great progress." They also predicted that it would be possible during the next two years to train South Vietnamese so that they could be responsible for their own national security and to withdraw most U.S. advisers by the end of 1965. The president endorsed this training effort and, on October 11, directed the preparation of plans to withdraw 1,000 American troops from South Vietnam by the end of 1963.

In June 1964 President Johnson selected Taylor to replace HENRY CABOT LODGE as ambassador to South Vietnam. Taylor concluded, shortly after arriving in Saigon, that the repressiveness of the

General Maxwell Taylor, chair of the Joint Chiefs of Staff and ambassador to South Vietnam, 1968 *(Photographed by Yoichi R. Okamoto; Lyndon Baines Johnson Library)*

South Vietnamese government was a serious impediment to the successful prosecution of the war. He pressed Major General Nguyen Khanh, who had replaced Diem as national leader following a November 1963 military coup, to arrange for the creation of a civilian-drawn constitutional charter. A provisional, civilian High National Council was established in September 1964, but in December it was overthrown by dissident military officers, led by, among others, Air Vice Marshal Nguyen Cao Ky and General Nguyen Van Thieu. Shortly afterward Taylor called a meeting of the officers and said, "I told you all clearly . . . we Americans were tired of coups. Apparently I wasted my words. . . . Now you have made a real mess." Despite Taylor's exhortations the officers refused to reestablish civilian rule.

Taylor supported the sustained American bombing of North Vietnam that began in March 1965. But when the bombing failed to alter North Vietnam's policies, he tried to resist the ensuing pressure from the U.S. military for sending large numbers of American combat troops to South Vietnam. In late March Taylor returned to Washington for a series of major strategy conferences. The Joint Chiefs of Staff and General WILLIAM WESTMORELAND favored the deployment of at least two American divisions on search-and-destroy missions in the South Vietnamese interior. Taylor argued for the dispatch of a much smaller number of troops to guard enclaves around U.S. bases. He maintained that the arrival of American combat forces would encourage the South Vietnamese army to slacken its efforts, arouse anti-Americanism, and lead to ever-increasing U.S. military involvement.

During the next few months General William Westmoreland, the commander of U.S. forces in South Vietnam, requested additional troops because of the deteriorating military situation. Taylor continued to express reservations, but, by July 1965, he changed his position. On July 28, the president announced the immediate dispatch of additional troops that would raise the number of U.S. forces in South Vietnam to 125,000. "Additional forces will be needed later," Johnson declared, "and they will be sent as requested."

In July 1965 Taylor was replaced as ambassador to South Vietnam by the returning Lodge. Later in the year President Johnson appointed him a special presidential consultant, but in that post Taylor no longer had a major influence on policy-making decisions.

Taylor consistently took a hawkish position on the Vietnam War during the remaining years of the Johnson administration. In March 1968, when the President convened a panel of senior advisers commonly known as the "Wise Men," Taylor was one of a minority who counseled against the beginning of disengagement. He told the president that he was confident that the American people would accept "the need for doing these very tough things that are facing us in Southeast Asia."

He published a book of memoirs, *Swords and Plowshares*, in 1972. He died on April 19, 1987.

—MLL

## Terry, Luther L(eonidas)
(1911–1985) *U.S. Surgeon General*

Terry, who was born in Red Level, Alabama, on September 15, 1911, earned his M.D. degree at Tulane University and specialized in cardiovascular medicine. He was assistant director of the National Heart Institute before President John F. Kennedy named him surgeon general in early 1961. As head of the Public Health Service, a division of the Department of Health, Education and Welfare, Terry was responsible for a variety of public health programs including the monitoring of the levels of radioactive fallout from Soviet and American above-ground nuclear explosions and the testing and distribution of polio and measles vaccines.

Terry won national prominence in January 1964, when he released a controversial study of the effect of smoking on health. He had commissioned the study 14 months earlier following a report by the Royal College of Physicians in Great Britain that cigarette smoking caused cancer and bronchitis.

The surgeon general's report, which Terry issued January 11, 1964, concluded that there was a definite correlation between cigarette smoking and lung cancer. It also suggested that the incidence of heart, respiratory, and circulatory diseases among smokers exceeded that of nonsmokers and asserted that "cigarette smoking is a health hazard of sufficient importance in the United States to warrant appropriate remedial action."

Following the release of the report, the value of tobacco stocks plummeted. Cigarette sales also declined but subsequently rose to levels only slightly below those of the previous year. Meanwhile PAUL RAND DIXON, chair of the Federal Trade Commission (FTC), announced that the FTC would require all cigarette packages and advertising to state: "Smoking is dangerous to health and may cause death from cancer and other diseases." Dixon's announcement was bitterly denounced by cigarette manufacturers and by many members of Congress from tobacco-growing states, who contended that the surgeon general's report was allegedly inaccurate and misleading because it was based on limited research. In August 1964 Dixon agreed to delay implementing his order pending congressional action.

In appearances before congressional committees in June 1964 and March 1965, Terry argued that HEW could more effectively enforce cigarette labeling provisions than the FTC. He asserted that Congress should grant HEW broad authority to determine the content of the smoking hazard warning. Congress, which was under great pressure from the tobacco interests, passed legislation in July 1965 requiring the following printed warning on cigarette packages and cartons: "Caution: Cigarette Smoking May Be Hazardous to Your Health," a statement which superseded the more ominous FTC warning. The new legislation prohibited any government agency from imposing an additional warning and postponed the warning requirement for cigarette advertisements until July 1969.

In the fall of 1965 Terry resigned as surgeon general to become vice president for medical affairs of the University of Pennsylvania. He was president of University Associates, a consulting firm from 1970 to 1983. He died on March 24, 1985.

—JLW

## Thomas, Norman (Mattoon)

(1884–1968) *spokesperson, Socialist Party*

Born on November 20, 1884, in Marion, Ohio, Thomas graduated from Princeton University in 1905 and earned a bachelor of divinity degree from Union Theological Seminary, a center of Social Gospel education. He became a minister in East Harlem and, in furtherance of his belief in the social responsibility of churches, directed a settlement house that provided social services in an immigrant neighborhood. In 1917 Thomas joined the Fellowship of Reconciliation, a religious pacifist group. He opposed American involvement in World War I.

Thomas joined the Socialist Party in 1918 and, in the same year, left his position in the East Harlem Church. During the 1920s he succeeded Eugene V.

Debs as the leader of the Socialist Party, and he headed its national ticket in every presidential election from 1928 through 1948. He garnered his greatest support in 1932, receiving almost 900,000 votes. In 1950 Thomas urged the party to abandon its increasingly ineffectual electoral efforts He supported Democrat ADLAI E. STEVENSON rather than the Socialists' national tickets in 1952 and 1956.

While believing in the moral superiority of the West over the Communist bloc, Thomas insisted during the 1950s that peaceful coexistence on the military level was necessary to avoid thermonuclear annihilation. In 1957 he was a founder of the Committee for a Sane Nuclear Policy (SANE). In 1961 Thomas helped found Turn Toward Peace, a league of peace and civic organizations. During the early 1960s he supported the civil rights movements and urged government action to ensure jobs for unskilled blacks in an age of increasing automation.

By the 1960s Thomas enjoyed the high esteem of most liberals and even some conservatives. Part of the reason was the good-humored, democratic character of his socialism. He had always favored the development of a "cooperative commonwealth" within the framework of constitutionalism, opposed violent revolution, and rejected the doctrines of class conflict and the dictatorship of the proletariat. But the great regard for Thomas also derived from his personal integrity. Furthermore, the compassion for the weak and the moral concern that formed the foundation of his views earned him wide admiration if not agreement with his ideas.

Thomas had given up his Socialist Party posts by the 1960s but remained the unofficial voice for the organization. However, the party no longer had any significant political influence, and Thomas's activities during the last years of his life centered on his individual advocacy of various liberal causes.

In 1964 Thomas campaigned actively for President LYNDON B. JOHNSON, praising his record on civil rights and poverty while denouncing the Republican candidate. Senator BARRY M. GOLDWATER (R-Ariz.), as "the greatest evil" in American politics. But Thomas was one of the earliest critics of the president's escalation of the American military involvement in Vietnam. In January 1965 Thomas warned against intervention in what he regarded as a civil war in Southeast Asia. The following June he contended that American efforts to act as the world's police officer would unify an increasingly polycentric

Communist bloc. Thomas assisted in the organization of a November 1965 antiwar rally in the District of Columbia at which he denounced the Indochina conflict as "cruelly immoral and politically stupid." However, Thomas opposed an abrupt unilateral withdrawal from Vietnam because of his fear of a massacre of Vietnamese opponents of the National Liberation Front. He praised the young people who opposed the war but expressed concern over what he felt were the excesses of the New Left. In 1968 Thomas backed the candidacy of Senator EUGENE J. MCCARTHY (D-Minn.) for the Democratic presidential nomination.

A supporter of the right of Soviet Jews to emigrate freely, Thomas joined civil rights leader BAYARD RUSTIN, John C. Bennett, president of Union Theological Seminary, and others in March 1966 to hold public hearings as the Ad Hoc Committee on the Rights of Soviet Jews. At the conclusion of its investigation in December, the committee urged the Soviet Union to permit Soviet Jews to settle in Israel or any other country.

As chair of the Institute for International Labor Research, created in 1957 to train democratic leaders in Latin America, Thomas denounced American intervention in the Dominican Republic in April 1965 during an uprising against that country's military junta. In June of the following year, Thomas and other observes went to the Dominican Republic to ensure that a scheduled presidential election would be conducted fairly. Although the country's leading democratic political figure, Juan Bosch, was defeated, Thomas and his colleagues were satisfied that the election was fair.

In February 1967 it was revealed that the institute had been receiving Central Intelligence Agency (CIA) funds. Thomas denied any knowledge of the CIA financing and expressed surprise that the agency had supported an organization promoting liberal democracy.

During the fall of 1967 Thomas suffered a stroke. He died in a nursing home on December 19, 1968.

—MLL

## Thompson, Frank, Jr.
(1918–1989) *member of the House of Representatives*
Thompson, who was born on July 16, 1918, in Trenton, New Jersey, served in the navy during both World War II and the Korean War, practiced law in Trenton, and won election to the state assembly in 1949. He won a House seat as a self-styled "New Deal–Fair Deal Democrat of the Adlai Stevenson school" in 1954. Assigned to the Education and Labor Committee, Thompson was a principal sponsor of several major education acts, including controversial proposals in 1959 and 1961 to provide federal grants to increase teachers' salaries. In 1959 Thompson cofounded the Democratic Study Group, which sought to develop a liberal legislative program and reform such "antiquated and obstructive" House procedures as the seniority system.

Thompson's efforts to fund the arts and humanities bore fruit in September 1965, when Johnson signed a bill, sponsored by Thompson, establishing the National Foundation on the Arts and Humanities. During the House debate Thompson described the United States as "the last civilized nation on the earth to realize that the arts and humanities have a place in our national life."

During the Johnson years, Thompson was a vigorous supporter of legislation that organized labor endorsed. In 1966 he was floor manager of the labor-endorsed bill permitting "common-site" picketing on construction jobs. The chair of the Education and Labor Committee, ADAM CLAYTON POWELL, JR. (D-N.Y.) kept the bill from coming to a vote because he insisted that unions first had to meet his requirements to eliminate practices that were racially discriminatory.

Powell's obstruction of this bill and his high-handed ways of using his powers as chair angered Thompson and other committee members. Thompson became a leader of committee members who challenged Powell's leadership. Thompson was the principal author of new rules that restricted Powell's authority as chair. The adoption of the new rules in September 1966 brought to the surface widespread congressional opposition to Powell on other issues. This hostility, combined with revelations of misuse of government funds on Powell's staff, resulted in the March 1, 1967, vote to exclude him from the 90th Congress.

In 1976 Thompson became chair of the powerful House Administration Committee. But his congressional career ended in ignominy several years later. In 1980 a jury convicted him of bribery and conspiracy charges arising from the Abscam scandal, in which federal agents posing as rich Arabs offered cash payments to members of Congress.

Thompson lost his bid for reelection shortly after his conviction, and he served two years in jail from 1983 to 1985. He died on July 22, 1989.

—DKR

## Thompson, Llewellyn E.

(1904–1972) *ambassador at large and special adviser on Soviet Affairs to the secretary of state, ambassador to the Soviet Union*

Thompson, who was born on August 24, 1904, in Las Animas, Colorado, graduated from the University of Colorado in 1928 and then enrolled in the Georgetown University School of Foreign Service. He entered the foreign service in 1929, serving in Ceylon (now Sri Lanka) and Switzerland. He went to the U.S. embassy in Moscow in 1941, and this assignment began his specialization in Soviet affairs. As second secretary of the embassy, he remained in Moscow when many foreign diplomats evacuated the Soviet capital because of the danger of German invasion. He began learning Russian at that time and earned the respect of Soviet officials for enduring the hardships of war.

Thompson left Moscow in 1944 for a two-year assignment in the embassy in London. He then went to the State Department, where he held a series of positions in Eastern European affairs. He served in the embassy in Rome for two years and then became in 1952 U.S. high commissioner and, later, ambassador to Austria. As high commissioner, he helped to negotiate the Italian-Yugoslav Trieste settlement and to formulate the treaty restoring Austria's full independence.

In April 1957 President DWIGHT D. EISENHOWER selected Thompson to succeed CHARLES E. BOHLEN. He served in that position during five eventful years. He traveled with Nikita Khrushchev in 1959 to a meeting with President Eisenhower at Camp David, Maryland, the first visit ever by a Soviet leader to the United States. He contributed to the preparations for the ill-fated summit conference in Paris in May 1960 between Khrushchev, Eisenhower, and the leaders of France and Great Britain, which dissolved in acrimony because of the Soviet downing two weeks earlier of a U.S. U2 spy plane. Thompson nevertheless continued to enjoy good relations with the Soviet leadership and helped to arrange the summit in Vienna in June 1961 between Khrushchev and President John F. Kennedy. As ambassador in

Moscow and then as ambassador at large and special adviser to the State Department on Soviet affairs beginning in autumn 1962, Thompson counseled Kennedy on a variety of important foreign policy issues, including Berlin, disarmament, and the Cuban missile crisis.

Thompson continued in his post during the early years of the Johnson administration. He attended all high-level Soviet-American talks, including those held in December 1964 between Secretary of State DEAN RUSK and Soviet foreign minister Andrei Gromyko. He also conducted congressional briefings on major Soviet developments, including the ouster of Premier Nikita S. Khrushchev from power in October 1964. Thompson's own standing with Russian leaders was so high that after an American RB-66 was shot down over East Germany in March 1964 President Johnson asked Thompson to deny personally Soviet charges that the plane was on a spy mission.

In January 1967 President Johnson asked Thompson to return as ambassador to Moscow to try to repair relations that were being increasingly strained by the Vietnam War and to attempt to interest the Soviet Union in promoting Vietnam peace negotiations. Thompson never achieved this goal and, indeed, never had a single serious talk with Communist Party first secretary Leonid I. Brezhnev. He did, however, help lay the groundwork for the inconclusive but cordial summit conference between Premier Aleksei N. Kosygin and President Johnson that took place in Glassboro, New Jersey, in June 1967.

Following his resignation as ambassador in January 1969, Thompson served as a foreign affairs consultant until his death on February 2, 1972.

—EWS

## Thurmond, (James) Strom

(1902–2003) *member of the Senate*

Thurmond, the oldest person ever to hold a seat in the U.S. Senate, was born on December 5, 1902, in Edgefield, South Carolina. After earning a B.S. from Clemson University in 1923, he taught high school and served on the Edgefield County Board of Education. Thurmond took a correspondence course, which allowed him to be admitted to the state bar in 1930. He was elected to the state senate in 1933 and five years later became a circuit court judge. He returned to the bench after serving in the army during World War II and in 1946 was elected governor of South Carolina.

In 1948, after the Democratic National Convention adopted a civil rights plank in its platform, Thurmond became the presidential candidate of the States' Rights, or Dixiecrat, Party. Thurmond campaigned on the issue of halting federal intervention that would endanger state and local control over racial segregation and carried four southern states for a total of 39 electoral votes. Thurmond lost a primary election in 1950 for a U.S. Senate seat, but he ran successfully four years later as a write-in candidate.

Independent, irascible, and occasionally vituperative, Thurmond was a leading opponent of antidiscrimination measures on Capitol Hill. Yet he stood somewhat apart from his southern colleagues because of his displays of flamboyance which some opponents of civil rights considered detrimental to their cause. Thurmond was one of many southern members of Congress who opposed social welfare legislation and favored a strongly anticommunist foreign policy and large defense appropriations. Yet he was one of few to endorse the causes of extreme right-wing groups like the John Birch Society in the early 1960s.

Thurmond transferred his affiliation from the Democratic to the Republican Party in 1964 so that he could work openly for the presidential candidacy of conservative senator BARRY M. GOLDWATER (R-Ariz.). During each of the remaining four years of the Johnson presidency, Thurmond was among the five leading Republican supporters of the Senate's conservative coalition.

A foe of all of the Johnson administration's civil rights proposals, he asserted that the voting rights bill of 1965 would usurp the constitutional authority of the states to establish voter qualifications and would create a "totalitarian" federal government. He denounced a 1967 measure to protect civil rights workers from harassment, stating that it would give "added protection to roving fomenters of violence, such as 'Stokely Carmichael and H. Rap Brown.' " Opposed to most Great Society programs, Thurmond attacked such measures as the 1965 housing bill and the 1967 elementary school aid bill as promoting dangerous expansion of federal power.

A hard-line opponent of what he regarded as unrelenting communist expansionism, Thurmond favored the unrestrained use of military force in Viet-nam. He charged in August 1966 that the administration was following a "no-win" policy in Southeast Asia. The following April he criticized an East-West treaty governing the peaceful exploration and use of outer space as "another step in the artificial and unrealistic atmosphere of détente with communism."

In 1968 Thurmond backed RICHARD M. NIXON for the Republican presidential nomination and was credited with convincing most southern Republican delegates to the party's national convention to vote for Nixon instead of conservative governor RONALD REAGAN of California. The Nixon administration, sometimes relying on the senator's advice, pursued a "southern strategy" of building Republican strength by following policies on such controversial issues as busing designed to appeal to white southern voters. By the time that Republicans took control of the Senate in 1981 for the first time in 28 years, Thurmond, who became chair of the Judiciary Committee, could take satisfaction in the increase of GOP senators from the 11 former confederate states from only two, when Thurmond switched parties in 1964, to nine at the beginning of the Reagan presidency.

Thurmond, who celebrated his 100th birthday at the end of his Senate service, retired in January 2003 and died a few months later on June 26. Shortly after his death, it was revealed that Thurmond, who had supported racial segregation during much of his political career, had a daughter whose mother was an African-American maid who had worked in his family's home during the 1920s.

—MLL

## Tower, John G(oodwin)
### (1925–1991) *member of the Senate*

Born in Houston on September 29, 1925, John G. Tower served in the navy during World War II and earned a bachelor's degree from Southwestern University and a master's degree from Southern Methodist University. Beginning in 1951, he taught political science at Midwestern University in Wichita Falls. He became involved in politics as a Republican, and, in 1960, he ran for the U.S. Senate against LYNDON B. JOHNSON, who was taking advantage of a Texas law that permitted him to run for the vice presidency and the Senate at the same time. Tower lost, but he exceeded expectations by taking more than 40 percent of the vote. In May 1961, he won a special election to fill Johnson's vacated seat, becoming the first Republican from Texas in the upper chamber since Reconstruction and the first Republican senator from a former confederate state since the beginning of popular election of senators in 1913. His victory was a harbinger of the growth of Republican strength in the South during the 1960s.

Tower gained considerable attention because of his conservative views and his close political relationship on Capitol Hill with Senator BARRY GOLDWATER (R-Ariz.). Like Goldwater, he favored an uncompromising anticommunist foreign policy and believed that President Kennedy was too conciliatory toward the Soviet Union. During the Kennedy years the two senators, as members of the Senate Labor and Public Welfare Committee, often issued joint minority reports expressing opposition to administration-sponsored social welfare proposals.

In 1964 Tower was chair of the unanimously pro-Goldwater Texas delegation to the Republican National Convention. On the eve of the convention, he declared that the Republicans had an excellent chance of capturing the White House if they nominated Goldwater. However, the selection of the Arizona senator proved to be a disaster for Texas Republicans. The Johnson sweep in Texas led to the defeat of the party's two U.S. representatives. Tower, however, won reelection in 1966 with 56 percent of the ballots.

Tower continued to compile a consistently conservative record on Capitol Hill during the Johnson administration. In 1964 he unsuccessfully opposed the granting of agricultural credits to Communist nations. Tower was an ardent supporter of America's Vietnam War effort. In March 1967 Senate Majority Leader MIKE MANSFIELD (D-Mont.) offered an amendment to a war appropriations bill urging international negotiations as a means of resolving the Vietnam conflict. Tower denounced the proposal, asserting that "if there is any way to strengthen the will of our opponents, it is to attach to an authorization of an appropriation to take care of our forces in the field another plaintive plea for peace."

In domestic policy Tower remained a foe of social welfare measures, maintaining that they represented an encroachment of federal power on state or individual rights. He joined Goldwater in the summer of 1964 to denounce a bill for extending a defense education act as representing "the slow but relentless advent of federal regulation of education

carried out on the installment plan and seeking to remain undetected under the protective cloak of 'national defense.' " The following year he opposed the Johnson administration's housing and Medicare bills, and in 1966 he voted against Demonstration Cities and mass transit measures. In 1968 the Americans for Democratic Action gave Tower's voting record a zero percent rating, while the Americans for Constitutional Action, a conservative group, supported 94 percent of his key votes.

Tower was reelected in 1972 and 1978, but decided to leave the Senate at the end of his term in 1985. Two years later he headed what was popularly known as the Tower Commission to investigate the Iran-contra scandal. In 1989 President George H. W. Bush nominated him to be secretary of defense. But amid charges that he was a womanizer and heavy drinker and that he had relations with defense industries that might present conflicts of interest, he did not gain Senate confirmation, the first time that an upper chamber had failed to approve a cabinet nominee of a president who had just been elected. He died in a plane crash on April 5, 1991.

—MLL

## Truman, Harry S.
### (1884–1972) *president of the United States*

Truman, who became president during a critical period in international affairs, spent most of his first 50 years in his native state of Missouri. He was born in Lamar, Missouri, on May 8, 1884, grew up in Independence, and managed a farm near Grandview. He served as a captain in an artillery regiment that fought in France during World War I. After the war, he started a haberdashery business in Kansas City with a partner, but it closed in 1922.

His political career began that same year, when he won election as a district judge of the Jackson County Court. He failed to gain reelection at the close of his two-year term. But in the election of 1926, and with the backing of the powerful Pendergast Democratic machine, he won the position of presiding county judge, an office that he held for eight years. In 1934 he won a U.S. Senate seat, and he consistently supported the Roosevelt administration. Truman got national attention during World War II, when he chaired the "Truman Committee" investigating abuses in the defense program. In 1944 Truman was chosen at the Democratic

Former president Harry S. Truman meeting with Lyndon Johnson for the signing of the Medicare Act, 1965 *(Lyndon Baines Johnson Library)*

defend South Korea against a North Korean attack. The Korean War soon settled down into a deadlock but it remained a deadly war that continued until after Truman left the White House.

In domestic affairs Truman sought to extend the New Deal with his own social welfare program. In 1948 he took some bold steps in civil rights, including the issuance of an executive order requiring the desegregation of the armed forces. This step, as well as many others, were controversial; still, Truman won an upset victory over New York governor Thomas E. Dewey in the election of 1948. Yet even though he gained election in his own right and Democratic majorities controlled both houses of Congress, Truman was unable to secure passage of most of his domestic proposals, which he called the Fair Deal, owing to the opposition of a conservative coalition of southern Democrats and Republicans. And in his second term, despite having implemented a sweeping loyalty program designed to eliminate security risks from government positions, Truman faced sensational charges from Senator Joseph R. McCarthy (R-Wisc.) and other Republicans that Communist subversives had infiltrated his administration. McCarthy never proved any of his charges, yet persistent accusations of a domestic Communist conspiracy offered a simple and powerful explanation to many Americans for U.S. difficulties in the cold war. In addition, the stalemated war in Korea and Truman's decision in April 1951 to relieve General Douglas MacArthur of his command of U.S. forces further undermined the president's popularity. In early 1952 Truman announced that he would not seek another term. He left office in January 1953.

Following his return to Independence in 1953. Truman issued numerous public statements throughout the decade, usually attacking Republican policies or politicians, defending his own record, or supporting Democratic candidates. He backed Governor AVERELL HARRIMAN's unsuccessful candidacy for the Democratic presidential nomination in 1956. After endorsing Senator STUART SYMINGTON's (D-Mo.) effort in 1960, Truman campaigned for the Kennedy-Johnson ticket. Although he disliked the Kennedy family, he had an even stronger aversion to the Republican candidate, Vice President RICHARD M. NIXON.

Truman was a strong supporter of the Johnson-Humphrey ticket in 1964 and expressed general support for the Great Society legislative program.

convention to replace Vice President Henry A. Wallace as President Franklin D. Roosevelt's running mate. Elected in November, Truman became president upon Roosevelt's death in April 1945.

Truman took office as World War II was ending in Europe and U.S.-Soviet relations were deteriorating. Although he tried to find some basis for continued Soviet-American cooperation, he concluded by late 1945 that there was no way to do so without making unacceptable concessions. During 1946 the cold war emerged, and the Truman administration developed a strategy of containment to halt Communist advances. The Marshall Plan and the North Atlantic Treaty Organization (NATO) were the twin pillars of this policy in Europe. But the cold war soon became a global contest, with confrontations in the Middle East and East Asia. In 1950, Truman committed U.S. military forces to

President Johnson flew to Independence in July 1965 to sign the law creating Medicare at a ceremony honoring Truman, who had been the first president to propose federal health insurance financed through the Social Security system. He endorsed the civil rights legislation of the Johnson administration, although he spoke critically of some civil rights demonstrators. In April 1964 Truman attacked those engaging in stalling and sit-in tactics at the New York World's Fair. He called the March 1965 civil rights march in Selma, Alabama, a "silly" bid to attract attention, and the next month he characterized Dr. MARTIN LUTHER KING, JR., as a "troublemaker"

Truman was a consistent public supporter of Johnson's Vietnam policy. In February 1965 he stated that U.S. troops were in South Vietnam "to help keep the peace and to keep ambitious aggressors from helping themselves to the easy prey of certain newly formed independent nations." Truman derided "irresponsible critics" and "sideline hecklers" of Johnson's policies. In October 1967 he joined the Citizens Committee for Peace with Freedom in Vietnam, a pro-war group opposing "surrender, however camouflaged" and advocating continued resistance to "naked aggression." Truman served as honorary chair of the Humphrey-for-President committee in April 1968. He died on December 26, 1972, at the age of 88.

—TO

## Turner, Donald F(rank)

(1921–1994) *assistant attorney general, Antitrust Division*

Born on March 19, 1921, in Chippewa Falls, Wisconsin, Donald Turner obtained a Ph.D. in economics from Harvard in 1947. He next earned a law degree from Yale in 1950 and then worked for a year as law clerk to Supreme Court justice TOM C. CLARK. Turner practiced in Washington, D.C., until 1954, when he returned to Harvard to teach law.

In collaboration with Harvard economist Carl Kaysen, Turner published *Antitrust Policy: An Economic and Legal Analysis* in 1959. *Antitrust Policy* became a standard text and, along with an array of important articles in professional journals, established Turner's reputation as the leading academic expert in the field of antitrust. At the recommendation of Attorney General NICHOLAS KATZENBACH, who had attended Yale Law School with Turner, President Johnson appointed Turner assistant attorney general in charge of the Antitrust Division in April 1965.

Katzenbach and Turner shared a less aggressive attitude toward antitrust enforcement than Turner's immediate predecessors, Lee Loevinger and William Orrick, Jr. In light of recent Supreme Court decisions that had greatly expanded the Justice Department's power to stop mergers, Katzenbach asserted in May 1965 that the department might have "more power than is necessary" and "may be able to block more mergers than it makes economic sense to block." He felt a "breathing spell" for business was needed. Turner had frequently argued before his appointment that antitrust law, a mass of legal precedents, was inconsistent, vague, and lacking in any guiding philosophy.

Resolving to "rationalize antitrust," Turner upgraded the division's Policy Planning and Evaluation Section, whose function was to review all cases sent up by the trial staff with the aim of formulating a unified division policy. Turner's application of greater manpower and meticulous care in the preparation of cases was generally credited with the improved quality of the division's briefs. In fiscal 1967, for example, 47 civil and nine criminal cases were terminated without any being lost in the courts. But another result was a significant decline in the average annual number of cases filed.

Turner also sought to rationalize enforcement with the promulgation of "Merger Guidelines," released on May 28, 1968, Turner's last day in office. In an effort to clarify antitrust law for the benefit of corporations, the guidelines listed those market percentages below which mergers were permissible. In general, corporate lawyers welcomed the greater predictability of antitrust policy. Some antitrust advocates criticized the new guidelines, insisting that an effective antitrust law should not be too precise, or it would eliminate that uncertainty which in their belief forestalled many contemplated mergers.

Turner's single most significant antitrust victory came in blocking a proposed merger between the International Telephone and Telegraph Corporation (ITT) and the American Broadcasting Companies, Inc. (ABC). The Federal Communications Commission approved the merger, but Turner refused to drop his objection. The department opposed the merger on several grounds, including a fear ITT's international interests might affect the integrity of ABC's news operations. ITT canceled the planned merger in January 1968.

Despite this suit and another filed in 1966 against the merger of the First National City Bank of New York and Carte Blanche, Turner exhibited a notable tolerance toward conglomerate mergers. He believed that bigness per se was not harmful and that the increase in the percentage of industrial assets controlled by the top firms was not necessarily dangerous.

The greatest wave of corporate mergers in American history up to that time occurred during Turner's tenure. During the first six years of the decade an average of 1,664 mergers took place annually; from 1967 through 1969 the annual average increased to 3,605 mergers, 80 percent of which were conglomerates. Turner approved a series of major mergers within the energy industry: Pure Oil Co. and Union Oil Co., Atlantic Co. and Richfield Co. and the Continental Oil Co. and the Consolidation Coal Co.

Turner followed an erratic course against the nation's two largest corporate giants, General Motors (GM) and the American Telephone and Telegraph Co. (AT&T). He personally negotiated a settlement in the decade-old GM bus case in November 1965. The agreement permitted GM to retain its 85 percent monopoly of the intercity bus market, with a provision requiring compulsory licensing of new firms entering the market. Turner dropped a court case pending against GM's monopoly of the locomotive market, an action that earned criticism from Loevinger, who had initi-

ated the suit. Turner maintained that GM's monopoly was due simply to greater efficiency. He also declined to bring a criminal action suit against the automobile manufacturers for conspiracy to suppress the development of pollution control devices. A Los Angeles grand jury had been prepared to indict in the case, and Turner reportedly admitted he could have obtained a conviction from a jury. Regarding AT&T, Turner sent a proposed complaint against its 1956 acquisition of Western Electric Co. to Katzenbach's desk in July 1966. The complaint charged monopolization of telephone equipment since 1956, but no action occurred.

Turner investigated the possibility of testing the limits of the Sherman Act with suits against "shared monopolies," or oligopolies. He had in mind industries like automobile production—dominated by GM, Ford and Chrysler—and soap marketing, in which Procter and Gamble, Lever Brothers, and Colgate predominated. In June 1966 Turner broached the possibility of suing against excessive advertising on the grounds that it raised entry barriers to new competitors and preserved oligopolies. No shared monopoly or excessive advertising cases were filed during Turner's tenure, however. Turner resigned in June 1968 and returned to teaching at Harvard. He later practiced law and in 1988–89 was a senior fellow at the Brookings Institution. He died on July 19, 1994.

—TO

# U

## Udall, Morris K(ing)

(1922–1998) *member of the House of Representatives*

Udall was born on June 15, 1922, in St. Johns, Arizona, into a prominent family. His father became chief justice of the Arizona Supreme Court; his mother was an author. He served in the U.S. Army Air Forces during World War II. Despite the loss of an eye in a knife accident when he was a child, he played professional basketball in 1948–49. After earning a law degree in 1949, he opened a law practice with his brother Stewart.

During the 1950s Udall participated in local Democratic politics. He served first as chief deputy attorney for Pima County and then as county attorney. After Stewart Udall gave up his seat from Arizona's Second Congressional District to become secretary of the interior in President Kennedy's cabinet, Morris Udall won a special election in May 1961 to fill the vacancy. He served on the Post Office and Civil Service and the Interior and Insular Affairs Committees. As chair of the former panel's Compensation Subcommittee, he sponsored the House version of the 1965 federal pay raise bill.

Udall usually supported the Johnson administration's Great Society legislation. But he was a critic of the president's Vietnam policies. In an October 1967 speech delivered in Tucson, Arizona, he declared that the United States was on "a mistaken and dangerous road" in Vietnam and should stop further escalation and "start bringing American boys home and start turning this war back to the Vietnamese." Udall said that his previous support of administration Vietnam policies had been a "mistake."

In 1968 Udall played a vital role in gaining passage of the $1.3 billion Colorado River Project, which was the culmination of a legislative battle fought for half a century over allocation of the waters of the Colorado River. Udall earlier had clashed with the California-based Sierra Club over a proposal, initially made in 1963, for construction of the Bridge Canyon and Marble Canyon hydroelectric dams in a section of the Grand Canyon in northern Arizona. He later said of the Sierra Club's successful effort to block the dams' construction, "I can't think of any group in this country that has had more power in the last eight years."

The final Colorado River bill was a compromise facilitated by a series of skillful legislative maneuvers, in which Udall was a crucial figure. He set up his own whip system in the House and contacted members of Congress in order to establish their voting preference on the measure. Principally as a consequence of Udall's efforts, the Colorado River Project passed Congress on September 12, 1968, and was signed into law by President Johnson on September 30.

In December 1968 Udall announced his candidacy for Speaker of the House, a post held by Representative JOHN MCCORMACK (D-Mass.). In a letter to all House Democrats, Udall expressed "genuine respect and affection" for McCormack but stated that there was an overriding need for new leadership. In January Udall lost his bid for the speakership by a vote of 178 to 58.

Udall was reelected in 1970, 1972, and 1974. He ran an unsuccessful campaign for the Democratic presidential nomination in 1976. He resigned from Congress in May 1991 because of poor health. He died on December 12, 1998.

## Udall, Stewart L(ee)

(1920–   ) *secretary of the interior*

Udall was born into a prominent family on January 31, 1920, in St. Johns, Arizona. His grandfather had been a Mormon pioneer in Arizona; his father eventually became the chief justice of the Arizona Supreme Court. He served in the U.S. Army Air Forces during World War II and in 1948 earned an LL.B. from the University of Arizona. Udall was elected to the U.S. House of Representatives in 1954, and won three successive reelection contests easily. In the House Udall was one of the Interior and Insular Affairs Committee's most vigorous proponents of conservation, reclamation, and national park improvement legislation. He helped sponsor "seminars" for freshman representatives and was a member of the liberal Democratic Study Group.

An early supporter of Senator John F. Kennedy's presidential aspirations, Udall was named Kennedy's secretary of the interior in December 1960. In his first three years in the cabinet, Udall strongly favored public over private power in his efforts to meet the nation's rapidly expanding water and energy needs. "The Eisenhower Administration regarded public power as something of a necessary evil," Udall declared. "We regard it as a necessary good." Believing that the nation's population and standard of living would continue to rise, he asserted that the federal government should assume a larger role in meeting the nation's energy needs. As secretary of the interior, he took important steps toward enlarging the federal role in protecting the environment as well as conserving natural resources and preserving areas of unique natural beauty. In his book *The Quiet Crisis* (1963), he called for greater public efforts to control pollution and preserve unspoiled wilderness areas.

During Udall's tenure as secretary of the interior, 2.4 million acres were added to the National Park Service, compared to only 30,000 acres added in the entire decade before 1960. Four entirely new national parks were created. Seven of the 11 National Recreation Areas were established in the three years after 1965 alone.

In his efforts to add new land to the park system, Udall often found himself attacked by conservationists, on the one hand, and timber, mining, and cattle interests, on the other. Final establishment of the Redwood National Park in 1968 culminated a four-year dispute involving lumber companies, the state of California, the Agriculture Department's

Forest Service, and conservationist groups. Environmentalists, led by the Sierra Club, succeeded in getting a park that was larger and located farther south than Udall's original proposal. Meanwhile, California governor RONALD REAGAN ensured that the state received compensation for its lands lost to the park.

Two other important conservation-recreation measures, both passed in 1968, were the National Trails System, the result of a three-year study supervised by Udall, and the Wild and Scenic Rivers System. The National Trails System established national scenic trails in wilderness areas for hiking and camping and national recreation trails near urban areas for jogging, bicycling, and similar activities. The rivers system prohibited incompatible water resource development, pollution, or commercialization of certain stretches of rivers. In some cases land around the rivers was to be set aside for limited recreational uses.

In 1967 Udall recommended federal measures to regulate surface mining operations and reclaim lands already damaged by harmful mining techniques. President Johnson proposed a surface mining reclamation bill in 1968, but Congress did not act on it. In 1967 Udall also offered a program to tap the immense oil shale deposits of the Green River Formation in the Rocky Mountains. The deposits, 80 percent of which were government-owned, were estimated to contain enough shale to produce 2 trillion barrels of oil. Udall's proposal to lease government land to individuals, corporations, and municipalities for research and production was attacked by congressional liberals led by Senator WILLIAM PROXMIRE (D-Wisc.). They believed that development should be turned over to a quasi-public corporation or a government agency. In 1968 Congress took no action on bills aimed at providing "the orderly leasing of publicly owned oil shale."

The drought that afflicted the Northeast from 1961 to 1965 bolstered Udall's view that the government ought to take steps to ensure that water supply and quality would keep pace with the nation's increasing needs. The Water Resources Planning Act of 1965, which furthered federal-state cooperation in developing water resources, also established a Federal Water Resources Council. As council chair, Udall directed a survey of Northeast drought conditions in August 1965. In his report the secretary was extremely critical of New York City, which, he said, had the reputation "of having one of the leakiest and most loosely managed water systems." In contrast, he praised Philadelphia's metered water system, telling the Senate Interior Committee that Congress "had every right to insist that U.S. cities do what Philadelphia is doing" to qualify for drought assistance. Congress voted emergency funds to increase the storage capacities of northeastern reservoirs. In addition, following Udall's survey, New York City and Philadelphia made an agreement for establishing a "strategic water bank" of 200 million gallons to be utilized in emergencies.

Although the drought ended soon after Udall's study, the secretary believed that its lesson for the public and legislators was clear. He persistently urged the creation of a National Water Commission to develop long-range plans on water resources. Congress finally established the commission in 1968. Udall also supported continuation and expansion of the government's desalination program. In 1967 Congress authorized the Interior Department to participate in construction of a nuclear-powered desalting plant in Southern California. Probably the most important piece of water legislation was the Water Quality Act of 1965, which set purity standards for all interstate waters, making it easier for government authorities to take action against polluters. A 1966 bill made funds available to states and communities to enforce the standards.

Although reclamation projects did not figure as prominently in the Johnson-Udall programs as they had under President Kennedy, few public works bills aroused as much controversy as the Colorado River Basin Project of 1968. At a cost of $1.3 billion, it was the largest reclamation program ever authorized in a single piece of legislation. Designed to divert the Colorado's waters to south-central Arizona, the plan had been long delayed because of disagreement among the southwestern states over the allocation of Colorado River water. Meanwhile, rapid population growth in the arid Southwest threatened the region's water supply. In 1963 Udall proposed the Southwest Water Plan, a regional development scheme that included two dams on the Colorado River. By 1966 all seven Colorado River basin states had finally agreed to implement the plan. However, the Sierra Club and other environmental organizations undertook an intensive lobbying effort against the proposal, directing most of their campaign against Udall's proposal to build two hydroelectric dams on a section of the Colorado that ran through the Grand Canyon. Because of the Sierra Club's pressure, Udall dropped both dams and suggested, instead, that the government buy an interest in a joint public-private thermal power plant. This plan was incorporated into the administration's Colorado River Basin Project bill.

Udall, at times took notable steps to accommodate critics. In April 1966, for example, he agreed with critics who charged that the Bureau of Indian Affairs had been "lethargic" and "rigid" in coping with Indian economic problems and promised a reorganization of the bureau, a greater emphasis on Indian education, a larger voice for Indians in their own affairs, and greater access to modern business techniques. In June 1968 Udall accepted safety critic RALPH NADER's assertion that the Bureau of Mines had been lax in protecting the health of coal miners. In September of the same year President Johnson proposed a Federal Coal Mine Safety and Health Act, and, in December, Udall formed a national Conference to Make Coal Mining Safe.

Near the end of the Johnson administration, Udall tried to persuade the president to add over 7.5 million acres to the National Park System under the provisions of the Antiquities Act of 1906. The president, however, yielded to the demands of Representative WAYNE ASPINALL (D-Colo.), chair of the House Interior Committee and a foe of conservationists, in adding only 384,500 acres to the park system Johnson defended the proclamation, arguing that to add more than 7 million acres "would strain the Antiquities Act beyond its intent."

In 1969 Udall became board chair of the Overview Corporation, an environmental consulting firm. In 1970 he began to write a syndicated column on the environment. In addition, Udall published a number of books, including *America's National Treasures* (1971) and *The National Parks* (1972). After resuming his law practice in the late 1970s, he represented clients who had been exposed to radiation as a result of the U.S. atomic testing program. His activities helped lead to the passage in 1990 of legislation that made possible compensation to these radiation victims.

—JCH

## Unruh, Jesse M(arvin)

(1922–1987) *speaker, California State Assembly*
Jesse Unruh was born on September 30, 1922, in Newton, Kansas, and experienced poverty and deprivation during his childhood in the Dust Bowl

of West Texas during the depression. He served in the navy during World War II, and he graduated from the University of Southern California in 1948. He became involved in politics as a Democrat while he was a student. In 1954, after two unsuccessful campaigns, he won election to the state assembly from a district in Los Angeles.

Despite his lack of seniority, Unruh quickly became one of the most powerful members of the assembly. By 1961 Unruh was speaker of the assembly and the Kennedy administration's chief ally in California, even though the governor, EDMUND G. BROWN, was a Democrat. Political analysts considered Unruh to be the most powerful state legislator in the country. Unruh, professionalized the assembly and improved the size and quality of its staff in an effort to make it equal in power to the executive branch. In July 1963, at the height of his power, he suffered a great loss of prestige by keeping Republican assembly members sequestered inside the assembly chamber until they agreed to vote on the state budget. The adverse public and press reaction to "The Lockup" eventually led Unruh to alter his "boss" image and trim his enormous waistline, which had earned him the nickname "Big Daddy."

Even though they were both Democrats, Unruh and Brown became public antagonists. Unruh developed assembly programs in ways that Brown thought challenged the executive's prerogatives. Sensing a conservative trend in the California electorate, Unruh became less inclined than Brown to aggressively back liberal legislation. He refused to support consistently the interests of organized labor and sought to reduce the influence of the liberal California Democratic Council (CDC) within the state Democratic Party. Both the unions and the CDC remained loyal to Brown while attacking Unruh's leadership.

In 1964 California Democrats began to vie for the U.S. Senate seat of the ailing Senator Clair Engle (D-Calif.). Brown supported the CDC's founding president, state controller Alan Cranston, and Unruh tacitly backed PIERRE SALINGER, formerly President John F. Kennedy's press secretary and a native Californian. Salinger won the primary, and Brown reluctantly appointed him to take over Engle's Senate seat following the latter's death. Salinger, however, lost in general election to Republican GEORGE MURPHY in one of the few notable Democratic defeats that November.

In 1965 relations between Unruh and Brown deteriorated even further. When Brown announced his intention to run for a third term in 1966, Unruh, who believed Brown had made a commitment to give him a chance for the governorship, hesitated before endorsing Brown. He made a point of spending the month before the November 1966 elections abroad, only returning to California after the victory of Republican RONALD REAGAN. Brown later blamed Unruh for his defeat.

During Governor Reagan's first term Unruh transformed his public image from that of an aggressive, political boss into that of a master of political strategy. However, his efforts to oppose Reagan on issues involving the University of California were generally unsuccessful. He failed to stop Reagan from persuading a majority of the university's Board of Regents to dismiss CLARK KERR as president of the university in January 1967. In August of the same year he again opposed Reagan when the governor sought to impose tuition in the state university system. Reagan succeeded in doubling the university's fee schedule without employing the unpopular term *tuition*. Although he attacked campus radicalism as forcefully as Reagan, Unruh won the praise of many of California's teachers, students, and liberals by demanding that the university's high standards be maintained while liberalizing its admissions policies.

In March 1968 Unruh became one of the first Democrats to support the presidential candidacy of Senator ROBERT F. KENNEDY (D-N.Y.), and he quickly adopted Kennedy's criticism of President Johnson's Vietnam policies. The Unruh staff played a key role in Kennedy's campaign in the crucial California primary in June, but on the evening of his victory Kennedy was assassinated in a Los Angeles hotel. As leader of the California delegation to the Democratic National Convention, Unruh decided not to impose a unit-voting regulation on the delegates and opened all state caucus meetings at the convention to the news media. He cast his own delegate vote for antiwar candidate Senator EUGENE MCCARTHY (D-Minn.) after his efforts to initiate a draft in favor of Senator EDWARD M. KENNEDY (D-Mass.) had failed. Unruh was widely praised for the democratic manner in which he led his delegation and for his effective leadership of dissident elements within the national party. During the fall campaign, he gave wholehearted support to the senatorial candidacy of his old enemy, Alan Cranston, but did not announce his endorsement of the Humphrey-Muskie ticket until late in September.

Since the Democrats lost their majority in the assembly in the 1968 elections, Unruh was forced to step down as speaker in January 1969. In 1970 he relinquished his assembly seat to run against Ronald Reagan in the gubernatorial contest. Following his loss to Reagan, Unruh devoted himself to college teaching and became a popular figure on the lecture circuit. In 1974 he was elected California state treasurer, and served three four-year terms in that office. He died on August 4, 1987.

—JCH

## Valenti, Jack J(oseph)

(1921–    ) *White House special assistant*

Jack Valenti grew up in Houston, where he was born on September 5, 1921. He was a bomber pilot during World War II and then earned a B.A. from the University of Houston in 1946 and an M.B.A. from Harvard in 1948. In 1952 Valenti opened an advertising and public relations firm in Houston. He was named Houston's Outstanding Young Man in 1956.

In 1956 Valenti met Senator LYNDON B. JOHNSON at a business reception. Valenti gained a favorable impression of Johnson and wrote a laudatory column about him for a Houston newspaper. Johnson enlisted Valenti's firm to handle the advertising in Texas for the Kennedy-Johnson ticket during the campaign of 1960.

Valenti developed a friendship with Johnson while the latter served as vice president. On November 22, 1963, Valenti rode in the motorcade when President John F. Kennedy made his final trip to Dallas. After Kennedy's murder that day, Johnson asked Valenti to fly back to Washington with him aboard Air Force One. Valenti then became an indispensable assistant to the new president.

Valenti's duties as a White House special assistant ran the gamut from tasks that were substantive and sensitive to those that were prosaic and mundane. Valenti was often at Johnson's side, in the Oval Office as well as the president's bedroom. He drafted much of the president's routine correspondence, such as thank-you notes for gifts. Yet he also, at times, took charge of the president's appointments, helped to draft policy speeches, and offered advice on both foreign and domestic matters. Some contemporary observers misunderstood his role and dismissed him as a "glorified valet." Valenti, how-

ever, was one of a handful of the most important White House assistants, even if, at times, he dealt with rather ordinary matters.

Valenti was unswervingly loyal, something that Johnson demanded, and often praised the president in public remarks. But he also offered candid and critical advice, especially on the growing U.S. military involvement in Vietnam. In December 1965 Valenti told Johnson that he favored a pause in the bombing of North Vietnam, a step that the president ultimately approved. "We are in quicksand," Valenti wrote to Johnson. "We need to do all we can now to end the fighting before we are in so deep we can never get out." In April 1966 Valenti again urged the president "to find some way out of Vietnam." Military advisers, he said, asked for a doubling of U.S. troops, yet "still they give you no prophecy of victory." Valenti asserted that the continuation of the war jeopardized the administration's Great Society—"all that you strive for and believe in." Yet while Johnson was keenly aware of this danger, he could find no acceptable way out of Vietnam.

In spring 1966 Valenti announced his resignation to become president of the Motion Picture Association of America, a position he held until his resignation on September 1, 2004.

## Vance, Cyrus R(oberts)

(1917–2002) *secretary of the army, deputy secretary of defense, deputy delegate to the Paris Peace Talks*

Vance, who became a versatile assistant to President Johnson and who dealt with a variety of volatile international issues, was born in Clarksburg, West Virginia, on March 27, 1917. After earning his law degree from Yale in 1942, Vance served in the navy and then entered private law practice. In 1958 he worked as a special counsel to the Preparedness Investigating Committee, a panel created by a Senate resolution in the aftermath of the Soviet launching of the *Sputnik* satellite in October 1957. Senator LYNDON B. JOHNSON was the chair of the committee, which recommended the creation of what became the National Aeronautics and Space Administration. Vance's work with that committee paved the way for his appointment as general counsel for the Department of Defense at the beginning of the Kennedy administration.

At the Defense Department Vance developed a close working relationship with Secretary of Defense ROBERT S. MCNAMARA, who asked Vance to aid him in the reorganization of the Pentagon bureaucracy. Vance became secretary of the army in July 1962. He then succeeded ROSWELL GILPATRIC as deputy secretary of defense in January 1964; he served at that post until June 1967, when ill-health forced him to resign.

Vance was one of Johnson's closest aides and throughout the administration acted as "presidential troubleshooter" in many important foreign crises. In January 1964 Johnson sent him to Panama to help quell the violence after American troops fired on rioters protesting the U.S. presence in the Canal Zone. Shortly after intervention by American marines in April 1965, Vance was part of a team that Johnson sent to the Dominican Republic to try to establish a coalition government satisfactory to both sides in that nation's civil war. The mission failed, but peace was finally restored in August as a result of the diplomatic efforts of ELLSWORTH BUNKER and the Organization of American States. Two years later Vance worked with representatives of the North Atlantic Treaty Organization (NATO) and the United Nations to establish a temporary truce in the civil war in Cyprus. Following North Korean raids on Seoul and the seizure of the USS *Pueblo*, Vance went to South Korea in February 1968 to assure the government of continuing American support. He also informed the South Korean leadership that the United States alone would try to negotiate the release of the ship's crew and that the South Korean government should refrain from unilateral actions, which might only inflame a volatile situation.

In July 1967, shortly after Vance's resignation from the Pentagon, Johnson asked him to be his on-the-scene representative during the Detroit riots. In consultation with Governor GEORGE ROMNEY and Mayor Jerome Cavanagh, Vance recommended that the president call in federal troops on the night of July 25, when local authorities failed to contain the growing violence. Several months after the incident, in September 1967, Vance wrote a report on his mission known as the "Detroit Book." This document became the source of a series of recommendations designed to minimize the danger of shooting civilians when dealing with urban riots. His report called for the use of "overwhelming law enforcement manpower" coupled with military and police restraint and the heavy use of tear gas instead of gunfire.

Vance was not one of the president's principal advisers on Southeast Asia, but he did participate in some of the meetings that transformed what had been primarily an advisory mission into a combat role in Vietnam during 1964–65. He supported a reprisal air strike after the alleged North Vietnamese attack in the Gulf of Tonkin on August 4, 1964. After a deadly raid by National Liberation Front (NLF) forces against a U.S. base in Pleiku on February 7, 1965, he recommended that the president approve retaliatory bombing attacks. Those bombing missions soon became a sustained campaign known as Rolling Thunder. By the spring of 1967, however, Vance, like Secretary of Defense McNamara, had doubts about the effectiveness of the bombing and the overall U.S. war effort. Like McNamara, he favored concentrating the bombing missions on infiltration routes that led into South Vietnam.

After leaving the Defense Department Vance continued to advise the president on Vietnam. Following the enemy's Tet offensive and the U.S. military's February 1968 request for over 200,000 additional troops, Vance became a member of the Senior Advisory Group on Vietnam commonly known as the "Wise Men." In meetings held on March 25 and 26 Vance, along with DEAN ACHESON, GEORGE BALL, and MCGEORGE BUNDY, among others, advocated de-escalation of the war, fearing that the political, social, and economic life of the United States would be torn apart by continued escalation. Johnson announced on March 31 that he had imposed restrictions on the bombing campaign against North Vietnam and hoped that his action would lead to the prompt opening of peace talks.

When the Paris peace talks between the United States and North Vietnam began in May 1968,

Vance became a deputy delegate. In that role he handled the organizational meetings associated with the talks, including those dealing with delegation size, languages to be used, and seating arrangements. In December, when discussions for holding the enlarged conference between United States, North Vietnam, South Vietnam, and the NLF bogged down over seating arrangements, Vance negotiated the compromise settlement. Instead of the rectangular table demanded by Hanoi, (which would have implied that the NLF was of equal status with the other members), or the round table suggested by the United States (which would have left the status of the NLF ambiguous), the conference agreed to a round table with two rectangular tables placed flanking it.

Vance resigned his post in February 1969 to resume law practice in New York. Vance served as secretary of state during the Carter administration. He resigned in April 1980 to protest the president's authorization of a military mission to rescue U.S. hostages in Iran. During the 1990s, as a representative of the United Nations, he tried to negotiate a settlement in the Bosnian war. He died on January 12, 2002.

—EWS

## Vanik, Charles A(lbert)

(1913–    ) *member of the House of Representatives*

Born in Cleveland on April 7, 1913, Charles A. Vanik received both bachelor's and law degrees from Western Reserve University. He entered politics as a Democrat and won a seat on the Cleveland City Council in 1938 and a term in the state senate in 1940. After serving in the navy during World War II, he resumed his political career by gaining election to a municipal judgeship. In 1954 he won a seat in the U.S. House by upsetting a Republican incumbent who had served 19 terms.

During the Johnson years, Vanik consistently supported Great Society legislation. In January 1965, he was in a position to help secure passage of the administration's medicare program because his committee assignment changed from Banking and Currency to Ways and Means. Vanik's presence helped increase pressure on committee chair WILBUR D. MILLS (D-Ark.), who had reservations about the administration proposal, to incorporate it into an expanded compromise plan that passed later in the

year. Vanik also supported the administration's plan to impose an income tax surcharge in October 1967 to offset the increasing costs of the Vietnam War. Vanik, however, was one of only five members of the Ways and Means Committee who voted to approve the administration proposal. Mills, who insisted on large budget cuts as his price for supporting the surcharge, joined with 19 other committee members to vote down the Johnson tax increase.

Vanik at first endorsed the administration's Vietnam policy, writing in December 1965 that "America has not turned its back on the plea for democracy and freedom on the Asiatic mainland." But in the early spring of 1968, he came out against American involvement; in May he won election as a delegate supporting Senator EUGENE J. MCCARTHY (D-Minn.) for president at the Democratic National Convention. Together with five other Democratic colleagues in October, he voted against the Defense Department appropriation bill for fiscal 1969, which passed 213 to 6.

In 1968 Vanik ran for reelection in a new Cleveland district. A year earlier the Ohio state legislature had redrawn Cleveland's four congressional districts. In the process it had created an overwhelmingly black district that included Vanik's old one. Declaring that his district should now have a black representative (in this instance Louis B. Stokes, the brother of Mayor CARL B. STOKES, Vanik filed in the adjacent district of 83-year-old Representative FRANCES P. BOLTON (R-Ohio), who had served in Congress since 1940. In a hotly contested election, Vanik charged that his wealthy opponent possessed "the provincial views of the hunt-club set." With 55 percent of the total vote, Vanik defeated Bolton.

Vanik easily won reelection to five more terms. In 1974, along with Senator HENRY M. JACKSON (D-Wash.), he cosponsored an amendment to a trade bill that denied normal trade relations to nations that imposed restrictions on the emigration of their nationals. The Nixon administration opposed the enactment of this Jackson-Vanik amendment, which was designed to facilitate the emigration of Soviet Jews because it complicated efforts to pursue a strategy of détente with the Soviet Union. Vanik left Congress at the end of his term in January 1981 and made an unsuccessful run the next year for the Democratic nomination for governor of Ohio.

—JLB

## Vaughn, Jack H(ood)

(1920–   )  *ambassador to Panama; secretary of state for inter-American affairs and coordinator of the Alliance for Progress; director, Peace Corps*

Born in Columbus, Montana, on August 18, 1920, Vaughn grew up in Mexico and Montana, where his father worked as a ranch hand. After service in the marines during World War II, he studied at the University of Michigan, receiving an M.A. in Latin American studies in 1947. Vaughn entered government service one year later as program director for the United States Information Agency (USIA) in La Paz, Bolivia. He spent four years with the USIA in Bolivia and Costa Rica before joining the International Cooperation Administration (ICA), a planning agency for U.S. foreign aid projects. Vaughn worked for the ICA in Latin America, western Africa, and in the agency's Washington headquarters. In 1961 he became director of Latin American projects for the newly formed Peace Corps.

Vaughn remained at the Washington headquarters of the Peace Corps until April 1964, when President LYNDON JOHNSON appointed him ambassador to Panama. This post had been vacant for seven months following violent demonstrations by Panamanians against U.S. control of the Canal Zone. Hoping to improve U.S.-Panamanian relations, Vaughn toured the countryside extensively, acquiring a reputation as "the peasant ambassador." He urged Panamanians to concentrate on rural development, rather than the canal, as their main source of economic growth. At the same time he conducted negotiations for revision of the Panama Canal treaty, expressing U.S. willingness "in principle" to recognize Panamanian sovereignty over the canal and to cooperate with Panama in managing the waterway.

In 1965 Vaughn left Panama to become an assistant secretary of state and U.S. coordinator of the Alliance for Progress. He served in these posts largely as a roving envoy to Latin America, attempting to reassure heads of state who feared that U.S. interest in the region had declined during the Johnson administration. The Alliance for Progress, Vaughn claimed, remained as vigorous during the mid-1960s as at the time of its creation in 1961. Back in Washington, however, he urged the administration to pay closer attention to specific Alliance programs; he especially favored community development projects of the kind undertaken by the Peace Corps.

Vaughn's enthusiasm for the Peace Corps, which had never wavered since the early 1960s, was rewarded when he became the agency's director in early 1966. He replaced SARGENT SHRIVER, who had resigned to devote full time to the administration's antipoverty program. Vaughn served for three years as Peace Corps director, for the most part administering and developing existing programs. He aroused controversy in 1967 by demanding that 92 Peace Corps volunteers in Latin America disassociate themselves from a statement opposing the Vietnam War. One year later, however, he endorsed the right of volunteers to oppose U.S. foreign policy while serving overseas.

Vaughn's forthrightness on controversial issues made him important enemies in Congress. Representative OTTO PASSMAN (D-La.) demanded his resignation for supporting dissent within the Peace Corps, while Senator WAYNE MORSE (D-Ore.) accused him of favoring authoritarian governments in Latin America. Vaughn resigned from the Peace Corps in March 1969. Two months later he was appointed ambassador to Colombia by President RICHARD NIXON, but he left this post after one year.

During the early 1970s Vaughn served as president of the National Urban Coalition, a research and funding agency for community development projects, and as dean of international studies at Florida International University. Later he became director of foreign development for the Children's Television Workshop, a communications firm.

—SLG

## Vinson, Carl

(1883–1981)  *member of the House of Representatives*

Vinson, who was born on November 18, 1883, in Baldwin County, Georgia, earned a law degree from Mercer University in Macon. After serving two terms in the Georgia House of Representatives, he was elected a county court judge. Two years later Vinson won a race for a vacant seat in the U.S. House of Representatives. He became chair of the House Naval Affairs Committee in 1931. He was champion of the enlargement of the navy, arguing that it "must be strong enough to defend our possessions and to support our territories."

In 1949 Vinson became chair of the recently formed Armed Services Committee, which had superseded the Naval Affairs Committee. In that position, Vinson established himself as a crucial force in shaping defense-related legislation. He centralized power over the committee in his hands. Rather than establish subcommittees with defined jurisdictions, he divided the panel into three equal groups and decided which would receive each bill. He was a master of the legislative process and a skillful floor manager. Almost all bills that cleared his committee gained approval in the House.

Vinson favored a large and powerful military and particularly emphasized the importance of conventional forces in the nuclear age. He was a critic of the Eisenhower administration's New Look, which emphasized nuclear deterrence at the expense of ground troops. During the early 1960s, he resisted the Kennedy administration's plans to substitute missiles for piloted bombers. Although he praised the abilities of Secretary of Defense ROBERT S. MCNAMARA, he criticized the secretary's centralization of power in the Defense Department at the expense of the individual services.

Vinson's power was coming to an end soon after LYNDON JOHNSON succeeded Kennedy as president. In early 1964 Vinson announced that he would not seek election to a 26th consecutive term. Yet he still wielded considerable influence over defense matters in his last year in Congress.

Vinson continued to advocate, over Defense Department opposition, the appropriation of funds for piloted bombers. In February his committee added to administration defense authorization requests $92 million for the development of strategic aircraft to replace the B-52 and B-58 bomber fleets. During floor debate he asserted that if those planes were retired "we will be in the position of depending entirely on missiles, a thing none of us wants to do." The final bill, passed by both houses, appropriated $52 million for developing new bombers.

In April 1964 Vinson opposed a legislative stipulation, first established in 1962, requiring that at least 35 percent of all funds for naval ship repair be assigned to private rather than navy shipyards. Noting that the Defense Department planned to close a number of navy shipyards by the end of the year, he urged a return to the earlier practice of assigning at least 75 percent of repair funds to the navy yards in order to preserve their existence. The formula, however, was not altered.

On March 20, 1964, President Lyndon B. Johnson, in a tribute to Vinson, stated, "No man in the history of this republic knows more about the posture of our defense, and no man has done more to improve it." On November 14, 1964, Vinson became the first representative to serve in the House for 50 years. He died on June 1, 1981.

—MLL

## Wagner, Robert F(erdinand), (Jr.)
(1910–1991) *mayor*

Robert F. Wagner, the mayor of New York City for 12 years, was involved in politics from his childhood. His father, Senator Robert F. Wagner (D-N.Y.), was a powerful figure in Democratic politics during the New Deal. The elder Wagner allowed his son, at times, to attend political meetings even when he was a boy. The senator's popularity was a major factor in the son's political advancement.

Wagner was born in New York City on April 20, 1910, and attended the Taft School and Yale University. After receiving a law degree from Yale in 1937, he was elected to the New York Assembly. He resigned his seat in 1941 to serve in the U.S. Army Air Forces in Europe. After the war, with the support of Tammany Hall, the regular New York City Democratic organization, Wagner advanced rapidly in politics.

He served successively as tax commissioner, commissioner of housing and buildings and chair of the city planning commission. In 1949 he was elected Manhattan borough president. In 1953 he defeated Vincent Impelliteri, the incumbent, in the primary election for the mayoral nomination. In the November general election Wagner swept to an easy victory.

Wagner's three terms as mayor coincided with an important transition in the city's development. From the mid-1950s to the mid-1960s New York enjoyed a period of relative prosperity. A boom in the construction of luxury apartments and office buildings enlarged the city's tax base and permitted it to finance a larger police force, higher teacher salaries, and improved social services. Yet that decade was also a time when a growing number of city residents lived in poverty, in part because many poor African Americans and Puerto Ricans moved to the city as middle-class whites left for the suburbs. Wagner experienced some of the tensions and difficulties associated with these demographic and economic changes during his final years in office, but they were generally not as persistent or severe as in the decade after he left office.

In his first two terms Wagner enjoyed many achievements. He gained passage from the city council of the first legislation barring racial discrimination in the sale or rental of housing, and, by executive order, he gave city workers—with the exception of police—the right to join unions and enter into collective bargaining with the city.

Wagner was probably at the height of his power at the beginning of his third term. To retain the support of an increasingly powerful Manhattan reform movement, he broke with the regular Democratic leadership in 1961, defeated his Tammany opponent in the September primary, and easily won reelection. He subsequently dominated the Tammany organization. Voters that year approved a new charter that increased the mayor's power relative to that of the borough presidents and the Board of Estimate. Wagner maintained close relations with New York City labor leaders and was instrumental in settling a number of major labor disputes, notably the 114-day 1962–63 newspaper strike.

During Wagner's last two years in office the city experienced increasing racial tension. On July 16, 1964, an off-duty white police officer, Lt. Thomas Gilligan, shot and killed 15-year-old James Powell, a black student who had allegedly threatened him with a knife. This incident aggravated already troubled relations between the police and the black community. Rioting broke out in Harlem on July 18 and later spread to the predominantly black Bedford-Stuyvesant section of Brooklyn. In four consecutive nights of rioting, hundreds of store windows were smashed and debris was often hurled at the police. One black was shot to death, five others were wounded, and 81 civilians and 35 police officers were injured. Wagner, who had been vacationing in Europe, flew home and in a July 22 televised address appealed for calm.

In the aftermath of the rioting, Wagner met with MARTIN LUTHER KING, JR., to discuss ways of ending violence in the black community. The mayor subsequently proposed to create 1,500 new city jobs for unemployed black youths and to recruit more black police officers. Black leaders, including King, were disappointed by Wagner's refusal to support creation of a board independent of the police department to review cases of alleged police brutality.

The 1964 Harlem riots were particularly disheartening to the mayor because his administration had taken the initiative in financing special programs to aid young people in slum neighborhoods. In 1961 the city, federal government, and Ford Foundation had pooled funds to support Mobilization for Youth (MFY), an organization that provided job counseling and retraining to hundreds of young people on the Lower East Side. MFY became the prototype for the "community action" antipoverty programs later funded by the Johnson administration's Office of Economic Opportunity and by cities throughout the country.

In June 1964 Mayor Wagner announced that the city would provide $3.4 million in addition to the federal government's $1 million contribution for the establishment of a major antipoverty program in Harlem to be administered by Harlem Youth Opportunities Unlimited and Associated Community Teams. (The two groups merged in 1964 to form HARYOU-ACT.)

The New York City antipoverty programs soon came under impassioned attack from politicians of both the left and the right. Conservative critics cited an August 1964 FBI report that charged that 30 of MFY's 300 employees had previous links to the Communist Party or Communist-front organizations. The Wagner administration's own Antipoverty Operations Board reported in November that the MFY had hired 20 persons with subversive connections and that the organization was badly managed. Some African-American leaders, including Harlem's

Representative ADAM CLAYTON POWELL (D-N.Y.), argued that the Wagner administration's failure to give neighborhoods control over their antipoverty organizations violated Title II of the 1964 Economic Opportunity Act. In April 1965 Powell asked the federal government to withhold antipoverty funds from New York until the program was reorganized. The mayor denied Powell's charges but, in response to increasing community and federal pressure, replaced his Antipoverty Operations Board with a new 17-member agency consisting of 11 mayoral appointees and six members from local antipoverty groups.

In June 1965 Wagner submitted a record $3.8 billion expense budget that contained a $250-million deficit. Wagner proposed to cover some of the deficit through the sale of "revenue anticipation notes" (RANS). The city had issued these notes for many years to pay its bills prior to the collection of taxes and receipt of federal and state aid, but New York's ability to issue these notes was limited by state law to the amount of money actually collected the previous year. To permit the city to borrow at unprecedented levels, the state legislature in June 1965 nullified the restrictive legislation and permitted the city to issue RANS on the basis of *estimated* anticipated revenues. The new legislation also permitted the city to borrow against taxes and fees that, though owed, were not scheduled for repayment during the upcoming fiscal year. A 1975 *Fortune* magazine analysis of the New York City fiscal crisis suggested that this legislation had been of monumental importance because it permitted the city to engage in the heavy deficit financing that, in the course of the next decade, brought it close to bankruptcy.

Early in December 1965, less than a month before his departure from office, Wagner appointed a three-member panel to negotiate a settlement between the Transport Workers Union and the New York City Transit Authority. Wagner did not play a direct role in the talks nor did Mayor-elect JOHN V. LINDSAY, who was reluctant to become directly involved in the negotiations until he was sworn into office. On December 31, 1965, Wagner, in a surprise move, flew to Acapulco for a vacation. On January 1, 1966, Lindsay's first day in office, 33,000 transit workers struck, shutting down New York's subways and buses.

After leaving office Wagner practiced law but he remained engaged in politics. President Johnson appointed him ambassador to Spain, and he held that position from 1968 to 1969. Later in 1969, he lost the primary election for the Democratic mayoral nomination. He served as President Carter's unofficial representative to the Vatican in 1978. He died on February 12, 1991.

## Wallace, George C(orley)
*(1919–1998) governor, American Independent Party candidate for president*

George C. Wallace, an important, combative, and polarizing political figure during the 1960s, was born in Clio, Alabama, on August 25, 1919. As a youth he was an excellent boxer, winning the Alabama Golden Gloves championship as a bantamweight in 1936 and 1937. His interest in politics arose from his service as a page in the state legislature during the summer of 1935. He earned a law degree from the University of Alabama in 1942 and served in the U.S. Army Air Forces during World War II. After his discharge, he became an assistant state attorney general and then won election in 1946 to the state legislature. He considered himself a populist, and he took a moderate position on racial issues. An alternate delegate to the Democratic National Convention in 1948, he did not join with southerners who walked out to protest the adoption of a progressive civil rights plank. He also served from 1950 to 1952 as trustee of historically black Tuskegee Institute. He was elected circuit judge in 1952 and held that position until 1959.

In 1958 Wallace entered the Democratic primary for governor. In his campaign, he emphasized improved social services and public works, while his opponent played to white voters' fears of racial desegregation. Wallace lost the primary and concluded that he would never again allow an opponent to take a more ardent stand than he did in favor of segregation.

After three years of preparation Wallace ran in the 1962 Democratic gubernatorial primary, promising to resist all efforts "of the federal courts, the Justice Department and the Civil Rights Commission to destroy our social and educational order." He won the primary, although he failed to get a majority, and then prevailed in the runoff with 56 percent of the vote. In his inaugural address as governor on January 14, 1963, Wallace promised "segregation now—segregation tomorrow—segregation forever."

Presidential candidate George C. Wallace, 1968 *(Photographed by Yoichi R. Okamoto; Lyndon Baines Johnson Library)*

Wallace repeatedly defied federal court orders for school integration in his first year in office. In June 1963 he personally blocked the entry of two black students to the University of Alabama at Tuscaloosa and stepped aside only after President Kennedy had federalized the Alabama National Guard and ordered several units onto the campus. In September 1963 Wallace delayed court-ordered desegregation of elementary and secondary schools in four Alabama cities for eight days, and again Kennedy had to intervene to end Wallace's defiance. The governor's actions brought him extensive national publicity and made him a symbol of southern resistance to racial integration.

Contending that the leadership of both national parties had strayed from "the principles on which this country was founded," Wallace launched a campaign for the presidency in the spring of 1964. Repeatedly denying charges that he was a racist, Wallace campaigned against big government and the federal bureaucracy. He declared that the "federal government in Washington is reaching into every facet of society and encroaching on the rightful powers of the state." He denounced the pending civil rights act as yet another usurpation of individual liberty and local government authority and condemned the federal courts as a "judicial oligarchy," manipulating the American people "as cogs in a gigantic socialist pattern."

Wallace entered three Democratic primaries in April and May, capturing 34 percent of the vote in

Wisconsin, 30 percent in Indiana, and 43 percent in Maryland. The size and source of the Wallace vote thoroughly impressed political observers as it indicated that he had substantial appeal outside the Deep South. He scored heavily in working-class neighborhoods in Milwaukee and Baltimore and carried every white precinct in the industrial city of Gary, Indiana. Wallace withdrew from the race on July 19, four days after the Republicans nominated Senator BARRY M. GOLDWATER (R-Ariz.), declaring that his "mission" of helping "conservatize" the national parties was accomplished.

Wallace continued to defend segregation during the rest of his term as governor. Early in 1965 MARTIN LUTHER KING, JR., made Selma the site of a major voter registration drive among blacks. On February 2 King announced plans for a march from Selma to Montgomery to protest the denial of voting rights to Alabama's blacks. Wallace asserted on March 6 that "such a march cannot and will not be tolerated," and the next day state troopers, acting under his orders, broke up the march as it left Selma. Television networks interrupted regular programming to show scenes of the violence in what became known as "Bloody Sunday." State troopers turned back a second march attempt on March 9.

In the midst of this standoff Wallace traveled to the White House to meet with President Johnson. Wallace desired Johnson's help to defuse the crisis, lest further violence belie his claims that he was only an opponent of an intrusive federal government, not a racist. Johnson, in turn, wanted Wallace's cooperation, lest federal intervention with overwhelming force during a violent confrontation alienate moderates and conservatives even as it satisfied liberal demands for protection of the marchers. During their three-hour discussion Johnson used his famous skills at persuasion and manipulation to outmaneuver the governor. When a federal court approved a new plan for a march a few days later, Wallace requested federal assistance. Johnson then placed contingents of the Alabama National Guard under federal supervision, allowing the marchers to complete a five-day journey to Montgomery on March 25.

In the final year of his term Wallace continued to resist integration efforts. In April 1966 Wallace ordered the resegregation of state mental hospitals, which had been integrated in March by the State Hospitals Board. In the same month he announced that Alabama would not comply with the school

desegregation guidelines recently issued by the federal Office of Education, and, in September, Wallace won passage of a law declaring those federal guidelines "null and void" in Alabama.

During his term as governor Wallace increased state education appropriations, inaugurated a large school construction program, and expanded the state's free textbook system. He improved the state's mental health facilities, sponsored a clean water act, and started the largest road building project in the state's history. These measures were generally applauded, but Wallace's critics noted that his tax program was regressive, that old age pensions, unemployment compensation, and welfare payments remained well below the national average during his administration and that Alabama had no minimum wage statute and weak child labor laws.

Because the Alabama constitution barred a governor from serving two consecutive terms, Wallace announced in September 1965 that he would seek a constitutional amendment to change this provision. He called a special session of the state legislature; while the House rapidly passed the succession bill, the Senate voted it down. Wallace circumvented his possible political eclipse by having his wife, Lurleen Wallace, run for governor in 1966. Announcing her candidacy on February 24, Wallace said that if his wife were elected, he would be "by her side" as governor and would "make the policies and decisions affecting the next administration." Lurleen Wallace won 52 percent of the vote in the May 1966 Democratic primary, defeating nine other candidates, and won the November election by a two-to-one margin. When his wife was sworn in as governor in January 1967, Wallace became her special assistant and served as de facto governor, continuing the policies of his own administration, until she died of cancer on May 7, 1968.

Throughout 1966 Wallace indicated he would run again for the presidency in 1968. He began organizing a new campaign in the spring of 1967 and formally announced his third-party candidacy on February 8, 1968. In this campaign, Wallace struck many of the same themes he had in 1964. Alleging that "there's not a dime's worth of difference" between national Democratic and Republican leaders, Wallace said the central issue of his campaign was whether the federal government "can take over and destroy the authority of the states." He denounced the growing federal bureaucracy and said the average man—"the steel worker, the paper worker, the rubber worker, the small businessman, the cab driver"—was "sick and tired of theoreticians in both national parties and in some of our colleges and some of our courts telling us how to go to bed at night and get up in the morning." Portraying himself as the defender of the workingman, Wallace promised to end the trend "toward the solution of all problems with more federal force and more takeover of individual liberty and freedom." Wallace summarized these popular themes by emphasizing that he would work for the ordinary American, who he said government overlooked. His campaign slogan—a national version of the one he had used in running for governor—was "Stand Up for America." Wallace again said he was not a racist, but he attacked federal civil rights laws as a denial of property rights and an infringement on states rights and personal liberty. He attacked the national news media and, as a strong "law and order" advocate, blamed the federal courts for an increase in crime. "If you are knocked in the head on a street in a city today," he complained, "the man who knocked you in the head is out of jail before you get to the hospital" because the courts had "made it impossible to convict a criminal."

Wallace's campaign had a major impact on the 1968 elections. His supporters succeeded in getting his name on the ballot, usually as the candidate of the American Independent Party, in all 50 states. By September both the Gallup and Harris polls gave Wallace 21 percent of the vote. It seemed that Wallace might be able to carry enough states to deny either major party candidate an electoral vote majority, throwing the election into the House of Representatives, where Wallace could influence the choice of a president.

Wallace's prospects began to decline in October. His biggest problem was his running-mate, former Air Force General CURTIS E. LEMAY. At the press conference at which Wallace introduced him, LeMay declared that he thought that the United States could win the Vietnam War without resorting to an atomic attack. But, he continued, Americans, in his view, had "a phobia" about the use of nuclear weapons, something that LeMay thought they should overcome. While Wallace and his aides desperately tried to get the general to cease his comments, LeMay blurted out that because of his controversial views, he would be fortunate not to appear to be a "drooling idiot." Wallace also had difficulties because of the protests and disorders that

often occurred during his campaign appearances and because of an intensive union campaign to diminish his appeal to workers.

Despite these problems Wallace still made an impressive showing on election day. He won 13.5 percent of the national vote in November and carried five states—Arkansas, Louisiana, Mississippi, Alabama, and Georgia. Over 4 million of Wallace's 9.9 million votes came from northern and western states. Wallace supplied his own assessment on the day after the election. Claiming victory in defeat, he contended that he had been "the bellwether for the two national parties" on campaign issues. He asserted his movement was still alive since President-elect Nixon had said "almost identically" the same things in his campaign that Wallace had.

Following the election Wallace became an outspoken critic of the Nixon administration, charging that its economic and tax policies hurt the "little man" and that Nixon was not doing enough to end busing for school desegregation. Wallace won reelection as Alabama governor in 1970, defeating incumbent governor Albert P. Brewer in a close Democratic runoff primary. He announced his candidacy for the Democratic presidential nomination on January 13, 1972. Between March and May he won the Democratic presidential primaries in Florida, Tennessee, North Carolina, Michigan, and Maryland and placed second in primary elections in Wisconsin, Pennsylvania, Indiana, West Virginia, and Oregon. Wallace was shot and seriously wounded on May 15, 1972, while campaigning in Maryland; the attack left him a paraplegic. He remained a contender for the Democratic nomination despite his injuries and placed third in the balloting in the July Democratic National Convention. Saying his doctors advised against it, Wallace did not run as a third-party candidate in 1972 but made another unsuccessful presidential bid in 1976. Wallace won four-year terms as governor of Alabama in 1974 and 1982. At the end of the latter term, he retired from politics. He died on September 13, 1998.

—CAB

## Warnke, Paul C(ulliton)

(1920–2001) *Defense Department general counsel, assistant secretary of defense for internal security affairs*

Born in Webster, Massachusetts, on January 31, 1920, Warnke graduated from Yale in 1941 and then joined the Coast Guard, serving until 1946. Two years later he received his law degree from Columbia University and joined the prestigious Washington law firm of Covington and Burling, where he spent the next 18 years, first as an associate and then as a partner. From 1962 until 1966 he served as a member of the Maryland and Washington, D.C., committees advising the U.S. Commission on Civil Rights.

Warnke left Covington and Burling to become general counsel for the Defense Department in August 1966. At the Pentagon he developed a close working relationship with Secretary of Defense ROBERT S. MCNAMARA and assisted him on several legal and technical problems, particularly those that dealt with the TFX fighter/bomber.

In June 1967 Warnke was appointed assistant secretary of defense for international security affairs. Two months later he helped McNamara, Deputy Secretary of Defense PAUL H. NITZE, and Undersecretary of State NICHOLAS KATZENBACH to write the "San Antonio Formula," a proposal that modified the administration's previous demand for North Vietnamese restraint before peace negotiations could begin. The proposal, sent privately to Hanoi, stated that the United States was "willing immediately to stop all aerial and naval bombardment of North Vietnam when that led promptly to productive discussions." On October 3 North Vietnam rejected the plan.

During the first months of 1968 Warnke stepped up his efforts to reduce the level of U.S. military activity in Vietnam. Following the Tet offensive of January and February, he served as a member of a special committee, headed by the incoming secretary of defense, CLARK CLIFFORD, that the president called together to examine the military's request for over 200,000 more troops. In meetings held at the beginning of March, Warnke opposed a troop increase and questioned the military's interpretation of the Communist offensive as an act of desperation or an attempt to precipitate a popular uprising against the government of South Vietnam. He thought that the offensive was designed to show American citizens that the United States was not winning the war and could not without undermining its foreign and domestic interests. In his opinion the United States should not attempt to win a military victory but should use only the degree of force necessary to achieve a compromise political settlement. Warnke, therefore, objected to further troop increases and suggested instead a strategy designed to protect population centers rather than extend areas of control. The committee rejected Warnke's recommendation and backed the military's request.

On March 31 the president announced new restrictions on the bombing in the hope that they would lead to the opening of negotiations. He wrote to Clifford suggesting that Hanoi had recently given indications that it now accepted the provisions of the "San Antonio Formula." In light of this, he recommended that the United States begin a policy of de-escalation as a sign of good faith. Warnke's advice in the committee meetings and in his correspondence with Clifford had an important influence on the secretary of defense, who in turn played a large role in convincing President Johnson of the need for de-escalation. Warnke nevertheless continued to make his case for a change in policy.

Once the Nixon administration came to power, Warnke left his defense post for private law practice. During the Carter administration, he served as director of the Arms Control and Disarmament Agency and as chief negotiator in the Strategic Arms Limitation Talks with the Soviet Union from 1977 to 1978. He resigned and resumed his law practice. He died on October 31, 2001.

—EWS

## Warren, Earl
### (1891–1974) *chief justice of the United States*

Earl Warren, by most estimates the greatest chief justice of the 20th century, was born in Los Angeles on March 19, 1891. He worked at various jobs to finance his education at the University of California, Berkeley, where he earned a B.A. in 1912 and a law degree two years later. He enlisted in the army during World War I, and then became a city attorney in Oakland and a deputy district attorney in Alameda County in 1920. In 1925 he became—first by appointment and then by election a year later—county district attorney. Reelected twice, he held that position until he won election as California's attorney general in 1938. In that state office he favored the relocation and internment in 1942 of Japanese Americans, an opinion he later regretted and considered wrong. In 1942 he won the first of three terms as governor of California, the only chief executive in the state's history elected three times. He was the vice presidential running mate of

Thomas E. Dewey during a losing campaign in 1948. He made a bid for the Republican presidential nomination in 1952 and then vigorously supported the party's choice, DWIGHT D. EISENHOWER. The new president considered Warren for a cabinet position, but instead promised to nominate him to the first vacancy on the Supreme Court. The death of Chief Justice Fred Vinson allowed Eisenhower to name Warren to the bench in September 1953.

Although no one could anticipate it at the time, Warren's appointment marked the beginning of a period of exceptional judicial activism that produced many landmark rulings from what people soon commonly called the Warren Court. The first such decision came in May 1954 in the case of *Brown v. Board of Education* in which the Court held that racial segregation in public schools was unconstitutional. This ruling helped launch a significant change in American race relations and also served as the base from which the Supreme Court went on to outlaw all public discrimination during the 1960s. The Court's unanimous ruling in the *Brown* case was an indication of Warren's unusual political acumen; he was determined that on a matter of such national significance the Court would speak with one voice. His opinion, while lacking rigorous constitutional analysis, had the virtue of stating in language that anybody could understand that racial segregation was immoral.

In the early 1960s the Court rendered other far-reaching decisions. In *Baker v. Carr* (1962), the justices took on the first of a series of cases that dealt with legislative apportionment and announced the standard of "one person, one vote." In a subsequent opinion written in 1964, Warren declared, "legislators represent people, not trees or acres." The Court's rulings resulted in the redrawing of congressional and legislative districts across the country. In April 1968 the Court extended the one person, one vote principle to local units of government. Another landmark case, *Griswold v. Connecticut* decided in 1965, established a right to privacy in the Constitution that led to overturning of state laws prohibiting the use of birth control.

During the Johnson years the Court extended its rulings on civil rights issues. In December 1964 the Court unanimously sustained the public accommodations section of the 1964 Civil Rights Act. The chief justice also wrote the majority opinion in a March 1966 case upholding seven major parts of the 1965 Voting Rights Act. Warren spoke for the Court in an April 1965 decision that invalidated a Virginia law substituting a special registration procedure for the poll tax outlawed by the Twenty-fourth Amendment. In June 1967 Warren, speaking for a unanimous Court, found unconstitutional state antimiscegenation laws, one of the last bastions of legalized segregation. In June of the next year the Court upheld an 1866 federal statute that prohibited racial discrimination in the sale or rental of housing and other property. The Court consistently overturned state convictions of civil rights demonstrators on a variety of legal grounds up until 1966. However, in November of that year a five-justice majority upheld the trespass convictions of protesters who had gathered outside a Florida jail. Warren dissented from this judgment and from a similar Court ruling in June 1967.

In the area of the rights of suspects in criminal investigations and trials, the Warren Court broke new ground. In June 1961, with Warren in the majority, it held that illegally seized evidence could not be used in state courts. In the 1963 case of *Gideon v. Wainwright* a majority of the justices declared that all criminal defendants had a constitutional right to an attorney. One of the Court's most important and familiar rulings occurred in 1966 in *Miranda v. Arizona*, which specified that police officers had to advise suspects they arrested in criminal cases of their right to remain silent and to have legal counsel.

These decisions aroused considerable controversy, including charges that the Court had gone too far in interfering with law enforcement efforts to bring criminals to justice. Warren, however, insisted that the Court's actions reflected a view that government must be fair and follow procedures that insured the protection of the constitutional rights of all citizens. Yet the criticism persisted.

Republican presidential candidate RICHARD M. NIXON made *Miranda* and other Court rulings on criminal rights a major issue in his 1968 campaign. Yet, other observers noted that although the Court enhanced the rights of the accused, it also upheld the right of police to use informants and made it clear that both wiretapping and eavesdropping would be approved if properly authorized by judicial warrants. An opinion written by Warren in June 1968 also upheld police authority to stop and frisk dangerous-looking persons for weapons.

The court also decided some controversial First Amendment cases. In December 1966 Warren spoke for a unanimous Court in ruling that the Georgia House of Representatives had violated JULIAN BOND's right of free speech when it excluded him from his seat in the legislature because of his opposition to the draft and the Vietnam War. Although he normally favored expanding the right to free expression, the chief justice proved to be less tolerant in the realm of obscenity. He dissented from several Court decisions that restricted government suppression of allegedly obscene materials and that resulted in much greater freedom of expression in this area. In May 1968 Warren, speaking for a seven-justice majority, upheld a provision in the Selective Service Act that made it a criminal offense to burn one's draft card and rejected the argument that this type of conduct was a form of symbolic speech protected by the First Amendment.

In addition to his work on the Court, Warren, at the urging of President Johnson, reluctantly agreed in November 1963 to head a commission to investigate the assassination of John F. Kennedy. After 10 months of work, which Warren later called "the unhappiest time of my life," the commission produced a unanimous report, concluding that Lee Harvey Oswald, acting alone, had killed Kennedy. The Warren Commission report at first enjoyed considerable public confidence. Over time, though, it became clear that there were gaps in the commission's investigation, arising from such problems as the withholding of information on the part of the CIA. Warren also decided out of respect for the privacy of the dead president's family not to interview JACQUELINE KENNEDY. These omissions led critics to dispute the commission's methods and findings. Even though new technologies have verified much of the reasoning that led to the commission's finding that Oswald was the sole assassin, critics persist in advancing conspiracy theories that purport to explain Kennedy's killing.

On June 13, 1968, Warren submitted his resignation to President Johnson, who accepted it pending confirmation of a new chief justice. The timing of Warren's resignation arose from his desire to keep Richard Nixon, Warren's longstanding political rival, from having an opportunity to name the next chief justice. Warren's effort failed, however, after President Johnson withdrew the nomination of Associate Justice ABE FORTAS in the fall of 1968 following allegations of financial irregularities. Fortas resigned from the Court, and Nixon designated Warren Burger as Warren's successor in 1969. In his last opinion for the Court on June 16, 1969, Warren reversed an appeals court decision written by Burger, and held that the House of Representatives had acted unconstitutionally in excluding ADAM CLAYTON POWELL from membership in March 1967.

A thoughtful man with a friendly affable manner, Warren devoted a part of his retirement years to public speaking and to the fishing, hunting, and spectator sports he so enjoyed. He died in Washington on July 9, 1974.

During his years on the bench, Earl Warren served as a symbol for the entire Court to both its admirers and its critics. Denunciations of the Court's rulings often turned into attacks on Warren personally. Picketers and hecklers harassed him when he delivered public speeches. The John Birch Society, an extreme right-wing organization, carried on a national campaign to impeach him. His actual role in making the Warren Court the activist, liberal body it became has been widely debated. While some observers contended that he played no greater part than his fellow liberal justices, a larger number have argued that his leadership and his political and administrative skills were essential for establishing cohesion and direction on the Court. With the single exception of obscenity, Warren supported every major change in constitutional doctrine made by the Court, and thus placed the weight of his reputation behind the Court's innovative trends. Although not considered a great legal scholar or judicial philosopher, Warren has been ranked as one of America's greatest chief justices, usually second only to John Marshall.

Legal scholars made their strongest criticism of Warren's methods. He was so oriented toward achieving desirable results, they charged, that he too often disregarded precedents, failed to explain or justify his rulings with solid legal reasoning, and left himself open to the charge that he interpreted the Constitution on the basis of political preferences.

Yet Warren has also earned substantial praise for his dedication to the ideal of equal justice for all Americans and to the protection of individual liberties. He presided over a court that had enormous effect on American law and life, giving impetus to and providing support for fundamental social change.

—CAB

## Washington, Walter (Edward)

(1915–2003) *executive director, National Capital Housing Authority; director, New York Housing Authority; Washington, D.C., mayor-commissioner*

Washington was born on April 15, 1915, in Dawson, Georgia, and raised in Jamestown, New York. In 1934 he moved to the District of Columbia to begin studies at Howard University. After graduating from Howard with a major in sociology and public administration, Washington joined the National Capital Housing Authority in 1941. As a member of an agency charged with the construction and management of low-rent housing, Washington served in a variety of capacities until named executive director in 1961. He remained in that post until November 1966, when New York mayor JOHN V. LINDSAY named him to head the New York Housing Authority. In September 1967 Washington left that position to become the first modern mayor of Washington, D.C., which had previously had a commission form of government.

Washington, who became the first African-American chief executive of a major U.S. city, faced significant obstacles in his new position. Congress retained control over the city's finances, yet some legislators were wary of relinquishing even limited power to the new mayor. In a time of racial tensions, many southern members of Congress did not easily accept Washington's appointment because he was African American, even though the city's population at the time was 70 percent black. Washington later recollected that it took years before some members of Congress would address him by his title rather than his name. Washington faced even greater challenges in trying to govern a city with the highest infant mortality in the country, poor schools, dismal housing, and a high rate of unemployment.

Washington, however, eagerly accepted the challenge of bringing what President Johnson called the capital's "wagon-wheel government into the jet age." He faced an early challenge when riots occurred in Washington after the assassination of MARTIN LUTHER KING, JR., on April 4, 1968. The mayor refused to accede to FBI director J. EDGAR HOOVER's demand that looters be shot on sight. Washington's efforts to quell the disturbances helped quiet critics who doubted his ability to lead the city. During his first year in office Washington took steps to recruit African Americans to the predominantly white police force and to hire blacks for other city positions. Problems, however, continued, including a high crime rate and persistent poverty.

Washington was appointed to two more terms as mayor-commissioner by President RICHARD M. NIXON. In 1974, after Congress granted the district home rule, Washington was elected to a four-year term as mayor. He lost his reelection bid in 1978. He then practiced law, but remained involved in district politics. He died on October 27, 2003.

—TJC

## Watson, W(illiam) Marvin

(1924–  ) *White House special assistant, U.S. Postmaster General*

Born on June 6, 1924, in Oakhurst, Texas, W. Marvin Watson studied at Baylor University but did not complete his studies before joining the marines during World War II. After the war he returned to Baylor, where he earned an M.B.A. degree in 1950. From 1957 until 1965 he worked in Dallas as an executive assistant to E. B. Germany, the president of Lone Star Steel Company.

Watson first met LYNDON B. JOHNSON in 1948 during Johnson's campaign for a U.S. Senate seat in Texas. Watson, then still a student at Baylor, was favorably impressed and supported Johnson. During the 1950s he became involved in Texas Democratic politics. He organized the first Johnson-for-President club in Texas and then joined the senator's campaign staff in 1960. Four years later he served as the president's convention coordinator when the Democrats met in Atlantic City to nominate Johnson in 1964. After the convention he was elected the Democratic state chair in Texas and was deeply involved in the fall campaign.

On February 1, 1965, Watson joined the White House staff as special assistant to the president. Watson had a host of responsibilities, including supervising the president's schedule, maintaining liaison with the Democratic National Committee and with governors and mayors, and interviewing nominees for staff positions. Although contemporaries often described him as the president's appointments secretary, Watson maintained that he had an understanding with the president that he would function as White House chief of staff, even though Johnson never gave that title to any of his aides. Watson later said that his typical workday started in the president's bedroom as he reviewed memoranda and messages that had accumulated overnight and decided which the president should see. At the beginning of the day, he usually would get from the president a long list of tasks that might require telephone calls or messages to see that Johnson's instructions were carried out. Watson usually did not depart the White House until the president was ready to retire at night.

Watson's responsibilities included maintaining contact with the FBI, a task that meant that intelligence reports intended for the president usually first went to him. Watson insisted that both he and the president had great confidence in the FBI director, J. EDGAR HOOVER, and the reports about the dangers to internal security that Hoover provided. Watson contended that Hoover's analyses, which many critics considered distorted, exaggerated, or unfounded, persuaded him that the country's enemies had "infiltrated, financed, and encouraged" the anti–Vietnam War movement. Watson also concluded, on the basis of FBI wiretaps and surveillance, that Dr. MARTIN LUTHER KING, JR., was taking advice from Communists.

Watson was one of a small number of the president's trusted aides and personal friends who knew during the winter of 1968 that Johnson was uncertain about whether to run for another term. Watson believed that Johnson was not worried about gaining renomination, even after Senator ROBERT F. KENNEDY (D-N.Y.) announced his candidacy on March 16. Watson believed that the loss of public support for the administration's Vietnam War policies was a major reason for Johnson's decision not to seek renomination. Also important was the president's health, including what Watson said was the president's fear that because of his family history he might not live out another term. According to Watson, Johnson even seriously considered resignation in October 1965, when he made a slow recovery from gall bladder surgery. On the evening of March 31, as Johnson began his televised address in which he revealed his plans, Watson called important public officials, including Vice President HUBERT H. HUMPHREY, so they would get a few minutes' advance notice of the president's dramatic announcement.

In April 1968, following the resignation of LAWRENCE F. O'BRIEN to work in Senator Robert F. Kennedy's campaign for the Democratic presidential nomination, Johnson nominated Watson to serve as U.S. Postmaster General. Watson held that position until the president left office in January 1969.

In April 1969 Watson became a top executive with responsibility for international activities of the Occidental Petroleum Corporation. In 2004, in collaboration with his White House assistant, Sherwin Markman, he published a memoir entitled, *Chief of Staff: Lyndon Johnson and His Presidency.*

—FHM

## Weaver, Robert C(lifton)

(1907–1997) *administrator, Housing and Home Finance Agency; secretary, Department of Housing and Urban Development*

The first African-American cabinet secretary, Robert C. Weaver was born on December 29, 1907, in Washington, D.C. He grew up in a middle-class suburb of Washington and attended Harvard University, where he studied economics and received a B.A. in 1929 and a Ph.D. in 1934. Weaver's work in economics persuaded him that economic opportunity was essential to racial equality. He also believed that federal action was a key to providing African Americans with a chance for success. During the New Deal, Weaver worked in a variety of federal agencies and was a member of President Franklin D. Roosevelt's informal "Black Cabinet." After leaving the federal government in 1944, Weaver served as director of the Mayor's Committee on Race Relations in Chicago. During the 1940s and 1950s he taught at Northwestern University, Columbia University, New York University, and the New School for Social Research. He published *Negro Labor: A National Problem* in 1946 and *The Negro Ghetto* in 1948. From 1949 to 1955 he headed the opportunity fellowships program of the John Hay Whitney Foundation.

Weaver served as New York State's rent commissioner in the late 1950s and as vice chair of the New York City Housing and Redevelopment Board in 1960. An expert on black labor and urban renewal problems as well as housing, Weaver was chosen as administrator of the Housing and Home Finance Agency (HHFA) by President-elect John F. Kennedy in December 1960. In that post he oversaw the main housing, home finance, and community development functions of the federal government and the operations of five subordinate agencies, including the Urban Renewal Administration and the Federal Housing Administration. Weaver helped draft the Kennedy administration's June 1961 omnibus housing bill and lobbied for the 1962 Senior Citizens Housing Act.

Continuing to serve as HHFA administrator in the Johnson administration, Weaver helped write all of President Johnson's housing and urban renewal programs, many of which were part of the administration's larger antipoverty effort. In the summer of 1964 he lobbied for the president's housing act. Passed in August it provided $1.1 billion to augment urban renewal grants, federal assistance for improvement of slum properties, housing loans for the handicapped and elderly, and other programs. Weaver also worked in 1965 for the $7.8 billion omnibus housing bill, which greatly expanded public housing and rent supplement programs for low-income families. He defended the bill's controversial rent supplement provisions, which sought to guarantee that individuals below the poverty level would not pay more than 25 percent of their incomes in rent. Despite strong resistance from Republicans and southern Democrats in Congress, the bill passed in August 1965.

Both Presidents Kennedy and Johnson repeatedly urged congressional authorization of a cabinet-level department of housing and urban affairs. The proposal made no headway during the Kennedy administration, in part because southern Democrats opposed the president's announced intention to name Weaver head of the new department. President Johnson gave no advance indication of his choice for such a post, and, in September 1965, a law was finally adopted creating a Department of Housing and Urban Development (HUD). On January 13, 1966, Johnson named Weaver the first secretary of HUD. With Senate confirmation of his appointment four days later, Weaver assumed the highest office in the executive branch of the federal government held by an African American to that time. HUD subsumed the HHFA; thus, Weaver's responsibilities initially remained largely unchanged in his new position.

As secretary of HUD, Weaver helped promote the administration-backed Demonstration Cities and Metropolitan Development Act in November 1966 and then implemented the Model Cities program that it created. Administered by HUD, the program was designed to demonstrate in selected poor neighborhoods how various federal and local programs could be coordinated and concentrated to eliminate urban blight and restructure the total environment of the neighborhoods' residents.

In July 1967 Weaver spoke out against a plan advanced by Senator CHARLES PERCY (R-Ill.) to promote home ownership among the poor. Weaver contended that many poor families had incomes that were too low or too irregular to meet the mortgage payments and maintenance costs of home ownership, and he called for better funding of existing housing programs. However, the administration's Housing and Urban Development Act of 1968 did include a program to help the poor buy their own homes, although the methods used differed from those outlined in Percy's proposal. Weaver lobbied for the 1968 bill, which became law on August 1. The act also authorized a three-year program to supply new and rehabilitated housing for low-income families, federal underwriting of the insurance industry against losses due to riots, and other new urban renewal programs.

In August 1966 Weaver encountered criticism of federal urban renewal efforts when he testified before a Senate government operations subcommittee investigating the problems of the cities. Subcommittee chair senator ABRAHAM A. RIBICOFF (D-Conn.) and Senator ROBERT F. KENNEDY (D-N.Y.) both asserted that urban redevelopment was not being achieved under existing federal programs. The many programs inaugurated during the Johnson administration and directed in part by Weaver expanded both the size and the scope of federal housing and urban renewal activities and often redirected their focus along lines favored by urban planning experts. Nonetheless, most commentators agreed that although individual projects were successful, federal programs in the 1960s failed to check the spread of urban decay.

During his tenure Weaver also strongly backed the administration's open housing bill, arguing that it would "fill a void" in the nation's policy against discrimination. On May 14, 1968, he announced that he would leave government following the presidential election. He submitted his resignation in November, effective January 1, 1969. From 1969 to 1971 Weaver served as president of Bernard Baruch College, a branch of the City University of New York. In 1971 he became professor of urban affairs at Hunter College in New York City. He died on July 17, 1997.

—CAB

### Webb, James E(dwin)

(1906–1992) *director, National Aeronautics and Space Administration*

Born on October 7, 1906, in Tally Ho, North Carolina, Webb earned a B.A. from the University of

North Carolina in 1928. He joined the U.S. Marine Corps Reserves, earning a commission as a second lieutenant and learning to fly during his training. He completed a law degree at George Washington University in 1936 and then joined the Sperry Gyroscope Corporation, which produced aeronautical instruments, and rose to the position of vice president by 1943. His work in the law office of former North Carolina governor O. Max Gardner led to his appointment in 1946 as President Truman's director of the Bureau of the Budget. Three years later, he became undersecretary of state, concentrating more on administrative matters than foreign policy questions. He resigned that position in 1952.

Webb counseled Oklahoma senator Robert Kerr (D-Okla.) on international questions during the senator's unsuccessful effort in 1952 to the secure the Democratic nomination for president. He worked as a director of Kerr-McGee Oil Industries in Oklahoma City during the 1950s. Kerr succeeded Senator LYNDON B. JOHNSON as chair of the Senate Aeronautical and Space Sciences Committee after Johnson became vice president in 1961. Kerr's recommendation was instrumental in President Kennedy's appointment of Webb as head of the National Aeronautics and Space Administration (NASA) in 1961.

The space program unexpectedly became a higher national priority than Kennedy imagined when he named Webb as NASA administrator. Kennedy was skeptical of approving the costs of an accelerated program to put humans in space until the Soviets launched the first spacecraft in April 1961 with a cosmonaut, Yuri Gagarin, aboard. This Soviet success occurred at almost the same time as another blow to U.S. prestige, when a CIA-sponsored invasion of Cuba aimed at overthrowing Fidel Castro ended in disaster at the Bay of Pigs. Webb recommended to the president that space flight could provide an opportunity to demonstrate U.S. power and technological achievement. NASA scientists advised Kennedy that the United States had a chance to be the first nation to send an astronaut to the Moon. Some of the president's science advisers, however, questioned the scientific significance of human space flights as well as their safety. Webb joined with Secretary of Defense ROBERT S. MCNAMARA in urging the president to give new priority to a program of space flights with astronauts. A memorandum to Kennedy on May 8 maintained, "It is man, not merely machines, in space, that captures the imagination of the world." NASA proposed a broad space program, including the launching of communications and weather satellites as well as a human flight to the Moon. Webb, who realized the complexity of the latter objective, recommended that the president avoid a commitment to achieving a Moon landing by a specific year. On May 25, Kennedy declared in a speech that space travel had a profound effect on international attitudes in the cold war "battle that is going on around the world between freedom and tyranny." He then set as a national goal the landing and safe return of an astronaut from a Moon mission by the end of the decade.

As NASA administrator, Webb oversaw the development of Project Apollo, the name of the Moon landing effort. Congress was receptive to the idea of making human space travel a national priority and raised NASA's annual budget from less than $1 billion to over $5 billion by the mid-1960s. Webb announced in 1962 that NASA had decided that it would put astronauts on the Moon in a landing vehicle that would descend from lunar orbit. This method avoided the need for the development of a huge rocket with enormous thrust, which would have been necessary for a direct flight between the Earth and the Moon. But the lunar-orbit method required precise maneuvers in order to get the astronauts safely to their destination and back.

Webb was highly effective in securing both presidential and congressional support for the Apollo project during the Johnson years. President Johnson had played a major role as a senator in the creation of NASA and took a special interest in the space program as vice president. As president, he continued to give high priority to the goal of a Moon landing by the end of the 1960s. Webb, however, cultivated the president's support through such actions as going to Capitol Hill to press for the passage of the Civil Rights Act of 1964, a key element of the president's domestic program. Webb was also effective at securing strong congressional backing for NASA budget requests. During 1965–66, the success of Gemini space flights, with two astronauts aboard each flight performing spectacular tasks such as space walks, facilitated Webb's task of securing enthusiastic congressional and public support for NASA.

In January 1967 disaster struck when a flash fire in an Apollo spacecraft killed three astronauts in a rehearsal for that program's first scheduled launching. During hearings in the House of Representatives, Webb maintained that NASA's capability "demonstrated in Project Mercury and in Project Gemini . . . has not all been consumed in one Apollo fire. . . . Whatever our faults, we are an able-bodied team." However, Major General Samuel C. Phillips, NASA's Apollo program director, testified that he had put forth a different view in a report he had written in 1965. Representative WILLIAM F. RYAN (D-N.Y.) obtained a copy of the "report" and asserted that it indicated "incredible mismanagement" of the Apollo program. The report, Ryan said, showed unsatisfactory equipment, ineffective planning and program control, and an inability to meet schedules.

Webb asked Johnson to allow a NASA review board, rather than a presidential commission or a congressional panel, to have primary responsibility for investigating the Apollo fire. The review board's report was released in March 1967 and showed among the conditions that contributed to the fire was a sealed cabin with pressurized oxygen, combustible materials in the cabin; vulnerable electrical wiring and plumbing; and inadequate provisions for escape, rescue, and medical assistance. The report did not assign responsibility for the fire. "Our object," Webb said, "was to get ready to fly again." Webb presented these findings to congressional committees. He often faced sharp questioning as well as critical commentary in the news media. His efforts helped to restore essential support for the Apollo project, even if his own prestige as NASA administrator remained diminished. He resigned from NASA in October 1968, nine months before the *Apollo 11* mission brought the first human explorers to the Moon. He resumed the practice of law in 1968 and died on March 27, 1992.

—MDB

## Welch, Robert H(enry) W(inborne), Jr.
### (1899–1985) *founder, John Birch Society*

Born on December 1, 1899, in Chowan County, North Carolina, Welch graduated from the University of North Carolina in 1916. In succession, he dropped out of graduate school at his alma mater, the U.S. Naval Academy, and Harvard Law School and then went into the candy business. His business prospered and Welch wrote a book about his success in 1941 entitled, *The Road to Salesmanship.*

Communism rather than candy became his main concern in the years after World War II. Like many Americans, Welch believed there was an internal communist threat to U.S. security as the cold war emerged. He briefly entered politics when he made an unsuccessful bid for the Republican nomination for lieutenant governor in the early 1950s. By the middle of the 1950s he concentrated on disseminating his anticommunist views in various writings and speeches. In 1956 he began publishing a magazine, which two years later he renamed *American Opinion*. In the pages of this journal and elsewhere, Welch expressed what had become an extremist perspective that there was an international Communist conspiracy that had infiltrated the highest levels of the U.S. government. In 1958 he founded an organization devoted to spreading this idea, as well as Welch's belief that the United States should break diplomatic relations with the Soviet Union, withdraw from the United Nations, and quit the North Atlantic Treaty Organization. Welch named the organization the John Birch Society after a U.S. intelligence officer whose death in China in 1945 constituted, in his view, the first casualty of the cold war. He located the society's headquarters in Belmont, Massachusetts.

During the early 1960s the John Birch Society gained national attention with campaigns to impeach Supreme Court justice EARL WARREN and to halt the fluoridation of local water systems, which Welch and others said deprived citizens of their liberty. Welch himself stirred controversy because of his allegations in a book entitled the *Politician*, first published in 1958, that President DWIGHT D. EISENHOWER was a Communist agent. Welch retreated in the face of intense criticism, maintaining in the early 1960s that he believed that Eisenhower and other high officials in his administration had only been exploited by Communists.

Fears about the strength and influence of the John Birch Society reached a peak in the mid-1960s. Welch appointed JOHN H. ROUSSELOT to handle the society's public relations efforts in 1964. Rousselot tried to play down the society's more extreme positions, and he spearheaded a recruitment effort that brought the society's membership to an estimated 80,000 in the middle of the decade. The success of Senator BARRY GOLDWATER (R-Ariz.) in winning the Republican presidential nomination heightened concerns about the society, especially after Goldwater proclaimed in his acceptance speech at his party's national convention that "extremism in the defense of liberty is no vice."

Goldwater's overwhelming defeat helped alleviate some of the concerns about whether the society's positions would affect public policy. In addition, Rousselot's public relations effort, no matter how sophisticated, could not overcome a widely shared view that the John Birch Society was a radical-right fringe organization.

During the late 1960s other controversies diminished the John Birch Society's limited appeal. In July 1966 national council member Revilo P. Oliver, a professor of classics at the University of Illinois whose academic credentials were prized by Welch, made anti-Semitic remarks at a Birch Society rally. Oliver resigned later in the month, and Welch denounced anti-Semitism, but the incident damaged the organization. During the same year another national council member, Dr. S. M. Draskovich, whom Welch had praised as "one of the five best-informed anticommunists in the world," resigned from the society, charging that it did little more than sell anticommunist books. These events, and the resignation of Rousselot in 1967, helped thwart further membership growth.

In the late 1960s and early 1970s Welch advanced increasingly obscure conspiracy theories. As a conservative movement gained wide appeal in American politics during the 1970s, the John Birch Society lost influence. Welch died on January 6, 1985.

—MLL

## Westmoreland, William C(hilds)
(1914–2005) *commander, U.S. Military Assistance Command, South Vietnam; army chief of staff*

Born on March 26, 1914, in Spartanburg, South Carolina, Westmoreland, attended the Citadel, a South Carolina military college, before winning appointment to West Point. Following his graduation in 1936, he was commissioned a second lieutenant in the artillery. During World War II he fought in North Africa and Sicily. As a colonel and executive officer of the Ninth Infantry, he fought in the Normandy landing and in the assault on Germany. During the Korean War, he commanded a regimental combat team and gained promotion to brigadier general. He was named commander of the elite 101st Airborne Division in 1958. Two years later President Eisenhower appointed him superintendent of West Point.

In January 1964 Westmoreland went to South Vietnam as deputy to General Paul D. Harkins, the head of the U.S. Military Assistance Command, Vietnam. In June, he succeeded Harkins. At that time, U.S. troops in South Vietnam were serving in the declared role of advisers to the South Vietnamese forces. Some of the American advisers, however, had experienced combat and a few had died in action. Westmoreland was determined to raise the effectiveness of the pacification programs and the antiguerrilla operations of the Saigon government. Yet he complained about a lack of South Vietnamese cooperation that was harming the war effort against the National Liberation Front (NLF). He wrote to the U.S. ambassador, General MAXWELL TAYLOR, that the Saigon government suffered from "inefficiency, corruption, disinterest and lack of motivation." As a result, the South Vietnamese "were not winning the war." Westmoreland thought it was essential "to lay things on the line," in order to make clear that increases in U.S. aid required Saigon's cooperation and reform.

During the end of 1964 and early 1965 President Johnson's top national security advisers wrestled with the question of how to reverse the deterioration in the war effort and raise the effectiveness of the South Vietnamese government. In February 1965 Johnson approved a recommendation for a graduated bombing campaign against North Vietnam, one aimed both at applying pressure that would induce the North Vietnamese to halt its support of military operations in the South and at reassuring Saigon leaders of U.S. support so that they would invigorate their efforts to fight the Communists. Soon after the beginning of this sustained air campaign, Westmoreland secured approval for the dispatch of two U.S. marine combat units, which landed at Danang on March 8, 1965, to protect the American airbase. During the next several months, Westmoreland pressed for the dispatch of more U.S. troops to take the offensive against the enemy. On July 28, 1965, Johnson announced at a press conference that he was ordering an increase in the U.S. troop strength in South Vietnam to 125,000. "Additional forces will be needed later," the president declared, "and they will be sent as requested." While Johnson maintained that there had been no change in policy, his actions had transformed an advisory mission into a combat effort. By the end of 1965 Westmoreland commanded more than 184,000 U.S. troops.

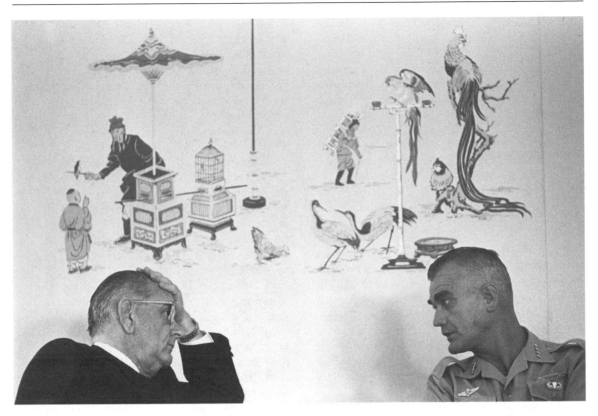

Military Assistance Commander and U.S. Army chief of staff William C. Westmoreland meeting with President Johnson in the White House, 1967 *(Photographed by Yoichi R. Okamoto; Lyndon Baines Johnson Library)*

Westmoreland used the growing number of U.S. forces to undertake "search-and-destroy" operations against the main enemy units. He insisted that the enemy's big units, not its guerrilla fighters, posed the greatest danger to South Vietnamese security. Westmoreland waged a war of attrition, hoping to use advantages in mobility and firepower to inflict casualties faster than the enemy could replace them. In the hope of reaching this crossover point—enemy losses that exceeded the availability of fresh troops—Westmoreland kept requesting reinforcements. Until the spring of 1967 the president authorized the dispatch of those forces. By early 1967 there were more than 400,000 U.S. troops in Southeast Asia. Even though Johnson refused to authorize U.S. ground operations into North Vietnam, Westmoreland remained optimistic that the combination of search-and-destroy missions in the South and bombing attacks in the North would eventually force the enemy to halt its efforts to overthrow the Saigon

government by force. U.S. intelligence estimates revealed, however, that Hanoi had increased its supply of troops and equipment to the South and had the resources to continue its war effort indefinitely.

As U.S. casualties mounted, Westmoreland's search-and-destroy tactics came under increasing criticism. Some critics charged that Westmoreland's troops became easy targets for enemy ambush when they went into the jungles. During 1967 Westmoreland was also criticized for his decision to defend U.S. base camps at Con Thien and Khe Sanh in Quang Tri Province. Some members of Congress who had become skeptical of the general's strategy suggested that Westmoreland was wasting troops and materiel in defending bases of little strategic importance.

Throughout the course of the war, Westmoreland issued optimistic progress reports, and he became a symbol of American determination in Southeast Asia. Amidst growing concern about the war, President Johnson brought him home in April

1967 to address a joint session of Congress. "Backed at home by resolve, confidence, patience and determination," he said, "we will prevail over the Communist aggressor." Some senators and representatives stood and applauded. In November, at a time when the Johnson administration was making a determined effort to reverse the decline in public support for the president's Vietnam policies, Westmoreland spoke at the National Press Club in Washington, D.C., and declared that "we have reached an important point when the end begins to come into view." Westmoreland predicted that U.S. troops would start to come home within two years if the progress in the war effort continued.

The enemy offensive on January 30, 1968, at the start of the traditional Tet holiday season in Vietnam seemed to belie Westmoreland's claims of progress. Communist forces launched a series of assaults on Saigon, Hue, and more than 100 other locations in South Vietnam. Westmoreland had expected enemy attacks to coincide with Tet, but he thought that the U.S. base at Khe Sanh would be the target. He did not anticipate attacks throughout the country, including raids on such symbols of authority as the U.S. embassy in Saigon and the South Vietnamese presidential palace. In most places, enemy fighters withdrew or retreated with heavy casualties, although hard fighting continued for weeks in such locations as Hue and Khe Sanh. Westmoreland declared that the Tet offensive was a desperate enemy maneuver that had ended in failure with devastating losses. Yet the surprise, audacity, and power of the enemy attacks during the Tet holidays brought a sharp drop in U.S. public support for the administration's war policies. And Westmoreland's request for more than 200,000 additional troops, which leaked to the news media in early March, raised new and even stronger objections to his strategy of search and destroy that seemed to require ever more increments of troops. In March 1968 the new secretary of defense, CLARK CLIFFORD, undertook a review of U.S. strategy and urged the president not to grant the troop request. The president decided only to send Westmoreland modest reinforcements. He decided as well to restrict the U.S. bombing of North Vietnam in the hope of gaining Hanoi's agreement to peace talks. Johnson announced these decisions in his televised address of March 31, revealing at the same time that he would not seek or accept the Democratic nomination for another term as president. Days earlier, the White House announced that Westmoreland would leave

South Vietnam to succeed General Harold K. Johnson as army chief of staff. General CREIGHTON ABRAMS became the new commander of U.S. troops in South Vietnam.

As the army's top uniformed officer, Westmoreland spoke frequently at military bases and civic functions to increase public support for the war. Westmoreland retired from the army in June 1972. In July 1974 he lost in a bid for the South Carolina Republican gubernatorial nomination.

In retirement Westmoreland openly attacked the Johnson administration's management of the war. He bitterly denounced former secretary of defense ROBERT S. MCNAMARA and his civilian aides who had refused to permit the air force to carry out the sustained and intensive bombing that he maintained could have brought the defeat of North Vietnam. He criticized these same officials for refusing to permit him to destroy Communist forces in their Cambodian sanctuaries. "What special audacity," he asked, "prompted civilian bureaucrats to deem they know better how to run a military campaign than did military professionals?" In 1982 Westmoreland sued CBS for libel over a documentary that alleged he had suppressed intelligence information about the size of enemy forces in Vietnam. He reached an out-of-court settlement with the network. He died on July 18, 2005.

—JLW

## Wheeler, Earle G(ilmore)

(1908–1975) *army chief of staff; chair, Joint Chiefs of Staff*

Born in Washington, D.C., on January 13, 1908, Wheeler graduated from West Point in 1932. An infantry officer, he saw combat in Germany during the final months of World War II. He held a variety of staff positions during the next 15 years, including director of the Joint Staff in the Pentagon. President Kennedy nominated him to be army chief of staff; his responsibilities began on October 1, 1962.

As army chief, Wheeler established a good professional rapport with Secretary of Defense ROBERT S. MCNAMARA for his implementation of the secretary's program of expansion and modernization of the army and for his articulate public defense of the nuclear test ban treaty in 1963.

President Johnson nominated Wheeler to be chair of the Joint Chiefs of Staff in July 1964. Wheeler became increasingly involved in the Vietnam. War both as an adviser to the president and as a liaison between the Joint Chiefs and civilian decision makers. Speaking for the Joint Chiefs in early 1965, Wheeler urged the bombing of North Vietnam in retaliation for enemy attacks on U.S. facilities and troops in South Vietnam. The president authorized such action following an enemy strike on an American base at Pleiku on February 7, and the air attacks became a sustained program of bombing of North Vietnam targets by early March. Although he was an ardent supporter of the bombing missions, Wheeler reported in early April that they had not reduced North Vietnamese military capabilities "in any major way." Wheeler also informed McNamara on March 20 that the Joint Chiefs believed that the military situation in South Vietnam was so "critical" that "if present trends are not reversed," the South Vietnamese government would lose the war and its failure "would be recognized world-wide" as "a U.S. defeat." To "turn the tide," the Joint Chiefs recommended that U.S. troops engage in combat missions against the enemy. During the next several months the president made a series of decisions culminating in his announcement at a press conference on July 28 that he was ordering additional troops to Vietnam that would bring the U.S. force level to 125,000 immediately and that more troops would follow that deployment.

Despite substantial increases in the U.S. war effort during the next two years, Wheeler thought the president should approve the dispatch of additional forces. In April 1967 General WILLIAM C. WESTMORELAND, the commander of U.S. forces in Vietnam, met with Johnson in Washington and urged the president to order the deployment of 200,000 troops beyond the level already authorized for the end of 1967, which would have brought total U.S. strength to 670,000. Wheeler participated in the meeting and, speaking for the Joint Chiefs, recommended an invasion of North Vietnam and the mining of North Vietnamese harbors. Johnson

General Earle Wheeler (left) speaking as General Creighton Abrams (center) and others listen, 1968 *(Photographed by Yoichi R. Okamoto; Lyndon Baines Johnson Library)*

demurred, however, and asked "where does it all end?" A few months later, Wheeler was so discontented that he briefly contemplated joining with other members of the Joint Chiefs to protest the president's Vietnam policies by resigning. Even though Wheeler and the other military leaders decided not to quit, civil-military relations had become severely strained because of differences over the war.

After the enemy's Tet offensive in early 1968, Wheeler went to South Vietnam to consult with Westmoreland and to make recommendations for future actions. In his report to the president on February 27, Wheeler described the enemy offensive as a failure that had nonetheless come close to success—"a very near thing." To "regain the initiative through offensive operations" Wheeler recommended an additional 206,000 troops. This request, which came as a shock to many Pentagon civilians, served as a catalyst for a reappraisal of U.S. policy.

During the discussions of the high-level ad hoc task force set up to study the proposal, several of civilian advisers, such as PAUL NITZE and NICHOLAS KATZENBACH opposed the troop increase. Despite this resistance, the task force report, issued on March 7, endorsed Wheeler's proposals. President Johnson, who initially approved of the recommendations, never put them into effect. The new secretary of defense, CLARK M. CLIFFORD, advised the president that even Wheeler could not guarantee that the 206,000 troop increase could bring the war to an end. And in the last week of March, the president's panel of senior advisers, commonly known as the "Wise Men," recommended that Johnson begin to disengage U.S. forces from the war. On March 31 Johnson announced new restrictions on U.S. bombing of North Vietnam in the hope that these actions would lead toward the opening of peace negotiations.

Throughout the conflict Wheeler strongly criticized those who protested the war at home. He thought that the single most important factor in prolonging the conflict was Hanoi's perception of America's weakness of purpose. Although Wheeler steadfastly believed that the United States could win the war in Vietnam, his definition of victory changed over the years. In 1965 he thought that it was possible to drive the Communists out of South Vietnam; by 1967 he echoed the administration's position that the U.S. goal was to bring Hanoi to the conference table under conditions favorable to the United States.

Wheeler retired from the army and from his position as chair of the Joint Chiefs of Staff in July 1970 and became a director of the Monsanto Corporation. He died on December 18, 1975.

—EWS

## White, Byron R(aymond)
### (1917–2002) *associate justice, U.S. Supreme Court*

Born on June 8, 1917, White grew up in Wellington, a small town in Colorado, where the main crop was sugar beets. He graduated in 1938 from the University of Colorado, where he was valedictorian of his class and an All-American in football. "Whizzer" White played professional football for the Pittsburgh Steelers in 1938 and the Detroit Lions in 1940 and 1941. A Rhodes Scholar at Oxford University in 1939, White served in the navy during World War II and then graduated from Yale Law School in 1946. He served as law clerk to Supreme Court chief justice Fred Vinson during the 1946–47 term. In 1947 White joined a prestigious Denver law firm, eventually becoming a partner and working primarily on corporate cases.

A friend of John F. Kennedy's since 1939, White was an early supporter of Kennedy's bid for the 1960 Democratic presidential nomination. White led Kennedy forces in Colorado prior to the Democratic national convention and headed a national Citizens for Kennedy-Johnson organization during the 1960 campaign. As deputy attorney general in the Kennedy administration, White helped recruit attorneys for the Justice Department, evaluated candidates for federal judicial appointments, and oversaw much of the day-to-day administration of he department. He was nominated as an associate justice of the Supreme Court in March 1962 and took his oath of office in April.

White surprised those who expected him to vote in most cases with the liberal justices on the Warren Court. He tended to give priority to law enforcement authorities rather than individual rights in cases that involved criminal investigations. He dissented, for example, in two 1964 decisions where the majority extended the right to counsel to include preliminary police investigation of a suspect and held the Fifth Amendment's privilege against self-incrimination applicable to the states. White also dissented from the 1966 *Miranda*

v. *Arizona* ruling, in which the majority placed restrictions on police interrogation of arrested suspects. White accused the Court of making "new law and new public policy" and warned that the decision would result in the return of "a killer, a rapist, or other criminal to the streets . . . to repeat his crime."

White also voted consistently to sustain federal laws regarding citizenship and Communists. He dissented in May 1964 when the Court nullified a law canceling the citizenship of naturalized Americans who returned to their native lands for three years and when it overturned a provision in the 1950 Internal Security Act denying passports to members of the Communist Party. He was again with the minority in June 1965 when the Court overturned a provision in the Landrum-Griffin Act that barred Communist Party members from serving as labor union officials. Justice White also dissented in January 1967, when the majority held unconstitutional three New York State laws requiring public school and state college teachers to sign oaths disavowing membership in the Communist Party and ordering the removal of teachers for treasonous or seditious acts or statements.

White voted to uphold the public accommodations section of the 1964 Civil Rights Act in December 1964, but he dissented when the Court ruled that the law barred state prosecution of peaceful demonstrators who had tried to desegregate the places covered by the act prior to the law's passage. In May 1966 White wrote the majority opinion in *Reitman v. Mulkey*, overturning a California state constitutional amendment that had nullified earlier legislation prohibiting racial discrimination in the sale or rental of housing.

Justice White spoke for the majority in a 1967 decision holding that a routine municipal housing inspection of a private dwelling, conducted without a warrant, was an unreasonable search in violation of the Fourth Amendment. White wrote for a six-member majority in June 1968 upholding a New York State law that required public school districts to loan textbooks to private and parochial schools. From 1964 through 1968 White consistently voted in favor of the Court's one-person, one-vote rule for reapportionment of legislative districts. In an April 1968 decision, White's majority opinion extended the reapportionment rulings to local elections where representatives were elected on a district basis.

During the Nixon administration, as the activist and liberal Warren Court gave way to the more conservative Burger Court, White occupied a centrist position on the high bench and was often a "swing" justice, providing the deciding vote in cases dividing the Court's liberal and conservative factions. He retired from the Court in 1993 and died on April 15, 2002.

—CAB

## White, F(rederick) Clifton
### (1918–1993) *political consultant*

F. Clifton White was born on June 13, 1918, in Leonardville, New York, and graduated from Colgate University in 1940. During World War II he rose to the rank of captain in U.S. Army Air Forces. He was a navigator on bombing missions. After the war, while teaching political science at Ithaca College, White made an unsuccessful primary bid for an upstate New York Republican House seat. After failing in his one try for elective office, White became involved in Republican politics in New York. He worked in the 1948 presidential campaign of New York governor Thomas E. Dewey and headed the New York Young Republicans. He also worked in DWIGHT D. EISENHOWER's presidential campaign organization in 1952.

A public relations consultant between 1955 and 1960, White remained active in state politics. He managed the 1958 gubernatorial campaign of state senate leader Walter Mahoney, who lost the GOP nomination to NELSON A. ROCKEFELLER. In 1960 he worked in the presidential campaign of RICHARD M. NIXON. But he became discontented with what he thought were Nixon's unnecessary concessions on issues to win Rockefeller's support prior to the Republican National Convention. He also disagreed with Nixon's decision not to contest the results of the November election in view of evidence of voting irregularities in Illinois and other states.

In 1961 White became a leader of a group of conservatives whose goal was to take control of the Republican Party. At the first meeting in Chicago in October 1961, White told about two dozen conservatives that they should not just aim at securing a platform that reflected their views on public policy. White instead emphasized the importance of organizing on the state and local level to win majorities at the caucuses and conventions where most of the delegates were chosen to attend the national nominating convention. At a second meeting in December 1961, White proposed a detailed organizational plan, which he would oversee from an office in New York City, which members of his group called Suite 3505. During the following year, White and his coworkers recruited new members, mastered the delegate selection procedures in each state, and raised funds.

In April 1963 White made a public announcement that his group had become the "National Draft Goldwater Committee." Senator BARRY M. GOLDWATER (R-Ariz.) had been the first choice of White and his associates from the time of their first meeting. Although public opinion polls showed the conservative senator lagging far behind the liberal Rockefeller, White insisted that Goldwater could win the Republican presidential nomination. To concede the nomination to Rockefeller, White also believed, might be to lose any chance for the next generation to make the GOP into an ideologically conservative party. Yet despite White's optimism about Goldwater's chances, the senator would not cooperate with the "National Draft Goldwater Committee." Goldwater was interested in the presidency, but thought that the best political strategy in early 1963 was to avoid any declared efforts to advance his prospects. Even more important, Goldwater distrusted White, considering him nothing more than a public relations expert who lacked conservative principles.

Despite Goldwater's coolness to their efforts, White and his followers were undeterred. Developments in 1963 raised Goldwater's prospects in ways that White could never have expected. In May, Rockefeller, who had divorced his wife two years earlier, married a woman who was 20 years his junior, who herself had been divorced only a month earlier, and who relinquished custody of her four children to her former husband. Many Republicans sharply disapproved of Rockefeller's actions, and his standing in the polls plummeted. According to the Gallup poll, Republicans preferred Rockefeller over Goldwater for the party's nomination by a margin of 44–21 percent a month before his remarriage. By June 1963 Goldwater led Rockefeller by 38-28 percent. The governor, who hoped that the adverse reaction would be temporary, never regained his advantage.

Although White expanded his efforts on Goldwater's behalf, the senator did not put aside his suspicion of White when he formally announced his candidacy in January 1964. Goldwater entrusted leadership of his campaign to friends and political associates from Arizona. White got only a subordinate position. Yet White's strategy for securing the nomination guided Goldwater's campaign. Goldwater partisans flooded precinct, municipal, county and district party delegate selection meetings throughout the country. While the news media and Republican leaders watched Goldwater lose the March New Hampshire primary, the Goldwater forces slowly and quietly amassed 400 delegates in nonprimary states where a majority of delegates were chosen. Not until early May did the anti-Goldwater Republicans begin to comprehend what had occurred. Goldwater's victory in the California primary and subsequent endorsement by the heads of the large Illinois and Ohio delegations assured his first ballot nomination at the Republican Convention in San Francisco in July.

Goldwater designated White as national director of the Citizens for Goldwater-Miller Committee. Designed to lure independent and Democratic voters to the Goldwater camp, the group did not play a major role in the general election. Instead, Goldwater ran his campaign through the Republican National Committee.

One month prior to the election, White became involved in a controversy over a Goldwater campaign film. A subcommittee of the Citizens Committee, "Mothers for a Moral America," had produced a 30-minute program, entitled "Choice," for national television. "Choice" dealt with the alleged moral decline of the nation; it highlighted racial rioting, women in topless bathing suits, and a brief sequence of an unidentified Texan—apparently intended to be identified as President Johnson—driving a Lincoln Continental at high speed while tossing beer cans out the window. Journalists who previewed the film were highly critical. After watching the film Goldwater publicly denounced it and forbade its use in his campaign.

After Goldwater's overwhelming defeat in November, White continued his efforts to promote conservative Republican candidates. Returning to his New York City public relations office, White worked for Governor RONALD REAGAN's (R-Calif.) campaign for the presidential nomination in 1968. Following White's counsel, Reagan avoided the spring primaries and instead sought to win southern and western delegates uncommitted or leaning toward Richard Nixon. By the time of the August 1968 convention, however, Nixon appeared so close to a first-ballot victory that White privately cooperated with leaders of the Rockefeller campaign. Their alliance failed. Most southern delegates held fast to Nixon, and the former vice president won on the first ballot.

Following the convention White managed the U.S. senatorial campaign of New York Conservative Party nominee James L. Buckley, brother of conservative writer WILLIAM F. BUCKLEY, JR. Although Buckley lost to liberal senator JACOB K. JAVITS (R-N.Y.), he amassed an impressive 1.1. million votes. His 1968 margin aided him in his successful campaign for the Senate, also managed by White, two years later.

White remained involved in campaign consulting. His clients included JESSE HELMS, who won election to the U.S. Senate from North Carolina in 1972. White died on January 9, 1993.

—JLB

## White, Kevin H(agan)

(1929–    ) *secretary of state of Massachusetts, mayor*

White was born on September 5, 1929, into a politically active Boston family. Both his mother and father had served as president of the Boston City Council. He studied at Williams College and Boston College, earning an LL.B. in 1955. Beginning in 1960 White served three terms as Massachusetts secretary of state, a post that gave him considerable publicity.

White's greatest political challenge came in 1967, when he ran as a Democrat for mayor of Boston. The city was then strongly polarized along racial lines over issues of crime and school integration. White's opponent, board of education member Louise Day Hicks, sought to exploit the "backlash" of Boston's large white ethnic community against desegregation and growing job competition from blacks. White argued in his campaign that all of Boston's residents suffered from "alienation" and a "breakdown of morale," which he promised to correct as mayor. Supported by blacks, liberals, and prosperous whites in outlying areas, he narrowly defeated Hicks in November by 12,000 votes.

In office White instituted a series of summer youth programs, appointed African Americans to top-level municipal posts, and named a woman who was receiving public assistance to sit on the public welfare board. He also succeeded in persuading Boston banks and loan companies to provide $50 million for low-income housing. His efforts helped him win the confidence of many ethnic whites who had earlier supported Hicks. In the mayoral election of 1971, White surprised many observers by defeating Hicks by a 42,000-vote margin.

White gained increasing exposure in national politics during the early 1970s. In 1970 he joined New York mayor JOHN LINDSAY and eight other big-city mayors to lobby in Washington for "congressional and state action to meet city needs." Among the programs the group favored were federal revenue sharing, welfare reform, mass transit subsidies, and crime-control measures. White also ran for governor of Massachusetts in 1970 but lost to incumbent Francis W. Sargent. During the mid-1970s he was frequently mentioned as a possible Democratic vice presidential candidate. White was reelected mayor of Boston in 1975, at a time when the city was again suffering racial violence resulting from court-ordered school busing. White won a final term as mayor in 1979.

—TJC

## Wiggins, J(ames) R(ussell)

(1903–2000) *editor, ambassador to the United Nations*

For 21 years an editor of the *Washington Post*, Wiggins served as U.S. ambassador to the United Nations during the last four months of the Johnson administration. Unlike most of the editors of major U.S. newspapers, he never went to college. Instead, Wiggins, who was born on December 4, 1903, in Luverne, Minnesota, worked on various midwestern newspapers. From 1946 to 1947 he served as assistant to the publisher of the *New York Times* and in May 1947 became managing editor of the *Washington Post*. From 1961 until his appointment as ambassador, Wiggins was editor and then executive vice president of that paper.

While editor Wiggins was credited with helping to build the *Post* from a small capital daily to a major national paper. A strong supporter of "the people's right to know," Wiggins fought against "national security" policies inimical to freedom of the press and opposed efforts to limit news coverage of crimes and trials.

During the Johnson administration Wiggins's editorials supported both the domestic Great Society program and the Americanization of the war in

Vietnam. Wiggins maintained that military intervention was justifiable if it "encouraged other small countries around the world to retain their independence in the face of aggression." The editor did not share the pessimism of many liberals that characterized the later years of the Johnson administration.

When GEORGE BALL resigned as ambassador to the United Nations in September 1968, President Johnson chose Wiggins to succeed him. While at the United Nations Wiggins maintained a middle-of-the road, conciliatory position. He condemned what he considered both Arab and Israeli aggression, asserted that Soviet expressions of its desire for peace were made in good faith, and deplored the efforts of Afro-Asian delegations to strip South Africa of its vote. No nation, he thought, should be deprived of a voice in the international body.

In January 1969 Wiggins resigned. Afterward he moved to Maine, where he edited the Ellsworth *American* until 2000. He died on November 19, 2000.

—EWS

## Wilkins, Roy
### (1901–1981) *executive secretary, NAACP*

Born on August 30, 1901, in St. Louis, Wilkins grew up in the home of an aunt and uncle in St. Paul, Minnesota, after his mother died when he was a child. He graduated from the University of Minnesota in 1923 and then moved to Kansas City later that year and became an editor of an African-American newspaper, the *Kansas City Call*. His work in the local NAACP chapter persuaded the organization's national leadership to hire him in 1931 to work as assistant secretary in its national headquarters in New York City. Upon the death of NAACP executive secretary Walter White in 1955, Wilkins became his successor.

Under Wilkins, the NAACP maintained its longstanding emphasis on political and legal action to end racial discrimination and to integrate African Americans fully into American society. During the early 1960s, Wilkins was disappointed with the slow and limited civil rights actions of the Kennedy

Executive secretary of the NAACP Roy Wilkins meeting with President Johnson in the Oval Office, 1965 *(Photographed by Yoichi R. Okamoto; Lyndon Baines Johnson Library)*

administration. Wilkins was piqued that it took the president until November 1962 to issue an executive order that Kennedy had promised during his campaign for the White House two years earlier and that barred racial discrimination in federally financed housing. He also disliked the president's desire to avoid submitting civil rights bills to Congress and to rely instead on executive action. Wilkins was pleased, however, when Kennedy decided after the demonstrations and violence in Birmingham, Alabama, to submit a civil rights bill in June 1963 that banned racial discrimination in public accommodations. During the March on Washington on August 28, 1963, Wilkins urged passage of that legislation and the establishment of a fair employment practices commission.

During the Johnson years Wilkins and the NAACP were deeply involved in helping to secure passage of major civil rights legislation. The greatest achievements were the passage of the Civil Rights Act of 1964 and the Voting Rights Act of 1965. In 1966, however, Congress did not act on another NAACP-supported bill that would have outlawed racial discrimination in the sale and rental of housing and the selection of juries.

As the volume of civil rights legislation increased, Wilkins and the NAACP gave more attention to fully implementing existing legal rights. In January 1965 Wilkins announced plans for creation of a national network of "citizenship clinics," intended to acquaint blacks with the provisions of new laws and educate them for "the assumption of full citizenship responsibilities." The NAACP subsequently sponsored voter registration drives in a number of cities. Wilkins also participated in several civil rights marches in Mississippi and Alabama during the mid-1960s. The NAACP leader, however, was generally skeptical of direct action to advance civil rights.

Developments of the mid- and late 1960s put the NAACP in the midst of a growing controversy within the civil rights movement. Convinced that the most effective strategy was to work through Congress and the courts, Wilkins condemned the call for Black Power, first raised by STOKELY CARMICHAEL in June 1966. An NAACP convention in July 1966 attacked Carmichael's advocacy of racial separatism and his justification of the use of violence by blacks in self-defense. Wilkins joined other moderate black leaders, including MARTIN LUTHER KING, JR., and WHITNEY YOUNG, in con-

demning the outbreak of rioting in many northern cities during the summer of 1967. Wilkins also resisted the growing opposition of many civil rights activists to the Vietnam War, claiming that civil rights and peace issues should be kept separate.

Wilkins's consistently moderate stand drew considerable criticism within the civil rights movement. More militant black leaders derided the NAACP's reformist strategy as "outmoded." The Student Nonviolent Coordinating Committee and the Congress of Racial Equality refused to join the NAACP in supporting the civil rights bill of 1966, which they viewed as a "sham." In 1967 Wilkins was the target of an abortive assassination plot by the Revolutionary Action Movement, a small black terrorist group.

Within the NAACP a group of militants known as the Young Turks sought to reduce Wilkins's influence and change what they viewed as the organization's "middle-class" image. Strongest in the northern and western chapters of the NAACP, the Young Turks favored closer ties to the peace movement and a more positive attitude toward Black Power. They attempted to gain control of the NAACP Board of Directors in 1967 and one year later demanded the right to function as an autonomous group within the organization. Wilkins defeated both challenges to his leadership but at the price of numerous resignations from the NAACP.

Despite the criticism of him as a moderate, "establishment" figure, Wilkins remained uncompromising in his condemnation of racial bigotry and his desire to advance equal opportunity. Soon after the riot in Detroit that resulted in the deaths of 43 people, Johnson established a bipartisan National Advisory Commission on Civil Disorders to investigate the causes of the urban riots and to recommend actions to prevent further disturbances. Wilkins contributed to the language of the commission's alarming conclusion: "our nation is moving toward two societies, one black, one white—separate and unequal." The commission called for new programs with "unprecedented levels of funding" that could end the segregation and poverty in inner cities that produced the riots. He was distressed that President Johnson failed to take action to implement the commission's recommendations.

During the early 1970s the NAACP continued to work for government action in housing, school desegregation, and job opportunities for blacks. The Nixon administration was less responsive than its predecessors, however, and NAACP officials took the unusual step of denouncing it as "anti-Negro" in 1970. Wilkins remained aloof from other civil rights leaders who espoused Black Power, but he continued to provide financial and legal support for community action programs in inner cities. He retired as executive secretary of the NAACP in 1977 and died on September 8, 1981.

—SLG

## Williams, Harrison A(rlington), Jr.
### (1919–2001)  *member of the Senate*

Born on December 10, 1919, and raised in Plainfield, New Jersey, Williams received his B.A. from Oberlin and his law degree from Columbia. After losing New Jersey state and municipal races as a Democrat in 1951 and 1952, Williams announced his candidacy for Congress after Representative CLIFFORD CASE (R-N.J.) resigned in August 1953. Williams borrowed the money to finance his campaign and in November 1953 defeated a conservative Republican to become the first Democratic representative in the Sixth Congressional District's 21-year history. Williams lost his seat in 1956, but two years later New Jersey governor Robert Meyner helped him secure the Democratic senatorial nomination. His victory in November made Williams New Jersey's first Democratic senator since 1938.

In August 1959 Williams became chair of the Senate Labor and Public Welfare Committee's newly formed Subcommittee on Migratory Labor. Williams introduced a series of bills in February 1961 designed to upgrade the quality of migrant life, but the only proposal enacted during the 87th Congress was a bill passed in September 1962 appropriating $3 million per year for migrant health programs.

In 1964 several programs based on Williams's earlier proposals were incorporated into President Johnson's Great Society legislative program. The administration's Economic Opportunity Act of 1964 authorized $15 million in fiscal 1965 for housing, education, child day-care, and sanitation services for farm workers. The 1964 omnibus housing bill included a $10 million grant program to pay up to two-thirds of the development cost for low-rent housing for domestic farm workers. In addition, Williams's bill requiring annual registration of farm labor contractors passed separately and was signed into law on September 7, 1964.

Williams's more far-reaching proposals for the establishment of a federal minimum wage for agricultural workers, a federal farm recruiting and placement service, farm-worker coverage under collective bargaining, and other labor laws were not acted upon by Congress. In 1968 Williams was unable to get his bill permitting strikes by agricultural workers out of committee, and he announced plans to attach the measure to the administration's farm program bill. Williams withdrew his amendment after intense lobbying against it by the American Farm Bureau Federation and other grower organizations.

Williams was a Democratic Party loyalist. *Congressional Quarterly* credited Williams with the highest "party unity" score among all Democratic senators in 1968. Although he was one of 15 senators who signed a January 27, 1966, letter to the president calling for continued suspension of air strikes against North Vietnam, Williams voted for the 1967 and 1968 Vietnam War appropriations.

Williams won reelection three times, but his conduct brought about two notable scandals. His behavior at a meeting of the New Jersey NAACP in 1968 led that organization to pass a resolution of censure. Williams said that his actions were the result of his drinking, and he promised to refrain from the use of alcohol. In 1981 he was convicted of bribery and conspiracy as a result of the Abscam scandal in which undercover investigators posed as wealthy Arabs. Facing expulsion, Williams resigned from the Senate on March 11, 1982, and served three years in prison. He died on November 17, 2001.

—DKR

## Williams, John B(ell)
### (1918–1983)  *member of the House of Representatives, governor*

Born on December 4, 1918, in Raymond, Mississippi, Williams graduated from the University of Mississippi in 1938 and earned a law degree two years later. A pilot in the U.S. Army Air Forces during World War II, he suffered severe injuries, including the loss of part of his left arm, in a plane crash. Elected to Congress in 1946, he was the youngest representative that Mississippi had ever sent to Capitol Hill. Although he was a Democrat, he consistently refused to support his party's national ticket because of his extreme opposition to civil rights. A racist, he referred to the day of the

Supreme Court's ruling on May 17, 1954, in *Brown v. Board of Education* that declared racial segregation unconstitutional as "Black Monday." He won reelection with little, if any, opposition.

During the 1960s Bell repeatedly denounced civil rights measures, often in vitriolic rhetoric. He called the Voting Rights Act of 1965 "a rape of the Constitution." He was also an ardent foe of foreign aid programs, and he consistently voted against New Frontier and Great Society legislation.

In 1964 Williams declared his support for the Republican presidential candidacy of Senator BARRY M. GOLDWATER (R-Ariz.). During the following January the House Democratic Caucus retaliated against Williams and Representative ALBERT W. WATSON (D-S.C.), the two Democratic representatives who had supported Goldwater, by censuring them and stripping them of their seniority. Williams thereby lost his second-ranking position on the Interstate and Foreign Commerce Committee and his fifth-ranking post on the District of Columbia Committee. In the same month the predominantly black Mississippi Freedom Democratic Party challenged the seating of all five of the state's representatives on the grounds that blacks had been excluded from participation in the previous year's election. The House rejected the challenge in September 1965 by a vote of 228 to 143.

After an unsuccessful effort to restore his seniority, Williams entered the Mississippi gubernatorial race in 1967. In the first round of the Democratic primary, he defeated former governor Ross Barnett, who had unsuccessfully tried to block the enrollment of the first African-American student at the University of Mississippi in 1962. Williams charged that Barnett was a "traitor," who had sold out to the Kennedy administration. In the primary runoff, he beat state treasurer William Winter and then won the general election.

In his inaugural address, in January 1968, Williams declared that he would seek funds for federal education, poverty and, welfare programs, which he had opposed in Congress. The governor asserted, "For right or wrong, whether we like it or not, federal programs have become a way of life in America." He subsequently established a federal-state programs office to seek such aid.

Although Williams, in the same address, denounced the perpetrators of violence against blacks, as governor he continued to support racial segregation. During July 1968 he denounced

HUBERT HUMPHREY for asserting that blacks could not freely participate in Mississippi Party proceedings. At the Democratic National Convention the following month, Humphrey supported a successful black challenge to the regular Mississippi delegation, which was led by Williams. In September the governor endorsed the third-party presidential candidacy of GEORGE C. WALLACE.

After Hurricane Camille struck Mississippi in August 1969, Williams appointed an all-white emergency council to coordinate federal and state relief. Responding to black protests, the federal government refused to provide assistance until the governor added blacks to the council. In 1970 Williams defended the Jackson police after they shot and killed two African Americans during a demonstration at all-black Jackson State College in May. After his term as governor was over in 1972, he worked to build the Republican Party in Mississippi. He died on March 26, 1983.

—MLL

## Williams, John J(ames)
(1904–1988) *member of the Senate*
Williams, who was born on May 17, 1904, in Frankford, Delaware, owned a chicken-feed business before entering national politics. He ran for the Senate in 1946 as a Republican on a conservative platform advocating the reduction of government control over the economy. While in the Senate, Williams voted against most domestic social welfare legislation and foreign aid measures. He was a consistent opponent of large-scale government spending and of measures that increased the powers of the executive branch in domestic affairs.

Shortly after coming to the Senate, Williams became involved in investigations of corruption, a topic that would become his major political interest throughout his career. In 1947 he was on a committee that investigated defense spending. Four years later, Williams opened a campaign against corruption in the Internal Revenue Service. Later in the decade he demanded an investigation of influence-peddling by presidential adviser Sherman Adams. During the Kennedy administration, Williams opposed the ambassadorial appointments of two business executive because of their involvement in questionable financial dealings and scored Representative ADAM CLAYTON POWELL (D-N.Y.) for using public funds for private expenses.

In 1963 Williams, spurred by press reports of Senate majority secretary BOBBY BAKER's involvement in questionable business activities, began a private investigation of Baker's affairs. His probe, uncovering information on possible tax frauds and influence-peddling in the awarding of government contracts, provided much of the information for the subsequent Senate Rules Committee hearings. Although not a member of the committee, Williams was invited to sit in on its sessions during the 16-month investigation. His insistence on a thorough probe of all those involved in Baker's activities, including senators, often brought him into conflict with the committee and its staff. In reaction to a committee ruling that limited its examination to Senate staff members, excluding senators, Williams introduced a resolution to expand the scope of the probe. After angry debate the resolution was killed.

In 1967 Williams moved to repeal the 1966 Presidential Election Campaign Fund Act that established a tax checkoff system to finance presidential campaigns. Williams opposed the measure because it had been passed without any attempt to reform campaign finance practices. The senator's proposal that the checkoff system be suspended until Congress adopted guidelines governing the distribution of money was accepted by the Senate. The system was eventually approved by Congress in 1971.

In 1971 Williams retired after 24 years on Capitol Hill. He died on January 11, 1988.

—EWS

## Williams, William A(ppleman)
(1921–1990) *historian*

Williams, one of the most influential U.S. historians of the 20th century, was born in Atlantic, Iowa, on June 12, 1921, graduated from the U.S. Naval Academy in 1944, and served in the Pacific theater during World War II. With the assistance of the GI Bill, Williams entered the University of Wisconsin in 1947 and earned a doctorate in history three years later.

Williams's scholarship aroused controversy beginning with the publication of his first book in 1952, entitled *American-Russian Relations, 1784–1947*. Williams argued that Soviet-American antagonism had developed over decades and provided a critique of the U.S. strategy of containment that emerged at the beginning of the cold war. His interpretation

went against standard scholarly and popular understandings of the cold war, which emphasized Soviet expansionism and a defensive U.S. reaction. Writing at the height of McCarthyism, Williams endured allegations that he was pro-communist. Such charges foreclosed the possibility of tenure at the University of Oregon, where Williams had begun teaching in 1952. In 1957 he took a faculty position at the University of Wisconsin.

During the next several years, Williams published books that offered a new, distinctive, and controversial interpretation of U.S. foreign policy. Williams's most important book, *The Tragedy of American Diplomacy* (1959) argued that since the end of the 19th century American leaders had believed that access to international markets was essential to domestic prosperity. U.S. foreign policy, according to Williams, was guided by open door expansionism, a policy first applied to China in the 1890s and then throughout the world. Williams maintained that the United States was an imperial power that built an informal empire based on its global economic power rather than an extensive formal empire that consisted of colonies. Despite professed anticolonialism, U.S. policy generally opposed revolutionary movements, according to Williams, lest nationalistic or leftist governments restrict U.S. access to markets, resources, and investment opportunities. Williams also explained the origins of the cold war as a result of U.S. efforts to apply the open door to Eastern Europe. In *The Contours of American History* (1961), Williams pressed his arguments back to the early days of the U.S. republic, insisting that government leaders used imperial expansion to avoid or resolve internal political strife.

During the early and mid-1960s Williams applied the ideas he had developed in his historical writings to current problems. His book *The United States, Cuba and Castro*, published in 1962, attributed the crisis in U.S.-Cuban relations to problems resulting from North American economic domination of the island. Williams later attacked American involvement in Vietnam and participated in an early teach-in against the war at the University of Wisconsin. Marx's analysis of capitalism, he claimed at this time, was more applicable to contemporary America than was generally acknowledged. "It becomes increasingly clear," Williams wrote in 1967, "that many of the policies and activities of the New and Fair Deals, and of the upper-class Daniel Boones of the New Frontier, are producing something less than happiness and security." His own solution, proposed in *The Great Evasion* (1964), was a system of "democratic socialism" that would place primary authority on the local and regional levels to encourage individual autonomy.

Coming at a time of intellectual ferment, Williams's revisionist interpretation of U.S. foreign policy aroused great controversy. Writing in 1967, historian ARTHUR SCHLESINGER, JR., a critic of Williams, attacked revisionism for ignoring the rigidity of Soviet ideology and the paranoid ambitions of Stalin. Yet with the escalation of U.S. involvement in Vietnam, Williams's revisionist interpretations reached a wider audience and won influential advocates. Williams contributed frequent articles to *Studies on the Left*, the *New York Review of Books*, and other leftist journals. A group of Williams's former students and followers at the University of Wisconsin, including Walter LaFeber, Thomas J. McCormick, Lloyd Gardner, and Ronald Radosh, formed the "Wisconsin school" of diplomatic history during the mid-1960s. Other prominent revisionist historians, including Gabriel Kolko, also acknowledged Williams's influence. A survey undertaken in 1971 by the Organization of American Historians indicated that Williams had far greater influence than any other scholar in spreading ideas "sharply critical of U.S. foreign policy."

During the late 1960s and early 1970s Williams extended his analysis of American expansionism with three books: *The Roots of the Modern American Empire* (1969), *The Shaping of American Diplomacy* (1970), and *Some Presidents: From Wilson to Nixon* (1972). In these works he traced the traditional American association of "freedom and prosperity" with expansion into foreign markets, stressing that this was a tenet of popular culture as well as a goal of policy makers. The reform efforts of the Kennedy and Johnson administrations, in Williams's view, were the latest in a series of efforts to ease social tensions in the United States by accumulating a greater share of the world's wealth. Williams denied, however, that such a policy could be sustained in the long run; the end of the Great Society program, he claimed, signaled the failure of "the orthodoxy which [Johnson] had been taught."

Williams taught at Oregon State University from 1969 to 1986. He was elected president of the Organization of American Historians in 1980. He died on March 5, 1990.

—SLG

## Willis, Edwin E(dward)
(1904–1972) *member of the House of Representatives*

Born on October 2, 1904, in Arnaudville, Louisiana, Willis earned a law degree in 1926 from Loyola University in New Orleans and practiced law before entering politics as a Democrat and winning election to the state senate in January 1948. Later that year, he won the first of 10 consecutive terms in the U.S. House of Representatives. He was appointed to the House Un-American Activities Committee (HUAC) in 1955 and became its chair in 1963, Willis led widely publicized HUAC investigations of unauthorized travel to Cuba by American citizens in September 1963 and of the Illinois Communist Party in May 1965. In October 1966 he announced plans for a committee study of urban rioting, and, a year later, HUAC held seven days of hearings on the possible contribution of subversive elements to the riots. A May 1968 committee report charged that pro-Communist splinter groups had aligned with extremist black nationalist organizations to wage revolutionary warfare and named Students for a Democratic Society, the Revolutionary Action Movement, and the Progressive Labor Party, among others, as advocates of revolutionary violence.

HUAC also initiated a major investigation of the Ku Klux Klan on March 30, 1965. After a six-month preliminary study, a five-member subcommittee headed by Willis opened hearings in October. The probe focused on Klan finances, the extent to which the Klan engaged in organized violence and connections between the Klan and local law enforcement agencies. The 36 days of hearings lasted into February 1966 and uncovered evidence of Klan involvement in intimidation and violence directed against blacks and civil rights workers. Willis, who once declared Klanism "incompatible with Americanism," was burned in effigy at Klan rallies in the South during the investigation, but Attorney General NICHOLAS KATZENBACH commended the subcommittee for its "careful and illuminating" study of the Klan. The hearings eventually led to the conviction and imprisonment of ROBERT M. SHELTON, JR., imperial wizard of the United Klans of America, for contempt of Congress.

In August 1967 Willis introduced a bill to redefine the functions and procedures of the Subversive Activities Control Board (SACB), which had little to do by then because of Supreme Court rulings holding many of its powers and procedures unconstitutional. Passed by Congress late in 1967 and signed into law on January 2, 1968, the SACB proposal was only the sixth HUAC-reported bill ever to become law.

A reserved and soft-spoken man, Willis had a favorable reputation among many House colleagues for his leadership of the committee. Nonetheless, HUAC remained a target of criticism during the 1960s for many liberals and civil liberties organizations on the grounds that it frequently abused witnesses, held hearings aimed at exposure rather than at producing legislation, and often exceeded its jurisdiction.

Also a member of the House Judiciary Committee, Willis opposed all civil rights bills and led southern Democratic efforts to defeat or dilute the 1964 Civil Rights Act on the House floor. A supporter of U.S. policy in Vietnam, Willis had a relatively conservative record on domestic issues. He did, however, vote for some Great Society legislation, such as the Economic Opportunity Act of 1964, elementary and secondary school aid bills, and the Housing and Urban Development Act of 1968.

Willis was defeated for renomination in a Democratic runoff primary in September 1968. He died in St. Martinville, Louisiana, on October 24, 1972.

—CAB

## Wirtz, W(illiam) Willard

(1912–   ) *secretary of labor*

Wirtz, who was born in De Kalb, Illinois, on March 14, 1912, was a 1937 graduate of the Harvard Law School. He taught law at the University of Iowa and Northwestern University before joining the War Labor Board, where he earned a reputation as an able mediator in labor disputes. After World War II, Wirtz chaired the National Wage Stabilization Board and then returned to teaching at Northwestern. In 1955 Wirtz entered private law practice in Chicago and was a partner with ADLAI E. STEVENSON. Wirtz served as an aide in Stevenson's 1956 presidential campaign. President Kennedy nominated Wirtz for undersecretary of labor in January 1961. When Kennedy chose Labor Secretary ARTHUR GOLDBERG to be a justice of the Supreme Court, Wirtz succeeded him as head of the department in September 1962.

As labor secretary, Wirtz was involved directly or indirectly in efforts to settle major strikes involving rail, airline, and dock workers during the early 1960s. He also appeared frequently before congressional committees to speak in favor of key domestic legislation that had the backing of the Kennedy administration and organized labor. In 1963 he won approval of amendments to the Manpower Training and Development Act that gave to the secretary of labor the authority to establish job training programs for high school dropouts.

During the Johnson years, Wirtz was involved in many efforts to settle major labor disputes, including threatened walkouts of rail workers in 1964 and a 42-day strike of airline mechanics in 1966. In the rail dispute, which centered on wages and train-crew sizes, President Johnson announced in April 1964 that a settlement had been reached between management and labor. The settlement was considered a personal triumph for the president, and Wirtz admitted that Johnson rather than his office had played the key role. In 1967, however, neither Johnson nor Wirtz was able to negotiate a settlement and a two-day walkout tied up the nation's railroads. The strike ended when Congress, at Johnson's request, passed a bill mandating compulsory arbitration of the dispute.

During the 1960s Wirtz worked for the enactment of the Johnson administration's major social programs, including federal aid to education, Medicare, antipoverty, and civil rights measures. He also helped win enactment in 1966 of a Johnson-supported minimum wage bill, which increased by stages the existing $1.25 nonfarm wage floor to $1.60 and extended minimum wage coverage to an estimated 9.1 million new employees. However, Wirtz and other members of the administration failed to win approval of two measures strongly favored by organized labor: a bill to repeal section 14(b) of the Taft-Hartley Act, which permitted states to pass "right-to-work" laws banning the union shop, and a bill to permit an individual building trades union having a dispute with a single subcontractor to picket an entire construction site and thereby shut it down.

Wirtz was a strong advocate of administration antipoverty programs, but he and Secretary of Health, Education and Welfare ANTHONY J. CELEBREZZE argued in 1965 that their departments were capable of managing antipoverty programs without the creation of a separate Office of Economic

Opportunity. However, President Johnson favored the creation of such an office under the direction of Peace Corps head R. SARGENT SHRIVER, and the administration's 1964 antipoverty legislation reflected the president's wishes.

A strong proponent of administration efforts to reduce unemployment through job-training programs, Wirtz in July 1967 called for the funding of Labor Department programs for the training of between 100,000 and 150,000 persons. He was cool to the suggestion of Senator ROBERT F. KENNEDY (D-N.Y.) that government provide tax incentives to businesses for establishing plants and jobs in inner cities. "The most immediate problem," said Wirtz, "is a training problem not job development."

An advocate of liberalized immigration laws, Wirtz argued that an end of the national origins quota system with a consequent increase in immigration would not seriously affect employment opportunities for American workers. (Such a measure passed in 1965.) He did argue, however, that the importation of Mexicans to work in the fields at harvest time undercut the wage scale of American laborers. In 1965 Wirtz ended the "bracero" farm labor program, thereby cutting the number of such workers in the United States from 200,000 to 50,000. This move was bitterly denounced by senators and representatives from southern and western agricultural states, particularly Florida and California. In September 1965 Vice President HUBERT H. HUMPHREY broke a tie vote and prevented the Senate from stripping Wirtz of his power over agricultural workers. Florida and California farmers soon learned, however, to rely on "greencard workers" (temporary immigrants) and Mexicans who entered the country illegally.

Although Wirtz supported legislation favored by organized labor, his relations with union officials were not entirely cordial. AFL-CIO president GEORGE MEANY referred to Wirtz as that "blasted egghead" and complained of the secretary's "damned superior" attitude. During 1964–65 Wirtz attempted to remove John Henning from his post as undersecretary of labor. Henning, the top-ranking labor official in government, had been appointed to his position with Meany's blessing. Henning argued that teenagers in the poverty program should be paid the minimum wage. Wirtz was opposed because he felt that the poverty program's role should be primarily to provide job training for private employment. He asked for Henning's removal

but President Johnson, under pressure from Meany, retained Henning in the Labor Department.

Meany also charged that Wirtz and the administration had failed to make sufficient effort to win repeal of 14(b). Moreover, in January 1965 Meany promised Wirtz that, while organized labor opposed the administration's official wage-price guidelines, "if the President is going to hold prices in line we have got to do our part" on wages. Meany later charged, however, that the administration had not kept its bargain and had permitted prices to soar.

Despite his increasing opposition to American involvement in Vietnam, Wirtz remained in the Johnson cabinet until the inauguration of Richard Nixon. Thereafter, he practiced law in Washington and then taught at the University of San Diego School of Law.

—JLW

## Wurf, Jerry (Jerome)
(1919–1981) *president, American Federation of State, County and Municipal Employees*

Born on April 18, 1919, in New York City, Wurf attended New York University for two years, but dropped out in 1940 and then took a job as an organizer for the Hotel and Restaurant Employees Union. Because of disagreements with union leadership, Wurf lost his job. But in 1947, he was hired as an organizer for the American Federation of State, County, and Municipal Employees (AFSCME) by union president Arnold Zander. The following year, he became head of District Council 37 in New York City.

In the 1950s public employment increased rapidly and AFSCME membership rose as well. The union doubled its membership between 1953 and 1960, when it numbered 182,000. Striving to close the gap in wages paid by public and private employers, AFSCME began to abandon its traditional reliance on political lobbying and adopted more typical labor tactics. Citywide collective bargaining was established in Philadelphia, and District Council 37 made a major breakthrough in 1954 when New York's mayor ROBERT WAGNER signed an executive order requiring municipal departments to bargain with unions that had established majority representation. Meanwhile, rank-and-file pressure for more aggressive tactics increased as did members' impatience with Zander, the union's president since its birth in 1937. In 1962 Wurf, until then a spokesperson for Zander, mounted an unsuccessful challenge against him. Two years later Wurf tried again and this time defeated Zander.

Upon taking office Wurf discovered that Zander had involved the union in Central Intelligence Agency (CIA) activities abroad. In 1967 Zander admitted that between 1958 and 1964 he had accepted more than $100,000 annually from the CIA for anticommunist activities, including the support of strikes that helped topple Cheddi Jagan's government in British Guiana. Following his election in 1964 Wurf severed the union's connections with the CIA. When, in 1967, several unions were revealed to have accepted CIA funding, Wurf was found to be the only labor leader who had extracted his union from such international activity.

AFSCME continued to grow rapidly during Wurf's early years as president, reaching 400,000 members in 1968, about two-thirds of them blue-collar workers. Although Wurf believed that firefighters and law enforcement officers "should not and cannot strike," he opposed legal prohibitions against strikes by other public employees. Antistrike laws "are not simply ineffectual," said Wurf. "They warp this vital process. They bring employees to the bargaining table, but as inferiors."

The New York area, an AFSCME stronghold, became a testing ground for public employees' strikes. Inspired in part by the success of strikes by New York City teachers, 8,000 members of AFSCME and the Social Service Employees Union struck the New York City Welfare Department in January 1965 in defiance of the state's Condon-Wadlin Act. Over 5,400 workers were dismissed for violating the act, and Wurf charged that Wagner used the law's provisions to break the strike. However, the dismissals were delayed, and the following year the state legislature exempted the strikers from the penalties required by the act. In 1967 Wurf and other leaders of public employee unions vehemently opposed the Taylor Law, New York governor NELSON ROCKEFELLER's replacement for Condon-Wadlin. Although the new law guaranteed organizing

and collective bargaining rights for public workers, it also included heavy fines and penalties for striking unions and their members. AFSCME defied the act in November 1968, when 3,000 nonprofessional workers struck New York State mental hospitals. Although strike leaders were jailed under the Taylor Law, the strike forced Rockefeller to accede to the union's demands.

A strike by African-American sanitation workers in Memphis drew national attention to AFSCME and to Wurf's leadership in 1968. Blacks comprised 30 percent of AFSCME's national membership, and racial issues were at the heart of the Memphis dispute. Seeking union recognition, a grievance procedure, promotions "without regard to race" and a 15¢ raise over the $1.60 hourly minimum, the AFSCME local called a strike on February 12. The black community in Memphis quickly rallied behind the strike. Wurf brought in he union's top leadership and, with local church groups, organized protests and daily marches through downtown Memphis. Wurf was among those arrested at a city hall sit-in. Following the April 4 assassination of MARTIN LUTHER KING, JR., who had come to Memphis to support the strikers, Wurf helped lead marches and protests that continued for two more weeks. On April 16 the city signed a contract with AFSCME in which it recognized the union and agreed to a dues checkoff, promotions based on seniority, a two-step 15¢-an-hour raise, and a "no-strike" clause. Wurf called it "a good settlement that couldn't have been achieved without the coalescence of the union and the Negro community."

Wurf, who became an AFL-CIO vice president and a member of the federation's Executive Council in 1969, dissented from the council's endorsements of the Nixon administration's Vietnam policy. By the end of the 1970s, AFSCME, with a membership of over 1 million, was the largest union in the AFL-CIO. Wurf was still president of AFSCME when he died on December 10, 1981.

—MDB

# Y

## Yarborough, Ralph W(ebster)

(1903–1996) *member of the Senate*

Yarborough, who was born on June 8, 1903, in Chandler, Texas, attended the U.S. Military Academy at West Point for one year before earning a law degree from the University of Texas in 1927. He served as an assistant state attorney general from 1931 until 1934 and was elected as a district judge in Austin, a position he held from 1936 to 1941. During World War II he was an army infantry officer in Europe and a member of the occupation forces in Japan.

In the 1950s Yarborough emerged as the leader of the liberal wing of the Texas Democratic Party. The liberals consisted of a coalition of intellectuals, trade unionists, African Americans, Mexican Americans, and East Texas populists. At odds with the state's powerful business interests, the liberals opposed Texas's restrictive labor laws and its widespread racial discrimination while favoring social welfare measures to aid the poor. Yarborough lost gubernatorial primaries to conservative Democrats in 1952, 1954, and 1956. His margin of defeat, however, grew progressively smaller in each election. In April 1957 he won a special election to fill a vacated Senate seat. The next year, he was elected to a full term.

Factional disputes continued to divide Texas Democrats in the early 1960s. JOHN B. CONNALLY, who had been secretary of the navy during the Kennedy administration, resigned his position and defeated a liberal Democrat in the Texas gubernatorial primary in 1962. The Connally-Yarborough rivalry, which had existed for several years, only grew worse after Connally's election as governor in November 1962. President Kennedy, who believed

that the factional dispute among Texas Democrats was one of several problems impairing his chances of carrying the state when he sought reelection in 1964, decided to travel to Texas on November 21, 1963, in hopes of raising his popularity with voters and closing the rifts in the state party.

Following Kennedy's assassination in Dallas during that trip, Johnson tried to act as a conciliator among Texas Democrats. Johnson had previously had close relations with Connally, but the president's support of civil rights caused strains with the governor. Johnson and Yarborough had disagreed over many issues over several years. The new president, nonetheless, dissuaded the conservatives from making a major challenge to Yarborough as he sought reelection in 1964. In return the liberals refrained from mounting a full-scale effort against Connally's reelection bid. As a result of the truce both Yarborough and Connally won easy primary and general election victories in 1964.

In the Senate Yarborough continued to back major administration-supported civil rights and social welfare measures. He was the only Senator from the Deep South who voted for the Civil Rights Act of 1964 and one of only five southern Democratic senators who voted for the 1965 Voting Rights Act. During the latter year Yarborough injected Texas politics into a Senate debate over a bill to extend President Johnson's antipoverty program of the previous year. A supporter of the War on Poverty, Yarborough argued in August that the power of governors to veto some of the antipoverty projects should be eliminated and charged Governor Connally with attempting to "defeat and destroy" the program in Texas. The following month Congress adopted a bill that modified the veto power without eliminating it.

In 1968, with Johnson a lame-duck president and the nation sharply divided over the Vietnam War, the truce between liberal and conservative Democrats in Texas disintegrated. When Connally announced that he would not run for a fourth term as governor, Yarborough was inclined to enter the gubernatorial primary. He was dissuaded from doing so by his supporters in organized labor, who wanted him to remain in Washington. Once more a conservative prevailed in a hard fought primary runoff.

Meanwhile, in the race for the Democratic presidential nomination, Yarborough supported antiwar candidate senator EUGENE MCCARTHY (D-Minn.), and Connally endorsed Vice President HUBERT H. HUMPHREY. At the August Democratic National Convention in Chicago a delegation led by Yarborough challenged the credentials of Connally's regular Texas delegation, but the challenge was rejected. Yarborough endorsed Humphrey after the convention selected the vice president as the party's nominee.

Lloyd Bentsen, Jr., one of the conservatives whom President Johnson had deterred from entering the 1964 senatorial primary, challenged Yarborough in the 1970 race. Armed with a substantial campaign treasury, Bentsen appealed to "law-and-order" sentiment and accused the liberal Texas senator of being insufficiently firm in his opposition to school busing. Yarborough lost to Bentsen, who defeated George H. W. Bush in the November election. After leaving the Senate, Yarborough practiced law in Austin. He died on January 27, 1996.

—MLL

## Yarmolinsky, Adam

(1922–2000) *special assistant to the secretary of defense, deputy assistant secretary of defense for international security affairs*

Yarmolinsky was born in New York City on November 17, 1922. His father, Avraham Yarmolinsky, a distinguished scholar of Russian literature, was chief of the Slavonic division of the New York Public Library; his mother, Babette Deutsch, was a well-known poet and critic who taught at Columbia University. Yarmolinsky earned an A.B. from Harvard University in 1943, after which he served in the U.S. Army Air Forces. Following the end of World War II he received a law degree from Yale University and was a clerk for Supreme Court Justice Stan-

ley Reed from 1949 to 1951. He then practiced law in Washington, D.C., and worked as an editor for Doubleday.

Shortly after won the election of John F. Kennedy in 1960, Yarmolinsky joined a task force headed by SARGENT SHRIVER, Kennedy's brother-in-law, to screen candidates for posts in the new administration. In January 1961, Secretary of Defense ROBERT S. MCNAMARA named Yarmolinsky his special assistant. While in the Defense Department Yarmolinsky served as temporary head of the national fallout shelter program and worked on a White House study that recommended that the Defense Department ban off-base discrimination against black service men and women.

Early in 1964 Yarmolinsky took a leave from the Defense Department to join a task force under Shriver that framed legislation for the Johnson administration's antipoverty programs. Yarmolinsky, with the support of McNamara, proposed that abandoned army camps be used as centers for educating semi-literate school dropouts. The idea won the support of Shriver but was bitterly denounced by Secretary of Labor WILLARD WIRTZ, Secretary of Agriculture ORVILLE FREEMAN, and ANTHONY CELEBREZZE, secretary of the Department of Health, Education and Welfare. They argued that the use of military bases for educational purposes would give the poverty program an unhealthy military cast. President Johnson agreed, and the program was dropped. Wirtz, Freeman, and Celebreeze also argued that their respective departments could better manage the various poverty programs than the new Office of Economic Opportunity (OEO) proposed by Shriver and Yarmolinsky. Johnson, however, believed that the OEO should control most antipoverty programs, and the legislation that the administration presented to Congress reflected that belief.

Yarmolinsky hoped that he would soon be named deputy director of OEO. However, in August 1964, eight southern members of Congress informed the White House that they would vote for the Johnson antipoverty program only if the administration promised not to appoint Yarmolinsky to OEO. This opposition to Yarmolinsky arose from his role in desegregating military bases in southern towns, his abrasive manner in dealing with Congress on military issues, and a general mistrust of his liberal and intellectual background. After President Johnson made the promise, the antipoverty bill became law; however, it would have passed even without the votes of Yarmolinsky's opponents. When questioned about Yarmolinsky in August 1964, Johnson denied even considering him for an appointment in the antipoverty program.

In the fall of 1964 Yarmolinsky returned to the Defense Department. He worked for a time on defense problems relating to the Panama Canal and later served on a task force studying economic problems in the Dominican Republic. In October 1965 he became deputy assistant secretary of defense for international security affairs, but this was a junior appointment that did not require congressional approval, and a disappointment to him.

Yarmolinsky left the Defense Department in September 1966 to teach at the Harvard Law School and the John F. Kennedy School of Government at Harvard.

In 1971 Yarmolinsky completed a book, sponsored by the Twentieth Century Fund, in which he documented the extraordinary impact of the military establishment on American life. He argued that a large military establishment was unavoidable but feared that neither Congress nor the president had exercised proper control over it. He questioned whether the military should always have the primary claim on scarce economic and social resources and deplored the tendency of state and local government to rely on federal troops to put down domestic disorders. He served as counselor to the Arms Control and Disarmament Agency during the Carter administration. Yarmolinsky died on January 5, 2000.

—JLW

## Yorty, Sam(uel William)

### (1909–1998) *mayor*

Yorty, who was born on October 1, 1909, in Lincoln, Nebraska, grew up in a home where William Jennings Bryan and Woodrow Wilson were family heroes. He moved to Los Angeles in 1927 after finishing high school and then studied law, gaining admission to the California bar in 1939. During the depression he was involved in a variety of alternative political and social movements, but he eventually won election as a Democrat to the state assembly and served from 1936 until 1940. In the assembly, he supported progressive social legislation, and he also sponsored the law that created the nation's first state un-American activities committee.

Yorty made an unsuccessful race for the U.S. Senate in 1940 and then practiced law. During World War II he served in the U.S. Army Air Forces in the Pacific. In 1945 he ran for mayor of Los Angeles, placing sixth among 13 candidates. He returned to the state assembly in 1949, and then won a seat in the U.S. House of Representatives, which he held for four years. In 1954 he lost another race for the U.S. Senate. Two years later, the Democratic Party leadership kept him from making a third try for the Senate.

Yorty's political views had grown more conservative, and he became discontented with the state Democratic organization. In 1960 he challenged the party directly when he endorsed Republican RICHARD M. NIXON over John F. Kennedy in the presidential election of 1960. Yorty remained a Democrat, however, and capitalized on his reputation as a maverick to win an upset victory in the Los Angeles mayoral race in 1961. He was adept at using television to lessen the difficulties of campaigning in a decentralized city that sprawled over a large area.

Yorty became mayor when the southern Californian economy was booming. He was able to attract new business to the city, lower property taxes, and undertake the renewal of the downtown area. Yorty kept his name before the California public through frequent appearances on popular television shows and a series of worldwide tours as a representative of the city. With greater support from the city's business community than he enjoyed in 1961, Yorty defeated Representative James Roosevelt (D-Calif.)—Los Angeles elections were nonpartisan by law—and six other candidates in the May 1965 mayoral contest. Yorty won 60 percent of the vote and, most important, helped carry his political allies to seats on the city council.

Yet only a few months later, in August 1965, Yorty again was at the center of controversy when a riot occurred in Watts, a predominantly African-American section of Los Angeles, resulting in 34 deaths, thousands of injuries and extensive property damage. Soon after the week of violence was over, Yorty traded public attacks with state and federal officials. The mayor criticized Governor EDMUND BROWN's lieutenant governor, Glenn M. Anderson—Brown was vacationing out of the state during the riot—for not responding quickly enough to a call for National Guard help. Yorty defended his police chief, William H. Parker, and the city force from charges of brutality, claiming that state police exacerbated the riot in its early stages.

When federal officials charged that Yorty had failed to cooperate with them to prevent such disturbances, he replied that the antipoverty program and the liberal Brown administration had raised poor people's expectations beyond what the authorities were able to fulfill. A few months before the riot Yorty had criticized the federal Office of Economic Opportunity (OEO) for excluding city officials from direction of OEO's antipoverty projects. He now charged that the OEO's withholding of funds from Los Angeles until the city met OEO criteria contributed to riot conditions.

In January 1966 the California Advisory Committee to the U.S. Civil Rights Commission, headed by Episcopal bishop JAMES A. PIKE, praised Lieutenant Governor Anderson, but singled out Yorty for "gross negligence" and "attitudes and actions" that contributed to riot conditions. Yorty saw the report as a personal "political attack" based on the "false charge that the police department caused the rioting".

In August 1966 hearings before a subcommittee of the Senate Government Operations Committee, Senator ABRAHAM RIBICOFF (D-Conn.) and Senator ROBERT F. KENNEDY (D-N.Y.) repeated the charge that Yorty had done little to improve conditions in Watts. Noting the restrictions in the Los Angeles city charter that he had long sought to revise, Yorty claimed that he lacked authority in areas such as education, health, and housing that were essential to effecting the changes the senators desired. Later, Yorty asserted that Kennedy was merely using the subcommittee hearings to further his political campaign against President Johnson. He added, "Bobby is an upstart who is trying to ride on his brother's fame and his father's fortune to take over the country."

Yorty's political battle with Governor Brown continued through the mid-1960s. In the June 1964 primaries he had unsuccessfully opposed Brown's slate of pro-Johnson delegates to the Democratic National Convention with his own slate also pledged to the president. Hoping to capitalize on the popularity his role in the Watts riot earned him among many California whites, Yorty unsuccessfully challenged Brown for the gubernatorial nomination in 1966.

Yorty's flamboyant style and blunt statements continued to inspire support and arouse opposition.

In 1967 the mayor hosted his own local television show. Yorty professed outrage when it was cancelled, especially because its replacement was *Hee Haw*. In 1969 Yorty ran for a third term against Thomas Bradley, a member of the city council and a former police lieutenant. Yorty's handling of the Watts riot had lost him much of the black electoral support that he had enjoyed during his earlier, victorious mayoral campaigns. Former vice president HUBERT H. HUMPHREY and Senator EDWARD M. KENNEDY (D-Mass.) both endorsed Bradley. Yorty tried to compensate by making racial appeals to secure white votes. The bitter campaign ended with Yorty's victory in a runoff election. Four years later, in a vitriolic race in which Yorty accused his opponent of being friendly with the Black Panthers, Bradley unseated the mayor. After leaving office, Yorty hosted a radio talk show and made a last, unsuccessful attempt in 1981 to win another term as mayor. He died on June 5, 1998.

—JCH

## Young, Milton R.

### (1897–1983) *member of the Senate*

Born on December 6, 1897, in Berlin, North Dakota, Young attended North Dakota State Agricultural College and Graceland College in Iowa without completing a degree. A farmer, he entered politics as a Republican when he won a seat on the local school board in 1924. He served in the North Dakota House of Representatives and then the state senate from 1932 until 1945. In 1945 he was appointed to a vacant seat in the U.S. Senate and then won a special election to complete the balance of the term. He was reelected in 1950 and in four more consecutive elections.

Despite his long service in the Senate, Young was not well known except on Capitol Hill and in his home state. He maintained his popularity in North Dakota by taking conservative positions of most issues while working diligently to bring federal benefits to his state.

Young's conservatism was reflected in his opposition to Medicare and antipoverty programs during the Johnson years and his support of cuts in labor and health, education and welfare spending. Although he voted for the Civil Rights Act of 1964, he opposed the Voting Rights Act of 1965 and voted against the use of federal funds to achieve integration through busing. Young, however, favored worker training programs and voted against deleting $900 million from the Model Cities program in 1966.

During the 1960s Young consistently supported legislation to aid farmers, including measures to extend crop insurance and improve marketing conditions for farm products. Concerned by North Dakota's loss of population and low per-capita income, he was instrumental in obtaining lucrative military projects for his state, including the construction of antiballistic missile bases. Young later said that of his accomplishments in the Senate, he was proudest of his success in bringing federal projects to North Dakota.

As early as 1954 Young spoke out against U.S. military intervention in Asia and throughout the 1960s continued to express opposition to the war in Vietnam on the ground that the area was "military untenable." Despite his reservations about the use of American troops in Asia, Young consistently voted in favor of appropriating funds for the war. He justified his stand by saying that he intended "to support the president of the United States when we are in war whether he [the president] agrees with my views or not."

In his final campaign for the Senate in 1974, Young, then 76, answered charges that he was too old with a television commercial that showed him demolishing a board with a karate chop. He retired from the Senate at the end of his term in January 1981. He died on May 31, 1983.

—EWS

## Young, Stephen M(arvin)

### (1889–1984) *member of the Senate*

Young, who was born on May 4, 1889, in Norwalk, Ohio, earned a law degree from Western Reserve University in 1911. He first ran for public office in 1912 as a Democrat, winning a seat in the state legislature and becoming, to date, the youngest Ohioan ever to serve in that body. Military service in Mexico during 1916 and in an artillery unit during World War I interrupted his political career. After his discharge from the military, Young served as a prosecutor in Cuyahoga County and then ran an unsuccessful race for the office of state attorney general in 1922. He practiced law for a decade and then won an at-large seat from Ohio in the U.S. House of Representatives, serving two terms from 1933 to 1937 and supporting New Deal programs. He gave up his seat to make a losing run for the Democratic

nomination for governor in 1936, but returned to Congress for a single term by winning election in 1940. Young failed in his bid for reelection in 1942 and then enlisted in the army, serving in North Africa and Italy. Young once more won Ohio's at-large seat in Congress in 1948 only to lose it in the election two years later. His defeat in 1956 in the race for state attorney general seemed to dim his prospects for securing elective office. Two years later, however, he scored an upset over incumbent senator John W. Bricker (R-Ohio) and took a seat in the upper chamber.

Young survived two difficult challenges to his Senate seat in 1964. In January JOHN J. GLENN, the first American astronaut to orbit the Earth, announced his candidacy for Young's seat in the May Democratic primary. Democratic Party strategists, concerned that the 74-year-old incumbent would lose in November, encouraged Glenn to make the race against Young. The senator experienced a major setback in January when the state Democratic convention, in a thinly veiled move on Glenn's behalf, declined to endorse him for reelection. The astronaut's victory appeared certain until an ear injury compelled him to withdraw from the race in late March. Young easily won the primary.

Young's good fortune continued through the general election. His Republican opponent in the senatorial race, Representative Robert Taft, Jr. (R-Ohio), possessed a famous name in Ohio politics and was 27 years Young's junior. But the Republican presidential campaign of Senator BARRY M. GOLD-WATER (R-Ariz.) fared badly in Ohio, and by closely associating his campaign with that of President Johnson, Young narrowly defeated Taft in November.

Young voted for every major piece of Great Society legislation while pursuing his own battles against some domestic and military spending programs. Young attacked civil defense appropriations, but lost in annual efforts taken to reduce the program's funding between 1964 and 1968. A member of the Senate Armed Services Committee, Young opposed the development of the Sentinel antiballistic missile system (ABM). In June 1968 he described the administration's request as "an utter waste of taxpayers' money . . . the deployment of antiballistic missile systems ringing some cities of our nation have been fruitless and wasteful."

Although his state's economy benefited from increased military production, Young criticized the Johnson administration's policies of deepening U.S.

military involvement in South Vietnam. In February 1966 he demanded that Johnson replace Secretary of State DEAN RUSK, complaining that he could not sleep well with Rusk running the State Department. In June 1968 Young and Senator LEE METCALF voted against a bill to enable the President to retain General EARLE G. WHEELER as chair of the Joint Chiefs of Staff. On the Senate floor in September 1968, Young defended antiwar protesters in a debate over the disturbances outside the August 1968 Democratic National Convention. "Democracy was clubbed to death," Young cried, "by Mayor [RICHARD J.] DALEY's police."

Young decided not to seek reelection in 1970, but took satisfaction in the election of his former campaign manager, Howard Metzenbaum, to the Senate in 1976. He died on December 1, 1984.

—JLB

## Young, Whitney M(oore), Jr.
### (1921–1971)  *executive director, National Urban League*

A graduate of Kentucky State College, Young, who was born on July 31, 1921, in Lincoln Ridge, Kentucky, served in the army during World War II. After receiving an M.A. in social work from the University of Minnesota, Young worked for the St. Paul Urban League from 1947 and 1950 and then became executive secretary of the Omaha Urban League. He was named dean of Atlanta University's School of Social Work in 1954 and served there until his appointment as executive director of the National Urban League in 1961. Young took charge of the Urban League at a time of intensified efforts to secure civil rights, most notably through sit-in demonstrations to gain integration of lunch counters and freedom rides to desegregate interstate bus lines and terminals. The Urban League had not favored such forms of direct action, but Young broadened its programs and gave it more aggressive and outspoken leadership, even if it remained among the most conservative of the major civil rights organizations. Urbane and articulate, Young presented an ambitious proposal for a "domestic Marshall Plan" in June 1963. His plan called for a massive and wide-ranging social, economic, and educational programs to provide African Americans with "first-class citizenship" and to prevent the "racial unrest" in northern cities from "taking flame."

One of the first civil rights leaders to be consulted by President Johnson in December 1963, Young cooperated closely with the Johnson administration in the planning and passage of its War on Poverty legislation. Testifying in support of the program at congressional hearings in April 1964, Young asserted that African Americans were "wary lest they find themselves with a mouthful of civil rights and an empty stomach." Following the passage of the Economic Opportunity Act in August 1964, Young organized a Community Action Assembly in Washington in December. Over 350 black leaders gathered to hear league officials explain in detail the provisions of the 1964 civil rights and antipoverty laws and ways in which local black organizations could implement the legislation and secure antipoverty funds. The league sponsored a series of similar workshops throughout 1965. With its own $8 million contract from the Labor Department, the league developed a major job training program for unemployed blacks.

Young supported Johnson in the 1964 presidential election and called the Republicans' nomination of Senator BARRY GOLDWATER (R-Ariz.) "an attempt to appeal to all of the fearful, the insecure, prejudiced people in our society." With three other civil rights leaders, Young signed a July 1964 statement urging a "moratorium" on mass civil rights demonstrations during the 1964 campaign.

Young participated in the march from Selma to Montgomery, Alabama, organized by MARTIN LUTHER KING, JR., in March 1965. When JAMES MEREDITH was shot in June 1966 while on a protest march in Mississippi, Young refused to sign a "manifesto" containing strong criticism of American society and government drafted by those who planned to continue the march. He objected to the slogan of "Black Power," which STOKELY CARMICHAEL frequently repeated during the continuation of the march. At an Urban League convention in July, Young deprecated Black Power as meaning "all things to all men." With six other black leaders he signed an October 1966 advertisement in the *New York Times* that repudiated the Black Power concept and reaffirmed his commitment to nonviolence, integration, and the "democratic process" as the major tenets of the civil rights movement. In July 1967 Young also joined in a statement appealing for an end to riots in northern inner cities. At an Urban League convention the next month, he added that the choice blacks faced was not one of "moderation vs. militancy" but of "militancy vs. extremism."

Young's emphasis on "responsible militancy" presaged a shift in his views on Black Power. Speaking at the July 1968 convention of the Congress of Racial Equality, Young endorsed a Black Power concept that emphasized "control of one's destiny and community affairs." He supported "as legitimate and historically consistent a minority's mobilization of its economic and political power to reward its friends and punish its enemies." At an Urban League convention the same month, Young launched a "New Thrust" program of community action in black neighborhoods. Labeling the program a "constructive Black Power" effort, Young explained that the league would now provide "technical assistance to the ghetto to help it organize, document its needs, select its own leadership and arrange for creative confrontations with appropriate officials." The "New Thrust" program signaled a major shift for the league to grassroots organizing to build black economic, social and political power. Over the next several years, Young directed a major rehabilitation program among the black poor which spent an average of $25 million per year.

Throughout the Johnson years Young frequently consulted with White House officials and served on seven presidential commissions, including a national advisory council for the antipoverty program. Young went to South Vietnam in July 1966 to investigate the condition of black troops. When Martin Luther King, Jr., made a strong statement in opposition to the Vietnam War in April 1967, Young opposed King's linking of the antiwar and civil rights movements, stating that the "limited resources and personnel" of the civil rights movement "should not be diverted into other channels." Young also joined a delegation of 22 prominent Americans who went to South Vietnam to observe the September 1967 elections. He later said he was "terribly impressed" with the elections. In 1969, however, Young came out strongly against the Vietnam War, arguing that it divided the nation and used funds which could best be spent in the nation's cities.

During the Nixon years Young criticized the administration for permitting what he called a "massive national withdrawal" from urban and racial problems. He also opposed an administration proposal for pretrial detention of "dangerous" criminals. Young endorsed bills for a national health insurance program and continued to call for greater aid to the poor. On March 11, 1971, Young was stricken while swimming in Lagos, Nigeria, and drowned.

—CAB

# Z

## Zablocki, Clement J(ohn)

(1912–1983) *member of the House of Representatives*

Clement J. Zablocki, who was born on November 18, 1912, and raised in Milwaukee, attended parochial schools and later studied at Marquette University, where he received a B.A. in 1936. He taught high school in Milwaukee during the late 1930s and served in the Wisconsin Senate from 1942 and 1948. He was elected to Congress in 1948 and for many years had little difficulty winning reelection.

Zablocki's district included a large white working-class area in Milwaukee's South Side and some nearby suburbs. His voting record generally reflected the views of organized labor, which gave him heavy support. In domestic affairs he usually voted for the Johnson administration's social welfare legislation, including antipoverty, Medicare, and education bills. The Pentagon could also rely on Zablocki to support its requests for increased arms appropriations; as the second-ranking member of the House Foreign Affairs Committee, he consistently backed the administration's Vietnam War policy.

Zablocki supported civil rights legislation, but in August 1966 he came into conflict with the Youth Council of the NAACP, whose adviser was Father JAMES E. GROPPI, when it demanded that Zablocki and other politicians resign from the Fraternal Order of Eagles, a national fraternity that excluded blacks. In September, demonstrators from Groppi's group picketed the Zablocki home to protest his membership. Zablocki refused to resign, arguing that he preferred to try to reform the organization from within.

In 1968 Zablocki headed President Johnson's Wisconsin primary campaign. On March 31 Johnson announced that he would not seek reelection. Zablocki nevertheless urged Democrats to vote for Johnson as a statement of confidence in the administration. On April 2 the president lost in Wisconsin to Senator EUGENE J. MCCARTHY (D-Minn.) by 150,000 votes.

During the Nixon years Zablocki remained a staunch supporter of the administration's Vietnam War policy. He died while still a member of Congress on December 3, 1983.

—JLW

## Zinn, Howard

(1922–   ) *civil rights and antiwar activist*

Zinn, who was born on August 24, 1922, in New York City, served in the U.S. Army Air Forces in World War II and then attended New York University, where he earned a bachelor's degree in 1951 and Columbia University, where he completed a Ph.D. in political science in 1958. He began teaching history in 1956 at Spelman College, a small African-American women's school in Atlanta where he became professor and chair of the department of history and social sciences. In 1964 Zinn took a position at Boston University, where he became professor of political science.

Zinn combined political conviction and social activism with his scholarly work. He became involved in the civil rights movement while teaching at Spelman and worked closely with the Student Nonviolent Coordinating Committee (SNCC), a civil rights group. In 1962 he participated in an unsuccessful desegregation drive in Albany, Georgia, and subsequently wrote a SNCC report that attacked the federal government for "abandoning its responsibility" to protect black demonstrators against white violence. Zinn's experience in the civil rights movement encouraged him to write *SNCC: The New Abolitionists*, published in 1964. The book's enthusiastic description of SNCC activities in the Deep South helped popularize the organization.

During the mid-1960s Zinn joined the growing peace movement, participating in the National Mobilization Committee to end the war in Vietnam. His book *Vietnam: The Logic of Withdrawal* appeared in 1967. Zinn was also known for his continuing activism. In February 1968 he flew to Hanoi with the Reverend DANIEL BERRIGAN, to receive three U.S. prisoners of war released by the North Vietnamese government. One year later Zinn participated in a conference of antiwar scientists and scholars at the Massachusetts Institute of Technol-

ogy, where he urged researchers to stop work on federally funded projects as a means of resisting "the lawlessness of government."

Zinn's efforts to stimulate campus activism during the 1960s made him increasingly impatient with the traditional "ivory tower" detachment of academics. He argued in numerous articles that the separation of knowledge from action is "immoral"; scholars make a political statement in their choice of subject matter, he claimed, for by ignoring controversial issues they play into the hands of reactionary forces. He elaborated those arguments in *The Politics of History*, published in 1970.

Zinn continued teaching at Boston University until his retirement in 1988. In 1980 he published *A People's History of the United States*. He participated in demonstrations against the U.S. war in Iraq in 2003 and 2004.

—SLG

# APPENDICES

# CHRONOLOGY

## 1963

**November 22**—Kennedy is assassinated in Dallas, Texas, by Lee Harvey Oswald. Lyndon Johnson is sworn in as the 36th president.

**November 24**—Jack Ruby kills Oswald in Dallas. The incident is seen live on TV.

**November 26**—In a railroad work-rules dispute a government arbitration board calls for the elimination of 40,000 jobs.

**November 27**—Johnson addresses a joint session of Congress and pledges continued support of Kennedy's programs. He asks Congress for the "earliest possible passage" of a civil rights program.

**November 29**—The Warren Commission is set up to investigate Kennedy's assassination.

**December 17**—The Senate ratifies the El Chamizal Treaty settling a longstanding boundary dispute with Mexico over land near the Rio Grande.

## 1964

**January 3**—Arizona senator Barry Goldwater announces his candidacy for the Republican presidential nomination.

**January 3**—Johnson establishes the President's Committee on Consumer Interests and appoints Esther Peterson its chair.

**January 8**—Johnson delivers his first State of the Union message and calls for a War on Poverty.

**January 9–12**—U.S. troops fire on anti-U.S. rioters in the Panama Canal Zone.

**January 10**—Panama breaks diplomatic ties with the United States.

**January 11**—U.S. Surgeon General Luther Terry's committee reports the use of cigarettes "contributes substantially to mortality."

**January 23**—The Twenty-fourth Amendment barring the use of a poll tax in federal elections is ratified.

**January 25**—*Echo II*, the first U.S.-USSR cooperative space venture, is launched.

**February 17**—The Supreme Court rules that congressional districts must be apportioned on a "one-person, one-vote" basis.

**February 26**—Johnson signs a $11.5 billion tax cut bill.

**March 4**—James Hoffa is found guilty of jury tampering.

**March 10**—Henry Cabot Lodge, Jr., wins the New Hampshire Republican presidential primary on a write-in vote.

**March 14**—Jack Ruby is found guilty of the murder of Lee Harvey Oswald.

**April 4**—The United States and Panama resume diplomatic ties and pledge negotiations on the Canal Zone treaty.

**April 7**—Alabama governor George Wallace receives 34.1 percent of the Democratic vote in the Wisconsin presidential primary.

**April 9**—Railroad workers agree to postpone a scheduled nationwide railroad strike over work-rules changes after a personal plea from Johnson.

**April 11**—Johnson signs a farm bill providing for major changes in federal wheat and cotton price subsidies.

**May 15**—New York governor Nelson A. Rockefeller wins an upset victory over Lodge and Goldwater in the Oregon Republican presidential primary.

**May 19**—Wallace polls 42.8 percent of the vote in the Maryland Democratic presidential primary.

**June 2**—Goldwater defeats Rockefeller by 59,000 votes in the California Republican presidential primary.

**June 10**—The Senate invokes cloture on ending the longest filibuster since the adoption of the cloture rule in 1917.

**June 14**—The United Steelworkers of America and 11 steel companies agree not to practice racial discrimination in the industry.

**June 15**—The Supreme Court rules that state legislative districts must be apportioned according to population.

**June 21**—Three civil rights workers, participants in the Mississippi Freedom Summer Project, are murdered in Neshoba County, Mississippi.

**July 2**—Johnson signs a civil rights bill providing for the integration of public accommodations.

**July 8**—The Senate Rules Committee finds Bobby Baker "guilty of many gross improprieties" while secretary to the Democratic majority.

**July 9**—Johnson signs the urban mass transportation bill providing $375 million to help public and private transit companies provide and improve urban mass transportation.

**July 15**—Barry Goldwater is nominated as the Republican candidate for president on the first ballot at the Republican National Convention. William Miller is chosen as the vice presidential candidate at the following session.

**July 18**—Racial violence breaks out in Harlem and Brownsville, two predominately black sections of New York City. During the summer riots occur in Rochester, New York, suburban Chicago, Jersey City, Elizabeth and Paterson, New Jersey, and Philadelphia, as well.

**August 4**—Johnson instructs the navy to take retaliatory action against North Vietnam for its alleged attack on the U.S. destroyer *Maddox in* the Gulf of Tonkin.

**August 7**—Congress passes the Tonkin Gulf Resolution authorizing Johnson to take "all necessary measures" to "repel any armed attack" against U.S. forces in Southeast Asia and approves in advance

"all necessary steps, including the use of armed force," that the president might take to aid U.S. allies in the region.

**August 20**—Johnson signs the economic opportunity bill of 1964, authorizing 10 separate programs, under the supervision of the director of the Office of Economic Opportunity, designed to make a coordinated attack on the causes of poverty—illiteracy, unemployment, and lack of public services.

**August 20**—Johnson signs a bill providing free legal counsel for indigents accused of federal crimes.

**August 26**—Johnson is nominated as the Democratic candidate for president on the first ballot of the Democratic National Convention. Minnesota senator Hubert Humphrey is chosen vice presidential candidate at the following session.

**August 31**—Johnson signs a bill establishing the federal food stamp program on a permanent basis.

**September 2**—Johnson signs a housing bill providing for urban and rural renewal programs to alleviate blight.

**September 3**—Johnson signs a bill establishing a permanent national wilderness system.

**September 3**—Johnson signs a bill creating a National Council of the Arts.

**September 24**—The Warren Commission issues its report concluding that Lee Harvey Oswald "acted alone" in assassinating Kennedy.

**October 14**—Martin Luther King, Jr., is awarded the Nobel Peace Prize.

**October 14**—Presidential aide Walter Jenkins resigns following his arrest on a morals charge.

**November 3**—Johnson wins reelection by a record plurality of almost 16 million votes and captures 486 electoral votes from 44 states. Democrats win 17 governorships and increase their majorities in Congress.

**November 25**—U.S. planes airlift Belgian paratroopers into Stanleyville to rescue white hostages held by Congolese rebels.

**November 28**—*Mariner 4* is launched to transmit close-up pictures of Mars.

**December 14**—The Supreme Court unanimously upholds the constitutionality of the public accommodations section of the 1964 Civil Rights Act.

# 1965

**January 4**—The House, 224-201, adopts a 21-day rule weakening the power of the Rules Committee to block legislation.

**January 11**—The International Longshoremen's Association begins a strike paralyzing Atlantic and Gulf Coast shipping operations until March 5.

**February 7**—Communist forces attack the U.S. air base at Pleiku.

**March 2**—The United States begins Operation Rolling Thunder, the sustained bombing of North Vietnam.

**March 4**—The U.S. Information Agency announces it will close its facilities in Indonesia because of harassment. The Peace Corps withdraws the following month.

**March 7**—About 500 blacks, beginning a protest march from Selma to Montgomery, Alabama, are attacked by sheriff's deputies and state troopers.

**March 8–9**—The first declared U.S. combat troops land in Vietnam.

**March 9**  Johnson signs an Appalachia aid bill.

**March 15**—Johnson addresses a joint session of Congress and calls for swift passage of voting rights legislation.

**March 21**—The civil rights march from Selma to Montgomery, Alabama, begins under the protection of federal troops.

**March 23**—The first Gemini flight carrying astronauts is launched.

**March 24**—*Ranger 9* transmits pictures of the Moon's surface to Earth.

**April 6**—Early Bird, the world's first commercial satellite, is launched.

**April 11**—Johnson signs the elementary and secondary education bill, granting aid to schools with large concentrations of children from low-income families and providing funds for educational materials and the creation of educational centers.

**April 26**—Secretary of Defense Robert McNamara states that the Vietnam war effort costs the United States about $1.5 billion a year.

**April 28**—U.S. Marines land in the Dominican Republic allegedly to protect American lives during the civil war.

**April 29**—U.S. Commissioner of Education Francis Keppel announces that public school districts receiving federal aid will be required to start desegregating their schools by the autumn of 1967.

**May 2**—In a televised address Johnson states that Marines were sent to the Dominican Republic to prevent a Communist takeover as well as to protect American lives.

**May 16**—A four-member U.S. fact-finding team arrives in Santo Domingo in an unsuccessful attempt to help form a coalition government.

**June 3**—Major Edward White takes the first U.S. "space walk."

**June 7**—The Supreme Court voids a Connecticut law prohibiting the use of birth control devices.

**June 8**—The State Department reports that Johnson has authorized the use of U.S. troops in direct combat if the South Vietnamese army requests assistance.

**June 15**—Three unions begin a 76-day maritime strike idling more than 100 ships in Atlantic and Gulf ports.

**June 17**—B-52s stage the first mass bombing raid in South Vietnam.

**June 30**—The Senate Rules Committee recommends indicting Bobby Baker for violation of conflict-of-interest laws.

**July 27**—The 17-nation disarmament conference resumes talks in Geneva.

**July 27**—Johnson signs a bill requiring health warnings on cigarette packages after January 1, 1966.

**July 30**—Johnson signs the Medicare bill, providing medical care for the aged financed through the Social Security system.

**August 4**—A proposed constitutional amendment to modify the Supreme Court's "one-person, one-vote" decision fails to receive a two-thirds majority in the Senate.

**August 6**—Johnson signs the voting rights bill suspending the use of literacy and other voter qualification tests.

**August 10**—Johnson signs the housing and urban development bill, providing $30 million in rent subsidies for low-income families.

**August 11**—Rioting breaks out in the predominantly African-American Watts section of Los Angeles. In a five-day period over 30 people are killed in the United States's most destructive outbreak of racial violence in decades.

**September 3**—A three-year steel pact is signed immediately before a nationwide strike is scheduled to begin.

**September 4**—The United States recognizes a provisional government established in the Dominican Republic with the support of both junta and insurgent representatives.

**September 7**—The United States suspends military aid to India and Pakistan as a result of the two countries' border clash.

**September 9**—Johnson signs a bill creating the Department of Housing and Urban Development.

**October 3**—Johnson signs an immigration bill eliminating the 1924 national origins quota system.

**October 11**—An administration effort to repeal Section 14(b) of the Taft-Hartley Act fails when the Senate rejects a motion to invoke cloture against a filibuster.

**October 15–16**—Nationwide demonstrations against U.S. policy in Vietnam are held in about 40 cities.

**October 22**—Johnson signs a highway beautification bill.

**November**—Ralph Nader's indictment of the auto industry, *Unsafe at Any Speed*, is published.

**November 8**—Johnson signs a higher education bill providing a three-year $23 billion program of college scholarships and college building construction grants.

**November 15**—The Supreme Court holds unconstitutional a provision of a 1950 law requiring members of the Communist Party to register with the federal government.

**November 27**—In a demonstration initiated by the National Committee for a Sane Nuclear Policy (SANE), over 15,000 marchers converge on the White House to protest U.S. involvement in Vietnam.

**December 5**—The Federal Reserve Board raises the discount rate from 4 percent to 4 1/2 percent.

**December 15**—*Gemini 6* and *Gemini 7* achieve man's first rendezvous in space.

**December 24–January 31**—The U.S. halts the bombing of North Vietnam in an effort to get peace talks started.

**December 31**—U.S. forces in Vietnam total 184,314.

# 1966

**January 1**—New York City transit workers begin a 13-day strike.

**January 7**—Martin Luther King, Jr., announces the beginning of a campaign in Chicago to attack the problems of inner-city residents.

**January 13**—Johnson nominates Robert C. Weaver as secretary of housing and urban development, making Weaver the first African American ever to serve in a cabinet post.

**January 17**—Four nuclear devices are released in a collision between a B-52 and a refueling tanker over Spain. All are recovered by April 7.

**January 19**—Johnson asks Congress for a supplemental appropriation of $12.8 billion mainly for the war in Vietnam.

**February 4**—The Senate Foreign Relations Committee begins televised hearings on U.S. policy in Vietnam.

**February 6–8**—At the Honolulu Conference Johnson announces renewed emphasis on "The Other War," the attempt to provide the Vietnamese rural population with local security and develop positive economic and social programs to win their active support.

**March 1**—The Senate rejects an amendment repealing the Tonkin Gulf Resolution.

**March 7**—The Supreme Court upholds the constitutionality of seven major provisions of the 1965 Voting Rights Act.

**March 16**—*Gemini 8* achieves the first successful space docking and then makes a safe emergency landing in the Pacific.

**March 21**—In three decisions the Supreme Court upholds the obscenity convictions of Ralph

Ginzburg and another New York publisher but rules the 18th-century novel *Fanny Hill* is not obscene.

**March 25**—The Supreme Court voids the use of poll taxes for state elections.

**April 12**—B-52 bombers are used for the first time against targets in North Vietnam.

**April 21**—Senate Foreign Relations Committee chair J. William Fulbright warns that the United States is "succumbing to the arrogance of power."

**April 24**—The Newspaper Guild begins a strike against New York's World-Journal-Tribune Inc., which lasts until September 11. It is the longest newspaper strike in a major city.

**April 27**—The Interstate Commerce Commission authorizes a merger between the Pennsylvania and New York Central railroads, the biggest corporate merger to date in U.S. history.

**April 30**—The U.S. shells Communist targets in Cambodia.

**June 1**—The White House Conference on Civil Rights opens.

**June 2**—*Surveyor I* lands on the Moon.

**June 3–13**—One of the largest battles of the Vietnam War is fought in the Central Highlands province of Kontum.

**June 6**—James Meredith is shot during a protest march in Mississippi.

**June 7**—Stokely Carmichael, of the Student Nonviolent Coordinating Committee demands "Black Power."

**June 13**—The Supreme Court lays down guidelines for police interrogation of arrested suspects in *Miranda v. Arizona.*

**June 28**—Johnson begins removal of U.S. forces as inter-American peacekeeping troops start leaving the Dominican Republic.

**June 29**—Johnson orders the bombing of oil installations at Haiphong and Hanoi.

**July 12**—Racial violence breaks out in Chicago. During the summer of 1966 over 20 cities, including New York, Los Angeles, Atlanta, Omaha, and Detroit, experience riots or serious disturbances.

**August 26**—Civil rights leaders and Chicago officials agree on a program to end housing discrimination in Chicago.

**August 30**—The United Farm Workers, headed by Cesar Chavez, win a representation election at the DiGiorgio Corporation in central California.

**September 18–24**—The U.S. records 970 casualties in Vietnam, a record for a single week.

**September 19**—An administration civil rights bill, including a controversial open housing provision, fails when the Senate refuses to invoke cloture against a filibuster.

**September 23**—Johnson signs a bill increasing the minimum wage to $1.60 an hour and extending coverage to 8 million additional workers.

**October**—The Black Panther Party is formed by Huey P. Newton and Bobby Seale in Oakland, California.

**October 15**—Johnson signs the bill creating the Department of Transportation.

**October 26**—Johnson visits U.S. troops in Vietnam, which number over 400,000.

**November 3**—Johnson signs an omnibus urban assistance and housing bill establishing a Demonstration Cities program.

**November 8**—President Johnson signs an anti-inflation act that suspends the 7 percent investment tax credit.

**November 8**—The Republicans gain three Senate seats, 47 House seats, and eight governorships in the mid-term elections. Edward W. Brooke is elected U.S. senator from Massachusetts, becoming the first black elected to the Senate in 95 years.

**November 14**—By a vote of 5 to 4, the Supreme Court for the first time sustains the state convictions of nonviolent civil rights demonstrators.

**November 29**—Johnson announces that $5.3 billion in federal programs are being canceled or postponed to save money.

**December 2–4**—Johnson escalates the fighting in Vietnam by ordering heavy air strikes on the Hanoi area.

# 1967

**January 10**—The House repeals the 21-day rule, adopted in January 1965.

**January 27**—Astronauts Virgil I. Grissom, Edward H. White, and Roger B. Chaffee are killed by a fire in their *Apollo I* capsule during ground tests at Cape Kennedy.

**January 27**—The United States signs a 62-nation treaty prohibiting the orbiting of nuclear weapons and forbidding territorial claims on the Moon and the planets.

**January 29**—Bobby Baker is convicted of income tax evasion, theft, and conspiracy to defraud the government.

**February 11**—The Twenty-fifth Amendment to the Constitution, dealing with presidential disability and providing for the filling of a vice presidential vacancy, is ratified.

**February 13**—The National Student Association admits that it received funds form the Central Intelligence Agency between 1952 and 1966 for projects overseas.

**March 1**—The House of Representatives votes 307-116 to deny Adam Clayton Powell his seat in Congress for improper use of government funds and other misconduct.

**March 6**—Svetlana Alliluyeva, Stalin's only child, asks asylum at the U.S. embassy in New Delhi.

**March 9**—Johnson asks Congress to restore the 7 percent investment tax credit sooner than originally planned.

**April 4**—The military announces the loss of the 500th plane over North Vietnam since bombing raids began in 1964.

**April 15**—One hundred thousand in New York City and 50,000 in San Francisco march to protest U.S. policy in Vietnam.

**May 15**—The Supreme Court extends to children in juvenile court proceedings the right to counsel and other procedural safeguards afforded in adult trials.

**May 17**—Sixteen senators critical of administration policy in Vietnam warn Hanoi, in a letter drafted by Senator Frank Church, that they are opposed to unilateral American withdrawal.

**May 19**—U.S. planes bomb a power plant in Hanoi in the fist strike at the heart of North Vietnam's capital.

**May 29**—The Office of Civil Operations and Revolutionary Development Support (CORDS) is formed, placing the Vietnam pacification program under military control.

**June 5**—War breaks out in the Middle East between Israel and Egypt, Jordan, and Syria.

**June 6**—Johnson praises a UN Security Council resolution calling for a cease-fire in the Mideast war.

**June 19**—U.S. District Court judge J. Skelly Wright orders an end to de facto segregation in Washington, D.C., public schools by the opening of the autumn term.

**June 23**—The Senate votes 92-5 to censure Connecticut senator Thomas Dodd for improper use of campaign funds.

**June 23–25**—Johnson and Soviet premier Alexei Kosygin hold a summit conference at Glassboro State College in New Jersey.

**July 6**—Congress's Joint Economic Committee issues a report stating that the Vietnam War created "havoc" in the U.S. economy during 1966 and predicting that the war will cost $4 to $6 billion more in 1967 than the administration's request.

**July 12**—Rioting breaks out in Newark, New Jersey. During the "long, hot summer" of 1967, racial violence disrupts 50 American cities.

**July 17**—Congress enacts an administration bill ending a two-day national railroad strike and providing for a compulsory settlement by a presidentially appointed panel if no voluntary agreement is reached within 90 days.

**July 23**—In a plebiscite Puerto Rico chooses to remain a commonwealth of the United States.

**July 23**—A riot breaks out in Detroit, Michigan, resulting in 43 dead.

**July 24**—Federal troops enter Detroit to help curb disorders.

**July 29**—Johnson appoints a special advisory committee on civil disorders to probe urban race riots.

**August 3**—Johnson asks Congress to enact a 10 percent income tax surcharge to combat inflation.

**September 29**—In a speech at San Antonio, Texas, Johnson modifies the U.S. position on Vietnam negotiations, saying that the United States is willing to stop all bombing if it will promptly lead to negotiations.

**October 2**—Thurgood Marshall is sworn in as the first African-American Supreme Court justice.

**October 13**—Johnson issues an executive order barring sex discrimination in government jobs and in employment with federal contractors and subcontractors.

**October 18**—The House Ways and Means Committee votes 20-5 to postpone action on the 10 percent surcharge recommended by Johnson and demands budget cuts as well.

**October 21**—An estimated 50,000 persons participate in a march to the Pentagon to protest U.S. policy in Vietnam.

**November 7**—Black mayors are elected in two northern cities, Carl B. Stokes in Cleveland and Richard G. Hatcher in Gary, Indiana.

**November 21**—General William C. Westmoreland declares in a speech before the National Press Club in Washington, D.C., that if progresses continue in Vietnam, U.S. forces could begin coming home in 18 to 24 months.

**November 22**—In one of the bloodiest battles of the Vietnam War, U.S. forces capture Hill 875 near Dak To.

**November 23–28**—U.S., UN, and NATO representatives meet with Turkish and Greek leaders in an effort to avert a war over Cyprus. An agreement is reached December 1.

**November 30**—Senator Eugene McCarthy (D-Minn.) announces that he will challenge Johnson in five or six Democratic primaries because of his concern "that the administration seems to have set no limit on the price it's willing to pay for a military victory" in Vietnam.

**December 18**—The Supreme Court holds electronic surveillance subject to the Fourth Amendment and rules judicial warrants necessary to authorize bugging.

**December 31**—U.S. forces in South Vietnam reach 485,600.

# 1968

**January 3**—Minnesota senator Eugene McCarthy announces that he will enter the New Hampshire Democratic presidential primary.

**January 23**—North Korea captures the U.S. spy ship *Pueblo.*

**January 30**—During the Tet holiday the Communists launched a major offensive with attacks in 150 cities, towns, and hamlets.

**February 1**—Richard M. Nixon formally announces his candidacy for the Republican presidential nomination.

**February 8**—Former Alabama governor George Wallace announces he will enter the presidential race as a third-party candidate.

**February 20**—The Senate Foreign Relations Committee begins hearings on the events leading to the passage of the Tonkin Gulf Resolution.

**February 27**—U.S. military leaders request 206,000 additional troops for Vietnam.

**March 2**—The National Advisory Commission on Civil Disorders (Kerner Commission) issues its final report, asserting that "white racism" is chiefly responsible for black riots and warning that the United States is "moving toward two societies, one black, one white—separate and unequal."

**March 11–12**—Secretary of State Dean Rusk testifies before the Senate Foreign Relations Committee on American policy in Vietnam.

**March 12**—In the New Hampshire Democratic primary, Eugene McCarthy wins a surprising 41.4 percent of the vote against Johnson's 49.6 percent.

**March 16**—New York senator Robert Kennedy announces his candidacy for the Democratic presidential nomination.

**March 17**—Representatives of the United States and the London Gold Pool work out a two-price system for gold.

**March 22**—Johnson announces that General William Westmoreland will leave his post as commander of U.S. forces in Vietnam to become army chief of staff.

**March 25–26**—The Senior Advisory Group on Vietnam commonly known as the "Wise Men," meets to discuss proposed troop increases and recommends against further escalation.

**March 31**—In a televised speech Johnson announces that he has ordered a partial halt to the bombing of North Vietnam. He also announces that he will not run for reelection.

**April 1**—The Supreme Court extends the "one person, one vote" standard of apportionment to local units of government that elect representatives on a district basis.

**April 4**—Martin Luther King, Jr., is assassinated in Memphis, Tennessee. The killing leads to riots in Washington, Chicago, and numerous other cities.

**April 11**—24,500 military reservists are called to active duty.

**April 11**—Johnson signs a civil rights bill barring discrimination in the sale or rental of about 80 percent of the nation's housing. The bill also contains antiriot and gun control provisions.

**April 23**—Students for a Democratic Society (SDS) at Columbia University leads the occupation of the college dean's office to protest proposed construction of a gymnasium by the university on a Harlem park site.

**April 26**—Two hundred thousand students in the New York metropolitan area boycott classes to protest the Vietnam War.

**April 27**—Vice President Hubert Humphrey announces that he will seek the Democratic presidential nomination.

**April 30**—New York governor Nelson Rockefeller announces that he will seek the Republican presidential nomination.

**May 2**—The Poor People's March departs Memphis for Washington, D.C. Later in the month 3,000 marchers camp near the Washington Monument on a site called "Resurrection City."

**May 3**—Johnson announces that the United States and North Vietnam have agreed to begin formal peace talks in Paris.

**May 6**—Norman Mailer's *Armies of the Night* is published.

**May 13**—Vietnam peace talks begin in Paris.

**May 28**—Eugene McCarthy wins the Oregon Democratic presidential primary with 45 percent of the vote.

**May 29**—Johnson signs a truth-in-lending bill.

**June 4**—Robert F. Kennedy wins the California Democratic presidential primary with 46 percent of the vote.

**June 5**—Sirhan Bishara Sirhan assassinates Robert F. Kennedy in Los Angeles.

**June 13**—President Johnson ratifies the U.S.-USSR consular treaty.

**June 13**—Chief Justice Earl Warren submits his resignation effective upon the approval of a successor. On June 26 Johnson nominates Justice Abe Fortas as Warren's replacement.

**June 17**—The Supreme Court rules that an 1866 civil rights law prohibits racial discrimination in the sale and rental of housing and other property.

**June 19**—Johnson signs an omnibus crime control and safe streets bill.

**June 24**—The police clear Resurrection City after the protesters' permit expires.

**June 28**—Johnson signs the income tax surcharge bill, which Congress had tied to a $6 billion budget cut.

**July 1**—Johnson signs the Nuclear Non-Proliferation Treaty.

**August 1**—Johnson signs a housing and urban development bill encouraging home ownership for low-income families.

**August 8**—The Republican National Convention nominates Richard M. Nixon for president on the first ballot. Maryland governor Spiro T. Agnew is chosen vice presidential candidate at the following session.

**August 10**—Senator George McGovern declares his candidacy for the Democratic presidential nomination.

**August 20**—The Credentials Committee of the Democratic National Convention votes to unseat the regular Mississippi delegation and seat instead a biracial challenge delegation.

**August 21**—Soviet troops invade Czechoslovakia.

**August 28**—Antiwar protestors clash with police outside the Democratic National Convention. Police tactics are denounced from the rostrum and floor of the convention.

**August 28**—Hubert Humphrey wins the Democratic nomination for president. Maine senator Edmund Muskie is chosen as his running mate the following day.

**September 23**—Agnew apologizes for having used the terms "Fat Jap" and "Polack" earlier in the month.

**October 2**—Abe Fortas asks Johnson to withdraw his name from consideration as chief justice following a filibuster by senators objecting to his advisory services to Johnson.

**October 31**—Johnson announces a halt to all bombing of North Vietnam as prelude to expanded peace talks.

**November 5**—Richard Nixon wins the presidential race with 43.4 percent of the popular vote and 301 out of 538 electoral votes.

**November 6**—San Francisco State College students shut down campus to protest suspension of an English instructor who is a member of the Black Panther Party.

**December 1**—The National Committee on the Causes and Prevention of Violence issues a report concluding that law enforcement officers at the Democratic National Convention in Chicago in August 1968 engaged in a "police riot."

**December 23**—North Korea releases the 82 crew members of the *Pueblo*.

**December 27**—*Apollo 8* completes a mission that included circling the Moon 10 times.

**December 31**—The total number of Americans killed in Vietnam in 1968 reaches 14,589.

## 1969

**January 14**—Johnson delivers his final State of the Union address.

**January 20**—Johnson leaves office; Richard M. Nixon is inaugurated as 37th President of the United States.

# Principal U.S. Government Officials of the Johnson Years

## Supreme Court

Earl Warren, Chief Justice 1953–69
Hugo L. Black 1937–71
William J. Brennan 1956–90
Tom C. Clark 1949–67
William O. Douglas 1939–75
Abe Fortas 1965–69

Arthur J. Goldberg 1962–65
John Marshall Harlan 1955–71
Thurgood Marshall, 1967–91
Potter Stewart 1958—81
Byron R. White 1962–93

## Executive Departments

**Department of Agriculture**
*Secretary of Agriculture*
   Orville L. Freeman, 1961–69
*Undersecretary*
   Charles S. Murphy, 1961–65
   John A. Schnittker, 1965–69
*Deputy Undersecretary*
   James L. Sundquist, 1963–65
*Assistant Secretary—Rural Development and
   Conservation*
   John A. Baker, 1962–69
*Assistant Secretary—Marketing Consumer Services*
   George L. Mehren, 1963–68
   Ted J. Davis, 1968–69
*Assistant Secretary—International Affairs*
   Roland R. Renne, 1963–65
   Dorothy H. Jacobson, 1964–69
*Assistant Secretary for Department Administration*
   Joseph M. Robertson, 1961–71

**Department of Commerce**
*Secretary of Commerce*
   Luther H. Hodges, 1961–65

John T. Connor, 1965–67
Alexander B. Trowbridge, 1967–68
Howard J. Samuels, (acting) 1968
Cyrus R. Smith, 1968–69
*Undersecretary*
   Franklin D. Roosevelt, Jr., 1963–65
   LeRoy Collins, 1965–66
   J. Herbert Holloman, (acting) 1967
   Howard J. Samuels, 1967–68
   Joseph W. Bartlett, 1968–69
*Undersecretary for Transportation*
   Clarence D. Martin, Jr., 1961–65
   Alan S. Boyd, 1965–67
   Reorganized under Department
      of Transportation, 1966
*Deputy Undersecretary for Transportation*
   Frank L. Barton, 1961–64
   Lowell K. Bridwell, 1964–67
   Reorganized under Department of
      Transportation, 1966
*Assistant Secretary for Administration*
   Herbert W. Klotz, 1962–65
   David R. Baldwin, 1965–69

*Assistant Secretary for Domestic and International Business*
  Jack N. Behrman, 1962–64
  Thomas G. Wyman, 1964–65
  Alexander B. Trowbridge, 1965–67
  Lawrence C. McQuade, 1967–69
*Assistant Secretary for Science and Technology*
  J. Herbert Holloman, 1962–67
  John F. Kincaid, 1967–69
*Assistant Secretary for Economic Affairs*
  Richard H. Holton, 1963–65
  Andrew F. Brimmer, 1965–66
  William H. Shaw, 1966–68
  William H. Chartener, 1968–70
*Assistant Secretary for Economic Development*
  Ross D. Davis, 1966–69

## Defense Department

*Secretary of Defense*
  Robert S. McNamara, 1961–68
  Clark M. Clifford, 1968–69
*Deputy Secretary of Defense*
  Roswell L. Gilpatric, 1961–64
  Cyrus R. Vance, 1964–67
  Paul H. Nitze, 1967–69
*Secretary of the Air Force*
  Eugene M. Zuckert, 1961–65
  Harold Brown, 1965–69
*Secretary of the Army*
  Cyrus R. Vance, 1962–64
  Stephen Ailes, 1964–65
  Stanley R. Resor, 1965–71
*Secretary of the Navy*
  Paul H. Nitze, 1963–67
  John T. McNaughton, 1967
  Paul R. Ignatius, 1967–69
*Assistant Secretary (Comptroller)*
  Charles J. Hitch, 1961–65
  Robert N. Anthony, 1965–68
  Robert C. Moot, 1968–73
*Assistant Secretary (Installations and Logistics)*
  Thomas D. Morris, 1961–64
  Paul R. Ignatius, 1964–67
  Thomas D. Morris, 1967–69
*Assistant Secretary (International Security Affairs)*
  William P. Bundy, 1963–64
  John T. McNaughton, 1964–67
  Paul C. Warnke, 1967–69
*Assistant Secretary (Manpower)*
  Norman S. Paul, 1962–65
  Thomas D. Morris, 1965–67

  Alfred B. Fitt, 1967–69
*Assistant Secretary (Public Affairs)*
  Arthur Sylvester, 1961–66
  Phil G. Goulding, 1967–69
*Assistant Secretary (Civil Defense)*
  Steuart L. Pittman, 1961–64
*Assistant Secretary (Administration)*
  Solis Horwitz, 1964–69
*Assistant Secretary (Systems Analysis)*
  Alain C. Enthoven, 1965–69
*Director of Defense Research and Engineering*
  Harold Brown, 1961–65
  John S. Foster, Jr., 1965–73

## Joint Chiefs of Staff

*Chair*
  Gen. Maxwell D. Taylor, U.S. Army, 1962–64
  Gen. Earle G. Wheeler, U.S. Army 1964–70
*Chief of Staff, U.S. Army*
  Gen. Earle G. Wheeler, 1962–64
  Gen. Harold K. Johnson, 1964–68
  Gen. William C. Westmoreland, 1968–72
*Chief of Naval Operations*
  Adm. David L. McDonald, 1963–67
  Adm. Thomas H. Moorer, 1967–70
*Chief of Staff, U.S. Air Force*
  Gen. Curtis E. LeMay, 1961–65
  Gen. John P. McConnell, 1965–69
*Commandant of the Marine Corps*
  Gen. David M. Shoup, 1960–63
  Gen. Wallace M. Greene, Jr., 1964–68
  Gen. Leonard F. Chapman, Jr., 1968–72

## Department of Health, Education and Welfare

*Secretary of Health, Education and Welfare*
  Anthony J. Celebrezze, 1962–65
  John W. Gardner, 1965–68
  Wilbur J. Cohen, 1968–69
*Undersecretary*
  Ivan A. Nestingen, 1961–65
  Wilbur J. Cohen, 1965–68
  James H. McCrocklin, 1968–69
*Assistant Secretary*
  James M. Quigley, 1961–66
*Administrative Assistant Secretary*
  Rufus E. Miles, Jr., 1961–65
  Donald F. Simpson, 1966–69
*Assistant Secretary (Education)*
  Francis Keppel, 1965–66
  Paul A. Miller, 1966–68
  Lynn M. Bartlett, 1968–69

*Assistant Secretary (Health and Scientific Affairs)*
Philip R. Lee, 1965–69
*Assistant Secretary (Individual and Family Service)*
Lisle C. Carter, Jr., 1966–68
*Assistant Secretary (Comptroller)*
James F. Kelly, 1966–70
*Assistant Secretary (Program Coordination)*
William Gorham, 1965–68
Reorganized as Planning and Evaluation 1968
*Assistant Secretary (Planning and Education)*
Alice M. Rivlin, 1968–69

## Department of Housing and Urban Development*
*Secretary*
Robert C. Weaver, 1966–68
Robert C. Wood, 1969
*Undersecretary*
Robert C. Wood, 1966–68
*Deputy Undersecretary for Policy Analysis and Program Evaluation*
William B. Ross, 1966–69
*Assistant Secretary for Mortgage Credit and Federal Housing Commissioner*
Philip N. Brownstein, 1966–69
*Assistant Secretary for Metropolitan Development*
Charles M. Haar, 1966–69
*Assistant Secretary for Renewal and Housing Assistance*
Don Hummel, 1966–69
*Assistant Secretary for Demonstrations and Intergovernmental Relations*
H. Ralph Taylor, 1966–69
*Assistant Secretary for Administration*
Dwight A. Ink, 1966–69
*Director, Office for Equal Opportunity*
Walter B. Lewis, 1968–69
*Established by law, September 9, 1965

## Department of the Interior
*Secretary of the Interior*
Stewart L. Udall, 1961–69
*Undersecretary*
James K. Carr, 1961–64
John A. Carver, Jr., 1965–66
Charles F. Luce, 1966–67
David S. Black, 1967–69
*Assistant Secretary—Fish and Wildlife*
Frank P. Briggs, 1961–65
Reorganized as Fish and Wildlife and Parks, 1965

Stanley A. Cain, 1965–68
Clarence F. Pautzke, 1968–69
*Assistant Secretary—Mineral Resources*
John M. Kelly, 1961–65
J. Cordell Moore, 1965–69
*Assistant Secretary—Public Land Management*
John A. Carver, Jr., 1961–64
Harry R. Anderson, 1965–69
*Assistant Secretary—Water and Power Development*
Kenneth Holum, 1961–69
*Assistant Secretary—Walter Pollution Control*
Frank C. DiLuzio, 1966–67
Max N. Edwards, 1968–69
*Administrative Assistant Secretary*
D. Otis Beasley, 1952–65
Robert C. McConnell, 1967–69

## Department of Justice
*Attorney General*
Robert F. Kennedy, 1961–64
Nicholas deB. Katzenbach, 1965–66
Ramsey Clark, 1967–69
*Deputy Attorney General*
Nicholas deB. Katzenbach, 1962–64
Ramsey Clark, 1965–67
Warren M. Christopher, 1967–69
*Solicitor General*
Archibald Cox, 1961–65
Thurgood Marshall, 1965–67
Erwin N. Griswold, 1967–73
*Assistant Attorney General/Antitrust Division*
William H. Orrick, Jr., 1963–65
Donald F. Turner, 1965–68
Edwin M. Zimmerman, 1968–69
*Assistant Attorney General/Civil Division*
John W. Douglas, 1963–66
Harold B. Sanders, Jr., 1966–67
Carl Eardley, (acting) 1967
Edwin L. Weisl, 1967–69
*Assistant Attorney General/Criminal Division*
Herbert J. Miller, Jr., 1961–65
Fred M. Vinson, Jr., 1965–69
*Assistant Attorney General/Internal Security Division*
J. Walter Yeagley, 1959–70
*Assistant Attorney General/Lands Division*
Ramsey Clark, 1961–65
Edwin L. Weisl, 1965–67
Clyde O. Martz, 1967–69
*Assistant Attorney General/Tax Division*
Louis F. Oberdorfer, 1961–65
Mitchell Rogovin, 1966–69

*Assistant Attorney General/Civil Rights Division*
Burke Marshall, 1961–65
John Doar, 1965–67
Stephen J. Pollak, 1967–69
*Assistant Attorney General/Office of Legal Counsel*
Norbert A. Schlei, 1962–66
Frank Wozencraft, 1966–69
*Assistant Attorney General/Administration*
Ernest C. Friesen, Jr., 1966–68
Leo Pellerzi, 1968–73

## Department of Labor
*Secretary of Labor*
W. Willard Wirtz, 1962–69
*Undersecretary*
John F. Henning, 1962–67
James J. Reynolds, 1967–68
*Deputy Undersecretary*
Millard Cass, 1955–71
*Assistant Secretary for Labor-Management Relations*
James J. Reynolds, 1961–67
Thomas R. Donahue, 1967–69
*Assistant Secretary for International Labor Affairs*
George L. P. Weaver, 1961–69
*Assistant Secretary for Labor Standards*
Esther Peterson, 1961–69
*Assistant Secretary for Policy Planning and Research*
Daniel P. Moynihan, 1963–65
*Assistant Secretary for Manpower*
Stanley H. Ruttenberg, 1966–69

## Post Office Department
*Post Master General*
John A. Gronouski, 1963–65
Lawrence F. O'Brien, 1965–68
W. Marvin Watson, 1968–69
*Deputy Post Master General*
Sidney W. Bishop, 1963–64
Frederick C. Belen, 1964–69
*Assistant Post Master General/Bureau of Operations*
Frederick C. Belen, 1961–64
William M. McMillan, 1964–69
*Assistant Post Master General/Bureau of Transportation*
William J. Hartigan, 1963–68
Frederick E. Batrus, 1968–69
*Assistant Post Master General/Bureau of Finance*
Ralph W. Nicholson, 1961–69
*Assistant Post Master General/Bureau of Facilities*
Amos J. Coffman, (acting) 1963–64
Tyler Abell, 1964–67

John L. O'Marra, 1967–69
*Assistant Post Master General/Bureau of Personnel*
Richard J. Murphy, 1961–69
*Assistant Post Master General/Research and Engineering*
Leo S. Packer, 1966–69
*Assistant Post Master General/General Counsel*
Timothy J. May, 1966–69

## State Department
*Secretary of State*
Dean Rusk, 1961–69
*Undersecretary*
George W. Ball, 1961–66
Nicholas deB. Katzenbach, 1966–69
*Undersecretary for Economic Affairs*
Thomas C. Mann, 1965–66
*Undersecretary for Political Affairs*
W. Averell Harriman, 1963–65
Eugene V. Rostow, 1966–69
*Deputy Undersecretary for Administration*
William J. Crockett, 1963–67
Idar Rimestad, 1967–69
*Deputy Undersecretary for Political Affairs*
U. Alexis Johnson, 1961–64
Llewellyn E. Thompson (acting), 1964–65
U. Alexis Johnson, 1965–66
Foy D. Kohler, 1966–67
Charles E. Bohlen, 1967–69
*Assistant Secretary for Public Affairs*
Robert J. Manning, 1962–64
James L. Greenfield, 1964–66
Dixon Donnelley, 1966–69
*Assistant Secretary for Congressional Relations*
Frederick G. Dutton, 1962–64
Douglas MacArthur II, 1965–67
William B. Macomber, Jr., 1967–69
*Assistant Secretary for Inter-American Affairs*
Thomas C. Mann, 1963–65
Jack H. Vaughn, 1965–66
Lincoln Gordon, 1966–67
Covey T. Oliver, 1967–69
*Assistant Secretary for European Affairs*
William R. Tyler, 1962–65
John M. Leddy, 1965–69
*Assistant Secretary for Far Easter Affairs*
Roger Hilsman, Jr., 1963–64
William P. Bundy, 1964–69
*Assistant Secretary for Near Eastern and South Asian Affairs*
Phillips Talbot, 1961–65

Raymond A. Hare, 1965–66
William J. Handley, (acting) 1966–67
Lucius D. Battle, 1967–68
Parker T. Hart, 1968–69
*Assistant Secretary for African Affairs*
G. Mennen Williams, 1961–66
Joseph Palmer II, 1966–69
*Assistant Secretary for International Organization Affairs*
Harlan Cleveland, 1961–65
Joseph J. Sisco, 1965–69
*Assistant Secretary for Administration*
Dwight J. Porter, 1963–65
*Assistant Secretary for Educational and Cultural Affairs*
Lucius D. Battle, 1962–64
Harry C. McPherson, Jr., 1964–65
Charles Frankel, 1965–67
Edward D. Re, 1968–69
*Assistant Secretary for Economic Affairs*
G. Griffith Johnson, Jr., 1962–65
Anthony M. Solomon, 1965–69

## Department of Transportation*

*Secretary*
Alan S. Boyd, 1967–69
*Undersecretary*
Everett Hutchinson, 1967–68
John E. Robson, 1968–69
*Deputy Undersecretary*
Paul L. Sitton, 1967–68
*Assistant Secretary for Policy Development*
Maurice Cecil Mackey, Jr., 1967–69
*Assistant Secretary for Public Affairs*
John L. Sweeney, 1967–69

*Assistant Secretary for International Affairs*
Donald G. Agger, 1967–69
*Assistant Secretary for Administration*
Alan L. Dean, 1967–71
*Assistant Secretary for Research and Technology*
Frank W. Lehan, 1967–69
*Established by law, October 15, 1966

## Department of the Treasury

*Secretary of the Treasury*
Douglas Dillon, 1961–65
Henry H. Fowler, 1965–68
Joseph W. Barr, 1968–69
*Undersecretary*
Henry H. Fowler, 1961–64
Joseph W. Barr, 1965–68
*Undersecretary for Monetary Affairs*
Robert V. Roosa, 1961–64
Frederick L. Deming, 1965–69
*Deputy Undersecretary for Monetary Affairs*
Paul A. Volcker, 1963–65
Peter D. Sternlight, 1965–67
Frank W. Schiff, 1968–69
*Assistant Secretaries*
Stanley S. Surrey, 1961–69
James A. Reed, 1961–65
John C. Bullitt, 1962–64
Robert A. Wallace, 1961–69
Merlyn N. Trued, (acting) 1964–65; 1965–66
William T. Davis, Jr., 1965–68
Winthrop Knowlton, 1966–68
Joseph M. Bowman, Jr., 1968–69
John R. Petty, 1968–72

# REGULATORY COMMISSION AND INDEPENDENT AGENCIES

## Atomic Energy Commission

Mary I. Bunting, 1964–65
Francesco Costagliola, 1968–69
Wilfrid E. Johnson, 1966–72
Samuel M. Nabrit, 1966–67
John G. Palfrey, 1962–66
James T. Ramey, 1962–73
Glenn T. Seaborg, 1961–71; Chair, 1961–71
Gerald F. Tape, 1963–69
Robert E. Wilson, 1960–64

## Civil Aeronautics Board

John G. Adams, 1965–71
Alan S. Boyd, 1959–65; Chair, 1961–65
John H. Crooker, Jr., 1968–69; Chair, 1968–69
Whitney Gillilland, 1959–76
Chan Gurney, 1951–65; Chair, 1954
G. Joseph Minetti, 1956–74
Charles S. Murphy, 1965–68; Chair, 1965–68
Robert T. Murphy, 1961–77

## Federal Communications Commission

Robert T. Bartley, 1952–72
Kenneth A. Cox, 1963–70
Frederick W. Ford, 1957–64; Chair, 1960–61
E. William Henry, 1962–66; Chair, 1963–66
Rosel H. Hyde, 1946–69; Chair, 1953–54, 1966–69
Nicholas Johnson, 1966–73
H. Rex Lee, 1968–73
Robert E. Lee, 1953–81; Chair, 1981
Lee Loevinger, 1963–68
James J. Wadsworth, 1965–69

## Federal Power Commission

Carl E. Bagge, 1965–70
David S. Black, 1963–66
Albert B. Brooke, Jr., 1968–75
John A. Carver, Jr., 1966–72
Lawrence J. O'Connor, Jr., 1961–71
Charles R. Ross, 1961–68
Joseph C. Swidler, 1961–65; Chair, 1961–65
Lee C. White, 1966–69; Chair, 1966–69
Harold C. Woodward, 1962–64

## Federal Reserve Board

C. Canby Balderston, 1954–66
Andrew F. Brimmer, 1966–74
J. Dewey Daane, 1963–74

Sherman J. Maisel, 1965–72
William McC. Martin, Jr., 1951–70; Chair, 1951–70
A. L. Mills, Jr., 1952–65
George W. Mitchell, 1961–76
James L. Robertson, 1952–73
Charles N. Shepardson, 1955–67
William W. Sherrill, 1967–71

## Federal Trade Commission

Sigurd Anderson, 1955–64
Paul R. Dixon, 1961–81; Chair, 1961–69
Philip Elman, 1961–70
A. Leon Higginbotham, 1962–64
Mary G. Jones, 1964–73
Everette MacIntyre, 1961–73
James M. Nicholson, 1967–69
John R. Reilly, 1964–67

## Securities and Exchange Commission

Hamer H. Budge, 1964–70; Chair, 1969–71
William L. Cary, 1961–64, Chair, 1961–64
Manuel F. Cohen, 1961–69; Chair, 1964–69
Hugh F. Owens, 1964–73
Richard B. Smith, 1967–71
Francis M. Wheat, 1964–69
Jack M. Whitney II, 1961–64
Byron D. Woodside, 1960–67

# HOUSE OF REPRESENTATIVES

## Alabama

George W. Andrews (D) 1944–71
Tom Bevill (D) 1967–97
Carl Elliot (D) 1949–65
George M. Grant (D) 1938–65
George Huddleston, Jr. (D) 1955–65
Robert E. Jones (D) 1947–77
William Nichols (D) 1967–88
Albert Rains (D) 1945–65
Kenneth A. Roberts (D) 1951–65
Armistead J. Selden, Jr. (D) 1953–69
Glenn Andrews (R) 1965–67
John H. Buchanan (R) 1965–81
William L. Dickinson (R) 1965–93
Jack Edwards (R) 1965–85
James D. Martin (R) 1965–67

## Alaska

Ralph J. Rivers (D) 1959–66
Howard W. Pollock (R) 1967–71

## Arizona

George F. Senner, Jr. (D) 1963–67
Morris K. Udall (D) 1961–91
John J. Rhodes (R) 1953–83
Sam Steiger (R) 1967–77

## Arkansas

E. C. Gathings (D) 1939–69
Oren Harris (D) 1941–66
Wilbur D. Mills (D) 1939–77
David Pryor (D) 1966–73

James W. Trimble (D) 1945–67
John Paul Hammerschmidt (R) 1967–93

## California
George E. Brown, Jr. (D) 1963–71; 1973–99
Everett G. Burkhalter (D) 1963–65
Philip Burton (D) 1964–83
Ronald B. Cameron (D) 1963–67
Jeffery Cohelan (D) 1959–71
James C. Corman (D) 1961–81
Ken W. Dyal (D) 1965–67
Don Edwards (D) 1963–95
Harlan Hagen (D) 1953–67
Richard T. Hanna (D) 1963–74
Augustus F. Hawkins (D) 1963–91
Chet Holifield (D) 1943–74
Harold T. Johnson (D) 1959–81
Cecil R. King (D) 1942–69
Robert L. Leggett (D) 1963–79
John J. McFall (D) 1957–78
George P. Miller (D) 1945–73
John E. Moss (D) 1953–78
Thomas M. Rees (D) 1965–77
James Roosevelt (D) 1955–65
Edward R. Roybal (D) 1963–93
John F. Shelley (D) 1949–64
Harry R. Sheppard (D) 1937–65
B. F. Sisk (D) 1955–79
John V. Tunney (D) 1965–71
Lionel Van Deerlin (D) 1963–81
Jerome R. Waldie (D) 1966–75
Charles H. Wilson (D) 1963–81
John F. Baldwin, Jr. (R) 1955–66
Alphonso Bell (R) 1961–77
Don H. Clausen (R) 1963–83
Del Clawson (R) 1963–78
Charles S. Gubser (R) 1953–74
Craig Hosmer (R) 1953–74
Glenard P. Lipscomb (R) 1953–70
Paul N. McCloskey, Jr. (R) 1967–83
William S. Mailliard (R) 1953–74
Pat M. Martin (R) 1963–65
Robert B. Mathias (R) 1967–75
Jerry L. Pettis (R) 1967–75
Edwin Reinecke (R) 1965–69
H. Allen Smith (R) 1957–73
Burt L. Talcott (R) 1963–77
Charles M. Teague (R) 1955–74
James B. Utt (R) 1953–70
Charles E. Wiggins (R) 1967–79

Bob Wilson (R) 1953–81
J. Arthur Younger (R) 1953–67

## Colorado
Wayne N. Aspinall (D) 1949–73
Frank E. Evans (R) 1965–79
Roy H. McVicker (D) 1965–67
Byron G. Rogers (D) 1951–71
Donald G. Brotzman (R) 1963–65, 1967–75
J. Edgar Chenoweth (R) 1941–49; 1951–65

## Connecticut
Emilio Q. Daddario (D) 1959–71
Robert N. Giaimo (D) 1959–81
Bernard F. Grabowski (D) 1963–67
Donald J. Irwin (D) 1959–61; 1965–69
John S. Monagan (D) 1959–73
William L. St. Onge (D) 1963–70
Thomas J. Meskill (R) 1967–71
Abner W. Sibal (R) 1961–65

## Delaware
Harris B. McDowell, Jr. (D) 1955–57; 1959–67
William V. Roth, Jr. (R) 1967–70

## Florida
Charles E. Bennett (D) 1949–93
Dante B. Fascell (D) 1955–93
Don Fuqua (D) 1963–87
Sam M. Gibbons (D) 1963–97
James A. Haley (D) 1953–77
A. Sydney Herlong, Jr. (D) 1949–69
D. R. (Billy) Matthews (D) 1953–67
Claude Pepper (D) 1963–89
Paul G. Rogers (D) 1955–79
Robert L. F. (Bob) Sikes (D) 1945–79
J. Herbert Burke (R) 1967–79
William C. Cramer (R) 1955–71
Edward J. Gurney (R) 1963–69

## Georgia
Jack Brinkley (D) 1967–83
John W. Davis (D) 1961–75
John F. Flynt, Jr. (D) 1954–79
E. L. Forrester (D) 1951–65
G. Elliot Hagan (D) 1961–73
Phil M. Landrum (D) 1953–77
James A. Mackay (D) 1965–67
Maston E. O'Neal, Jr. (D) 1965–71

J. L. Pilcher (D) 1953–65
Robert G. Stephens, Jr. (D) 1961–77
W. S. Stuckey, Jr. (D) 1967–77
J. Russell Tuten (D) 1963–67
Carl Vinson (D) 1914–65
Charles L. Weltner (D) 1963–67
Benjamin B. Blackburn (R) 1965–75
Howard H. (Bo) Callaway (R) 1965–67
Fletcher Thompson (R) 1967–73

## Hawaii
Thomas P. Gill (D) 1963–65
Spark M. Matsunaga (D) 1963–77
Patsy T. Mink (D) 1965–77; 1990–2002

## Idaho
Ralph R. Harding (D) 1961–65
Compton I. White, Jr. (D) 1963–67
George V. Hansen (R) 1965–69; 1975–85
James A. McClure (R) 1967–73

## Illinois
Frank Annunzio (D) 1965–93
William L. Dawson (D) 1943–70
Edward R. Finnegan (D) 1961–64
Kenneth J. Gray (D) 1955–74
John C. Kluczynski (D) 1951–75
Roland V. Libonati (D) 1957–65
William T. Murphy (D) 1959–71
Thomas J. O'Brien, (D) 1933–39, 1943–64
Barratt O'Hara (D) 1949–51; 1953–69
Melvin Price (D) 1945–88
Roman C. Pucinski (D) 1959–73
Daniel J. Ronan (D) 1965–69
Dan Rostenkowski (D) 1959–95
Gale Schisler (D) 1965–67
George E. Shipley (D) 1959–79
Sidney R. Yates (D) 1949–63; 1965–99
John B. Anderson (R) 1961–81
Leslie C. Arends (R) 1935–74
Harold R. Collier (R) 1957–75
Edward J. Derwinski (R) 1959–83
John N. Erlenborn (R) 1965–85
Paul Findley (R) 1961–83
Elmer J. Hoffman (R) 1959–65
Robert McClory (R) 1963–83
Robert T. McLoskey (R) 1963–65
Robert H. Michel (R) 1957–95
Tom Railsback (R) 1967–83
Charlotte T. Reid (R) 1963–71

Donald Rumsfield (R) 1963–69
William L. Springer (R) 1951–73

## Indiana
John Brademas (D) 1959–81
Winfield K. Denton (D) 1949–53; 1955–66
Lee H. Hamilton (D) 1965–99
Andrew Jacobs, Jr. (D) 1965–73; 1975–97
Ray J. Madden (D) 1943–77
J. Edward Roush (D) 1959–69; 1971–77
E. Ross Adair (R) 1951–71
William G. Bray (R) 1951–75
Donald C. Bruce (R) 1961–65
Charles A. Halleck (R) 1935–69
Ralph Harvey (R) 1947–59; 1961–66
John T. Myers (R) 1967–97
Richard L. Roudebush (R) 1961–71
Earl Wilson (R) 1941–59; 1961–65
Roger H. Zion (R) 1967–75

## Iowa
Bert Bandstra (D) 1965–67
John C. Culver (D) 1965–75
Stanley L. Greigg (D) 1965–67
John R. Hansen (D) 1965–67
John R. Schmidhauser (D) 1965–67
Neal Smith (D) 1959–95
James E. Bromwell (R) 1961–65
H. R. Gross (R) 1949–75
Charles B. Hoeven (R) 1943–65
Ben F. Jensen (R) 1939–65
John H. Kyl (R) 1959–65; 1967–73
Wiley Mayne (R) 1967–75
William J. Scherle (R) 1967–75
Fred Schwengel (R) 1955–65; 1967–73

## Kansas
William H. Avery (R) 1955–65
Robert Dole (R) 1961–69
Robert F. Ellsworth (R) 1961–67
Chester L. Mize (R) 1965–71
Garner E. Shriver (R) 1961–77
Joe Skubitz (R) 1963–78
Larry Winn, Jr. (R) 1967–85

## Kentucky
Frank Chelf (D) 1945–67
Charles P. Farnsley (D) 1965–67
William H. Natcher (D) 1953–94
Carl D. Perkins (D) 1949–84

Frank A. Stubblefield (D) 1959–74
John C. Watts (D) 1951–71
Tim L. Carter (R) 1965–81
William O. Cowger (R) 1967–71
Eugene Siler (R) 1955–65
M. G. Snyder (R) 1963–65; 1967–87

## Louisiana
Hale Boggs (D) 1941–43; 1947–73
Edwin W. Edwards (D) 1965–72
F. Edward Hébert (D) 1941–77
Gillis W. Long (D) 1963–65; 1973–85
Speedy O. Long (D) 1965–73
James H. Morrison (D) 1943–67
Otto E. Passman (D) 1947–77
John R. Rarick (D) 1967–75
T. Ashton Thompson (D) 1953–65
Joe D. Waggoner, Jr. (D) 1961–79
Edwin E. Willis (D) 1949–69

## Maine
William D. Hathaway (D) 1965–73
Peter N. Kyros (D) 1967–75
Clifford G. McIntire (R) 1951–65
Stanley R. Tupper (R) 1961–67

## Maryland
George H. Fallon (D) 1945–71
Samuel N. Friedel (D) 1953–71
Edward A. Garmatz (D) 1947–73
Richard E. Lankford (D) 1955–65
Clarence D. Long (D) 1963–85
Hervey G. Machen (D) 1965–69
Carlton R. Sickles (D) 1963–67
Gilbert Gude (R) 1967–77
Charles McC. Mathias, Jr. (R) 1961–69
Rogers C. B. Morton (R) 1963–71

## Massachusetts
Edward P. Boland (D) 1953–89
James A. Burke (D) 1959–79
Harold D. Donahue (D) 1947–74
John W. McCormack (D) 1928–71
Torbert H. Macdonald (D) 1955–76
Thomas P. (Tip) O'Neill, Jr. (D) 1953–87
Philip J. Philbin (D) 1943–71
William H. Bates (R) 1950–69
Silvio O. Conte (R) 1959–91
Margaret M. Heckler (R) 1967–83
Keith Hastings (R) 1959–73

Joseph W. Martin, Jr. (R) 1925–67
F. Bradford Morse (R) 1961–72

## Michigan
Raymond F. Clevenger (D) 1965–67
John Conyers, Jr. (D) 1965–
Charles C. Diggs, Jr. (D) 1955–80
John D. Dingell, Jr. (D) 1955–
Billie S. Farnum (D) 1965–67
William D. Ford (D) 1965–95
Martha W. Griffiths (D) 1955–74
John Lesinski, Jr. (D) 1951–65
John C. Mackie (D) 1965–67
Lucien N. Nedzi (D) 1961–81
James G. O'Hara (D) 1959–77
Harold M. Ryan (D) 1962–65
Neil Staebler (D) 1963–65
Paul H. Todd, Jr. (D) 1965–67
Weston E. Vivian (D) 1965–67
John B. Bennett (R) 1943–45; 1947–64
William S. Broomfield (R) 1957–93
Garry E. Brown (R) 1967–79
Elford A. Cederberg (R) 1953–78
Charles E. Chamberlain (R) 1957–74
Marvin L. Esch (R) 1967–77
Gerald R. Ford (R) 1949–73
Robert P. Griffin (R) 1957–66
James Harvey (R) 1961–74
Edward Hutchinson (R) 1963–77
August E. Johansen (R) 1955–65
Victor A. Knox (R) 1953–65
Jack McDonald (R) 1967–73
George Meader (R) 1951–65
Donald W. Riegle, Jr. (R) 1967–73; (D) 1973–76
Philip E. Ruppe (R) 1967–74
Guy Vander Jagt (R) 1966–93

## Minnesota
John A. Blatnik (D) 1947–74
Donald M. Fraser (D) 1963–79
Joseph E. Karth (D) 1959–77
Alec G. Olson (D) 1963–67
Odin Langen (R) 1959–71
Clark MacGregor (R) 1961–71
Ancher Nelson (R) 1959–74
Albert H. Quie (R) 1958–79
John M. Zwach (R) 1967–75

## Mississippi
Thomas G. Abernethy (D) 1943–73
William M. Colmer (D) 1933–73

Charles H. Griffin (D) 1968–73
G. V. (Sonny) Montgomery (D) 1967–97
Jamie L. Whitten (D) 1941–95
John B. Williams (D) 1947–68
Arthur Winstead (D) 1943–65
Prentiss Walker (R) 1965–67

**Missouri**
Richard Bolling (D) 1949–83
Clarence A. Cannon (D) 1923–64
W. R. Hull, Jr. (D) 1955–73
William L. Hungate (D) 1964–77
Richard H. Ichord (D) 1961–81
Paul C. Jones (D) 1948–69
Frank M. Karsten (D) 1947–69
William J. Randall (D) 1959–77
Leonor K. Sullivan (D) 1953–77
Thomas B. Curtis (R) 1951–69
Durward G. Hall (R) 1961–73

**Montana**
Arnold Olson (D) 1961–71
James F. Battin (R) 1961–69

**Nebraska**
Clair Callan (D) 1965–67
Ralph J. Beermann (R) 1961–65
Glenn Cunningham (R) 1957–71
Robert V. Denney (R) 1967–71
Dave Martin (R) 1961–74

**Nevada**
Walter S. Baring (D) 1949–53; 1957–73

**New Hampshire**
J. Oliva Huot (D) 1965–67
James C. Cleveland (R) 1963–83
Louis C. Wyman (R) 1963–65; 1967–74

**New Jersey**
Dominick V. Daniels (D) 1959–77
Cornelius E. Gallagher (D) 1959–73
Henry Helstoski (D) 1965–77
James J. Howard (D) 1965–88
Charles S. Joelson (D) 1961–69
Paul J. Krebs (D) 1965–67
Thomas C. McGrath (D) 1965–67
Joseph G. Minish (D) 1963–85
Edward J. Patten (D) 1963–81
Peter W. Rodino, Jr. (D) 1949–89

Frank Thompson, Jr. (D) 1955–80
James C. Auchincloss (R) 1943–65
William T. Cahill (R) 1959–70
Florence P. Dwyer (R) 1957–73
Peter H. B. Frelinghuysen (R) 1953–75
Milton W. Glenn (R) 1957–65
John E. Hunt (R) 1967–75
Frank C. Osmers, Jr. (R) 1939–43; 1951–65
Charles W. Sandman, Jr. (R) 1967–75
George M. Wallhauser (R) 1959–65
William B. Widnall (R) 1950–74

**New Mexico**
Joseph M. Montoya (D) 1957–64
Thomas G. Morris (D) 1959–69
E. S. Johnny Walker (D) 1965–69

**New York**
Joseph P. Addabbo (D) 1961–86
Jonathan B. Bingham (D) 1965–83
Frank J. Brasco (D) 1967–75
Charles A. Buckley (D) 1935–65
Hugh L. Carey (D) 1961–74
Emanuel Celler (D) 1923–73
James J. Delaney (D) 1945–47; 1949–78
John G. Dow (D) 1965–69; 1971–73
Thaddeus J. Dulski (D) 1959–74
Leonard Farbstein (D) 1957–71
Jacob H. Gilbert (D) 1960–71
James M. Hanley (D) 1965–81
James C. Healey (D) 1956–65
Edna F. Kelly (D) 1949–69
Eugene J. Keogh (D) 1937–67
Richard D. McCarthy (D) 1965–71
Abraham J. Multer (D) 1947–67
John M. Murphy (D) 1963–81
Leo W. O'Brien (D) 1952–66
Richard L. Ottinger (D) 1965–71; 1975–85
Otis G. Pike (D) 1961–79
Bertram L. Podell (D) 1968–75
Adam C. Powell, Jr. (D) 1945–67; 1967–71
Joseph Y. Resnick (D) 1965–69
John J. Rooney (D) 1944–74
Benjamin S. Rosenthal (D) 1962–83
William F. Ryan (D) 1961–72
James H. Scheuer (D) 1965–73; 1975–93
Samuel S. Stratton (D) 1959–89
Herbert Tenzer (D) 1965–69
Lester L. Wolff (D) 1965–81
Robert R. Barry (R) 1959–65

Frank J. Becker (R) 1953–65
Daniel E. Button (R) 1967–71
Barber B. Conable, Jr. (R) 1965–85
Steven B. Derounian (R) 1953–65
Paul A. Fino (R) 1953–68
Charles E. Goodell (R) 1959–68
James R. Grover, Jr. (R) 1963–75
Seymour Halpern (R) 1959–73
Frank J. Horton (R) 1963–93
Clarence E. Kilburn (R) 1940–65
Carleton J. King (R) 1961–74
Theodore R. Kupferman (R) 1966–69
John V. Lindsay (R) 1959–65
Robert C. McEwen (R) 1965–81
William E. Miller (R) 1951–65
Harold C. Ostertag (R) 1951–65
John R. Pillion (R) 1953–65
Alexander Pirnie (R) 1959–73
Ogden R. Reid (R) 1963–72; (D) 1972–75
R. Walter Riehlman (R) 1947–65
Howard W. Robison (R) 1958–75
Katherine St. George (R) 1947–65
Henry P. Smith III (R) 1965–75
J. Ernest Wharton (R) 1951–65
John W. Wydler (R) 1963–81

## North Carolina
Herbert C. Bonner (D) 1940–65
Harold D. Cooley (D) 1934–66
L. H. Fountain (D) 1953–83
Nick Galifianakis (D) 1967–73
David N. Henderson (D) 1961–77
Walter B. Jones (D) 1966–92
Horace R. Kornegay (D) 1961–69
Alton Lennon (D) 1957–73
Ralph J. Scott (D) 1957–67
Roy A. Taylor (D) 1960–77
Basil L. Whitener (D) 1957–69
James T. Broyhill (R) 1963–86
James C. Gardner (R) 1967–69
Charles R. Jonas (R) 1953–73

## North Dakota
Rolland Redlin (D) 1965–67
Mark Andrews (R) 1963–81
Thomas S. Kleppe (R) 1967–71
Don L. Short (R) 1959–65

## Ohio
Thomas L. Ashley (D) 1955–81
Michael A. Feighan (D) 1943–71

John J. Gilligan (D) 1965–67
Wayne L. Hays (D) 1949–76
Michael J. Kirwan (D) 1937–70
Rodney M. Love (D) 1965–67
Walter H. Moeller (D) 1959–63; 1965–67
Robert T. Secrest (D) 1949–54; 1963–66
Robert E. Sweeney (D) 1965–67
Charles A. Vanik (D) 1955–81
Homer E. Abele (R) 1963–65
John M. Ashbrook (R) 1961–82
William H. Ayres (R) 1951–71
Jackson E. Betts (R) 1951–73
Frances P. Bolton (R) 1940–69
Oliver P. Bolton (R) 1953–57; 1963–65
Frank T. Bow (R) 1951–72
Clarence J. Brown (R) 1939–65
Clarence J. Brown, Jr. (R) 1965–83
Donald D. Clancy (R) 1961–77
Samuel L. Devine (R) 1959–81
William H. Harsha (R) 1961–81
Delbert L. Latta (R) 1959–89
Donald E. Lukens (R) 1967–71; 1987–90
William M. McCulloch (R) 1947–73
Clarence E. Miller (R) 1967–93
William E. Minshall (R) 1955–74
Charles A. Mosher (R) 1961–77
Carl W. Rich (R) 1963–65
Paul F. Schenck (R) 1951–65
J. William Stanton (R) 1965–83
Robert Taft, Jr. (R) 1963–65; 1967–71
Charles W. Whalen, Jr. (R) 1967–79
Charles P. Wylie (R) 1967–93

## Oklahoma
Carl Albert (D) 1947–73
Ed Edmondson (D) 1953–73
John Jarman (D) 1951–75; (R) 1975–77
Jed Johnson, Jr. (D) 1965–67
Tom Steed (D) 1949–81
Victor Wickersham (D) 1941–47; 1949–57;
    1961–65
Page Belcher (R) 1951–73
James V. Smith (R) 1967–69

## Oregon
Robert B. Duncan (D) 1963–67; 1975–81
Edith Green (D) 1955–75
Al Ullman (D) 1957–81
John R. Dellenback (R) 1967–75
Albin W. Norblad, Jr. (R) 1946–64
Wendell Wyatt (R) 1964–75

## Pennsylvania
William A. Barrett (D) 1945–47; 1949–76
James A. Byrne (D) 1953–73
Frank M. Clark (D) 1955–74
N. Neiman Craley, Jr. (D) 1965–67
John H. Dent (D) 1958–79
Joshua Eilberg (D) 1967–79
Daniel J. Flood (D) 1945–47; 1949–53; 1955–80
Joseph M. Gaydos (D) 1968–93
William J. Green, Jr. (D) 1945–47; 1949–63
William J. Green III (D) 1964–77
Elmer J. Holland (D) 1942–43; 1956–68
William S. Moorhead (D) 1959–81
Thomas E. Morgan (D) 1945–77
Robert N. C. Nix (D) 1958–79
George M. Rhodes (D) 1949–69
Fred B. Rooney (D) 1963–79
Herman Toll (D) 1959–67
Joseph P. Vigorito (D) 1965–77
Edward G. Biester, Jr. (R) 1967–77
Robert J. Corbett (R) 1939–41; 1945–71
Willard S. Curtin (R) 1957–67
Paul B. Dague (R) 1947–66
Edwin D. Eshleman (R) 1967–77
James G. Fulton (R) 1945–71
George A. Goodling (R) 1961–65; 1967–75
Albert W. Johnson (R) 1963–77
John C. Kunkel (R) 1939–51; 1961–66
Joseph M. McDade (R) 1963–99
William H. Milliken, Jr. (R) 1959–65
John P. Saylor (R) 1949–73
Herman T. Schneebeli (R) 1960–77
Richard S. Schweiker (R) 1961–69
G. Robert Watkins (R) 1965–70
James D. Weaver (R) 1963–65
J. Irving Whalley (R) 1960–73
Lawrence G. Williams (R) 1967–75

## Rhode Island
John E. Fogarty (D) 1941–44, 1945–67
Fernand J. St. Germain (D) 1961–89
Robert O. Tiernan (D) 1967–75

## South Carolina
Robert T. Ashmore (D) 1953–69
W. J. Bryan Dorn (D) 1947–49; 1951–74
Tom S. Gettys (D) 1964–74
Robert W. Hemphill (D) 1957–64
John L. McMillan (D) 1939–73
L. Mendel Rivers (D) 1941–70
Albert W. Watson (D) 1963–65; (R) 1965–71

## South Dakota
E. Y. Berry (R) 1951–71
Ben Reifel (R) 1961–71

## Tennessee
William R. Anderson (D) 1965–73
Ross Bass (D) 1955–64
Ray Blanton (D) 1967–73
Clifford Davis (D) 1940–65
Robert A. Everett (D) 1958–69
Joe L. Evins (D) 1947–77
Richard Fulton (D) 1963–75
George W. Grider (D) 1965–67
Tom Murray (D) 1943–66
Howard H. Baker (R) 1951–64
Irene B. Baker (R) 1964–65
William E. Brock III (R) 1963–71
John J. Duncan (R) 1965–88
Dan Kuykendall (R) 1967–75
James H. Quillen (R) 1963–97

## Texas
Lindley Beckworth (D) 1939–53; 1957–67
Jack Brooks (D) 1953–95
Omar Burleson (D) 1947–78
Earle Cabell (D) 1965–73
Bob Casey (D) 1959–76
Eligio (Kika) de la Garza (D) 1965–97
John Dowdy (D) 1952–73
Bob Eckhardt (D) 1967–81
O. C. Fisher (D) 1943–74
Henry B. González (D) 1961–99
Abraham Kazen, Jr. (D) 1967–85
Joe M. Kilgore (D) 1955–65
George H. Mahon (D) 1935–79
Wright Patman (D) 1929–76
J. J. Pickle (D) 1963–95
W. R. Poage (D) 1937–78
Joe R. Pool (D) 1963–68
Graham Purcell (D) 1962–73
Ray Roberts (D) 1962–81
Walter Rogers (D) 1951–67
Olin E. Teague (D) 1946–78
Albert Thomas (D) 1937–66
Lera M. Thomas (D) 1966—67
Clark W. Thompson (D) 1933–35; 1947–66
Homer Thornberry (D) 1949–63
Richard C. White (D) 1965–83
Jim Wright (D) 1955–89
John Young (D) 1957–79
Bruce Alger (R) 1955–65

George H. W. Bush (R) 1967–71
James M. Collins (R) 1968–83
Ed Foreman (R) 1963–65; 1969–71 (New Mexico)
Robert D. Price (R) 1967–75

## Utah

David S. King (D) 1959–63; 1965–67
Laurence J. Burton (R) 1963–71
Sherman P. Lloyd (R) 1963–65; 1967–73

## Vermont

Robert T. Stafford (R) 1961–71

## Virginia

Walkins M. Abbitt (D) 1948–73
Thomas N. Downing (D) 1959–77
J. Vaughan Gary (D) 1945–65
Porter Hardy, Jr. (D) 1947–69
W. Pat Jennings (D) 1955–67
John O. Marsh, Jr. (D) 1963–71
David E. Satterfield III (D) 1965–81
Howard W. Smith (D) 1931–67
William M. Tuck (D) 1953–69
Joel T. Broyhill (R) 1953–74
Richard H. Poff (R) 1953–72
William L. Scott (R) 1967–73
William C. Wampler (R) 1953–55; 1967–83

## Washington

Brock Adams (D) 1965–77
Thomas S. Foley (D) 1965–95
Julia B. Hansen (D) 1960–74
Floyd V. Hicks (D) 1965–77
Lloyd Meeds (D) 1965–79
Walt Horan (R) 1943–65

Catherine May (R) 1959–71
Thomas M. Pelly (R) 1953–73
K. William Stinson (R) 1963–65
Thor C. Tollefson (R) 1947–65
Jack Westland (R) 1953–65

## West Virginia

Ken Hechler (D) 1959–77
Maude E. Kee (D) 1951–65
James Kee (D) 1965–73
John M. Slack, Jr. (D) 1959–80
Harley O. Staggers (D) 1949–81
Arch A. Moore, Jr. (R) 1957–69

## Wisconsin

Lester R. Johnson (D) 1953–65
Robert W. Kastenmeier (D) 1959–91
John A. Race (D) 1965–67
Henry S. Reuss (D) 1955–83
Lynn E. Stalbaum (D) 1965–67
Clement J. Zablocki (D) 1949–83
John W. Byrnes (R) 1945–73
Glenn R. Davis (R) 1947–57; 1965–74
Melvin R. Laird (R) 1953–69
Alvin E. O'Konski (R) 1943–73
Henry C. Schadeberg (R) 1961–65; 1967–71
William A. Steiger (R) 1967–78
Vernon W. Thomson (R) 1961–74
William K. Van Pelt (R) 1951–65

## Wyoming

Teno Roncalio (D) 1965–67; 1971–78
William H. Harrison (R) 1951–55; 1961–65;
    1967–69

# SENATE

## Alabama

Lister Hill (D) 1938–69
John J. Sparkman (D) 1946–79

## Alaska

E. L. Bartlett (D) 1959–68
Ernest Gruening (D) 1959–69
Theodore F. Stevens (R) 1968–

## Arizona

Carl Hayden (D) 1927–69

Paul J. Fannin (R) 1965–77
Barry M. Goldwater (R) 1953–65; 1969–87

## Arkansas

J. William Fulbright (D) 1945–75
John L. McClellan (D) 1943–77

## California

Clair Engle (D) 1959–64
Pierre Salinger (D) 1964
Thomas H. Kuchel (R) 1953–69
George Murphy (R) 1965–71

**Colorado**
Gordon Allott (R) 1955–73
Peter H. Dominick (R) 1963–75

**Connecticut**
Thomas J. Dodd (D) 1959–71
Abraham A. Ribicoff (D) 1963–81

**Delaware**
J. Caleb Boggs (R) 1961–73
John J. Williams (R) 1947–71

**Florida**
Spessard L. Holland (D) 1946–71
George A. Smathers (D) 1951–69

**Georgia**
Richard B. Russell, Jr. (D) 1933–71
Herman E. Talmadge (D) 1957–81

**Hawaii**
Daniel K. Inouye (D) 1963–
Hiram L. Fong (R) 1959–77

**Idaho**
Frank Church (D) 1957–81
Len B. Jordan (R) 1962–73

**Illinois**
Paul H. Douglas (D) 1949–67
Everett McKinley Dirksen (R) 1951–69
Charles H. Percy (R) 1967–85

**Indiana**
Birch Bayh (D) 1963–81
Vance Hartke (D) 1959–77

**Iowa**
Bourke B. Hickenlooper (R) 1945–69
Jack Miller (R) 1961–73

**Kansas**
Frank Carlson (R) 1950–69
James B. Pearson (R) 1962–78

**Kentucky**
John Sherman Cooper (R) 1952–55, 1956–73
Thruston B. Morton (R) 1957–68

**Louisiana**
Allen J. Ellender (D) 1937–72
Russell B. Long (D) 1948–87

**Maine**
Edmund S. Muskie (D) 1959–80
Margaret Chase Smith (R) 1949–73

**Maryland**
Daniel B. Brewster (D) 1963–69
Joseph D. Tydings (D) 1965–71
J. Glenn Beall (R) 1953–65

**Massachusetts**
Edward M. Kennedy (D) 1962–
Edward W. Brooke (R) 1967–79
Leverett Saltonstall (R) 1945–67

**Michigan**
Philip A. Hart (D) 1959–76
Patrick V. McNamara (D) 1955–66
Robert P. Griffin (R) 1966–79

**Minnesota**
Hubert H. Humphrey (D) 1949–64, 1971–78
Eugene J. McCarthy (D) 1959–71
Walter F. Mondale (D) 1964–76

**Mississippi**
James O. Eastland (D) 1941, 1943–78
John Stennis (D) 1947–89

**Missouri**
Edward V. Long (D) 1960–68
Stuart Symington (D) 1953–76

**Montana**
Mike Mansfield (D) 1953–77
Lee Metcalf (D) 1967–78

**Nebraska**
Carl T. Curtis (R) 1955–79
Roman L. Hruska (R) 1954–76

**Nevada**
Alan Bible (D) 1954–74
Howard W. Cannon (D) 1959–83

**New Hampshire**
Thomas J. McIntyre (D) 1962–79
Norris Cotton (R) 1954–74

**New Jersey**
Harrison A. Williams, Jr. (D) 1959–82
Clifford P. Case (R) 1955–79

**New Mexico**
Clinton P. Anderson (D) 1949–73
Joseph M. Montoya (D) 1964–77
Edwin L. Mechem (R) 1962–64

**New York**
Robert F. Kennedy (D) 1965–68
Charles E. Goodell (R) 1968–71
Jacob K. Javits (R) 1957–81
Kenneth B. Keating (R) 1959–65

**North Carolina**
Sam J. Ervin, Jr. (D) 1954–74
B. Everett Jordan (D) 1958–73

**North Dakota**
Quentin N. Burdick (D) 1960–92
Milton R. Young (R) 1945–81

**Ohio**
Frank J. Lausche (D) 1957–69
Stephen M. Young (D) 1959–71

**Oklahoma**
J. Howard Edmondson (D) 1963–64
Fred R. Harris (D) 1967–73
A. S. Mike Monroney (D) 1951–69

**Oregon**
Maurine B. Neuberger (D) 1960–67
Mark O. Hatfield (R) 1967–97
Wayne Morse (R) 1945–52; (Ind.) 1952–55; (D)
    1955–69

**Pennsylvania**
Joseph S. Clark (D) 1957–68
Hugh D. Scott, Jr. (R) 1959–77

**Rhode Island**
John O. Pastore (D) 1950–76
Claiborne Pell (D) 1961–97

**South Carolina**
Ernest F. Hollings (D) 1966–2005
Olin D. Johnston (D) 1945–65

Donald S. Russell (D) 1965–66
Strom Thurmond (D) 1955–64; (R) 1964–2003

**South Dakota**
George McGovern (D) 1963–81
Karl E. Mundt (R) 1948–73

**Tennessee**
Ross Bass (D) 1964–67
Albert Gore (D) 1953–71
Herbert S. Walters (D) 1963–64
Howard H. Baker, Jr. (R) 1967–85

**Texas**
Ralph W. Yarborough (D) 1957–71
John G. Tower (R) 1961–85

**Utah**
Frank Moss (D) 1959–77
Wallace F. Bennett (R) 1951–74

**Vermont**
George D. Aiken (R) 1941–75
Winston L. Prouty (R) 1959–71

**Virginia**
Harry Flood Byrd, Sr. (D) 1933–65
Harry Flood Byrd, Jr. (D) 1965–71 (I)
    1971–83
A. Willis Robertson (D) 1946–66
William B. Spong, Jr. (D) 1966–73

**Washington**
Henry M. Jackson (D) 1953–83
Warren G. Magnuson (D) 1944–81

**West Virginia**
Robert C. Byrd (D) 1959–
Jennings Randolph (D) 1958–85

**Wisconsin**
Gaylord Nelson (D) 1963–81
William Proxmire (D) 1957–89

**Wyoming**
Gale W. McGee (D) 1959–77
Clifford P. Hansen (R) 1967–78
Milward L. Simpson (R) 1962–67

# GOVERNORS

## Alabama
George C. Wallace (D) 1963–67
Lurleen B. Wallace (D) 1967–68
Albert P. Brewer (D) 1968–71

## Alaska
William A. Egan (D) 1959–66, 1970–74
Walter J. Hickel (R) 1966–69, 1990–94

## Arizona
Paul Fannin (R) 1959–65
Samuel P. Goddard, Jr. (D) 1965–67
John R. Williams (R) 1967–75

## Arkansas
Orval E. Faubus (D) 1955–67
Winthrop Rockefeller (R) 1967–71

## California
Edmund G. Brown (D) 1959–67
Ronald Reagan (R) 1967–75

## Colorado
John A. Love (R) 1963–73

## Connecticut
John N. Dempsey (D) 1961–71

## Delaware
Elbert N. Carvel (D) 1949–53, 1961–65
Charles L. Terry, Jr. (D) 1965–69

## Florida
Farris Bryant (D) 1961–65
Haydon Burns (D) 1965–67
Claude R. Kirk, Jr. (R) 1967–71

## Georgia
Carl E. Sanders (D) 1963–67
Lester G. Maddox (D) 1967–71

## Hawaii
John A. Burns (D) 1962–74

## Idaho
Robert E. Smylie (R) 1955–67
Don Samuelson (R) 1967–71

## Illinois
Otto J. Kerner (D) 1961–68
Samuel H. Shapiro (D) 1968–69

## Indiana
Matthew E. Welsh (D) 1961–65
Roger D. Branigin (D) 1965–69

## Iowa
Harold E. Hughes (D) 1963–69

## Kansas
John Anderson, Jr. (R) 1961–65
William H. Avery (R) 1965–67
Robert B. Docking (D) 1967–75

## Kentucky
Edward T. Breathitt (D) 1963–67
Louie B. Nunn (R) 1967–71

## Louisiana
Jimmie H. Davis (D) 1944–48, 1960–64
John J. McKeithen (D) 1964–72

## Maine
John H. Reed (R) 1959–67
Kenneth M. Curtis (D) 1967–75

## Maryland
J. Millard Tawes (D) 1959–67
Spiro T. Agnew (R) 1967–69

## Massachusetts
John A. Volpe (R) 1961–63; 1965–69
Endicott Peabody (D) 1963–65

## Michigan
George W. Romney (R) 1963–69

## Minnesota
Karl F. Rolvaag (D) 1963–67
Harold LeVander (R) 1967–71

## Mississippi
Ross R. Barnett (D) 1960–64

Paul B. Johnson (D) 1964–68
John Bell Williams (D) 1968–72

**Missouri**
John M. Dalton (D) 1961–65
Warren E. Hearnes (D) 1965–73

**Montana**
Tim M. Babcock (R) 1962–69

**Nebraska**
Frank B. Morrison (D) 1961–67
Norbert T. Tiemann (R) 1967–71

**Nevada**
Grant Sawyer (D) 1959–67
Paul Laxalt (R) 1967–71

**New Hampshire**
John W. King (D) 1963–69

**New Jersey**
Richard J. Hughes (D) 1962–70

**New Mexico**
Jack M. Campbell (D) 1963–67
David F. Cargo (R) 1967–71

**New York**
Nelson A. Rockefeller (R) 1959–73

**North Carolina**
Terry Sanford (D) 1961–65
Daniel K. Moore (D) 1965–69

**North Dakota**
William L. Guy (D) 1961–73

**Ohio**
James A. Rhodes (R) 1963–71, 1975–79

**Oklahoma**
Henry Bellmon (R) 1963–67, 1987–91
Dewey F. Bartlett (R) 1967–71

**Oregon**
Mark O. Hatfield (R) 1959–67
Tom McCall (R) 1967–75

**Pennsylvania**
William W. Scranton (R) 1963–67
Raymond P. Shafer (R) 1967–71

**Rhode Island**
John H. Chaffee (R) 1963–69

**South Carolina**
Donald S. Russell (D) 1963–65
Robert E. McNair (D) 1965–71

**South Dakota**
Archie M. Grubbrud (R) 1961–65
Nils A. Boe (R) 1965–69

**Tennessee**
Frank G. Clement (D) 1953–59, 1963–67
Buford Ellington (D) 1959–63, 1967–71

**Texas**
John B. Connally, Jr. (D) 1963–69

**Utah**
George Dewey Clyde (R) 1957–65
Calvin L. Rampton (D) 1965–77

**Vermont**
Philip H. Hoff (D) 1963–69

**Virginia**
Albertis S. Harrison, Jr. (D) 1962–66
Mills E. Godwin, Jr. (D) 1966–70, 1974–78

**Washington**
Albert D. Rosellini (D) 1957–65
Daniel J. Evans (R) 1965–77

**West Virginia**
William W. Barron (D) 1961–65
Hulett C. Smith (D) 1965–69

**Wisconsin**
John W. Reynolds (D) 1963–65
Warren P. Knowles (R) 1965–71

**Wyoming**
Clifford P. Hansen (R) 1963–67
Stanley K. Hathaway (R) 1967–75

# SELECTED PRIMARY DOCUMENTS

# 1. Address Before a Joint Session of the Congress, November 27, 1963

*Public Papers of the Presidents of the United States: Lyndon B. Johnson, 1963–64, Vols. 1–2 (Washington, D.C.: U.S. Government Printing Office, 1965), 1: 8–10.*

Mr. Speaker, Mr. President, Members of the House, Members of the Senate, my fellow Americans:

All I have I would have given gladly not to be standing here today.

The greatest leader of our time has been struck down by the foulest deed of our time. Today John Fitzgerald Kennedy lives on in the immortal words and works that he left behind. He lives on in the mind and memories of mankind. He lives on in the hearts of his countrymen.

No words are sad enough to express our sense of loss. No words are strong enough to express our determination to continue the forward thrust of America that he began.

The dream of conquering the vastness of space—the dream of partnership across the Atlantic—and across the Pacific as well—the dream of a Peace Corps in less developed nations—the dream of education for all of our children—the dream of jobs for all who seek them and need them—the dream of care for our elderly—the dream of an all-out attack on mental illness—and above all, the dream of equal rights for all Americans, whatever their race or color—these and other American dreams have been vitalized by his drive and by his dedication.

And now the ideas and the ideals which he so nobly represented must and will be translated into effective action.

Under John Kennedy's leadership, this Nation has demonstrated that it has the courage to seek peace, and it has the fortitude to risk war. We have proved that we are a good and reliable friend to those who seek peace and freedom. We have shown that we can also be a formidable foe to those who reject the path of peace and those who seek to impose upon us or our allies the yoke of tyranny.

This Nation will keep its commitments from South Viet-Nam to West Berlin. We will be unceasing in the search for peace; resourceful in our pursuit of areas of agreement even with those with whom we differ; and generous and loyal to those who join with us in common cause.

In this age when there can be no losers in peace and no victors in war, we must recognize the obligation to match national strength with national restraint. We must be prepared at one and the same time for both the confrontation of power and the limitation of power. We must be ready to defend the national interest and to negotiate the common interest. This is the path that we shall continue to pursue. Those who test our courage will find it strong, and those who seek our friendship will find it honorable. We will demonstrate anew that the strong can be just in the use of strength; and the just can be strong in the defense of justice.

And let all know we will extend no special privilege and impose no persecution. We will carry on the fight against poverty and misery, and disease and ignorance, in other lands and in our own.

We will serve all the Nation, not one section or one sector, or one group, but all Americans. These are the United States—a united people with a united purpose.

Our American unity does not depend upon unanimity. We have differences; but now, as in the past, we can derive from those differences strength, not weakness, wisdom, not despair. Both as a people and a government, we can unite upon a program, a program which is wise and just, enlightened and constructive.

For 32 years Capitol Hill has been my home. I have shared many moments of pride with you, pride in the ability of the Congress of the United States to act, to meet any crisis, to distill from our differences strong programs of national action.

An assassin's bullet has thrust upon me the awesome burden of the Presidency. I am here today to say I need your help; I cannot bear this burden alone. I need the help of all Americans, and all America. This Nation has experienced a profound shock, and in this critical moment, it is our duty, yours and mine, as the Government of the United States, to do away with uncertainty and doubt and delay, and to show that we are capable of decisive action; that from the brutal loss of our leader we will derive not weakness, but strength; that we can and will act and act now.

From this chamber of representative government, let all the world know and none misunderstand that I rededicate this Government to the unswerving support of the United Nations, to the honorable and determined execution of our commitments to our allies, to the maintenance of military strength second to none, to the defense of the strength and the stability of the dollar, to the expansion of our foreign trade, to the reinforcement of our programs of mutual assistance and cooperation in Asia and Africa, and to our Alliance for Progress in this hemisphere.

On the 20th day of January, in 1961, John F. Kennedy told his countrymen that our national work would not be finished "in the first thousand days, nor in the life of this administration, nor even perhaps in our lifetime on this planet. But," he said, "let us begin."

Today, in this moment of new resolve, I would say to all my fellow Americans, let us continue.

This is our challenge—not to hesitate, not to pause, not to turn about and linger over this evil moment, but to continue on our course so that we may fulfill the destiny that history has set for us. Our most immediate tasks are here on this Hill.

First, no memorial oration or eulogy could more eloquently honor President Kennedy's memory than the earliest possible passage of the civil rights bill for which he fought so long. We have talked long enough in this country about equal rights. We have talked for one hundred years or more. It is time now to write the next chapter, and to write it in the books of law.

I urge you again, as I did in 1957 and again in 1960, to enact a civil rights law so that we can move forward to eliminate from this Nation every trace of discrimination and oppression that is based upon race or color. There could be no greater source of strength to this Nation both at home and abroad.

And second, no act of ours could more fittingly continue the work of President Kennedy than the early passage of the tax bill for which he fought all this long year. This is a bill designed to increase our national income and Federal revenues, and to provide insurance against recession. That bill, if passed without delay, means more security for those now working, more jobs for those now without them, and more incentive for our economy.

In short, this is no time for delay. It is a time for action—strong, forward-looking action on the pending education bills to help bring the light of learning to every home and hamlet in America—strong, forward-looking action on youth employment opportunities; strong, forward-looking action on the pending foreign aid bill, making clear that we are not forfeiting our responsibilities to this hemisphere or to the world, nor erasing Executive flexibility in the conduct of our foreign affairs—and

strong, prompt, and forward-looking action on the remaining appropriation bills.

In this new spirit of action, the Congress can expect the full cooperation and support of the executive branch. And in particular, I pledge that the expenditures of your Government will be administered with the utmost thrift and frugality. I will insist that the Government get a dollar's value for a dollar spent. The Government will set an example of prudence and economy. This does not mean that we will not meet out unfilled needs or that we will not honor our commitments. We will do both.

As one who has long served in both Houses of the Congress, I firmly believe in the independence and the integrity of the legislative branch. And I promise you that I shall always respect this. It is deep in the marrow of my bones. With equal firmness, I believe in the capacity and I believe in the ability of the Congress, despite the divisions of opinions which characterize our Nation, to act—to act wisely, to act vigorously, to act speedily when the need arises.

The need is here. The need is now. I ask your help.

We meet in grief, but let us also meet in renewed dedication and renewed vigor. Let us meet in action, in tolerance, and in mutual understanding. John Kennedy's death commands what his life conveyed—that America must move forward. The time has come for Americans of all races and creeds and political beliefs to understand and to respect one another. So let us put an end to the teaching and the preaching of hate and evil and violence. Let us turn away from the fanatics of the far left and the far right, from the apostles of bitterness and bigotry, from those defiant of law, and those who pour venom into our Nation's bloodstream.

I profoundly hope that the tragedy and the torment of these terrible days will bind us together in new fellowship, making us one people in our hour of sorrow. So let us here highly resolve that John Fitzgerald Kennedy did not live—or die—in vain. And on this Thanksgiving eve, as we gather together to ask the Lord's blessing, and give Him our thanks, let us unite in those familiar and cherished words:

America, America,
God shed His grace on thee,
And crown thy good
With brotherhood
From sea to shining sea.

## 2. Remarks at the University of Michigan, May 22, 1964

*Public Papers of the Presidents of the United States: Lyndon B. Johnson, 1963–64, Vols. 1–2. (Washington, D.C.: U.S. Government Printing Office, 1965), 1: 704–707.*

President Hatcher, Governor Romney, Senators McNamara and Hart, Congressmen Meader and Staebler, and other members of the fine Michigan delegation, members of the graduating class, my fellow Americans:

It is a great pleasure to be here today. This university has been coeducational since 1870, but I do not believe it was on the basis of your accomplishments that a Detroit high school girl said, "In choosing a college, you first have to decide whether you want a coeducational school or an educational school."

Well, we can find both here at Michigan, although perhaps at different hours.

I came out here today very anxious to meet the Michigan student whose father told a friend of mine that his son's education had been a real value. It stopped his mother from bragging about him.

I have come today from the turmoil of your Capital to the tranquility of your campus to speak about the future of your country.

The purpose of protecting the life of our Nation and preserving the liberty of our citizens is to pursue the happiness of our people. Our success in that pursuit is the test of our success as a Nation.

For a century we labored to settle and to subdue a continent. For half a century we called upon unbounded invention and untiring industry to create an order of plenty for all of our people.

The challenge of the next half century is whether we have the wisdom to use that wealth to enrich and elevate our national life, and to advance the quality of our American civilization.

Your imagination, your initiative, and your indignation will determine whether we build a society where progress is the servant of our needs, or a society where old values and new visions are buried under unbridled growth. For in your time we have the opportunity to move not only toward the rich society and the powerful society, but upward to the Great Society.

The Great Society rests on abundance and liberty for all. It demands an end to poverty and racial injustice, to which we are totally committed in our time. But that is just the beginning.

The Great Society is a place where every child can find knowledge to enrich his mind and to enlarge his talents. It is a place where leisure is a welcome chance to build and reflect, not a feared cause of boredom and restlessness. It is a place where the city of man serves not only the needs of the body and the demands of commerce but the desire for beauty and the hunger for community.

It is a place where man can renew contact with nature. It is a place which honors creation for its own sake and for what it adds to the understanding of the race. It is a place where men are more concerned with the quality of their goals than the quantity of their goods.

But most of all, the Great Society is not a safe harbor, a resting place, a final objective, a finished work. It is a challenge constantly renewed, beckoning us toward a destiny where the meaning of our lives matches the marvelous products of our labor.

So I want to talk to you today about three places where we begin to build the Great Society—in our cities, in our countryside, and in our classrooms.

Many of you will live to see the day, perhaps 50 years from now, when there will be 400 million Americans four-fifths of them in urban areas. In the remainder of this century urban population will double, city land will double, and we will have to build homes, highways, and facilities equal to all those built since this country was first settled. So in the next 40 years we must rebuild the entire urban United States.

Aristotle said: "Men come together in cities in order to live, but they remain together in order to live the good life." It is harder and harder to live the good life in American cities today.

The catalog of ills is long: there is the decay of the centers and the despoiling of the suburbs. There is not enough housing for our people or transportation for our traffic. Open land is vanishing and old landmarks are violated.

Worst of all expansion is eroding the precious and time honored values of community with neighbors and communion with nature. The loss of these values breeds loneliness and boredom and indifference.

Our society will never be great until our cities are great. Today the frontier of imagination and innovation is inside those cities and not beyond their borders.

New experiments are already going on. It will be the task of your generation to make the American city a place where future generations will come, not only to live but to live the good life.

I understand that if I stayed here tonight I would see that Michigan students are really doing their best to live the good life.

This is the place where the Peace Corps was started. It is inspiring to see how all of you, while you are in this country, are trying so hard to live at the level of the people.

A second place where we begin to build the Great Society is in our countryside. We have always prided ourselves on being not only America the strong and America the free, but America the beautiful. Today that beauty is in danger. The water we drink, the food we eat, the very air that we breathe, are threatened with pollution. Our parks are overcrowded, our seashores overburdened. Green fields and dense forests are disappearing.

A few years ago we were greatly concerned about the "Ugly American." Today we must act to prevent an ugly America.

For once the battle is lost, once our natural splendor is destroyed, it can never be recaptured. And once man can no longer walk with beauty or wonder at nature his spirit will wither and his sustenance be wasted.

A third place to build the Great Society is in the classrooms of America. There your children's lives will be shaped. Our society will not be great until every young mind is set free to scan the farthest reaches of thought and imagination. We are still far from that goal.

Today, 8 million adult Americans, more than the entire population of Michigan, have not finished 5 years of school. Nearly 20 million have not finished 8 years of school. Nearly 54 million—more than one-quarter of all America—have not even finished high school.

Each year more than 100,000 high school graduates, with proved ability, do not enter college because they cannot afford it. And if we cannot educate today's youth, what will we do in 1970 when elementary school enrollment will be 5 million greater than 1960? And high school enrollment will rise by 5 million. College enrollment will increase by more than 3 million.

In many places, classrooms are overcrowded and curricula are outdated. Most of our qualified teachers are underpaid, and many of our paid teachers are unqualified. So we must give every child a place to sit and a teacher to learn from. Poverty must not be a bar to learning, and learning must offer an escape from poverty.

But more classrooms and more teachers are not enough. We must seek an educational system which grows in excellence as it grows in size. This means better training for our teachers. It means preparing youth to enjoy their hours of leisure as well as their hours of labor. It means exploring new techniques of teaching, to find new ways to stimulate the love of learning and the capacity for creation.

These are three of the central issues of the Great Society. While our Government has many programs directed at those issues, I do not pretend that we have the full answer to those problems.

But I do promise this: We are going to assemble the best thought and the broadest knowledge from all over the world to find those answers for America. I intend to establish working groups to prepare a series of White House conferences and meetings—on the cities, on natural beauty, on the quality of education, and on other emerging challenges. And from these meetings and from this inspiration and from these studies we will begin to set our course toward the Great Society.

The solution to these problems does not rest on a massive program in Washington, nor can it rely solely on the strained resources of local authority. They require us to create new concepts of cooperation, a creative federalism, between the National Capital and the leaders of local communities.

Woodrow Wilson once wrote: "Every man sent out from his university should be a man of his Nation as well as a man of his time."

Within your lifetime powerful forces, already loosed, will take us toward a way of life beyond the realm of our experience, almost beyond the bounds of our imagination.

For better or for worse, your generation has been appointed by history to deal with those problems and to lead America toward a new age. You have the chance never before afforded to any people in any age. You can help build a society where the demands of morality, and the needs of the spirit, can be realized in the life of the Nation.

So, will you join in the battle to give every citizen the full equality which God enjoins and the law requires, whatever his belief, or race, or the color of his skin?

Will you join in the battle to give every citizen an escape from the crushing weight of poverty?

Will you join in the battle to make it possible for all nations to live in enduring peace—as neighbors and not as mortal enemies?

Will you join in the battle to build the Great Society, to prove that our material progress is only the foundation on which we will build a richer life of mind and spirit?

There are those timid souls who say this battle cannot be won; that we are condemned to a soulless wealth. I do not agree. We have the power to shape the civilization that we want. But we need your will, your labor, your hearts, if we are to build that kind of society.

Those who came to this land sought to build more than just a new country. They sought a new world. So I have come here today to your campus to say that you can make their vision our reality. So let us from this moment begin our work so that in the future men will look back and say: It was then, after a long and weary way, that man turned the exploits of his genius to the full enrichment of his life.

Thank you. Goodbye.

NOTE: The President spoke at the graduation exercises at the University of Michigan at Ann Arbor after receiving an honorary degree of Doctor of Civil Law. His opening words referred to Harlan H. Hatcher, president of the university, Governor George Romney, senators Pat McNamara and Philip A. Hart, and representatives George Meader and Neil Staebler, all of Michigan.

## 3. Telephone Conversation, with Senator Richard B. Russell (D-Ga.), May 27, 1964

*Transcript of Telephone Conversation between Lyndon B. Johnson and Senator Richard Russell, May 27, 1964, 10:55 A.M., Citation #3519–21, Recordings and Transcripts of Conversations and Meetings, Lyndon B. Johnson Library, Austin, Texas.*

Richard Russell[1]: How are you, Mr. President?

Lyndon B. Johnson: Oh, I got lots of troubles.

Russell: Well, we all have those.

Johnson: What do you think about this Vietnam thing? I'd like to hear you talk a little bit.

Russell: Frankly, Mr. President, if you were to tell me that I was authorized to settle it as I saw fit, I would respectfully decline and not take it.

Johnson: [Laughs]

Russell: It's the damn worst mess I ever saw, and I don't like to brag. I never have been right many times in my life. But I knew that we were going to get into this sort of mess when we went in there. And I don't see how we're ever going to get out of it without fighting a major war with the Chinese and all them down there in those rice paddies and jungles. I just don't see it. I just don't know what to do.

Johnson: That's the way I been feeling for six months.

Russell: It appears that our position is deteriorating. And it looks like the more we try to do for them, the less they're willing to do for themselves. It's just a sad situation. There's no sense of responsibility there on the part of any of their leaders. . . . It's a hell of a situation. It's a mess. And it's going to get worse. And I don't know what to do. I don't think the American people are quite ready to send our troops in there to do the fighting. And if it came down to an option of just sending Americans in there to do the fighting, which will, of course, eventually lead into a ground war and a conventional war with China, we'd do them a favor every time we killed a coolie, whereas when one of our people got killed, it would be a loss to us. If it got down to that or just pulling out, I'd get out. But then I don't know. There's undoubtedly some middle ground somewhere. If I was going to get out, I'd get the same crowd that got rid of old Diem[2] to get rid of these people and get some fellow in there that said he wished to hell we would get out. That would be a good excuse for getting out. . . .

Johnson: How important is it to us?

Russell: It isn't important a damn bit, with all this new missile . . .

---

[1]Russell had been Johnson's mentor in the Senate, and they forged an extremely close relationship. Once Johnson became president, they were at odds over civil rights. Russell was one of the leaders in the filibuster against the civil rights bill of 1964 that was then going on in the Senate at the time of this conversation. But Johnson maintained a close relationship with Russell and often discussed major issues, such as Vietnam, with him.

[2]Ngo Dinh Diem, was murdered during a coup that overthrew his government in South Vietnam on November 1–2, 1963.

Johnson: Well, I guess it's important to us—

Russell:—from a psychological standpoint—

Johnson: I mean, yes, from the standpoint that we are party to a treaty.[3] And if we don't pay any attention to this treaty, why, I don't guess they think we pay attention to any of them.

Russell: Yeah, but we're the only ones paying any attention to it.

Johnson: Yeah, I think that's right.

Russell: You see, the other people are just as bound to that treaty as we are. I think there are some twelve or fourteen other countries.[4]

Johnson: That's right, there are fourteen of 'em . . .

Russell: Other than a question of our word and saving face, . . . I don't that think anybody would expect us to stay in there. Some old freebooter down in there—I've forgotten his name—. . . sort of a hellraiser—. . . I think that if he were to take over, he'd ask us to get out. Of course, if he did, under our theory of standing by self-determination of people, I don't see how we can say we're not going to go, if he were in charge of the government. The thing is going to be a headache to anybody that tries to fool with it. Now you got all the brains in the country, Mr. President. You better get a hold of them. I don't know what to do about this. I saw it all coming on. But that don't do any good now. That's water over the dam—under the bridge. We're there. You've got over there McNamara.[5] He was up here testifying yesterday before the committee.[6] . . . He's been kicked around on it, so where I'm not sure he's as objective as he ought to be in surveying the conditions out there. He feels like it's of up to him personally to see that the thing goes through. And he's a can-

do fella. But I'm not too sure he understands the history and background of those people out there as fully as he should. But even from his picture, the damn thing ain't getting any better and it's getting worse. And we're putting more and more in there. And they're taking more and more away from the people we're trying to help, that we give them. You better get some brains from somewhere. . . . I don't know what to do with it.

Johnson: Well, I spend all my days with Rusk and McNamara and Bundy and Harriman and Vance and all those folks that are dealin' with it[7], and I would say that it pretty well adds up to them now that we've got to show some power and some force and that they do not believe—they're kinda like MacArthur in Korea—they don't believe that the Chinese Communists will come into this thing. But they don't know and nobody can really be sure. But their feeling is that they won't. And in any event, that we haven't got much choice, that we're treaty-bound, that we're there, that this will be a domino that will kick off a whole list of others, and that we've just got to prepare for the worst. Now I have avoided that for a few days. I don't think the American people are for it. I don't agree with Morse[8] and all he says, but—

Russell: No, neither do I, but he's voicing the sentiment of a hell of a lot of people.

Johnson: I'm afraid that's right. I'm afraid that's right. I don't think the people of the country know much about Vietnam, and I think they care a hell of a lot less.

Russell: Yeah, I know, if you go to send a whole lot of our boys out there—

Johnson: . . . That's what I'm talking about. . . . We had thirty-five killed—and we got enough hell over thirty-five—this year.

Russell: More than that have been killed in Atlanta, Georgia—been killed this year in automobile accidents.

---

[3]The Southeast Asia Treaty Organization, created in 1954, committed each member nation, including the United States, in the event of an armed attack in the area covered by the treaty, "to meet the common danger in accordance with its constitutional processes." South Vietnam was part of the area covered under the treaty.
[4]Actually, there were seven other members of SEATO beside the United States—France, the United Kingdom, Australia, New Zealand, Thailand, the Philippines, and Pakistan.
[5]Robert S. McNamara, secretary of defense.
[6]Russell was referring to the Senate Armed Services Committee, which he chaired.

---

[7]Dean Rusk, secretary of state; McGeorge Bundy, special assistant to the president for national security affairs; W. Averell Harriman, undersecretary of state for political affairs; Cyrus Vance, deputy secretary of defense.
[8]Senator Wayne Morse (D–Ore.), an opponent of deepening U.S. involvement in South Vietnam.

Johnson: That's right, . . . but that doesn't make any difference. . . . The Republicans are going to make a political issue out of it, every one of them, even Dirksen.[9]

Russell: It's the only issue they got.

Johnson: . . Hickenlooper[10] said that we just had to stand and show our force and put our men in there and let come what may come. And nobody disagreed with him. Now Mansfield,[11] he just wants to pull up and get out. Morse wants to get out, and Gruening[12] wants to get out. And that's about where it stops. I don't know.

Russell: There's others here that want to get out, but haven't said much about it. Frank Church[13] has told me two or three times that he didn't want to make a speech on it. He just wished to God we could get out of there. I don't know whether he's told you that or not.

Johnson: No, I haven't talked to him. . . . Who are the best people we have that you know of to talk about this thing? I don't want to do anything on the basis of just the information I got now. . . . I've talked to Eisenhower[14] a little bit.

Russell: I think that the people that you have named have all formed a hard opinion on it. . . .

Johnson: Rusk has tried to pull back. . . . But he's about to come to the conclusion now that Laos is crumbling and Vietnam is wobbly—

Russell: Laos, Laos, Laos. Hell, it ain't worth a damn. . . . That Laotian thing is absolutely impossible. It's a whole lot worse than Vietnam. There are some of these Vietnamese, after they beat 'em over the head, that'll go in there and fight. But Laos is an impossible situation. It's just a rathole there. I don't know. Before I took any drastic action, I think I'd get somebody about like old Omar Bradley[15] and one or two

perhaps senior people that have had some government experience—not necessarily military. . . . Let them go out there and fool around for a few days and smell the air and get the atmosphere and come back here and tell you what they think. They are new in it—would not have a great many preconceived ideas in approaching it.

Johnson: Now one of our big problems, Dick, the biggest between us—and I don't want this repeated to anybody—is Lodge.[16]

Russell: I know it!

Johnson: He ain't worth a damn. He can't work with anybody. . . . Now we got the best USIA[17] man to put on all the radios and try to get 'em to be loyal to the government and to be fighting and quit deserting and he calls in the USIA and says, "I handle the newspapers and magazines and radio myself, so the hell with you." So that knocks that guy out. Then we send out the best CIA man we got and he said, "I handle the intelligence. To hell with you." Then he wants a new deputy chief of mission. We get him to give us some names and we pick one of those[18], the best we got, send him out to run the damn war and he gets where he won't speak to the deputy chief of mission. Then we get General Harkins[19] out there and we thought he was a pretty good man and he gets where he can't work with him. So we send Westmoreland[20] out. And it's just a hell of a mess. You can't do anything with Lodge, and that's where McNamara's so frustrated. He goes out and they get agreements and he issues orders and he sends his stuff in there and Lodge just takes charge of

---

[9]Senator Everett M. Dirksen (R–Ill.), the minority leader in the Senate.

[10]Senator Bourke Hickenlooper (R–Iowa).

[11]Senator Mike Mansfield (D–Mont.), the majority leader in the Senate.

[12]Senator Ernest Gruening (D–Ak.).

[13]Senator Frank Church (D–Idaho).

[14]Former president Dwight D. Eisenhower.

[15]General of the Army Omar N. Bradley was chair of the Joint Chiefs of Staff from 1949 until 1953.

[16]Henry Cabot Lodge, the U.S. ambassador to South Vietnam. Lodge was a Republican who had been his party's nominee for vice president in 1960. He had won the Republican primary in New Hampshire in March 1964 as a write-in candidate, but refused to return to the United States to campaign for the presidential nomination. Still, Johnson and Russell believed that Lodge had political aspirations that might affect his support of administration policy in Southeast Asia.

[17]United States Information Agency.

[18]David G. Nes was the deputy chief of mission.

[19]General Paul D. Harkins was commander of the U.S. Military Assistance Command Vietnam, until June 20, 1964.

[20]General William C. Westmoreland was deputy commander of the U.S. Military Command, Vietnam, January 27–June 19, 1964. On June 20, he succeeded Harkins as commander.

it himself and he's not a take-charge man and it just gets stacked up.

Russell: He never has followed anything through to a conclusion since I've known him and I've known him for twenty-odd years. . . . He's a bright fellow, an intelligent fellow, but . . . he thinks he's dealing with barbarian tribes out there, that he's an emperor and he's gonna tell 'em what to do. There ain't any doubt in my mind but that he had old Diem killed out there himself—[21]

Johnson: That was a tragic mistake. It was awful, and we've lost everything.

Russell: Why don't you get somebody who's more pliant than Lodge, who'd do exactly what he said, right quick? He's living up on cloud nine. . . . I don't know. Probably the best thing you could do would be to ask Lodge if he don't think it's about time to be coming home.

Johnson: Well, he'd be back home campaigning against us on this issue, every day.

Russell: God Almighty, he's gonna come back anyhow when the time comes. I'd give him a reason for doing it. He's gonna come back. If you bring him back now, everybody'll say he's mad 'cause Johnson removed him out there. . . . You needn't worry. Lodge'll be in here. In my judgment, he'll be on that ticket in some way. I don't think they'll nominate him for president, but they may put him on there for vice president. Whether they do or don't, he'll be back here campaigning before that campaign's over. . . . I better take that back. This thing is so hopeless for the Republicans. . . . He certainly has got enough political sense not to get his head chopped off. It would be perfectly foolish. . . .

Russell: I just don't know. It's a tragic situation. It's just one of those places where you can't win. Anything you do is wrong. . . . I have thought about it. I have worried about it. I have prayed about it.

Johnson: I don't believe we can do anything—

Russell: It's something that frightens me 'cause it's my country involved over there and if we get into there on any considerable scale, there's no doubt in my mind but that the Chinese will be in there

and we'd be fighting a danged conventional war against our secondary potential threat and it'd be a Korea on a much bigger scale and a worse scale. . . . If you go from Laos and Cambodia into Vietnam and bring North Vietnam into it too, it's the damndest mess on earth. The French report that they lost 250,000 men and spent a couple billion of their money and two billion of ours down there and they just got the hell whipped out of them. And they had the best troops in there. . . .

Johnson: You don't have any doubt but that if we go in there and get 'em up against the wall, the Chinese Communists are gonna come in?

Russell: No sir, no doubt about it.

Johnson: That's my judgment, and my people don't think so. . . .

Russell: There's no doubt in my mind about it that you'll find Chinese volunteers in there as soon as you get—or very shortly after we have active combat units engaged.

Johnson: . . . Well, we are ready to confer with anybody, any time. But conferences ain't gonna do a damn bit of good. They ain't gonna take back and give us the territory and behave. We tell 'em every week, we tell Khrushchev,[22] we send China and Hanoi and all of 'em word that we'll get out of there and stay out of there if they'll just quit raiding their neighbors. And they just say, "Screw you."

Russell: That's right.

Johnson: So a conference won't do it. So the whole question, as I see it, is, is it more dangerous for us to let things go as they're going now, deteriorating every day—

Russell: I don't think we can let it go, Mr. President, indefinitely.

Johnson: —than it would be for us to move in?

Russell: We either got to move in or move out.

Johnson: That's about what it is.

Russell: You can make a tremendous case for moving out, not as good a one for moving in, but—

Johnson: Well, you take Nixon, Rockefeller[23]—

---

[21]Lodge had been an advocate of a coup to oust Diem.

[22]Soviet chairman Nikita S. Khrushchev.

Russell: It would be more consistent with the attitude of the American people and their general reactions to go in—they could understand that. But getting out, even after we go in and get bogged down in there in a war with China, it's going to be a hell of a mess. It would be worse than where we are now, to some extent, and that's what makes it so difficult. . . . I don't know how much Russia—they want to cause us all the trouble they can—but is there any truth in the theory that they are really at odds with China?

Johnson: . . . They wouldn't forsake that Communist philosophy.

Russell: We might get them to take an active part in getting the thing straightened out.

Johnson: We're doing all we can on that, but she doesn't show any signs of contributing.

Russell: They'd be foolish to . . . because we are just continuing to pour money in there and get nothing back out of it. We don't even get good will back out of that. . . . McNamara is the smartest fellow that any of us know, but he's got so damn—He is opinionated as hell, and he's made up his mind on this.

Johnson: I'll tell you what he's done, Dick. I think he's a pretty flexible fellow. He's gone out there, and he got Khanh[24] to agree that we cannot launch a counteroffensive or hit the North until he gets more stabilized and better set in the South and he thought he was buying us time and we could get by till November. But these politicians got to raise hell. . . . All the senators, Nixon and Rockefeller and Goldwater[25] all saying let's move, let's go in the North. . . . They can always get an isolated example of the bad things that McNamara says. But that's not generally true. They've had too many damned people being killed every day. And they're flying the sorties and they're getting some results and they're killing thousands of their people. But we're losing more. I mean, we're

losing ground. And he was hoping that we could avoid moving into the North and thereby provoking the Chinese for a few months.

Russell: Hell, there ain't any way you can move into the North. You know as well as I do we've tried that from infiltration, guerrilla war standpoint, with disastrous results.

Johnson: Lodge, Nixon, Rockefeller, Goldwater all say move. Eisenhower—

Russell: Bomb the North and kill old men, women, and children?

Johnson: No, no no. They say pick out an oil plant or pick out a refinery or something like that. Take selected targets. Watch this trail they're coming down.[26] Try to bomb them out of there, when they're coming in.

Russell: Oh, hell. That ain't worth a hoot. That's just impossible. . . . We tried it in Korea.[27] We even got a lot of old B-29s to increase the bomb load and sent 'em over there and just dropped millions and millions of bombs, day and night, and in the morning—they would knock out the road at night—and in the morning the damn people would be back traveling over it. . . . We never could actually interdict all their lines of communication in Korea although we had absolute control of the seas and the air, and we never did stop them. And you ain't gonna stop these people either.

Johnson: Well, they'd impeach a president, though, that'd run out, wouldn't they? I just—outside of Morse, everybody I talk to says you got to go in, including Hickenlooper, including all the Republicans. None of them disagreed with him yesterday when he made the statement that you got to take a stand. And I don't know how in the hell you're gonna get out unless they[28] tell you to get out.

Russell: If we had a man running the government over there that told us to get out, we could sure get out.

Johnson: That's right, but you can't do that, . . . Wouldn't that pretty well fix us in the eyes of the world, though, and make it look might bad?

---

[23]Former vice president Richard M. Nixon and New York governor Nelson A. Rockefeller. The latter was a candidate for the Republican presidential nomination in 1964.

[24]Major General Nguyen Khanh, prime minister of South Vietnam.

[25]Senator Barry Goldwater (R–Ariz.), the eventual Republican nominee for president in 1964.

[26]The Ho Chi Minh Trail.

[27]During the Korean War.

[28]Johnson seems to be referring to the South Vietnamese government.

Russell: Well, I don't know. [laughs] We don't look too good right now. At least, you'd look pretty good, I guess, going in there with all the troops and sending them all in there, but I tell you it'll be the most expensive venture this country ever went into.

Johnson: I've got a little old sergeant that works for me over at the house, and he got six children. And I just put him up as the United States Army and Air Force and Navy every time I think about making this decision and think about sending that father of those six kids in there. And what the hell are we going to get out of his doing it? And it just makes the chills run up my back.

Russell: It does me. I just can't see it.

Johnson: I haven't got the nerve to do it, and I don't see any other way out of it.

Russell: Not much sense to do it. It's one of these things where, "heads I win, tails you lose."

Johnson: Well, think about it, and I'll talk to you again. I hate to bother you, but I just—

Russell: I wish I could help you. God knows I do, 'cause it's a terrific quandary that we're in over there. We're just in the quicksands up to over very necks. And I just don't know what the hell is the best way to do about it.

Johnson: I love you, and I'll be calling you.

## 4. Special Message to Congress, March 15, 1965

*Public Papers of the Presidents of the United States: Lyndon B. Johnson, 1965, Vols. 1–2. (Washington, D.C.: U.S. Government Printing Office, 1966), 1: 281–287.*

Mr. Speaker, Mr. President, Members of the Congress:

I speak tonight for the dignity of man and the destiny of democracy.

I urge every member of both parties, Americans of all religions and of all colors, from every section of this country, to join me in that cause.

At times history and fate meet at a single time in a single place to shape a turning point in man's unending search for freedom. So it was at Lexington and Concord. So it was a century ago at Appomattox. So it was last week in Selma, Alabama.

There, long-suffering men and women peacefully protested the denial of their rights as Americans. Many were brutally assaulted. One good man, a man of God, was killed.

There is no cause for pride in what has happened in Selma. There is no cause for self-satisfaction in the long denial of equal rights of millions of Americans. But there is cause for hope and for faith in our democracy in what is happening here tonight.

For the cries of pain and the hymns and protests of oppressed people have summoned into convocation all the majesty of this great Government—the Government of the greatest Nation on earth.

Our mission is at once the oldest and the most basic of this country: to right wrong, to do justice, to serve man.

In our time we have come to live with moments of great crisis. Our lives have been marked with debate about great issues; issues of war and peace, issues of prosperity and depression. But rarely in any time does an issue lay bare the secret heart of America itself. Rarely are we met with a challenge, not to our growth or abundance, our welfare or our security, but rather to the values and the purposes and the meaning of our beloved Nation.

The issue of equal rights for American Negroes is such an issue. And should we defeat every enemy, should we double our wealth and conquer the stars, and still be unequal to this issue, then we will have failed as a people and as a nation.

For with a country as with a person, "What is a man profited, if he shall gain the whole world, and lose his own soul?"

There is no Negro problem. There is no Southern problem. There is no Northern problem. There is only an American problem. And we are met here tonight as Americans—not as Democrats or Republicans—we are met here as Americans to solve that problem.

This was the first nation in the history of the world to be founded with a purpose. The great phrases of that purpose still sound in every American heart, North and South: "All men are created equal"—"government by consent of the governed"—"give me liberty or give me death." Well, those are not just clever words, or those are not just empty theories. In their name Americans have fought and died for two centuries, and tonight around the world they stand there as guardians of our liberty, risking their lives.

Those words are a promise to every citizen that he shall share in the dignity of man. This dignity cannot be found in a man's possessions; it cannot be found in his power, or in his position. It really rests on his right to be treated as a man equal in opportunity to all others. It says that he shall share in freedom, he shall choose his leaders, educate his children, and provide for his family according to his ability and his merits as a human being.

To apply any other test—to deny a man his hopes because of his color or race, his religion or the place of his birth—is not only to do injustice, it is to deny America and to dishonor the dead who gave their lives for American freedom.

## THE RIGHT TO VOTE

Our fathers believed that if this noble view of the rights of man was to flourish, it must be rooted in democracy. The most basic right of all was the right to choose your own leaders. The history of this country, in large measure, is the history of the expansion of that right to all of our people.

Many of the issues of civil rights are very complex and most difficult. But about this there can and should be no argument. Every American citizen must have an equal right to vote. There is no reason which can excuse the denial of that right. There is no duty which weighs more heavily on us than the duty we have to ensure that right.

Yet the harsh fact is that in many places in this country men and women are kept from voting simply because they are Negroes.

Every device of which human ingenuity is capable has been used to deny this right. The Negro citizen may go to register only to be told that the day is wrong, or the hour is late, or the official in charge is absent. And if he persists, and if he manages to present himself to the registrar, he may be disqualified because he did not spell out his middle name or because he abbreviated a word on the application.

And if he manages to fill out an application he is given a test. The registrar is the sole judge of whether he passes this test. He may be asked to recite the entire Constitution, or explain the most complex provisions of State law. And even a college degree cannot be used to prove that he can read and write.

For the fact is that the only way to pass these barriers is to show a white skin.

Experience has clearly shown that the existing process of law cannot overcome systematic and ingenious discrimination. No law that we now have on the books—and I have helped to put three of them there—can ensure the right to vote when local officials are determined to deny it.

In such a case our duty must be clear to all of us. The Constitution says that no person shall be kept from voting because of his race or his color. We have all sworn an oath before God to support and to defend that Constitution. We must now act in obedience to that oath.

## GUARANTEEING THE RIGHT TO VOTE

Wednesday I will send to Congress a law designed to eliminate illegal barriers to the right to vote.

The broad principles of that bill will be in the hands of the Democratic and Republican leaders tomorrow. After they have reviewed it, it will come here formally as a bill. I am grateful for this opportunity to come here tonight at the invitation of the leadership to reason with my friends, to give them my views, and to visit with my former colleagues.

I have had prepared a more comprehensive analysis of the legislation which I had intended to transmit to the clerk tomorrow but which I will submit to the clerks tonight. But I want to really discuss with you now briefly the main proposals of this legislation,

This bill will strike down restrictions to voting in all elections—Federal, State, and local—which have been used to deny Negroes the right to vote.

This bill will establish a simple, uniform standard which cannot be used, however ingenious the effort, to flout our Constitution.

It will provide for citizens to be registered by officials of the United States Government if the State officials refuse to register them.

It will eliminate tedious, unnecessary lawsuits which delay the right to vote.

Finally, this legislation will ensure that properly registered individuals are not prohibited from voting.

I will welcome the suggestions from all of the Members of Congress—I have no doubt that I will get some—on ways and means to strengthen this law and to make it effective. But experience has plainly shown that this is the only path to carry out the command of the Constitution.

To those who seek to avoid action by their National Government in their own communities; who want to and who seek to maintain purely local control over elections, the answer is simple:

Open your polling places to all your people.

Allow men and women to register and vote whatever the color of their skin.

Extend the rights of citizenship to every citizen of this land.

## THE NEED FOR ACTION

There is no constitutional issue here. The command of the Constitution is plain.

There is no moral issue. It is wrong—deadly wrong—to deny any of your fellow Americans the right to vote in this country.

There is no issue of States fights or national rights. There is only the struggle for human rights.

I have not the slightest doubt what will be your answer.

The last time a President sent a civil rights bill to the Congress it contained a provision to protect voting rights in Federal elections. That civil rights bill was passed after 8 long months of debate. And when that bill came to my desk from the Congress for my signature, the heart of the voting provision had been eliminated.

This time, on this issue, there must be no delay, no hesitation and no compromise with our purpose.

We cannot, we must not, refuse to protect the right of every American to vote in every election that he may desire to participate in. And we ought not and we cannot and we must not wait another 8 months before we get a bill. We have already waited a hundred years and more, and the time for waiting is gone.

So I ask you to join me in working long hours—nights and weekends, if necessary—to pass this bill. And I don't make that request lightly. For from the window where I sit with the problems of our country I recognize that outside this chamber is the outraged conscience of a nation, the grave concern of many nations, and the harsh judgment of history on our acts.

## WE SHALL OVERCOME

But even if we pass this bill, the battle will not be over. What happened in Selma is part of a far larger movement which reaches into every section and State of America. It is the effort of American Negroes to secure for themselves the full blessings of American life.

Their cause must be our cause too. Because it is not just Negroes, but really it is all of us, who must overcome the crippling legacy of bigotry and injustice. And we shall overcome.

As a man whose roots go deeply into Southern soil I know how agonizing racial feelings are. I know how difficult it is to reshape the attitudes and the structure of our society.

But a century has passed, more than a hundred years, since the Negro was freed. And he is not fully free tonight.

It was more than a hundred years ago that Abraham Lincoln, a great President of another party, signed the Emancipation Proclamation, but emancipation is a proclamation and not a fact.

A century has passed, more than a hundred years, since equality was promised. And yet the Negro is not equal.

A century has passed since the day of promise. And the promise is unkept.

The time of justice has now come. I tell you that I believe sincerely that no force can hold it back. It is right in the eyes of man and God that it should come. And when it does, I think that day will brighten the lives of every American.

For Negroes are not the only victims. How many white children have gone uneducated, how many white families have lived in stark poverty, how many white lives have been scarred by fear, because we have wasted our energy and our substance to maintain the barriers of hatred and terror?

So I say to all of you here, and to all in the Nation tonight, that those who appeal to you to hold on to the past do so at the cost of denying you your future.

This great, rich, restless country can offer opportunity and education and hope to all: black and white, North and South, sharecropper and city dweller. These are the enemies: poverty, ignorance, disease. They are the enemies and not our fellow man, not our neighbor. And these enemies too, poverty, disease and ignorance, we shall overcome.

## AN AMERICAN PROBLEM

Now let none of us in any sections look with prideful righteousness on the troubles in another section, or on the problems of our neighbors. There is really no part of America where the promise of equality has been fully kept. In Buffalo as well as in Birmingham, in Philadelphia as well as in Selma, Americans are struggling for the fruits of freedom.

This is one Nation. What happens in Selma or in Cincinnati is a matter of legitimate concern to every American. But let each of us look within our own hearts and our own communities, and let each of us put our shoulder to the wheel to root out injustice wherever it exists.

As we meet here in this peaceful, historic chamber tonight, men from the South, some of whom were at Iwo Jima, men from the North who have carried Old Glory to far corners of the world and brought it back without a stain on it, men from the East and from the West, are all fighting together without regard to religion, or color, or region, in Viet-Nam. Men from every region fought for us across the world 20 years ago.

And in these common dangers and these common sacrifices the South made its contribution of honor and gallantry no less than any other region of the great Republic—and in some instances, a great many of them, more.

And I have not the slightest doubt that good men from everywhere in this country, from the Great Lakes to the Gulf of Mexico, from the Golden Gate to the harbors along the Atlantic, will rally together now in this cause to vindicate the freedom of all Americans. For all of us owe this duty; and I believe that all of us will respond to it.

Your President makes that request of every American.

## PROGRESS THROUGH THE DEMOCRATIC PROCESS

The real hero of this struggle is the American Negro. His actions and protests, his courage to risk safety and even to risk his life, have awakened the conscience of this Nation. His demonstrations have been designed to call attention to injustice, designed to provoke change, designed to stir reform.

He has called upon us to make good the promise of America. And who among us can say that we would have made the same progress were it not for his persistent bravery, and his faith in American democracy.

For at the real heart of battle for equality is a deep-seated belief in the democratic process. Equality depends not on the force of arms or tear gas but upon the force of moral right; not on recourse to violence but on respect for law and order.

There have been many pressures upon your President and there will be others as the days come and go. But I pledge you tonight that we intend to fight this battle where it should be fought: in the courts, and in the Congress, and in the hearts of men.

We must preserve the right of free speech and the right of free assembly. But the right of free speech does not carry with it, as has been said, the right to holler fire in a crowded theater. We must preserve the right to free assembly, but free assembly does not carry with it the right to block public thoroughfares to traffic.

We do have a right to protest, and a right to march under conditions that do not infringe the constitutional rights of our neighbors. And I intend to protect all those rights as long as I am permitted to serve in this office.

We will guard against violence, knowing it strikes from our hands the very weapons which we seek—progress, obedience to law, and belief in American values.

In Selma as elsewhere we seek and pray for peace. We seek order. We seek unity. But we will not accept the peace of stifled rights, or the order imposed by fear, or the unity that stifles protest. For peace cannot be purchased at the cost of liberty.

In Selma tonight, as in every—and we had a good day there—as in every city, we are working for just and peaceful settlement. We must all remember that after this speech I am making tonight, after the police and the FBI and the Marshals have all gone, and after you have promptly passed this bill, the people of Selma and the other cities of the Nation must still live and work together. And when the attention of the Nation has gone elsewhere they must try to heal the wounds and to build a new community.

This cannot be easily done on a battleground of violence, as the history of the South itself shows. It is in recognition of this that men of both races have shown such an outstandingly impressive responsibility in recent days—last Tuesday, again today,

## RIGHTS MUST BE OPPORTUNITIES

The bill that I am presenting to you will be known as a civil rights bill. But, in a larger sense, most of the program I am recommending is a civil rights program. Its object is to open the city of hope to all people of all races.

Because all Americans just must have the right to vote. And we are going to give them that right.

All Americans must have the privileges of citizenship regardless of race. And they are going to have those privileges of citizenship regardless of race.

But I would like to caution you and remind you that to exercise these privileges takes much more than just legal right. It requires a trained mind and a healthy body. It requires a decent home, and the chance to find a job, and the opportunity to escape from the clutches of poverty.

Of course, people cannot contribute to the Nation if they are never taught to read or write, if their bodies are stunted from hunger, if their sickness goes untended, if their life is spent in hopeless poverty just drawing a welfare check.

So we want to open the gates to opportunity. But we are also going to give all our people, black and white, the help that they need to walk through those gates.

## THE PURPOSE OF THIS GOVERNMENT

My first job after college was as a teacher in Cotulla, Tex., in a small Mexican-American school. Few of them could speak English, and I couldn't speak much Spanish. My students were poor and they often came to class without breakfast, hungry. They knew even in their youth the pain of prejudice. They never seemed to know why people disliked them. But they knew it was so, because I saw it in their eyes. I often walked home late in the afternoon, after the classes were finished, wishing there was more that I could do. But all I knew was to teach them the little that I knew, hoping that it might help them against the hardships that lay ahead.

Somehow you never forget what poverty and hatred can do when you see its scars on the hopeful face of a young child.

I never thought then, in 1928, that I would be standing here in 1965. It never even occurred to me in my fondest dreams that I might have the chance to help the sons and daughters of those students and to help people like them all over this country.

But now I do have that chance—and I'll let you in on a secret—I mean to use it. And I hope that you will use it with me.

This is the richest and most powerful country which ever occupied the globe. The might of past empires is little compared to ours. But I do not want to be the President who built empires, or sought grandeur, or extended dominion.

I want to be the President who educated young children to the wonders of their world. I want to be the President who helped to feed the hungry and to prepare them to be taxpayers instead of taxeaters.

I want to be the President who helped the poor to find their own way and who protected the right of every citizen to vote in every election.

I want to be the President who helped to end hatred among his fellow men and who promoted love among the people of all races and all regions and all parties.

I want to be the President who helped to end war among the brothers of this earth.

And so at the request of your beloved Speaker and the Senator from Montana; the majority leader, the Senator from Illinois; the minority leader, Mr. McCulloch, and other Members of both parties, I came here tonight—not as President Roosevelt came down one time in person to veto a bonus bill, not as President Truman came down one time to urge the passage of a railroad bill—but I came down here to ask you to share this task with me and to share it with the people that we both work for. I want this to be the Congress, Republicans and Democrats alike, which did all these things for all these people.

Beyond this great chamber, out yonder in 50 States, are the people that we serve. Who can tell what deep and unspoken hopes are in their hearts tonight as they sit there and listen. We all can guess, from our own lives, how difficult they often find their own pursuit of happiness, how many problems each little family has. They look most of all to themselves for their futures. But I think that they also look to each of us.

Above the pyramid on the great seal of the United States it says—in Latin—"God has favored our undertaking."

God will not favor everything that we do. It is rather our duty to divine His will. But I cannot help believing that He truly understands and that He really favors the undertaking that we begin here tonight.

# 5. Commencement Address at Howard University, June 4, 1965

*Public Papers of the Presidents of the United States: Lyndon B. Johnson, 1965, Vols. 1–2. (Washington, D.C.: U.S. Government Printing Office, 1966), 2: 635–640.*

Dr. Nabrit, my fellow Americans:

I am delighted at the chance to speak at this important and this historic institution. Howard has long been an outstanding center for the education of Negro Americans. Its students are of every race and color and they come from many countries of the world. It is truly a working example of democratic excellence.

Our earth is the home of revolution. In every corner of every continent men charged with hope contend with ancient ways in the pursuit of justice. They reach for the newest of weapons to realize the oldest of dreams, that each may walk in freedom and pride, stretching his talents, enjoying the fruits of the earth.

Our enemies may occasionally seize the day of change, but it is the banner of our revolution they take. And our own future is linked to this process of swift and turbulent change in many lands in the world. But nothing in any country touches us more profoundly, and nothing is more freighted with meaning for our own destiny than the revolution of the Negro American.

In far too many ways American Negroes have been another nation: deprived of freedom, crippled by hatred, the doors of opportunity closed to hope.

In our time change has come to this Nation, too. The American Negro, acting with impressive restraint, has peacefully protested and marched, entered the courtrooms and the seats of government, demanding a justice that has long been denied. The voice of the Negro was the call to action. But it is a tribute to America that, once aroused, the courts and the Congress, the President and most of the people, have been the allies of progress.

## LEGAL PROTECTION FOR HUMAN RIGHTS

Thus we have seen the high court of the country declare that discrimination based on race was repugnant to the Constitution, and therefore void. We have seen in 1957, and 1960, and again in 1964, the first civil rights legislation in this Nation in almost an entire century.

As majority leader of the United States Senate, I helped to guide two of these bills through the Senate. And, as your President, I was proud to sign the third. And now very soon we will have the fourth—a new law guaranteeing every American the right to vote.

No act of my entire administration will give me greater satisfaction than the day when my signature makes this bill, too, the law of this land.

The voting rights bill will be the latest, and among the most important, in a long series of victories. But this victory—as Winston Churchill said of another triumph for freedom—"is not the end. It

is not even the beginning of the end. But it is, perhaps, the end of the beginning."

That beginning is freedom; and the barriers to that freedom are tumbling down. Freedom is the right to share, share fully and equally, in American society—to vote, to hold a job, to enter a public place, to go to school. It is the right to be treated in every part of our national life as a person equal in dignity and promise to all others.

## FREEDOM IS NOT ENOUGH

But freedom is not enough. You do not wipe away the scars of centuries by saying: Now you are free to go where you want, and do as you desire, and choose the leaders you please.

You do not take a person who, for years, has been hobbled by chains and liberate him, bring him up to the starting line of a race and then say, "you are free to compete with all the others," and still justly believe that you have been completely fair.

Thus it is not enough just to open the gates of opportunity. All our citizens must have the ability to walk through those gates.

This is the next and the more profound stage of the battle for civil rights. We seek not just freedom but opportunity. We seek not just legal equity but human ability, not just equality as a right and a theory but equality as a fact and equality as a result.

For the task is to give 20 million Negroes the same chance as every other American to learn and grow, to work and share in society, to develop their abilities—physical, mental and spiritual, and to pursue their individual happiness.

To this end equal opportunity is essential, but not enough, not enough. Men and women of all races are born with the same range of abilities. But ability is not just the product of birth. Ability is stretched or stunted by the family that you live with, and the neighborhood you live in—by the school you go to and the poverty or the richness of your surroundings. It is the product of a hundred unseen forces playing upon the little infant, the child, and finally the man.

## PROGRESS FOR SOME

This graduating class at Howard University is witness to the indomitable determination of the Negro American to win his way in American life.

The number of Negroes in schools of higher learning has almost doubled in 15 years. The number of nonwhite professional workers has more than doubled in 10 years. The median income of Negro college women tonight exceeds that of white college women. And there are also the enormous accomplishments of distinguished individual Negroes—many of them graduates of this institution, and one of them the first lady ambassador in the history of the United States.

These are proud and impressive achievements. But they tell only the story of a growing middle class minority, steadily narrowing the gap between them and their white counterparts.

## A WIDENING GULF

But for the great majority of Negro Americans—the poor, the unemployed, the uprooted, and the dispossessed—there is a much grimmer story. They still, as we meet here tonight, are another nation. Despite the court orders and the laws, despite the legislative victories and the speeches, for them the walls are rising and the gulf is widening.

Here are some of the facts of this American failure.

Thirty-five years ago the rate of unemployment for Negroes and whites was about the same. Tonight the Negro rate is twice as high.

In 1948 the 8 percent unemployment rate for Negro teenage boys was actually less than that of whites. By last year that rate had grown to 23 percent, as against 13 percent for whites unemployed.

Between 1949 and 1959, the income of Negro men relative to white men declined in every section of this country. From 1952 to 1963 the median income of Negro families compared to white actually dropped from 57 percent to 53 percent.

In the years 1955 through 1957, 22 percent of experienced Negro workers were out of work at some time during the year. In 1961 through 1963 that proportion had soared to 29 percent.

Since 1947 the number of white families living in poverty has decreased 27 percent while the number of poorer nonwhite families decreased only 3 percent.

The infant mortality of nonwhites in 1940 was 70 percent greater than whites. Twenty-two years later it was 90 percent greater.

Moreover, the isolation of Negro from white communities is increasing, rather than decreasing as Negroes crowd into the central cities and become a city within a city.

Of course Negro Americans as well as white Americans have shared in our rising national abun-dance. But the harsh fact of the matter is that in the battle for true equality too many—far too many—are losing ground every day.

## THE CAUSES OF INEQUALITY

We are not completely sure why this is. We know the causes are complex and subtle. But we do know the two broad basic reasons. And we do know that we have to act.

First, Negroes are trapped—as many whites are trapped—in inherited, gate-less poverty. They lack training and skills. They are shut in, in slums, without decent medical care. Private and public poverty combine to cripple their capacities.

We are trying to attack these evils through our poverty program, through our education program, through our medical care and our other health programs, and a dozen more of the Great Society programs that are aimed at the root causes of this poverty.

We will increase, and we will accelerate, and we will broaden this attack in years to come until this most enduring of foes finally yields to our unyielding will.

But there is a second cause—much more difficult to explain, more deeply grounded, more desperate in its force. It is the devastating heritage of long years of slavery; and a century of oppression, hatred, and injustice.

## SPECIAL NATURE OF NEGRO POVERTY

For Negro poverty is not white poverty. Many of its causes and many of its cures are the same. But there are differences—deep, corrosive, obstinate differences—radiating painful roots into the community, and into the family, and the nature of the individual.

These differences are not racial differences. They are solely and simply the consequence of ancient brutality, past injustice, and present prejudice. They are anguishing to observe. For the Negro they are a constant reminder of oppression. For the white they are a constant reminder of guilt. But they must be faced and they must be dealt with and they must be overcome, if we are ever to reach the time when the only difference between Negroes and whites is the color of their skin.

Nor can we find a complete answer in the experience of other American minorities. They made a valiant and a largely successful effort to emerge from poverty and prejudice.

The Negro, like these others, will have to rely mostly upon his own efforts. But he just cannot do it alone. For they did not have the heritage of centuries to overcome, and they did not have a cultural tradition which had been twisted and battered by endless years of hatred and hopelessness, nor were they excluded—these others—because of race or color—a feeling whose dark intensity is matched by no other prejudice in our society.

Nor can these differences be understood as isolated infirmities. They are a seamless web. They cause each other. They result from each other. They reinforce each other.

Much of the Negro community is buried under a blanket of history and circumstance. It is not a lasting solution to lift just one corner of that blanket. We must stand on all sides and we must raise the entire cover if we are to liberate our fellow citizens.

## THE ROOTS OF INJUSTICE

One of the differences is the increased concentration of Negroes in our cities. More than 73 percent of all Negroes live in urban areas compared with less than 70 percent of the whites. Most of these Negroes live in slums. Most of these Negroes live together—a separated people.

Men are shaped by their world. When it is a world of decay, ringed by an invisible wall, when escape is arduous and uncertain, and the saving pressures of a more hopeful society are unknown, it can cripple the youth and it can desolate the men.

There is also the burden that a dark skin can add to the search for a productive place in our society. Unemployment strikes most swiftly and broadly at the Negro, and this burden erodes hope. Blighted hope breeds despair. Despair brings indifferences to the learning which offers a way out. And despair, coupled with indifferences, is often the source of destructive rebellion against the fabric of society.

There is also the lacerating hurt of early collision with white hatred or prejudice, distaste or condescension. Other groups have felt similar intolerance. But success and achievement could wipe it away. They do not change the color of a man's skin. I have seen this uncomprehending pain in the eyes of the little, young Mexican-American schoolchildren that I taught many years ago. But it can be overcome. But, for many, the wounds are always open.

## FAMILY BREAKDOWN

Perhaps most important—its influence radiating to every part of life—is the breakdown of the Negro family structure. For this, most of all, white America must accept responsibility. It flows from centuries of oppression and persecution of the Negro man. It flows from the long years of degradation and discrimination, which have attacked his dignity and assaulted his ability to produce for his family.

This, too, is not pleasant to look upon. But it must be faced by those whose serious intent is to improve the life of all Americans.

Only a minority—less than half—of all Negro children reach the age of 18 having lived all their lives with both of their parents. At this moment, tonight, little less than two-thirds are at home with both of their parents. Probably a majority of all Negro children receive federally-aided public assistance sometime during their childhood.

The family is the cornerstone of our society. More than any other force it shapes the attitude, the hopes, the ambitions, and the values of the child. And when the family collapses it is the children that are usually damaged. When it happens on a massive scale the community itself is crippled.

So, unless we work to strengthen the family, to create conditions under which most parents will stay together—all the rest: schools, and playgrounds, and public assistance, and private concern, will never be enough to cut completely the circle of despair and deprivation.

## TO FULFILL THESE RIGHTS

There is no single easy answer to all of these problems.

Jobs are part of the answer. They bring the income which permits a man to provide for his family.

Decent homes in decent surroundings and a chance to learn—an equal chance to learn—are part of the answer.

Welfare and social programs better designed to hold families together are part of the answer.

Care for the sick is part of the answer.

An understanding heart by all Americans is another big part of the answer.

And to all of these fronts—and a dozen more—I will dedicate the expanding efforts of the Johnson administration.

But there are other answers that are still to be found. Nor do we fully understand even all of the problems. Therefore, I want to announce tonight that this fall I intend to call a White House conference of scholars, and experts, and outstanding

Negro leaders—men of both races—and officials of Government at every level.

This White House conference's theme and title will be "To Fulfill These Rights."

Its object will be to help the American Negro fulfill the rights which, after the long time of injustice, he is finally about to secure.

To move beyond opportunity to achievement.

To shatter forever not only the barriers of law and public practice, but the walls which bound the condition of many by the color of his skin.

To dissolve, as best we can, the antique enmities of the heart which diminish the holder, divide the great democracy, and do wrong—great wrong—to the children of God.

And I pledge you tonight that this will be a chief goal of my administration, and of my program next year, and in the years to come. And I hope, and I pray, and I believe, it will be a part of the program of all America.

### WHAT IS JUSTICE

For what is justice?

It is to fulfill the fair expectations of man.

Thus, American justice is a very special thing. For, from the first, this has been a land of towering expectations. It was to be a nation where each man could be ruled by the common consent of all—enshrined in law, given life by institutions, guided by men themselves subject to its rule. And all—all of every station and origin—would be touched equally in obligation and in liberty.

Beyond the law lay the land. It was a rich land, glowing with more abundant promise than man had ever seen. Here, unlike any place yet known, all were to share the harvest.

And beyond this was the dignity of man. Each could become whatever his qualities of mind and spirit would permit—to strive, to seek, and, if he could, to find his happiness.

This is American justice. We have pursued it faithfully to the edge of our imperfections, and we have failed to find it for the American Negro.

So, it is the glorious opportunity of this generation to end the one huge wrong of the American Nation and, in so doing, to find America for ourselves, with the same immense thrill of discovery which gripped those who first began to realize that here, at last, was a home for freedom.

All it will take is for all of us to understand what this country is and what this country must become.

The Scripture promises: "I shall light a candle of understanding in thine heart, which shall not be put out."

Together, and with millions more, we can light that candle of understanding in the heart of all America.

And, once lit, it will never again go out.

NOTE: The President spoke at 6:35 p.m. on the Main Quadrangle in front of the library at Howard University in Washington, after being awarded an honorary degree of doctor of laws. His opening words referred to Dr. James M. Nabrit, It., president of the University. During his remarks he referred to Mrs. Patricia Harris, U.S. ambassador to Luxembourg and former associate professor of law at Howard University.

## 6. Memorandum from the President's Special Assistant for National Security Affairs (Bundy) to President Johnson, Notes of Meeting, Washington, July 21–22, 1965 (excerpts)

*Foreign Relations of the United States, 1964–1968, volume III: Vietnam, June–December 1965 (Washington, D.C.: U.S. Government Printing Office, 1996)*

*Document 71, Notes of Meeting, Washington, July 21, 1965, 10:40 a.m., pp. 189–97.*

*Document 76, Notes of Meeting, Washington, July 22, 1965, Noon–2:15 p.m. pp. 209–17.*

*Document 78, Notes of Meeting, Washington, July 22, 1965, 3–4:20 p.m., pp. 218–20.*

Washington, July 21, 1965, 10:40 a.m.[1]

---

[1]Source: Johnson Library, Meeting Notes File, Box 1. No classification marking. The meeting was held in the Cabinet Room of the White House. The notes were originally handwritten by Valenti and later transcribed. They are quoted extensively in Valenti, A Very Human President, pp. 319–40. For another account of this meeting, see Document 72; more information on attendance is in footnote 1 thereto. For other firsthand accounts of the White House meetings on Vietnam on July 21 and July 22, see Johnson, Vantage Point, pp. 147–48; and Ball, The Past Has Another Pattern, pp. 399–403. William Bundy also wrote an account of the meetings. (Johnson Library, Papers of William P. Bundy, Chap. 27, pp. 30–33)

SUBJECT
Viet Nam

PRESENT
McNamara
Rusk
Vance
Mac Bundy
Gen. Wheeler
Geo. Ball
Bill Bundy
Len Unger
Helms
Raborn
Lodge
Rowan
McNaughton
Moyers
Valenti

(McNamara passed Top Secret paper to all in room to read. The paper was returned to McNamara.)

McNamara made it clear that the paper was his own view of the situation—his specific recommendations had been concurred in by Lodge, Sharp, Taylor, Johnson, Westmoreland but the rest of the paper had not—he did not seek or receive their concurrence.

Lodge: If I thought a diplomatic move would be successful, I would be for it. Now, it would harden the enemy. This is not the time to do it. Clarifying objectives is good for the world public, but not necessary for governments. They understand it.

McNamara: Seems to me our call-up and increase in budget is evidence that we are not taking over North Vietnam.

M. Bundy: Our public utterances will make it clear that we are not trying to take over North Vietnam.

McNamara: Our public actions must do this. We must show that we are not in with Ky's objective to invade NVN. We are building such a force that NVN might think that is what we are trying to do.

Lodge: Remember this "on to NVN" movement is part of a propaganda move and nothing more.

M. Bundy: Isn't it true that most of the diplomatic moves come from other nations rather than the U.S. (in rebuttal to Lodge's hard position).

McNamara: This is exactly what I am talking about.

Lodge: The President has done a remarkable job of forming public opinion so far. Very skillful.

M. Bundy: Are there divergences between GVN and US in troop use?

McNamara: GVN wants us to use troops in the highlands. This is unacceptable to us. While GVN originally recommended this, they are now in agreement with us.

Rusk: What is the capability of GVN to mobilize their own forces?

McNamara: They are trying to increase by 10,000 per month. Our country team is optimistic. I am not. Desertion rate is high. They say it is lessening, but I do not agree. We did not find any thread of discontent among our troops. U.S. morale is of the highest order. Proud of their dedication and devotion. It reflects the belief they are doing something worthwhile.

Wheeler: Agree. Advisors are pleased with Vietnamese. They speak very highly of Vietnamese common soldier. Officer corps very different. Some officers are not of highest quality. Not total however. Weakness in VN's forces are lack of adequate officer corps—in their training and attitude—but they are getting better.

Rusk: Any summary of enemy troubles?

McNamara: No, nothing more than we already know. They are suffering heavy losses. They are well supplied with ammunition. I suspect much of inflow of supplies is water-borne. Only part of our action that is unsatisfactory is our patrol of the seashore. But even if we did have tight control, it should make little difference in the next six to nine months.

Rusk: What is the timing on how we should proceed?

McNamara: There ought to be a statement to the American people no later than a week.

Bundy: It is quite possible the message to Congress will be a message to the public.

Rusk: We ought to get civilians in the Congressional testimony to abuse [disabuse] the feeling that the military is making the decisions.

Bundy: Perhaps Rusk should follow up the President's speech with statement of total unanimity.

Ball: It is one thing to ready the country for this decision and another to face the realities of the decision. We can't allow the country to wake up one morning and find heavy casualties. We need to be damn serious with the American public.

McNamara: We discussed the command arrangements—they are to be left as they are—parallel commands.

The President entered the meeting at 11:30 a.m.

McNamara: To support an additional 200,000 troops in VN by first of the year the reserves in the US should be reconstituted by like amount. I recommend calling up 235,000 a year from now, replace the reserves with regulars.

In mid-1966 we would have approximately 600,000 additional men.

President: What has happened in recent past that requires this decision on my part? What are the alternatives? Also, I want more discussions on what we expect to flow from this decision. Discuss in detail.

Have we wrung every single soldier out of every country we can? Who else can help? Are we the sole defenders of freedom in the world? Have we done all we can in this direction? The reasons for the call up? The results we can expect? What are the alternatives? We must make no snap judgments. We must consider carefully all our options.

We know we can tell SVN "we're coming home." Is that the option we should take? What flows from that.

The negotiations, the pause, all the other approaches—have all been explored. It makes us look weak—with cup in hand. We have tried.

Let's look at all our options so that every man at this table understands fully the total picture.

McNamara: This is our position a year ago (shows President a map of the country with legends). Estimated by country team that VC controls 25%—SVN 50%—rest in white area, VC in red areas.

VC tactics are terror, and sniping.

President: Looks dangerous to put US forces in those red areas.

McNamara: You're right. We're placing our people with their backs to the sea—for protection. Our mission would be to seek out the VC in large scale units.

Wheeler: Big problem in Vietnam is good combat intelligence. The VC is a creature of habit. By continuing to probe we think we can make headway.

Ball: Isn't it possible that the VC will do what they did against the French—stay away from confrontation and not accommodate us?

Wheeler: Yes, but by constantly harassing them, they will have to fight somewhere.

McNamara: If VC doesn't fight in large units, it will give ARVN a chance to re-secure hostile areas.

We don't know what VC tactics will be when VC is confronted by 175,000 Americans.

Raborn: We agree—by 1965, we expect NVN will increase their forces. They will attempt to gain a substantial victory before our build-up is complete.

President: Is anyone of the opinion we should not do what the memo says—If so, I'd like to hear from them.

Ball: I can foresee a perilous voyage—very dangerous—great apprehensions that we can win under these conditions. But, let me be clear, if the decision is to go ahead, I'm committed.

President: But is there another course in the national interest that is better than the McNamara course? We know it's dangerous and perilous. But can it be avoided?

Ball: There is no course that will allow us to cut our losses. If we get bogged down, our cost might be substantially greater. The pressures to create a larger war would be irresistible. Qualifications I have are not due to the fact that I think we are in a bad moral position.

President: What other road can I go?

Ball: Take what precautions we can—take losses—let their government fall apart—negotiate—probable take over by Communists. This is disagreeable, I know.

President: Can we make a case for this—discuss it fully?

Ball: We have discussed it. I have had my day in court.

President: I don't think we have made a full commitment. You have pointed out the danger, but you haven't proposed an alternative course. We haven't always been right. We have no mortgage on victory.

I feel we have very little alternative to what we are doing.

I want another meeting before we take this action. We should look at all other courses carefully. Right now I feel it would be more dangerous for us to lose this now, than endanger a greater number of troops.

Rusk: What we have done since 1954–61 has not been good enough. We should have probably committed ourselves heavier in 1961.

Rowan: What bothers me most is the weakness of the Ky government. Unless we put the screws on the Ky government, 175,000 men will do us no good.

Lodge: There is no tradition of a national government in Saigon. There are no roots in the country. Not until there is tranquility can you have any stability. I don't think we ought to take this government seriously. There is no one who can do anything. We have to do what we think we ought to do regardless of what the Saigon government does.

As we move ahead on a new phase—it gives us the right and duty to do certain things with or without the government's approval.

President: George, do you think we have another course?

Ball: I would not recommend that you follow McNamara's course.

President: Are you able to outline your doubts—and offer another course of action? I think it is desirable to hear you out—and determine if your suggestions are sound and ready to be followed.

Ball: Yes. I think I can present to you the least bad of two courses. What I would present is a course that is costly, but can be limited to short term costs.

President: Then, let's meet at 2:30 this afternoon to discuss Ball's proposals. Now let Bob tell us why we need to risk those 600,000 lives.

(McNamara and Wheeler outlined the reasons for more troops.) 75,000 now just enough to protect bases—it will let us lose slowly instead of rapidly. The extra men will stabilize the situation and improve it. It will give ARVN breathing room. We limit it to another 100,000 because VN can't absorb any more. There is no major risk of catastrophe.

President: But you will lose greater number of men.

Wheeler: The more men we have the greater the likelihood of smaller losses.

President: What makes you think if we put in 100,000 men Ho Chi Minh won't put in another 100,000?

Wheeler: This means greater bodies of men—which will allow us to cream them.

President: What are the chances of more NVN men coming?

Wheeler: 50-50 chance. He would be foolhardy to put 1/4 of his forces in SVN. It would expose him too greatly in NVN.

President: (to Raborn) Do you have people in NVN?

Raborn: Not enough. We think it is reliable.

President: Can't we improve intelligence in NVN?

Raborn: We have a task force working on this.

1:00 p.m.—Meeting adjourned until 2:30 p.m.[2]
Resume same meeting at 2:45 p.m.

Ball: We can't win. Long protracted. The most we can hope for is messy conclusion. There remains a great danger of intrusion by Chicoms.

Problem of long war in US:

1. Korean experience was galling one. Correlation between Korean casualties and public opinion (Ball showed Pres. a chart) showed support stabilized at 50%. As casualties increase, pressure to strike at jugular of the NVN will become very great.

---

[2]William Bundy later recalled that the president had a private meeting with McNamara and Rusk before the second full meeting convened at 2:30. (Johnson Library, *Papers of William P. Bundy*, Chap. 27, p. 31) No other record of this meeting has been found.

2. World opinion. If we could win in a year's time—win decisively—world opinion would be alright. However, if long and protracted we will suffer because a great power cannot beat guerrillas.

3. National politics. Every great captain in history is not afraid to make a tactical withdrawal if conditions are unfavorable to him. The enemy cannot even be seen; he is indigenous to the country.

   Have serious doubt if an army of westerners can fight orientals in Asian jungle and succeed.

President: This is important—can westerners, in absence of intelligence, successfully fight orientals in jungle rice-paddies? I want McNamara and Wheeler to seriously ponder this question.

Ball: I think we have all underestimated the seriousness of this situation. Like giving cobalt treatment to a terminal cancer case. I think a long protracted war will disclose our weakness, not our strength.

   The least harmful way to cut losses in SVN is to let the government decide it doesn't want us to stay there. Therefore, put such proposals to SVN government that they can't accept, then it would move into a neutralist position—and I have no illusions that after we were asked to leave, SVN would be under Hanoi control.

   What about Thailand? It would be our main problem. Thailand has proven a good ally so far—though history shows it has never been a staunch ally. If we wanted to make a stand in Thailand, we might be able to make it.

   Another problem would be South Korea. We have two divisions there now. There would be a problem with Taiwan, but as long as Generalissimo is there, they have no place to go. Indonesia is a problem—insofar as Malaysia. There we might have to help the British in military way. Japan thinks we are propping up a lifeless government and are on a sticky wicket. Between long war and cutting our losses, the Japanese would go for the latter (all this on Japan according to Reischauer).

President: Wouldn't all those countries say Uncle Sam is a paper tiger—wouldn't we lose credibility breaking the word of three presidents—if we set it up as you proposed. It would seem to be an irreparable blow. But, I gather you don't think so.

Ball: The worse blow would be that the mightiest power in the world is unable to defeat guerrillas.

President: Then you are not basically troubled by what the world would say about pulling out?

Ball: If we were actively helping a country with a stable, viable government, it would be a vastly different story. Western Europeans look at us as if we got ourselves into an imprudent fashion [situation].

President: But I believe that these people are trying to fight. They're like Republicans who try to stay in power, but don't stay there long.
(aside—amid laughter—"excuse me, Cabot")

Ball: Thieu spoke the other day and said the Communists would win the election.

President: I don't believe that. Does anyone believe that?
(There was no agreement from anyone—McNamara, Lodge, B. Bundy, Unger—all said they didn't believe it.)

McNamara: Ky will fall soon. He is weak. We can't have elections until there is physical security, and even then there will be no elections because as Cabot said, there is no democratic tradition. (Wheeler agreed about Ky—but said Thieu impressed him)

President: Two basic troublings:

1. That Westerners can ever win in Asia.
2. Don't see how you can fight a war under direction of other people whose government changes every month.

   Now go ahead, George, and make your other points.

Ball: The cost, as well as our Western European allies, is not relevant to their situation. What they are concerned about is their own security—troops in Berlin have real meaning, none in VN.

President: Are you saying pulling out of Korea would be akin to pulling out of Vietnam?

Bundy: It is not analogous. We had a status quo in Korea. It would not be that way in Vietnam.

Ball: We will pay a higher cost in Vietnam.

This is a decision one makes against an alternative.

On one hand—long protracted war, costly, NVN is digging in for long term. This is their life and driving force. Chinese are taking long term view—ordering blood plasma from Japan.

On the other hand—short-term losses. On balance, come out ahead of McNamara plan. Distasteful on either hand.

Bundy: Two important questions to be raised—I agree with the main thrust of McNamara. It is the function of my staff to argue both sides.

To Ball's argument: The difficulty in adopting it now would be a radical switch without evidence that it should be done. It goes in the face of all we have said and done.

His whole analytical argument gives no weight to loss suffered by other side. A great many elements in his argument are correct.

We need to make clear this is a somber matter—that it will not be quick—no single action will bring quick victory.

I think it is clear that we are not going to be thrown out.

Ball: My problem is not that we don't get thrown out, but that we get bogged down and don't win.

Bundy: I would sum up: The world, the country, and the VN would have alarming reactions if we got out.

Rusk: If the Communist world finds out we will not pursue our commitment to the end, I don't know where they will stay their hand.

I am more optimistic than some of my colleagues. I don't believe the VC have made large advances among the VN people.

We can't worry about massive casualties when we say we can't find the enemy. I don't see great casualties unless the Chinese come in.

Lodge: There is a greater threat to World War III if we don't go in. Similarity to our indolence at Munich.

I can't be as pessimistic as Ball. We have great seaports in Vietnam. We don't need to fight on roads. We have the sea. Visualize our meeting VC on our own terms. We don't have to spend all our time in the jungles.

If we can secure their bases, the VN can secure, in time, a political movement to (1) apprehend the terrorist and (2) give intelligence to the government.

The procedures for this are known.

I agree that the Japanese agitators don't like what we are doing but Sato is totally in agreement with our actions.

The VN have been dealt more casualties than, per capita, we suffered in the Civil War. The VN soldier is an uncomplaining soldier. He has ideas he will die for.

Unger: I agree this is what we have to do. We have spotted some things we want to pay attention to.

President: How can we get everybody to compete with McNamara in the press? We are trying to do so many other things with our economic and health projects. Constantly remind the people that we are doing other things besides bombing.

Unger: Took this question up with Zorthian and press people.

Document 76. Notes of Meeting[1]
Washington, July 22, 1965, noon–2:15 p.m.

PRESENT
President
McNamara
Vance
Gen. Wheeler
Gen. Johnson
Secy. Resor
Gen. McConnell
Gen. Greene
Adm. McDonald
Clifford[2]
Secy. Nitze
Secy. Zuckert
Secy. Brown
Bundy

---

[1]Source: Johnson Library, Meeting Notes File, Box 1. No classification marking. The meeting was held in the Cabinet Room of the White House. The notes were originally handwritten by Valenti and later transcribed. They are quoted extensively in Valenti, *A Very Human President*, pp. 340–52. Valenti recalled that before this meeting, President Johnson told him: "All these recommendations seem to be built on a pretty soft bottom. Everything blurs when you get almost to the gate." (Ibid., p. 341)

[2]Clark Clifford was invited to this meeting at the president's request. (Ibid., p. 340)

President: I asked McNamara to invite you here to counsel with you on these problems and the ways to meet them.

Hear from the Chiefs the alternatives open to you and then recommendations on those alternatives from a military point.

Options open to us

1. Leave the country—with as little loss as possible—the "bugging out" approach.
2. Maintain present force and lose slowly.
3. Add 100,000 men—recognizing that may not be enough—and adding more next year.

Disadvantages of #3—risk of escalation, casualties will be high—may be a long war without victory.

President: I would like you to start out by stating our present position and where we can go.

Adm. McDonald: Sending Marines has improved situation. I agree with McNamara that we are committed to extent that we can't move out. If we continue the way we are it will be a slow, sure victory for the other side. By putting more men in it will turn the tide and let us know what further we need to do. I wish we had done this long before.

President: But you don't know if 100,000 will be enough. What makes you conclude that if you don't know where we are going—and what will happen—we shouldn't pause and find this out?

McDonald: Sooner or later we'll force them to the conference table. We [They?] can't win an all out war.

President: If we put in 100,000 won't they put in an equal number?

McDonald: No. If we step up our bombing—

President: Is this a chance we want to take?

McDonald: Yes, when I view the alternatives. Get out now or pour in more men.

President: Is that all?

McDonald: I think our allies will lose faith in us.

President: We have few allies really helping us.

McDonald: Thailand, for example. If we walk out of Vietnam, the whole world will question our word. We don't have much choice.

President: Paul, what is your view?

Nitze: In that area not occupied by US forces, it is worse, as I observed on my trip out there.

We have two alternatives—support VN all over this country—or fall out from secure position we do have. Make it clear to populace that we are on their side. Gradually turn the tide of losses by aiding VN at certain points.

If we just maintained what we have—more the Pres. problem than ours—to acknowledge that we couldn't beat the VC, the shape of the world will change.

President: What are our chances of success?

Nitze: If we want to turn the tide, by putting in more men, it would be about 60/40.

President: If we gave Westmoreland all he asked for what are our chances? I don't agree that NVN and China won't come in.

Nitze: Expand the area we could maintain. In the Philippines and Greece it was shown that guerrillas lost.

President: Would you send in more forces than Westmoreland requests?

Nitze: Yes. Depends on how quickly they—

President: How many? 200 instead of 100?

Nitze: Need another 100 in January.

President: Can you do that?

Nitze: Yes.

McNamara: The current plan is to introduce 100,000—with possibility of a second 100,000 by first of the year.

President: What reaction is this going to produce?

Wheeler: Since we are not proposing an invasion of NVN, Soviets will step up material and propaganda—same with Chicoms. Might have NVN introduce more regular troops.

President: Why wouldn't NVN pour in more men? Also, call on volunteers from China and Russia.

Wheeler: First, they may decide they can't win by putting in forces they can't afford. At most would put in two more divisions. Beyond that they strip their country and invite a counter move on our part.

Secondly, on volunteers—the one thing all NVN fear is Chinese. For them to invite

Chinese volunteers is to invite China's taking over NVN.

Weight of judgment is that NVN may reinforce their forces, they can't match us on a build-up.

From military view, we can handle, if we are determined to do so, China and NVN.

President: Anticipate retaliation by Soviets in Berlin area?

Wheeler: You may have some flare-up but lines are so tightly drawn in Berlin that it raises risks of escalation too quickly. Lemnitzer thinks no flare-up in Berlin. In Korea, if Soviets undertook operations, it would be dangerous.

President: Admiral, would you summarize what you think we ought to do?

McDonald: 1. Supply forces Westmoreland has asked for.
2. Prepare to furnish more (100,000) in 1966.
3. Commensurate building in air and naval forces, step up of air attacks on NVN.
4. Bring in needed reserves and draft calls.

President: Any ideas on cost of what this would be?

McNamara: Yes—$12 billion—1966.

President: Any idea what effect this will have on our economy?

McNamara: It would not require wage and price controls in my judgment. Price index ought not go up more than one point or two.

McConnell: If you put in these requested forces and increase air and sea effort—we can at least turn the tide where we are not losing anymore. We need to be sure we get the best we can out of SVN—need to bomb all military targets available to us in NVN. As to whether we can come to satisfactory solution with these forces, I don't know. With these forces properly employed, and cutting off their supplies, we can do better than we're doing.

President: Have results of bombing actions been as fruitful and productive as we anticipated?

McConnell: No sir, they haven't been. Productive in SVN, but not as productive in NVN because we are not striking the targets that hurt them.

President: Are you seriously concerned when we change targets we escalate the war?

They might send more fighters down. Can't be certain if it will escalate their efforts on the ground.

Would it hurt our chances at a conference if we started killing civilians?

McConnell: We need to minimize civilian killings.

President: Would you go beyond Westmoreland's recommendations?

McConnell: No sir.

President: How many planes lost?

McConnell: 106 all types—small percentage of total.

President: How many out there?

McConnell: 146 combat. We have lost 54 combat.

President: How many Navy planes?

McConnell: In the 30's—about 125 combat.

Zuckert: It's worth taking a major step to avoid long run consequences of walking away from it.

President: Doesn't it really mean if we follow Westmoreland's requests we are in a new war—this is going off the diving board.

McNamara: This is a major change in US policy. We have relied on SVN to carry the brunt. Now we would be responsible for satisfactory military outcome.

President: Are we in agreement we would rather be out of there and make our stand somewhere else?

Johnson: Least desirable alternative is getting out. Second least is doing what we are doing. Best is to get in and get the job done.

President: But I don't know how we are going to get that job done. There are millions of Chinese. I think they are going to put their stack in. Is this the best place to do this? We don't have the allies we had in Korea. Can we get our allies to cut off supplying the NVN?

McNamara: No, we can't prevent Japan, Britain, etc. to charter ships to Haifong.

President: Have we done anything to get them to stop?

McNamara: We haven't put the pressure on them as we did in Cuba but even if we did, it wouldn't stop the shipping.

Brown: It seems that all of our alternatives are dark. I find myself in agreement with the others.

President: Is there anything to the argument this government is likely to fail, and we will be asked to leave? If we try to match the enemy, we will be bogged down in protracted war and have the government ask us to leave.

Brown: Our lines of communication are long.

President: How long?

Brown: 7000 miles from the West Coast, but not too much greater than China's. Biggest weakness of political base is lack of security they can offer their people.

President: Are we starting something that in 2–3 years we can't finish?

Brown: It is costly to us to strangle slowly, but chances of losing are less if we move in.

President: Suppose we told Ky of requirements we need—he turns them down—and we have to get out and make our stand in Thailand

Brown: The Thais will go with the winner.

President: If we didn't stop in Thailand where would we stop?

McNamara: Laos, Cambodia, Thailand, Burma, surely affect Malaysia. In 2–3 years Communist domination would stop there, but ripple effect would be great—Japan, India. We would have to give up some bases. Ayub would move closer to China. Greece, Turkey would move to neutralist position. Communist agitation would increase in Africa.

Greene: Situation is as tough as when it started. But not as bad as it could be. Marines in 1st Corps area is example of benefits.

Stakes:

1. National security stake. Matter of time before we go in some place else.
2. Pledge we made.
3. Prestige before the rest of the world.

If you accept these stakes, there are two courses of action:

1. Get out
2. Stay in and win.

How to win:

1. South—
2. North

The enclave concept will work. Would like to introduce enough Marines to do this. Two Marine divisions and one air wing. Extend. 28,000 there now—additional 72,000.

McNamara: Greene suggests these men over and above the Westmoreland request.

President: Then you will need 80,000 more Marines to carry this out.

Greene: Yes. I am convinced we are making progress with the SVN—in food and construction. We are getting evidence of intelligence from SVN.

In the North—we haven't been hitting the right targets. We should hit POL storage—essential to their transportation. Also airfields destroyed, MIGs and IL28's. As soon as SAM installations are operable.

President: What would they do?

Greene: Nothing. We can test it by attacking POL storage.

Then we should attack industrial complex in NVN. Also, they can be told by pamphlet drop why we are doing this. Then we ought to blockade Cambodia—and stop supplies from coming down.

How long will it take? 5 years—plus 500,000 troops. I think the US people will back you.

President: How would you tell the American people what the stakes are?

Greene: The place where they will stick by you is the national security stake.

Johnson: We are in a face-down. The solution, unfortunately, is long-term. Once the military solution is solved, the problem of political solution will be more difficult.

President: If we come in with hundreds of thousands of men and billions of dollars, won't this cause them to come in (China and Russia)?

Johnson: No. I don't think they will.

President: MacArthur didn't think they would come in either.

Johnson: Yes, but this is not comparable to Korea. Same situation—China bases and communications—

President: But China has plenty of divisions to move in, don't they?

Johnson: Yes, they do.

President: Then what would we do?

Johnson: (long silence) If so, we have another ball game.

President: But I have to take into account they will.

Johnson: I would increase the build-up near NVN—and increase action in Korea.

President: If they move in 31 divisions, what does it take on our part?

McNamara: Under favorable conditions they could sustain 31 divisions and assuming Thais contributed forces, it would take 300,000 plus what we need to combat VC.

Resor: I'm a newcomer—(interrupted by President)

President: But remember they're going to write stories about this like they did the Bay of Pigs—and about my advisors. That's why I want you to think very carefully about alternatives and plans.
Looking back on the Dominican Republic would you have done anything any differently, General?

Johnson: I would have cleaned out part of the city and gone in—and with same numbers.

President: Are you concerned about Chinese forces moving into NVN?

Johnson: There is no evidence of forces—only teams involved in logistics. Could be investigating areas which they could control later.

President: What is your reaction to Ho's statement he is ready to fight for 20 years?

Johnson: I believe it.

President: What are Ho's problems?

Johnson: His biggest problem is doubt about what our next move will be. He's walking a tightrope between the Reds & Chicoms. Also, he's worrying about the loss of caches of arms in SVN.

President: Are we killing civilians along with VC?

Wheeler: Certain civilians accompanying the VC are being killed. It can't be helped.

President: The VC dead is running at a rate of 25,000 a year. At least 15,000 have been killed by air—half of these are not a part of what we call VC. Since 1961 a total of 89,000 have been killed. SVN are being killed at a rate of 12,000 per year.

Resor: Of the three courses the one we should follow is the McNamara plan. We can't go back on our commitment. Our allies are watching carefully.

President: Do all of you think the Congress and the people will go along with 600,000 people and billions of dollars 10,000 miles away?

Resor: Gallup Poll shows people are basically behind our commitment.

President: But if you make a commitment to jump off a building, and you find out how high it is, you may withdraw the commitment.

President: I judge though that the big problem is one of national security. Is that right?

(murmured assent)

President: What about our intelligence? How do they know what we are doing before we do it? What about the B-52 raid—weren't they gone before we got there?

McNamara: They get it from infiltration in SVN forces.

President: Are we getting good intelligence out of NVN?

McNamara: Only reconnaissance and technical soundings. None from combat intelligence.

President: Some Congressmen and Senators think we are going to be the most discredited people in the world. What Bundy will now tell you is not his opinion nor mine (I haven't taken a position yet) but what we hear.

Bundy: Argument we will face:

For 10 years every step we have taken has been based on a previous failure. All we have done has failed and caused us to take another step which failed. As we get further into the bag, we get deeply bruised. Also, we have made excessive claims we haven't been able to realize.

Also, after 20 years of warnings about war in Asia, we are now doing what MacArthur and others have warned against.

We are about to fight a war we can't fight and win, as the country we are trying to help is quitting.

The failure on our own to fully realize what guerrilla war is like. We are sending conventional troops to do an unconventional job.

How long—how much. Can we take casualties over five years—aren't we talking about a military solution when the solution is political. Why can't we interdict better—why are our bombings so fruitless—why can't we blockade the coast—why can't we improve our intelligence—why can't we find the VC?

President: Gerald Ford has demanded the President testify before the Congress and tell why we are compelled to up the reserves. Indications are that he will oppose calling up the reserves.

McNamara: I think we can answer most of the questions posed.

Clifford: If the military plan is carried out, what is the ultimate result if it is successful?

Wheeler: Political objective is to maintain SVN as free and independent. If we follow the course of action, we can carry out this objective.

Wheeler: Probably after success, we would withdraw most of our forces; [some?] international or otherwise, would have to stay on.

If we can secure the military situation, it seems likely that we can get some kind of stable government.
Meeting adjourned at 2:15 p.m.

Document 78 Notes of Meeting[1]
Washington, July 22, 1965, 3–4:20 p.m.

---

[1]Source: Johnson Library, Meeting Notes File, Box 1. No classification marking. The notes were originally handwritten by Valenti and later transcribed. The meeting was held in the Cabinet Room of the White House.

PRESENT
President
McNamara
Rusk
Ball
Busby
Clifford
Gen. Wheeler
Cy Vance
Moyers
Valenti
Bundy
Cater
John McCloy
Arthur Dean

President: I don't think that calling up the reserves in itself is a change of policy. There is a [no?] question though that we are going into a new kind of activity in VN. Basic objective is to preserve the independence and freedom of VN. This is not necessarily tied in with calling up reserves.

Rusk: The essence of policy is why we are there and what our war aims are. Moving from 75,000 to 185,000 men is a change of policy. Much is to be said for playing this low key.

President: That one point needs to be stressed with Congressional leadership—also to explain with candor what we are doing to the American people. But when we do, we help the NVN get their requests fulfilled by China and Russia.

McNamara: We can stay away from "change of policy" but it is a change in risk and commitment. We need to explain why it is in our interest to do it.
Services have submitted budget request by [of?] $12 billion. We can cut this down by half or more.

Moyers: I don't think the press thinks we are going to change basic policy, but the requirements to meet that policy.

President: That's right and we ought to say it.

Ball: I hope we can avoid a debate on whether it is a change. We always lose on this. We are becoming co-defendants with SVN.

McCloy: The country is looking to getting on with the war.

President: There are three alternatives:

1. Sit and lose slowly
2. Get out
3. Put in what needs to go in.

Rusk: If we bring out our message of decision while the Bucharest meeting is going on—it might bring them closer together. What we do in SVN is not of great concern to China. But a progressive step-up in bombing increases risk of China intrusion.

President: But the Chiefs say what we are doing in the North is not enough, only pin pricking them, just goosing them.

Rusk: But it is contradictory to do this when we can't find anybody in the South.

Both China and the Soviets have pressure on them. A commitment in SVN is one thing, but a commitment to preserve another socialist state is quite another. This is a distinction we must bear in mind.

We have a 1 in 5 chance of Russia's staying out if we make our commitment and if we bomb Hanoi. A commitment of large forces by us will lead to pressures on us to destroy Hanoi. This is the key point.

McCloy: Do you think they will let go if they still have sanctuary?

Rusk: Their only sanctuary is 1/5 of the country.

A. Dean: What do you do if the war drags on—with mounting casualties—where do we go? The people say if we are not doing what is necessary to end it, why don't we do what is necessary?

McNamara: We are begging the questions. If we bomb Haifong, would this end the war? and the answer is "No." We have only destroyed so far about 20% of the ammunitions capacity and a lesser percentage of barracks capacity.

Dean: If this carries on for some years, we'll get in the same fix we were in Korea and the Yalu.

Rusk: We were under no pressures to make it a larger war until the war was practically over.

McCloy: If we could define our objectives specifically, what are our objectives in a discussion? What do we have to negotiate?

Rusk: 1. Infiltration from the North must stop.
2. We have no interests in a permanent military base there.
3. 1954–1962 agreements ought to be solved by peaceful means and not . . .

McCloy: When do the troops get withdrawn?

Rusk: When proof of infiltration—stopping.

Bundy: If we really were the ones for free elections, it would be good. It is difficult for Saigon to sign on.

McCloy: Would we be willing to take a Tito government or a VC victory?

Bundy: That's where our plan begins to unravel.

Now—how to keep a reasonable peace offensive going—

President: We have got to keep peace proposals going. It's like a prizefight. Our right is our military power, but our left must be our peace proposals. Every time you move troops forward, you move diplomats forward. I want this done. The generals want more and more—and go farther and farther. But State has to supply me with some, too.

We need Ernie Pyle out there interviewing soldiers who can tell how proud they are to do their duty.

Rusk: Thinking of Bucharest meeting, I suggest you meet with the leadership on Tuesday and make a statement on Wednesday.

Ball: We have big problem of disarmament meeting on Tuesday in Geneva.

McNamara: We can't delay this from the public.

President: Congress ought to be briefed on Saturday or Sunday and go up Monday to Congress. We ought to decide what our decision is, write it, brief Ambassadors and then tell the people.

Is the message a personal talk to the Congress or a normal message? Possibly a normal message.

Meeting adjourned at 4:20 p.m.

## 7. The President's Address to the Nation on Civil Disorders, July 27, 1967

*Public Papers of the Presidents of the United States: Lyndon B. Johnson, 1967, Vols. 1–2. (Washington, D.C.: U.S. Government Printing Office, 1968), 2: 721–724.*

My fellow Americans:

We have endured a week such as no nation should live through: a time of violence and tragedy.

For a few minutes tonight, I want to talk about that tragedy—and I want to talk about the deeper questions it raises for us all.

I am tonight appointing a special Advisory Commission on Civil Disorders.

Governor Otto Kerner of Illinois has agreed to serve as Chairman. Mayor John Lindsay of New York will serve as Vice Chairman. Its other members will include Fred R. Harris, Senator from Oklahoma; Edward W. Brooke, United States Senator from Massachusetts; James C. Corman, U.S. Representative from California, 22d District, Los Angeles; William M. McCulloch, the U.S. Representative from the State of Ohio, the 4th District; I. W. Abel, the president of the United Steel Workers; Charles B. Thornton, the president, director, and chairman of the board of Litton Industries, Inc.; Roy Wilkins, the executive director of the NAACP; Katherine Graham Peden, the Commissioner of Commerce of the State of Kentucky; Herbert Jenkins, the chief of police, Atlanta, Georgia.

The Commission will investigate the origins of the recent disorders in our cities. It will make recommendations—to me, to the Congress, to the State Governors, and to the mayors—for measures to prevent or contain such disasters in the future.

In their work, the Commission members will have access to the facts that are gathered by Director Edgar Hoover and the Federal Bureau of Investigation. The FBI will continue to exercise its full authority to investigate these riots, in accordance with my standing instructions, and continue to search for evidence of conspiracy.

But even before the Commission begins its work, and even before all the evidence is in, there are some things that we can tell about the outbreaks of this summer.

First—let there be no mistake about it—the looting, arson, plunder, and pillage which have occurred are not part of the civil rights protest. There is no American right to loot stores, or to burn buildings, or to fire rifles from the rooftops. That is crime—and crime must be dealt with forcefully, and swiftly, and certainly—under law.

Innocent people, Negro and white, have been killed. Damage to property—owned by Negroes and whites—is calamitous. Worst of all, fear and bitterness which have been loosed will take long months to erase.

The criminals who committed these acts of violence against the people deserve to be punished—and they must be punished. Explanations may be offered, but nothing can excuse what they have done.

There will be attempts to interpret the events of the past few days. But when violence strikes, then those in public responsibility have an immediate and a very different job: not to analyze, but to end disorder.

That they must seek to do with every means at their command: through local police, State officials, and—in extraordinary circumstances where local authorities have stated that they cannot maintain order with their own resources—then through Federal power that we have limited authority to use.

I have directed the Secretary of Defense to issue new training standards for riot control procedures immediately to National Guard units across the country. Through the Continental Army Command, this expanded training will begin immediately. The National Guard must have the ability to respond effectively, quickly, and appropriately, in conditions of disorder and violence.

Those charged with the responsibility of law enforcement should, and must, be respected by all of our people. The violence must be stopped, quickly, finally, and permanently.

It would compound the tragedy, however, if we should settle for order that is imposed by the muzzle of a gun.

In America, we seek more than the uneasy calm of martial law. We seek peace that is based on one man's respect for another man—and upon mutual respect for law. We seek a public order that is built on steady progress in meeting the needs of all of our people.

Not even the sternest police action, nor the most effective Federal troops, can ever create lasting peace in our cities.

The only genuine, long-range solution for what has happened lies in an attack—mounted at every level—upon the conditions that breed despair and violence. All of us know what those conditions are: ignorance, discrimination, slums, poverty, disease, not enough jobs. We should attack these conditions—not because we are frightened by conflict, but because we are fired by conscience. We should attack them because there is simply no other way to achieve a decent and orderly society in America.

In the past 3 1/2 years, we have directed the greatest governmental effort in all of our American history at these ancient enemies. The roll call of those laws reveals the depth of our concern: the Model Cities Act, the Voters Rights Act, the Civil Rights Acts, the Rent Supplement Act, Medicare and Medicaid, the 24 educational bills, Head Start, the Job Corps, the Neighborhood Youth Corps, the Teacher Corps, manpower development and training. And many, many more acts too numerous to mention on television tonight.

We will continue to press for laws which would protect our citizens from violence, like the Safe Streets and Crime Control Act now under consideration in the Congress, and the Gun Control Act.

Our work has just begun. Yet there are those who feel that even this beginning is too much. There are those who would have us turn back even now, at the beginning of this journey.

Last week in Congress, a small but important plan for action in the cities was voted down in the House of Representatives. The Members of that body rejected my request for $20 million to fight the pestilence of rats—rats which prowl in dark alleys and tenements, and attack thousands of city children. The passage of this legislation would have meant much to the children of the slums. A strong Government that has spent millions to protect baby calves from worms could surely afford to show as much concern for baby boys and girls.

There are some tonight who feel that we cannot afford a model cities program. They reduced my request for funds this year by two-thirds.

There are some who feel that we cannot afford additional good teachers for the children of poverty in urban areas. Or new efforts to house those who are most in need of housing. Or to aid in education to those who need to read and write. Theirs is a strange system of bookkeeping.

I believe we should be counting the assets that these measures can bring to America: cities richer in opportunity; cities more full of promise; cities of order, progress, and happiness. Instead, some are counting the seeds of bitterness.

This is not a time for angry reaction. It is a time for action: starting with legislative action to improve the life in our cities. The strength and promise of the law are the surest remedies for tragedy in the streets.

But laws are only one answer. Another answer lies in the way our people will respond to these disturbances.

There is a danger that the worst toll of this tragedy will be counted in the hearts of Americans: in hatred, in insecurity, in fear, in heated words which will not end the conflict, but prolong it.

So let us acknowledge the tragedy; but let us not exaggerate it.

Let us look about tonight. Let us look at ourselves. We will see these things:

—Most Americans, Negro and white, are leading decent, responsible, and productive lives.
—Most Americans, Negro and white, seek safety in their neighborhoods and harmony with their neighbors.
—Nothing can destroy good will more than a period of needless strife and suspicion between the races.

Let us condemn the violent few. But let us remember that it is law-abiding Negro families who have really suffered most at the hands of the rioters. It is responsible Negro citizens who hope most fervently—and need most urgently—to share in America's growth and prosperity.

This is no time to turn away from that goal.

To reach it will require more than laws, and much more than dollars. It will take renewed dedication and understanding in the heart of every citizen.

I know there are millions of men and women tonight who are eager to heal the wounds that we have suffered; who want to get on with the job of teaching and working and building America.

In that spirit, at the conclusion of this address, I will sign a proclamation tonight calling for a day of prayer in our Nation throughout all of our States. On this Sunday, July 30, I urge the citizens in every town, every city, and every home in this land to go into their churches—to pray for order and reconciliation among men.

I appeal to every Governor, every mayor, every preacher, and every teacher, and parent to join and give leadership in this national observance.

This spirit of dedication cannot be limited to our public leaders. It must extend to every citizen in this land. And the man who speaks to break the peace must feel the powerful disapproval of all of his neighbors.

So tonight, I call upon every American to search his own heart.

And to those who are tempted by violence, I would say this: Think again. Who is really the loser when violence comes? Whose neighborhood is made a shambles? Whose life is threatened most?

If you choose to tear down what other hands have built,

—You will not succeed;

—You will suffer most from your own crimes;

—You will learn that there are no victors in the aftermath of violence.

The apostles of violence, with their ugly drumbeat of hatred, must know that they are now heading for ruin and disaster. And every man who really wants progress or justice or equality must stand against them and their miserable virus of hate.

For other Americans, especially those in positions of public trust, I have this message:

Yours is the duty to bring about a peaceful change in America. If your response to these tragic events is only "business as usual"—you invite not only disaster, but dishonor.

So, my fellow citizens, let us go about our work. Let us clear the streets of rubble and quench the fires that hatred set. Let us feed and care for those who have suffered at the rioters' hands—but let there be no bonus or reward or salutes for those who have inflicted that suffering.

Let us resolve that this violence is going to stop and there will be no bonus to flow from it. We can stop it. We must stop it. We will stop it.

And let us build something much more lasting: faith between man and man, faith between race and race. Faith in each other and faith in the promise of beautiful America.

Let us pray for the day when "mercy and truth are met together: righteousness and peace have kissed each other." Let us pray—and let us work for better jobs and better housing and better education that so many millions of our own fellow Americans need so much tonight.

Let us then act in the Congress, in the city halls, and in every community, so that this great land of ours may truly be "one nation under God—with liberty and justice for all." Good night and thank you.

# 8. The President's News Conference, November 17, 1967

*Public Papers of the Presidents of the United States: Lyndon B. Johnson, 1967, Vols. 1–2. (Washington, D.C.: U.S. Government Printing Office, 1968), 2: 1,045–1,055.*

The President. Good morning, ladies and gentlemen, I will be glad to take your questions.

## QUESTIONS

### FORCE LEVELS IN VIETNAM

[1.] Q. Do you think that at this point our force levels in Vietnam will begin to level off in authorized strength, or do you think more troops may be needed in the future?

The President. We have previously considered and approved the recommendations of the Joint Chiefs of Staff for the force level.

General Westmoreland discussed this at some length with me last night and this morning. He anticipates no increase in that level.

### APPRAISING CRITICISMS OF THE PRESIDENT

[2.] Q. Mr. President, we are getting close to the end of your 4th year in office. You have been subjected to a great deal of personal criticism, ranging from a Senator in your own party planning to run—

The President. I am generally familiar with that.

Q. —to the preacher in Williamsburg. I wonder how you appraise this personally?

The President. It is not a surprise. I am aware that this has happened to the 35 Presidents who preceded me. No public official, certainly not one who has been in public life 35 years as I have been, would fail to expect criticism.

There is a different type of criticism. There is a difference between constructive dissent and storm trooper bullying, howling, and taking the law into your own hands.

I think that the President must expect that those in the other party will frequently find it necessary to find fault and to complain—to attempt to picture to the people that the President should be replaced.

It is also true in all parties that there are divisions. We don't all think alike. If we did, one man would be doing all the thinking.

So you have divisions in parties. We have perhaps more than our share sometimes. But I am sure the Republicans think that, too.

When you get into a political year, with the help and advice and the abetting that the press can do, and the assistance that the opposing party can do—because it is to their interest to try to destroy you in order to have a place for themselves—and you take the divisions in your own party, and they concentrate, then it does seem to mount up and at times occupy a great deal of public attention.

But I don't think it is unusual for a President to be criticized. That seems to be one of the things that goes with the job.

Not many of us want to say, "I failed," or "I made a mistake," or "We shouldn't have done that," or "This shouldn't have happened."

It is always easier to say that someone over there is wrong. The President is more or less a lightning rod. At least I have seen that in this country.

I remember, to take one or two illustrations, when President Truman very courageously and, I think, very wisely went into Korea.

One of our pollsters dashed out with a poll—Dr. Gallup—and found that that position was approved by about 81 percent. Six months later, when the sacrifices were evident and the problems began to appear, the same pollster, talking to the same people, found that this had dropped from 81 to 26 percent.

Now, those things have happened in all of our crises—economic, domestic, and international. A President learns to expect them and learns to live with them.

The important thing for every man who occupies this place is to search as best he can to get the right answer; to try to find out what is right; and then do it without regard to polls and without regard to criticism.

## THE BOMBING OF NORTH VIETNAM

[3.] Q. Mr. President, a good many Americans have said that a stop to the bombing is worth trying just to see if North Vietnam will respond. What is your view on this?

The President. North Vietnam has responded. Their statement this week in the Hanoi newspaper in response to my statement from the Enterprise is very clear and very compelling. It should answer any person in this country who has ever felt that stopping the bombing alone would bring us to the negotiating table.

Hanoi made it very clear in response to my appeal from the Enterprise that their position, in effect, was the same as it has always been. It was the same as enunciated in Ho Chi Minh's letter to me which Ho Chi Minh made public.

There are some hopeful people and there are some naive people in this country—and there are some political people.

But anyone who really wants to know what the position of North Vietnam is should read what the spokesmen of North Vietnam say.

That is best summarized in Mr. Ho Chi Minh's letter to the President that he made public, that is on the record, that he has never changed.

So all of these hopes, dreams, and idealistic people going around are misleading and confusing and weakening our position.

## THE VIETCONG'S WILLINGNESS TO NEGOTIATE

[4.] Q. Do you have any evidence that the Vietcong might be moving toward the position of wanting to negotiate separate from Hanoi and, if so, what would be your attitude toward negotiating with them?

The President. I would prefer to handle our negotiations through diplomatic channels with whomsoever we may negotiate.

I don't think this is the place to do our negotiating. We are very anxious to find a solution that will bring an end to the war.

As we have stated so many times, we are ready to meet and discuss that with the officials of Hanoi and the Vietcong will have no problem in having their voice fully heard and considered.

But I think that it would be better if we would wait until opportunity develops along that line and then do it through our trained diplomats.

## REFLECTIONS AFTER 4 YEARS IN OFFICE

[5.] Q. Mr. President, a minute ago you talked about the job of being President. This Wednesday you are going to complete 4 years in the Office of the President. I wonder if you could reflect for a moment on the Presidency and what have been your greatest satisfactions and what are your greatest disappointments.

The President. Well, I think we had better do that a little later. I can't tell all the good things that have happened or the bad ones, either, in these 4 years in a 30-minute press conference. I would be charged with filibustering.

But we primarily want to think of the future—and not the past.

It has been almost two centuries since our Revolution and since we won our freedom. We have come a long way during that period. But we have much farther to go, as you can see from our education and health and city statistics, and farm statistics.

As long as there are four people out of every ten in the world who can't spell "cat," or can't write "dog," we have much to do.

I am particularly proud of what we have done in education—from Head Start to adult education, where men and women past 70 are learning to read and write for the first time.

I am very pleased, for instance, that we have raised our contributions from the Federal Government to higher education from 16 percent to 24 percent in the last 4 years, while the States have remained practically static.

We have made revolutionary strides in education, in health, in conservation, where we are probably taking in as much land in the public domain for the first time in years as we are letting out.

We feel that we have brought a degree of stability into our international relations to this hemisphere through the Alliance for Progress and our meetings at Punta del Este.

Working with other nations, we have made material advances in helping underdeveloped nations in Africa.

We are very pleased with what has come out of our meetings with the Germans and with the British in connection with our trilateral talks; what has come out of our Kennedy Round meetings; the several treaties that we have negotiated with the Soviet Union, and the one that we are working on so hard now—the nonproliferation treaty.

We are happy that 9 million more people have good-paying jobs today than had them when I came into this office.

But these are things of the past, and we should accept. They are here. We want to preserve them.

But the important problems are ahead. What is the next century going to be like? What is the third century going to be like?

As long as the ancient enemies are rampant in the world—illiteracy, ignorance, disease, poverty, and war—there is much for government to do.

We are working on that now. We will be talking more to you about that in the months ahead.

## ASSESSMENT OF SITUATION IN VIETNAM

[6.] Q. Mr. President, in view of your talks this week with General Westmoreland, Ambassador Bunker, and others, what is your present assessment of our progress and prospects in Vietnam?

The President. Well, I will repeat to you their assessment, because they are the ones who are in the best position to judge things locally. I will give you my evaluation of what they have said.

First, I think every American's heart should swell with pride at the competence and capacity of our leadership in Vietnam.

I believe, and our allied people believe, that we have a superior leadership. I think it is the best that the United States of America can produce—in experience, in judgment, in training, in general competence.

I have had three meetings with Ambassador Bunker and three with General Westmoreland. I had coffee with him at length this morning, just before I came here.

Our American people, when we get in a contest of any kind—whether it is in a war, an election, a football game, or whatever it is—want it decided and decided quickly; get in or get out.

They like that curve to rise like this [indicating a sharp rise] and they like the opposition to go down like this [indicating a sharply declining line].

That is not the kind of war we are fighting in Vietnam.

We made our statement to the world of what we would do if we had Communist aggression in that part of the world in 1954.

We said we would stand with those people in the face of common danger.

The time came when we had to put up or shut up. We put up. And we are there. We don't march out and have a big battle each day in a guerrilla war. It is a new kind of war for us. So it doesn't move that fast.

Summarizing and trying to be fully responsive to your question in the time allotted, we are moving more like this [indicating gradual rise]. They are moving more like this [indicating decline], instead of straight up and straight down.

We are making progress. We are pleased with the results that we are getting.

We are inflicting greater losses than we are taking.

Amidst the horrors of war—and more people have been killed trying to vote in South Vietnam than have been killed by bombs in North Vietnam, according to the North Vietnam figures—in the midst of all the horrors of war, in guerrilla fighting in South Vietnam, we have had five elections in a period of a little over 14 months. There was great doubt whether we could have any. It took us from 1776 to 1789—not 13 months but 13 years—to get a Constitution with our Anglo-Saxon background and all the training we had.

To think that here in the midst of war, when the grenades are popping like firecrackers all around you, that two-thirds or three-fourths of the people would register and vote, and have 5 elections in 13 months—and through the democratic process select people at the local level, a constituent assembly, a house of representatives, a senate, a president and a vice president—that is encouraging.

The fact that the population under free control has constantly risen, and that under Communist control has constantly gone down, is a very encouraging sign.

The improvement that has been made by the South Vietnamese themselves in putting in reforms, in announcing other programs, and in improving their own Army, is a matter of great satisfaction to Ambassador Bunker and to General Westmoreland.

We have a lot to do yet. A great many mistakes have been made. We take two steps forward, and we slip back one. It is not all perfect by any means.

There are a good many days when we get a C-minus instead of an A-plus.

But overall, we are making progress. We are satisfied with that progress. Our allies are pleased with that progress. Every country that I know in that area that is familiar with what is happening thinks it is absolutely essential that Uncle Sam keep his word and stay there until we can find an honorable peace.

If they have any doubts about it, Mr. Ho Chi Minh—who reads our papers and who listens to our radio, who looks at our television—if he has any doubts about it, I want to disillusion him this morning.

We keep our commitments. Our people are going to support the men who are there. The men there are going to bring us an honorable peace.

## HANOI'S INTERPRETATION OF PUBLIC OPINION IN THE UNITED STATES

[7.] Q. Mr. President, Hanoi may be interpreting current public opinion polls to indicate that you will be replaced next year. How should this affect the campaign in this country?

The President. I don't know how it will affect the campaign in this country. Whatever interpretation Hanoi might make that would lead them to believe that Uncle Sam—whoever may be President—is going to pull out and it will be easier for them to make an inside deal with another President, then they will make a serious misjudgment.

## THE PRESIDENT'S PLANS FOR 1968

[8.] Q. Are you going to run next year?

The President. I will cross that bridge when I get to it, as I have told you so many times.

## PROSPECTS FOR PASSAGE OF TAX BILL

[9.] Q. Mr. President, there are increasing statements from Capitol Hill that say your tax bill is dead for this session of Congress. Is there any plan on the part of your administration to try and revive this before Congress leaves; and, secondly, if not, what plans might you have next year to avert this inflationary trend that we are told will be coming?

The President. We want very much to have a tax bill just as quickly as we can get it. We think the sound, prudent, fiscal policy requires it. We are going to do everything that the President and the administration can do to get that tax bill.[1]

I would be less than frank if I didn't tell you that I have no indication whatever that Mr. Mills or Mr. Byrnes[2] or the Ways and Means Committee is likely to report a tax bill before they adjourn.

I feel that one of our failures in the administration has been our inability to convince the Congress of the wisdom of fiscal responsibility and the necessity of passing a tax bill not only for the effect it will have on the inflationary developments, but the effect it will have on the huge deficit that we are running.

I think one of the great mistakes that the Congress will make is that Mr. Ford[3] and Mr. Mills have taken this position that they cannot have any tax bill now. They will live to rue the day when they made that decision. Because it is a dangerous decision. It is an unwise decision.

I think that the people of America—none of whom want to pay taxes—any pollster can walk out and say, "Do you want to pay more tax?" Of course you will say, "No, I don't want to pay tax."

But if you ask him: "Do you want inflation; do you want prices to increase 5 or 6 percent; do you want a deficit of $30 or $35 billion; do you want to spend $35 billion more than you are taking in?" I think the average citizen would say, "No."

Here at the height of our prosperity when our gross national product is going to run at $850 billion, when we look at the precedents of what we have done in past wars—in Korea when President Truman asked for a tax increase, people supported it.

This request has been before the Congress since last January. They have finished most of the appropriations bills. I read the story this morning. It looks like out of $145 billion they will roughly cut a billion dollars in expenditures.

But they will cut several billion from revenues because of inaction, because people don't like to stand up and do the unpopular thing of assuming responsibility that men in public life are required to do sometime.

I know it doesn't add to your polls and your popularity to say we have to have additional taxes to fight this war abroad and fight the problems in our cities at home. But we can do it with the gross national product we have. We should do it. And I think when the American people and the Congress get the full story they will do it.

We have failed up to now to be able to convince them. But we are going to continue to try in every way that is proper.

## INTENTIONS OF SENATOR EUGENE MCCARTHY

[ 10.] Q. Senator McCarthy has said he is considering opposing you in the presidential primaries because he believes it would be a healthy thing to debate Vietnam in the primaries, for the party and for the country, too. Do you agree with him? What effect do you think this would have on your own candidacy?

The President. I don't know how I am going to be, after all this opposition develops, so far as my state of health is concerned. But I am very healthy today. I don't know whether this criticism has contributed to my good health or not.

I don't know what Senator McCarthy is going to do. I am not sure that he knows what he plans to do. I think we had better just wait and see, until there is something definite there, and meet it when it is necessary.

## PUBLIC OPINION ON VIETNAM

[11.] Q. Why do you think there is so much confusion, frustration, and difference of opinion in this country about the war in Vietnam?

The President. There has always been confusion, frustration, and difference of opinion when there is a war going on.

There was in the Revolutionary War when only about a third of the people thought that was a wise move. A third of them opposed it, and a third were on the sideline.

That was true when all of New England came down to secede in Madison's administration in the War of 1812, and stopped in Baltimore. They

---

[1]The Revenue and Expenditure Control Act of 1968 was approved by the President on June 28, 1968 (Public Law 90-364, 82 Stat. 251).
[2]Representative Wilbur D. Mills of Arkansas, chair of the House Ways and Means Committee, and Representative John W. Byrnes of Wisconsin, ranking Republican member of the Committee.
[3]Representative Gerald R. Ford of Michigan. House Minority Leader.

didn't quite make it because Andrew Jackson's results in New Orleans came in.

They were having a party there that night. The next morning they came and told the President they wanted to congratulate him—that they had thought he was right all along, although they had come from Boston to Baltimore in a secessionist move.

That was true in the Mexican War when the Congress overwhelmingly voted to go in and later passed a resolution that had grave doubts about it. Some of the most bitter speeches were made. They were so bitter they couldn't be published. They had to hold up publication of them for 100 years.

I don't have to remind you of what happened in the Civil War. People were here in the White House begging Lincoln to concede and work out a deal with the Confederacy when word came to him of his victories. They told him that Pennsylvania was gone; that Illinois had no chance. Those pressures come to a President.

You know what President Roosevelt went through, and President Wilson in World War I. He had some Senators from certain areas then that gave him very serious problems until victory was assured.

Now, when you look back upon it, there are very few people who would think that Wilson, Roosevelt, or Truman were in error.

We are going to have this criticism. We are going to have these differences.

No one likes war. All people love peace. But you can't have freedom without defending it.

## THE CUTBACK IN FOREIGN AID

[12.] Q. Mr. President, the foreign aid authorization has been cut back nearly a third from what you requested. What is the impact of this economy?

The President. At a time when the richest nation in the world is enjoying more prosperity than it has ever had before, when we carefully tailor our requests to the very minimum that we think is essential—the lowest request that we have had in years—and then Congress cuts it 33 1/3 percent; I think it is a mistake. It is a serious mistake.

When you consider that $1 billion that we are attempting to save there, out of the $850 billion that we will produce, we ought to reconsider that decision. Because what we are doing with that

money not only can give great help to underdeveloped nations; but that, in itself, can prevent the things that cause war where you are required to spend billions to win it.

I would rather have a little preventive medicine. Every dollar that we spend in our foreign assistance, trying to help poor people help themselves, is money well spent.

I don't think we overdid it. I don't think we went too far. But I think the Congress has, in the reductions it has made.

Again, it is popular to go back home and say, "Look what I did for you. I cut out all these foreign expenditures."

But when the trouble develops—the people who are starving, the people who are ignorant, illiterate, and diseased—and wars spring up and we have to go in, we will spend much more than we would if we had taken an ounce of prevention.

## THE VIETNAM DISSENTERS

[13.] Q. Mr. President, some people on the air and in print accuse you of trying to label all criticism of your Vietnam policy as unpatriotic. Could you tell us whether you have guidelines in which you are enabled to separate conscientious dissent from irresponsible dissension?

The President. No, I haven't called anyone unpatriotic. I haven't said anything that would indicate that.

I think the wicked fleeth when no one pursueth, sometimes.

I do think that some people are irresponsible, make untrue statements, and ought to be cautious and careful when they are dealing with the problem involving their men at the front.

There is a great deal of difference, as I said a moment ago, between criticism, indifference, and responsible dissent—all of which we insist on and all of which we protect—and storm trooper bullying, throwing yourself down in the road, smashing windows, rowdyism, and every time a person attempts to speak to try to drown him out.

We believe very strongly in preserving the right to differ in this country, and the right to dissent. If I have done a good job of anything since I have been President, it is to insure that there are plenty of dissenters.

There is not a person in this press corps that can't write what he wants to write. Most of them do write what they want to. I say "want" advisedly. I want to protect that. Our Congress wants to protect it.

But if I, by chance, should say: "Now, I am not sure that you saw all the cables on this and you are exactly right; let me explain the other side of it," I would hope that you wouldn't say I am lambasting my critics, or that I am assailing someone.

What I am trying to do is to preserve my right to give the other side. I don't think one side ought to dominate the whole picture.

So what I would say is, let's realize that we are in the midst of a war. Let's realize that there are 500,000 of our boys out there who are risking their lives to win that war. Let's ask ourselves what it is we can do to help.

If you think you can make a contribution and help them by expressing your opinion and dissenting, then do it.

But then if the Secretary of State starts to explain his viewpoint, don't send out instructions all over the country and say: "When he starts to talk and says 'Mr. Chairman,' stamp your feet. When he comes to the end of a sentence, all of you do this, and at the third sentence, all of you boo."

I am amazed that the press in this country, who insist on the right to live by the first amendment, and to be protected by it, doesn't insist that these storm trooper tactics live by the first amendment, too, and that they be wiped out.

I think the time has come when it would be good for all of us to take a new, fresh look at dissent.

We welcome responsible dissent. But there is a great deal of difference between responsible dissent and some of the things that are taking place in this country which I consider to be extremely dangerous to our national interest, and I consider not very helpful to the men who are fighting the war for us.

Now, everyone must make that judgment for himself.

I have never said anyone was unpatriotic. I don't question these people's motives. I do question their judgment.

I can't say that this dissent has contributed much to any victories we have had.

I can't say that these various proposals that range from a Senator to a county commissioner to a mayor of a city have really changed General Westmoreland's plan much, or Ambassador Bunker's approach. The papers are filled with it every day.

So I think you have to consider it for what you think it is worth and make your own judgment. That is the theory of the first amendment. We don't stop the publication of any papers. We don't fine anyone for something they say. We just appeal to them to remember that they don't have the privilege at the moment of being out there fighting.

Please count to 10 before you say something that hurts instead of helps.

We know that most people's intentions are good. We don't question their motives. We have never said they are unpatriotic, although they say some pretty ugly things about us.

People who live in glass houses shouldn't be too anxious to throw stones.

## U.S. AIMS IN VIETNAM

[14.] Q. Mr. President, is your aim in Vietnam to win the war or to seek a compromised, negotiated solution?

The President. I think our aims in Vietnam have been very clear from the beginning. They are consistent with the SEATO Treaty, with the Atlantic Charter, and with the many, many statements that we have made to the Congress in connection with the Tonkin Gulf Resolution. The Secretary of State has made this clear dozens and dozens of times—and I made it enough that I thought even all the preachers in the country had heard about it.

That is, namely, to protect the security of the United States. We think the security of the United States is definitely tied in with the security of Southeast Asia.

Secondly, to resist aggression. When we are a party to a treaty that says we will do it, then we carry it out.

I think if you saw a little child in this room who was trying to waddle across the floor and some big bully came along and grabbed it by the hair and started stomping it, I think you would do something about it.

I think that we thought we made a mistake when we saw Hitler moving across the landscape of Europe. The concessions that were made by the men carrying umbrellas at that time—I think in retrospect we thought that was a mistake.

So as a consequence, in 1954 under the leadership of President Eisenhower and Secretary Dulles, we had a SEATO Treaty.

It was debated, it was considered and it was gone into very thoroughly by the Senate. The men who presented that treaty then said: This is dangerous. The time may come when we may have to put up or shut up.

But we ought to serve notice in Asia now as we refused to serve notice in Europe a few years ago that we will resist aggression—that we will stand against someone who seeks to gobble up little countries, if those little countries call upon us for our help. So we did that.

I didn't vote for that treaty. I was in the hospital. Senator Kennedy didn't vote for it—the late President—he was in the hospital. Senator Dirksen didn't vote for it. But 82 Senators did vote for it. They knew what was in that treaty.

The time came when we had to decide whether we meant what we said when we said our security was tied in to their security and that we would stand in unison in the face of common danger.

Now, we are doing that. We are doing it against whoever combines out there to promote aggression. We are going to do whatever we think is necessary to protect the security of South Vietnam—and let those people determine for themselves what kind of a government they have.

We think they are moving along very quickly in that direction to developing a democratic procedure.

Third, we are going to do whatever it is necessary to do to see that the aggressor does not succeed.

Those are our purposes. Those are our goals. We are going to get a lot of advice to do this or to do that. We are going to consider it all. But for years West Point has been turning out the best military men produced anywhere in the world.

For years we have had in our Foreign Service trained and specialized people. We have in 110 capitals today the best brains we can select.

Under our constitutional arrangements the President must look to his Secretary of State, to his foreign policy, to his Ambassadors, to the cables and views that they express, to his leaders like the Joint Chiefs of Staff, and to General Westmoreland and others—and carefully consider everything they say and then do what he thinks is right.

That is not always going to please a county commissioner, or a mayor, or a member of a legislature. It never has in any war we have ever been in been a favorite of the Senate.

The leaders on the military committees and the leaders in other posts have frequently opposed it.

Champ Clark, the Speaker of the House, opposed the draft in Woodrow Wilson's administration. The Chairman of the Foreign Relations Committee—with the exception of Senator Vandenberg—almost invariably has found a great deal wrong with the Executive in the field of foreign policy.

There is a division there, and there is some frustration there.

Those men express it and they have a right to. They have a duty to do it.

But it is also the President's duty to look and see what substance they have presented; how much they thought it out; what information they have; how much knowledge they have received from General Westmoreland or Ambassador Bunker, whoever it is; how familiar they are with what is going on; and whether you really think you ought to follow their judgment or follow the judgment of the other people.

I do that every day. Some days I have to say to our people: "Let us try this plan that Senator X has suggested." And we do.

We are doing that with the United Nations resolution. We have tried several times to get the United Nations to play a part in trying to bring peace in Vietnam.

The Senate thinks that this is the way to do it. More than 50 of them have signed a resolution. The Senate Foreign Relations Committee had a big day yesterday. They reported two resolutions in one day.

I have my views. I have my views about really what those resolutions will achieve. But I also have an obligation to seriously and carefully consider the judgments of the other branch of the Government. And we are going to do it.

Even though we may have some doubts about what will be accomplished, that they think may be accomplished, if it is a close question we will bend to try to meet their views because we think that is important. We have already tried the United Nations before, but we may try it again because they have hopes and they believe that this is the answer. We will do everything that we can to make it the answer.

I don't want to hurt its chances by giving any predictions at this moment.

We will consider the views that everyone suggests.

Merriman Smith, United Press International: Thank you, Mr. President.

## 9. The President's Address to the Nation Announcing Steps to Limit the War in Vietnam and Reporting His Decision Not to Seek Reelection, March 31, 1968

*Public Papers of the Presidents of the United States: Lyndon B. Johnson, 1968–69, Vols. 1–2. (Washington, D.C.: U.S. Government Printing Office, 1970), 1: 469–476.*

Good evening, my fellow Americans:

Tonight I want to speak to you of peace in Vietnam and Southeast Asia.

No other question so preoccupies our people. No other dream so absorbs the 250 million human beings who live in that part of the world. No other goal motivates American policy in Southeast Asia.

For years, representatives of our Government and others have traveled the world—seeking to find a basis for peace talks.

Since last September, they have carried the offer that I made public at San Antonio. That offer was this:

That the United States would stop its bombardment of North Vietnam when that would lead promptly to productive discussions—and that we would assume that North Vietnam would not take military advantage of our restraint.

Hanoi denounced this offer, both privately and publicly. Even while the search for peace was going on, North Vietnam rushed their preparations for a savage assault on the people, the government, and the allies of South Vietnam.

Their attack—during the Tet holidays—failed to achieve its principal objectives. It did not collapse the elected government of South Vietnam or shatter its army—as the Communists had hoped.

It did not produce a "general uprising" among the people of the cities as they had predicted.

The Communists were unable to maintain control of any of the more than 30 cities that they attacked. And they took very heavy casualties.

But they did compel the South Vietnamese and their allies to move certain forces from the countryside into the cities.

They caused widespread disruption and suffering. Their attacks, and the battles that followed, made refugees of half a million human beings.

The Communists may renew their attack any day.

They are, it appears, trying to make 1968 the year of decision in South Vietnam—the year that brings, if not final victory or defeat, at least a turning point in the struggle. This much is clear:

If they do mount another round of heavy attacks, they will not succeed in destroying the fighting power of South Vietnam and its allies.

But tragically, this is also clear: Many men—on both sides of the struggle—will be lost. A nation that has already suffered 20 years of warfare will suffer once again. Armies on both sides will take new casualties. And the war will go on. There is no need for this to be so. There is no need to delay the talks that could bring an end to this long and this bloody war.

Tonight, I renew the offer I made last August—to stop the bombardment of North Vietnam. We ask that talks begin promptly, that they be serious talks on the substance of peace. We assume that during those talks Hanoi will not take advantage of our restraint.

We are prepared to move immediately toward peace through negotiations.

So, tonight, in the hope that this action will lead to early talks, I am taking the first step to deescalate the conflict. We are reducing—substantially reducing—the present level of hostilities. And we are doing so unilaterally, and at once.

Tonight, I have ordered our aircraft and our naval vessels to make no attacks on North Vietnam, except in the area north of the demilitarized zone where the continuing enemy buildup directly threatens allied forward positions and where the movements of their troops and supplies are clearly related to that threat.

The area in which we are stopping our attacks includes almost 90 percent of North Vietnam's population, and most of its territory. Thus there will be no attacks around the principal populated areas, or in the food-producing areas of North Vietnam.

Even this very limited bombing of the North could come to an early end—if our restraint is matched by restraint in Hanoi. But I cannot in good conscience stop all bombing so long as to do so would immediately and directly endanger the lives of our men and our allies. Whether a complete bombing halt becomes possible in the future will be determined by events.

Our purpose in this action is to bring about a reduction in the level of violence that now exists.

It is to save the lives of brave men—and to save the lives of innocent women and children. It is to permit the contending forces to move closer to a political settlement.

And tonight, I call upon the United Kingdom and I call upon the Soviet Union—as cochairmen of the Geneva Conferences, and as permanent members of the United Nations Security Council—to do all they can to move from the unilateral act of deescalation that I have just announced toward genuine peace in Southeast Asia.

Now, as in the past, the United States is ready to send its representatives to any forum, at any time, to discuss the means of bringing this ugly war to an end.

I am designating one of our most distinguished Americans, Ambassador Averell Harriman, as my personal representative for such talks. In addition, I have asked Ambassador Llewellyn Thompson, who returned from Moscow for consultation, to be available to join Ambassador Harriman at Geneva or any other suitable place—just as soon as Hanoi agrees to a conference.

I call upon President Ho Chi Minh to respond positively, and favorably, to this new step toward peace.

But if peace does not come now through negotiations, it will come when Hanoi understands that our common resolve is unshakable, and our common strength is invincible.

Tonight, we and the other allied nations are contributing 600,000 fighting men to assist 700,000 South Vietnamese troops in defending their little country. Our presence there has always rested on this basic belief: The main burden of preserving their freedom must be carried out by them—by the South Vietnamese themselves.

We and our allies can only help to provide a shield behind which the people of South Vietnam can survive and can grow and develop. On their efforts—on their determination and resourcefulness—the outcome will ultimately depend.

That small, beleaguered nation has suffered terrible punishment for more than 20 years.

I pay tribute once again tonight to the great courage and endurance of its people. South Vietnam supports armed forces tonight of almost 700,000 men—and I call your attention to the fact that this is the equivalent of more than 10 million in our own population. Its people maintain their firm determination to be free of domination by the North.

There has been substantial progress, I think, in building a durable government during these last 3 years. The South Vietnam of 1965 could not have survived the enemy's Tet offensive of 1968. The elected government of South Vietnam survived that attack—and is rapidly repairing the devastation that it wrought.

The South Vietnamese know that further efforts are going to be required:

—to expand their own armed forces,
—to move back into the countryside as quickly as possible,
—to increase their taxes,
—to select the very best men that they have for civil and military responsibility,
—to achieve a new unity within their constitutional government, and
—to include in the national effort all those groups who wish to preserve South

Vietnam's control over its own destiny. Last week President Thieu ordered the mobilization of 135,000 additional South Vietnamese. He plans to reach—as soon as possible—a total military strength of more than 800,000 men.

To achieve this, the Government of South Vietnam started the drafting of 19-year-olds on March 1st. On May 1st, the Government will begin the drafting of 18-year-olds.

Last month, 10,000 men volunteered for military service—that was two and a half times the number of volunteers during the same month last year. Since the middle of January, more than 48,000 South Vietnamese have joined the armed forces—and nearly half of them volunteered to do so.

All men in the South Vietnamese armed forces have had their tours of duty extended for the duration of the war, and reserves are now being called up for immediate active duty. President Thieu told his people last week: "We must make greater efforts and accept more sacrifices because, as I have said many times, this is our country. The existence of our nation is at stake, and this is mainly a Vietnamese responsibility."

He warned his people that a major national effort is required to root out corruption and incompetence at all levels of government.

We applaud this evidence of determination on the part of South Vietnam. Our first priority will be to support their effort.

We shall accelerate the reequipment of South Vietnam's armed forces—in order to meet the enemy's increased firepower. This will enable them progressively to undertake a larger share of combat operations against the Communist invaders.

On many occasions I have told the American people that we would send to Vietnam those forces that are required to accomplish our mission there. So, with that as our guide, we have previously authorized a force level of approximately 525,000.

Some weeks ago—to help meet the enemy's new offensive—we sent to Vietnam about 11,000 additional Marine and airborne troops. They were deployed by air in 48 hours, on an emergency basis. But the artillery, tank, aircraft, medical, and other units that were needed to work with and to support these infantry troops in combat could not then accompany them by air on that short notice.

In order that these forces may reach maximum combat effectiveness, the Joint Chiefs of Staff have recommended to me that we should prepare to send—during the next 5 months—support troops totaling approximately 13,500 men.

A portion of these men will be made available from our active forces. The balance will come from reserve component units which will be called up for service.

The actions that we have taken since the beginning of the year

—to reequip the South Vietnamese forces,

—to meet our responsibilities in Korea, as well as our responsibilities in Vietnam,

—to meet price increases and the cost of activating and deploying reserve forces,

—to replace helicopters and provide the other military supplies we need, all of these actions are going to require additional expenditures.

The tentative estimate of those additional expenditures is $2.5 billion in this fiscal year, and $2.6 billion in the next fiscal year.

These projected increases in expenditures for our national security will bring into sharper focus the Nation's need for immediate action: action to protect the prosperity of the American people and to protect the strength and the stability of our American dollar. On many occasions I have pointed out that, without a tax bill or decreased expenditures, next year's deficit would again be around $20 billion. I have emphasized the need to set strict priorities in our spending. I have stressed that failure to act and to act promptly and decisively would raise very strong doubts throughout the world about America's willingness to keep its financial house in order.

Yet Congress has not acted. And tonight we face the sharpest financial threat in the postwar era—a threat to the dollar's role as the keystone of international trade and finance in the world.

Last week, at the monetary conference in Stockholm, the major industrial countries decided to take a big step toward creating a new international monetary asset that will strengthen the international monetary system. I am very proud of the very able work done by Secretary Fowler and Chairman Martin of the Federal Reserve Board.

But to make this system work the United States just must bring its balance of payments to—or very close to—equilibrium. We must have a responsible fiscal policy in this country. The passage of a tax bill now, together with expenditure control that the Congress may desire and dictate, is absolutely necessary to protect this Nation's security, to continue our prosperity, and to meet the needs of our people.

What is at stake is 7 years of unparalleled prosperity. In those 7 years, the real income of the average American, after taxes, rose by almost 30 percent—a gain as large as that of the entire preceding 19 years.

So the steps that we must take to convince the world are exactly the steps we must take to sustain our own economic strength here at home. In the past 8 months, prices and interest rates have risen because of our inaction.

We must, therefore, now do everything we can to move from debate to action—from talking to voting. There is, I believe—I hope there is—in both Houses of the Congress—a growing sense of urgency that this situation just must be acted upon and must be corrected.

My budget in January was, we thought, a tight one. It fully reflected our evaluation of most of the demanding needs of this Nation.

But in these budgetary matters, the President does not decide alone. The Congress has the power and the duty to determine appropriations and taxes.

The Congress is now considering our proposals and they are considering reductions in the budget that we submitted.

As part of a program of fiscal restraint that includes the tax surcharge, I shall approve appropriate reductions in the January budget when and if Congress so decides that that should be done.

One thing is unmistakably clear, however: Our deficit just must be reduced. Failure to act could bring on conditions that would strike hardest at those people that all of us are trying so hard to help.

These times call for prudence in this land of plenty. I believe that we have the character to provide it, and tonight I plead with the Congress and with the people to act promptly to serve the national interest, and thereby serve all of our people.

Now let me give you my estimate of the chances for peace:

—the peace that will one day stop the bloodshed in South Vietnam,
—that will permit all the Vietnamese people to rebuild and develop their land,
—that will permit us to turn more fully to our own tasks here at home.

I cannot promise that the initiative that I have announced tonight will be completely successful in achieving peace any more than the 30 others that we have undertaken and agreed to in recent years.

But it is our fervent hope that North Vietnam, after years of fighting that have left the issue unresolved, will now cease its efforts to achieve a military victory and will join with us in moving toward the peace table.

And there may come a time when South Vietnamese—on both sides—are able to work out a way to settle their own differences by free political choice rather than by war.

As Hanoi considers its course, it should be in no doubt of our intentions. It must not miscalculate the pressures within our democracy in this election year.

We have no intention of widening this war.

But the United States will never accept a fake solution to this long and arduous struggle and call it peace.

No one can foretell the precise terms of an eventual settlement.

Our objective in South Vietnam has never been the annihilation of the enemy. It has been to bring about a recognition in Hanoi that its objective—taking over the South by force—could not be achieved.

We think that peace can be based on the Geneva Accords of 1954—under political conditions that permit the South Vietnamese—all the South Vietnamese—to chart their course free of any outside domination or interference, from us or from anyone else.

So tonight I reaffirm the pledge that we made at Manila—that we are prepared to withdraw our forces from South Vietnam as the other side withdraws its forces to the north, stops the infiltration, and the level of violence thus subsides.

Our goal of peace and self-determination in Vietnam is directly related to the future of all of Southeast Asia—where much has happened to inspire confidence during the past 10 years. We have done all that we knew how to do to contribute and to help build that confidence.

A number of its nations have shown what can be accomplished under conditions of security. Since 1966, Indonesia, the fifth largest nation in all the world, with a population of more than 100 million people, has had a government that is dedicated to peace with its neighbors and improved conditions for its own people. Political and economic cooperation between nations has grown rapidly.

I think every American can take a great deal of pride in the role that we have played in bringing this about in Southeast Asia. We can rightly judge—as responsible Southeast Asians themselves do—that the progress of the past 3 years would have been far less likely—if not completely impossible—if America's sons and others had not made their stand in Vietnam.

At Johns Hopkins University, about 3 years ago, I announced that the United States would take part in the great work of developing Southeast Asia, including the Mekong Valley, for all the people of that region. Our determination to help build a better land—a better land for men on both sides of the present conflict—has not diminished in the least. Indeed, the ravages of war, I think, have made it more urgent than ever.

So, I repeat on behalf of the United States again tonight what I said at Johns Hopkins—that North Vietnam could take its place in this common effort just as soon as peace comes.

Over time, a wider framework of peace and security in Southeast Asia may become possible. The new cooperation of the nations of the area could be a foundation-stone. Certainly friendship with the nations of such a Southeast Asia is what the

United States seeks—and that is all that the United States seeks.

One day, my fellow citizens, there will be peace in Southeast Asia.

It will come because the people of Southeast Asia want it—those whose armies are at war tonight, and those who, though threatened, have thus far been spared.

Peace will come because Asians were willing to work for it—and to sacrifice for it—and to die by the thousands for it.

But let it never be forgotten: Peace will come also because America sent her sons to help secure it.

It has not been easy—far from it. During the past four and one-half years, it has been my fate and my responsibility to be Commander in Chief. I have lived—daily and nightly—with the cost of this war. I know the pain that it has inflicted. I know, perhaps better than anyone, the misgivings that it has aroused.

Throughout this entire, long period, I have been sustained by a single principle: that what we are doing now, in Vietnam, is vital not only to the security of Southeast Asia, but it is vital to the security of every American.

Surely we have treaties which we must respect. Surely we have commitments that we are going to keep. Resolutions of the Congress testify to the need to resist aggression in the world and in Southeast Asia.

But the heart of our involvement in South Vietnam—under three different presidents, three separate administrations—has always been America's own security.

And the larger purpose of our involvement has always been to help the nations of Southeast Asia become independent and stand alone, self-sustaining, as members of a great world community—at peace with themselves, and at peace with all others.

With such an Asia, our country—and the world—will be far more secure than it is tonight.

I believe that a peaceful Asia is far nearer to reality because of what America has done in Vietnam. I believe that the men who endure the dangers of battle—fighting there for us tonight—are helping the entire world avoid far greater conflicts, far wider wars, far more destruction, than this one.

The peace that will bring them home someday will come. Tonight I have offered the first in what I hope will be a series of mutual moves toward peace.

I pray that it will not be rejected by the leaders of North Vietnam. I pray that they will accept it as a means by which the sacrifices of their own people

may be ended. And I ask your help and your support, my fellow citizens, for this effort to reach across the battlefield toward an early peace.

Finally, my fellow Americans, let me say this:

Of those to whom much is given, much is asked. I cannot say and no man could say that no more will be asked of us.

Yet, I believe that now, no less than when the decade began, this generation of Americans is willing to "pay any price, bear any burden, meet any hardship, support any friend, oppose any foe to assure the survival and the success of liberty."

Since those words were spoken by John F. Kennedy, the people of America have kept that compact with mankind's noblest cause.

And we shall continue to keep it.

Yet, I believe that we must always be mindful of this one thing, whatever the trials and the tests ahead. The ultimate strength of our country and our cause will lie not in powerful weapons or infinite resources or boundless wealth, but will lie in the unity of our people. This I believe very deeply.

Throughout my entire public career I have followed the personal philosophy that I am a free man, an American, a public servant, and a member of my party, in that order always and only.

For 37 years in the service of our Nation, first as a Congressman, as a Senator, and as Vice President, and now as your President, I have put the unity of the people first. I have put it ahead of any divisive partisanship.

And in these times as in times before, it is true that a house divided against itself by the spirit of faction, of party, of region, of religion, of race, is a house that cannot stand.

There is division in the American house now. There is divisiveness among us all tonight. And holding the trust that is mine, as President of all the people, I cannot disregard the peril to the progress of the American people and the hope and the prospect of peace for all peoples.

So, I would ask all Americans, whatever their personal interests or concern, to guard against divisiveness and all its ugly consequences.

Fifty-two months and 10 days ago, in a moment of tragedy and trauma, the duties of this office fell upon me. I asked then for your help and God's, that we might continue America on its course, binding up our wounds, healing our history, moving forward in new unity, to clear the American agenda and to keep the American commitment for all of our people.

United we have kept that commitment. United we have enlarged that commitment.

Through all time to come, I think America will be a stronger nation, a more just society, and a land of greater opportunity and fulfillment because of what we have all done together in these years of unparalleled achievement.

Our reward will come in the life of freedom, peace, and hope that our children will enjoy through ages ahead.

What we won when all of our people united just must not now be lost in suspicion, distrust, selfishness, and politics among any of our people.

Believing this as I do, I have concluded that I should not permit the Presidency to become involved in the partisan divisions that are developing in this political year.

With America's sons in the fields far away, with America's future under challenge right here at home, with our hopes and the world's hopes for peace in the balance every day, I do not believe that I should devote an hour or a day of my time to any personal partisan causes or to any duties other than the awesome duties of this office—the Presidency of your country.

Accordingly, I shall not seek, and I will not accept, the nomination of my party for another term as your President.

But let men everywhere know, however, that a strong, a confident, and a vigilant America stands ready tonight to seek an honorable peace—and stands ready tonight to defend an honored cause—whatever the price, whatever the burden, whatever the sacrifice that duty may require. Thank you for listening. Good night and God bless all of you.

## 10. The President's Address to the Nation upon Announcing His Decision to Halt the Bombing of North Vietnam, October 31, 1968

*Public Papers of the Presidents of the United States: Lyndon B. Johnson, 1968–69, Vols. 1–2. (Washington, D.C.: U.S. Government Printing Office, 1970), 2: 1,099–1,103.*

Good evening, my fellow Americans:

I speak to you this evening about very important developments in our search for peace in Vietnam.

We have been engaged in discussions with the North Vietnamese in Paris since last May. The dis-cussions began after I announced on the evening of March 31st in a television speech to the Nation that the United States—in an effort to get talks started on a settlement of the Vietnam war—had stopped the bombing of North Vietnam in the area where 90 percent of the people live.

When our representatives—Ambassador Harriman and Ambassador Vance—were sent to Paris, they were instructed to insist throughout the discussions that the legitimate elected Government of South Vietnam must take its place in any serious negotiations affecting the future of South Vietnam.

Therefore, our Ambassadors Harriman and Vance made it abundantly clear to the representatives of North Vietnam in the beginning that—as I had indicated on the evening of March 31st—we would stop the bombing of North Vietnamese territory entirely when that would lead to prompt and productive talks, meaning by that talks in which the Government of Vietnam was free to participate.

Our ambassadors also stressed that we could not stop the bombing so long as by doing so we would endanger the lives and the safety of our troops.

For a good many weeks, there was no movement in the talks at all. The talks appeared to really be deadlocked.

Then a few weeks ago, they entered a new and a very much more hopeful phase.

As we moved ahead, I conducted a series of very intensive discussions with our allies, and with the senior military and diplomatic officers of the United States Government, on the prospects for peace. The President also briefed our congressional leaders and all of the presidential candidates.

Last Sunday evening, and throughout Monday, we began to get confirmation of the essential understanding that we had been seeking with the North Vietnamese on the critical issues between us for some time. I spent most of all day Tuesday reviewing every single detail of this matter with our field commander, General Abrams, whom I had ordered home, and who arrived here at the White House at 2:30 in the morning and went into immediate conference with the President and the appropriate members of his Cabinet. We received General Abrams' judgment and we heard his recommendations at some length.

Now, as a result of all of these developments, I have now ordered that all air, naval, and artillery bombardment of North Vietnam cease as of 8 a.m., Washington time, Friday morning.

I have reached this decision on the basis of the developments in the Paris talks.

And I have reached it in the belief that this action can lead to progress toward a peaceful settlement of the Vietnamese war.

I have already informed the three presidential candidates, as well as the congressional leaders of both the Republican and the Democratic Parties of the reasons that the Government has made this decision.

This decision very closely conforms to the statements that I have made in the past concerning a bombing cessation.

It was on August 19th that the President said: "This administration does not intend to move further until it has good reason to believe that the other side intends seriously"—seriously—"to join us in deescalating the war and moving seriously toward peace."

And then again on September 10th, I said: "The bombing will not stop until we are confident that it will not lead to an increase in American casualties."

The Joint Chiefs of Staff, all military men, have assured me—and General Abrams very firmly asserted to me on Tuesday in that early, 2:30 a.m. meeting—that in their military judgment this action should be taken now, and this action would not result in any increase in American casualties.

A regular session of the Paris talks is going to take place next Wednesday, November 6th, at which the representatives of the Government of South Vietnam are free to participate. We are informed by the representatives of the Hanoi Government that the representatives of the National Liberation Front will also be present. I emphasize that their attendance in no way involves recognition of the National Liberation Front in any form. Yet, it conforms to the statements that we have made many times over the years that the NLF would have no difficulty making its views known.

But what we now expect—what we have a right to expect—are prompt, productive, serious, and intensive negotiations in an atmosphere that is conducive to progress.

We have reached the stage where productive talks can begin. We have made clear to the other side that such talks cannot continue if they take military advantage of them. We cannot have productive talks in an atmosphere where the cities are being shelled and where the demilitarized zone is being abused.

I think I should caution you, my fellow Americans, that arrangements of this kind are never foolproof. For that matter, even formal treaties are never foolproof, as we have learned from our experience.

But in the light of the progress that has been made in recent weeks, and after carefully considering and weighing the unanimous military and diplomatic advice and judgment rendered to the Commander in Chief, I have finally decided to take this step now and to really determine the good faith of those who have assured us that progress will result when bombing ceases and to try to ascertain if an early peace is possible. The overriding consideration that governs us at this hour is the chance and the opportunity that we might have to save human lives, save human lives on both sides of the conflict. Therefore, I have concluded that we should see if they are acting in good faith.

We could be misled—and we are prepared for such a contingency. We pray God it does not occur.

But it should be clear to all of us that the new phase of negotiations which opens on November 6th does not—repeat, does not—mean that a stable peace has yet come to Southeast Asia. There may well be very hard fighting ahead. Certainly, there is going to be some very hard negotiating, because many difficult and critically important issues are still facing these negotiators. But I hope and I believe that with good will we can solve them. We know that negotiations can move swiftly if the common intent of the negotiators is peace in the world. The world should know that the American people bitterly remember the long, agonizing Korean negotiations of 1951 through 1953—and that our people will just not accept deliberate delay and prolonged procrastination again.

Well then, how has it come about that now, on November 1st, we have agreed to stop the bombardment of North Vietnam?

I would have given all I possess if the conditions had permitted me to stop it months ago; if there had just been any movement in the Paris talks that would have justified me in saying to you, "Now it can be safely stopped."

But I, the President of the United States, do not control the timing of the events in Hanoi. The decisions in Hanoi really determine when and whether it would be possible for us to stop the bombing.

We could not retract our insistence on the participation of the Government of South Vietnam in serious talks affecting the future of their people—the people of South Vietnam. For though we have allied with South Vietnam for many years in this struggle, we have never assumed and we shall never demand the role of dictating the future of the people of South Vietnam. The very principle for which we are engaged in South Vietnam—the principle of self-determination—requires that the South Vietnamese people themselves be permitted to freely speak for themselves at the Paris talks and that the South Vietnamese delegation play a leading role in accordance with our agreement with President Thieu at Honolulu.

It was made just as clear to North Vietnam that a total bombing halt must not risk the lives of our men.

When I spoke last March 31st, I said that evening: "Whether a complete bombing halt becomes possible in the future will be determined by events."

Well, I cannot tell you tonight specifically in all detail why there has been progress in Paris. But I can tell you that a series of hopeful events has occurred in South Vietnam:

—The Government of South Vietnam has grown steadily stronger.
—South Vietnam's Armed Forces have been substantially increased to the point where a million men are tonight under arms, and the effectiveness of these men has steadily improved.
—The superb performance of our own men, under the brilliant leadership of General Westmoreland and General Abrams, has produced truly remarkable results.

Now, perhaps some or all of these factors played a part in bringing about progress in the talks. And when at last progress did come, I believe that my responsibilities to the brave men—our men—who bear the burden of battle in South Vietnam tonight, and my duty to seek an honorable settlement of the war, required me to recognize and required me to act without delay. I have acted tonight.

There have been many long days of waiting for new steps toward peace—days that began in hope, only to end at night in disappointment. Constancy to our national purpose—which is to seek the basis for a durable peace in Southeast Asia—has sustained me in all of these hours when there seemed to be no progress whatever in these talks.

But now that progress has come, I know that your prayers are joined with mine and with those of all humanity, that the action I announce tonight will be a major step toward a firm and an honorable peace in Southeast Asia. It can be.

So, what is required of us in these new circumstances is exactly that steady determination and patience which has brought us to this more hopeful prospect.

What is required of us is a courage and a steadfastness, and a perseverance here at home, that will match that of our men who fight for us tonight in Vietnam.

So, I ask you not only for your prayers but for the courageous and understanding support that Americans always give their President and their leader in an hour of trial. With that understanding, and with that support, we shall not fail.

Seven months ago I said that I would not permit the Presidency to become involved in the partisan divisions that were then developing in this political year. Accordingly, on the night of March 31st, I announced that I would not seek nor accept the nomination of my party for another term as President.

I have devoted every resource of the Presidency to the search for peace in Southeast Asia. Throughout the entire summer and fall I have kept all of the presidential candidates fully briefed on developments in Paris as well as in Vietnam. I have made it abundantly clear that no one candidate would have the advantage over others—either in information about those developments, or in advance notice of the policy the Government intended to follow. The chief diplomatic and military officers of this Government all were instructed to follow the same course.

Since that night on March 31st, each of the candidates has had differing ideas about the Government's policy. But generally speaking, however, throughout the campaign we have been able to present a united voice supporting our Government and supporting our men in Vietnam. I hope, and I believe, that this can continue until January 20th of next year when a new President takes office. Because in this critical hour, we just simply cannot afford more than one voice speaking for our Nation in the search for peace.

I do not know who will be inaugurated as the 37th President of the United States next January. But I do know that I shall do all that I can in the next few months to try to lighten his burdens as the contributions of the Presidents who preceded me have greatly lightened mine. I shall do everything in my power to move us toward the peace that the new President—as well as this President and, I believe, every other American—so deeply and urgently desires.

Thank you for listening. Good night and God bless all of you.

NOTE: The president recorded the address on October 30, 1968, in the Family Theater at the White House for broadcast over nationwide radio and television at 8 p.m. on October 31. In his address he referred to W. Averell Harriman and Cyrus R. Vance, U.S. representatives at the Paris peace talks with North Vietnam, General Creighton W. Abrams, commander, U.S. Military Assistance Command, Vietnam, and General William C. Westmoreland, army chief of staff who preceded General Abrams as U.S. commander in Vietnam.

# SELECTED BIBLIOGRAPHY

Anderson, Terry H. *The Movement and the Sixties.* New York Oxford University Press, 1995. A study of cultural and social activists and what they achieved.

Berman, Larry. *Planning a Tragedy: The Americanization of the War in Vietnam.* New York: W. W. Norton, 1982.

———. *Lyndon Johnson's War: The Road to Stalemate in Vietnam.* New York: W. W. Norton, 1989. Berman provides engrossing accounts of Johnson's Vietnam decisions based on extensive archival research.

Bernstein, Irving. *Guns or Butter: The Presidency of Lyndon Johnson.* New York: Oxford University Press, 1996. Examines the effects of foreign policy on Great Society programs.

Beschloss, Michael, ed. *Reaching for Glory: Lyndon Johnson's Secret White House Tapes, 1964–65.* New York: Simon and Schuster, 2001.

———, ed. *Taking Charge: The Johnson White House Tapes, 1963–64.* New York: Simon and Schuster, 1997. Both Beschloss volumes contain edited transcripts of the president's telephone conversations.

Branch, Taylor. *Pillar of Fire: America in the King Years, 1963–65.* New York: Simon and Schuster, 1998. A study of two critical years in the civil rights movement that focuses on Martin Luther King, Jr.

Brands, H. W. *The Wages of Globalism: Lyndon Johnson and the Limits of American Power.* New York: Oxford University Press, 1995. A useful study by a prolific historian of both Johnson's international policies and his relationships with his foreign policy advisers.

Cohen, Warren I., and Nancy Bernkopf Tucker, eds. *Lyndon Johnson Confronts the World: American Foreign Policy, 1963–68.* These essays probe the many dimensions beyond Vietnam of Johnson's foreign policy.

Conkin, Paul K. *Big Daddy from the Perdernales: Lyndon Baines Johnson.* Boston: Twayne Publishers, 1986. A brief, if at times thin, but useful biography.

Dallek, Robert A. *Flawed Giant: Lyndon Johnson and His Times, 1961–1973.* New York: Oxford University Press, 1998. Excellent, balanced, and extensively researched study of Johnson and his presidency.

DeBenedetti, Charles. *An American Ordeal: The Antiwar Movement of the Vietnam Era.* Syracuse, N.Y.: Syracuse University Press, 1990. The most thorough study of the opposition to the war.

Farber, David. *Chicago '68.* Chicago: University of Chicago Press, 1988. Excellent study of the confrontation at the 1968 Democratic National Convention that includes the perspectives of antiwar activists as well as Mayor Daley and the Chicago police.

———, ed. *The Sixties; From Memory to History.* Chapel Hill: University of North Carolina Press, 1994. Wide-ranging essays on liberalism, the women's movement, the sexual revolution, television news and Vietnam, and other topics.

Graham, Hugh Davis. *The Civil Rights Era: Origins and Development of National Policy, 1960–1972.* New York: Oxford University Press, 1992. An important study of presidential and congressional actions.

Herring, George C. *America's Longest War: The United States and Vietnam, 1950–1975.* 4th ed. New York: McGraw-Hill, 2002. The best overview of U.S. involvement in Vietnam.

Johnson, Lyndon Baines. *The Vantage Point: Perspectives on the Presidency, 1963–1969.* New York: Holt, Rinehart and Winston, 1971. Johnson's memoir of his White House years.

Kearns, Doris. *Lyndon Johnson and the American Dream.* New York: Harper and Row, 1976. A study of Johnson's life and presidency by a former White House fellow and post-presidential aide.

Kunz, Diane, ed. *The Diplomacy of the Crucial Decade: American Foreign Relations during the 1960s.* New York: Columbia University Press, 1994. Essays on many dimensions of Kennedy's and Johnson's cold war policies.

Lerner, Mitchell B. *The Pueblo Incident: A Spy Ship and the Failure of American Foreign Policy.* Lawrence: University Press of Kansas, 2002. A fascinating study based on declassified documents of the hostage crisis during Johnson's last year in the White House.

Logevall, Fredrik. *Choosing War: The Lost Chance for Peace and the Escalation of the Vietnam War.* Berkeley: University of California Press, 1999. A provocative study of the "long 1964" in which Johnson's decisions changed a U.S. advisory effort into what the author sees as an unnecessary war in Vietnam.

Matusow, Allen J. *The Unraveling of America: Liberalism in the 1960s.* New York: Harper and Row, 1984. Analyzes what the author sees as the shortcomings of liberal reform.

Schwartz, Thomas Alan. *Lyndon Johnson and Europe: In the Shadow of Vietnam.* Cambridge, Mass.: Harvard University Press, 2003. An engaging study that portrays Johnson as an effective leader of the Western alliance.

Unger, Irwin, and Debi Unger. *LBJ: A Life.* New York: John Wiley and Sons, 1999. A brisk, synthetic overview of Johnson's life and public career in Congress and the presidency.

Source: *Public Papers of the Presidents of the United States*

# INDEX

**Boldface** page numbers indicate primary discussions. *Italic* page numbers indicate illustrations. An italicized *c* following a page number indicates chronology.